Filtration and Purification in the Biopharmaceutical Industry

Drugs and the Pharmaceutical Sciences

A Series of Textbooks and Monographs
James Swarbrick
PharmaceuTech, Inc. Pinehurst, North Carolina

RECENT TITLES IN SERIES

Filtration and Purification in the Biopharmaceutical Industry, Third Edition
Maik W. Jornitz

Handbook of Drug Metabolism, Third Edition
Paul G. Pearson and Larry Wienkers

The Art and Science of Dermal Formulation Development
Marc Brown and Adrian C. Williams

Pharmaceutical Inhalation Aerosol Technology, Third Edition
Anthony J. Hickey and Sandro R. da Rocha

Good Manufacturing Practices for Pharmaceuticals, Seventh Edition
Graham P. Bunn

Pharmaceutical Extrusion Technology, Second Edition
Isaac Ghebre-Sellassie, Charles E. Martin, Feng Zhang, and James Dinunzio

Biosimilar Drug Product Development
Laszlo Endrenyi, Paul Declerck, and Shein-Chung Chow

High Throughput Screening in Drug Discovery
Amancio Carnero

Generic Drug Product Development: International Regulatory Requirements for
Bioequivalence, Second Edition
Isadore Kanfer and Leon Shargel

Aqueous Polymeric Coatings for Pharmaceutical Dosage Forms, Fourth Edition
Linda A. Felton

Good Design Practices for GMP Pharmaceutical Facilities, Second Edition
Terry Jacobs and Andrew A. Signore

For more information about this series, please visit: www.crcpress.com/Drugs-and-the-Pharmaceutical-Sciences/book-series/IHCDRUPHASCI

Filtration and Purification in the Biopharmaceutical Industry

Third Edition

Edited by

Maik W. Jornitz

CRC Press
Taylor & Francis Group
Boca Raton London New York

CRC Press is an imprint of the
Taylor & Francis Group, an **informa** business

CRC Press
Taylor & Francis Group
6000 Broken Sound Parkway NW, Suite 300
Boca Raton, FL 33487-2742

First issued in paperback 2022

ISBN-13: 978-1-138-05674-9 (hbk)
ISBN-13: 978-1-03-233828-6 (pbk)
DOI: 10.1201/9781315164953

Library of Congress Cataloging-in-Publication Data

Names: Jornitz, Maik W., 1961- editor.
Title: Filtration and purification in the biopharmaceutical industry / [edited by] Maik W. Jornitz.
Description: Third edition. | Boca Raton, Florida : CRC Press, 2019. |
Series: Drugs and the pharmaceutical sciences |
Includes bibliographical references and index.
Identifiers: LCCN 2018060549 | ISBN 9781138056749 (hardback : alk. paper) |
ISBN 9781315164953 (ebook)
Subjects: LCSH: Biological products—Separation. | Filters and filtration. |
Pharmaceutical biotechnology—Methodology.
Classification: LCC RS190.B55 F54 2019 | DDC 615.1/9—dc23
LC record available at https://lccn.loc.gov/2018060549

Visit the Taylor & Francis Web site at
http://www.taylorandfrancis.com

and the CRC Press Web site at
http://www.crcpress.com

With love and respect

I dedicate this work to those who inspire and support me, especially

my mentor and former co-editor Theodore H. Meltzer.

To my family, Dorette, Lisa, and Philip for their patience, tireless

encouragement, and the joy they bring to my life

—M.W.J.

Contents

Foreword

The use of membrane filters for clarification and control of contamination has been a key tool in the arsenal of pharmaceutical and biopharmaceutical manufacturing. It is incumbent on the users of this technology to understand its mechanisms and limitations. This book provides a thorough explanation of the types of filters, considerations for their use, and discussion of their applications, as well as regulatory considerations.

The use of membrane filters has never been more important. With the rise of the numbers of large molecule and injectable products, more and more users are employing this technology. More large molecule products are being developed, and with biosimilars the market is expanding. The availability, cost, and quality of these products are important to the health care for an increasing number of patients worldwide. It is critical that these users educate themselves on this technology so that the application is successful.

Despite the long history of filtration in our industry, there continues to be misunderstanding and debate on the mechanisms and use of membrane filtration. This newest edition will address some of these "hot topics." From the improvement in the manufacturing and control of membrane filters themselves to their incorporation into and expanding portfolio of single-use systems, the capabilities of filters to deliver performance and value are improving. There are different uses for membrane filters, which have implications for new downstream purification technologies. But there continues to be disagreement over the basic functionality of membrane filters, and this edition with address some of these, especially the requirement for "Pre-use, post-sterilization" integrity testing.

Richard M. Johnson
President and CEO
Parenteral Drug Association
Bethesda, MD, USA
"Connecting People, Science and Regulation®"

Acknowledgments

This book is the third edition of the "Filtration Book" series, starting with *Filtration in the Pharmaceutical Industry* (1987), *Filtration in the Biopharmaceutical Industry* (1998), and *Filtration and Purification in the Biopharmaceutical Industry* (2008). This time the title stayed the same, but with the rapid evolution of our industry, this may change in the future renditions. This book revision includes a chapter on single-use technologies, a process technology that receives a tremendous adoption rate and changes the process and facility designs. We have seen application specific separation and purification developments and process intensification. Our industry is changing constantly, even conservatively so. These changes were addressed in this revision, informing about advancements and innovations, which garner higher efficiencies and yields. This revision certainly could only be undertaken by the experts of the particular processing steps and equipment.

I would like to express my sincere appreciation to the contributing authors of this book. Their expertise and experience contributed to this book is invaluable for me, and for the editors, and the pharmaceutical and biopharmaceutical end users searching for precious information and support. The contributions of these experts to this book establish an overview of know-how and necessary tips, important for manufacturing process requirements.

My thoughts and deepest gratitude go to my mentor and former co-editor/-author, Dr. Theodore H. Meltzer. Ted has been instrumental to my technology learning, the trainings given, and the writings published. I treasured the discussions we had, which were constant and starting as soon as we met. Filtration has been our passion and many probably wondered, how much one can talk, deliberate, examine, and interact about filtration. Well, for Ted and myself, it never stopped. Too many aspects of filtration are still unanswered and too many new facets were discovered. Ted had a never-ending inquisitive nature and brought it forward with ease to any potential source of information. His inquires, most commonly spiced with some sort of humor, were always answered with diligence and patience as one could not but like him. Unfortunately, Ted passed in 2011; as he would express, "one day I will go to the great Bubble Point." He is missed tremendously, as an expert and human!

I would like to recognize Hilary Lafoe and Jessica Poile of CRC Press/Taylor & Francis Group, our publisher, for their inexhaustible patience and support to accomplish this book.

Sincerely
Maik W. Jornitz, M.Eng.
Manorville, NY
May 2019

Summary

Filtration and Purification in the Biopharmaceutical Industry, Third Edition

This third edition greatly expands its focus with extensive new material on the critical role of purification and the significant advances in filtration science and technology. This new edition provides state-of-the-science information on all aspects of filtration and purification, including the current methods, processes, technologies and equipment, and brings you up-to-date with the latest industry standards and regulatory requirements for the pharmaceutical and biopharmaceutical industries. Additionally, it also includes new process technologies like single-use process equipment, which receives a high adoption rate.

An essential, comprehensive, source for all professionals involved in pharmaceutical and biopharmaceutical processing and compliance, this text

- Addresses recent biotechnology-related processes and advanced technologies, such as viral retentive filters, membrane chromatography, downstream processing, cell harvesting, single-use technologies, and media and buffer filtrations
- Presents detailed updates on the latest FDA and EMA regulatory requirements involving filtration and purification practices
- Describes current industry and supplier quality standards and validation requirements and provides guidance for compliance

Editor

Maik W. Jornitz is the President and CEO of G-CON Manufacturing Inc., and Principle Consultant of BioProcess Resources LLC., Jornitz has over 30 years of experience in separation, filtration and single-use technologies, process and facility designs, the related regulations and validation requirements respectively. His subject matter expertise in sterilizing grade filtration supports regulators as much as the industry. As a former member of the PDA Board of Directors (former Chair of the Board of Directors) and Chair of the Science Advisory Board (SAB), Jornitz has been part of multiple PDA task forces, for example the Technical Report # 26, #40, #41, #45, mycoplasma task forces, and Program Co-Chair for the 2008, 2013, and 2016 Annual Meeting and Co-Chair of the Aging Facility Task Force. He is also a member of the ISPE, ASTM, ASME E55, BPOG, and is a faculty member of PDA TRI and Global Compliance. Jornitz authored and co-authored over 100 scientific papers. He is co-editor and author of 10 books, including *Filtration and Purification in the Biopharmaceutical Industry*, published by Informa in 2008, *Sterile Filtration. A Practical Approach*, published by Marcel Dekker in 2001, and *Pharmaceutical Filtration*, published by PDA/DHI in 2006. He has contributed in total 15 chapters to various technical books, including the *Encyclopedia of Pharmaceutical Technology*, published by Marcel Dekker in 2002. He holds over 30 patents related to biopharmaceutical process equipment (single-use technology) and integrity testing. He received 5 distinguished author awards, 2 PDA Special Service, the Michael S. Korczynski, J. Agalocco, F. Carlton and Martin Van Trieste award, and he has been in the Medicine Maker top ten influencer list. He formerly worked for Sartorius Stedim in various positions for over 25 years, and he is Science Advisory Board member of Interphex and ICAV, and member of the Biotechnology Industry Council. Mr. Jornitz received his M.Eng. in Bioengineering at the University of Applied Sciences in Hamburg, Germany and accomplished the PED program at IMD Business School in Lausanne, Switzerland.

Contributors

Ross Acucena
GE Healthcare
Westborough, Massachusetts

James A. Akers
Akers & Kennedy
Kansas City, Missouri

Hazel Aranha
Sartorius Stedim North America, Inc.
Bohemia, New York

Todd E. Arnold
Cuno, Inc.
Meriden, Connecticut

Denise G. Bestwick
Validation Resources, LLC
Bent, Oregon

Uwe Beuscher
W. L. Gore & Associates, Inc.
Newark, Delaware

Carl Breuning
Sartorius Stedim North America, Inc.
Bohemia, New York

Raymond H. Colton
Validation Resources, LLC
Bent, Oregon

Robert S. Conway
Cuno, Inc.
Meriden, Connecticut

Michael Debes
W. L. Gore & Associates, Inc.
Newark, Delaware

Sherri Dolan
Sartorius Stedim North America, Inc.
Bohemia, New York

Michael Dosmar
Sartorius Stedim North America, Inc.
Bohemia, New York

Lynn P. Elwell
BioNetwork Capstone Learning Center
Wake Technical Community College
Cary, North Carolina

Uwe Gottschalk
Lonza AG
Basel, Switzerland

Olivier Guenec
Sartorius Biohit Liquid Handling Oy
Laippatie 1, 00880 Helsinki
Finland

Bryce Hartmann
W. L. Gore & Associates, Inc.
Newark, Delaware

Elisabeth Jander
Pall Corporation
Dreieich Germany

Maik W. Jornitz
G-CON Manufacturing, Inc.
College Station, Texas

Joseph Manfredi
GMP Systems, Inc.
Fairfield, New Jersey

Peter Makowenskyj
G-CON Manufacturing, Inc.
College Station, Texas

Susan Martin
Sartorius Stedim North America, Inc.
Bohemia, New York

Marc W. Mittelman
Mittelman and Associates, LLC
Brookline, Massachusetts

Eugene A. Ostreicher
Cuno, Inc.
Meriden, Connecticut

Steven Pinto
Sartorius Stedim North America, Inc.
Bohemia, New York

George T. Quigley
ErtelAlsop
Kingston, New York

Cherish Robinson
W. L. Gore & Associates, Inc.
Newark, Delaware

Scott Ross
W. L. Gore & Associates, Inc.
Newark, Delaware

Kirsten Jones Seymour
Sartorius Stedim North America, Inc.
Bohemia, New York

Magnus Andreas Stering
Sartorius Stedim SA
Aubagne, France

Paul S. Stinavage
Pfizer, Inc.
Kalamazoo, Michigan

Michael Wikol
W. L. Gore & Associates, Inc.
Newark, Delaware

1

Prefiltration in Biopharmaceutical Processes

George Quigley
ErtelAlsop

CONTENTS

Prefiltration Principles

Prefiltration can be described simply as any filtration step incorporated into a manufacturing process prior to the final filtration. The usual purpose in conducting pharmaceutical filtrations is to remove objectionable particles from a fluid drug preparation. In effecting such a purification there is a concern for the rate at which the filtration takes place, and the extent to which it proceeds before the retained particles block the filter's pores sufficiently to render further filtration so slow as to be impractical. An adequacy of particle removal is the principle goal. The rate of filtration and throughput are secondary considerations. Nevertheless, the accrual of particles on the final filter relative to its porosity and extent of filter surface determines the ongoing rate of filtration as well as its ultimate termination.

In practically all pharmaceutical and biotech processes, the final filter is a microporous membrane, which is manufactured from high-tech polymers. It is commercially available in pore size designations of $0.04-8\,\mu m$, and due to its mode of manufacture is of a narrow pore size distribution. Consequently, these filters presumably retain particles of sizes larger than their pore size ratings with great reliability,* the mechanism of particle retention being sieve retention or size exclusion. Being extremely effective at removing submicronic particles, they retain so thoroughly that with heavily loaded liquids they may not have a significant capacity to remove large volumes of particulates while maintaining sufficient fluid flow across the filter. More importantly, the more particulate matter with which the final filter is challenged and retained, the higher the differential pressure across the filter will become. This is undesirable because it is widely known that a filter performs at its highest particle retention efficiency when operated at low differential pressures (Δp). At a low Δp, the filter retains small particles through the mechanism of adsorptive sequestration. Lower operating pressure differentials will provide greater throughputs than will high Δp, because the higher pressure differentials tend to compress the filter cakes rendering them less permeable to liquids. The problem can be solved by the use of larger effective filter areas (EFAs). However, this entails the cost of the additional membrane filters. The use of prefilters accomplishes essentially the same purpose, but at a lesser expense.

In reality, therefore, the only reason for prefiltration is based on economic constraints. There are no particulate contaminants in a fluid stream that could not, at least in principle, be removed by the final sterilizing grade filter. However, the cost of filtration would increase significantly under this situation, due to the larger amount of final filtration area that would be required. Prefiltration, by this definition, is a more cost-effective means of removing the majority of the contaminants from the fluid stream prior to the final filter removing the remainder. It, therefore, becomes important to incorporate one or more levels of prefiltration so that the particulate challenge to the final filter is minimized, allowing it to operate at the highest level of efficiency.

Prefilters are not intended to be completely retentive (if they were, they would by definition be final filters). Prefilters are designed to accommodate only a portion of the particulate load, permitting the remainder to impinge upon the final filter. In the process, the life of the final filter is prolonged by the use of the prefilter, whose own service life is not unacceptably shortened in the process. Overall, the service life of the prefilter(s)/final filter assembly is extended to the point where the rate of fluid flow and its throughput volume meet practical process requirements.

Depth-type filters are usually used for prefiltrations. However, microporous membranes of higher pore size ratings may serve as prefilters for final filters of finer porosities. In such cases, it was best, however, that the liquid not be highly loaded, or that more extensive EFA be used to forestall premature filter blockage (Trotter et al., 2002; Jornitz et al., 2004).

Cellulose-Based Depth Filters

One of the most common prefilters used in biopharmaceutical processes is the cellulose-based depth filter, which is used in either a sheet format or in a lenticular cartridge format. These are very cost-effective prefilters due to the relatively inexpensive raw materials used in their manufacture and the

---

* This is a popular view of the pore size ratings. It is known, however, that the assigned numerical pore designations are not dimensional measurements. Among other factors, the particle shapes may importantly influence their capture.

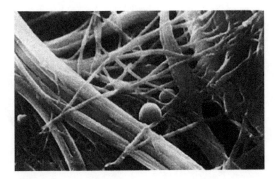

FIGURE 1.1 Cellulse fiber matrix.

thickness and structure of the filter matrix that is formed during the manufacturing process. The basic raw materials used in the production of these filters are cellulose fibers, inorganic filter aid, and a polymeric wet-strength resin (Figure 1.1).

Cellulose pulp is available as either hardwood or softwood. Hardwood is primarily comprised of short fibers, which provide a smooth filter sheet surface. However, the short fibers create a dense structure with minimal void volume. Softwood has a longer fiber structure, which provides greater void volumes and a mechanically stronger filter sheet with a rough surface.

The void volume of the cellulose and particle retention capacity of the cellulose component of the filter is controlled by refining the cellulose fibers. Pulling the fibers apart creates more and more surface area as the cellulose fibers are fibrillated to a lower freeness. Freeness is a measurement of the ability of water to flow through the fibers; the lower the freeness, the tighter the matrix of cellulose fibers and the smaller the particle retention capacity of the filter media.

The Filter Aid

The next primary component of the filter sheet is the filter aid. The overwhelming majority of filter sheets contain Diatomaceous Earth (DE) and/or Perlite as a filter aid (Figure 1.2). These two inorganic substances are naturally occurring and mined from deposits in various parts of the world.

Perlite is volcanic ash that has a glass-like, smooth structure. The particles are relatively homogeneous in shape and they form densely within the matrix of cellulose fibers. The powder is available in various particle sizes to provide a range of porosity.

FIGURE 1.2 Example of Perlite structure.

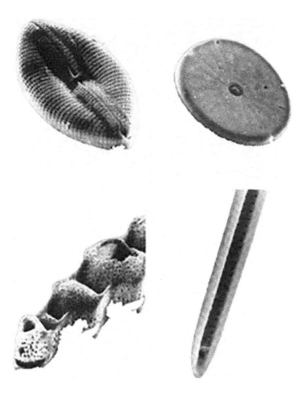

FIGURE 1.3   Diatoms in diatomaceous earth.

DE is comprised of diatoms, which are fossilized remains of plankton. The fresh water variety of this product contains less than 20 different diatoms, while salt water DE is made up of thousands of different species. This broad range of shapes creates a less dense matrix in the cellulose fibers and therefore a greater void volume in the filter sheet. The trade-off is that the variety of shapes creates a filter sheet with less mechanical strength than a sheet made with perlite. Like perlite, DE is available in a variety of grades for various particle retention capabilities (Figure 1.3).

The Wet-Strength Resin

The final component of the filter sheet is the wet-strength resin. This ingredient serves two purposes; the first is to hold the sheet together and the second is to impart a positive charge to the internal surfaces of the filter sheet. The positive charge is referred to as zeta-potential and it allows the filter to retain particles that are smaller than the pore size by attracting them to these positively charged sites (Figure 1.4).

The components can be mixed together in different ratios to affect the performance qualities of the filter sheet, the most important of which are flow capacity and particle retention. Cellulose-based filter sheets can provide effective particle retention down to 0.1 μm. The retention rating of depth filters is stated as a nominal value, essentially meaning that it will remove at least one particle of the stated size. Most manufacturers, however, provide the rating based upon a certain percentage of particles of the stated size under standard conditions. The rating is usually based upon the filter's ability to retain a fixed-size spherical particle at a constant differential pressure. In practice, most particles are not spherical and filtration studies should be carried out to define the ability of the filter to provide an acceptable filtrate.

FIGURE 1.4 Wet strength resin.

Retention Mechanisms

Sieve Retention

There are a number of retention mechanisms employed by depth filters. Among them are: sieving, inertial impaction, Brownian motion, and adsorption.

Sieving is the simplest form of particle retention, and results from the removal of particles that are larger than the pores that they are trying to pass through. The retention is independent of the number of particles or pores, and it is independent of the filtration conditions. For example, unless it is high enough to deform the suspended particle, the differential pressure does not affect the particle removal. The nature (polymeric) of the filter, as also that of the particle, is of no concern unless the physicochemistry of the fluid vehicle reduces the particle size or enlarges the pore size. Each of these is a real possibility under certain conditions (Figure 1.5).

The particle may be large enough to be retained at a pore entrance or it may become trapped at a restriction within the pore. If it is deformable; as the differential pressure increases it may become further embedded in the fiber matrix. It is conceivable that if the differential pressure gets high enough the particle could be forced through the pore restriction, deeper into the matrix, and possibly through the matrix back into the fluid stream. Therefore, it is very important to adhere to the pressure limitations as provided by the filter media manufacturer. There are practical limits to the thickness of the filter sheet. The thickness of the filter medium plays an important role in its particulate holding capacity;

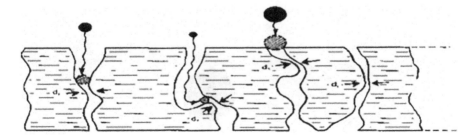

FIGURE 1.5 Sieve retention mechanism.

the thicker the sheet, the more likely the retention. However, depending upon the filter porosity, higher differential pressures may be required in the filtration. Filter manufacturers formulate filter sheets to a thickness sufficient to provide effective filtrations. Sheets that are unnecessarily thick will be too costly to dry following the vacuum formation step of their manufacture. Both economics and practicality are involved.

Inertial Impaction

The inertial impaction of a particle upon a filter surface can occur when the fluid bearing the particle changes its direction of flow as it is deflected into and through the filter pores. The inertia of the particle may continue it on its original path to collide with the filter surface where adsorptive forces can cause its arrest.

This inertial force depends directly upon the mass of the particle, and the square of its velocity. It is, therefore, more important with heavier particles. The inertial force is attenuated by the viscosity of the fluid and is consequently influenced by temperature that is inversely related to viscosity. For this reason, it is less effective in liquid than in gaseous contexts (Figure 1.6).

Brownian Motion

Smaller particles, less heavy, are less influenced by inertia. However, they are more affected by Brownian motion wherein they are vectored from the fluid pathway to the pore surface by collisions with the fluid's molecules (Figure 1.7). The result is retention of the particles by the filter surfaces they impact.

At all temperatures above absolute zero the various sections of all molecules are in constant motion: the various bonds being flexed, rotated, stretched, etc. The higher the temperature, the greater the amplitude of the molecular motion. The significance of absolute zero is that only at that temperature or below is all molecular movement frozen. In their frenetic activity, the fluid molecules collide, perhaps repeatedly, with suspended particles. The latter are directed to new directions of travel within the fluid stream. As a result of their induced random and erratic movements, the particles have opportunities to encounter pore surfaces. This is the nature of Brownian or diffusional interception. It is favored by small size particles, and by the lower viscosities of the suspending fluids.

Inertial impaction

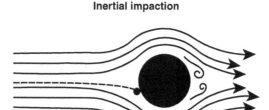

FIGURE 1.6　Intertial impaction separation mechanism.

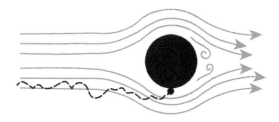

FIGURE 1.7　Brownian motion or diffusive separation.

Adsorptive Interactions

The donating of electrons by one atom, possibly already part of a molecule, to another, results in a strong bonding between the two atoms. This is the nature of the chemical bond. The same occurs from the sharing of electrons between two atoms. The atomic interactions resulting from electron sharing is called covalent bonding. By convention, electrons each represent a full negative charge. Thus, possessing more electrons than in its neutral state confers a negative charge upon an atom. Having fewer than the normal number of electrons in its possession gives an atom a plus or positive electrical charge. Opposite electrical charges attract one another and combine to form a valence or chemical bond. Similar electrical charges repel one another.

It is also possible for atoms, whether individual or as part of a molecular structure, to acquire a partial-electric charge.* The oppositely partially charged atoms can also combine to form a stable union, albeit weaker than the chemical bond just discussed. This is often referred to as a "physical" bond. It is similar in its electrical nature but involves only partial charges; it is weaker than the "chemical" bonds derived from full electrical charge interactions. The distinction between chemical and physical is one of degree. The motivating force is identical.

It is the partial charges that are mostly involved in adsorptions. In the case of particles being adsorptively bonded to filter surfaces, the partial charge on an atom constituting the particle surface interacts with an oppositely charged atom on the filter surface (pore wall). The result is the adsorption of one surface to the other. The particle adheres to the filter, and in the process is removed from the fluid stream that flows unimpeded through the filter pores.

Adsorption is the bonding of particulates to the surfaces of the pore walls of a filter by any of several electrical charge phenomena. Often referred to as electrokinetic forces, these may be in the nature of strong plus charges resident on a quaternary nitrogen atom that is part of a molecular grouping. This is the case of the depth filters here considered. The adsorptive interaction between the particle surface and the pore surface is accomplished via the electrokinetic charge on the wet-strength resin which is used to cross-link the cellulose fibers. Its plus charge connects with partial-negative charges on the particle surfaces. This enables the removal of particles smaller than the filter pores by bonding them to the oppositely plus-charged nitrogen atoms of the resin molecules that are components of the depth filter surface (Figure 1.8). In this manner, particles smaller than the pores are rendered immobile by their adsorption to the resin molecules; they are not removed from the fluid stream by sieve retention.

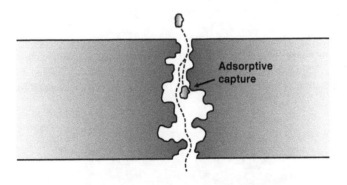

FIGURE 1.8 Adsorptive capture within the torterous path.

---

* Partial charges derive from several causes: hydrogen bonding; van der Waal forces; dipoles, both permanent and induced; hydrophobic adsorptions; etc. The various influences, e.g., zeta potential, ionic strengths, Debye lengths, etc. that are operative in the double electric layer phenomenon may be involved. (Please refer to Meltzer and Jornitz [2006] for details and references.)

Charge-Modified Filters

The resin with its quaternary nitrogen atom is in effect a charge-modified filter. There are, of course, limitations to the use of charge-modified filters. Their performance is stoichiometric in character. Their removal efficiency is strongly dependent upon the encounters between the charged sites fixed on the filter surface and the oppositely charged particles being carried by the flowing fluid. It is heavily influenced by the rate of flow, particularly as the charged sites become increasingly occupied. The performance is limited by the finite capacity of the charge entities. Breakthrough becomes increasingly possible as the number of the charge sites decreases. Thus, where adsorption is dependent on quaternary charge sites, the filter's ability to remove particles through this adsorption mechanism is exhausted when all the fixed-charge sites are occupied. Any additional particles smaller than the pore sizes will pass through the filter and into the filtrate. The use of charge-modified filters is an important technique but requires careful operations.

Activated Carbon

Activated carbon presents an enormous extent of surface for the adsorptive interactions leading to the removal of many different types of impurities. Activated carbon is prepared by the thermal degradation of carboniferous materials in an atmosphere limited in its oxygen content. It has strong adsorptive capacities. This is a consequence of its enormous surface area when in finely divided form. Additionally, the thermal decomposition in a restricted oxygen atmosphere introduces certain oxygenated molecules onto the carbon's surface that are conducive to adsorptions. This furnishes an impressive extent of surface area for adsorptive interactions leading to the removal of many different types of impurities (Figure 1.9).

As such, activated carbon is commonly used for the removal of metal catalysts in conjunction with a horizontal plate filter. It serves as well for the removal of organic substances, and of color-bearing (chromophoric) molecules.

The use of finely divided activated carbon risks its undesired dissipation throughout a filtration system. Its fine size makes easy its distribution by the flowing fluid. Its use requires careful management. One option is to utilize filter sheets containing activated carbon used as an ingredient in the formulation of the filter medium. This can eliminate the use of loose powdered carbon, but the lower amounts present in the filter sheets may offer a more restricted capacity.

Filter Forms

Cellulose-based depth filters are available in three configurations, single-use capsules, flat sheets, and lenticular cartridges. These three configurations are used in capsule chassis; plate and frame filter presses, and filter housings, respectively. Plate and frame filters have been used for over 100 years and

FIGURE 1.9   Active carbon filter pads.

provide the ability to build and wash filter cakes. They utilize flat sheets which are less expensive than lenticular cartridges by a factor of approximately 5:1 based on cost per unit area of filtration.

The plate and frame filter requires the opening and closing of the filter in order to load and unload the filter sheets, and this is time-consuming and the design tends to leak. Plate and frame filters are available in either an internally ported or externally ported design (Figure 1.10).

With an externally ported filter press the filter sheet has no holes and the flow channels are external to the filter plate dimension. This requires the use of eyelet gaskets to seal the flow port channels. The individual sheets must also be sealed between the plates and frames which mean that there are five independent sealing surfaces between each plate (Figure 1.11).

Internally ported filter presses have holes in the filter sheets and the flow channels are internal of the plate and frame. This design will have less active filtration area than an externally ported filter with the same plate dimension. However, due to the internal ports, only the filter sheet is required to be sealed between each plate and frame (Figure 1.12).

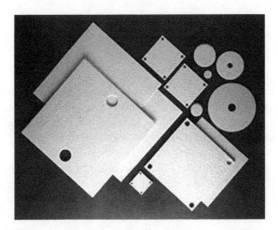

FIGURE 1.10   Plate and frame filters.

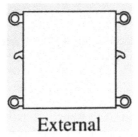

FIGURE 1.11   Externally ported filter sheet.

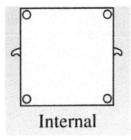

FIGURE 1.12   Internally ported filter sheets.

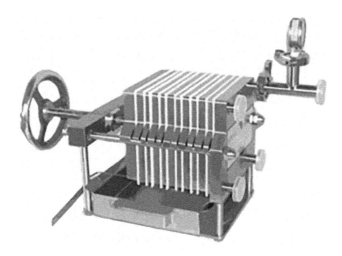

FIGURE 1.13   Plate filter press.

Filter presses are commonly used in the Cohn fractionation process to collect precipitated paste, which is subsequently washed with a solvent to resolubilize the precipitate for further processing. Plate and frame filters are also used in the filtration of oral syrups and other pharmaceutical preparations that are manufactured in high volumes and have relatively low value per unit volume.

Another type of plate filter is the horizontal plate filter which can use filter paper or filter sheets, and is commonly used for catalyst recovery in active pharmaceutical ingredient applications.

Use of the horizontal plate filter is even more labor intensive than the open vertical plate and frame filter. It consists of a plate stack that is assembled outside of a vessel and held together with tie-rods that are tightened around the outside diameter of the stack. The assembled unit must then be hoisted in the air and lowered into the vessel where it is secured in place. The vessel is closed and the filtration process can commence (Figure 1.13).

Lenticular Configuration

The lenticular configuration was introduced in the 1940s by Alsop Engineering, and was specifically designed to provide an enclosed version of the plate and frame filter that was easier to change than a horizontal plate filter.

Lenticular filter cartridges are available in three nominal diameters, 8, 12, and 16 in. The cartridges are made up of a series of cells that are stacked on top of one another with plastic rings between them to prevent bypass between the cells. Endcaps are then placed at the top and bottom of the assembly and held in place with either stainless steel straps or a polypropylene core. The endcaps can be provided to accept either flat gaskets or dual O-rings (Figure 1.14).

The filter housings that these filters are placed in are available in vertical or horizontal orientations and can hold up to 20 cartridges. The two primary advantages of this design are the enclosed aspect of the operation, and the ease of filter replacement between batches. This makes the lenticular design very popular in the filtration of many pharmaceutical and biotech products (Figure 1.15).

Single-Use Disposable Devices

A more recent development in fermentation processing is the use of disposable filter devices in the several steps from the bioreactor through the final fill. These filters are also finding their way into more traditional pharmaceutical manufacturing process, given the ease of disposal and reduction in cleaning validation requirements. Disposable depth filters are available for use in these systems in different formats such as encapsulated lenticular filters and cassettes.

FIGURE 1.14 Lenticular filter units.

FIGURE 1.15 Lenticular filter housing.

Fibrous Materials

Glass Fibers

The type of filtration applications utilizing depth filters is large and varied. Use is made of fibers of many compositions in addition to the cellulosic prefilters. Glass fibers find application in serum filtrations. These include borosilicate glass fibers, some with special coatings such as of nitrocellulose polymers. These coatings are very effective in the removal by adsorption of process impurities, especially of protein-like matter, and of lipids. The nitrated polymer likely performs its adsorptive removal of impurities through the agency of hydrogen bonding.

Polypropylene

Polypropylene fibers are widely used. They can be formed into fleeces and mats of various fiber diameters that are bonded together and are permanently cross-linked by heat, being joined by melting, to minimize or eliminate media migration. The melt-spinning method of permanently fixing the fibers to one another, satisfactory in its own right, replaced the adhesives and mechanical manipulations of earlier and less effective methods of mat formation. In turn, the melt-blown technique now supersedes even this fabrication of polypropylene fleeces by varying the mean fiber size during the fashioning of the prefilter. This enables the progressive changing of the mat's pore size while it is being constructed. The result is a highly graded asymmetric composition having a constant packing density. One advantage is that, in effect, a series of prefilters is combined into the making of the single prefilter composite. The asymmetric morphology provides less resistance to flows, requires lower differential pressures in their operations, provides for the accommodation of higher particle loadings, and offers greater particle removal due to the efficiency of thinner fibers. Fibers of diameters as small as $0.3\,\mu m$ in their mean size provide the retention of particles from a fluid stream down to $1\,\mu m$ in size. The graded pore size format is derived by decreasing the fiber diameters rather than by increasing the mat's density by tighter packing. This enhances the prefilter porosity and provides the additional advantages of lower operational differential pressures, and larger load accommodations.

Examples of Applications

The use of prefilters is applied to numerous applications; indeed, almost universally in process filtrations, so helpful is the beneficial effect of prefiltration. Following are some examples of applications wherein prefiltration plays an important role.

Active Pharmaceutical Ingredients

Depth filters are primarily utilized in two locations in active pharmaceutical ingredients (API) processes, namely, catalyst removal, and as prefilters to final membrane filtration. In many API applications, activated carbon is used to remove metal catalysts. The activated carbon can be added as a loose powder retained on the surface of a filter paper or depth filter sheet. Or the activated carbon can be included in the depth filter formulation to eliminate the use of the loose powder. In this application, contact time with the carbon is the most critical factor in achieving a successful filtration. This can be accomplished by maintaining low flow rates per unit filtration area and low differential pressures across the filter. The activated carbon adsorbs the metal ions remaining after the catalysis. The catalyst and its value are recovered after the process is complete.

Another application into which depth filters are incorporated into a filtration step is prior to crystallization of the API. In this phase of the process, the depth filter is used as a prefilter to a membrane filter. Its primary purpose is to protect the membrane filter from fouling during the processing of the entire batch. This is usually performed using a lenticular cartridge configuration upstream of the membrane (Figure 1.16).

Blood/Plasma Products

Filtrations perform a very necessary function in the preparation of therapeutic blood proteins. The practice has a three-part purpose, namely, to clarify the filtrate, to remove particulates in the prefiltration stage that might otherwise block the final filter, and to sterilize filtratively the treated preparation.

Let us first consider the need for clarification. An example of such a requirement occurs at the end of the Fraction IV centrifugation; the precipitate is found not to be removed with complete efficiency. The supernatant solution does contain suspended matter; nephelometry is used to determine the extent. Filtration with depth-type filters is resorted to in order to achieve clarity.

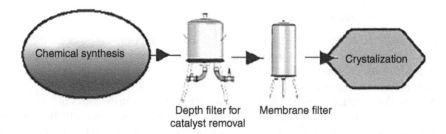

FIGURE 1.16 Depth and membrane filters incorporated into a filtration step prior to crystallization of the API.

The depth-type filters most commonly used are the positive charge-induced prefilters, those having positive zeta potentials; mixed esters of cellulose-coated paper prefilters; and course and/or fine glass fiber layers, in conjunction with a $0.8\,\mu m$-rated microporous membrane consisting of a vinyl acrylate copolymer coating deposited on a nylon or polyester mat support. Filter aids, in particular DE, are often used in conjunction with the prefilter treatment to increase the dirt-holding capacity of the filter system.

Pretreatment and Prefiltration

In large-volume parenteral filtrations, prefilter action is often the key to successful filter operations. This is particularly true where heavily laden liquids, such as serum and plasma, are concentrated. The particulate load is best reduced by pretreatments involving adsorbents, such as DE, or finely divided fumed silica, followed by depth-type prefiltration, before the liquid is permitted to encounter the final, sterilizing microporous membrane filter. Otherwise, premature clogging of that filter will occur.

The purpose of the pretreatments is to present large surface areas on which adsorption and impurity retention may occur. Hence, the use of fumed silica, a finely divided particulate material especially suited for removing lipids and lipoproteins (Condie and Toledo-Pereyra, 1976). The depth-type prefilters likewise offer large surface areas for impurity depositions, e.g., fiberglass prefilters. Additionally, however, prefilters consisting of mixed esters of cellulose coatings on paper (cellulose fiber mats) promote purifying adsorptive sequestrations through hydrogen bonding to their nitro group moiety, as stated above. Positive charge-modified depth filters are especially suitable as prefilters in serum/plasma prefiltration. They offer positive-charged sites for particle capture, as well as large surface areas for particle adsorption. In consequence, asbestos filters, previously used extensively, are now at least partially successfully substituted for with success by the charge-modified depth filters (Holst et al., 1978).

Pretreatment Agents

Fiori et al. (1980) describe successful applications of pretreatments and prefiltrations relative to therapeutic blood protein preparation. Fumed silica and DE are used as pretreatment aids. The fumed silica (Degussa Aerosil) has a surface area of 200 m^2/g, diatomite a surface area of approximately 2 m^2/g. Condie and Toledo-Pereyra (1976) advise that lipoproteins, triglycerides, cholesterol, fibrinogen, and the plasminogen-plasmin system present in 1 L of plasma are adsorbed onto 40 g of fumed silica within a contact time of 60 min. This is significant, because Olson and Faith (1978) report that lipoproteins serve to clog microporous filters. Similarly, fibrinogen has a clogging action on such membranes, particularly as it may form fibrous deposits of fibrin in the operation of the blood-clotting mechanism. The adsorptive pre-removal of these substances renders more practicable subsequent filtration of plasma/serum. Diatomite has long been utilized in the pretreatment of plasma (Cohn et al., 1946). Depending on how heavily laden the plasma/serum is, how difficult it is to filter, from 2.5 to 5 g are used per liter of the liquid. Removal of the silica or diatomite can be effected in several ways, such as by filtration utilizing prefilters of the type herein discussed. The efficiency of such "filter aid" pretreatments is judged by the clarity of the plasma/serum filtrate as determined by nephelometry (Cohn et al., 1946; Holst et al., 1978).

Prefilters for Plasma/Serum

As stated in a separate chapter in this text, the development of positive charge-modified prefilters permitted the replacement of asbestos filters for the prefiltrative purification of plasma/protein, the handling of asbestos having become interdicted by the Environmental Protective Agency on account of the carcinogenicity of certain of its manifestations.

Cohn Fraction IV4 supernatant is a material that usually requires clarifications not easily achieved. Sheet filtration has often been relied on for this purpose. According to Fiori et al. (1980), Seitz 1 micron sheets in a plate-and-frame arrangement, $2 ft^2$ of surface per 40–45 L of supernatant IV4, do the job. Fiori et al., also list Ertel, Cellulo, and Alsop filter media as being essentially equivalent. In a typical operation, the plate-and-frame arrangement is prerinsed with 40% aqueous ethanol solution at –5°C; some $5 L/ft^2$ of filter pad are used. Filtration of the supernatant fraction IV4 is then commenced at a differential pressure of 5–7 psi or less. DE in the amount of 2.5–5 g/L of supernatant Fraction IV4 may be added to the rinse solution to form a precoat on the pads. Also, a similar amount of diatomite may be stirred into the supernatant fraction IV4 itself. Since such filter pad constructions inevitably exhibit filter medium migration, the filtrate that issues initially is refiltered, such as by recycling, to have the fibers that were set loose in the filtration removed by the pad filter action. The temperature during this filtration is kept at –5°C.

Substitution of a positive charge-modified prefilter, such as one composed of cellulose and diatomite in the charge-modified form, is comparably effective in its clarifying action (Holst et al., 1978). The charge-modified prefilter is prerinsed with water for injection to which 2.5–5 g of diatomite is added per liter of supernatant fraction IV4 to be filtered. (A diatomaceous precoat is thus formed on the prefilter surface.) Some 7 L of prerinse is used per square foot of prefilter surface. To the fraction IV4 supernatant is then added 2.5 L of diatomite, and filtration, using a bell housing is, performed at an applied differential pressure of approximately 5–7 psi at –5°C. About 1000 L can be filtered through a prefilter cartridge of $11 ft^2$ of effective filtration area.

Holst et al. (1978) report that using suitable pore size-rated positive charge-modified prefilters supernatant fraction IV1, ordinarily difficult to clarify, can be treated effectively, 40 L being processed per square foot of filter. Similarly, fraction IV4 and fraction V paste, reconstituted to a strength of 5% protein after lyophilization to remove residual alcohol, and subsequent to certain processing steps, can be filtered at –5°C and pH 7.1 to an extent of $15 L/ft^2$ of filter surface at an applied differential pressure of about 10 psi. The clarity of the filtrate is thus improved to 10 nephelometric units from 40 in the unfiltered feedstock.

Prefilters of fiberglass, are reported to be effective for plasma/serum, particularly so for the removal of denatured proteins, and lipoproteins, especially of the beta and pre-beta varieties. For this reason, pleated cartridge constructions of a course glass fiber upstream of a fine glass fiber are widely used as plasma/serum prefilters.

Serum Filtration

In one example of serum filtration, the serum is first treated prefiltratively with DE. A cake is made of the diatomite in a 273-mm Buchner funnel. The formation of this filter cake is an artful practice. If the cake is too tightly packed, the rate of plasma flow may be too slow, and the throughput may become abbreviated by premature clogging of the small pores of the compacted cake. If the cake is too open, insufficient adsorptive purification of the serum may result. Such a "Jello" cake is undesirable. It yields a cloudy serum filtrate where clarity is being sought. In accordance with adsorptive purifications, the thicker the diatomite cake, the greater the product clarity, but also the larger the loss of expensive serum by inclusion within the cake.

The proper cake formation of the DE slurry, and its mode of distribution within the Buchner funnel, are all important. The successful exercise of building a cake of the desired consistency is one based largely on experience. Its purpose is to remove lipids, triglycerides, lipoprotein, and cholesterol from the serum.

The temperature of the filtration is important. The serum is usually maintained at 2°C–8°C, but may be kept at room temperature during filtration, depending on the concerns regarding organism growth. The rate of filtration is about 18 L over a 20-min period.

Following treatment with the filter aid, the clarified serum is prefiltered through successive disks of extra thick fiberglass, namely, 2 μm-rated and 1.2 μm-rated fiberglass. Membrane filtration is then undertaken using 0.8 μm-rated, and 0.45 μm-rated membrane filters in series. The first 10 L of effluent serum are recycled.

The filtered serum usually contains fewer than 100 organisms per milliliter, as determined by the pour-plate technique using blood agar. The organisms of concern are the *E. coli, Pseudomonas*, and possibly other in-plant flora. In order to stabilize the filtered serum, proprietary preservatives, such as sodium azide, and broad-range antibiotics are added. Lyophilization of the serum serves to increase its shelf life.

Plate-and-Frame Filtration of Serum

Plate-and-frame assemblies utilizing cellulose pads have been used to remove the lipid and lipoprotein components prior to membrane filtration. A 20-plate assembly has sufficed to filter some 200 L of serum; 10 L of serum being factored per plate. Prior to the introduction of the serum, the plate assembly is prewashed with saline, sodium citrate solution, or whatever liquid is appropriate to that particular serum application; an air blowdown of the press to eliminate as much as possible of the washing solution follows; serum filtration is then commenced. The first quantities of serum collected are recycled to minimize the diluting effect of the remainder of the prewash solution.

Plasma Fractionation

Blood plasma can be separated into several components for therapeutic products. Many plasma processors use the Cohn Fractionation process to separate the various components. This procedure selectively precipitates out certain components while allowing others to stay in solution. The residual "paste," which is typically retained in a plate and frame filter press fitted with filter paper, contains the precipitated fractions. The precipitates are then resolubilized with a washing procedure and recollected for further processing. This method is used on each of the plasma fractions in a similar fashion. Depth filters are also used as prefilters to sterilizing grade filters prior to the final fill. Once again the depth filter is used to remove the majority of the remaining particulate to protect the sterilizing filter and prevent it from fouling (Figure 1.17).

Cohn Fractionation Procedure

Human plasma is collected and is immediately frozen to minimize compositional alterations and bacterial growth. Testing of the collected plasma is conducted to ensure its freedom from such infections as hepatitis, syphilis, etc. The variously collected plasma is then thawed and pooled in a holding tank at 4°C ± 1°C. A crypoprecipitate is formed and is separated by centrifugation. It contains the antihemophilic factor (AHF), fibronectin (cold-insoluble globulins), and fibrinogen.

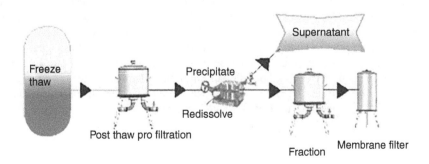

FIGURE 1.17 Plasma fractionation example.

The cryo-poor plasma pool is then adjusted with regard to pH, and cold ethanol is added to a specific concentration. The pH is usually 7.4 ± 0.2, the alcohol concentration 8%, and the temperature $-2°C \pm 0.5°C$. This treatment yields a fraction I precipitate, and a supernatant I.

Treatment of supernatant I with 20% ethanol at pH 6.8–6.9 at $-5°C \pm 1.0°C$ yields fraction II and III precipitate plus supernatant II and III. Adjustment of the pH of supernatant to 5.2 ± 0.1 at $-5°C \pm 1°C$ results in fraction IV precipitate. If treated at pH 5.9 ± 0.05 at the same temperature with ethanol at 40%, the fraction IV4 followed by pH adjustment to 4.6–4.8 at $-5°C \pm 0°C$ and the addition of ethyl alcohol at 40% yields fraction V as a precipitate along with the supernatant V.

Another common procedure for obtaining the plasma protein fractions is to combine fractions I, II, and III at 20% ethanol, fractions IV1 and IV4 at 40% alcohol, and fraction V at 40% alcohol. The point being made is that there are variations of the original Cohn Fractionation that are practiced.

Albumin

In essence, fraction V is crude human albumin. It contains salts and residual alcohol. It is dissolved in distilled water, and made up to 10% ethanol concentration at pH 4.6–4.8 at $-3°C \pm 1°C$. It is then passed through a depth filter to remove any extraneous, insoluble proteins. The filtered solution is readjusted with alcohol to 40% strength at pH $5.2 + 0.1$ at $-6°C \pm 1°C$. A supernatant is removed by centrifugation to leave a precipitate of albumin.

The reworked albumin precipitate is dissolved in distilled water, prefiltered through 3–8 μm-rated depth filters, and final filtered through 0.2 μm-rated membranes. The albumin solution is then concentrated, usually by one of three methods, namely, lyophilization followed by reconstitution with sterile water, by thin-film evaporation, or by ultrafiltration. Where lyophilization and reconstitution are utilized, the resulting nonsterile bulk solution is stabilized and again filtratively sterilized by passage through depth and final filters into a final sterile bulk tank. Where thin-film evaporation is used, the resulting fraction V precipitate is dissolved in distilled water, stabilized, and clarified by use of prefilters before being subjected to the thin-film evaporator. Following this, the concentrated solution is again prefiltered and final filtered through a sterilizing membrane. Where ultrafiltration is employed as the means of concentration, the procedure is the same except that ultrafiltration is substituted for the thin-film evaporator.

The sterile bulk albumin preparations are assayed for suitability in terms of their protein concentrations, sterility, non-pyrogenicity, pH, purity, turbidity, and safety; after which they are sterile-filled into their final containers subject to QC release and submission to the Bureau of Biologics.

In one operation wherein albumin is prepared in 5% and 25% strengths, some 700 L of the preparation is sterilized by filtration through a steam autoclaved, 0.2 μm-rated membrane filter at an applied differential pressure of 20–25 psi maximum. Cotton plugs are used as the vent filters on the tanks.

Factor 9

AHP-poor plasma at $3°C–9°C$ is freed of sodium and other salts, for example, by electrodialysis. The pH is adjusted to just below neutral and the temperature is maintained at $5°C \pm 2°C$. An ion-exchange resin is mixed into the plasma to bind the coagulation factors II, VII, IX, and X. The resin with its adsorbed coagulation factors is separated in a basket-type centrifuge. The resin is then suspended and washed with buffer of pH 6.7 ± 0.1 and placed into a column. Elution is then made from the ion exchanger using cold buffer. The eluted fractions containing the coagulation factors are filtered through a 0.2 μm-rated filter and bottled for storage in frozen condition. Concentration of the frozen factor 9 solution can be had by permitting its thawing to $3°C–5°C$ followed by ultrafiltration. Its pH is adjusted to 6.5–7.0, and it is prefiltered through mixed esters of cellulose-coated paper prior to its filtrative sterilization through a 0.2 μm-rated membrane to yield the sterile bulk solution of factor 9.

Oral Syrups

In the filtration of oral syrups, the depth filter is used to clarify the solution prior to filling and is generally followed by a cartridge filter to protect from any particulate that might pass through the depth filter.

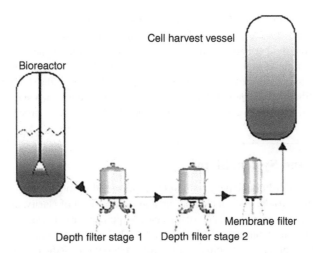

Cell harvest vessel

Bioreactor

Membrane filter

Depth filter stage 1   Depth filter stage 2

FIGURE 1.18   Cell harvest filtration.

Fermentation Solutions

Particulate from bioreactor offloads can be significant and broad in particle size. The particle size is largely a function of the cell type used in the fermentation process. For instance, with mammalian cells, there is a component of the cell debris that is 6–12 μm in size and another in the 0.5–2 μm range. This creates a need for multiple stages of separation. In some instances, a centrifuge will be placed at the outlet of the bioreactor, followed by a depth filter to remove the remainder of the particulate for protection of the chromatography stage. The other option is to use two stages of depth filters to effectively remove the wide range of particle sizes (Figure 1.18).

Depth filters can also reduce virus levels in process streams and are very effective in prolonging the life of virus removal membrane filters.

Filter Selection

When selecting an appropriate prefilter, the following characteristics should be considered:

- The ability to protect downstream processes and final filters
- Chemical compatibility of the filter
- Thermal characteristics of the process

Cellulose-based depth filter sheets are capable of withstanding temperatures in excess of 300°F (150°C). However, when configured in a lenticular cartridge the polypropylene components limit the thermal stability of the filter to that of the polypropylene or other polymer that may be used.

A filter that is chemically compatible with the process fluid is one that will maintain its integrity and structure under the process conditions of the application. Most filter manufacturers provide chemical compatibility information, but trials should always be performed to assure suitability of the filter in the fluid to be filtered. Tests to make this determination could be a soak test for an extended period of time at the process temperature or a forward flow test with the unfiltered fluid under conditions that are the same as the process. Following a soak test the mechanical strength of the filter can be tested, or it can be placed in a filter holder and tested for particle retention efficiency. When running a forward flow test the filtrate can be tested for quality. Of course, if the filter sheet falls apart following the test or pieces of the filter are found in the soak fluid or the filtrate, the filter should be deemed to be incompatible with the fluid under the current process conditions.

By its definition, a prefilter should remove sufficient particulate from the feed stream to protect the downstream filters for the duration of the entire batch. This can be determined by performing a particle analysis of the unfiltered fluid stream and then running trials with a filter sheet that fits the profile of the particle analysis. That filtered liquid should then be processed through the appropriate filter in the next stage of processing to assure the device will be adequately protected for the duration of the batch. If the particle size distribution is wide enough it may be necessary to include two stages of prefiltration, or a prefilter to the prefilter, in order to effectively prepare the fluid for the next process stage.

Filtration Trials and System Sizing

Choosing the proper depth filter and determining the required filtration area can be accomplished using basic laboratory filtration trials. First decide on the appropriate level of clarity, and then choose a grade of filter medium that should provide this clarity, as based upon either particle distribution data or manufacturer's recommendation. A number of filter grades might be evaluated before a selection is made. A minimum amount of the preparation being readied for processing is dedicated to trial testing. Properly performed, such evaluating tests can provide the data necessary to ensure the correct size filtration system for full-scale production. Determine how much effective filtration area is required to perform the testing. The smaller the EFA, the less product need be expended to complete the testing. If the area of filter medium is too small, surface tension effects may result. A 47-mm diameter filter disk is a common trial- size for flat filter media. In a 47-mm diameter housing (i.e., 13.5 cm^2 of filtration area) every milliliter of product filtered can equate with 0.8 L/m^2 of throughput in the production mode using appropriately larger filters.

The selection by trial can next be made of the filter medium in terms of porosity. The choice of a membrane filter of the correct pore size rating can be determined by testing several different possibilities. If necessary, compatibility can be assayed using membranes of different polymeric composition.

Cellulose-based depth filters can be formulated with a variety of filter materials, allowing for multiphase separations. As mentioned, if the primary goal of the filtration is color or catalyst removal, use a carbon-based filter medium or an activated carbon treatment step in union with the filtration. For haze removal, DE-containing filter pads may provide the best results. Finally, for basic, general particulate removal, almost any formulation of filter pad can be used. Pretest by first utilizing small volumes, approximately 50 mL, of unfiltered liquid through the filter to determine whether the grade of medium is capable of providing the clarity, often measured in NTU (Nephelometric Turbidity Units), that the process specifications require. The coarsest or highest flowing filter medium that fits this criterion, should be chosen for its suitability for scale-up testing.

In the struggle between productivity and the optimal ability of the filter to remove particulate, productivity usually wins. The lower the differential pressure during filtration, the longer the filter life will be in terms of total volume filtered per unit area; also, the more efficient the filter medium will be. However, most production processes operate under time and cost constraints. Thus, the operating pressures in the scaled-up process will be greater than the ideal lowest possible pressure. For realistic results, many filtration tests are conducted at approximately 10 psi (0.8 bar) to provide some balance between the two. Pressure can be supplied by a constant supply of compressed air or by a pump operating at a constant flow that can be set to supply 10 psi of pressure. This method is acceptable with any low viscosity liquid. However, maintaining acceptable flow rates with liquids of viscosities higher than 100 centipoises, requires a more practical approach. Either an increase in pressure during the testing or choosing a filtration device with a larger effective filtration area should be resorted to.

The bench scale trial testing should be considered finished when flow through the filter essentially stops or no longer conforms to a desired rate. During the testing, the length of time required to perform the filtration should be noted. When the testing is completed, two important informational items should be available, namely, the total throughput, i.e., the amount of liquid that has passed through the filter. This will provide the volume per unit filtration area, using that specific filter media under the stipulated test conditions of temperature, pressure, particulate content in the unfiltered liquid, and the fluid viscosity. The other important factor determined will be the flow capacity per unit area, or flux rate.

These two calculations will allow the user to determine the filtration area and amount of time required to filter the entire production batch.

Batch sizing: $At = 1/T \times V_b$ or flow rate sizing: $At = 1/F_x \times F_s$ where: At = total required system filtration area; T = throughput; V_b = volume of batch; F_x = flux rate and F_s = system flow rate. The two numbers rarely coincide; the more critical of the two most often determines the size of the filtration system required.

The same approach can be taken for the optimization of preexisting filtration processes. If the current processes have not been addressed in many years, and are still operating under their original conditions, parameters may have changed. A new experimental investigation may disclose potential improvements. Perhaps EFA, the filtration area can be reduced; filtration costs saved, or faster batch times yielded. The trials can be performed at the end user's site, at the supplier's local technical service facility, or at the filter medium manufacturer's laboratory. Attempts at updating processing operations merit encouragement.

REFERENCES

Cohn AJ, Strong LE, Hughes WL Jr., Mulford DJ, Ashworth JN, Melin N, Taylor HL. A system for the separation into fractions of the protein and lipoprotein components of biological tissues and fluids. *J Am Chem Soc* 1946: 68:459–475.

Condie RM, Toledo-Pereyra LH. Fibrinogen-Free Plasminogen Plasmin-Free Plasma and Method of Preparing Same. U.S. Patent 1976, 3998946.

Fiori JV, Olson WP, Holst SL. Depth Filtration. In: Curling JM, ed. *Methods of Plasma Protein Fractionation.* New York: Academic Press, 1980.

Holst SM, Martinez M, Zarth B. Alternatives to asbestos in Cohn fractionation. *J Parenter Drug Assoc* 1978: 32(1):15–21.

Jornitz MW, Meltzer TH. Sterilizing filtrations with microporous membranes. *Pharmacopeial Forum* 2004: 30(5):2–9.

Meltzer TH, Jornitz MW. *Pharmaceutical Filtration: The Management of Organism Retention.* PDA-DHI Publishers, Bethesda, MD, 2006.

Olson WP, Faith MW. Lipoprotein removal from serum and plasma by membrane filtration. *Prep Biochem* 1978: 8(5):378–386.

Trotter AM, Rodriguez PJ, Thoma LA. The usefulness of 0.45 µm-rated filter membranes. *Pharm Technol* 2002: 26(4):60–71.

2

Charge-Modified Filter Media

Eugene A. Ostreicher, Todd E. Arnold, and Robert S. Conway
Cuno, Inc.

CONTENTS

Introduction

This chapter focuses on filtration developments, specifically charged filter media, as applied to primarily pharmaceutical and beverage applications. There are many examples where the use of charged filter media has been applied to additional fluid purification areas including microelectronic integrated circuit manufacture (Stone and Parekh, 1993), wastewater remediation (Hagg, 1998), water treatment (Mika et al., 1999), and others. Several reviews addressing the charged filtration media development and implementation are available in the literature (Zeman and Zydney, 1996). Further, the use of charge-enhanced media has been applied to nearly the full range of filtration types, encompassing microfiltration, ultrafiltration, nanofiltration, and even reverse osmosis membranes (Ebersold and Zydney, 2004). Charged media has also been used in "non filtration" applications such as chromatographic separation (Zhou and Tressel, 2006).

Early developments to improve upon filter media comprising naturally occurring materials involved investigations to create synthetic filter media or "engineered" filter media consisting of natural components. The need to develop synthetic filter media was driven by requirements generated by the beverage and pharmaceutical industries. Prior to 1960s, pharmaceutical and beverage products were clarified or sterilized using filter media composed of cellulose and asbestos. Asbestos-containing filters were used extensively in the sterile filtration of many pharmaceutical products, particularly biological products (e.g., fractionated blood products). Even after the advent of sterilizing membrane filters in the early 1950s, cellulose-asbestos prefilters were found necessary to reduce the contaminant loading on the membranes. In the production of fractionated blood products, the use of asbestos filters was uniquely critical for the removal of lipids, denatured protein, and bacterial endotoxins (pyrogens). The use of these filters dates back to a paper by Cohn et al. (1946) on the fractionation of human blood, the basis for what is now a major health industry. In the alcoholic beverage industry, cellulose-asbestos sheet media, or asbestos-based filter precoat mixtures, were used for final polishing and sterilization (Rose, 1977). In the late 1960s, asbestos was being recognized as a potential health hazard and the drive to develop non-asbestos-containing filter media was born. Although the link to pulmonary disease was associated with inhalation of aerosolized fibers of asbestos (Selikoff and Lee, 1968), elimination of this material from filter media used for liquid filtration applications was being pursued. In 1973, the Food and Drug Administration (FDA) 23 proposed restrictions on the use of asbestos filters in the manufacture of parenteral drugs (FDA, 1973) and issued appropriate regulations in 1975 (FDA, 1975, 1976).

Charge-Modified Depth Filter Development

Most early (pre-1950) filter media consisted of natural materials such as cellulose and other fibers. These filter media were manufactured by mechanical means such as vacuum formed wet laydown methods to produce relatively thick filter sheets. This type of filter media is known as "depth filtration media" to distinguish it from more recent filter developments of membrane or surface filters involving precipitation of organic polymers.

It had long been recognized that adsorptive effects can enhance the capture of particulate contaminants. Contaminant particles and a porous filter medium can interact with two types of adsorptive forces: van der Waals forces, which are short ranged and always attractive; and, the electrical double-layer interactions, which may be attractive or repulsive depending on the surface charge of the contaminant particle and that of the pore surface. These interactions determine whether a particle will be attracted to or repulsed by the pore surface. If the contaminant particle and the pore surface are of the same charge, and the double layers of the particle and the surface interact in a repulsive manner, then the capability of a filter medium to remove particles physically smaller than the pores of the medium is limited. On the other hand, if the contaminant particle and the pore surface are oppositely charged, and there is at least no repulsive interaction between the electrical double layers of the particle and the pore surface, then particles physically smaller than the pore size of the medium are capable of being removed by adsorption by the process called electrokinetic capture. Since most contaminants encountered in nature are electronegative, this suggests that in order to increase retention of smaller particles, the filter medium should have a positive zeta potential.

As in 1971, an evaluation of asbestos had given strong indication that the unique filtration properties of asbestos depended on its electropositive surface charge. It became obvious that if a substitute were to be developed, it would have to be possible to modify the surface charge characteristics of other types of fibers and/or particulate materials. A review of the technical and patent literature revealed that the concept of chemically modifying the surface of a filter medium to provide enhanced filtration characteristics was not a particularly new one. The earliest reference was a 1936 patent (Cummings, 1936) that described the treatment of diatomaceous earth to produce an electropositive, insoluble aluminum hydroxide coating. Such treated diatomaceous earth, when used as a filter aid, acted as a flocculent for colloidal contaminants. In 1938, another patent (Elliott and Elliott, 1938) was issued describing the treatment of filter sand with rosin. While there is nothing in the chemistry of rosin that would lead one to believe that it could function as a charge modifier, the inventors appeared to believe that there was such an effect, and their patent states, "Sometimes this coating carries an electrical charge; either positive or negative, and opposite to that of suspended colloid particles." In 1952, a patent (Rodman, 1952) was issued describing the use of a modified aliphatic amine to treat filter media intended for use in oil filtration. That patent attributed enhanced sludge removal to cellulose fiber filters so treated.

In the early 1960s, synthetic polyelectrolytes were developed for use in water treatment. These polyelectrolytes are water-soluble, high molecular weight, synthetic organic polymers containing a series of repeating monomeric units. The monomeric units are characterized by having ionizable functional groups that dissociate in water to produce charged sites along the polymer chain. Initially, these polyelectrolytes were used as coagulants to improve the filterability of suspended solids. In such applications, they function by destabilizing colloid particles, through charge neutralization and/or bridging, so as to induce flocculation. In 1966 and 1967, Dow Chemical was awarded patents (Guebert and Laman, 1966; Guebert and Jones, 1967), which describe the use of cationic polyelectrolytes to charge modify filter aids and the use of such charge-modified filter aids in removing microorganisms from water. In the early 1970s, Baumann and his coworkers at the University of Iowa did extensive work on the use of polyelectrolytes as a pretreatment to provide an adsorbed charge modifier coating on filter aids and filter media (Baumann and Oulman,1970; Burns et al., 1970). Their work is particularly significant because they were the first experimenters to use electrokinetic (streaming potential) measurements to quantify the level of charge modification achieved.

This prior technology demonstrated that it was feasible to charge modify the surfaces of normally anionic filter materials so as to produce a cationic surface characteristic and that such charge modification resulted in enhanced filtration properties. This knowledge allowed the definition of a set of developmental guidelines for the production of commercially useful depth filter media:

1. The basic filter material should be a fine, high-surface area fiber, or particulate with an ionic surface charge.
2. This material should be dispersible in water slurry with cellulose fiber and being vacuum-formed into a thick sheet structure.
3. The chemical charge modifier should have a strong cationic functionality and should be capable of being chemically bonded to the anionic high-surface area substrate.

This latter requirement was based on the needs of the pharmaceutical and beverage industries for a "clean" (low extraction) and "safe" (no toxicological problems) filter medium. Finding the appropriate charge modifier system to satisfy this requirement was the innovative step that moved development beyond all of the prior technology, which was based on the adsorption of a charge-modifying agent.

Unfortunately, adsorption is a reversible process, and such adsorbed charge modifiers exhibited high extraction levels. In practice, this meant that the charge-modifying agent must have an appropriate cross-linking functionality in addition to its cationic functionality. During the period 1972–1976, several basic types of filter media employing this method of creating charge-enhanced filter media were developed and commercialized (Ostreicher, 1977a, b, 1982; Hou and Ostreicher, 1981; Ostreicher and Hou, 1981).

Success in duplicating the performance of cellulose-asbestos filter media is most easily demonstrated by comparing the laboratory performance of a Zeta Plus media grade (Figure 2.1a) with that of the

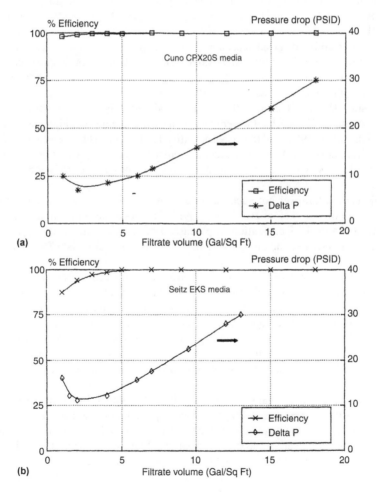

FIGURE 2.1 (a) Comparative filtration characteristics for Zeta Plus medium. (b) Comparative filtration characteristics of cellulose-asbestos medium.

corresponding Seitz cellulose-asbestos grade (Figure 2.1b). These laboratory results were soon verified by the success of Zeta Plus in replacing cellulose-asbestos in a broad range of industrial filtration
applications.

Because of the low wet strength of cellulose-asbestos, this medium had been limited to use as a sheet
medium in filter presses, with all of the associated problems of leakage, sterilization, and lengthy change
out time and correspondingly high labor costs. In addition to having equivalent or superior filtration
performance, Zeta Plus exhibited significantly better wet strength. This was an additional benefit of the
cross-linking characteristics of the charge modifier systems used, and it allowed the development of a
new generation of radically improved disposable depth filter cartridges. In the intervening years, such
cartridges have significantly displaced the use of filter presses.

Polymeric Microfiltration Membrane Development

Rising out of the development of positively charged depth filter media, the concept of charge modification of polymeric microporous membranes was first proposed in the early 1970s by Ostreicher.
It was believed at that time that there was no advantage to trying to embellish the performance of
an "absolute" filter that was already capable of achieving the level of performance demanded by the
application. In the late 1970s, however, the reliability of such membrane filters came into question
with several investigators reporting bacterial passage through such supposedly "absolute" membranes
(Wallhäusser, 1979; Howard and Duberstein, 1980). In addition, the medical industry was coming to
realize that other contaminants besides bacteria, viruses, and bacterial endotoxins (pyrogens), had to
be removed from parenteral drugs for patient safety (Brown, 1980). Significant success was achieved
in removing both viruses and bacterial endotoxins (Sobsey and Jones, 1979; Gerba et al., 1980; Hou
et al., 1980) by use of the charge-modified Zeta Plus filter medium, and it appeared that such enhanced
performance could also be achieved with a charge-modified polymeric membrane. The new nylon
membrane charge-modified filter media were based on the unique morphology and surface chemistry
of nylon (Ostreicher et al., 1984) and the very specialized requirements of the pharmaceutical industry
(low organic extractions) and the semiconductor industry (low-ionic extractions). This necessitated
the development of two new two-component charge modifier systems (Barnes et al., 1984; Ostreicher
et al., 1984).

The primary market, however, for such membranes was in filtration and sterilization of pharmaceutical products. In this market, microporous polymeric membranes of 0.2 mm nominal rating have
found widespread use in the sterilization of parenteral drugs. For this purpose, their performance
was characterized in terms of the complete removal of the microorganism *Pseudomonas diminuta*
(Pall, 1975).

The existence of the adsorptive phenomena in conventional microporous membranes is recognized
(Tanny and Meltzer, 1976; Tanny et al., 1979). The effect of such adsorptive phenomena on the performance of "sterilizing" membranes was treated as a secondary and unremarkable attribute of the base
polymer used to produce the membrane. Perhaps exaggeratedly, mechanical sieving was defined as the
primary mode of filtration. All of the commonly accepted modes of membrane characterization con-
cerned themselves with the determination of pore size distributions (especially maximum pore size) and
the correlation of such physical parameters with the bacterial rejection characteristics exhibited by the
membranes.

Historically, membranes were characterized as surface-type filters. In an SEM study, Knight et al.
(1982) were able to demonstrate rigorously that a charge-modified nylon membrane functions as an
adsorptive depth filter by virtue of the electrokinetic capture and adsorption function provided by the
combination of charge modification and high internal membrane pore surface area. Figure 2.2 shows a
cross-section of such a charge-modified membrane after it was subjected to a 0.109-mm monodisperse
latex (MDL) bead challenge. This photograph demonstrates the reality of electrokinetic capture and
adsorption with the MDL particles adhering to the surfaces of the relatively larger pore structure. That

such removal is quantitative is shown graphically in Figure 2.3, which presents the particle removal efficiencies of a charge-modified 0.2 mm membrane and unmodified 0.1 and 0.2 mm membranes. The pressure drop characteristics for each of these membranes are shown superimposed on the efficiency curves in Figure 2.4.

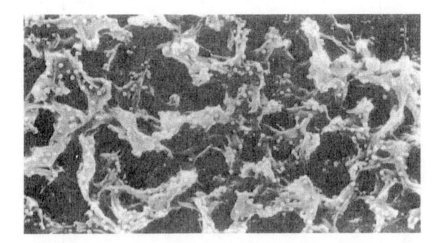

FIGURE 2.2 Electrokinetic capture of 0.109 mm particles on a charge-modified membrane.

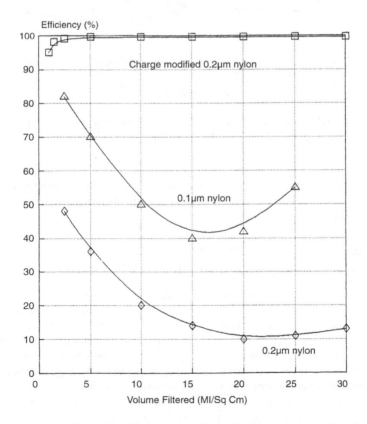

FIGURE 2.3 Filtration characteristics of modified and unmodified nylon 66 membranes, subjected to 0.109-mm MDL bead challenge.

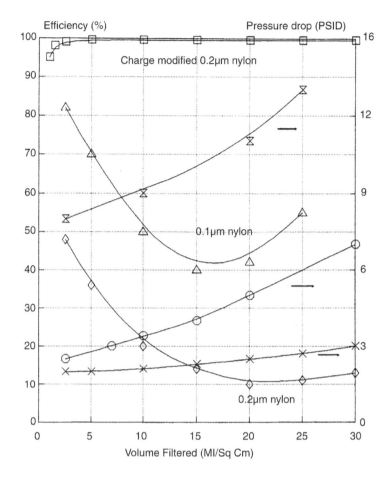

FIGURE 2.4 Filtration characteristics of modified and unmodified nylon 66 membranes subjected to 0.109-mm MDL bead challenge. ⋈, ΔP 0.1 mm nylon; ○, ΔP charge-modified 0.2 mm nylon; ×, 0.2 mm nylon.

Initially, Cuno was the only filter manufacturer producing a charge-modified filter medium. Pall Corporation (nylon 66), Gelman, and Millipore have since joined in this technology. Gelman produced a positively charged polyethersulfone sulfate membrane, while Millipore produces a charge-modified (poly vinylidene difluoride (PVDF)) membrane.

Theoretical Basis of Charge-Modified Filter Media

New test methods had to be developed to evaluate and quantify the performance of candidate charge-modified media and, eventually, to provide process and quality control criteria for the final product. The primary performance characteristics for any filter medium are capture efficiency and capacity. The test techniques that had been developed to measure these characteristics in unmodified submicrometer filter media, such as bubble point, diffusion flow, and sterilization testing with specific microorganisms, dealt strictly with mechanical straining. They were not useful in measuring the efficiency and capacity of charge-modified media.

It was necessary that the contaminant particle size be smaller than the pore size of the medium being tested. In addition, it was necessary that the contaminants used have consistent and reproducible surface charge and particle size distribution characteristics. These requirements were necessary so that consistent and reproducible evaluation could be made of the electrokinetic capture and adsorption characteristics of the media independent of mechanical straining effects. The following test methods were developed to meet these requirements.

MDL bead testing, the "workhorse" of the developmental efforts, consists of challenging the filter medium sample, at a specified constant flow rate, with an aqueous dispersion of single-size monodisperse polystyrene latex beads adjusted to a specified turbidity, pH, and resistivity. The effluent turbidity and medium pressure drop are measured and recorded as a function of the throughput. The particle removal efficiency of the media sample, for the specific particle size used, can be calculated directly from the inlet and effluent turbidity values (Knight and Ostreicher, 1981). These tests use relatively high contaminant challenge levels to reduce the time to breakthrough to an acceptable value for reasons of practicality as shown in Figure 2.5. It is evident from the curves shown in this figure that at modest challenge concentrations, one is dealing with a billion particles per milliliter to evaluate filter media. It is also evident that to evaluate media with different sizes of MDL beads, a constant number of particles should be used rather than a constant concentration. These MDL particles are commercially available in a number of diameters ranging from 0.021 to >2.0 mm. The results shown in Figures 2.1, 2.3, 2.6–2.8 are based on the use of this particular MDL bead test technique.

As developmental efforts led to the surface charge modification of ever finer pore size media, even the MDL test was impacted by interference from mechanical straining effects. To deal with this situation, a test technique was developed based on the use of metanil yellow, a water-soluble anionic dye with a molecular weight of approximately 375. The dimensions of this molecule are approximately 18 Å × 9 Å (Graham, 1955), allowing it to be used as a test contaminant for almost any charge-modified media down into the microfiltration range without interference from mechanical straining effects. In this test method, the media sample is challenged, at a specified constant flow rate, with an aqueous dispersion of metanil

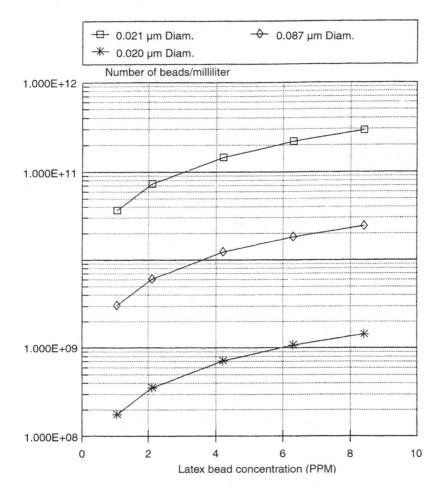

FIGURE 2.5 Number of latex per milliliter versus latex bead concentration for beads of different diameters.

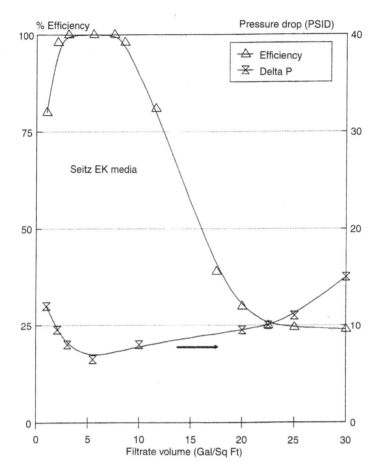

FIGURE 2.6   Filtration characteristics of cellulose-asbestos filter medium.

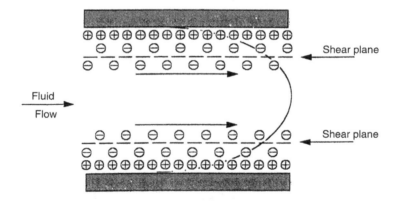

FIGURE 2.7   Ion distribution near the wall of a positively charged capillary.

yellow adjusted to a specified pH and resistivity, and light transmittance is measured with a spectrophotometer. The light transmittance of the effluent is measured and recorded as a function of throughput.

Surface charge cannot be measured directly or quantified by indirect techniques. Such indirect techniques as streaming potential (Knight and Ostreicher, 1981) for porous filter media allow the measurement of the potential at the hydrodynamic shear plane (zeta potential). The zeta potential is an important indicator of the electrokinetic status of a filter material and can be used to determine the capacity of a

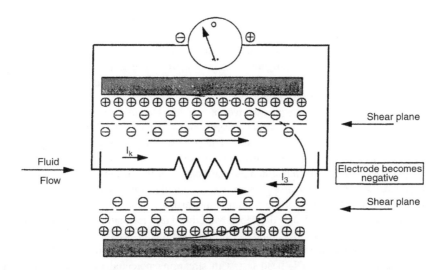

FIGURE 2.8   Ion distribution near the wall of a positively charged capillary with measuring circuit.

medium for contaminant and to determine its efficiency, as is shown later. Zeta potential is defined as the potential at the surface of shear between a liquid and a particle or a surface. It cannot be directly measured but can be calculated, for example, from streaming potential measurements, which is one of a series of four electrokinetic effects, the others being electrophoresis, electroosmosis, and sedimentation potential. All these effects are due to the disturbance of the static equilibrium conditions in the electrical double layer that exists at a solid/liquid interface.

The capillary pore model is used to demonstrate the concept of charge-modified membrane and is shown in Figure 2.7. In this case, the capillary represents one pore of a network of pores. The wall of the capillary is shown as having a layer of positively charged ions attached to the capillary wall, with an equal number of ions of opposite charge loosely distributed in the second layer. The surface of shear, as indicated in Figure 2.7, creates an imbalance in charge due to laminar flow of fluid through the capillary.

Streaming potential is the electric potential that is developed when a liquid is forced through a capillary or a network of capillaries such as a microporous membrane. It is due to the pressure drop across the end of a capillary or a porous plug such as a microporous membrane containing a liquid. The fluid flow created by the pressure drop across the capillary creates a disturbance in the electrical double layer, which sets up an electric potential across the ends of the capillary or porous medium. This potential can be measured directly by using a pair of inert electrodes in an external circuit of high impedance, so that all the current is forced to flow back through the system being measured, in this case a capillary. An apparatus for measuring streaming potential on a charged glass capillary is shown in Figure 2.8. It should be obvious from Figure 2.8 that a simple test apparatus can easily be assembled to evaluate the charge characteristics of filter material, whether it is a microporous membrane, felted filter medium, or granular material.

The relationship between the zeta potential and the surface potential is, however, a subjective one that depends on the ionic species and their concentrations in the test fluid. These test techniques are suitable for qualitative evaluations of the filtration mechanism and the effect of pH on both the charge modification process and the filtration process.

The MDL bead and dye tests are capable of providing a quantitative measure of the adsorptive capacity of a charge-modified filter medium. For reasons that are discussed later, the test results are sensitive to both the ionic content (species and concentration) and the pH of the test contaminant dispersion. Precise control of these two factors is critical to the reproducibility of the test results. Because of the abbreviated time frame, they are sensitive to the initial short-term pH shift and ionic extractions induced by the filter medium sample. Streaming potential measurements (Knight and Ostreicher, 1981) show that a potentially significant period of time is required for the media double layer to come into equilibrium with the bulk solution. Experimental precision requires that these factors be recognized and dealt with accordingly.

The electrokinetic behavior of colloidal particles, especially as it influences particle interactions and stability, has been the subject of a great deal of theoretical and experimental investigation, and there is an extensive literature available dealing with this aspect of electrokinetic phenomena. Unfortunately, no similar effort has been expended to investigate the electrokinetic interactions between colloidal particles and porous filter media. Cuno investigators were able to develop a "working" model of these interactions based on empirically derived understandings.

Wnek (1979), using the electrokinetic perspectives of colloidal chemistry, proposed that asbestos owed its unique filtration characteristics to the strong positive surface charge that it possessed at neutral and lower pH. He further proposed an operative filtration mechanism for such positively charged filter media that consisted of electrokinetic capture (via attractive double-layer interaction) and adsorption of negatively charged particles, which in turn resulted in modification of the surface charge on the media from positive to negative. This, he further proposed, would eventually inhibit additional electrokinetic capture, allowing eventual breakthrough of the contaminant particles.

With the development of the previously described MDL bead test, it became possible to experimentally verify the breakthrough phenomena for cellulose-asbestos filter media (see Figure 2.6) and, subsequently, for other forms of charge-modified filter media as shown, for example, in Figures 2.1, 2.3, and 2.7.

Further testing combined the MDL bead test with streaming potential measurements (Knight and Ostreicher, 1981). This use of simultaneous streaming potential and particle removal efficiency measurements allowed the defining of the real-time relationship between the electrokinetic condition of the media and the particle removal efficiency, as shown in Figure 2.9. For a positive surface charge-modified depth filter (Zeta Plus CPX-50S), the 0.109 mm negatively charged mono. The capillary pore model is used to demonstrate the concept of charge-modified membrane and is shown in Figure 2.7. In this case, the capillary

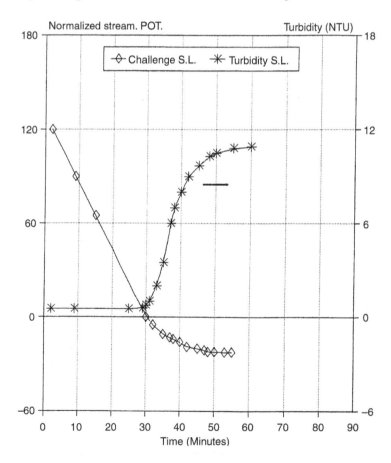

FIGURE 2.9   Results of 0.109-mm MDL bead challenge to single-layer-type 50S Zeta Plus medium.

represents one pore of a network of pores. The wall of the capillary is shown as having a layer of positively charged ions attached to the capillary wall, with an equal number of ions of opposite charge loosely distributed in the second layer. The surface of shear, as indicated in Figure 2.11, creates an imbalance in charge due to laminar flow of fluid through the capillary kinetic capture and adsorption. The interaction between the constant-rate latex bead challenge and the medium gives a normalized streaming potential that decays linearly from a negative value (positive zeta potential) through zero and then asymptotically approaches a final positive normalized streaming potential (negative zeta potential). Only when the normalized streaming potential approaches and passes through zero does the particle removal efficiency, as measured by effluent turbidity, start to decrease. Finally, the particle removal efficiency asymptotically approaches zero (inlet turbidity = effluent turbidity) as the normalized streaming potential similarly approaches its final value. These results appear to verify the model proposed by Wnek, perhaps subject to some minor modifications. On the basis of Wnek's model, it was anticipated that the streaming potential would asymptotically approach zero with contaminant breakthrough starting at a low negative normalized streaming potential and going to zero filtration efficiency at zero streaming. These tests, however, showed that the filtration efficiency did not approach zero until the normalized steaming potential approached the high positive values exhibited by the unmodified filter medium. This actual performance appears to be indicative of a discrete, rather than uniform, positive charge deposition resulting in a grossly amphoteric surface, that is, a surface possessing a heterogeneous distribution of anionic and cationic charge functionalities.

At first glance, it would appear that the adsorptive capacity of a medium might be predictable from the initial equilibrium value of the normalized streaming potential. To examine this question, a test series was run comparing the streaming potential and 0.109-mm MDL capacity of single- versus double-layer media samples. The results, shown in Figure 2.10, demonstrated that although the adsorptive capacity is additive, the normalized streaming potentials for the single-layer and double-layer media samples were

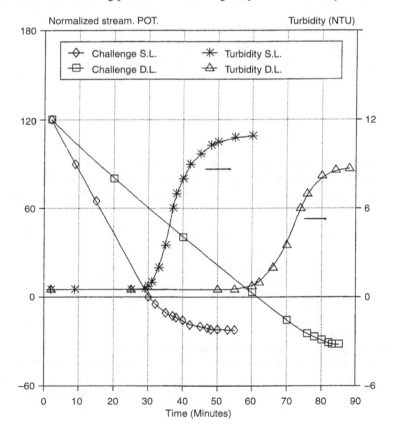

FIGURE 2.10 Results of 0.109-mm MDL bead challenge to single- and double-layer-type 50S Zeta Plus medium. SL, single layer; DL, double layer.

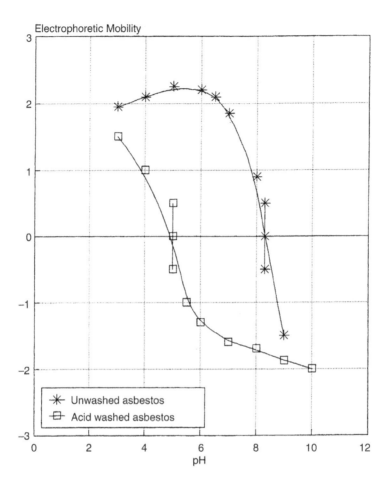

FIGURE 2.11   Electrophoretic mobility of chrysolite asbestos.

identical. At least in this case, therefore, the normalized steaming potential did not correlate with the adsorptive capacity. The correlation between effective medium thickness and adsorption capacity did appear to indicate that total charge-modified surface area might be the primary determinant of capacity.

Early characterizations of the surface charge characteristics of asbestos (see Figure 2.11) show a strong relationship between the electrokinetic characteristics and the pH of the water in which the asbestos fibers were dispersed. This relationship is the result of the effect of pH on the relative levels of dissociation of the various surface functional groups that, in a composite, determine the surface charge characteristics. More often than not, the surface chemistry of the systems with which we are dealing are amphoteric; that is, both anionic and cationic functional groups exist at the surface.

Increasing the pH will suppress the dissociation of the cationic groups and increase the dissociation of the anionic groups, and vice versa.

Unmodified nylon 6,6 membrane, for example, has surface charge characteristics determined by the carboxyl and amine end groups of the nylon 6,6 molecule as shown conceptually in Figure 2.12 and assumes that the carboxyl and amine end groups are uniformly distributed throughout the wetted pore surface.

In Figure 2.13, it is shown that the unmodified nylon 6,6 membrane exhibits a negative surface charge at pH > 6.0. Charge-modifying the nylon membrane surface with a strong quaternary amine charge modifier elicits a radical change in this characteristic, providing a positively charged surface which is stable up to pH 11.0.

One might expect that electrokinetic capture and adsorption performance would be impacted by pH, and in fact this is the case. The results of a metanil yellow dye challenge test on nylon microporous

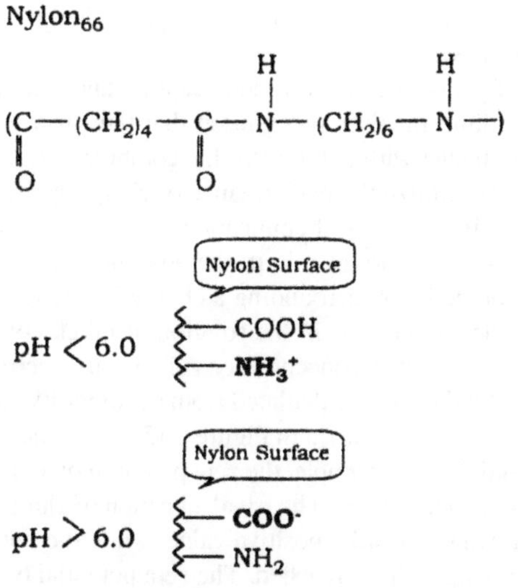

Nylon₆₆

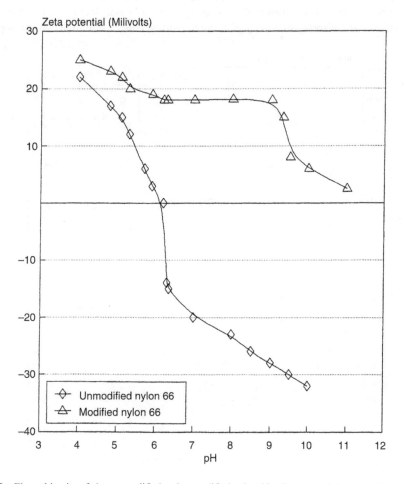

FIGURE 2.12   Surface charge characteristics of nylon 66.

FIGURE 2.13   Electrokinetics of charge-modified and unmodified nylon 66—Zeta potential versus pH.

membrane are shown in Figure 2.14. The effect of pH and type of charge modifier on membrane metanil yellow dye capacity is clearly shown.

Understanding the impact of pH on the electrokinetic capture and adsorption characteristics of a surface charge-modified filter medium involves recognition that the surface charge characteristics of the medium and the contaminant change with pH. Given this combined effect, it becomes evident that pH can be adjusted to enhance and optimize the performance of charge-modified filter media, and, indeed, such techniques have been used in a number of applications.

The ionic environment plays an important role in the adsorptive capacity of charge-modified filter media. The size of the ionic double layer surrounding a charged particle or surface is controlled by the concentration and valence of the counterions in the solution. Riddick (1968) measured the electrophoretic mobility for a silica colloid in various concentrations of various electrolytes. The colloid concentration used was 100 ppm. Zeta potentials were calculated from the mobility values and were plotted against electrolyte concentration. The curves are shown in Figure 2.15. Inorganic electrolytes can have a significant impact on the zeta potential. In this example, the zeta potential of a dilute solution of colloidal silica was modified by adding different electrolytes. The trivalent cation of aluminum chloride easily sends the zeta potential from a negative value toward a positive value, while the potassium sulfate, a monovalent cation, goes more negative until a plateau is reached. The zeta potential begins to rise because the high-ionic concentration begins to compress the double layer.

Increased ionic concentration and higher valence counterions reduce the thickness of the double layer and vice versa. This has a significant impact on the repulsive or attractive interactions between particles and between a particle and the filter pore surface. The net effect of ionic concentration and valence can be, for evaluative purposes, quantified in terms of the resistivity of the solution. Decreasing the resistivity of the solution will increase the adsorptive capacity of a charge-modified filter medium. It does so, apparently, by

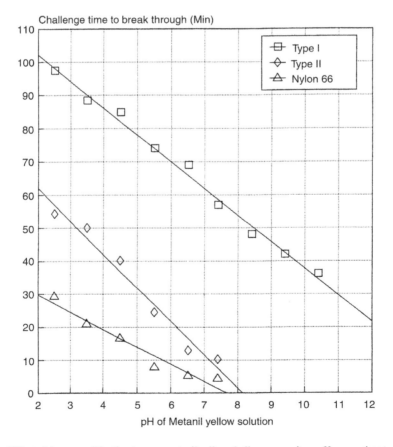

FIGURE 2.14   Effect of charge modification type on metanil yellow challenge capacity—pH versus time to breakthrough.

reducing the thickness of the double layer surrounding the contaminant particles. Since there is a repulsive double-layer interaction between particles, this reduction allows the particles to approach each other more closely and decreases the amount of "space" occupied by an adsorbed particle on the oppositely charged filter medium pore surface. In one particularly interesting test, a Zeta Plus sample was subjected to a low conductivity 0.109-mm MDL bead challenge and run until breakthrough occurred. At that point, a salt was added to the contaminant dispersion to significantly increase the conductivity. As shown in Figure 2.16, the effect of this salt addition was to restore the ability of the sample to absorb contaminant particles.

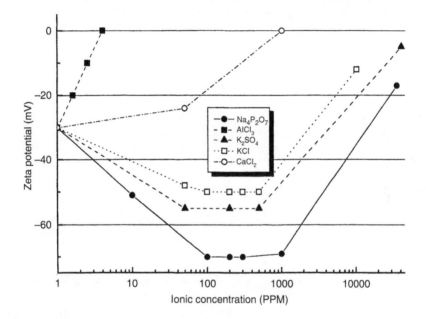

FIGURE 2.15 Zeta potential versus concentration curves. (Reconstructed from Riddick, 1968.)

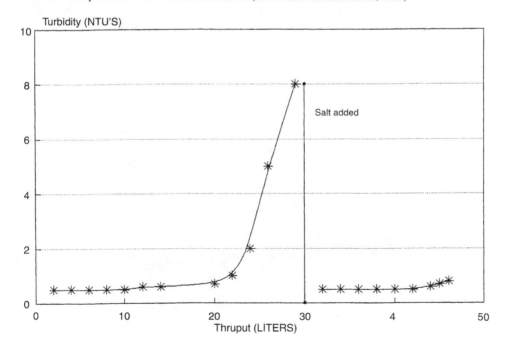

FIGURE 2.16 Effect of salt addition on adsorptive capacity.

Charge-modified cartridges have demonstrated an exceptional ability to retain high concentrations of particles in semiconductor UPW systems. The electropositive charge modification to the nylon microporous membrane enables such cartridges to remove particles much smaller than the rated pore size of the membrane. The electrokinetic adsorption and mechanical sieving have proven to be effective in removing contaminants such as colloidal silica and fragmented ion-exchange resin beads from UPW systems. The ability of such 0.04-mm membranes to adsorb 0.021-mm MDL beads is illustrated in Figures 2.17 and 2.18.

Figure 2.17 shows the equilibrium flush out of a 0.04-mm Zetapor microporous membrane subsequently challenged with a 4.2 ppm (1×10^{11} beads/mL) suspension of 0.21-mm MDL beads. Figure 2.18 is a scanning electron photomicrograph of the membrane challenged in Figure 2.17.

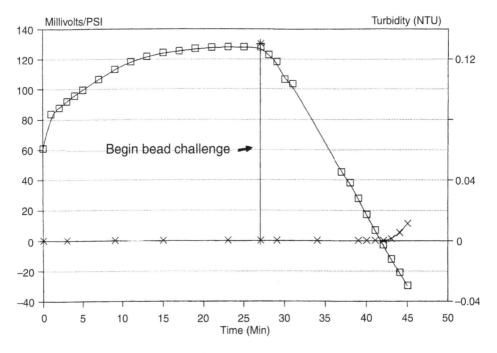

FIGURE 2.17   Streaming potential challenge curve. Challenged with 0.021 mm MDL (4.2 ppm).

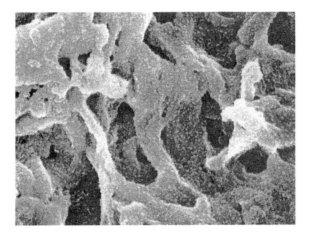

FIGURE 2.18   Micrograph of a 0.04 mm Zetapor membrane subjected to 0.021-mm MDL bead challenge.

Recent Applications of Charged Membranes

The development of pharmaceuticals produced by biotechnology has created an increased need for critical separations. Biologic therapeutic pharmaceuticals are complex, high molecular weight, amphoteric compounds. Charge-modified depth filters, microporous membranes, and ultrafiltration membranes have been developed to facilitate separation and purification of these complex biomolecules. The paragraphs below reference some recent applications of charged microporous membranes and depth filters in biological separations. Referred to are endotoxin and DNA removal, clearance of virus from biological solutions, discrete separations of low molecular weight proteins, and peptides by charged ultrafiltration membranes and removal of protein aggregates and contaminating host cell proteins (HCPs) from monoclonal antibody preparations. In addition to these applications, there are emerging separation applications involving membrane chromatography (Zhou and Tressel, 2006) and other methods of effecting charged-based separations including pore-filled membranes. Although these recent developments are beyond the scope of this chapter, several references are provided (Brandt et al., 1988; Charcosset, 1999).

Charge-modified filter media are now widely used in the pharmaceutical industry for the removal or control of negatively charged contaminants such as endotoxins. Carazzone et al. (1985) investigated charge-modified filter media to determine if they were able to retain substances of opposite charge in solutions of different composition, that is, in both electrolytes and nonelectrolytes. The endotoxin used in this study was extracted from gram negative Escherichia coli B5. Carazzone et al. found that (a) the removal of pyrogens to below detectable limits from distilled water is possible using both 0.2 and 1.2-mm charge-modified membranes and (b) in the presence of 0.9% NaCI solution, neither the 0.2 nor 1.2-mm membrane depyrogenated the challenge solution and, similarly, neither set of charge-modified membranes removed the endotoxin in a 2% peptone solution.

Evaluation of the same charge-modified filters with Serratia marcescens produced similar results in that organism retention was higher for charge-modified filters than for conventional membrane filters and the presence of electrolytes or peptone significantly reduced the efficiency of the charge-modified membrane.

Carazzone concluded that: "the efficiency of positively charged filter media to remove pyrogenic substances and to improve microorganism removal from solutions varies with the composition of the solution to be filtered and with the pre-filter and final filter used."

Wickert (1993) reviewed the work of Barker and coworkers, who conducted a validation study to quantify the endotoxin removal capacity of charge-modified filters in water systems while evaluating the effect of flow rate, temperature, and steam sterilization conditions. The test system consisted of a 0.45-mm positively charged prefilter, a 0.2-mm positively charged filter to remove the endotoxin, and an additional 0.2-mm positively charged filter to retain endotoxin that might break through. All three filters were connected in series. The system was challenged with E. coli B5 purified endotoxin suspended in 0.5 mm EDTA at a challenge level of 8×10^7 EU. Variations in pH > 3 did not significantly affect the filter performance, but reducing the flow rate appeared to increase the filters' capacity for endotoxin. The effect of temperature and steam sterilization interval did not have an effect on endotoxin removal and therefore did not affect the stability of the charge modifier. Wickert concludes, "the information on the effect of varying process parameters also demonstrates the capability of this technology and confirms its flexibility."

Nagasaki (1988) evaluated nylon 6,6 charge-modified and unmodified filter cartridges after 5 months of identical service in a semiconductor high purity water system. He found that one of the key benefits of charge modification is that the membranes are much less susceptible to hydrolysis, speculating that the protection mechanism was the cross-linking of the charge modifier and the nylon. Hot water exposure testing was performed on both charge-modified and unmodified membranes. The result showed that the charge-modified membranes maintained elasticity, whereas the unmodified membranes became brittle after 2000 h of exposure. He concluded that "the added stability of the charge modified membrane is therefore another important factor to be taken into account in selecting a filtration system."

In a study of calf thymus DNA retention by depth filters published by Dorsey et al. (1997), the authors found depth filter-mediated retention of DNA was attributed to both mechanical separation and electrokinetic attraction. The data showed, however, that the primary retention mechanism of nucleic acid was due to electrokinetic forces. Figure 2.19 shows retention of 100 ng/mL calf thymus DNA at pH 7.4 using depth filter media with varying concentrations of cationic resin. Percent retention of DNA increases with

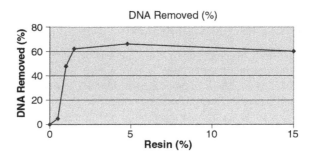

FIGURE 2.19   Effect of increasing cationic resin concentration on DNA retention by charge-modified filter n.

increasing resin content to a maximum of 5% resin. Further DNA retention was believed to be limited by steric hindrance. Retention of nucleic acids is significant to biotherapeutic protein purification as production methods involve the use of cell culture and contaminating host cell nucleic acids require removal to low levels in fished drug product.

In addition to use in cell clarification and bioburden reduction, depth media has been shown to be useful during bioprocessing application to remove HCPs and nucleic acids. A study performed by Yigzaw et al. (2006) demonstrated that depth media having a high level of positive zeta potential was able to remove HCP to a level that protected chromatography columns downstream and reduced the frequency of protein aggregation.

Data were presented indicating that the primary mode of operation was electrostatic adsorption of the HCP by charged depth media.

An increasingly critical need for production of biologic drugs is viral clearance. There are numerous methods for achieving viral clearance including inactivation or aggregation, size exclusion retention by fine microporous membranes and adsorptive retention by chromatographic resins and filtration media. An example of adsorptive depth filter viral clearance was published by Tipton et al. (2002). The study involved investigation of viral clearance from an affinity column eluate pool. The viruses used in the study were porcine parvovirus (PPV) with a mean diameter of 18–26 nm and xenotropic murine leukemia virus (XMuLV) with a mean diameter of 80–100 nm. Two depth filters were employed with respective tertiary and quaternary amine resin charge modification and both depth filter media having a mean pore size of 300 nm. The log reduction value (LRV) for PPV varied from 0.9 to 1.1 with the lower charge (tertiary amine) depth filter and from 1.4 to 2.0 with the stronger charged (quaternary amine) depth filter. For the slightly larger virus, XMuLV, an LRV of >4.8 was observed with both depth filter types. The slightly higher retention of the larger virus may suggest increased retention contribution due to mechanical size exclusion effects. Nonetheless, viral clearance by adsorptive depth filtration is an effective means of reducing viral contamination.

Novel techniques of separating proteins using ultrafiltration membrane, as opposed to microporous membranes or depth filters have recently been published (Ebersold and Zydney, 2004; Mehta and Zydney, 2006). In experiments involving a process termed high performance tangential flow filtration (HPTFF), highly selective protein separations can be obtained by manipulating both membrane pore size distribution and electrostatic charge interactions. In one instance, Ebersold and Zydney (2004) demonstrated that HPTFF was able to separate protein differing by a single amino acid residue (Ebersold and Zydney, 2004). Zydney's group also published charge-based protein separation involving charge modification of both the membrane and target protein. In this study, a small negatively charged dye was linked to protein followed by filtration through an ultrafiltration membrane. The protein charge modification enhanced protein passage through the membrane. The technique also allows for subsequent removal of the dye charge modifier, allowing protein separation to be affected in further membrane separation processes.

Charge modification techniques can also be used to reduce membrane fouling. While microporous membranes which possess a positive zeta potential capture particles having a net negative charge, there are numerous references in the literature indicating that the addition of a negative charge to membranes, primarily ultrafiltration media and microporous media used in tangential flow applications, reduces membrane fouling by preventing nonspecific binding to the membrane surface (Rao and Zydney, 2005; Mehta and Zydney, 2006; Kumar et al., 2005).

Conclusions

The current understanding of normal electrokinetic phenomena offers a particularly comprehensible or technically satisfying definition of why a given charge-modified medium functions at all, let alone so well. Understanding asbestos allowed us to create a significant new technology. We can only believe that further understanding of the mechanisms involved will lead to the creation of both new products and new applications.

Understanding of the mechanisms involved has been, for the most part, empirically derived. Much work remains to be done in terms of optimizing both the products and the applications. This, in turn, demands a more rigorous understanding of the chemical and electrokinetic phenomena involved both in producing a surface charge-modified medium and in applying such media to both existing and new applications. It is known from practical experience that charge-modified filter media provide unique separation capabilities in systems on which "normal" electrokinetic phenomena are probably not operative. The use of surface charge-modified filter media to provide improved filtration performance has become an accepted technology.

REFERENCES

Barnes RG, Chu C, Emond GT, Roy AK. Charge modified microporous membrane process for charge modifying said membrane, and process for filtration of fluids. U.S. Patent 4473475; 1984.

Baumann ER, Oulman CS. Polyelectrolyte coatings for filter media. *Filtr Sep* 1970; 7(6): 689.

Brandt S, Goffe RA, Kessler SB, O'Connor JL, Zale SE. Membrane-based affinity technology for commercial scale purifications. *Bio/Technol* 1988; 6: 779–782.

Brown DG. Microbial contamination associated with hospital fluids. *CRC Crit Rev Environ Control* 1980; 9: 279–299.

Burns DE, Baumann ER, Oulman CS. Particulate removal on coated filter media. *J AWWA* 1970; 62: 121.

Carazzone M, Arecco D, Fava M, Sancin P. A new type of positively charged filter: preliminary test results. *J Parent Sci Technol* 1985; 39(2): 69–74.

Charcosset C. Purification of proteins by membrane cheomatography. *J Chem Technol Biotechnol* 1999; 71(2): 95–110.

Cohn AI, Strong LE, Hughes WL, Mulford DJ, Ashworth JN, Melin M, Taylor HL. A system for the separation into fractions of the protein and lipoprotein components of biological tissues and fluids. *J Am Chem Soc* 1946; 69: 459–475.

Cummings AB. Electropositive composition and method of making the same. U.S. Patent 2036258; 1936.

Dorsey N, Eschrich J, Cyr G. The role of charge in the retention of DNA by charged cellulose-based depth filters. *BioPharm* 1997; 10(1): 46–49.

Ebersold MF, Zydney AL. The effect of membrane properties on the separation of protein charge variants using ultrafiltration. *J Membr Sci* 2004; 243: 379–388.

Elliott RD, Elliott MJ. Filtering. U.S. Patent 2106318; 1938.

FDA. Asbestos particles in food and drugs: notice of proposed rulemaking. *Food Drug Admin Fed Reg* 1973; 38(188): 27076.

FDA. Asbestos-form particles in drugs for parenteral injection. *Food Drug Admin Fed Reg* 1975; 40(51): 11865.

FDA. Human and veterinary drugs. *Food Drug Admin Fed Reg* 1976; 41(31): 6878.

Gerba CP, Hou KC, Babineau RA, Fiore JV. Pyrogen control by depth filtration. *Pharm Tech* 1980; 4: 83.

Graham D. Characterization of physical adsorption systems. III. The separate effects of pore size and surface acidity upon the adsorbent capacities of activated carbon. *J Phys Chem* 1955; 59: 896–900.

Guebert KW, Laman JD. Removal of microorganisms from fluids. U.S. Patent 3242073; 1966.

Guebert KW, Jones IC. Coated filter aids. U.S. Patent 3352424; 1967.

Hagg MB. Membranes in chemical processing- a review of applications and novel developments. *Sep Purif Methods* 1998; 27(1): 51–168.

Hou KC, Ostreicher EA. Method for removing cationic contaminants from beverages. U.S. Patent 4288462; 1981.

Hou K, Gerba CP, Goyal SM, Zerda KS. Capture of latex beads, bacteria, endotoxin and viruses by charge modified filters. *Appl Environ Microbiol* 1980; 40: 892.

Howard G, Duberstein R. A case of penetration of 0.2 fJ.m rated membrane filters by bacteria. *J Parenter Drug Assoc* 1980; 34(2): 95.

Knight RA, Ostreicher EA. Measuring the electrokinetic properties of charged filter media. *Filtr Sep* 1981; 18(1): 30.

Knight RA, Fiore JV, Rossitto JV. Microporous membranes as depth filters. *Presented at World Filtration Congress III* (Filtration Society); 1982.

Kumar R, Zhu C, Belfort G. Low fouling synthetic membranes by photon induced graft polymerization- new monomers and exciting properties. *AIChE Annual Meeting*, paper 465d; 2005.

Mehta A, Zydney AL. Effect of membrane charge on flow and protein transport during ultrafiltraion. *Biotechnol Prog* 2006; 22(2): 484–492.

Mika AM, Childs RF, Dickson JM. Ultra-low pressure water softening: a new approach to membrane construction. *Desalination* 1999; 121: 149–158.

Nagasaki I. Charge-enhanced membranes for water filtration. *Solid State Technol* 1988.

Ostreicher EA. Particulate filter medium and process. U.S. Patent 4007113; 1977a.

Ostreicher EA. Fibrous fIlter medium and process. U.S. Patent 4007114; 1977b.

Ostreicher EA. Process of making an improved filter media. U.S. Patent 4321288; 1982.

Ostreicher EA. Charge modified Filter media. U.S. Patent 4981591; 1991.

Ostreicher EA, Hou KC. Filter and method of making same. U.S. Patent 4305782; 1981.

Ostreicher EA, Knight RA, Fiore JV, Emond GT, Hou KC. Charge modified microporous membrane, process for charge modifying same, and process for filtration of fluids. U.S. Patent 4473474; 1984.

Pall DB. Quality control of absolute bacteria removal filters. *Bull Parenter Drug Assoc* 1975; 29: 142.

Rao S, Zydney AL. Controlling protein transport in ultrafiltration using small charged ligands. *Biotechnol Bioeng* 2005; 91: 733–742.

Riddick TM. *Control of Colloid Stability through Zeta Potential.* Ann Arbor, Michigan, United States: Zeta-Meter Inc.; 1968.

Rodman CA. Method of filtration by attracting sludge particles. U.S. Patent 2613813; 1952.

Rose AH. *Alcoholic Beverages.* London: Academic Press; 1977: 374.

Selikoff IJ, Lee DHK. *Asbestos and Disease.* New York: Academic Press; 1968.

Sobsey MD, Jones BL. Concentration of poliovirus from tap water using positively charged microporous filters. *Appl Environ Microbiol* 1979; 37: 588.

Stone T, Parekh B. *Charged Microporous Membranes, Microelectronics Applications Note MA033.* Bedford, MA, Millipore Corporation; 1993.

Tanny G, Meltzer TH The dominance of adsorptive effects in the filtrative purification of flu vaccine. *J Parenter Drug Assoc* 1976; 32(6): 258.

Tanny GB, Strong DK, Presswood WG, Meltzer TH. Adsorptive removal of Pseudomonas diminuta by membrane filters. *J Parenter Drug Assoc* 1979; 33(1): 40.

Tipton B, Boose JA, Larsen W, Beck J, O'Brien T. Retrovirus and parvovirus clearance from and affinity column product using adsorptive depth filtration. *BioPharm* 2002; 15: 43–50.

Wallhäusser KH. Is the removal of microorganisms by filtration really a sterilization method. *J Parenter Drug Assoc* 1979; 33(3): 156.

Wickert K. Validation of positively charged filters used for endotoxin control. *Pharm Eng* 1993; 13: 41–45.

Wnek W. Electrokinetic and chemical aspects of water filtration. *Filtr Sep* 1979; 11(3): 237.

Yigzaw Y, Piper R, Tran M, Shukla A. Exploitation of the adsorptive properties of depth filters for host cell protein removal during monoclonal antibody purification. *Biotechnol Prog* 2006; 22: 288–296.

Zeman LJ, Zydney AL. *Microfiltration and Ultrafiltration: Principles and Applications.* New York: Marcel Dekker, Inc.; 1996.

Zhou JX, Tressel T. Basic concepts in Q membrane chromatography for large scale antibody production. *Biotechnol Prog* 2006; 22(2): 341–349.

3

Filter Designs

Maik W. Jornitz
G-CON Manufacturing, Inc.

CONTENTS

Introduction

Filtration, membrane, or depth filtration has been used for centuries, although the first modern filters for sterilizing filtration only started to appear in the 1920s. These membrane filters were casted on glass plates and afterwards cut to discs. The disc filter designs were used as a multi-stack filter system to sterilize fluids, till the pleated filter cartridge design was developed. That design was a major breakthrough, as one could establish a large amount of filtration area in a fairly confined space. This design is still the prevalent format used for sterilizing grade membrane filter systems, although many other things changed, like the pleat density and format, as well as the welding of the membrane to the endcap area.

Other filtration designs like lenticular- or pod-like designs are used mainly for depth filtration purposes, to create a larger surface area for such filters, as these filter materials typically cannot be pleated. Pod-like structures are used for single-use, encapsulated designs, so the end user does not come in contact with the separated material, neither is the surrounded environment affected by an exchange of such filter and cleaning requirements are greatly reduced or eliminated.

Disc Filter Membranes

Disc or flat filters were the first filter configuration used within the pharmaceutical industry, mainly as 293-mm discs within large stainless steel holding devices. Multiple membrane discs were assembled in a multi-stack filter housing. The assembly of such housing was/is difficult as one works with wetted flat filters and has to be extremely careful not to damage the filter membrane. Also wrinkles or folds during assembly might cause problems during the filtration process or the sterilization of the filter assembly in an autoclave. These "process" filtration devices were replaced by pleated filter cartridge formats (Technical Report 26, 2008). Disc filters are cut from the casted membrane sheet and are, available in a large variety of size, either builds into a disposable plastic housing or placed into a filter holder. Common diameter sizes to be placed in filter holders are 4, 25, 47, 50, 90, 142, and 293 mm. Any of the different sizes are used for different type of applications. The most common 47 and 50 mm are utilized as microbial (analytical) assessment filter (Figure 3.1) and can have different colors or colored grids printed on

FIGURE 3.1   Different flat filter sizes and types.

the membrane. The grid structure on the membrane helps counting organisms per defined filtration area and previous filtered volume. Such analytical filters commonly have a pore size of 0.45 μm and utilize adsorptive polymeric materials, for example, nylon or cellulose nitrate (Badenhop, 1983; ASTM, 1988; Carter and Levy, 1998). The reason for the material choice is the requirement of adsorptive capture of the organisms. The pore size is chosen to be 0.45 μm to assure the nutrient, on which the membrane is placed, penetrates through the membrane surface to feed the captured organisms. The 0.45-μm adsorptive filters are also used as the capture filter during the bacteria challenge test with the similar purposes that described microbial filters.

Typically, these flat filter membranes are installed in either polymeric or stainless steel filter holders, separated by an O-ring seal to the filtrate side. The installation of flat filter membranes into the filter holder can be tricky and is attached with potential flaws. For this reason, some filter manufacturers started supplying flat filter units which are welded into a polymeric housing. These types of filter units are much more user friendly and reliable, separating the upstream from the filtrate side.

Since disc filters are restricted within its effective filtration area (EFA) pleated filter cartridge designs were developed to increase the filtration area without increasing the footprint of the filtration system or filter holder. The pleated filters also had an advantage over its sealing toward the filtrate side. The pleat pack was welded, whereby the flat filter discs are all sealed via an O-ring seal.

Pleated Cartridge Filters

The primary motivation to develop pleated membrane cartridges was the need of an increase in the filter area sufficient to secure the engineering advantages of lower applied differential pressures and larger volume flows (particularly advantageous with more viscous liquids). Achieving this goal in the pleated filter cartridge form meant, moreover, that less plant space needed to be allocated for filter installations. As described above, 293-mm discs utilized before pleated filter cartridges required large floor space due to the low effective filtration are of 0.5 ft² (0.05 m²). To replace a common 10″ filter cartridge and to achieve its same EFA, 15 293-mm discs would be needed to gain the equal amount of filtration area. Therefore, the footprint of such system is by far larger than the need of a 10″ filter housing. Moreover, every disc filter required O-ring sealing, therefore, the assembly was time-consuming and insecure. Whereby, pleated filter unit has the pleated membrane or filter media welded to the top and bottom endcap, therefore, creates a much more reliable and robust seal to the filtrate side.

It is not easy to pleat a filter membrane, as it can break or be damaged, such instances were experienced during the development of these filter units. To avoid the potential break of pleatings, the pleat density, respectively, membrane area was restricted to 4 ft² (0.4 m²). This still represented a close to tenfold filtration area improvement over 293-mm discs. The filtration area is achieved within the cylindrical pleat pack, which was resin bonded to the endcaps (Figure 3.2).

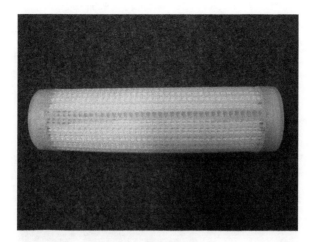

FIGURE 3.2   Resin-bonded pleated filter cartridge.

Polyester material was commonly used as pre- and support fleece. Both, the polyester and the resin used to bond the membrane to the endcap were reasons for the low chemical and thermal resistance of such filters, not to mention extractable/leachable levels, which would be unacceptable in today's standards (FDA, 1987; Jornitz and Meltzer, 1998, 1999). The first membrane materials were cellulose acetate, cellulose nitrate, polyamide, and polyvinylidene fluoride (PVDF). Often, these membrane materials were surface treated to achieve pleatability, wettability, and stability of the membrane, which required large water flush volumes to remove leachables from the filter matrix before the filter could be used. Pleating polymeric membranes has been a major achievement due to the possibility of pleat breaks, which happens once so often if the right pleat parameters, methodologies, and chemical composition have not been found. Unique treatments during the pleating process are required to be used to make sure the pleating is performed without potential damage. Furthermore, the pleat edges are required to be robust; otherwise, the membrane could be damaged during the filtration process, for example, due to pressure pulses or water hammer (Figure 3.3.)

Nowadays, available are pleated filters composed variously of cellulose acetates, Teflons, PVDF, polysulfone, polyethersulfon, nylon, etc. The pleating arrangement, the back-and-forth folding of the flat membrane filter upon itself, permits the presentation of a large filter surface area within a small volume. A pleated membrane cartridge of some 2.75″ (70 mm) plus in diameter and 10″ (254 mm) in length can contain from 5 to 8 ft^2 (0.5 to 0.8 m^2) of filter surface, depending on the membrane thickness, prefiltration layers, and construction detail. Track-etched polycarbonate of 10 µm thicknesses has been offered in cartridges containing some 20 ft^2 (2 m^2) of membrane surface, required due its low porosity. Pleated membrane cartridges are also offered in various lengths from 2″ to 40″ and EFAs from 0.015 to 36 m^2 (Figure 3.4). This range of sizes and EFAs are required for scale-up and down within the process and development steps. A pleated filter device should be able to scale-up linear from the pre-clinical volume size to process scale (Technical Report 26, 2008). Trial work by the filter suppliers assured specific designs, which fulfill this need. Typically, filterability or filter scaling trials are performed using flat filter discs (indicator trial). Once the right filter combination has been found another test, with the narrowed filter combination, is performed using small-scale pleated devices to assure that the preliminary result is correct (verification trial). These small pleated devices require to be scalable to the large-scale pleated filter system used in the production setting.

Pleated filter elements introduced the opportunity to combine various prefilter fleeces or membranes in front of the final filter membrane. Instead of stacking flat filter discs on top of each other with the risk of leaking due to insufficient sealing or unutilized EFA due to air entrapment between the membranes, pleated filters already will have these prefilter combinations build into the element. The manufacturers gained the flexibility to combine filter combinations determined in filterability trials into a welded filter element, which meant filtration applications could be optimized (Datar et al., 1992).

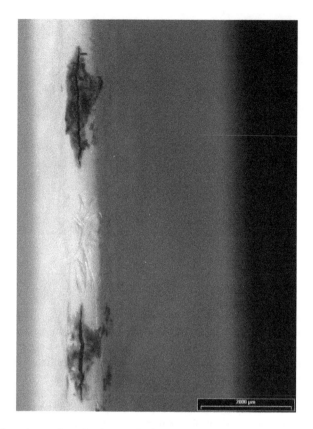

FIGURE 3.3   Damaged membrane pleat edge due to pulsation.

FIGURE 3.4   Different filter cartridge structures and types.

Typical construction components of the pleated filter cartridge are as follows:

Endcaps are the terminals for the cartridge and the pleat pack and are responsible for holding the cartridge contents together. The endcaps are also responsible for providing the seal of the membrane pleat pack between upstream and downstream side of the filter. Also the adapters which are used to fit the filter element into a filter housing are welded onto the endcaps. Polypropylene endcaps are frequently adhered to the membrane pleat pack, by ultrasonic welding, which is the current status quo and most robust weld form. In the past, the use of a polypropylene melt softened preferably by fusion welding or polypropylene heated up to the melt point and the pleat pack dipped into it were the weld mechanisms. These welding techniques resulted often in excessive polypropylene melt running up the filter pleats, which caused either hydrophobic spots or weakened membrane areas. Ultrasonic welding of the endcap to the inner core, outer support area and the membrane pleat pack avoid such behavior. In instances, polypropylene endcapping can cause hydrophobic areas on the pleat pack, for example, with nylon membranes. They, therefore, use polyester endcaps and melts, which is not completely unproblematic due to the lower chemical and thermal compatibility of the polyester. It has been reported that the polyester material became so brittle that one could rub it to dust. Therefore, such filter cartridge should be inspected on a regular basis, if used in applications with multiple uses. In the past, polyurethane adhesives were also used in endcap materials. In conjunction with polyurethane sealant, the use of polypropylene endcaps has sometimes resulted in the falling off of end-caps; therefore, ultrasonic welding is the most common bondage of end-caps nowadays. Besides using similar components, means also a low extractable level. Polysulfone endcaps are also used when required, as an inert polymeric material that can be adhered dependably to the pleat pack/outer support cage without creating hydrophobic spotting problems.

In the past, a stainless steel ring stabilized the cartridge filtrate outlet against steam-induced dimensional changes and hence preserved the integrity of the O-ring seal to the filter housing base. The use of such dimension-stabilizing rings is made in the construction of pharmaceutical-grade cartridges intended for sterilization(s), especially when polypropylene end caps are involved. Nevertheless, it has been also found that such stainless steel ring, with different expansion rates during temperature changes can also cause problems in respect to hairline cracks and fissures within the adapter polymer or the welding sites. This could go so far that the adapter damage does not allow any longer proper O-ring sealing (Figure 3.5). This effect often has been seen with adapter, which has not been molded from one piece, but are two pieces welded together. The welding starts cracking, liquid penetrates into the stainless steel ring cavity and expand during the next steaming (Jornitz and Meltzer, 2000). To avoid the differences in expansion of the support ring and the adapter polymer, most of the adapters are constructed with a polymer support ring.

The outer support cage is responsible for forming the outer support structure of the cartridge and for holding the pleated internal contents together. The outer support cage also provides for a backpressure guard in preventing loss of filter medium integrity as a result of fluid flowing in the opposite direction under excessive backpressure. Additionally, it eases the handling of the filter cartridge during installation. The user does not come in direct contact with the pleats and damage can be avoided.

The outer filter pleated support layer serves as a multipurpose constituent. Pleating, and the assembly of the membrane into cartridge form, requires its inclusion in the cartridge. The supportive outer pleated layer aids in protecting the filter medium throughout the cartridge pleating and assembly operation. The material also serves as a prefilter to extend the useful service life of the final membrane that lies beneath it. Lastly, the support maintains the structure throughout fluid processing. Without this layer, the pleats under pressure might be compressed, limiting the filter area available to the fluid processing.

FIGURE 3.5 Filter cartridge adapter damage.

The drainage or downstream screen, similar to the outer filter pleat support, stabilizes the pleating of the pleat pack. Additionally, it keeps the filter medium pleats separated during fluid processing to assure that maximum filtration area is open for optimum flow rates and drainage of remaining filtrate, i.e., reducing the dead volume or otherwise trapped fluids. The filter arrangement of the microporous membrane sandwiched between the support and drainage layers, all simultaneously pleated, is often called the "filter pack" or the "pleat pack" (Figure 3.6).

Ultrasonic welding is widely used as the sealing between the pleat pack, drainage fleeces, inner core and outer cage, and the endcaps. Early potting work with melted polypropylene on nylon cartridges attributed to the generation (possibly through wicking) of hydrophobic spots that frustrated attempts to bubble-point the sealed cartridge. At least one company, therefore, adopted polyester sealants as a potting agent. A less general heating of a more restricted area seems to avoid the (wicking) problem. Use of a low-melting sealant may involve some ½ in. of the pleat pack at each end of the filter assembly. A newer sealing technique utilizing polyolefin endcaps relies on fusion welding of the cap to approximately 1/8 in. of each of the pleat pack. Valuable EFA is retained thereby. The tendency in cartridge sealing is to utilize as few different materials as possible. Polytetrafluoroethylene (PTFE) or PVDF microporous membranes are applied for their hydrophobicity (vent and air filters) or for their chemical compatibility to certain solvents and oxidizers, or to hot acids (semiconductor etchants). Thermoplastic fluorinated polymers, preferably as fluorinated as possible, are used for the cartridge components and in its sealed construction.

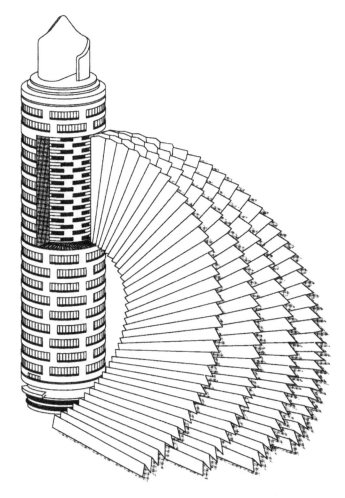

FIGURE 3.6 Schematic representation of filter cartridge (outer support fleece, upstream membrane, final membrane, and inner support fleece).

The melts supported are then usually made of a porous Teflon® material or of PVDF, as is also the remainder of the cartridge hardware from the like polymer in its solid, impervious form.

The filter cartridge inner core serves as the inner hollow tube on which the pleated pack is supported. It confers strength upon the cartridge assembly. This component also determines the final assembly length of the cartridge. Lastly, the core is the outlet port of the cartridge. Through its perforations of the inner core, the filtered fluid passes to be guided to the outlet of the filter housing (filtrate side). The cartridge core should not be flow limiting, but can be in high flow applications, for example, in air filtration or water filtration with prefilter cartridges. It can be seen that the flow rate will not drastically increase by using a 30″ filter size to a 20″ air filter (Figure 3.7), as the flow is restricted by the inner core diameter. The only benefit here is a higher service life, but not an increase in flow. For this reason, air filtration systems are commonly sized with 20″ filter cartridges.

The filter membrane is the heart of the filter cartridge, responsible for removal of the contaminants. Solutions permeate into and through the filter medium and into the cartridge core, then proceed through the outlet assembly and filtrate piping. Once the filter medium has become fully wetted, processing can be continued until one of several flow decay indicators signals the need for cartridge replacement, as customer preference dictates. When the filter is used as the sterilizing or terminal filter, the filter sizing is of importance, as the filter shall never prematurely block before the batch of fluid is filtered. The sizing of the filter system is therefore a very important exercise and typically performed with the support of the filter supplier.

Cartridge designs can be manifold and fit for the application. Not only size differences are applicable, but also cartridge adapters, i.e., plug-ins, which fit into filter housings sockets and recesses (Figure 3.8). A single cartridge with an end plug is used as a 10″ filter. Otherwise, it can be joined by adapters to as many 10″ double open-end cartridges as are necessary to form the ultimate unit length desired. The filter user needs stock only three items, namely, the double open-end cartridges, the adapters, and end plugs. Nevertheless, joining such 10″ element together manually include also the risk of bypasses around the O-rings or gaskets used. Consequently, these types of designs are undesirable in today's applications.

Single open-ended filter cartridges with double-bayonet lock are mostly used for sterilizing grade filter cartridges due to the reliability of the fit into the housing and the form hold of the filter by the bayonet lock. Bypass situations have to be avoided, which can only be accomplished, if the sealing between the filter cartridge and its holder is smug and stays as such. In the case of the string-wound prefilter cartridges, no endcaps are used, because the avoidance of product bypass is not as critical as in sterilizing grade filtration (Technical Report 26, 2008). Having said this, it is always desirable that any filter cartridge element is firmly fit in the housing and properly sealed, as bypass situations in prefilter application could foul the sterilizing grade filter following. Again that premature fouling is very undesirable.

In microporous membrane applications, frequent use is made of the single open-end 10″ cartridge, usually in T-type housings. Such a unit is manufactured with an integral endcap and also constructed in

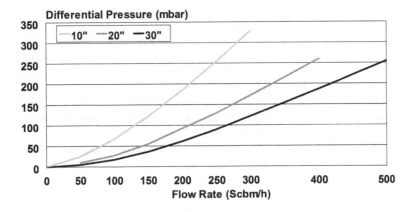

FIGURE 3.7 Flow rate curves of 10″, 20″, and 30″ filter cartridges sizes.

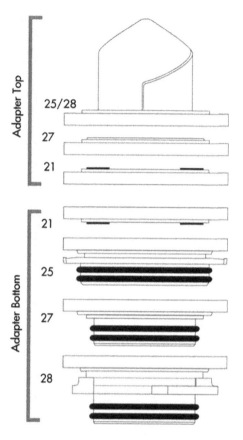

FIGURE 3.8 Different filter cartridge adapter types and designs.

20″ and 30″ lengths. Attempts have been made to offer pharmaceutical manufacturers the versatility of 10″ single and double open-end units to be assembled via adapters with O-rings. As such an arrangement increases the critical sealing area, its acceptance has been limited. The more widespread use in critical pharmaceutical manufacture is of single open-end 10″, 20″, and 30″ properly welded cartridges.

The O-ring materials used are also of critical importance, as the chemical compatibility of the O-ring material has to be determined toward the fluid to be filtered and the time and mode of use. The O-ring is the critical area of the separation between up- and downstream side; therefore, any incompatibility might be a hazard to the filtrate quality. Furthermore, in instances of multiple steam sterilization, the O-ring material has to be checked for so-called heat-set. The O-ring experiences the pressure points from the housing wall and the cartridge adapter. When the temperature is elevated, as in the steaming process, the O-ring starts deforming at the pressure points. If the O-ring material is not flexible enough, the deformation (heat-set) will be upheld. The O-ring will commonly show an oval shape. In applications, where the filter is used over a long time with multiple steam cycles, it is recommended that O-rings are visually inspected on a routine basis to see whether the O-ring is deformed. Any heat-set might result into a bypass situation. ethylene propylene diene methylene (EPDM) O-ring materials showed so far, the highest heat-set tendency, nevertheless are very compatible to chemicals. Silicone has commonly a high flexibility and low heat-set (Meltzer and Jornitz, 1998).

In the past, the dimensions of the membrane cartridges were derived from those of the string-wound filters, roughly 10″ length × 2.5″ diameter. Increasing the diameters of these cartridges serves to increase their EFA (per unit number of pleats). Most manufacturers supply cartridges with a 2.75″ (70 mm) diameter. Diameters as well as adapter types are commonly standardized or similar, which create the opportunity for the filter user to choose. Additional capital investments into different filter housings are not necessary due to the common adapter types utilized.

The resulting increase in the EFA reflects two factors in addition to the cartridge diameter. The first consideration is the diameter of the inner core of the cartridge with its effect on the pleat structure. Each pleat consists of a membrane layer or of multiple membrane layers, sandwiched between two protective layers whose presence is necessary to avoid damage to the membrane in the pleating process, and which serve usefully in the finished cartridge as pleat separation and drainage layers. As a consequence of this sandwich construction, each pleat, naturally, has a certain thickness. Fewer of these thicknesses can be arranged around an inner core of narrower diameter. Therefore, increasing the diameter of the center core increases the extent of its perimeter and the number of pleats that can surround it. This governs the number of pleats possible in the pleat pack that can comprise the membrane cartridge, thus increasing its EFA.

One other consideration favors the use of inner cores with larger diameters. Particularly in longer cartridges, 20″ or 30″ used under elevated applied differential pressures, the liquid flow through the microporous membrane may be so great as to find restrictions to its passage through long inner cores of narrower diameters. Thus, in pleated cartridge constructions intended for the high water flows of the nuclear power industry, the outer cartridge diameter may be 12″ to accommodate a maximum number of high pleats or greater arranged around a center core dimensioned at a 10″ diameter. The concern, exclusive of pleat heights, is to increase the service life, the throughput of the filter, by increasing its EFA. (In this application, high flow rates are accommodated within the 10″ core diameter.)

Such restrictions to flow within cartridge center cores are generally not the concerns in critical pharmaceutical filtrations, except in air filtration, where large volumes of air are passed through the membrane into the inner core with the possibly lowest pressure loss. Here the inner core may play a possible restrictive factor, which has to be investigated.

To define a cartridge, designations must be made of such considerations as its pore size designation (FDA, 1987), its diameter, its length, the type of outlet, for example, the O-ring(s) sizes, the configuration of the outer end, e.g., open or closed, with or without fin, the type of O-ring or gasket seal, e.g., silicone rubber, EPDM rubber, and any nonstandard features. Manufacturer product numbers serve as shorthand substitutes for the detailed specifications.

The second factor governing the EFA of a cartridge, in addition to its overall diameter and center core diameter, is the pleat height. Obviously, for any given pleat, the greater its height, the longer its surface area. Present pleating machines cannot fashion pleat heights beyond 1″ or so. The designing of a cartridge usually begins with a defining of its overall outside diameter. Given a maximum pleat height of 1″, the maximum size of the center core becomes determined. But if the pleat height is diminished in order for the center core diameter to be increased, the greater overall number of pleats that can be arranged around the wider core may more than compensate in EFA for that lost through pleat height diminution.

The optimum number of pleats to be arranged about a center core of a filter cartridge may reflect the filtrative function for which it is intended (Meltzer, 1986; Jornitz and Meltzer, 2000). In the handling of rather clean, prefiltered liquids, as in most pharmaceutical final filtrations, relatively few particles require removal. A crowding of as large a number of pleats as possible in order to enhance the filter area may be acceptable because the pleat separation layers will operate to make even the crowded surfaces individually available to the liquid being filtered. Where there are high solid loadings in the liquid, or a viscous fluid, a different situation may result. The particles being removed may be large enough to bridge across a pleat, to block the interval between two adjacent pleat peaks. Or, being small, they may, after their individual deposition on the filter, secrete and grow large enough to cause bridging. Whatever the mechanism, the bridging serves to deny the liquid being processed access to useful flow channels bordered by membrane. The EFA would restrict itself to the surface of the pleat edges. In air filtration a too dense pleat pack can also create capillary action which would trap water between the pleats and reduce the EFA by water logging.

In practice, pleated cartridges are built for general usage in what is still an artful construction (Jornitz and Meltzer, 2000; Meltzer and Jornitz, 1998). Nevertheless, there is said to be available an empirically developed formula that relates the outer cartridge diameter to the maximum core diameter, and to the number of pleats of given height that should be used.

Care must be taken to protect the surface of the membrane during the pleating operation, and to avoid damage to the filter structure. Both these objectives are furthered by sandwiching the membrane between two support layers and feeding the combination to the pleater. The outlying support layers protect the membrane surfaces. Nevertheless, the fleeces have to be chosen properly, for example, a fleece too coarse could press too much on the membrane, at the pleating curvation and starts pressing into the membrane. In Figure 3.9, one can see the result of coarse fleece compression on a PTFE membrane, which weakens the membrane and might be detrimental in long-term use of the filter. Especially air filters are used over a long period and experience multiple in-line steam sterilization. If the membrane shows impressions by the coarse filter fleece, this commonly means that the filter membrane in this area is thinning. Multiple steam sterilization could exaggerate this thinning and flaws can develop. On the other hand, a fleece, which is too soft, will not support the membrane sufficiently. Usually soft fleeces have a high fiber density and a small fiber diameter, which means liquid, for example, condensate, would be bound within the fiber structure. Such phenomenon needs to be avoided, for example, in air filtration, because it could cause water logging.

Additionally, the pleat sandwich in its thickness minimizes opportunities for the membrane to be too strongly compressed at the pleat. What is required is a pleat having some radius of curvature rather than a sharp, acute angle of fold. This prevents the membrane from being subjected, at the pleat line, to forces in excess of its mechanical properties as expressed in the magnitude of its tensile and elongation values. Different polymeric materials will, of course, have different tensile and elongation qualities; various materials differ in their brittleness. Pleating of asymmetric membrane requires attention, as the membrane structures will act differently at the different pleat formations. The open asymmetric upstream structure may be stretched to a degree that it breaks or opens up. Any pleating of asymmetric membranes undergoes thorough quality checks to show the pleat edge is not too sharp but rounded. Sharp pleat edges or pleatings with a high pleat density will have a gap in between the pleats, which would result into capillary activity, i.e., in air filtration condensate could potentially be trapped in between the pleats and the air filter might experience water blockage. Therefore, filter designs and construction require thorough investigation in development to achieve the best performance ratios. In instances, the highest effective filtration is in the confined construction of a filter cartridge might not be the optimal solution, as the pleat density becomes too high. However, EFA should also not be too low as it will influence the flow rate and total throughput. Decreasing the diameter of the center core will serve to lessen the number of pleats, although in applications which require a high flow, for example, air, the inner core becomes the flow restrictor. Therefore, the inner core again needs to be optimized to the filter cartridge utilization. For example, a 28-mm core diameter will require a 40%–50% higher differential pressure than a 35-mm inner core to achieve an air flow rate of 100 scbm. This differential pressure increase might not seem to be high, but the costs involved running such pressure difference is substantial.

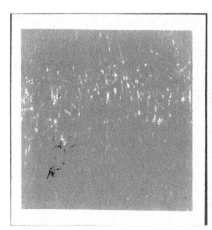 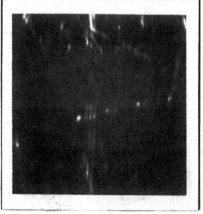

FIGURE 3.9   Prefilter fleece impression on a PTFE membrane.

Capsule Filters

The disk and cartridge filters of commerce are usually disposables. It is their housings and holders, usually of metal, that are permanent. However, filters encapsulated into plastic housings have been devised wherein the entire unit is disposable (Figure 3.10).

There are advantages to these devices. Among them is that many are available in presterilized conditions, by gamma irradiation, steam or ethylene oxide, which bares the advantage that these units are ready to use. They are in a standby condition on the shelf, available when needed. That they are disposables does not necessarily militate against the economics of their usage. Calculations show that where labor costs are reckoned, the installation of a single 293-mm filter disk in its housing and the cleaning, which follows the filtration process, is more costly than the equivalent filtration area in the form of a disposable filter device. The use of the disposables entails very little setup time, and no cleanup time. There is no need to sterilize the already presterilized units. Disposal after the single usage eliminates risks of cross-contamination.

One small volume parenteral (SVP) manufacturer adopted the use of disposable filter devices embodying flat disk filter design of essentially the same EFA as a 293-mm disk to replace the latter. The cost savings, reckoned largely as labor, was considered significant. In making the substitution, there were such factors as flow rate versus differential pressure, throughput, rinse volume, time effect wetting and extractable removal, ability to be heat sterilized, confirmation by vendor of product nontoxicity, and freedom from pyrogenic substances (FDA, 1987; Technical Report 26, 2008). Another SVP manufacturer opted for the same type of replacements, selecting, however, the required EFA in pleated filter capsule form. In both cases, the disposable device was equipped with sanitary connections, enabling a straightforward substitution. Pleated disposable device show commonly better performance due to the prefilter fleeces and sometimes prefilter membrane in front of the final filter membrane. Therefore, 293-mm disc filters could potentially also be replaced by 150 or 300 cm^2 disposable devices, even when such have a smaller EFA.

In one application involving the filtration of serum through a 0.1 μm-rated membrane (Jornitz and Meltzer, 1999), a pleated filter capsule replaced a 293-mm disk because a steam-autoclaved disk holder assembly required a much longer period to cool down to use-temperature than did the plastic-housed disposable filter. The savings in time was judged substantial enough to merit being addressed.

FIGURE 3.10 Different types and styles of disposable capsule filters.

The venting of disposable filter devices has been the recipient of good design considerations. One disposable capsule manufacturer has taken care to so position the vents that they are on the highest point of the containing shell, exactly where they are most effective. Another design utilizes a self-venting device in the form of a hydrophobic membrane. This permits the self-venting of air while safeguarding against the passage of liquid or contaminants (in either direction). This is particularly useful in water installations, where intermittent use serves repeatedly to introduce air to the system. The self-venting feature reduces maintenance and increases the system efficiency.

There are often ancillary advantages to the use of disposable filter devices. Some manufacturers construct their shells of transparent polymers so that the filtration process is observable. The instruments are compact and relatively lightweight, hence, easy to handle. Nor does their construction lack the sophistication of their metal housing-contained counterparts. Thus, many of the disposable units are equipped with vent plugs and drain plugs. The identifying description they bear on their outer casings, make their traceability, in accordance with FDA record requirements rather certain (FDA, 1987). Product and batch numbers become part of the permanent operational record. Above all, the use of these disposables obviates the need to expense or amortize stainless steel filter holders. No capital expenditures are involved.

Furthermore, the use of disposable filters can reduce costs in respect of cleaning, which would occur with stainless steel filter housings after every use. Cleaning validation, which needs to be performed with fixed equipment like filter housings, will be greatly reduced. The disposable filters do not go through such cleaning regime and therefore the validation of cleaning exercises is avoided. For this reason and the convenience of the use of disposable filters, the biopharmaceutical industry switches more and more to capsule filters instead of filter housings. That use of disposable equipment becomes more common can also be seen in the fact that bags replace glass or stainless steel holding and storage vessel. Commonly a disposable capsule filter is connected to such bag; both are available in different sizes for the individual purpose. Once the capsule filter is connected the bag and filter are gamma irradiated to sterilize the entire setup. Single-use process equipment or filter-bag assemblies become widely used within the industry. The benefits of faster processing cycles have been recognized, as well as the possibility to assign the assembly as a closed system, due to sterile aseptic connectors. Single-use process technology is prevalently installed within new processes and converted into older, established processes. Certainly, the filter material and polymers need to be gamma stabile otherwise particle shedding or an excess amount of extractable can occur.

Another advantage is the fact that the user will not encounter the product filtered. This certainly could be the case when using cartridge filters within a housing. The cartridge has to be removed from the housing at the end of the filtration run, i.e., the user probably comes in contact with the filtered product remaining on the filter cartridge and housing, which may need to be avoided due to health hazards or biological activity. Disposable filters create the opportunity to replace a filter without being in contact with the product.

The single-use filter devices are available in a large variety of constructions, whether disk, multidisc, pleated cylinders of various lengths and of different EFAs. Their expanse of filter surface runs from 4-mm discs suitable for affixing to hypodermic needles to 30″ capsules of about 180 ft^2 (1.8 m^2) (Figure 3.11). The filters are made of a variety of polymeric filter materials, both hydrophilic and hydrophobic, namely, cellulose esters, PVDF, polysulfone, polyethersulfone (Meltzer, 1986), nylon, polyethylene, Teflon, etc. Their shells are composed variously of polycarbonate, polyethylene, but most often polypropylene.

The versatility of these single-use filter units is increased by constructions involving integral prefilters, as in one capsule unit having approximately the EFA of a 293-mm disk. This is appropriate, as single-disk filtrations most often involve applications that require the use of a prefilter. Repetitive final filter constructions are also available in disposable unit form. These are used, for instance, in tissue culture medium filtrations where repetitive final filter arrangements are common.

The increase in the tailoring of disposable filter device constructions to specific application needs helps explain the mounting popularity of their usage and heightens predictions of their continuing replacement of at least part of the more conventional filter/holder market.

The use of most cartridge filters accords with FDA emphasis on record keeping. Despite all the care with which filter manufacturers pack flat disk filters, the membranes themselves are unlabeled. Cartridge filters are, however, available with identifying data (Technical Report 26, 2008). Most are identified with

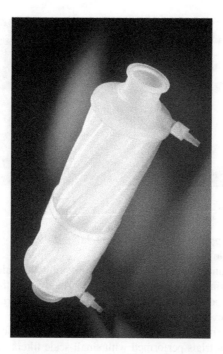

FIGURE 3.11 Large-scale disposable capsule filters.

some code, if not on the cartridge itself then on its container. Some manufacturers stamp or dot matrix code the cartridge endcap with the part number, its pore size identity, and its lot number as well and often manufacturers even number each cartridge consecutively within each lot. Should the need ever arise to trace the components and history of these filters, and of their components, the ability to do so exists. Batch records in concert with the appropriate manufacturing QC records make this possible.

Because of the criticality of use of membrane filters, appropriate and even extreme care is to be used in their handling. In the case of cartridge filters, this practice continues. However, the actual membrane surface of these instruments is out of reach of ordinary handling. There is, therefore, far less possibility of damage to the filters. Overall, cartridges are used mostly for the more rapid flow rates and/or the large-volume filtration productions they enable, a consequence of their aggrandized EFAs.

Cartridges are increasingly constructed so that their *in situ* sterilization can be affected by the convenient use of the steam-in-place technique.

Lenticular Prefilter Designs

Lenticular filter designs are mainly used as clarifying filters in cell harvest applications or very typical in the beverage industry. Highly adsorptive cellulosic or kieselgur-containing depth filter pads are welded together in a plate format (Figure 3.12). These plate formats commonly have a diameter of 12″ or 16″ and are welded together in stacks of 4–16 to create a depth filter unit.

The benefits of these depth filter materials are the tremendous dirt load capacity (total throughput). These filters are commonly used to prefilter solutions, which would blind membrane filters rapidly. The adsorptive depth filter material is ideal to separate colloidal substances and lipids; therefore, these filters are very often found in plasma and serum applications. Furthermore, these filters also find their use in the cell harvest step in downstream processing after the bioreactor. Again, the high dirt load capacity is appreciated within such application. When compared to the traditional technologies of centrifugation or cross-flow microfiltration, the combination of dirt hold capacity and reduction of the filtrates turbidity show better results than the quoted alternative technologies. Nevertheless, the selection of the separation technology of choice within the cell harvest application requires performance analysis, as the results

FIGURE 3.12   Lenticular depth filter stack design.

can vary from application to application. It is detrimental to test the performance in small-scale trials to utilize later in the process scale the optimal technology.

As with pleated membrane and prefilter cartridges, the possibility to scale the filter element is essential (Meltzer, 1987). Large-scale trial most often cannot be performed due to the lack of product and more so financial burden. The filter products require to be scaled-down to perform optimization and validation trials at the lowest possible burden on product volume requirements. The ability to scale-down the filter is one side of the story. More importantly, the results gained in small-scale trials require to be linear scalable to process scale. Any trials performed with small-scale filters, which have a different design in process scale, are of no value, as the more tests are required in large scale due to the design change. For this reason, filter manufacturers designed specific small-scale devices which mirror the larger-scale process filter (Figure 3.13).

Since such filters are utilized in biopharmaceutical processes, these filters required to be in-line steam sterilized and fully validated. Especially leachable levels of the filters need to be low or the flush volume required to achieve regulatory requirements need to be a slow as possible. These critical parameters have been picked up by the filter manufacturers and current lenticular filters have a far higher mechanical and thermal stability than in the past. The construction and design of the support cages and fleeces, the welding and adapter technology evolved. The filters reached with these design changes a higher stability and safety level. Since most of the filter pads utilized in lenticular filters are resin bonded, the filters are pre-flushed within the manufacturers production process to achieve the low leachable level required. Nevertheless, as with pleated filter devices, the leachable level should be determined within the filter user's production facility to evaluate any product or production process influences. Most of the filter

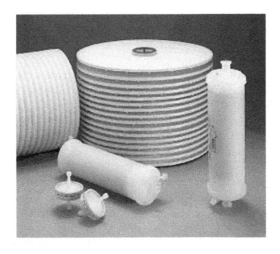

FIGURE 3.13   Scalable lenticular depth filter types.

manufacturers testing conditions are very specific and are commonly achieved utilizing water as a test fluid. As some products can have a different influence on the filter's matrix and operating parameters on the stability of the filter, the filter requires to be validated into these conditions. Again, small-scale device might help in this exercise.

When lenticular filter combinations are tested, the tests do not only involve the total throughput of the filter element as it is commonly the case with pleated prefilter cartridges, but an important factor is the turbidity measurement of the filtrate. The turbidity measurement will create an indication of the protective properties of the lenticular filter retention rating used and how much of the contaminants are separated by the particular filter rating. Since the applications for lenticular filters vary, these filters have to undergo tests, which include the process conditions. The retentivity efficiency of these filters is very much dependent on the fluid contact time within the filter matrix. The longer the contact time the better the separation of contaminants, as the main separation force of these filters is adsorptive retention. Therefore, the process conditions especially pressure and flow conditions require evaluation to find the optimal total throughput combination with the lowest turbidity level within the filtrate. At the beginning of a trial the lowest possible differential pressure is used, which fulfills the flow requirements. Samples are taken in specific time intervals and the turbidity measured. This gives an indication of which pressure conditions is the optimal for the filtration task, but also might show the exhaustion of the filter media, if after a certain filtered volume, the turbidity of the filtrate starts rising. These tests will determine the process conditions required that the filter needs to be used at. To determine which turbidity level is the optimal filtrates with specific turbidities are utilized with membrane filters, which commonly follow the lenticular prefilter. These trials will show, at which turbidity level the next membrane filter step will obtain the highest total throughput. Once the optimal process parameters are determined they are locked in the filtration protocol and the standard operating procedures.

Conclusion

A multitude of filter designs, past and current, have been used and established. Filter designs fulfill specific application and performance requirements. The design of a filter for a specific application is intricate and requires to be evaluated thoroughly instead of being blindly installed. Every filtration application has its optimal filter, whether it is the chemical compatibility, the particulate load, the flow requirements, unspecific adsorption, hold-up volumes, multi-use, etc. All the different technical aspects need to be utilized as scope for the designs' respective choice as which filter system should be used. For the benefit of the industry with its wide array of different applications, the filter suppliers developed a similar wide array of filter designs and specifications. Nowadays, the choice of high-quality, robust filters is staggering very much to the appreciation of the end user.

REFERENCES

American Society for Testing and Materials (ASTM) (1988). Standard F838-83, Standard Test Method for Determining Bacterial Retention of Membrane Filters Utilized for Liquid Filtration. Revised 1988.

Badenhop, C.T., (1983). The Determination of the Pore Distribution and the Consideration of Methods Leading to the Prediction of Retention Characteristics of Membrane Filters. D. Eng., University of Dortmund.

Carter, J.R. and Levy, R.V., (1998). Microbial retention testing in the validation of sterilizing filtration. In *Filtration in the Biopharmaceutical Industry.* Meltzer, T.H. and Jornitz, M.W., Eds., Marcel Dekker, New York.

Datar, R., Martin, J.M. and Manteuffel, R.I., (1992). Dynamics of protein recovery from process filtration systems using microporous membrane filter cartridges, *J. Parenter. Sci. Technol.* 46(2): 35–42.

FDA, Center for Drugs and Biologics and Office of Regulatory Affairs (1987). Guideline on Sterile Drug Products Produced by Aseptic Processing.

Jornitz, M.W. and Meltzer, T.H., (1998). Sterile double filtration, *Pharm. Tech.* 22(10): 92–100.

Jornitz, M.W. and Meltzer, T.H., (1999). Addressing Uncertainties in Sterile Filtrations; Substituting Double Filters and 0. 1 for 0.2 μm Rating.

Jornitz, M.W. and Meltzer, T.H., (2000), *Sterile Filtration—A Practical Approach*, Marcel Decker, New York.

Meltzer, T.H. and Jornitz, M.W., Eds., (1998), *Filtration in the Biopharmaceutical Industry*, Marcel Dekker, New York.

Meltzer, T.H., (1987). Chapter 1: Depth-filters, particles and filter ratings. In *Filtration in the Pharmaceutical Industry*. pp. 3–60, Marcel Dekker, New York.

Meltzer, T.H., (1986). The advantages of asymmetric filter morphology, *Ultrapure Water* 3(6): 43–48.

Technical Report No. 26 (revised 2008). Sterilizing filtration of liquids, *PDA J. Pharm. Sci. Technol.* 52.

4

Membrane Pore Structure and Distribution

Maik W. Jornitz
G-CON Manufacturing, Inc.

CONTENTS

Membrane Filter Pore Formation

The microporous filter membrane analogy is that of a polymeric sponge. Little is known about the exact sizes and shapes of the pores throughout the membrane structure. An oversimplified picture of the pore passageways is that of irregular and tortuous interconnected spaces extending through the depth of the polymer matrix. As just explained, the structure derives from a polymer solution being casted or quenched on specified steel belts. The chain segments are separated from one another by distances that reflect its dilution. It is the intersegmental distances among the polymeric chains that in their interconnections prefigure the pores of the finished membrane. Formulae of different polymer concentrations give rise to different intersegmental separations, ultimately to different porosities, when by proper manipulations the polymer is precipitated as a gel, to be either washed or dried to its solid, microporous membrane state. There is inevitably a pore size distribution, and some anisotropic pore shape formation (Kesting 1985). The pore size depends on different parameter variables, like polymeric component concentrations, casting speed, and environmental conditions. The recipes for such membrane formation processes are highly guarded and controlled diligently to obtain quality consistency.

The casting solution, as stated, consists of polymer dissolved in a mixture of solvent and high-boiling, typically aqueous, non-solvent. In terms meaningful to the polymer chemist, pore formation occurs as follows: As solvent progressively evaporates from the casting solution, the non-solvent increases in content to the point where phase separation takes place. Non-solvent droplets separate within the polymer/solvent phase, and polymer comes out of solution to concentrate at the phase interfaces. The swollen polymer shells surrounding the non-solvent droplets thicken as continuing solvent loss occasions of more polymer deposition. The eventual disappearance of the polymer/solvent phase brings the polymer-surrounded droplets into mutual contact. They consolidate into clusters and distort into polyhedral cells filled with non-solvent under the impetus of area-minimizing forces. Finally, the edges of the cells accumulate polymer at the expense of the cell walls. Thinning of the walls of the polyhedra leads to their rupture, and interconnection. The reticulation of the discrete cells of the polymeric matrix permits the removal of the non-solvent, as by washing or drying. Not the polyhedral cells, but their interconnecting openings, thus formed, comprise the metering pores of the membrane (Kesting 1985). The described process happens when the polymeric dough is cast on a belt and run through an evaporation process. Other casting processes, called quenching, happen by casting a polymeric dough on a rotary belt and immerse the dough into a chemical bath which allows precipitation of the polymer. The pore forming solvent is washed out and creates the porous structure. Both casting procedures are used for different types of polymers. Evaporation casting is mainly used for cellulosic polymers and immersion casting of polyamide, polyvinylidene fluoride, and polyethersulfone.

Pore Shapes

As stated, the filter pores are usually pictured as being irregular and tortuous capillaries composed of interconnected spaces within the polymer matrix. As stated, casting formulae of different polymer concentrations give rise to different intersegmental separations, ultimately to different porosities.

Williams and Meltzer (1983) hypothesize the formation of the microporous membrane structure according to known "soap bubble clustering." The reasons for this resemblance are that in both cases there is the coming together of spheres whose spatial clustering is under the influence of area-minimizing forces. The geometric consequences of these forces are known from the study of soap bubbles (Almgren and Taylor 1976). Polygonal facets characterize the resulting spaces of a free-floating cluster of soap bubbles, as shown in Figure 4.1. In the pore formation, non-solvent takes the place of the air of the bubbles. Figure 4.2 is of detergent foam confined between glass plates. The polyhedral spatial structures are obvious. Figure 4.3 is of a reticulated polyurethane (polymeric) foam. The cellular pores are seen to be polygonal in shape. The phenomenon of clustering through polyhedral spatial arrangements is manifest in other settings. It is a trait of zeolitic molecular sieves whose interconnection is through the open panels common to contiguous polyhedra, although caused by crystal-packing rather than area-minimizing forces.

In the case of the membranes, the pores are formed from the open areas prefigured in the casting solution. They are hypothesized to be of various polygonal shapes, framed by polymeric struts and walls, and to be, like the zeolites, interconnected by openings in their common walls. It is these openings that are seen to be the metering and retaining pores of the membranes.

FIGURE 4.1   Connected soap bubble cluster.

FIGURE 4.2   Detergent foam cluster between glass plates.

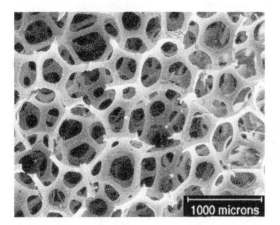

FIGURE 4.3   Polyurethane foam.

Porosity and Pore Numbers

The porosity of the filter, its total open pore structure, is difficult to measure. Mercury porosimetry is not adequate; surface area measurements are not suitable; scanning electron micrographs (SEMs) are not representative (Figure 4.4). It is generally assayed, though with some inexactness, by comparing the weight of an area of dry membrane with one whose pores are filled with water, making allowances for the different fluid densities. The set of largest pores can be identified by bubble point determinations. The number of pores, however defined, is estimated on the basis of oversimplified assumptions. The values arrived at are consequently unreliable. The number of the all-important retentive pores, or of the largest pores, cannot be assessed with any degree of confidence. The pore size distribution, an important structural feature, is seldom assayed although an ASTM method (F-316–1980) based on air flow rates exists for so doing. Automated equipment for this purpose was devised by Badenhop in 1983 (Badenhop et al. 1970; Badenhop 1983; Meltzer 1987, Chap. 3). Porometers based on the Badenhop design are commercially available and at least can create comparability results of different membranes and membrane structures.

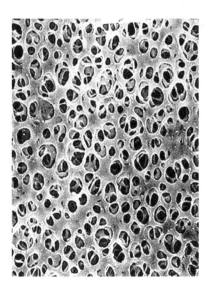

FIGURE 4.4   Cellulosic membrane structure.

The various techniques for measuring porosity offer a way of disclosing the morphological structure of a membrane that flow measurements alone cannot reveal. For example, if the density of a given filter is high, it may indicate that a degree of compaction of the membrane has occurred. The static flow measurements may not have been materially affected, but the membrane may show a rapid clog rate during filtration runs. These evaluations are of prime interest to the membrane manufacturer in establishing effective process control of the casting processes as a consistent reliable membrane propensity is of utmost desire. Filter manufacturers have, therefore, improved the control mechanisms and meet the quality consistency requirements of the industry.

Commercially Available Membranes

Microporous membranes are available from several filter manufacturers in a series of pore sizes ranging from 0.04 to 8 μm. The ratings are assigned individually by each manufacturer; there was no true industry standard. Consequently, the same pore size ratings from the various manufacturers may actually be different. The resolve to avoid random labeling of filter membrane and determine a distinct performance attribute, a group of filter manufacturers and industry experts defined a specific microbial challenge test to determine the sterilizing grade filter, typically being a 0.2 or 0.22 μm membrane. The challenge standard, first known as HIMA standard, has been evolved and recently republished by ASTM as F838-15. It created the first standard cluster of membrane filters, which were comparable and could be consistently evaluated by the end user. This comparison was not possible with 0.1 μm membrane filters, resulting in erroneous performance claims.

In any case, the pore size ratings do not have dimensional significance. Each pore size rating group is prepared using a different casting formula. However, their preparation does not yield distinct quanta, although the variations within a class are less than those between classes. Each batch of membranes is labeled by a single pore size value, although each of the individual filters comprising the group has its variance within that rating. Therefore, a given membrane may more accurately be described as a "tight 0.2" or as an "open 0.1." Yet it will be labeled with either one or the other pore sizes. In the actual event, one manufacturer could call it the one pore size; another could label it the other, and the very same membrane would be evaluated differently on the basis of its label. In the one case, it might be classified as "a slow flowing 0.2/0.2 micron filter." In the other, it would be "a fast flowing 0.1 micron filter." Performance comparisons with other 0.1s or 0.2/0.2s, especially of other manufacturers, may become skewed; as for example, 0.1 µm-rated membranes seemingly flowing faster than 0.2/0.2 µm-rated filters. This may not be a surprise for a filter expert, realizing that a single layer 0.1 µm membrane has a lower flow resistance than a homogenous double-layer 0.2/0.2 µm membrane. To make matters worse there was no comparison standard for 0.1 µm membrane, which resulted in the tight or open type of pore structure claims. Microbial challenge tests take these terms out of the equation, as the filter either retains the organism under specific challenge conditions or not.

Three important performances by which filters are often judged are particle retention, total throughput and flow rate. It would be expected that membranes of identical pore size ratings and porosity should give rather equal performances of flow and possibly of retention. That, however, is not the case. Pore and particle shapes, both largely unknown, are among the reasons. A lack of standards in rating is another. The influences of particle retention mechanisms also have an effect. As is shown in Table 4.1, Tolliver and Schroeder (1983) found that the retention of 0.198 µm latex particles by five commercially available 0.2 or 0.22 µm-rated membranes differed significantly.

Lindenblatt et al. (2002) report (Figure 4.5) that the flow rates exhibited by four 0.2 or 0.22 µm-rated membranes, as also of four 0.1 µm-rated filters differed markedly. Moreover, as indicated in Figure 4.6, the throughput volumes to a 95% extent of blocking also differed. Jornitz et al. (2004) offer comparable data.

The dissimilarity in flow rate performance can be rationalized as reflecting differences in membrane thinness, total porosities, novel filter design, or membrane configuration. A double-layer 0.2/0.2 µm filter membrane configuration is thicker than a single 0.1 µm filter, which result in a higher flow resistance. However, the total throughput of the 0.1 µm filter will be much lower, as there is no protective prefilter membrane in front of the end filter membrane. Yet, such factors are not mentioned in the manufacturers'

TABLE 4.1

Retentivity of Different Membrane Polymers with Different Fluids

Filter Type	In Water	In 0.05% Triton X-100
Polycarbonate	100.0	100.0
Asymmetric Polysulfone	100.0	100.0
Polyvinylidene Fluoride	74.8	19.2
Nylon 66	82.1	1.0
Cellulose Esters	89.4	25.1

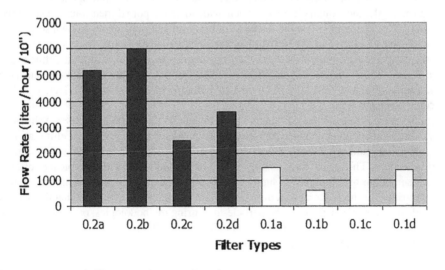

FIGURE 4.5 Flow rates of different membrane configurations.

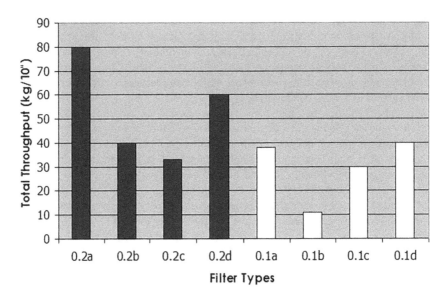

FIGURE 4.6   Total throughput of different membrane configurations.

descriptions of their membranes, as would be expected for an exceptional property. Consequently, it becomes an unrewarding exercise to try to compare even identically labeled filters from their catalogue descriptions. As is usually the case in the physical sciences, reliable evaluations and comparisons must be derived from performance data obtained through experimental investigation. This is especially true since there is no perfect filter unit available, but specific, optimal filter systems for the individual applications. It is of need to determine which filter is the ideal for the specific application and process parameters at hand.

Pore Size Ratings

Numerous methods have been utilized to assess pore size (See Meltzer 1987, Chap. 3). Early on mercury porosimetry was the method of choice (Honold and Skau 1954; Rootare and Spencer 1972; Williams 1984). Not surprisingly, substantial efforts had been made to define pore dimensions by way of the retention of particles. Pore sizing based on the retention of organisms of presumably known sizes was widely investigated (Rogers and Rossmore 1970; Wallhäusser 1979; Pall et al. 1980). The results of these efforts supported the establishment of the described challenge standards, helpful to at least define a sterilizing grade filter. However, such filters are typically labeled as 0.2 or 0.22 μm membrane filters, but a measurement of the true pore may not reveal a 0.2 pore size, but adsorptive retention is effective and the pore structure could be larger.

Sizing studies were also made based on latex bead retentions (Wrasidlo et al. 1983; Schroeder 1984) (Figure 4.7). These, in conjunction with the use of surfactant, have the advantage of eliminating adsorptive effects. The undertakings assumed the exclusivity of sieve retentions and ignored the existence of pore size distributions. The results were usually judged of limited value. This is typical of efforts where simplifying assumptions are employed in support of a hypothesis; the very conclusions are limited by the inherent arbitrariness of the necessary premises. They are complicated by the fact that the definitions of the particles themselves may depend on the particle-measuring methodologies; on the procedural protocols; and on the measuring devices used (Rogers and Rossmore 1970). The all-too-vague understanding of the "pore" structure complicates the situation.

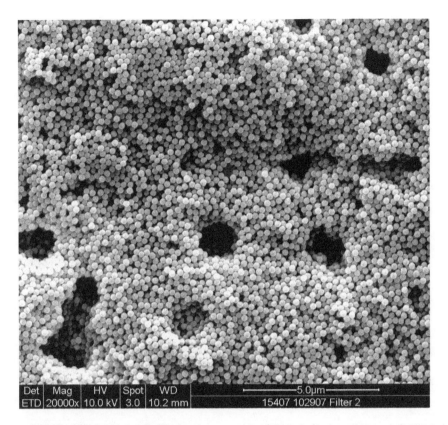

FIGURE 4.7 Membrane challenged with latex beads.

Mean Flow Pore

The ASTM (1980) sized the pore in terms of its flow rate capabilities, namely, as the mean flow-pore. This appellation has the advantage of not automatically implying, as measurements with particles do, that sieve retention and the relationship of pore and particle sizes alone correctly define the rating. The mean flow pore can be arrived at by way of graphical plotting (Figure 4.8). The straight-line relationship of air flow rate versus applied differential pressure is plotted for a dry membrane. The procedure is then repeated for a wet membrane (pores filled with water). The applied differential air pressure will cause no frank air flow through the wet membrane at pressures below the "bubble point." At the bubble point, the water is forced out of the set of largest pores, and air flow, thus, begins. Increasing the air pressure will cause the set of next smaller pores to open, and so on, until the air pressure is sufficient to open all the pores of the membrane. These pores are so opened as to form an inversely proportional relationship between pore size and the pressure required for evacuation of the pores. Plotting air flow through the wet membrane as a function of the applied pressure yields a sigmoidal curve whose upper reaches become asymptotic to the dry membrane air-flow curve. The rate of air flow through the dry membrane represents the total air flow at any applied differential pressure, all the pores being open to accommodate that flow. Therefore, half the total air flow is represented by a line drawn to bisect into halves the angle separating the dry-air flow rate from the differential pressure axis, the abscissa. Extension of the drawn line to the wet-flow curve followed by extrapolation from that point to the pore size scale, also on the abscissa, reveals the mean flow-pore value of the filter.

PORE SIZE RATINGS
MEAN FLOW-PORE MEASUREMENT

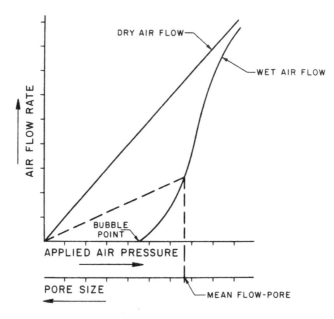

FIGURE 4.8 Mean flow pore determination.

Absence of Rating Standards

Each filter manufacturer is free to use his own pore sizing method. There being no industry standard, the different rating methods need not agree, and some confusion inevitably results. Indeed, one manufacturer of polyamide membranes advised that on the basis of latex particle retention his 0.2 μm-rated filter deserved a 0.48 μm rating, while his 0.1 μm-rated membrane should be listed as 0.26 μm-rated (Krygier 1986). Pall et al. (1980) state that nylon and cellulose ester membranes that are labeled 0.2/0.22 μm-rated, on the not-unusual basis that they retain the ASTM standard challenge of 1×10^7 cfu of *B. diminuta* per cm^2 of effective filtration area (EFA), would be labeled 0.4–0.6 μm rated on the basis of latex particle retentions, and that a particular 0.1 μm-rated nylon 66 membrane would be classified as being 0.286 μm-rated.

The pore size ratings are not found on direct mensuration and do not represent actual pore dimensions. Nevertheless, on the basis of experience, the assigned pore size numbers do offer a level of practical guidance to particle retentions. This is of importance as the end user requires an indication of the potential retention performance of the filters. However inexactly, they bear a relationship to particle sizes. As catalogue or parts numbers, they serve as an administrative tool for the filter suppliers and end user alike.

Early exaggerated reports of pore size uniformity confused the meaning of the pore size rating. Meant to signal the mean pore size, it was translated also as identifying the largest pores, those that are the concern in particle retentions. Experts in the membrane field advised, "The membrane filter functions primarily as a screen filter. It retains all particles larger than the pore size of the filter" (Dwyer 1966). This is now known not to be so, nor, as stated, does the pore size rating value represent the pore dimensions. This erroneous concept sustained belief in the exclusivity of sieve retention, and catered to the comforting, though erroneously, reliance on absolute filters. The series of experimental findings in the 1970s and 1980s, referenced below corrected the record. Absoluteness cannot be claimed, when fluid compositions, microorganism type, or process parameters may have an influence on the retention performance of a particular filter. This fact is the main reason why process validation of the sterilizing grade filter is required. Within the validation exercise the true performance of the filter is confirmed.

Latex Particles

Rigid cross-linked polystyrene spheres are available in rather precise narrow size ranges. These particles are spherical because they are produced by emulsion polymerization. The styrene and divinylbenzene of which they are polymerized are insoluble in the suspending aqueous medium. Vigorous stirring disperses this liquid organic material into emulsified micro-quantities that, being immiscible with water, assume spherical form. Once polymerized, the latex particles are rigid, which is to say, relatively incompressible because the styrene is cross-linked with the divinylbenzene to make them so. The standard spheres are not perfectly mono-sized but do have an extremely narrow Gaussian particle size distribution predetermined by the conditions of the emulsification (largely the rate of stirring) and verified by a variety of instrumental and microscopic methods. The median particle size is defined as that point at which one-half of the particles are larger and one-half smaller. These spherical particles have been employed in defining filter pore size ratings by offering calibrations of the pore size just sufficient to sieve retain them.

Latex Particle Applications

Attempts to size pores were made involving the retention of latex particles of known size in the presence of surfactant (0.1% non-ionic Triton X-100). The surface active agent was employed because of its ability to neutralize adsorptive effects of either the membrane or the latex beads (Wrasidlo et al. 1983; Wrasidlo and Mysels 1984; Tolliver and Schroeder 1983). Elimination of the complications posed by simultaneous organism adsorptions and sieve retentions was sought.

Pall et al. (1980) used such monodispersed latex spheres in a comparative study of a nylon membrane and a filter of mixed esters of cellulose. These investigators employed a special holder to contain a 47-mm disk filter on a wire mesh support with an O-ring so positioned as to define precisely $10\,cm^2$ of filter test area that could be bubble point tested and subjected to challenge by the latex particles. The retained spheres were counted using an ISI Model 40 scanning electron microscope at $7,000 \times$ magnification. (Approximately 1×10^{11} latex particles could be counted over a 1-h period.) The second method of sphere quantification involved measurement of solution turbidimetry using ultraviolet adsorption by the filtrate at 310 nm and employing a Beckman 26 spectrophotometer.

Pall et al. (1980) found that the efficiency of latex bead retention by membranes was affected by pH; more so at lower pHs. This is in line with the effect of high ionic strengths on adsorptions. The larger hydronium ion concentrations increased the electrokinetic charge effects. As will shortly be explained, this encourages the adsorptive retention of latex particles. To the contrary, the effect of surfactant discourages adsorptions, either by decreasing the surface's adsorption-propensities, or alternatively, by attaching surfactant molecules to, and coating the latex particles. This increases their effective diameters to the extent where the distances separating them, the Debye length, become too large for the weak adsorptive forces to bridge. This is described as being an example of steric stabilization. When Triton X-100 was absent, the retention results, although erratic, were higher, because adsorptive separation influences were permitted to manifest themselves as a reinforcement to the sieve retention.

Wrasidlo et al. (1983) encountered similar influences of pH, and of surfactants, using 0.1% Triton X-100, on latex particle retentions (Tables 4.1 and 4.2), as also did Lee et al. (1993). Other surfactants provided somewhat different amounts of latex retentions in studies by Emory et al. (1993).

Kaczmarek et al. (1978) at IITRI of Illinois Institute of Technology addressed this point with scanning electron microscopy. The investigators used 0.23 μm Dow latex spheres in concentrations of 10^5–10^9/mL in conjunction with *B. diminuta* at the 10^8/mL level at an applied differential pressure level of 10 psi ($0.7\,kg/cm^2$) to challenge 0.2 μm-rated membranes. They found that all of the membranes investigated withstood the bacterial challenge; none was absolute against the passage of latex particles. Zeman (Zeman and Zydney

TABLE 4.2

Microbial Penetration of Various Organisms in Different Solutions

Organism	Source Reference	Growth Medium	Length (μm)	Width (μm)
Brevundimonas diminuta	ATCC 19146	SLB	0.68	0.31
Pseudomonas cepacia	ATCC 35254	DI H$_2$O	1.11	0.46
P. cepacia	ATCC 25416	SLB	1.15	0.42
P. cepacia	Process isolate	Saline	1.00	0.43
P. fluorescens	Process isolate	SLB	0.90	0.53
P. fluorescens	Process isolate	SLB	1.17	0.46
P. fluorescens	Process isolate	DI H$_2$O	1.02	0.22
P. luteola	Process isolate	SLB	0.72	0.39
P. luteola	Process isolate	DI H$_2$O	0.86	0.33
P. maltophilia	Process isolate	DI H$_2$O	0.88	0.44
P. maltophilia	Process isolate	Product	1.40	0.52
P. pickettii	CDC-Anderson	DI-H$_2$O	1.37	0.48
P. pseudoalcaligenes	Process isolate	RPMI	1.06	0.32
P. stutzeri	Process isolate	SLB	1.22	0.50
P. testoseroni	Process isolate	SLB	0.99	0.38
Xanthamonas maltophilia	Process isolate	DI H$_2$O	1.28	0.37
Bacillus cereus	Process isolate	Media fill	1.19	0.36

1996, p. 277) plots the log reduction value (LRV) of Pall et al. (1980) alongside the *B. diminuta* retention data (LRV) given by Sladek and Leahy (1981) against a (Zeman) calculated particle/pore diameter ratio. Zeman concludes that the bacterial retention mechanism is different from that of the latex. Conceivably, the bacterial retention involves adsorptive sequestration as well as sieving. The latex retention is the result of sieving alone, but only at specific surfactant concentrations. The latex beads tend to carry an electrical partial charge which, unless rendered inoperative, as by surfactant, makes them amenable to adsorptions.

Surfactant Molecular Action

The surface of the latex bead, being of a divinylbenzene cross-linked polystyrene composition, is essentially hydrophobic. As such, it is subject to hydrophobic adsorptions. The uniqueness of surfactant molecules is their ability to mediate simultaneously between polar and nonpolar molecular structures. Their distinctive action as detergents is due to their being polar at one end, and nonpolar at the other. The nonpolar end, often an alkylated aromatic structure, such as dodecylbenzene, adsorbs to the nonpolar latex bead surface. Its repetitive ethylene oxide or propylene oxide units consisting of repetitively spaced etheryl oxygens, --0--, feature the electronegativity of their unshared electrons. The positive partially charged hydrogen atoms of the water molecules bond to these oppositely charged portions of the surfactant molecule-dipole. The practical result is a water layer grafted by hydrogen bonding to a hydrophobic surface whose wetting is the purpose of the exercise. In the matter at hand, the surface wettability of the latex bead is not the objective. That derives from the hydrophobic adsorption of the surfactant's nonpolar surface to the nonpolar latex particle. The polar other end of the surfactant molecule forms hydrogen bonds with the water molecules. By means of its (partially) charged and uncharged areas, the surfactant molecule mediates between the polar water and the nonpolar latex sphere.

Pore Size Distribution

The casting process of membrane manufacture produces filters having pores with a size distribution that, in the few cases investigated, are Gaussian in shape (Figure 4.9) (Marshall and Meltzer 1976). The pore

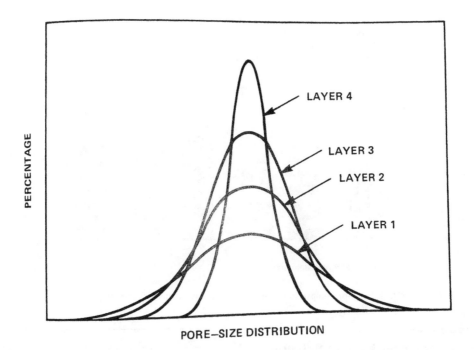

FIGURE 4.9 Depiction of narrowing pore size distribution with increasing membrane layer and thickness.

size distributions among 0.2/0.22 μm-rated membranes prepared of different polymers by six different filter manufacturers is illustrated in Figure 4.10. Latex beads were employed by Wrasidlo et al. (1983) in retention studies at attempts to obtain the flow pore size distributions of membranes. Mostly, the pore size distribution remains a subsidiary concern despite its influence on the retention picture (Zahke and Grant 1991; Jornitz and Meltzer 2001, pp. 34–37). Assuming sieve retention, if all of a filter's pores were of the same size the retention of organisms, also essentially of a given but somewhat larger size, would be independent of the challenge density. The widespread ignorance of pore size distributions helped promote the belief, for all practical purposes, in the exclusivity of sieve retentions.

One factor in particular had delayed explanation of the dependence of organism retention on the challenge density as being due to pore size distribution. It was believed that the pore size distribution was of negligible importance. The pore size distribution of membranes had been explored by mercury porosimetry and had been reported to be a narrow ±5%. The 0.45 μm-rated membrane was said to be ±0.02 μm in its distribution: "It reflects an extraordinary degree of uniformity" (Dwyer 1966). Subsequently, Marshall and Meltzer (1976) demonstrated the actual value to be closer to ±100%.

Pore size distribution wherein the number of smaller pores far outweighs the fewer large pores can explain why the efficiency of particle removal in filtrations varies inversely, in certain instances, with the challenge density. Only when so great a number of organisms is present as to enable confrontations with the few larger pores, do the organisms escape capture. However, hydrodynamic flows do favor the larger pores.

The attention, especially in sterilizing filtrations, is so focused on restraining bacterial passage that only the largest pores, those which the organisms can negotiate on a size basis, are a matter of concern. Hence, the emphasis is on the bubble point measurement of the set of largest pores. There is reason to believe that, despite their relative paucity, the larger pores are early on engaged because of the preferential flow through larger orifices (Jornitz and Meltzer 2004; Mouwen and Meltzer 1993; Grant and Zahke 1990). As will be seen, this is not necessarily so, but when it is organism passage may occur. In any case, in this view, the smaller pores, those adequate for the sieve retention of the organisms, can safely be ignored.

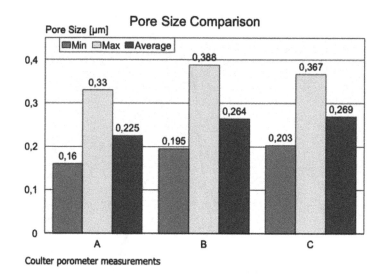

FIGURE 4.10   Pore size distribution comparison of three 0.2 micron rated membrane filters.

Pore size Distribution and Retention

Neither porosity nor pore size ratings nor their combination suffice to explain particle retentions. Pore size distributions play an important role so might membrane thickness. Consider Figures 4.11 and 4.12. (Note: mean flow pore is by definition represented at that graphical point, A′ and C′, which, when extended back to the pore size axis, divides the area under the distribution curve in half. Total flow porosity is represented by the distribution curve when the curve is the result of a differentiation of the wet flow to pressure ratio with respect to pressure.) Some views of a relationship between particle and pore sizes can be pictured if it is assumed (unrealistically) that the pore openings are round and the particles are spherical. In that case, the particles that are only slightly larger than the actual pore openings would fit more precisely into and over them and would block them with great efficiency. Filters that have a comparatively large percentage of their flow porosity concentrated at the size of the particles tend to yield

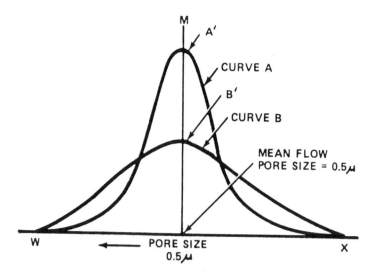

FIGURE 4.11   Two membrane with same mean pore size, but different pore size distribution.

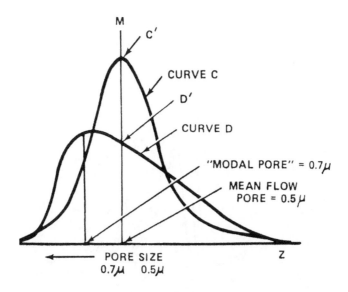

FIGURE 4.12   Two membrane with different mean pore size and different pore size distribution.

small throughputs. Larger particles, like marbles being retained by window screen, pack differently to leave a less blocked surface. The more open spaces, thus provided, would shelter the pores within them against precipitous blocking.

Figure 4.11 shows the comparative flow pore distributions of two different membrane filters that have equal flow porosities and equal mean flow pores and thus exhibit the same flow-rate properties with clean fluids The membrane represented by Curve-A can be expected to exhibit better retention of 0.5-µm bacteria than that represented by Curve-B. This difference occurs as a result of Curve-A's comparatively smaller number of flow pores in the larger-than-0.5-µm region. However, its larger number of flow pores in the 0.5-µm region means that Curve A will exhibit a comparatively faster blockage and lower through-put than Curve B. Incidentally, the 0.5-µm level is the mean flow pore for both membranes in this case.

Figure 4.12 shows the pore distributions of two membranes, C and D, which have the same flow poros-ity, the same mean pores, and the same bubble points. However, in the filtration of 0.7-µm particles, the filter represented by Curve C will clog more slowly than will the filter represented by Curve D. This is explained by the comparatively large number of flow pores at or near 0.7 µm in membrane D.

Pore Size Distributions during Filtrations

In an elegant exercise in experimentation, Thomas et al. (1992) devised an apparatus that enabled them to determine the alterations in pore size distribution that a membrane undergoes during an ongoing filtration. The apparatus is designed to measure changes in the pore distribution function as a result of the increase in bacterial challenge over time. This is achieved by the incorporation of a gas flow meter into the arrangement for challenging the filter. This is done by way of a three-way valve located above the inlet to the vessel that contains the bulk challenge solution. The digital flow meter operates in ranges from 6.0 mL/min to 100 L/min with an accuracy of 3%. A filter membrane is placed into a filter holder by means of suitable piping and turbulence-free connections. The downstream side of the filter holder is exposed to the atmospheric pressure. The upstream side of the holder is connected by the flow meter to a pressure controller. The challenge suspension is exposed to a gradual increase in pressure, and the resulting flow is measured.

Thomas et al. (1992) confronted a 0.45 µm-rated nylon membrane with a 1.8×10^7 cfu/cm² EFA challenge of *P. aeruginosa*. The pore size distribution of the filter was measured at regular intervals during the bacterial challenge. Figure 4.13 from Thomas et al. (1992) presents the successive changes

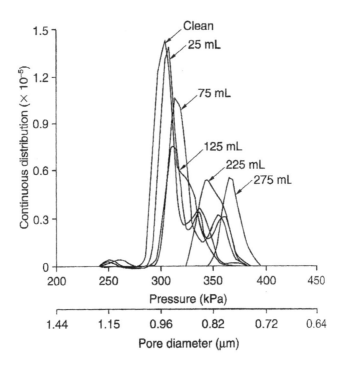

FIGURE 4.13   Pore size distribution shift due to pore blocking.

that the filter's pore size distribution underwent as the filtration progressed. Initially as 50-mL incremental volumes were filtered, the pore size distribution changed relatively little, although the total porosity decreased as would be expected. As the total effluent volume increased, the effect of the 50-mL increments became more manifest, the decrease in the pore diameter becoming more pronounced. This may be taken as evidence that the large pores are less immediately engaged in retaining suspended particles.

Trotter et al. (2002) confirmed that a filter's flow decay caused by continuous organism deposit resulted in an increase in bubble point and a decrease in diffusive airflow. These changes in integrity test values reflect the shifts in pore size distribution that a membrane undergoes consequent to heavy degrees of loading. One has to realize though that such heavy filter loads are typically not found within the majority of applications. The tests performed pushed the filter unit to block, undesirable in actual process conditions.

In high contamination applications, single-point diffusive airflow testing might not prove reliable because the decrease in the diffusive flow caused by the accumulated particles may not reveal flaw, especially in multi-round filter housings (Meltzer et al. 1999). However, whether a pore size shift occurs depends on the filter design and contamination levels. It has been found (unpublished studies) that such shifts in integrity testing may result when a single-layer filter configuration is used but will not occur when a double-layer format is involved. In the latter case, the upstream membrane of the double layer acts in the capacity of a prefilter. This results in a reduced quantity of particles being deposited on the downstream membrane, which functions as the final filter. The sacrificial use of the prefilter in prolonging the service life of the final filter is the very purpose of the prefilter arrangement. The lesser amount of loading on the final filter results in an absence of that amount of pore blockage that might otherwise have caused bubble point elevation and diffusive airflow depression.

Fortunately, drug preparations presented for final filtrations are ordinarily relatively free of particles. However, if that were not so, a better case could be made for the European Medicinal Agency (EMA)'s preference for the final filter to be confronted with no more than 10 cfu/100 cm³ of solution. It was best that final filters should be used to further cleanse already clean solutions.

Membrane Homogeneity

As judged from their successful performances, the microporous membranes available on the market have the high degrees of homogeneity necessary for their applications. Nevertheless, the membranes are characterized by largely unknown pore size distributions. The largest pores in an expanse of membrane may be so few in number that as filters of smaller areas are cut from the master roll, some of the smaller size filters will not contain them. It was found by Sundaram et al. (1999) that *R. pickettii* penetrated large-area filters of 0.2/0.22 membranes of nylon 66, and of PVDF, but did not pass through every 47-mm sample disc of those very compositions that were tested. These investigators ascribe the cases of non-passage to the "stochastic (i.e., governed by the rules of probability) nature of the retention mechanisms."*

However, the situation likely reflects the inhomogeneity of the membrane product resulting from the pore size distribution. The smaller and more numerous the filter areas cut from a filter roll, the more likely it is that the scattered few larger pores will be present within some, but not all, the 47-mm discs. Larger areas are more likely each to contain some such larger pores, making for their more consistent encounter and, therefore, for their being less evident as aberrations. Such situations may explain, in part, the "stochastic nature of the retention mechanisms" referred to by Sundaram et al. These investigators also noted the influence of possible pore size distribution effect.

Such membrane inhomogeneity, in terms of porosity, resulting from pore size distributions would, in any case, be of very limited significance in pharmaceutical processing operations. Its manifestation would bear some inverse relationship to the EFA of flat disc membranes, but only after a certain low level of EFA is attained. Therefore, it would assert itself only in flat membranes having the low EFA of 47-mm discs, possibly somewhat larger. The EFAs of pleated cartridges that are utilized in pharmaceutical processing contexts would seem to be too large to be affected.

REFERENCES

Almgren, F.J. and Taylor, J.E. (1976), Geometry of soap films and soap bubbles, *Scientific American*, 235(1): 82–93.

American Society for Testing and Materials (1980), *Pore-Size Characteristics of Membrane Filters for Use with Aerospace Fluids*, ASTM Standard F-316, ASTM, West Conshohocken, PA.

ASTM F 838-15 (2015), *Standard Test Method for Determining Bacterial Retention of Membrane Filters Utilized for Liquid Filtration*, ASTM International, West Conshohocken, PA.

Badenhop, C.T. (1983), The Determination of the Pore Distribution and the Consideration of Methods Leading to the Prediction of Retention Characteristics of Membrane Filters, D. Eng., University of Dortmund.

Badenhop, C.T., Spann, A.T., and Meltzer, T.H. (1970), A consideration of parameters governing membrane filtration, In J.E. Flinn, Ed., *Membrane Science and Technology*, Plenum, New York, pp. 120–138.

Dwyer, J.D. (1966), Membrane filtration, pp. 262–265, In *Contamiation Analysis and Control*, Reinhold Publishing Corp., New York.

Emory, S.F., Koga, Y., Azuma, N., and Matsumoto, K. (1993), The effects of surfactant type and latex-particle feed concentration on membrane retention, *Ultrapure Water*, 10(2): 41–44.

Grant, D.C. and Zahke, J.G. (1990), Sieving capture of particles by microporous membrane filters from clean liquids, *Swiss Contamination Control*, 3(4a): 160–164.

Honold, E. and Skau, E.L. (1954), Application of mercury-intrusion method for determination of pore-size distribution to membrane filters? *Science*, 120: 805–806.

Jornitz, M.W. and Meltzer, T.H. (2001), *Sterile Filtration—A Practical Approach*, Marcel Dekker, New York.

Jornitz, M.W. and Meltzer, T.H. (2004), Sterilizing filtrations with microporous membranes, *Pharmacopeial Forum*, 30(5): 1903–1910.

Jornitz, M.W., Meltzer, T.H., and Lindenblatt, J. (2004), The filtration debate, *Pharmaceutical Formulation & Quality*, 89–93.

---

* It seems a somewhat illogical contradiction to attribute variations in experimental results to the Laws of Chance in contexts where achieving dependability of retention is the objective, and where validation of its attainment is sought.

Kaczmarek, A.J., Fochtman, E., and Klein, M. (1978), *Private Communication*, I.I.T. Research Institute, Chicago, IL.

Kesting, R.E. (1985), Chapter 7: Phase-inversion membranes, In *Synthetic Polymeric Membranes—A Structural Perspective*, 3rd Ed., Wiley-Interscience, New York.

Krygier, V. (1986), Rating of Fine Membrane Filters Used in the Semiconductor Industry, *Transcripts of Fifth Annual Semiconductor Pure Water Conference*, pp. 232–251, San Francisco, CA.

Lee, J., Liu, B.Y.H., and Rubow, K.L. (1993), Latex sphere retention by microporous membranes in liquid filtration, *Journal of the IES*, 36(1): 26–36.

Lindenblatt, J., Jornitz, M.W., and Meltzer, T.H. (2002), Filter pore size versus process validation—a necessary debate? *European Journal of Parenteral Science*, 7(1).

Marshall, J.C. and Meltzer, T.H. (1976), Certain porosity aspects of membrane filters, their pore size distributions and anisotropy, *Bulletin of the Parenteral Drug Association*, 30(5): 214–225.

Meltzer, T.H. (1987), *Filtration in the Pharmaceutical Industry*, Marcel Dekker, New York.

Meltzer, T.H., Madsen, Jr., R.E., and Jornitz, M.W. (1999), Considerations for diffusive airflow integrity testing, *PDA Journal of Pharmaceutical Science and Technology*, 53(2): 56–59.

Mouwen, H.C. and Meltzer, T.H. (1993), Sterlizing filters; pore-size distribution and the $1 \times 10^7/cm^2$ challenge, *Pharmaceutical Technology*, 17(7): 28–35.

Pall, D.B., Kirnbauer, E.A., and Allen, B.T. (1980), Particulate retention by bacteria retentive membrane filters, *Colloids and Surfaces*, 1: 235–256.

Rogers, B.G. and Rossmore, H.W. (1970), Determination of membrane filter porosity by microbiological methods, In C.J. Corum, Ed., *Developments in Industrial Microbiology*, 2, American Institute of Biological Sciences, Washington, DC, pp. 453–459.

Rootare, H.M. and Spencer, J. (1972), A computer program for pore volume and pore area distribution calculations from mercury porosimetry data on particulate and porous materials, *Powder Technology*, 6: 17–23.

Sladek, K.J. and Leahy, T.J. (1981), Retention of Bacteria in Membrane Filters, *Proceedings of the Second World Congress of Chemical Engineers*, Vol. IV, pp. 1–6, Montreal, Quebec.

Thomas, A.J., Durkheim, H.H., and Alpark, M.J. (1992), Validation of filter integrity by measurement of the pore distribution function, *Pharmaceutical Technology*, 16(2): 32.

Tolliver, D.L. and Schroeder, H.G. (1983), Particle control in semiconductor process streams, *Microcontamination*, 1(1): 34–43 and 78.

Trotter, A.M., Rodriguez, P.J., and Thoma, L.A. (2002), The usefulness of 0.45 µm—rated filter membranes, *Pharmaceutical Technology*, 26(4): 60–71.

Schroeder, H.G. (1984), *Selection Criteria for Selection of Sterilizing Grade Filters*, Society of Manufacturing Engineers, Philadelphia, PA.

Sundaram, S. (1999), Retention of Diminutive Water-Borne Bacteria by Microporous Membrane Filters, *Presented at PDA National Meeting*, Washington, DC.

Wallhäusser, K.H. (1979), Is the removal of microorganisms by filtration really a sterilization method? *Journal Parenteral Drug Association*, 33(3): 156–171.

Williams, R.E. (1984), *Bubble Point Testing and Its Importance to the End User*, Filtration Society, Monterey, CA.

Williams, R.E. and Meltzer, T.H. (1983), Membrane structure: The bubble point and particle retention: A new theory, *Pharmaceutical Technology*, 7(5): 36–42.

Wrasidlo, W. and Mysels, K.J. (1984), The structure and some properties of graded highly asymmetric porous membranes, *Journal of Parenteral Science and Technology*, 38(1): 24–31.

Wrasidlo, W., Hofmann, F., Simonetti, J.A., and Schroeder, H.G. (1983), Effect of Vehicle Properties on the Retention Characteristics of Various Membrane Filters, *PDA Spring Meeting*, San Juan, PR.

Zahke, J.G. and Grant, D.C. (1991), Predicting the performance efficiency of membrane filters in process liquids based on their pore-size ratings, *Microcontaminants*: 23–29.

Zydney, A.L., (1996), Membrane fouling, In Zeman, L.J. and Zydney, A.L, Eds., *Microfiltration and Utrafiltration: Principles and Applications*, Marcel Dekker, New York.

5

Filtrative Particle Removal

Ross Acucena
GE Healthcare

CONTENTS

Introduction

That a particle larger than an opening cannot possibly fit through it without being distorted has been so commonly experienced that it is regarded as being self-evident. It is on the basis of this axiomatic understanding that the mechanism for the separation of particles from fluids by filter action is universally comprehended. Particles suspended in fluids are restrained by their size from negotiating the pores of the filter while the suspending liquid flows through unimpeded at a rate that is most usually a direct function of the applied differential pressure.

The pores, being tortuous, are longer than the membrane's thickness which for most microporous membranes is about 15 microns. The operative particle retention phenomenon is described variously as "sieve retention" or "size exclusion," or some like descriptive term. So apt is this portrayal that assaying the pore size is attempted from measurements of the rate of fluid flow through an orifice. Likewise, the arrest of a particle by a filter pore serves to quantify the size of one relative to the size of the other. In its simplest form, this relationship assumes that both the pores and particles are each monosized. The particle shape and its orientation relative to that of the pore are important. It is conveniently assumed that the pores are circular in diameter and that the particles are spherical in shape. These oversimplified assumptions are rarely in accord with reality. Where nonspherical particles are involved, the frame-of-reference method of determining the average projected area of the particle is by particle counters that program the projected area and deduce from it the diameter of a circle of equal area. Other type counters disclose either the average projected area of a tumbling particle, or its volume. Correction factors must be developed for use with either type particle counter (Johnston and Swanson 1982).

Actually, not too much is known about the pore structures, nor is enough known about the shapes of the particles undergoing restraint by the filter. The pore shapes are described as being tortuous. Usually, the particles being arrested are neither spherical nor monosized. The filter pores, too, are not all of one diameter, and probably no pore, being sinuous, is uniform in diameter. Each pore is likely to periodically feature constricted areas, whether at its entrance at the filter surface or within its interior. It is at these smallest diameters that the particles undergo size exclusion.

The pore structures of the microporous membranes represent the paths of least resistance to fluid flows. They are not firmly established integral pathways extending through the filter from one surface to the other as in a sieve. Excepting track-etched membranes, they are assemblies of spatial vacancies in the filter matrix that, depending upon filtration conditions such as the degree of particle loading and viscosity, may periodically become blocked by particle accumulations. At such times, an ad hoc synthesis of available openings forms a new path of least resistance through the filter.

The Sieve Retention Mechanism

The sieving mechanism is perhaps the most familiar manifestation of filter action. The particle is retained because it is too large to fit through the filter mesh or pores. For monosized particles and a filter of identically sized pores, the retention is independent of the number of particles or pores. It is independent of the filtration conditions. For example, the differential pressure motivating the fluid's flow, unless it is high enough to deform the suspended particle, does not affect the particle removal. The nature (polymeric) of the filter, as also that of the particle, is of no concern unless the physicochemistry of the fluid vehicle reduces the particle size or enlarges the pore size. Each of these is a real possibility under certain conditions. Filter efficiency is then threatened.

Filter action becomes complicated when there is a spread to the size particles and pores. In the real-world, both the particle size and pore size are characterized by size distributions. The selection of the filter is made largely in the expectation that its pores are sufficiently small to retain the particles while generous enough in size to minimally restrain the rate of flow. At best, making the choice depends upon some relevant experience. If the basis of the filter selection is rendered inappropriate by changes in size of either pore or particle, a probability factor then governs the filter efficiency. It depends upon the likelihood of small particle/large pore encounters; which in turn depends upon the ratio of smaller particles (organisms) to enlarged pores. In essence, the size alterations create a size distribution situation.

The particle shape, especially in conjunction with the rate of flow as produced by a pressure differential, may well have an effect on retention. An elongated, slim particle may more likely be oriented longitudinally to the direction of flow by increasingly higher flow rates. Its likelihood of being retained would depend upon the size and shape of the pore and upon the flow velocity. It could tend to escape capture were it is directed to the brief (1 mil), straight-through columnar pores of a track-etched membrane. The shapes of particles and pores are rarely known. Approximations of how particles and pores interact with regard to their sizes are usually based on assumptions that particles are spherical and pores are circular.

Statements are made on occasion to the effect that membrane filters are absolute. The term "absolute filter" signifies an unqualified success to its utilization; a freedom of its performance from dependency on particular conditions. Even in situations where there are particle and pore size distributions, as long as the smallest particle is larger than the largest pore, the filtration is absolute. But *only* in that circumstance may the filter be so characterized. Seldom in a filtration operation is either the particle or pore size distribution known. The term "absolute filter" is a marketing term. It does not belong in the technical literature. Absoluteness is a relationship of a filter's pores to a collection of confronting particles. It is not a filter property.

The sieve retention mechanism is easily understood; the particles larger than the filter pores they encounter are restrained by size exclusion; the smaller particles and fluid are not so retained. Its effectiveness depends solely upon the numbers and sizes of the particles and pores, and to that extent may be probabilistic, depending upon what size particle meets which size pore.

The sieve retention mechanism is relied upon in a variety of applications. Effecting the clarification of fluids is an ancient filtration practice that removes visible particles, variously described as being from 20 or 40 μm in size. Among the most demanding application is the filtrative sterilization of pharmaceutical preparations. This is an important activity whose performance is commonplace and reliable. The segregation of different size particles from mixture can be managed by using sieves of different mesh sizes (Figure 5.1).

FIGURE 5.1   Depiction of sieve retention.

Pore Size Distribution

Early on there was the belief that size exclusion was the sole mechanism of particle removal by filters. If that were so, namely, if all of a filter's pores were of the same size, the retention of organisms, also essentially of a given but somewhat larger size, would be independent of the challenge density. It was known, however, that retention efficiencies could vary inversely with the organism density of the challenge (Wrasidlo et al. 1983; Wallhäusser 1979).

Pore size distributions, wherein the number of smaller pores outweighs the fewer large pores explains why the efficiency of particle removal in filtrations is dependent upon the challenge density. Only when so great a number of organisms is present as to enable confrontations with the few larger pores, do the organisms escape capture; this is despite the fact that hydrodynamic flows do favor the larger pores.

Particles in Dilute Suspensions

Interesting results were forthcoming from filtration studies involving dilute suspensions. Their implications seem important enough to warrant experimental confirmation being undertaken. Organism challenges to membrane filters are generally based on the total colony-forming units (cfus) that confront each square centimeter of effective filtration area (EFA). There is reason to believe, however, that the retention results reflect not the total count alone, but also the state of dilution in which the challenge is presented to the filter.

Grant and Zakha (1990) challenged 0.45 µm-rated Polyvinylidene fluoride (PVDF) membranes with latex particles of different sizes in dilute suspensions. The latex particles averaged 0.605, 0.652, and 0.662 µm in size. The particle concentrations were from 1.2×10^8 to 1.4×10^9 particles per liter. Grant and Zahka associated log reduction values (LRVs) with the concentration of the particles removed by the filters. This was done by periodically measuring the (particle) population in the successive portions of effluent. Grant and Zahka found that the capture of particles initially showed complete retention. This was followed by particle penetration of the filter. This decline in retention, however, gradually slowed to the point where the retention improved with further filtration. These phenomena can be rationalized as follows: hydrodynamic flow tends to direct the suspended particles to the larger pores; the flow rate being a function of the pore radius to the fourth power. However, larger pores are far less numerous than the smaller retaining pores of the pore size distribution. On the basis of probability, the particles initially encounter and are retained by the many smaller pores. As these become progressively blocked, small pore availability decreases. The relatively fewer large pores proportionately increase in number. The particles, hydrodynamically directed, begin to find and penetrate them. As filtration continues, pore clogging, and bridging gradually diminish the dimensions of the larger pores. The larger pores having become smaller, the retentivity increases (Figure 5.2).

A similar finding was made by Roberts et al. (1990), and Roberts and Velazquez (1990) using latex particles. Emory et al. (1993) confirmed that cross-linked polystyrene latex bead "retention is strongly dependent on particle feed concentration" (Figure 5.3).

The course of the curves can be rationalized as follows: the more numerous the particles and the larger their size, the faster is the recovery of the retention from its low point. That is because both size and number tend to more rapidly block the larger pores. When the blockage develops slowly, the observed particle penetration becomes more obvious. A more rapid reduction in the size of the larger pores gives the appearance of less discernable penetrations within the time period. It is a matter of the rate at which a sufficient mass of particles reaches the larger pores to block them, and of the number of unretained particles that are counted in that period of time. So large a number and/or of so large a size can simultaneously arrive at the pores as to give the appearance of immediate blockage. In effect, the period during which the larger pores are open enough to permit particle penetration is so foreshortened as not to allow the penetration of enough particles to be noticed. Thus, the same total number of particles impacting the membrane at different rates can elicit different retentions.

The dilution effect not having been investigated to any great extent with organisms, nor even fully with latex particles, remains hypothetical. However, Trotter et al. (2000) in an inquiry regarding the rate at

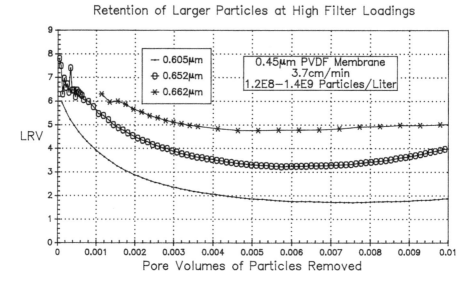

FIGURE 5.2   Retention of larger particles at high filter loading.

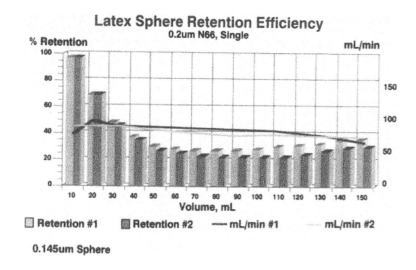

FIGURE 5.3   Latex sphere retention.

which organism loading affected both the bubble point and the diffusive airflow of a membrane found data supportive of the thesis. Trotter et al. demonstrated the same occurrences attending the filtration of *Brevundimonas diminuta* organisms.

Figure 5.4 is a plot of diffusive airflow versus bacterial loading at 45 psi (3 bar). Initially the airflow rate is constant, but it subsequently decreases gradually as the extent of organism loading increases. Nevertheless, such test behavior depends on the membrane configuration. Double filters are not thus affected because of the upstream filter's acting as a prefilter in reducing the load on the downstream final filter. This decrease in airflow confirms the Grant and Zahka's (1990) findings that organisms initially engage the smaller pores because of their greater numbers. The consequent blocking of the smaller pores decreases the filter's porosity relatively little until significant numbers become occluded to air passage. This results in increasing the proportion of larger pores, which in turn, leads to particle passage. Furthermore, the greater the concentration of the organism challenge, the briefer is the interval before

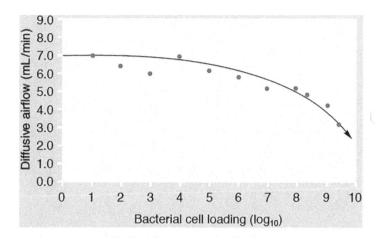

FIGURE 5.4 Diffusive air flow drop with bacteria load.

TABLE 5.1

Dependence of Organisms Breakthrough on Initial Organism Concentration

Initial *P.diminuta* concentration	10^3/mL		10^4/mL		10^5/mL	
Filtrate (mL)	0.2-µm rated	0.45-µm rated	0.2-µm rated	0.45-µm rated	0.2-µm rated	0.45-µm rated
100	0	0	0	1	1	1,000
200	–	–	2	4	4	
1000	0	0	9	25	17	(10^4)
Filtration time for 1000 ml	6'52"	2'27"	2'12"	2'30"	3'15"	8'

Source: From Wallhäusser (1976).

the larger pores are obstructed. This equates with the higher latex particle concentrations more speedily causing the clogging that diminishes the diameters of the larger pores, thus, telescoping the time interval for the latex penetration and reducing the possibilities for penetration to occur. This, too, accords with the observations made by Grant and Zahka.

A confirmation of this hypothesis is forthcoming from Duberstein (1979) who reports that "short-term tests with *high concentration challenge levels* [emphasis added] using *P. diminuta* as test organisms" resulted in so large a pressure drop as to effect a blockage of a 0.2 µm-rated membrane without compromise of the effluent's sterility. The blockage occurred at a level of about 10^{13} test organisms per ft^2 of membrane surface. Wallhäusser (1976) reported that organism breakthrough took place as the total challenge number increased at concentrations of over 10^4/mL (Table 5.1).

Elford (1933) found, and confirmed that higher total organism densities resulted in greater probabilities of organism passage (Figure 5.5). Thomas et al. (1992) during bacterial challenge experiments with *P. aeruginosa* periodically determined the pore size distribution of the challenged membrane. These investigators computed the numerical integral of the pore distribution function obtained during the challenge interval. A relationship became evident between these values and the volume filtered. From this, the number of organisms challenging the membrane was deduced. Thomas et al. conclude, "Assuming only the sieve retention mechanism is at work, the membrane's pore-size distribution then assumes a higher degree of importance, because it provides a measure of the probability that such bacteria will encounter pores large enough to allow their passage." The influence of the challenge dilution, previously demonstrated for latex spheres and silica particles, is now shown as conceivably applying to organisms as well.

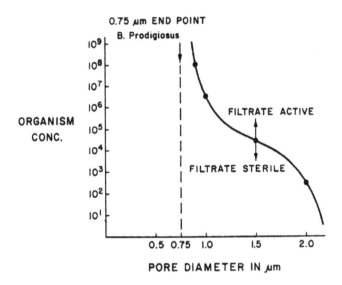

PORE-DIAMETER VERSUS BACILLUS PRODIGIOSUS
CONCENTRATION

STERILE OR ACTIVE EFFLUENT ARE A RESULTANT
OF THESE PARAMETERS.

ELFORD, W. J. PROC. OF ROYAL SOC. (LONDON) 112 B
384-406 (1932-1933)

FIGURE 5.5   Retentivity at different pore sizes.

Dilute Challenge Implications

There are at least two conclusions to be drawn from the dilute challenge effect. First, the EMEA requirement that final filters not be confronted with more than 10 cfu/mL could be a greater test of the retention
capabilities of a filter than the FDA's 1×10^7 cfu/cm^2 EFA which is usually performed with only some
2 L of water. With reference to the choice of 0.1 μm-rated or 0.2/0.22 μm-rated membranes as sterilizing
filters, it was stated that the unnecessary use of the tighter filter would result in decreased flow rates
and their accompaniments of possible premature blockage, etc. However, the pore and organism size
relationship that underlies making an intelligent selection posits knowing what the organism size will
be in its suspending liquid, given that size shrinkage may occur. This would require a prefiltration sizing of the organism(s) of interest after exposing them to the liquid vehicle for a duration at least equal to
that required for the processing step itself. This, in turn, would necessitate a far more diligent bioburden
assessment than is customarily performed. In short, an educated choice of the filter would rely upon a
performance validation.

The Largest Pores

Mostly, the pore size distribution remains a subsidiary concern despite its influence on the retention
picture (Zahka and Grant 1991; Jornitz and Meltzer 2001, pp. 34–37). This is so because the focus is on
particle passage which is seen as occurring through the largest pores regardless of the overall distribution. Hence, the emphasis on the bubble point measurement of the set of largest pores. There is reason
to believe that, despite their relative paucity, the larger pores are early on engaged because of the preferential flow through larger orifices (Jornitz and Meltzer 2004; Mouwen and Meltzer 1993; Grant and
Zahke 1990). This is not necessarily so, but when it is organism passage may occur. In this view, the
measurement of the smaller pores, those adequate for the sieve retention of the organisms, can safely be

ignored. One factor in particular had delayed acceptance of the dependence of organism retention on the challenge density as being due to pore size distribution.

Early-on in membrane usage, it was held that the pore size distribution was of negligible importance. The pore size distribution had been explored by mercury porosimetry and had been reported to be a narrow ±5%. The 0.45 μm-rated membrane was said to be ±0.02 μm in its distribution. "It reflects an extraordinary degree of uniformity" (Dwyer 1966). Subsequently, Badenhop et al. (1970) and Marshall and Meltzer (1976) determined that the casting process of membrane manufacture produces filters having pores with a relatively narrow pore size distribution that, in the few cases investigated, are essentially Gaussian in shape (Figure 5.6). Marshall and Meltzer's measurements showed that the largest pore was about double the size of the mean flow–pore value for the membranes examined.

As said, the widespread early-on ignoring of pore size distributions helped promote the belief, for all practical purposes, in the exclusivity of sieve retentions. The pore size distributions among 0.2/0.22 μm-rated membranes prepared of different polymers by seven different filter manufacturers is illustrated in Figure 5.7 (Meltzer and Lindenblatt 2002). Latex beads were employed by Wrasidlo et al. (1983) in retention studies to obtain the flow pore size distributions of membranes (Table 5.2).

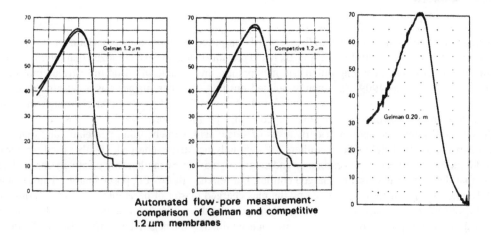

Automated flow-pore measurement-comparison of Gelman and competitive 1.2 um membranes

FIGURE 5.6   Mean pore size measurement of different membranes.

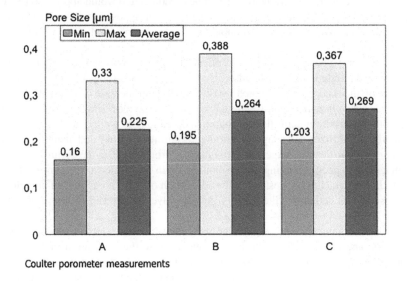

Coulter porometer measurements

FIGURE 5.7   Pore size distribution of different 0.2 micron membranes.

TABLE 5.2

Retention of Various Size Latex Particles for 0.2 µm-Rated Membranes

Latex Particle Size (µm)	0.091	0.198	0.305	0.460
Membrane Type		Percent	Retention	
Asymmetric Polysulfone	54.3	100	100	100
Charge-modified nylon	10.5	100	100	100
Polycarbonate (track-etched)	6.3	100	100	100
Polyvinylidene difluoride	23.4	19.2	84.5	100
Cellulose esters	17.7	25.1	48.6	100
Nylon 66	1.0	1.0	1.0	100

Source: From Wrasidlo et al. (1983).
All solutions 0.04% latex in 0.05% Triton X-100.

Adsorptive Effects

Although adsorptive sequestration was first seriously proposed as an important mechanism of organism retention only in the late 1970s by Tanny et al., it had previously long been recognized that filters of many chemical compositions, including polymeric membranes, are capable of adsorbing various molecular entities. As far back as 1909, Zsygmondy pointed out that the filter surface has a certain adsorbing capacity that must be satisfied before unhindered passage of the dispersed phase through the filter occurs. Numerous investigators have since noted many specific adsorptions. In 1927, Kramer worked with "bacterial filters" composed of derivatives of silicic acid, namely, sand, porcelain, and diatomaceous earth. Such Berkefeld siliceous filters are definitely negatively charged. He also used plaster of paris filters composed of calcium carbonate and magnesium oxide. Such filters are positively charged. He found that the filters passed same-charged entities, but retained those of opposite charge. Thus, Congo Red dye, negatively charged, is retained by the plus charged plaster of paris filters, but passes through the siliceous filters of minus charges. Congo Red upon slight acidification is altered to its blue-colored manifestation that is positively charged. As such, it is retained by the negatively charged Berkefeld filters, but passed through the plus charged MgO and $CaCO_3$ filters. The charge relationships in filtrations are evident. Kramer worked with viruses and bacterial toxins, not with bacteria. He makes clear, nonetheless, that he believes the charge neutralization effect he demonstrated would apply also to bacteria. The mechanism of the adsorptive retention is the attractive forces of opposite charges. Kramer explains the mechanism as being due to the Helmholtz double layer. Also known as the electric double layer, it is discussed below.

Elford (1933) reported that dyes could adsorptively be removed from true solutions by collodion membranes; cellulose nitrate being a most adsorptive material. The strong adsorption tendencies of the cellulose nitrate polymer had also been noted by Elford (1931) in the case of viruses. The use of membrane filters to adsorptively collect and isolate nucleic acids, enzymes, single-strand DNA, ribosomes, and proteinaceous materials in scintillation counting operations is well established. Moreover, such adsorptive retentivity is utilized nowadays by introducing chromatography and membrane adsorber steps into the downstream purification stages of fermentation processes. Bovine serum, antigen/antibody, antibody complex, and specific binding and receptor protein adsorption to cellulose nitrate has been shown to occur. Berg et al. (1965) investigated the adsorption of both inorganic and organic compounds upon polymerics such as cellulosic filter papers, nylon, polyethylene, and cellulose diacetate dialysis membranes.

That water-soluble organics could adsorptively be removed from aqueous solutions by filters was observed by Chiou and Smith (1970). These investigators were thus led into a rather thorough study of such adsorptions by filters. Udani (1978) and Brose et al. (1994) studied the adsorptive sequestration of such preservatives as benzalkonium chloride, chlorocresol, and chlorhexidine acetate from their solutions by membrane filters. The adsorptive removal of flu vaccine impurities and antibodies onto membrane filters has been reported (Tanny and Meltzer 1978). Inorganic particulate matter can be removed filtratively through the adsorption mechanism. It is thus well documented that molecules and materials can be adsorbed onto filters, to become filtratively removed thereby.

Adsorption of Organisms

The adsorptive bonding of numerous entities, including organisms, to solid surfaces is noted in the literature. Some 80 years ago, Kramer (1927) indicated that size exclusion was not the exclusive mechanism whereby membranes retained organisms. Four decades ago, Nash et al. (1967) stated, "These filters do not act as mechanical sieves alone, since the electrical charge on the particle (bacterium, virus, etc.) and the composition of both filter and the suspending medium will play a part in determining filterability. The ability to pass through filters is related to particle size in only a crude way." Pertsovskaya and Zvyagintsev (1971) found that different groups of different bacteria are adsorbed by polymeric films composed of polyamides, polyacrylates, polyethylenes, or cellulose acetate. That various bacteria adsorb onto various surfaces was also disclosed by Gerson and Zajic (1978). Hjertin et al. (1974) studied the adsorption of yeasts on nonionogenic, hydrophobic agarose, and the column adsorption of *S. typhimurium*.

Zierdt and his associates in 1977 at the National Institutes of Health noted that both gram-negative and gram-positive organisms were retained on the surfaces of polycarbonate, and cellulose acetate membrane filters of pore sizes much larger than the bacteria. The organisms involved in the studies were *escherichia coli* and *staphylococcus aureus*. The adsorptive bonding of the bacteria to the polymeric filter surface withstood the mechanical and desorptive actions of washings with buffer solutions (Zierdt et al. 1977). scanning electron microscope (SEM) photographic evidence is shown in (Figure 5.8) of 0.8 μm *S. aureus* organisms retained on the horizontal surface of the membrane, and upon the vertical lips of its pores. The membrane was a (track-etched) polycarbonate of 12 μm-rated pore size. Zierdt et al. (1977) found that a higher percentage of organism retentions occurred at challenge levels as low as 500 cfu–1,000 cfu/mL than took place at the higher levels of 10^8–10^9 cfu/mL.

At the higher densities increasing number of *escherichia coli* passed through the filter, although more were retained. Again, these findings accord with adsorptive sequestration effects, not with sieve retentions. Leahy and Sullivan's (1978) SEM shows *Brevundimonas diminuta* pendant from glass fibers in circumstances unattributable to sieve retention (Figure 5.9). The SEM photographs of organisms retained by filters despite the absence of sieving conditions confirm that other capture mechanisms are operative.

Tanny et al. (1979) demonstrated that the ability of 0.45 μm-rated membranes to contain challenge densities of 2×10^7 cfu/cm² of filter area depended upon the pressure differential being reduced to 0.5 psi (0.3 bar) (Table 5.3). Sterile effluent was not obtained at the higher delta pressures of 10 and 15 psi. This dependence of organism capture upon the transmembrane pressure accords with

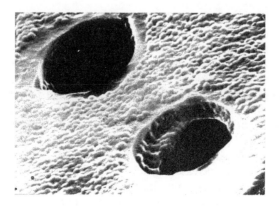

FIGURE 5.8   Organism retained on a 0.8 micron membrane.

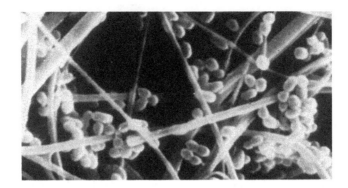

FIGURE 5.9   Organisms retained on a glass fiber matrix.

TABLE 5.3

Organism Retention at Different Differential Pressures

Operating Pressure (psi)	Total Filteration Time for 2,000 mL min: s	500 mL	1,000 mL (organism 100/mL)	1,500 mL	2,000 mL	Average No. of. Organisms in Filtrate/mL
5	189:30	0	0	0	0	0
5	75:00	4	12	7,200	7,200	
5	304:00	0	0	0	0	
15	108:27	0	13	19	39	10–20
15	69:30	3	2	0	7,200	
15	43:58	6	15	12	11	
30	18:35	93	91	61	66	50–100
30	16:12	38	34	39	52	
30	50:02	7,200	7,200	7,200	7,200	

adsorptive sequestration effects, but not with sieve retentions. These investigators, therefore, challenged the exclusivity of sieve retention as the mechanism of organism removal. They postulated that the retention of *B. diminuta* by 0.45 µm-rated cellulose acetate membranes involved adsorptive sequestration.

Some Operational Influences

Differential Pressure

To the extent that particle removal is dependent upon sieve retention, the filter efficiency, in terms of the percentage of the total particles that are removed, should not be affected by the differential pressure. This is because sieving is essentially independent of the challenge level, or of the flow rates as dictated by the differential pressure. There are some negative effects, however. Compactions caused by higher differential pressures may render filter cakes less penetrable by the fluid. Foreshortened throughputs may result. Slower rates of flow may also result from the densification of the diffused polarized particle layer suspended in front of the filter (Figure 5.10). Where particles smaller than the pores are present, filter cake densification, as also cake buildup, should progressively increase the filter efficiency by retaining smaller particles. Differential pressure can have a profound effect upon filter efficiency where particles are subject to adsorptive removals. Increased liquid flow rates, the product of higher ΔPs, reduce the residence time of the particle in the pore passageway. This diminishes the prospects for its adsorptive sequestration to take place. The longer the mutual exposure of particles and pore wall surfaces, the greater the chances of their adsorptive connection. Lower delta pressures increase retentions where

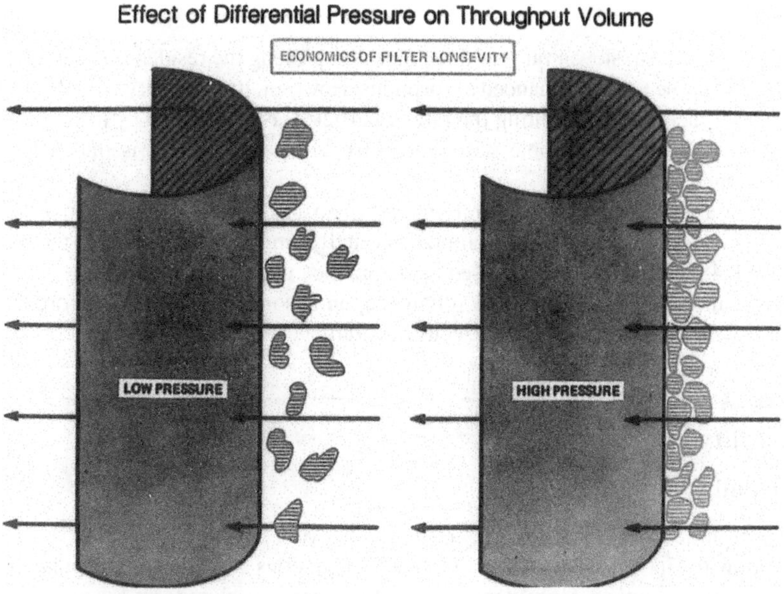

Effect of Differential Pressure on Throughput Volume

ECONOMICS OF FILTER LONGEVITY

LOW PRESSURE

HIGH PRESSURE

FIGURE 5.10 Differential pressure effect on the filter cake.

the adsorption mechanism is involved because longer residence times increase the probabilities of pore wall encounter, and of resulting particle captures. This accords with the experience that employing lower ΔPs tends to increase filter efficiencies.

The overall effect of higher ΔPs on filter efficiencies will vary depending upon the extent of particle loading, and the proportion of smaller and larger particles relative to the filter's pore size distribution. The permeability of a filter cake depends also upon the packing pattern of the retained particles. This, in turn, reflects the numbers, sizes, and shapes of the particles involved (Meltzer 1987, Chap. 10, p. 429; Wrasidlo and Mysels 1984). This touches upon the choosing of prefilters, a subject beyond the scope of this chapter.

Temperature

Temperature has several effects that require consideration. Temperature gives a greater amplitude to particle diffusion, promoting the likelihood of adsorptive pore wall encounters. On the other hand, at a given differential pressure a fluid will flow faster at more elevated temperatures, thereby reducing the residence time within the filter and thus working against adsorption. By reducing the duration of the filtration, higher temperatures become the equivalent of higher differential pressures. Nevertheless, overall, adsorption from aqueous solutions seems generally favored by higher temperature. It results in a more rapid rate of adsorption to a lower degree or capacity.

Temperature has been shown to enhance the efficiency with which the smaller particles of an AC fine test-dust suspension in water are removed by membrane filters. This was experimentally determined in a study wherein, to eliminate the effect of viscosity, polypropylene glycol was added to the aqueous solution to keep its viscosity constant even as its temperature was raised (Johnston 1985). The increase in the efficiency of small-particle captures caused by temperature is ascribed to the increased amplitude of the diffusion of these particles as caused by their higher thermal energies. Increased pore wall encounters and concomitant adsorptive sequestrations result.

If the sizes of pores and organisms are presumed to be unaffected by temperature, the sieve removal of organisms should not be affected. If so, it would seem, therefore, that it is the adsorptive effects that must be reduced by temperature elevations. The rationalization has the higher temperature reducing the viscosity that, in turn, reduces the particle's resident time within the pore's passage way that reduces the amount of retention. Higher temperature in this regard has the same effect as increasing the differential pressure.

Viscosity

Viscosity finds expression in slower rates of flow. This will prolong the residence time of particles within pores. This should incline toward enhanced adsorptions. However, the viscosity will also reduce the likelihood of pore wall encounter by limiting the rate of particle travel imparted by the collisions produced by Brownian motion. Inertial impactions will be similarly affected. Viscosity is amenable to moderation by increase in temperature.

The viscosity of a pharmaceutical preparation may be so sufficiently high as to make impractical its flow rate through the 0.2/0.22 μm-rated membranes usually employed in filtration sterilizations. In the event, repetitive 0.45 μm-rated are often used. This practice could compromise the sieve retentions of given organisms, and may impose stronger reliance upon adsorptive arrests. Such organism removals will be favored by the slower flows of the viscous material.

Water Solubility

Hydrophilic and Hydrophobic

The terms "hydrophilic" and "hydrophobic," respectively, from the Greek, denote a fondness or love of water, and an antipathy to water. Molecules exhibit these qualities according to the polarity or nonpolarity of their constituting atomic arrangements. Generally, polarity derives from oxygen atoms such as are present in ethers, esters, alcohols, carboxylic acids, etc. The oxygen atom is strongly electronegative. In its participation in covalent bonding, it retains more than its share of the bonding electrons. The polar areas result from the partial charges caused by such unequal sharing of bonding electrons. The partial electrical charges (to be detailed below) result in hydrations, in aqueous solubility, and in other manifestations of hydrogen bonding. The nonpolar molecules, lacking obvious electrical charges, have no affinity for H- bonding, or, presumably, for the mutual interactions of opposite electrical charges. However, complex structures such as proteins, polymers, and the organism and filter surfaces composed of them may have multiple sites of polar and nonpolar character.

It is possible to generalize regarding the adsorption of materials from aqueous media by viewing the adsorptive phenomenon as being in competition with the tendency of the material to remain in solution. Water solubility derives from the polarity, the partial electric charges, of molecules that enable their adsorptive interactions with oppositely charged sites on water molecules. The hydrogen bond, soon to be explained, is the agency of this interaction. The less attraction its molecules have for water molecules, the less water-soluble is a substance and the easier it is to remove it from solution by adsorption. By this measure, less ionized or less-polar molecules are easier to adsorb from aqueous solutions. They have fewer or no alliances with water molecules to hold them back from the attractions of stronger adsorptive sites such as may exist on filter surfaces.

The Wetting Action of Surfactants

The hydrogen bond is the source of water-wetting and thus influences the action of wetting agents. These are molecular structures which are polar at one end or site and nonpolar at another. The molecule of a classic-type wetting agent or surfactant consists of a very hydrophobic alkylated aromatic moiety, such as dodecylbenzene, attached to a highly hydrophilic portion composed of repetitious units of ethylene oxide or propylene oxide. The nonpolar hydrophobic end of the surfactant molecule is hydrophobically adsorbed onto the hydrophobic surface of the suspended particle whose water-wetting is ultimately desired.

The hydrophilic portion of the surfactant molecule extends into the aqueous solution where its repetitively spaced etheryl oxygens, (--O--), the seat of its polarity, feature the electronegativity of their unshared electrons that form hydrogen bonds with the water molecules.

The surfactant molecules mediate between the particle's hydrophobic, nonpolar surface and the water, the hydrophilic medium. In effect, the arrangement is a water-wettable surface adsorptively grafted onto the hydrophobic particle which, as a result, is now amenable to the aqueous medium.

Surfactant Particle Size—Enlargement

The findings of Bowman et al. (1967) wherein penicillinase occupied the adsorptive sites of a filter that would otherwise have served to retain *B. diminuta,* has been discussed. Surfactants can likewise preempt the adsorptive sites of filters to deny latex particles their access. In studies involving the retention of latex particles serving as surrogates for organisms, it was found that retention efficiencies decreased in the presence of surfactants. An alternate explanation is possible, namely, that surfactant deposited on the latex particles increases the energy barrier to their coming together. The resulting steric stabilization, also called entropic stabilization, enlarges the distance of their separation to such an extent that the weak forces of attraction cannot overcome it.

Pall et al. (1980) in reporting that the presence of surfactant diminished the latex bead retention, noted that different surfactants did so to different extents. Emory et al. (1993) corroborated that not all surfactants have the same effect on a given membrane. Confirmation of Pall et al.'s findings were made by Wrasidlo et al. (1983), in respect to both pH and surfactant (Tables 5.4 and 5.5). Tolliver and Schroeder (1983) compared the retention of 0.198 μm latex beads suspended in water, with those suspended in an aqueous solution of 0.05% Triton X-100.

The comparisons were made using various commercially available 0.2 μm-rated membranes. Table 5.6 shows differences in results between the two vehicles. The dissimilarity is greatest for the nylon 66 membrane. The polyamide polymers are known to exhibit adsorptive interactions with surfactants that

TABLE 5.4

0.198-μm Latex Percent Retention for Various 0.2 μm-Rated Membranes as a Function of pH

Filter Type	Bubble Point	pH 4	pH 6	pH 8	pH 9
Asymmetric polysulfone	51	100	100	100	100
Polycarbonate (track-etched)	63	100	100	100	100
Polyvinylidene difluoride	55	86.8	74.8	79.5	67.3
Cellulose esters	58	36.3	89.4	23.0	31.3
Nylon 66	45	99.9	82.1	23.7	28.4

Source: From Wrasidlo et al. (1983).

TABLE 5.5

Retention (%) of 0.198 μm Spheres by various 0.2 μm-Rated membrane

Filter Type	In Water	In 0.05% Triton X-100
Polycarbonate	100.0	100.0
Asymmetric polysulfone	100.0	100.0
Polyvinylidene fluoride	74.8	19.2
Nylon 66	82.1	1.0
Cellulose esters	89.4	25.1

Courtesy Tolliver and Schroeder (1983) and Microcontamination.

TABLE 5.6

Impact of Pressure on Passage (β Ratio)

Filter Type	Pore Size (μM)	β Ratio		
		0.5 psid	5 psid	50 psid
GS	0.22	$>10^{10}$	$>10^{10}$	$>10^{10}$
HA	0.45	10^8	10^7	10^6
DA	0.65	10^4	10^4	10^3
AA	0.80	10^2	10^1	10^0

interfere with, for example, the uptake of proteins. The action of surfactant in differentiating among the extents of latex particle retentions in otherwise similar situations is taken as a confirmation of the adsorptive sequestration mechanism.

Significance of Mechanism

Size exclusion is so dominantly the mechanism of particle retention that it is erroneously still regarded by some to be the exclusive mode of organism (particle) retentions. This is the situation despite that some 70 years ago Elford (1933) wrote, "The importance of adsorption in filtration has long been recognized." Nevertheless, the presumed absolute certainties of sieve retention retain their blandishments. There are advantages to the sieve retention mode of particle arrests. Where the mechanism of particle retention can be selected, sieve retention or size exclusion should be the choice. Its certainty is less conditional than the alternative mechanisms. Its restraint on the passage of an organism through a pore depends essentially only on their size relationship. Indeed, the selection of a filter for an application is commonly made with the aim that its pore size rating will be suited to the sieve removal of the suspended particles.

Sieving is free of the many influences that govern adsorptive sequestrations, such as the number of pores, the challenge density, the adsorptive propensity of the polymeric filter, the differential pressure, temperature, viscosity, ionic strength of the solution. The axiomatic nature of the size exclusion mechanism is assuring in its simplicity. Thus, when non-sterile effluent results from the use of 0.2/0.22 µm-rated membranes (Sundaram et al. 2001, Part I), the advocacy is made to use membranes of lower pore size ratings, more assertive of size exclusions. The 0.1 µm-ratings are championed as alternatives to the more conventional use of the 0.2/0.22 µm variety despite that the organisms escaping capture by the latter are not necessarily retained by the former. There are applications that do require the use of tighter filters. However, a needless penalty in flows is incurred when the proposed substitution is gratuitous (Kawamura et al. 2000).

The use of membranes that are tighter than needed to perform desired organism removals unnecessarily invite reduced throughputs; as also premature filter blockage resulting from retained particles whose removal is not considered necessary for the drug's purity or efficacy. The rate of flow is ineluctably reduced. Its restoration to practical levels may require longer processing times, higher applied pressures, or more extensive filter areas. As a guiding rule, a membrane of as large a pore size rating as will assure the desired extent of particle retention should be used. The flow that follows this choice is accepted as an inherent consequence.

Absoluteness in the sense that employing a given filter, of whatever pore size rating, will invariably yield sterile effluent is probably unattainable. The ultimate filtration results depend upon the specifics of the membrane, of the organism type, of the fluid's composition, and of their interactions, plus the choice of the filtration conditions.

It is not necessary to understand the adsorption effects, provided that the omission does not equate with an ignorance of their influences. If one understood only the operation of sieve retention, then it would be possible to conclude that the challenge density is not an important factor in filtrations (especially when pore size distribution is seldom of concern). It may even be concluded that differential pressure is not a prime determinant of retention (unless its level is high enough to distort the particle, allowing for its permeation of the filter). The efficacy of low differential pressure applications in achieving enhanced retentions is well understood by filter practitioners, but perhaps largely as a rule of thumb. As such it has value. However, comprehending that the differential pressure governs the residence time of the microbe within the pore pathway; that this in turn reflects on the probability of pore wall encounters; and that this can influence the likelihood of adsorptive captures offers the advantages that derive from understanding the phenomena involved.

It might not have mattered if Bowman and her associates could have filtered *B. diminuta* from a penicillinase solution without understanding the retention mechanism. It turned out to be important, however, to learn that proteinaceous materials, by way of a different mechanism, could interfere with the retention of *B. diminuta*, and to understand how by use of a second mechanism this interference could be avoided.

Achieving maximization of adsorptive retentions is conditional, as stated, upon attaining certain stipulations, namely, the use of membranes of suitable polymeric compositions, amenable organism types, the imperviousness of both organisms and pores to size alterations by the fluid, and securing the proper filtration conditions. Not enough is yet known about the interactions and relative importance of these factors to permit their optimization. By contrast, the certainty of sieve retention seems utterly simple. However, it too has its unexplored dimensions, e.g., pore size distributions, particle-concentration effects, particle deformations under pressure, rates of organism size alterations, etc.

The adsorptive sequestration mechanism is not compromised by the complexity of its background. Where particle retention by either mechanism takes place, it remains viable and dependable given the fulfillment of the necessary operational conditions. In any case, the attainment of organism retentions by whatever mechanism requires validation, confirmation forthcoming from documented experimental evidence. As regards the filtrative removal of organisms by adsorptive sequestration, a fuller substantiation of the mechanism will be detailed below.

Supportive Experimental Findings

The dependence of adsorptive sequestration on the differential pressure is illustrated in (Table 5.3) and by (Figure 5.11). In the latter illustration, an organism small enough to enter the membrane pore can meet one of two fates; it can either emerge with the convective stream, or, because of Brownian motion, it can contact the pore wall to become adsorptively attached. The longer its residence time within the pore, the greater the probability of its pore wall encounter, and adsorptive interaction. Thus, differential pressure is a process condition that influences a filter system's retention qualities. The lower the stream velocity, as governed by the differential pressure, the longer the residence time. The viscosity of a fluid in its capacity to attenuate the mean free-path of Brownian motion is also a property that influences adsorptive captures. So, too, is temperature, in that it is a moderator of viscosity.

The retention of particles of different sizes and shapes may be affected differently, and to different extents by these fluid properties. Sieving, the size-discriminating mechanism, is independent of the challenge level. Its only requirement is that all the particles be larger than the largest pores. However, the adsorptive particle arrests depend upon a conjunction of the several conditions that define a filtration, including the adsorptive bonding of the particle and membrane surfaces. Lacking the certainty of a conjoining of the two surfaces introduces a probability factor into the adsorptive sequestration operation. Its results do depend upon the challenge density. The larger the number of organisms that essay passage of the filter, the more will emerge with the effluent. Thus, the higher challenge densities do more severely test the filter.

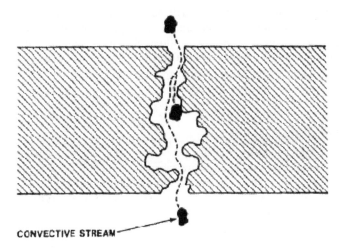

CONVECTIVE STREAM

FIGURE 5.11   Adsorptive capture due to the torturous path.

Elford's Findings

Elford (1933) confronted filters of different pore size ratings with organism challenges of different severities. He observed, as depicted in Figure 5.5, that below a certain pore diameter the filter completely retain as many as 10^9 *Bacillus prodigiosus* (now called *Serratia marcescens*). Only at pore diameters larger than necessary for sieve retention is the efficiency of filtration dependent upon the organism challenge level. Above Elford's "end-point" or critical pore size, adsorptive sequestration becomes the capture mechanism, reinforcing the effects of sieve retention, but subject to the number of the particles that are present. The filter efficiency is greatest where the challenge level is lowest. Particle capture is then a matter of probability; the larger the number of particles, the more likely that some will escape capture. For this reason, too, final filters can be regarded as polishing filters; cleaning fluids already cleaned by prefilters.

Investigators have noted the dependence of retention upon the particle density. Such ought not be the case with sieve retentions where the organism/pore size relationship is the determining factor unless a pore size distribution is involved. The rationalization is that the organisms must be so numerous as to ensure the probability of an encounter with the occasional large pore. Likewise, the dependence of the extent of retention upon the differential pressure probably bespeaks an adsorptive arrest. It could occur also in a sieving context if the organisms were distorted and forced through the filter pores by the pressure differential, although this is an unlikely event (see the section "Wallhäusser's Findings").

Bowman et al.

An early indication that sieve retention was not the universal means of filtratively removing organisms resulted from investigations by Bowman et al. (1967). It was found that 0.45 µm-rated membranes composed of the mixed esters of cellulose, then considered the "sterilizing" filters, retained *B. diminuta* except when penicillinase was present in the preparation. It is difficult to account for the action of the penicillinase in terms meaningful to the sieving phenomenon. In the presence of the protein it required the then newly devised 0.22 µm-rated membrane to sterilize the preparation. It was rationalized that the tighter filter affected retention by the sieving mechanism, whereas the more open membrane retained more so by adsorption, provided the adsorptive sites were not competitively occupied by the protein molecules. This experience provided an early recognition of the adsorptive sequestration mechanism's relevance to pharmaceutical filtrations. It also marked the origin of the 0.22 µm-rated membrane as the "sterilizing filter," and the acceptance of *B. diminuta* as the model for small organisms likely to be present in pharmaceutical bioburdens.

Wallhäusser's Findings

Shown in (Table 5.1) are Wallhäusser's findings (1976a,b, 1979) that confirm that organism retentions can reflect the inverse of their numbers. At the time of this experimental investigation the exclusivity of sieve retention and the absoluteness of membrane filtration were in vogue. Wallhäusser's work proved the actual situation to be otherwise. The compromising of sieve retention can be explained on the basis of pore size distribution. Enough organisms need be present to encounter the fewer larger pores in order to avoid capture.

Leahy and Sullivan

The work of these investigators (1978) provides a concise relationship among pore size ratings, applied differential pressures, and organism challenge levels for mixed esters of cellulose membranes. As shown in Table 5.7, mixed esters of cellulose membranes of 0.22 µm-rating exhibit LRVs of 10 against *B. diminuta* challenges whether at applied differential pressures of 0.5 or 50 psi (0.33 or 3.3 bar). That the capture mode for the 0.22 (0.2) µm-rated membrane is sieve retention is attested to by its freedom from the pressure differential influence. Interestingly, Aicholtz et al. (1987) demonstrated the complete retention of *B. diminuta* ATCC-19146 by 0.22 (0.2) µm-rated membrane, even at 55 psid (3.7 bar), confirming sieve retentions by the less open membranes.

TABLE 5.7

Flu-Vaccine Filtration Volume in mLs/s

0.45 μm Mixed Cellulose Esters			Mixed Cellulose Esters		
Manufacturer I			**Manufacturer II**		
36/90	38/90	33/90	28/90	25/90	30/90
38/120	41/120 (Titers 64%, 65%)	34/120	31/120 (Titers 64%, 65%)	27/120	34/120
0.45 μm Cellulose Triacetate			**0.45 μm Dynel-Type**		
40/90	46/90	40/90	64/90	48/90	52/90
42/120	50/120	42/120	70/120	53/120	57/120
45/180	55/180	43/150	78/180	57/180 (Titers 89%, 87%)	63/180
	58/210 (Titers 90%, 91%, 91%)		80/210		

However, Leahy and Sullivan found that the same type of filter in its 0.45 μm-rated manifestation shows a LRV of 8 at 0.5 psid, a LRV of 7 at 5 psid, and a LRV of 6 at 50 psid. The 0.65 μm-rated membrane, and its 0.8 μm-rated counterpart show the progressively increasing influence of the applied differential pressure level on the organism retention. This is a manifestation of adsorptive sequestration.

Leahy and Sullivan (1978) confronted the 0.45 μm-rated membrane with 10^{10} *B. diminuta*, some 10 million organisms. At 0.5 psi (0.13 bar), only about 100, at most, failed to be retained. At 50 psi (2.3 bar), some 10,000 escaped arrest. If one assumes that the difference in the numbers retained at 0.5 and 50 psi may be considered those captured due to adsorption, then even for the 0.45 μm-rated filter, retention of *B. diminuta* is essentially due to sieving. As Carter and Levy point out (1998), microbial retention efficiency is directly proportional to bubble point values, indicating the prevalence of sieve retention as the capture mechanism. Adsorptive sequestration serves as a reinforcing mechanism, making more certain the organism removal by the filter.

Tanny et al.

The contribution of Tanny et al. (1979) was the illustration that 0.45 μm-rated cellulose acetate membranes sustained challenges of 2×10^7 cfu/cm^2 EFA at a pressure differential of 0.5 psi (0.3 bar) but not at higher delta pressures (Table 5.3). This dependence of organism capture upon the transmembrane pressure accords with adsorptive sequestration, but not with sieve retentions. This finding challenged the then credited belief in the exclusivity of sieve retention as the mechanism of organism removal. Tanny et al. postulated that the retention of *B. diminuta* by 0.45 μm-rated cellulose acetate membranes involved adsorptive sequestration.

Definition of "Mechanism of Retention"

Present understanding of the particle retention mechanisms is strongly based on the sieving effect that results from size exclusions wherein the particle's larger size makes impossible its passage through the pore. There is also the recognition that adsorptive influences, electrical in nature, play a role in the retention of smaller particles. Some consider a mechanism to be the manner in which the particle and filter surfaces come into contact with one another. Thus, there is the "gravitational mechanism" of particle capture; so-called because it explains the settling of a particle onto a *horizontal* filter surface. It is not necessary to postulate a bonding force between the two surfaces other than that exercised by gravity itself. But how is one to explain the stabilization of a particle's coupling with a *vertical* surface? Such contacts result from Brownian motion or inertial impactions. But what explains the continuance of their connecting relationship once initiated by contact? The usage of the term "mechanism" should perhaps explain why the particle/surface relationship continues and persists. It should reference the strength of the adsorptive bond that is established between the particle's and the filter's surfaces, albeit such information is rarely available. It is an explanation of these bonding mechanisms that will here be attempted in a more detailed hypothetical manner.

The mechanistic forces are understood to be electrical in nature. The physical behavior of molecules toward one another is expressed through the electrical forces involved in electrostatics and electrodynamics. They are consequences of electrical charges of various origins. Even the hydrophobic interactions that do not derive from obvious ion or dipole features that could initiate electrical interactions are, nevertheless, considered by some to be electrical in their influence. However complex, the adsorptive forces operational in the bonding of separate surfaces result from mutual electrical attractions. Almost certainly, other factors perhaps not yet known, are also involved. It is, however, the electrical interactions that will be considered here.

Filter Cake Formation

Cake filtration has been listed as a retention mechanism (Lee et al. 1993). Particles retained by a filter build a filter cake to a height commensurate with the fluid's extent of loading. Obviously, the greater the height of the filter cake, the greater its resistance to flow. The flow decay, the reduction in flow rate thus occasioned, depends upon the number, sizes, and shapes of the constituting particles, and also on their hardness. The permeability of a normal packing pattern of discrete, hard silica-sand particles will better resist compaction. Cakes of softer, more gelatinous particles will more easily be deformed by pressure to undergo a loss in permeability. The many type particulates that are likely to be encountered will, thus, exhibit a spectrum of flow decays reflecting particle rigidity and shape.

Mathematical formulae have been developed by which different rates of decay may be interpreted in terms of the mechanisms by which the particles were assembled. In essence, the sites and manners of particle depositions can be deduced from flow decay studies. Given our paucity of knowledge concerning pore structures, the conclusions reached are at best highly conjectural. Nevertheless, they are not totally devoid of significance. Differences in the rates of flow decay are interpreted as resulting chiefly from sieve retentions or mainly from adsorptive sequestrations. The faster decays are believed to be the products of size exclusions, the slower rates are seen to result from adsorptive captures. Flow decays marked by intermediate rates are taken to indicate mixtures of the particle arresting mechanisms.

The logic involved has the larger particles rather completely blocking the flow-restrictive areas of the pores, whether at the pore openings at the filter surface or within the passageway itself. The latter occurs when the particle is small enough to enter the pore but is large enough to block it internally. Particles too small to precipitously block the liquid flow adsorb to the pore surfaces such as the pore walls. The adsorptive captures serve to clog the pores, eventually to block them by bridging. Their accumulation is a function of time. Thus, the slower rates of reductions in flows characterize the adsorptive sequestration operations. The more sudden blockages are ascribed to the sieving mechanism. Mixtures of both mechanisms of particle removal are signaled by flow declines whose rates are between the two extremes. Such intermediate rates of decay depend upon the particle size proportions of the mixture.

The Modeling of Particle Captures

The differentiation between particle retentions by sieving and by adsorptive sequestration may be sought through mathematical modeling. It is assumed that bacterial retention is the controlling occurrence; the one leading to the eventual blinding of the filter. Particle retention takes place to build an ever-increasing filter cake. Its limiting permeability decreases as it builds over time. This introduces a growing hydrodynamic resistance to flow at constant pressure. The mathematical treatment leads to a distinction between the two capture mechanisms. It distinguishes between the rate of change in flows that eventuate from sieving and from adsorption. Size exclusion is assumed to cause pore blockage rather rapidly by particles too large to enter pores. The same results from particles small enough to enter pores, but large enough to block the constricted areas within them. Adsorptive sequestrations are also presumed to take place progressively. The accumulation of smaller particle within pores serves increasingly to clog them by reducing the total pore volume. The end result is a clogging of the passageways more slowly to the point of complete blockage. The surface adsorption of smaller particles followed eventually by bridging of the pores also occurs. This differs from the more precipitous blockage of cake formation by the larger particles. The relevant factors are expressed mathematically by Ruth et al. (1933) in the case of pore blockage. The mathematics pertaining to particle adsorption and pore clogging were elucidated by Hermans and Bredee (1936).

The mathematical treatments, as said, embody certain assumptions. Where bacterial removal is the concern, it is assumed that bacterial retention is the eventually cause of filter clogging and blocking. Also assumed is the non-compressibility of the filter cake, an assumption that is rather suited to more rigid particulates than bacteria. The assumption made from time-to-time that sieve retention is solely a surface phenomenon can be challenged. Thin though the membrane is, particle retention need not necessarily be confined to the filter's outside surface. It may occur upon the pore walls to cause clogging.

This type of flow decay or flux decline study is performed using constant-pressure conditions. Plotting is periodically made of the volume or throughput as a function of time. Flux decline during filtration will be a consequence of any retention mechanism but will follow different time-volume relationships depending on the mechanism governing the filter's clogging and/or blocking. Given its numerous assumptions and several uncertainties, the mathematics involved in interpreting the plotting of the flow decay data may lead to non-rigorous results. However, they are not without significant implications.

Bowen et al. (1976) derived and applied mathematical equations to differentiate between the effects of size exclusion and adsorption. The assumptions inherent in their approach are more fully treated in the final section of this report.

For Sieve Retention

The most commonly used model (Ruth et al. 1933) for bacterial filtration by sieve retention is that of a porous matrix whose pores are smaller than that of the organisms. In such a situation, the bacteria create a filter cake that grows in thickness as the filtration progresses. The cake will add a resistance to the flow at constant pressure, the instantaneous rate of filtration at time t, $J_V(t)$, and the total volume of filtrate up to time t, $V(t)$, will change in a disproportionate manner as a function of time. Assuming an incompressible cake and a constant pressure differential across the filter, the relation is:

$$t = k\left[V(t) + 2V_f V(t)\right]$$

where V_f is the volume of filtrate required to produce a change in total resistance equal to that of the filter; k is a "filtration constant" that depends on pressure, ΔP; viscosity, η; filter area, A; cake resistance, R_c; and particle concentration, C, in the following way:

$$k = 2A^2 \Delta P / \eta C R_c$$

From these simple relations, it follows that a plot of $t/V(t)$ versus $V(t)$ should yield a straight line with a slope of k and an intercept of kV_f. Such a plot constitutes a first verification of the sieve retention, or, as also called, the surface retention model. The term surface signifies the particle's arrest at the restrictive pore site, whether at the filter surface or within the pore.

For Adsorptive Sequestration

Adsorptive capture, whether of a particle or of a soluble or near-soluble entity from the solution, involves the entry of that particle, viable or otherwise, into the pore channel. In these situations, the particle being adsorptively retained is smaller than the filter's pore. (Even though the pore entrance is larger than the organism, sieve statistics dictate that a substantial fraction of the bacteria will be excluded, approximately 99.9% for pores 10% larger in diameter than the particle.) The convective flow situation existing within the pores will tend to transport the entering particles through the membrane. However, the attractive forces, when sufficient in strength, act between the bacteria and the pore walls against the convective flow and promote interception of the particles (Figure 5.11). In terms of the model, all these forces are combined and treated as a first-order reaction between the particle and the wall.

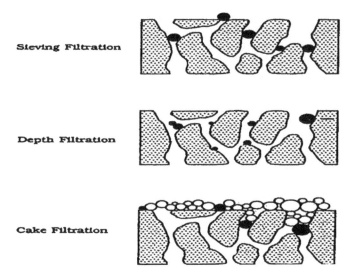

FIGURE 5.12 Particle capture mechanisms in membranes.

Each particle "reacting" within the pore cavity, i.e., being adsorbed, reduces the total pore volume. Where k is a filtration constant related to the internal pore area and the particle concentration, the equation expressing the adsorptive model of flux decrease is:

$$\frac{t}{V(t)} = \frac{kt}{2} + \frac{1}{J_V(0)}$$

or

$$\frac{1}{J_V(t)} - \frac{1}{J_V(0)} = kt$$

where k is a filtration constant related to the internal pore area and the particle concentration.

A plot of $t/V(t)$ versus t should yield a straight line with a slope of $k/2$, and such behavior constitutes a test of the model, wherein the particles are retained within the pores by adsorption. Smaller particles must first gather to bridge the choke points of the pores (Figure 5.12). The particle accretions build a filter cake that is permeable until the differential pressure is exceeded by the pressure drop resulting from the cake's resistance to flow. The permeability of the cake can be foreshortened by its compaction under increased pressure. The onset of impermeability depends upon the structure of the cake and its resulting compressibility as determined by the particles' sizes, shapes, numbers, and pattern of packing.

Straight-Line Plotting

The data reported by Wallhäusser (1979) (Table 5.1) were plotted in accord with the sieve retentive model and also with the adsorptive model. Figure 5.13 shows a straight line indicating the particle capture to be the result of an adsorptive mechanism. The nonlinear line resulted from plotting the data for sieve retention. This signaled that sieve retention was not the mechanism at work.

The data obtained by Tanny et al. (1979) were plotted for adsorptive captures of *B. diminuta*. Both a 0.2/0.22 μm- rated and a 0.45 μm-rated membrane were used in separate but identical tests. The straight line obtained for the 0.45 membrane denoted that adsorptive capture was operative. The nonlinear, curved line signified that adsorptive interactions did not govern *B. diminuta* retention by the 0.2/0.22 membrane (Figure 5.14). The results forthcoming from the plotted data were what might have been predicted from the relative pore size ratings and the size of the organisms.

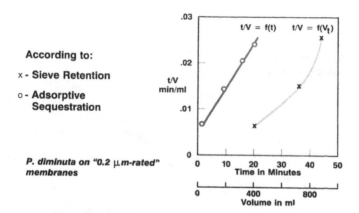

According to:

x - **Sieve Retention**

o - **Adsorptive Sequestration**

P. diminuta **on "0.2 μm-rated" membranes**

FIGURE 5.13   Plotting of Wallhäeuser data.

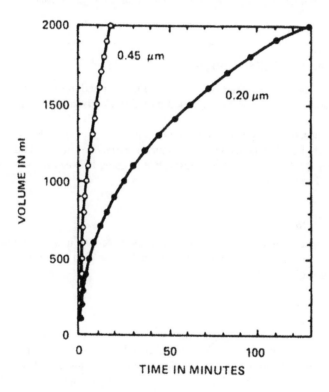

FIGURE 5.14   Flow decline data for 0.45 and 0.2 micron membranes.

An interesting set of curves resulted from challenging 0.45 μm-rated cellulose acetate membranes with different quantities of *B. diminuta*, namely, 1×10^4 and 1×10^5. The lesser challenge showed the straight line plot indicative of adsorptive captures. The early reaches of the 1×10^5 challenge likewise yielded a linear curve of the same significance. However, as more organisms were filtered from the challenge stream, the line began deviating from its straight course (Figure 5.15). This signaled a departure from the mechanism of adsorption. Tanny et al. (1979) rationalized the results as follows: The early removal of the *B. diminuta* from the 1×10^5 challenge was accomplished by adsorptive sequestration. This resulted in a clogging of the filter pores. Thereafter, the organism removal became an exercise in sieve retention.

One may conclude from the above examples that the mechanism of retention responsible for organism removals in particular filtrations may indeed be identified by a proper plotting of flow decay data.

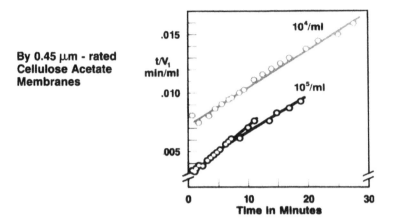

By 0.45 μm - rated Cellulose Acetate Membranes

FIGURE 5.15 Total throughput curve of 0.45 micron membranes at different bacteria load.

Retentions by Particle/Filter Contacts

Gases, like liquids, operate largely by size exclusion in being separated from their particulates. Adsorptive sequestrations can come into play when suspended particles are given motion that culminates in their encounter with a filter surface. The several ways in which particles directly encounter filter surfaces, such as through inertial impactions, Brownian motion, gravitational force, may also be considered retention mechanisms. The particles become fixed to the membrane surface by electrical attractive forces, subsequently to be explained. These constitute the adsorptive bonding between the surface of the impacting particle and the surface of the filter.

Gravitational Settling

Such gravitational impacts can come about when particles suspended in a flowing fluid atop a filter are heavy enough to settle out in response to the force of gravity in accord with Stoke's Law: The larger the particle, the faster its settling rate.

Inertial Impaction

The inertial impaction of a particle upon a filter surface can occur when the fluid bearing the particle changes its direction of flow as it is deflected into and through the filter pores. The inertia of the particle may continue it on its original path to collide with the filter surface where adsorptive forces can cause its arrest (Figure 5.16). This inertial force depends directly upon the mass of the particle, and the

INERTIAL IMPACTION

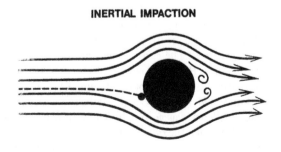

FIGURE 5.16 Inertial impaction retention mode.

square of its velocity. It is, therefore, more important with heavier particles. The inertial force is attenuated by the viscosity of the fluid. Consequently, it can be influenced by temperature which is inversely related to viscosity. For this reason, it is less effective in liquid than in gaseous contexts.

Brownian Motion

Smaller particles, less heavy, are less influenced by inertia. However, they are more affected by Brownian motion wherein they are vectored from the fluid pathway to the pore surface by collisions with the fluid's molecules. The result is retention of the particles by the filter. The nature of the bonding that adheres one surface to the other, the actual mechanism, will shortly be elucidated. At all temperatures above absolute zero the various sections of all molecules are in constant motion; the various bonds being flexed, rotated, stretched, etc. The higher the temperature, the greater the amplitude of the molecular motion. The significance of absolute zero is that only at that temperature or below is all molecular movement frozen. In their frenetic activity, the fluid molecules collide, perhaps repeatedly, with suspended particles. The latter are impelled to new directions of travel within the fluid stream. As a result of their induced random and erratic movements the buffeted particles have opportunities to encounter pore surfaces and to become attached thereto by electrical forces we have yet to describe. This is the nature of Brownian or diffusional interception (Figure 5.17). It is favored by the small size of the particles, and by the lower viscosities of the suspending fluids. Thus, it is more important in gas rather than in liquid filtrations.

Relative Retention Efficiency of Gases and Liquids

All molecules and their component atoms and linkages are, under normal conditions, in constant motion. Their bonds flex, stretch, and rotate in response to temperature. The motion diminishes with decline in temperature and ceases only at absolute zero. Indeed, this is a definition of absolute zero. Thus, the molecules of a fluid medium are in constant collision with one another, and with any particles suspended therein. The mean free paths of the molecules in motion are less restricted in gaseous contexts than in liquid because of the relatively fewer interruptions by collisions with other molecules, the gas molecules being more widely separated from one another than molecules in liquids. Therefore, Brownian motion and inertial impactions that vector suspended particles to filter surfaces are more effective in gases than in liquids. The attenuation of particle movements caused by the viscosity of the suspending fluid that reduces the opportunities for encounters between filter surfaces and particles is an impediment to adsorptive bonding. This accounts for the findings of Megaw and Wiffen (1963) that relatively large pore size rated filters are capable of removing particles some two magnitudes smaller than their ratings with very high efficiencies. These investigators showed that 0.05 μm particles are retained by 0.8 μm-rated membranes. Leahy and Sullivan (1978) challenged equivalent filters in liquid media using organisms larger than the Megaw and Wiffen particles by a factor of 10. Despite the larger sizes, the particle capture efficiencies in liquid were of lower magnitudes.

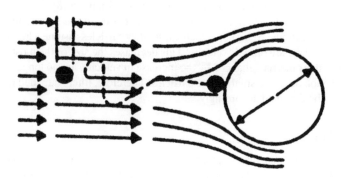

FIGURE 5.17 Brownian motion retention.

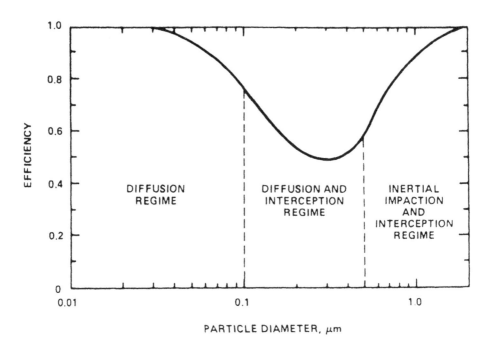

FIGURE 5.18   Most particle penetration point curve.

Most Penetrating Particle

For both inertial impactions and Brownian motion the consequences of the particle's connecting with the filter surface is attenuated by the viscosity of the liquid medium; not so in the case of gases with their low viscosities. These impact mechanisms are, therefore, of greater influence in removing particles from gas streams than from liquids. The particle's mass is very important to the effectiveness of inertial impactions; the Brownian motion, diffusive by nature, is far less influential on these larger particles. The inertia of the smaller particles is too minor to have a significant effect. According to Liu et al. (1983), it is the diffusional interceptions of these smaller particles, the result of Brownian motion, that is responsible for the high filtration efficiencies of air filters. The rate of particle capture is inversely proportional to the square root of the particle's diameter. This is especially true for particles below 0.3 μm in size, particularly in dry air, and at low air stream velocities. The opposite is true for the larger particles because their mass, especially as multiplied by their squared velocity, has so important an effect on their inertia. As the particle mass decreases, the inertial impactions diminish in influence. It turns out that particles of about 0.3 μm in size, modified somewhat by their velocity, are the least retained by either of these two types of impactions. Therefore, particles of this size are the most likely to penetrate an air filter. This, then, by definition, is the size of the most penetrating particles (Figure 5.18).

Modifications in filter design are necessitated by the increases in the air stream velocities that are required in specific applications. At higher velocities, smaller particles assume a higher inertia, the product of their mass, and the square of their velocity. This decreases the size of the most penetrable particle. The 0.3 μm particles, their inertia enhanced by the increase in velocity, are no longer the least possible to capture. That designation passes to smaller size particles. Therefore, filters intended for such applications as vent filters need to be designed accordingly.

The Adsorptive Bonding

The conjoining of a particle and filter surface by way of size exclusion need not necessarily result in an organic union between the two. Their adjacency may involve nothing more than the particle having been deposited passively at the filter surface by the flowing fluid. Aside from the accidents of geometry and gravity, other ways of two surfaces interacting involve some exercise of a bonding force. By the term "adsorptive sequestration" the authors means to characterize whatever forces result in a bonding strong enough to remain viable following the separate surfaces having made contact. Depending upon semantics, one can choose to describe the situation as resulting from different types of adsorptions, or one can speak of the one adsorption mechanism and its several manifestations. Either view is acceptable to the authors.

The theme of this writing is the coming together of two surfaces, namely, that of a particle (more explicitly of an organism), and that of a filter in a union that is the result of bond formation. The situation is that of a particle carried by a flowing fluid stream into contact with a fixed-in-place filter. The particle remains attached to the filter, thus fulfilling the purpose of the filtration. Our inquiry pertains to the origin and nature of the bonding forces. The particle removal is complex in that there are conflicting forces simultaneously in operation: One produces a mutual attraction between the two surfaces whereas the other exerts a mutually repulsive influence. The desired interaction requires the attenuation of the stronger repulsive force to enable the dominance of the weaker attractive action.

Briefly, to be elaborated upon later, the repulsion arises chiefly from strong charges of the same sign, namely, the Coulombic forces. The genesis of the attractive forces is several. Zydney (1996, Chap. 9) lists one source as being quantum-mechanical in nature. The second is electrostatic in its action. It derives from interactions between fixed charges and/or fixed dipoles. The third type of attractive force is the product of molecular polarizations caused by induced dipole—induced dipole interactions. These are the so-called dispersion forces also known as the London–van der Waals (VDW) forces. The respective forces differ in their origins; more importantly, they differ in their strengths. The formation of the adsorptive bond requires the balancing of the strengths and directions of the several operating forces. This determines the distance at which the influences of the attractive forces become effective. It is known as the Debye length. The means whereby the Debye length is reduced to the point where the attractive forces prevail is the addition of salts to achieve a high ionic content. At its culmination is the adsorptive bonding of separate surfaces, such as of an organism and a filter surface.

The mechanism responsible, in its successive stages, for this achievement was first elucidated in the destabilization of colloidal systems.

Colloidal Destabilization

In its simplest form, the colloidal state is a suspension of discrete particles that resist settling out even over long periods of time. Colloids, of whatever composition, consist of particles from 0.001 to 1 μm ($10^{-7} - 10^{-4}$ cm) in size, too small to be visible under an optical microscope. Colloidal particles are too small in size, (and hence in mass), to be responsive to Stoke's Law*. Colloidal particles are subject to Brownian motion. They are given erratic movements through collisions with the ions in solution. This helps prevent their settling out. The colloidal particle has a large surface area. This encourages the adsorption of ions and the concomitant acquisition of electrical charges. (Colloidal charges can also result from the ionization of molecules on the surface of a particle, or from the dissolution of ions from the solid into the liquid state.) Since like-charges repel, and since all the particles constituting a colloid bear the same charge, the discrete particles repel one another and do not agglomerate to form a sediment.

The adsorptive joining of one colloidal particle to another involves the same forces of attraction that regulate the adsorption of dissolved molecules by membranes, or of organisms from their suspensions. Both attractive and repulsive forces manifest themselves simultaneously. The attractive forces have

---

* Stoke's Law relates to the settling of suspended particles. It reflects two factors: The density differences between the particle and fluid, and the size of the particles. The greater the density differences, the faster the settling. The larger the particle, the faster its settling rate. The gravitational force acting upon a particle to cause its settling varies with the square of the particle diameter.

$$V_{Stokes} = (d_1 - d_2) a^2 g / V = \text{settling velocity},$$

where a = particle diameter, g = gravitational constant, d_1 = particle density, d_2 = liquid density, η = liquid viscosity.

only a short-range effectiveness; the repelling forces are stronger and operate over a longer distance. The adsorptive process is essentially one of overcoming the repulsive, long-range, forces. A most important consideration, then, is the distance separating the molecules or particles being adsorbed and the adsorbing sites on the filter. It is over this distance, the Debye length, that the attractive forces between the separated surfaces must operate in order for them to come together to form the adsorptive bond. This is not achievable at great distances. However, at shorter distances the attractive forces, whether of hydrophobic or more overt charge-related origins, prevail. Increasing the ionic strength of the suspending liquid by the addition of salts interposes ions between the charged particles. This reduces the charge density, the zeta potential, and the distance over which it has influence. The attractive forces are enabled to assert their powers over the reduced distance. The solid surfaces of the particles then undergo adsorptive bonding with one another, and agglomeration results.

An intriguing view of the effects of the zeta potential, the measure of the electrokinetic effect, *vis-à-vis* colloids is given by Pall et al. (1980). These investigators point out that colloidal suspensions are stabilized when their particles are endowed with net surface charges of similar sign in the magnitude of 30–40 mV or more. The mutually repulsive forces then suffice to repel the particles from one another. The double-layer distance is then large enough to frustrate the shorter range attractive VDW forces. Therefore, no flocculation occurs, and the colloidal dispersion is stabilized. Below about 30 mV the double layer extent shortens, and the zeta potentials begin to reflect the growing involvement of the attractive secondary valence forces. Marshall (1992) considers the critical Debye length to be from 10 to 20 nm, at which point ". . . long range (sic) van der Waal attractive forces can exceed 'the' electrical repulsion forces . . .." Over and at the zero-charge level, attraction dominates and flocculation occurs: the colloid becomes destabilized.

Consideration will now be given to the dispersion stabilizing theory (DLVO) theory, in its development from the established Debye–Hückel theory accounting for the electrical charge phenomena that govern the filtrative removal of particles from their suspensions. The designation DLVO derives from the initials of the theoreticians' family names: Derjaguin, Landau, Vervey, and Overbeek.

Electron Sharing and Electrical Charge

In an oversimplified view, an atom consists of a very dense nucleus that comprises its mass and is positively charged because it contains positively charged (+) subatomic particles. Surrounding, but relatively far removed, are concentric rings of negatively (−) charged electrons. Often referred to as the "electron cloud," the implication is of continuous movement of the electrons at such speeds as to blur their momentary positioning. The electrons in the outermost shells are the least firmly bound. They are characterized by having the highest quantum numbers. They are the valence electrons whose activities are involved in chemical reactions between atoms. The remainder of the atom is known as the "core" or "kernel." Atoms are uncharged, possessing just enough electrons (−) to neutralize the nucleus' (+) positive charges. Each ring is limited to an exact number of electrons; usually eight except for the lighter elements, most notably hydrogen. The outermost ring is mostly incompletely filled. An atom in forming a molecule will completely fill or empty its outermost shell by transferring (accepting or donating) electrons to another atom that is under the same compulsion, or by sharing the two bonding electrons with another atom to the same purpose.

Since the electron, by convention, is negatively charged; atoms that come to possess more electrons than they do in their neutral state, are labeled as being negatively charged. If they contain fewer electrons than in their neutral state, they are designated as being positively charged. Atomic and molecular entities react to one another in response to their plus or minus electrical status. It is generally comprehended that opposite electrical charges attract and bond to one another, whereas like-charges mutually repel.

Bond Types

Electron transference or sharing occurs as a response to valence requirements. The formation of a valence bond lowers the energy of the formed structure, making it more stable. The ionic bond that is formed by the donation of an electron by one atom and its acceptance by another is strongly charged electrically.

Being strong, it exercises its influence over relatively longer distances. It is often called a primary bond. The covalent bonds fashioned by electron sharing are not, unlike the ionic bonds, structurally and inherently charged. Although not so strong as the ionic bond, the covalent bond too is considered a "primary bond." These two types of bonds, namely, the ionic and covalent, are the valence bonds. They differ from the bonding that is caused by the partial sharing of electrons. Although respectively called "primary" and "secondary" or "strong" and "weak," or even "chemical" and "physical," these bonds cover an entire spectrum of strengths. There is perhaps "no sharp dividing line between the true bonds and the weaker interactions described in different terms" (Wheland 1947).

The Ionic Bond

The ionic bond, as said, involves the complete transfer of an electron from one atom to another. It is characteristic of inorganic salts. They mirror the electrical charges that result from the electron's change of location. Consider the union of a sodium atom and a chlorine atom. In the electron transfer described, the electrically neutral sodium atom, now bereft of an electron, becomes changed into a positive-charged sodium cation. The neutral chlorine atom, having acquired an electron, is now negatively charged. It is now a chloride anion. The transfer of the electron that creates the ionic bond is total and complete. The electron whose transfer created the negative charge stays completely with the chloride ion. It is not shared with the sodium ion. The two oppositely charged ions interact on the basis of the mutual attraction of their opposite charges to create a molecule that is a salt, sodium chloride.

The molecular combination consists of an aggregate of positively charged sodium ions in lattice form juxtaposed to an assembly of negatively charged chloride ions in lattice form; the lattices being connected by the strong attractions of their opposite electrical charges. The two oppositely charged ion lattices are separated when the salt is dissolved in water, it being a polar medium. The water molecule carries partial positive charges on its hydrogen, and a partial negative charge on its oxygen atom. The orientation of the water dipoles in an alignment of plus-ends to minus-ends serves to moderate the full Coulombic charges of the ions. This attenuation allows their separation. Nevertheless, although now separated, the ionic charges are strong enough to exert their attractive or repulsive powers over long distances.

This is in contrast to the weaker forces that result from the partial charges arising from the unequal sharing of covalent bonding electrons, or from other phenomena associated with covalent bonding. (See below.)

The Fuoss Effect

The positive effect of ionic strengths on adsorptive sequestrations is forthcoming from the field of water treatment and involves the adsorption of organic substances by activated carbon. This is greatly enhanced by the presence of calcium and magnesium ions. According to Weber et al. (1983), the adsorption of humic materials by activated carbon is pH-dependent and is influenced by the presence of inorganic ions in the solution (Figure 5.19). Calcium is slightly more effective than magnesium, and divalent ions are more influential than monovalent ions by an order of magnitude; potassium ions are slightly more effective than sodium ions. The salutary effects of lower pH on increasing adsorption had previously been remarked upon by Schnitzer and Kodama (1966). A plausible explanation may derive from the Fuoss effect as discussed by Ong and Bisque (1966) and as advanced by Ghosh and Schnitzer (1979).

The Fuoss effect states that large polymeric electrolytes, such as derived from humic acids, exist in solution in a coiled configuration, as indeed do all polymers. Polymeric molecules increasingly unwind and extend themselves the diluter the solutions (Figure 5.20).

Increasing ionic strengths, to the contrary, promote the tightening of such coiling. The contractions of the humic acid molecules under the influence of higher ionic strengths have two adsorption-promoting consequences. The size of the polymer molecules decreases as they become progressively more coiled (Figure 5.21). In the process, the folding of the polymeric chains increasingly confine their hydrophilic moieties, and more openly present their hydrophobic constituents, of which tryptophane, tyrosin, and phenylalanine are the most extreme. The first effect further increases the ease of interstice penetration; the second promotes hydrophobic adsorptions. Thus, the presence of ions such as hydronium, calcium,

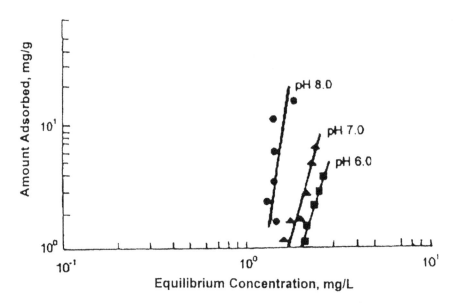

FIGURE 5.19   Adsorption isotherm of humic acid at different pH.

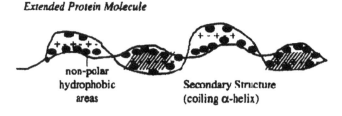

FIGURE 5.20   Secondary structure protein.

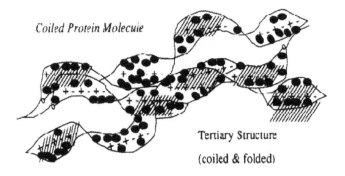

FIGURE 5.21   Tertiary structure protein.

and magnesium promote the molecular coiling. Both the capacity for adsorption and the rate of adsorption are increased. This is significant because adsorption is rate-dependent.

Evidence that the adsorption onto active carbon surfaces of organic materials derived from humic substances is promoted by lower pH was furnished by Weber et al. (1983) and by Schnitzer and Kodama (1966) and was stated also by Michaud (1988). Weber et al. (1983) found that the adsorption isotherm for humic acid on an activated carbon, although increased somewhat by going from pH 9.0 to 7.0, increases markedly when the pH is lowered to 3.5.

Endotoxin Adsorption by Ionic Interaction

As stated, the transfer of the electron that creates the ionic bond is total and complete. The resulting ions combine with ions of opposite charge. This type of bonding has been exploited to develop membrane absorbers which contain a polymeric membrane that has a covalently bonded hydrophobic interaction ligand. Such filters have found use in the biomanufacturing process for polishing purification where high throughputs can be achieved with low fouling feeds and alleviate the need for traditional chromatographic columns and the preparatory packing and other labor-intensive preparation that is required. The pyrogenic lipopolysaccharidic endotoxins are retained by such filters bearing positively charged functional substituents. The adsorptive interaction involves the attractive forces operating between the positive charges on the membrane and the negatively charged surfaces of the endotoxin aggregates, which behave as anions at pH >2. (See the section: "Hydrophobic Adsorption: Ultrafilters.")

Carazzone et al. (1985) showed that charge-modified nylon membranes remove pyrogenic substances from solutions with an efficiency that depends upon the composition of the liquid. The endotoxins used were extracted from *E. coli* 055:B5. The removed pyrogens are firmly adsorbed. They are not released during continuation of the filtration process. However, the charged nylon filters exhibit a finite adsorption capacity; the pyrogen removal efficiency decreasing with the successive aliquot being filtered. The capture mechanism is charge mediated on a stoichiometric basis. As the positive charges become progressively neutralized, the capture efficiency decreases, and endotoxin breakthrough becomes more likely. At any stage of the filtration, the removal efficiency which reflects the encounters between the anchored positive ions and the endotoxin units, is very dependent upon the rates of flow, and the progressively diminishing number of positive charges. The higher the flow rate proportional to the remaining number of positive charges, the more likely it is that the removal efficiency will diminish. The endotoxin unit may exit the filter before the positive-charged site is collided with. Endotoxin breakthrough is the first indication of insufficient numbers of remaining charges, whether through their exhaustion, or too high flow rates. In sum, the main factors affecting this type of charge-retention are: the EFA, the total volume filtered, and the rates of flow as determined by the delta pressure. Other factors, such as pH, viscosity, and temperature also contribute to the final outcome.

To avoid the impracticalities of endotoxin breakthrough, two filtration units in series with a sampling port in between, enables ascertaining, through the use of periodic sampling, when the upstream filter permits endotoxin penetration. At this point, the relatively unused downstream filter reassures against unretained endotoxin contaminating the final effluent. Replacement of the exhausted filter and reversing the direction of flow through the filters enables the replacement filter to safeguard the purity of the effluent (Figure 5.22). Validation is required to determine the time of exhaustion for the upstream filter. Evaluation of endotoxin breakthrough necessitates using the fluid product under process conditions.

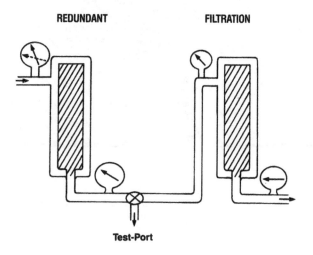

FIGURE 5.22 Redundant filtration set-up.

Hydrophobic Adsorption: Ultrafilters

Ultrafilters of various molecular weight cutoffs (MWCOs) were tested for their abilities to remove endotoxins. The membranes were composed of polysulfone and of cellulose triacetate (Wolber et al. 1998). Log reductions of 4–5 were obtained using filters having MWCOs of 10,000.

All known endotoxins have a hydrophobic lipid A core as well as a hydrophilic polysaccharide appendage. It is the lipid A core that is responsible for the pyrogenic activity of the endotoxin and for its hydrophobic character (Galanos et al. 1972). Its nonpolar nature reflects the 16–20 carbon chain that it contains. This nonpolar chain furnishes the site for the hydrophobic interaction between the lipopolysaccharide (LPS) and the like-bonded segments of filter surfaces, the nonpolar polypropylene molecules.

Lipid A, being nonpolar, is incompatible in terms of phase separation with aqueous solutions. It spontaneously aggregates in such media to form small micelles or larger bilayered vesicle arrangements (Sweadner et al. 1977). In these formations, the negatively charged hydrophilic groups lie on the surfaces of the molecule exposed to the aqueous solutions. The core of the micelle or vesicle is composed of the hydrophobic lipid A portion of the endotoxin. The exposed anionic groups on the outside attract their oppositely charged counterions to form an electrically neutral double layer that also includes water molecules bound by dipole–dipole interactions.

Robinson et al. (1982) (Figure 5.23) illustrates the LPS (endotoxins) pyrogenic bacterial being adsorptively retained by hydrophobic membranes through the hydrophobic interaction of the uncharged filter surface and the nonpolar lipid A core of the endotoxin. The enclosed nonpolar lipid

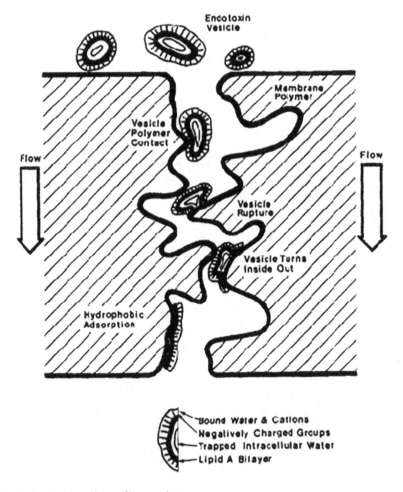

FIGURE 5.23   Endotoxin adsorption on filter membrane.

A core establishes contact with the nonpolar polypropylene pore walls and so becomes hydrophobically adsorbed upon rupture of the charged hydrophilic pellicle. At the bottom of the hydrophobic effect is the entropically driven tendency of hydrophobic structures to interact with one another in order to reduce the area of their contact with water. The probability of this occurrence is enhanced by ultrafilters of lower pore sizes.

Hydrophobic Adsorption; Microporous Membranes

Table 5.8 illustrates that the adsorptive removal of the endotoxin, as measured by LRV, is indeed inversely proportional to the pore size of the membrane. As Table 5.8 also shows, deaggregation of the endotoxin micelles and vesicles by the action of ethlenediaminetetraacetic acid (EDTA) results in the removal of the endotoxin by the nonpolar membrane, but not by weakly polar cellulose triacetate membranes. These latter filters retain the aggregated pyrogens, but only because of pore size, through sieve retention.

The use of 0.2 μm-rated inverse-phase (temperature-governed) polypropylene membranes reduce the endotoxin concentration of solutions filtered through them by an LRV of 1–3. The use of a 0.1 μm rated polypropylene membrane of similar inverse phase structure reduces the endotoxin by an LRV of 3–4. Thus, endotoxin removal by hydrophobic adsorption requires both a hydrophobic filter and intimate contact with the LPS (aggregate or no), as ensured by the use of small pore size-rated membranes. The microporous polypropylene membranes produced by the temperature-governed phase inversion process meet both requirements (Hiatt et al. 1985).

Competition among Ions

Carazzone et al. (1985) found that in the case of a deionized water-containing pyrogen concentration comparable to 12 ng of *E. coli* endotoxin, the adsorptive removal by the charged nylon filters can be accomplished. Pyrogen removal from 5% glucose solutions is not interfered with. However, the presence of 2% peptone solution, at either pH 3.8 or 8.3, inhibits the removal of endotoxin from solutions. This bears a similarity to the experience of Bowman et al. (1967), who found that the protein penicillinase, by preempting the adsorption sites, interfered with the adsorptive removal of *B. diminuta* by non-charged membranes filters. Perhaps surprisingly, electrolytes, and specifically 0.9% sodium chloride solution prevent the removal of the endotoxin by the positive-charged membranes. To this should be added that the stoichiometric relationship between charge site and the endotoxin unit results in the loss of two positive charges when one sulfate ion, having a double negative charge, is neutralized at a single site. This very situation explains the charge reversal that these membranes may undergo, releasing their captured endotoxin in the bargain. Carazzone et al. conclude, "Positively charged media are interesting, but need careful preliminary studies in order to define their suitability and operational procedures."

TABLE 5.8

Influence of Pore Size and Endotoxin Aggregation State on Endotoxin Adsorption to Filters

Polymer Type	Pore Size (μm)	Endotoxin Aggregation State	Endotoxin LRV
Polypropylene	Prefilter	DI	0.1
	0.2	DI	1–3
	0.1	DI	3–4
Cellulose acetate	0.2	DI	0.1
	0.025	DI	3.0
Polypropylene	0.2	EDTA	1.0
	0.1	EDTA	1.0
Cellulose acetate	0.2	EDTA	0.1
	0.025	EDTA	0.1

Source: From Robinson et al. (1982), Courtesy of Membrane Company.

Notes: (1) Deionized water (DI) solutions of endotoxin are mixtures of vesicular and micellar structures; (2) 0.005 M EDTA solutions have only micellar structures.

Fajan's Rule

It may be that there is a hierarchal order governing anionic attractions to the membrane's positive charges. If so, it may be similar to Fajan's Rule that governs ion-exchanges, namely, it depends on the charge density of the ion. This, in turn, is the ratio of the charge to the ion size. The greater the charge density of the ion, and the smaller the ion, the more closely it can approach the opposite, fixed-ionic charge involved in the exchange reaction, and the greater its selectivity. However, in aqueous media, the ion radius is not its isolated or crystallographic radius, but is rather that of its hydrated state. The smaller the isolated ion, the more closely it can approach water molecules and the more plentifully it can be hydrated by them. Thus, the proton, the smallest of all cations, becomes surrounded by many waters of hydration, and conversely acquires the largest radius. The potassium ion is crystallographically larger than the hydrogen ion, but can increase its size by only 5 or 6 waters of hydration. Its effective radius in its hydrated state is, therefore, smaller than that of the hydrated proton. That ion, being relatively small crystalligraphically, acquires a large skirt of water molecules.

This finds reflection in the selectivity of the cation-exchange reactions. The larger the hydrated ion, the weaker is its bonding, and the more easily is it exchanged. In the case of anions, the hydroxyl ion, being relatively small crystallographically, acquires a large skirt of water molecules. It is the largest anion in its hydrated form, and is, therefore, the least preferred in anion-exchange reactions. This would also explain the effect of pH on the removal of endotoxin by charge-modified membranes.

The Covalent Bond and Partial Charges

The covalent chemical bond is formed by a sharing of two electrons by two atoms. It is typical of organic molecular structures. The covalent bond forms when the electrons in the outer shells of the electron clouds of the two constituting atoms overlap in a complementary fashion. The overlap enables the electron sharing that satisfies the fulfilling of the outer shells of both atoms. This establishes a bonding that connects the two atoms. (By contrast, strong repulsive forces result from incompatible electron cloud overlapping.)

The bond strength depends upon the two particular atoms involved, as does the degree of their sharing the bonding electrons. The sharing need not be equal, the propensity of different atoms for attracting electrons not being the same. Atoms are neutral in charge. An electron, by convention, is negatively charged. Therefore, the atom acquiring the greater share of the two bonding electrons than the one it contributed takes on a negative charge. The partner atom with its smaller share assumes a partial positive charge. The partial charges attract their opposite partially charged equivalents present in other molecules. Being only partial in their extent of charge, their attractions form bonds that are relatively weak. Their force extends over lesser distances, and when in opposition to repulsive forces arising from full charges are easily surpassed. Thus, they are called "secondary" bonds. However, they are important factors in adsorptive bonding such as are operative between organisms and filters that culminate in organism removals. (The symbol for the partial charge is the lower case Greek letter delta, δ.)

Polarization and Dipoles

Molecular structures possessing dielectric properties manifest through the magnitude of their dielectric constant how much of their presence will reduce the strength of an electric field. The polarization of dielectric materials is managed by way of an external electric field. The molecular polarity arising from the partial or unequal sharing of bonding electrons, or from other polarizing effects, results in a number of bond types. This includes bonds arising from van der Waal forces, and also from dipole structures, the most important of which are the hydrogen bonds or H-bonds. Polarity can be inherent in the molecular structure or can be induced by outside charge influences. Normal fluctuations in an atom's electron-cloud density cause instantaneous but constantly altering dipoles in that atom.

Dipoles are neutral molecules characterized by permanent and separate polar sites of positive and negative charges that do not coincide. They are characterized by this unsymmetrical arrangement of electrical charges. The dipole moment is a measure of the polarity of the molecule. It is defined as the distance between the charges, multiplied by the magnitude of one of the charges.

Their significance is that their induced polarity, in turn, induces dipoles into surrounding molecules. The VDW forces are of this character. Being induced dipoles, induced by induced dipoles, they act between transient dipoles on separate molecules, not on permanent dipoles. Albeit effective at only short distances, they are very important influences in adsorption bonding at sufficiently short Debye lengths. The polarization of an isotropic dielectric is directly related to the strength of the external electric field that is its cause (Gabler 1978, Chap. 4).

Polarization results from the alignment of permanent dipoles and/or induction of dipoles in the affected molecules or atoms. Permanent dipoles undergo better alignment. Moreover, the molecule's plus and minus charge centers are separated further. Larger induced dipoles result.

As stated, the several electrical forces differ in their origins, whether by valence or by different degrees of electron sharing, etc., and, thus, find expression in a spectrum of strengths. The chemical or valence bonds are the stronger. The weaker bonds, more easily disrupted, are the ones represented in adsorptions. Although weaker than the chemical bonding, the consequences of their effects are often profound, and include the many manifestations of hydrogen bonding, such as are important in protein chemistry. Both arise from particular arrangements of electrons and from the electrical charges that result. The very surface interactions that are operative in the adsorptive sequestration of organisms apply also to the agglomeration of colloidal particles, and to the fouling by proteins of filters; the latter by hydrophobic adsorptions.

The Dipole Structure

Molecules may be charge-neutral overall but may be complex enough to simultaneously contain positive and negative sits, whether ions or partial charges. As stated above, the partial charges leading to interactions can arise from several sources. In polar molecules, fixed dipoles may represent the finite distance that exists between the centers of positive- and negative-charged functional groups. An unequal sharing of electrons may be induced in a neutral molecule by the proximity of a dipolar molecule. As a result of this polarization, the molecule with the induced dipole will by its electronic imbalance be able to exercise its partial charge influences on other neutral molecules, etc. An even greater polarization or electron-pair dislocation leading to a greater partial charge would be induced in a heretofore electrically neutral neighbor by the full electrical charge of an ion. At the other extreme, as will be discussed, VDW forces are hypothesized to be induced dipoles, induced by induced dipoles. They are instantaneous dipoles that average over time to zero. These are weak but significant electrical forces that are considered responsible for the charge interactions (adsorptive connections) between molecular structures that possess no obvious polar features. A common interaction is one between two bipolar molecules, whether of fixed structural origin, or induced. The hydrogen bond is an example. Following are some examples of the importance of hydrogen bonding.

The Hydrogen Bond

The hydrogen bond or H-bond is an important feature in the structure of water. What is known about the structure of water derives from studies involving such arcane subjects as neutron and X-ray absorption spectroscopy, and X-ray Raman scattering. More recently, time-resolved infrared spectroscopy has been utilized to determine the equilibrium position of the oxygen and hydrogen atoms on the attosecond (10^{-18} s) time scale by studying the time variations of vibrational frequencies. Comprehension of the hydrogen bond (H-bond) is gained from studies of water in both its liquid and solid states using such esoteric techniques.

The hydrogen bond arises from a dipole/dipole interaction. It is the most important of such interactions. The water molecule, H_2O, consists of two hydrogen atoms each bonded to the same oxygen atom. The nucleus of the oxygen atom pulls the bonding electrons more strongly to itself and away from the hydrogen atoms. The bonding is not disrupted, but the bonding elements become partially charged. The unequal sharing of the electrons makes the electron-richer oxygen partially negative and the proportionately deprived hydrogen atoms partially positive. This creates the $O^- H^+$ dipole (Tanford 1980, Chap. 5). There are two hydrogen atoms originating from two different water molecules that connect to a single

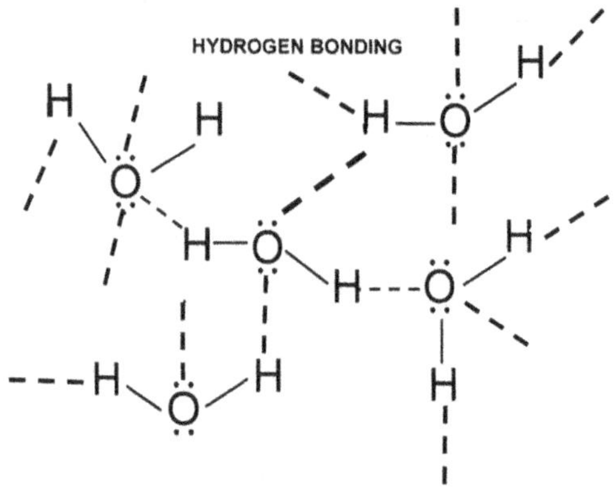

FIGURE 5.24   Hydrogen bonded molecular network.

oxygen atom of one of those molecules. One hydrogen atom is of the pair chemically bonded to the oxygen atom to comprise the water molecule. The other forms the hydrogen bond that bridges one water molecule to the other. Interestingly, the two hydrogen atoms are not equidistant from the oxygen atom. The one attached by valence forces to the oxygen atom is at a distance of 1.00 Å from it. The H-bonded hydrogen is 1.76 Å apart from that oxygen. The oxygen atoms of the two interacting water molecules are 2.76 Å apart, while the two nearest non-hydrogen bonded oxygen atoms are 4.5 Å distant from one another. The chemically bonded hydrogen is more closely attached; perhaps an indication of the relative strengths of the two types of bonds.

The attractive forces of the oppositely signed partial charges decrease rapidly with the distance between the dipoles. Only the proton (hydrogen atom, of atomic weight 1) is small enough to approach the electronegative oxygen atom closely enough to establish the H-bond. Moreover, the electromagnetic associations involving hydrogen atoms in dipole arrangements are only strong enough to be formed with the most electronegative elements, namely, fluorine, oxygen, and nitrogen in decreasing order. The H-bond strength is on the order of 4.5 kcal/mol; the range being from 2 to 10 kcal/mol. The covalent O–H bond has a strength of 110 kcal/mol (Zydney 1996). Typically, the covalent bond strengths is about 100 kcal/mol, approximately the same as an ionic bond in a crystal of NaCl (Gabler 1978, Chap 5). Nevertheless, the H-bond, although weak in its energy of attraction, figures significantly in many fields of chemistry, and has importance especially in protein chemistry. The water molecule is tetrahedral in shape. The molecules of water in its solid (ice) state exist as tetrahedral hydrogen-bonded structures. Much of this ordered form persists even in the mobile liquid. Each of the tetrahedral corners holds either a pair of electrons or a hydrogen atom. Each of the partly positive hydrogen atoms of one water molecule can form a hydrogen bond with a partly negative oxygen atom of each of two different water molecules. This commonly accepted view based on the interpretations of neutron and X-ray diffraction patterns holds that water molecules have the capacity to bond hydrogen with each of four other water molecules, but that fewer than that number are simultaneously present. This process, repeated throughout the water volume, creates an interconnected molecular network that includes H-bonded rings and chains of dynamically altered arrangements (Figure 5.24).

Effect upon Vaporization

Consider its effects upon the physical properties of various substances. As a general rule, the smaller a molecule, the more easily it is vaporized from its liquid state. That is, if it is a liquid, it has a lower boiling point. Conversely, if it is a gas, it requires greater pressures to compress it into a liquid. On this basis, three rather simple molecules can be compared for assessing the influence of hydrogen bonding on physical properties. Hydrogen cyanide (HCN) has a molecular weight of 14; hydrogen sulfide (H_2S) has a molecular weight of 34; and water (H_2O) has a molecular weight of 18. In conformity with their mass, H_2O should have the lowest boiling point; HCN should be next; and H_2S should be the least volatile.

However, water boils at 100°C at atmospheric pressure; hydrogen cyanide, at 26°C; while hydrogen sulfide boils at −59.6°C.

In vaporizing so readily (at −60°C), H_2S fits the rule that so simple a molecule should easily exist in the gaseous state at room temperature. HCN, being of a lower molecular weight, would vaporize even more readily were it not for the hydrogen bonds that form between the H of one HCN molecule and the N of another. The molecules joined by the hydrogen bonding comprise a larger mass, and, therefore, volatilize more slowly; heat being necessary to first break the H-bonds. The hydrogen bonds that are established among water molecules are dipolar associations of the H of one water molecule with the O of another. These are stronger than the dipolar H to N intermolecular bonds of HCN. Therefore, water requires the more considerable heat of 100°C temperature to break its hydrogen bonds enough to become the gaseous molecule it should be at a molecular weight of 18. Even at that, much of the vaporous form of water is as a dimer, a combination of two water molecules joined by a single H-bond. Thus, hydrogen bonding accounts for many of the properties of water, such as its wetting and solution properties, etc. Its density/ temperature relationship is among them.

Density of Water

Hydrogen bonding accounts for many of the singular properties of water, such as its high boiling point, its high surface tension, its wetting and solution properties, etc. Its density/temperature relationship is among them. Water is one of few substance (diamonds are another) all of which are in the tetrahedral crystalline shape, whose molecular arrangements in the solid, crystalline state (ice) are less dense than they are in the liquid state. As a result, ice floats on water, with enormous effects upon terrestrial life. The hydrogen bond is a weak bond, on the order of 4.5 kcal/mol as compared to a covalent bond at 110 kcal/mol for an O–H bond. However, it is an extremely important bond. It has a prominence in protein chemistry, having strong influences in the associative bonding common to proteins, and it plays a major role in maintaining the structural integrity of many biological macromolecules.

The hydrogen bond, represented formally by three dashes, is weak enough to be broken easily by the molecular mobility of the liquid state, only to be reformed immediately with new neighboring water molecules. Facile though the bond may be, it represents a definite force. Thus, water molecules being electromagnetically associated, are not gaseous at room temperature as their molecular weight of 18 would suggest but form a rather high boiling liquid (100°C).

Solvating Effects

An example of the water molecules' wetting and solvating capability follows: The electrolytic salt molecules considered above are ions that exist as molecular entities as long as the electrical ionic bond created by the attractions of opposite charges persists. The ionic bond can, however, be weakened and disrupted by the insinuation of electrically charged structures between the sodium and chlorine moieties, thus attenuating their strong mutual attraction. The addition of water to an electrolyte, such as salt, affects this ion/dipole interaction. Water, because of the electronegativity of its oxygen atom and the electropositivity of its hydrogen atoms , is a dipolar molecule with a high dielectric charge; its oxygen atom has a partial, hence weak, negative charge, and its two hydrogen atoms have each a partial positive charge (Tanford 1980, Chap. 5).

The water molecules, by way of their partial charges, respond to the electrical charge forces of the ions, causing them to become hydrated. That is, the ions acquire skirts of water molecules attached by the electrical attractions of opposite charges. These new electrical alliances compete with and dilute and weaken the power of the primary ionic bonds forming the salt molecule. Heretofore, the electrical needs of the ionic charges had been exclusively satisfied by the counterions, but these interactions are now compromised by the competing dipolar influences of the many water molecules. The water separates the ionic lattices by displacing the ionic bonds with its own dipolar alliances. This brings the salt into solution. That is to say, each ion is now individual, released from its ionic lattice, and separated from the others by an envelope of water molecules that are attached to one another within their hydrogen-bonded structures. The ion size is increased by its hydration. This can have implications where the ion-size is a consideration. The charge density of the hydrated ion is less than that of the ion itself; the mass over which the charge is spread being greater. Organic compounds can also acquire waters of hydration if they contain partial charges that interact with their opposites on the water molecules.

An interesting view of the adsorptive bond formation that ultimately attaches the particle to the filter involves a competition between two forces. Hydrophilic sites on surfaces become wetted because of their strong mutual attraction with water molecules. In order for two such wet solid surfaces to interact with one another, the water molecules bonded to each of them must be displaced. This dislodgment can only be effected by stronger surface-to-surface forces.

VDW Forces

There are charge/charge (ion/ion) interactions; ion or charge/dipole, and dipole/dipole charge interactions. There are also charge/induced-dipoles, and dipole/induced dipoles. Overall, the strength of the bonding is greatest where charges are involved, less for permanent dipoles, and least for induced dipoles. The strength of the bonding depends upon the asymmetry of the molecule's charge distribution, the distance of separation, and the value of the dielectric constant (Gabler 1978, Chap. 5). In all these cases some molecular polar entity can be recognized as being the originating cause. However, a similar imbalance of electrons may come about in molecules where no polar influence is evident. These are ascribed to induced-dipole/induced-dipole electrostatic forces. They are the London-VDW dispersion forces, named for their early investigators. They serve as a weak but very important attraction mechanism. They were deduced from experimental investigations of departures from the Perfect Gas Law. The noble gases* are inert because their outer electron orbitals are completely filled. Therefore, they do not form covalent bonds, not being in need of electron donating or borrowing. It was found, nevertheless, that they exhibit electronic attractions. This, it is theorized, is the result of partial charge interactions not involving valence bond formation.

As a consequence of their obscurity, but with an appreciation of their reality, there are widespread mistaken references in the technical literature to the VDW forces as regards their genesis. All attractive forces of partial charge origins are often referred to as VDW forces or as "secondary valence" effects. Albeit incorrectly designated, the end result serves in that there is recognition that unsatisfied electronic expressions are at work. The VDW forces are universally operative but are seen to be of prime importance among nonpolar molecules, such as hydrocarbons, whose nonpolar structures would seem not to hold possibilities for inducing dipole formation.

The VDW forces are fundamentally different from the classical models of the electrical interactions just considered. The VDW attractions are ascribed to *transient dipoles* that result from an "instantaneous non-zero dipole moment" that induces a momentary dipole in a neighboring molecule (Gabler 1978, Chap.6). Electrons are in constant circulation around their nucleus. Therefore, the charge distribution, over a time period, is not in one fixed position. It is described in terms of a "cloud" to emphasize its ubiquitous positioning. However, although constantly changing, the molecule does at any instance have an immediate dipole moment. It is this that induces dipoles in adjacent molecules. The VDW forces operate as attractive influences, albeit weak and effective over only short distances. However, in their multitude they are of substantial import. A molecule is not limited to a single fluctuating dipole, but may have many transient dipoles, each capable of inducing a dipole in another molecule. The VDW, therefore, has a cumulative effect (Gabler 1978, Chap. 6).

It may be of interest to know that in addition to being responsible for the adsorption of organisms and other particles to filter surfaces, and its similar action in destabilizing colloids, VDW forces govern the condensation of gases into liquids by their induced-dipole, induced-dipole interaction. For instance, in the gaseous state, water molecules, like all vapors, are widely separated and remain so. When, however, they are squeezed together by pump action, the attractive forces acting among them become operative over the compressed intermolecular distances and overcome the ever-present repulsive forces. Liquid water is thus created. (This is the operative principle of the vapor compression still whose external pressure brings together the water vapor molecules and coalesces them into the greater intimacy of

---

* The noble gases are helium, argon, neon, krypton, and radon.

the liquid state.) The closer molecular proximity of the liquid state accounts for its higher density. The dipole/dipole attractive force resulting from the thermal condensation of steam has the same effect, as does also the induced VDW. Because of its effect, the VDW has been described as being an internal pressure. VDW forces are involved in lipid–lipid interactions, in interactions among hydrocarbons, and even, as stated, among the noble gases.

Bonds of Partial Charges

Obviously, there are numerous bond configurations that result from the partial sharing of the covalent electrons. These differ in their origins and strengths. Not all are significant to the desired particle retentions by filters. The presently accepted theory accounting for a filter's ability to remove particles focuses upon those interactions that are governing. In addition to the ionic bonding there is a variety of partial charge interactions: charge–charge arrangements, charge–dipole combinations, dipole–dipole reactions, charge-induced dipole interactions, and induced dipole–induced dipole dispositions (Gabler 1978). Three of these bond types in addition to the ionic types are generally considered to be the influences that in their interplay of repulsions and attractions achieve the balance necessary for particle retentions. These interactions differ in their strengths and in the distances over which they exercise their powers.

Of the two interactions that exhibit the repulsive behavior of like-charged entities, the more powerful is the mutual reaction of full ionic charges. Coulomb's Law describes the situation. It holds that the electrical force between two poles is the direct result of the difference in the charge between them, and that its action is direct and strong enough to operate over long distances. The law established that like-charges repel, and unlike-charges attract. In the case of organism and filter, both acquire the same charge designations from the solution that surrounds them. Its influence decays inversely as the square of the distance between the poles. Another repulsive force is the more general repulsion exercised when any two atoms are brought together close enough for their (negatively charged) electron clouds to overlap. These forces are limited to the short distances at which they are generated. The mutual repulsions of the like-charges of the strong primary (ionic) forces that are operative over the longer distances are dominant.

The interactive forces that project an attraction between organism and filter surfaces are seen to be the result of the mutual responses of unlike-charged atoms or molecules. These are generally ascribed to forces arising from quantum mechanical origins, from electrostatic interactions, and from VDW forces.

The distance separating the two surfaces is of prime importance. The long-range Coulombic mutual rejections overwhelm the attractive short-range powers. At low ionic strengths the attractive influences become dominant only at a very short distance of separation between the two surfaces. The separation distance is termed the Debye length. The greater the Debye length as caused by a sizable (zeta) potential, the greater the influence of the mutual repulsion involving like-charged surfaces. As will be discussed, the Debye lengths can be shortened to the point where the attractive forces compel the surface-to-surface bonding of particle and filter.

To summarize, the attractive forces are short range, whether electrostatic, quantum mechanical, etc. They are the products of interactions that include the VDW forces. When the two surfaces are at a distance, the repulsive forces, being stronger, dominate. With decreasing separation distances, the attractive impulses increase relative to those that repel. When the distance separating the two surfaces is reduced sufficiently, the attractive forces can assert themselves. At this point, the adsorption of particles to filters, or other solid-surface interactions occur. Adamson (1982, p. 232) states that at a separation distance of a particle's diameter the attractive forces are at a maximum. Beyond this point repulsions again set in. The cause of this repulsion is the overlapping of the electron clouds. It is of a very short range and manifests itself rapidly as atoms or molecules come within a certain distance of one another.

Quantum-Mechanical Forces

Although the valence needs are satisfied by the union of two atoms, the molecule thus formed may still attract others around it due to the partial charges just discussed. These residual weaker forces have a strength of about 0.5–5 kcal. This force level, associated with a two-atom molecule, is too small to effect bonding. However, these forces are additive. Where the molecule is composed of many atoms, as in the case of polymers, the residual force can be considerable. It is then conducive to bonding. As Zydney (1996, p. 399), describes, it is these quantum-mechanical forces that operate at short ranges to attract affected surfaces to one another. This leads to electron sharing and bonding between the partnering atoms. This type of interaction exerts an attractive force helpful in particle removals. Electrostatic attractions and the VDW forces are two other phenomena that exercise attractions between surfaces.

There is, however, a potential and practical downside to this interaction. It can occur between macromolecular species present in the solution leading them to aggregate into larger entities that may contribute to filter fouling. Be that as it may, such positive quantum-mechanical interactions are among the attractive forces that adhere particles to filters.

Electrostatic Interactions

Aside from the electrical charges that derive from their molecular structures, surfaces of macromolecular units such as filters, organisms, and other large elements acquire fixed charges from their exposure to aqueous solutions that almost certainly contain ions. Negative ions seem to undergo preferential adsorptions onto surfaces especially at neutral pHs. At alkaline pHs anion (negative) adsorptions predominate. Negative surface charges may also result from the ionic dissociation of carboxylic acids created by the oxidation of organic molecules.

Electrically charged surface atoms, whether of ionic or covalent origins generate electrostatic responses in the atoms of adjacent molecules. Mutual attractions or repulsions result, respectively, from unlike or like-charged neighbors. Thus, interactions arise, as stated, from the fixed charges of opposite signs and from fixed and charge-induced dipoles (Gabler 1978, p. 180). The negative charges adsorbed and fixed to the filter, and/or other particle surfaces attract and firmly bind a layer of counterions. The formation of a layer of ions of opposite charge is in accord with the Debye–Hückel theory. This layered combination of fixedly adsorbed ions and counterions forms the first of the electric double-layer arrangement that is central to the adsorptive bonding phenomenon (Figure 5.25).

The attractive forces that are ultimately responsible for the bonding of particle surfaces to filter surfaces derive from such electrostatic interactions. The accepted accounting for the adsorptive interaction of surfaces, shortly to be discussed, is named the DLVO theory. As already stated, the name derives from the initials of its authors' surnames: Derjaguin, Landau, Vervey, and Overbeek. It can be considered an extension or an elaboration of the Debye–Hückel theory. Adamson (1982, p. 215) depicts a detailed model of the double layer (Figure 5.26).

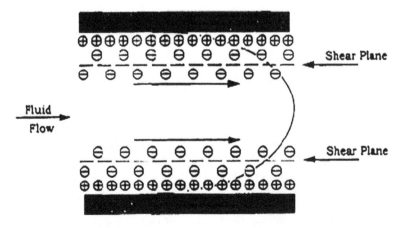

FIGURE 5.25   Ion distribution near a positively charged surface.

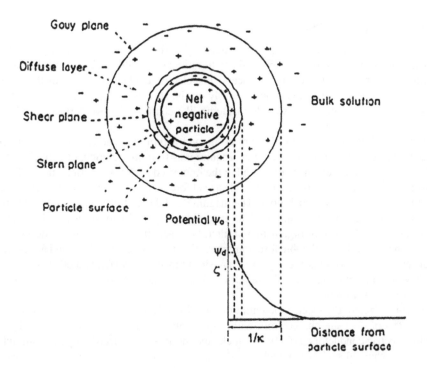

FIGURE 5.26   Charge distance depiction.

Free Surface Energy

As a result of the surface interaction between filter and particle there is a reduction in the system's free surface energy. The result is a more stable molecular arrangement. A proper treatment of the subject of free surface energy requires the application of thermodynamics. A less ambitious effort is being made here to set forth the concept of free surface energy in a less rigorous manner. The beneficiaries will be those who, like the authors, are limited in their ability to probe the occult and mysterious.

The situation being considered is that of a filter and of an organism both immersed in an aqueous solution. All molecules have a certain energy available for interactively relating to their surroundings, neighboring molecules provided proper conditions exist. Common to all surfaces, their molecules differ from those within the mass because they interface with a surrounding gas phase, namely, the air. Being a gas, air has a low density. It is sparse in its molecular population. The surface layer of the solid object is, thus, molecularly unsaturated. The molecules composing it possess a residual field that is high in Gibbs' free surface energy.

Consider a droplet of water. Every water molecule within its depth will interact with its neighbors to the full extent of its powers to undergo bonding. As a result, a given volume of water will, in effect, consist of a network of water molecules connected to one another by hydrogen bonds. (See the section: "Hydrogen Bonding.") The propensity of the water molecules to H-bond is a measure of the energy available to them for interaction with other (suitable type) molecules.

However, the water molecules situated on the spherical boundaries of the water droplet and constituting its interface with non-water molecules have few neighbors on the droplet's periphery suitable for bonding. The unexpended energy remaining in their nonbonded region is the free surface energy being discussed. When a liquid is dispersed into discrete multi-droplets the mass of water assumes a proportionally larger surface area, and, therefore, a larger total free surface energy. The free surface energy of the multi-droplets expended in bonding interactions serves to coalesce them into larger volumes with a consequent diminishment in the liquid's total surface area. A loss results in the total free surface energy. This is a consequence of the adsorptive interaction.

Attractive and Repulsive Forces

It may be advantageous to again address the balancing of the attractive and repulsive forces whose management can culminate in particle removals by filtration; especially so for those of us for whom the "electric double layer" is a relatively new concept. The electric double layer governs the adsorption of organisms to filter surfaces. It forms simultaneously on the surfaces of both the filter and the particle when they are exposed to an aqueous medium. Being like-charged, the two surfaces exhibit a mutual repellency.

In a filtration both the particle and filter are positioned within the aqueous stream. As is inevitable, both surfaces, because of their higher energies, acquire ions from the solution, or gain charges induced thereby. The acquired ions become firmly fixed to the immersed surfaces. In effect, the surfaces of both filter and organism simultaneously accumulate electrical forces of both stronger and weaker powers, and of both attractive and repulsive capabilities. The magnitude of these effects is proportional to the charge density on the individual adsorbing surface. The acquired ions give rise to strong and, hence, long-range Coulombic forces. In the case of organism and filter, both acquire the same charge designations from the solution. Therefore, the Coulombic forces are mutually and strongly repellant and are exercised over long distances. The concurrent attracting forces are short range, e.g., VDW, and others of partial charge origins. They are too weak to redress the repulsion. That they are effective only at short distances is a measure of their weaker influences.

As would be expected, the electric potential of the adsorptively fixed ionic surface charges attracts counterions, ions of opposite charge from within the solution that become fixedly attached to them. These, being electric conductors, effectively shield and moderate the electrically repellant interactions between the two charged surfaces, namely, of filter and of organism. In consequence, the electrostatic forces are reduced in potential. However, not all of the fixed surface charges are neutralized or shielded by the inseparably attached counterions. Consequently, additional ions of opposite charge, intermingled with *their counterions,* are attracted by the fixed surface charges that remain un-neutralized. However, these augmenting counterions remain mobile within the solution because, although responsive to the fixed surface charges, they are increasingly distant from them, and the interactive forces diminish sharply with distance. The mobile ions, by definition, can be caused to migrate by the impress of an electric current.

The fixed surface charges and their *firmly held* countersigned ions constitute the first layer of the electric double layer. The second layer is composed of the *mobile* counterions. The double-layer potential extends from the line of counterion separation as far into the liquid as is necessary in its search to include enough countersigned ions to satiate the remaining unsatisfied fixed charges on the solid's surface. The electrical force generating the attraction of the mobile counterions is called the zeta potential. The distance it extends into the solution in its seeking after counterions is known as the Debye length (symbol K^{-1}).

The zeta potential will shortly be treated in detail. Postponing its consideration permits a less disjointed account of how the electric double layer functions.

Attenuation of Repulsive Forces

It is evident from the foregoing that empowering the attractive VDW forces requires the shortening of the Debye length. This can be accomplished by the addition of ions in the form of salts. Contrarily, the low ionic content of dilute solutions results in extending the Debye lengths. This renders the weak attractive forces impotent against the strong long-range Coulombic forces of repulsion. The addition of ions to the solution makes possible the dominance of the attractive forces. The ionic strength of a solution is a measure of its salt or ion content. Upon the reduction of the Debye length as occasioned by the addition of ions, the short-range attractive VDW forces enable the appropriate surface sites on the organism to interact with those on the filter. Since there are as many opportunities for the VDW force orientations to exercise repulsions, as there are to encourage attractions, the domination by the attractive tendencies requires explanation. Actually, both the attractive and repulsive forces are reduced by the addition of ions, but the repulsive power is the one more affected. On balance the attractive forces emerge the stronger.

It turns out that two factors incline in favor of the attractive forces. First, when placed in an electric field the induced dipoles that are the VDW forces can align themselves either in a head-to-head and tail-to-tail, or head-to-tail sequence. This reflects a probability factor. The head-to-tail arrangement, alternating the positive and negative partial charge interactions involves a lower energy level and thereby signals its greater stability. The greater stability, therefore, favors this orientation, and it is this orientation that more effectively shields and neutralizes the zeta potential. Instituting a chain of subsidiary or partial charge interactions, in the form of an array of dipoles, between two like-charged repulsive forces such as reside on particle and filter, serves to attenuate the mutual antagonistic, repellent interactions.

This is abetted by a polarization factor. The VDW force, also called the London dispersion force, affects the size of the dipole moment by influencing the spatial separation of the plus and minus charges. These exist in each molecule in proportion to the dipole sizes. In the electrostatic attraction mode, polarization increases the interaction between the two molecules. In the repulsive orientation, the polarization decreases the molecular moments; hence, the repulsive force. As stated by Wheland (1947), "The attractive orientations on the average, are more attractive than the repulsive orientations are repulsive." As a result of these two factors, the short-range VDW forces exert an attractive influence, and bring about the desired filtrative removal of organisms by an adsorptive interaction.

Incidentally, the equilibrium point where the attractive and repulsive forces balance one another defines the space that exists between the atoms composing molecules, and also between the overlapping segments of long polymeric chains.

Perhaps the influence of ionic strength can be made more apparent by focusing on the effects of the "ion cloud" created by the addition of salts. "The counterions screen the central molecule and reduce the strength of its net charge," according to Gabler (1978); also, "The (electron) cloud shrinks about the macromolecules making the entire unit more compact." Its size is reduced. The ions of the opposite polarity tend to cluster closer to the macromolecule. In so doing, they dilute or shield its effective charge. The crowding grows proportionately closer as the concentration of counter-charged ions increases. A more effective screening of the charge takes place. This compression enables the charged macromolecules to approach each other closely enough to overcome the repulsive forces.

The exemption of the attractive forces from the shielding powers of the electron cloud is more apparent than real. The attractive forces are also reduced. However, "The counterion cloud dilutes the net charge on the macromolecule more so than it does the VDW forces." The attractive VDW forces created by the dipole oscillation from one orientation to another are, unlike the net charges, not disrupted because the counterion distribution cannot orient fast enough to conform to the dipole oscillations.

Gabler states, "The key to the whole explanation is the fact that as the salt concentration increases, the Debye length, which measures the radius of the shell of counterions about the macromolecule, decreases." As a result of the greater diminishment of the repulsive forces, the countervailing forces of attraction assert themselves, and the two surfaces attain interaction by way of the adsorptive sequestration mechanism.

It is this effect that minimizes the strength of the (repelling) zeta potential. This, then, describes the working of the electric double layer in furthering the filtration operation in its adsorptive removal of particles from suspensions.

Debye Length-Associated Phenomena

Fletcher (1996) describes the attractive and repulsive forces involved in the interactions between organisms and the filter or other surfaces, and offers quantification of the approximate distances at which they are significant: At distances greater than 50 nm, called the "secondary minimum," VDW attractive forces do cause the positioning of the bacteria nearer the surface, but so weakly that they are readily removed by shear forces. At distances of 10–20 nm, repulsive electrostatic forces still dominate. Here the Debye length is too great for the weaker VDW attractive forces to prevail. At between 2 and 10 nm both repulsive and electrostatic attractive forces are manifest, the distance is now small enough to allow the weaker attractive forces to begin asserting themselves. At between 0.5 and 2 nm, the water adhering to the surfaces is still a barrier to specific surface interactions. However, if the two surfaces include nonpolar areas or patches, these may coalesce to form hydrophobic adsorptions concomitant with the

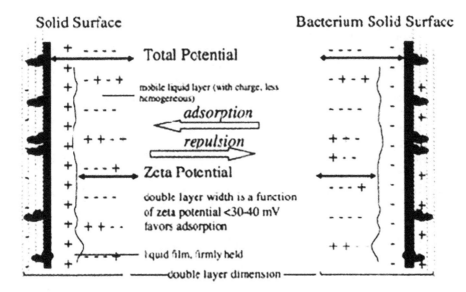

FIGURE 5.27 Different charge influences and interactions.

elimination of the intervening water. At less than 1.0 nm, the attractive forces are strong enough to cause specific organism-surface interactions to take place (Figure 5.27).

In agreement with this observation, Pall et al. (1980) state that when the Debye length corresponds to a zeta potential of less than 30 mV, the VDW forces are able to effect the adsorptive interaction. Colloids are stabilized when their particles are endowed with net surface charges of similar sign in the magnitude of 30–40 mV or more.

There are, however, limitations to attaining the required small Debye lengths. As mentioned, the adsorption of a surfactant molecule onto a macromolecule's surface increases its size. This steric hindrance may keep it too far from the other surface to yield a sufficiently short Debye length. Nonionic surfactants in particular contribute to such a condition. The two surfaces are, thus, sterically stabilized against adsorptive coalescence. Spatial interferences can also result from the hydration barriers created by the increase in an ion's size by its acquisition of waters of hydration. Such steric interferences can create an energy barrier sufficient to frustrate adsorptions.

Bacterial Adhesion to Surfaces

It would seem that the adsorption of organisms from their suspensions onto solid surfaces would involve the same forces of attraction and repulsion that regulate the adsorptive joining of one colloidal particle's surface to that of another, as just discussed. The process involving organisms would explain their retention by filters. It would also seem to be central to the establishment of biofilms, concentrations of microbes, dead and alive, nutrients, and their metabolic products. Organisms seem compelled to seek attachment to surfaces. It acts as a survival mechanism. As attachments to surfaces, organisms secure protection from sterilants such as active chlorine preparations. The extracellular polymeric substances (EPSs) within which the organisms are embedded in the biofilm serve to shield them from antagonistic agents, including a free chlorine residual of several ppm (Le Chevallier et al. 1984; Ridgway and Olson 1982; Seyfried and Fraser 1989).

Marshall (1992) points out that in conformity with accepted theory, bacteria, as also particles in general, are kept from contact with surfaces by electrostatic forces. This includes the surfaces of other organisms. The repulsive forces involved, as discussed, are effective at long range, and prevail over the weaker attractive forces that are simultaneously present. As described in the discussion of the electric double layer, the repulsions are attenuated by higher electrolyte concentrations. The attractive forces, albeit weaker, can then assert their influence. The adsorptive interactions that follow result in the formation of a biofilm.

However, according to Marshall, the repulsive forces may still be strong enough to keep relatively larger bacteria from directly contacting the surface to which they are attracted. Steric hindrance, a result of the organism's large size, would be the cause. Were this the case in the matter of forming biofilm, some authorities believe that the too large separation distances could be bridged by an extracellular slime (EPS) exuded by the organisms. The EPS is constituted of complex molecular structures such as heteropolysaccharides and glycoproteins. Presumably, these exudates overarch the too large separation distances to establish the biofilm. Nevertheless, there is also the opposite view, namely, that the attachments are other than a result of such metabolic processes as the exopolymer-mediated bridging. In this view, the adsorptive attachments are exactly those resulting from the electric double-layer phenomenon. In this manner, it is believed, the organisms become attached to the filter surface, and to one another. Biofilm development is the result.

The Electrical Double Layer

The formation of the electrical double layer and its consequences in terms of charge distributions and the distances over which they hold sway are basic to the understanding of the adsorption mechanism. To recapitulate in the interest of clarity, all surfaces, whether of filters or organisms, etc., acquire a net surface charge of fixed ions when immersed in an aqueous solution (certain to contain ions). This may eventuate from the adsorption of specific ion from the solution, or from the ionic dissociation of functional groups that are part of the surface's molecular structure. According to Zydney (1996) at neutral pH most microporous membrane surfaces preferentially adsorb negative ions, such as carboxylic acids, and become negatively charged. The carboxylic acid group on a surface is likely to result from the almost inevitable time-dependent oxidation of organic molecules that form parts of the particle or filter surface. Alternatively, positive charges may become adsorbed to become a permanent part of the filter surface.

Regardless of the origin or sign of the charge, its presence endows the surface with an electrical potential that is a function of the charge density. These surface charges will alter the arrangement of the ion concentration within the solution by attracting ions of opposite charge. Such counterions will form a fixedly joined layer to the acquired surface charges already bonded in an inseparable union. This will, by dint of its opposite charge, attenuate the original electrical potential of the surface charges. The result is a single but biphasic overlay of oppositely charged sites on the surface. However, the attracted and fixedly held counterions within this overlay are deficient in number to the surface charges that attract them.

The negative charges on the surface, remaining unshielded by counterions, represent the net electric potential of this biphasic layer. The as yet unappeased surface charge extends its influence into the liquid for additional positive ions to more completely fulfill its charge needs, and vice versa if positively charged. This potential will project into the solution to a distance known as the Debye length attracting additional counterions within the solution. The counterions, the electrical load carriers, will form successive charge-neutralizing zones throughout the liquid; more diffused but with increasingly less charge homogeneity as the charge attractions progressively attenuate with distance.

The counterions fixed to the surface charges are immobilized. They are firmly bonded, whether to the organism or filter surface. However, the attracted counterions more distant within the solution become increasingly less firmly bonded according to their distance from the fixed surface charges. Within a certain zone, there is a line (more properly a band) of separation between the fixed counterions and those that could exhibit mobility in response to an imposed direct electric current. Were such to be applied, a line or zone of separation would become manifest between the mobile and immobile counterions. The zeta potential extends within the solution from this line of separation in its search for ions of opposite charge to satisfy its unassuaged fixed charges. The more dilute the solution, i.e., the fewer the ions, the larger the Debye length.

It may be useful to consider the disposition of the charges as being in the form of a capacitor. Gabler (1978) provides a necessary source. The subject arrangement consisting of two connected plates oppositely charged by an electrical source but separated by a vacuum extensive enough to insulate one plate from the other. Consider the introduction of a dielectric between the plates. Although the dielectric molecule remains electrically neutral, opposite charges build on its surfaces next to the plates. The dipoles, originally randomly arranged, align themselves so that their electrical fields oppose the field causing the orientation. This polarization of the dielectric structures neutralizes or dilutes the charges on the plates. The upshot is a reduction in the voltage or electric field between them. The field of a charge reflects its surrounding medium. Therefore, the presence of water, or any other dielectric, reduces a charge's electrical field to a level less than it would exhibit in a vacuum. It is this moderation of the zeta potential that enables the diminution of the Debye length to the point where adsorptive bonding between surfaces can take place.

The Zeta Potential

The first part of the electrical double layer consists, as said, of the charges sited on the boundary surface of the solid (filter), and the (hydrated) counterions that are permanently attracted and bound to it. It is called the Stern layer or Helmholtz layer. The second layer, measured from the line of separation, consists of the diffuse, less strongly bound layer of less homogeneous ions assembled within the solution in response to the zeta potential. It is called the Gouy or Gouy-Chapman layer (Figure 5.28). The application of an electric current upon this arrangement causes the migration within the Gouy layer of the less firmly fixed counterions ions it contains. A line of shear will form, as stated, between the fixed counterions, and those present and migrating in the liquid bulk. The Debye length measures the distance over which the zeta potential extends within the solution to satisfy its need for ions of opposite sign.

The same phenomenon manifests itself on both the filter and organism surfaces. The larger the zeta potential as caused by the paucity of fixedly attached counterions, the greater the Debye length separating the two surfaces, and the stronger their mutual repulsion.

The net effect of the double layers is the development of the zeta potential. Of similar sign on both the filter and organism surfaces, its repellant force inhibits the mutual approach of the particle surfaces to that of the filter. In the case of colloids, it prevents the approach of one colloidal particle to another.

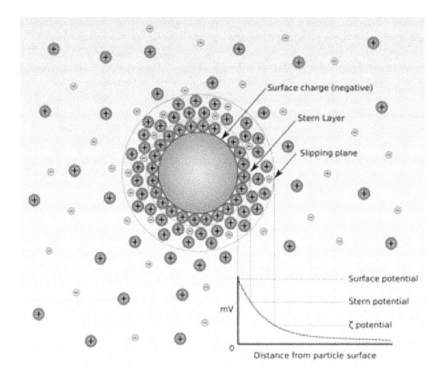

FIGURE 5.28   Charge distance.

This preserves the stability of colloidal suspensions, and countervails organism adsorption to filters. The capacities for attractive and repulsive forces between any two surfaces are simultaneously present. The attractive forces can act only over smaller distances because they are relatively weak. Their more limited powers reflect their origins as being derived from partial charges, namely VDW forces, and hydrophobic adsorptions. At moderate to large distances, the electrical potential arising from the partial charges decay exponentially in an electrolyte solution with a characteristic length scale equal to the thickness of the double layer (Zydney 1996). They operate at the twelfth power of the distance. Thus, these electrostatic attractive forces become negligible when the surfaces are separated by more than a few Debye lengths. However, the repulsive forces are stronger. They mirror the stronger influence of full charges.

The interposition of ions between the two repelling charges attenuates their mutual repulsion. Thus, the zeta potential, can be moderated by managing the ionic strength of the solution, as by the addition of electrolytes. The ions from the dissolved electrolytes provide an electrostatic shielding of the zeta potential, causing its diminishment, and the shortening of the Debye length. The magnitude of the electrostatic interactions between the charges on the membrane surface and the ions of the second layer is, therefore, a strong function of the ionic strength of the solution. The zeta potential reduction by the addition of ions is the customary practice in water treatments utilizing coagulation with alum to settle colloids. The zeta charge-moderating ions being made available, a shorter Debye length obtains. The diminishment of the double-layer distance, by the addition of Al^{+3} ions, promotes the colloid destabilization and agglomeration that is the water purification's objective. The adsorptive sequestration of particles to filter surfaces results from a like-effect enabled by solutions of high ionic strengths or high osmolarities to moderate the long-range repulsive forces and to permit the short-range VDW attractive forces to dominate.

Restatement and Elaboration

The measure of the zeta potential represented by the symbol ζ is the difference in the electrokinetic potential that exists within the Gouy layer over the entire mobile counterion expanse. It is a measure of the charge on the filter surface that is not satisfied by the permanently bound counterions (Figures 5.25 and 5.27). The counter charges required for electrical balance must, therefore, come from the mobile, less tightly bound ions within the liquid phase. Commencing at the line of shear, the zeta potential extends within the bulk of the solution encompassing the mobile counterions it influences.

The thickness of the double layer relative to the particle diameter is very small. In a 10.3 molar monovalent ion solution, the thickness is approximately 100 Å or 0.01 μm (American Water Works Association 1969). Nevertheless, a reduction to such a Debye length is needed as it enables the attractive forces to take over. Its magnitude is inversely related to the ease of destabilizing colloid particles, and/or encouraging adsorptions. Both are exercises that involve double-layer shrinkage and charge neutralization. The lower the zeta potential, the smaller the distance, the Debye length, between the permanent charges of the first surface and the fixed, opposite charges of the second surface. Adsorption follows from the interaction of the two (opposite) charges. The precise location of the shear plane, the Stern layer, is not known with exactness since it depends on the adsorbed ions and their degrees of hydration. Nevertheless, zeta potential measurements are useful in characterizing the surfaces of particles, including bacteria. Its values relate to the coagulation-flocculation process, to colloid destabilizations, but only when charge-neutralization is the only consideration (Bratby 1980, Sec. 2.8). This is not always the case, and its predictions may differ from the classical jar test results (Bratby 1980, Sec. 8.1). There are, then, limitations to zeta potential predictions of performance.

According to Cohn's Rule, a particle suspended in water acquires a zeta potential that reflects both its and the water's dielectric constant (Johnston 2004, Chap. 9.2). Water has a dielectric constant of 72. If the particle has a higher dielectric value, its zeta potential in water is positive. (Asbestos is a case in point.) If the dielectric charge of the particle is lower, its zeta potential is negative. Most particles suspended in water bear negative charges.

An intriguing view of the effects of the zeta potential, the measure of the electrokinetic effect, *vis-à-vis* colloids is given by Pall et al. (1980). These investigators point out that colloidal suspensions are stabilized when their particles are endowed with net surface charges of similar sign in the magnitude of 30–40 mV or more. The mutually repulsive forces then suffice to repel the particles from one another.

The double-layer distance is then large enough to frustrate the shorter range attractive VDW forces. Therefore, no flocculation occurs, and the colloidal dispersion is stabilized. Below about 30 mV the double-layer extent shortens, and the zeta potentials begin to reflect the growing involvement of the attractive secondary valence forces. Marshall (1992) considers the critical Debye length to be from 10 to 20 nm, at which point "... long range (*sic*) van der Waal attractive forces can exceed 'the' electrical repulsion forces . . .." Over and at the zero charge level, attraction dominates and flocculation occurs: the colloid becomes destabilized.

To be sure, the ionic strength of the suspending solution, like its pH, exerts a restraining influence on the magnitude of the mutually repelling like-charges. Low pH (high hydronium ion, $H_2O–H^+$), and/or high ion concentrations serve to attenuate the repulsive forces. They shorten the Debye length, and so usually promote flocculation in colloids. They also tend to influence adsorptive particle arrests. Nonionic surfactants also exert an influence. The particles are enlarged in size by the hydrophobic adsorption of an enveloping nonionic-surfactant coating. The increase in their size abbreviates the charge density which now becomes dispersed over a larger area. This shortens the Debye length, making it possible for the attractive forces to come into play. The separating effect of the repulsive potential energy barrier that prevented the attractive oppositely charged particles from approaching one another is overcome at the shortened distances. The phenomenon is referred to as steric stabilization. It has also been called entropic stabilization. The spatial barrier effect, or Debye length may be of a considerable magnitude. Nonionic surfactants in particular can exert a significant influence on overcoming its colloid stabilization effect; likewise, on the adsorptive sequestration of particles by filters.

Jaisinghani and Verdegan (1982) provide a discussion of how to measure the zeta potential of a filter medium. However, the measurements of zeta potential, even by the zeta meters devised for that purpose, are time-consuming to a degree that reduces their practicality in assaying, for example, the quantity of alum needed for the clarification of water to rid it, by agglomeration, of its colloidal content. The time-honored jar tests are often used for this purpose. Their results are considered more dependable (Bratby 1980, Sec. 8.1). As stated, there are limitations to the reliability of predictions of performance based on zeta potential. Some consider zeta meters as less than perfect instruments, and view their use as troublesome (Mandaro 1987, pp. 187–193). They prefer to measure the streaming current potential.

Streaming Current Potential

In the measurement of zeta potential, the core particle with its attached charges is caused to separate from its charge envelope by being moved electrically through the suspending (non-flowing) water toward an electrode. The same separation of the electrical double layers can be obtained by anchoring the particles, as by adsorption to surfaces, and causing the liquid to flow past them. This is called the streaming current potential technique.

It is easier to perform than zeta potential measurements, and it too measures the voltage necessary to separate the double layers and, hence, helps determine the ease of colloid destabilization or particle adsorption. It does so by providing a measurement of the net surface charge of the colloidal particles. This correlates with how much coagulant must be added to the colloidal suspension to cause it to agglomerate. The coagulant, such as alum, supplies multivalent cations, Al^{+3}, to neutralize the negative charges of the first electrical layer. This charge neutralization destabilizes the colloidal suspension, *reducing the double-layer dimension*, the Debye length, and thus permitting the particles to agglomerate and to become large enough to be responsive to gravitational settling.

Streaming current measurements are more speedily performed, and the results are less subjective. They offer the advantage of being immediately expressed as the average for the system. This technique reads an alternating current on a direct current meter. The polarity of the output is adjusted to indicate the surface charge. Streaming current measurements are relative, and are dependent on the very streaming current detector used. In general, however, their values correspond to the optimum destabilization points given by jar tests using particular coagulants.

Knight and Ostreicher (1981) described a suitable instrument, and reported on the use streaming-current potential measurements. In potable water treatment plants, such devices are relied upon to assess the coagulation requirements of water-containing colloids, i.e., to gauge the amount of alum needed to destabilize the colloids. The findings are, however, usually confirmed by coagulation jar tests. Knight and Oestreicher (1981) also formulated an equation that relates streaming potential to zeta potential, and translates the zeta potential to the application need. This is described by Mandaro (1987).

Hydrophobic Adsorptions

Theories on Hydrophobic Adsorptions

Given its abstruse nature, it is not surprising that there are several explanations for the phenomenon of hydrophobic adsorption. No challenges are posed to its reality, but there are differences concerning its cause and effects. Adamson (1982) writes, "The term 'hydrophobic bonding' is appropriate to conditions wherein there is an enhanced attraction between two surfaces (as of a particle and filter) exposed to a liquid if the liquid-particle interaction is weaker than the liquid-liquid interaction." The term "hydrophobic" implies an antipathy for water. This derives from an absence of polar groups capable of hydrogen bonding to water. It is demonstrated by an extreme immiscibility with water. Molecular structures, such as ester, and carboxylic groups that contain oxygen atoms, give rise to dipoles on account of the strong electronegativity of their oxygen atoms. The dipole/dipole and other electrical interactions account for the attractions between solid surface sites that result in adsorptive sequestrations, and also colloidal agglomerations.

Such polar features are, however, absent from hydrocarbon molecules that, nevertheless, do interact in the manner that suggests adsorptive influences. The apparent contradiction requires clarification. It will be remembered that the VDW forces that operate among hydrocarbons bereft of oxygen or other polarizing features were hypothesized as being due to "instantaneous non-zero dipole moments" that resulted in attractions, albeit weak ones. This explains the hydrocarbon interaction as also being charge related. In this view, hydrocarbon molecules, here taken as the archetypical nonpolar substances, are motivated by the opposite signs of their VDW-type partial charges to connect with other hydrophobic molecules in hydrophobic adsorptions.

A hypothesis that does not rely upon charge interactions between hydrocarbon molecules is also possible. In agreement with time-honored alchemists' observations, namely, "like prefers like," it is accepted that hydrocarbon molecules do connect with other hydrophobic molecules. The implication is that the hydrocarbon molecules' VDW *attraction of the one for another* is the key driver in hydrophobic adsorptions.

This seems also to be the view of Fletcher (1996, p. 3). He sees the water separating (adsorbed to) the bacterium and filter surfaces as a barrier to their coming together. Moreover, removal of the water is "energetically unfavorable." However, if either surface "has non-polar groups or patches," the resulting hydrophobic interaction will displace the water and allow a closer approach of the two surfaces. This more orthodox explanation does not rely upon charge interactions between hydrocarbon molecules. It cites the reduction in free surface energy that is an accompaniment of hydrophobic adsorptions. The implication is that this is the force that motivates the coalescence of the dispersed hydrophobic phase.

The gathering of the hydrophobic material and its separation from the water is perhaps more distinctly explained by Tanford (1980) who quotes G.S. Hartley as stating, "The antipathy of the paraffin-chain for water is, however, frequently misunderstood. There is no question of actual repulsion between individual water molecules and paraffin chains, nor is there any very strong attraction of paraffin chains for one another. There is, however, a very strong attraction of water molecules for one another in comparison with which the paraffin-paraffin or paraffin-water attractions are very slight." Thus, Tanford (1980, Chap. 5) expostulates that it is the water molecules' alliances among themselves that rejects interactions with the hydrocarbon molecules, causing a concentration of the latter: "The free energy is representative of the attraction between the substances involved. The free energy of attraction between water and hexane or octane obtained at 25°C is about −40 erg/cm^2 of contact area; the free energy of attraction of the hydrocarbons for themselves at the same temperature is also about −40 erg/cm^2; but the free energy of attraction of water for itself is −144 erg/cm^2. It is clearly the latter alone that leads to a thermodynamic preference for elimination of hydrocarbon-water contacts; the attraction of the hydrocarbon for itself is essentially the same as its attraction for water." The driving force of the hydrophobic adsorptions, then, is the reduction in free surface energy that results from the strong mutual attractive forces that manifest themselves in hydrogen bonding among the water molecules.

In the above discussion on the hydrogen bond it was stated "The water molecule is tetrahedral in shape. Each of its corners holds either a pair of electrons or a hydrogen atom. Each of the partly positive hydrogen atoms of one water molecule can form a hydrogen bond with a partly negative oxygen atom of each of four different water molecules, etc. Actually, two or three is the usual number. This process, repeated throughout the water volume, in effect creates an (imperfect) interconnected network. Thus, the molecules of water in its solid state (ice) exist as tetrahedral hydrogen bonded structures. Much of this ordered form persists even in the mobile liquid."

The hydrocarbon molecules with little affinity for the water molecules are rebuffed from intruding among these spatially, tetrahedrally ordered arrangements. It is the network formed by the water molecules among themselves that in expelling the hydrocarbon molecules causes their segregation. These may conjoin also to the hydrophobic areas of solid surfaces they encounter, such as of pipes or filters. In their coming together, the hydrocarbon molecules, as also the water molecules, effect a reduction in the total free surface energy. It is likely that micellar groupings are involved under the influence of area-minimizing forces.

With regard to hydrophobic adsorptions to filter membrane surfaces, Zydney (1996) describes the phenomenon as follows: "Solute-membrane interactions can occur only if sufficient energy is provided to displace the H-bonded water molecules from the surface of both the membrane and the macrosolute. In contrast, the removal of unbonded water molecules from the surface of a hydrophobic membrane or macrosolute, is energetically very favorable, leading to a very strong 'attractive' interaction between hydrophobic surfaces in aqueous solutions." Although referred to variously as hydrophobic adsorption, or hydrophobic bonding, "it really reflects the change in energy or entropy due to the dehydration of the two surfaces, and the formation of additional hydrogen bonds among water molecules.

It is possible to generalize regarding the adsorption of materials from aqueous media by viewing the adsorptive phenomenon as being in competition with the tendency of the material to remain in solution, the less water-soluble the material, i.e., the less the interaction between the macrosolute and water, the easier it is to remove it from solution by the adsorptive interaction. By this measure, less ionized or nonpolar molecules are easier to adsorb because they have less affinity for the water molecules than the water molecules have for themselves. Hydrophobic adsorption assumes its importance as a particle retention mechanism on the basis of the relative strengths of the several interactions that are possible in a given situation, namely, particle to particle; water to particle; and water to water; with the last being the strongest.

Adsorption of Proteins

The strong tendency of nylon filters to remove proteins from their solutions by adsorptive sequestration is here demonstrated in Figure 5.29 with specific reference to Iso gamma globulin.

The adsorption of proteins by filters has received much study (Marshall et al. 1993; Zydney 1996, pp. 424–436). The subject is of special interest in the biotech industry. The loss of products of costly fermentations, e.g., monoclonal antibodies, is an expense to be avoided. Such loss can take place during the purification process by adsorption to filters. Yield losses due to unspecific adsorptions result in production capacity losses, and translate very specifically to market values. A gram of a monoclonal antibody product may have a market value of up to $1 million. Any milligram loss due to unspecific adsorption will accumulate over a year's production to intolerable values. It is, therefore, important to evaluate individual membrane polymers and filter designs to achieve the lowest possible yield loss.

A similar opportunity exists to effect the hydrophobic interaction of a microporous polypropylene membrane with lipopolysaccharidic endotoxin molecules to attain their removal from aqueous solutions. Figure 5.29 illustrates the differences in the avidity with which different polymeric membranes adsorb certain proteins. Each polymeric material has its own individual propensity for adsorptions. Also demonstrated is the fact that given the same polymer, different proteins adsorb to different extents. This may

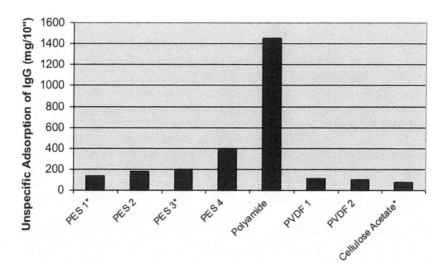

FIGURE 5.29 Unspecific adsorption of different membrane polymers.

have utilitarian significance to bacterial fouling. The attachment of organisms to surfaces, often in the form of biofilms, is a major problem in many situations, and has, accordingly, also been widely studied (Characklis 1990; Ridgway 1987; Mittelman et al. 1998).

However, the mechanisms of protein adsorptions have perhaps been probed even more extensively. It is the hope in this writing that the experimental elucidations of protein adsorptions can serve as a guide to the better understanding of bacterial adsorptions. As expressed by Mittelman et al. (1998), the molecules of proteins and organisms are complex enough to present areas of both polar and nonpolar character. In the similarity of their mechanism of retention by filters may lie a commonality of their management. Encouragement is given this expectation by the findings of Fletcher and Loeb (1979) showing that marine bacteria attach most readily to hydrophobic plastics. By contrast, the smallest number attaches to negatively charged hydrophilic surfaces (Zydney 1996, p. 440).

Isoelectric Point and Hydrophobicity

Analysis of data derived from experimental studies of protein uptake by membranes indicates that sieve retention, especially of aggregated or denatured protein, is an operational mechanism (Sundaram 1998, p. 548; Kelly et al. 1993). By far, however, protein uptake by filters is an adsorption phenomenon (Zydney 1996). This negative charge increases in alkaline solution, whether from an increase in anion adsorption; an increase in ionization of acidic groups; or the deprotonation of basic groups, such as amines (e.g., $-NH_3^+ \rightarrow -NH_2$). The reverse behavior is true in acidic solution. Thus, as the solution pH is lowered, most amphoteric species will eventually pass through a point at which they have no net charge. The pH at which this occurs is referred to as the isoelectric point or pI. The isoelectric points of proteins range from a low of pI < 1 for pepsin to a high of pI = 11 for lysozyme. This wide range of pI reflects the impressive heterogeneity of amino acid compositions among different proteins (Zydney 1996).

Such proteins as the serum albumins undergo hydrophobic interactions with the long nonpolar chains of fatty acids that terminate in hydrophilic carboxylic acid groups. In the case of the interactions between the fatty acids and serum proteins, the opportunity for hydrophobic interaction is increased by muting the polarity of the protein. This is done by adjusting the pH to the isoelectric point of the particular protein, because at that point the electrostatic charges inherent in the amphoteric protein molecules are neutralized. The heightened interactions of filters with proteins at the charge-free isoelectric points of the latter are taken to indicate hydrophobic adsorptions.

Conformational Changes

Truskey et al. (1987) measured protein adsorption, circular dichroism, and the biological activity of a variety of protein solutions, i.e., insulin, iso-gamma globulin (IgG), and alkaline phosphatase, The solutions' properties were measured before and after passing the proteins through a variety of membranes. Shifts in circular dichroism and decreases in the activity of the enzymes were determined to be the result of conformational changes of the protein structure that are attendant upon adsorption. This study showed that membranes with the greatest degree of hydrophobicity had the greatest effect on protein adsorption. This, in turn, effectuated a strong conformation with concomitant denaturation. The protein–membrane interaction resulted in the protein's exposing its internal hydrophobic sites, which were folded within its structure during its exposure to aqueous solution. This bespeaks a relationship between protein shape and function. The exposed hydrophobic sites that engaged in the membrane–protein binding, protein–protein binding, and protein denaturation were likely the more hydrophobic amino acids. (See: The Fuoss Effect.)

Opportunities may exist for the shearing of protein molecules as they negotiate a microporous membrane's tortuous passageways. A loss of the protein's properties may result. (Such, at least, are the fears of wine aficionados who decry wine filtration for the taste changes they allege to occur, presumably as a result of protein shearing.) Shearing in general is, however, seen as being less responsible for functional losses through denaturations than are the conformational changes that follow the adsorptions of proteins to polymer surfaces.

Qualitative Measurement of Protein Binding

That specific proteins exhibit differences in their adsorptive proclivities has been remarked upon. The usefulness of a means of measuring this tendency is obvious. Badenhop et al. (1970) have devised and utilized such a test method. A standardized drop of an aqueous solution of serum albumin was placed upon the surface of each of three membrane filters. The extent to which the water-drop spread was evidenced by the area of wetness. This was essentially the same for the three filters: cellulose triacetate, cellulose nitrate, and an experimental PVC. However, the spread of the albumin within the wet area differed. The visual detection of the albumin was made possible by the use of Ponceau S stain. It was found that the albumin spread along with the water over the cellulose triacetate when the bovine albumin concentration was 100 mg percent. At that concentration level, the albumin spread only very little on the cellulose nitrate and even less on the experimental PVC. At a concentration of 700 mg percent, the spread of albumin over the experimental PVC filter did not increase much, but did so for the cellulose nitrate.

This experience is interpreted as indicating the relative binding forces for the three polymers for serum albumin in aqueous solution. The cellulose triacetate is seen as exerting the least interaction; hence, the least binding and the least impeded in spreading along the membrane surface. The experimental PVC by this measure binds the strongest of the three polymers examined. The nitrocellulose binds albumin strongly, but the attractive forces at a given area are saturated at the 700-mg-percent level, permitting the further spreading of the protein. The interaction strength of membranes is, thus, expressible in terms of its fixative properties relative to specific proteins, both in terms of the quantity of protein it can bind and the extent of localization the bound protein exhibits.

Overcoming Protein Binding

Hydrophilization of membranes is commonly deployed to allow filters to be constructed of robust materials which may be hydrophobic in nature such as PVDF of PES while minimizing protein binding due to adsorption. Such modifications can limit the useable range of filters in pH or temperature environments that their membrane polymer could withstand thus, care should be made in filter selection. The modification of Polyethersulfon (PES) and the ability to cast asymmetric membranes has improved the efficiency of aqueous filtrations in biomanufacturing.

That proteins tend to adhere to hydrophobic surfaces by way of the hydrophobic adsorption mechanism seems an established fact. It is, however, not the only mechanism for such attachments. H-bonding may also be involved.

Protein Fouling of Filters

The ease of filtering serum depends largely upon the animal species from which the serum is obtained. Several of the many components of sera add to the difficulty of their filtration. Fetal calf serum is relatively easy, and porcine serum is relatively difficult to filter. The most troublesome components are the lipids, and proteins. When their depositions and adsorptions block and clog the filters, the occurrence is called "fouling." It is perhaps curious that an anthròpomorphism is used as a pejorative term to characterize physicochemical phenomena such as molecular interactions when the consequences are not desired.

The contribution made to filter blockage by the membrane's polymeric composite is pronounced when bovine serum is the filtration fluid. Comparison was made between a 0.22-μm-rated cellulose triacetate membrane and a 0.45-μm-rated experimental PVC membrane as a filter for bovine serum. In order to minimize clogging due to particulate matter, the bovine serum was prefiltered through a 0.8-μm-rated cellulose triacetate membrane. It was found that the cellulose triacetate membrane, although characterized by a smaller mean-pore size, yielded double the throughput of the experimental PVC filter. The difference in performance is ascribed to filter interaction with the serum proteins. Protein binding "fouls" the hydrophobic (PVC) membrane and reduces the throughput. Such proteins as the serum albumins undergo hydrophobic interactions with the long nonpolar chains of fatty acids that terminate in hydrophilic carboxylic acid groups. In the case of interactions between the fatty acids and serum proteins, the opportunity for hydrophobic interaction is increased by muting the polarity of the protein. This is done by adjusting the pH to the isoelectric point of the particular protein, because at that point the electrostatic charges inherent in the amphoteric protein molecules are neutralized.

Practical Implications of Adsorptive Sequestration

The loss of permeability with continuing filtration has been probed by several investigators. The findings were expressed in mathematical equations depicted as plotted curves whose analysis led the experimenters to conclusions. As an example of such efforts, Johnston constructed log/log plots of a constant pressure filtration wherein volume filtered over time, V versus time, t, was expressed for each of four different circumstances: (a) cake filtration, (b) intermediate blocking, (c) standard blocking, and (d) complete blocking (Johnston 2003, p. 104). In this, the author's writing, conclusions derived from Bowen et al. (1967) are set forth.

Bowen et al. (1976) investigated the mathematics of particle capture within pores of fine capillaries. Although complex, the key parameters can be summarized. The first is a reduced Peclet number, γ, which is a dimensionless parameter containing the average fluid velocity, V_m, the pore radius, R, the solution diffusion coefficient of the particle, D, and the length of the capillary, x, and is defined as:

$$\gamma = \left(\frac{D}{2V_m R} \right)\left(\frac{x}{R} \right)$$

The two terms in parentheses represent two effects. The first is the competition between diffusion, tending to move the particle toward the wall, and convection tending to carry the particle down the capillary and out the filter. The second, expressed by the ratio x/R, can be regarded as the number of chances that diffusion will have to carry out its task.

Bowen et al. (1976) present an interesting treatment of retentivity, or of its equivalent, the collection efficiency that is at work in adsorptive sequestrations. They plot this parameter as a function of γ for different values of the particle-wall reaction constant K. When K is infinitely large, all particles are captured at all fluid velocities. When K is simply large (i.e., a strong attractive interaction existing between the bacterium particle and the pore wall), then a range of conditions is present wherein the capture efficiency will be less than unity; an organism could "slip through." The equation predicts that as the mean fluid velocity, V_m, increases, γ will decrease, as will the capture efficiency. Thus, higher pressures which increase V_m and produce faster filtration times, also decrease the absolute retentivity of a membrane that is operated by adsorptive sequestration. Furthermore, for a given bacteria/wall interaction and a fixed set of flow conditions, the capture efficiency is independent of the total volume of fluid passed.

Thus, a membrane operating by this mechanism at bacterial levels low enough to yield absolute collection efficiencies will be independent of the total challenge per square centimeter of membrane surface; in contrast to the membrane operating by sieve retention alone, wherein the total bacterial challenge is important (presumably in relation to the number of pores present in the filter).

By contrast, neither the thickness of the membrane, the concentration of particles, the fluid velocity, nor the applied pressure will affect the selectivity of a surface (filter cake), sieve-retaining filter toward bacteria. Only the pore size is important, and if all pores are equal in size to, or less than, the organism, the filter will be absolutely retentive. *However, all commercial membrane filters have pore sizes distributed about some mean.* Thus, it is conceivable that there exists at least one set of pores sufficiently large to allow the passage of a single organism. Hence, the rationalization that if the number of organisms filtered per square centimeter of membrane approaches or exceeds the number of pores per square centimeter, the membrane is unlikely to prove absolutely retentive. For sieve capture, the critical parameter for testing the membrane's absolute retentivity is:

$$\text{Total Final challenge} = \frac{\text{no. of organisms filtered}}{\text{Area of filter}} = \frac{\text{Total cfu}}{A}$$

The practical implications of the pressure differential employed in filtrations merits being repeated. Higher applied differential pressures will result in higher rates of flow. The price may, however, be paid in terms of reduced filter efficiencies and shorter service lives.

A. The equation indicates that as the mean fluid velocity, V_m, increases, γ will decrease, as will the capture efficiency. Thus, higher pressures which increase V_m and produce faster filtration times, also decrease the absolute retentivity of a membrane that operates by adsorptive sequestration.

   The inverse relationship of differential pressure with retention, presumably not an expression of sieve retention, fits in with adsorptive sequestration. This was demonstrated by Tanny et al. (1979).

B. For a given bacterium/wall interaction, (i.e., adsorption), and a fixed set of flow conditions, the capture efficiency is independent of the total volume of fluid passed. Thus, a membrane operating by this mechanism at bacterial levels low enough to yield absolute collection efficiencies will be independent of the total challenge per square centimeter of membrane surface; in contrast to the membrane operating by sieve retention alone, wherein the total bacterial challenge is important, presumably in relation to the number of pores present in the filter.

   The statement suggests that retentions by adsorptive sequestration would be independent of the bacterial dilution, whereas sieving which relies upon pores, would not give independent results. Jornitz and Meltzer (2001), commenting on work reported by Grant and Zahka (1990) using silica particles, and by Roberts et al. (1990) using latex beads, state that dilute challenges would not be problematic to adsorptive captures, but would be a worst case scenario for sieving. Experimentation establishing the dilution effect of organism suspensions has yet to be performed.

C. By contrast, neither the thickness of the membrane, the concentration of particles, the fluid velocity, nor the applied pressure will affect the selectivity of a surface (filter cake), sieve-retaining filter toward bacteria. Only the pore size is important, and if all pores are equal in size to, or less than, the organism, the filter will be absolutely retentive. Indeed, this is the definition of an absolute filter. It does assume incompressible particles.

D. An initial high concentration of organisms is not essential to less-than-absolute retention. The ultimate level of the total viable organism challenge is the important factor. Thus, a sufficiently large volume of low bacterial concentration could, in principle, predispose toward non-sterile filtration where sieve retention is the sole capture mechanism, and where all the organisms are not necessarily larger than the largest pores.

   It is assumed that "all the organisms are not necessarily larger than the largest pores" equates with a situation wherein the organism challenge confronts a filter with a pore size distribution. As detailed below, Jornitz and Meltzer (2001, pp. 562–564) commented on work reported by Grant and Zahka (1990) using silica particles and by Roberts et al. (1990) using latex beads.

They state that dilute challenges would not be problematic to adsorptive captures, but would be a worst case scenario for sieving. Detailed experimentation investigating the dilution effect of organism suspensions have yet to be performed.

The practical implications of the pressure differential employed in filtrations merits repeating. Higher applied differential pressures will result in higher rates of flow. The price may, however, be paid in terms of reduced filter efficiencies and shorter filter service lives.

Summary

The appellation "sterilizing" filter, conferred by the filter manufacturer on the basis of integrity test values correlated with organism retentions, qualifies a filter for trial. Whether its promised potential is fulfilled in a given processing context can be judged only by accomplishing filter validation studies utilizing product-related bacterial challenge testing. The meaning of "sterilizing filter" is relevant only when applied to a specific filter, with a particular fluid, and a defined microbial content under stipulated conditions. Extrapolations to other conditions, however, circumspect that fail to recognize that it is the unique attributes of the individual filtration that are paramount in the ability to provide a sterile effluent, are inherently unwarranted.

It is now appreciated that organism retention by a filter is governed by an interaction of influences more complex than the proportion of pore and organism sizes alone. In any case, the physical and chemical properties of the suspending liquid contribute to adsorptive and impactive arrests and are certainly capable of altering filter pore and microorganism sizes. Consequently, integrity test measurements, based upon the assumption of both fixed pore and organism sizes, cannot unerringly signal the reliability of organism removal by size exclusion. This reduces their heretofore assumed uniqueness as categorical indicators of filter validations (Jornitz 2002). Their critical and decisive function as arbiters of filter integrity remains unimpaired.

The misleading imputation of organism (particle) retentions as arising solely from size exclusion origins should be abandoned. Adsorptive/impactive mechanisms of organism retention compel consideration.

The definition of "sterilizing" filter becomes restricted to that filter which, under specific operating conditions, removes all organisms of interest known to be present in the given preparation. The achievement of sterility is decided in terms of the specific organism(s) whose complete removal is validated by documented experimental evidence. The attestation requires positive outcomes to the isolation, cultivation, and measurement of the target organism(s). As in the case of *Brevundimonas diminuta*, the subject organism(s) may be assumed to be a model for others whose presence or absence is not assessed. Such assumptions may prove unjustified. Where the sterility of drug preparations is involved, assumptions will not suffice. Validation is necessitated.

Increased dependence now devolves upon bioburden studies, recognized to be under strong limitations themselves. Nevertheless, bioburden investigations, demanding though they be, are required for the validation of sterile filtrations. One must be able to identify and quantify the organisms whose removal is the object of the filtration exercise.

The attainment of a sterilizing filtration requires validation of the filter and the filtration process. Documented experimental evidence is essential to the process.

REFERENCES

Adamson A.A. (1982) *Physical Chemistry of Surfaces*, 4th Edition, Wiley Interscience, New York.

Aicholtz P., Wilkins R., Gabler R. (1987) Sterile filtration under conditions of high pressure and bacterial challenge levels. *J. Parenteral Drug Assoc.* 41: 117–120. Nanobacteria—Novel Biofilm Producing Organisms in Blood. Scanning Vol. 15, Suppl. III.

American Water Works Association (1969) Chapter 12: Theory and control of coagulation-flocculation, In Cohen J.H., Hannah H. (Eds.) *Coagulation and flocculation*, IWA Publishing, pp. 11–22.

Badenhop C.T., Spann A.T, Meltzer T.H. (1970) A consideration of parameters governing membrane filtration, In Flinn J.E. (Ed.) *Membrane Science and Technology*, Plenum, New York, pp. 120–138.

Berg H.F., Guess W.L., Autian J. (1965) Interaction of a group of low molecular weight organic acids with insoluble polyamides I. Sorption and diffusion formic, acetic, propionic, and butyric acids into nylon 66. *J. Pharm. Sci.* 54(1): 79–84.

Bowen B.D., Levine S., Epstein N. (1976) Fine particle deposition in laminar flow through parallel plates and cylindrical channels. *J. Colloid Interface Sci.* 54(3): 375–390.

Bowman F.W., Calhoun M.P., White M. (1967) Microbiological methods for quality control of membrane filters. *J. Pharm. Sci.* 56(2): 453–459

Bratby J. (1980) Chapter 8: Coagulation and flocculation tests, In Cohen J.H., Hannah H. (Eds.) *Coagulation and flocculation*, Uplands Press, Croyden, UK, p. 268.

Brose D.J., Cates S., Hutchison F.A. (1994) Studies on the scale-up of microfiltration devices. *PDA Pharm. Sci. Tech.* 48: 184–188.

Carazzone M., Orecco D., Fava M., Sansin P. (1985) A new type of positively charged filter: Preliminary test results. *J. Parenteral Sci. Tech.* 39(2): 69–74.

Carter J.R., Levy R.V. (1998) Microbial retention testing in the validation of sterilizing filtration. In Meltzer T.H., Jornitz M.W. (Eds). *Filtration in the Biopharmaceutical Industry*, Marcel Dekker, New York.

Characklis W.G. (1990) Microbial biofouling control, In Characklis W.G., Marshall K.C. (Eds.) *Biofilms*, Wiley, New York, pp. 585–633.

Chiou L., Smith D.L. (1970) Adsorption of organic compounds by commercial filter papers and its implication on quantitative-qualitativechemical analysis. *J. Pharm. Sci.* 59(6): 843–847.

Duberstein R. (1979) Mechanisms of bacterial removal by filtration, *J. Parenteral Drug Assoc.* 33(95): 250–256.

Dwyer J.D. (1966) Membrane filtration. In Dwyer J. (Ed.) *Contamination Analysis and Control*, Reinhold Publishing Corp., New York, pp. 262–265.

Elford W.J. (1931) A new series of graded colloidion membranes suitable for general microbiological use especially in filterable virus studies. *J. Path. Bact.* 34: 505–521.

Elford W.J. (1933) The principles of ultrafiltration as applied in biological studies, *Proc. Royal Soc.* 112B: 384–406.

Emory S.F., Koga Y., Azuma N., Matsumoto K. (1993) The effects of surfactant type and latex-particle feed concentration on membrane retention. *Ultrapure Water* 10(2): 41–44.

Fletcher M. (1996) Bacterial attachments in aqueous environments, In Fletcher M. (Ed.) *Bacterial Adhesion*, John Wiley, New York, pp. 1–24.

Fletcher M., Loeb G.L. (1979) Influence of substratum characteristics on the attachment of a marine *Pseudomonas* to solid surfaces. *Appl. Environ. Microbiol.* 37: 67.

Gabler R. (1978) *Electrical Interactions in Molecular Biophysics*, Academic Press, New York.

Galanos C.E., Rietschel E.T., Ludertiz O., Westphol O., Kim Y.B., Watson D.W. (1972) Biological activity of lipid a complexed with bovine serum albumin. *Eur. J. Biochem.* 31:230–233.

Gerson D.F., Zajic, J.E. (1978) The biophysics of cellular adhesion, In Ven Katsubram K. (Ed.) *Immobilized Microbiological Cells*, American Chemical Society, Washington, DC, pp. 29–53.

Ghosh K., Schnitzer H. (1979) UV and visible absorption spectroscopic investigations in relation to macromolecular characteristics of humic substances. *J. Soil Sci.* 30: 735.

Grant D.C., Zahka J.G. (1990) Sieving capture of particles by microporous membrane filters from clean liquids. *Swiss Contam. Control* 3(4a): 160–164.

Hermans P.H., Bredee H.L. (1936) Principles of the mathematical treatment of constant-pressure filtration. *J. Soc. Chem. Ind. Trans. Commun.* 55: 1–4.

Hiatt W.C., Vitzthum G.H., Wagener K.B., Gerlach K., Josefi C. (1985). Microporous membranes via upper critical temperature phase separation, In Lloyd D.R. (Ed.) *Material Science of Synthetic Membranes*, American Chemical Society, Washington, DC.

Hjertin S., Rosengren J., Pahlman S. (1974) Hydrophobic luracion chromatography: The synthesis and the use of some alkyl and aryl derivatives of agarose. *J. Chromatogr.* 101: 281–288.

Jaisinghani R., Verdigan B. (1982) Electrokinetics in Hydraulic Oil Filtration—The Role of Anti-Static Additives. *World Filtration Congress III*, Vol. II, pp. 618–626. Filtration Society, UK.

Johnston P.R. (1985) Fluid filter media: Measuring the average pore size and correlations with results of filter tests. *J. Testing Evalu.* 13(4): 308–315.

Johnston P.R. (2003) Capacity of a filter medium in constant-pressure filtration, In Johnston P.R. (Ed.) *Fluid Sterilization by Filtration*, 3rd Edition, Interpharm/CDC, Boca Raton, FL.

Johnston P.R. (2004) *Fluid Sterilization By Filtration*, 3rd Edition, Interpharm/CRC, New York, NY.

Johnston P.R., Swanson, R. (1982) A correlation between the results of different instruments used to determine the particle-size distribution in AC fine test dust, *Powder Technol.* 32:119–124

Jornitz, M.W., Meltzer, T.H. (2001) *Sterile Filtration - A Practical Approach*, Marcel Dekker, New York, NY.

Jornitz M.W. (2002) Filters and filtration, In William Andrew (Ed.) *Pharmaceutical Encyclopedia*, Marcel Dekker, New York.

Jornitz M.W., Meltzer T.H. (2002) The mechanics of removing organisms by filtration: The importance of theory. *Pharm. Tech. Eur.* 14(5): 22–27.

Jornitz, M.W., Meltzer, T.H. (2004), Sterilizing filtrations with microporous membranes. *Pharmacopeial Forum* 30(5): 2–9.

Kawamura K., Jornitz M.W., Meltzer T.H. (2000) Absolute or sterilizing grade filtration—What is required? *PDA J. Parenteral. Sci. Technol.* 54(6): 485–492.

Kelly S.T., Opong W.S., Zydney A.L. (1993) The influence of protein aggregates on the fouling of microfiltration membranes during stirred cell filtration. *J. Membr. Sci.* 80: 175–187.

Knight R.A., Ostreicher E.A. (1981) Measuring the electrokine tic properties of charged filter media. *Filtr. Sep.* 18: 30–34.

Kramer S.P. (1927) Bacterial filters. *J. Infect. Dis.* 40: 343–347.

Leahy T.J., Sullivan M.J. (1978) Validation of bacterial retention capabilities of membrane filters. *Pharm. Technol.* 2(11): 64–75.

LeChevallier M.W., Hasenauer, T.S., Camper, A.K., McFeters, G.A. (1984) Disinfection of bacteria attached to granular activated carbon. *Appl. Environ. Microbiol.* 48: 918–992.

Lee J., Liu B.Y.H., Rubow K.L. (1993) Latex sphere retention by microporous membranes in liquid filtration. *J. IES.* 36(1): 26–36.

Liu B.Y.H., Pui D.Y.H., Robow K.L. (1983) Characteristics of air sampling filter media, In Marple V.A., Liu B.Y.H. (Eds.) *Aerosols in the Mining and Industrial Work Environments*, Vol. III, Butterworth Press, Woburn, MA.

Mandaro R.M. (1987) Chapter 5: Charge-modified depth filters: Cationic-charge-modified nylon filters, In T.H. Meltzer (author) *Filtration in the Pharmaceutical Industry*, Marcel Dekker, New York.

Marshall K.C. (1992) Biofilms: An overview of bacterial adhesion, activity, and control at surfaces. *Am. Soc. Microbiol. News* 58(4): 202–207.

Marshall J.C., Meltzer T.H. (1976) Certain porosity aspects of membrane filters, their pore distributions and anisotropy. *Bull. Parenteral Drug Assoc.* 30(5): 214–225.

Marshall A.D., Munro P.A., Tragdgardh G. (1993) Effect of protein fouling in micro-filtration and ultrafiltration on permeate flux, protein retention and selectivity: A literature review. *Desalination* 91: 65–108.

Megaw W.J., Wiffen W.D. (1963) The efficiency of membrane filters. *Int. J. Air Water Pollut.* 7: 501–509.

Meltzer, T.H. (1987) *Filtration in the Pharmaceutical Industry*, Marcel Dekker, New York.

Meltzer T.H., Lindenblatt J. (2002) Selecting 0.1 or 0.2/0.22-rated filters: Consideration of rates of flow. *Eur. J. Parenteral Sci.* 7(4):111–114.

Michaud D. (1988) Granulated activated carbon. A series of three papers. *Purification*. June: 20–26; July: 38–50; August: 36–41.

Mittleman M.W., Jornitz M.W., Meltzer, T.H. (1998) Bacterial cell size and surface charge characteristics relevant to filter validation studies. *PDA J. Pharm. Sci. Tech.* 52(1): 37–42.

Mouwen H.C., Meltzer T.H. (1993) Sterlizing filters; Pore-size distribution and the $1 \times 10^7/cm^2$ challenge. *Pharm. Technol.* 17(7): 28–35.

Nash R.A., Haeger B.E., Powers J.T., Personeus G.R. (1967) An evaluation of membrane filters for sterile processing, *Bull. Parenteral Drug Assoc.* 21:165–183.

Ong H.L., Bisque R.E. (1966) Coagulation of humic colloids by metal ions. *Soil Sci.* 106(3): 220.

Pall D., Kirnbauer E.A., Allen B.T. (1980) Particulate retention by bacteria retentive membrane filters. *Colloids Surf.* 1: 235–256.

Pertsovskaya A.F., Zvyagintsev D.G. (1971) Adsorption of bacteria on glass, modified glass surfaces, and polymer films. *Biol. Nauk.* 14(3): 100–105.

Ridgway H.F. (1987) Chapter 6: Microbiological fouling of reverse osmosis membranes: Genesis and control, In Mittelman M.W., Geesey G.G. (Eds.) *Biological Fouling of Industrial Water Systems: A Problem Solving Approach*, Water Micro Associates, San Diego, CA.

Ridgway H.F., Olson, B.H. (1982) Chlorine resistance patterns of bacteria from two drinking water distribution systems. *Appl. Environ. Microbiol.* 44: 972–987.

Roberts K.L., Velazquez D.J. (1990) Characterizing the rating and performance of membrane filter for liquid applications using latex sheres. *Swiss Contam. Cont. Quar.* 3: 71–74.

Roberts K.L., Velazquez D.J., Stofer D.M. (1990) Challenging the membrane filter ratings. *Semicond. Int.* 13(11): 80–84.

Robinson J.R., O'Dell M.D., Takacs J., Barnes T., Genovesi C. (1982) *Removal of Endotoxins by Adsorption to Hydrophobic Microporous Membrane Filters*, PDA, Philadelphia, PA.

Ruth B.F., Montillon G.H., Montanna R.E. (1933) Studies in filtration: Part I, Critical analysis of filtration theory. *Ind. Eng. Chem.* 25: 76–82.

Schnitzer M., Kodama H. (1966) Montmorillonite: Effect on pH on its adsorption of a soil humic compound. *Science* 153: 70.

Seyfried P.L., Fraser, D.I. (1980) Persistence of *Pseudomonas aeruginosa* in chlorinated swimming pools. *Can. J. Microbiol.* 26, 350–355.

Sundaram S. (1998) Chapter 17: Protein adsorption in microporous membrane filtration, In Meltzer T.H., Jornitz M.W. (Eds.) *Filtration in the Biopharmaceutical Industry*, Marcel Dekker, New York.

Sundaram S., Eisenhuth J., Howard G.H. Jr., Brandwein H. (2001) Part 1: Bacterial challenge tests on 0.2 and 0.22 micron rated filters. *PDA J. Pharm. Sci. Technol.* 55(2): 65–86.

Sweadner K.J., Forte J., Nelsen L.L. (1977) Filtration removal of endotoxin (Pyrogens) in solution in different states of aggregation. *Appl. Environ. Microbiol.* 34: 382–385.

Tanford C. (1980) *The hydrophobic effect—Formation of micelles and biologic membranes*, 2nd Edition, Wiley–Interscience, New York.

Tanny G.B., Meltzer T.H. (1978) The dominance of adsorptive effects in the filtrative sterilization of a flu vaccine. *J. Parent. Drug Assoc.* 32(6):258–267.

Tanny G.B., Strong D.K, Presswood G., Meltzer T.H. (1979) The adsorptive retention of *Pseudomonas diminuta* by membrane filters. *J. Parenteral Drug Assoc.* 33(1): 40–51.

Thomas A.J., Durkheim H.H., Alpark M.J. (1992) Validation of filter integrity by measurement of the pore distribution function. *Pharm. Tech.* 16(2): 32.

Tolliver D.L, Schroeder H.G. (1983) Particle control in semiconductor process streams. *Microcontamination* l(1):34—43 and 78.

Trotter A.M., Meltzer T.H., Feng B., Thomas L. (2000) Integrity test measurements—Effects of bacterial cell loadings. *Pharm. Tech.* 24(3): 72–80.

Truskey G.A., Gabler R., DiLeo A., Manter T. (1987) The effect of membrane filtration upon protein confirmation. *J Parenter Sci Technol.* 41(6): 180–193.

Udani G.G. (1978) Adsorption of Preservatives by Membrane Filters During Filter Sterilizations, Thesis for B.Sc. Honours (Pharmacy), School of Pharmacy, Brighton Polytechnic, Brighton, UK.

Wallhäusser K.H. (1976a) Preservation and sterility of ophthalmic preparations and devices, In Deasey P.B., Timoney R.F. (Eds.) *The Quality Control of Medicines*, Elsevier/North-Holland Biomedical Press, Amsterdam.

Wallhäusser K.H. (1976b) Bacterial filtration in practice. *Drugs Made in Germany* 19: 85–98.

Wallhäusser K.H. (1979) Is the removal of microorganisms by filtration really a sterilization method? *J. Parenteral Drug Assoc.* 33(3): 156–171.

Weber W.H., Voice T.C., Jodellah A. (1983) Adsorption of humic substances: The effects of heterogeneity and system characteristics. *J. Am. Water Works Assoc.* 75(12): 612–619.

Wheland G.W. (1947) Chapter 2: Some fundamental *concepts*, In Francis Carey (Ed.) *Advanced Organic Chemistry*, 2nd Edition, John Wiley and Sons, New York.

Wolber P., Dosmar M., Banks J. (1988) Cell harvesting scale-up: Parallel-leaf cross-flow microfiltration methods. *Biopharm Manuf.* 1(6): 38–45.

Wrasidlo W., Hofmann F., Simonetti J.A., Schroeder H.G. (1983) Effect of Vehicle Properties on the Retention Characteristics of Various Membrane Filters. *PDA Spring Meeting*, San Juan, PR.

Wrasidlo, W., Mysels, K.J. (1984) The structure and some properties of graded highly asymmetric porous membranes. *J. Parenteral Sci. Technol.* 38(l): 24–31.

Zahke J.G., Grant D.C. (1991) Predicting the performance efficiency of membrane filters in process liquids based on their pore-size ratings. *Microcontaminants*: 23–29.

Zierdt C.H., Kagan R.L., MacLawry J.D. (1977) Development of a lysis-filtration blood culture technique. *J. Clin. Microbiol.* 5(1): 46–50.

Zsigmondy R. (1909) *Colloids and the Ultramicroscope*, Chapman & Hall, London, p. 153.

Zydney A.L. (1996) Chapter 9: Membrane fouling, In Zeuman L.J., Zydney A.L. (Eds.) *Microfiltration and Utrafiltration: Principles and Applications*, Marcel Dekker, New York, pp. 397–446.

6

Microbiological Considerations in the Selection and Validation of Filter Sterilization

James A. Akers
Akers and Kennedy

CONTENTS

Background

Treatises on the filtration of liquids with the objective of achieving a sterile effluent are typically replete with detailed discussions of the physical and chemical characteristics of filters and the various mechanisms at play in retention. Rarely does one find a careful consideration of the microbiological considerations of filtration in spite of the simple truth that the retention of microorganisms is a nearly all-consuming component of the filter validation exercise. It must also be said that "sterility" of the effluent is arguably the aspect of filtration that receives the greatest regulatory scrutiny both in product dossier review and in plant inspection.

The purpose of this chapter is to examine microbiological considerations of filtration in depth. This contrast with the typical treatment of microbiology in filtration science, which is sad to say rather superficial. Everyone involved in aseptic validation knows that a model organism has been chosen and that it is *Brevundimonas diminuta* (ATCC-19146). Knowing this, they will be aware that Food and Drug Administration (FDA) has defined a proper challenge as not less than 1×10^7 colony-forming unit (cfu) of this organism per square centimeter of available filter surface area. It is certainly tempting to believe that there is some significance to the selection of 107 cfu/cm^2 of filter surface, and that perhaps it relates in some manner to the 10^{-6} "sterility assurance level" that applies to physical sterilization. However, the origins of the 10^7 cfu/cm2 challenge level are not completely clear, perhaps their genesis relates in part to the notion that a concentration one order of magnitude greater than 10^6 would result in a satisfactory "worst-case" condition. "Worst-case" in the realm of microbiological validation of filters can be a very difficult condition to define, and in the author's opinion careful scientific analysis regarding appropriate microbial titers for the challenge have been lacking.

Sterilizing Grade Filters—A Microbiological Perspective

Filter sterilization can be strictly defined as the complete elimination of viable organisms of any species from a fluid. A liquid, containing suspended microorganisms would be rendered free of contaminating microbes by separation of these organisms from the 151 liquid. Presently, filters with a 0.2 or 0.22-mm pore size rating are considered sterilizing grade filters, although FDA defines a sterilizing filter as one that can retain the aforementioned 107 cfu/cm^2 of effective filter area challenge with *B. diminuta* (ATCC # 19146) a result of no recoverable cfu in the effluent.

It seems appropriate to ask if this definition is really valid from a scientific perspective. First, one might ask if *B. diminuta* is indeed a representative model organism, the answer would appear to the author to hinge upon the objective of the validation test. If the desire is to conduct a risk-based analysis to determine if the filter will retain, with a high level of safety, typical bacterial and mycological flora likely to be present in a fluid prepared under reasonably controlled compounding conditions, the answer in most cases would be yes. However, if the challenge with *B. diminuta* is intended to demonstrate absolutely and without equivocation the ability of the filter to produce a sterile effluent, defined as an absolute the answer would quite obviously be no. Actually, it might very well be impossible to claim that a 0.2-mm filter could even be defined unequivocally as a bacterial-retentive filter.

For example, organisms of the family Rickettsiaceae number among them numerous important human pathogens (a pathogen being defined as an organism known to produce disease). Among the diseases produced by members of this family are typhus, Rocky Mountain spotted fever, trench fever, and psittacosis (*Coxiella burnetti*). Fortunately, the majority of organisms in this family would not be expected to survive in dry powder active ingredients or excipients, nor in the typical compounding environment. However, some *Coxiella* spp. can survive heat and drying and all of these organisms can survive at −70°C for extended periods of time and in lyophilized materials. These organisms lack rigid cell walls and as a result are pleomorphic, which means they are variable in size and shape. These organisms can be found in nature in the 0.3- to 0.6-mm size range which is to say that they could be at least as difficult to filter as *B. diminuta*.

If we leave the realm of true bacteria when can find another class of highly pleomorphic prokaryotic organisms-mycoplasma. These organisms lack the true cell wall characteristic of true bacteria and typically range in size from 0.2 to 0.8 mm, although smaller examples among the family mycoplasmataceae have been reported. In the last 10 years, the filtration of mycoplasmas has become an issue, particularly with respect to the manufacturing of biotechnology and biological products. Largely, this is because mycoplasma can be endemic in some of the ingredients used in the preparation of cell culture and tissue culture media. Studies published by Sundaram et al. clearly indicate that if a challenge level of 107 cfu was used in conjunction with many commercial 0.2-mm filters complete retention will not occur. This led to the suggestion that perhaps filters in the range of 0.1-mm pore size rating should be considered sterilizing grade filters rather than 0.2 or 0.22 mm pore size rating filters.

If we move not only away from true bacteria but in fact away from prokaryotes in general, we can identify no shortage of organisms can still fall under the category of microbes which would not be absolutely retained by even 0.1-mm filters. These organisms are of course viruses. Viruses are obligate intracellular parasites which lack even the most basic of metabolic capability. Viruses in fact are not arguably alive at all until or unless they are in contact with a cell which is permissive to infection by a particular viral species. Unless they are in the process of replicating a virus is in fact biologically inert.

Because viruses are not possessed of metabolic apparatus, they have a remarkably simple and efficient structure. In their most basic configuration, they can consist of nothing more than a rather small single strand of genetic material and a handful of structural proteins. For example, the *enteroviruses*, a collection of several hundred distinct viral serotypes, contains among its numbers a significant array of human and animal pathogens. Two notable examples are the polioviruses and their close relatives the *Coxsackie* viruses as well as the foot and mouth disease virus. The reader may recall a significant outbreak of foot and mouth disease virus in Great Britain in 2001 and 2002, which resulted in tremendous public health concerns and billions of dollars of loses in the food animal industry in that country. These viruses consist of a single strand of RNA with a total size of ~1×10^6 D, but in comparison a typical bacteria would contain genetic material (double-stranded DNA) with a mass of >10^{12} D. These viruses have an icosahedral shell made up of four structural proteins and a small nucleic acid-associated protein. Not surprisingly, these viruses can be quite small in fact on average they are roughly 25–30 nm in diameter. A nanometer is 10^{-9} m or 1,000 times smaller than a micrometer. Thus, it seems unlikely that a filter with a mean pore size rating of 0.2-mm would fare well against a challenge by *Enterovirus*, at least in terms of separation by sieve retention.

There are smaller and larger viruses than the *Enterovirus*, for example. The largest virus, the poxviruses are in the range of 400 nm. Other viruses known by name to the reader would include Herpes viruses, which are typically 150–180 nm in diameter and the human immunodeficiency virus which is just slightly smaller. However, none of these viruses would be expected to be efficiently retained by sieve mechanisms by 0.2-mm filters. During my years as a research virologist, I had occasion to use 0.22-mm nylon 66 or cellulose acetate filters to clarify solutions containing up to 10^8 plaque-forming units of various species of poxvirus per mL. On average the virus titer was notably reduced, in some cases by 50%–90%, which of course meant that the post-filtration titer was still 10^7 plaque forming units or more. The filtered solutions were probably bacteria free, but were obviously not virus free and therefore not sterile. So, in the work described above a filter often defined in the pharmaceutical industry as sterilizing grade was used to clarify a solution of virus and to remove bacteria specifically because it would not remove viruses. Thus, a "sterilizing grade filter" can be used specifically because it will not yield a sterile effluent under some use conditions.

Actually, medical microbiology played a central role in the development of filtration and in the use of filters was critical to the discovery of viruses. In the late 19th century, alternatives to heat sterilization of bacterial media were sought and it occurred to scientists that it could be possible to develop filters which would retain bacteria leaving only sterile effluent. Chamberland and Pasteur working independently developed unglazed porcelain filters and efforts to develop cellulose fiber filters proved unsuccessful. By 1891, bacterial-retentive filters using Kieselguhr (diatomaceous earth) had been developed. Shortly thereafter in 1892, Iwanowski demonstrated that the agent that caused tobacco mosaic disease retained infectivity even after a solution containing this agent passed through a bacterial-retentive filter. In 1898, Loeffler and Frosch demonstrated that the agent which caused foot and mouth disease in cattle was also "filterable." Initially, the organisms we now know as viruses were called "filterable agents" and by the early 20th century, it was understood that all three of the major groups of viruses, plant, animal, and bacteria were small enough in size to pass through bacterial-retentive filters.

During our lives we have witnessed the emergence of a new category of disease-producing entities which are smaller and simpler than viruses—in fact much smaller and simpler. These entities are called prions and are now widely accepted as the etiological agents of an array of transmissible spongiform encephalitides. These entities lack even genetic material in the form of RNA or DNA and are in fact proteins with the ability to replicate in brain tissue. These are fairly rapidly progressive diseases which are uniformly fatal. Obviously, "sterilizing" grade filters would not retain them, even if we define sterilizing grade as 0.1 mm. There could of course be new categories of disease caused by similar agents, or by viruses or even by components of microbes that have not yet been detected. The world of infectious diseases is a constantly changing, or one might rightly say evolving one, in which new discoveries are often made.

With the foregoing in mind, it can be concluded that one cannot merely select a filter of 0.2 mm or "better" in the jargon of validation and be certain that the result will be a sterile effluent under all possible conditions. This holds true even if that filter is subject to the standard microbial challenge test at a "worst case" microbial level of $>10^7$ cfu/cm^2 effective filter area. This holds true even if the challenge test was conducted in a solution that mimics product and the challenge level was slightly higher to ensure the "most challenging conditions" again in jargon of validation.

The ability of viruses and certain families of bacteria to penetrate filters has been understood by research scientists for a very long time. However, the reader could reasonably ask if there is any evidence of filters having been penetrated under actual use conditions. Leo et al. (1997) reported that *Ralstonia pickettii* (formerly *Burkolderia pickettii* and *Pseudomonas pickettii*) had in a manufacturing setting penetrated 0.2-mm filters. Articles by Sundaram et al. (1999) reported that 0.2-mm filters might not reliably remove "diminutive" bioburden organisms and that 1 mm could provide a safer solution.

The author is also aware through personal communications of studies in which bioburden organisms (bacteria) have penetrated 0.2-mm filters at concentrations of 10^7 cfu/cm^2 effective filter area. It is not surprising from a scientific perspective that under some conditions "diminutive" bacteria can penetrate "sterilizing" grade filters.

A Risk-Based Approach to Filter Evaluation

It seems obvious after considering the full spectrum of disease-producing microorganisms that defining a filter by virtue of its pore size rating alone, as a sterilizing grade filter, is too simplistic. The traditional method of filter evaluation is akin, and probably intellectually related, to the overkill approach often chosen for the validation of physical sterilization processes. However, filtration and moist heat sterilization are two very different processes and technically there are no significant parallels. Resistance of moist heat biological indicators, for example, has no real relationship to size of a filter challenge organism although both resistance and size are thought to be important to achieving "worst case" challenge conditions. The reason that no relationship exists is that filters retain, they do not kill, whereas physical sterilization methods kill but leave remnants of the killed (as defined by the ability to reproduce) behind. Therefore, it can be said the filtration works in a manner that is almost exactly the opposite of physical sterilization.

What is very clear is that in both physical sterilization and filter sterilization the nature of and number of the presterilization bioburden is critical. In the case of physical sterilization by moist heat or radiation the fact that microbial remnants including toxins could be left behind as contaminants (although most toxins are denatured by heat sterilization). In filter sterilization, the type and quantity of the bioburden are also vital to performance and hence mitigation of risk.

The brute force approach to filter evaluation can and has created the impression that because filters can retain heroic numbers of the model challenge organism, bioburden control is only moderately critical. It is often thought that provided a solution is beneath a product's acceptable level of endotoxin postfiltration, prefiltration bioburden must have been adequately controlled. Actually, bioburden control may be the most important single risk-mitigating factor in filter sterilization. Particularly since the selection of a sterilizing grade filter of 0.2 mm or smaller is a given and choosing a filter of appropriate effective filter area relates to volume to be filtered, desired flow rate, and of course, bioburden.

An alternative approach to proving the efficacy of a filter sterilization process is to demonstrate that bioburden is consistently controlled to a predetermined safe level. EU (CPMP/QWP/486/95) provides clear guidance by setting a recommended prefiltration bioburden level of 10 cfu/100 mL. The FDA on the other hand appears to allow more flexibility stating only that prefiltration bioburden should be controlled. It is self-evident that the lower the bioburden the lower the risk of an effluent containing microbial contaminants. From this perspective alone the EU recommendation, which is the same as the compendial limits for water for injection, seems appropriate. It is important to note that 10 cfu/100 mL is a challenge level applied to the sterilizing filter, thus this level could be achieved through the use of prefiltration, if necessary. While it may not be possible to achieve 10 cfu/100 mL in every case, it is reasonable to think that it may be possible in many if not most cases with appropriate care, process knowledge and physical controls in place.

Bioburden Control

Given the central importance of bioburden control to risk mitigation and process control, it seems reasonable that microbiologists should carefully study all aspects of product formulation upstream of the filtration step. The purpose of this study is to ensure that appropriate controls are in place to ensure that microbiological control is sufficient to ensure that a low target bioburden level can be attained. Among the principle issues that must be considered are:

1. Facility design: Including proper zoning of clean rooms, barriers or isolators, personnel and materials flow, decontamination and sterilization of vessels and utensils, decontamination of environments, gowning requirements, utilities services, and temperature and humidity control.
2. Equipment selection: Ensuring that materials are easily cleanable and can withstand repeated and rigorous antimicrobial treatments.

3. Definition of control conditions: Establishing frequencies of antimicrobial treatments to process equipment and the facility, putting in place control points where risk of microbial contamination is found to be high. Controls could include refrigeration, prefiltration and definition of appropriate hold times.

4. Sampling and monitoring: Microbiological monitoring of the environment and sampling of product at various steps in the process to ensure that controls are working as they should. It is critical to note that all monitoring and sampling must be done under aseptic conditions to ensure that the collected samples are representative and remain as unaffected as possible by human intervention during the sampling process.

5. Microbiological evaluation of incoming active pharmaceutical ingredients and excipients: It is often critical to know that the producers of bulk pharmaceutical actives and excipients have adequate process controls in place to minimize bioburden and that they are able to package and ship the product in a manner that minimizes contamination risk. Among points to consider are the nature of the chemicals, for example, are they inherently antimicrobial or would they support survival or even growth? It is also critical to consider how chemicals are packaged and bagged, microorganisms have been found between layers of bags and corrugate packaging can harbor microbes. Finally, the integrity of chemical containers and their ability to withstand the shipping process without loss of integrity should be considered.

Control of bioburden at the compounding level is too often thought to be noncritical in terms of microbiological safety, or "sterility assurance." This is often defended by the seemingly logical argument that validation of the filter system and process is accomplished under worst case conditions. It seems logical, at least superficially, that if a filtration process is capable of retaining 10^7 cfu/cm^2 controlling bioburden to very low levels is unnecessary and perhaps wasteful of time. In cases where the characteristics of the product ensure that microbiological risk is minimal perhaps this is true. However, some scientists have been surprised to learn that even products that appear upon inspection to be very low risk in terms of microbial growth or survival can under normal production conditions have far higher than expected bioburden levels.

Establishing a Bioburden Acceptance Criterion

The previously mentioned recommendation of a 10 cfu/100 mL target level for pre filtration bioburden may work in many cases, but certainly not all cases. However, it is important to consider the inherent variability of microbiological analysis. Most microbiologists would agree that a reasonable and therefore acceptable level of variability in microbiological analysis is on the order of 30% or more. As a note of caution one should not assume that the rapid microbiological methods, which are becoming increasingly important to industry, are inherently more accurate, precise, or reproducible than traditional growth and recovery-based microbiological methods.

Given levels of variability inherent in microbial analysis and considering also that microorganisms are not homogeneously distributed in most environments or materials it is not appropriate to, for example, set a target level of X cfu/mL and reject the material at a level of X$þ$1 cfu/mL. The cfu is not a direct measure or count of microorganisms present. The cfu is exactly what its name implies: it is a "unit" of microorganisms capable of growing into a single visible colony on solid medium. Said unit may consist of 10 viable cells or it may contain 30 viable cells. It is quite possible that a large unit of cells could break into two or more smaller groups and manifest as two or three cfu rather than one. Therefore, some latitude should always be given regarding microbiological limits. The recently implemented harmonized compendial microbial limit tests (USP <61>, <62>, and <1111> 2017a–c) state that in the case of an established level of 10 cfu the maximum acceptable count should be 20 cfu. Similarly, if the established target level is 10^3 cfu the maximum acceptable count should be 2000 cfu. In general, a membrane filtration approach to bioburden testing will be easier for most users to implement and with the majority of products more suitable than direct plating methods in the evaluation of prefiltration bioburden.

Frequency of Bioburden Sampling

The frequency of sampling should also be a risk-based decision predicated upon product and process knowledge. Products that are known to be inherently low risk in terms of microbial survival or proliferation may not require testing on a lot-by-lot basis. Products that are extremely antimicrobial or which contain a preservative system may not require routine testing at all. On the other hand, products that are supportive of microbial growth should be tested on a lot-by-lot basis.

The importance of proper physical controls for bioburden cannot be overemphasized. Bioburden sampling is generally a nonspecific growth and recovery study with the aim of generating a total aerobic count. As such this is a general screen and is unlikely to recover all microorganisms that could be present in the material. Therefore, the microbiologist is well advised to focus upon the implementation of controls that will reduce risks from all microorganisms that could be present in the product or the environment. One must always remember that even a count of zero cfu does not mean the absence of contamination but rather that any contaminants present were not recovered. Zero recovery certainly implies very low risk, but it is impossible to establish that zero means no risk at all.

Further Consideration on the Microbial Challenge

Mechanisms of Microbial and Particulate Retention

The mechanics of membrane filtration are too complex to discuss in detail in a brief chapter focused on microbiology, however, no discussion of filtration process development, control of validation can be complete without some consideration as to how filters retain microorganisms. Although the image that most individuals have is one of microorganisms being separated by uniformly spaced pores of identical size, much like insects on a window screen, reality is considerably more complex.

Actually, there are several mechanisms by which organisms are removed from a process stream by filters. The most important is sieve retention, also known as "direct interception" or "size exclusion." Particles are restrained from passing through the filter because their size is larger than the restrictive cross-sections of the convoluted filter pores through which the conveying fluid flows unimpeded.

However, it is possible for organisms too small to be removed by sieve retention to become attached to a pore surface by adsorptive effects. In general, these absorptive effects are related to electrical charges. They may originate from full ionic charges, or from molecular structures characterized by dipoles, whether permanent or induced. Most frequently, the partially charged atoms of such structures result from the unequal sharing of the covalent bonding electrons. These find expression in any of several different bonding interactions. Among the better known of these are hydrogen bonding, the van der Waals forces, and hydrophobic adsorptions. As is well known, oppositely charged entities attract one another to form adsorptive interactions. It is such electrical bonding that attaches the partially charged atoms on an organism surface to molecular structures of opposite charge sited on the surface of a filter. The molecular structures of both organisms and filters are complex enough to provide ample sites for such mutual adsorptive bondings.

Microorganisms may be found as free-living single cells in nature, but it is far more common for them to be attached together in clumps. The surfaces of microorganisms may be inherently sticky as a result of capsular structures, which can provide environmental advantages in terms of protection against damage and in repelling a host's immune response. Fortuitously, bacteria smaller than *B. diminuta* would be a minority among the bioburden found in typical process streams. Also, beneficial is the fact that under no circumstances should the bioburden approach the filter challenge level of 10^7 cfu/cm^2 of effective surface area. Historically, the assumption has been made that viruses are not a significant risk factor in the filter sterilization of drugs and biologics. The prevailing data may bear this assumption out, but given the absence of analytical data it is not possible to discern whether there have been adverse reactions that could be attributed to virus, microbial toxins, diminutive bacteria, or nonbacterial prokaryotes that could have passed through a filter.

Microbial Challenge Testing of Filters

Filters used in the production of sterile products are always 0.2-μm pore size rating. This physical characteristic is always a primary requirement for a filter to be considered acceptable for use in the production of a sterile product stream. Further, confirmation of a filter's suitability is established by means of the challenge with *B. diminuta* discussed previously in Chapter 6. The FDA has defined a proper challenge as one that confronts every square centimeter of the available filtration area with 1×10^7 cfu of this model organism. As previously mentioned, it is important to consider that this challenge test does not confirm the unequivocal ability of a filter to produce a process stream that is always free of microbial contamination. The true mission of the filter is to adequately abate microbiological risk in terms of infection of the end user, absolute sterility being impossible to establish by this or any other widely applied test including the so-called "sterility test." The sterility test is of course, itself often dependent upon filter sterilization.

Sampling

The proper management of the sampling technique is itself an important subject deserving a full but separate discussion. The size of the effluent sample or the number of samples that are analyzed should be large enough to offset the heterogeneity that is typical of suspensions, and to yield a count of some reliability to be made. The suspended organisms will over time adsorb to the surfaces of the sample container regardless of its material of construction, and quite possibly to each other. The bacterial titer can be diminished by binding of organisms to each other and to surfaces and also by die-off. If the analysis is not to be performed promptly, refrigerated storage must always be utilized to prevent, or minimize organism growth or loss in viability. The size of an organism changes as it develops through its growth stages during its cultivation. Typically, the growth curve for most organisms placed in a new environment extends through three phases. During the first or lag phase the organism adjusts to its environment and particularly to the nutrient conditions to which it is exposed. There is an increase in the individual cell size before there is an increase in numbers as the individual cell activates the enzymatic apparatus necessary to replicate its genetic material, structural components, and metabolic machinery. In the second or exponential growth or log phase, attached cells begin to divide, and under appropriate growth conditions a logarithmic increase in cell population occurs. The cell numbers increase more rapidly than does the cell mass. Thus, the cell numbers are increasing, but the size of the individual cells typically is decreasing. Newly replicated cells are smaller than their parent cells and as the nutrient supply diminishes, cells are unable to continue to replicate at a logarithmic rate. The rapid buildup of toxic waste materials during the so-called "log phase" of population expansion further slows growth. There follows the third "stationary phase" wherein the number of new cells equals the number that are dying. In the later stages of this phase, there are increasing amounts of dead organisms and cell debris. The early stages of the stationary phase are, therefore, optimal for the selection of bacteria for use in the challenge of filters. Procedures for enumeration of the culture on solid medium and microscopic evaluation of the bacteria follow standard microbiological laboratory practices.

Given the difficulties associated with the preparation of cultures of *B. diminuta* that are at the proper concentration and also within the most desirable size range filter challenge testing is often contracted to specialized laboratories which possess experience in the conduct of these assays. While the methods employed are by no means beyond the capability of most microbiological analytical laboratories, they are sufficiently unique that they are often left to laboratories operated by the filter manufacturers themselves. This has led to concerns that in many, if not most cases, the filter vendors are allowed to determine the adequacy of their own product's performance. In general, when the challenge testing is contracted to an outside laboratory to perform, the customer's microbiologist(s) should conduct a thorough scientific evaluation and compliance audit of the facility and its personnel.

Challenge tests are conducted using actual product if possible, if this cannot be done because of the inability of the organisms to survive in the solution than a placebo as similar as possible to the product is used in lieu of actual product. This may not in all cases be a perfect test since the tonicity of product may change the size of bacteria in the challenge culture. However, realistically this is acceptable since the test is being conducted in conditions that approximate those that will apply in actual production. Another consideration that must often be included in the challenge test is filtration time since in products that are supportive of microbial growth population increases are theoretically possible during processing. If microbial proliferation in product is a concern it may be advisable to filter the product first into a sterile holding tank to mitigate risk, and then to further manage risk from aseptic connections a second filter can be used immediately upstream of the filling system.

The acceptance criterion applied to the challenge test is that no growth of *B. diminuta* can be recovered from the challenge test effluent. Realistically, this means that the actual retention required to pass the challenge test is often slightly greater than 10^7 cfu/cm^2. It is considered that a filter passing this challenge test is in fact a "sterilizing" filter.

Actually, this conclusion is based upon assumptions that are arguably too general. That the filter performed as desired under given circumstances does not ensure that it will necessarily act similarly with other types of organisms, or even with the same organism under different filtration conditions. The earlier belief that sterility resulted exclusively from the particles being too large to negotiate the filter's pores is now known to be far too simplistic. Each filtration is an individual expression of several factors whose balanced influences govern the outcome of the organism/filter interaction.

Factors that May Influence Retention

The retention of an organism by a filter represents a nexus of many interdependent factors. These include the filter pores, their numbers and size distribution, and restrictive diameters; as also the types and sizes of the organisms, their numbers, sizes, and structural makeup. It is the matching of the sizes and shapes of the pores and organisms that is the determinant in the sieve retention or size exclusion mechanism. It is axiomatic that a particle larger than a pore cannot penetrate it unless compressively deformed by excessive differential pressures. Although membranes are classified in terms of single pore size ratings, they are actually characterized by pore size distributions, albeit usually of an unknown magnitude. Thus, it is conceivable that an organism that could be retained by a pore of one of the sizes characterizing the distribution would not be retained should it confront a pore at the large end of the size distribution curve. Absolute retention is possible only when the smallest particle of the particle size distribution is larger than the largest pore of the pore size distribution. Given the usual application of filters, of unknown pore size distributions, to the removal of organisms of unknown size distributions, it would be presumptuous, and misleading to declare that a particular filter will be absolute in its action.

Sieving, the chief mechanism of particle removal, can be reinforced by the adsorptive sequestration of the particles. The electrical charges on the surfaces of the organisms and filters manifest mutually attractive forces. The result is the arrest and removal of the organisms as the fluid flows through the filter pores. The polymeric composition of the filter matrix in terms of its polarity determines its surface charge and, hence, its tendency to undergo adsorptive effects. However, the physicochemical nature of the suspending liquid can so modify the electrical attractive and repulsive forces by its ionic strength, pH, surfactant content, etc. as to promote or hinder adsorptions. Thus, the same organism and filter may interact differently in solutions of various compositions; a desired organism removal may or may not result. An example of such an occurrence was noted by Bowman (1966): A 0.45-mm rated mixed cellulose ester membrane could be used to sterilize a preparation by the recovery bacteria in sterility testing. However, the addition of penicillinase to the same preparation enabled bacteria to migrate through the same filter. This proteinaceous enzyme preempted the adsorptive sites of the filter, preventing the sequestration of the organisms. That adsorptive influences were at work was shown by the eventuation of a sterile effluent from the penicillinase preparation when a 0.22-rated membrane was employed. Sieve retention was the effective mechanism when a tighter membrane was used.

The differential pressure is especially influential in its effect on adsorptive interactions. The higher it is, the faster the liquid flow and the shorter the residence time of the particle within the pore passageway. This reduces the particle's opportunity to encounter the pore wall and, thus, minimizes the likelihood of adsorptive sequestrations. Intriguingly, as reported by Mouwen and Meltzer in 1993, there is reason to believe that the concentration of organisms, aside from their total numbers, can influence the attainment of sterile effluent.

Other chemical conditions present during filtration can have an influence on organism removals. For example, the viscosity of a solution may be high enough to prevent an organism within the liquid stream from reaching an adsorptive site on the pore wall before it is carried out of the filter by convective flow. Given the reciprocal relationship of viscosity and temperature, the opposite effect can result when the same filtration is performed with the liquid preparation at a higher temperature.

Also, the ratio of organisms to pores can strongly affect the rates of flow and their consequences in terms of throughputs and filter efficiency. Thus, even the effective filtration area may impact on the likelihood of obtaining sterile effluent. In fact, there continues to be some debate as to whether higher bacterial titer challenge levels actually represent worst case conditions or whether more dilute concentrations may actually prevent rapid clogging of pores which would be expected to increase apparent filtration efficiency.

The sterilization of a fluid by a filter is, as can be seen from the preceding brief overview is exceedingly complex and is influenced by a staggering array of factors, some more important than others. Most influential are the relative sizes and numbers of the organisms as compared to a filter's restrictive pores. The physicochemical nature of the fluid in terms of its ionic strength, pH, osmolarity, and viscosity, are other obvious influencing factors. The possibilities for the adsorptive sequestration of organisms by the filter depend upon the polarity of both their surfaces as expressed by the partial charge-induced van der Waals forces. The polymeric nature of the filter may also govern its tendency to arrest certain organisms via hydrophobic adsorptions. Additionally, susceptibility of the filter's pore sizes to alterations by contact with given solutions bears consideration. The organism size is of obvious influence. The relative amphiphilic nature of both the filter and organism surfaces can affect absorption. Common ingredients of liquid preparations such as surfactants, proteins, and charged entities such as colloids can affect the filter's ability to retain microorganisms. As previously, albeit briefly explained, filtration conditions including but not limited to temperature, viscosity, and especially differential pressure will influence filter process performance.

Summary

The effective removal of microorganisms from a process stream is anything but simple. In the author's view, the definition of a sterilizing filter and belief structure that has evolved around filter function is both simplistic. Filtration is all too often taken for granted in terms of both performance and outcome due to an overly optimistic belief in worst case challenge testing and a certain naivety regarding the true nature of the microbiological world. What is required is a realistic appraisal of filtration, which accepts that the actual demonstration of unequivocal "sterilization" is not currently possible.

It seems quite clear that risk mitigation in filter sterilization can only be achieved when control of bioburden is given equal or perhaps even greater weight than the successful completion of a biological filter challenge. Hence, there is obvious merit in the suggestion that control of bioburden to consistently low levels through proper process design, facility design, and process control, is not just essential but mandatory. Finally, one should always bear in mind that there is firm evidence that passing the challenge test alone is no reason for a feeling of absolute safety and security. A holistic approach to the selection, validation, and use of filters in aseptic manufacturing based upon careful risk analysis and contamination control is the only way to achieve the level of confidence that production of sterile products requires.

REFERENCES

Bowman FW. Application of membrane filtration to antibiotic quality control sterility testing. *J Pharm Sci* 1966; 55:818–821.

Iwanowski D. Concerning the mosaic disease of the tobacco plant. *St Petersb Acad Imp Sci Bul* 1892; 35:67–70. Translation published in English as Phytopathological Classics Number 7 (1942). American Phytopathological Society Press, St. Paul, Minnesota.

Loeffler F, Frosch P. Berichte der Kommission zur Erforschung der Maul- und Klauenseuche bei dem Institute fuer Bakterilogie. *Parasitenkunde und Infectionkrankheiten, Abt I* 1898; 23:371–391.

Leo F, Auiremman M, Ball P, Sundaram S. 1997. Application of 0.1 um filtration for enhanced sterility assurance. Pharmaceutical Filling Operations. Paul Scientific and Technical Report. PPD-SFR-30.

Mouwen HC, Meltzer TH. Sterilizing Filters; pore-size distribution and the $1 \times 10E7$ challenge. *Pharm Technol* 1993; 17(7):28–35.

Sundaram S. 1999. Retention of diminutive water-borne bacteria by microporous membrane filters. *Presented at PDA National Meeting*, Washington DC. December 7.

USP. 2017a. <61> Microbiological Examination of Nonsterile Products: Microbial Enumeration Tests, The United States Pharmacopeial Convention, 12601 Twinbrook Parkway, Rockville, MD.

USP. 2017b. <62> Microbiological Examination of Nonsterile Products: Tests for Specified Microorganisms, The United States Pharmacopeial Convention, 12601 Twinbrook Parkway, Rockville, MD.

USP. 2017c. <1111> Limits for Non-Sterile Products, The United States Pharmacopeial Convention, 12601 Twinbrook Parkway, Rockville, MD.

7

Filter Configuration Choices and Sizing Requirements

Maik W. Jornitz
G-CON Manufacturing, Inc.

CONTENTS

Introduction

Over the last decade, filtrative separation of contaminants became a prevalent processing step in the bio-pharmaceutical industry. With the rise of sterilizing-grade filter use, the need for application specific filter devices also increased. In the years before the filter manufacturer's product portfolio had one or two types of filters present, but with the need to gain optimal performance in a variety of processing steps and fluid streams, the filtration systems had to be adapted to the specific of such application. The filter configurations gained an innovative boost within the development of filter manufacturers and new pleat designs, filter membrane configurations, dimensions and combinations were made available. These new choices of filter devices require to be tested within the specific application to define the optimal choice and size of filter.

The filtrative processing of a fluid suspension requires an adequate expanse of effective filtration area (EFA). The volume of the preparation and its degree of loading are the factors. Knowing the rate of filtration is important if the operation is to be designed for a batch size to meet a particular time schedule. Such may be required for compliance with regulatory needs, or out of concern for product stability, or from considerations of economy of time and/or labor, or even of convenience. The sufficiency of the filter's size to accommodate the extent and nature of the preparation's particle load needs to be known. Too small a filter will necessitate augmentation of the filtration operation in order to complete it. Mid-process interferences, for example, filter changes, can be seriously disruptive, if not prohibited, especially where sterile effluent is the goal of the filtration. Using an unnecessarily large filter would be wasteful of yield, hold up volume and filter material, and an indication of poor system design.

To this end the throughput of the filtration system, however defined, requires being known. Throughput will reflect the amount of particulate material to be removed, and the resulting filter-clogging and blocking characteristics under the selected filtration conditions of temperature, differential pressure, viscosity, pressure pulses, etc. This typically cannot be calculated. It is learned from the processing of a small volume of the preparation followed by an extrapolation to its actual volume. The more extensive the extrapolation, the less certain is its conclusion. Specific test procedures and verifications can reduce the extrapolation and make scaling of filter more reliable. Where costly product is being processed, departures from the optimum filter usage can be very expensive. In addition to its EFA, the contribution of the filter's design and construction requires careful assessment. For this reason, particularly in the current production of expensive biopharmaceuticals, an upgrade in the conventional sizing practices is warranted.

Choice of Filter Rating

The ideal filter would ensure the required particle removal while providing as rapid a rate of flow as possible. A more open filter could be less efficient and permit the escape of some lower size particles whose capture was desired. A too tight filter, in addition to unnecessarily restricting the flow rate, could retain finer particles whose presence is not seen as being objectionable. This could lead to an earlier and needless restriction of the throughput. The choice of the membrane filter is, therefore, worthy of deliberation.

Perhaps the best choice of the pore size rating to be used is made on the basis of a relevant experience. Where this is lacking, the selection is predicated on an estimation of the smallest particle size one wishes to remove. Experimental trial and error with different filters are then relied upon for confirmation. The pore size rating of the filter is chosen on the assumption that the size exclusion mechanism of particle retention is operative. In the case of filtration sterilizations, the 0.2/0.22 micron-rated membrane is traditionally chosen. In instances of possible mycoplasma removal needs, like cell culture media or determined microbial breakthrough of a 0.2 micron filter, 0.1 micron-rated filters become the choice. As these filters are very tight, protection is needed, which is typically achieved using various prefiltration steps.

The realization of filtration sterilizations is not confined to any particular pore size rating. Process operational parameters and other factors govern. The attainment of sterility employing 0.45 micron-rated membranes has been shown to be possible under appropriate conditions; chiefly low differential pressures, 5 psi (0.33 bar) in work by Tanny et al. (1979). Log reduction values of 8 were forthcoming at 30 psi (2 bar) differential pressure from each of two brands of 0.45 micron-rated membranes tested in *Brevundimonas diminuta* challenge studies (Trotter et al., 2002). The filtrative sterilization of preparations too viscous to yield practical rates of flow through 0.2 micron-rated membranes, may be managed utilizing repetitive 0.45 micron-rated membranes. This practice is rarely needed or utilized, but not necessarily opposed by regulators as long as reason for such filtration setup is given and the filtration process being process validated. (FDA, 2004).

It is understood that the pore size ratings are not the actual pore dimensions. Unlike the columnar pores of the track-etched membranes, the "pores" of the casting-process membranes are not integral passageways. The concept of "pore" is an artificial construct of individual spaces or vacancies within the microporous polymeric matrix that under the impetus of the partial pressure composes a pathway of least resistance to the fluid flow. Should parts of this chain of spaces becomes blocked by particle arrests, the fluid, differential pressure directed, on an *ad hoc* basis utilizes the available next-best adjacent spaces to continue the chain of flow (Johnston, 1992, pp. 41–45)

Like-rated membranes of different manufacture are not identical in pore size, there being no established rating standard to which pore size designations are to conform (Meltzer and Lindenblatt, 2002; Jornitz and Meltzer, 2001, Chapter 1). Moreover, the optimum filter choice is made less certain by the lack of knowledge concerning the pore size distribution, as also of the particle size distribution. Despite the absence of such pertinent data, the matching of filters to applications in the industry is usually performed successfully. The conventional technique of "trial and error," running filterability trials, suffices for proper "pore size" choices to be made. Another beneficial factor for potential filter choice may be the long experience and in-depth knowledge by filter suppliers. The accumulated data on basis of the suppliers create guidance of which filter system would be most appropriate for specific applications.

Rate of Flow

The insertion of a filter into a fluid stream creates an obstruction to flow. To overcome the resistance, a higher pressure must be enacted upstream of the filter. The difference in the pressures, differential pressure, delta P or ΔP, upstream and down, determines the rate of flow. For Newtonian fluids, flow rate (Q) is directly related both to the differential pressure (ΔP) and the EFA. For a constant flow rate of a clean liquid (i.e., absent particles), differential pressure and EFA bear an inverse relationship. It follows that changing one of these parameters involves alterations in one of the others. These relations are proportionate. Changes in one parameter by some percentage or multiple will necessitate a change in a second parameter by the same percentage or multiple.

Flow rate per differential pressure per EFA equals a definite value. To double the flow rate requires either doubling the ΔP or the EFA while keeping the other constant. To decrease the ΔP but to maintain the same flow rate demands an increase in EFA. The required increase in flow rate achieved at a reduced pressure could, in a case where the particulate loading is high, result in a greater throughput by minimizing compaction of the filter cake of retained matter. The desired increase in EFA can be arranged by the use of parallel filtration, larger filter elements, or different filter designs. Filtration costs will inevitably increase. Alternatively, the EFA could be kept unchanged along with gaining the advantages of lower differential pressures if a lower flow rate were accepted. This would incur an increase in processing time. Concerns regarding product stability or microbial proliferation may dictate faster processing times (Priebe et al., 2003). In short, the relationship among flow rate (Q), EFA, and differential pressure (ΔP) can be utilized in filtration design to attain particular goals (Green and Meltzer, 1987).

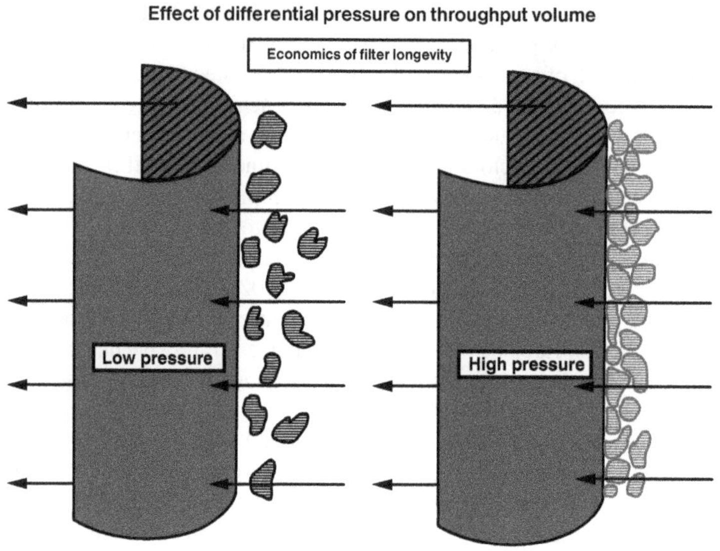

Effect of differential pressure on throughput volume

FIGURE 7.1   Filter cake compaction depiction.

The Filter Area

In designing a filter system, a large enough EFA should be provided to permit completion of the filtration within the span of time allotted to it. Using a larger EFA than necessary needlessly sustains the wasting of filters. An insufficiency of filtration area is even less desirable. It may force a mid-process change-out of filters, a most disruptive action, and prohibited when the process is a terminal filtration step. Expeditious filtrations are usually desired. Filter blockage by retained particles is the usual cause of flow rate reduction that may prolong a filtration. However, slower flow rates motivated by reduced differential pressures may be selected deliberately for the advantages they offer. These include the avoiding of filter cake compactions, as also of the polarized particle layer in front of the filter surface (Figure 7.1). Permeate-reducing compactions may limit throughputs. In addition, lower differential pressures increase the possibilities of enhancing the adsorptive retentions of smaller particles. Slower flows will more leisurely bring to the filter the particles that will be retained. Ultimately, the same number of particles will be removed by the filter, and the final throughput will not be encumbered. However, care must be taken that the processing of the production batch should be completed within the time allotted.

Larger expanses of membrane may have purposes other than accommodating larger particulate loads. As just stated, they may substitute for higher differential pressures in supplying more effluent volume per unit time. In this role they will yield a more diffuse particulate deposit less susceptible to permeability reductions. However, unlike direct reductions in ΔP they will not increase filter efficiency by favoring adsorptive sequestrations since the rate of flow will remain the same.

Viscosity

Flow rate is the easiest to measure from among the filter properties of interest, namely, flow rate, throughput, and retentivity. The other two properties are discerned by experimentation, but flow is, for most fluids, a product directly defined by the differential pressure, and inversely moderated by viscosity. Viscosity, in turn, is reciprocal in relation to temperature. Rates of flow can be varied by manipulating the differential pressure, and the temperature/viscosity relationship.

Flow information is normally given for water. Since the rate of flow varies inversely with viscosity the flow rates for more viscous liquid media will be reduced proportionately and must be corrected for.

Water, the standard, has an assigned numerical viscosity value of one. A liquid having a viscosity of 3 centipoise (cP) will flow one-third as fast; a liquid whose viscosity is 36 cP will flow 1/36th as rapidly; etc. The viscosity effect on rates of flow is not exact, as it ignores liquid/filter interactions which, in their extreme, manifest themselves in filter swelling and other incompatibility expressions. Fortunately, substituting other liquids for water generally minimizes these aberrations. Compatibility is also a condition of proper filter choice. Generally, liquids tend to be less viscous at elevated temperatures, and to filter more rapidly. The heating of liquids to effect more rapid filtration is usually not used, however, particularly where protein denaturation poses a threat. Some note of the liquid temperature should, nevertheless, be made.

Membrane Filter Structure Influences

An increase in membrane area results in a proportionate increase in flow rate. Higher flows are also proportional to higher pressures, as also to lower viscosities. With regard to filter structure, fluid flows are enhanced by larger EFAs, and shorter pores, as derived from thinner membranes, and wider diameters (higher pore size ratings). The filter's porosity, not too easily measured, is the ratio of void space to solid matrix that composes the filter. Cast microporous membranes are generally 70%–80% porous. Thin filters are markedly proficient in rates of flow. Their manufacture by the casting technique does incur larger risks of imperfections due to their thinness. Integrity testing attests to their proper and acceptable construction. Furthermore, thinner membranes may not have consistent retentivities in prolonged filter applications, as the torturous path through the membrane is minimized.

The flow characteristics of single pores are described by the Hagen–Poiseuille Law wherein a fluid of viscosity η, with an average velocity u, of the fluid is related to the tube diameter d (in this case pore), and pressure drop ΔP along a length.

Equation:

$$d^2/32 = u * \eta * z/\Delta P \text{ (Johnston 2003)}$$

This stands on the comparison of filters for their flow qualities. Consider a fluid of a given viscosity flowing at the same average velocity through two pores of similar length, under the impetus of an identical pressure differential. All the factors being equal except for the pore diameters, the rate of flow for the pores of the two membranes will differ as the squares of their diameters, or as the fourth power of their radii. If, however, the diameters of the pores are the same, differences in the flow velocities must derive from differences in porosity. However, this measurement of flow does not reveal either filter's retention properties.

The flux of a membrane describes the effluent flow in terms of volume (e.g., mL) per unit of pressure (psi or bar), per unit time (s or min), per filter area (cm^2 or in.^{2}).

Pressure Units

The chief motivator of liquid flow is the applied differential pressure, the difference between the upstream and filtrate side pressure. There is room for ambiguity because "pressure" is referred to in many different terms:

- Inlet Pressure is the pressure entering the inlet (upstream) side of the filter as displayed on the inlet pressure gauge. It is also called the upstream, or line, or gauge pressure. In a closed filtration system gauges will be used upstream and downstream from the filter. The applied differential pressure is that of the difference between the readings of the two gauges. In a vented or open system, the downstream pressure is the ambient pressure. It equals that of the atmosphere, usually taken as being 14.5 psi (1 bar). When gauge pressure is being used, the downstream pressure is zero. The differential pressure is then equal to the line pressure. The inlet pressure is, therefore, usually expressed as gauge pressure.

- Outlet Pressure: The pressure exiting the downstream side of the filter. It is also called the downstream or filtrate side pressure.
- Gauge Pressure: The pressure registered on a pressure gauge at that particular line location. Since the gauges are meant to be unresponsive to atmospheric pressures, they register the pressure over that of the 14.5 psi (1 bar). If the gauge is located upstream of the filter, and the system downstream is open to the atmosphere, the gauge pressure is read as being the indicated value, but it is actually at that level plus 14.5 psi or 1 bar. However, the gauge reading is the actual differential pressure driving the flow. It is symbolized as psig.
- Absolute Pressure is the pressure above a vacuum. Symbolized as psia, it would read 14.5 psi above gauge pressure.
- Differential Pressure: The difference between the inlet and outlet pressures. Also called ΔP, psid, or pressure drop. As a filtration proceeds in its particle removal function, filter cake builds and increasingly raises the resistance to flow. The difference between the up- and downstream gauges diminishes progressively; hence, the term "pressure drop." It is a measure of the filter's blockage and an indicator of how much of the membrane's capacity to accommodate particulate has been consumed, or (its reciprocal) how much yet remains available. Green and Scheer (1998) also define additional differential pressures.
- Maximum Differential Pressure: The maximum differential pressure available for filtration after the system restrictions and the pump limitations are accounted for. Also referred to as the available differential pressure, it is typically greater than the ΔP actually used in the filtration.
- Operating Pressure: Typically the filter suppliers describe the maximum allowable operating pressure for the filtration system. This pressure shall not be exceeded, as otherwise damage may occur. The maximum allowable operating or differential pressure are both also temperature dependent. The pressure conditions require being lower at elevated temperature conditions, as higher temperatures weaken the polymeric membrane of filter construction system.
- Initial Differential Pressure: The differential pressure at the start of the filtration. It has significance as the clean differential pressure, unencumbered by particle depositions.
- Final Differential Pressure: The differential pressure at the filtration's conclusion, the dirty differential pressure.

Constant Pressure Filtration

Most filtration processes are carried out under constant pressure conditions. It is not the differential pressure that is constant. The pressure referred to is a constant inlet pressure supplied by a pump whose operational setting is fixed for the duration of the filtration. The particle retention will inevitably cause a growing resistance to flow even as the inlet pressure remains constant. This results in a sequential diminution in the flow rate. The gauge pressure after the filter will indicate the growing blockage by registering progressively higher pressure readings. This leads to ongoing decreases in the differential pressure since the inlet pressure remains at its constant set level. The phenomenon is referred to as "pressure drop." Its consequent reduction in flow rate continues, in accord with the developing pressure drop, to where it no longer suffices for a meaningful rate of flow. Usually, the filtration is terminated when the flow has decreased to some 20% of its starting value (Figure 7.2). However, this can be decided as being where the flow stream becomes broken, falls below a given rate, or at any other arbitrary point.

Pump Pressure Setting

In certain cases, the inlet pressure level may be limited by the pump capacity or by considerations of the sufficiency of other components of the system. Usually, the pump is set to deliver from 1 to 2 bar (15–30 psi), as when transferring from a formulation kettle through a sterilizing filter to a holding or storage tank. The rate of flow will decrease with time to the extent that filter blockage occurs, but the diminution in flow rate is of no consequence provided that at the end of the filtration, the batch has been put through the filter within the allotted production time. What is required of the filter, other than that it display the necessary particle-trapping efficiency, is that it accommodates the required throughput volume within the time interval designated for the filtration. As stated, parallel arrangements can be utilized to help achieve desired goals.

Where filling machines are involved, they may be fed from storage tanks open to atmospheric pressure, their vents protected by hydrophobic vent filters. The filling-machine pump draws the liquid to the filling needle. The filtered liquid may, in some instances, however, flow directly to a filling machine without the mediation of a storage tank. In such cases, pressure regulators are used to govern the differential pressure across the filter, as well as to control the necessary pressure to the filling machine. In applications, where the applied differential pressure level are not critical to filter performance (such as where filter efficiency is not critical), the pump may be set in an inlet pressure of 3 or even 4 bars (45–60 psi). The filling-machine pressure regulator will then come into play to ensure proper inlet pressure to the filling machine, simultaneously defining the outlet pressure from the filter and the differential pressure across the filter.

Selection of Inlet Pressure

Trade-offs are involved in the selection of the initial differential pressure level. The higher the inlet pressure selected, the larger is the pressure drop that can result. Advantageously, this offers the largest extent of pressure loss before the filtration is terminated. Filter cartridge constructions can accommodate direct differential pressures of 72.5 psi (5 bar), back-pressures of 30 psi (2 bar), and at least 24,000 pulsations at 72.5 psi (5 bar). Leahy and Sullivan (1978) (Table 7.1) found that *Brevundimonas diminuta* were retained completely and equally well by a 0.22 micron-rated membrane at 50 psi as at 5 psi. Aicholtz et al. (1987) confirmed that such membranes in cartridge form responded equivalently at 50 psi. However, filter efficiency, defined as percentage particle retention, as also throughput, or service life, can vary inversely with ΔP.

Higher inlet pressures will initially produce higher rates of flow, but will reduce the opportunities for adsorptive removals, and by compaction of the filter cake, as well as of the polarized particle layer sited in front of the filter will likely abbreviate the throughput, depending upon the degree of loading and fouling. The use of higher initial ΔPs reaches their culminations more speedily but is otherwise not beneficial. At lower ΔPs, the flow rates being lower, it will take longer for the retained particles to build up to the same filter blocking level. However, the total throughput volumes will be identical, except for the differences made by filter cake compaction. Thus, higher ΔPs may produce foreshortened throughputs within a briefer service life. The trade-off is between throughput volume and operational time. It may be a requirement that the batch be filtered and completed within one shift.

In conducting a filtration, the highest filter efficiency is sought, especially when filtration sterilizations are the goal. For this reason, filtrations are generally not conducted at differential pressures above 30 psi (2 bar). This accords with the recommendation's forthcoming from HIMA (1982). This is also the ΔP level at which the bacterial challenges performed by filter manufacturers in qualifying membranes as being of sterilizing quality are carried out, at 30 psi (2 bar). Prudently, most filtrations are conducted at constant delta pressures at that level or even lower, at 10–20 psi.

TABLE 7.1

Impact of Pressure on Passage (β Ratio)

Filter Type	Pore Size (Hm)	β Ratio		
		0.5 psid	5 psid	50 psid
GS	0.22	$>10^{10}$	$>10^{10}$	$>10^{10}$
HA	0.45	$>10^8$	10^7	10^6
DA	0.65	10^4	10^4	10^3
AA	0.80	10^2	10^1	10^0

Assessment of Remaining Filter Capacity

In addition to achieving the required particle retention level, the throughput volume is also of importance in a given filtration. Both of these qualities are reflective of the rate of flow. As stated, flow rate (Q), is related to both the differential pressure (ΔP), and to the EFA. Therefore, if a change occurs in one of these parameters, one of the others must have undergone alteration. Thus, if at a particular differential pressure, a given rate of flow decreases by half, it signifies that half of the EFA has been consumed, i.e., 50% of the porosity blocked by retained particulate. At this point, a doubling of the ΔP will restore the flow to its previous level, although influences of filter cake compaction require to be evaluated. The point being made is that the loss in flow rate is also a measure of the remaining EFA. If operational alterations are to be instituted for whatever reasons, this EFA value should serve as the point of departure.

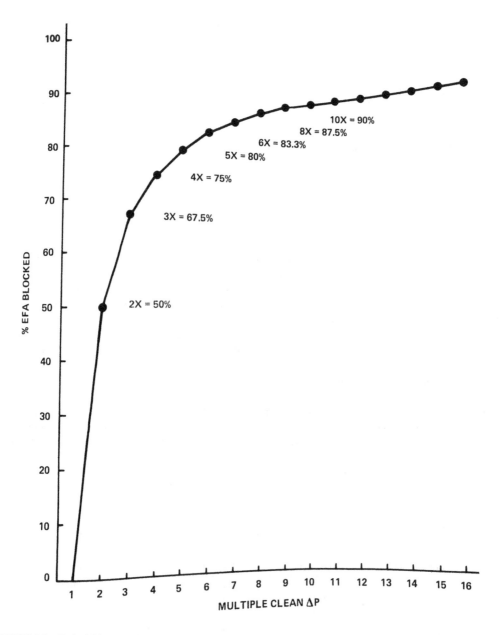

FIGURE 7.2   Typical filter blocking curve.

Termination Point

Once the maximum ΔP has been decided upon and the pump has been set accordingly, the flow that results is inevitably fixed. The maximum differential pressure, however defined, having been utilized from the very beginning, there remains no margin for increase. Inevitably, the flow will progressively diminish as the filter blocks. The inlet pressure setting remains unchanged. Each halving of the flow signals a 50% loss of filter capacity in terms of EPA. After the second halving of the initial flow rate, the filter capacity is down to 25%, and so on. The slope of the curve describing the accumulating throughput volume, or EFA reduction as a function of the pressure drop increases at a steadily diminishing rate; a geometric progression that becomes asymptotic at about 80%.

Figure 7.2 illustrates this law of diminishing returns. The added throughput volume gained after 80% or so of the filter capacity has been utilized is generally not judged worth the time required to secure it. To optimize the filter economics, some threefold doubling of the initial ΔP is allowed for. Thus, one-half of 30 psi (1 bar) is 15 psi; one-half of which is 7.5 psi, which then halves to 3.75 psi. At this point, 87.5% of the filter capacity has been consumed. To achieve the point of diminishing returns, the filtration should be terminated when the pressure differential reaches 5 or 6 psi (0.4 bar) or the flow drops to 20%.

In sum, the rate of flow in constant pressure filtrations starts at a maximum, and decreases in accordance with the filter-blocking propensities of the liquid suspension. Generally, the filtration is ended when the rate of flow has decreased to some 20% of its original value, or to the point where the filtrate becomes a broken stream, or in accordance with some other user preference. No matter how much one increase the differential pressure typically the filter at that stage is blocked and consumed.

If the differential pressure decreases to an unproductive level due to filter blockage caused by particle accretion, and a constant or at least a continuing flow is desired, either the EFA or the upstream pressure must be increased proportionately. The latter, however, changes a constant pressure filtration into a constant volume filtration.

Constant Volume or Flow Filtrations

The operational conveniences of constant pressure filtrations do not always suit. Thus, in filtering serum, where throughput rather than rate of flow is important, low initial inlet pressures are used. As the rate of flow decreases to an unacceptable level, the impediment to flow is overcome by *moderately* increasing the inlet pressure. Filter clogging needs to be avoided. Once experienced, it may be impossible to reverse or remove. By means of such progressive incremental boosting of inlet pressure, the differential pressure is increased, and the flow rate is restored. Thus, filtrations are maintained at realistic levels while enabling an optimum throughput to be achieved, albeit slowly.

Constant Volume Serum Filtrations

In one instance, the use of an initial 26–39 psi inlet pressure caused an almost immediate flow cessation in a serum filtration. Lowering the initial inlet pressure to 7 psi resulted in flow resumption. Usually, however, in serum filtrations, once cessation caused by excessive pressure has ensued, flow will not be revived by a lowering of pressure.

Serum filtrations require time and large filter areas. Constant volume filtrations are usually employed because, although the rates of flow are of secondary importance, the maintenance of a low but constant rate of flow serves to control and regulate the impress of harmful higher inlet pressure levels on the filtration. Elevated pressures in these applications show a higher, more rapid fouling rate. This can be due to higher polarization rates due to higher flows, but also gel formation on the membrane and cake compression. One requires to be sensitive in regard to the utilized differential pressure. The inlet pressure is varied periodically over the filtration process only enough to overcome the increasing resistance to flow caused by the progressive blockage of the filter, as signaled by decreasing flow.

In the constant volume mode of filtration, then, one seeks to maintain a steady rate of flow by manipulating the inlet pressure as a means of controlling the applied differential pressure to minimize the flow decay occasioned by progressive filter blockage.

It cannot be overemphasized that proper filter system design requires the operational assessments of flow decay studies. Where these are not possible, approximations can be forthcoming from data presented in filter manufacturers' catalogs.

Parallel Filter Arrangements

If, at the maximum differential pressure, still yielding satisfactory particle/organisms retentions, the rate of flow is insufficient, the filter efficiency should not be put at risk by increasing ΔP. Rather, additional filter area should be utilized in a parallel configuration to increase the flow rate and the throughput level.

As is illustrated in Figure 7.3, the purpose of a parallel filter arrangement is to enhance the rate of flow and the throughput by use of more extensive EFA. In effect, the particulate deposition is dispersed over a larger area. Each filter confronts less of the total particle load. Blockage of the individual filter is thereby minimized. The realization of extending the throughput volume by managing the wider dispersal of the retained particulate matter depends upon the degree of loading.

In pharmaceutical settings such constructions providing the additional EFA in the form of additional filters being fed from the same liquid source and exiting to a common pool are called parallel arrangements. They are especially useful for filtering highly loaded fluids. The additional cartridges may be utilized in their separate housings. However, the term is not applied to multi-housed filters although they manage the same flow process to the same effect (Figure 7.4). Essentially, a greater area of membrane is supplied to prevent (or slow) filter blockage by particle accretion.

Each filter operates at full differential pressure to give a total rate of flow whose value is the appropriate multiple of one individual unit. The pressure drop across each of the individual parallel flow paths is equal. The pressure drop is not increased by the added membranes, because the number of parallel filtration paths does not increase the overall applied differential pressure of the system. Indeed, the more parallel paths, the lower the ΔP necessary to provide a given total rate of flow and throughput volume. The parallel flow arrangement can, therefore, be used to increase the rate of flow of a filtration at a given differential pressure.

Parallel filtration, while maintaining a constant rate of flow from a filtration, can be used to reduce the applied differential pressure over a given filter area, thus increasing both filter efficiency and longevity. For example, consider a filtration whose purpose is the sterilization of a batch of small-volume parenteral preparation on its way from the batch preparation vessel to a dwell tank prior to the filling machine. The filter indicated will, therefore, be of a 0.2 micron pore size rating, requiring autoclave sterilization and integrity testing, such as by the bubble-point procedure. Ambient temperature will prevail; the liquid viscosity is that of water, 1 cP. Assume that a product flow of not less than 10 gal./min (37.9 L/min) will be required, and the initial inlet pressure used is to be set at a constant 20 psi (1.4 bar) differential, the initial drop being from 20 psig (1.4 bar), to ambient pressure.

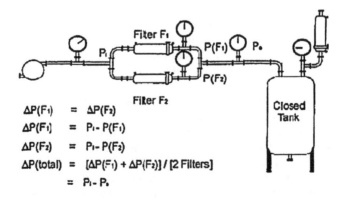

$$\Delta P(F_1) = \Delta P(F_2)$$
$$\Delta P(F_1) = P_i - P(F_1)$$
$$\Delta P(F_2) = P_i - P(F_2)$$
$$\Delta P(total) = [\Delta P(F_1) + \Delta P(F_2)] / [2 \text{ Filters}]$$
$$= P_i - P_o$$

FIGURE 7.3   Parallel filter configuration.

FIGURE 7.4 Multi-round filter housing.

Of the many filters available for this purpose from the several manufacturers, one could choose a cartridge that has a flow rate in the 10-in. or 24.9-cm length of some 8 gal. or 30 L/min at 20 psi or 1.4 bar differential pressure. Alternatively, one can read the flow rate per 1 psi differential from the filter manufacturer's catalog, namely, 0.4 gal./min (1.5 L/min) and multiply by 20 psi (1.4 bar) to yield 8 gal./min (30.4 L/min) per 10-in. (24.9-cm) cartridge. The viscosity of this small-volume parenteral preparation being 1 cP, the same as that of water, no correction for viscosity is required. The flow through a 10-in. (24.9-cm) cartridge will be 8 gal./min (30.4 L/min). However, the desired flow is 10 gal./min (37.8 L/min) more filter area than that provided by one 10-in. (24.9-cm) cartridge is required.

The necessary filter area can be provided best and most simply by the use of one 20-in. (49.8-cm) cartridge in a single holder. If such a 20-in. length cartridge were not available, two 10-in. cartridges could be mounted in a parallel arrangement, as shown in Figure 7.3.

Each 10-in. (24.9-cm) cartridge operates at the full differential pressure of 20 psi (1.4 bar) and independently delivers 8 gal./min (30.4 L/min) of product (except if this quantity becomes progressively decreased by ensuing filter blockage).

A general formula applies:

$$\text{Flow required} = \frac{\text{Number of 10 in. } \left(24.9\text{-cm cartridges psi or kg/cm}^2\right) \left(\text{liquid viscosity}\right)}{\text{Flow per 10-in. } \left(24.9\text{-cm cartridge at 1 psi or 0.7 bar}\right) \text{actual differential needed}}.$$

Parallel flows can be used to increase the total rate of flow and the total throughput volume over a given time at a constant pressure. They also permit the attainment of a given volume of filtrate at a lower differential pressure. Filtrations performed at lower differential pressures tend to increase the filtration efficiency in addition to prolonging the filter system's service life.

Series Arrangements

Filter arrangements in which fluid flows from one filter through another is termed a serial filtration (Figure 7.5). It provides the prefilter (PF)/final filter (FF) combination with enhanced total throughput. In effect, the PF increases the EFA to the extent that it distributes the particulate load between two or more

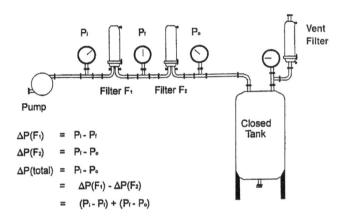

FIGURE 7.5   Series filtration configuration.

filters. This prolongs the service life of the filtration unit as measured by its throughput. The rate of flow decay is diminished. As a result, the rate of filtration may be improved. The extent of improvement depends upon the preparation's total suspended solids (TSS) load. The efficiency of the FF is thereby increased. Correctly sized, the serial arrangement avoids the troublesome change-out of filters during the filtration process.

Alternatively, the serial filtration may be intended to ensure against imperfect particle retention on the part of the FF. In this type of application, the filter combination is a special case of repetitive filtrations or redundant filtration. Prefiltration is a frequent practice with high fouling fluid stream like cell culture media. It extends the service life of the filter couple, increases the throughput, and minimizes the interference with the flow rate by the retained particles.

The serial coupling of the filters, for whatever purpose, inevitably increases the pressure drop across the filter train. The pressure drop is the chief penalty of the series arrangement. It increases the pumping costs and may require the expense of additional housings. Again, depending upon the TSS, the improvements in the rates of flow occasioned by the distribution of the load over a larger filter area may be negated by the lower differential pressures that result from the two filters being in a serial alignment.

Double-Layered Filters

Double-layer filters are a special case of the repetitive filter arrangement wherein the two membranes are included within a single cartridge. Two types of double-layered filter constructions are available. The two different constructions are intended for different purposes. Both are, however, in the form of serial filters.

The heterogeneous type consists of layers of membrane of dissimilar pore size ratings. An example of a heterogeneous cartridge construction would be a 0.45 micron-rated membrane upstream from a 0.2/0.22 micron-rated FF (Figure 7.6). The homogeneous type is composed of two membranes of the same pore size, e.g., both 0.2 micron rated (Figure 7.7).

Heterogeneous Filters

An example of a heterogeneous cartridge construction, as said, would be a 0.45 micron-rated membrane upstream from a 0.2/0.22 micron-rated FF. The more open filter, in its position upstream of the tighter, serves in the protective role of PF, accepting a portion of the particulate load, and thereby prolonging the service life of the final downstream membrane. The rate of flow is slowed by the longer overall flow path of the double construction. It is reduced from that of either single membrane. However, the PF effect is to prolong the throughput by dispersing the particulate burden between two filters. Depending upon the numbers, sizes, and shapes of the particles, the effect should be the prolongation of the throughput volume.

By way of automated integrity testing machines that avoid invasions of the filtration train downstream of the FF, the integrity testing of a filter can be performed without endangering the asepsis of the system.

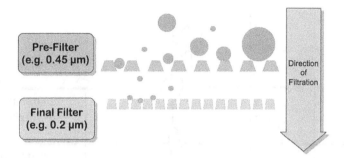

FIGURE 7.6 Heterogenous double-layer membrane configuration.

FIGURE 7.7 Homogenous double-layer membrane configuration.

When repetitive filters are used, each in its own housing, neither filter can be tested without invading the space separating them unless some very unusual arrangements are devised. This is one disadvantage of relying on repetitive filters. With heterogenous double-layer membrane configurations in one filter device, that filter device can be tested in its entirety without interjection on the filtrate side.

Homogeneous Filters

The homogeneous double constructions contain two membranes of like pore size ratings. This double-layer construction reduces the probability of particle passage. The intention is to ensure that even if an inappropriate or flawed membrane were somehow included, the second filter would serve as a safeguard. Likewise, when single membranes cannot be cast to thicknesses sufficient to retain the target organisms, they too are used in double constructions. The second filter serves as an assistant to the first, reinforcing its intended action of particle retention.

The clean rate of flow through double-filter constructions is less than that through single membrane layers. This is due to the pressure drop that results from the overall pore lengths being longer. The clean rate of flow through homogeneous arrangements is greater than through heterogeneous double filters because in the former combination both membranes have the tighter restrictions of the FF.

Repetitive Filters

The pore is modeled as being a convoluted, irregular capillary. Because of its tortuosity, it is necessarily longer than the depth of the filter. Its restrictive dimensions may occur anywhere along its length. This assumption explains certain views regarding repetitive filters. It would be expected that lengthening a pore might proportionally increase the pressure drop, i.e., decrease the differential pressure across its span. This should reduce its flow rate and promote its adsorptive particle-trapping abilities, but probably not alter its throughput. The actual situation wherein membranes are superimposed in intimate contact on one another in effect does prolong the pore length. The consequences just detailed follow.

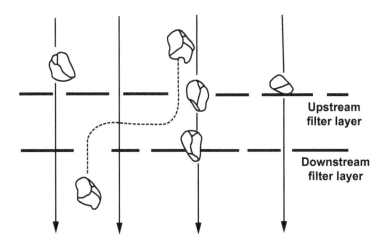

FIGURE 7.8   Effect of repetitive layers of retention.

The congruent positioning of the filter layers will cause a narrowing of the pore size distribution. Fewer large size pores will result because such pores in the one filter will likely superimpose those of smaller ratings in the other since there are many more of the smaller. The result will be a diminution in the overall pore size, and in their distribution. This should assist sieve retentions. Moreover, the pore paths are doubled in their lengths, as are also their surfaces. This encourages adsorptive sequestrations as particles being carried through the pore passages more frequently undergo Brownian-type collisions likely to cause their impactions with the pore walls. The filter efficiency is enhanced thereby.

Where use is made of two membranes that are separated from one another, a different result is obtained. Between the two membranes there exists a space wherein the fluid exiting the first membrane forms a pool from which it is hydrodynamically directed to the larger pores of the second membrane. The hydrodynamic flows preferentially convey particles to the more open pores. This detracts from the narrowing of the pore size distribution's doubling of the single filter's pore length (Reti et al., 1979) (Figure 7.8).

Again, the log reduction values (LRVs) of individual filters are not additive in their combinations (Trotter et al., 2000; Reti et al., 1979). The exact sum depends upon the probabilities of given size organisms meeting an appropriately sized pore within the pore size distribution. Whether by encounter with a larger pore, or with a flaw, the likelihood is that the organisms penetrating the upstream filter will be the smaller of the organism present in the feedwaters. This will decrease the size distribution of the organisms downstream of the first filter in the direction of overall smaller sizes. This, in turn, makes more likely a lower LRV for the downstream filter.

Redundant Filtration

This term is often used to designate a repetitive, for example, 0.2 and 0.2 micron, or two filter arrangement wherein the two filters, each in its own cartridge, are housed separately. The term "redundant" often conveys a negative cast to the usage as being wasteful or unnecessary. Its intended meaning in filtration is to imply "enough and to spare." The first filter, as is common to repetitive filters, is expected to fulfill the retention requirement. The second filter serves as insurance. It is a safeguard that by its very presence is worth the cost of the greater certainty it supplies. As already observed, the LRVs of repetitive filters are not twice the value of a separate filter.

Redundant filtration incurs the cost of two housings, but the separate housings permit the integrity testing of each filter, albeit the risks to asepsis inherent in prefiltration integrity testing still apply. Within a single housing the upstream testing of the downstream filter is manageable, but will require the isolation of the upstream filter.

Regulatory Recommendations

As regards the EU and Food and Drug Administration (FDA), both the guideline CPMP, April 1996, and EC Annex 1, as well as the FDA's Aseptic Guide (2004) recommend the use of redundant 0.2/0.22 micron-rated membranes. *FDA's new aseptic guideline states, "Use of redundant filtration should be considered in many cases."* The placement of the filters is to be "as close as possible" (or practical) to the filling needles; to this will minimize the likelihood of their function being affected by random biofilm shedding. The usual location is indeed just before the filling needles or before the reservoir that feeds them. In practice, the "recommendations" may be enforced as if they were law.

The recommendation is not based on any known survey or experimental data, nor have the regulatory authorities explained their reasoning. Those responsible for the public safety are often obliged to make decisions when adequate supporting data are not yet available. Overdesign is a normal response to uncertainties. By way of automated integrity testing machines that avoid invasions of the filtration train downstream of the FF, the integrity testing of a filter can be performed without endangering the asepsis of the system. When repetitive filters are used, each in its own housing can be integrity tested separately. When in the same holder, neither filter can be tested without invading the space separating them unless some very unusual arrangements are devised. This is one disadvantage of relying on repetitive filters.

PF Action

What is required of a FF is that it reliably retains the particles or microorganisms it is proposed to remove from the fluid stream being processed. In pursuit of this reliability, membrane filters, characterized by their narrow pore size distribution, are usually selected for critical operations. The pore size designation is made on the basis of the presumed particle size. This is seldom known with certainty, but experience with the application can serve as a guide. Membranes are available in smaller pore size ratings than are depth-type filters, their ratings are more dependably defined, and, as said, their pore size distributions

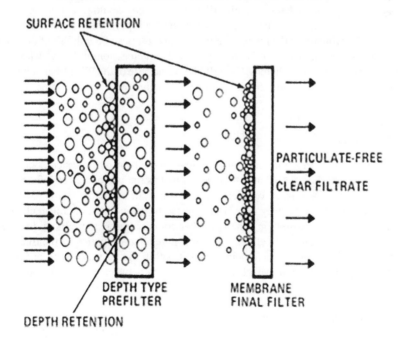

FIGURE 7.9 PF/FF combination.

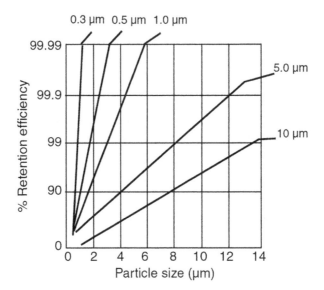

FIGURE 7.10   Retention efficiency curves for multiple PF cartridges.

are narrower as a consequence of their technologies of manufacture. As a result, their particle retentions are more thorough. However, in retaining higher particle loads they may sooner undergo blockage, leading to a troublesome need for mid-process filter replacements. Alternatively, more extensive filter area can be used at the outset. Also, a PF(s) may be employed. Its function is the acceptance of part of the particle load, thereby sparing the FF that burden, and prolonging its service life (Figure 7.9). Depth-type filters are usually used for prefiltrations. However, membranes of higher pore size ratings may serve as PFs to FFs of finer porosities. In such cases, it were best, however, that the liquid not be highly loaded, or that more extensive EFA be used to forestall premature filter blockage (Trotter et al., 2002; Jornitz and Meltzer, 2001, Chapter 4).

PFs are not intended to be completely retentive (if they were, they would by definition be FFs). PFs are designed to accommodate only a portion of the particulate load, permitting the remainder to impinge upon the FF. Figure 7.10 illustrates the retention efficiency for a series of depth PFs of different pore size ratings. In the process, the life of the FF is prolonged by the intercession of the PF, whose own service life is not unacceptably abbreviated thereby. Overall, the service life of the PF(s)/FF assembly is extended to the point where the rate of fluid flow and its throughput volume meet practical process requirements.

PFs and FF Efficiency

Not only does the use of PFs serve the function of increasing the EFA of the system, but it may increase the filter efficiency as well. Filter efficiency may be defined as the percentage of influent particles that are retained by the filter. When the sieve retention mechanism of particle arrest is not the sole means of organism capture, the filter efficiency may be an inverse function of the organism challenge level. It depends on the particle size distribution. The two-filter combination is more likely to arrest particles small enough to penetrate one filter. In effect, the longer pore length supplied by the filter pair provides greater opportunity for a smaller particle being carried within the passageway to encounter the pore wall in response to Brownian motion. An adsorptive interaction between particle and pore surface could result.

By accepting a portion of the load, the PF attenuates the rate of flow decay of the FF, thereby increasing the throughput. In reducing the challenge level of larger particles to the FF, it may leave available the smaller pores of that filter that might otherwise be preempted. This could increase the filter's efficiency for adsorptive captures.

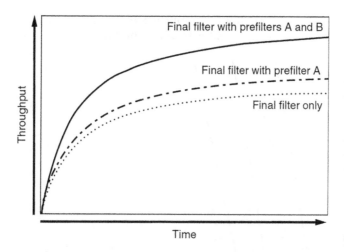

FIGURE 7.11 FF life extension due to the use of a PF.

PF Selection by Flow Decay

A filter's clean rate of flow, i.e., that is characterized by the use of a clean fluid mirrors such fluid characteristics as viscosity, temperature, etc., and its degree of interaction, if any, with the filter. The rates of flow of fluids containing particles reflect the progressive pore blocking caused by the filter's retention of the particles, especially as aggravated by the differential pressure's compaction of the filter cake they form. This (dirty) rate of flow is the rate of flow decay. The total throughput volume given by a filter will chiefly depend upon the particle-size/pore size relationship. The filtration conditions, the differential pressure in particular, will strongly affect the results. The determinants are the filter's EFA, its thinness, its total porosity (the number and sizes of its pores), and the number and sizes of the particles it retains, which is to say upon the TSS content and its concentration. It may be that a given filter/liquid combination may not yield the required throughput, or that the flow rate may not produce it in a timely fashion. In such instances, reliance may be made upon the use of PFs to correct the situation. A proper PF selection can be made by the use of flow decay measurements.

Flow decay measurements, the plotting of flow (throughput to time t) as a function of time, will reveal the flow-limiting effects of the particle load. This is first performed for the proposed processing filter. From this will be learned whether the selected (final) filter will yield adequate flow rates, retentions, and throughputs.

The same type of determination following the use of a PF, will illustrate the effect of the PF on the rate of decay. Comparison of both flow decay curves will show the ameliorating effect of employing the PF. What is desired of a PF is that it should so modify the flow decay curve as to enable acceptable throughputs over an acceptable interval of time (Figure 7.11). The assaying of different PFs allows comparisons to be made regarding their relative efficiencies. If necessary, more than one PF can be used in concert with the final membrane in composing the filter assembly. Illustrated in Figure 7.12 is the optimization by PFs of a 1.25% trypticase soy broth preparation.

Using Filter Models

Flow decay or filterability trials are traditionally performed using volumes of the drug preparation small enough to be assayed using 47-mm flat disc filters. The results obtained are then extrapolated to the membrane EFA that will be needed for the drug volume being processed. It is the employment of just such flow decay investigations that can be used to estimate the best filter combinations.

Obviously, flow decay models as apt as possible should be used to obtain data whose extension will lead to reliable filter scale-ups. It is convenient and economical, both in terms of effort and material

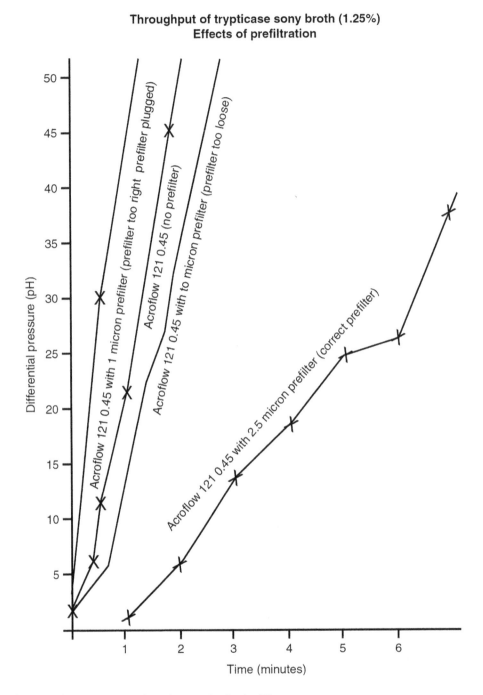

FIGURE 7.12 Throughput curves of trypticase soy broth using PFs.

costs, to use the 47-mm flat discs, for "indicator trial" measurements of throughputs. However, it is too often assumed that in the sizing of filters an extrapolation can be made from small flat discs to pleated filter cartridges large enough to handle production requirements. Meaningful scale-up or sizing to meet the needs of the process that will rely on pleated cartridges can only be done with pleated filter devices. Flow cannot adequately be measured and extrapolated from flat stock to pleated membranes due to influences inherent in the pleating process. The measurement of the EFAs of flat disc filters is uncomplicated. That of pleated filters is appreciably more complex. The flow rate scale-up using 47-mm flat discs reflects only the influences of the membrane thickness and its porosity. The modifications in EFA resulting from pleat-pack constructions must not be neglected. These derive from the flow-attenuating influences of the cartridge's support and drainage layers. To this must be added the reduction in flow caused by the occurrence of pleat compaction. The utmost caution has to be exercised when filter choices are made by evaluating flow rates using 47-mm flat disc filters. The flow data will not extrapolate well from flat stock to pleated filter cartridges.

A more responsible action is to follow the "indicator trials" using 47-mm discs with "verification trials" wherein the flow rate measurements are obtained by the use of pleated devices. Small pleated membrane units, such as capsules or mini-cartridges are available for this purpose. These "verification trials" are needed to more quantitatively confirm the results gained from using 47-mm disc filters. It is from the "verification trials" with small pleated devices that extrapolations to pleated cartridges can be extended to full productions.

Where expensive preparations are being dealt with, as in the biopharmaceutical industry, an even more accurate scale-up operation should be based on full scale "assurance trials." These should be undertaken before the full production run is ventured. If necessary, a full 10-in. cartridge should be employed as a model. If the drug preparation is too expensive for such trials, water, or an aqueous fluid compounded to a viscosity similar to that of the preparation should be relied upon.

It should be pointed out in passing that the wrong perceptions derived from inappropriate tests may prove expensively misleading. Failures to properly assess correct choices in the scale-up process may result in the rejection of filters that could perform appropriately in production runs.

Pleating Effect on Throughput and Flow Decay

Production runs will probably require pleated cartridges to supply the larger EFA that will be needed. The projection of flow decay data from flat discs, as said, is inappropriate in determining the required EFA when it is to be secured as pleated cartridges. Cartridges are more complex in their construction than are simple flat disks. The pleating will indeed furnish the added EFA that is its purpose. However, the flow dynamics, the pleat architecture itself, the number of pleats and their heights, the nature of the support and drainage layers, and possibly more subtle performance parameters may detract from the full potential offered by the pleating. Figure 7.13 illustrates some of the different pleated filter designs that are available, conceivably for different effects. Densification of the filter-pack may conceivably contribute to a greater retention of particles. Were this to lead to an earlier filter blockage, the throughput would be negatively affected. In essence, it would be as if less EFA than had been expected were at hand. This may be one reason why conclusions forthcoming from flow decay studies, while accepted, are paired with the caveat of a generous safety margin (Jornitz et al., 2004). Therefore, following the preliminary 47-mm disc "indicator trials" identification of the proper filter combination necessitates follow-ups with assurance trials employing pleated filter devices.

The practice of sizing the production filter by an ultimate reliance on 47-mm discs is still experienced within the industry. It should not be. It may suffice where the filtration deals with relatively inexpensive products whose mishandling occasioned by unsuitable sizing operations will be relatively inconsequential. It is surely inappropriate in the biopharmaceutical industry where the products are of a significant value and where their losses will be costly. The 47-mm disc usage can lead to estimates of flow rates and throughput values. However, only pleated elements can reliably be used to predict the performance of pleated cartridges. Required, at least, is the use of small-scale pleated devices. Such are available as capsules or mini-cartridges.

The Importance of the Filtration Area of 47-mm Discs

The EFAs of a 47-mm flat disc filter is $17.4\,cm^2$ in area. Use is made of this number in system sizing work wherein this expanse of filter surface yielding a given amount of throughput is employed to determine by way of ratios what expanse of filter area would be needed to produce a specified volume of product in actual productions. The use of the 47-mm discs for this purpose is widespread although the operational details may differ among its users, there being no standardized operational steps.

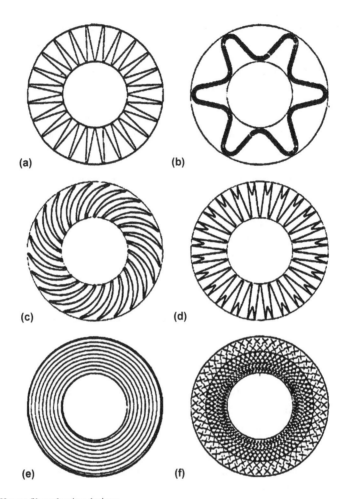

FIGURE 7.13   Different filter pleating designs.

In the classic usage of 47-mm disc filters, a membrane is removed from its package, and is inserted into a stainless steel holder wherein it is held in position, sealed by the compressive action of O-rings. The EFA of the 47-mm disc is 17.4 cm². However, in the holder the O-rings preempt some of the disc's peripheral space. The actual effective filter area of such an assembly available to the liquids being treated was identified by filtering a staining solution of acridine yellow. The stained area measured 41-mm in diameter. Its area was calculated ($\pi/4\,d^2$) to be 13.2 cm². This accords with the defined meaning of EFA as the effective area used for filtration is the uncovered membrane area and not the total area.

It is not known what number value the many users of 47-mm disc filters may individually employ in their sizing protocols. The area measurement of filter EFAs by acridine staining seems not to be a widely recognized procedure. It is little discussed or published. Certainly, its application to the use of 47-mm disk filter in the present context is hardly universal.

If the EFA value used for the 47-mm flat filter is that of the full 47 mm dimension, while its actual use area in the application is 13.2 cm², then the extrapolations made would lead to expectations of larger flows than will actually be realized.

The absence of industry standards in this instance is exacerbated by the appearance on the market of a "47 mm disc" pre-sealed in a disposable holder. The staining technique reveals its diameter to be 48 mm. This is equivalent to an EFA of 18.4 cm². Were its diameter to be exactly 47 mm, its EFA would be 17.4 cm². This compares with the replaceable individual inserts' EFA of 13.2 cm². This EFA mix-up of supposedly same 47-mm test filter device can cause detrimental scaling effects. Therefore, one requires to determine precisely the actual EFA of the test filter used (Jornitz et al., 2009).

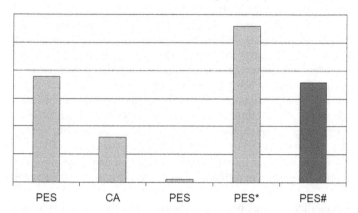

FIGURE 7.14 47-mm disc area differences influencing the total throughput result.

The opportunities for inaccuracies in sizing decisions based on the use of 47-mm disc filters argues for follow-up "verification testing" with larger filter units (Figure 7.14). This could be the prelude to the infinitely more reliable "assurance testing" wherein full-scale modeling would be relied upon.

Inhomogeneity Consequences

Some degree of filter inhomogeneity, in terms of porosity, could eventuate from membrane pore size distributions. Its manifestation would bear some inverse relationship to the EFA of flat disc membranes, but only after a certain low level of EFA is attained. The fewer larger pores of the pore size distribution may not be numerous enough to be part of every small area of membrane that may be cut from the membrane role. Therefore, as previously stated, the homogeneity would assert itself only in membranes of low EFA, e.g., flat discs of 47, or so, mm size.

Such inhomogeneity would be of very limited significance in pharmaceutical processing operations where the large EFAs of pleated cartridges are utilized. However, it could perhaps have some negative consequences where the sizing of filters is performed by flow decay measurements on 47-mm filters. The probability of such a situation would be minimized by trial replications. This possibility argues for the use of test filters larger than the 47-mm discs customarily employed. In any case, the use of membranes of larger EFAs would involve the measurement of larger volumes of test liquids. The data, consisting of larger integers, should result in more reliable extrapolations.

Flow Decay Procedure

Number of Housings

Tests are sometimes conducted by placing simultaneously as many different filter/PF disks into a single holder as will fit while still providing adequate sealing and freedom from interference. This method is simpler than using individual holders for each filter, but it will not reflect as much useful data. By using a single disk holder, the flow decay determination will, by experimental design, yield equivalent areas for the PFs and FF. This limits the utility of the flow decay to providing information on the proper pore size and material selection. It will not provide any information on the ratio of PF/FF areas. The suggested method is to use a separate filter holder for each simulated filter, to obtain data on the individual units, collect the effluent, and to filter the solution through the next filter unit in series. Using this approach will generate data both the next filter unit in series. Using this approach will generate data both on proper pore size rating selections and relative PF/FF areas.

However, when a serial or double-layer design cartridge filter is being considered, this construction must be reflected in the flow decay test. In this case, the multiple layers should be placed in the same disk holder, since this will automatically yield the equivalent areas inherent in the serial cartridge design.

Two 47-mm filter holders are connected in series. One end of this arrangement is connected to the source of the fluid whose filtration is being tested. The effluent end of the filter combination leads to a collecting vessel with volume calibrations so that filtered liquid volumes can be read. A 2-L graduated cylinder serves nicely where water samples are being tested. For fluids such as serum, a 100- or 250-mL graduated cylinder suffices. The applied pressures should be measurable. A stopwatch or timer is also required. The flow decay should be monitored by recording data at preselected time intervals. The intervals may be modified as the decay progresses. It is suggested that either flow rate versus time (in a constant differential pressure system) or differential pressure versus time (in a constant flow rate system) be recorded.

Recently, these filterability test rigs became automated, i.e., the filtered volume is measured with a balance, the differential pressure is evaluated with pressure transducers and the data are processed with a data acquisition system. A software program calculates a certain square foot predictor and plots the graphs of differential pressure, flow, and volume. These systems are extremely accurate filterability devices, and work very well also in regard to retaining and storing the evaluated data within a computer system.

The liquid is passed through a filter placed in the downstream filter holder. For the moment, the upstream holder remains without a filter. The filter used is of the degree of fineness required for the ultimate treatment of the liquid. Flow is continued until the point of filter insufficiency or of shutdown is reached. During the flow, measurement of the time interval to pass a given small volume of the liquid is frequently made. Alternatively, the volume of flow per fixed time interval is measured. Either way, the ongoing rate of flow is frequently checked and plotted. A slowdown in rate signals the advent of filter insufficiency. This endpoint is most reliable when the applied pressure is kept constant. The total volume that is filtered to the point of shutdown is recorded, as is also the corresponding length of time.

The point of filter insufficiency is reached when the rate of liquid flow, its volume per unit time, falls below a certain desired amount. Usually a decrease in the rate of flow to about 20% of its initial value signals an endpoint. In different contexts other indicators may be used as appropriate. This cutoff point is regarded as the point of diminishing returns.

The procedure is then repeated, but this time with a more open filter in the upstream holder along with the ultimate fine filter in the downstream holder. The upstream filter serves as a PF to the other. The efficacy of its prefiltering role is indicated by how much added volume of liquid is filtered before the shutdown point is reached.

The procedure is again repeated using various combinations of different PFs and the ultimate filter. The qualities of the more open filters (serving as PFs) can also be assessed individually.

For each filter or filter combination, the volume of liquid passed is then plotted as a function of time. Comparisons can then be made, leading to a selection of the optimum PF-filter couple.

If flow decay studies are carried out on the FF and individually on each PF, it becomes possible correctly to proportion the EFAs of the required PF (s)/FF combination. This is done in keeping with the formula:

$$\text{Number of PF per FF} = \frac{\text{FF throughput per unit EFA}}{\text{PF throughput per unit EFA}}$$

Arithmetical Calculations

An elementary arithmetic example can be given illustrating the calculations involved in determining the EFA needed to filter a given batch of a preparation. An extrapolation is made from the base-throughput obtained by use of a 47-mm disc. The 47-mm disc has a filter area of 1.49 in.^{2} A cartridge composed of the same filter medium and porosity will be assumed to contain an area of 6 ft^2. Therefore, the volume throughput relative to a 47-mm filter of the same filter medium is:

$$\frac{6\,\text{ft}^2 \times 144\,\text{in.}^2\,/\,\text{ft}^2}{1.49\,\text{in.}^2} = 580$$

Thus, if the total throughput given by the 47-mm disc is 2,500 mL, then 25 × 580 = 1,450 L or 383 gal. will flow through the cartridge, assuming the filter medium to be similar, before it shuts down, there being 3.79 L to the gallon. The rate of flow measured on the 47-mm disc will indicate how many cartridges would be required to complete the filtration in a timely manner. However, 47-mm disc trials can only create a hypothetical, noncommittal value. Any scaling with 47-mm discs has to be considered with caution due to its unreliability as regards cartridge constructions. In particular, the translation of flow rates cannot reliably be made in like fashion to pleated cartridges. Small pleated filter should be used as models for pleated cartridges.

To determine the total throughput and best filter combination one commonly utilizes 47-mm test filter composites. The first test establishes the base-throughput. It is always performed with the FF. Multiple tests can be performed with different PF discs to see how the initially established base-throughput increases. Once the optimal combination is found, pleated small-scale filter devices of the same combination should be used to scale the required total throughput and the size of the filter area.

As stated, the flow decay should be performed at the differential pressure and fluid temperatures to be used in the final system. This will allow the filter/fluid interaction best to simulate operating conditions. Changing these parameters, such as by the common method of accelerating the flow decay by raising the pressure, may adversely affect the accuracy of the data due to factors such as particle impact.

By such use of disciplined flow decay studies intelligent PF choices can be made. These should yield filter systems with rates of flow and total throughputs that will satisfy the practical requirements of the filtrative practice.

Order of Pore Size Trials

In assessing the optimizing effect of the PF(s) on the ultimate pore blockage of the FF, some advocate the first use of membrane of the just-next-larger pore size rating as PFs to remove the small particles that are likely to cause a more sudden blockage. The more usual practice, for the same reason, is to rely upon depth-type filters rather than membranes for PFs, but also in an ascending order of pore size ratings.

Being of a larger pore size rating than the FF, the PF will more likely permit the smaller particles to impact the FF. The concern is that these may so resemble the pore sizes they encounter in the FF as to cause its plugging in the fashion of a cork-in-a-bottleneck. This would lead to a catastrophic and precipitous decline in flow. To avoid this occurrence, the pore size of the PF is chosen to be on the smaller side among PFs. The tightest PF available, but larger in its nominal retention than the FF, is tried first to reduce the quantity of smaller particles that are passed. It should be noted, however, that the pore size rating systems are not standardized, and that depth-type PFs are, in any case, sized differently from membranes. Typically, PFs are labeled with nominal retention ratings; therefore, some uncertainty attends this effort.

The lack of information about the pore and particle sizes, and their distributions make essential the experimental assessment of the PF/FF couple. It cannot otherwise be predicted. Thus, Figure 7.15 shows a perhaps un-predictable effect of particle sizes on filter pore blockage. The assumption of a portion of the particle load is the PF's purpose. More precisely, its function is to pass only enough of the load to the FF to provide an acceptable and timely rate of fluid flow and throughput to meet practical process requirements. In practice, this means that the filter cake that builds on the FF must remain permeable to the fluid. This necessitates avoiding both its extensive buildup and compaction. Figure 7.15 illustrates a case in point. Wrasidlo and Mysels (1984) employed a 0.2 micron nominal-rated string-wound cartridge in conjunction with a 0.2/9.22 micron-rated membrane in a water filtration application. This provided

FIGURE 7.15   Fractionate retention by pre-, serial and final filtration.

the PF/FF combination with only one-third the service life obtained from the same FF protected by a 5 micron nominal-rated string-wound cartridge filter.

The finding is explained as follows: Empirically it is known that filters having a comparatively large percentage of their pores in sizes similar to those of the particles tend to yield lower throughputs. This occurrence is rationalized by an oversimplified assumption, namely, that the pore openings are round and regular, and that the particles are spherical. If that were the case, the particles that are only slightly larger than the actual pore openings would fit more precisely into them and would plug them with great efficiency (complete pore plugging). Larger particles, like marbles being retained on a window screen, would pack differently (cake formation). Although contiguous, the larger spheres would shelter those pores located on portions of the filter surface sited beneath the protective overhang of their spherical shapes. The pores within this shielded area would be less accessible to precipitous blockage by like-sized particles. To prevent the cork-in-the bottleneck situation, the succession of PF trials is initiated using a PF just larger than the pore size rating of the FF. The object is for the PF to withhold a substantial portion of the particles conducive to a rapid blockage of the downstream filter.

In the subject example, the 0.2 micron nominally rated string-wound filter removed enough of the larger size particles to allow the nearly exclusive passing of the smaller ones to form a dense and impermeable filter cake. The resulting pore blockage of the final membrane thereby abbreviated its service life in terms of throughput. However, using the 0.5 micron nominally rated string-wound filter permitted a portion of larger particles to pass along with the smaller ones. In consequence, the filter cake in its mix of particle of various sizes was irregular enough in its packing pattern to remain permeable to the liquid. If this, in fact, were to establish a general rule, then what would be required is that the PF should permit a proper mixture of particle sizes to deposit on the FF. The attainment of this goal can be ascertained only by flow decay studies. The studies would also determine the ideal differential pressure condition to maintain a porous filter cake.

Translation of Findings

If the PF flow decay pattern is rather close to that of the FF, then the brevity of the interval between the two flows offers only small possibilities for improvement. In effect, the PF is itself acting as the FF. It is too similar in its particle capture and flow propensities to offer advantages in throughput to the designated FF. A larger pore size-rated PF is indicated. In cases where this is not enough, coupling the FF with a PF serves to prolong the period of meaningful flow rates. A second PF, to protect the first, can give an additional period of useful life to the filtration system. In these situations, the area under each appropriate curve represents the total throughput volume. On the other hand, a very high flow rate for the PF being tried signals that it is too open to significantly protect the FF; its pore size rating is too high. In depth filter trials, the retentivity efficiency of the depth filter can be determined by measuring the turbidity of the filtrate. The better the retentivity the clearer the filtrate, although the right balance between retention of the depth and the FF needs to be found. The ideal scenario is the blockage of the PF and FF at the same time at the filtration of the total desired fluid volume.

Housing Considerations in Flow Decay

When properly interpreted the PF(s)/FF combination is extrapolated to the equipment scale needed for processing. Some general observations may be helpful. Filter manufacturers publish graphs of flow rates that are fairly linear within a range. Within this range, most of the differential pressure is being used to drive the fluid through the filter and only a small portion is used to overcome the flow resistance of the housing. When the recommended flow rate is exceeded, however, deviations can occur. First, filter efficiency and throughput may be decreased due to the high-velocity impact of particles on the filter media. Pore plugging may result.

Additionally, differential pressure will increase in a curvilinear fashion at a level higher than predicted by straight-line extrapolation. While the filter may still behave in a linear manner, the housing inlet, cartridge core, and outlet become increasingly restrictive to fluid flow, because of the relatively small orifices involved. Also, the increased frictional losses and turbulence will generate heat. This can have a stabilizing effect on proteinaceous and/or other solution components. Specifically, it has been calculated that 3/4-in. (19-cm) pipe can accommodate flows to a maximum of 80 L/min. Differential pressures intended to be productive of higher flow rates will avail nothing. Regardless of the higher differential pressure, the maximum rate of water flow through a 3/4-in. pipe will essentially remain 80 L (ca. 29 gal./min).

Some filter/filter housing manufacturers list the flow resistance of their filter/housing assemblies to pure water, permitting a more accurate prediction to be made from catalog graphs relating liquid flow rates to applied differential pressures.

Filter manufacturers generally supply data concerning the rates of flow through their various filters (and housings) as a function of incremental pressure differential, e.g., 4 L/min/Δ psi for a 0.2 micron-rated membrane. One must choose as a limit that differential pressure which, through the filter selected, will not exceed the flow capabilities of the filter housing. Different filter ratings (their various degrees of openness) will correspond to different ΔP levels conducive to attaining the maximum allowable liquid flow.

Possible Processing Operation

Based on restrictions of the sort just discussed, certain specific filter flow rate limitations can be recommended for the processing operation:

1. When possible, maintain a flow rate of 1–3 gal./min/ft^2 (4–12 L/min/929 cm^2) EFA.
2. The maximum flow rate should be 5 gal./min ft^2 (20 L/min/cm^2) EFA.
3. The filter cartridge-to-housing interface will normally be the most restrictive area to flow. The flow per interface should be maintained at 5–15 gal./min (20–57 L/min) when possible.
4. The maximum flow rate per interface should be 25 gal./min (95 L/min). This implies that a single cartridge housing should have a flow rate not exceeding 25 gal./min (95 L/min whether the cartridge length is 10 in. (24.9 cm), 20 in. (49.8 cm), or 30 in. (74.7 cm). If a flow rate of 25 gal./min (95 L/min) can be achieved with a 10-in. (24.9-cm) cartridge, increased lengths should be used to increased throughput, the service life of the filter, rather than its flow rate. Equivalent maxima for three-round and seven-round housings should be 75 gal./min (285 L/min and 175 gal./min (665 L/min), respectively.

As discussed, filter efficiency almost always is inversely proportionate to ΔP, as also most usually to the flow rate. It is directly related to service life (longevity or throughput). Thus, considerations of filter efficiency should be paramount. Subject to such dispensations as may be derived from specific validation studies, it would seem advisable to conform to the HIMA (1982) recommendations of not utilizing applied differential pressure levels of 30 psi (2 bar).

Repetition of Inlet Pressure Effects

Again, consider constant pressure filtrations. When the rate of flow has decreased to one-half its original value, one-half of the filter can be said to have been consumed. When half of that flow rate is reached, another half of the remaining filter, or three-quarters of its original, has been utilized, etc. For each halving of the flow rate, there is a proportionate decrease in the remainder of yet-available filter area. The 80% diminution in the initial flow rate, at whatever constant inlet pressure level, being regarded as the economical cutoff point for a filtration, this point is reached when there has been a three- to fivefold halving of the initial rate of flow.

It makes no difference what the constant inlet pressure level is; halving the initial flow rate implies a 50% reduction in the initially available EFA. At higher inlet pressure levels, there will be larger initial liquid flows. These will more speedily supply the number of particulates that will block 50% of the filter EFA. At whatever rate the particles are supplied, however, the eventuation of the 50% EFA blockage will be signaled by a 50% decrease in flow rate. This assumes that particle deformation, or high velocity impactions caused by the differential pressure has not resulted in pore blockage.

At lower inlet pressure levels, it will merely take longer for the same volume of liquid to deliver the same number of blocking particles to 50% of the filter EFA. The flow decay curves, plots of rates of flow versus time, are dissimilar for different constant inlet pressure levels, but the total throughput volumes, the areas under the curves, are essentially the same.

Essentially but not exactly, for as already stated the effects of higher differential pressures may serve to decrease filter service life by compacting the filter cake and by tending to cause surface blockage of the filter pores by compaction of the particulates. This would attenuate the rates of flow, and, almost certainly, the throughput volume of the filter. The use of higher inlet pressure creates higher pressure differentials across the filter and produces shorter filter service lives with foreshortened throughput volumes.

There is, therefore, an economic trade-off to the use of higher inlet pressure levels. A filter's throughput volume, abbreviated to whatever extent by the effects of higher differential pressures, is more rapidly attained at higher inlet pressures. The trade-off is between throughput volume and time. It will be advantageous to secure the larger throughput volumes characteristic of lower inlet pressures in constant pressure filtrations only to the extent of longer time.

Overdesign

There is always an area of uncertainty regarding the accuracy of extrapolations made from small trials to larger operations. Flow decay measurements are no exception. In addition to the variables of EFA and operating conditions mentioned previously, two other factors can seriously affect the accuracy of the tests. These are changes in particle distribution/burden/cleanliness of the fluid, and fluid/system dynamics. To account for these variables, filtration engineers often will "oversize" the calculation by a factor of 1 1/2–2 times. Their intention is the commendable one of avoiding costly underdesign, which entails interim, often prohibited, filter changes and insufficient housing capacity. Far more economical, it is commonly reasoned, to spend unnecessarily, but not extravagantly so, for added filters than to be saddled with an installed system insufficient for its purposes. However, justified the practice, it should not serve as a substitute for responsible conclusions being drawn from precise flow decay determinations, as oversizing systems has in itself detriments, for example, yield losses due to higher unspecific adsorption and hold-up volumes. It is suggested that any appropriate correction of this type be factored into the equation after completing system sizing, rather than after the flow decay.

It is very possibly that the degree of overdesign may become stipulated by the filter holder hardware. Thus, if a water purification system were to require five 10-in. (24.9-cm) cartridges in parallel to deliver the necessary flow, then a seven-cartridge housing would be indicated (assuming that five- or six-cartridge housings were not available in the market). Automatically, the five-cartridge system would become oversized by two cartridges or 1.4 times. Here the degree of overdesign would be permitted to rest, particularly if the next larger available housing were for 14 cartridges.

When the system becomes sized, its EFA will usually reflect the most arduous demands, such as the peak flow rates. The accommodation of these conditions obviously requires a larger filter area than would an averaged or more modest constant rate of flow. There are engineering alternatives to such problems. Thus, the use of a storage vessel, where such a device can be tolerated and properly maintained, may permit system sizing on the basis of averaged rates of flow. The filter requirements would then be diminished.

Conclusion

A filterability trial is the most cost-effective method for selecting filter types, pore sizes, and filter areas, particularly in a new system. The purpose of a flow decay is to provide information on the particle distribution of the fluid to be filtered, as also on the interaction between the fluid and the filter media. Flow decays can be performed quickly and easily in "indicator trials" in a matter of hours using small-disk filters and are often performed by the filter manufacturer's application specialists. These experts not only run the small scale, filter disc indicator trials effectively, but also often have the experience to choose certain filter combinations for specific application at hand. Even with the expertise of the specialists and, nowadays automated filterability test systems, small-disc filter trials cannot be linearly scaled to the commercial size filter system. Thus, "verification trials" should follow to more quantitatively confirm the results gained from using 47-mm disc filter indicator trials. It is from the "verification trials" with small pleated devices that the flow and blocking modifications introduced by cartridge constructions can be evaluated and allowed for. The results forthcoming from the more focused "verification trials" are then extrapolated to the full-scale pleated cartridges needed to accommodate full productions.

The completion of this series of preliminary filterability or flow decay evaluations, designed to progressively and realistically address production requirements, will provide objectively accurate data leading to the choice of proper PF/FF combinations in the appropriate ratio of their filter areas.

REFERENCES

Aicholtz, P., Wilkins, R., and Gabler, R. (1987). Sterile filtration under conditions of high pressure and bacterial challenge levels, *J Parenter Drug Assoc 41*: 117–120.

CPMP—EMEA (April 1996). Note for Guidance in Manufacture of the Finished Dosage Form.

FDA (2004). *Guideline on Sterile Drug Products Produced by Aseptic Processing*, Center for Drugs and Biologics and Office of Regulatory Affairs. Food and Drug Administration, Rockville, MD.

HIMA (1982). *Microbial Evaluation of Filters for Sterilizing Liquids*, Document No. 3, Volume 4, Health Industry Manufacturers Association, Washington, D.C.

Green, H. and Meltzer, T.H. (1987). Chapter 10, Flow & Pressure, Filter Sizing and Filter System Design, in Meltzer, T.H. *Filtration in the Pharmaceutical Industry*, Marcel Dekker, New York.

Green, H. and Scheer, L.A. (1998). Chapter 12, Sizing Microporous Membrane Filter Systems, in Meltzer, T.H. and Jornitz, M.W. *Filtration in the Biopharmaceutical Industry*, Marcel Dekker, New York.

Johnston, P.R. (1992). Liquid Flow through a Single Tube, in Johnston, P.R. (Ed.) *Fluid Sterilisation by Filtration* p. 29, Interpharm Press, Buffalo Grove, IL.

Johnston, P.R. (2003). *Fluid Sterilization By Filtration*, 3rd Edition, pg. 7, Interpharm/CRC, New York, NY.

Jornitz, T.H. and Meltzer, T.H. (2001). Chapter 4, Flow Decay, Filter Sizing, in Jornitz, T.H. and Meltzer, T.H. (Eds.) *Sterile Filtration: A Practical Approach*, Marcel Dekker, New York.

Jornitz, M.W., Meltzer T.H., and Lindenblatt J. (2004). The Filtration Debate. *Pharmaceutical Formulation and Quality.* May, pp. 89–93.

Jornitz, M.W., Meltzer T.H., Bromm H., and Priebe P.M. (2004). Testing for the optimal filter membrane, required prerequisites, *Genet Eng News* 24(13): 89–93.

Jornitz, M.W., Meltzer T.H., and Garafola, W. (2009). The proper use of 47-mm flat disc filters in filter sizing studies, *BioPharm Int* 22(9).

Leahy, T.J. and Sullivan, M.J. (1978). Validation of bacterial retention capabilities of membrane filters, *Pharm Technol* 2(11): 64–75.

Meltzer, T.H. and Lindenblatt, J. (2002). Selecting 0.1 or 0.2/0.22-rated filters: Consideration of rates of flow, *Eur J Parenter Sci* 7(4): 111–114.

Priebe, P.M., Jornitz, M.W., and Meltzer, T.H. (2003), Making an Informed Membrane Filter Choice, *Bioprocess International*, October 2003: 64–66.

Reti, A.R., Leahy, T.J., and Meier, P.M. (1979). The Retention Mechanism of Sterilizing and Other Submicron High Efficiency Filter Structures, *Proceedings of the Second World Filtration Congress*, pp. 427–436, London.

Tanny, G.B., Strong, D.K, Presswood, W.G., and Meltzer, T.H. (1979). The adsorptive retention of pseudomonas diminuta by membrane filters, *J Parenter Drug Assoc* 33(1): 40–51.

Trotter, A.M., Meltzer, T.H., Bai, F., and Thomas, L. (2000). Integrity test measurements—Effects of bacterial cell loadings, *Pharm Technol* 24(3): 72–80.

Trotter A.M., Rodriguez P.J., and Thoma L.A. (2002). The usefulness of 0.45 μm—Rated filter membranes, *Pharm Technol* 26(4): 60–71.

Wrasidlo W. and Mysels K.J. (1984). The structure and some properties of graded highly asymmetric porous membranes, *J Parenter Sci Technol* 38(1): 24–31.

8

Stainless Steel Application and Fabrication in the Biotech Industry

Joseph Manfredi
GMP Systems, Inc.

CONTENTS

Introduction

When viewed against the scale of world history, both biopharmaceuticals and stainless steel are virtual newborns. Notwithstanding, however, since its discovery little more than a hundred years ago, stainless steel has become a significant material choice for numerous and varied processing industries including food, beverage, drugs, and cosmetics, yet these represent only the tip-of-the-iceberg when one considers the breath of its application range in medical devices, power generation, automotive systems, architecture, maritime use, chemicals, kitchen appliances, barbecues, furniture, transportation, and aerospace.

Within this chapter, a brief history of the pharmaceutical industry will partially parallel the development of stainless steel alloys to provide background and allow for an understanding of their convergence. In addition, a basic explanation of stainless steel metallurgy, corrosion resistance, and application will be provided prior to discussion of fabrication and polishing.

Since the breadth and depth of this subject cannot be fully explored within the confines of a small section of this text, only general summary information will be offered primarily as a companion to the other materials which are the real subject matter of this volume. Much of this information has been simplified for that reason, and there may be instances where this summarization will result in explanations that will be less than fully correct from a rigorous scientific or technical perspective.

A Brief History of Pharmaceuticals

The recorded history of pharmaceutical products dates to at least as far back as 3,000 BC based on the discovery of Sumerian tablets from that era inscribed with human prescriptions. Over the course of the ensuing 5,000 years, events throughout the centuries crisscross the globe from Baghdad to New York City as the efficacy, quality, and safety of pharmaceutical products evolve, struggling through ethical and developmental crises, constantly improving both the duration and quality of life we enjoy today and expect to enjoy even more fully in the future.

Often, the process has been painfully slow with the vast majority of significant improvement in drug discovery, development, processing, and delivery occurring during the last 100 years.

The student of pharmaceutical history will find more than ample material for further study in topics such as the Magna Carta of Pharmacy, the first Pharmacopeia, Germ Theory, Paracelsus, and Variolation, as well as a plethora of other events, individuals, and activities that have ever so painstakingly moved the pharmaceutical industry from a black art to a serious and critical science. Those with an interest can easily find substantial data to detail this development including especially important ethical and legal milestones.

During ancient times, as might be expected, drugs and their ingredients were natural substances obtained from plants, animals, and the earth. They were stored in what were then suitable and appropriate containers, including earthenware vessels, animal skin pouches, and bone, rock, or wood receptacles fabricated using implements that we would undoubtedly consider extremely crude, by today's standards.

Certainly, during those times, the interaction between the ingredients and their containers was of little or no concern and undoubtedly the mere ability to enclose and somewhat protect these materials was their most significant benefit.

Thankfully, as time unfolded, humankind developed tools, materials, and techniques that would spur further advancement, and is reflected in the birth of modern chemistry, metallurgy, manufacturing, and medicine.

Not surprisingly however, the field of medicine has often lagged behind many of the other areas of science. This was especially evident during wartime periods when developments in transportation, munitions, and armament were put to use, far exceeding the ability of physicians and pharmacists to care for those surviving the carnage. Of note, there were less than 24 effective drugs known prior to 1700, and most of those were plant based including such items as aloe, figs, and *senna*. Additionally, alcohol predominated in most early remedies obviously because of its numbing and/or euphoric effects.

During the ensuing post-Sumerian millennia one might have expected to see significant improvement in pharmaceutical products and medical technology; however, as late as 1878, it was still relatively common for prescriptions to have little or no scientific merit, such as this script written by Dr. H. C. Wood for peritonitis, an inflammation of the stomach lining (Dowling, 1970) (Figure 8.1).

During much of medical history, societies endured in spite of the treatments and their practitioners. Medical care was often the purview of witchdoctors, priests, minstrels, traveling salesmen, carnies, and other charlatans, making healthcare a source of concern, uncertainty, and most often, fear for the patient.

Drugs, primarily from plant and animal sources, were variable in their effectiveness at best and in the hands of the unscrupulous, ranged from ineffectual to lethal.

Dr. H.C. Wood-1878
Prescription for Peritonitis

- Bleed patient until faint.
- Apply leeches to the abdomen.
- Multiple doses of calomel (laxative).
- Render unconscious with opium.

FIGURE 8.1 Past treatment example of peritonitis.

Neither practitioners nor patients understood drug activity within the body and the study of pharmacokinetics and pharmacodynamics had yet to come into existence.

Fortunately, over time, advances in materials allowed for somewhat improved formulation and storage of products and ingredients. Elegant constructs such as glass and ceramic were pressed into service, although certain more basic and traditional materials remained prevalent.

As we approached the 20th century, in a practical sense, we had moved significantly ahead, but in a real sense, our medicines and understanding remained primitive.

By this time, drug product development had become the realm of the chemist and pharmacist, although processes had been improved and refined, a huge gap remained between the chemistry capable of producing active entities and our ability to formulate, dose, and safeguard patients.

Many of the issues faced in the drug arena were also stumbling blocks for the food and beverage industries, and it may be surmised that similar challenges combined with the U.S. Food and Drug Administration (FDA) as a common regulatory base, led to parallel solutions and the ability to apply technology across marketplaces.

One of the most significant and defining moments for pharmaceuticals came in large part as a result of events involving the food processing industry, based on the publication of *The Jungle* by Upton Sinclair in 1906. Unsanitary and dangerous conditions in the Chicago meat packing industry were exposed by Sinclair, and when word of these problems was made public, and in light of other known and serious cases of food and drug adulteration, enactment of the Pure Food and Drug Act under then President Teddy Roosevelt was inevitable.

During the same general historical timeframe, humankind's development of implements advanced from Stone Age to Bronze Age and eventually to the modern era. During the 18th and 19th centuries, the use of iron and the development of steel allowed for the fabrication of machinery and tools; however, these materials were susceptible to atmospheric corrosion and had limited application in wet environments especially when salts were present.

Hence, as early as 1821, scientists and metallurgists, recognizing the need for noncorroding metals especially for cutlery, began experimentation using chromium to enhance the properties of iron and steel. Dozens of alloys were created, throughout much of that century, ranging from Ferrochromium to numerous types of steel containing varying amounts of chrome, nickel, carbon, and other alloying materials.

Unfortunately, much of the early work missed its mark based on crude investigations, weak research, and bad luck. The most significant issues related to the failure to properly understand the interaction between alloying substances and development of appropriate test methodology.

Finally, during the late 1800s scientists began to recognize these gaps in exploring mid-range alloy formulations and the relationships between alloying materials. As a result, early forms of the family of alloys we today call "stainless steels" began to emerge.

Interestingly, as we began the 20th century, glass, ceramic, tin, and other fairly common materials continued to be mainstays in drug manufacture while differing "schools of thought" began to emerge in other industries, especially food processing.

In spite of the relative inertness of glass and ceramics, these materials were perceived, albeit inappropriately, to be weak and susceptible to breakage. This, coupled with their limited options for fabrication, opened the door to other materials better suited to market requirements wherein dairies and food processing plants were among the earliest users of stainless steels.

Stainless Steel Development

Stainless steel itself is not an alloy, but rather it is a family or group of alloys based on the addition of greater than 10%–12% chromium to iron or steel which imparts resistance to chemical attack similar to noble metals such as gold (Zapffe, 1949).

The quest to develop stainless steels was not based on a burning need within the healthcare industry but was based on the cost of corrosion of iron and steel which had been estimated to average approximately $3.5 billion annually between 1900 and 1950 (Zapffe, 1949). It was that cost that motivated scientists and metallurgists to seek an alloy that would not rust or corrode under normal atmospheric conditions. Little did they know how successful they would be once the alloying puzzle was completed, "enabling a new era in engineering," (Zapffe, 1949) that would go far beyond the basic corrosion-resistant features of stainless steel.

Initial work begun by Bertier in 1821 resulted in the creation of Ferrochromium, but it would take another 100 years before the primary grades of stainless would be determined and their characters understood. During this period, dozens contributed significantly including such prominent names as Guillet, Monnartz, Giesen, Brearley, Portevin, Maurer, Strauss, Becket, Dantsizen, Field, and Monypenny.

When considering stainless steels of any type, the underlying principle that must be recognized is passivity, for it is passivity that gives stainless steel its stainlessness and corrosion resistance. Passivity is ultimately based on a chromium-enriched (iron-depleted) oxide film that occurs on the surface of the metal. Chrome/iron ratios in the range of 0.8–1.2 are fairly common, with higher ratios more desirable. Passivity will be discussed in further detail in subsequent pages; however, it will remain the most important underpinning for the application and use of stainless steels.

The discovery of stainless steels and those responsible has been chronicled by numerous authors; however, it is appropriate to make specific note of the text, *Stainless Steels*, written by Carl A. Zapffe (1949), that this author has used extensively as a reference. Zapffe makes note of the discovery of the constitution, corrosion resistance, and industrial usefulness of stainless steels including assignation of those individuals that were most responsible. *Stainless Steels* remains an extremely valuable reference volume in spite of its 1949 date of publication and it is well worth the effort to locate and obtain a copy.

Stainless steels are often classified by their structure using roman numerals, and Zapffe identifies three classes. Class I stainless steels are referred to as "martensitic stainless steels" because martensite characterizes their microstructure when hardened. This particular feature also gives rise to alternative nomenclature such as "hardening" or "hardenable" stainless steels, typically by way of heat treatment.

Class II alloys are characterized by an extremely low carbon content resulting in an iron-chrome alloy more appropriately defined as a type of iron than as a type of steel. Notwithstanding, this group is designated "ferritic stainless steel," again based on its microstructure, comprised primarily of ferrite.

Finally, Class III alloys include the grade commonly referred to as 18-8 stainless steels with approximately 18% chromium and 8% nickel. These grades are designated "austenitic stainless steels" with a microstructure based on "austenite."

Details of the exact structure, formation, phase transition, and subphases for each of the classes are beyond the scope of this text. Extensive research has been performed in these areas and an abundance of material is available for anyone interested in expanding their knowledge base.

Class I stainless steel usually includes chromium in the range of 12%–17%, while Class II grades have chromium between 18% and 30%. Class III alloys include chromium in the range of 8%–30%; however, this group introduces nickel as another major alloying material and may also include molybdenum as well as other lesser-used materials.

Microstructure designations will be reviewed more fully on subsequent pages along with additional detail, while remaining true to the simplifications applied thus far.

Passivity

Returning to the subject of passivity, it should be made clear that passivity is a condition of negligible corrosion rather than noncorrosion, and passivity is relative since material that is passive with regard to a particular medium may not be passive, or may corrode, in another.

The passive layer, or film, that protects the stainless steel is extremely thin, estimated on the order of 5–50 Å (1 Å = 1 ten billionth of a meter), yet is capable of endowing the material with corrosion resistance near that of noble metals such as gold, silver, and platinum. This passive film occurs when the chromium content of the steel nears 12% and improves to some extent with increasing chromium levels as well as with the addition of nickel and possibly other substances to the alloy.

It should also be noted that damage to a passive surface results in de-passivation, or activation, of the material allowing chemical attack to occur. Hence, in dynamic applications, such as those within a pharmaceutical environment, passivity must be monitored and periodically re-passivation must occur to ensure a stable surface condition remains.

It is well recognized that passivity is naturally occurring in air; however, the rate and degree of passivation may be inadequate for a particular application depending on individualized circumstances.

Materials which have had adequate time to achieve passivity after fabrication will typically achieve a relatively high degree of passivity; however, naturally occurring passivity is still usually less robust than passivity artificially induced via a deliberate and methodical treatment process. Materials that have recently undergone fabrication of one type or another that disturbed the passive layer will most likely require re-passivation prior to being put into service, especially if the period prior to use is small or if the material might be inhibited in any way from achieving natural passivity.

Artificially induced passivity is usually implemented via a multistep process that includes a cleaning of the material surface to remove any grease, oil, or other contaminant that might interfere with passivation, typically using a mild caustic cleaner. The cleaning is followed by a passivation step whereby an oxidizing acid such as nitric, phosphoric, or citric, occasionally with additives such as chelants, contacts the metal surface expediting its passivation. Rinsing steps will most likely occur at various points in the process using water, keeping in mind that the quality of both the chemicals and the water must be appropriate for the application to avoid introduction of contaminants.

Passivation can be verified using an indirect test such as Ferroxyl (copper sulfate) as well as via electrochemical spot tests, readily in the field. Alternatively, direct tests such as Auger Electron Spectroscopy (AES) and X-Ray Photoelectron Spectroscopy (XPS), are also available for use; however, both are significantly more expensive, may require sample destruction and are more difficult to implement.

Since artificially induced, or assisted, passivation involves the handling and disposal of dangerous chemicals that may contain heavy metals, it is usually recommended that only firms with proper expertise perform the procedures, especially if they are required in a field setting rather than in a controlled manufacturing environment.

Preoperational passivation is a common requirement in the pharmaceutical and biotech industries and is accomplished in a relatively easy fashion as the metal has not been degraded, as yet, in any way by product contact. Re-passivation is often complicated by the presence of rouge on the surface of the stainless steel, which must be removed before any attempt at re-passivation should be made, as the rouge will typically not allow the required intimate contact between the passivating chemicals and the metal surface.

Passivity cannot be overemphasized as it is the singular primary reason that stainless steels exhibit their corrosion resistance. Incorrect alloying based on too little chromium, too much carbon, or improper levels of other constituents will result in a material unable to form a suitable film and not qualified to function as, or be termed, stainless steel. If insufficiently passive, any stainless steel will be subject to corrosion in varying degrees based on the condition of the surface film, the corrosive media, and other important factors such as temperature.

Corrosion

The corrosion resistance of stainless steel, as aforementioned, is based primarily on the passive film or coating that develops on the surface of the metal, hence retardation, destruction, or removal of the passive layer renders the surface nonpassive or active, and subject to corrosive attack. Although there were many who shared in the honor of discovering stainless steel, four names stand out as the most significant including Giesen, Guillet, Monnartz, and Portevin. Within that small group, it was Monnartz whose writings provided key insight into the nature of stainless steel by discovering that: (a) the corrosion resistance of 12% chromium steels increased dramatically; (b) passivity was responsible for the improved corrosion resistance; (c) passivity depended upon oxidation of the surface metal; (d) preoperational passivation improved performance in corrosive environments; (e) a relationship existed between passivity and the temperature of a corrosive environment; (f) formation of carbide precipitates retarded or prevented passivity; (g) carbon stabilized with other alloying elements such as molybdenum can be kept from interfering with corrosion resistance; and (h) addition of molybdenum had an especially favorable effect in enhancing corrosion resistance Zapffe (1949).

Stress corrosion cracking (SCC) or environmentally assisted cracking (EAC) of stainless steel can result in catastrophic failure and should obviously be avoided at all cost. This failure is typically the result of interaction between stress, the environment, and the materials microstructure. Failures of this type often involve chlorides and have occurred in the vicinity of swimming pools and as a result of chloride-containing insulation on stainless steel tanks and piping. Insulation-related failures have caused the shutdown of nuclear reactors and resulted in the rupture of tanks containing hot U.S. Pharmacopeia (USP) grades of water, causing serious personal injury to operations personnel.

Generally accepted theory today holds that pit corrosion may be the most common form of corrosive attack on stainless steel in pharmaceutical product contact applications. This type of corrosion is typically more subtle beginning with a surface defect or fault in the passive layer. As a result, the underlying metal begins to dissolve, leading to a buildup of positively charged metal ions. This in turn attracts negatively charged ions, most likely chlorides, to the vicinity, causing the local pH to drop to as low as 2–3, even in a neutral solution, and retards reformation of the passive film.

Pit initiation is not well understood; however, it is thought by Ryan et al. (Bhadeshia and Sourmail, 2005) that MnS (Manganese sulfide) inclusions, difficult to avoid in the manufacturing process, coincide with chromium depletion at the pit boundary. Pitting indexes can be calculated for the various grades of stainless steel and should be considered when making application selections.

Stainless alloys can become sensitized, and the resultant sensitization can allow stainless steel to undergo changes resulting in decreased corrosion resistance. The change that occurs is the formation and precipitation of chromium-rich carbides. The resulting chromium depletion at the grain boundaries results, even under stress-free conditions, in anodic intergranular attack.

Rouge

Rouge is an iron-based contamination on the surface of the stainless steel occurring most notably in aqueous environments, in varying colors, textures, and levels of adherence. The amount and degree of rouging is commonly based on temperature with higher temperatures resulting in darker colors and significantly stronger adherence. Rouge, in its initial stages, is typically orange or reddish-brown in color and loosely attached, often with a powdery look, and which may be removed by wiping using only a soft cloth. As rouge continues to develop, colors darken and surface bonding increases such that removal using chemical dissolution is required. In its worst stages, often found in clean steam systems, rouge is black in color and adhered so tightly that the aggression required to remove it will most probably damage the material surface significantly so as to require repolishing, if thinning has not progressed too far, or even replacement. Although research into the details of the rouging phenomenon is incomplete, it is believed that once rouge has adhered to the stainless surface pitting eventually commences, de-passivating and activating the surface of the metal, allowing further corrosion to occur. Hence, it is accepted practice to periodically derouge and then re-passivate the in-service metal initially based upon visual inspection techniques, and subsequently by extrapolation of historical data to determine a reliable and predictable schedule, as rouge formation is not usually erratic. Alternatively, rouge-monitoring equipment can be installed that will definitively measure the levels of rouge and its rate of progression, potentially reducing cost. Rouge removal may not be consistent from application to application or system to system, making it prudent to construct systems with removable coupons that can be tested offline for the purpose of determining a completely reliable removal procedure for a specific situation.

In spite of its unappealing look, rouge seldom causes purified water quality degradation and often only causes contamination of the products it contacts when it sloughs off of the stainless steel surface as undesirable particulate, and as is obvious, in all cases foreign particulate is undesirable and unacceptable in pharmaceutical and biotech products.

Tverberg (1998) has written extensively on rouge and metallurgical aspects of stainless steel and is an excellent reference for additional insight into these alloys as well as expanded understanding of the degrees, implications, and nature of stainless steel rouge, based on his in-depth research and substantial industrial experience.

Stainless Steel Classification

Returning to the discussion of microstructure, the division of stainless steels by class results in delineation of the primary types along with their basic characteristics; however, it should be noted that within each class Zapffe defines subclasses (typically three for each) which further differentiate the alloys within each group. Sequential lettering added to the numeral designation as in Class IIIa, IIIb, IIIc allows for the further classification as work hardenable, free spinning, and modified, respectively. It is also important to note that many of the categorizations used are generalizations which cannot be absolutely applied, but rather are provided for simplification purposes and to aid general understanding. As well, more current classifications alter slightly this subclass structure as will be mentioned in the following pages.

The terms ferrite, martensite, and austenite, previously mentioned, refer to the microstructure of the metal. Iron does not occur environmentally in its pure form because of its tendency to combine with other elements such as oxygen. Once extracted from its ore, if unprotected, iron will rapidly react in a reversion process, such as rusting, to its pre-purified form. Iron, in its pure form can exist with either a ferritic crystalline structure, depicted as a body-centered cubic atomic model, or as austenite represented by a face-centered cubic atomic model (Figure 8.2).

This allotropic character results in many technical nuances related to the atomic density; however, these issues are beyond the scope of this discussion. The third structure mentioned, martensite, can only occur in impure or alloyed iron and is "actually a distorted and unstable arrangement of atoms caught in transition from austenite to ferrite" (Zapffe, 1949). However, it is the very character of martensite that allows for hardening by heat treatment and its designated uses.

The family of alloys known as stainless steel is commonly depicted using a tree as the model. The basis for this appears to be with Zapffe, since *Stainless Steels*, published in 1949, begins with this artwork and includes no acknowledgment. However, it is interesting that many subsequent writers also utilize the "tree model" without assignment of credit to Zapffe or others.

In his graphic of the tree, Zapffe shows a simple trunk and limb structure emblazoned with the various classifications of stainless steel. The simplicity of the tree concept is superb for visualizing how the different classes and grades of stainless steel increase with the height of the tree, along with increasing chromium and cost. Without the benefit of hindsight, and recognizing the infancy of the industry, Zapffe refers to the limbs as branches; hence, the following explanations will continue that reference, at least in the short term.

Class I stainless steels as mentioned previously, are primarily martensite. The members of this class are hardenable via heat treatment, with corrosion resistance higher in the hardened forms, and as a result they are very well suited to uses such as surgical instruments, knives, fasteners, turbine parts, bearings, shafts, and springs. Also called "straight chromium" stainless steels, they exhibit lower corrosion resistance based on the chromium (12%–17%) and carbon (< 1% typically) constituent levels with few grades having other significant alloying materials. A number of the 400 series stainless steels are considered Class I including 403, 410, 414, 416, 420, 431, and 440. Class I members are usually magnetic and can be difficult to weld or fabricate while maintaining their martensitic structure. It is also worth noting that most Class I stainless steels require stress-relieving in their fully hardened condition, and

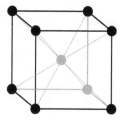
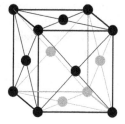

Body-Centered Cubic Model   **Face-Centered Cubic Model**

FIGURE 8.2   Microstructure atomic models.

that stress-relieving via heating will, of necessity, occur below the temperatures which might modify the martensitic structure of the material. Also, Class I stainless is often sensitive to embrittlement from hydrogen gas, particularly in the hardened condition. This can occur from moisture in the manufacturing process or from pickling solutions used in posttreatment. Class I stainless is represented as the "first branch" of Zapffe's tree although it is more appropriately described as the trunk, rooted in the ground where it connects to its iron source.

Class II stainless steels are typically referred to as ferritic or nonhardenable stainless steels based on the primarily ferrite crystalline structure that exists in the metal. These 400 series grades, including 405, 409, 430, 442, 443, and 446 contain chromium in the range of 12%–27% with carbon usually below 0.2% (except for 446 with 0.35% carbon maximum). These alloy variants are magnetic, cannot be hardened by heat treatment, although some can be work hardened, and are also difficult to weld. Applications vary widely including uses such as cooking utensils, architectural trim, chemical processing equipment, heating elements, automotive exhausts, fasteners, bank vaults, decking, and household appliances. Alloying substances beyond chromium are used, including aluminum, copper, tungsten, and silicon for benefits including improved weldability, greater hot strength, and higher oxidation resistance. These are the second branch of the Zapffe tree, having both higher corrosion resistance and higher cost, as depicted by their elevation on the tree.

The third and final branch of the Zapffe tree is the Class III alloys which are austenitic in structure. This group of materials includes 300 series stainless steels and utilizes additional alloying materials, most importantly nickel and molybdenum, for increased corrosion resistance and improved workability.

Austenitic alloys are typically nonmagnetic in the annealed condition and cannot be hardened by heat treatment although hardening by cold working is common. These grades, highest on the tree, represent the best corrosion resistance (especially 310, 316, and 317 grades) and have the added benefit of being easily welded. In addition, excellent cleanability and exceptional resistance to both high and low temperatures make these stainless steels well suited for application in food processing, kitchens/restaurants, architecture, pharmaceutical/biopharmaceutical manufacture, chemical processing, ovens, heat exchangers, marine applications, and hospitals. Of note, the substantial amount of 18-8 stainless steel designed into the Art Deco ornamental top of the Chrysler building in New York City by William Van Alen and completed in 1930 remains in excellent condition after many decades exhibiting remarkably little corrosion. Grades comprising Class III include 302, 304, 308, 310, 316, 317, 321, and 347 that typically fall into the 18-8 category with 18% chromium and 8% nickel. Grades such as 316 also include molybdenum represented, albeit incorrectly, as 18/8/3, for increased resistance to chloride corrosion. Carbon for these grades is kept typically in the range of 0.08%–0.20% although low carbon grades with 0.02%–0.03% maximum, discussed later in more detail, have grown in use significantly.

Sensitization, one potential weakness of these grades, should be recognized because of the potential formation of carbide precipitates and will be discussed again relative to welding and fabrication. As might be expected, the alloys in this class represent the more expensive of the basic grades of stainless steel.

As noted earlier, the depiction of stainless steel as a tree has continued extensively and as the industry has grown, so has the tree. Today, the primary tree remains as generally described by Zapffe; however, the original three classes are now better classified as limbs, rather than branches, and new limbs have "grown" and from these limbs new branches have also been added. This can be seen in Figure 8.3, reproduced with the kind permission of the Specialty Steel Industry of North America (SSINA)

This revised tree includes a fourth branch (limb) representing Duplex Stainless Steels, reclassified (modified) since Zapffe's time. These grades, such as 2205, are comprised of 18%–26% chromium and 4%–7% nickel, with a resulting crystalline structure that is a combination of ferrite and austenite, hence the name "Duplex." In addition, duplex grades generally have a higher resistance to stress corrosion and chloride attack making them more suitable than the 300 series for application with sea water, pickling, and desalination operations. Duplex stainless formulations exhibit excellent weldability and have the added benefit of increased strength, although relatively expensive.

The SSINA revised tree also depicts new branches representing development of "super" grades of ferritic, duplex, and austenitic stainless steel including alloys such as AL6XN shown below in Table 8.1 as compared to 304, 304L, 316, and 316L stainless steels.

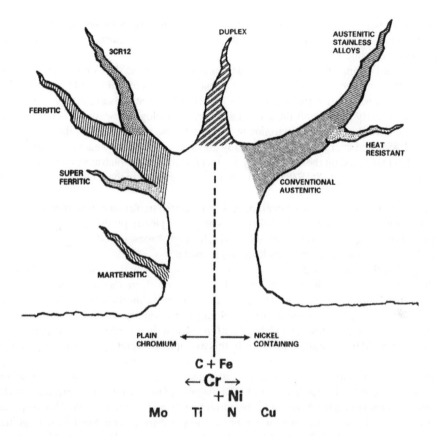

FIGURE 8.3 The stainless steel tree.

TABLE 8.1

Common Stainless Steels Compared by Composition

Material Grade	Percent Chromium	Percent Nickel	Percent Carbon (maximum)	Percent Iron	Percent Molybdenum
304SS	18–20	8–12	0.08	65–71	0
304LSS	18–20	8–12	0.03	65–71	0
316SS	16–18	10–14	0.08	62–69	2–3
316LSS	16–18	10–14	0.03	62–69	2–3
AL6XN	20–21	23–25	0.02	46–51	6–7

Application and Welding of Stainless Steel

As noted previously, the food and beverage industries quickly adopted stainless steel for use in processing because of its corrosion resistance, especially considering the heavy added stress imposed by routine cleaning regimens. Based on relatively low price and ease of fabrication, 304 stainless became the predominant material for use in these applications with vendors specializing in all manner of sanitary components that evolved to meet the demand of a constantly increasing population. In parallel with developing materials technology was the genesis of sanitization and sanitary design. The ability to clean and maintain stainless steel without the fear of corrosion coupled with a better understanding of microbiology and sanitation allowed for equipment and component design that would result in a quality revolution. Organizations such as the International Association of Milk, Food and Environmental

Sanitarians, then a part of the U.S. Public Health Service, developed a series of accepted standards and practices designated as "3A" to ensure the quality, consistency, and cleanability of equipment used in food and dairy processing.

This drive toward cleanability and sanitary design ensured that the developing industry would take full advantage of the properties of stainless steel especially during fabrication and finishing. It is prudent to mention, at this juncture, that the use of series 304 stainless steel was eventually transferred to the pharmaceutical industry along with the related sanitary technology; however, 304SS was considered inadequate for the tougher pharma environment. Eventually the pharmaceutical industry standardized on the use of 316SS, and later 316LSS, for virtually all stainless process contact applications. This may have occurred in part based on the use of stainless steel for high purity pharmaceutical water and steam systems, operating at or above 185°F (85°C) temperature, since water in these circumstances can become very aggressive.

The actual manufacture of stainless steel, often in an electric arc furnace, is beyond the scope of this discourse; however, the resulting ingots, billets, or slabs are typically produced and used subsequently, via forging or hot rolling, to form various standard sizes and shapes, of rod, bar, sheet, and plate. It is from these forms that most secondary fabrications are made.

For example, in the case of a processing vessel 8′ in diameter with 8′ sidewall, multiple standard size sheets of stainless would most likely be welded together to form the body, or shell of the vessel. Assuming for this example standard sheets of 4′ × 8′, more than six sheets would be required to form the body, and as well, the top and bottom of the vessel might also require fabrication from more than one sheet. It should be noted that sheet and plate differ typically in their thickness and depending upon the application, plate could be substituted for sheet in this example, if operating pressure so dictated.

Another example is the stainless steel tube and pipe used throughout pharmaceutical and biopharmaceutical processing plants as structural members, to transfer ingredients, finished product, and utilities, and even to serve as conduit for electrical wires. The majority of this material is fabricated from flat stock of appropriate thickness that has been cut to the correct width and is often coiled. This strip material is then processed through a set of dies that form it into the proper shape prior to longitudinal welding to create the finished tubular product. Tubing, 1.5″ and larger, is typically made in this fashion based on cost; however, tubing below 1.5″ may also be welded or may be seamless based on economics. Large diameter (>1″) seamless tubing is available in very limited supply and seldom used due to the extremely high cost on a per-foot basis. It should be noted that tubing is typically defined by its outer diameter such that 2″ tubing measures exactly 2″ OD, whereas pipe is typically defined by its interior diameter making 2″ pipe only nominally 2″ on the ID. As well, tube wall is most often referred to by gauge, such as 16 gauge (measuring 0.065″ for 2″ OD size) whereas pipe is typically produced in schedules such as Schedule 5 (measuring 0.065″ for 2″ Schedule 5 pipe size).

Since the tolerances for tubing are frequently more stringent, tubing has become the standard for polished sanitary materials, as control of wall thickness can be better achieved. Specifications that provide for dimensional tolerances of both pipe and tube were developed by the American Society for Testing Materials (ASTM) including standards such as ASTM-A312, ASTM-A269, and ASTM-A270, the latter of which defines specific tolerances for tube that will be polished, primarily for sanitary application.

Another important aspect of sanitary materials is the method by which fittings and accessories are created. Elbows used to construct transfer systems are made from the tubing described above that has been cut into sections specifically for that purpose and then bent appropriately to create the proper shape. Tees that allow for connection of instruments and which also serve to split flow are also manufactured from the same tubing. Cut sections are placed into a fixture and a hole is drilled in the side. A forming sphere of the correct size is then pulled through the hole creating a collar on which an extension is welded. This method is less expensive and provides a higher quality than alternatives such as saddle welding to create the same type tee fitting. Additional types of fittings such as reducers, adapters, caps, and sanitary flanges (ferrules) are manufactured by various techniques including machining, forming, and in the case of clamps used to join two sanitary flanges, forging.

It should also be noted that the requirements for dimensional accuracy of sanitary materials goes beyond that needed simply for polishing. Sanitary fittings are specially designed to create a cleanable interior surface. Sanitary flanges are constructed to align precisely when assembled to minimize any hold-up of product or cleaning chemical, as even minute amounts can result in bacterial proliferation, cross contamination, or contamination byproducts that might adulterate subsequent batches. It is for this reason that standard threaded connections, flanges, and other non-sanitary joining components and methods are unacceptable in virtually all pharmaceutical product contact applications. Sanitary fittings must be dimensionally accurate so that they also align perfectly for welding, especially with automated equipment, which will be discussed later, for the same reasons as when assembling via clamps and gaskets. Gaskets for sanitary applications are specially designed to ensure proper alignment and minimal gasket intrusion into the product area, providing proper torque is applied. Notwithstanding, sanitary fittings for assembly of components should be used sparingly and appropriately to facilitate disassembly for service, repair, and replacement. Even though sanitary fittings are designed to provide a high level of cleanability and reliability, their use should be weighed carefully against the use of welding and applied only as needed to suit the application since welding is far superior in joint integrity without the requirements for gasket replacement and retightening of clamps on a continuing life cycle basis.

Polishing of stainless steel is another critical aspect of producing high-quality sanitary materials. Polishing can be accomplished either mechanically, using abrasives or electrochemically in a process called electropolishing, although electropolishing is usually applied over a high-quality mechanical finish. Polishing will be discussed in further detail in subsequent sections.

Stainless steels can be joined by most conventional techniques including welding, brazing, and soldering; however, welding provides the highest quality and strongest joint especially when polishing is required. Welding is the only practical way to permanently join multiple pieces of stainless steel together so that they act as a single piece.

Welding as defined by the American Welding Society (AWS) and quoting Cary, is "a localized coalescence of metals or nonmetals produced either by heating the materials to suitable temperature with or without the application of pressure or by the application of pressure alone with or without the use of filler material" (Cary, 1979).

Welding using the Oxy-Fuel Gas process is typically the only gas process utilized and is limited to sheet typically not thicker than 3 mm. This limitation is based on slower heating and the large area affected by the flame. Other techniques often utilized are electrically driven and include shielded metal arc welding (SMAW) and gas tungsten arc welding (GTAW); however, it should be noted that no less than 12 alternative methods are also in use, based on the material grade, thickness, desired speed, and quality requirements. Electrically driven welding can be configured as straight polarity where the electrode is negative, focusing maximum heat at the electrode or reverse polarity with the electrode positive, focusing maximum heat at the workpiece. As noted, many welding processes may be capable of performing the work; however, the determination of which welding process is most suitable for an application may be driven by cost or quality considerations. For most commercial applications, speed translates to lower cost with value measured by "deposition rates" based on the amount of filler metal deposited during the welding process. Yet it may surprise those unfamiliar with the breath of the welding industry that 500,000 tons of filler materials were sold along with $1.2 billion in welding equipment during 1976 alone (Cary, 1979).

SMAW is also termed "stick" welding and involves a coated consumable electrode, the core of which becomes part of the finished weld. The coating on the outside of the "stick" protects the molten metal from the atmosphere and results in slag formation that is typically chipped away after the weld is completed. The welder wears a helmet (also called a shield) with a filtered lens that provides protection for the face, neck and eyes from heat, radiation, and spatter that would cause injury.

The other process mentioned is GTAW (or just GTA) called alternatively, tungsten inert gas (TIG) welding that utilizes a nonconsumable tungsten electrode and inert gas for shielding in lieu of the coating used with SMAW. The electrodes are usually alloys themselves with materials such as thorium and cesium added to increase their effectiveness. These radioactive additives can cause safety concerns and must not be overlooked especially where large volumes of the material might be stored. Tungsten, with the highest melting point of all metals, at 6,170°F (3,410°C), is ideally suited for service as a welding electrode. Electrodes for manual welding are typically ground to a sharp point to create a small precisely focused arc and their length is of minimal concern since the arc gap is controlled by the welder. Alternatively, for most sanitary orbital welding, dimensional control of the electrode is more critical.

Arc gap is a function of electrode length hence precise control is necessary for proper welding and required by the equipment. In addition, the tip is ground parallel to its length and a flat is added in lieu of a point. These modifications serve to direct and control the arc more fully.

The inert gases utilized are typically argon or helium (sometimes also referred to as Heli-Arc); however, other gases such as nitrogen, even though not inert, are occasionally used for specialized applications. Argon predominates in sanitary stainless applications and can also be applied as a mixture with helium or hydrogen. These mixture gases provide the attraction of reduced heat input required to accomplish the same function as would be accomplished with only pure argon with higher heat. In addition, the purity of welding gases can impact the quality of the finished weld. Industrial grades of gas, termed "pre-purified" may have purity levels of 99.996%; however, it is not uncommon for levels 99.998% or higher to be specified. Shielding gases can be supplied either in liquid form or as a compressed gas. Containers or cylinders used for compressed gas are typically smaller than those designed for liquid materials making justification of liquid more difficult for smaller projects even though liquid materials typically offer higher purity levels and are less costly per cubic foot.

GTA/TIG has numerous advantages when compared to SMAW as it allows for more precise control, a cleaner weld exterior, and the flexibility to use filler material or to simply fuse the parts together. There are also advantages relative to automation as well.

The welding processes discussed above are traditionally manual, requiring a skilled welder to control every aspect of the process. This is no small feat as there are a significant number of variables requiring simultaneous action. As noted above, a welder will typically require a helmet with protective lens as the arc that is developed is so bright that extended direct viewing would cause blindness. In addition, the lens is often so dark as to block all ambient light prior to arc strike. Hence, the welder is unable to see the torch or the part before welding commences, making setup extremely difficult. To alleviate this problem, most helmets either tilt or have lenses that tilt so the welder is able to get into position and then lower the shield. Newer electronic helmets have become available in the last 10 years. These helmets offer the advantage of viewing through a clear lens until the instant of arc strike with automatic dimming in milliseconds to protect the welder's eyes.

Traditionally, GTA/TIG welding required electrode contact with the part to initiate the arc, often termed "scratch starting." This process was difficult, as contact longer than an instant resulted in fusing of the electrode to the part with resulting contamination of both the electrode and the stainless material. Newer high frequency "arc starters" function in a fashion similar to lightning by ionizing the local gas allowing the arc to "jump" from the torch to the workpiece without direct contact, provided they are in reasonable proximity and based on the voltage potential.

During the welding process the arc gap must be maintained relatively constant as the welder traverses the seam to be welded. Virtually any size or shape part must be accommodated, requiring the welder to move longitudinally at a constant speed while maintaining a constant arc gap. Hence, for our purposes, it should be sufficient to note that high-quality welding requires, at a minimum, excellent eye-hand coordination, superior reactions, significant stamina, adequate training, and continued practice.

The standardization by pharma on 300 series stainless reminds us of the issues relating to sensitization that can occur. When many austenitic stainless steels remain in the temperature range of 400°C–800°C for more than 2–3 min, sensitization occurs, resulting in carbide precipitation and significantly reduced corrosion resistance of the material. There are methods that can be employed to minimize the potential for sensitization including rapid welding, with minimum heat buildup, which allows the material to cool quickly enough so that time spent in the sensitization range is below that where carbide precipitation would occur. In addition, low carbon grades of stainless, designated with the suffix "L" can be employed, that by their nature alone, minimize the potential for carbide precipitates, and when applied in conjunction with techniques such as precision welding, multiply the benefit.

A third method is the implementation of automated welding to eliminate the variability created by the manual welding process and ensure, via precise control of heating, the time spent at the sensitization temperature is below that required for carbide precipitation to occur.

Over the decades, numerous methods for automating various welding processes have been implemented. These have ranged from simple fixtured torches to welding lathes, to today's laser-guided computer-controlled robots. In a factory environment and based on production scale quantities, many component and equipment manufacturers have invested in automated machinery that can improve quality, precision, and yield. Whether creating seam-welded tubing, process vessels, machine components, fittings, or filter housings, automated welding is applied to ensure the products produced meet the highest quality standards and are done so reliably. One particular variation of automatic welding, originally developed for the aerospace industry, is termed orbital welding and is used in the welding of circular materials, most typically tube, pipe, and components similarly shaped.

Orbital welding power supplies typically utilize electronics to control both the power supplied for welding and the action of the special torch that is required for the process. Controllers can range from simple microprocessors to sophisticated computers; however, the overall process is relatively consistent from vendor to vendor and relies on the basics of TIG with improvements over the recognized manual process.

Torches for orbital welding have been in existence for more than 40 years and are available in two basic types, open and closed. Open orbital weld torches, or heads, utilize a fairly common TIG torch configuration with electrode holder surrounded by a ceramic cup that is used to distribute the inert gas. The torch is attached to a fixture that clamps onto a circular part and precisely rotates the torch head around the part during the welding process. Weld quality is extremely high; although the outside of the weld is typically oxidized since the gas cup only provides coverage immediately adjacent to the electrode. Torches of this type are suitable for tube and pipe applications, structural parts, and machinery components, but do not offer the highest quality available and are therefore not commonly used for pharmaceutical product contact materials unless subsequent machining, polishing, or rework is involved. Alternatively, the enclosed weld torch offers a far superior level of quality based on its unique design. Closed weld heads surround the weld joint a full 360° with inert gas, minimizing any exterior discoloration and oxidation. Some designs even assist by using the exterior purge gas to provide support for the molten puddle, minimizing possible sag that might result in irregularity of the interior surface. In addition to the inherent advantages of these more sophisticated torches, a technique for precise temperature control is commonly employed, termed pulsed arc, whereby the power source pulses the arc at predetermined increments from a high current to a lower, or background current. These pulsations occur in rapid succession allowing the molten metal to cool on each low pulse, effectively creating many overlapping spot welds. The pattern that is created, when graphed, resembles a square wave, and cycle times of 1/10 s are fairly common. For thicker materials this process can be augmented by a stepping function, called step pulsing that stops the electrode rotation during high pulse allowing greater penetration. Alternatively, for very light gauge materials, speed ramping can accentuate the pulsed arc process by increasing the rotational speed as the material is heated so as to avoid overheating or damage to the part.

Every type of orbital weld head rotates the electrode around the circumference of the part maintaining a precise arc gap, while also offering excellent rotational speed accuracy for superb control of heating. The heads themselves do not rotate and are generally small and compact in size allowing welds to be made in extremely restricted spaces and in virtually any position. Weld heads are designed such that each head can accommodate a range of sizes, minimizing the cost of automation and the amount of hardware required. Control for the torch comes from programming within the power supply, typically downloaded into the machine's memory by the factory or input by the operator. Programming variations range from simple hard-wired thumb wheels, to factory "burned" EPROMS (erasable, programmable, read-only memory) to simple electronic programmers, to computer interfaces, to flash memory cards or memory sticks.

Programming allows for the weld to be divided into segments, typically by degrees, with precise control of current, voltage, rotational speed, and time in each segment. Power supplies are often equipped with printers that can provide data that may be useful in validating the quality of the work and may also include feedback electronics to alarm in the event of a problem. Programming override by operators is typically limited to minimize the potential for error and ensure consistency.

Open weld heads have the ability, as with manual TIG, to fuse two parts together with or without the use of filler metal, which if used, must of course be proper. However, closed weld heads are autogenous in that only butt fusion occurs since the use of filler material is not an option due to their nature. The joint configuration is commonly termed square-butt based on AWS standard terminology and requires precise end preparation so as to avoid gaps that would thin the wall or cause blow-through when welding with an autogenous process. In addition, burrs that would change the arc gap, improperly created tack welds, tungsten inclusions, surface contaminants, and beveled edges can negatively impact the finished weld quality ultimately resulting in rejection.

Automated welding has served to reduce the likelihood of sensitization significantly and, when used in conjunction with "L," or low carbon, grades of stainless, such as 316LSS, has almost completely eliminated carbide precipitation as a concern for most light gauge applications commonly found in healthcare product manufacturing facilities.

In spite of the small amount of carbon in stainless steel, its ability to interfere with the corrosion resistance of the alloy is substantial and warrants repeated mention. Worthy of note as well is that other minor constituents can also significantly impact the function of stainless steel. Sulfur for one, at levels below those specified, impedes the welding process by changing the material's heat transfer characteristics, ultimately resulting in widened weld beads that do not penetrate through the metal thickness, potentially causing rejectable weld defects associated with incomplete fusion. As already mentioned, autogenous orbital welding requires very high dimensional tolerances since any small gap between the parts can result in failure, thinning that causes structural weakening, and/or depressions in which organisms may proliferate. To overcome this and other potential problems, specialized tools have been designed to support orbital welding units including cutting and facing tools that prepare the ends to be welded so that they are square and true. Other tools, such as oxygen analyzers, to ensure elimination of oxygen from the weld zone, and borescopes, for internal inspection, are needed to ensure the quality of the finished weld. It is also worth noting that virtually every aspect of the welding process is precisely controlled from verification of materials via material (or mill) test reports (MTRs), to confirmation of test welds, to the cleanliness of wipes used in preparation, to purity of gas that shields the weld. This is especially necessary for pharmaceutical ingredient or product distribution systems since these welds cannot be polished after they are made and hence must be reliably of the highest quality.

Although discussion of support tools cannot be addressed in full detail within these confines, two specific types justify further comment, including cutting/facing tools and inspection equipment.

Tools used to cut or face materials in preparation for welding must typically accomplish two goals; the first of which is creating an edge or surface suitable for the process. This might involve straight cuts, bevels, tapers, or other suitable configuration. Some methods lack the required accuracy or may, by their function, create an undesirable condition. For example, flame cutting typically results in a very irregular surface unsuitable for welding unless additional finishing is performed. Another example is common roller-type tube cutters that deform the edge of the material making alignment for welding difficult. The second goal is to avoid contamination or damage to the material. Carbide saws heat the material excessively while creating a substantial burr and often imbed particulate in the surface with a final result particularly difficult to overcome.

Cutting and facing operations that operate at relatively low temperatures and without imparting contamination are most suitable. Some of these are able to cut only while others are used for final facing and yet others can do both in a single step. Shop or factory-based activity can employ lathes and other machine tools, while field work can be more difficult especially when repairs in congested areas and difficult to access areas are the objective. Properly designed equipment is extremely important to ensuring a high-quality joint can be completed.

Inspection tools are needed when direct viewing of the weld is not possible, and devices range from dental mirrors to expensive and fragile electronic machinery. In any event, care must be taken so that any inspection device that is used does not damage the finish on the material's surface. This is especially of concern when a device must be inserted into a part that has been polished previously and where repolishing is not possible. Early borescopic equipment utilized mirrors and required insertion of a small high powered light into the part, with viewing via an eyepiece much like a telescope. Their design required rigidity, they were unable to navigate corners or bends, and bulbs often broke during contact with surfaces potentially leaving glass shards behind. Advances in fiber optics allowed for remote light transmission, keeping bulbs external to the inspected area, and allowed for flexibility of movement and review of remote previously inaccessible locales. The most advanced equipment in use today employs miniaturized video cameras for high-quality viewing on an electronic display as well as recording with data entry capability.

Finishing

Stainless steels after manufacture, exhibit a dull gray matte finish that may be suitable as-is for use in chemical plants, power generation, and other applications where corrosion resistance is the sole reason for their selection. However, in addition to their chemical resistance qualities, stainless steels when polished provide an extremely pleasant cosmetic appearance as well as offering a surface that can be easily cleaned for hygienic purposes including that required for food preparation, medical care, and pharmaceutical production. This is not true for all specialized or corrosion-resistant alloys, as Hastelloy C-22, often used to replace 316LSS in extremely corrosive environments, is extremely difficult to polish to required levels because of its tendency to foul the polishing tools. Finishing of stainless steel for esthetic appeal can be accomplished using various methods including blasting or peening (as might result from impaction by sand or beads), mechanically using machine tools or abrasives such as emery, or electrochemically using a process known as electropolishing.

It is the latter two that are most appropriate for pharmaceutical product contact and the ones on which we will focus.

The surface finish of materials such as strip, plate, and rod is typically the result of processing, secondary to formulative manufacture, such as forging, hot rolling, or even cold rolling. This finish is commonly referred to as a "mill finish" and although fairly smooth it most likely is granular in makeup similar to that depicted in the photomicrograph (Figure 8.4).

This quality or level of finish has not been approved in most instances involving food, drugs, or cosmetics primarily because of the crevices that are believed to impede cleanability and sanitation.

Through the application of graduated abrasives, applied using various types of belts, pads, disks, wheels, and bobs, the finish can be enhanced so as to be suitable for architectural requirements including hand rails and door frames, for household appliances and furniture, for marine uses including boat railings and trim, for use in food and drug processing, etc. The requirements for these varied and diverse needs range from basic shininess to precise polishes measured by calibrated instruments to ensure consistent hygienic conditions.

To create a high-quality mechanical finish, abrasives of decreasing size are progressively applied starting with the coarsest and ending with the finest. Typical finishing for pharmaceutical components will begin with coarse finishing (50–80 grit) with subsequent steps increasing approximately 40–60 grit each until the final required finish is achieved. Grit is used here only to offer the reader a familiar reference since common sand paper is typically specified and labeled by grit size.

Much of the finishing technology used today originated in support of the food and dairy industry where polished stainless steel was utilized for food contact surfaces needing to be hygienic and cleanable. Finishes during that period were typically designated by number such that a dairy finish was considered to be #4 or, 150 grit. This meant that the surface, when viewed under a microscope, appeared to

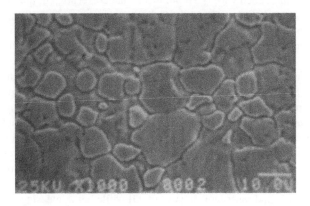

FIGURE 8.4 Photomicrograph of mill-finished stainless steel sheet magnified 1,000×. Note 10 μm reference at bottom right.

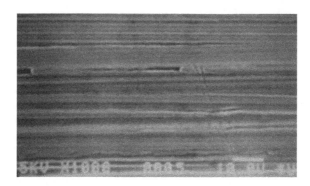

FIGURE 8.5 Photomicrograph of 180 Grit (20 Ra) mechanically polished stainless steel sheet magnified 1,000×. Note 10 μm reference at bottom right.

have 150 scratches or grit lines across 1″ of area, corresponding to the same number of particles of grit on the abrasive tool.

This can be seen clearly in the following photomicrograph, Figure 8.5, which also shows the scouring and smearing of the metal that actually occurs. As is obvious, abrasives used in polishing are aggressive and have a tendency to increase the surface area by creating minute peaks and valleys that increase reflectivity while scoring the surface, much like that of the bygone phonograph record.

Since finishes cannot be evaluated by the naked eye, products of substandard quality often found their way into the marketplace through unscrupulous vendors trying to gain a competitive edge or buyers hoping for a bargain. Hence, finishes improperly applied as a result of skipped steps, untrained personnel, or from the use of abrasive tools kept in service beyond their reasonable life, were often indistinguishable from materials with high-quality properly applied finishes. One of the significant contributions made by the pharmaceutical industry to sanitary technology was the standardization on roughness average (Ra) surface measurement using the microinch (μm in Europe and elsewhere) scale. This occurred through the joint efforts of vendors and users who desired to create a standard that would ensure equivalent quality and measurable acceptance levels.

In addition, it should be noted that the finishes demanded by pharmaceutical users were higher than that needed by food and dairy facilities, forcing vendors to stock multiple lines of products that were almost indistinguishable, making the need for surface measurement even more critical. As well, measuring tools known as profilometers, that had, in years past, been impractical for other than factory floor use, became available as inexpensive handheld field-friendly devices allowing buyers to confirm the quality of their purchases. Today, it is common for buyers to insist that the products they purchase are supplied with documentation verifying the quality of both the material and the finish via MTRs and "finish maps." Materials are coded with "heat numbers" that correspond to the MTRs' and finish maps that show the location and value of surface measurements taken at the factory, and can be field verified if necessary or desirable. Today, most materials are physically engraved with much of this information to ensure long-term tracking as part of validation is possible. One note of interest is that testing by profilometer imparts a small scratch on the material surface where the test was performed.

Mechanical finishing can be automated, such as for long lengths of tubing, and can also be accomplished by machining as part of a single fabrication process; however, not all parts can be automatically polished and items such as the interiors of fabricated tees may require manual finishing. The finesse needed to complete this work requires the operator to not only polish to achieve a smooth finish but to blend with adjacent surfaces to create an appealing final product. More importantly, finishers can easily remove excess material, thinning the wall of the part if too much pressure is applied, or if the tool is allowed to remain in the same position excessively as a result of distraction or inattention. Hence, mechanical finishing remains a combination of art and science as the finished product must meet measurable standards and must look consistent, all while being pleasing to the eye.

Alternative to mechanical polishing is electropolishing, discovered in France in 1929. Electropolishing is an electrochemical metal removal process in which the part to be polished is made the anode and placed into a solution, usually acidic, with a current applied. Metal is removed by dissolution starting from the highest points and with increasing current becomes more aggressive. Electropolishing can also be utilized to electro-machine parts to extremely precise tolerances, as well as for deburring and smoothing in preparation for coating or plating. Common surface reductions of 0.001″–0.002″ during polishing are achieved; however, more significant reductions can be accomplished. Electropolishing has also occasionally been termed reverse plating and develops an extremely reflective surface finish resembling a mirror when aggressively applied or when applied over a high-quality mechanical finish as is common in most pharmaceutical applications. Electropolished surfaces are distinct in appearance, not at all resembling mechanical finishes, and are extremely smooth with improved cleanability when used with products that adhere to mechanically polished surfaces. Electropolishing offers the added advantage of creating an extremely passive condition on the metals surface; however, there is debate as to whether preoperational passivation is necessary for materials that have been electropolished. This debate may be appropriate for parts small enough to have been bath electropolished or for assemblies requiring mechanical attachment with minimal chance of damaging the passive surface; however, in many instances, it is purely an academic discussion relative to a defined surface condition. Let us take, for example, a liquid product distribution network of 500 linear feet constructed of 1.5″ diameter sanitary electropolished tube and fittings. This material will require field assembly by welding; however, the surface area disturbed by the welding process will be extremely small compared to the entire surface in contact with the product. Discounting fittings to simplify calculations, tubing alone accounts for approximately 179 ft^2 of surface area that will be in product contact. Based on experience, the number of welds required can be approximated conservatively at 100 with each heat affected zone (HAZ) measuring approximately 0.5″ in width. Calculation reveals that the area disturbed by welding will amount to 1.49 ft^2 or approximately 0.8% of the entire surface. With less than 1% of the total electropolished surface compromised, it may appear that the risks are minimal; however, the failure to perform a preoperational passivation will result in potential compromise of the entire system and not nearly worth the relatively small savings.

In practical field applications, preoperational passivation, ideally *in situ*, is a far safer and practical solution. The following photomicrograph, shown in Figure 8.6, of an electropolished surface applied over a mechanical finish readily shows the level of increased smoothness that can be achieved.

Smoothness had always been associated with cleanability and assumed to serve as a counteracting force against biofilm formation. There is, however, much debate regarding this subject. In a recent article published in Medical Device & Diagnostic Industry (MD&DI), Rokicki states that a new process termed magnetoelectropolishing, which uses a magnetic field to enhance dissolution during the electropolishing process improved the properties of 316L stainless steel and "…found that the magnetoelectropolishing process can add many useful properties, including lubricity and antimicrobial peculiarity to metals used in blood contacting devices. Antimicrobial peculiarity refers to the fact that magnetoelectropolished 316L stainless steel is less prone to bacteria attachment and biofilm formation than standard electropolished 316L steel " (Rokicki, 2006). However, many microbiologists take a contrarian's position positing that no surface can successfully resist biofilm formation. Rokicki goes on to state "One big advantage of magnetoelectropolished surfaces of 316L-stainless-steel blood-contacting implants is their improved

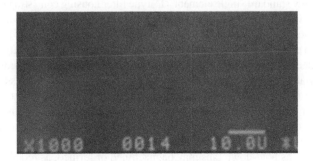

FIGURE 8.6 Photomicrograph of stainless steel sheet with 180 Grit (20 Ra) mechanical polish followed by electropolish, magnified 1,000×. Note 10 μm reference at bottom right.

hydrophilic character. The improvement can be seen in the water contact angle… It is well documented that hydrophilic metallic surfaces are hemo-compatible and bacteria resistant." As a result of this debate, most likely much research is yet to follow. One very interesting opposing hypothesis concerns the "lotus effect," (Riedewald, 2006) which is based on the surface morphology of the lotus plant. The surface of this particular genus is relatively rough and appears to self-clean using water, which is unable to adhere to the surface, to remove other surface contaminants, thus allowing its surface to remain far cleaner than other plant types. It has been postulated that this geometric phenomenon, if properly applied to a stainless steel surface would render it more likely to resist both contamination and bacterial colonization resulting in biofilm formation.

This theory certainly challenges conventional wisdom and is not the first challenge that has occurred regarding this particular subject and most likely it will not be the last.

An in-depth discussion of microbiology would be inappropriate here; however, to allow for a complete understanding of the related issues we can simplistically state that organisms occur in either the free-floating planktonic state or preferentially as participants in a colonized biofilm, which affords a more safe and secure environment for propagation. Planktonic organisms reproduce more slowly than their colonized counterparts as a result of their mobile state, are more susceptible to sanitizing materials, and may be more likely to be captured when a sample is taken. Conversely, organisms participating in a biofilm have more abundant nutrients, are protected to significant degree from sanitants, and in their stationary state are relatively secure from sampling, entrapment, or other exposure to system hardware. Biofilm occurs ubiquitously in nature and is most readily recognized by anyone attempting to cross a brook by stepping on submerged rocks. The incredibly slippery surface that exists usually results in a fall since firm footing cannot be achieved.

Most biologists believe that biofilm cannot be avoided without continuous sanitizing conditions (i.e., heat or ozone); however, frequent sanitization of one form or another can reduce its rate of development. There has been significant research in this field although pharma-specific information does not appear to be abundantly available and this suggests further biofilm-related research would be appropriate. Based on available information and historical performance of pharma water systems, this author believes that biofilm formation can be significantly retarded when continuous sanitization is employed such as for systems operating continuously above 165°F, and that there is a direct correlation between occurrences of sanitization and biofilm formation.

Fabrication of Stainless Steel

Welding is the primary method of permanently joining pieces of stainless steel and results in homogeneity that can be subsequently finished to create a smooth cleanable surface if properly created and polished. Alternatively, stainless can be fabricated using numerous other techniques, such as machining, drawing, and bending, alone or in concert, and also in conjunction with welding. In fact, it is common for assemblies to be the result of multiple fabrication steps which can include many of those listed above.

Take, for example, any standard single element "T" type filter housing consisting of base/tubesheet and dome/head. The base assembly is the point of connection of the element and usually contains the connection fittings. It is most likely constructed from an appropriately sized piece of plate that is machined, possibly on automated equipment. Connecting the base to the process requires fittings and these may be internal ports machined into the base, usually threaded for non-sanitary applications, or fittings welded and polished appropriately for sanitary applications. In addition, hold-down tabs and other accessories may also be required for the particular application. Alternatively, the base may be constructed as a stamping from thinner material, or may be completely machined including fittings, from a single cast or forged piece. Either of these options impact the cost with higher prices associated with the machined component and lower associated with the stamping.

Accessory parts, such as hold-down tabs may be machined or formed, as required by the application, for welding and subsequent polishing. Dome or head assemblies can be fabricated from parts or may be formed from a single sheet possibly using a deep drawing operation. Head fabrication from parts can include the body, cap, fittings, valves, mounting fitting/flange, and other specialized items typically welded and polished for sanitary and even non-sanitary units.

Where possible, standard subcomponents will reduce the cost of manufacture and hence, improve competitiveness. Housing body material can range from standard diameter pre-polished tube and pipe to virtually any custom diameter created from sheet that is rolled and welded, and can even be fabricated in sections if required. Caps can be closed or open, depending on the need for fittings, and can be formed, machined, or drawn. In some product lines, reducers can serve to simplify manufacturing or for more complex designs, special fabrications may be necessitated that incorporate centering devices or retainers.

For non-sanitary applications, parts could be threaded, bolded, welded, or assembled in any fashion that accomplishes the physical prerequisites including mechanical and hydraulic integrity, serviceability, and operating pressure. For sanitary applications the added requirements of cleanliness dictate the use of sanitary fittings, polished surfaces, drainability, appropriate sealing, and possibly integrity testing.

Vendors may require specialized equipment to facilitate the fabrication of their products which may or may not be commercially available. Special welding fixtures as well as unique tools for polishing may be the only practical solutions to overcoming fabrication difficulties and allowing a product to arrive in the marketplace.

Stainless steel will remain our primary focus; however, it should be noted that alternative materials are certainly suitable for housing construction, including various other metals as well as a multitude of plastics, all based on process worthiness. For drug product contact, however, stainless steel remains the most widely accepted.

The example housing included above is simple and appropriate for discussion of pharmaceutical products, but is hardly representative of the entire range of products available. It would take the reader only moments using the Internet to locate dozens of manufacturers and to view the myriad of designs, styles, sizes, shapes, and applications that exist; however, it should be recognized that the vast majority of these are not accepted for use in sanitary environments.

As with most other applications for stainless steel, the primary issues are formability, welding, and polishing. Welding as discussed before is performed primarily by the TIG process, using both manual and automated configurations, although specialty welding including welding lasers, resistance welding, and plasma arc welding (PAW) are also employed. Advantages can be gained from the use of specialized welding as often increased speed, reduced HAZ, smaller weld bead (for ease of polishing), and minimized warping result in higher-quality product and decreased cost.

The physical characteristics of stainless steel dictate that welding be performed more quickly and with less heat input so as to minimize distortion that can become problematic if uncontrolled. With its melting point below that of common carbon steels and with lower coefficient of thermal conductance, higher coefficient of thermal expansion and higher electrical resistance, distortion can easily become a fabricator's dilemma. Even simple functions, such as welding two tubes together, can result in difficulty if consideration to the nature of stainless is ignored. Many tube welding failures have occurred when untacked or lightly tacked materials pull apart because of shrinkage and distortion. Plate and sheet materials also often distort during fabrication such that they are rendered unusable, especially if the fabricator is unfamiliar with proper techniques. Maintaining dimensional accuracy when fabricating stainless, is a unique challenge that can be overcome only by experience, knowledge, and proper equipment.

In addition, it is not uncommon for stainless welding to be improved by a stepwise approach rather than creation of a single bead. When welding stainless steel, regardless of the thickness, it is prudent to consider this approach to avoid warpage that might otherwise occur. Many vendors of parts recommend a crisscross approach that requires (using a clock face for explanation) division of the weld into a number of segments that distribute the heat to avoid damage to, or warpage of, the part. For example, welding might begin with approximately 1/12 of the weld created at 3 o'clock, and subsequent equal sized sections welded sequentially at 9, 6, 12, 4, 10, 7, 1, 5, 11, 8, and 2 until the seam is completed.

This process has proven extremely useful in welding large pieces of plate, small light gauge parts, or components of differing thicknesses, although the exact pattern of creating the joint may vary from part to part, fabrication to fabrication, and welder to welder.

Stainless exhibits excellent mechanical workability such that it can be drawn, bent, and machined with relative ease. Hence, it is common to see stainless components ranging from ductwork to punches and dies, to step ladders, all more expensive on a first-cost basis but with far superior overall life expectancy.

For this reason, stainless can form the tubesheet, head, fittings, clamp, and even the accessories for a common filter housing with little fanfare.

In addition, the physical properties of stainless also allow finishing, either mechanically or electro-chemically, to a superior quality and offers brightness when finished, substantially above most other materials, including platinum, with the notable exception of silver.

Finishes applied to stainless are done so in a cost-effective manner providing benefits that can offset the better corrosion resistance of more exotic alloys such as Hastelloy. It is the corrosion resistance, ease of fabrication, relatively low cost, and availability of stainless steel that makes it such an attractive over-all alloy, with few competitors offering a challenge to its position as material of choice for pharmaceutical, biotech, food, beverage, cosmetic, and dairy applications.

Conclusions

When compared to other metals, especially steel and iron, the entire family of stainless steels accounts for a very small portion of the world's overall metal usage, so small in fact that stainless steel accounts for significantly less than 5% of the overall volume. This should not be surprising as the largest applications for metals such as steel and iron involve bridges, buildings, transportation (cars, trucks, buses, trains, ships, etc.), machinery, and other applications that consume incredibly huge amounts of material on an annual basis. Stainless steel is unique, multifaceted, and surprisingly inexpensive, yet there are few industries that can justify the added cost or overcome the obstacles that range from planned obsolescence, to personal preference, although stainless does tend to be viewed as a modernistic material of construction.

It would indeed be an interesting exercise to compare the cost of bridge construction in stainless steel against the life cycle cost of steel including maintenance, parts replacement due to rusting and repeated paintings with its associated environmental impact. Likewise, machinery, automobiles, trucks, trains, and ships would seldom corrode and would never require painting if they were made from stainless steel as is the case of the Chrysler building and even the DeLorean automobile, although admittedly, it might get a bit tiresome if everything lasted indefinitely and only came in one color.

In closing this section, it is worth mentioning that stainless steel is a remarkably unique material with an extremely long life compared to mild steel. Many stainless components, used by industry and by homeowners, even though repairable or reusable, will outlive their practical usefulness and require replacement. Often this material is discarded into landfills and other inappropriate dumpsites.

Stainless steel is 100% recyclable, and as such, its disposal as basic garbage is a deplorable waste that can be avoided through public education.

REFERENCES

Bhadeshia, HKDH and Sourmail, T. (2005) Stainless Steels. University of Cambridge. June 27, 2006: p. 3. http://www.msm.com.ac.uk/phase-trans/2005/stainless-steel/stainless.html

Cary, H.B. (1979) *Modern Welding Technology*. Englewood Cliffs, NJ: Prentice-Hall Inc.

Dowling, H.F. (1970) *Medicines for Man*. New York: Alfred A. Knopf, Inc.

Riedewald, F. (2006) Bacterial adhesion to surfaces: The influence of surface roughness. *PDA Journal of Pharmaceutical Science and Technology* 60(3), 164–171.

Rokicki, R. (2006) Machining: Magnetic fields and electropolished metallic implants. *Medical Device & Diagnostic Industry* 28(3), 116–123.

Tverberg, J. (1998) Ensuring quality in electropolished stainless steel tubing. *Tube & Pipe Journal* 9(5), 46–50.

Zapffe, C.A. (1949) *Stainless Steels*. Cleveland, OH: The American Society of Metals.

BIBLIOGRAPHY

"3-A Sanitary Standards." (1981) International Association of Milk, Food and Environmental Sanitarians: US Public Health, The Dairy Industry Committee.

"Austenitic Stainless Steel." (2006) Know Stainless Steel. June 27, 2006. http://www.jindalstainless.com/stainlesssource/know-stainless-steel/austenitic-steels.html

Avis, K.E. and Wu, V.L. (1996) *Drug Manufacturing Technology Series Volume 2: Biotechnology and Biopharmaceutical Manufacturing, Processing, and Preservation*. Englewood, CO: IHS Health Group.

Banes, P.H. (1999) Passivation: Understanding and performing procedures on austenitic stainless steel systems. *Pharmaceutical Engineering* 19, 44–58.

"Basic Branches: The Family Tree of Stainless Steel." (2006) The Stainless Steel Information Center. June 20, 2006. http://www.ssina.com/overview/branches.html

"Benefits." (2006) The Stainless Steel Information Center. June 20, 2006. http://www.ssina.com/overview/benefits.html

Bhadeshia, HKDH and Sourmail, T. (2005) "Stainless Steels." University of Cambridge. June 27, 2006. http://www.msm.com.ac.uk/phase-trans/2005/stainless-steels/stainless.html

Cary, H.B. (1979) *Modern Welding Technology*. Englewood Cliffs, NJ: Prentice-Hall Inc.

"Chemical Composition." (2006) The Stainless Steel Information Center. June 20, 2006. http://www.ssina.com/overview/chemical.html

Connor, L.P. (1987) *Welding Handbook: Welding Technology* (8th Edition). Miami, FL: American Welding Society.

"Corrosion: Galvanonic Corrosion." (2006) The Stainless Steel Information Center. June 20, 2006. http://www.ssina.com/corrosion/galvanic.html

"Crystal Lattice Structures: The Body Centered Cubic (A2) Lattice." (2004), 1. August 14, 2006. http://cst-www.nrl.navy.mil/lattice.struk/a2.html

Dowling, H.F. (1970) *Medicines for Man*. New York: Alfred A Knopf, Inc.

"Ferritic Stainless Steel." (2006) Know Stainless Steel. June 27, 2006. http://www.jindalstainless.com/stainlesssource/know-stainless-steel/ferritic-steels.html

"First Branch." (2006) The Stainless Steel Information Center. June 20, 2006. http://www.ssina.com/overview/firstbranch.html

"Fourth Branch." (2006) The Stainless Steel Information Center. June 20, 2006. http://www.ssina.com/overview/fourthbranch.html

Gonzalez, M.M. (2006) Biopharmaceutical water systems: Materials of construction for biopharmaceutical water systems, part 2. *American Pharmaceutical Review* 9(3), 68–74.

"History of Steel." (2006) Know Stainless Steel. June 27, 2006. http://www.jindalstainless.com/stainlesssource/know-stainless-steel/index.html

"How is it made?" (2006) The Stainless Steel Information Center. June 20, 2006. http://www.ssina.com/overview/how.html

"Martensitic Stainless Steel." (2006) Know Stainless Steel. June 27, 2006. http://www.jindalstainless.com/stainlesssource/know-stainless-steel/martensitic-steels.html

Post, R.C. (1999) "Alloyed Steel." The Facts on File of Science, Technology, and Society. Science Online New York. June 27, 2006. http://www.fofweb.com

O'Brien, R.L. (1991) *Welding Handbook: Welding Processes* (8th Edition, Volume 2). Miami, FL: American Welding Society.

Oates, W.R. (1996) *Welding Handbook: Materials and Applications-Part 1* (8th Edition, Volume 3). Miami, FL: American Welding Society.

Oates, W.R. and Saitta, A.M. (1998) *Welding Handbook: Materials and Applications-Part 2* (8th Edition, Volume 4). Miami, FL: American Welding Society.

Riedewald, F. (2006) Bacterial adhesion to surfaces: The influence of surface roughness. *PDA Journal of Pharmaceutical Science and Technology* 60(3), 164–171.

Rokicki, R. (2006) Machining: Magnetic fields and electropolished metallic implants. *Medical Device & Diagnostic Industry* 28(3), 116–123.

"Second Branch." (2006) The Stainless Steel Information Center. June 20, 2006. http://www.ssina.com/overview/secondbranch.html

"Stainless Steel: An introduction to a versatile, aesthetically pleasing and 'full life cycle' material." (2006) The Stainless Steel Information Center. June 20, 2006. http://www.ssina.com/overview/intro.html

"Stainless Steel Overview: History." (2006) The Stainless Steel Information Center. June 20, 2006. http://www.ssina.com/overview/history.html

"Third Branch." (2006) The Stainless Steel Information Center. June 20, 2006. http://www.ssina.com/overview/thirdbranch.html

Tverberg, J. (1998) Ensuring quality in electropolished stainless steel tubing. *Tube & Pipe Journal* 9(5), 46–50.

"Updates." (2006) The Stainless Steel Information Center. August 3, 2006. http://www.ssina.com/index2.html

Zapffe, C.A. (1949) *Stainless Steels*. Cleveland, OH: The American Society of Metals.

9

Protein Adsorption on Membrane Filters

Maik W. Jornitz
G-CON Manufacturing, Inc.

CONTENTS

Introduction

The adsorption of proteins onto polymeric filters is of considerable practical interest. The technique of preparing new drugs by way of fermentation processes includes their downstream purification by separation procedures such as filtration or liquid–solid chromatography. Separation of the extracellular products from the cell remnants is achieved by filtration in a clarification step: microporous membranes are employed. The debris is retained by the filter; the effluent contains the desired proteins. Ultrafiltration by way of tangential flow operations is a technique often used to concentrate the sought-after products. Alternatively, liquid–solid chromatography is utilized to bond the proteinaceous products to a carrier surface. Subsequently, the desired (protein) product is released in purer form.

Purifying activities based on filters can be complicated by blockage of the filter pores caused by protein, and/or other, depositions. The same may result when preparations containing proteins undergo filtrations designed for sterilizations, and for virus removal. The hindrance of the filtration process by protein adsorption is termed "fouling," a word whose pejorative implication is one of unwelcome interference. Actually, fouling is a poorly understood phenomenon. Protein adsorptions studies are undertaken in pursuits of its enhancement. The loss of time and effort attendant upon a filter blockage translates to a monetary loss. An even greater direct loss may occur when valuable proteins, the product of present biochemical efforts, are irreversibly adsorbed to a filter to become discarded with it. The strong interest in securing high yields of high-value proteins is self-apparent and much needed to serve the patient base.

The technical literature is not as clear as it might be regarding the type(s) of filters most responsive to protein bonding. Commercial competition for the filter market may, on occasion, tend to blur differences among filters regarding their adsorptive properties. One purpose of this writing is to pursue technical guidance that may be of value in reaching independent judgments.

The factors that govern protein adsorptions to filters are broadly understood. A review of the mechanisms involved will be made with an eye toward matching them with salient features of the filters' polymeric structures. A clearer understanding of the adsorptive bonding of proteins to filters is its goal.

Proteins and Adsorptions

The adsorption of proteins can occur whenever any surface comes in contact with a protein solution. Protein adsorption to filters is hardly a singular or exceptional event. Various particle types such as organisms; colloidal particles; humic acids; and numerous molecular substances of organic-chemical origins, preservatives, stabilizers, endotoxins, etc. undergo similar bonding. Nor do filters supply the only surfaces for adsorptions. In fact, large surfaces, whether of activated carbon, or beds of ion-exchange resins, or polymeric bags, qualify equally. It is the extent of surface area and charge, among other factors, that governs the quantities of materials adsorbed. However, the particular properties of a given molecular structure also exert an influence on how it behaves in the adsorption process. Thus, silica glass made from silica sand, despite its greatly reduced surface area compared with the sand granules, is also available for adsorptive interactions. Therefore, the loss of protein from solutions stored in glass vessels also deserve appraisal.

When an organism adsorbs to a filter, or when colloidal particles agglomerate, the result is seen as a surface-to-surface reaction. A different terminology is needed to describe the adsorption of a molecule to a filter surface. Albeit three dimensional, molecules are ordinarily not thought of as having surfaces. Yet the forces that adsorptively unite the two entities are of an identical nature. The interacting molecules may each be part of a surface. They may also be macrosolutes in solution, certain atomic arrangements of which mutually attract and bond by way of adsorptive mechanisms that will be described below.

It is proteins in the form of solutions that are processed by filtration. Often, however, because of their structural complexity, proteins occur as amorphous or colloidal particles. They are essentially rather complex combinations of amino acids, sometimes including linkages to other type molecules. The amino acids, as the name implies, are each characterized by their terminal groups: one is an amine ($-NH_2$) and the other a carboxylic acid group ($-COOH$). As a result of being amphoteric, they combine respectively, with both acids and bases. The amine and carboxylic acid groups of separate amino acid molecules can be interacted to form amides. The resulting larger polypeptide molecules may also be characterized by terminal amine and carboxylic acid groups. A cascade of repetitive interactions with other amino acids can yield convoluted long chains of high molecular weights composed of the various linked amino acids and possibly of other substituent groups of atoms. The resulting proteins are repetitive units of their constituting amino acids transformed into polyamide chains, all connected by a series of amide linkages ($-C-N-$).

Isoelectric Point

All large molecular structures and membranes adsorb ions, both positive and negative, from their contact with aqueous solutions. As a result their surfaces come to bear net electrical charges. Most membranes preferentially adsorb negative ions (Zeman 1996, Chap. 9). Such may also result from the ionization of the carboxylic acid groups which form when organic molecules are oxidized. Thus, at neutral pHs most membranes have a net negative charge. At the higher pH ranges these minus charges are of a greater magnitude because the carboxylic acids' rate of dissociation increases to more plentifully produce the carboxylic anion ($-COO^-$). The same results at the higher pHs from greater anionic adsorption, as well as from the deprotonization of ammonium groups $(-NH_3^+) \rightarrow (-NH_2)$. Some membranes are deliberately positively charged to enhance the adsorptive separation of contaminants. For example, in the past positively charged membranes were used to adsorptively retain endotoxins, a practice which is not any longer encouraged by regulatory agencies.

In the acidic range below pH 7, the opposite reaction takes place with increasing quantities of plus charges being adsorbed or generated by way of ionic dissociations that yield hydrogen ions. These through hydrogen-bonding (explained below) with water molecules form hydronium ions (H_2O---H).

The transition from the negative charge to positive charge stages passes through the point where there are essentially no charged molecules. This is the p*I* or isoelectric point of the molecule. It differs from the neutral pH point because of the effects of the adsorbed or generated charges discussed above.

The pH of protein ambiances determines the sign of their electrical charge and the extent to which they will react as an acid or base. As stated above, in the acidic pH range the amine groups carry a plus charge. In the higher pH regions the carboxylic acid group bears a negative charge. Proteins and peptides may variously contain different amounts of amine and carboxylic acids. At the pH that marks their electrical neutrality they are without overt electrical charge. This is the protein molecule's isoelectric point, the p*I*. The zero potential is practically null, and there is, therefore, little if any, tendency for the molecule to migrate in an electrical field. Free of electric charge influences, the isoelectric point identifies the pH at which the particular protein is to a maximum degree responsive to adsorptive influences. The shift of the isoelectric point is very effectively used in the chromatographic purification process steps of a biologic downstream process. Different ligands on a matrix create different charges or attractive forces, which will be used to separate different fluid contaminants and purify protein solutions.

Given the importance of proteins, it is perhaps not surprising that they have undergone considerable investigation, both experimental and theoretical. Consequently, there exists a body of knowledge concerning how these entities undergo interactions resulting in their adsorption to one another, and to surfaces such as they encounter in filtrations. Protein adsorption is a multifaceted process. It is dependent upon the individual protein, upon other proteins that may be present, the protein concentrations, the makeup of the specific liquid vehicle such as its ionic strength, pH, etc., and upon the process conditions, such as buffer composition, temperature, etc.

Conformational Changes of Adsorbed Proteins

In being adsorbed, the protein's molecular structure tends to conform to the shapes of the adsorbing surfaces. In so doing, its shape and certain of its properties may be altered. This includes a reduction in the extent of biological activity. The degree of conformation presumably is a measure of the strength of the adsorptive bonding. There is a direct commonality between a protein's hydrophobicity and its adsorptive conformation to the substrate. In attaching to a site on the filter surface the pliable protein molecule may folds on itself. In so doing, it exposes small portions of its more hydrophobic amino acids. These are shielded when the protein is in aqueous surroundings. The resulting increase in its hydrophobicity may promote additional folding and shape-alteration as the protein molecule interacts with more adsorption sites.

In addition to the initial steric factor, the hydrophobicity of a protein progressively increases in several successive stages of folding. Its primary structure reflects its molecular composition. Its secondary, tertiary, and quaternary stages represent its three-dimensional structures wherein the hydrophobicity increases as also its conformation. Under strong adsorptive interactions at hydrophobic sites, given time, protein molecules tend to flatten into a very dense layers to an extent shorter in length than that of the molecule in solution (Sundaram 1998). They increasingly undergo more avid surface interactions as expressed by greater extents of conformation. Conformational changes are favored by an increase in a protein's flexibility, as shown by adiabatic compressibility studies.

The protein deposit once formed is not necessarily reversible. Under conditions that favor strong adsorption, desorptions may prove irreversible. Such reversibility is more likely where the adsorption is of a hydrophilic type, presumably because such are less tightly held. The adsorption can be reversed by changing the solution conditions to those that are promotive of hydrophilicity. This can be affected by the presence or additions of alcohols, glycols, and surfactants to the aqueous solution. Such will be changing the character of the adsorption from hydrophobic to hydrophilic. Desorption has a higher possibility. Following desorption, the protein may recover its original conformation either partly or completely. The greater strength of the hydrophobic adsorptions is indicative of the greater stability of the protein in those very conditions.

Truskey et al. (1987) measured protein adsorption, circular dichroism, and the biological activity of a variety of protein solutions, i.e., insulin, iso-gamma globulin (IgG), and alkaline phosphatase. The solutions' properties were measured before and after passing the proteins through a variety of membranes. Shifts in circular dichroism and decreases in the activity of the enzymes were determined to be the result of conformational changes of the protein structure that are attendant upon adsorption. This study showed that membranes with the greatest degree of hydrophobicity had the greatest effect on protein adsorption. This, in turn, effectuated a strong conformation with concomitant denaturation. The protein–membrane interaction resulted in the protein's exposing its internal hydrophobic sites, which were folded within its structure during its exposure to aqueous solution. This bespeaks a relationship between protein shape and function. The exposed hydrophobic sites that engage in the membrane–protein binding, protein–protein binding, and protein denaturation are likely the more hydrophobic amino acids; the most hydrophobic of which are tyrosine, phenylalanine, and tryptophane.

Opportunities exist for the shearing of protein molecules as they negotiate a microporous membrane's tortuous passageways or flowing over a tangentially located membrane in the diafiltration step. A loss of the protein's properties may result. Shearing in general is, however, seen as being less responsible for functional losses through denaturations than are the conformational changes that follow the adsorptions of proteins to polymer surfaces, temperature conditions, or prolonged processing times.

Adsorption Isotherms and Fouling

According to accepted theory, the atoms composing the surface of a solid are arranged in the orderly fashion of a crystalline lattice in a checkerboard pattern. Each atom comprising the surface has available free valence electrons capable of interacting with one, and only one, molecule from its surrounding phase, be it a gas or a solution. The rate of molecular adsorption depends upon the rate at which molecules collide with the surface, the fraction that adhere, and the extent of surface area that becomes covered. The relationship of these several factors is known as the Langmuir isotherm. In its accord with the data from many adsorption studies, it is considered the archetype of the classical adsorption. The data forthcoming from the studies of protein adsorptions onto filter surfaces would have been expected to fit the Langmuir isotherm equation. One of its assumptions holds that only the one layer of protein molecules directly in contact with a filter's surface is adsorbed upon it. This is not found to always be the situation.

Experimental investigations indicate that elements of protein adsorptions to filters do fit the Langmuir equation. This argues in favor of its underlying assumption, namely, then only one layer of molecules can be adsorbed. However, so thin a deposition ought not be enough to lead to membrane fouling. Also experienced are fouling situations wherein filters speedily suffer flux decay consequent to adsorbing only minute quantities of aggregated or insolublized, or denatured protein. The more orthodox view of fouling is the progressive building of an adsorbed layer to the point of pore-blockage over a longer-term filtration. Such an occurrence is not expected in Langmuir-type one-layer adsorptions. As will later be discussed, Bowen and Gan (1991) made use of the standard Langmuir model in analyzing their adsorption isotherms. It did not provide a reasonable fit for their data. The present situation is far from clear.

Adsorptive Forces

According to Zeman and Zydney (1996, Chap. 9), the interactions between filter and adsorbent arise from a number of causes. Electrostatic influences involve the molecule that is adsorbed sharing the partial electric charge of one of its atom-sites with a partially charged atom of a molecule of opposite sign on the filter's surface. The partial charges are generated by fixed charges, as of ions, or by fixed dipoles, also to be explained. It is this interaction that marks the adsorptive bond. Adsorptions may also result from forces that, according to some authorities, are not necessarily charge related. These are known as hydrophobic adsorptions. Their motivation is ascribed to reductions in Gibbs' free surface energy.

There are also polarization, or London-van der Waals (VDW), forces that derive from induced dipole–dipole reactions. To these should be added quantum mechanical interactions between smaller entities in solution that result in covalent bond formations that create molecular structures large enough to block filter pores. The nature of the covalent bond will presently be described. Although known as dispersive forces, they are generally attractive in their influence. Conformational changes are favored by an increase in a protein's flexibility, as shown by adiabatic compressibility studies.

Heterogeneity of Surfaces

The bonding interactions that characterize adsorptions are understood to be electrical in nature. (There is some disagreement regarding the hydrophobic adsorption mechanism.) Electrical charge considerations, partial charges, hydrogen bonding, dipoles, VDW forces are all involved. The electrical potentials that result may empower given atoms with positive or negative charge characteristics. The resulting opposite or like-charges are essential parts of the adsorption phenomenon. Adsorptions to filters can be considered as interactions between their surface molecules and certain features of the molecules present in their surrounding environment. The chemistry of proteins and of surfaces to which they adsorb are often heterogeneously complex to an extreme. Various sites on surface may be partially charged and can be of like- or of opposite signs. The extent of charge-site hydration, for example, is influenced accordingly. Their electric potential, and the hydrophobic/hydrophilic character of given atomic sites on any of two surfaces may differ considerably. Importantly, their tendency for adsorption may also manifest itself to different extents.

Protein adsorption is a sum total of many phenomena. In consequence it is difficult to predict. Protein surfaces can contain differences in hydrophobicity, charge, and degree of hydration, and can change with protein conformation, and solution characteristics (Zydney 1996). The filter surface to which it bonds in its adsorptive interaction may have similar differences. Neither surface need be uniform with regard to surface charge or surface composition. Opportunities simultaneously exist, therefore, for both hydrophilic and hydrophobic adsorptions to take place. The former involves electric charge interactions; the latter presumably are free of such influences. Both may simultaneously be possible in a given situation. It is possible to ascribe a given adsorption to either one of these causes, or to both.

Adsorption of proteins on polymeric filter membranes is complex and so is the choice of the membrane materials in regard to adsorptive properties, the process operating parameters, which may enhance such adsorptive capture, the fluid conditions, and possible pretreatment of the filter. In critical applications, it is of utmost importance to evaluate all the influences and gain appropriate knowledge to find the ideal filter system and process condition.

Hydrophobic versus Hydrophilic Bonding

It is possible to make an assessment regarding the relative strengths of the charge-involved hydrophilic adsorptions and those of the hydrophobic interactions that are, presumably, charge-free. A number of situations suggest that the hydrophobic adsorptions are the more effective:

- The adsorptive interaction of a protein and a surface increases as the hydrophobicity of both filter surface and protein increase. Moreover, as electrical charges on the protein and on the adsorbing surface decrease, adsorption generally increases. Therefore, protein-filter interactions are generally believed not to depend upon electrostatic attractions. They are credited to hydrophobic forces. (Hydrophobic adsorption is considered by many authorities to operate free of such electric charge influences.)

- Desorption is a function of the rate of evaporation from a completely covered surface. As stated above, the reversibility of an adsorption is more likely where it is of a hydrophilic type, presumably because such are less tightly held. Desorption may result from changing the solution conditions to those promotive of hydrophilicity: as by additions of alcohols, glycols, and surfactants to the aqueous solution. Desorption from the hydrophilic bonding is then more possible. The greater strength of the hydrophobic adsorptions is indicative of the greater stability of the protein in those very conditions.

- It is known that adsorptions are greatest when proteins are at their p*I* points, at which pHs they are essentially free of the ionic charges gained them by their amphoteric amine and carboxylic acid groups.

An exception arises when the dominant ionic groups on the protein and filter surfaces are of opposite electrical signs. In this case, an increase in protein adsorption follows directly from a decrease in the repulsive aspect of the zeta potential. The attractive forces are then enabled to exert their influences. This situation results from the "screening" of the repulsive charge by high ionic strengths such as eventuate from salt additions (utilizing buffers), or from the higher hydronium ions of lower pHs.

Protein Shape Alterations

The picture of the absorption process is not one of particles or protein molecules encountering and becoming bonded by chance to a surface in some static fixation. Molecular movement is involved. The attractive forces making for adsorption, both VDW and hydrophobic, are effective only at very short ranges. Where the distance between the two surfaces is small enough for bonding to occur, the protein molecule will attach end-on. Conformational changes, movement within the protein molecules, will then result. The protein molecule will tend to collapse by undergoing progressive stages of folding, and to flatten out into dense layer on the membrane or other solid surface. In the process, its hydrophilic/hydrophobic character may alter, as has been described.

Charge attractions may not become manifest because the distance separating them are too great. Even so, they can become operative in high ionic strength situations. This is so because high ionic values, in effect, condense the electrical double layers, as stated above, shrinking them to distances wherein charge or hydrophobic attractions can assert themselves. Movements, both inter- and intramolecular, are part of the adsorption picture. In this type of dynamic setting there are possibilities for adsorptive bonding to take place.

It is intriguing that the outermost atoms (surfaces) of a complex molecular structure presented by a complex protein molecule may undergo significant property changes depending upon the degree to which its convoluted molecule becomes extended or contracted in solution. Protein molecules display their most hydrophilic character in their extended, if sinuous, forms in aqueous solutions. Their solubility in water derives from the prominence of their hydrophilic amino acids in aqueous solutions. In the situation, their constituting hydrophobic amino acids are least exposed to the water. As their structures fold progressively to where their more hydrophobic amino acids become more openly exposed, they undergo an increasing hydrophobicity. In consequence, this tends to encourage hydrophobic adsorptions; soon to be discussed.

As discussed below in the section entitled, "Fuoss Effect," this very alteration of molecular structure mirrors the prolongation of humic acid adsorptions onto activated carbon surfaces by the presence of ions. This exemplifies the wide application of the adsorption process that also governs the protein-filter picture.

Another example of the general nature of the adsorptive interaction was related by Brose and Waibel (1996) while discussing their work on protein adsorptions by filters. That preservatives can be adsorbed by filters is known. These investigators reference their findings with regard to the adsorption of certain preservatives, namely, benzalkonium chloride and benzododecinium chloride to filters. The subject adsorptions and concentrations reflected linear relationship at the 0.02–0.25 wt % level. Preservatives being utilized within ophthalmic solutions, require to be present at specific concentrations within the filled container. When adsorptive filter materials are used, such filters can minimize or alter the concentration, resulting in an out-of-specification fill. Evaluation of how to saturate the filter surface-charged sites is necessary, and starting volumes discarded or specific fluid volumes first recirculated over the membrane before the actual filling cycle starts. Once the adsorptive sites have been saturated, the adsorption of the preservative is prevented.

Hydrophobic Adsorption: Serum

A number of protein-to-filter adsorptions will be discussed with a view toward identifying the operational factors, such as were just described.

The ease of filtering serum depends largely upon the animal species from which the serum is obtained, as well as the collection location and season. Several of the many components of sera add to the difficulty of their filtration. Fetal calf serum is relatively easy, and porcine serum is relatively difficult to filter. The most troublesome components are the lipids and proteins. When their depositions and adsorptions block and clog the filters, the occurrence is called "Fouling." The contribution made to filter blockage by the membrane's polymeric composition is pronounced when bovine serum is the filtration fluid. Comparison was made between a 0.2 μm-rated cellulose triacetate membrane and a 0.45 μm-rated experimental Polyvinyl chloride (PVC) membrane as a filter for bovine serum. In order to minimize clogging due to particulate matter, the bovine serum was prefiltered through a 0.8 μm-rated cellulose triacetate membrane. It was found that the cellulose triacetate membrane, although characterized by a smaller mean pore size, yielded double the throughput of the experimental PVC filter. The difference in performance is ascribed to filter interaction with the serum proteins. Protein binding "fouls" the hydrophobic (PVC) membrane and reduces the throughput.

Such proteins as the serum albumins undergo hydrophobic interactions with the long nonpolar chains of fatty acids that terminate in hydrophilic carboxylic acid groups. In the case of the interactions between the fatty acids and serum proteins, the opportunity for hydrophobic interaction is increased by muting the polarity of the protein. This is done by adjusting the pH to the isoelectric point of the particular protein, because at that point the electrostatic charges inherent in the amphoteric protein molecules are neutralized. That the elimination of partial charge effects does not vitiate protein adsorption based on hydrophilic surfaces serves as support for the hydrophobic adsorption mechanism.

Hydrophobic Adsorption: Ultrafilters

A similar situation enabled the hydrophobic interaction of a microporous polypropylene membrane with lipopolysaccharidic endotoxin molecules to attain their removal from aqueous solutions.

All known endotoxins have a hydrophobic lipid A core as well as a hydrophilic polysaccharide appendage. It is the lipid A core that is responsible for the pyrogenic activity of the endotoxin and for its hydrophobic character (Galanos et al., 1972). Its nonpolar nature reflects the 16–20-carbon chain that it contains. This nonpolar chain furnishes the site for the hydrophobic interaction between the lipopolysaccharide and the like-bonded segments of filter surfaces, the nonpolar polypropylene molecules.

Lipid A, being nonpolar, is incompatible in terms of phase separation with aqueous solutions. It spontaneously aggregates in such media to form small micelles or larger bilayered vesicle arrangements (Sweadner et al., 1977). In these formations, the negatively charged hydrophilic groups lie on the surfaces of the molecule exposed to the aqueous solutions. The core of the micelle or vesicle is composed of the hydrophobic lipid A portion of the endotoxin. The exposed anionic groups on the outside attract their oppositely charged counterions to form an electrically neutral double layer that also includes water molecules bound by dipole–dipole interactions.

Robinson et al. (1982) (Figure 9.1) illustrates the lipopolysaccharides (LPS; endotoxins) pyrogenic bacterial being adsorptively retained by hydrophobic membranes through the hydrophobic interaction of the uncharged filter surface and the nonpolar lipid A-core of the endotoxin. The enclosed nonpolar lipid

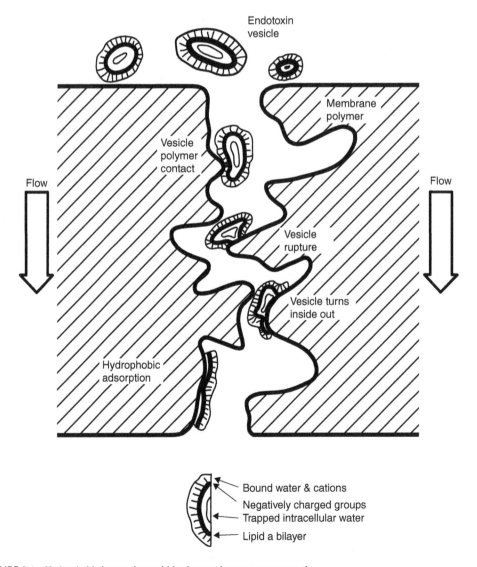

FIGURE 9.1 Hydrophobic interactions within the membranes torturous path.

A-core establishes contact with the nonpolar polypropylene pore walls and so becomes hydrophobically adsorbed upon rupture of the charged hydrophilic pellicle. At the bottom of the hydrophobic effect is the entropically driven tendency of hydrophobic structures to interact with one another in order to reduce the area of their contact with water.

Hydrophobic Adsorption and Sieve Retention

The endotoxin in the above example was removed through hydrophobic adsorption and not by sieve retention. This is demonstrated by removal of the pyrogenic agent when a microporous filter of higher pore size rating was used. However, the probability of free surface energy reduction is enhanced by using ultrafilters of lower pore sizes.

Table 9.1 illustrates that the adsorptive removal of the endotoxin, as measured by log reduction value (LRV), is indeed inversely proportional to the pore size of the membrane. As Table 9.1 also shows, de-aggregation of the endotoxin micelles and vesicles by the action of ethylenediamine tetraacetic acid (EDTA) results in the removal of the endotoxin by the nonpolar membrane but not by weakly polar cellulose triacetate membranes. These latter filters could retain the aggregated pyrogens through sieve retention, but only because of their small pore size. Being polar, the *hydrophilic* cellulose acetate (CA) filter is presumed not to participate in hydrophobic adsorptions.

By contrast with the *hydrophilic* CA filter, the use of *hydrophobic* 0.2 μm-rated inverse-phase (temperature-governed) polypropylene membranes could reduce the endotoxin concentration of solutions filtered through them by either mechanism. Utilizing a polypropylene membrane of 0.2 μm-rating, the reduction attained an LRV of 1–3. The use of a 0.1 μm-rated polypropylene membrane of similar inverse phase structure reduced the endotoxin by an LRV of 3–4. It would seem that the use of smaller pore size-rated hydrophobic filters could utilize both sieve retention and hydrophobic adsorption in retaining the pyrogenic agent. Thus, the simultaneous removal of endotoxin by both hydrophobic adsorption and sieve retention can be ensured by the use of hydrophobic small pore size-rated membranes. The proper pore-sized microporous polypropylene membranes produced by the temperature-governed phase inversion process meet both requirements (Hiatt et al., 1985).

Models for Organism Adsorptions

The focus on protein adsorptions to filters may well be extended to parts of surfaces similarly agreeable to adsorptive bonding. Interspersed among different and varied molecular arrangements such areas, if sufficiently extensive and influential, should react accordingly in being conducive to hydrophobic

TABLE 9.1

Influence of Pore Size and Endotoxin Aggregation State on Endotoxin Adsorption to Filters

Polymer Type	Pore Size (μm)	Endotoxin Aggregation State	Endotoxin LRV
Polypropylene	Prefilter	DI	0.1
	0.2	DI	1–3
	0.1	DI	3–4
CA	0.2	DI	0.1
	0.025	DI	3.0
Polypropylene	0.2	EDTA	1.0
	0.1	EDTA	1.0
CA	0.2	EDTA	0.1
	0.025	EDTA	0.1

Notes: (1) Deionized water (DI) solutions of endotoxin are mixtures of vesicular and micellar structures; (2) 0.005 M EDTA solutions have only micellar structures.

adsorptions. This broadens our consideration to other phenomena usually not considered as involving adsorptions.

Molecular complexities characterize proteins, and also the polymeric structures of filters employed in sterilizing filtrations. Long-chain structures of atomic constituents in varied arrangements are common to both. This allow for the simultaneous presence of different hydrophobic/hydrophilic groups or areas within large and complex molecular arrangements. This, it is speculated, may apply to the structures of organisms as well as to those of proteins. The bacterial cell surface consists of a peptidoglycan layer covalently linked to a variety of membrane proteins and anionic polymers. Although much of this surface is hydrophilic, some hydrophobic areas are simultaneously present as well (Zydney 1996). Through hydrophobic adsorptions, those areas on the proteins join and bond with hydrophobic areas on filter surfaces (Dumitriu and Dumitriu-Medvichi 1994). In the case of the proteins, the areas of hydrophobicity reflect that of the constituting amino acids. As stated, the most hydrophobic of which are tyrosine, phenylalanine, and tryptophane.

There is a hope in this writing that the experimental elucidations of protein adsorptions can serve as a guide to the better understanding of bacterial adsorptions. As expressed by Mittleman et al. (1998), the molecules of proteins and of organisms are complex enough to present areas of both polar and nonpolar character. In the similarity of their mechanism of retention by filters may lie a commonality of their management. Encouragement is given this expectation by the findings of Fletcher and Loeb (1979), showing that marine bacteria attach most readily to hydrophobic plastics. By contrast, the smallest number attach to negatively charged hydrophilic surfaces (Zydney 1996, p. 440).

Organism Adsorption to RO Polymer

Encouragement is given to the concept that organism attachments to filter surfaces may be imitative of those of proteins. Using radioisotopically labeled *Mycobacerium* BT2-4 cells, Ridgway et al. (1984a,b, 1985, 1986) studied biofilm formation on CA RO membranes. The adhesion of the organisms without the impress of a differential pressure was surprisingly rapid. It showed no log phase and was biphasic: An initial rapid adhesion, straight line with respect to time, was followed by a much slower rate of attachment, also linear with time. The first phase of adhesion took place over a 1–2 h period; the slower phase proceeded indefinitely. Typical saturation adsorption kinetics were involved in keeping with the Langmuir adsorption isotherm equation.

Colonization of CA membranes by the microbes was quite rapid, 3×10^5 cfu/cm^2 over a 3-day period. The greater degree of adhesion was to the nylon (polyamide) membrane by five- or tenfold (Ridgway et al., 1984a,b).

The adsorption was interfered with by nonionic surfactant. It is presumed that the surfactant molecules attach to the adsorptive sites of both organisms and membranes, and constitute a steric buffer between the hydrophobic ligands. Ridgway concludes from this that the adsorption phenomenon is hydrophobic in nature.

Interestingly, inactivation of the bacteria by monochloramine did not decrease their adsorption to the membrane surfaces. The implication is that the bacterial attachments are physicochemical rather than the result of such metabolic processes as exopolymer-mediated bridging of the electric double layer, or the result of chemotactic responses. In any case, the different polymeric materials adsorbed organisms to different extents.

The individuality of an organism with regard to the different polymers is mirrored by that of a given polymeric material for different organisms. Thus, *Mycobacterium* adheres 25 times greater than does a wild strain of *Escherichia coli*. The adsorption of *E. coli* and *Mycobacterium* correlates with their surface hydrophobicity; similarly, for hydrophilic *Acinetobacter phosphadevorus* and a more hydrophobic strain.

Biofilm Adhesions to Surfaces

Figure 9.2 illustrates the eagerness with which different polymeric membranes adsorb certain proteins. Each polymeric material has its own individual propensity for adsorptions; also, given the same polymer, different proteins adsorb to different extents.

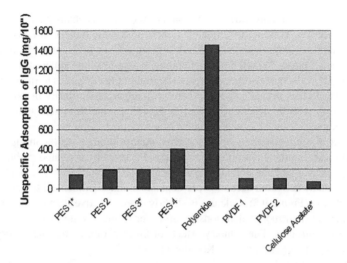

FIGURE 9.2 Unspecific adsorption of different membrane materials.

This may have significance to bacterial fouling. The attachment of organisms to surfaces, often in the form of biofilms, is a major problem in many situations, and has, accordingly, also been widely studied (Characklis 1990; Ridgway 1987; Mittleman 1998). It is a considerable stretch to equate protein adsorption to biofilm formation. However, to the extent that areas of proteinaceous compositions may characterize organisms, they may react equivalently. Surface heterogeneity implies such independence of action regardless of the character of the remainder of the surface of which they are part. Such serves to justify this speculation. Ridgway (1984) showed the different extents to which *Brevundimonas diminuta* adsorbes to a polyamide RO filter, and to one composed of CA.

Biofilm Similarities to Protein Adsorption

It can be hypothesized that the formation of biofilms involves the very mechanism that characterizes protein-to-filter attachments. Biofilms are formed by planktonic organisms attaching to the solid surfaces. It is speculated that the organisms in adhering to the solid surfaces may utilize as an adhesive an extracellular polymeric substances produced by them. Alternatively, the adsorptive attachments may result from the influence of the electric double layer. Indications of hydrophobic adsorptions in biofilm formation has been suggested. More importantly, reductions in free surface energy are involved in the attachments. This latter quality is a result, if not a cause, of hydrophobic adsorptions, as will be discussed. From the foregoing, it seems there is a degree of commonality between biofilm formation and protein adsorption.

The adsorption of organisms from their suspensions onto solid surfaces would involve the same forces of attraction and repulsion that regulate the adsorptive joining of one colloidal particle's surface to that of another. The process involving organisms would manifest itself in their adsorptive retention to the filter surfaces.

Marshall (1992) points out that bacteria, as also particles in general, are kept from contact with surfaces by electrostatic forces. This includes the surfaces of other organisms. The repulsive forces involved are effective at long range, and prevail over the weaker attractive forces that are simultaneously present. As will be described in the forthcoming discussion of the electric double layer, the repulsions are attenuated by higher electrolyte concentrations. The attractive forces, albeit weaker, can then assert their influence. The adsorptive interactions that follow would result in the formation of a biofilm.

Fuoss Effect

In suggesting a similarity between protein adsorptions to polymeric filter surfaces and organism attachments to the same type of surfaces, it is speculated that the term "adsorption" as used in the phrase "protein adsorption" includes a more varied expression of the same mechanisms that fixedly bond other surfaces to one another. The bonding to activated carbon of organic molecular substances, whether in the form of vapors, liquids, or particles, as utilized in gas masks or in water purification contexts, is a classical example of adsorption. As will be seen, the ionic strengths of the aqueous solutions from which proteins may be adsorbed also govern the adsorptive bonding of the organics to the surfaces of the activated carbon particles. In this instance as well, there is an apparent similarity in cause and effect. It is speculated that the adsorption of organic compounds including proteins to activated carbon surfaces is part of a like operation.

The positive effect of ionic strengths on adsorptive sequestrations is forthcoming from the field of water treatment and involves the adsorption of organic substances by activated carbon. This is greatly enhanced by the presence of calcium and magnesium ions. According to Weber et al. (1983), the adsorption of humic materials by activated carbon is pH-dependent and is influenced by the presence of inorganic ions in the solution (Figure 9.3). Calcium is slightly more effective than magnesium, and divalent ions are more influential than monovalent ions by an order of magnitude; potassium ions are slightly more effective than sodium ions. The salutary effects of lower pH on increasing adsorption had previously been remarked upon by Schnitzer and Kodama (1966).

A plausible explanation may derive from the Fuoss effect as discussed by Ong and Bisque (1966) and as advanced by Ghosh and Schnitzer (1979). The Fuoss effect states that large polymeric electrolytes, such as derived from humic acids, exist in solution in a coiled configuration, as indeed do all polymers. Polymeric molecules, as also protein structures, increasingly unwind and extend themselves the diluter the solutions (Figure 9.4). Higher ionic strengths, to the contrary, promote the tightness of such coilings. The contractions of the humic acid molecules under the influence of higher ionic strengths has two adsorption-promoting consequences. The size of the polymer molecules decreases as they become progressively more coiled (Figure 9.5). In the process, the folding of the polymeric chains increasingly confine their hydrophilic moieties, and more openly present their hydrophobic amino acid constituents, of which tryptophane, tyrosin, and phenylalanine are the most extreme. The first effect further

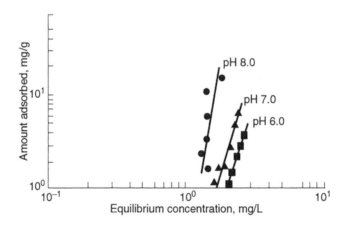

FIGURE 9.3 Adsorption isothermes for humic acid on carbon effect of pH.

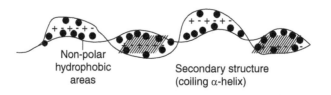

FIGURE 9.4 Unwind polymer structure.

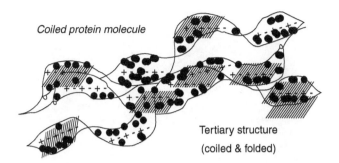

FIGURE 9.5 Densely coiled polymer structure.

increases the ease of interstice penetration; the second promotes hydrophobic adsorptions. Thus, the presence of ions such as hydronium ($H-H_2O$ or H_3O), calcium, and magnesium promote the molecular folding. Both the capacity for adsorption and the rate of adsorption are increased. The adsorption is rate-dependent.

Evidence that the adsorption onto active carbon surfaces of organicmaterials derived from humic substances is promoted by lower pHs was furnished by Weber et al. (1983) and by Schnitzer and Kodama (1966) and was stated also by Michaud (1988). Weber et al. (1983) found that the adsorption isotherm for humic acid on an activated carbon, although increased somewhat by going from pH 9.0 to 7.0, increases markedly when the pH is lowered to 3.5. As will be discussed, lower pH values, equivalent to higher hydronium ion concentrations, also promote the adsorption of proteins to hydrophilic filter surfaces.

Qualitative Measurement of Protein Binding

That specific proteins exhibit differences in their adsorptive proclivities has been remarked upon. The usefulness of a means of measuring this tendency is obvious. Badenhop et al. (1970) have devised and utilized such a test method. A standardized drop of an aqueous solution of serum albumin was placed upon the surface of each of three membrane filters. The extent to which the water-drop spread was evidenced by the area of wetness. This was essentially the same for the three filters: cellulose triacetate, cellulose nitrate, and an experimental PVC. However, the spread of the albumin within the wet area differed. The visual detection of the albumin was made possible by the use of Ponceau S stain. It was found that the albumin spread along with the water over the cellulose triacetate when the bovine albumin concentration was 100 mg percent. At that concentration level, the albumin spread only very little on the cellulose nitrate and even less on the experimental PVC. At a concentration of 700 mg percent, the spread of albumin over the experimental PVC filter did not increase much, but it did so for the cellulose nitrate. This is interpreted as indicating the relative binding forces of the three polymers for serum albumin in aqueous solution. Another adsorption level experiment is the use of Coomassie Blue. The deeper the blue, the higher the unspecific adsorption (Figure 9.6). These small-scale trials can be used as an indication of the protein adsorptive behavior of specific polymers.

The cellulose triacetate is seen as exerting the least interaction. Its saturation point is satisfied with a small amount of albumin, leaving enough to spread and adsorb to larger areas. Thus, it is the least adsorbing and the least interfering in the albumin's spreading along the membrane surface. The experimental PVC by this measure adsorbs the most strongly of the three polymers examined. It adsorbs so strongly and to such an extent that it serves totally to saturate the contact spot. None is left available for spreading even at the 700-mg percent level.

The nitrocellulose binds albumin strongly, but its attractive forces at a given area are not as avid as those of PVC in attaining saturation. Thus, at the 700-mg percent level, unlike the PVC, some of the albumin remains to spread further.

The adsorptive strength of a membrane is, thus, expressible in terms of its adsorption to a specific protein, both in terms of the quantity of protein it binds to the point of saturation, and in the extent available for adsorpion beyond the point of contact.

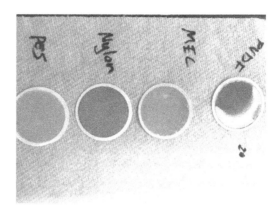

FIGURE 9.6   Different membrane adsorption using Coomassie Blue.

Hydrophilization of Membranes

Protein studies have generally shown that filters composed of polar structures, such as cellulose tri-acetate, exhibit minimal tendencies toward adsorption. (Nitrocellulose membranes, as stated, disclose a higher tendency toward adsorption, possibly through the agency of hydrogen bonding.) Inherently hydrophobic filters, such as an experimental PVC, manifest the highest proclivity of these filter types to interact with proteins. In an effort to minimize the fouling of filters by protein depositions, hydrophobic filters generally available from filter manufacturers have been modified by chemical grafting to convert them to filters characterized by hydrophilic surfaces. The methods by which the "hydrophilizing" alteration is managed are largely proprietary. It is known, however, that methyl methacrylate, probably under free radical attack, can react with given molecular structures to introduce polar ester groups onto the otherwise hydrophobic substrate surface. The reaction is catalyzed by cobalt 60 gamma emanations. The heretofore hydrophobic filter, liable to fouling by proteins, is essentially prevented from so being by conversion of its surface to one that is hydrophobic.

Kim et al. (1994) modified the surface of a polyethylene membrane by introducing 5–7 mol alcoholic hydroxyl group per kilogram; enough to cover the entire polyethylene surface. The filter's saturation capacity for bovine λ-globulin was reduced from 7 mg/m^2 to under 1 mg/m^2 as a result of the filter's surface having been hydrophilized. The change in surface character was from nonpolar and hydrophobic to hydrophilic. The difference in the adsorptive response resulted from the presence of the O–H atomic couple that characterizes alcohols. The oxygen atom of that atomic pair in its acquisitive and unequal sharing of the bonding electrons with the partnering hydrogen atom assumes a partial negative electric sign. The partial loss of the bonding electrons by the hydrogen atom leaves it with a partial but positive electrical charge. It is this partial charge that transforms what would otherwise have been a hydrophobic bonding into one that is dependent on the attraction of opposite electrical signs, albeit only of partial electrical potential.

That the hydrophilization of membranes composed of hydrophobic polymers makes them less receptive to protein adsorption is a relatively recent understanding within the pharmaceutical industry. However, it was demonstrated over three decades ago by filtration practitioners in the brewing industry. Badenhop et al. (1970) showed that coating a hydrophobic experimental PVC membrane with a hydrophilic coating resulted in a significant increase in the filtrative throughput of heavy beers. This resulted from a reduction in the protein fouling of the filters. This argues for an awareness of solutions to problems that may be forthcoming from applications outside of the pharmaceutical industry.

Newer membrane filter surface treatments are forthcoming, which are either designated to reduce the protein adsorption on the surface-treated membrane or create a high bond with the membrane matrix to avoid washing off resulting in hydrophobic spots. Polymer science has not only focused on the stability of the membrane polymers used or the leachable level reduction, but also in the creation of membrane surfaces with lower and lower adsorptive properties.

Competitive Adsorptions

Certain agents competitively preempt the adsorptive sites to block the adsorption of other molecules. This blocking effect is particularly noticed in protein work. Hawker and Hawker (1975) found that gamma globulin is retained in smaller amounts than is fibrinogen. The same action adsorbed IgG from antisera, as measured by nephelometry. Interestingly, addition of polyethylene glycol to the antisera or polyethylene glycol prewashing of the filters prevented such losses. As stated, such shielding effects, ascribed to the preferential adsorption of the polyethylene glycol to the membrane and to consequent blockage of the adsorptive sites have been used in electrophoresis work. The membrane strip used in electrophoresis may be coated with various wetting agents or with albumin solution, etc. The serum proteins being electrophoresed plate out in different spread patterns than they do on the untreated strip.

Surfactants are particularly efficient at preempting the adsorptive sites and blocking them from other type of molecules. This can be considered as resulting from a competitive action that favors the stronger and, thus, the more stable bonding.

Blocking of Adsorptions by Surfactants

Wrasidio and Mysels' (1984) findings that the nonionic surfactant rinsing (with Triton X-100) or polystyrene latex spheres renders their retention less complete by conventional 0.2 μm-rated membrane was taken to indicate adsorptive influences. Hawker and Hawker (1975) showed that membrane treatment with a nonionic surfactant (Tween 20) rinses presumably similar block adsorptions. Prewashing with dilute plasma has almost the same effect. However, the adsorption site-blocking adsorbed plasma leaves some charged protein bound within the filter. This serves to attract and bind additional protein. Thus, prewashing with protein is somewhat less effective than Tween 20 at preventing fibrinogen retention by 0.2 μm-rated membranes (Hawker and Hawker 1975). Pitt et al. (1985) showed that various membranes adsorbed proteins differently and that the same polymeric material, possibly influenced by a different wetting agent, yielded disparate results.

The use of surfactant in conjunction with latex particle retention minimizes adsorption effects and counters particle flocculation. Emory et al. (1993) investigated the effects of three different types of surfactants—nonionic, anionic, and cationic—on the retention of latex particles by each of four types of membranes. The membranes tested were of polysulfone, nylon 66, hydrophilic PVDF, and mixed esters of cellulose; the latter free of its usual wetting agent content.

For all the surfactants, the retention of the 0.198 μm beads by the 0.2 μm- rated membranes decreased asymptotically with surfactant concentration. This can be taken as an index of the blocking of the adsorptive sites by preemptive surfactant adsorption (Figure 9.7). The surfactants tested gave somewhat different retentions for the several membranes. Generally, the anionic surfactant yielded lower retentions, the cationic higher, i.e., less adsorptive, blocking. In the case of the nylon 66 filter, the nonionic and cationic agents produced the least retention, the most blockage. The different filters might possibly have received different ratings had they all been characterized by a single method. Variations in the retention effect could conceivably reflect actual differences in the pore sizes.

Retention (%) of 0.198 um - Spheres by Various 0.2 um - Rated Membrane

Filter Type	In water	In 0.05% Triton X-100
Polycarbonate	100.0	100.0
Asymmetric Polysulfone	100.0	100.0
Polyvinylidene Fluoride	74.8	19.2
Nylon 66	82.1	1.0
Cellulose Esters	89.4	25.1

FIGURE 9.7 Adsorptive separation effected by surfactants.

Within monoclonal antibody processes, Polysorbate 20 is utilized, which is an important stabilizer added to the final formulation. The Polysorbates can compete with adsorptive retentivity, but also may avoid protein adsorption, though this means that the Polysorbate will be adsorbed and diminished within the final formulation. It has to be determined whether this is the case or not. Trial work has shown that PVDF membranes have a lower adsorption than some of the Polyethersulfons (Zhou et al., 2008; Mahler et al., 2009).

Mechanisms of Adsorption

Hydrophobic Adsorptions

Given its abstruse nature, it is not surprising that there are several explanations for the phenomenon of hydrophobic adsorption. No challenges are posed to its being a reality, but there are differences concerning its cause and effects. Adamson (1982) writes, "The term 'hydrophobic bonding' is appropriate to conditions wherein there is an enhanced attraction between two surfaces (as of a particle and filter) exposed to a liquid if the liquid-particle interaction is weaker than the liquid-liquid interaction." The term "hydrophobic" implies an antipathy for water. It is demonstrated by an extreme immiscibility with water. This derives from an absence of polar groups capable of hydrogen bonding to water by way of electrical partial charge interactions. Hydrophobic adsorption is, therefore, believed by some authorities to be *free* of partial charge involvements. As will shortly be seen, the driving force of the adsorption phenomenon is believed by these authorities to result from diminutions in free surface energy that accompany such adsorptions, as explained below.

The rebuttal of this hypothesis holds that electric charges *are* involved, although in a less than obvious fashion. The more apparent electric double-layer actions involving electrical charges do arise from molecular structures, such as ester, and carboxylic groups that contain oxygen atoms. They do give rise to dipoles on account of the strong electro-negativity of their oxygen atoms. The dipole/dipole and other electrical interactions account for the attractions between solid surface sites that result in adsorptive sequestrations, and also colloidal agglomerations. However, although such polar features are absent from hydrocarbon molecules, the latter, nevertheless, do interact in the manner that suggests adsorptive influences based on electrical charges. The apparent contradiction requires clarification.

The VDW forces that exercise attracting interactions among hydrocarbons bereft of oxygen atoms or other polarizing features are hypothesized as being due to "instantaneous non-zero dipole moments" that result in attractions, albeit weak ones. This would explain the hydrocarbon interaction as also being charge related. In this view, hydrocarbon molecules, here taken as the archetypical nonpolar substances, are motivated by the opposite signs of their VDW-type partial charges to adsorptively connect with other hydrophobic molecules in hydrophobic adsorptions.

The simpler hypothesis that does not rely upon charge interactions between hydrocarbon molecules is possible. In agreement with time-honored alchemists' observations, namely, "like prefers like," it is accepted that hydrocarbon molecules do tend to connect with other hydrophobic molecules. The implication is that the hydrocarbon molecules' VDW attraction of the one for another is the key driver in hydrophobic adsorptions.

This seems also to be the view of Fletcher (1996, p. 3). He sees the water adsorbed to the bacterium and filter surfaces as a (separating) barrier to their coming together. Moreover, removal of the water is "energetically unfavorable." However, if either surface "has non-polar groups or patches," the resulting hydrophobic interaction will displace the water and allow a closer approach of the two surfaces. This more orthodox explanation does not rely upon charge interactions between hydrocarbon molecules. It cites the reduction in free surface energy that is an accompaniment of hydrophobic adsorptions. The implication is that this is the force that motivates the coalescence of the dispersed hydrophobic phase.

Nevertheless, the gathering of the hydrophobic material and its separation from the water is more distinctly explained by Tanford (1980) who quotes G.S. Hartley as stating, "The antipathy of the paraffin-chain for water is, however, frequently misunderstood. There is no question of actual repulsion between individual water molecules and paraffin chains, nor is there any very strong attraction of paraffin chains for one another. There is, however, a very strong attraction of water molecules for one another in comparison with which the paraffin-paraffin or paraffin-water attractions are very slight." Thus, Tanford (1980, Chap. 5) expostulates that it is the water molecules' alliances among themselves that rejects interactions with the hydrocarbon molecules, causing a concentration of the latter: "The free energy is representative of the attraction between the substances involved. The free energy of attraction between water and hexane or water and octane obtained at 25°C is about -40 erg/cm^2 of contact area; the free energy of attraction of the hydrocarbons for themselves at the same temperature is also about $\underline{-40}$ erg/cm^2; but the free energy of attraction of water for itself is -144 erg/cm^2. It is clearly the latter alone that leads to a thermodynamic preference for elimination of hydrocarbon-water contacts; the attraction of the hydrocarbon for itself is essentially the same as its attraction for water." The driving force of the hydrophobic adsorptions, then, is the reduction in Gibbs' free surface energy that results from the strong mutual attractive forces that manifest themselves in hydrogen bonding among the water molecules. Partial charge influences need not be involved.

At this point, we are obliged to briefly consider the hydrogen bond, covalent bonding, partial charges, and the electric double layer. A fuller treatment will follow subsequently.

The water molecule is tetrahedral in shape. Each of its corners holds either a pair of electrons or an hydrogen atom. Each of the partly positive hydrogen atoms of one water molecule can form a hydrogen bond with a partly negative oxygen atom of each of four different water molecule, etc. Actually, two or three is the usual number. This process, repeated throughout the water volume, in effect creates an (imperfect) interconnected network. Thus, the molecules of water in its solid state (ice) exist as tetrahedral hydrogen-bonded structures. Much of this ordered form persists even in the mobile liquid.

The hydrocarbon molecules with little affinity for the water molecules are rebuffed from intruding among these spatially, tetrahedrally ordered arrangements. It is the network formed by the water molecules among themselves that in *expelling* the hydrocarbon molecules causes their segregation. These may conjoin also to the hydrophobic areas of solid surfaces they encounter; such as of pipes or filters. In their coming together, the hydrocarbon molecules, as also the water molecules, effect a reduction in the total free surface energy. It is likely that micellar groupings are involved under the influence of area-minimizing forces.

With regard to hydrophobic adsorptions to filter membrane surfaces, Zydney's (1996) view seems closer to that of Fletcher (1996). He describes the phenomenon as follows: "Solute-membrane interactions can occur only if sufficient energy is provided to displace the H-bonded water molecules from the surface of both the membrane and the macrosolute (protein). In contrast, the removal of unbonded water molecules from the surface of a hydrophobic membrane or macrosolute, is energetically very favorable, leading to a very strong 'attractive' interaction between hydrophobic surfaces in aqueous solutions." Although referred to variously as hydrophobic adsorption, or hydrophobic bonding, "It really reflects the change in energy or entropy due to the dehydration of the two surfaces, and the formation of additional hydrogen bonds among water molecules."

Significance of Solubility

It is possible to generalize regarding the adsorption of materials from aqueous media by viewing the adsorptive phenomenon as being in competition with the tendency of the material to remain in solution. Solubilization involves partial charge interactions between the water molecules and the molecules being brought into solution. This is the same type of bonding that result in the hydration of ions. The adsorptive union is between the full charge on the ion and the partial charge of opposite sign on the atoms of the water molecule. The less extensive the bonding with water, the less water-soluble the material; i.e., the smaller the interaction between the given molecular entity and water, the easier it is to remove it from solution by hydrophobic adsorptive interaction. By this measure, less ionized or nonpolar molecules are easier to adsorb because they have less affinity for the water molecules than the water molecules have for themselves. Hydrophobic adsorption assumes its importance as a particle retention mechanism on the basis of the relative strengths of the several interactions that are possible in a given situation, namely, particle to particle, water to particle, and water to water, with the last being the strongest.

Free Surface Energy

A proper treatment of the subject requires the application of thermodynamics. An effort is being made here to set forth the concept of free surface energy in a less rigorous manner. The beneficiaries will be those who, like the authors, are limited in their ability to probe the occult and mysterious.

Consider a droplet of water. Every water molecule within its depth will interact with its neighbors to the full extent of its powers to undergo bonding. As a result, a given volume of water will, in effect, consist of a network of water molecules connected to one another by hydrogen bonds. The propensity of the water molecules to bond is a measure of the energy available to them for interaction with other (suitable type) molecules.

However, the water molecules situated on the spherical outside boundaries of the water droplet and constituting its interface with non-water molecules have no neighbors on the droplet's periphery suitable for bonding. The unexpended energy remaining in their nonbonded region is the free surface energy being discussed. Liquid water dispersed in discrete droplet form has a proportionally large surface area, and, therefore, a large total free surface energy. The energy expenditure undergone in bonding interactions serves to coalesce the droplets into larger volumes with a consequent diminishment in total surface area. A loss in the total free surface energy is the result.

The Electrical Double Layers and Partial Charges

Adsorptive effects can be explained by considering the electrical aspects of surface chemistry (Adamson 1982, Chap. V). Largely, these form the basis of the Debye–Hückel theory, contributed to and enlarged upon by notable authorities in the field. It is sufficiently recondite in its mathematics to frustrate its presentation by the authors of this chapter except as a generality.

As a prelude to explaining the electrical double layer it may be timely to review the nature of the partial charges that are commonly considered to be of pertinence in the formation of adsorptive bonding interactions.

Adsorptive Forces

Atoms in their neutral state are each characterized by a set number of electrons. In interacting with one another to form various molecules, two atoms become mutually bonded by strong electrical forces. These result from one atom acquiring an electron from the other. The electron is conventionally regarded as bearing a negative electrical sign. Thus, the atom that accepts the electron is said to be negatively charged (–), since it now has one electron (negatively charged) more than it has in its neutral state. The recipient atom in donating its electron departs from its neutral status by losing an amount of negative electricity, namely, an electron. It thus becomes plus charged. The two partnering atoms sharing in this electron-exchange are said to be chemically bonded, united by the attraction that oppositely electrical charges have for one another. This, the ionic bond, is the product of an electron being transferred from one atom to another.

Covalent Bonding

The two electrons that commonly constitute a covalent chemical bond are each donated by one of the interacting atoms. However, the two-bonding electrons are not shared equally. An atom, as a consequence of its size, may draw the electron pair closer to itself and so acquires a greater portion of the negative charge. Accordingly, the other bonding atom, bereft of a portion of the negative charge, in effect becomes plus charged. It is from such unequal sharing of the bonding electrons that the partial charges originate. The partial charge on an atom of one molecule will tend to connect with (adsorb onto) an oppositely charged atom on another molecule. The hydrogen bond is an example of such an interaction.

Hydrogen Bond

Aspects of the hydrogen bond were discussed above. The hydrogen bond arises from a dipole/dipole interaction (Figure 9.8). It is the most important of such interactions. The water molecule, H_2O, consists

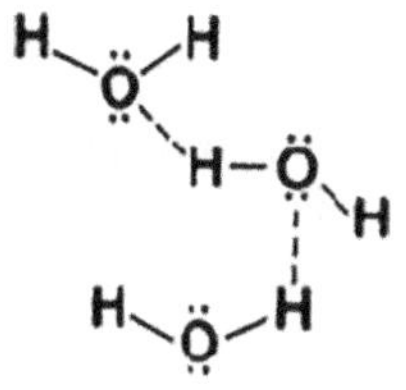

FIGURE 9.8 Hydrogen bonding model.

of two hydrogen atoms each bonded to the same oxygen atom. The nucleus of the oxygen atom pulls the bonding electrons more strongly to itself and away from the hydrogen atoms. The bonding is not disrupted, but the bonding elements become partially charged. The unequal sharing of the electrons makes the electron-richer oxygen partially negative, and the proportionately deprived hydrogen atoms partially positive. This creates the O^- H^+ dipole (Tanford 1980, Chap. 5). There are two hydrogen atoms originating from two different water molecules that connect to a single oxygen atom of one of those molecules. One hydrogen atom is of the pair chemically bonded to the oxygen atom to comprise the water molecule. The other forms the hydrogen bond that bridges one water molecule to the other. Interestingly, the two hydrogen atoms are not equidistant from the oxygen atom. The one attached by valence forces to the oxygen atom is at a distance of 1.00 Å from it. The H-bonded hydrogen is 1.76 Å apart from that oxygen. The oxygen atoms of the two interacting water molecules are 2.76 Å apart, while the two nearest non-hydrogen-bonded oxygen atoms are 4.5 Å distant from one another. The chemically bonded hydrogen is more closely attached, perhaps an indication of the relative strengths of the two types of bonds.

The attractive forces of the oppositely signed partial charges decrease rapidly with the distance between the dipoles. Only the proton (hydrogen atom, of atomic weight 1) is small enough to approach the electronegative oxygen atom closely enough to establish the H-bond. Moreover, the electromagnetic associations involving hydrogen atoms in dipole arrangements are only strong enough to be formed with the most electronegative elements, namely, fluorine, oxygen, and nitrogen in decreasing order. Nevertheless, the H-bond, although weak in its energy of attraction, figures significantly in many fields of chemistry, and has importance especially in protein chemistry.

As stated, the water molecule is tetrahedral in shape. In its solid (ice) state, it exist as tetrahedral hydrogen-bonded structures. Much of this ordered form persists even in the mobile liquid. Each of the tetrahedral corners holds either a pair of electrons or an hydrogen atom. Each of the partly positive hydrogen atoms of one water molecule can form a hydrogen bond with a partly negative oxygen atom of each of two different water molecule. This process, repeated throughout the water volume, creates an interconnected molecular network that includes H-bonded rings and chains. The network of H-bonded water molecules requires the heat energy of boiling water to break the adsorptive bonding to set free the individual water molecules in vapor form, namely, steam.

The bond strengths of partial charges are less than those of the fuller electrical forces that characterize the chemical bonds. They are sometimes referred to as physical bonds. It is largely this type bonding that motivates the adsorptive interactions among the partially charged atom of different signs sited on different molecules.

Hydrogen-Bonding Interactions

That proteins tend to adhere to hydrophobic surfaces by way of the hydrophobic adsorption mechanism seems an established fact. In agreement with that explanation, studies on protein fouling of filters have generally shown that filters composed of polar structures, such as cellulose triacetate, exhibit minimal tendencies toward protein adsorptions. Hydrophobic adsorption is, however, not the only mechanism for such attachments. Thus, nitrocellulose membranes disclose a higher tendency toward protein adsorption, possibly through the agency of hydrogen bonding.

The efficacy of hydrophilization has not been restricted to pharmaceuticals. This practice has been put to good use in certain other applications including one considered by many to be of high purpose. Hydrophilization ameliorates the filter clogging (fouling) caused by the interactions of the filter polymer with the protein (albumin) present in beers. Larger production throughputs of the beverage are gained from hydrophilization of the filter.

The mechanism of the intermolecular attraction is believed to result from hydrogen bonding between the partial negatively charged atoms of the nitro groups and the partial positively charged hydrogen atoms of the protein molecule. However, by contrast, the throughput of beer utilizing an experimental Dynel microporous membrane was even more restrictive. Dynel, being a copolymer of vinyl chloride and acrylonitrile, is strongly hydrophobic. It likely favored protein adsorption through the exercise of its hydrophobicity, rather than through hydrogen bonding although its nitrogen atoms are amenable to hydrogen bonding. Hydrophobic filters, such as the experimental PVC membrane previously mentioned, manifest the highest proclivity of these filter types to interact with the proteins present in beers.

Vaccine Adsorption to Filters

As shown in Table 9.2 the filtration of influenza vaccine through microporous polymeric membranes results in the loss of titer, a costly and undesirable consequence of vaccine purification by filtration. The loss of titer with a mixed ester of cellulose membrane was 35%, with CA it was 9%. A membrane composed of vinyl chloride acrylonitrile copolymer lost 11% of titer. Moreover, the effect on the filter in terms of throughput was significant. The CA filter in 47-mm disc form yielded an average of 38 mL over a 120 s interval, the copolymer produced 80 mL over 210 s, and the mixed esters gave 58 mL in a period of 210 s. The influence of the polymeric composition of the filter is evident (Tanny and Meltzer 1978).

It is essential to test different filter membrane polymers in the initial stages (commonly preclinical phase) to evaluate not only throughput, but especially unspecific adsorption. Most commonly, unspecific adsorption is responsible for excessive yield losses. The filtration device needs to be balanced toward the application. It should, therefore, be tested accordingly.

Protein-Filter Adsorptions

The study of protein adsorption to filters makes use of "the filter saturation curve." What is measured is the concentration of the filtrate as a function of the volume filtered per unit area of filter. Initially the rate of adsorption is highest, while the filtrate's protein concentration is the lowest. As the filter approaches saturation, the adsorption rate decreases. The effluent's protein content increases until it approaches that of the feedstream. At this point, by definition, no additional adsorption can occur. The data reveal the volume of a given protein solution needed to saturate the particular filter. In addition, the quantity of protein required to saturate per unit area of filter, the filter's effective filtration area (EFA) becomes known. Generally, this approximates 5–50 L/10-in. filter cartridge, which translates to 0.5–10 mL/cm². The concentration of the protein solution and the area of the filter being known, the protein adsorption

TABLE 9.2

Flu-Vaccine Filtration Volumes

0.45-μm Mixed Cellulose Esters			Mixed Cellulose Esters		
Manufacturer I			Manufacturer II		
36/90	38/90	33/90	28/90	25/90	30/90
38/120	41/120 (Titers 64, 65%)	34/120	31/120	27/120 (Titers 64, 65%)	34/120
0.45-μm Cellulose Triacetate			**0.45-μm Dynel Type**		
40/90	46/90	40/90	64/90	48/90	52/90
42/120	50/120	42/120	70/120	53/120	57/120
45/180	55/180	43/150	78/180	57/180	63/180
	58/210		80/210		
(Titers 90%, 91%, 91%)				(Titers 89%, 87%)	

value per unit filter area at the point of saturation can be calculated. For a solution of a given protein concentration, the volume necessary to be filtered for the effluent to achieve parity with the concentration of feedstream becomes known.

Sundaram (1998) points out that in most cases the filter saturation curve indicates that a comparatively small amount of protein serves to saturate the filter to attain the steady state of quantitative recovery in the effluent. To the extent that the adsorptive propensities of the different filter types are investigated to learn which adsorb least, the effort is largely unnecessary because so little protein is lost regardless. The attendant economic concerns would still hold for filling containers with very dilute protein contents, or with very expensive protein, or where small batch sizes are involved. Sundaram further calls attention to the potential loss of protein by adsorption to the surfaces of the processing equipment other than the filters. Prefilters, tanks, rubber, or metal piping, even filter holders, etc. need to be considered. To avoid this overall adsorptive loss, careful system design is required.

Undissolved Protein

There are instances where at steady state the effluent's protein concentration does not recover fully to that of the feed solution. The phenomenon of not achieving "saturation" may result from the sieve removal of proteinaceous gels or particulates, or from undissolved protein. Protein deposited during filtrations using microporous membrane may have been generated as small quantities of aggregated or denatured protein caused by foaming, extreme pHs, high shear stresses, or extreme temperatures (Sundaram 1998). This is more likely to occur the finer the pore size rating of the filter, as would be used in organism or virus removal. The condition may also stem from multilayered adsorption wherein the saturating mono-layer of protein participates in protein–protein interactions to build in depth.

The latter possibility is disagreed with, especially by those who define "adsorption" by way of the Langmuir adsorption isotherm wherein only one layer of adsorbed material is considered possible. The disagreement may reflect differences in semantics. Some hold that the term "adsorption" pertains only to the partitioning of a macrosolute between a solvent and a surface, thus, defining the adsorbed material as being that limited to intimate contact with the adsorbing surface. Be that as it may, in the forthcoming discussion of the electric double layer it will be seen that while the adsorptive forces do indeed hold the primary adsorbed layer fixedly, a more distant layer is also held, albeit not as fixedly. The point being made is that in actuality the adsorptive forces extend further than just to the first layer, although in less strength. The differentiation among adsorptive effects by way of definitions may satisfy attempts at classifications. A more meaningful differentiation will result from characterizations based on the effects that are manifested by the mechanisms of adsorption.

To make certain that protein in particle form is not classified as being protein adsorbed from solution, filters of smaller pore size ratings may be employed to remove such non-dissolved matter. Adsorption studies based on this usage are obliged to assume that the extent of pore wall surface is the same for the filters of different pore size ratings. Such an assumption may be unwarranted. The numbers used in listing filter porosity values are likely approximations. This tends to render as unreliable the adsorption data based on unit surface area studies.

A similar consideration likely extends to the sometimes advocated substitution of 0.1 μm-rated membranes for the 0.2/0.22 μm-rated filters. Quite probably, the finer pores of the 0.1 μm-rated filter of the same porosity present larger pore wall surface areas than do their 0.2/0.22 μm-rated counterparts.

Dynamic or Static Wetting-Out

Pitt (1987) in his investigative work brought the filter into contact with the protein solution by dipping. Filter disks of 8-mm diameter having $0.5\,cm^2$ nominal area, dipped in 1 mL of protein solution for 18 h at ambient temperature were utilized. The protein, partly labeled by iodine, was used with filters of hydrophilic PVDF, hydrophilic polysulfone, and cellulose diacetate. These filters showed low protein binding on the order of $<10\,μg/cm^2$ nominal area for bovine serum albumin (BSA), and IgG from sheep. This is what would be expected from hydrophilic surfaces comparatively incapable of hydrophobic adsorptions. Polyamide (nylon), and cellulose nitrate filters exhibited high-protein binding for these proteins, namely,

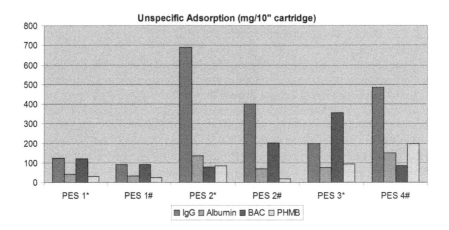

FIGURE 9.9 Unspecific adsorption difference on the same membrane polymer of different suppliers.

~190 and ~250 µg/cm² nominal area, respectively. These findings could also be expected from the adsorptive mechanism based on hydrogen bonding, especially in the case of the nitrocellulose polymer.

Long experience with the relative difficulty of wetting filters demonstrates the inefficiency of this static method. It may prove difficult to expel the air from the smaller filter pores. What is required is the dynamic flow of the protein solution through the filter. The complete involvement of all the pore surfaces should not be assumed. It may necessitate prolongation or repetition.

Pitt (1986) compared the static method of dipping with the active or dynamic method of passing the protein solution through the filter's pores by filtration. Only the nylon (polyamide) filter among a group of three, including hydrophilic polysulfone, and hydrophilic PVDF, showed a difference in the amount of protein adsorbed in terms of the mass per unit area uptake of insulin or of human growth hormone. The nylon filter adsorbed a much higher amount of protein by using by the dynamic rather than the static method, namely, >1,000 µg/cm² nominal area. Certain nylon filters are reputed to be somewhat "open." Perhaps, it may be speculated that such a "more open" filter responds more strongly to the greater efficiency of the dynamic method of exposure to the protein solution.

Figure 9.9 illustrates that filters made of the same polymer and having the same pore size rating, but made by different manufacturers exhibit different adsorption characteristics. The variations may well result differences in the pore or membrane structure, but probably finds its prominence in the surface treatment of the membrane.

The Electrical Double Layer

The situation being considered is that of two surfaces, both immersed in an aqueous solution. One may be of a particle or large molecule; the other that of a filter. Common to all surfaces, the surface molecules differ from those within the mass because they interface with a surrounding phase that contains relatively few molecules that are similar enough to bond with. The surface layer is, thus, molecularly unsaturated. This gives rise to a residual field that finds expression in a surface energy. As is inevitable, the surfaces, because of their higher energy, acquire ions from the solution, or gain charges induced thereon. The acquired ions become fixed to the immersed surfaces.

In effect, they simultaneously endow the surfaces of both filter and protein (or other entity), with electrical forces of both stronger and weaker powers, and of both attractive and repulsive capabilities. The magnitude of these effects is in accordance with the charge density on the individual adsorbing surface resulting from the fixed charges. The acquired ions give rise to the strong and, hence, long-range Coulombic forces. When the surfaces of both organism and filter bear charges of like sign, their mutual repulsion ensues. The attractive forces of opposite signs are effective only at shorter ranges. Like the VDW forces, they cannot redress the repulsion. The limitation to the effectivity of the VDW forces to short distances is a measure of their weaker influences. They avail only at shorter distances.

As would be expected, the electric potential of the surface charges just described is moderated by counterions from within the solution that become fixedly attached to them. These intervening counterions effectively shield the electrical interactions between the charged surfaces. In consequence, the electrostatic forces are reduced in potential.

Not all of the surface charges are neutralized or shielded by the inseparably attached counterions. Therefore, more ions of opposite charge, intermingled with their counterions, are attracted by the fixed surface charges that remain unshielded. However, these counterions remain mobile because they are increasingly distant from the fixed surface charges, although responsive to them. The interactive forces diminish sharply with distance. Other than the first layer of counterions that becomes firmly attached, the remainder of the counterions involved, although attracted, are sufficiently distant from the surface charge to remain mobile within the solution. They can be caused to migrate by the impress of an electric current. This establishes a line of separability between the fixedly attached counterions and those that are mobile.

The electric potential that from this line of counterion separation extends further into the liquid to satisfy the un-neutralized portion of the surface-fixed charges is called the zeta potential. The distance it extends is known as the Debye length. In effect, the zeta potential measures the unsatisfied electric charge of the single layer comprised of the ions of the surface and the somewhat fewer counterions they fixedly attracted and bonded to. The layer of fixed surface charges and their tightly bound counterions is the first of the double layers. The mobile counterions in the solution constitute the second of the double layers. In combination they form the electric double layer.

It should be remembered that the electric potential characterizes both the filter and particle or protein surfaces. The larger the Debye length, the greater the electric potential, and the more extensive the distance between both surfaces. Although attractive like-charges and repulsive opposite charges are simultaneously active, the stronger repelling like-charges dominate at the longer Debye lengths. The repulsion derives from the influences of the strong primary forces that are operative over longer distances. The other repulsive force is more general. It results when any two atoms are brought together close enough for their (negatively charged) electron clouds to overlap.

For the attractive influences to exercise their powers the repulsive forces require attenuation. This situation is invoked by the addition of salts to the solution. As the ions thus supplied increase in concentration, the counterionic cloud around each surface increases as well. The enveloping ions shield the zeta potential, and the Debye length decreases proportionally. This enables the weaker attractive forces to assert their powers. The attractive forces are short range and electrostatic. They are the products of various dipole interactions, including VDW forces. The result is an adsorptive joining of the two surfaces, namely, that of the protein or particle and that of the filter.

Exactly the same phenomenon applies to the different particles constituting a colloid. The colloidal particles separated by the zeta potential are enabled to agglomerate and precipitate when salted out, as by the addition of the multi-ions of aluminum sulfate in water clarification contexts.

Incidentally, the equilibrium point where the attractive and repulsive forces balance one another defines the space that exists between the atoms composing molecules, and also between the overlapping segments of long polymeric chains.

When placed in an electric field, dipoles will tend to orient themselves in head-to-tail chain-like fashion alternating their positive and negative partial charge interactions. Such an array of dipoles intervening between two like-charged repulsive forces serves to attenuate their mutual antagonism by substituting a chain of subsidiary or partial charge interactions. As a result of the diminishment of the repulsive forces, the countervailing forces of attraction assert themselves, and the two surfaces become united by the adsorptive sequestration mechanism.

At distances of 10–20 nm, repulsive electrostatic forces dominate. Here the Debye length is too great for the weaker VDW attractive forces to participate. At between 2 and 10 nm both repulsive and electrostatic attractive forces are manifest, the distance now being small enough to allow the weaker attractive forces to begin asserting themselves. At between 0.5 and 2 nm, the water adhering to the surfaces is still a barrier to specific surface interactions. However, if the two surfaces include non-polar areas or patches, these may coalesce to form hydrophobic adsorptions concomitant with the elimination of the interfering water. At less than 1.0 nm, the attractive forces are strong enough to cause specific organism/surface interactions to take place.

Pall et al. (1980) state that when the Debye length corresponds to a zeta potential of less than 30 mV, the VDW forces can affect the adsorptive interaction. The adsorptive union is stabilized when the particles are endowed with net surface charges in the magnitude of 30–40 mV or more.

Dipole Alignment

Upon the reduction of the Debye length as occasioned by the addition of ions, the short-range attractive VDW forces enable the appropriate surface sites on the organism to interact with those on the filter. Since there are as many opportunities for the VDW force orientations to exercise repulsions, as there are to encourage attractions, the domination by the attractive tendencies requires explanation. It turns out that two factors incline toward the attractive forces. The induced dipoles that are the VDW forces in a molecule can align themselves either in a head-to-head and tail-to-tail, or head-to-tail sequence. This reflects a probability factor. The head-to-tail arrangement involves a lower energy level. This orientation is, therefore, favored.

This is abetted by a polarization factor. Also called the London dispersion force, it affects the size of the dipole moment by influencing the spatial separation of the plus and minus charges is each molecule in proportion to the dipole sizes. In the electrostatic attraction mode, polarization increases the interaction between the two molecules. In the repulsive orientation, the polarization decreases the molecular moments, and, hence, the repulsive force. As stated by Wheland (1947), "The attractive orientations on the average, are more attractive than the repulsive orientations are repulsive." As a result of these two factors, the short-range VDW forces exert an attractive influence, and bring about the desired filtrative removal of organisms by an adsorptive interaction.

This phenomenon can also be stated slightly differently. When placed in an electric field, dipoles will tend to orient themselves in head-to-tail chain-like fashion alternating their positive and negative partial charge interactions. Such an array of dipoles intervening between two like-charged repulsive forces serves to attenuate their mutual antagonism by substituting a chain of subsidiary or partial charge interactions. As a result of the diminishment of the repulsive forces, the countervailing forces of attraction assert themselves, and the two surfaces become united by the adsorptive sequestration mechanism. This is perhaps best illustrated by the colloidal destabilization phenomenon by way of which study it was elucidated. It is also this effect that minimizes the strength of the (repelling) zeta potential.

Debye Length Phenomena

Fletcher (1996) describes the attractive and repulsive forces involved in these interactions between organism and the filter or other surfaces, and offers quantification of the approximate distances at which they are significant: At distances greater than 50 nm, called the "secondary minimum," VDW attractive forces do cause the positioning of the bacteria nearer the surface, but so weakly that they are readily removed by shear forces. At distances of 10–20 nm, repulsive electrostatic forces dominate. Here the Debye length is too great for the weaker VDW attractive forces to participate. At between 2 and 10 nm both repulsive and electrostatic attractive forces are manifest, the distance now being small enough to allow the weaker attractive forces to begin asserting themselves. At between 0.5 and 2 nm, the water adhering to the surfaces is still a barrier to specific surface interactions. However, if the two surfaces include nonpolar areas or patches, these may coalesce to form hydrophobic adsorptions concomitant with the elimination of the interfering water. At less than 1.0 nm, the attractive forces are strong enough to cause specific organism/surface interactions to take place.

Pall et al. (1980) state that when the Debye length corresponds to a zeta potential of less than 30 mV, the VDW forces can affect the adsorptive interaction. Colloids are destabilized when their particles are endowed with net surface charges of similar sign in the magnitude of 30–40 mV or more.

There are, however, limitations to attaining the required small Debye lengths. The adsorption of a surfactant molecule, or of a macromolecule, onto a surface increases its size. This steric hindrance may keep it too far from the other surface to yield a short Debye length. Nonionic surfactants in particular contribute to such a condition. The two surfaces are, thus, sterically stabilized against adsorptive coalescence. Spatial interferences can also result from the hydration barriers created by the increase in an ion's size by its acquisition of waters of hydration. Such steric or geometric interferences can create an insurmountable energy barrier sufficient to frustrate adsorptions.

Recent Cartridge Testing

A plentiful literature is available on protein adsorption and its effects. Its accumulation over time spans periods when factors presently considered important were then not recognized to be so. Thus, the value of some earlier studies can be questioned. Additionally, much exploratory work dealt with filters in small disk form. While often appropriate for experimentation, they obviously do not suit processing needs. Consequently, the forthcoming review of recent work will be confined to investigations involving filters in cartridge form.

Conclusions drawn from such studies should be made with care. Investigations made using only membranes and proteins are designed to evaluate the adsorptive tendencies of the constituting polymers. This could enable filter choices to be made based on the polymer's character with regard to adsorptions. The results obtained using small disk filters can be extended to measure the contributions of the filter holders, and of ancillary equipment exposed to the protein test solutions. At best, only the polymeric interactions are assayed.

However, the uncomplicated simplicity of the small filter disk may not translate sufficiently well for cartridge usage in processing operations. The more complex cartridge constructions involve pleating of the filter; the pleat densities and their heights and patterns along with the nature of the separation and drainage layers that are used along with its endcaps, and core and cage of whatever materials of construction deserve consideration. These several items all contribute to the totality of the cartridge's adsorptions.

The performance of a cartridge regarding its protein adsorption is at the most a characterization of cartridges of its type. Its performance may be compared for whatever reason and by any standard, however arbitrary, with cartridges of a different type. However, in making comparisons there should be an awareness that the construction features of the tested cartridges are unalike. Tests reported in the literature distinguish the subject cartridges according to the filter's polymeric identity. They are further identified as being hydrophilized or not. It should be remembered that if the surface's conversion will totally insulate the underlying polymeric membrane from contact with the protein. Care must be taken not to misidentify the polymeric material that is in actual contact with the protein solution.

Filter Saturation Curve

Plotting protein recovery (in percentage) against volume throughput (in L) will show a straight horizontal line when the filtrate's protein concentration attains the steady state equal to that of the feed stream. A continuation of the line's upward slope to the end of the test signifies that the filter's adsorptive capacity had not yet been assuaged to that point.

A straight horizontal line from the onset to the end of the filtration test signals that there is no adsorption, or so little that the rate and/or extent of adsorption is not noticeable enough to affect its effluent concentration over the course of the filtration. The likely interpretation would be that only a miniscule amount of adsorption took place over a very short time period.

An initial downward direction of the plotted line indicates the rate of protein adsorption by the magnitude of its angle from the horizontal. A subsequent upturn of the plotted trace signals by its steepness the diminishing rate of protein uptake by the filter. Its eventual return to the horizontal bespeaks the steady state of saturation.

Where protein adsorption is the concern, that filter would be considered best that indicated from the start the least deviation from a straight horizontal line.

The filter saturation data can be plotted differently. Thus, the plotting of the Langmuir adsorption equation, illustrated by Figure 9.10, usually identifies protein adsorption as a function of the filtrate mass (g), or volume (L). An upturn of the line from its very origin represents the region of protein adsorption. As the rate of adsorption decreases, the line tends to level on its way to the horizontal. It does so at the point of saturation. The failure of the plotted line to achieve a horizontal position means that the protein

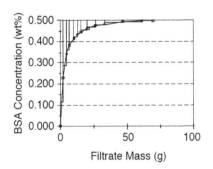

FIGURE 9.10   Adsorption of BSA versus filtrate volume.

uptake never reached saturation over the duration of the test. The area under the curve is a measure of the amount of protein adsorbed over the test's duration. In the case of cartridges this includes the amount of protein adsorbed by all components and appurtenances in contact with the protein test solution.

Studies Directed to Capsules

Protein adsorption studies involving cartridges and disposable capsules suitable for processing purposes have been reported in the literature. The data garnered in such experimentation will here be reported by way of the graphs or tables constructed by their investigators. Except where necessary to explain our conclusions, experimental details will not be dealt with. Interested parties can secure the experimental details, and from the published papers. This will enable readers to make their own evaluations.

Brose and Waibel (1996) studied the uptake of BSA, and of immunoglobulin-G using commercially available filter capsules constructed with a polypropylene shell. The capsule designs differed to a degree: the polyvinylidene fluoride (PVDF) capsule did not utilize a prefilter, while the CA device included a 0.45 μm-rated CA prefilter along with a 0.2/0.22 μm-rated CA final filter. These filter units consisted of membranes of either PVDF, nylon, or CA of 0.2/0.22 μm-rated pore size. Dynamic flow-through exposed the membranes to the protein solutions at 24°C under <1 psi over a time period that usually terminated when protein adsorption/desorption attained equilibrium.

Figure 9.11 shows that the BSA (wt %) adsorption data plotted against the BSA concentration (wt %) was linear for all three capsule types. However, the BSA adsorption, at about 220 μg/cm^2/wt %, by the nylon (polyamide) filter device was almost double the capacity of either the CA or PVDF filters. These equaled one another at about 120 μg/cm/wt %.

The substantially greater adsorption of both BSA and IgG by nylon in capsule form is in line with findings by Pitt (1987). His earlier work was based on the testing of nylon filters in the form of single pieces of membranes unencumbered by considerations of holders, etc. With regard to IgG, the nylon capsule does not respond in linear fashion at low IgG levels. It does attain the saturation stage of the adsorb/desorb equilibrium at a high adsorption level.

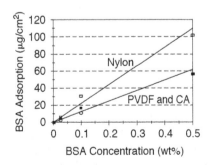

FIGURE 9.11   BSA adsorption on different filter materials.

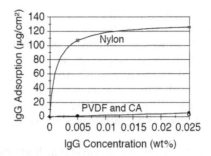

FIGURE 9.12 IgG adsorption on different filter membrane materials.

Figure 9.12 indicates that IgG adsorption (μg/cm^2) is linearly related to its concentration (wt %) for the CA and the PVDF membranes, the level adsorbed being $\approx$200 μg/cm^2/wt %. The nylon filter adsorbed each protein in a nonlinear fashion until saturated with it. Brose and Weibel attribute the high protein adsorption of the nylon to the strong hydrogen bonding of the amide groups of the 6,6 nylon polymer.

In each case, the nylon showed itself to be the most adsorptive of the tested filters for both the BSA and IgG proteins. This agrees with Pitt (1987) findings. BSA demonstrates an adsorption relationship that is linear with respect to its concentration for all the tested capsules. However, at 220 μg/cm^{2}wt%, it is almost double the 120 μg/cm^2 value exhibited for the cellulose ester and PVDF instruments. In the case of the IgG adsorption, it too is linear relative, at 200 μg/cm^2, to its concentration for the CA and PVDF capsules. For the polyamide (nylon) device, the adsorption increased linearly from its starting level to the point of saturation.

It is evident that protein adsorption by filters occurs, that it is manifested differently by different proteins and filters, and that its control, where desired, is variously managed in separate ways that do not find universal application to all proteins or to every filter.

Studies Directed to Cartridges

The performance of various polymer-type pleated membranes in 10″ cartridge form in the retention of protein was investigated by Datar et al. (1992). The use of cartridge filters instead of flat membrane disks (13 or 47 mm) enabled the protein retention influences of the conventional support and drainage layer construction to be assessed. The effect of prefilters could also be measured as four different types were evaluated along with four final filters. Certain prefilter–final filter combinations were also tested. The protein used was BSA in 90 μg/mL concentration. Protein concentration was measured absorption units at wavelength 280 nm and converted to concentration units as μg/mL.

The filter types examined were:

a. polypropylene membrane rated 1.2 μm.

b. polypropylene depth filter rated 0.5 μm.

c. nylon 6,6 membrane rated 0.2 μm.

d. hydroxyl-modified polyamide membrane rated 0.2 μm.

e. hydrophilic PVDF rated 0.2 μm.

f. mixed cellulose ester depth filter {not rated}.

g. CA membrane rated 0.2 μm.

h. polysulfone membrane rated 0.2 μm.

The protein saturation curves depict the pattern of protein adsorption forthcoming from the tested cartridges. The CA unit, as well as the hydroxylated polyamide, and the hydrophilic PVDF were essentially equal in their small uptake and their swift saturation with the BSA. The results are in agreement with the known experience wherein hydrophilic membranes are found not to favor protein adsorptions.

The membrane identified as being constructed of polysulfone polymer shows, within 1 or 2 L of flow-through, so very thorough a recovery as to have been extraordinarily fast in becoming saturated with whatever small quantity of BSA it adsorbed. Polysulfone is sufficiently hydrophobic, however, to have been expected to be more avid in its hydrophobic adsorptions. Albeit real, the behavior may simply be inexplicable for now. It is also possible that additives, such as wetting agents, are part of its formulation, and are responsible for its unexpected behavior. Possibly being considered subsidiary, the additive may not been mentioned. They may even not have been known by the experimenters. This changed as the Polysulfone or Polyethersulfone membranes are surface treated nowadays, which reduced the unspecific adsorption greatly.

Notice should be taken of the BSA adsorption by the nylon 6,6. It was strong from the very start, recovered its concentration somewhat slowly, and achieved its saturation more gradually than did the other polymeric cartridges. Of the cartridges tested nylon was the most adsorptive of BSA. This conclusion affirms the common view regarding nylon 6,6 as being strongly adsorbing of proteins.

The prefilters tested as follows: despite its innate hydrophobicity, polypropylene in both pleated membrane and depth filter form caused significant protein loss. Both cartridge types attained maximum concentration recovery after a flow-through of 1 or 2 L.

The cartridge of mixed cellulose esters initially adsorbed high amounts of protein. Its recovery to the protein concentration of the test solution was the most gradual of all the cartridges tested. Although identified by way of its manufacturer and catalogue title, its polymeric composition was not specified. The mixed esters are a mixture of CA and cellulose nitrate. The adsorptive take-up of protein by CA is generally low. That of the cellulose nitrate is very high, due to the hydrogen bonding by the nitro group of atoms. The slow recovery shown by this cartridge may be explained as resulting from two different polymers, each distinctive in its own rate of achieving saturation. Had the description of the cartridge's polymeric identity been made plain, the results of the protein adsorption and its recovery would have been evident. This argues for a fuller characterization of the filters used in investgations to include their polymeric identity, and that of additives. This could assist reaching proper experimental conclusions.

Having tested both prefilters and final filters, Datar et al. (1992) assayed various combinations of both in an effort to construct a filter system least conducive to protein adsorption. The nylon prefilter (single layer)/nylon final filter (double layer) combination, as also the hydroxyl-modified polyamide prefilter (single layer)/final filter of the same material in a double layer were examined. In essence, each set of filters exhibited, with only slight differences, if any, the protein adsorption characteristics shown by the final single filter alone. As might have been expected, the prefilter/final filter combination composed of membranes hydrophilized to present hydrophilic surfaces were the least involved in protein (BSA) adsorption.

Conclusion

What was sought in this exercise was an understanding of the filter cartridge properties important to the adsorptive retention of proteins and/or preservatives. The literature pertinent to the subject is impressive in both quantity and quality. Our selection and treatment of it was directed primarily to the polymeric materials comprising the filters in terms of their tendency toward adsorptions in general and toward proteins in particular. Comparisons among filters on this basis are plentiful, but the techniques applied vary in their degrees of sophistication. Anticipating an address to production needs, our focus was extended to the modification, if any, of the polymer's contribution by the features of cartridge construction. On this point, the literature is sparse.

The conclusions confirmed that hydrophobic areas within a heterogeneous surface were promotive of protein adsorption. The hydrophilic, charge-involving areas of filter surfaces were significantly less encouraging to protein uptake. To the minor extent examined, neither membrane pleating nor the cartridges' drainage and separation layers exerted a notable influence on the adsorption of proteins. In our judgment, the prefilter contribution to protein adsorption did not modify, in proportion to its added area, that of the final filter.

Much remains to be systematically investigated. In designing a filtration system that would minimize protein adsorption, an optimum ratio of prefilter to final filter would require experimental definition. The extent of filter area to be used in a production run would necessitate an experimentally defined EFA. Where the minimum adsorptive losses would be desired, the smallest EFA should be used. This would be of particular concern where high-value protein would be at stake, or where dilute protein solutions undergo filtrations, as for organism or viral sterilizations.

Strategies for minimizing losses, for designing appropriate sampling protocols, for the testing and assaying of samples, and for the formulation of the process fluid's composition are needed. These strategies have to find themselves in the tests performed to determine how a particular filter membrane polymer, structure, combination, and filter configuration will work best with a specific application. There is no ideal filter, but the empirical study of which filter fits best into a specific application.

REFERENCES

Adamson, A.A., (1982). *Physical Chemistry of Surfaces*, 4th Edition, Wiley Interscience, New York.

Badenhop, C.T., Spann, A.T., and Meltzer, T.H., (1970). A consideration of parameters governing membrane filtration, In J.E. Flinn, Ed., *Membrane Science and Technology*, Plenum, New York, pp. 120–138.

Bowen, R.W. and Gan, Q., (1991). Properties of microfiltration membranes: Adsorption of BSA at Polyvinylidene fluoride membranes, *J. Colloid Interface Sci.*, 144: 254–261.

Brose, D.J. and Waibel, P., (1996). Adsorption of protein in commercial microfiltration capsules, *BioPharm.* 9(1): 36–39.

Characklis, W.G., (1990). Microbial biofouling control, In W.G. Characklis and K.C. Marshall, Ed., *Biofilms*, Wiley, New York, pp. 585–633.

Datar, R., Martin, J.M., and Manteuffel, R.I., (1992). Dynamics of protein recovery from process filtration systems using microporous membrane filter cartridges, *J. Parenter. Sci. Technol.*, 46(2): 35–42.

Dumitriu, S. and Dumitriu-Medvichi, C., (1994). Hydrogel and general properties of biomaterials, In S. Dimitriu, Ed., *Polymeric Biomaterials*, Marcel Dekker, New York, p. 1.

Emory, S.F., Koga, Y., Azuma, N., and Matsumoto, K., (1993). The effects of surfactant type and latex-particle feed concentration on membrane retention, *Ultrapure Water*, 10(2): 41–44.

Fletcher, M., (1996). Bacterial attachments in aqueous environments, In M. Fletcher, Ed., *Bacterial Adhesion*, John Wiley, New York, pp. 1–24.

Fletcher, M. and Loeb, G.L., (1979). Influence of substratum characteristics on the attachment of a marine *Pseudomonas* to solid surfaces, *Appl. Environ. Microbiol.*, 37: 67.

Galanos, C.E., Rietschel, E.T., Ludertiz, O., Westphol, O., Kim, Y.B., and Watson, D.W., (1972). Biological activity of lipid a complexed with bovine serum albumin, *Eur. J. Biochem.*, 31: 230–233.

Ghosh, K. and Schnitzer, H., (1979). UV and visible absorption spectroscopic investigations in relation to macromolecular characteristics of humic substances, *J. Soil Sci.* 30: 735.

Hawker, J. and Hawker, L.M., (1975). Protein losses during sterilization by filtration, *Lab. Practice*, 24: 805–807.

Hiatt, W.C., Vitzthum, G.H., Wagener, K.B., Gerlach, K., and Josefi, C., (1985). Microporous membranes via upper critical temperaturephase separation, In D.R. Lloyd, Ed., *Material Science of Synthetic Membranes*, *American Chemical Society*, Washington, DC.

Kim, M., et al., (1994). Reduction of nonselective adsorption of proteins by hydrophilization of microfiltration membranes by radiation-induced grafting, *Biotechnol. Prog.* 10(1): 114–120.

Mahler, H.C., Huber, F., Kishore, R., Reindl, J., Rueckert, P., and Mueller, R. (2009). Adsorption behavior of a surfactant and a monoclonal antibody to sterilizing-grade filters, Published online January 20, 2010 in Wiley Inter Science (http://www.interscience.wiley.com). DOI 10.1002/jps.22045.

Marshall, K.C., (1992). Biofilms: An overview of bacterial adhesion, activity, and control at surfaces, *Am. Soc. Microbiol. News*, 58(4): 202–207.

Michaud, D., (1988). Granulated Activated Carbon, A Series of Three Papers, *Water Conditioning and Purification*, June pp. 20–26, July pp. 38–50, and August pp. 36–41.

Mittleman, M.W., Jornitz, M.W., and Meltzer, T.H., (1998). Bacterial cell size and surface charge characteristics relevant to filter validation studies, *PDA J. Pharm. Sci. Tech.*, 52(1): 37–42.

Ong, H.L. and Bisque, R.E., (1966). Coagulation of humic colloids by metal ions, *Soil Sci.*, 106(3): 220.

Pall, D.B., Kirnbauer, E.A., and Allen, B.T., (1980). Particulate retention by bacteria retentive membrane filters, *Colloids Surf.*, 1: 235–256.

Pitt, A., (1987). The non-specific protein binding of poly mereic microporous membranes, *J. Parenteral Sci. Technol.*, 41: 110.

Pitt, A.M., Melia, J.A., and McElhinney, S.A., (1985), *The Non-Specific Protein Binding of Polymeric Microporous Membranes*, PDA, Philadelphia, PA, Poster Session.

Ridgway, H.F., (1987). Microbiological fouling of reverse osmosis membranes: Genesis and control, In G.G. Geesey and M.W. Mittelman, Eds., *Biological Fouling of Industrial Water Systems: A Problem Solving Approach*, Water Micro Association, San Diego, CA, p. 151.

Ridgway, H.F., Rigby, M.G., and Argo, D.G., (1984a). Adhesion of a mycobacterium to cellulose diacetate membranes used in reverse osmosis, *Appl. Environ. Microbiol.*, 47: 61–67.

Ridgway, H.F., Rigby, M.G., and Argo, D.G., (1984b). Biological fouling of reverse osmosis membranes: The mechanism of bacterial adhesion, *Proceedings of the Water Reuse Symposium III., The Future of Water Reuse*, Vol. 111: San Diego, CA, 1314–1350.

Ridgway, H.F., Rigby, M.G., and Argo, D.G., (1985). Bacterial adhesion and fouling of reverse osmosis membranes, *J. Am. Water Works Assoc.*, 77: 97–106.

Ridgway, H.F., Rogers, D.M., Argo, D.G., (January 16–17, 1986). Effects of surfactants on the adhesion of mycobacteria to reverse osmosis membranes. *Transcripts of Fifth Annual Semiconductor Pure Water Conference*, San Francisco, CA.

Robinson, J.R., O'Dell, M.D., Takacs, J., Barnes, T., and Genovesi, C. (1982) Removal of endotoxin by adsorption to hydrophobic microporous membrane filters, *PDA November Meeting*, Philadelphia, PA.

Schnitzer, M. and Kodama, H., (1966). Montmorillonite: Effect on pH on its adsorption of a soil humic compound, *Science* 153: 70.

Sundaram, S., (1998). Protein adsorption in microporous membrane filtration, In T.H. Meltzer and M.W. Jornitz, Ed., *Filtration in the Biopharmaceutical Industry*, Marcel Dekker, New York.

Sweadner, K.J., Forte, J., and Nelsen, L.L., (1977). Filtration removal of endotoxin (Pyrogens) in solution in different states of aggregation, *Appl. Environ. Microbiol.*, 34: 382–385.

Tanny, G.B. and Meltzer, T.H., (1978). The dominance of adsorptive effects in the filtrative sterilization of a flu vaccine, *J. Parent. Drug Assoc.*, 32(6): 258–267.

Tanford, C., (1980). *The Hydrophobic Effect: Formation of Micelles and Biological Membranes*, 2nd Edition, Wiley, New York.

Weber, W.H., Voice, T.C., and Jodellah, A., (1983). Adsorption of humic substances: The effects of heterogeneity and system characteristics, *J. Am. Water Works Assoc.*, 75(12): 612–619.

Wheland, G.W., (1947). Chapter 2: Some fundamental concepts, In *Advanced Organic Chemistry*, 2nd Edition, John Wiley and Sons, New York.

Wrasidlo, W. and Mysels, K.J., (1984). The structure and some properties of graded highly asymmetric porous membranes, *J. Parenter. Sci. Technol.*, 38(1): 24–31.

Zeman, L.J., (1996). Chapter 4: Characterization of MF/UF membranes, In L.J. Zeman and A.L. Zydney, Eds., *Microfiltration and Ultrafiltration: Principles and Applications*, Marcel Dekker, New York, pp. 180–291.

Zhou, J.X., Qiu, J., Jiang, G., Zhou, C., Bingham, N., Yeung, H., Dransart, B., Wadhwa, M., and Tressel, T., (2008). Non-specific binding and saturation of Polysorbate-20 with aseptic filter membranes for drug substance and drug product during mAb production, *J. Membr. Sci.*, 325: 735–741.

Zydney, A.L., (1996). Chapter 9: Membrane fouling, In L.J. Zeman and A.L. Zydney, Eds., *Microfiltration and Utrafiltration: Principles and Applications*, Marcel Dekker, New York, pp. 397–446.

10

Integrity Testing

Magnus Andreas Stering
Sartorius Stedim SA

CONTENTS

Background

The integrity testing of filters is one of a series of interdependent activities that in their proper combination result in the preparation of sterile drugs. Integrity testing, quality management by the filter supplier, bioburden studies and process validation are the building blocks of this practice. Each of these components has its own complexities, and not all of their influencing factors are presently understood.

The integrity testing of filters is central to the practice of sterile filtration. The exercise is seen to stand between certainty and potential failure. Because of their frequent usage the integrity tests that are available are generally well known. What is less well comprehended is their underlying physics, their operational requirements and what could generate a false passed* or a false failed test,* and finally a deeper understanding of when a given test is particularly suited for a given application.

The key requirement of an integrity test is that it establishes a quantitative correlation between a property or characteristic of the filter of interest with its organism retention capabilities. This would, for example, address the needs of sterilizing filtration practitioners to identify filters of a particular pore size rating having the necessary bacterial retention capability. Present integrity test procedures for hydrophilic membrane filters enable this to be done by way of interpreting measured airflows through water-, product- or solvent-wet membranes.

The purpose of this writing is to help clarify the situation.

Nondestructive Testing

An important application of the filtration process is the production of sterile drugs. A method of identifying a "sterilizing grade" filter, one suitable for *trial* in a sterilizing filtration, is made by way of integrity testing. The Food and Drug Administration (FDA) has defined a sterilizing filter as one that retains the classic challenge of at least 1×10^7 colony-forming units (cfus) of *Brevundimonas diminuta* ATCC-19146 per cm^2 effective filtration area (EFA) at pressures up to 30 psi (2 bar). The challenge concentration of at least 1×10^7 cfus per cm^2 provide a safety margin well beyond what would be expected in production. It should be understood, however, that a filter thus qualified does not automatically ensure a sterile effluent. That achievement is the result of several factors whose successful culmination requires the documented experimental evidence that constitutes validation (Thomas et al., 1991). In the performance of the sterilization exercise it is necessary to ensure that a proper filter, a "sterilizing grade" filter, is being utilized, one capable of retaining the FDA-defined organism challenge.[†] This is best assessed by a direct confrontation of the membrane by a proper organism challenge. However, the filter, thus tested, is contaminated by the organisms and may not subsequently be employed as a process filter. What is required is a nondestructive integrity test, based on correlation of pore size with the log reduction value (LRV) indicative of organism retention; therefore, a surrogate test is used that is nondestructive to filters, and whose values will correlate with organism retention.

In the present practice, the membrane's largest pore size is probed by the bubble point test. Its value can be correlated with the membrane's ability to sustain the $1 \times 10^7/cm^2$ *B. diminuta* confrontation made by the use of a standard ASTM 838-15 microbiological challenge procedure. On this basis such membranes are experimentally qualified to be of the "sterilizing grade," and are thus labeled as being of the 0.2/0.22 μm-rated pore size. They may then be selected for trials in actual product filtration sterilizations to ascertain their suitability to so perform in given filtration contexts.

It must, therefore, be understood that the pore size rating is not directly reflecting the actual pore size but rather the performance of the filter membrane, especially as a membrane does not have "one" pore size but a pore size distribution. Additionally, different membrane types from the same manufacturer with the same pore size ratings will display different pore size distributions based on the membrane polymer and manufacturing process.

Filter manufacturers have measured and correlated bubble point/diffusive flow values and LRVs for the commercially available membranes. It is this correlation that serves as a nondestructive test for

---

* The terms "false positive" and "false negative" are sometimes mistakenly used to designate a false passed or a false failed test or vice versa. To avoid confusion the terms "false positive" and "false negative" should be used for sterility testing results but not for integrity testing results.

[†] The stipulated challenge of 1×10^7 of *B. diminuta* per cm^2 was proposed by HIMA (1982) for flat disc membranes, to be achieved at 30 psi (2 bar). *The total effluent was to be assayed.* In the case of cartridges, the effluent volume required being limited, for practical purposes, to that quantity produced at rates of flow of 3.86 L/min/ 0.1 m^2 EFA. A cartridge containing 7 ft^2. (6503 cm^2) of EFA would require that a flow of 5.4 L/min be used in a challenge to define a "sterilizing grade" filter.

determining a given filter's organism retention capabilities. This is precisely the information needed to ensure the proper choice of membrane for use in filtrative sterilizations.

Regulations

So important is integrity testing that it is required by the regulating authorities responsible for overseeing pharmaceutical processing practices worldwide. Examples follow:

- FDA Guidance for Industry sterile drug products produced by aseptic processing (2004): "Normally, integrity testing of the filter is performed prior to processing, after the filter apparatus has already been assembled and sterilized. It is important that integrity testing be conducted after filtration to detect any filter leaks or perforations that might have occurred during the filtration. Forward flow and bubble point tests, when appropriately employed, are two integrity tests that can be used. A production filter's integrity test specification should be consistent with data generated during filtration efficacy studies."
- Guide to Good Pharmaceutical Manufacturing Practice (Orange Guide 1983), p. 62 9.82: The integrity of the filter assembly should be checked by an appropriate method, such as bubble point pressure test or forward-flow pressure test immediately before and after use. Abnormal filtration flow rates should be noted and investigated. Results of these filter integrity checks should be recorded in the batch record.
- ISO/DIS 13480 2, 2003-03-15, "Aseptic Processing of Health Care Products
  - Part 2: Filtration" Section 7: Filtration Process
    - 7. 1.2—Written integrity test procedures shall be established including acceptance criteria and methods of failure investigation and conditions under which the filter integrity test can be repeated.

  Notes: Information from the filter manufacturer can be useful in designing and validating integrity test procedure(s) based on gas flows through wetted filters.
- It should be demonstrated that the integrity test conditions can be supported by standardized bacterial retention testing. The standard bacterial retention tests should use a challenge level of at least 10^7 cfus per square centimeter, with filters representative of standard production filters approaching the acceptance test limit.
  - 7.1.3—One or more wetting fluids shall be selected. These shall be the filter manufacturers' recommended reference wetting fluid or the actual fluid to be filtered. In the latter case, the appropriate integrity test value specification shall be established and validated.
  - 7.1.4—For air and gas filters, appropriate frequency for physical integrity testing shall be established.

Practical Concerns Apropos of Regulations

The regulators in fulfilling their obligation to protect the public may establish rules likely to reduce risk to a minimum. Such may, however, encounter practical limitations.

For example: ISO/DIS 13408, Section 8.10 states:

"The filtration system should be designed to permit in-place integrity testing as closed system prior filtration." However, Wallhäuser (1985) believed that the diffusion test would be impractical as a pre-use integrity test where steaming is used as the sanitizing agent. Given the sensitivity of diffusive airflows to temperature, the testing would require being delayed until the system, filter, and housing, cooled to the level proper for measurement; a matter of many hours. Scheer et al. (1993) explored the effects of temperature on the diffusion test; it is the least subjective of the integrity tests. These investigators found that serious errors in test results are possible unless temperature and volume factors are recognized and accommodated. They observed, "The exigencies of field filter testing may only rarely allow the needed degree of control." Similar caution has to be taken with bubble point measurements as the bubble point depends on the surface tension of the wetting fluid, which, respectively, depends on the its temperature. When integrity tests are performed the temperature of wetting fluids, test gas, and the environment need to be diligently observed as temperature changes have a detrimental influence that could generate both false passed and false failed integrity test results.

The alternative to a substantial time delay would be to integrity test the filter under aseptic conditions outside its holder, and to install it under the same conditions. This would eliminate the testing delay occasioned by the need for steam-sterilized filters to cool to where they could be used for accurate air-flow measurements. Several filters could simultaneously be sanitized outside the filtration system and be allowed to cool in an aseptic ambiance until one was needed for installation.

To comply with its recommendation the filter would be sanitized after its installation, but prior to its being integrity tested in-place. Ironically, manual testing of the already installed filter would be accomplished by downstream measurement of the airflow rate. Such would risk asepsis. However, upstream integrity testing can be performed with automated integrity test equipment.

When to Perform Integrity Testing

Another example of regulations, at times, being in opposition to practicality is given in answering an often asked question, namely, when integrity testing should be performed. Most often the regulations require the filter's integrity testing to be conducted "immediately before and after use." However, regulatory guidance regarding pre- and post-use integrity testing is a bit ambiguous. For example, FDA's aseptic processing guidance (2004) states, "Integrity testing of the filter(s) can be performed prior to processing, and should be routinely performed post-use." Annex 1 of the European GMP (EudraLex 1996, 2008) regulations states, "The integrity of the sterilised filter should be verified before use and should be confirmed immediately after use by an appropriate method such as a bubble point, diffusive flow or pressure hold test." Clearly, regulators expect a post-use integrity test to be performed, while a pre-use integrity test appears to be optional, at least in the United States.

Irrespective of the regulatory guidance, pre-use and post-use integrity testing is desired to demonstrate the integrity of the filter and to ensure the filter device has not been damaged, for example, during steam sterilization or even transportation. Ideally, the pre-use integrity test should be performed by the filter user with the filter installed in the housing of intended use; however, it could be possible under certain conditions to accept the filter manufacturer's integrity test value as the pre-use test. This could be done if the individual filter has been integrity tested by the manufacturer (and is accompanied by certification to that effect) and the transportation conditions have been validated and monitored, the installation and sterilization processes have been validated and monitored, and the personnel appropriately trained by the filter user to assure, insofar as possible, that these operations are well controlled and do not result in seal leakage or damage to the filter. In the event of a post-use integrity test failure, the filtered batch must be rejected.

Pre-Use Integrity Testing

After sterilization of the filter cartridge, e.g., by steam, it is recommended (FDA 2004) that it be integrity tested prior to filtration. (Post-filtration integrity testing is a requirement.) There are good reasons for this recommendation. Stresses, possibly induced to the filter during its manufacture, are relaxed by the steam heat. This may result in altering the sizes of some pore.

The initial integrity testing may be performed as soon as the membrane is thoroughly wet. Integrity testing can be performed offline prior to the filter's installation in its housing. However, aseptic installation is then necessitated. This involves risk. Integrity testing after installation introduces its own problems. Manual testing compels invasion of the system downstream of the filter. Serious risks to the system's asepsis are involved. The use of automated test machines avoids this problem. They all utilize test methodologies which operate from the upstream side and, therefore, avoid such compromises. The available automated machines utilize either pressure decay, or direct flow measurements, making it unnecessary to attach anything to the downstream side.

Since the steam sterilization process is commonly the most stressful process experienced by the filter, it would be advantageous to test the filter after steam sterilization but before use. Any potential damage resulting from excessive sterilization parameters or incorrect handling would be determined by such test. However, since the filter requires wetting and testing with an atmospheric pressure condition on the filtrate side, the filtrate side at that point requires appropriate engineering designs to allow the flush and test process. These designs are, in instances, not easily fulfilled, and the risk of a secondary contamination of the filtrate side might be higher than the risk of filter damage. Especially in the case of, e.g., single-use systems requiring manual opening and closing of pinch valves there is a great risk of operator errors. The automation of the pre-use integrity testing process would reduce this risk. The decision should therefore ideally lie within the hands of the filter user and risk management perspectives. Nevertheless the Pre-Use Post Sterilization Integrity Testing, commonly called the PUPSIT, is a requirement in Annex 1 of the European Guidelines as mentioned above.

Post-Use Integrity Testing

Other than convenience, there is no reason to delay the post-use integrity testing. There is not a sufficient experience on which to formally base a time limit on the commencing of the test. Nevertheless, delayed testing can only encourage time-related alterations, if any, in the filter's condition; nor need any be elucidated. What is wanted is the knowledge of the post-use integrity of the filter. Delaying the analysis can only occasion change, from whatever cause, which can modify the filter's immediate after-filtration condition from what it was, e.g., product precipitation.

Integrity Test Purposes

Integrity testing serves several purposes. One important function is to make certain the identity of the selected filter; by affirming the correctness of its identifying label. Each pore size rating of a filter is characterized by the filter manufacturer as having a distinct integrity test value. At the moment when a filter is removed from its shipping container preparatory to use, only the proper performance of an integrity test attests to its identity. Even its identifying label is no guarantee; mistakes do occur. Integrity testing provides the needed confirmation that the selected filter is the proper one.

The filter and the liquid vehicle being filtered may be incompatible. Such may result in pore size changes consequent to the membrane's exposure to the fluid over a time period peculiar to the specific membrane (polymer)/liquid couple (Lukaszewicz and Meltzer 1980). Integrity testing is sensitive enough to disclose whether a filter has undergone even subtle incompatibilities that can impair its retentivity.

It is not uncommon to steam-sterilize a filter prior to its use. As stated, the heat may release stresses, if any, built into the filter during its fabrication. Alterations in the pore structure may result. Moreover, the steaming cycle itself with its heating and cooling phases is a stressful experience for any filter given the different rates of expansions and contractions of its several components. It may induce stresses in the membrane. Repeated steaming may lead to anomalous results. A series of repeated steam sterilization cycles according to validated process conditions, each followed by integrity testing, can be used to learn how many sterilization cycles a given filter may endure. Regardless, prudence and the risk for release of cell debris in the case of multiple use, if not economics, suggest that cartridges be confined to a single steam sterilization cycle. A comparison of pre-use and after-use integrity test values can show by their constancy or lack thereof whether the membrane has undergone morphological alteration.

In the validation exercise it might be necessary to establish a relationship between the water-wetted and the product-wetted membrane. This is accomplished by way of integrity testing whereby the water-wetted integrity test value is quantified to that of the product-wetted integrity test value.

Integrity testing can be performed either manually or by utilizing automated test machines. The self-evident objectivity of the automated machines offers a significant advantage. Additionally, the automated testers enable upstream measurement manipulations that finesse exposure of the filtration system to risking the system's asepsis. More important, the automated testers are magnitudes higher in the sensitivity of their measurements of airflows and displacement volumes. These greatly enhance the reliability of the bubble point's identification.

Integrity Test Prerequisite Conditions

Integrity test results can be greatly influenced mainly by temperature and temperature variations but also by the nature of the wetting liquid and the test gas. The effect of temperature change is complex, and cannot be explained by the ideal gas law alone. The influence on test results also depends on whether the sample is made of stainless steel (multiuse filter housing) or plastic, such as a polypropylene (PP) filter capsule or single-use bag in ethylene vinyl acetate, since different materials react differently to temperature changes depending on their thermal expansion factors and heat conductivity (Stering 2017) Risk assessment for thermal influences on filter and container closure integrity testing). Different test methods also react differently to temperature variations. In order to work under optimal conditions the following prerequisite conditions should be fulfilled:

- The type of wetting liquid

    Only wetting liquid for which validated test parameters and test values are available must be used.

- The temperature of the wetting liquid

    The wetting liquid should be at the same temperature as the environment +/- 1K. If specific thermal conditions have been validated, e.g., bubble point with cold liquid in an ambient environment, the thermal conditions and waiting time before starting the test must be as validated.

- The temperature of the environment

    The temperature of the environment should typically be around 72 °F/22 °C (e.g., 68 to 77/20 to 25 °C) but different filter suppliers give different ranges. Testing under conditions that are outside specified prerequisites may require specific validation of test parameters and test values, e.g., integrity testing in a cold room.

- The temperature of the filter sample being tested

    The temperature of the filter sample being tested including its housing/capsule should be at the same temperature as the environment +/- 1K unless specifically validated.

- The temperature variation of the environment

    The temperature of the environment must be stable and should ideally not vary by more than +/- 1K per 5 min or per test time, whichever is the lowest. Drafts or direct sunlight are prohibited.

- The test gas type

    Both compressed air and nitrogen are commonly used. Standard integrity testing values for diffusion/forward flow are typically given for compressed air. The use of nitrogen requires a correction factor for diffusion values. When using water as wetting liquid the correction factor is $\text{Diffusion}_{maxN_2} = \text{Diffusion}_{maxAir} \times 0.82$. Other wetting liquids may require different correction factors.

- The temperature of the test gas

    The test gas is typically supplied at 72.5–101.5 psi/5–7 bar gauge and should be at ambient temperature, more precisely at the same temperature as the environment +/- 1K.

Also the performance of the integrity testing device may be affected by factors like particles in the supplied test gas and its humidity.

To avoid any impact on the functionality of the device it is recommended to use compressed gas with the following characteristics:

- Particle free, e.g., filtered with a hydrophobic 0.2/.022 rated filter
- Oil free
- Dry with a dew point of −4°F/−20°C

The characteristics of the test gas quality can also be referred to ISO 8573-1 class 3, or better.

Integrity Test Reliability and Risk Assessment

The reliability of the integrity test results is fundamental for the release of the drug. A false passed test result can put the patients' lives in danger—and false failed test results, which may quarantine otherwise acceptable product and contribute to drug shortages.

Even though the quality manager and the operator strive to fulfill prerequisite conditions deviations may accidently occur. Additionally operators may do mistakes, especially when doing repetitive routine-based operation for which there are no standard operating procedures.

To improve reliability of integrity testing it is important to identify risks, to understand and quantify the impact on the integrity test result by doing a risk assessment, e.g., failure mode effects analysis. If there is a risk of generating a false passed test the potential deviation must be seen as critical. The likelihood of the event would then partly determine if the risk is acceptable or not.

Under all circumstances, it is of highest importance to understand how to detect the deviation. This may include, but not exclusively, regular training of operators and quality people and specific alarm parameter settings in the integrity testing device for automatic detection of operator mistakes.

The establishment of a comprehensive risk assessment for filter integrity testing will reduce operator mistakes and may greatly improve the reliability of the test results and would comply to the request for Quality Risk Management of all process related steps in the new version of Annex 1 of the European GMP which is expected to be released in 2019.

Filtrative Sterilizations

It is perhaps in conjunction with sterilizing filtrations that integrity testing finds a most important application. It affirms that a filter used in a sterilizing filtration is of a "sterilizing grade." And it verifies that the filter underwent no alteration in its organism-retention qualities during the entire filtration. This is done by a show of identity between the pre-use and after-use integrity test values.

The concern in conducting a filtrative sterilization is that during its employment the filter may, for whatever cause, develop a pore or flaw large enough to allow the passage of organisms. One would, therefore, wish to measure the size of the set of largest pores present in the filter before and after its use to make certain that no pore enlargement occurred. Pore size determinations cannot realistically be conducted under such use conditions. But a technique for approximating the size of a filter's largest pores is available. It consists of the bubble point test. Correlation of a filter's bubble point value and its degree of retentivity is key. It makes possible the use of integrity testing to judge the appropriateness of a filter for application in filtration sterilizing contexts. The bubble point concept will presently be elaborated upon. If the bubble point value of a filter's post-use test is the same as that of its pre-use reading, the sizes of its largest pores did not undergo enlargement during the filtration. That they remained the same throughout the filtration exercise affirms the filter's integrity (Meltzer and Jornitz 2006, Chapter 1).

Each of the differently rated pore sizes of the different filter types is distinguished by its bubble point values, and each is characterized by its particular propensity for organism retentions, namely, their LRVs. The filter's selection for the sterilization is made on the basis of its LRV. The "sterilizing grade" filter should have an LRV of 7, meaning that the filter will sustain the challenge of 1×10^7 cfus of *Brevundimonas diminuta ATCC-19146* per square cm of EFA. This accords with the FDA's definition of a "sterilizing filter" (FDA 1987, 2004). The filter is particularized by its bubble point. Its value remaining unchanged by the filtration attests to its being of a "sterilizing grade." It has the potential to perform as a sterilizing filter under the proper operational conditions.

Similar to the bubble point, diffusive flow test limits differ with pore size ratings and polymeric structures. The larger the pore size rating the lower the test pressure of a diffusive flow test. The test pressure commonly depends on the bubble point value, and is measured at around 80% of it. The membrane polymer influences both the wettability and test pressure limits. Therefore, it is necessary for filter manufacturers to determine and correlate the bubble point and diffusive flow limits for every individual filter type.

The "Sterilizing Grade" Filter

By definition, a sterilizing filter is one that produces a sterile effluent when confronted with the *B. diminuta* challenge, just enumerated, in a standard filtration exercise based on an ASTM procedure (ASTM F 838-15) and conducted by the filter manufacturers (Meltzer and Jornitz 2006, Chapter 1). This does not mean that its use will necessarily produce sterile effluent in other trials. Passing the standard challenge test qualifies the filter to be of a "sterilizing grade." Its actual performance in any given application remains to be seen. Until rather recently, it was believed that the sterilization of fluids could be achieved by their filtration through a "sterilizing" membrane whose proper and pertinent identity was confirmed by its pore size rating, which was itself determined by integrity testing. Developments in filtration practices showed this belief to be too generally founded. Conclusions based on pore size ratings are subject to modification by the physicochemical specificity of the organism-suspending fluid; by the individuality of the organism type in its size-changing response to the fluid; in the possible change in pore size induced by the fluid; and by the adsorptive qualities of the filter resulting from its particular polymeric composition; all influenced by the filtration conditions in their numerous varieties, especially by the transmembrane pressure.

A filter may not sterilize the same preparation under different filtration conditions, especially under dissimilar differential pressures (Leahy and Sullivan 1978). A given membrane may or may not retain a particular organism type suspended in a different drug vehicle (Bowman et al 1967). The organism type need not remain constant in size, but may alter in response to its suspending fluid (Gould et al 1993; Leo et al 1997; Meltzer et al 1998). The effect of the vehicle upon the polymeric membrane may cause a change in its pore sizes (Lukaszewicz and Meltzer 1980). The complex of influences governing the outcome of an intended sterilizing filtration necessitates a careful validation of the process, including that of the filter (PDA Technical Report # 26). The very drug preparation of interest, the exact membrane type, the precise filtration conditions, and the specific organism type(s) of concern are to be employed in the validation.

A sterilizing filter can be judged only by its performance in the removal of identifiable and culturable organisms known to be present in the drug preparation (Agalloco 1998). Not finding any of the subject organisms of interest in a microbiological testing can be indicative of their absence, as due to their complete removal by filtration. This assumes, however, that were they present, the method used for culturing and counting them would be known, and that their proper nutrition, incubation, and adequate time for growth would have been provided for. Failing this assumption, the non-discovery of organisms does not equate with their being none.

Certainly, there is no known absolute filter, one that will retain all organisms under all conditions, especially if viruses are included (Aranha 2004).

LRV

Prior to use of the term LRV, now rather widely accepted, a filter's organism retentivity was signified by the symbol T_R meaning "Titer Reduction." It referred to the ratio of particles in the influent stream to those in the effluent. This is also the definition of filter efficiency (Pall and Kirnbauer 1978). The concurrent term beta ratio described the filter efficiency of the removal of AC Fine Test Dust from hydraulic fluids. Reti (1977) and Leahy and Sullivan (1978) applied that term to organism retentions as well. LRV, a filter's LRV, is an expression adapted by HIMA, the Health Industry Manufacturers Association (now known as AdvaMed) in an effort to standardize a code word for the predilection of a filter to retain organisms. The LRV is the logarithm to the base 10 of the ratio of the organisms in the influent stream to those that emerge in the filtrate. Thus, if a filter has an LRV of 7, it is capable of diminishing the number of test organisms by seven orders of magnitude. Expressed as a percent reduction in the number of microorganisms, the number would be 99.99999%.

To determine the specific LRV of a filter, a test challenge level has to be used that will cause some passage of organisms through the filter, in order to supply a denominator for the LRV expression. Sterilizing membrane filters do not ordinarily permit the passage of test organisms. Therefore, the LRV of such filters is described solely in terms of the numerator, the influent or challenge level, as being greater than the $\log_{10}$ of that total challenge.

The "Pores"

The filtrative removal of organisms by a filtration depends primarily on the size of the organisms relative to the size of the restraining pores. Some characterization of the filter pore sizes is, therefore, indicated.

As the name "microporous membranes" implies, pores are intersperse within the polymeric matrices of these filters. The separating of particles, both organisms and others, from fluid suspensions takes place at the pore sites, the size of which determines the particle sizes retained by the mechanism of size exclusion or sieve retention.

Too little is known about the numbers, sizes, and/or shapes of the pores of microporous membrane. The membrane structure is usually pictured as being analogous to that of a polymeric sponge. A hypothesized oversimplification of the pore passageways is that of irregular and tortuous capillaries that are, therefore, more extended in length than the filter's surface-to-surface thickness. The pores are marked by irregularly restricted diameters, whether at their entrances or within their channels that provide the choke points that interfere with particle passage. Nevertheless, however complex, the pores are conveniently pictured as being essentially cylindrical and composed of interconnected spaces extending as pathways through the depth of the polymer matrix.

A more explicit pore architecture is hypothesized wherein the pores are not columnar passageways, but are rather aggregations of polyhedral open-walled chambers or cells of different proportions, the "pore sizes" of which are defined by the dimensions of polygonal apertures leading from one hollow cell to another (Williams and Meltzer 1983). This reasoning envisages pore formation as the coming together of hollow spheres. These eventuate from the membrane-casting process whose spatial clustering is under the influence of area-minimizing forces. The phenomenon of clustering through polyhedral spatial arrangements is known from the studies of contiguous soap bubbles whose structural formation is under the same constraints (Figure 10.1; Almgren and Taylor 1976).

According to Johnston (2003, Chapter 3), the very concept of a definable "pore" is an artificiality when applied to microporous membranes other than the straight-through columnar pores that characterize the track-etched variety. The complex geometry of the sponge-like membrane results in the pores having ratios of cross-sectional areas to perimeters, called the hydraulic parameters. These vary over the entire thickness of the membrane. A membrane's depth can be considered to be constructed of a number of superimposed unit planes which in their aggregate impose their effect on retention and flow rates (Piekaar and Clarenburg 1967). These vary over the entire thickness of the membrane (Johnston 2003). The "pores" so considered are presumably connected throughout the unit planes to constitute pathways for fluid flows. However, where blockages by particle retentions interfere, flow redistributions may result through new "pore" alignments.

The "pores" so considered are, however, hypothetical constructs useful in understanding filter performance. Unlike the track-etched pores they are *not* integral, structural pathways for fluid flow. Nevertheless, the events taking place at the pores are depicted as if they were continuous and integral paths through the depth of the filter.

FIGURE 10.1   Polyhedral soap bubble structure.

Particles are separated from the fluid by adsorptions to pore surfaces, as well as by the size exclusion mechanism. The adsorptive sequestration mechanism can serve to remove suspended matter that is smaller in size than the pores. Thus, the meaning of the average pore size as reflecting organisms retained exclusively by the size exclusion mechanism is necessarily an oversimplification (Trotter et al., 2000).

Sieve Retention Mechanism

As noted, in sterilizing filtrations, for the drug preparation to emerge as a sterile effluent, the filter needs to have the capability of withstanding the direct confrontation of 1×10^7 cfus of *Brevundimonas diminuta ATCC-19146* per square cm of EFA in a standard test. This accords with the FDA's concept of a "sterilizing filter" (FDA 1987, 2004) "The microorganism *Brevundimonas diminuta* (ATCC 19146) when properly grown, harvested and used, is a common challenge microorganism for 0.2 μm rated filters because of its small size (0.3 μm mean diameter)." The *B. diminuta* serves as a model organism for the microbes likely to be encountered in pharmaceutical contexts.

Filter selection is made essentially on the premise that sieve removal is the exclusive mechanism of particle retention; adsorptive effects, being difficult to predict, are ignored. It is conveniently assumed that even the filter's largest size pores will restrain the passage of the smallest of the challenging *B. diminuta* organisms. The correlation of a filter's bubble point value, related to the largest size pores, with its quantified capability to retain the *B. diminuta* test organisms is experimentally determined by the filter makers using a standardized test.

The filter's classification as suitable for a filtrative sterilization is postulated on this relationship. The filter's pre-use bubble point and/or diffusive flow value is assessed by the user although its level is already known from measurements made by the filter manufacturers. Filter manufacturers integrity test each sterilizing grade filter cartridge prior to release. The release test methods of the manufacturers often underestimate the bubble point value and overestimates the diffusion value thus bringing added safety margin (the bubble point release criterion being a minimal value and the diffusion release criterion being a maximal value). Nevertheless, the user may be obligated by the regulations to confirm the identity and propriety of the particular filter selected for use. The integrity of the filter is affirmed by the post-use test's value.

Theoretical Basis for the Integrity Tests

The integrity testing of a hydrophilic filter depends upon the interpretation of the flow rates of a test gas issuing from the downstream side of its water-filled pores exposed to its differential pressure at successively higher applied upstream pressure levels. The endpoint sought is the differentiation of a diffusive airflow from that of a viscous or bulk airflow. The measurement relied upon to recognize the distinction is the bubble point, so called because its appearance is manifested by a stream of bubbles on the downstream side when its outlet is put into a cup filled with water. Its value in the pressure terms of psi or bars is individual for each of the various filter types, and for the pore size rating classifications within each type. The former derives from the filter type's particular molecular composition; the latter, from the pore's restricted diameters. This appertains also to the integrity testing of hydrophobic filters using liquids of lower surface tensions such as aqueous alcoholic solutions in place of water as the wetting fluid.

Consider the course of a procedure involving a progressive increase in the differential pressure of a gas upon a water-filled membrane. The resulting increasing rate of gas passage through the filter will progress in stages. The initial gas flow will occur by diffusion through the water-filled pores. This will be followed by a bulk or viscous airflow through pores blown empty of water at the bubble point pressure. This point marks the transition from diffusive to viscous airflow. It identifies the largest pores of the filter by way of the lowest differential pressure needed to blow them clear. The implications are to the smallest organisms the filter can retain by sieve retention. It is the largest pores that are emptied first. The next smaller size pores follow progressively. In agreement with the bubble point equation, they exhibit the inverse relationship of the bubble point pressures to the sizes of the largest pores.

The various filter types differ in their bubble points because their particular molecular structures require dissimilar and distinct force levels to separate (and expel) the water molecules from the individuality of the polymeric pore walls. The sizes of the largest pores, so revealed, are not measured in dimensional units, but are rather approximated by their inverse connection to pore size as identified by their bubble points. Correlating the various differential pressures with their corresponding organism retention capabilities (LRVs) establishes the desired integrity test. It relates a filter's putative pore size to its organism removal ability. If a filter identified by its pre-use bubble point value suffices to perform a particular organism removal, and its bubble point value measured post-use is found to be unaltered and within the manufacturers' limit, its integrity is confirmed as being unblemished.

The Capillary Rise Phenomenon

An understanding of the phenomenon governing the rise of water in glass capillaries and the subsequent emptying thereof explains the relationship of a filter's largest pores to the bubble point integrity test.

Water will rise in a glass capillary tube to an extent governed by its diameter. If one of the ends of a number of glass capillaries of different diameters were dipped into water, the liquid would rise highest in the narrowest tube. The narrower the diameter of the capillary, the greater the rise. The hydrophilicity of the (polar) silicate material constituting the tube, and the polarity of the water influence the extent of rise. Water will not rise in a polyethylene (hydrophobic) tube or capillary, nor will mercury rise in glass capillaries (see the section: "Wetting of Pore Surfaces").

The reason for the rise of water in glass is the hydrogen bonding that is cohesive among the water molecules. Similar partial charge influences create an adhesive bond between the water molecules and the silicate anions of the glass. It causes the one to spread over the other. It results from the attractive forces existing between partial charges of opposite signs. One such is situated on an atom that is part of a molecule of the glass surface; its opposite partial charge is sited on an atom, whether hydrogen or oxygen, of a water molecule. The presence of such an intermolecular bonding action is signaled by the concavity of the liquid meniscus within the capillary. The interaction of the water and the silicate surfaces pulls the liquid film upward along the glass walls. The liquid molecules not in intimate touch with the glass constitute, in effect, a free-standing column of water. Hydrogen bonding only with one another is less affected by the rise in proportion to their distance from the capillary walls. The mass of hydrogen-bonded water is lifted by these cohesive forces operating within the water bulk, as expressed by the surface tension, gamma (λ), the term in the equation responsible for the capillary rise.

Within the capillary this chain of mutually hydrogen-bonded molecules is manifested by a concave meniscus. The water rises until it is balanced by the opposing force of gravity. Such attractive forces are absent between water and polyethylene capillaries, or between mercury and glass because of the dissimilarities in the surface tensions of the liquids and solids. In cases involving non-wetting liquid within a capillary the meniscus is convex. This is the upper crescent-shaped part of Langmuir's spherical free-falling drop. The liquid drop falling through the air is spherical because its molecules are dissimilar in their solubility parameters from those of the air that constitute their ambient surroundings. The free surface energy of the molecules comprising the drop's surface is expressed as surface tension. This results in a sphere, the geometric form which encloses the largest volume possible within its minimum extent of surface.

Voiding the Water-Filled Capillaries

For the purpose of integrity testing it is assumed that the pores of microporous filters act as do capillaries when they are wetted with water. To expel the water from the membrane pores requires a countervailing force to destabilize the capillary rise equilibrium. At the peak of the water's height in the capillary, the upward force resulting from surface tension effects is balanced by the force of gravity. Air pressure applied to the surface of a wetted membrane contained in a suitable holder will upset this equilibrium. Enough pressure will have to be exerted to overcome the bonding forces adhering to the water molecules to the pore surfaces. At this differential pressure, the bubble point, the water will be ejected from the membrane's largest pores.

Bubble Point Test

Pore Size and Pore Shape

It is the bubble point that is relied upon to gauge pore sizes. This teaching stems from an examination of the capillary rise phenomenon. However, dimensional pore sizes cannot with accuracy be calculated from the bubble point equation:

$$P = 4\gamma \cos \Theta / d,$$

where P is the pressure required to expel the liquid from the filter pore whose diameter is d; while γ is surface tension (test liquids other than water may be used) and theta, Θ, is the angle of wetting.

For example, assuming a pore size of 0.2/0.22 µm, the calculated theoretical pressure needed to expel a liquid like water would be 14.4 bar; at γ for water of 0.072 N/m at 20°C; and cos Θ = 1. Certainly, this is not the case. The bubble point pressure commonly found for 0.2/0.22 µm-rated filter membranes is around 50 psi (3.5 bar).

The reason for the differences between the calculated and measured dimensions (or pressure levels necessary to cause liquid to be expelled from the pores) derives, as stated, from the assumption inherent in the equation that the pores are circular in cross section (see the section The "Pores.") Shown in Figure 10.2 is a scanning electron micrograph of a typical inverse phase microporous membrane. The convoluted polygonal shapes of the pores make it impossible to directly measure their perimeters or the areas they enclose.

In the one instance where calculations based on the shape factor can be performed—for woven metallic cloth of the Dutch twill design, wherein the pores are skewed equilateral triangles—calculated and measured values agree (SAE 1968). A capillary rise equation that more generally treats the shape of the pore includes a shape factor, L, for the length of the pore perimeter, and A for the area it encloses instead of $2\pi r$ and πr^2 terms correctly applicable to circles alone:

$$P = L\gamma \cos \Theta / A,$$

The pore shapes importantly influence the pore diameter values. Pores having the irregular outlines that characterize membrane voids are smaller in their extent of open volume than are those of a similarly sized spherical periphery. This is so because the area within a circle is the largest expanse that can be enclosed by a given perimeter. If the same size perimeter assumes any shape other than circular, the area it encloses must be smaller. It is, thus, safe to say that particles much smaller than the numerical pore ratings will be sieve-retained by membrane filters (Ferry 1935; Petras 1967).

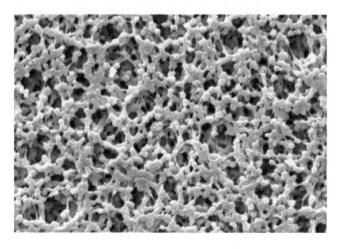

FIGURE 10.2 Scanning electron microscope (SEM) of evaporation-casted membrane.

In any case, the bubble point method based on capillary rise yields only relative values of the membranes largest pore sizes. This accord with the previously quoted statement of the Aerospace Recommended Practice (SAE 1968), "No bubble point test measures actual pore size but only allows correlation of the measured capillary pressure with some dimensional characteristics of the pore structures." Nevertheless, however roughly, the bubble point is indicative of the sizes of the filter's largest pores.

Sensitivity of Bubble Point Measurements

The bubble point is the measurement of prime interest where filters are engaged to produce sterile effluent in processing operations. For example, for filtrative sterilizations, an LRV is required of a membrane sufficient to sustain a *B. diminuta* bacterial challenge of 1×10^7 cfu/cm^2 of EFA. Pore size and organism retention are directly related (Williams and Meltzer 1983). The higher the bubble point's differential pressure, the smaller is the pore (diameter), and the larger is its LRV. This relationship is illustrated in Figure 10.3. The data plotted (Johnston and Meltzer 1979) are LRVs and corresponding bubble point

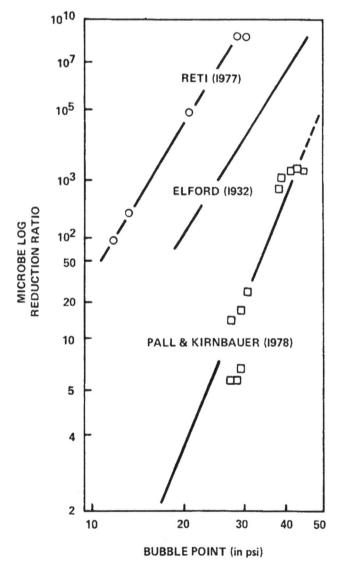

FIGURE 10.3 Relationship between bubble point value and retentivity.

values reported by Reti et al. (1979), Elford (1933), Pall and Kirnbauer (1978), and Leahy and Sullivan (1978). The correlation is evident from the straight lines having essentially the same slopes, as obtained from the three groups of data.

Figure 10.4 shows that a ~10% change in bubble point (and subsequent changes in permeability and pore size) results in a tenfold change in the bacterial reduction ratio. The figure posits the conclusion that when one attempts both to measure such large reduction ratios and to reproduce the results within ±10%, one should expect to see tenfold variations in the microbe reduction ratio. In other words, if 10^7 is a true value, one may find numbers anywhere between 10^6 and 10^8. An uncertainty of 10% inheres to the bubble point measurement, as it is manually conducted.

Hofmann (1984) on the basis of hypothesized dimensions calculates that the bubble point's detection for a 47-mm disc will involve a gas flow rate of ~20–50 μL/min, equivalent to a linear gas flow of 6–16 mm/min within the 2-mm diameter tubing downstream. To attain the same measurement sensitivity for a 296-mm diameter disc, the same viscous gas flow of 20–50 μL/min would be involved, in addition to the diffusive background flow of 1.5 mL/min. To achieve the same sensitivity for a 10-in. sterilizing grade cartridge, the detection of the 20–50 μL/min bulk airflow against a diffusive gas flow background of 12 mL/min would be required; clearly not possible with the present instrumentation.

Measuring test points on a curve generally decreases the accuracy of their readings. This is one reason for not measuring the differential pressure points at above 80% or so of the bubble point. Accordingly, the bubble point's identification of the filter's largest pores is tenuous, as also is the uncertainty of its location on the curve. Given the importance of the bubble point's indication of the differential pressure level that motivates bulk airflow, its position on the curve and the differential pressure that quantifies it requires a more sensitive evaluation than is available (Hofmann 1984).

The pursuit of a more exact locating of the bubble point by way of identifying its differential pressure level led to an investigation of other testing technique, and to subsequent efforts at improving test operations. The diffusive flow integrity test, soon to be discussed, was designed to integrity test filters based on a single-point analysis.

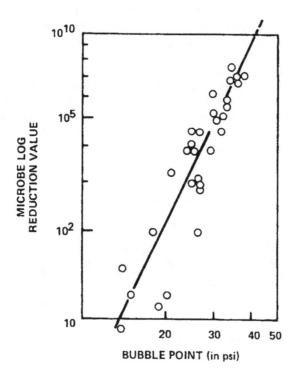

FIGURE 10.4 Bubble point value and retentivity.

Bubble Points: Perceived and Intrinsic

The gas passing through the filter enters a pool of water and is made visible as a stream of bubbles (Figure 10.5). Hence, the name "bubble point." In manual testing, the *intrinsic* bubble point is likely not to be noticed immediately. The mini-quantities of air emerging from solution must first collect in sufficient quantity to form the bubbles. What is first noticed is the *perceived* bubble point; the exact instance at which the bulk air becomes apparent to the eye or automated test instrument. It is probably always at a higher differential pressure than the intrinsic point whose early detection requires great sensitivity. The larger the filter area, the less accurate and the more subjective the bubble point becomes. The so-called bubble point, perceived at a higher pressure, is taken to represent a pore smaller than it really is. Organism retentions based on particle size/pore size relations, therefore, gain an undeserved but helpful safety margin derived from the mistaking of the perceived bubble point as being the intrinsic.

Johnston et al. (1981) found that a seven-member panel differed markedly in identifying the perceived bubble points of 10-in. cartridges. The range of values varied between 5 and 50 mL/min of gas flow. A similar range, 20–70 mL/min was found by Hofmann. This equaled an increase of 10–60 mL/min over the 10 mL/min diffusive flow expected at that differential pressure level. At so insensitive a detection level, a 10% departure from the intrinsic value would result in an error of two orders of magnitude in the LRV. If the desired LRV of a filter is seven (7), the bubble point reading would be between an LRV reading of from six (6) to eight (8). This bespeaks the strong dependence of obtaining useful results from the fine-tuning of measurements. The automated test machines do incorporate instruments of greater sensitivity.

The Knee Area of the Curve

The curvilinear trace, the knee area of the curve just discussed, is important enough to merit a sharper focus. It represents a mixture of air originating from both diffusive and viscous or bulk air passage. The initial break in the straight line's diffusive airflow leading into the knee curve occurs when the applied differential pressure is strong enough to force water from the group of largest filter pores in accord with the teachings derived from the voiding of water-filled capillaries. This is the bubble point. It marks the beginning of bulk air passage. As the differential pressure increases successively, it is followed in series by the voiding of the next-smaller set of pores, etc. until all the pores are blown empty of the liquid. This causes successively increasing rates of air exiting the filter as a bulk flow, in addition to the diffusive flow that remains ongoing until all the pores are emptied of water.

The breadth of the curvilinear region is largely the product of the filter's pore size distribution which presents a spectrum of pore sizes, the emptying of which occurs stepwise over a span of increasing differential pressures. The wider the distribution, the more extensive the area of curvature. Membranes of narrower pore size distributions show sharper transitions; both from the diffusive airflow to the emptying of the pores, and from that to the completely viscous airflow at still higher differential pressures (Pall and Kirnbauer 1978). However, the presence of anisotropic pore structures, more easily voided, also

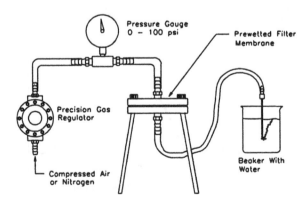

FIGURE 10.5   Manual bubbler point measurement.

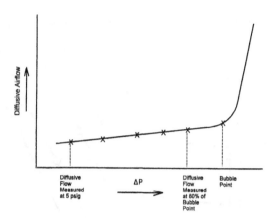

FIGURE 10.6   Test pressure curve.

contribute by diffusion to the increasing airflow, and confuse the recognition of the "true" bubble point, and its exact initiation point (Kesting et al. 1981).

What is desired is the unambiguous identification of the bubble point, described in differential pressure units. This requires knowing exactly when bulk air passage commences. However, as detailed above in the section: "Diffusive Airflow Influence on Bubble Point," at that very point the diffusive airflows from filters having an EFA larger than about that of a 47-mm disc obscure the sharp edge of the bulk airflow's beginning. Adding to the uncertainty is the diffusive flow contributed by the anisotropic pores. It is more likely that the thinning of the water layers in the anisotropic pores occurs earlier at lower differential pressures than the emptying of the largest pores. This occurrence would speed the rate of diffusion and add to the bubble point's obfuscation. Therefore, diffusive flow testing is preferred over bubble point when integrity testing asymmetric membranes (Meltzer 1986).

Nevertheless, because of practical considerations it is common to assume that the initial break in the straight diffusive airflow line marks the bubble point. It is so assumed by the automated testers where the sensitivity of measurement is already of a superior quality. The assumption focuses and makes more evident the curve's break from the linearity of its upward progression. At this point, the filter's bubble point value has increased to where it signifies smaller pores, and its correlated LRV level has also increased to where the potential for organism passage is no longer possible for reasons of size interferences (Figure 10.6).

Concerns that the bubble point's arbitrary placement at the onset of the curve may lead to improper judgments and/or actions, are assuaged by the safety margins added to the experimentally defined bubble point level by the filter manufacturers. The membranes thus characterized are of a somewhat tighter diameter. They are, therefore, more retentive of smaller organisms. They do exhibit some reduction in flow rates and are likely more restrained in their throughputs against more heavily loaded suspensions. Users are obliged to respect the filter manufacturer's stipulated bubble point values in their membrane applications.

Normalized Bubble Points

Interestingly, the bubble point of a given type filter may upon measurement seem to increase as the filter's pore size decreases. Johnston and Meltzer (1980) illustrated that this is an artifact occasioned by the larger volume of air produced per area of filter by a given differential pressure. This quantity of air, being larger, is earlier perceived as bubbles, and is, therefore, earlier identified as the bubble point. Figure 10.7 shows that although the perceived bubble point does seem to differ reciprocally with the filter area, the inherent bubble point of the membrane type wetted by the same liquid remains constant. Dividing the apparent (perceived) bubble point values by the filter areas serves to normalize the data, converting it to its inherent value. However, in practice bubble point data are seldom normalized. Instead, the bubble point is simply reported along with the size of the filter for which it was obtained.

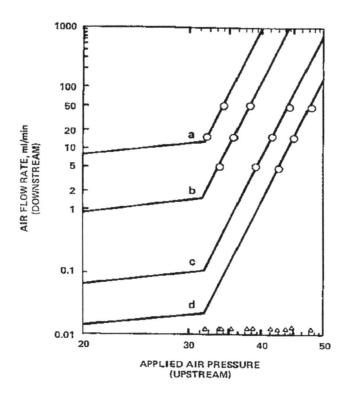

FIGURE 10.7 Bubble point shift as a function of area. The membrane was 130-μm thick, 0.2 μm rated. Filtration area $a = 4545\,cm^2$ (pleated device), $b = 589\,cm^2$ (disc), $c = 44\,cm^2$ (disc), and $d = 9.6\,cm^2$ (disc).

The Bubble Point's Significance

The basis for the integrity testing of filters depends upon the interpretation of airflows through membranes wetted by water. The bubble point measurement identifies the largest (diameter) pores present in a membrane by the differential pressure required to empty them of their water. The largest (diameter) pores are vacated first. The pores thus sized are correlated with their ability to restrain the passage of organisms. It is this correlation that enables a filter to be characterized and selected for an application requiring a given pore retention value. The differential pressure supplies the work function necessary to disrupt the bonding between the water molecules and the molecules of the hydrophilic pore surface that constitutes wetting, and to forcibly separate the water from the pore walls. The bonding strength of the wetting interaction to be overcome is peculiar to each particular filter/fluid combination and is different for each pore size rating of each of the different type of filters.

Given that the dominant mechanism of particle removal by filters depends on size discrimination, the concern in conducting a sterilizing filtration is that the filters not have pores large enough to enable organisms to escape capture. To address this concern a filter's pore sizes should be known. However, the pore size designations assigned by the filter manufacturers will not do because two filters labeled identically may, in fact, not be so.

In the absence of industry standards, pore size ratings are assigned by the filter manufacturers on an individual basis. Filters from different manufacturers may bear identical pore size labels, but, regardless, may differ and cannot really be compared on the basis of their assigned ratings. The bubble point technique offers a different approach to filter sizing in that it quantifies a filter's largest pores in specific differential pressure units.

Consider: By definition, groups, however assembled, differ from one another more greatly than do members within a group. Thus, the filter groups classified by pore size ratings do differ from one another. But the individual members of each group are also unalike, albeit to some lesser amount. Hence, such descriptions as: An "open" 0.2/0.22 µm, or a "tight" 0.2/0.22 µm. Both bear the same pore size label but do differ to an extent that may be significant in a given application. Therefore, comparing two filters of a given filter type and pore size classification involves some uncertainty. But comparing two filters its terms of their "largest pores," each identified individually by a specific differential pressure value, is a less ambiguous situation. This is an advantage of the bubble point designation. Its comparisons among filters of a given type are more credible.

However, the comparison of organism retentions among different types of filters based on bubble point values remains elusive. The number of their pores, their sizes and size distributions, and especially their pore shapes may not be assumed to be the same.

The Largest Pores: What They Portend

The utility of the bubble point derives from its identifying a filter's largest pores as measured by the differential pressure required to expel the water from a wetted filter. The flow of bulk air through the emptied pores produces the stream of bubbles that marks the endpoint. The bubble point equation follows:

$$P = 4\gamma \cos\Theta/d,$$

P is the pressure required to expel the liquid (test liquids other than water may be used) from the filter pore whose diameter is d, while γ is surface tension, and Θ is the angle of wetting. The integer serves as a correction factor necessary for the better conformance of the equation with actual measurements. Its presence acknowledges our imperfect understanding of the phenomena involved.

Laplace's Law is descriptive of pores with the shapes of ideal cylinders. Nevertheless, as applied here, it makes plain in equation form the inverse relationship of P, the bubble point pressure, and d, the pore's diameter. The bubble point value is the applied differential pressure level just sufficient to expel the water from the largest pores. However, the value calculated by way of the Laplace equation is always lower than would be expected. The differences are ascribed to imperfect wetting of the pore surfaces. This increases theta, Θ, the angle of wetting, and affects the results. The differences also may be due to the irregular shapes of the pores, and the pore size distribution. As said, the bubble point equation applies to regular cylinders, not to the irregularly shaped pores of the microporous membranes.

Different type of filters may differ in their completeness of wetting, in their pore size distributions, in the shapes of their pores, and even in their pore sizes as classified by the nonstandard systems of the individual filter manufacturers (Hofmann 1984). Consequently, the bubble point is not an absolute measure of a filter's largest pores. Comparisons of bubble point values among filters of different type but of identical pore size ratings do not lead to useful results. However, the bubble point does serve, for the same type of filter, as a relative measure of its largest pore size against which retention data can be correlated (Johnston et al. 1981).

Hofmann (1984), making enabling simplified assumptions, details mathematically the sensitivity with which differential pressures and flow volumes must be measured to differentiate between the diffusive and bulk airflows contributing to the total quantity of air passing through a wetted membrane. The precise identification of the bubble point depends upon the sensitivity in measuring differential pressures, and/or gas volumes. This is best achieved using automated test machines.

In the striving for exactness during the development of the bubble point test, different approaches were advocated and explored for their possible advantages. The presently accepted integrity tests arose from such efforts.

Diffusive Airflow Influence on Bubble Point

The bubble point measurement can be replicated at multiple differential pressure points in ascending order. The plot of this series of test points, each of which represents the rate of *diffusive airflow* as a direct function of its particular differential pressure, produces an upward-trending straight line of moderate slope. It extends to some level above the differential pressure value attained at about 80% of the bubble point level. Above this point the line begins to curve upward. This is taken to mark the bubble point. At its advent, bulk airflow commences through the largest pores emptied of water by the attained differential pressure. The airflow is then a mixture of bulk air plus the air diffusing through the smaller pores still filled with water. What is sought is the exact point when bulk airflow begins. However, the accuracy of the measurements is clouded by the simultaneously occurring large diffusive airflows. For small area filters (EFA), e.g., flat 47-mm discs, the visual sensitivity of manual determinations suffices to define the bubble point. The diffusive airflows of larger area filters overwhelm the bulk airflow, and obfuscate the bubble point (Johnston et al 1981).

According to Hofmann (1984), the transition pressure, where the increase in the rate of gas bubble appearance ceases to be proportional to the incremental increase in challenge pressure, necessitates "subjective" bubble point determinations.

The bubble point differs for each pore type. This reflects the different and specific molecular composition comprising the filter, and the strength of its adhesive bonding to water molecules. Thus, various combinations of liquids and solid surfaces coupled in the wetting action result in distinct and different bonding strengths. The various pore size ratings of a given filter type also differ in bubble point readings because the narrower the pore, the greater the force necessary to expel its liquid content. The differential pressures are needed to surpass the wetting interaction, the cohesive bonding strength, between the solid molecules of the pore walls and the liquid. Attaining the differential pressure level of a wetted filter's bubble point results in its largest pore's being emptied of the water. The result is a clear channel available to bulk airflows.

Advantages and Disadvantages of Bubble Point Testing

As for every test methodology, there are benefits but also limitations to the bubble point test. This certainly is also valid for the other described integrity test methods.

Advantages

The bubble point test can be directly correlated to membrane pore size. It detects the largest pore by forcing the liquid from such pores and creating a bulk air flow which can be detected. It is relatively easy to perform on small- to medium-scale filters. It is the only test, which can be performed on small-scale filtration devices, which cannot be tested via the diffusive flow measurement or the pressure hold test. The test duration can be brief due to short stabilization periods and faster pressure rises. The correlation between the bubble point and the bacteria challenge, as well as the water-wetted bubble point and the product-wetted bubble point is reliably and easy to establish. Temperature influences are not as critical as for the diffusive flow or pressure hold test. The temperature influence restricts itself to the surface tension of the wetting medium. A temperature increase of the air upstream volume does not have such an effect as in diffusive flow or pressure hold testing due to the fact that the bubble point method consists of several consecutive short measurement steps (typically less than 10 s for each measurement) with a short stabilization step in between, combined with a relative comparison between subsequent values.

Disadvantages

When performing a manual bubble point test, one has to manipulate the downstream, i.e., filtrate sides of the filter, which one wants to avoid. Furthermore, a high degree of the test person's subjectivity is involved, when the test is performed manually. Both such disadvantages can be avoided, using automated integrity test machines. The sensitivity of the bubble point test decreases with increasing filtration area, due to the fact that the diffusive flow will obliterate the bubble point's detection. Also specific failures (i.e., microflaws) generating a slightly increased flow would only displace the linear portion of the test curve upwards without changing the pressure at which the transition from diffusion to bulk flow appears. Such failures should not be able slip through the quality control of the filter manufacturer as both diffusion and bubble point are used for the manufacturing release test in addition to comprehensive control points of the membrane quality.

The use of the bubble point becomes more critical with smaller pore size-rated filter membranes. The bubble point values of such pore size rating may be above the maximum allowable differential pressure of such membranes, or above the allowable operating pressure of a filter device. Bubble point measurement does not take the membrane thickness into account. This can be critical for the retentive capabilities of such membranes (Pall and Kirnbauer 1978).

Assymetric Diffusive Flow Test

Fick's Law of Diffusion

The diffusive airflow is an expression of Fick's Law of Diffusion (Reti 1977; Waibel et al 1996; Jornitz and Meltzer 1998):

$$N = DH(P_1 - P_2)r/L$$

Where N = the permeation rate; D = diffusivity of the gas in the liquid; H = solubility coefficient of gas in the liquid; L = the membrane thickness; $(P_1 - P_2)$ = differential pressure; ρ = total porosity.

The diffusive flow permeates the pores of all sizes, large and small. It should be noted that the sizes of the pores do not enter into the equation; in their aggregate they comprise L, the thickness of the liquid layer, the membrane being some 80% porous. The critical measurement of a flaw is the thickness of the liquid layer. Therefore, a flaw or an oversized pore would be measured by the thinning of the liquid layer due to the elevated test pressure on the upstream side. The pore or defect may not be large enough for the bubble point to come into effect, but the elevated test pressure will force liquid out of the pore.

Besides the thickness of the liquid layer, the EFA is a critical parameter for diffusive flow measurement. The measurement of the diffusive flow will be impossible at a too small filter size, because the restricted filter area would not allow enough air volume to be diffused through the wetting liquid layer to be measured accurately. Therefore, a filter element that shows less diffusion will not necessarily retain better. It may mean only that this filter element contains less membrane area or that the membrane has a reduced total porosity, or that it is thicker than stated.

The Single-Point Diffusive Airflow Integrity Test

A simplified integrity test for filters based on a single-point determination was proposed for use by Dr. David Pall (Pall 1973). He observed that the line traced by multipoint diffusive airflow measurements *is invariably straight and of constant upward slope* in its direct and undeviating reach to the bubble point. He named it the forward flow bubble point test, abbreviated to the forward flow test (Pall 1975).

Plotting the diffusive airflow rates as functions of differential pressures for the various filter types results in lines that extend straight and direct to the bubble point. This signifies that the diffusive airflow, uncomplicated by bulk flows, can be identified equally well by testing at any differential pressure level lower than that of the bubble point.

If the test point for a newly assayed filter melds into the diffusive airflow line previously established by multipoint testing as being characteristic of that filter type, then the filter's integrity is confirmed. A higher diffusive airflow than expected is interpreted as a failed integrity test due to a flaw or larger pore that is untypical for that type of membrane. A lower rate of diffusive airflow signifies structural aberrations in the filter, whether thicker membrane, a lower porosity, some unforeseen pore blockage, etc. Thus, the single point serves as a positive integrity test for that filter type.

The original test point selected by Dr. Pall at ~5.25 psi (0.35 bar) was changed to a differential test pressure of about 80% of the bubble point level (Reti 1977). The alteration increased the test's sensitivity. Hofmann (1984) reports that testing at a differential pressure of 2.7 bar instead of at 320 mbar increased the test sensitivity 20-fold.

Some experimenters in conducting the single-point testing believe that it is unnecessary to measure the bubble point itself because the straight-line slope inevitably leads to it. However, the single point determination for a given filter does presupposes the availability for comparative purposes of the diffusive airflow line. This will already have been constructed from multipoint tests, for that membrane type.

Single-Point Plus Bubble Point

An obvious advantage of the single-point test is the time and effort saved in making diagnoses, a worthwhile goal, especially in process filtrations. However, added advantages may be available to those who still prefer the routine of multipoint analyses, but who desire the speed of single-point testing. Schroeder (2001) questions whether multipoint airflow integrity testing needs to entail excessive time investments. He suggests that the straight-line reliability of multipoint testing can be obtained by utilizing two test points instead of the one single point. The point of origin at zero differential pressure already exists. To this initial point would be added the single point being discussed, plus measurement at the bubble point.

The flow rate is a function of a filter's total porosity. The single-point testing is measured at the differential pressure level equivalent to 80% of the bubble point. It is based on the assumption that its results would fall on the straight line that would have been traced to the bubble point level characteristic of integral filters of its type had the testing been performed at multipoint pressures. Were the test point to fall below the line it would indicate a tighter membrane; above the line would signify a failed filter.

Testing at 80% of Bubble Point

In proposing the "Forward Flow Bubble Point Test" Dr. Pall had performed the testing at the differential pressure of 5.25 psi. Presumably, any differential pressure would suit as well for in-process testing given that it is a point on the straight line, as are all of the multipoints composing the plot. All the differential pressure points are equivalent in this regard.

As can be seen from Figure 10.8, however, absent bubble point testing, integrity failures may escape detection. Testing only at about 5 psi could disclose nothing about the filter's integrity at pressures above that level. Failures would not be disclosed unless the bubble points were also assessed as points of reference. It was realized that without actually assaying the bubble point, assuming a straight line from a point so far removed from the bubble point entailed far more risk than one performed as close to the bubble point as possible (Reti 1977). As a result, the single point selected for testing was adjusted to ~80% of the bubble point's differential pressure level; as close as possible to the break in linearity, while avoiding the uncertainties of measuring on a curve (Reti 1977). Nevertheless, the advantages of single-point testing can perhaps best be utilized when the multipoint line against which the single test is referenced is already available.

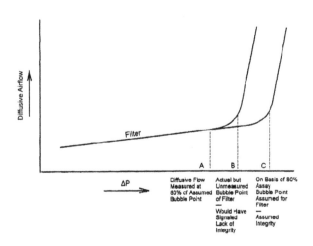

FIGURE 10.8 Diffusive flow curve.

Correlation of Diffusion and Retention

As in bubble point measurement, the numbers obtained from diffusive airflow tests have significance only because they can be correlated with organism retentions. The measurements are usually stipulated to be performed by the filter manufacturer, at the defined test pressure that was used in securing the correlation with organism retentions, usually at ~80% of the bubble point value.

The diffusive airflow integrity test does not confine its measurements solely to the set of largest pores or through a single flaw, as does the bubble point. Rather, it measures the airflow diffused through all the available pores. A larger pore or flaw will be evidenced by a higher total diffusive flow, possibly over the allowable limit set by the bacterial correlation itself. A higher rate of diffusion caused by the differential pressure then being applied may also be due to an anisotropic effect. At higher differential pressures, a thinning of the liquid layers in the larger inverted "V" shaped, or downstream—pointed funnel-shaped pores takes place. These are inevitably present to some extent in cast membranes (Kesting 1985). These thinner aqueous barriers are more readily diffused.

For reasons of prudence, filter manufacturers commonly add a safety margin onto the point of bacterial breakthrough, the true correlation point. The resulting limiting value is the actual maximum diffusive airflow level described in the user's manual or validation documentation. Any integrity test limits not directly correlated to a bacteria challenge test can only be quantitative but not qualitative. It is necessary, however, that users observe and respect the limits of these nondestructive tests, the safety margins included.

Advantages and Disadvantages of Diffusive Flow testing

Advantages

The diffusive airflow test has a high sensitivity which increases with larger filter surface areas. A thinning of the liquid layer takes place in the larger pores or flaws as the differential pressure mounts. This results in an increase of the diffusive flow. The diffusive flow measures the entire pore volume of the membrane matrix, including flaws, if any. The test pressures of the diffusive flow assay can be sensitive enough to identify the above-mentioned thinning of the wetting liquid layer within a larger pore. This anisotropic effect may not be detectable with the bubble point test, but will be detected by the diffusive flow test, especially when automated machines are used. Furthermore, the diffusive flow test is very well suited for membranes with small pore size, e.g., 0.1 micron-rated filters. If one uses the bubble point test for such filter pore size ratings, the maximum operating or differential pressure allowable for the membrane can be exceeded and the filter damaged. In such cases, it is advisable to use the diffusive flow test.

Diffusive airflow measurements have their advantages in addition to serving as indicators of filter integrity. They can more precisely reveal filter incompatibilities. They can be used to gauge the completeness of a filter's wettability, and they are more revealing of a filter's clean water flow properties. Usually smaller pores are wetted with more difficulties than larger pores. This would not be detected by the bubble point measurement but can be evaluated by the diffusive flow test.

Additionally, the diffusive flow test can be correlated to the bacteria challenge test as described in the paragraph above. Such correlation is easier to accomplish, when the filter's pore size distribution is narrow. The correlation is then very well defined and easy to perform.

Disadvantages

Being more sensitive at testing larger filtration areas creates a problem in itself, in testing multi-round filter housings. In an effort to provide a safety margin, filter manufacturers may fashion cartridges that have diffusive airflows of less than the maximum acceptable rate, say 15 mL/min at the given test pressure. Consider an assembly of nine 10-in. cartridges. Assume that eight of these elements have acceptable diffusive airflows of 10 mL/min but the ninth one, lacking integrity, has a diffusional airflow rate of 55 mL/min. The total diffusive airflow rate for the nine-element assembly would be 135 mL/min, undistinguishable from the 135 mL/min expected for the integral nine 10-in. cartridge arrangement.

A single-point diffusive airflow determination would not reveal the presence of the flawed cartridge. However, multipoint diffusive testing, as shown in Figure 10.9, could make evident a single filter's flaw even within a multielement arrangement (Waibel et al. 1996; Jornitz and Meltzer 1998). The diffusive airflow rate differs directly with the differential pressure, whereas the bulk airflow, as through flaws, reflects also the fourth power of the pore radius. Therefore, at higher pressure levels the flows through the flaw would increase markedly in deviating from the straight line of the diffusive airflow. If, consequently, the diffusive airflows are plotted from multipoint pressure data, the rate of climb of the resulting curve would reveal in its increase what a single point cannot. The increased slope of the linear section of the multipoint diffusion curve would allow for experimental investigation. Such evaluation of the slope can only be done by multi-plotting the entire graph through to the bubble point.*

A reduction of the overall max diffusion value fur such multi-round housings based on statistical measurements would also serve the cause of risk mitigation for false passed test results.

Due to their sensitivity, temperature deviations during the test's duration will have a high impact on the result. Any temperature influence during the test should be avoided and eliminated. Even touching a hand to the filter housing or keeping such close to an air conditioning system, will cause wrong integrity test result, with the danger of a false passed integrity test result. A thermal variation of only 1K inside the filter housing/capsule could result in an impact of 25% on the measured diffusion value based on a pressure drop value of 0.73 psi/50 mbar under stable conditions. For this reason, automated integrity test systems plot diffusive flow or pressure drop, which reveal the occurrence of deviations during the test. Monitoring environmental temperature variations if any also adds reliability to the test result.

Automated integrity test machine has also the advantage that the diffusive flow test can be performed from the upstream side of the filter system. The manual diffusive flow test causes the disadvantage of a downstream, filtrate side manipulation, which carry the risk of a secondary contamination. Furthermore, the manual test lacks accuracy, compared to an automated test system.

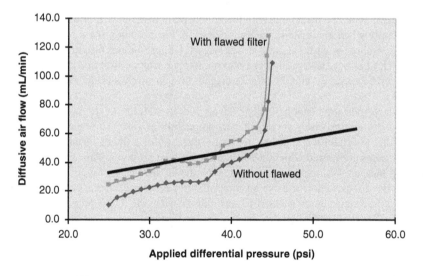

FIGURE 10.9   Multipoint diffusion test curves.

---

* This is also the basis for the Flow Ratio Test advocated by Hofmann (1984) for distinguishing by way of the diffusive airflow an integral filter from one that is flawed. The gas flow is determined at a high pressure, 2.7 bar, and at a low pressure, 0.5 bar. When the ratio of the high-pressure diffusion is compared with that of the low, the nonintegral filter is seen to have the higher ratio. See the section "Flow Ratio Test" below.

Multipoint Diffusive Flow Test

Multipoint Integrity Test

The gas flow being discussed is motivated by differential pressures, which can be arranged in ascending order. The airflow is proportional to the differential pressure. In the case of a multipoint diffusion test, the points plotted in pressure units, psi or bars, against flow rates, in mL/min, trace a straight line having a moderate upward slope until at a point it departs from its linearity to begin forming an upward curve. Until this point, the airflow consists totally of air diffused through the water-filled pores. At this point, or approximate to it, bulk airflow joins the effluent air stream. The benefit of a multipoint diffusion test is the fact that one can test multiple filters and check their diffusive flow behavior precisely by reviewing the slope of the graph achieved. The multipoint diffusion test finds its use in determining product-wet diffusive flow test points, or in testing multi-round filter housings. The multipoint test makes apparent the trend developing during the progression of the diffusive airflow toward the bubble point. This presents an advantage when investigations of failures are undertaken.

Anisotropic Pore Structures

In instances, there may be uncertainty about the origin of the increasing air flow rate that initiates the break in the plotted line. It need not necessarily be the bubble point onset. It may be the result of the partial voiding of anisotropic pores (Reti 1977). Anisotropic pore structures, according to Kesting (1985), are inevitable accompaniments of the membrane casting process. These funnel-shaped pores, if pointed downstream, thin their water contents under increasing differential pressures, thereby augmenting the rates of gaseous diffusion (Figure 10.10). The multipoint diffusive airflow plots of these filters, by their deviations from the linear diffusive airflow line, reveal the presence of anisotropic membrane structures. The bubble point may not distinctly be differentiated from the anisotropic contribution. Both occurrences cause deviations from the straight diffusive airflow lines. The ejection of water from pores at the bubble point would seem logically to follow the anisotropic thinning of the water barrier within the pores. Each of these occurrences marks departures from the strictly diffusive airflows. The automated test machines signal these departures from the linear as being the bubble point. This assumption, possibly unwarranted, causes no problem as regards the correlation with organism retentions, given the modification of the bubble point values by the safety margins provided by the filter manufacturers.

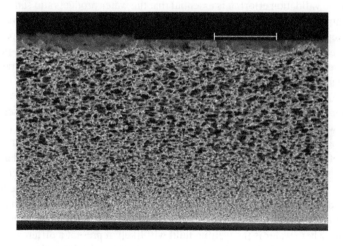

FIGURE 10.10 Asymmetric membrane structures.

Distinguishing Airflows: Diffusive and Bulk

Diffusive airflows can be distinguished from those resulting from flaws. Multipoint log/log plotting will show an ascending straight line of slope 1.0 for the diffusive flows. They are proportional to the differential pressure, whereas flow through a flaw increases nonlinearly with the test pressure. Bulk gas flow is proportional to the test pressure, but also to the ratio of absolute test gas pressure to atmospheric pressure. Judging a filter's integrity requires a distinction to be made between the two types of flow; the bulk flow must be sufficiently above that resulting from diffusion to be quantified. Helpfully, the difference between the diffusive and viscous airflows increases with the applied test pressure. Hofmann found that the change in test pressure from 320 mbar to 2.7 bar increased the sensitivity of the test by more than 20-fold.

Nonetheless, according to the findings in one study, single-point testing dealing with an additional bulk flow of 1.5 mL/min due to a flaw was not at 2.7 bar sensitive enough to discriminate between the perceived and actual bubble points (Hofmann 1984). He suggests the application of a flow ratio test to address the problem.

Flow Ratio Test

With respect to the sensitivity of differentiating between viscous and diffusive airflows, Hofmann (1984) champions a "Flow Ratio Test." His advocacy is based on the diffusive airflow rates being linear, whereas the airflow through a flaw is not. He suggests that a most certain way of ascertaining whether a filter is flawed is to measure its diffusive airflow at a low differential pressure followed by a measurement at an elevated differential pressure. If the flow at the higher differential pressure is not proportionate to the increase in the test pressures, then a *flaw* is indicated. Pores larger than usual for the type filter should be apparent at any differential pressure from the airflow being greater than customary. However, to achieve discernable and disproportionate flows from the high and low differential pressure tests, larger test pressure differentials should be invoked. The larger the pressure difference, the higher the sensitivity of the flaw detection.

Comparing Slopes of Diffusive Airflow Lines

The airflow is the product of structural features common to all filters, namely, the porosity and characteristics of the pores: their numbers, lengths, widths, and points of constriction. These are the very structural features that characterize the several membrane types regarding particle retentions, flow rates, and, where relevant because of particle content, throughputs. Differences in these structural features create distinctions among the membrane types. The airflow lines are constructed of multipoints, each of which reflects a particular mix of these very same features. The sum result is revealed in the slope of the line. Therefore, the comparison of the line slopes of different membranes can make plain their identity or their individuality.

In particular, in the validation effort, it is essential that the water/product ratio sanctioning the translation of the minimum water-wet integrity test value into the minimum product-wet value be valid (PDA 2008, Technical Report #26). The water-wet diffusive airflow line should be compared in its entirety with the product-wet curve. The two lines should be completely congruent. Single-point comparisons, however informative, simply will not suffice; the slope of the line is wanted. The same is true as regards comparing pre-use and post-use integrity tests. Single-point comparisons have value but are perhaps less informative than multipoints.

Neither the bubble point test nor the single diffusive airflow determination by itself serves the purpose of integrity testing as well as do the multipoint analyses. However, once the slope of the product airflow line is at hand, single-point diffusive airflow testing can be accepted in processing contexts. The likelihood in such cases of a dereliction between the 80% test point and the bubble point is judged acceptably reduced by the fuller characterization of the filter type. Interpretations can then be made on the basis of whether the single-point reading is on, over, or under the diffusive airflow line characteristic of the filter type.

When a drug product is used to wet the filter the bubble point will change from that of water; usually decreasing due to the difference in the surface tensions of the liquids involved. Consequently, the 80% of bubble point level where water is the wetting fluid will likely represent a different level when product is used as the wetting liquid. However, there need be no problem in determining the product-specific bubble point. Its value may have undergone a shift from the water bubble point, merely because of the surface tension effect. A simple numerical displacement may not, however, be assumed in deriving the single point diffusive air flow. The diffusive airflow displacement reflects not only the shift in bubble point occasioned by the liquid's surface tension, but it may be raised or lowered by the solubility differences of air (or nitrogen, where this is used) in the product as compared to that in water.

Pressure Hold/Decay Testing

The pressure hold test, also called the pressure decay or drop test, is still a common test, where a manual test is performed. The pressure hold test is a variant of the diffusive airflow test. All is arranged as in the diffusion test: when the stipulated applied pressure is reached and has been stabilized for a predefined time, the pressure source is valved off. The decay of pressure within the holder is then observed over a predetermined time interval by using a precision pressure gauge or pressure transducer. The difference to the diffusion test comes from the fact that the diffusion test uses either an algorithm to convert the pressure decay into a diffusion value or injects the required quantity of gas to get back to the initial pressure.

The decrease in pressure can come from two sources; the first being diffusive loss across the wetted filter. The upstream pressure in the holder decreases progressively all the while diffusion takes place through the wetted membrane. The second source of pressure decay could result from a leak in the filter system. Indeed, one virtue of the pressure hold test is that it does test the integrity of the plumbing: valves, gaskets, etc. In this function it serves as a leak tester. That is why it is often used as the initial integrity test. However, it can serve as an integrity test only because its correlation with the organism retention capabilities of the filter has been established by way of converting its test values to those of a multipoint diffusive airflow test. This enables its correlation with the organism retention values determined for the multipoint diffusion assay.

Pressure Decay Basis

The pressure hold test measures the loss of air from within the filter housing. The perfect gas law governs the air loss measurement:

$$PV = nRT$$

Where: n = moles of gas, R = universal gas constant, T = temperature, P = gas pressure, V = gas volume on the upstream side of the filter.

The decrease in gas pressure is influenced strongly by the upstream volume of the filter holder (Figure 10.11). It depends on the particular holder-filter combination and the exact details of the filter and

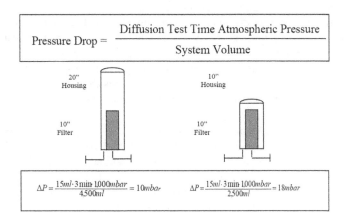

FIGURE 10.11 Influence of upstream volume on the pressure hold value.

housing being used. Even the placement of the valve and any tubing volume must be considered, because this can affect the total volume within which the pressure decay takes place. Changing either the filter size or the housing necessitates a redetermination of the pressure hold value, for this may change the total volume surrounding the filter in its housing.

$$\text{Pressure drop} = \frac{\text{diffusion vol} \times \text{test time} \times \text{atm pressure}}{\text{System volume}}$$

For the same diffusion volume per identical time the pressure drop would be different as a function of the system volume, as demonstrated by the 2 following calculations (a) and (b):

$$\text{(a)} \quad \Delta P = \frac{15\,\text{mL}^3 \times 3\,\text{min} \times 1,000\,\text{mbar}}{4500\,\text{mL}^3} = 10\,\text{mbar}$$

$$\text{(b)} \quad \Delta P = \frac{15\,\text{mL}^3 \times 3\,\text{min} \times 1,000\,\text{mbar}}{2500\,\text{mL}^3} = 18\,\text{mbar}$$

The test is most often performed using automated testing equipment which, using appropriate (software) algorithms, converts pressure hold/decay data into diffusive flow data for which there are correlations to organism retention.

An advantage of the pressure hold/drop (or decay) test is that it determines the integrity of the entire filtration train including the filter. This test investigates the possibilities for leaks or improper seals in the filtration system before the filtrative action is initiated. Performed using automated equipment connected upstream of the filter, it avoids risks to the membrane's asepsis and minimizes human subjectivity and operational errors. The pressure hold/drop test is described by PDA (2008) Technical Report #26, Trotter and Meltzer (1998); and in Jornitz and Meltzer (2001, pp. 426–434).

In the semiconductor and beverage industries, where integrity tests are used to signal confirmation to the filter's specifications (rather than to reflect precise organism retention levels as required by FDA regulations in pharmaceutical processing), the pressure hold test can serve very well, provided that the measurement of the pressure decay is sensitive enough and that a use history is developed for the given holder-filter combination employed.

In a personal communication, Ian Hart (1998) suggested the use of a manual pressure hold test at the bubble point level, performing the test post-sterilization but before filtration. Due to the fact that the manual pressure hold test can be performed on the upstream side, this test can be performed post-sterilization without risks to asepsis. Steam sterilization is most stressful to the filter integrity; therefore, an integrity test should be performed after steaming. Raising the test pressure slowly to the minimum allowable bubble point limit given by the filter manufacturer, one only has to define the maximum allowable pressure decay level. This maximum pressure decay can be evaluated during the qualification stage of point tests at the same time. After filtration, the test is repeated and the before and after values are compared. This eliminates the risk of inaccuracies in determining the pressure drop via a pressure gauge, due to the higher test pressure level. Furthermore, it also creates the possibility of evaluating the filter system in terms of leaks from improperly sealed housings before filtration. This provides higher security for the process overall.

To be reflective of a filter's organism retention capabilities, the integrity test measurement, of pressure decay, for example, must be correlated to the measured property. Hango et al. (1989) describe the use of the pressure hold method as an integrity test under conditions of having the exact volume of the holder-filter combination and the relevant diffusive airflow defined by the filter supplier (Figure 10.12). Under these circumstances, the pressure decay measured under pressure hold conditions (in the absence of plumbing leaks) can be correlated to ordinary diffusive airflow data that are in turn correlated with specific retention values.

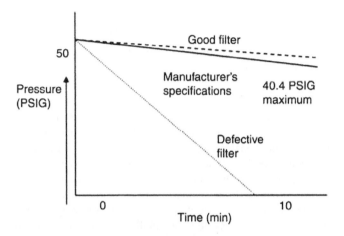

FIGURE 10.12   Diffusive flow of different filter states.

Conversion of Pressure Decay into Diffusive Flow

The conversion of the pressure decay readings into diffusive flow values enables the transformation of the test into an integrity test qualified for sterilizing grade membrane filters. This can be done by calculating the diffusive flow of a filter element based on the pressure drop during test time *t* with a known upstream volume and reference pressure (1 atm or 1 bar) according to industrial standard DIN 58 356, part 2, and as shown in PDA Technical Report #26 Appendix D (Trotter and Meltzer 1998).

Gas diffusion and the phenomenon of diffusive airflow are in accord with Fick's law,

$$N = \frac{DH}{L}(p_1 - p_2)\rho$$

where:

N = permeation rate; moles of gas per unit time; $(p1 - p2)$ = transmembrane pressure

H = Henry's law solubility coefficient for the liquid-gas system; L = thickness of the membrane

ρ = void volume of the membrane, usually around 0.8

The pore path being tortuous (i.e., the pore is modeled as being a convoluted, irregular capillary), L is longer than the membrane is thick; thus, the correction factor. The equation above demonstrates that the air diffusion involves the solubility coefficient. H in Henry's law addresses the solubility of test gases in various wetting fluids. Other factors that directly affect diffusive flow include differential pressure, the specific liquid/gas diffusion coefficient, the inverse relationship to membrane thickness, and, to a lesser degree, a correction factor for pore path tortuosity and other restrictions to fluid flow.

The significance of these factors dictates that the different wetting liquids and test gases will result in different diffusive flow values. Therefore, testing must be performed using the actual test gas and wetting liquid to show the direct and precise correlation of pressure decay with the calculated diffusive flow measurements.

The correlation to bacterial challenge tests and to the bacterial retentiveness of the filter must also be demonstrated. This is done by bacterial challenge testing on filters that were previously qualified by the diffusion test. Using filters with gradually increasing diffusional flows, one may elucidate at which value the filter will begin to pass test microbes. Using these diffusive flow data, a correlation to the calculated diffusive flow may be made and thus to the pressure drop/decay test.

$$D = \frac{P_1 V_1 \ln p}{p_0 t p_2 - \Delta p}$$

where:

D = diffusion in mL/min; V_1 = upstream volume of filter system

p_1 = starting test pressure; p_0 = atmospheric pressure of 1.0 bar

p_2 = ending test pressure; t = test time

$\Delta p = p_1 - p_2$ in pressure units

This formula compensates for the diffusive flow decrease as a result of the progressive pressure drop during the test time. This may become a significant factor when filter systems with high diffusive air/gas flow are encountered. This methodology is used by filter manufacturers to validate the pressure decay test and to qualify the various integrity test devices in performing these tests.

The translation of the pressure hold (decay) curve into the straight line of the diffusive airflow plot that relates to organism retention can be accomplished mathematically, as just shown. It is, however, performed automatically by the automated test machines designed for integrity testing. Moreover, these devices have the sensitivity essential for detecting the small pressure losses that may be involved.

Determinations of the pressure decays by means of the pressure gauges normally employed in the manual pressure hold tests are woefully inadequate. Conventional pressure gauges lack the sensitivity required for the pressure hold test. If there are no sealing leaks, the pressure in a housing will decline about 1 psig over a 10-min period. After 20 min, it is to be hoped that such a drop can be noticed. In the event of system leaks, the pressure drops more precipitously. Small pressure drop readings may be of value in determining whether filter seating or housing O-ring leaks exist. Such readings are too insensitive to reveal much about the filter. Larger diameter gauges would be more useful but these and their periodic calibration are expensive.

Most of the automated integrity test devices use pressure transducers to measure the pressure drop in the upstream side of the housings. These measurements can be made with great accuracy. Pressure transducers typically have an accuracy of 0.1 to 0.3% full scale. That is why the automated instruments have the requisite detection sensitivity.

Pressure Hold Test: Pros and Cons

One advantage of the pressure hold test is that it is capable of revealing imperfections in the assembly and sealing of the housing and filters and disclosing flaws in the filters, just like the diffusion test. This is particularly useful in initial integrity testing for the early disclosure of filter seating failures or housing sealing leaks, avoiding a profitless undertaking of the filtration.

A second advantage is that the pressure decay reading central to the pressure hold test can be made on the upstream side of the filter, on the housing itself, without compelling invasion of the downstream side of the system, even when done manually. Aseptic invasions and connections are common; they are made successfully every day. They do, however, pose a risk to the system and are best avoided where possible.

The use of automated test devices helps avoid downstream invasions during the performance of the more conventional integrity tests.

The major disadvantage of the pressure hold test is that it is strongly influenced by temperature, to the same extent as the diffusive airflow method.

Integrity Test Scenarios

Integrity Test Preferences

Curiously, preferences for one particular test or another have been occasioned by the commercial rivalry that seems normal to competitive enterprises. Perhaps pride of innovation or of technical improvement motivates some to champion a given test. A reluctance to acknowledge a competitor's accomplishments may direct or misdirect the views of others. Then too there are always the possibilities of straightforward differences in evaluations and opinions.

In certain applications each of the integrity tests will serve equally well. The analyst may exercise his preference. There are, however, situations wherein the area of the filter, its EFA, compels the use of a particular test. Small filters, such as disc filters up to 296 mm in diameter, cannot produce diffusive airflows large enough to yield reliable results. The insufficiency can be overcome by the use of higher differential pressures, or by employing more sensitive measuring devices when available. But the practical need is best supplied by bubble point testing. Filters of larger EFAs can produce diffusive airflows so large as to obscure the bubble point readings. Bubble point assays, on the other hand, are best performed on smaller size filters where the interference of simultaneous diffusive airflow is minimized. Where both types of tests are possible, perhaps their mutual reinforcing actions should be sought to diminish the uncertainties of each.

Detecting Incompatibilities

Gross incompatibilities between membranes and fluids may be easy to discern. More subtle effects can be judged by their influence on the filter's bubble point. Any indication that contact between the filter and fluid tends to enlarge the pores is clear evidence of incompatibility. However, the bubble points can disclose incompatibilities that affect only the largest pores. Changes in the smaller pores are not made evident. The diffusive airflow readings mirror the influences of all the pores (total porosity). Thus, the use of diffusive airflow measurements may indicate potential fluid/filter incompatibilities with greater sensitivity than do bubble point determinations. Kinetic rates of change, as are involved in the size reductions of certain organisms exposed to particular liquid preparations, can be quantified by repeating the incompatibility testing along a time axis.

The pore size alterations caused by heating stresses can likewise be detected, as also the kinetics of the process. However, in these activities it was best that the slopes of the plotted multipoint lines be compared, rather than those of the single-point rate.

Figure 10.13 illustrates the diffusive airflow analysis revealing flaws induced in a membrane subjected to the stresses of repeated steam sterilization cycles. In diffusive flow measurements, what is sought is the point of departure from the constant slope of the diffusive airflow line. Automated test equipment measures the gas diffused over a period of, say, 5 min. If the maximum flow rate is not exceeded, the pressure is raised appropriately.

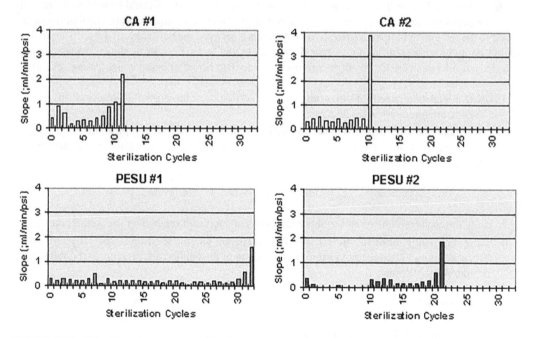

FIGURE 10.13 Filter flaws due to steam sterilization.

Diffusive flow measurements offer advantages where the phenomena being investigated relate to changes in total porosities rather than exclusively to the larger pores, as in incompatibility assessments. Gross incompatibilities between membranes and fluids may be easy to discern. Subtle effects can be judged by the influence of the medium being filtered upon the bubble point of the filter. Any indication that contact between the filter and fluid tends to enlarge the pores is clear evidence of incompatibility. Diffusive airflow measurements may here offer an even more sensitive indicator of incompatibility than bubble points. The bubble point values reflect the largest pores. Changes in the smaller pores do not become registered. However, the diffusive airflow readings mirror the influences of all the pores (total porosity). Therefore, the use of diffusive airflow measurements indicates potential fluid/filter incompatibilities with greater sensitivity than do bubble point determinations alone.

Integrity Testing Multi-Round Assemblies

A number of problems require resolution in the search for methods to determine the integrity testing of multiple cartridges in multi-round housings. One wishes to eschew the testing of the individual cartridges in the laboratory followed by their insertion into the housing under aseptic conditions. What is required is the clear determination of the assembled cartridges' bubble point. It is assumed that a single failed cartridge could be detected, and that this would suffice to impugn the integrity of the entire assemblage. Presumably, one might by selective assumptions calculate the chances for one failed filter not to affect the function of the others. An encouraging positive conclusion might then lead to calculations involving two faulty filters, etc.

There would still remain the problem of the combined diffusive flows from the assembled cartridges being large enough to make impossible the recognition of the filter combination's bubble point. Clearly, the larger the number of cartridges involved, their lengths, porosities, and the differential pressures involved would have to be balanced against the airflows resulting from the single or multiple flaws.

Even were it possible to hypothesize a realistic situation involving these several factors, the arbitrary, if necessary, assumptions would likely not represent the complex combination of flows that the situation actually offers.

As helpful as a solution to the stated problem would be, it is not likely that it will emerge from a hypothesized set of conditions involving perhaps two filters at the most. Where two filters are involved, the balancing of the combined bulk airflows against the combined diffusive flows could be achieved, but at the cost of assumptions that may not be realistic (Olson et al. 1981). The technique would be similar to that discussed in the section: "Filter Area Effects." The difference between the bulk flows and the diffusive flows would have to be so large as not to confuse the former by the latter. In order to reduce the risk for false passed test results there are mainly three approaches, classified hereafter based on increasing reliability:

1. Using a statistically reduced max diffusion value based on the normally expected diffusion values of the filter cartridges being tested

   One commonly used approach is to multiply the so-called individual typical diffusion value by the number of cartridges minus one, and then add the validated max value for one cartridge. The calculation would then be:

$$\text{Diffusion}_{maxTotal} = \text{Diffusion}_{Typ.Ind.} \times (n-1) + \text{Diffusion}_{maxInd.}$$

2. Using the combined diffusion test, also with statistically reduced values, plus the bubble point test
3. Using the multipoint diffusion test with max diffusion values based on statistically reduced diffusion values with linearized values as a function of the applied test pressure and finally the minimum bubble point

For further enhanced reliability there is no alternative otherwise to aseptically testing and housing the filters individually or having individual outlets of each filter, and, for example, measuring the pressure increase on the outlet of the filter against closed valves.

It should be kept in mind though that filter integrity testing by itself is insufficient for sterility insurance. Without a solid quality management by the filter supplier combined with a process validation the value of the integrity test result is nil.

Repetitive Filter Effects

The pore is modeled as being a convoluted, irregular capillary. Because of its tortuosity, it is necessarily longer than the depth of the filter. Its restrictive dimensions may occur anywhere along its length. This assumption explains certain observations regarding repetitive filters. It would be expected that lengthening a pore might proportionally increase the pressure drop, i.e., decrease the differential pressure across its span. This should reduce its flow rate, promote its adsorptive particle-trapping abilities, but probably not alter its throughput. The actual situation wherein membranes are superimposed in intimate contact on one another in effect does prolong the pore length. The expected consequences follow.

The congruent positioning of the filter layers will cause a homogenization of the pore size distribution. There will result fewer large size-rated pores because pores of large pore size ratings in either filter will likely juxtapose those with those of smaller ratings in the other because there are many more of the smaller. The result will be a diminution in the overall pore size. This should assist sieve retentions. Moreover, the pore paths are doubled in their lengths, as are also their surfaces. This encourages adsorptive sequestrations. The filter efficiency is enhanced.

Where use is made of two membranes that are separated from one another, a different result is obtained. Between the two membranes there exists a space wherein the fluid exiting the first membrane forms a pool from which it is hydrodynamically directed to the larger pores of the second membrane. The hydrodynamic flows preferentially convey particles to the more open pores. This detracts from the narrowing of the pore size distribution's doubling of the single filter's pore length (Figure 10.14) (Reti et al. 1979).

To repeat, the LRVs of individual filters are not additive in their combinations. The exact sum depends upon the probabilities of certain size organisms meeting an appropriately sized pore within the pore size distribution. Whether by encounter with a larger pore, or with a flaw, the likelihood is that the organisms penetrating the upstream filter will be the smaller of the organisms present in the infeed. This will decrease the size distribution of the organisms downstream of the filter in the direction of overall smaller sizes. This, in turn, makes more likely a lower LRV for the downstream filter.

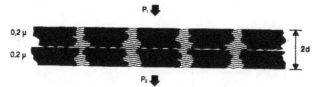

Thickness of the liquid film with a homogenous double layer (0.2 μm + 0.2 μm).

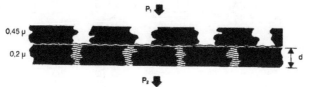

Thickness of the liquid film with a heterogenous double layer (0.2 μm + 0.45 μm).

FIGURE 10.14 Integrity test influence by multilayer membranes.

Redundant Filtration

This term is often used to designate a repetitive or two-filter arrangement wherein the two filters, each in its own cartridge, are housed separately. The term "redundant" often conveys a pejorative cast to the usage as being wasteful or unnecessary. Its intended meaning in filtration is to imply "enough and to spare." The first filter, as is common to repetitive filters, is expected to fulfill the retention requirement. The second filter serves as insurance. As already observed, the LRVs of repetitive filters are not twice the value of a separate filter (Figure 10.15).

Economics of Redundant Filtration

Redundant filtration incurs the cost of two housings, but the separate housings permit the integrity testing of each filter. Within a single housing the upstream testing of the downstream filter is manageable but will require the isolation of the upstream filter; not a simple undertaking.

The economics of using redundant filters depends upon the value of the loss of a batch of drug product, the frequency of batch failures, the total cost of the redundant filters to prevent the batch losses, and the expense in downtime and effort needed for filter replacement. The sum total of these costs is to be offset by the value of the saved drug batches. The likelihood of savings resulting from the reliance on redundant filters is more likely positive when the production of the more costly biotech drugs is involved.

Regulatory Recommendations

As regards the EU and FDA, both the Guideline CPMP, April 1996, and EC Annex 1, as well as the FDA's Aseptic Guide (2004) recommend the use of redundant 0.2/0.22 μm-rated membranes. FDA's latest aseptic guideline (2004) states, "Use of redundant filtration should be considered in many cases." The placement of the filters is to be "as close as possible" (or practical) to the filling needles. The usual location is indeed just before the filling needles or before the reservoir that feeds them. In practice, the "recommendations" of a double filter arrangement tend to be enforced as if they were law. In Europe this usage is becoming the common practice.

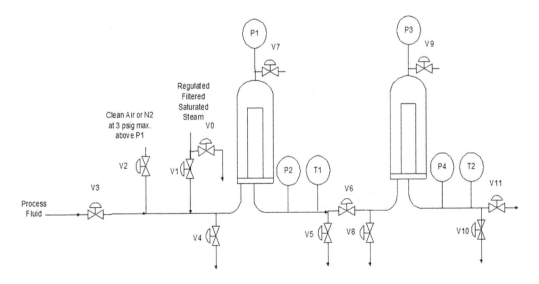

FIGURE 10.15   Redundant filtration setup.

Hydrophilic Filter Integrity Test Considerations

The Wetting of Surfaces

The wetting action of a solid by a liquid is illustrative of the bonding interaction between the molecules of the liquid and those of the solid surface. Bubble points reflect the cohesive force of such a wetting action between a specific liquid, e.g., water, in contact with a specific solid surface, as of a capillary or pore wall. Given the pairing of specific molecular entities, this particular cohesive force is unique. Its value depends upon the specific liquid and solid molecules involved.

The bubble point is universally applicable. Its measurements and correlations with a filter's qualities or properties are objectively independent of the analyst, or of the filter's manufacturer.

The strengths of the adhesive forces are expressions of the surface-free energies involved. The critical surface tension of a solid is identified by that of a liquid whose intimacy of wetting results in its spreading over the solid surface. The greater the surface tension similarity between liquid and solid, the more avid the molecular interaction (hydrophilic) and the more complete the wetting. Conversely, the more unalike the solid's surface tension is from that of water's 72 dynes/cm, the more difficult it will be to obtain water-wetting. The membranes employed in filtering aqueous compositions need to be hydrophilic. Their critical surface tensions should approach water's high value of 72 dynes/cm. Some frequently used polymers for hydrophilic filters such as polyethersulfone or PVDF do not meet this requirement and are in fact naturally hydrophobic. Coating agents that may or may not be covalently bound are then used to make the membrane hydrophilic.

The surfaces of the smaller pores are more difficult to wet because their narrow lumens are difficult to intrude.

The failure to obtain complete and total wetting will leave some pores filled with air not displaced by water in the wetting exercise. This will lead to error in measuring filter properties associated with flows and flow rates, including bubble points.

Complete wettability results in the liquid's spreading itself over the solid's surface. This occurs when the adhesion between the solid and liquid molecules is greater than the cohesion between the like molecules of the liquid. Less avid wetting tends toward the beading of the liquid in droplet form upon the solid. The hierarchy of wetting extends from the complete spreading of the liquid over the solid to its appearance as spherical beads on the solid surface. In less than perfect wetting, an angle is formed at the contact site of liquid and solid. It becomes more pronounced, the greater the imperfection of the wetting. The more spherical the liquid drop, the greater the angular space between the flat surface of the solid and the upward curvature at the bottom of the spherical liquid bead (Figure 10.16). Called the contact angle or the angle of wetting, it is symbolized by the Greek letter theta, Θ.

The degree of wetting imperfection reflects the differences in the cohesive energy densities (CEDs) more properly their solubility parameters, the square root values of the CEDs, of the liquid and solid molecules that determine their structural similarities; the less-alike their molecular architecture, the less

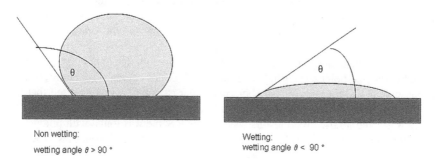

Non wetting:
wetting angle $\theta > 90°$

Wetting:
wetting angle $\theta < 90°$

FIGURE 10.16 Liquid surface interaction of different fluids.

their mutual attraction, and the greater their free surface energies. These find expression in surface tension values. Called the critical surface tension, the surface tension of the solid is revealed by that of the liquid that fully wets it. The significance of the critical surface tension will be made more evident below in see the section "Ensuring Complete Wetting."

Water-Wetting the Filters

The tests or test suited to the examination of hydrophilic filters require a *complete* wetting out of the filter. The pores most difficult for water to intrude and to wet are most likely the narrowest, or as commonly labeled, the smallest. Usually the air content is replaced by water which in combination with a pressurized gas enables measurements of the rate at which the gas passes through the wetted filter. The measured airflow quantities translate into assays of filter integrity. Ensuring constant temperature and complete wetting are basic requirements.

The incomplete wetting out of the filter is the most frequent cause of integrity test failures. The diffusive airflow rate is expected to be proportional to the differential pressure. When water does not fill all the pores, the unfilled pores, not blocked by liquid, permit premature bulk air flows. The flow, enhanced beyond the normal for its pressure differential level, is interpreted as indicating a flawed filter. Actually, the air flowing through the filter is a mixture of diffused air augmented by bulk or viscous air flows. The latter term describes a flow pattern within a range where the ratio of flow rate to the driving, or differential pressure is constant. The range of viscous airflow extends both above and below the velocity value of 10.5 ft/min.

Solid surfaces, such as pore walls, are wetted by liquids having surface tensions similar to their own. Water has the high surface tension of 72 dynes/cm. To wet filters that are less hydrophilic requires liquids of lower surface tensions, closer to the critical surface tensions of the less hydrophilic filter polymers. The critical surface tension of polyethylene is 32 dynes/cm, PP is 29.5, PVDF (polyvinylidene fluoride) is 25, and PTFE (polytetrafluoroethylene) is 18 dynes/cm. Aqueous alcoholic solutions exhibit surface tensions lower than that of water. Their numbers are those of water (high), moderated by admixture with the lower numbers of organic alcohols. For example, aqueous alcoholic solutions of ~ 60-70% v/v, methanol, ethanol, isopropanol, or (rarely) 25% v/v tertiary butanol are employed to wet completely filters that wet reluctantly with water alone. The subsequent elimination of the alcohol from the system is accomplished by a thorough water flush performed before the aqueous alcoholic solution evaporates from the membrane surfaces and leaves them dry.

Product as the Wetting Liquid

More often, post-filtration integrity testing is performed by using the product filtered as the wetting agent, due to the fact that a flush with water may need a copious amount of such. Certainly, the contact between certain membranes and various pharmaceutical preparations can produce depressed bubble points compared with the values for water (Table 10.1). The depressed bubble point can be restored, more or less, but mostly less, by copious washing of the filter with water, depending on the filter material and/ or product ingredients used. Some subtle wetting effects, adsorption, or fouling involving product ingredients may be at work here whose surface physics is not comprehended. In addition, the surface tension differences between the product and water are contributory to the anomaly.

Often, efforts are made to flush the filter with water before running the final integrity test, so that pre- and post-filtration bubble point tests using water are obtained for comparison. However, even copious water flushing may not restore the water bubble point. For example, it was reported that nylon membranes became fouled by proteins in an albumin filtration process, that often enough the filters were not wetted by water and a false failed results was obtained. Same was found with products containing tween. Even after large water flush volumes, the surface tension reducing properties were seen. In such cases, pre-and post-filtration comparisons may usefully be performed using product as wetting agent for the filters. The displacements in bubble values being ascribed to unknown wetting effects, but largely to the influences of the surface tension values of the product, are assumed not to reflect on the organism removal capabilities of the membrane.

TABLE 10.1

Bubble Point Values for Different Wetting Agents using Cellulose
Acetate 0.2 μm

Product	Bubble Point Value (bar)
Water	3.20
Mineral oil	1.24
White petrolatum	1.45
Vitamin B complex in oil	2.48
Procainamide HCl	2.76
Oxytertracycline in Polyethylene glycol (PEG) base	1.72
Vitamin in aqueous vehicle	2.07
Vitamin in aqueous vehicle	2.69
Iron dextran	2.83
Vitamin E in oil base	1.66
Solution preserved with benzyl alcohol	2.14
Diazepam in glycol base	1.93
Digoxin in glycol base	2.14

However, regulatory authorities also advocate performing bacteria challenge tests with the actual product under process conditions. Such challenge tests, involving also viability testing, confirm the filter's retentivity. Moreover, they reveal any negative influences of the product toward the challenge organism (Mittelman et al 1998).

Parker (1986) determined the acceptable minimum bubble point for a given type of filter using product as wetting medium in accordance with the formula

$$P_p = \frac{P_o P_m}{P_w}$$

where P_p is the minimum acceptable product bubble point, P_o is the observed bubble point using product, P_w is the average of the water bubble points observed for samples of the filters (commonly three filters from three different batches), and P_m is the filter manufacturer's stated minimum allowable bubble point. Enough filters or filter devices are secured from each lot of the subject filter type to yield an acceptable average value. Testing is performed for each product being filtered using 47-mm disk filters or small-scale pleated filter devices.

Desaulniers and Fey (1990) confirmed Parker's findings. Parker and Desaulnier and Fey describe the exact protocols by means of which the product bubble point may be determined. The latter authors also describe an apparatus suitable for the purpose.

More recently, the PDA Technical Report No. 26 describes such product integrity evaluation thoroughly. The formula, in itself the same as described by Parker, is with the recommended test procedure, described, in addition to a statistical approach, using Student´s t-distribution to obtain a "Corrected Product-wetted Bubble Point." Due to the fact that the evaluation of the product wet bubble point can include a high variability, the statistical evaluation is required to take account of such variabilities. Following equation is used:

$$\text{CPBP} = \text{PBP}_{min} - (t_{adf})s$$

where CPBP is the corrected product-wetted bubble point (bubble point limit used for production filters), PBP_{min} is the minimum product-wetted bubble point established by multiple integrity tests, using Parker´s formula, t_{adf} is the t-value from Student´s table associated with a confidence level α and degrees of freedom and s the standard deviation.

The report also quotes an example in Appendix E, using a one-sided Student´s test with a 95% confidence level, α. Seven bubble point tests were performed, the individual values are stated in Table 10.2.

TABLE 10.2

Example of Measured Product-Wetted and Water-Wetted Filters and the Resulting
Average Values and Correction Ratio

Water-Wetted Bubble Point (psi)	Product-Wetted Bubble Point (psi)	Ratio
53.1	43.7	
52.8	43.6	
53.1	43.5	
52.1	42.4	
52.1	42.8	
55.3	46.1	
55.4	46.5	
53.4 (average value)	44.1 (average value)	0.826

Source: Courtesy of PDA, Bethesda, MD.

The average water-wetted and product-wetted values were calculated by adding the measured values for
water and dividing it by 7 (same for the product values).

Now a correction ratio of 0.826 is calculated by dividing the product-wetted average bubble point value
(PBP_{avg}) 44.1 psi by the water-wetted average bubble point value (WBP_{avg}) 53.4 psi.

The minimum allowable water-wetted bubble point (WBP_{min}) is in this example 53.7 psi. These values
are usually given by the filter manufacturers and are correlated to bacteria challenge tests. The product-
wetted bubble point value (PBP_{min}), is now calculated by multiplying the correction ratio, 0.826, with the
minimum allowable water-wetted bubble point value (WBP_{min}) is 53.7 psi. Therefore, the product-wetted
bubble point value (PBP_{min}) is 44.4 psi (0.826×53.7 psi).

The standard deviation, s, for the product-wetted bubble point values in column 2 is 1.587 psi. The
t-value at 95% confidence level, for $n-1$ degrees freedom (in this example $n = 7$) is $t_{0.95,6} = 1.943$. Multiply
t by the standard deviation, s, to obtain the correction factor of 3.084 psi (1.943×1.587 psi).

Now the corrected product-wetted bubble point, using $CPBP = PBP_{min} - (t_{\alpha df})s$, can be calculated.
$CPBP = 44.4$ psi $- 3.084$ psi $= 41.3$ psi. This value admits a certain variability within the evaluation
without compromising the integrity test procedure and levels.

Usually the evaluation of the so-called product integrity test values requires three filter membranes or
devices of three different lots, i.e., nine tests in total. At one point it was recommended that one of these
filter lots must be close to the minimum allowable water bubble point value given by the filter manufacturer to ensure retentive capability at the established limit values. This factor is now included within the
corrected product-wetted bubble point value evaluation.

Wetting and Temperature Requirements

The water flow is always from the outside to the inside through the outer cage of the cartridge, through
the filter layers, to its exit by way of the inner core. A thorough wetting out of the filter is needed to prepare it for integrity testing. It needs to be completely wetted, as well, for steam sterilization, and for its
application of filtering aqueous preparations.

The majority of integrity test failures stem from the incomplete wetting out of the filter. There is no uniform standard procedure. It seems reasonable that the filter manufacturer's protocol should be followed.
Some recommend specific flush procedures suitable for their membrane polymers and filter configurations. Some filter purveyors provide pertinent advice by way of troubleshooting guides. Figure 10.17
shows such information presented as a wetting-tree recommended by one filter manufacturer.

Recalcitrant cases may benefit from the use of hot water (100°F–200°F; 38°C–84°C). However, the
influences of the higher temperature have then to be avoided, especially in integrity testing, by flushing
the filter system with cold water. Alternatively, the system is allowed to cool down before the integrity
test is performed.

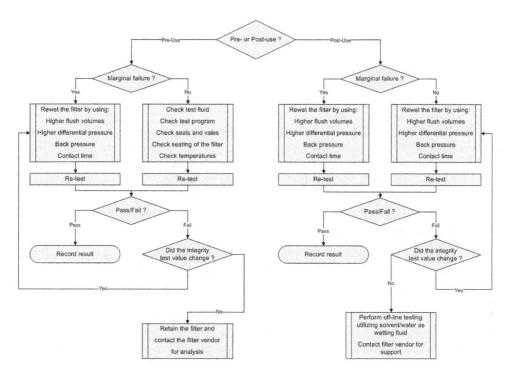

FIGURE 10.17   Filter manufacturers decisions tree.

Fluids, such as alcohols, with their lower surface tensions are more in accord with the critical surface tension of the polymers than is water with its high value of 72 dynes/cm. These can be used in combination with water and can then be removed by flushing to aid in complete wetting out the membrane.

The second most likely cause of failure is damage to the filter. Due to the delicacy of the membrane the damage is seldom subtle, and the failure is abrupt. Integrity test failures resulting from chemical incompatibilities can become progressively evident, depending on the severity of the chemical mismatch. As it involves filters, it is usually in the nature of a plasticization. It may be rate controlled by the diffusion of the liquid into the solid. Therefore, prior to testing, the contact time between filter and fluid should equal the processing duration.

An early confirmation of the filter's identity can be obtained. The compatibility of the filter and the drug preparation relative to organism retentions, such as pore size alterations, can be ascertained in an exploratory study by comparing the integrity test values before and after exposures of the filter to the drug product for a period of time equal to at least the duration of the processing filtration. Pore size modifications caused by steam sanitizations may also be assessed in an exploratory study after a steam/filter contact time equal to that of the processing step itself. It is necessary to allow the steamed assembly to cool (or to be cooled) to the proper temperature before the testing begins; the test results being temperature sensitive.

Gas Permeation of a Wetted Filter

Let us consider the origins of the gas flows generated in arriving at a filter's bubble point. Most commonly, air pressure is applied to the wetted filter, pores are filled with water. Nitrogen gas is to be preferred because of its lower moisture uptake (Hofmann 1984*). Carbon dioxide is not suitable because its high solubility in water produces a diffusive air flow rate too high to be useful in the measurements.

---

* Hofmann (1984) states that compressed air have a greater water-holding capacity than nitrogen. Its use, he believes, would excessively dry the membrane by affecting the distribution of the water within the membrane pores. This would add error to the test results. However, this has not materialized largely in practice.

Under the applied pressure, the gas molecules dissolve on the higher-pressured upside of the filter in accord with Henry's Law which states that a gas is soluble in proportion to its partial pressure above the solution. The dissolved gas exists in a true state of solution; its individual molecules disperse among the water molecules. From their high partial pressure at the point of their introduction upstream of the filter, the dissolved gas molecules diffuse to the lower partial pressure areas downstream of the filter, to equilibrate their concentration as dictated by solution physics. The differential pressure across the filter compels the attainment of this equilibration.

The elevated partial pressure at the inlet site undergoes a successive reduction to its lowest point at the atmospheric pressure side of the filter. The ensuing progressive decrease in the solubility of the gas reflects its decreasing partial pressure. This is sufficiently reduced at its exit from the filter for the gas to be less soluble, and to emerge from solution. It is seen as a stream of bubbles, measurable by their rate of collection as a gas, or as volume displacements of water from a burette.

Constant Temperature

To accommodate the requirement for constant temperature conditions in the pressure hold test, the appropriate automated testers include equipment to determine whether the temperature is within the acceptable range. Otherwise, temperature deviation can be seen on the graph printed by the machine. If the temperature is not constant enough, the machine displays a warning.

Figure 10.18 shows what can happen when a higher temperature source heats up the upstream volume of the filter's housing. Even a brief touch of the hand to the housing immediately shows on the printed graph (Hofmann 1984). Such influences may not be detected by a manual test. This poses a risk. An automated test machine is able to evaluate the status regarding temperature.

Temperature effects can be minimized by avoiding draft, direct sunlight and move away from nearby autoclaves. Monitoring the temperature at different locations could help finding the best place to fulfill the prerequisites for stable temperature. Using insulation on the filter housing/capsule should only be the last solution if temperature variations cannot be avoided.

Changing the volume could work in either direction: a larger volume would require a longer time to change it's temperature, but a smaller volume would generate a larger pressure drop thus being less impacted by the temperature drift. In any case the inaccuracy of an eventual manual volume determination would be carried over to the actual measurement of the pressure drop (Trotter and Meltzer 1998). It is, therefore, essential that the upstream volume be known with an exactness in order for the pertinent calculations to reveal their true significance.

Filter Area Effects

It is, for instance, not possible to completely separate the diffusive airflow component from the bulk airflow at the bubble point. Therefore, the bubble point examination is more suited to the testing of filters whose areas are small enough not to incur large diffusive flows that would overwhelm the detection of bubble points. The filter being assayed should, however, be large enough to produce a diffusive flow large enough to be measured with accuracy.

Whether the diffusive airflow given by a filter interferes with the accurate determinations of the filter's bubble point depends upon the EFA of the filter and the length of time necessary to arrive at the bubble point. During the progressive pressure increases on the way to the bubble point, diffusive airflow will be taking place. If, in the interval over which the bubble point is reached, enough air becomes diffused to substantially match the bulk airflow at the bubble point, the latter determination becomes uncertain. This effect becomes more noticeable when liquids of lower surface tension are involved, such as solvent-water mixtures.

Generally, the diffusive airflows from 10-in. cartridges begin significantly to interfere with the bubble point as it is commonly performed. However, even multiple 10-in. cartridges can and are successfully bubble pointed provided that the pressure is rapidly brought to just below the presumed bubble point, and then carefully, but not leisurely, raised to the actual bubble point. There are limits even to this helpful technique. At some point, the filter area is large enough to provide diffusive airflows that will interfere

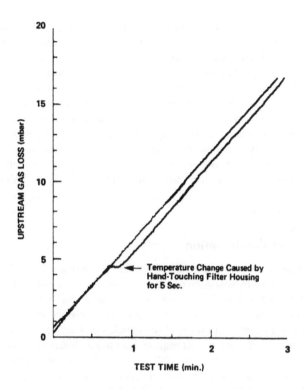

FIGURE 10.18 Temperature influences on pressure drop.

with the bubble point regardless of how expeditiously performed. The relevant area will differ for different filters, and, therefore, cannot be defined with exactness.

Consider a 10-in. cartridge with a diffusive airflow of 15 mL/min. At its bubble point it will have a certain bulk airflow, far in excess of 15 mL/min., perhaps about 540 mL/min. Three such cartridges joined into one 30-in. assembly will have a diffusive airflow of 45 mL/min but the same bulk airflow at the bubble point, namely, about 540 mL/min if only a single section were involved. (If the bubble point is simultaneously reached at more than a single cartridge, the air flow will be proportionately greater.) The bubble point is identifiable, 540 mL/min diluted by 45 mL/min.

An assembly of three individual 30-in. cartridges could have a diffusive airflow of about 136 mL/min and the viscous airflow at the bubble point of 540 mL/min or so. The difference between 135 and 540 mL/min is large enough not to confuse the two different airflows provided the time to reach the bubble point is minimized. If, however, it takes 4 or 5 min to reach the bubble point, then the diffusive airflow will not be distinguishable from the bubble point because the total diffusive airflow and the bulk airflow (at the bubble point) will be equal. The latter will be confused by the former. If an assembly of twelve 30-in. cartridges is involved, its diffusive airflow will be 540 mL/min. No matter how fast the bubble point is determined, it will be interfered with by the diffusive air flow emanating from the filter arrangement. Nevertheless, it should be noted that the impact on the accuracy of the bubble point measurement of the filter element having the lowest bubble point in a multi-round housing may be as small as one pressure step. This comes from the fact that as the additional pressure step is added the bulk flow of the cartridge with the lowest bubble point increases over proportionally.

Integrity Testing Hydrophobic Filters

The archetypical hydrophobic membranes find application as air filters, generally as vent filters. These protect the contents of the tanks or other containers against contamination by the air that enters or leaves them as occasioned by the addition or withdrawal of their stored liquids. The concern is with the possibility of water finding lodgment in the membranes as a result of splashing, foaming, or even by the condensation of water vapor. Liquid water would possibly impede air passage, conceivably leading to tank collapse upon out-pumping; moreover, water would encourage microbial growth. Contamination therewith is strongly to be avoided. The prescription against such an occurrence is to deny the presence of moisture. This can be done for hydrophilic filters using electrically heated or steam-jacketed filter housings. The temperature is raised above the dew point of the ambient air. Usually, steam at 1/3 bar (5 psi) pressure is enough. Unfortunately, the long-term passage of air through such heated arrangements will cause the oxidative degradation of certain filter cartridge components, such as PP, and may also oxidatively degrade the microporous membrane itself, depending upon its composition. Fluorinated polymers are relatively immune to oxidative alteration; PTFE extremely so, PVDF somewhat less so. That is why these polymers are so widely used in air filtration contexts. The greater hydrophobicity of PTFE offers substantial advantages.

Pore Blockage by Water Condensation

Mechanical considerations also favor the use of hydrophobic membranes for air filtration. Water intruding on air or vent filters, whether by splashing or condensation, can be removed from hydrophobic structures by the imposition of a pressure sufficient to overcome its bulk inertia. In the case of hydrophilic air (vent) filters, however, higher applied pressures are required to outweigh the adsorptive forces holding the water within the pores. Pressures in excess of the bubble point are needed to vacate even the largest pores, and pores of smaller diameters will require even more elevated pressures. The result is that water, splashed or condensed, within the hydrophilic membrane can cause serious blockages of pore passageways to the detriment of airflow. In the case of vent filter, tank implosions are risked when, under such conditions, liquid is pumped from storage tanks not protected by rupture disks or blowout patches. It is, therefore, considered advantageous to avoid the possibilities of such incidents through the use of hydrophobic air filters.

Testing with Lower Surface Tension Liquids

Hydrophobic materials are generally characterized by low critical surface tensions. They, thus, resist wetting by water with its high, 72 dynes/cm^2 surface tension. However, aqueous alcoholic solutions of the compositions given above are of lower surface tension values and can serve as the wetting fluids adequate to bubble pointing or forward flow/diffusion testing of the fluoropolymeric membranes. This technique requires, however, the subsequent disposition of the wetting liquid. Such can be accomplished, but by rather complex plumbing arrangements, or by risking asepsis downstream of the filter.

Water Penetration Test

It has long been understood that water can be forced through hydrophobic filters under extreme pressures. The pressure necessary for this action relates inversely to the diameters of the pores. This situation involves the same wetting considerations that govern the time-honored mercury porosimetry procedure of probing the diameters of microporous membranes. Non-wetting mercury permeates glass capillaries or other porous materials that are too different in their surface tension characteristics to be wetted by the liquid metal. However, defining the relationship between pore diameter and the pressure required to force water through a hydrophobic filter does not in itself constitute an integrity test. For that conjunction, a documented correlation must be demonstrated to exist between the intrusion pressure and acceptable levels of organism retention by the filter. Such a relationship has been reported, thereby establishing the water permeation test as an integrity test applicable to the integrity characterizations of hydrophobic filters.

However, the vent filter's pores having been permeated by water must then be made rid of the liquid by a drying operation. This requirement was time-consuming and costly in terms of heat. It was found that a better test to the same purpose resulted from measuring the intrusion pressure rather than the penetration pressure involving the hydrophobic filter material and the liquid water.

Water Intrusion Pressure

The water intrusion test (WIT) measures the decay rate of a pressure level imposed upon a hydrophobic filter enveloped by water. By means of an automated integrity tester, a particular decay level is identified as the point at which water enters the largest pores of the filter and also evaporates from the upstream to the downstream side of the membrane, which has been supported by the following trials:

1. WIT with salt water. After 30 min of pressurization small droplets can be recovered at the inner core of the filter. This liquid has much lower conductivity than the upstream water giving evidence for condensed humidity.
2. WIT against vacuum at 1.5 barg (thus respecting the normal 2.5 bar differential pressure) will generate reproducible test values without drying in-between and no water droplets are formed on the inner core as the humidity does not condensate under vacuum. These test values are identical to the first test under normal conditions whereas a second test under normal conditions without drying in between typically yields a 20% lower test value due to higher humidity/saturated conditions.

Hydrophilic Surface Deposits

The water intrusion test depends upon and measures the hydrophobicity of the filter. Only the experimentally demonstrated correlation of its values with the entrance of water into the hydrophobic pore structure establishes it as an integrity test. But the basic measurement of filter hydrophobicity is itself an inherent requirement in its pertinence to air filter reuse. Consider an integral air filter that contains hydrophilic accretions or deposits upon its surface. Their presence may encourage microbial growth and, ultimately, organism penetration. Solely ensuring air filter integrity, however essential, is not enough in air filter usage. The filter's full hydrophobicity must also be assessed to ensure freedom from compromising hydrophilic impurities.

Long-Term Air Filter Applications

As previously stated, in the usual air filtration or vent filter applications, the filter is so little exhausted by the depositions it collects that its reuse is compelled for economic reasons; hence, the need periodically to repeat its integrity verification before and after each individual use, ideally without removing it from its installation. The filter may remain integral, but if it collects, as it well may, deposits of hydrophilic matter, then as localized and limited as these may be, they can serve as loci for organism growth and penetration, defeating the very purpose intended by the use of a hydrophobic filter. If the intention of the integrity test in air filtration applications is solely to assess filter integrity, then the water intrusion test may, on occasion, mislead and be responsible for the discard of integral filters. If, however, the purpose of examining the filter is to gauge its suitability as a longer-term air filter, as in fermenter operations, for example, then the water intrusion test is sovereign for the purpose because it simultaneously measures the integrity and the hydrophobicity of the subject filter. Both of these properties are required in a filter dedicated to longer-term air filtration applications.

When the water intrusion test indicates an integral filter, it may be used (or reused) with confidence, even in long-term air applications. Failure to pass the water intrusion test signals a need for further filter assessment. A bubble point test or a forward flow/diffusion test subsequently performed and passed successfully may indicate that the filter is not sufficiently free of deposits to permit its safe reuse, albeit integral. Then, if considered desirable, a suitable filter-refurbishing effort may be undertaken.

In passing it can be remarked that hydrophobic membranes, widely employed as vent filters, are not wetted by water, and that a certain pressure is, therefore, required to force the water into them. This pressure, called the water penetration pressure (WPP), is different for different filter membrane polymers. For example, the typical WPP for an 0.2 μm rated PTFE membrane is around 4.5 bar (65 psi), and that for PVDF is around 2.8 bar (41 psi). WPP depends also on the pore size of the individual filter membrane.

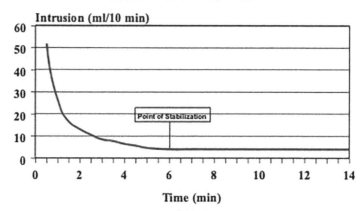

FIGURE 10.19   Test stabilization time.

The upstream side of the hydrophobic filter cartridge housing is flooded with water. Air or nitrogen gas is then forced into the upstream side of the filter housing above the water level to a defined test pressure by way of an automated integrity tester. A period of pressure stabilization is allowed over a time frame recommended by the filter manufacturer (Figure 10.19). During this interval the cartridge pleats adjust their positions under the imposed pressure. After the pressure drop thus occasioned stabilizes, the test time starts, and any further pressure drop in the upstream pressurized gas volume, as measured by the automated tester, signifies the beginning of water intrusion into the largest (hydrophobic) pores and evaporation from the upstream side to the downstream side, water being incompressible. The automated integrity tester is sensitive enough to detect the pressure drop. This measured pressure drop is converted into a measured intrusion value, which is compared to a set of intrusion limit, which has been correlated to the bacterial challenge test. This correlation has been demonstrated between the observed pressure drop and the organism retention characteristic of the hydrophobic membrane (Tarry et al. 1993; Dosmar et al. 1993; Meltzer et al. 1994; Jornitz et al. 1994; Tingley et al. 1995). This empirically established correlation serves as the validating authority for the water intrusion test.

Drying of Filters

When the test is over, the water is drained from the upstream side of the filter housing and the filtration can be started. In terms of a freeze dryer vent filter, one has to dry the filter after the WIT before the freeze drying can be started, because of the need to avoid residual water. Residual water would reduce the efficiency of the freeze drying process, but what is more important, the residual water would freeze and expand and thereby jeopardize the integrity of the hydrophobic membrane.

A water-intruded filter can be dried by generating a low pressure and using a heat exchanger creating a warm flow of dry air or nitrogen through the filter. Typical process parameters are an absolute pressure of 8.7 psi (600 mbar), a gas flow of 100 m³/h at 122 °F (50 °C). Lower pressure and higher flow rate will even furhter speed up the drying. The test setup is shown in Figure 10.20. The procedure has the advantage of being fast-working and efficient. Drying such filters by using heat-jacketed filter housings or pipework and running the warmed air along the filter or through the filter at atmospheric or even overpressure will not have the same effect. Drying with a heat jacket will take more than 5 h. By using this procedure, hydrophobic vent filters can be integrity tested *in situ* without the use of alcoholic solutions and the risk of downstream contamination.

To simplify the test for users, filter manufacturers offer fully automatic test units (Figure 10.21) that, once connected to the appliances, make it possible to run the test without user intervention. This saves time and increases the reliability of the test.

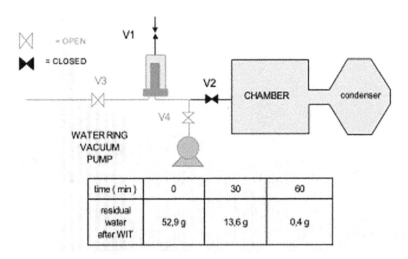

time (min)	0	30	60
residual water after WIT	52,9 g	13,6 g	0,4 g

FIGURE 10.20 Drying cycle of a water intrusion-tested vent filter.

FIGURE 10.21 Automated water intrusion test machine.

The water intrusion test, like other integrity tests, is sensitive to temperature and to the water purity in terms of surface tension. It is, however, less sensitive to temperature variations than the diffusive airflow measurements because of the large thermal mass represented by the water in the housing. Nevertheless, when a hand is placed on the housing wall containing the air volume above the housing, a temperature effect can be detected. The basis for this integrity test has already been discussed. To further enhance the robustness the fully automatic test can implement a temperature sensor into the gas volume of the filter housing. Temperature compensating algorithms can then correct the measured value to a certain extent and improve the overall reliability of the test (Stering et al 2011).

Correlations have been established between the organism retentions exhibited by a filter and the rates of pressure drop from a given pressure level as caused by water intruding into a hydrophobic filter (Figure 10.22 and Table 10.3). The greater the rate of pressure drop, the greater the extent of water intrusion into the pores, as measured by pressure drop over a given time interval. The lower the pressure drop,

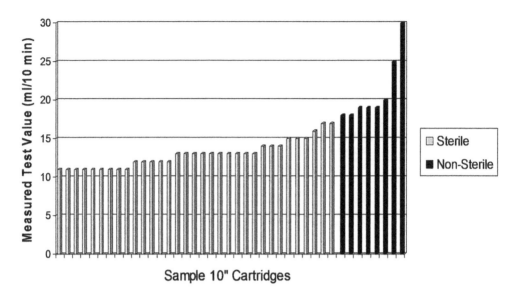

FIGURE 10.22   Water intrusion value correlation to bacteria challenge test.

the narrower the pore and the more retentive the filter. The principle underlying this integrity test is the same as the basis for mercury intrusion into porous materials except that pressures too low to cause polymeric pore distortions are involved. Nonintegral filters will actually have water forced into them, integral filters will not. The automated test machine is sensitive enough to detect the small pressure decrease that accompanies the incipient entry of water into and evaporation through integral filters.

   Since the water intrusion test involves wetting phenomena, it will reflect, in common with the other integrity tests, the influences of surface tension (therefore, water purity), temperature, and pore wettability, as already discussed. The importance of these factors in the operations of the bubble point, diffusive airflow, and pressure hold integrity tests has been detailed by Scheer et al. (1993). Filter manufacturers

TABLE 10.3

Overview of performed Bacteria Challenge Tests for Cartridges GA

Lot Number	H_2O Intrusion Rate* (mL/10 min)	Results B.C.T.**	LRV***
576/01	6	Sterile	≥11
576/01	7	Sterile	≥11
579/01	8	Sterile	≥11
579/01	8	Sterile	≥11
576/01	8	Sterile	≥11
577/01	8	Sterile	≥11
579/01	8	Sterile	≥11
576/01	8	Sterile	≥11
576/01	8	Sterile	≥11
577/01	8	Sterile	≥11
577/01	9	Sterile	≥11
576/01	9	Sterile	≥11
579/01	9	Sterile	≥11
576/01	9	Sterile	≥11
577/01	10	Sterile	≥11
579/01	11	Sterile	≥11

(Continued)

TABLE 10.3 (*Continued*)

Overview of performed Bacteria Challenge Tests for
Cartridges GA

Lot Number	H₂O Intrusion Rate* (mL/10 min)	Results B.C.T.**	LRV***
577/01	11	Sterile	≥11
576/01	11	Sterile	≥11
579/01	11	Sterile	≥11
579/01	11	Sterile	≥11
577/01	11	Sterile	≥11
579/01	11	Sterile	≥11
579/01	12	Sterile	≥11
577/01	12	Sterile	≥11
577/01	12	Sterile	≥11
577/01	12	Sterile	≥11
576/01	13	Sterile	≥11
577/01	13	Sterile	≥11
579/01	13	Sterile	≥11
577/01	13	Sterile	≥11
576/01	13	Sterile	≥11
577/01	13	Sterile	≥11
576/01	14	Sterile	≥11
020/11	15	Sterile	≥11
020/11	17	Non sterile	≈8.6
5042/01	18	Non sterile	≈8.3
576/01	19	Non sterile	<7
579/01	20	Non sterile	<7
5171/01	25	Non sterile	<7
5171/01	30	Non sterile	<7
5171/01	37	Non sterile	<7
576/01	49	Non sterile	<7

*Test parameters:
Test pressure: 2.5 bar|36 psi
Stabilization time: 10 min
Test time: 10 min
Test medium: Water 20 °C
**B.C.T. = Bacteria Challenge Test
***LVR = log reduction value

offering the water intrusion test also specify the maximum allowable water temperature and the water quality necessary to obtain an appropriate test result. Elevated water temperatures and contamination will lower the surface tension of the water, and in this case the test pressure required to push the water into the hydrophobic membrane will be lower. The higher evaporation at higher temperatures also generates higher intrusion values. Water at lower temperatures has higher surface tension and lower evaporation. This generates lower intrusion values with the risk for false passed test results. An application specific WIT validation at 14°C demonstrated about 23% lower values than at 24°C. For this reason, as in all other integrity test methodologies, test specifications have to be defined and kept.

Redrying of Air Filters

The reuse of air filters is common because their utility is so little compromised by the particulate deposits they accumulate in any individual application. Before reuse, the air filter is sterilized, customarily by steaming. The water film that is deposited on the membrane surfaces by the condensation of steam is removed by drying before reuse. This must be done to discourage organism growth and penetration. In this

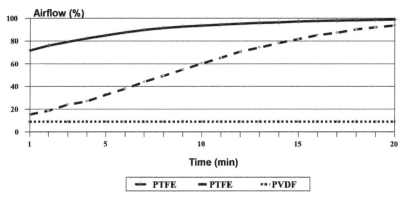

Measured at 200 mbar=dp, after steaming

FIGURE 10.23   Blowdown time of different filter units.

regard, membrane surface hydrophobicity is a prime consideration; the water requires being removed. This is more easily done for PTFE filters than for those composed of any other commercially available polymer, including PVDF. Figure 10.23 presents a comparison of blow-downs used to restore full airflow to hydrophobic membranes after steaming. As is evident, airflow recovery for the PTFE cartridge is achieved in 10–12 min; the PVDF cartridge is at only 25% of its initial flow rate at the end of this time period. The PTFE filter's construction contributes to this result, but the greater avidity of PVDF for water is a significant consideration. The more extreme hydrophobicity of PTFE allows for its more rapid drying. Compact pleating of the membrane and multilayer constructions may also contribute to a longer drying time.

Advantages and Disadvantages of Water Intrusion Testing

The water intrusion test offers several advantages. For example:

1. The test is highly sensitive because its test pressures for 0.2/0.22 μm-rated filters are in the range of the WPP of 0.45 μm-rated filters.
2. Contaminants such as solvent mixtures are avoided.
3. In addition to the integrity, the validated hydrophobicity is tested, i.e., any contaminants on the membrane can be discovered.
4. The test can be performed in place, after steam sterilization.
5. Test times are greatly reduced, because contaminants, i.e., solvents do not have to be flushed off and off-line testing is not necessary.

The specifications defined by the filter manufacturers have to be observed to achieve reliable test results. In most cases, the test is performed with automated test machines. This may be considered a disadvantage because of capital costs incurred. Nevertheless, automated test machines are usefully versatile and are also commonly used to perform other integrity tests such as the diffusive airflow and bubble point tests.

Prefilter Integrity Testing

Use of Prefilters

The interruption of a filtration by an insufficiency of filter area (EFA) can be avoided by the use of prefilters. The purpose of the prefilter is to accept part of the particle load, which otherwise would deposit on the final filter. A particulate deposit over a given area of final filter could indeed be large enough to interfere with or actually block further flow (Pall et al. 1980). The sacrificial role of the prefilter in accepting its share of the particle load spares the final filter. If the combined prefilter–final filter assembly is sized appropriately (utilizing flow decay measurements), the concentration of the accumulated particles per unit area would be reduced to where the flow would not become unduly restricted. Essentially, the prefilter would serve as an enlargement of the final filter area. The final filter's service life would be prolonged to where it would suffice for processing the entire preparation. In the preselection of the final filter, its ability to retain the entire load of the subject suspension without compromise of its final filter function would have been ascertained.

The purpose of the prefilter is to retain part of the total-suspended solids load. The nature of the filtration media (fibers versus membrane or a combination thereof), its retention rate and the involved retention mechanisms (size exclusion or adsorption or a combination thereof) will govern the number and sizes of the particles retained by it and/or passed through it to the final filter under the selected operational conditions. The prefilter presumably serves no other purpose. If it were, for example, also being counted upon to remove some particular entity in its defined entirety, then it would, in that respect, be a final filter. Its "final filter" status would, in that case, require its own validation.

Validation requirements for prefiltration commonly restrict itself to the testing of the compatibility of the filter to the product and process conditions. Such testing is performed by the evaluation of leachables from the filter and/or particulate matter.

The number of these larger pores is unknown. Pores may be large enough for organisms to penetrate them, but may be so few in number as to yield airflows small enough to escape immediate notice. The perceived bubble point is almost certain, therefore, to be higher than the intrinsic.* The difference is in the nature of a safety factor against bubble points that are too low.

Integrity Testing of Prefilters

The final filter as a consequence of its structural features and of the filtration conditions employed, imparts by its performance a distinct, and ultimate quality to the effluent. Its elimination of particles, including organisms, from a suspension, impacts the practical factors of rates of flow, and throughput volumes. The unique constructions of the final filter with regard to its porosity aspects, such as pore sizes, are depended upon to furnish the desired level of organism removals. It is these singular structural features that must remain unchanged over the entire filtration in order for the final filter's operational effects to be realized. It is for this reason that its pre-use and after-use integrity testing is required.

Prefilters made of fibers can effect organism removals, but their nominal ratings are relied upon only in a subsidiary fashion. It is the filtration conditions, chiefly the rates of flow, and the products of the motivating differential pressure that govern a prefilter's organism removal. These factors are assessed in the process validation step; they are not in the purview of integrity testing. For critical applications where precise performances are required prefilters made of membranes can be used. Membrane prefilters have better-defined retention rates based on size exclusion than prefilters made of fibers and may have a clearly defined bioburden reduction. If the prefilter is claimed to assure the reduction of the bioburden below 10 cfu/100 mL it is advisable to select a prefilter than can be integrity tested.

Nevertheless, for sake of discussion, let us assume that the prefilters made of fibers can be subjected to integrity testing, and that its failure would result in a higher bacterial challenge to the final filter. Would that so affect the final filter as to compromise its organism retention? By definition, the final filter is qualified to be a sterilizing filter by way of the classic 1×10^7 cfu/cm^2 EFA *B. diminuta* challenge. On that basis, the final filter's organism retention capability would not be affected even by the full brunt of the organism load. Therefore, prefilters in general do not require integrity testing.

The prefilter function is the prolongation of the final filter's service life by sacrificially assuming part of the total-suspended solids load. Integrity testing of prefilters is of interest because its compromise threatens the effluent quality with regard to organism content. Validation requirements for prefiltration are commonly restricted to investigating the compatibility of prefilters and fluid vehicles under process conditions, and to the evaluations of leachables. However, these considerations are evaluated in connection with choosing the membrane. They are independent of responsibilities addressed in the process validation. They would be dependent upon a filter's structural modifications only were they to permit organism penetrations of the filter along with compromise of the final filter's efficacy in organism retentions. Such might result if changes occur to the pore sizes and/or their distributions. Such alterations may increase the number and sizes of the particles passed through to the final filter. The final filter's flow rate and throughput may be affected accordingly, but not the integrity. Therefore, the integrity of the prefilter requires no confirmation. If, however, the final quality of the effluent, depended, for example, upon the removal of some particular entity, such as endotoxin, then it would, in that respect, be a final filter. Its "final filter" status would, in that case, require its own validation including integrity testing. Also, the concern regarding extractables from the prefilter warrants being addressed. But these, too, being water soluble, are most unlikely to be affected on the basis of structural changes discernable by integrity testing.

On occasion there may be a need for the filtration activity to be completed within a given time period; whether because of production schedules or concerns of grow-through. FDA in 1976 addressed the problem of grow-through by requiring that the mixing and filtration of a preparation be completed within the 8-h period of a single shift, an interval too brief for grow-through to take place. Alteration of drug quality is not the concern. Processing time is the focus of this situation. Assuming a delay caused by failure of the prefilter to sufficiently spare the final filter its burden of particulate matter, the failed effort to meet the time limitation, or its success in meeting the goal is the defining determination. Either outcome could be indicated by a clock; integrity testing would be superfluous.

Troubleshooting

This section will describe some of the problems which can occur, when performing any integrity test, whether manually or with an automatic test unit. In any case, one has to be aware that an automatic test device always avoids human subjectivity and creates a higher accuracy level.

Manual Integrity Test

Numerous things can go wrong during the integrity test which could have a negative impact on the test thus generating a false failed test or no result at all. In case of a failed integrity test or no result at all the operator needs to inspect the test setup and look for potential causes of failure. In general it is considered that not more than 3 test attempts are allowed before declaring a filter non-integral. The below list highlights potential causes for failed manual tests in addition to an actually failing filter.

- No test pressure buildup
  - Filter system leakage, i.e., damaged sealing, valve open, clamps improperly closed, damaged filter
  - Improperly wetted filter
  - Inappropriate wetting medium, e.g., solvent instead of water
  - Wrong filter pore size
  - Improper inlet valve setting and too speedy pressure increase
  - Pressure gauge works improperly
- Failure of Bubble Point
  - Damaged filter
  - Improperly wetted filter
  - Inappropriate wetting medium, e.g., solvent instead of water
  - Wrong filter pore size
  - Wrong filter size (too big)
  - Too speedy pressure increase
  - Pressure gauge works improperly
  - User subjectivity
  - Wrong test gas (other than air or nitrogen)

- Failure of diffusive flow
  - Damaged filter
  - Improperly wetted filter
  - Inappropriate wetting medium, e.g., solvent instead of water
  - Wrong filter pore size
  - Wrong filter size (too big)
  - Too speedy pressure increase
  - User subjectivity
  - Wrong test gas (e.g., air instead of nitrogen or CO_2 instead of air)
  - Temperature shifts during the test time
  - Improper test pressure setting
  - Insufficient stabilization time
  - Inappropriate downstream test tubing
- Failure of pressure decay
  - Filter system leakage, i.e., damaged sealing, valve open, clamps improperly closed, damaged filter
  - Improperly wetted filter
  - Inappropriate wetting medium, e.g., solvent instead of water
  - Wrong filter pore size
  - Wrong filter size (too big)
  - Too speedy pressure increase
  - Improper pressure gauge function
  - User subjectivity
  - Wrong test gas (e.g., air instead of nitrogen or CO_2 instead of air)
  - Temperature shifts during the test time
  - Improper test pressure setting
  - Insufficient stabilization time

Automatic Integrity Test

Numerous things can go wrong during the integrity test which could have a negative impact on the test thus generating a false failed test or no result at all. In case of a failed integrity test or no result at all the operator needs to inspect the test setup and look for potential causes of failure. In general it is considered that not more than 3 test attempts are allowed before declaring a filter non-integral. The below list highlights potential causes for failed automatic tests in addition to an actually failing filter.

- No test pressure buildup
  - Filter system leakage, i.e., damaged sealing, damaged tubing, valve open, clamps improperly closed, damaged filter
  - Improperly wetted filter
  - Inappropriate wetting medium, e.g., solvent instead of water
  - Wrong filter pore size
  - Gas supply to the unit blocked
  - Inlet tubing to the filter housing improperly installed
  - Excessive temperature drifts
  - Improper valve function within the test unit
  - Internal pneumatic leaks

- Continuous venting of the unit
  - Internal valve contamination and improper function
- Abortion of test during stabilization phase
  - Filter system leakage, i.e., damaged sealing, damaged tubing, valve open, clamps improperly closed, damaged filter
  - Improperly wetted filter
  - Contaminated filter
  - Wrong filter pore size
  - Wrong filter size (too big)
  - Excessive temperature drifts
  - Internal pneumatic leaks
- Abortion during upstream volume test
  - The filter system upstream volume is too large
  - The filter system upstream volume is too small
  - An external reference volume is connected inappropriately
  - Filter system leakage
  - Internal pneumatic leaks
  - Filter failure
- Measured volume is wrong
  - Wrong input of the reference volume
  - The wrong filter housing/sample is connected
  - Internal pneumatic leaks
- Failure of bubble point
  - Damaged filter
  - Improperly wetted filter
  - Inappropriate wetting medium, e.g., solvent instead of water
  - Wrong filter pore size
  - Wrong filter size (too big)
  - Internal pneumatic works improperly
  - Inlet tubing to the filter housing improperly installed
  - Wrong test gas (other than air or nitrogen)
  - Wrong test parameter setting
  - Wrong test code
- Failure of diffusive flow
  - Damaged filter
  - Improperly wetted filter
  - Inappropriate wetting medium, e.g., solvent instead of water
  - Wrong filter pore size
  - Wrong filter size (too big)
  - Internal pneumatic works improperly
  - Inlet tubing to the filter housing improperly installed
  - Wrong test parameter setting
  - Wrong test gas (e.g., air instead of nitrogen or CO_2 instead of air)
  - Temperature shifts during the test time
  - Insufficient stabilization time

- Failure of pressure decay
  - Filter system leakage, i.e., damaged sealing, valve open, clamps improperly closed, damaged filter
  - Improperly wetted filter
  - Inappropriate wetting medium, e.g., solvent instead of water
  - Wrong filter pore size
  - Wrong filter size (too big)
  - Internal pneumatic works improperly
  - Inlet tubing to the filter housing improperly installed
  - Wrong test parameter setting
  - Wrong test gas (e.g., air instead of nitrogen or CO_2 instead of air)
  - Temperature shifts during the test time
  - Insufficient stabilization time
- No pressure decay
  - Test tube to the housing improperly installed
  - Downstream valve closed
  - Blocked connector
  - Blocked internal pneumatic
- Inappropriate multipoint diffusion graph
  - Damaged filter
  - Improperly wetted filter
  - Inappropriate wetting medium, e.g., solvent instead of water
  - Wrong filter pore size
  - Wrong filter size
  - Internal pneumatic works improperly
  - Inlet tubing to the filter housing improperly installed
  - Wrong test parameter setting
  - Wrong test gas
  - Temperature shifts during the test time
  - Insufficient stabilization time
- Failure of water intrusion
  - Filter system leakage, i.e., damaged sealing, valve open, clamps improperly closed, damaged filter
  - Contaminated filter surface
  - Inappropriate or contaminated test medium, e.g., solvent instead of water or water with a lower surface tension
  - Inappropriate water temperature
  - Wrong filter material, with lower hydrophobicity
  - Wrong filter pore size
  - Wrong filter size (too big)
  - Internal pneumatic works improperly
  - Inlet tubing to the filter housing improperly installed
  - Wrong test parameter setting
  - Wrong test gas (other than air or nitrogen)
  - Temperature shifts during the test time
  - Insufficient stabilization time

REFERENCES

Agalloco, J.P. (1998) Guest editorial: It just doesn't matter. *PDA J. Pharm. Sci. Technol.* 52(4): 149–150.

Almgren, F.J. and Taylor, J.E. (1976) Geometry of soap films and soap bubbles. *Science American.* 235(1), pp. 82–93.

ASTM, American Society for Testing and Materials, Committee F-838-15 (2015, Reapproved) *Bacterial Retention of Membrane Filters Utilized For Liquid Filtration.* ASTM, West Conshohocken, PA.

Aranha H. (2004) *'How To' Guide: Viral Clearance Strategies for Biopharmaceutical Safety.* D and MD Publications, Westborough, MA.

Bowman F.W., Calhoun M.P., and White M. (1967) Microbiological methods for quality control of membrane filters. *J. Pharm. Sci.* 56(2): 453–459.

CPMP (1996) Note for Guidance on Virus Validation Studies: The Design, Contribution and Interpretation of Studies Validating the Inactivation and Removal of Viruses. CPMP/BWP/268/95.

Desaulniers, C. and Fey, T. (1990) The product bubble point and its use in filter integrity testing. *Pharm. Technol.* 42(10): 42–52.

Dosmar, M., Wolber, P., Bracht, K., Troger, H., and Waibel, P. (1993) A new in-place integrity test for hydrophobic membrane filters. *Filtration and Separation*, June 1993, pp. 305–309.

Elford W.J. (1933) The principles of ultrafiltration as applied in biological studies. *Proc. R. Soc.* 112B: 384–406.

EudraLex (1996, 2008) Volume 4, EU Guidelines to Good Manufacturing Practice Medicinal Products for Human and Veterinary Use, Annex 1, Manufacture of Sterile Medicinal Products, Brussels.

FDA (1987, 2004) *Guidance for Industry, Sterile Drug Products Produced by Aseptic Processing—CGMP.* Center for Drugs and Biologics and Office of Regulatory Affairs. Food and Drug Administration, Bethesda, MD.

Ferry, J.D. (1935) Ultrafilter membranes & ultrafiltration. *Chem. Rev.* 18(3): 373–447.

Gould, M.J., Dawson, M.A., and Novitsky, T.J. (1993) Evaluation of microbial/endotoxin contamination using the L.A.L. test. *Ultrapure Water* 10(6): 43–47.

Hango, R. A., Syverson, W.A., Miller, M.A., and Fleming, M.J., Jr. (1989). DI water point of use filter program for 1-MB DRAM semiconductor manufacture. *Transcripts of Eighth Annual Semiconductor Pure Water Conference*, Santa Clara, CA, January 18–20, pp. 73–94.

Hart, I. (1998) Private communication to M.W. Jornitz and T.H. Meltzer.

HIMA (1982) *Microbial Evaluation of Filters for Sterilizing Liquids.* Document No. 3. Vol. 4. Health Industry Manufacturers Association, Washington, D.C.

Hofmann, F. (1984) Integrity testing of microfiltration membranes. *J. Parenter. Sci. Technol.* 38: 148–159.

ISO/DIS 13480 2, 2003-03-15 (2003) *Aseptic Processing of Health Care Products—Part 2: Filtration' Section 7: Filtration Process.* ISO, Geneva, Switzerland.

Johnston, P.R. (2003) *Fluid Sterilization by Filtration*, 3rd Ed, p. 7. Interpharm/CRC, New York.

Johnston, P.R., Lukaszewicz, R.C., and Meltzer, T.H. (1981). Certain imprecisions in the bubble point measurement. *J. Parenter. Sci. Technol.* 35(l): 36–39.

Johnston, P.R. and Meltzer, T.H. (1979) Comments on organism challenge levels in sterilizing-filter efficiency testing. *Pharm. Technol.* 3(11): 66–70, 110.

Johnston, P.R. and Meltzer, T.H. (1980) Suggested integrity testing of membrane filters at a robust flow of air. *Pharm. Technol.* 4(11): 49–59.

Jornitz, M.W. and Meltzer, T.H. (1998) Validation of Filtrative Serilizations, *Filtrations in Biopharmaceutical Industry*, T.H. Meltzer and M.W. Jornitz, Eds., (Marcel Dekker, New York).

Jornitz, M.W. and Meltzer, T.H. (2001) *Sterile Filtration—A Practical Approach.* Marcel Dekker, New York.

Jornitz, M.W., Waibel, P.J., and Meltzer, T.H. (1994) The filter integrity test correlations. *Ultrapure Water* 11(7): 59–64.

Kesting R.E. (1985) Chapter 7. Phase-Inversion Membranes, *Synthetic Polymeric Membranes—A Structural Perspective*, Kesting, R.E., Ed., 3rd Ed. Wiley-Interscience, New York.

Kesting, R.E., Murray, A.S., Jackson, K., and Newman, J.M. (1981) Highly anisotropic microfiltration membranes. *Pharm. Technol.* 5(5): 52–60.

Leahy, T.J. and Sullivan, M.J. (1978) Validation of bacterial retention capabilities of membrane filters. *Pharm. Technol.* 2(11): 64–75.

Leo, F.M., Auriemma, M., Ball, P., and Sundaram, S. (1997) Application of 0.1 micron filtration for enhanced sterility assurance on pharmaceutical filling operations. *BFS News.* pp. 15–24.

Lukaszewicz, R.C. and Meltzer, T.H. (1980) On the structural compatibilities of membrane filters. *J. Parenter. Drug Assoc.* 34(6): 463–472.

Meltzer, T.H. (1986) *The Sterilizing Filter and Its Validation.* Proceedings of Institute of Environmental Sciences, Dallas/Fort Worth, TX.

Meltzer, T.H. and Jornitz, M.W. (2006) Chapter 1. The Sterilizing Filter, In Meltzer, T.H. and Jornitz, M.W. (Eds.), *Pharmaceutical Filtration: The Management of Organism Removal.* PDA/DHI Publishers, Bethesda, MD.

Meltzer, T.H., Jornitz, M.W., and Trotter, A.M. (1998) Application-directed selection 0.1μm or 0.2μm rated sterilizing filters. *Pharm. Technol.* 22(9): 116–112

Meltzer, T.H., Jornitz, M.W., and Waibel, P.J. (1994) The hydrophobic air filter and the water intrusion test. *Pharm. Technol.* 18(9): 76–87.

Mittelman, M.W., Jornitz, M.W., and Meltzer, T.H. (1998) Bacterial cell size and surface charge characteristics relevant to filter validation studies. *PDA J. Pharm. Sci. Technol.* 52(1): 37–42.

Olson, W.P., Martinez, E.O., and Kern, C.R. (1981). Diffusion and bubble point testing of microporous cartridge filters; preliminary results at production facilities. *J. Parenter. Sci. Technol.* 35(6): 215–222.

Orange Guide, UK (1983) Guide to Good Pharmaceutical Manufacturing Practice, London, UK

Pall, D.B. (1975) Quality control of absolute bacteria removal filters. *Bull. Parenter. Drug Assoc.* 20(4): 192–204.

Pall, D.B. and Kirnbauer, E.A. (1978). Bacteria removal prediction in membrane filters. *52nd Colloid and Surface Symposium,* University of Tennessee, Knoxville, TN.

Pall, D.B., Kirnbauer, E.A., and Allen, B.T. (1980) Particulate retention by bacteria retentive membrane filters. *Colloids Surf.* 1: 235–256.

Pall, D.H. (1973) Quality control of absolute bacteria removal filters. *Presentation at PDA Annual Meeting* 1973, November 2, 1973, New York.

Parenteral Drug Association (2008) Technical Report No. 26. Sterilizing filtration of liquids. *PDA J. Pharm. Sci. Technol.* 52 (Suppl 1): 1–31.

Parker, J.H. (1986) Establishment and use of minimum product bubble point in filter Integrity testing. *Pharm. Manuf.* 3: 13–15.

Petras, E. (1967) Comparative investigations of the efficiency of membrane filters. *Kolloid Z.* 218(2): 136–139.

Piekaar, H.W. and Clarenburg, L.A. (1967) Aerosol filters: Pore size distribution in fibrous filters. *Chem. Eng. Sci.* 22: 1399–1408.

Reti, A.R. (1977) An assessment of test criteria in evaluating the performance and integrity of sterilizing filters. *Bull. Parenter. Drug Assoc.* 31(4): 187–194.

Reti, A.R., Leahy, T.J., and Meier, P.M. (1979). The retention mechanism of sterilizing and other submicron high efficiency filter structures. *Proceedings of the Second World Filtration Congress,* pp. 427–436, London, UK.

Scheer, L.A., Steere, W.C., and Geisz, C.M. (1993) Temperature and volume effects on filter integrity tests. *Pharm. Technol.* 17(2): 22–23.

Schroeder, H.G. (2001) Rationalization and valid scale–up of integrity test parameters for sterilising grade filter cartridges. *Pharm. Technol.* 55(2): 134–142.

Society of Automotive Engineers (SAE) (1968). Bubble Point Test.Method, *Aerospace Recommended Practice* ARP–901.

Stering, M. (2017) Risk assessment for thermal influences on filter and container closure integrity testing. *Pharm. Eng.* 37(4): 56–61.

Stering, M., Debruyne, N., and Castiglioni, G. (2011) Water intrusion test integration: Accuracy and temperature qualification in freeze dryers. *Pharm. Technol.* 23(11): 30.

Tarry, S.W., Henricksen, J., Prashad, M., and Troeger, H. (1993) Integrity testing of ePTFE membrane filter vents. *Ultrapure Water* 10(8): 23–30.

Thomas, A.J., Durkheim, H.H., Alpark, M.J., and Evers, P. (1991) Detection of L-forms of *Pseudomonas aeruginosa* during microbiological validation of filters. *Pharm. Technol.* 15(1): 74–80.

Tingley, S., Emory, S., Walker, S., and Yamada, S. (1995) Water-flow integrity testing: A viable and validatable alternative to alcohol testing. *Pharm. Technol.* 19(10): 138–146.

Trotter, A.M. and Meltzer, T.H. (1998). The pressure hold/decay integrity test: Its correlation to diffusive flow. *PDA J. Pharm. Sci. Technol.* 52(4): 182–185.

Trotter, A.M., Meltzer, T.H., Bai, F., and Thomas, L. (2000) Integrity test measurements—Effects of bacterial cell loadings. *Pharm. Technol.* 24(3): 72–80.

Waibel, P.J., Jornitz, M.W., Meltzer, T.H. (1996). Diffusive airflow integrity testing. *PDA J. Parenter. Sci. Technol.* 50(5): 311–313.

Wallhäuser, K.H. (1985). Sterility assurance based on validation and in-process control for microbial removal, filtration, and aseptic filling. *Pharm. Ind.* 47(3): 314–319.

Williams, R.E. and Meltzer, T.H. (1983) Membrane structure: The bubble point and particle retention: A new theory. *Pharm. Technol.* 7(5): 36–42.

11

Filter Manufacturer's Quality Assurance and Qualifications

Maik W. Jornitz
G-CON Manufacturing, Inc.

CONTENTS

Introduction

The majority of sterilizing grade and prefiltration devices is supplied into the highly regulated biopharmaceutical industry. This means for the filter suppliers, that similar quality standards pertinent in the processes of the biopharmaceutical industry have to be applied to the supplier's processes. These standards start with the qualification of the production equipment during the development phase, the validation of the production process in its entirety, definitions of in-process controls and documentation during the production process, release criteria, specifications and tolerance settings, and complete traceability of the finalized product and product components. Standard operating procedures and training matrixes within the supplier's manufacturing processes are comparable with the end user's processes. No matter whether regulated or not, the quality management system requires to meet the stringent quality requirements of the industry served.

Besides validating/qualifying the entire process, suppliers are also asked to deliver qualification documentation, which supports the process validation requirements of the filter user. Depending on the equipment such qualification documentation can be elaborate due to the subcomponents of the device.

For single-use equipment, for example, raw material controls and definitions may be included in the qualification documentation or extractable profiles.

Once the equipment is ordered or supplied to the end user, most commonly the supplier will submit qualification documentation as described above, support qualification and acceptance testing and in instances offer product- or process-related validation services. The quality of the supplier's production processes often mirror the production processes of the relevant industry the supplier delivers to. Additionally, the suppliers establish appropriate technical support structures to be able to react rapidly to any support needs of the industry. This is of importance as the end user has to be able to answer to regulatory enquiries or when equipment requires maintenance, calibration, or repair. A production stand still cannot be tolerated as it would resolve in multimillion-dollar losses in revenue, stock-out situations and put drug product batches at risk.

Supplier's Development Cycle

Suppliers strive to improve their products and processes to be able to supply the industry with state-of-the-art equipment and improvements within the industries processes. For this reason, suppliers constantly invest 3%–8% of their revenue in the development of new product or improvement project of existing products. However, every time a product is newly developed a similar qualification and documentation trail as in pharmaceutical R&D has to be established.

Raw Material Supplies

The development cycle begins with the choice of a qualified sub-supplier and ends with a fully qualified product and validated production process. Supplier's development groups are multifunctional teams, which work together with sales and marketing, supply chain, and production to have an appropriate scope of what is required within the industry the supplier serves. For example, supply assurances of raw materials have to be given over a long-time span. Furthermore, is the raw material needed readily obtainable at the quality specification set and are the production capacities, as well as machineries available. Once these corner stones have been investigated, verified, and contractually fixed, the development of the product will start. Any effort to develop a piece of equipment without the knowledge of market need, supply assurance, and production feasibility is a wasted effort. As logical as it sounds, these corner stones are the first milestones, which are documented within a development process and typically mean that audits by the supplier's quality assurance and supply chain departments of the raw or sub-material supplier have taken place. These audits have to be documented and are commonly applicable to a minimum of two suppliers. Supply assurance for a supplier is as important as for the end user, as any supply change will result into a change notification, comparability studies, and in instances a possible revalidation of the equipment at the end user level and notification of the regulatory authorities. Therefore, changes require to be avoided. Critical raw materials and components fall under long-term supply assurance contracts and might have multiple year inventory levels within the sub-supplier and/or supplier level. Reasons for such multi-year inventory levels are the needs of potential post-approval change filings by the end user to a multitude of agencies, typically requiring 3–4 years to be globally established. Additionally, supplier development will involve quality assurance to analyze whether the sub-supplier's quality certification, systems and assurance meets the specification required to meet the industry's quality standards. As the end user audits the supplier's processes, the suppliers will do the same at the sub-supplier level. The more thorough the suppliers internal and external quality and supply investigations the better the supply quality to the end user. The trend is that the end users rely more and more on the supplier's quality system to assure the right quality is supplied from all the sub-suppliers. The end user has no desire to audit all the sub-suppliers but expects that the supplier has a proper handle on the sub-supplier base.

Prototype Testing

Once the sub-supplies have been firmly established and supplies and quality assured the supplier's development group will create prototypes and different versions of the equipment, which will be first

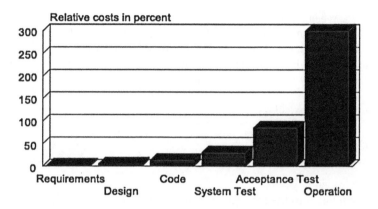

Relative costs in percent

FIGURE 11.1 Costs of software development.

tested in-house and at a later stage at a beta-sites, which is commonly an end users' process development or small-scale site. However, any stage of the pilot scale production and/or assembly has to be thoroughly documented to be able to assure consistency and improvement, if necessary. In instances of the development of source code within equipment, any development of such code or any change within the code has to be documented in name of the programmer, date, description of change, or progress (Figure 11.1). The entire source code establishment requires being auditable and needs to be well documented from the start, as the cost implications are much higher at the end-product level.

Prototypes will be tested and if these do not meet the specified requirements, the development requires getting back to the drawing board and improving the equipment to users' specifications. It is highly important to test the equipment thoroughly as it has to meet user requirement specification (URS) optimally, but also requires having reliable, repeatable performance fulfillment. The test data obtained will also help for validation purposes, for example, setting the specifications and troubleshooting advice, if it runs out of specification. As in any pharmaceutical process, the vendor processes are also defined within a specification band, which the process has to stay in with. However, during the development phase and small-scale testing the outer edges of the specification band will be checked to see how fast this event could happen and what the result would be. Once the specification band has been determined it will be locked in place and all process parameters and settings will be defined within a standard operating procedure (SOP) structure.

Besides the establishment of the specification and performance review of the newly developed prototype, a key success factor for the large-scale production of a new product is the communication and hand over of a product from development to production processes. The prototype production helps to establish appropriate communication channels and teamwork to make the transition into large-scale production as smooth and uneventful as possible. This also assures that there are no glitches in the future production process or, if so, that these can be rectified rapidly. If communication breaks down, typically the tech transfer breaks down and inevitably the large-scale production process will be hit with problems in future. The learning from the development phase has to be transferred to the production phase.

Validation—Qualification

When done, the raw material quality, product parts production, assembly, sterilization, packaging and transportation specifications require to be locked. This means that production parameters and tolerance are verified and set, most commonly by multiple production batches similar to the industry's practices. For example, machine setting, product formulations, production environments and flows have been defined and the personnel trained accordingly. Only the established and fixed production parameters create the assurance of reliable repeatability of the final product quality specification. The setting of production parameters also creates opportunities for analytical technologies to measure product specification during the production process. Process controls help to assure that the process is stabile and performs as defined. When all specification, process requirements, and controls are defined, validation protocols and SOPs have been instituted. Validation tests are commonly set by publicly available international standards, for example, sterilizing grade filters have to meet current pharmacopeial requirements and will be tested accordingly. In the case of sterilizing grade filters following qualification tests are typically performed, but may vary from supplier to supplier:

- USP plastic class VI toxicology
- Endotoxin release
- Particulates release
- Oxidizable substances
- pH/conductivity shift
- Integrity test limits correlated to bacteria challenge tests
- Steam sterilizability
- Physical dimensions
- Operating parameters, like maximum operating pressure/temperature
- Flow rates

Nevertheless, the suppliers have their own sets of tests, which equipment will undergo to verify performance criteria set by the supplier and user alike. For example, in instances also pulsation resistance is tested, or specific worst-case extractable tests are performed. The extractable data, as well as all other tested parameters, are conducted with model solvents und specific lab test conditions. Most commonly one could utilize the supplier-specific tests as indicators to check how the equipment might behave within certain environmental or process conditions. However, the indicator results obtained during the supplier's qualification stage has to be verified by appropriate process validation. The test results of the qualification tests can be found within the supplier's qualification documentation (erroneously called validation guides), which are supplied to the end user (Figure 11.2). In some instances, other more specific documents are made available by the supplier for specific products, for example, extractable guides for sterilizing grade filters. Filter suppliers also submit quality certificates with every filter, which list release criteria and the attainment of such.

The qualification documents, however, will not replace process validation or performance qualification (PQ) at the end user's site. These documented tests establish the basic requirements for the equipment to (a) be able to work within the biopharmaceutical environment and (b) verify that the equipment meets regulatory requirements. If this scientific basis will not be met by the developed product the product will be scrapped or will require major changes to meet the requirements.

Quality Control Parameter

Qualification tests and the validation of the supplier's production process will also set the standards of tests which quality control will use to determine product consistency and reliability. Most commonly suppliers have already standard quality assurance tests defined by other production processes or equipment specification. These can be utilized to a large degree; however, it could be that a specific piece of equipment requires additional tests or release criteria. For example, the in-process controls and release criteria for a sterilizing grade filter will differ to a membrane chromatography device or filter housing. Nevertheless, all the product categories have to have appropriate controls and release criteria established to meet quality and consistency standards.

Supplier's development departments have to work in close conjunction with multiple departments. Development not only creates a new or improved product, but has to assure sub-supplies, determines appropriate production specifications, tolerances, and the validation of such, which is commonly done with supply chain and quality assurance functions. Additionally, with the validation of the production process, close collaboration with quality control is required to create appropriate SOPs, validation and qualification documentation, and the review of the development documents, for example, for source

Table of Contents

FIGURE 11.2 Filter qualification documentation example.

code utilized is the controls and automation of certain equipment. Quality assurance works in close conjunction with development to assure consistent feasibility, performance, and quality. Finally, the supplier's product management and technical service departments are supplied with performance data and specifications of the new product by the development department. The data are compared to the

performance criteria set at the beginning of the product development cycle and the performance requirements set by the industry.

Supplier's Process Qualifications

Depending on the complexity of the supplier's products the production processes require process specific
validation. Most commonly supplier's production processes are multistep processes meaning every step
requires validation, appropriate operation procedures and qualification, training, and certification of the
personnel involved.

Example Filter Manufacturing

For example, membrane casting for a sterilizing grade filter is one step within the production of a sterilizing grade filter (Figure 11.3). This casting process requires very specific environmental conditions and
machine settings. These conditions can be humidity, temperature, solvent vapor saturation, casting belt
speed, dope thickness, etc. During the casting process the machine parameters are constantly monitored
and samples of the casted product are taken and tested frequently. Even before the casting process the
polymeric cast solution mixing and component concentration determines the success to cast a specific
membrane property. The component recipes and mixing parameters are highly guarded, as these are
the critical success criteria, which will not only determine the feasibility of a cast, but also of the latter
configuration. However, the parameters and recipes have to be well defined and controlled to create reliable repeatability. Same counts for the casting process; therefore, the cast and the environment within the
casting process are highly controlled and monitored.

All parameters and test results are documented within the batch records of this particular cast and can
be reviewed by auditors. The documented results also serve as a historical database to perform statistical
evaluations, evaluate process performance, or support development efforts. The casting process parameters determine the pore size of a membrane, but also its pore size distribution, i.e., the process has to be
closely adjusted and monitored to achieve a narrow or desired distribution. Other quality attributes are
membrane thickness, uniformity, pleatability, structure, etc.

Once the membrane batch is cast, it will be pleated, sealed, end-capped, welded, flushed, integrity
tested, bagged, and autoclaved. However, the procedures or individual production steps line-up does not
matter, every single step has defined process parameters in which the production step has to run. The
time frame between every step requires as much monitoring as the step itself. The process has to be

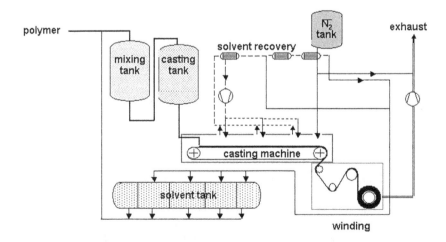

FIGURE 11.3 Membrane evaporation casting process.

validated as an individual step and in its entirety. This also includes the necessary personnel, material, and waste flow. Since the production process has individual steps and can run with a multitude of product items, it is of importance to have the process appropriately designed and controlled that any potential product mix-up is voided.

The production parameters and release criteria have to be defined for each step and described within SOPs. Every parameter, specification, and tolerance level is documented within a validation master file and cannot be changed without approval by multitude of departments, most important among them is quality assurance. Release criteria are established by in-process tests. These tests can be destructive and nondestructive integrity tests, tensile strength, NVR (nonvolatile residue), physical dimensions, pore size distribution, flow, throughput, etc. Once the criteria are met, the product can move to the next step of the process. However, if the product does not meet the criteria, an investigation will be instigated to analyze why the product is out of specification. Most commonly such investigations happen at the development of full-scale production, since the products are moved from development's pilot scale to full scale. Scaling within vendors process can be as difficult as in the end user's industry. This might be seen as a negative but should rather be seen positively as it is better to amend root causes of undesired product quality within the production validation processes, instead of established production processes. The more possibilities of failures can be eradicated during the validation and pilot scale process, the higher the likelihood for reliable compliance during commercial-scale production.

Once the production processes are established, maintenance protocols will assure that the production equipment is working as specified. Maintenance protocols are written during the validation phase as wear and tear can vary and specific tools are constantly inspected during the validation phase.

Example Automated Processes

Any automated equipment utilized in the production process has to undergo installation, operation, and PQ, especially in regard of the process and systems controls. For example, an injection molding system which is utilized to produce a specific part for a medical device requires as much qualification work and documentation as an autoclave within the pharmaceutical industry. The product component delivered by the molding machine has to be of consistent quality, complying with set tolerances and specifications. If any of these specified parameters is not met, the batch will not be released and an out of specification investigation will be performed. These tests are described and used as release parameters for validation batches and thereof commercially marketed batches. However, consistency in set quality parameters is the most important aspect in any stage of the production.

Example Manual Processes

In certain production process, the process cannot be automated and the production step is performed by personnel, for example, steel welding. The settings within welding can be described, but only as indicator specification, for example, the tube volume and material thickness which will determine the protective gas pressure and welding energy settings. However, due to the complexity and individuality of some equipment, for example, bioreactors or cross-flow systems, most welding might be done by pure experience of the welder. The welders require specific certification and most often have a multiyear experience. The welding itself will be analyzed and inspected before release, but this does not minimize the skill level required for such welding tasks. Similar skills are required for cutting, honing, bending, polishing, etc. The validation within these processes is the certification and routine training of the personnel, log books as well as the consistent quality of the raw materials used. Any raw material entering the facility will be inspected, documented, and requires specific certification and stamps. The raw material has to be traceable and of specified quality. Furthermore, release quality tests and the database of these release successes will also ensure that the personnel stay consistent within the quality specifications set. Release tests are of exceptional importance in any manual production process, as these are the most valuable qualification data points. A person cannot be validated; therefore, all parameters surrounding the personnel have to be stringently monitored.

Example Packaging

An additional piece of validation work on the vendors' part is packaging validations and transportation tests. The goods will be packed in specifically designed packaging which assures robustness during transport, as the finished product shall not be damaged during the transfer from the supplier's warehouse to the incoming goods warehouse of the end user. The supplier will test the packaging design using specific standards, e.g., ASTM D 4169 (2003) and D 4728-17 (2017). These tests are drop and vibration tests. ISO 12048 (1994) is a compression test, which will verify the stability of the packaging. As soon as the goods leave the factory, the vendor loses control over the handling of the goods. Therefore, packaging plays a major role to maintain the flawlessness and integrity of the goods shipped. Moreover, robustness is not only attached to mechanical stability, but also to thermal and chemical stability. Temperature changes during transport are not unusual, especially during overseas shipments. The packaging must be flexible enough to overcome any thermal expansion or shrinkage. It also should repel any condensation occurring due to temperature changes or changes in humidity. Oxidation due to sunlight is probably the most common photochemical attack to polymeric packaging. The packing has to be stabile under these circumstances; otherwise, polymeric degradation would result in weakening the packaging or particulate shedding of the packaging. This is specifically important for gamma sterilized packaging or products, as the packaging and product can degrade over time after the irradiation process. For this reason, shelf-life studies are always undertaken with gamma sterilized goods. The shelf life will be a guidance for the end user and should be observed to avoid any use of expired products, which may undergo an increase of particulate or extractable matter.

The ultimate tests for packaging are multiple shipments into the different regions supplied to and by different carriers. At the end, these tests will create a framework of test data of different means of transportation at different environmental conditions, which will result in a tolerance band for the designed packaging. Only such tests create practical data verifying the experimental lab data, as the transportation process is often not in the hands of the supplier. The transportation process can often not be specified or defined by a user leaflet, i.e., the handling is unknown and the only option to verify that the transport is not doing any harm to the packaged good is the actual test.

Supplier's In-Process Controls and Release Criteria

Depending on the suppliers' products the in-process controls and release criteria vary from narrowly defined step-by-step controls within the production process or as an end result control and release (Jornitz and Meltzer, 2001). Most commonly, individually produced components are tested when produced and again when the individual components are assembled. As previously described the control and release criteria and tests are established within the development process and depend also on the criticality of the product supplied to the end user. In instances, control and release criteria are fairly simple and encompass only a single test criterion, most of the time though product distributed to the pharmaceutical industry undergo multiple tests within the parts and final product production process.

Raw materials, supplied to the vendor, are checked first whether the quality documentation is complete. Again, depending on the criticality of the component the material might undergo specific tests to verify that the quality standards described are met. For example, polymer granulates undergo thermal profiles to check that the quality and type is the same as specified by the supplier to the sub-supplier. Granulates which are used for pharmaceutical purpose also undergo specific tests like endotoxin, particulate, and extractable tests. In other instances, the raw material is visually inspected, for example, stainless steel tubing in regard to surface finished, damages, flaws, and material stamps.

If the raw material does not meet one of the specifications the material will not be released into production. All raw material batch records are kept with the batch records of the resulting product. The product has to be completely traceable to allow appropriate investigation, if necessary. Raw material suppliers are generally audited once a year, depending on the significance of the raw material supplied. However, if there has been an incident the supplier will be audited immediately thereafter, and corrective

Identified Extractables of Different Membrane Filter Cartridges from Several Filter Manufacturers							
Cartridge A	Cartridge B	Cartridge C	Cartridge D	Cartridge E*	Cartridge F*	Cartridge G*	Cartridge H*
Dietyhlphthalate	Cyclohexan	Propionic acid	Dietyhlphthalate	Acrylic acid	Dimethylbenzen	Etherthioether	Caprolactame
Stearic acid	Ethoxybenzoic acid	Diphenylether	12 oligo. aliphates	2 phenolic oligo.	Etherthioether	Propionic acid	Butyrolactone
2,6-Di-tert.-butyl-cresol	2,6-Di-tert.-buty cresol	2,6-Di-tert.-butyl-cresol	Hydroxybenzoic aci	2,6-Di-tert.-butyl-cresol	2,6-Di-tert.-butylcresc	2,6-Di-tert.-butyl-cresol	Laurinlactame
2,2-Methylene-bis 4-ethyl-6-tert. Buty phenol	Cyclohexadiene 1,4-dion	4-Methyl-2,5-cyclohexadiene-1-on	Tert.-butyl-methyl-2,5-cyclohexadiene-1-on	3 oligo. Benzyl-di-phenylmethan	3,5-Di-tert. butyl-4-hydroxyphenyl propionate	3,5-Di-tert.-butyl-methyl-2,5-cyclo-hexadiene-1-on	Laurinlactame derivate
Hydroxybenzoic acid	Phenylisocyana	Hydroxybenzoic acid	2,4-Bis(1,1-di-methoxy-1-ethyl)-phenol	Triphenylphosphite	2 N-containing high MW compounds	4,4-Dichloro-diphenylsulfone	4-Methoxy-4-chlor-diphenylsulfone
7 oligo. Siloxanes	Palmitic acid	Palmitic acid	Succinic acid	Stearic acid	Acetamide	Benzothiazolone	Adipinic acid
Bis-(2-ethylhexyl)-phthalate	Stearic acid	Dimethoxydiphen sulfone	3 oligo, siloxanes	Bis-(2-ethylhexyl)-phthalate	N-cont. aromatic high MW comp.	4-Hydroxypropyl-benzoat	Dibutylphthalate
12 oligo. Aliphates	12 oligo. aliphates	11 oligo. aliphates	Polyether	Polyacrylate	3 oligo. amides	6 oligo. Aliphates	Ethylhexylphthalate
4-Methyl-2,5-cyclohexadiene-1-on	11 oligo. siloxanes	Methoxy-4-chloro-diphenylsulfone		Ethylacrylate	Bis-(2-ethylhexyl)-phthalate	Hydroxyphenyl acetamide	Dihydroethyl-phthalate
	Methyl-4-hydroxybenzoa	Bis-(2-ethylhexyl)-phthalate		Diphenylphthalate	10 oligo. siloxanes	Methoxy-4-chloro-diphenylsulfone	2,6-Di-tert.-butyl-cresole
	Etherthioether	Polyether		9 oligo. Siloxanes	2 oligo. aliphates	7 oligo. Siloxanes	Diisobutylphthalate
		7 oligo. siloxanes		6 oligo. aliphates		Cyclohexanone	Diacetylbenzene
		2,4-Bis(1,1-di-methoxy-1-ethyl)-phenol					Cyclotridecanone
							4-4-Dichlorodi-phenyl-sulfone
							Propionic acid
							4 oligo. siloxanes
							3 oligo. aliphates
* Identification of the RP-HPLC peaks by FTIR is still in progress—extractables list of marked cartridges may be incomplete.							

FIGURE 11.4   Table of extractable of eight different sterilizing grade filters.

action verified. At that point the audit frequency could also increase till reliability level is achieved required by the manufacturer.

For example, filter cartridges, whether pre- or membrane filter are tested for extractables (see Figure 11.4) to check whether there is any change within the profile, which might not meet release criteria (Meltzer and Jornitz, 1998). Similar tests are flow, throughput, mechanical and thermal robustness. Membrane filter are commonly individual integrity tested before release.

Stainless steel products also have specific definitions, which need to meet the biopharmaceutical requirements (Jornitz and Meltzer, 2001). These are individual stamping of the steel goods, welding certification, material qualification, and certification. The steel source can determine the quality of the steel. The steel components are required to be accurate, as these determine welding quality, corrosive robustness, and the electrolytic behavior within a system. Nowadays, stainless standards are set by the industry, which define, for example, the ferrite content or surface roughness.

Depending on the application the stainless steel equipment used differs greatly in the surface treatment. The smoother the surface, the greater the treatment steps and the costs involved. In some instances, surface treatments are not needed or are even undesirable; potentially a glass-beaded surface is sufficient. However, since cleaning is a major factor within the biopharmaceutical industry the surfaces require to be smooth and with a minimum groove rate. Any groove would allow pockets of microbial growth, which could potentially result in biofilm formation. Electropolishing, after high-grid polishing is utilized to cut any high peaks of material and avoid pockets (see Figures 11.5 and 11.6).

Electropolishing will remove any peaks or valleys within the surface structure. This is of importance as a buffing process after the electropolishing process could result in covered pockets which could result in microbial containment spaces. These pockets or caves could potentially protect microbial contaminants and would, therefore, be a starting point for a biofilm formation, growing out from that point. Therefore, any stainless steel pretreatment, abrasion, buffing, or polishing process has to be well qualified and requires to be adapted to the steel quality at hand and the end use of such equipment.

Most commonly, when automated equipment is supplied appropriate qualification documentation is required before the equipment is released and shipped to the client. Without such documentation the

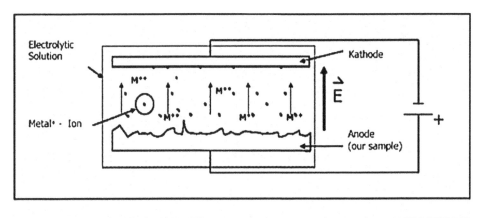

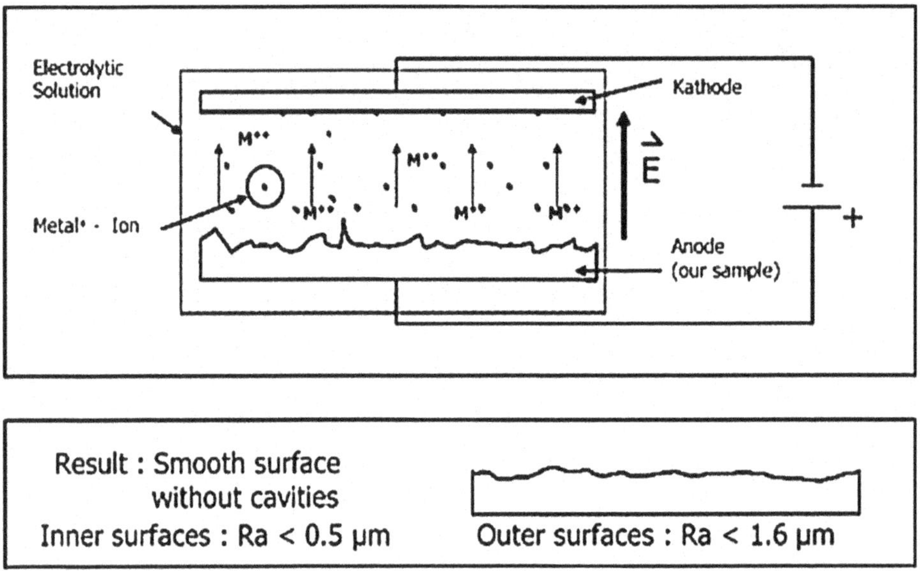

FIGURE 11.5   Schematic diagram of an electropolishing process.

Level	Description	Typical Applications
A-1	Grade #3 Diamond	Lens / Mirror – requires 420 SS material
A-2	Grade #6 Diamond	High Polish parts
A-3	Grade #15 Diamond	High polish parts
B-1	600 Grit paper	Medium polish parts
B-2	400 Grit paper	Medium polish
B-3	320 Grit paper	Med – Low polish
C-1	600 Stone	Low polish parts
C-2	400 Stone	Low polish parts
C-3	320 Stone	Low polish parts
D-1	Dry Blast Glass Bead	Satin finish
D-2	Dry Blast # 240 Oxide	Dull finish
D-3	Dry Blast # 24 Oxide	Dull finish

FIGURE 11.6   Table of different polishing methods and the end result.

equipment would be of no use and the shipment might be rejected. It is essential that these documents are sent to the client for preapproval. Once the approval is received only then the vendor can ship the equipment to the client. Appropriate qualification documentation is an essential release criterion nowadays. In instances of complex automated equipment, for example, fermentation equipment, factory acceptance tests (FATs) are crucial release criteria before the system is shipped to the client. These tests encompass a full-scale run of the equipment to see whether the equipment performs to URS. If there are points of concern, these will be adjusted to fulfill the defined criteria at the manufacturing site of the supplier. A release criterion, external to the manufacturer, but as critical, is a site acceptance test (SAT) of equipment. At that point the equipment is checked at the client's site, under the environmental conditions of the client.

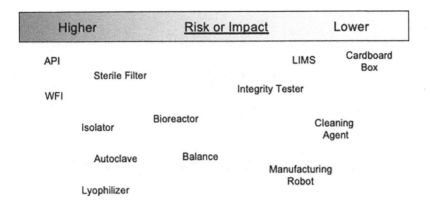

FIGURE 11.7 Possible example of risk and impact assessments.

From an end user's standpoint, the release criteria of the supplier have to meet the risk assessment criteria set by the end user (and more often the regulatory authorities). This means, depending on the quality impact of a specific component or equipment supplied, the release criteria on both sides, supplier and end user, will differ in stringency. The quality of supplied water for injection (if not produced within the facility) has a higher risk attached than a condensate valve on a tank. Different risk or impact classifications have to be defined for product and equipment supplies (see Figure 11.7). Some products have a direct impact on the quality of the end product, some have only a minor influence, some have no influence, but are used to check on a component with a quality influence. It is of importance to always review quality attributes in accordance to product quality as well as patient's safety. For example, an integrity test system does not have a direct influence, but is used to check the integrity, the quality of a sterilizing grade filter, which has an influence on the quality of the drug product and therefore patient's safety. Consequently, the calibration of such test system is essential. The release and test criteria for these products will differ and be defined in a way which will meet the necessary quality purpose. It would make no sense to use similar evaluation conditions for noncritical items. It would just raise costs and possible process delays. Therefore, these risk assessments have to be performed before release criteria are defined.

Qualification of Equipment

The probably most descriptive and utilized guidance on qualification mechanisms is the GAMP (Good Automated Manufacturing Practice, 2008) guidance published by the ISPE (International Society of Pharmaceutical Engineering). It describes thoroughly the individual, necessary steps required to fulfill the quality expectations of automated systems. This guidance is used for a multitude of equipment utilized within the biopharmaceutical industry, for example, autoclaves, lyophilizers, filling machines, integrity test systems, bioreactors, and others.

Within the GAMP documentation, specification steps are described, but also three main qualification requirements: installation qualification (IQ), operational qualification (OQ), and PQ. There are other qualification tests which are quoted randomly, for example, design qualification (DQ) and system qualification (SQ). However, the three major qualification segments are IQ, OQ, and PQ and are applicable to every automated piece of equipment supplied.

A system design and the qualification steps all start with the URSs. This is the foundation of any system which will be designed and if defined inappropriately the entire project might be prone to fail or at least will require rework with additional costs and delivery time delays involved. The URS can be seen as the foundation of a building, the better the foundation the better the construction on it. Any of the above-mentioned qualification step, are the verification of the URS, functional specification (FS) and design specification (DS).

IQ

IQ is the documented verification that all important aspects of hardware and software installation adhere to the system specification.

Within this qualification, the entire system is checked whether all components are correctly installed and whether the entire documentation for the individual components is available. Most often the IQ step runs through a thorough check list to evaluate that everything meets the requirements set within the design or hardware specifications (see Figure 11.8) (Spanier, 2001).

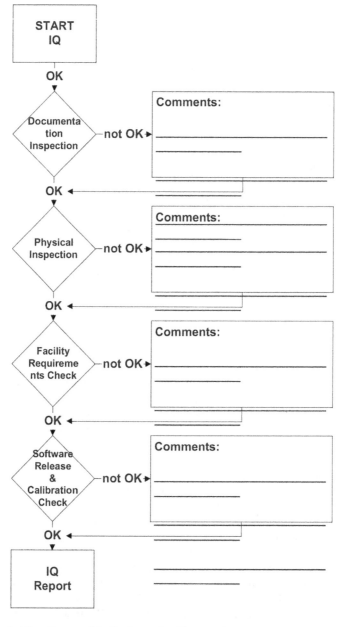

FIGURE 11.8 Typical flow diagram of the first layer of an IQ protocol.

The IQ documentation is delivered by the supplier but checked by the end user. Often and most practical would be to perform the IQ and OQ part during the FAT which verifies that the system is working.

OQ

OQ is the documented verification that the system operates in accordance with the system specification throughout all anticipated operating ranges (see Figure 11.9).

These tests verify that the FSs are met by empirically checking and testing against the manufacturer's recommended test sequences of all the critical operational and functional features and performance specifications of the machinery. These test sequences are performed within the supplier's facility, again most commonly during the FAT. Within this qualification phase the system will run at the specifications given by the user. Thus, suppliers are required to have all supplies necessary to run the system, for example, water and steam supplies. The OQ can be performed within few hours or weeks, depending on the complexity of the system build. Most commonly the OQ documentation is already established within the process of the FS, as every single function described requires to be tested during OQ. If a FAT

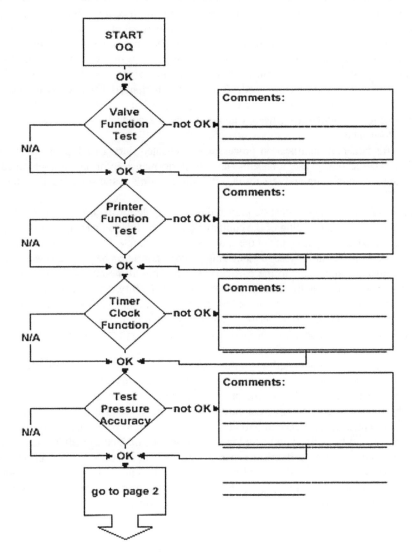

FIGURE 11.9 Typical flow diagram of the first layer of an OQ protocol.

happened and the documentation is not established at this point the workload will be tremendous and the precision will suffer.

Once the system run through the FAT and OQ and all documentation is established, the system can be shipped to the end user's site. At this point the PQ is performed as the final part. The PQ is often also part of the SAT or vice versa, depending on individual user procedures.

PQ

PQ is the documented verification that the system operates in accordance with the URS while operating in its normal environment and performing the function required by the process to be validated.

These records include batch records, routine calibration, and performance checks, which are commonly defined by the equipment used. Every piece of equipment has different requirements of compliance with specifications defined within the specification phase. Moreover, the environment within the end users' facilities varies. For this reason, PQs are run to check whether the equipment works within such an environment. Additionally, during the PQ phase, the equipment may be pushed to the limits to verify that it still performs and does not spiral out of control. In instances automated equipment might malfunction when, for example, the software is pushed to a limit. It could well be that the system shuts down or that certain controls and adjustments elevate themselves out of control or set tolerances. These stringent tests belong to a risk assessment program, which determines the functionality of the system. Will it still work in as robust way as requested, or will it perform in a way detrimental to the entire manufacturing process? The environment certainly has an influence on such functionality, as well as the process control system and its source code. It has been experienced that systems are not validatable due to commercially available software, adjusted to the purpose, but not fully compatible. Such software might not be able to cope with the stringency and demands of a production process and therefore show insufficient performance.

These three fundamental qualification processes are repeated during each phase of the validation process. In the qualification phase, a baseline level of performance information is obtained from the component manufacturers' data and test results, structural testing of the software, and the associated supplier documentation.

Equipment validation packages must be prepared and available for the user's own validation efforts and tests to verify proper functioning of the equipment. These validation packages are commonly very comprehensive and cover every function of the equipment. For example, the documentation for a complex fermentation system can result in close to 1,000 ring binders, nowadays being often electronic versions. In instances regulations applicable to the particular equipment will be quoted for the user to support other necessary validation or qualification processes within the facility. As described the equipment supplier can support, and commonly does, the end user with installation and OQ documentation; however, any process validation or PQ has to be performed within the facility and process environment. This will assure that the equipment is functioning properly aside the laboratory settings within the manufacturer's facilities.

Finally, maintenance and continued testing and verification are the responsibility of the end user, who may seek assistance from the equipment manufacturer or its own maintenance department. Service manual establishment is required before equipment is supplied to assure appropriate maintenance possibilities. Such service manuals' list spares required within specific frequencies. Commonly the supplier has experience at which interval certain parts of the system need to be exchanged or replaced. These essential spares need to be defined and listed within the service manual as well as maintenance intervals. It may be of advantage to stock critical spare parts to assure a speedy repair if critical equipment is not functioning. Maintenance tasks can also be performed by outside service organizations, though the qualification of these organizations has to be verified. Most often service contracts are established between the vendor service side and the user maintenance department.

Another important aspect should not be forgotten—training. All qualification and acceptance steps are good, but without use if the staff utilizing the equipment is not trained effectively. Training protocols and standard operating procedures (SOP) need to be described before the equipment is used. Both training manuals and SOPs should be reviewed to assure correctness.

Stages of Equipment Supplies and Qualifications

Stages of the individual specification and qualification segments are mainly visualized within the V-model of the GAMP guidance (2008). The V-model shows the different responsibilities, but also interactions of specifications versus qualifications (see Figure 11.10). It is often modified to meet different requirements of different equipment suppliers.

Within the V-model, the individual tasks or steps are described, but also responsibilities defined. In parts of the process the user is solely responsible, in other parts the supplier and specifically in the qualification phase, the user and supplier share responsibilities, as most often these tasks are performed jointly. Every single step is of utmost importance and has to be viewed with stringency and thoroughness, as every step following depends on the quality of the previous task. The entire system can only be as good as the starting quality; therefore, multiple other process control and approval steps are involved, which are not shown within the V-model. However, before a system is built each function, software and hardware design has to undergo critical review to verify that the URSs are met. In instances, specifications given might not be feasible to design or produce or subparts are not available or too costly. Sometimes, a cost focus might be not desirable, as cutting corners might result in a system which is not fulfilling the needs of the process defined. Examples have shown that shortcuts in respect to equipment or design qualities have resulted in higher adjustment costs at a later stage, typically resulting in change orders. In instances, inadequate attention to the design of the system has resulted in yield losses or dysfunctions. The costs resulting from such failures are tremendous. The recommendation has to be that the user and vendor work closely together to find an optimal solution for the particular need. Costs have to reasonable but should not be the main focus. The robustness of the process and delivery time depends upon the work and resources invested at the beginning. The more thorough the work performed at the start of a project the smoother it runs through the resulting steps.

The most important aspect is the URS, in which attention to detail is essential. Any rough idea given as URS will end in a back and forth between the user and supplier in the FS stage. Valuable man hours are wasted which is undesirable to both parties. Often forgotten, but always present is that the user is the specialist of the application and the supplier the specialist of the equipment. Utilizing both sets of experience will result in the best possible option. Yet, controls and measurements should be utilized

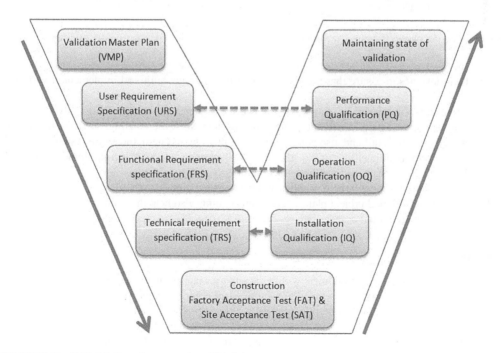

FIGURE 11.10 V-Model of requirement and qualification steps.

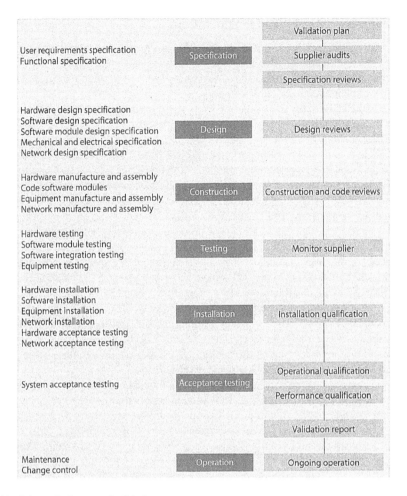

FIGURE 11.11   Schematic diagram of validation.

during the milestones to assure that the system will function once built and implemented within the facility.

As described, the V-model creates an overview; however, project flows and detailed activity descriptions require other tools, for example, specific project management software (see Figure 11.11). These tools will define activities in detail and also control points for parts of a system, the entire system, or just the raw materials (PDA Technical Report No. 15, 2009; Wolber et al., 1988). The time frames will also be reviewed on a frequent basis, as time pressures commonly will result in human error. Every supplier has experiences with their equipment supplies and knows what quality system requirements need to be established within a detailed project plan. These control points also help the vendor to avoid any errors, which would create additional costs.

Conclusion

Validation and qualification of equipment within the end user facility, under the process conditions is an essential need and regulatory requirement. Yet, suppliers of equipment, whether consumables or capital equipment, perform a multitude of qualification programs within their own facility. Such qualifications programs start during the development phase and commonly include not only the supplier's own processes, but also sub-vendor sites, processes, and product qualities. A supplier cannot just rely on the sub-supplies, but has to assure supply reliability and quality, just as any end user needs to do. Furthermore, the development team receives quality milestones by the end user. These specifications have to be kept, which means within the development phase, control mechanisms are defined which are used to verify that the specifications are met. These are typically also used as release criteria at full-scale production. Similarly, capital equipment receives URSs which are converted into FSs followed by software/hardware DSs. Again, the fulfillment of the URSs has to be controlled at every stage to avoid any surprises and noncompliance. The capital equipment runs through different specification stages like a consumable product runs through a development phase. At the end of the day, both product groups require compliance to the end user, respectively, regulatory specifications.

Once the goods have been developed or built, the performance has to be qualified within the end user's environment. Does the equipment perform under these circumstances? For example, sterilizing grade filters undergo process validation utilizing the actual or close at drug product and the process conditions. Evidence has to be given and documented to show the filter is performing to the set requirements under the environmental circumstances. The PQ stage does so for capital or automated equipment. The equipment might be pushed to its limit to assure that it functions under worst-case conditions reliably. The tests are performed onsite to guarantee that any environmental condition does not have an adverse effect on the performance of the equipment. Lab test at the vendor or pure quality certification cannot be accepted and will not meet regulatory requirements. Process validation and qualification is a must to meet regulatory needs.

Suppliers, nowadays, do not just produce and supply goods, but make sure that these goods meet the requirements of the biopharmaceutical industry and its regulatory authorities. Moreover, once an item is sold the suppliers' efforts do not stop; they support the end user with services to support any subsequent user qualification and validation effort. Both supplier's experiences and end user's know-how will optimize the process reliability and in combination assure that the specification of the equipment will meet the needs of the process. The vendor has to be more than half way toward the end user, by supplying qualification data of the goods supplied, which can be utilized to either make a choice of equipment or be utilized within the filing documentation.

REFERENCES

ASTM D 4169 (2003), *Standard Practice for Performance Testing of Shipping Containers and Systems*, ASTM International, West Conshohocken, PA.

ASTM D4728-17 (2017), *Standard Test Method for Random Vibration Testing of Shipping Containers*, ASTM International, West Conshohocken, PA.

ISO 12048 (1994), Packaging—Complete, filled transport packages—Compression and stacking tests using a compression tester, International Organization for Standardization ISO Central Secretariat Chemin de Blandonnet 8 CP 401-1214 Vernier, Geneva, Switzerland.

GAMP (2008), *Guide for Validation of Automated Systems in Pharmaceutical Manufacture: User Guide*, ISPE European Office, Brussels, Belgium.

Jornitz, M.W. and Meltzer, T.H. (2001), *Sterile Filtration—A Practical Approach*, Chapter 7, Filter integrity testing, Marcel Dekker, New York.

Meltzer, T.H. and Jornitz, M.W. (1998), *Filtration in the Biopharmaceutical Industry*, Marcel Dekker, New York.

Spanier, H.J. (2001), Qualification of a filter integrity test device, *Pharm. Tech. Europe*, Vol. 13, No. 12, pp. 45–52.

PDA Technical Report No. 15 (2009), *Validation of Tangential Flow Filtration in Biopharmaceutical Applications*, PDA, Bethesda, MD.

Wolber, W.P., Beech D. and McAllister, M. (1988), Validation of computerized membrane integrity test systems, *J. Parenter. Sci. Technol.*, Vol. 42, No. 4, pp. 106–110.

12

Validation of the Filter and of the Filtration Process

Paul S. Stinavage
Pfizer, Inc.

CONTENTS

Introduction

The validation of sterilizing filtrations and the sterilizing filters involved is critical to the production of a sterile drug product, or of a sterile active pharmaceutical ingredient (API). The sterility of the drug preparation cannot be ascertained by analysis of its samples. It is impossible to test every drug container to assess its sterility. Similarly, a statistical determination of sterility would require so large a sampling as to be impractical. Validation of a process provides the assurance that the product manufactured is sterile. Validation is a regulatory requirement (FDA 1985). Validation of the filters used to achieve a sterile API is also necessary. It serves to assure that they perform in the manner intended; this may also be a regulatory requirement if there are no further sterilizing steps for the ingredient after its being formulated into the final product. Validation of a sterilizing filtration involves determining the effect of the liquid on the filter, and the effect of the filter on the liquid, and demonstrating that the filter removes all microorganisms of interest from the liquid under the actual processing conditions.

One further point may need to be considered, namely, the interaction among the contaminating organisms, the solution, and the filter. Therefore, several studies are necessary to perform a complete filter validation. These include investigating extractables, chemical compatibility, initial filter performance, and bacterial retention testing. If the filter is to be post-use integrity tested in product-wet condition then validation of product-wet integrity test specifications is also necessary. It is important to note that sterilizing filters should not be reused for subsequent product processing.

Present Status

Until approximately 25 years ago, it was believed that the sterilization of fluids could unerringly be achieved by their filtration through a "sterilizing" membrane whose proper and pertinent identity was confirmed by its pore size rating, which was itself determined by integrity testing. Developments in filtration practices have showed this belief to be too generally founded. What had once seemed simple is now recognized as being quite complex. It was discovered that the positive conclusions based on pore size ratings were subject to modification by the physicochemical specificity of the organism-suspending fluid, by the individuality of the organism type in its size-changing response to the fluid, in the possible changes in pore size induced by the fluid's effect on the filter, and by the adsorptive qualities of the filter resulting from its particular polymeric composition; all influenced by the filtration conditions in their numerous varieties, but especially by the transmembrane pressure. A filter may not sterilize the same preparation under different filtration conditions, especially under dissimilar differential pressures (Leahy and Sullivan 1978). A given membrane may or may not retain a particular organism type suspended in a different drug vehicle (Bowman et al. 1967). The organism type does not remain constant in size, but alters in response to its suspending fluid (Gould et al. 1993; Leo et al. 1997; Meltzer et al. 1998). The effect of the vehicle upon the polymeric membrane may cause a change in its pore sizes (Lukaszewicz and Meltzer 1980).

The certainty of obtaining sterile effluent requires far more than the identification of a "sterilizing filter" by a pore size rating. The complex of influences governing the outcome of an intended sterilizing filtration necessitates a careful validation of the process, including that of the filter (PDA Technical Report # 26). The very drug preparation of interest, the exact membrane type, the precise filtration conditions, and the specific organism type(s) of concern should be employed in the necessary validation.

Given the complexity of the organism removal operation, it is doubtful whether a universal sterilizing filter can be devised. Certainly, there is no known absolute filter, one that will retain all organisms under all conditions, especially if viruses are included (Aranha 2004). Therefore, the successful attainment of a sterile filtration with regard to specified organisms of interest must in every individual case be attested to by the documented experimental evidence that constitutes validation.

Mechanisms of Retention

The retention of organisms by filters is central to achieving sterile effluents. The mechanisms whereby particles are removed from solutions by attachments to filters are variously characterized. How the organism and filter surfaces encounter one another, as by the influence of inertial impaction, Brownian motion, or gravitational settling, etc. are, in this writing, not as significant as the bonding that keeps the two in juxtaposition after the contact is established. The nature and strength of the mutual bonding that joins the two surfaces are the considerations of interest.

For the purposes of this discussion, each of two particular situations constitutes a mechanism. Sieve retention, also called size exclusion, size discrimination, or direct interception is the mechanism that is most relied upon, and that is operative in most filtrations. It results in particle captures because the particle is too large to pass through the restricted areas of the filter's pores. Mechanical in its function, it is, once joined, augmented by electrical effects derived largely from partial charges.

Adsorptive sequestration is the mechanism that retains particles small enough to enter and pass through the filter pores. Such small entities in their passage bond to the pore walls, thus effecting their retention. The adsorption of one solid surface, the particle, to that of another, the filter, is the consequence of electrically charged atoms. As is commonly known, like charges repel; unlike charges attract. Such unions can eventuate from full ionic charges such as are involved when quaternarized charge-modified filters are used. However, these adsorptions usually result from the mutual attraction of partial-charges of opposite signs. Such bonding phenomena as permanent dipoles, induced dipoles, hydrogen bonding, van der Waals forces, and hydrophobic adsorptions may be involved (Meltzer and Jornitz 2006; Gabler 1978).

Given a liquid with a sufficient degree of loading, the quantity of particles retained on a filter's surface may build a filter cake. Depending upon the packing density of the cake it may, in effect, function as a filter overlying the microporous membrane. Either or both of the above described mechanisms may operate to remove particles from the liquid as it permeates the interstices of the filter cake. Some consider "filter cake" formation to be a particle retention mechanism. Be that as it may, its formation is not likely from the lightly loaded liquids being readied for sterile filtrations.

The FDA's 2005 Aseptic Processing Guidance (September 2004) states: "A sterilizing grade filter should be validated to reproducibly remove viable microorganisms from the process stream producing a sterile effluent." This emphasizes the importance of bacterial retention validation of the sterilizing filter. Bacterial retention validation provides data verifying that the filtered product is safe from a microbiological perspective. Bacterial challenge testing is performed by the filter manufacturer to classify the retention capability of the filter (PDA Technical Report 26). The filter user is expected to perform testing to demonstrate that the intended filter construction will completely remove a challenge organism from a product or product family under process conditions. The validation of the intended process filter should simulate "worst case" production conditions, including the size of influent bioburden, and filter integrity test values. "Worst-case" conditions mean those circumstances that are least conducive to organism removals.

Similarly, the effect(s) of the product on resident bioburden and/or the standard challenge organism may not be well recognized. Organisms grown under nutritional stress conditions may have different characteristics from those cultured in rich, defined media. Poor nutritional conditions, such as those in many drug products, result in smaller organisms than those grown under optimal nutrient conditions (Geesey (1987), Gould et al. (1993), Sundaram (1999), Meltzer and Jornitz (2006). These characteristics should be accounted for during sterilizing filter validation testing.

Influences on Mechanisms of Retention

The retention of an organism by a filter represents a nexus of many interdependent factors. These include the filter pores, their numbers and size distribution, and restrictive diameters; as also the types and sizes of the organisms, their numbers, sizes, and structural makeup. It is the matching of the sizes and shapes of the pores and organisms that is the determinant in the sieve retention or size exclusion mechanism. It is axiomatic that a particle larger than a pore cannot penetrate it unless compressively deformed by excessive differential pressures. Although membranes are classified in terms of single pore size ratings, they are actually characterized by pore size distributions, albeit usually of an unknown magnitudes. Thus, it is conceivable that an organism that could be retained by a pore of one of the sizes characterizing the distribution would escape capture were it to confront one of the membrane's larger pores. Absolute retention is possible only when the smallest particle of the particle size distribution is larger than the largest pore of the pore size distribution. Given the usual application of filters, of unknown pore size distributions, to the removal of organisms of unknown size distributions, it would be inappropriate, and misleading to declare that a particular filter will be absolute in its action.

Sieving, the chief mechanism of particle removal, can be reinforced by the adsorptive sequestration of the particles. The electrical charges on the surfaces of the organisms and filters manifest mutually attractive forces. This interaction results when they are opposite in sign. The one surface will become adsorptively bonded to the other. The result is the arrest and removal of the organisms as the fluid flows through the filter pores. The polymeric composition of the filter matrix in terms of its polarity determines its surface charge and, hence, its tendency to undergo adsorptive effects. However, the physicochemical nature of the suspending liquid can so modify the electrical attractive and repulsive forces by its ionic strengths, pH, surfactant content, etc. as to promote or hinder adsorptions. Thus, the same organism and filter may interact differently in solutions of various compositions; a desired organism removal may or may not result. An example of such an occurrence was noted using a 0.45 μm-rated mixed cellulose ester membrane, a given preparation could be sterilized by the removal of its *Brevundimonas diminuta* content. However, the addition of penicillinase to the same preparation prevents the attainment of sterile effluent. The proteinaceous component preempts the adsorptive sites of the filter, preventing the sequestration of the organisms. That adsorptive influences were at work was shown by the eventuation of a sterile effluent from the penicillinase preparation when a 0.22 µm-rated membrane was employed. Sieve retention is the effective mechanism when the tighter membrane is used.

The differential pressure is especially influential in its effect on adsorptive interactions. The higher it is, the faster the liquid flow and the shorter the residence time of the particle within the pore passageway. This reduces the particle's opportunity to encounter the pore wall and, thus, minimizes the likelihood of adsorptive sequestrations. Intriguingly, there is reason to believe that the concentration of organisms, aside from their total numbers, influence the attainment of sterile effluent (Zahka and Grant 1991; Mouwen and Meltzer 1993).

The filtration conditions also have an influence on organism removals. For example, the solution's viscosity may be high enough to frustrate an organism ensconced within the liquid stream from reaching an adsorptive site on the pore wall before it is carried out of the filter by the convective flow defined by a given ΔP. Given the reciprocal relationship of viscosity and temperature, the opposite effect can result when the same filtration is performed with the liquid preparation at a higher temperature.

Also, the ratio of organisms to pores can strongly affect the rates of flow and their consequences in terms of throughputs and filter efficiency. Thus, even the effective filtration area (EFA) may impact on the likelihood of obtaining sterile effluent.

The sterilization of a fluid by a filter depends upon a number of factors; some more important than others. Most influential are the relative sizes and numbers of the organisms and the restrictive pores. The physicochemical nature of the fluid in terms of its ionic strength, pH, osmolarity, viscosity, etc. is another contributing factor. The possibilities for the adsorptive sequestration of organisms by the filter depend upon the polarity of both their surfaces as expressed by the partial charge-induced van der Waals forces. The polymeric nature of the filter may also govern its tendency to arrest certain organisms via hydrophobic adsorption. The type, number, concentration(s), and especially the size of the organisms whose removal is sought relative to the numbers and sizes of the restricted diameters of the filter pores is of obvious importance in determining the extents of organism removals. The susceptibility of the filter's pore sizes to alterations by contact with given solutions bears consideration. The organism size is of obvious influence. It too may be altered, whether increased or diminished, by contact with fluids of certain compositions. The ingredients of liquid preparations such as surfactants, various proteins, and charged entities such as colloids can affect the filter's sterilizing actions. The filtration conditions, e.g., temperature, viscosity, and especially differential pressure will influence the outcome of the filtration.

The mechanisms of organism removal being chiefly sieve retention, the size and numbers of the organisms and filter pores are important factors, as also the pore size distribution. Incompatibility between fluid and filter may result in pore size alteration, while incompatibility of fluid and organisms may be the cause of morphological changes in the latter. In either case, the organism removal by size exclusion or sieving may be compromised. A proper combination of all these factors is required to produce a sterilizing filtration.

Compatibility of Filter and Liquid

The compatibility of filter and liquid should not be assumed. Testing for compatibility investigates whether the drug product has a deleterious effect upon the filter membrane or its supporting materials. The goal of compatibility testing is to investigate whether the filter maintains its pore integrity following exposure to the product under the process conditions, and to ascertain that the filter medium is not adversely affected by the product or process conditions.

The liquid vehicle can alter the properties of the filter, including its pore sizes (Lukaszewicz and Meltzer 1980). The changes may derive from the relaxation of the casting strains undergone by the filter during its manufacture. The direction of the pore size change is unpredictable. Another consequence of plasticization could be a dimensional swelling of the polymeric matrix at the expense of the pore areas. Such occurrences could interfere with the expected pattern of sieve retentions. It is, therefore, required that the validation exercise assure that this means of particle removal, if operative in the filtration, remain reliably so during the entire filtration. A study of the filter performance is necessary to make certain that it remains unchanged and dependable during the entire filtration.

Gross incompatibilities, such as membrane degradations, e.g., dissolutions, hydrolyses, oxidations, may easily be recognized from changes in the filter's appearance. However, subtle alterations in the filter's structure will require experimental investigation. This can be achieved by way of integrity testing to see whether pertinent porosity alterations result from the exposure of the filter to the drug solution. The rate of such structural change being unknown, the testing should be performed after exposing the filter to the liquid for a period of time at least equal to the duration of the filtration processing step.

Comparing pre- and post-filtration values of bubble point determinations would reveal whether pore size alterations in the larger pores, signaling incompatibility, were caused by the filter/liquid contact. Such may be caused by the plasticizing action of liquid molecules intruding among the molecules of the solid polymeric filter. An enlargement of the polymer's intersegmental spaces by the liquid's plasticizing action could alter the particle retention expected from the sieving mechanism. Diffusive airflow testing would, however, more generally disclose changes caused to any of the pores regardless of their size. The polymer's intersegmental spaces are related to the filter's pores. The liquid molecules' intrusions into these spaces could serve to convert them into larger pores. This conceivable occurrence necessitates experimental investigation to make certain that it is not a realistic possibility.

Extractables

Contact between the molecules of the liquid and those of the filter polymer may result in a leaching of molecular substances from the filter into the drug solution. Such substances may consist of remnants of the casting formulae used to produce the filters, and of additives designed to protect the polymer molecules against chemical degradations during their fabrication and application as filters. Included are stabilizers against the oxidation of polymer molecules such as polypropylene; against the dehydro-dechlorinations of polyvinyl chloride as caused by ultraviolet light and oxygen; and to counter the physical degradations caused by the heating and shearing inherent in the milling, extrusion, and molding involved in working with polymers. The possibility of extractables being added to the filter's effluent deserves experimental investigation. The presence of leachables or extractables is a concern. They may be harmful to the drug's recipient. Their identity and avoidance is sought if at all possible. The likelihood of releasing extractables into the drug preparation during filtration is increased by plasticization of the filter polymer. The filter's reduction in viscosity by plasticization speeds the migration of substances from within the filter into the drug preparation. The time interval over which extractables are to be assessed should match the exposure of the filter to the liquid. Securing enough material for identification of the extractables, usually by way of ultraviolet or infrared spectral analyses, can be accelerated and accomplished by refluxing the extracting solvent through an appropriate area of the filter by the use of Soxhlet extractors.

It is necessary to generate extractable data to demonstrate that the filter does not add an unacceptable level of particles and/or chemical extractables to the product stream. Depending on the use of the filter, a variety of carriers may be tested. Usually the actual drug preparation is not used for extractable testing because of the possible interference of the product constituents with components extracted from the filter.

Water extractable data for filters are typically available from filter vendors. Typically, water extractable data are generated following a 4-h soak time of the filter in water. Additionally, filter vendors may generate water extractable data for filters after one or more sterilization cycles. Post-sterilization filter extractable data demonstrate the effect that sterilizations, either moist heat or irradiation, can have on the extractable level that are found. Since most (but certainly not all) pharmaceutical products are aqueous based, these extractable data have applicability to most products.

Further extractables validation may be required for filters used to filter APIs that are used with nonaqueous solvent systems. Extractable validation of these solutions may involve passing a model solvent system through the filter or soaking the filter followed by examination of the solvent system for filter components.

Flushing filters prior to use may be used to decrease the level of extractables present. If it is determined that flushing is necessary to limit extractables present in the product, validation should be conducted to establish the quantity of product that should be treated, by what volume of fluid, flushed over what interval of time, filtered and discarded, in order to achieve acceptable extractable levels in the filtrate. The ratios of product-treated to volume flushed at what rate, and totally discarded should be reflected in the standard operating procedure (SOP) used for product manufacture.

Extractable Test

In addition to the product bacteria challenge test, assays of extractable or leachable substances have to be performed. Previous reliance on nonvolatile residue (NVR) testing as a method of investigating extractable levels is discounted by the regulators as being too insensitive. Extractable/leachable analyses on membranes and other filter components are routinely done by appropriate separation and detection methodologies. Extractable measurements and the resulting data for their individual filter types are usually available from filter manufacturers (Reif 1998). These tests are performed using specific solvents such as, ethanol, or water at "worst case" conditions. Such conditions do not represent true processing realities. Therefore, depending on the process conditions and the solvents used, explicit extractable tests have to be performed as well. Formerly, these tests were done only with selected solvents, but not with the drug preparations themselves. There was concern lest the drug product's residues mask or interfere with the extractables undergoing measurement (Stone et al. 1994). Recent findings indicate the possibility of evaluating extractables utilizing the actual drug product as the extraction medium.

Such tests are conducted by the validation services of the filter manufacturers using such sophisticated separation and detection methodologies as GC-MS, FTIR, RP-HPLC, UV-VIS, GPC-RI, HPCE, and SFC.* These analytical techniques are employed in order to identify and quantify the individual components extracted from the filter. Their identities are required to judge the seriousness of their presence in the pharmaceutical preparation. Elaborate studies on sterilizing grade filters, performed by filter manufacturers show that there is not a release of high quantities of extractables. The range is from parts per billion to a maximum of parts per million per 10-in. cartridge element; nor have toxic substances been found (Reif et al. 1996; Reif 1998).

Model Organisms

The centerpiece of the subject validation is the assaying of the filter's efficiency in removing organisms from their liquid suspensions. The microbes whose removal from the drug preparation is the object of the filtration should be identified beforehand by microbiological analyses. The bioburden varies in its composition within the pharmaceutical experience. It would be helpful, for reasons of practicality, if the different organism types found to be present would respond uniformly to the filters. To the extent that this is so, the use of model organisms may be relied upon. The bacterium usually selected for challenging the "sterilizing grade" membranes rated 0.2/0.22 µm-rating is *Brevundimonas diminuta* ATCC 19146. While useful in its intent, this practice is not universally justified. In particular, the sieve retention mechanism is not applicable to those organisms that undergo size diminutions or shape alterations that permit their penetration of the 0.2/0.22 µm-rated "sterilizing" membranes. Other organisms are used in the testing of membranes of different sizes or characteristics, e.g., *Serratia marcescens* in the case of 0.45 µm-rated membranes.

Conclusions cannot be made regarding the sterile filtration of microorganisms unless methods of quantifying them by culturing and counting are available. Organisms such as the L-forms, nanobacteria,

---

* Gas Chromatography-Mass Spectometry, Fourier Transmission by Infrared, High Pressure Liquid Chromatography, Ultraviolet-Visible, High Pressure Chromatographic Extraction.

and "viable but non-culturable" entities may not be amenable to such analyses. Concerns about their presence may be justified, but absent the means to cultivate and count them, it is impossible to attest to their complete absence; obviously as determined within the limits of the assay. It follows that a sterilizing filter can be judged only by its performance in the removal of identifiable and culturable organisms known to be present in the drug preparation (Agalloco 1998).

Use of Isolates

An advantage is seen in the use of isolates obtained from the drug preparation itself. The use of organisms native to the drug composition lessens the artificiality of employing cultured *B. diminuta* as the test organism. The assay's endpoint involves culturing, growing, and counting the *live* organisms found present in the filtrate. If dead organisms were to penetrate the filter, they would not be detected in the effluent. An absence of live organisms will be taken to mean that the filter completely removed the challenging microbes; that the filter performed its sterilizing function. It is necessary, therefore, to make sure that the absence of live organisms is due to filtration sterilization and not to their being killed by the drug preparation. The very origin of the bioburden organisms shows that the isolates are able to survive in the process stream. This consideration in itself favors the use of process isolates; the concern need then not be entertained that the suspending liquid might be cidal. The possibility of erroneously concluding from the absence of live organisms in the effluent that the filter had restrained the passage of organisms when in actuality they had been killed by the drug preparation is eliminated.

It might have been thought that *B. diminuta* being killed by the drug would render moot the question of its filtrative removal. However, in its role as a model organism for assaying the filtration, it is required also to represent those bacterial types that might not be killed by the drug preparation. When *B. diminuta* are added to the drug solution, care is taken to determine their survival. If they are killed by the drug, the cidal component is removed, or other effective steps are taken, as will be described, to substitute a placebo compounded to mimic the properties of the drug preparation as closely as possible, but without its cidal effect. The absence of the live organisms from the effluent could then properly be credited to their filtrative sterilization.

Size and Shape

If the bioburden isolates can be cultured in the product to a level necessary to provide a challenge of at least 1×10^7 then their physiological state and size characteristics will be the same as in the process stream. If it is necessary to grow the challenge organisms in other than product, it still may be possible to allow them to equilibrate for several doubling times in the product solution so that they will still have the same physiological and size characteristics as organisms cultured in product.

The size of the test organisms is obviously important. It is, therefore, necessary to demonstrate that the bioburden organisms are of appropriate size. That the organisms challenging the test membrane, whose pores are 0.2/0.22 μm-rated, are neither individually too large nor in aggregated form are assured by their passage through a 0.45 μm-rated filter.

It is also necessary to culture the organisms as a monodispersed suspension in numbers adequate to challenge the test and control filters without the complications of filter cake buildup, such as may impose their particle retentions on the operation. Filters of large enough areas are obviously required to meet the challenge stipulation of 1×10^7 (or greater) colony-forming units (cfu)/cm^2 of EFA. In the ideal, no pore would escape challenge, and none would be confronted by more than one microbe. The numbers of pores constituting a filter is, in any case, not known. But even if the numbers of pores and organisms could be matched, the laws of probability via the Poisson distribution (Juran 1974) show that an attempt to lay down an average of two microbes per square micrometer of area will result in 15% of the squares being vacant while another 15% will contain three or more organisms (Johnston and Meltzer 1979).

Culturing

The challenge organisms can be obtained by introducing their sample into a proper volume of nutrient medium for the period of time suitable for their growth, to the point where they can be counted. The suitability of the growth medium must match the requirements of the particular microbial type(s); these may differ significantly for the various microbes. There is no growth medium that will serve all organism types. As said above, certain types are viable but not culturable. Their presence cannot be assessed by this technique. As already stated, it is only live organisms that can be cultivated to the point where they can be counted. Dead or living organisms that will not develop on the selected growth medium will escape detection. Therefore, of the various types of microbes that may be present, only those for which a suitable growth medium is available can be tested for. The inability to detect an organism type other than the organisms of interest reveals nothing concerning their presence or absence. The count of zero has significance only for the identifiable organisms. The sterility of the effluent is judged only as regards that particular organism type.

Bacteria Challenge Test

The choice of suspending fluid is important. If possible, the best choice is to suspend the challenge organisms in the product solution. The method is cited by the 2004 FDA Aseptic Processing Guidance as being preferred. However, in many cases, this is not possible, generally because the product is antagonistic to the challenge organism.

Before performing a product bacteria challenge test, it has to be assured that the liquid product does not have any detrimental, bactericidal, or bacteriostatic effects on the challenge organisms, commonly *Brevundimonas diminuta*, being suspended in it. This is necessitated because the microbial assaying is by the counting of live organisms. The assessment is done utilizing viability tests. The product is considered non-bactericidal, if, over the exposure time the viable organism count decreases by less than or equal to 1 log. The organism is inoculated into the product to be filtered at a certain bioburden level. At specified times, defined by the actual filtration process, the log value of this bioburden is tested. If the bioburden is reduced due to antagonistic fluid properties, different bacteria challenge test modes become applicable.

Filtration conditions (i.e., time, throughput, volume per unit filtration area, differential pressure, pressure cycling, flow rate, hydraulic shock) used for validation experiments should mimic, to the extent possible, "worst-case" processing conditions. These are the situations wherein the possibilities of removing organisms are minimal. "Worst case" processing conditions include high pressure, longer filtration time, and greatest volume filtered, and may include other parameters. When considering filtration conditions, as with the suspending fluid, concessions may be required in order to ensure challenge organism viability.

There are three bacteria challenge methods designed to confront the filter with the live organisms. They are described within the PDA Technical Report No. 26: higher organism challenges, placebo (modified product) challenge, and product recirculation through the filter followed by an organism challenge after recirculation. If the mortality rate is low, the challenge test will be performed with a proportionally higher bioburden, designed to permit the challenge level to decline to, but not below, $10^7/cm^2$ by the end of the processing time. In some cases, it is possible to modify the product (i.e., removal of preservative or other bactericidal component) to allow for the survival of the organisms in a product surrogate. If the mortality rate is too high, the common definition of which is >1 log during processing time, a placebo is fashioned by removing the toxic substance, or by modifying the filtration conditions, or product properties to the point where the challenge organisms are not adversely affected. Examples of possible modifications are pH, temperature, etc. If the organism can survive in the product for a period less than the entire filtration time, it may also be possible to shorten the exposure of the challenge organism. This could be accomplished by adding the challenge organisms after the product has been circulated through the test and control filters for a portion of the recirculation time.

In some cases, the only option left may be to circulate the product solution through the product filters for the processing time under "worst case" conditions, rinse the test and control filters, and challenge the filters with the challenge organism suspended in saline-lactose broth. However, this would not assess the effect of the product on the challenge organisms. In addition, the interplay of the organisms, product solution, and the filter would remain unexamined. Although this method is not to be preferred, it still provides an indication of what can be expected from the filter's performance during product sterilization.

Afterwards the filter is flushed extensively with water, and the challenge test, as described in ASTM F838-38, is performed. The rinse is followed by the bacterial challenge in saline lactose broth or other non-bactericidal carrier.

During filter validation studies, the entire filtrate must be assayed for the presence of the challenge organism. This is generally accomplished by a second assay filter placed in-line downstream of the test and control filters. This raises anew the question of whether 0.2/0.22- or 0.45 µm-rated membranes are the more suitable as assay filters. Originally, the rated pore size used was 0.45 µm. The 0.2/0.22 µm-rated size came to be used by some because it was thought more likely to retain smaller entities more reliably. Present practices, based on several if equivocal studies, sanction the use of either pore size rating.

Filtration conditions, i.e., high differential pressures, longer filtration times, and throughputs, i.e., greater volume filtered, along with volume per unit filtration area, flow rate, hydraulic shock, and pulsation studies used for validation experiments should mimic, to the extent possible, "worst-case" processing conditions. These are the situations wherein the possibilities of removing the organisms are minimal. "Worst case" processing conditions may include other parameters. When considering filtration conditions, as also the composition of the suspending fluid, concessions may be required in order to ensure a proper organism challenge.

Sampling

The proper management of the sampling technique is itself an important subject deserving of a full but separate discussion. The size of the effluent sample or the number of samples that are analyzed should be large enough to offset the heterogeneity that is typical of suspensions, and to yield a count of some reliability to be made. The suspended organisms will over time adsorb to the surfaces of the sample container regardless of its material of construction. The resulting cfu counts will be diminished thereby. If the analysis is not to be performed promptly, refrigerated storage may be utilized to prevent or minimize organism growth to the point where die-off or growth alters the original numbers.

The size of an organism changes as it develops through its growth stages during its cultivation. Typically, the growth curve for most organisms placed in a new environment extends through three phases. During the first or lag phase the organism adjusts to its new surroundings. There is an increase in the individual cell size before there is an increase in numbers. In the second or exponential growth or log phase, attached cells begin to divide, and a logarithmic increase in cells occurs. The cell numbers increase more rapidly than does the cell mass. Thus, the cell numbers are increasing, but the size of the individual cells is decreasing. This results from the decreasing food supply, and the accumulation of toxic waste products. There follows the third or maximum stationary phase wherein the number of new cells equals the number that are dying. In the later stages of this phase there are increasing amounts of dead organisms and cell debris. The early stages of the stationary phase are, therefore, better for the detection of the live organisms. Where the exponential growth curve enters the stationary phase, the early beginning of the growth curve, is where the exponential growth curve enters the stationary phase, the early beginning of the growth curve, is where the organism selection is best made.

Organism Counting

The organisms in the sample can be detected and/or counted in a number of ways. A liquid portion can be added to a suitable growth medium in liquid form. Following incubation at a temperature and for a time proper for the organism type of interest, the presence of organisms will be made apparent by a clouding of the mixture. When the selected assay involves the isolation of the sample's organisms by filtration, the filter cum organisms are placed on a nutrient medium for appropriately cultivation by incubation for the correct time and temperature. This technique requires samples large enough to furnish enough organisms for an accurate count to be made. The count should be from 20 to 100 cfu. The number is considered accurate, to plus or minus one-half log by some, while others set the limits as plus or minus one log. A cfu reading of 20 would by the latter reckoning represent a value from 0 to 100 or 150 cfu. To attain a confidence level of 95% some 22 samples would be needed. When records are kept of successive assays, the trending of the data over time impart to the results a significance that single readings do not have. Nevertheless, in individual tests the cfu counts of 20 or less are usually treated as if they were reliable in their quantification. Thus, assays reading zero organisms are, in effect, taken to signify sterility.

"Sterilizing Grade" Membrane

If the microbiological assay indicates that none of the challenging organisms escaped capture by the filter, it is designated as being a sterilizing filter. Actually, this conclusion is too general in its assumptions. That the filter performed as desired under given circumstances does not ensure that it will necessarily act similarly with other types of organisms, or even with the same organism under different filtration conditions. The earlier belief that sterility resulted exclusively from the particles being too large to negotiate the filter's pores proved simplistic. Each filtration is an individual expression of several factors whose balanced influences govern the outcome of the organism/filter interaction.

"Sterilizing grade" filters are characterized by a bacteria challenge test carried out by the filter manufacturer. This test is performed under strict parameters using a specified growth medium, etc. (ASTM F838–83). This filter manufacturers' organism testing defines the "sterilizing filter" in terms of its integrity test value correlating with a sufficiency of organism retention, namely, 10^7 cfu/cm^2 of EFA. This qualifies it for use in actual process filtrations. However, "sterilizing grade" filters are not necessarily capable of yielding sterilized product under all circumstances. The process parameters, fluid properties, the polymeric structure of the filter, and the nature of the bioburden will influence the outcome. Consequently, FDA requires validation, documented experimental evidence that the "sterilizing grade" filter does indeed yield a sterile effluent when conducted within stipulated process parameters with the actual drug product and actual bioburden (Jornitz 2002).

Need for Process Validation

A filter characterized as qualifying for the "sterilizing grade" designation bestowed upon 0.2/0.22 μm-rated membranes, as just discussed, may not fulfill that role in an actual processing operation. There are many reasons why this should be, given the numerous influences that impact the attainment of sterile effluent. For example, if the test organisms known to be smaller than *B. diminuta*, a tighter filter may be indicated (Kawamura et al., 2000). There are also several other reasons for requiring product bacteria challenge testing. First of all, the influence of the product and process parameters on the viability of the microorganism has to be determined. There may be cases of shrinkage in the size of the organisms due to a higher osmolarity of the product, or to prolonged processing times, or to starvation due to the extremely low assimilable carbon content of the suspending fluid. Second, the filter's compatibility with the product and process parameters has to be tested; it should not be assumed. The filter should not show any sign of degradation due to the product. Additionally, assurance is required that the filter will withstand the process parameters, especially the applied differential pressure. For example, pressure pulses, as from filling machines, should not influence the organisms' retention.

It should be remembered that there are two main separation mechanisms involved in liquid filtrations, namely, sieve retention and adsorptive sequestration. In sieve retention, when the smallest particle or organism is retained even by the largest pore within the membrane structure, the contaminant will be removed regardless of the process parameters. This would be the ideal situation of an absolute filtration. Retention by adsorptive sequestration, however, depends on the filtration conditions. Contaminating organisms smaller than the actual pore size can penetrate the filter, but may be retained by adsorptive attachments to the pore surfaces. This effect is enhanced by using highly adsorptive polymers for filter materials, for example, glass fiber as a prefilter, or polyamide as a membrane in protein processing. Certain liquid properties can, however, minimize adsorptive effects. Borderline compatibilities may enlarge pores, and the fluid's physiochemical properties may alter organism shapes and sizes. Any of these several situations may result in the penetration of the filter by organisms. Whether the fluid has properties that will lower the occurrence of adsorptive sequestration, and possibly allow penetration has to be evaluated using the specific product and specified conditions in the bacteria challenge tests.

Sterilization of Filters

To produce sterile effluent, it seems self-evident that the filter should itself be in a sterilized condition prior to its use. Pre-use sterilization of the sterilizing filter ensures that the filter medium is itself sterile and will not introduce organisms into the process stream. Filters are often sterilized prior to use, either by in-line steamed-in-place (SIP), or by steam autoclaving followed by aseptic installation.

Filters may also be sterilized by gamma irradiation. Less frequently, they may be sterilized using ethylene oxide. It is important that the filter membrane and support material remain undamaged under the conditions employed for sterilization (PDA Technical Report 26). Validation is necessitated for any method of sterilization that is utilized.

With regard to moist heat sterilizations, such as by steam, thermocouples and thermal-resistant biological indicators (BIs) are used. Generally, *Geobacillus stearothermophilus* spores are employed for the validation experiments. Empty-chamber runs are performed to identify and map the slowest-to-heat locations in the autoclave. If the filter is SIP, care must be taken to eliminate any opportunity for condensate to collect and for areas of entrapped air to be present in the lines or in the filter housings. The presence of water limits the temperature to 100°C, the equilibrium point of water in its liquid and vapor states. Unlike steam, entrapped air cannot impart a heat of condensation to the process. It could, on the contrary, act as an insulator. Heat penetration studies should be conducted to identify the slowest-to-heat locations even in the piping; these studies should also include the monitoring of any location that may be prone to collect condensate. During BI studies, the thermocouples and BIs are placed in the previously determined slowest-to-heat locations during the moist heat sterilization validation. These can provide evidence that the desired temperature was attained even at the sites most likely to be at lower temperatures. If possible, spores can be inoculated directly onto the filter and the filter placed in microbiological culture medium to investigate whether the filter membrane is sterile. Inactivation of the heat-resistant spores and adequate heat penetration attest to the sterilization of the filter by the process sterilization cycle.

The radiation dose necessary for sterilization may be calculated using the bioburden present on the filters to be sterilized according to (ANSI/AAMI/ISO 11137, 2006) criteria. Radiation exposure is measured using dosimetry. Biological indicators and/or dosimeters are placed in locations throughout the carrier including sites that are "difficult to penetrate." Following exposure the dosimeters and indicators are removed and examined to determine the adequacy of exposure throughout the carriers.

That a particular filter can serve as a sterilizing filter is established by confronting it with a meaningful organism challenge. The microbiological assessment of whether any of the challenge organisms escaped capture is made by examining the effluent for their presence. The FDA has defined a proper challenge as one that confronts every square centimeter of the EFA with 1×10^7 cfu of *Brevundimonas diminuta* ATCC-19146.

Ingredient and Product Adsorption

Filter and filtration validations may also address concerns that are independent of the matter of sterility, but that are important to the filtration process nonetheless. A particularly unwelcome tendency on the part of filters, depending upon their porosity and its disposition as pores of various lengths, widths, and tortuosities, is the volume of product they retain following the termination of a filtration. This can be an economic concern especially when expensive biopharmaceuticals are being processed. This volume of liquid can be freed from the pores by applied pressures larger than the bubble points of the several pores. However, the recovered liquid should be segregated from the filtered product. It may contain organisms released by the filter under the impetus of the pressure used in expelling the liquid. If not inappropriate, it should be combined and processed with the next batch of product of similar composition.

It was earlier stated that electrical charge phenomena were involved in the adsorptive interactions between filters and particles, such as organisms, suspended in the liquid vehicles. Likewise, the filters in response to exactly the same type of electrical forces can adsorb molecules from the solutions they process. As a result, the filter medium may adsorb and remove some amounts of certain components of the drug preparation undergoing filtration. Indeed, the active drug ingredient may itself be affected. This could result in some portion of the product batch containing a diminished level of active drug. Some filter polymers are more inclined to specific adsorptions than are others. Perhaps more pointedly, the molecular structure of certain ingredients containing charged or partially charged atoms will more avidly bond with the drug molecules that are categorized by their own partial charges.

Validation of the filter medium intended to filtratively sterilize a drug product, therefore, includes testing to determine whether the active ingredient is adsorbed by the filter medium. Generally, this is accomplished by passing the drug product solution, with its known concentration of the active ingredient(s), through the selected filter. The filtered material is then assayed for the level of active component present in the filtrate. A decreased level of active ingredient in the filtrate is indicative of the ingredient being adsorbed by the filter medium. Depending upon their polymeric nature, filter membranes can, in addition to active ingredients, adsorb, for example, preservatives such as benzalkonium chloride or chlorhexadine during a filtration of a product containing them. Likewise, the nonspecific adsorption of proteins by filters is an important matter. It is customary for testing of this type to be performed using some three-filter samples, each from a different lot of filters.

Often, the filter will become quenched, that is, the adsorptive sites on the filter surface will presumably become saturated, and the adsorptive removal of the ingredient will slow and ultimately cease. Testing should be performed to determine whether this does indeed occur after some volume has been filtered. If this is the case, then studies can be used to determine the volume of the filtrate to be discarded prior to filling the remaining portion of the product batch.

Such adsorptive losses from the product formulation can be slowed or avoided by saturating the membrane with the preservative, or with serum albumin in advance of the filtration. Preservative loss, particularly when the packaged product in repeatedly revisited in multiuse applications such as with contact lens solutions, can be dangerous. Long-term use and the possibilities for organism growth in the absence of sufficient preservative can be a serious matter (Udani 1978; Chiori et al. 1965).

Similarly, problematical would be the adsorptive removal of proteins from a biological solution. To ascertain the correct dosage of a protein preparation undergoing filtration, adsorption studies may have to be performed to define the most suitable filter in terms of its polymeric identity, and construction. In addition, determining the prerinsing procedure, and flow conditions necessary to its use should be included. Any yield losses caused by nonspecific adsorptions can be costly with respect to lost product and its market value. Adsorption studies can be helpful in optimizing downstream processes with regard to yield loss. Yield losses may also impact upon capacity problems, which are existent within the biotech industry. Yield losses have a detrimental influence. Most commonly, such losses can also be attributed to nonspecific adsorptions caused by the wrong choice of membrane polymer. Proteins adsorb avidly to filters composed of nitrocellulose, including the mixed cellulose esters, probably by hydrogen bonding. They adsorb strongly also to filters composed of polyamide polymers. It is understood that proteins undergo hydrophobic adsorptions. These are peculiar to filters of nonpolar polymeric structures; thus, the low adsorption of proteins exhibited by the cellulose acetate filters.

Particulate Matter

Particulates are critical in sterile filtration, specifically of injectables. The USP (United States Pharmacopeia) and BP (British Pharmacopoeia) quote specific limits of particulate-level contaminations of defined particle sizes. These limits, being regulatory requirements, must be met. Therefore, particle release from sterilizing grade filters necessitates measurement. Filters are routinely tested. Particle enumeration is performed with laser particle counters. Such tests are also performed on the actual product to prove that the filtration step, especially under process conditions, did not result in an increased level of particulates within the filtrate. Specific pre-use flushing protocols, if necessary, can be established for the filters being used, to flush out loose particulate debris. The flushes, singly or repetitive, whether by water, alcohol, or some other suitable liquid would be defined in terms of volume and rate of flow. Each flush would be followed by a particle count on the filter effluent to determine whether the particles still being shed had attained an acceptable level. These tests are also applicable to prefilters to reduce the possibility of particulate contamination generated within the process steps. USP standards for large-volume parenterals (LVPs) stipulate they are not to contain more than five particles/mL of sizes greater than 25 μm, and not more than 50/mL 10 μm or larger. This equates to 50,000 of 10 μm or larger, and 5,000 of 25 μm or larger per liter. In addition, no visible particles (haze) are permitted (USP 27). For small-volume parenterals (SVPs) intended for intravenous and certain other injections, the particulate level is confined to one-fifth the LVP limit on a dosage basis, regardless of its volume. This amounts to 10,000 particles of 10 μm or larger, and 1,000 of 25 μm or larger per dose. LVPs are preparations delivered through the skin in volumes larger than 100 and up to 1,000 mL. They include irrigation solutions and parenteral dialysis fluids which may be used in 1.5–2 L quantities. Also, included are flexible pouches for blood collection to which 5 mL anticoagulant have been added under LVP-operating conditions. SVPs are preparations below 100 mL in quantity. They are often administered in a piggyback arrangement by way of the LVP delivery set.

Filter Integrity Testing

So obvious are the outcomes of filtration exercises dependence upon the integrity of the filters that are employed, that calling attention to their integrity testing requirements seems superfluous. Post-use integrity testing of product sterilizing filters is a regulatory requirement. It represents the proof of the pudding, as it were. Its application and proper performance is indispensable to the entire picture of sterilizing filtrations. Pre-use, post-sterilization integrity testing of sterilizing filters is strongly urged by both the regulations and the regulators. The pre-use, post- sterilization demonstrates that the filter is properly installed and that the filter was not damaged during the sterilization process. However, its manual performance necessitates an invasion of the filter train downstream of the filter. This presents an important risk to the system's asepsis. Neglecting this particular testing represents a business risk to the drug preparer, but not a physiological risk to any drug recipient, because a compromised filter will be discovered after the batch is processed. Reworking or discarding the processed batch will then be required. Clearly, the integrity testing of sterilizing filters prior to use, but after installation, obliges that the testing method not involve breaking the sterile line downstream of the filter. If this cannot be accomplished, then pre-use integrity testing should not be performed and a risk assessment for not performing the test be developed. This can be managed by use of an automated integrity test machine; such performs the testing from the upstream side of the filter.

REFERENCES

Agalloco, J.P. (1998). Guest editorial: It just doesn't matter, *PDA J. Pharm. Sci. Technol.* 52(4): 149–150.
AAMI/ISO 11137-1:2006/(R)2015 & A1:2013 Sterilization of health care products.
Aranha, H. (2004). *'How To' Guide: Viral Clearance Strategies for Biopharmaceutical Safety.* D and MD Publications, Westborough, MA.
Bowman, F.W., Calhoun, M.P., and White, M. (1967). Microbiological methods for quality control of membrane filters, *J. Pharm. Sci.* 56(2): 222–225.
Chiori, C.O., Hambleton, R., and Rigby, G.J. (1965). Inhibition of spores of *B. Subtilis* by cetrimide retained on washed membrane filters, *J. Appl. Bacteriol.* 28: 122–330.
FDA (1985). *Guideline on General Principles of Process Validation.* Center for Drugs and Biologicals and Office of Regulatory Affairs, (1985). Food and Drug Administration, Rockville, MD.

Gabler, R. (1978). *Electrical Interactions in Molecular Biophysics*. Academic Press, New York.

Geesey, G.G. (1987). Survival of microorganisms in low nutrient waters. In Geesey, G.G. and Mittelman, M.W. (Eds) *Biological Fouling In Industrial Water Systems—A Problem Solving Approach*. Water Micro Associates, Long Beach, CA, pp. 103–122.

Gould, M.J., Dawson, M.A., and Novitsky, T.J. (1993). Evaluation of microbial/endotoxin contamination using the LAL test, *Ultrapure Water 10*(6): 43–47.

Johnston, P.R. and Meltzer, T.H. (1979). Comments on organism challenge levels in sterilizing-filter efficiency testing, *Pharm. Technol. 3*(11): 66–70, 110.

Jornitz, M.W. (2002). *Filters and Filtration, Pharmaceutical Encyclopedia*. Marcel Dekker, New York.

Juran, J.M., Ed. (1974). *Quality Control Handbook*, 3rd. ed. McGraw-Hill, New York, pp. 22–29; App. 2, p. 2.

Kawamura, K., Jornitz, M.W., and Meltzer, T.H. (2000). Absolute or sterilising grade filtration—What is required? *J. Pharm. Sci. Technol. 54*(6): 485–492.

Leahy, T.J. and Sullivan, M.J. (1978). Validation of bacterial retention capabilities of membrane filters, *Pharm. Technol. 2*(11): 64–75.

Leo F.M., Auriemma, M., Ball, P., and Sundaram, S. (1997). Application of 0.1 Micron Filtration for Enhanced Sterility Assurance on Pharmaceutical Filling Operations. *BFS News*. p. 15–24. (A publication of the Pall Corporation.)

Lukaszewicz, R.C. and Meltzer, T.H. (1980). On the structural compatibilities of membrane filters, *J. Parenter. Drug Assoc. 34*(6): 463–472.

Meltzer, T.H. and Jornitz, M.W. (2006). *Pharmaceutical Filtration: The Management of Organism Removal*. PDA/DHI Publishing, Parenteral Drug Association, Bethesda, MD.

Meltzer, T.H., Jornitz, M.W., and Trotter, A.M. (1998). Application-directed selection 0.1 μm or 0.2 μm rated sterilizing filters, *Pharm. Technol. 22*(9): 116–122.

Mouwen, H.C. and Meltzer, T.H. (1993). Sterlizing filters; pore-size distribution and the $1 \times 10^7/\ cm^2$ challenge, *Pharm. Technol. 17*(7): 28–35.

PDA Technical Report No. 26 (2008). Sterilizing filtration of liquids, *PDA J. Pharm. Sci. Technol.* Supplement; Vol. 52; Number S1.

Reif, O.W. (1998). Chapter 8: Filtration in the biopharmaceutical industry. In Meltzer, T.H. and Jornitz, M.W. (Eds) *Extractables and Compatibilities of Filters*. Marcel Dekker, New York.

Reif, O.W., Solkner, P., and Rupp, J. (1996). Analysis and evaluation of filter cartridge extractables for validation in pharmaceutical parantheses processing, *J. Pharm. Sci. Technol. 50*(6): 399–410.

Stone, T.E., Goel, V., and Leszczak, J. (1994). Methodology for analysis of filter extractables: VA model stream approach, *Pharm. Technol. 18*(10): 116–130.

Sundaram, S. (December 7, 1999). Retention of diminutive water-borne bacteria by microporous membrane filters, *Presented at PDA National Meeting*, Washington, DC.

Udani, G.G. (1978). Adsorption of Preservatives by Membrane Filters During Filter Sterilizations, Thesis for B.Sc. Honours (Pharmacy), School of Pharmacy, Brighton Polytechnic, Brighton, UK.

Zahka, J.G. and Grant, D.C. (December 1991). Predicting the performance efficiency of membrane filters in process liquids based on their pore-size ratings, *Microcontaminants 9*(12): 23–29.

13

Extractables and Leachables Evaluations for Filters

Raymond H. Colton and Denise G. Bestwick
Validation Resources, LLC

CONTENTS

Introduction

Sterile filtration is one example of a process using a polymeric component for which extractables and leachables are a concern. Ideally, sterile filtration removes unwanted particles and bacteria while allowing the formulation to remain unadulterated. Although hundreds of liters of pharmaceutical formulation may be filtered through just a few square meters of filtration area, the effect of leachables cannot be underestimated due to the intimate interaction of the formulation with the polymer. While the filtration area may be small, the surfaces that experience product contact are several thousand times larger due to the pore structure of the polymeric filter materials. In Figure 13.1, the top surface is the reported filter surface area. However, the solution contact surface also includes the surfaces of the porous "sponge" structures within the filter. Leachables may also come from filter housings, membrane support layers, O-rings, or any other polymeric components of the filter. Identifying and quantifying these contaminants can be an analytical, albeit necessary, challenge. The necessity is more apparent in the final steps of downstream processing, where impurities may have a greater effect on the product.

The evaluation of filters for leachables and extractables is both a regulatory requirement and an appropriate safety concern. A filter incompatibility may be identified by leachable and extractable testing even when other filter validation methods, such as bacterial challenge testing, show acceptable results.

Regardless of whether driven by regulatory or safety concerns, it is the responsibility of the drug manufacturer, not the filter vendor, to show a filter is compatible with the manufacturing process stream and does not add levels of contaminants that could alter the safety, identity strength, quality, or purity of the drug product.

Definitions

The terms extractables and leachables are often used interchangeably within the literature and regulatory guidances. However, in recent years, there has been an effort to standardize the terminology to differentiate leachables from extractables.

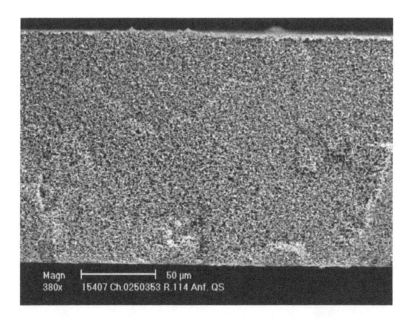

FIGURE 13.1 Cross-section of a polyethersulfone 0.2 mm filter. (Courtesy of Sartorius AG.)

Extractables

Extractables are defined as compounds that have the potential to be removed from a contact material by use of exaggerated extraction conditions. Extractables are usually detected by extracting a material with multiple solvents of varying polarity at elevated temperature. The temperature should be sufficient to enhance the migration of compounds out of the materials but not so high as to cause the material to become unstable, that is, it should not approach the glass transition point in the case of a polymer.

Leachables

Leachables are compounds that actually do migrate out of a contact material into the actual pharmaceutical formulation during normal use conditions with respect to key operating parameters including but not limited to time, temperature, pH, and any filter preparation steps such as sterilization and rinsing. Leachables are typically a subset of extractables.

Sources of Extractables and Leachables in Filters

Extractables and leachables can come from any material, for example, plastic, glass, or metal. However, they are most often associated with the use of elastomers and plastics. The evaluation of extractables and leachables has been well established in the pharmaceutical field when considering the use of plastics and rubber stoppers in container-closures as indicated by the guidance published in 1999 by the FDA for container closure systems (CDER, 1999). The discussion of extractables and leachables in pharmaceutical processing materials such as filters has become more acute as single-use disposable materials have become more common.

Polymer-based plastic materials would be difficult to process and unstable without the use of additives. Most polymeric additives are not covalently bonded to the polymer.

Therefore, they can migrate from the polymer to a contacting solution. Their actual migration depends on the nature of the contacting solution and the conditions during contact. Fortunately, most pharmaceutical formulations are aqueous-based and most polymers and their additives are, by nature, organic and hydrophobic. Consequently, polymeric components and additives do not readily migrate into water-based pharmaceutical formulations.

That does not mean polymeric additives cannot leach into an aqueous pharmaceutical formulation. While water for injection (WFI) may not be expected to leach very much out of a hydrophobic polymer, pharmaceutical formulations can have significantly different properties from WFI. One example of this is the use of solubilizing agents such as surfactants, which enhance the solubility of a pharmaceutical product. Biopharmaceuticals typically have more organic ingredients with the potential to leach compounds out of plastics.

Antioxidants

Plastics made of polymers that contain C–H, C–OH, or C O bonds are subject to oxidation. This is observed daily in the burning of fossil fuels to create energy. As a result, most pure polymers quickly degrade through oxidation. Polymers without these bonds, such as polytetrafluoroethylene, are the most resistant to oxidation. To reduce oxidation, polymers require the use of antioxidants. The most common type are phenolic antioxidants such as 2,4 di-t-butylphenol and hindered phenolics such as found in the Irgonox, Ethanox, and Lowinox product lines. The phenolic rings of the antioxidants capture free radicals before the free radicals oxidize the polymer that would cause additional polymer breakage.

Lubricants

Polymer additives can include internal lubricants (to lubricate the polymer chains during processing) and external lubricants (to lubricate interface between the polymer and the processing equipment during processing). Examples of lubricants are silicone and fatty acids such as stearic acid.

Oligomers and Monomers

Oligomers and monomers of the base polymer can be the result of incomplete polymerization or they can be the degradation product of oxidation of the fully formed polymer.

Plasticizers

Plasticizers, a common additive in polymers such as polyvinylchloride, to enhance flexibility are not common in filters. However, compounds such as di-2-ethylhexylphthalate are known to be associated with extractables from polyolefins (Jenke et al., 2005).

Wetting Agents

Wetting agents are compounds more common to filters than to other disposable polymeric components used in pharmaceutical processing. Many of the filter materials such as polyvinylidine fluoride and polyethersulfone are naturally hydrophobic. In order to make the filter hydrophilic, wetting agents are added during the manufacturing process. Wetting agents include polyvinyl pyrrolidone, polyethylene glycol, and polyacrylates. They can be coated, impregnated, or covalently bonded so as to make the filter surfaces hydrophilic.

Regulatory Requirements

The regulations, globally, for many pursuits lack clarity regarding the specific requirements. Industry must interpret to the best of their ability the actions needed to meet regulatory mandates. The interpretation and implementation activities are similar to solving a puzzle. The requirement to perform extractables and leachables testing on processing materials (including filters) is a perfect example of this puzzle. A few of the extractable/leachable puzzle pieces can be found in published guidances yet even these lack details and specifics needed to develop effective filter extractable/leachable validation programs. The best guidance truly comes from published papers and conferences sponsored by various organizations. With real-life examples, industry can find guidance to develop and implement filter extractable/leachable validation programs.

Under U.S. FDA regulations, there is no doubt filter users must validate filters for extractables and leachables. While FDA regulations and guidances lack clarity for the specific requirements of extractables and leachables testing, FDA Warning Letters (readily accessible on the FDA's website) demonstrate FDA's expectation on the evaluation of filters for extractables and leachables (FDA).

FDA Warning Letter dated August 16, 2005 (following inspection of a pharmaceutical manufacturing facility in Switzerland):

> …Further, it is unclear to us whether you have conducted filter extractable and leachable testing with product. If you have this data, provide it to us. If not, let us know when you will be able to provide it to us…

FDA Warning Letter dated September 30, 2005 (following inspection of a facility engaged in manufacturing sterile ophthalmic solutions):

> …You have failed to validate the [redacted] membrane filter used for filter sterilization for compatibility, *extractables* and microbial retention.

The Center for Drug Evaluation and Research (CDER) published an industry guidance in November 1994 referencing the requirement of extractables evaluation as part of process validation in applications for human drug products: the Guidance for Industry for the Submission Documentation for Sterilization Process Validation in Applications for Human and Veterinary Drug Products (CDER, 1994) states:

> The specific bulk drug product solution filtration processes, including tandem filter units, prefilters, and bacterial retentive filters, should be described. Any effects of the filter on the product

formulation should be described (e.g., adsorption of preservatives or active drug substance, or extractables).

This guidance describes the requirement for scientifically valid methods performed at conditions "fully representative and descriptive of the procedures and conditions proposed for manufacture of the product."

Similarly, FDA's pharmaceutical good manufacturing Practices (GMPs) mandate that materials used in the production of pharmaceutical products be compatible with the drug products (*Code of Federal Regulations, Food and Drugs* Title 21, Part 211.65). Title 21 of the Code of Federal Regulations (CFR) Part 211.65 states:

> Equipment shall be constructed so that surfaces that contact components, in-process materials, or drug products shall not be reactive, additive, or absorptive so as to alter the safety, identity, strength, quality, or purity of the drug product beyond the official or other established requirements.

The requirement for evaluation of extractables and leachables moved industry to begin its quest for clarity and definition in the early 1990s. Most of the early focus was on final container/closure systems but processing materials were also being considered. The Division of Manufacturing and Product Quality at CDER published a Human Drug cGMP notes memo in September 1994 containing policy questions and answers (Human Drug cGMP Notes, 1994). One of the policy questions was specifically: "Does a manufacturer need to test each drug product for filter extractables?" While the answer was "no" the discussion in the answer stated:

> This does not mean that the drug manufacturer does not need to have information concerning filter extractables. They must have data showing the identity, quantity and toxicity of the extractables. They should also have the methods and solvent systems used to obtain the amount of extractables per filter.

Since September 1994, the industry and regulating agencies have discussed, reviewed, examined, and clarified the expectations for extractables and leachables testing. As mentioned earlier in this chapter, even the respective definitions have evolved over time. At this time, there are no specific guidances for extractables and leachables but industry associations are collaborating with regulating agencies to define the standards of practice for this field of inquiry.

CDER published a Guidance for Industry entitled Container Closure Systems for Packaging Human Drugs and Biologics in May 1999 (CDER, 1999). This guidance, while not specifically addressing processing equipment, gives an indication of the types of drug products that the FDA considers to be the highest risk for extractables. In this guidance, the FDA classifies drug products on the basis of the risk of administration route (e.g., injectables, topical, oral) and on the level of intimate contact (solutions, aerosols, powders). A drug that is to be administered as an injectable or inhalant will have the highest level of regulatory concern. Oral or topical drugs will have lower concern. With regard to extractables testing, it states:

> When feasible, the preferred solvent (for extractables testing) would be the drug product or a placebo vehicle.

The Parenteral Drug Association (PDA) published Technical Report 26 "Sterilization Filtration of Liquids" to guide users with the selection and validation of sterilizing-grade filters (PDA, 1998). Section 4.4 of the report addresses extractables and specifies:

> It is the user's responsibility to demonstrate that the product does not contain objectionable levels of extractables from the filter.
> The filter user is responsible for obtaining extractable data for the drug product formulation.

Outside of U.S. regulations, Health Canada also speaks to the filter requirements in a Draft Guidance for Industry (Draft Guidance for Industry, 2001). In the section "Process Validation," it states:

> Filters used should be validated with respect to pore size, compatibility with the product, absence of extractables and lack of adsorption of the drug substance or any of the components.

The Canadian regulatory basis again comes from the GMPs. Part C, Division 2, in the Equipment section, C.02.005, states:

> The equipment with which a lot or batch of a drug is fabricated, packaged/labeled or tested shall be designed, constructed, maintained, operated and arranged in a manner that
>
> a. *permits the effective cleaning of its surfaces;*
> b. *prevents the contamination of the drug and the addition of extraneous material to the drug; and*
> c. *permits it to function in accordance with its intended use.*

The pharmaceutical industry in Europe faces the same challenging puzzle when it comes to finding clear guidance on filter validation for extractables and leachables. In the rules governing medicinal products (in the European Union), Volume 4 titled Good Manufacturing Practices, Chapter 3, paragraph 3.39 has a statement very similar to that in U.S. FDA and Canadian Food and Drug regulations:

> Production equipment should not present any hazard to the products. The parts of the production equipment that come into contact with the product must not be reactive, additive or absorptive to such an extent that it will affect the quality of the product and thus present any hazard.

As is the case in the United States, the European Union has better defined requirements related to packaging materials (final container/closure systems) and some guidance can be found by reviewing these documents. In 2004, the European Agency for the Evaluation of Medicinal Products (EMEA) published the Guideline on Plastic Primary Packaging Materials (EMEA, 2004). This guideline used in conjunction with several Committee for Proprietary Medicinal Products (CPMP) guidelines provides some basis for extractables/leachables testing (e.g., Notes for Guidance on Development Pharmaceutics (CPMP/QWP/155/96); Stability Testing: Stability Testing of New Drug Substances and Products (CPMP/ICH/2736/99) (Revision of CPMP/ICH/380/95); and Stability Testing: Stability Testing of Existing Active Substances and Related Finished Products (CPMP/QWP/122/02)) for European regulated products.

Clearly, filter users are required to validate their filters for extractables and leachables. It is the user's responsibility to develop and implement programs to meet this requirement. It is recommended that the user include key stakeholders in the planning and implementation process. Being familiar with the FDA's Pharmaceutical Quality Initiative as defined in its Pharmaceutical Quality Assessment System (PQAS) (CDER, 2004; FDA, 2004) is key to developing and implementing an acceptable filter validation program. Incorporating the concepts included therein can lead to a scientifically sound program allowing for increased process and product understanding. Quality by design can be a natural consequence if programs such as filter validation are addressed early in the product lifecycle. Regulating bodies have shown flexibility in how extractables/leachables can be addressed as long as sound scientific principles and innovative problem solving are used. In the end, users who clearly have an overarching goal of better understanding their process and product will likely have the most success.

Developing an Extractable and Leachable Program

Often a process uses many filters including feed stock filters, particulate filters, cross-flow (also referred to as tangential flow) cassettes along with the final sterile filters. It can be a daunting job to decide where to focus on extractable program and create a strategy to effectively implement and meet regulatory and safety requirements.

Product Lifecycle

It is suggested to start early in the product lifecycle. If extractable/leachable results are obtained which present safety and possibly efficacy issues then alternate filters can be considered and evaluated early in the development process. Alternate filters may need to be considered for possible changes later in the development cycle. Other factors in the drug development process may lead to necessary changes in filter types. Having options available could save time in fast-paced development programs.

Create a Team

It is important to identify key stakeholders in the filter validation program. Create a dedicated team of scientists, quality Assurance, validation specialists, etc., to plan and implement the program.

Filter Risk Assessment

Evaluate the particular regulatory and safety risks of process filters using a risk assessment approach. Consider different criteria that are appropriate to the application. Key risk factors to consider are the following:

1. *Drug Dosage Form*: The safety risk of a drug depends on the route of administration and the size of the dosage. Routes that allow a drug to pass into the blood stream more easily will be subjected to more scrutiny with regard to impurities. In general, the FDA Guidance on Container Closures (CDER, 1999) indicates the level of concern is:

   Inhaled Drugs > Parenteral Drugs and Ophthalmic Drugs > Topically Applied Drugs > Oral Drugs.

   In addition, the dosage of the drug will be factored into the regulatory and safety concern. A drug product that is administered in large quantities on a regular basis will have higher concern than a drug product that is only occasionally administered in a small quantity.

2. *Location of the Filter in the Process*: The closer a filter is to the finished product, the higher the safety and regulatory concern. The final sterile filtration will have the highest concern because any leachables will be contained in the final product. Filters further upstream will be less of a concern. Process steps that allow for impurities to be removed will lower the concern. An example is the use of cross-flow filters for diafiltration to remove known impurities. Often the diafiltration volume is many times larger than the retained fraction that gives solubilized leachables an opportunity to be flushed from the system. However, one should be prepared to address whether the leachables would rather partition into the retained portion because of the chemical nature of the drug product.

3. *Composition of Filtration Stream*: Since filters are usually made of organic polymers, process streams with high organic content tend to enhance leaching. A process stream that is organic or contains high proportions of an alcohol such as ethanol will be more of a safety and regulatory concern.

4. *Contact Time*: While filters generally have fairly short contact time compared to final container/closures or in-process storage materials, some filters may be used for several days as in the case of a blow/fill/seal operation. Longer contact time will generate a higher level of leachables.

5. *Processing Conditions*: High temperatures and pH extremes can potentially increase the level of leachables and lead to higher safety and regulatory concern. Contact time, i.e., processing time, plays a role in the opportunity of polymeric attack or leachable extraction.

6. *Pretreatment Steps*: Filters are often pretreated prior to use. Typical pretreatments are steam sterilization, gamma irradiation, and rinsing.

   a. *Gamma Irradiation*: Increases extractables and leachables. Organic materials can be degraded when exposed to gamma irradiation. The degradation continues over any storage time. Therefore, the shelf life for gamma-sterilized goods must be established.

   b. *Steam Sterilization*: Neutral affect on extractables and leachables. The high temperature during steam sterilization may bring extractables/leachables to the surface of the polymer. However, volatile extractables/leachables may be removed by steam sterilization.

   c. *Rinsing*: Decreases extractables and leachables. Rinsing, either with water or with product, is an effective method to reduce the level of extractables/leachables in a product.

A published example of the risk assessment approach can be found in the December 2002 BioPharm publication. Priority is established by assigning numerical risks to each of the categories to achieve a ranking of filters with the highest degree of concern (Bennen et al., 2002).

Obtain Information from Filter Manufacturers

Extractable data generated by filter manufacturers may prove helpful in planning the extractables/leachables program. This data may identify process parameters and those filters with more propensity to add leachables under the process conditions to the product stream. Additionally, it is important to obtain verification of the materials of construction from filter manufacturers, especially within different sizes of the same filter. Due to the design of many extractable/leachable tests, it may be necessary to perform the test with smaller filters than those used in the process. This also facilitates detection because the extractables/leachables are concentrated in the smaller volume of extractant used with the smaller filters.

A capsule should not be substituted for a cartridge because, while the filter material and support structures may be the same for each filter, the filter housing material changes the relative ratio of the materials of construction leading to differing levels of extractables/leachables and possibly even new extractables/leachables if the filter housing introduces a new material.

Results of the risk assessment and the information obtained from the filter manufacturers can be used to create a list of filters requiring validation.

Possibility of Grouping Filters

It is important to consider multiple manufacturing processes at one facility as well as redundancy within one manufacturing process. This allows for the development of grouping strategies. Efficiencies can be incorporated into the program if the same filters are used for similar process streams. Dependent upon the validation strategy employed by the organization, it may be possible to validate one type of filter used for the same type of media or process stream in multiple manufacturing processes.

Grouping Strategy Examples:

1. If the same filter type is used on five different concentrations of NaCl buffer then only the low and high concentration could be tested.
2. If different sizes of the same filter are used for the same process stream, then only one size is tested as long as the materials of construction are identical for the different sizes.
3. If the same product is filtered by the same filter in multiple filtration steps but each step uses different temperatures and contact times then testing the highest temperature and longest time could be acceptable.

The grouping strategy concept can possibly provide advantage by reducing the number of extractables/leachables studies. However, it is important to carefully review the materials of construction and obtain assurance from the filter manufacturer indicating this to be true.

As the extractable program is developed, the type of testing to be performed must be determined. Generally, extractables testing is done early in the program, before leachables testing. In some cases, it may be sufficient to do only one or the other. This decision would typically be based on the risk assessment and information obtained from the manufacturer.

Extractable Tests

The goal of extractables testing is to facilitate the extraction of as many compounds as possible under relatively extreme conditions. The goal is not to break down the polymer into individual components to the point of the polymer losing its integrity. Rather, the goal is to subject the polymer to "vigorous" conditions to maximize the number of compounds that can migrate out of the polymer.

Choice of Extractables Solvents

For filters, the extractions are normally performed with at least two solvents. The choice of solvents is dictated by:

1. the intended use of the filter and
2. the materials of construction of the filter.

For filters that are used in aqueous-based systems, the use of high purity water (e.g., WFI) and a low molecular weight alcohol such as ethanol or isopropyl alcohol (IPA) are appropriate.

For filters that are used with organic solutions, extraction with an organic solvent such as hexane is recommended along with a low molecular weight alcohol.

Another consideration is to choose a solvent with properties that make identification easier.

1. Solvents should be easy to work with for identification. For example, octanol is effective at extracting organics from polymers. However, due to certain chemical characteristics of octanol, it is difficult to concentrate the extractables found in the octanol using standard techniques such as evaporation and solid phase extraction.
2. Solvents without significant impurities should be chosen for a cleaner analysis.

Extraction Methods

The extraction of a filter can be performed by one of several methods.

1. Soak with (dynamic) or without (static) agitation. In this case, the filter can be submerged in (if it is a cartridge) or filled with (if a capsule) the chosen extraction solvent(s). Agitation can be achieved by shaking the filter with the extraction solution.
2. Recirculation. The extraction solvent can be recirculated through a filter. This will enhance the extraction because the flow causes a forced convection that minimizes the formation of a concentration gradient that can slow the migration of the extractables.

The effect of extraction technique on the rate and level of extractables obtained was studied in the following experiment.

1. *Extraction Technique Experiment*: Three identical filter capsules were extracted with IPA at room temperature for 48 h. Two were filled and placed on separate shakers with the ends plugged with glass stoppers. The third filter had IPA recirculated using a dual headed peristaltic pump. The control sample for the filters on the shakers was IPA in a glass flask. The control for the recirculation extraction was the second head of the peristaltic pump with tubing and flask but without the filter. The schematic diagram of each test is shown in Figures 13.2 and 13.3.

   Samples were taken from the shaken filter capsules, the shaken controls, and the solvent flasks of the recirculation extraction and control over a 48-h period. The samples were analyzed by reversed phase-high performance liquid chromatography (RP-HPLC). The level of the extractables was estimated by summing the peak areas of all the extractable peaks.

   The extractable peak areas versus time are shown in Figure 13.4. After 8 h, the filter capsule shaken at 180 rpm had a higher level of extractables than the filter capsule shaken at 120 rpm. After 24 and 48 h, there was negligible difference between the two shaken filters.
2. *Extraction Technique Experiment Results and Conclusion*: The filter capsule extracted using recirculation showed lower levels of extractables through the 48 h. This can be explained because the volume of IPA necessary to fill the capsule, tubing, and solvent flask was about double that required to fill the shaken capsule filters. It would be expected the mass of extractables removed from the filter would be higher than using recirculation because of the constant replacement of

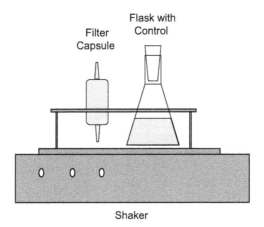

FIGURE 13.2   Schematic diagram of extractable test with shaking.

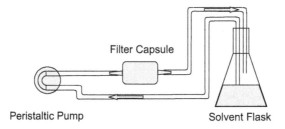

FIGURE 13.3   Schematic diagram of extractable test using recirculation.

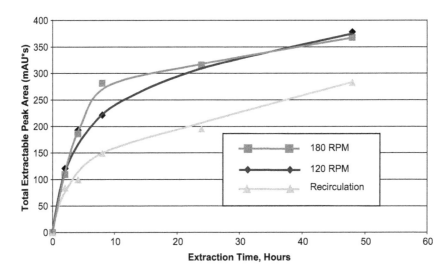

FIGURE 13.4   HPLC-UV peak area of extractables during a 48-h extraction for shaken filter at 120 and 180 rpm compared to recirculation.

solvent in the pores of the filter. This is true if the difference in volume is accounted for when comparing the sum of the peak areas. However, the detected concentration of the extractables as indicated by the total peak area is lower for the recirculation because the larger volume dilutes the extracted compounds.

This experiment demonstrated shaking is an acceptable extraction technique. It is vigorous enough to promote extractables in a relatively short period of time. Shaking may actually facilitate increased detection due to the lower volume required.

Leachable Tests

The goal of leachables testing is to determine what migrates out of the filter into the pharmaceutical formulation when exposed to process conditions that are typical or that test the extreme limits of acceptable conditions. Since leachables are typically a subset of extractables, some filter users perform only leachable tests. Whenever possible, the leachable tests should be performed with the same filter as is used in the process.

The conditions for leachables testing are determined by the maximum acceptable range of the process conditions. The test conditions are then chosen based on worst-case conditions. Table 13.1 shows how this might be done.

Test parameters and extraction conditions:

1. *Filter Size*: In the example shown in Table 13.1, the manufacturing process uses three 30-in. filters. It is acceptable to test with one 10-in. filter if the materials of construction can be verified to be equivalent in the two sizes. The filter manufacturer can usually provide a letter to this effect upon request.

2. *Filtration/Extraction Product Volume*: If the filter is used to process 2,000 L, it is considered advantageous for the extraction to be performed with a substantially smaller volume because the concentration of leachables will be higher with a smaller volume and therefore easier to detect and identify. The process volume and extraction volume cannot be directly compared because the process uses a 30-in. filter and the extraction will be performed with a 10-in. filter. To normalize the difference in filter surface areas, it is necessary to determine the ratio of the extraction volume to the surface area. In this case, testing a 10-in. filter in only 2 L of formulation leads to a volume/surface area ratio approximately 100 that of the process.

3. *Rinsing*: As mentioned previously, rinsing generally decreases the level of leachables. The rinsing volume should be no more than is used for the process after adjusting for the size of the filter. To make rinsing "worst-case," the rinsing step can be eliminated or, the rinsing volume can be significantly less than that used for the process. In this case, 2 L of rinse is used for a 10-in. filter compared to 20 L for three 30-in. filters.

4. *Sterilization*: The sterilization step performed in the leachables study should be comparable to the sterilization step used in the process. This is especially true for filters that have been gamma irradiated.

TABLE 13.1

Comparison of Process Conditions to Leachables Test Conditions

	Process Conditions	**Test Conditions**
Filter part number	Part number for 30-in. filter	Part number for 10-in. filter
Filter area	3 filters × 2.1 m^2 = 6.3 m^2	0.7 m^2
Product name	API name	API name
Filtration/extraction product volume	2,000 L	≤ 2 L
Product volume/surface area	2,000 L/6.3 m^2 = 320 L/m^2	2 L/0.7 m^2 = 2.9 L/m^2
Rinsing	20 L WFI	2 L WFI
Sterilization	125°C, 30 min	126° ± 1°C, 30 min
Contact time	Up to 4 h	At least 4 h
Temperature range	15°C–30°C	30°C ± 5°C

5. *Time*: The length of an extraction should generally be at least as long as the total contact time in the process.

6. *Temperature*: The extraction temperature should be close to the maximum temperature of the process filtration step. It may be acceptable to do an accelerated test at an elevated temperature. However, an accelerated test is subject to validation of the temperature/time correlation.

As with extractables testing, leachables testing can be performed with soaking (static or dynamic) or with recirculation. The control is a sample of the pharmaceutical formulation exposed to the same test conditions as the filter but with no filter contact. For a static or dynamic extraction, the control can be placed in a glass flask sealed with a ground glass stopper (use of rubber stoppers should be avoided). For a recirculation extraction, the control is the exact same recirculation system, ideally operated simultaneous to the filter recirculation. A dual-head peristaltic pump is well suited for this.

It is not usually necessary to test three lots of filters for leachables. While there can be lot-to-lot variation in the concentration of the individual leachables, it is rare for the number or identity of extractables/leachables to vary between lots. Still, there is no harm in testing three lots and it should be a consideration during the risk assessment phase.

Analytical Methodology

Extractables and leachables from filters are generally present at concentrations below 10 ppm and often below 1 ppm. At these low levels, sensitive analytical techniques must be used. In the case of leachables, the formulation components (active pharmaceutical, buffers, and other additives) are present in much greater concentrations than the leachables, thereby increasing the analytical challenges. A publication by Reif et al. (1996) presents the techniques for which extractables analysis from filters is based. In the referenced study, extractions were performed on eight types of filters, methodology was discussed and extractables were identified.

The analytical techniques can be either specific or nonspecific. Specific analytical techniques can separate the individual components of the samples. These include liquid and gas chromatography equipped with various detectors (e.g., ultraviolet-visible diode array, mass spectrometer, flame ionization, etc.). Nonspecific techniques look at the bulk solution. These include techniques such as total organic carbon (TOC) measurements, nonvolatile residue (NVR) measurements and Fourier- transform infrared (FTIR) spectroscopy.

Specific Analytical Techniques

Specific analytical techniques such as high performance liquid chromatography (HPLC) and gas chromatography-mass spectrometry (GC-MS) are the standards for extractable and leachable testing. Both techniques allow for separation of the sample components which is necessary for identification. For leachable testing, specific analytical techniques are necessary to separate the leachables from the components of the formulation. FTIR can be used successfully to facilitate identification of an extractable or leachable once the compound has been separated (isolated) and concentrated from the total sample.

No single analytical technique is capable of detecting all possible extractables and leachables. For this reason, a combination of two analytical techniques is recommended. The use of two techniques is supported in the ICH Q2(R1) guidance (Validation of Analytical Procedures, 2005) on analytical methods. While it is not the goal of this chapter to review analytical chemistry techniques in detail, a brief overview is provided. Most extractables and leachables analyses involve HPLC with UV detection, HPLC with MS detection, and GC-MS. Table 13.2 summarizes the advantages and limitations of the most common analytical techniques.

NonSpecific Analytical Techniques

Nonspecific tests such as TOC and NVR can give an indication of the total level of extractables in mass or concentration (Table 13.3).

TABLE 13.2

Specific Analytical Techniques for Extractables and Leachables Analysis

Method	Description	Advantages	Limitations
HPLC with UV detection	Compounds are injected into a chromatography column that separates based on polarity of molecule	• High sensitivity ~0.05 ppm • Able to detect wide range of molecular sizes	• Cannot detect molecules without a UV chromaphore such as saturated hydrocarbons
GC-MS	Sample is evaporated and injected into a chromatography column that separates based on polarity, molecular size, and vapor pressure	• High sensitivity ~0.1 ppm • Can detect non-UV active molecules • MS fragments are basis for identification	• Compounds must be at least semivolatile and thermally stable
LC-MS	An HPLC with mass spectrometer detector in place or in conjunction with a UV detector	• High sensitivity ~0.05 ppm • Can detect non-UV active molecules • Able to detect wide range of molecular sizes • MS fragments are basis for the identification	• Not all molecules can be ionized
FTIR	Infrared energy is passed through a purified compound. Absorbance pattern indicates the presence of specific chemical moieties	• FTIR of a pure compound can be matched with commercial databases to provide identification of compounds	• Minimal capability to analyze mixtures • Limited sensitivity • Can be helpful to identify extractables when used in conjunction with fractionation by HPLC

TABLE 13.3

Nonspecific Techniques for Extractables and Leachables Analysis

Method	Description	Advantages	Limitations
NVR	The extraction solvent is evaporated and the residual mass is weighed. NVR is described in USP <661> (2017) where sample is evaporated at 105°C	• Gives total mass of nonvolatile extractables • Relatively simple technique	• Any extractables that have significant vapor pressure at the boiling point of the solvent will be evaporated and therefore not measured accurately • Volatile compounds are ignored • Cannot be used with formulations that have significant nonvolatile components such as buffers • Thermally unstable compounds may be degraded
TOC	Inorganic carbon is purged and then organic carbon is oxidized to form carbon dioxide which is measured	• Measures concentration of carbon-based extractables	• Cannot be used with formulations or solvents with significant organic content
pH	• Measurement of pH before and after extraction	• For non-buffered solutions, a change in pH can indicate an extractable	• Does not indicate reason for pH change

Other Analytical Techniques

1. *Headspace GC*: The sample is heated in a closed system and volatile compounds in the sample are vaporized. Headspace-GC is able to detect residual solvents and volatile extractables.

2. *Inductively Coupled Plasma*: Mass Spectrometry (ICP-MS): Twenty or more metals can be analyzed. Metals are most often a concern when additives that contain metals such as fillers and colorants are used.

Identification of Extractables and Leachables

It is recommended to identify and quantitate detected extractables and leachables. LC-MS and GC-MS form the basis for identification because the retention times and mass fragments are usually correlated to an individual extractable/leachable. There are commercial databases to aid in identification with GC-MS. Individual laboratories will typically generate internal databases of commonly found extractables and leachables not found in the commercial databases.

The mass fragments from LC-MS and LC-MS-MS are also used to identify leachables and extractables although there are no commercial databases available. A qualified laboratory, however, can interpret the spectra to facilitate identification. Identification of HPLC peaks can also be accomplished by isolating the peak, concentrating it and then analyzing by GC-MS and FTIR. There are commercial databases containing over 200,000 FTIR and GC-MS spectra.

Ideally, once an extractable/leachable is identified, the compound is procured and the identity confirmed by comparing the mass spectra and retention times using LC-MS or GC-MS. With this information, the confidence of the identity is absolute.

Finally, it is not always possible to positively identify some extractables and leachables. This can occur when the unknown extractable/leachable is an oligomer or series of oligomers for which the precise molecular weight cannot be determined. Or, it may be a degradation product of an additive for which there is not a database match and for which a standard cannot be purchased. In such cases, in accordance with Impurities in New Drug Substance (2006), it is acceptable to show the efforts that have been made to identify the compound. When absolute identification is not possible, a general chemical classification can be made (e.g., siloxane, aliphatic acid).

Quantitation of Extractables and Leachables

If the identity of an extractable or leachable is confirmed by comparison to a procured reference standard, then the quantity in the filter extraction sample can easily be determined. A quantitation method should be validated according to the ICH Q2(R1) guidelines (Validation of Analytical Procedures, 2005). Alternatively, the quantity can be estimated by bracketing multiple injections of the filter extract with multiple injections of the same solution spiked with the identified extractable at high and low concentration. Appropriate statistics can be used to show that the concentration of the compound in the filter extract is bracketed by the high and low concentration standards.

If the compound cannot be procured, the identified leachable can be quantitated using a compound of similar chemical structure and/or character that will produce a similar peak response in the specific analysis method. For instance, an extractable/leachable that is an oligomer, can be quantified with the base monomer. Or, a degradation product of a phenolic antioxidant might be quantified with the antioxidant itself. It is important to scientifically justify any chemical substitutions made for quantitation.

FTIR of NVR

The analysis of the NVR from a filter extraction using FTIR has been discussed in the literature (Weitzmann, 1997a, b; Stone, 1994) as a way to both quantitate and identify extractables/leachables. The user is cautioned about this method because of limits to the scientific relevance.

1. Only analyzing NVR eliminates all volatile and many or most semivolatile extractables depending on the boiling point of the extraction solvent which can be as high as 187°C for propylene glycol.
2. FTIR can only distinguish the major nonvolatile components from the remaining mixture and only with limited certainty.
3. Components present in lower concentrations may not be detected at all.

FTIR is a powerful technique when used to analyze pure samples as discussed earlier. However, it has clear limitations when analyzing mixtures.

Example of HPLC Analysis of a Leachable Test Sample

Figure 13.5a and b show the HPLC chromatograms of the blank control (pharmaceutical formulation without filter) and the filter extract. In Figure 13.5a, there is a large product peak between 1 and 3 min and a small product peak at 34 min. In the filter extract (Figure 13.5b), the same two product peaks are detected. A unique peak at 18 min is also detected. The 18-min peak is related to a leachable from the filter.

It is possible for a filter leachable to elute within the first few minutes of the chromatographic analysis where the large product peak elutes. Since the chromatographic column used in this example does not retain hydrophilic compounds chemically, many product-related peaks elute rapidly and within the column void volume. The void volume is defined as the volume of mobile phase required to carry an unretained component through the HPLC system. Since most filter leachables are at least somewhat hydrophobic, it is not likely that a leachable will elute before or within the first product-related peak. The second product-related 34 min is sufficiently small whereby a co-eluting leachable would be detectable either due to a larger, broader peak, or a shoulder on the peak.

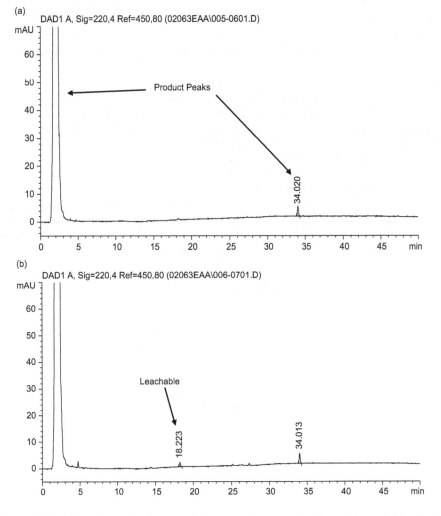

FIGURE 13.5 (a) HPLC with UV detection of a blank control from an actual formulation and (b) HPLC with UV detection of a filter extract from the same formulation.

Eliminating Analytical Interference in Leachables Testing

Most extractable solvents are chosen because they have minimal or at least predictable analytical interference. However, many pharmaceutical formulations used in leachables testing have compounds that can interfere with analytical techniques such as HPLC and GC-MS. Examples of compounds that cause analytical interference are proteins, surfactants, amino acids, and molecules that contain unsaturated carbon bonds. It is recommended to analytically prescreen suspect process streams in order to determine which may have irresolvable analytical interference. Once determined, alternative testing options for these specific process streams can be evaluated and determined. Since the alternatives may require more time to perform it is best to know this as early in the validation program as possible.

Technical Report 26 (PDA, 1998) also addresses the complications of detecting leachables in the presence of the components of the pharmaceutical formulation by stating:

> When the product formulation precludes the use of standard analytical methodology, a suitable model may be used to measure the levels of extractables.

It is possible to predict which process streams may produce analytical interference based on the chemical structure. Figure 13.6a shows the structure of histidine, a chemical which produces significant UV interference when analyzed by HPLC-UV. Figure 13.6b shows the structure of Triton X-100, a surfactant that produces significant UV interference even at fairly low concentrations. In both examples, the UV interference is caused by the presence of the ring structures.

There are several options to resolve problems with analytical interference. First, one can design the analytical method to separate potentially interfering compounds. For example, a reversed-phase HPLC method can be designed to allow the hydrophilic formulation components to pass through the HPLC column unimpeded while the column retains the leachables that have a more organic nature. This is an acceptable direction because most filter leachables are not hydrophilic.

Second, by using more than one analytical technique it is more likely a leachable will be detected. By using complementary methods such as HPLC and GC-MS the interfering compounds in one instrument may not interfere the same way in the other instrument.

Third, the interfering compound may be removed using a sample preparation technique. Standard techniques to remove the interfering compounds are solid phase extraction (SPE), liquid–liquid extraction (LLE), and size exclusion chromatography.

When preparing a sample to remove analytical interference, the method used must be qualified each time it is used. This can be accomplished by spiking the pharmaceutical formulation with compounds that are known to extract from the material being tested. The method is qualified if all of the spiked compounds are sufficiently recovered after sample preparation.

Example of Analytical Interference Removal

Histidine

Use of SPE demonstrates the removal of analytical interference from the histidine sample. SPE uses a column prepacked with silica beads that are treated with an organic layer with an 18 carbon chain length.

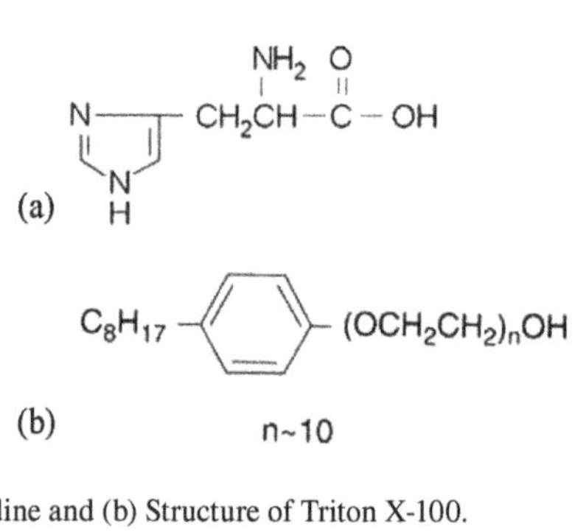

FIGURE 13.6   (a) Structure of histidine and (b) Structure of Triton X-100.

After the column is conditioned with water and methanol, a sample of the pharmaceutical formulation is pulled through the column with mild vacuum. The leachables adhere to the hydrophobic column while the more hydrophilic product passes through the column unimpeded. The leachables are then eluted with a solvent such as methanol, acetonitrile, or methylene chloride.

Figure 13.7a and b show an example of an aqueous solution containing 2.5% histidine. Figure 13.7a shows the direct injection analysis using RP-HPLC with UV detection. In the first 12 min, it is not possible to detect leachables because of the analytical interference. Figure 13.7b shows the formulation spiked with known potential leachables and the analytical interference removed using SPE.

Alternatives to Standard Leachables Testing

There are situations when it is not possible to test with the actual formulation. In these cases, it is wise to use the best available science to choose an alternative test method.

Cases where testing with the formulation cannot be done include:

1. Formulations which cause irresolvable analytical interference;
2. Formulations that are cytotoxic;
3. Formulations that are prohibitively expensive.

(a)

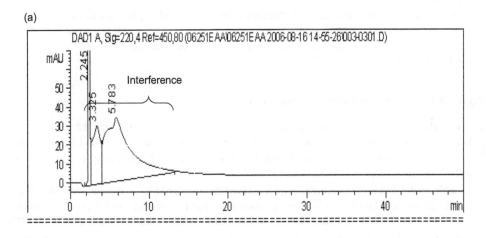

(b)

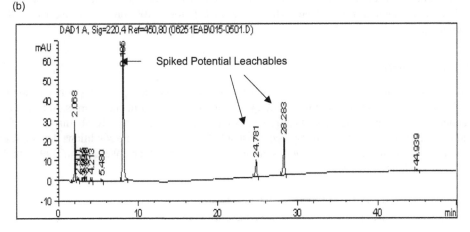

FIGURE 13.7 (a) HPLC-UV of histidine formulation and (b) HPLC-UV of histidine formulation with interference removed by SPE.

In these cases, it is often acceptable to modify the actual formulation slightly and allow for successful analysis. For example, removal of a cytotoxic compound that is present at a low concentration will likely have minimal effect on the potential of the formulation to leach organic compounds from the polymer. This is especially true if other ingredients in the formulation dominate the potential to extract leachables. The same approach may be used for formulations that are prohibitively expensive.

There are certain formulations that lead to irresolvable analytical interference or negatively alter the analytical performance of the instruments thereby making the results unreliable. An example of a common additive often used as a solubilizing agent in pharmaceutical formulations is Triton X-100. Triton X-100 (Figure 13.6b) is a surfactant with an eight-carbon alkyl chain (saturated hydrocarbon), a phenyl group (aromatic-ring), 10 unit polyoxyethylene chain (multiple ethyl esters), and a hydroxyl group. The combination of oliophilic (oil loving) groups and hydrophilic (water loving) groups make it ideal to keep drugs or biopharmaceutical ingredients that have limited water solubility in solution. The same properties that make Triton X-100 useful for solubilizing drugs also make it effective at solubilizing leachables from polymers. In addition, sample preparation steps such as SPE and LLE retain the Triton X-100 along with the leachables. Figure 13.8a shows an HPLC chromatogram of a 20% aqueous solution of Triton X-100. The analytical interference is dramatic and in this specific example, ruined the HPLC column and contaminated the entire HPLC system. Figure 13.8b shows the HPLC chromatogram for 0.1% (1,000 ppm) Triton X-100. There is substantial interference from 13 to 17 min. There is still significant interference at 0.01% (100 ppm) as shown in Figure 13.8c. Only when the concentration is reduced to 0.001% (10 ppm) is the analytical interference reduced to negligible as shown in Figure 13.8d.

When there is irresolvable analytical interference there are several approaches to meeting the leachables testing requirement. One approach is to substitute or mimic the interfering compound. A second approach is to use data from extractables modeling studies of the filter and estimate the correlation to the actual formulation.

Example of the Mimic/Substitute Approach

1. If the interference is restricted to a narrow range as in the case demonstrated by 0.1% Triton X-100 (Figure 13.8b), the leachable test with the actual formulation can still be performed knowing that a narrow range (4 out of 50 min) cannot be used to detect leachables. The remaining 46 min are unobstructed and therefore useful.
2. To address the 4 min of interference, a second extraction would be performed with the Triton X-100 substituted. The Triton X-100 concentration would be removed or lowered and another compound substituted as a mimic that has similar properties. In this case, ethanol or IPA would be substituted. To make it worst-case, the concentration of the mimic can be higher than the compound it is replacing. To mimic 0.1% Triton X-100, one might use 1% or 10% ethanol.

Modeling Leachables

A second approach to address leachables when the actual formulation precludes standard analytical techniques is to use existing extraction data that is provided by the filter manufacturers. In lieu of testing with actual product, some filter manufacturers have data from a variety of solvents that are performed at conditions more typically found in a process instead of the more extreme conditions that are used for standard extractables testing. This method is discussed in detail by others (Weitzmann, 1997a, b; Stone, 1994). Modeling follows these steps:

1. identify the significant constituents to be modeled;
2. examine the functional groups in each constituent;
3. assign each constituent or functional group within a constituent to a solvent group; and
4. apply data from the representative solvents to the worst case for each group.

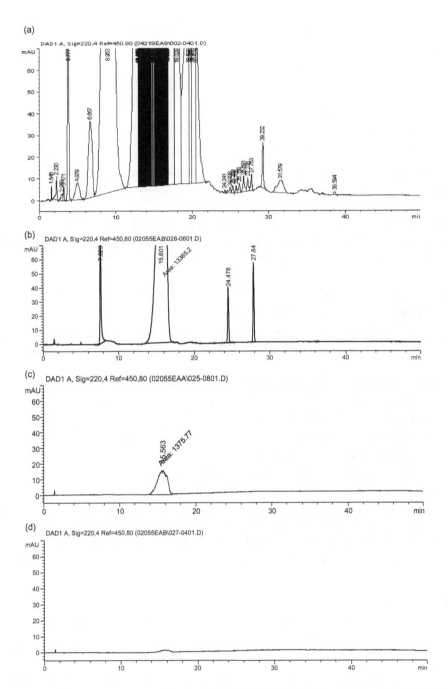

FIGURE 13.8 (a) HPLC-UV of 20% Triton X-100, (b) HPLC-UV of 0.1% (1,000 ppm) Triton X-100, (c) HPLC-UV of 0.01% (100 ppm) Triton X-100, and (d) HPLC-UV of 0.001% (10 ppm) Triton X-100.

Typical solvents and functional groups are suggested to be (Weitzmann, 1997a):

1. water (for groups such as cresols, fluoroalkanols);
2. ethanol (for aliphatic alcohols);
3. dimethylforamide (for amide, glycol ethers);
4. propylene glycol (for glycols);

5. methylene chloride (for methylene chloride and ethylene chloride);
6. 2-ethoxyethanol (for polyethers and dioxane);
7. acetone (for aliphatic esters and ketones).

One advantage of modeling is that the performance of leachables testing is usually not required because it relies on a database of extractions. Another consideration is there is historic record to modeling being accepted by the regulatory bodies.

Disadvantages of modeling include:

1. There is no scientific correlation between the model solvents and the actual drug formulation.
2. Use of solvents such as 100% ethanol, dimethyl foramide, and methylene chloride can lead to overprediction of the leachables.
3. The tested filter may not be the same configuration as the actual process filter.
4. Modeling is often used as a substitute to actual product testing even when standard analytical methods do not preclude the use of the actual product.

Extractables and Leachables Summary

In summary, start early in the product lifecycle to develop the filter validation program which includes extractables/leachables testing. Consider the following steps to create a successful program:

1. include critical stakeholders in the planning and implementation process;
2. perform a filter risk assessment;
3. obtain extractable data from manufacturers;
4. obtain verification of materials of construction from filter manufacturers;
5. determine which filters require validation;
6. do a grouping analysis to possibly reduce the number of tests;
7. understand the chemical nature of the process streams being validated;
8. consider prescreening process streams to find irresolvable analytical interferences so alternative testing can be decided and addressed early;
9. perform extractable and/or leachable testing using suitable analytical techniques;
10. identify and quantitate detected leachables.

REFERENCES

Bennen J, Bing F, Boone H, et al. Evaluation of extractables from product-contact surfaces. BioPharm International 2002 15(2): 22–34.
CDER Publication: Guidance for Industry for Container Closure Systems for Packaging Human Drugs and Biologics, May 1999.
CDER Publication: Guidance for Industry for the Submission Documentation for Sterilization Process Validation in Applications for Human and Veterinary Drug Products, November 1994a.
Draft Guidance for Industry, Quality (Chemistry and Manufacturing) Guidance: New Drug Submissions (NDSs) and Abbreviated New Drug Submissions (ANDSs), Section P3.5 Process Validation and/or Evaluation, p. 35, July 18, 2001.
EMEA, Guideline on Plastic Primary Packaging Materials, 2004.
FDA Warning Letters can be obtained through the Freedom of Information Act via the FDA website: http://www.fda.gov/foi/warning.htm, 2004.
Human Drug cGMP Notes, Division of Manufacturing and Product Quality, HFD-320, Office of Compliance, CDER, Volume 2, Number 3, September 1994b.
Impurities in New Drug Substance Q3A(R2) International Harmonized Tripartate Guideline, October 25, 2006.

Jenke D, Swanson S, Edgcomb E, Couch T, Chacko M, Carber MJ, and Fang L. Strategy for assessing the leachables impact of a material change made in a container/closure system. PDA J Pharm Sci Technol 2005 59: 360–380.

Office of New Drug Chemistry's New Risk-Based Pharmaceutical Quality Assessment System, CDER, September 29, 2004.

PDA. PDA Journal of Pharmaceutical Science and Technology, Technical Report No. 26, "Sterilizing Filtration of Liquids," 1998, Supplement, Volume 52, Number S1.

Reif OW, Soelkner P, and Rupp J. Analysis and evaluation of filter cartridge extractables for validation in pharmaceutical downstream processing. PDA J Pharm Sci Technol 1996 50: 399–410.

Stone TE. Methodology for analysis of filter extractables: a model stream approach. Pharm Tech 1994: 116–130.

USP. 2017. <661> Plastic Packaging Systems and Their Materials of Construction, The United States Pharmacopeial Convention, 12601 Twinbrook Parkway, Rockville, MD.

Validation of Analytical Procedures: Text and Methodology Q2(R1). ICH International Harmonized Tripartate Guideline, Incorporated November 2005.

Weitzmann CJ. The use of model solvents for evaluating extractables from filters used to process pharmaceutical products, part 1—practical considerations. Pharm Tech 1997a: 44–60.

Weitzmann CJ. The use of model solvents for evaluating extractables from filters used to process pharmaceutical products, part 2—assigning a model solvent. Pharm Tech 1997b: 72–99.

14

Media and Buffer Filtration Requirements

Maik W. Jornitz
G-CON Manufacturing, Inc.

CONTENTS

Introduction

Filtration applications are expanding and with the expansion, new filter designs and filtration purposes are evolving. Filter systems are not any longer standardized and limited to a tight filter-type portfolio but broadened with new requirements and needs by emerging applications. As such, filter designs experienced optimization, which met the specific process parameters required within specific applications. Two major applications, which differ greatly from each other, will be described within this chapter. The specifics and design needs of these two applications will be explained. Media filtration, one of the two, commonly focuses on a filter design which creates the highest total throughput and lowest fouling, influenced by unspecific adsorption. Buffer filtration with low fouling or blocking potentials is commonly high-flow applications. The processing of buffer batches needs to be fast and efficient, the design of the filtration system is very different than the one used in media filtration.

Potential parameters which determine specific design criteria are:

- Flow rate
- Total throughput
- Unspecific adsorption
- Retention rating
- Thermal and mechanical robustness
- Chemical compatibility
- Extractable/leachables

- Hold-up volume
- Disposability

All criteria have been considered and sterilizing grade filters evolved to high performance, high-tech products meeting biopharmaceutical and regulatory requirements. New welding and membrane treatment technologies reduced the extractable/leachable content greatly. Wetting agents formerly used are not required any longer due to enhanced membrane surface treatments. New polymeric developments and membrane structures created the possibilities of higher thermal and mechanical resistance. Support fleeces which sandwich the membrane formed a higher stability. Fleece choices and developments, as well as membrane enhancements resulted in improved flow rates and total throughputs. Comparing some of the performance data of 20 years ago, filter cartridges of high flow rate designs reach 5 times higher flow rates than its former counterparts. Total throughput increases reached a 3–4 times higher level both within the same dimensional structure. All these improvements were needed to be able to fulfill a growing stringency by specific applications. Furthermore, it produced the opportunity for the end user to optimize their processes and cut down costs or enhance production yields (Soelkner and Rupp, 1998; Jornitz et al., 2002, 2003, 2005; Cardona and Inseal, 2006).

Media Filtration

Application Considerations

Growth media are widely used in the biotech industry, for example, for microbiological tests, cell culture and fermentation processes or media fill runs. The major volume use for media is within cell culture and fermentation processes, which will be the focus of this writing. Growth media of the past were commonly standardized and animal derived. Since cell lines become more and more specialized, the media followed suit and nowadays over 70% of the media used are special media, which are developed for a specific cell lines and cell culture processes. These recipes are highly guarded secrets as the media is a major component to determine cell density, expression rate, performance, and downstream processing activities. Any change within the recipe of a specialty media can potentially influence the drug product outcome, yield, or volatility. This also means that filtration devices used within such specific media filtration applications should not be influential in regard to the media composition, i.e., neither adsorb a particular component to the membrane nor leach extractable into the media. Appropriate tests have to be performed to determine whether such possibility exists with the device and membrane polymer used. Process validation work is a key element to establish whether or not a filter fulfills the required performance parameters set. Such validation work starts with the media supplier and the filtration steps within their production processes and ends with an end user validation to manifest the filter performance in the end users' environment.

The incidences of transmissible spongiform encephalitis (TSE) caused the industry to take precautionary measurements, especially tracing the raw material back to the origin of the source, its region and potential for transmissible diseases. Still with pooling, batch to batch quality variations and difficulties of traceability, the media users started switching to plant-derived media (plant peptones). This switch caused another problem, which has become a widely discussed issue, mycoplasma contamination of the cell culture media. Mycoplasma contaminations are on the rise and require attention, as studies have found that not only the working, but also master cell banks are affected. Mycoplasma contaminants are difficult to detect, it takes a considerable amount of time, and challenging to remove such. Most commonly 0.1 micron-rated filters are used to remove a potential mycoplasma contamination; however, it is not and will not be the "silver bullet," i.e., process validation of the particular separation process is essential to assure retentive effectiveness. The advice is probably to use a multistep removal/inactivation process to be best-assured the contamination is eliminated. A Parenteral Drug Association (PDA) task force worked on multifaceted solution of these issues, which include novel detection methodologies, inactivation steps, and removal by filtration, including a microbial challenge standard for 0.1 micron filtration steps. The individual task force groups published comprehensive technical reports of their designated working group. These reports are a valuable tool of how to avoid or handle a potential mycoplasma contamination.

The other disadvantage of plant-derived media is the growth or expression rate, which might not be as effective as with animal-derived media. For this reason, growth promoters are added, for example, insulin or insulin-like growth factor (IGF) (Yandell et al., 2004). The growth promoters play an essential role and are a critical component of the media used. Therefore, any unspecific adsorption of the IGF on the membrane polymer would be detrimental to the media's quality and the cell culture growth. Once more the filter choice by testing for such unspecific adsorption is of importance.

Specific Requirements

Media are available in a large variety from different raw material sources and of different compositions. Additionally, the raw material quality experiences seasonal, dietary, growth, and regional variations, which makes it in instances difficult to define the exact performance of a raw material. This factor can be challenging when filtration systems have to be determined and sized. Therefore, the main performance criterion for filtration systems for media is total throughput or filter capacity, the total amount of fluid which can be filtered through a specified filtration area. Filters used in media filtration require to be optimized to achieve the highest total throughput and will be tested accordingly. To achieve reliable data, it is always of advantage when the test batch is at the lower end of the quality specification to gain a worse-case scenario. Temperature, differential pressure, and pretreatment of the filter play an important role in performance enhancement of the filter system (Meltzer, 1987; Jornitz and Meltzer, 2001). For example, it has been experienced that lower temperature of the media filtered and even the filter system might enhance the total throughput by 30%. The flow rate will be affected by the higher viscosity, but again the essential performance part is not flow, but total throughput. Too high flow rates in the filtration of biological solutions, showed the negative side effect of gel formation on the membrane and therefore premature blockage. To start with lower differential pressure has been seen advantageous, as again gel formation and/or cake compaction will be avoided. The lower the differential pressure at start of the filtration, the better the performance. A preflush of the filter system with preferably cold buffer, will also enhance the total throughput. Operating the filter with just the media, without preflush, has been found to foul the filter faster and therefore reduce the filter's capacity. In instances, it is necessary to utilize prefiltration combinations to avoid fouling or blocking of the sterilizing grade or 0.1 micron final filter element. These combinations need to be determined in filterability trials to gain the most optimal combination to filter the particular media and to size the system appropriately (Figure 14.1).

Another important, but often overlooked factor of media filtration is the influence of unspecific adsorption of the filter material. To separate lipids in the media raw material adsorptive filter media are desired. However, in cell culture media, especially containing growth promoters unspecific adsorption has to be avoided. Certain membrane polymers do have a higher unspecific adsorption (Figure 14.2). Sometimes the membrane polymer can be of similar type, but the surface treatment of the polymer is different or

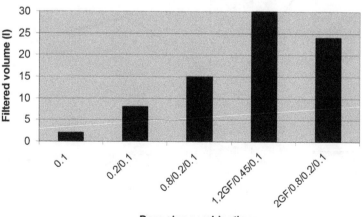

FIGURE 14.1   Total throughput determination of different pore size combinations.

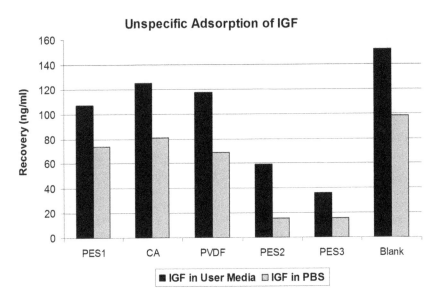

FIGURE 14.2   Unspecific adsorption of IGF to different filter devices.

the design of the filter device is different. In any case, high unspecific adsorption can have an influence on growth promoters like IGF.

A higher unspecific adsorption of the polymeric membrane material also has an influence on the total throughput performance of the filter; the higher the unspecific adsorption, the higher the fouling of the filter. Accelerated fouling will result in a lower filtered volume through the filter device (Figure 14.3). Often the fouling of the membrane will also result in difficulties to integrity test post-filtration. Copious amounts of water are required to flush the filter to achieve either complete wetting of the membrane or elimination of product residue which would negatively influence the integrity test. The last resort in

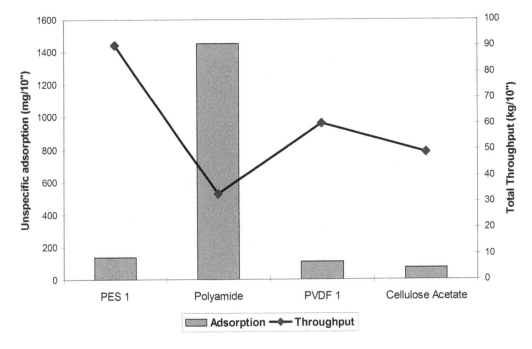

FIGURE 14.3   Influence of higher unspecific adsorption to performance.

these instances is to flush the filter with a solvent or solvent/water mixture and perform the integrity test afterwards.

Adsorptive removal of a constituent of the media is one factor which could hinder cell growth. The other factor is any release of leachables/extractables into the media. Extractables release from either the filter or other polymeric equipment could inhibit cell growth (Cahn, 1967; Jornitz, 2002). Filter devices these days have a very low extractable level, in the ppm range and commonly do not pose a risk (Reif, 1998). However, media filtration happens also with gamma irradiated, presterilized filter/holding bag assemblies. Since gamma irradiation can have degradative effects an increase in an extractable might happen. This factor has to be considered and evaluated. Past experiences showed that leachables from a gamma irradiate single-use bioreactor bag-created cell death. Such instances require thorough investigation to determine why the leachable levels occur, what leachable causes the cell death and what preventative measurements need to be taken. Most commonly though vendor's awareness resolved such issues and developed more applicable polymeric materials and film to be used in media application. Process validation, which includes extractable studies, will verify that the filter-holding vessel assembly fulfills the set specification.

As described, mycoplasma contaminations are not any longer a problematic topic of the past, but with the switch to plant-derived media, it became a current issue, which requires to be addressed. One possibility is to filter the media through a 0.1 micron-rated filter. In the past, there was no such standard as the ASTM F 838-15 (2015) 0.2 micron-rated filter challenge standard for 0.1 micron-rated filters. Therefore, one found varying retention capabilities of such filters (Figure 14.4). This conundrum has been resolved by the work of the PDA mycoplasma task force. A comparative challenge standard has been defined, which creates a better overview of the retentivity capabilities of different 0.1 micron-rated filters. The mycoplasma retentivity of a 0.1 micron filter does not only depend on the pore size distribution but also on the filter construction and thickness of the membrane. A double-layer membrane system reduces the bioburden toward the final filter membrane and commonly shows a higher retentivity. Tests have shown that at high bioburden level challenges organisms were found on the filtrate side. The likelihood of a mycoplasma penetration increases with decreasing membrane thickness. It is advisable to utilize a sufficiently thick mycoplasma retentive membrane layer, instead of aiming for improved flow rates and thinner membrane layers. Process conditions have a high influence on the separation of the organism. Higher pressure conditions or pressure pulsations might support mycoplasma penetration.

Mycoplasma removal by filtration with 0.1 micron-rated filters is one possible step within a process. Nevertheless, since the issue is as critical as viral removal, a process should have multiple removal/inactivation steps and filtration should be supported by other means like heat treatment. HTST (high temperature short time) exposure has been used in the dairy industry and found its use also in the cell culture media applications. Such treatment was necessary when Leptospira was found within cell culture media (Vinther, 2012). Since this pathogen penetrates 0.1 micron filters, it was necessary to use HTST to eliminate this unusual contaminant. Utilizing a multitude of separation or inactivation methods, the

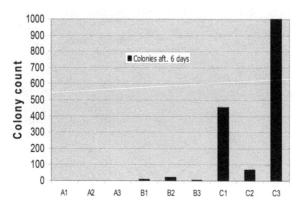

FIGURE 14.4 Mycoplasma retentivity of different 0.1 micron-rated filters (A, B, C) at same challenge conditions.

end user has to be encouraged to perform process validation to verify that the filter performs as expected within the end users' process. Process conditions require testing, as laboratory conditions can only be an indication.

The variation of the filter retention performance can be explained with the membrane configuration the different filters have, the adsorptive separation and membrane design.

Filter Designs

Total throughput, the measure of the total amount of filtrate that can be filtered before the filter element blocks, is probably the most widely required performance criteria in most of the applications, but specifically in media filtration. It is directly proportional to the filter surface area, system size, and prefilter combinations. Certainly, the impact on the total filtration costs can be substantial, if the filter is not optimized for total throughput or an inappropriate pre- and final filter combination is used. What may appear to be a less expensive filter could actually significantly increase the filtration costs.

The total throughput of a filter cartridge depends on the membrane filter polymer, pore structure, and filter design. As previously elaborated, some membrane polymers are highly adsorptive, which might be of use in specific applications. Nevertheless, higher adsorptivity is commonly associated with a higher fouling rate and therefore lower total throughput. Total throughput optimized filter element commonly utilizes a membrane polymer which is either moderately or low adsorptive.

Membranes with a higher asymmetric proportion, that is, a larger pore structure on the upstream side becoming finer throughout the membrane to the filtrate side (Figure 14.5). The overall result, in effect, is an assembly of "V" shaped pores. The filters cartridges are so constructed that the more open ends of the "V" shaped pores of the membrane are directed upstream. This enables them to accommodate larger deposits in their more open, upstream, regions. The result is a commonly larger total throughput than a symmetric membrane structure. Another side effect which asymmetric membranes showed is a higher flow rate, which might be a result of a lower resistivity.

High asymmetric filter membrane systems have shown higher total throughputs than symmetric membrane designs. However, as mentioned before filterability tests only will show whether the filter is the right one or not for the particular application. Trial work performed with asymmetric and symmetric membrane configuration showed surprises in cell culture media filtration, as a symmetric heterogeneous membrane filter configuration showed much better total throughput results than the asymmetric heterogeneous membrane configuration. The performance was 30% better than with an asymmetric membrane design. The filter membranes were also of different membrane materials, which may have had different adsorptive properties, meaning the low adsorptive membrane did not foul prematurely. Other trial results showed the influence of the pore size configurations causing better performances. For example, chemically defined media was filtered with high total throughput with a 0.8/0.2 micron combination, but a plant hydrolysate with a 0.45/0.2 micron combination. Trial work is essential.

FIGURE 14.5 Highly asymmetric polyethersulfone membrane.

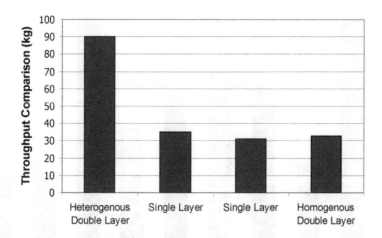

FIGURE 14.6 Total throughput differences of 0.2 micron-rated filters with different membrane combinations.

Another design improvement is the membrane combination within the filter element. A coarser prefilter membrane layer in front of the final filter membrane, the so-called heterogeneous double-layer membrane, has a distinctly higher total throughput due to the fractionate retention of the contaminants (Figure 14.6). The prefilter membrane, for example, 0.45 micron rated, creates a protective layer over the 0.2 micron-rated final filter membrane. A large load of contaminants is removed first before they reach the final filter membrane. This fact is similar to the utilization of prefilter combination in front of the final filter cartridge, except the prefilter membrane of a heterogeneous double-layer construct is contained within the filter cartridge element. This factor also avoids the need of two separate filter housings, respectively, the typical hold-up volume experienced with a two housing filtration system. Certainly, the prefilter layer within a heterogeneous filter design adds to flow resistance; therefore, the flow rate of a heterogeneous filter design is lower than its single-layer counterpart, but higher than a homogeneous (0.2/0.2 micron) filter cartridge. Flow, though, is not the main performance criteria within media filtration. High throughputs are the desired performance.

Further parameters to improve the total throughput within a filter cartridge design are the choices of prefilter fleeces and the effective filtration area (EFA), that is, the pleat design of the membrane within a filter element. Unique pleat designs can create a higher filtration area within the filter cartridge and therefore higher total throughputs (Soelkner and Rupp, 1998; Cardona et al., 2004). Thinner prefilter fleeces allow higher pleat amounts within a filter element; however, if too thin the flow channel between the pleats potentially be too tight and a complete filtration area utilization might not be given. A thicker fleece creates a wider flow channel and also protects the next filter layer. Nevertheless, thicker fleece constructs restrict pleat density and also might press into the membrane. A well-administered balance of construction criteria is required to be able to design a high performance filter. Vendors have optimized the filter design in this accordance.

All these construction parameters result in optimal total throughput performance and certainly differ from filter to filter (Figure 14.7). Such performance difference can even increase depending on the fluid to be filtered. Finding the optimal filter combination can mean potential savings of 50% of the total filter expenditure in the specific application or hundreds of thousands of dollars per annum.

The total throughput can be further advanced by evaluations of appropriate pre- and final filter combinations, if required. A lower cost prefilter might be used to protect the final filter and reduce the required final filter size.

Testing and Sizing Filters

Total throughput tests to determine the appropriate final filter and/or combination of pre- and final filter are performed with 47-mm flat filter composites. These composites have to have the same fleece and filter combination as the filter element to be used later at commercial scale. Commonly, multiple

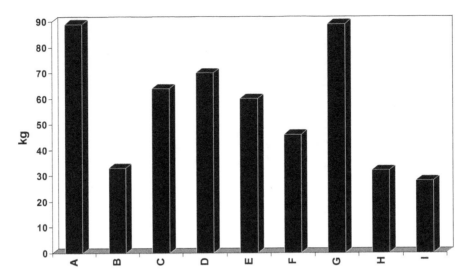

FIGURE 14.7 Total throughput (in kilogram (kg)) comparison of different 10-in. polyethersulfone filter, 0.2 micron sterilizing grade membrane filters using a model solution B, H, and I being single-layer filter).

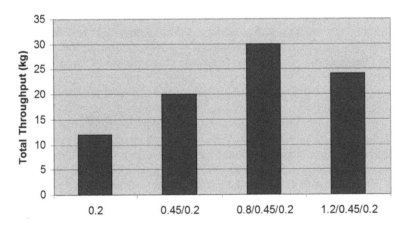

FIGURE 14.8 Total throughput comparison of different 47-mm flat disc pore size combinations using a model solution.

composites are tested to determine the appropriate final filter and to be able to test multiple prefilter options. These tests will determine the optimal combination that achieves the highest fluid throughput per EFA (Figure 14.8).

When 47-mm discs are used, venting of the test filter system is essential. If the filter device is not vented appropriately, the entire EFA is not used and the test result will be incorrect (Figure 14.9). If, and unfortunately it happens, the results of a 47-mm trial are used to size the required filter system, the system would be greatly oversized. The discs used during the filterability tests should be visually inspected to see that the entire area was used or for possible flaws.

Often filter combinations of different filter vendors are tested to establish the best possible filter combination and to potentially determine a second supply source. Such comparison tests need to be designed carefully, so the comparison is truly actual and not skewed due to wrong information, for example, filtration area. For example, 47-mm disc tests can be either performed by using a stainless steel filter holder or a small-scale single-use device. In instances, the tester believed that the filtration area of these two very different devices is the same and even has been informed as such by the vendor's technical literature. However, this is not the case, as the single-use test device commonly has a 36% larger filtration area (Figure 14.10). The tester would have thought that the throughput of the filter membrane combination

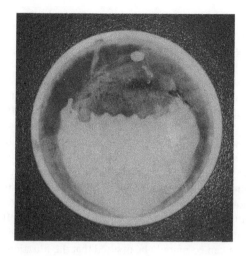

FIGURE 14.9 A 47-mm test filter which was incorrectly vented.

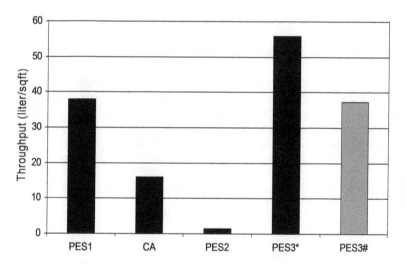

PES3* = disposable device w/o EFA correction; PES3# = with correction

FIGURE 14.10 Filterability results of different filter materials, one filter device being disposable with a larger surface area (PES 3*).

within the single-use device is far superior to the 47-mm filter composite in the stainless steel holder, not realizing that the performance of the single-use filter might be worse and only performs better due to the larger surface area. One can see in Figure 14.10, that the filter surface area correction of the single-use (disposable) device, PES3#, shows the true comparable performance. If the end user would have used the throughput of PES3* and scaled the filter system with this result using the same surface area as the stainless steel test device, the commercial-scale filter system would have been undersized, a detrimental scenario. For that reason, filterability tests require precise procedural definitions, information by the vendor and interpretation of the test results.

If there is sensitivity to unspecific adsorption, these small-scale trials can be utilized to sample the filtrate and determine any yield, activity, or constituent loss. Samples of the filtrate would be taken at frequent, prespecified intervals and assayed for eventual losses or filtrate alterations. These trials can determine the losses, which might occur in process scale, and therefore countermeasures can be taken. Besides, during the trial work with 47-mm discs, optimal processing conditions, for example, differential pressure or temperature and pretreatment protocols, or appropriate buffer flushing, can be determined. It should be noted that stand-alone 47-mm membrane adsorption studies may be of limited utility. Comparison of the membrane composite, which reflect the commercially used filter configuration and under identical operating conditions is recommended.

Yet, 47-mm tests can only suggest the best filter combination, i.e., serve as an indicator trial. To define the proper filter size required within the large-scale production process, small-scale pleated devices of the predetermined filter combination should be utilized. These tests are utilized to verify the findings of the 47-mm disc trials. Only these pleated devices offer linear scalability as these are of the same design with the same flow dynamics as the large-scale filter elements. It is necessary that the design of such filter devices be an exact replica of the final combination that will be validated in the full-scale process, otherwise linear scalability is impossible. Test data collected with 47-mm discs or during small-scale filter device evaluations might be used within a database system for future filter performance choices. The common procedure of testing starts with an indicator trial (47-mm discs) to find the best filter combination, followed by verification trials (pleated small-scale devices), which authenticate the findings of the indicator trials and create a possibility of sizing, and followed by confirmation trials (process scale) which validate the filter choice and size made in the verification trials. When this procedure is utilized the end user can commonly be assured that the filtration system is optimally tailored for the applications needs.

Validation Requirements

The filter vendors qualify any commercially available filter element or device within their laboratories to specific standards, for example, United States Pharmacopeia (USP). These tests encompass a multitude of tests which are required by regulatory authorities, but also additional tests to determine stability specification for the filter element. In the past, tests performed by the filter vendors were utilized as validation tests or data; however, the tests are performed within laboratory settings under standard conditions and therefore can only be classified as qualification tests. The vendor qualifies that the filter developed meets the defined specifications and stays within these specifications repeatedly and reliably. In addition, the filter supplier is also validating the manufacturing process, again to assure consistent quality output.

The common qualification trials and data comprise following measurements:

- Water flow rate
- Size/dimensions
- Temperature/pressure limits (maximum limits)
- Steamability or gamma sterilizability
- Correlation of the integrity test limits to bacteria retention
- Chemical compatibility
- Extractables
- Endotoxin release
- Particulates release
- Biosafety (Plastic Class VI test)
- pH/Conductivity
- Oxidizable substances
- For 0.1 micron-rated filters, mycoplasma retentivity

These test data are made available by the suppliers in qualification documentation. Within this documentation the filter suppliers are also adding other essential technical data, as well as item numbers, quality certificates, and product descriptions.

Since the data determined by the filter supplier are run at standard conditions, the end user requires performing process validation work, evaluating the filter device performance within the process environment under process conditions. Specific tests are described within the guidelines (FDA, 2004; ISO

13408-2, 2003), which require to be performed to verify the filters' performance within the production environment. These tests can include following activities:

- Viability testing in the product to be filtered
- Bacteria challenge testing with either the product or a placebo
- Leachable testing
- Particulate testing
- Chemical compatibility testing
- Unspecific adsorption tests

All tests should be performed under process conditions and with either the actual drug product, in this case media, or a placebo or model solution. The main reason to perform these tests is to verify that the filter performs as expected within the process. Filterability trials described previously are the first step to establish the optimal filter combination. Within these tests, when performed under process conditions, compatibility, extractables, and particulate matter can be tested. Especially compatibility requires immediate determination, as it is a knockout criterion. However, the next immediate steps need to be product bacteria challenge testing to evaluate that the filters' retentivity is not compromised by either influence of product or process conditions on the separation mechanisms, membrane stability, or organism structure or size. For example, high ionic strength of the solution could potentially shrink the organism and cause penetration of the filter membrane. Mycoplasma challenge tests are important to verify the filters' retention performance with the media used instead of a standard challenge solution and standard conditions. The process fluids and parameters can have an unfavorable impact on the filter's performance, for example, the adsorptive retentivity can be influenced. If so, such incidence needs to be determined.

Buffer Filtration

Applications

The variety of buffers and its applications is limitless (Table 14.1). However, most use of buffers is found for pH adjustment within the cell culture process or elution promoter or isoelectric point (pI) adjustment within the purification process. In cell culture processes, the buffer utilized to adjust the cultures' pH consist most often of basic buffer (glutamate, sodium carbonate) or acidic buffer (citric-, malic-, acetic-acid). The buffer is fed automatically into the cell culture or fermentation process to keep the pH level at an optimal setting for cell proliferation. The pH might also be of importance for extracellular product stability and therefore has to be considered within the development of a process. Strong pH adjustments are also used in viral inactivation within the downstream process. The process fluid is adjusted to a pH of 3.5–4 for 30 min at ambient temperature. The mixing during this process time is essential to achieve unified pH adjustment within the set time frame. Certainly, the appropriate pH specification, time, and temperature depend on the virus to be inactivated and the product itself. Process validation studies will determine which setting would be optimal to inactivate any target virus and to avoid any detrimental influence on the product. To stabilize products in the downstream process, for example, utilizing diafiltration for buffer exchange, phosphate buffers find their main use. Buffers function not only as pH adjustment, but also as adjustment of the ionic strength of the solution. In individual process steps, it is essential to either lower or eliminate the salt concentration within the fluid. The pH as well as salt concentration gradients are main function for chromatographic capture and elution. The fine-tuned balance established during the development of the process will be mainly adjusted by specific buffers used in the individual processing step. In instances, buffers are also used to pre-wet or flush either filtration systems or any equipment to avoid potential product alterations, degradation, or precipitation.

Buffers play an essential role in the mentioned process steps and are typically used in large volumes. Since buffers come in contact with the product or are introduced into the cell culture vessel, the buffers require being sterile to avoid any contamination of the culture or process. Buffer filtration with sterilizing

TABLE 14.1

Short List of Common Buffers

Industrial Term	Chemical Name	pK$_a$ @ 25°C	Buffer Range
Acetate		4.76	3.8–5.8
Bicine	N,N-bis(2-hydroxyethyl)glycine	8.35	7.6–9.0
HEPES	4-2-hydroxyethyl-1-piperazineethanesulfonic acid	7.48	6.8–8.2
MES	2-(N-morpholino)ethansulfonic acid	6.15	6.1–7.5
PIPES	Piperazine-N,N-bis(2-ethanesulfonic acid)	6.76	6.1–7.5
TAPS	3-{[tris(hydroxymethyl)methyl]amino} propansulfonic acid	8.43	7.7–9.1
Tricine	N-tris(hydroxymethyl)methylglycine	8.05	7.4–8.8
Tris	Tris(hydroxymethyl)methylamine	8.06	7.5–9.0

grade filters is probably one of the largest filter consuming process steps, since the buffer volumes required are substantial.

Specific Requirements

As described, buffers are employed in every step of a biopharmaceutical process. Whether considered critical, for example, in the formulation process or not does not matter, the buffer requires to be filtered, most often with a sterilizing grade filter. The filtration step will eliminate any impurity or contaminant, which otherwise would enter the process chain. If the contaminant is a microorganism it might proliferate within the process step and cause either biofilm or endotoxin problems in future.

Filtration of buffers happens most commonly from a mixing vessel into a hold vessel. The hold vessel is then stored within a cold room till the buffer is used. Stainless steel vessel systems are nowadays replaced by disposable mixing vessels and hold bags (Figure 14.11). The hold bags can also be designed in a manifold fashion, so the bag volumes are easy to handle and are available as required (Figure 14.12). Disposable devices have the benefit that these are gamma irradiated, ready-to-use, do not need to be cleaned, and are sealed systems. The storage of multiple bags of smaller volumes is easier than one large hold tank, which requires to be moved through the facility. However, when disposable systems are used the compatibility to the specific buffers requires to be determined by evaluating the extractable profile or at least a TOC (Total Organic Carbon) analysis. Data of compatibilities to different buffers can also be obtained from the disposable system supplier. Similarly, any filtration device applied to filter the specific buffer requires to be tested in regard to its compatibility under the process conditions of the specific practice.

Since buffers are commonly of high purity the filter performance criteria focus on flow rate and not total throughput. A premature blocking of the filter is often not experienced, as the solutions are non-fouling and lack the high quantity of contaminants typically found in other applications. Flow is the determining factor of process time within the buffer preparation process. The faster the flow rate of the filter, the higher the equipment utilization. The better the flow rate of the filter the lower the required EFA, respectively, the cost per liter will be reduced. For example, a low flow rate (2,500 L/h), 0.2 micron-rated filter would require 48 min to filter a 2,000 L volume versus only 20 min for a high flow filter (6,000 L/h). This would reduce equipment use time by half or the EFA could be reduced, which would cut filter costs.

Another important factor to consider is the buffer's pH range or the variety of buffers used. One can find in certain pharmaceutical processes that the pH ranges from 1–14, the full spectrum, which some polymers are capable to withstand and others not. Again, filter suppliers are aware about this fact and developed high flow filters most often with a polyethersulfone-base polymer as this material is compatible over the entire pH range.

Filter Designs

As mentioned above, flow rate is the key performance parameter in buffer filtration. However, to gain optimal flow rates from sterilizing grade membrane filters, there are limited parameters which can be controlled within the filtration process. Either the differential pressure can be raised, or larger filter

FIGURE 14.11   Disposable, levitating mixing system.

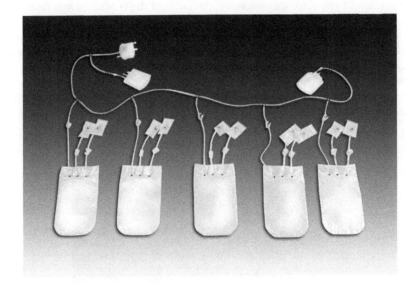

FIGURE 14.12   Disposable holding bag manifold.

surface can be applied, which raises the consumable and capital investment costs. In instances of higher viscosity buffers, the temperature could be raised to lower the viscosity. Every centiPoise of viscosity increase lowers the flow rate accordingly.

Since the process conditions are restrictive and might not be able to achieve optimal performance, specific high flow membrane filter designs have been developed by the filter vendors. Such filters are optimized in respect to the design of the filter membrane and the construction of the filter.

Flow rate increases due to membrane designs are commonly achieved by high porosity, low membrane thickness, and high membrane pleatability. The higher the porosity, the thinner the membrane, and the lower the flow resistances through the membrane in accordance to Darcy's law, in which permeability of the porous media is directly proportional to the fluid flow rate and inversely proportional to membrane thickness. However, thickness of a membrane has also an effect of long-term retentivity assurance and therefore a careful balance has to be observed (Pall et al., 1980). To lower flow resistance, many of the high flow filter devices use asymmetric membrane structures which seem to channel the fluid stream better through the membrane structure and thickness. Asymmetric membranes also include the additional benefit of fractionate retention and therefore distribution of the contaminant.

To achieve a larger EFA within the confinements of the filter cartridge construction, the membrane requires to be easy pleatable. If the pleatability of the membrane is not given, the EFA of such a filter is commonly low and/or the pleat edges are too weak to withstand pressure pulsation (Figure 14.13). Inappropriate membrane thickness or design can create a stretching of the pleat tips. This results in a weakness within the stretched membrane material and physical stress, like steaming or pressure pulsations can break the pleat tip open. Since both stress factors happen during filtration, such designed filter element might be undesirable as it could fail integrity after filtration.

Pressure pulsations caused by water hammer are not unusual in high flow applications. Any filling processes which utilize rapid valve action and therefore fluid flow and stoppage, might create excessive pressure pulses. The filter cartridge designs require to withstand such pulsations and are commonly tested within the filter supplier development facilities before released into the market (Figure 14.14).

Besides membrane design, filter cartridge design is a key element to achieve optimal flow rate conditions. For example, a single-layer membrane construction will achieve higher flow rates than a membrane double-layer combination, especially when such is of a homogenous (e.g., 0.2/0.2 micron) construct. The flow restriction of a homogenous double-layer design can be so high that a single-layer membrane filter of a smaller pore size, 0.1 micron rated, might reach a similar flow rate as the 0.2/0.2 micron rating (Figure 14.15), since the membrane thickness of the 0.2/0.2 micron membrane is much thicker.

Additionally, the support fleeces, which are layered on top and bottom of the membrane, require being of appropriate structure and thickness. If the structure, for example, fiber diameter is too large, the fleece structure could press into the membrane at the pleat tips and cause friction. One can see such fiber impressions in Figure 14.13. Fleece with large fiber structures are also difficult to pleat. When the support fleece is too thick, the pleat density will be lower and therefore the EFA. Conversely, when the fleece layer is too thin the pleat density might be too tight, uneven flow dynamics happen and only the

FIGURE 14.13 Membrane breaks at the pleat edges due to insufficient membrane design and pulsations.

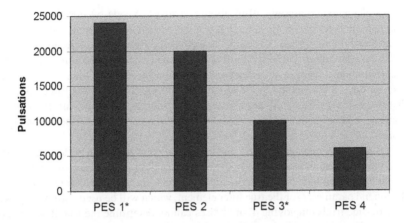

FIGURE 14.14 Pulsation resistance of different high flow filter cartridge at 5 bar differential pressure (*, Double layer filter).

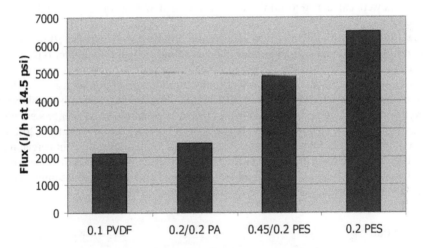

FIGURE 14.15 Flow rate comparison of different 10-in. filter cartridge configurations.

outer areas, the pleat tips, of the filter membrane will be used. The inner core of the filter cartridge would be the next restricting factor. The dimension of a filter cartridge is very specific and cannot be easily changed, the inner core being one of the dimensional structures. When the filter membrane is optimized for flow, the flow rate can be so high that the restricting factor becomes the inner core and filter cartridge adapter diameter. At one point, the diameter cannot handle more flow without increase in the pressure conditions. Again, such structural designs have to be well balanced and will take years of testing to optimize. Suppliers run a multitude of different performance trials before any design or component is defined for a specific filter. Only such trial basis will determine an optimal filter choice for a specific application.

Testing and Sizing Filters

As suppliers perform multiple tests within their development process, so has the filter user to test flow optimized filters of multiple suppliers: (a) to find the best possible filter for the particular application and (b) to qualify a second supply option.

Flow rate depends on the entire filter cartridge design and not solely on the membrane's porosity, thickness, and construction. If a membrane, with an exceptional flow rate, cannot be pleated it is futile within a filter cartridge construction. The optimization of filtration processes requires tests using comparable filter elements, commonly 10-in. filter cartridges. A side-by-side trial can be performed using only comparable filter elements; as such a test would take into account the entire design of the filter construction and the membrane structure, as well as the EFA, flow distribution due to pleat densities, and the fleece thickness. The test would be performed under the required or specified process conditions, i.e., commonly using a set inlet pressure, while the time to filter the fixed fluid volume will be measured. Such a test setup can be utilized for different filter types to be tested. Important, though, is that the process parameters are constant. For example, the same buffer composition, pressure, and temperature settings to have a comparable result in order to determine the optimal filter type or combination.

The 47-mm tests for flow rate can be performed as an indicator when the buffers have certain viscosity differences; nevertheless, most commonly the results are of no use when utilized as a process-scale indication, as such tests evaluate only the porosity and thickness of the membrane itself. Nevertheless, critical and beneficial parameters of the true filter element, which will be used within the process, are not evaluated. Side-by-side trials employing 47-mm discs cannot determine the true flow rate performance of the filter within the production process (Figure 14.16). The chart depicts the true flow rate measurements using 10-in. filter elements and tests performed with 47-mm discs. The tests have been performed at a set differential pressure of 0.5 bar with water at 20°C. The flow rate results of the 10-in. elements and 47-mm discs were calculated to L/m²/h to compare the flow rates of the disc and the true flow of process elements.

As Figure 14.16 shows, the 47-mm flow rate results differ greatly from the 10-in. element flows, i.e., 47-mm test discs are inappropriate for use in determining an appropriate filter type and scale. For example, the flow rate of 47-mm disc composite A could have a 20% higher flow rate than the 47-mm composite B. However, the 10-in. filter element of composite A has 0.5 m² filtration area and the composite B 0.7 m² filtration area, which represents a 40% higher filtration area, respectively, higher flow. The 47-mm flow rate test would have misguided the user to a filter composites and later process filter device, which seems to have a higher flow in the small-scale test, but truly has potentially a 20% lower flow rate. Moreover, if the process filter would be scaled with the 47-mm results, the commercial filter system would have been undersized. Comparisons of flow rate of different filters should not be performed with 47-mm discs as such tests just mislead the end user. Such tests are only time-consuming and are not of true value. Only large-scale trials can determine the best flow rate filter.

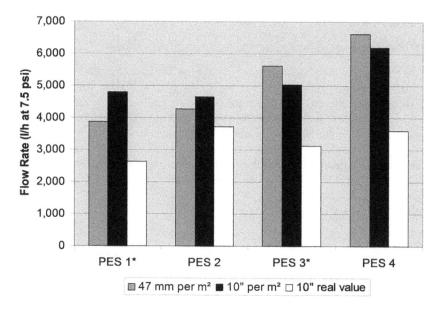

FIGURE 14.16 Flow rate comparisons of 47-mm discs and 10-in. elements (extrapolated to 1 m²) and actual 10-in. cartridge flow (*, Double-layer filter).

A benefit of 47-mm test composites is the possibility to check chemical compatibility with lower buffer volumes required. The chemical compatibility needs to be tested as some of the membrane polymers do not fit to certain buffer pH ranges. The 47-mm disc could be flushed with the buffer in a recirculation mode under the future process conditions to find out whether any subtle incompatibility exists. An integrity test, TOC or pH/conductivity test before and after filter contact can create an indication whether the filter polymer is the right choice or not.

High flow rate filters often find the restriction in flow also within the adapter or inner core design of a filter; the smaller the inner core or adapter diameter, the higher the resistivity to flow. Small-scale device trials would not be able to determine such influence. Only full-scale trials will reveal any potential slow-down of flow due to insufficient adapter or pipe diameters.

Another benefit given by large-scale trials with the actual filter device is the possibility of appropriate sizing. Even when safety factors could be used with 47-mm test devices, most commonly the system would be oversized. Some users might consider this as cost of business; however, the costs of such casual-sized system could be double as high as an accurately sized system. The costs are not only attached to the price of such filter devices, but also the hardware required, flush volumes, sterilization times, setup times, and cost of waste. The entire process requires to be evaluated before an inaccurate decision is made.

Conclusion

Years of use and testing have shown that there is no such thing as the perfect filter device, an overall encompassing filter which will serve every application optimally. The variety of applications and process settings require filters which are not developed to be the best in every performance aspect, but rather be the optimal in a specific performance criterion looked for in a specific application. This chapter touched two very specific applications, which require a completely different scope of filter designs and testing. It shows that in future filter devices, as well as any other equipment used within biopharmaceutical processes, will be developed according to application needs instead of product features. The one filter fits all approach is as obsolete as the one pharmaceutical process fits all. To find the optimal filter, filter users and vendors have to work together in a very close cooperation to achieve the goal to reduce the costs, maintain the yield, and meet the process requirements. Costs are not saved by discounts, but by optimizing the process step within the application and all parameters surrounding this step, including waste removal.

REFERENCES

ASTM F 838-15 (2015), *Standard Test Method for Determining Bacterial Retention of Membrane Filters Utilized for Liquid Filtration*, ASTM International, West Conshohocken, PA.

Cahn, R.D. (1967), Detergents in membrane filters, *Science*, Vol 155, pp 195–196.

Cardona, M. (2004), *Considerations for Buffer Filtration*, The Free Library, Advantage Business Media 27.

Cardona, M.; Inseal, O.G. (2006), Filtration designs remove processing bottlenecks for high-yield biotech drugs, *BioPharm International*, Vol 2006.

FDA (2004), *Guidance for Industry Sterile Drug Products Produced by Aseptic Processing—Current Good Manufacturing Practice*, FDA, Rockville, MD.

ISO 13408-2 (2003), *Aseptic Processing of Health Care Products—Part 2: Filtration*, ISO, Geneva, Switzerland.

Jornitz, M.W.; Meltzer, T.H. (2001), *Sterile Filtration—A Practical Approach*, Marcel Dekker, New York.

Jornitz, M.W. (2002), Optimising Biopharmaceutical Processing- Key Trends in Up and Downstream Operations, World Drug Summit, Copenhagen, April 10–12, 2002.

Jornitz, M.W.; Soelkner, P.G.; Meltzer, T.H. (2002), Sterile filtration—A review of the past and present technologies, *PDA Journal*, Vol 56, No 4, pp 192–196.

Jornitz, M.W.; Soelkner, P.G.; Meltzer, T.H. (2003), The economics of modern sterile filtration, *Pharmaceutical Technology*, Vol 27, No 3, pp 156–166.

Jornitz, M.W.; Meltzer, T.H.; Bromm, H.; Priebe, P.M. (2005), Choosing the appropriate membrane filter— Test requirements, *PDA Journal*, Vol 59, No 2, pp 96–101.

Meltzer, T.H. (1987), *Filtration in the Pharmaceutical Industry*, Chapter 20, Marcel Dekker, New York.

Pall, D.B.; Kirnbauer, E.A.; Allen, B.T. (1980), Particulate retention by bacteria retentive membrane filters, *Colloids and Surfaces*, Vol 1, pp 235–256.

Reif, O.W. (1998) Chapter 8. In *Filtration on the Biopharmaceutical Industry*. Meltzer, T.H., Jornitz, M.W., Eds. Marcel Dekker, New York.

Soelkner. P.; Rupp. J. (1998) Chapter 5. In *Filtration on the Biopharmaceutical Industry*. Meltzer, T.H., Jornitz, M.W., Eds. Marcel Dekker, New York.

Vinther, A. (2012) Novel Contamination Investigation in Upstream Drug Substance Manufacturing, *PDA Annual Meeting*, April 2012.

Yandell, C.; Lawson, J.; Butler, I.; Wade, B.; Sheehan, A.; Grosvenor, S.; Goddard, C.; Simula, T. (2004) An Analogue of IGF-I, *BioProcess International*, March, 2004.

15

Downstream Processing

Uwe Gottschalk
Lonza AG

CONTENTS

Introduction

Overview of Downstream Processing in the Biopharmaceutical Industry

Biopharmaceutical manufacturing is conventionally divided into upstream and downstream phases, the former dealing with the propagation of biological raw material and the latter with the extraction and purification of the desired product. Downstream processing can thus be defined as the series of operations that takes the output from the upstream process (e.g., fermentation broth, plant tissue, animal tissue/body fluids) and yields a stable, pure product (Kalyanpur 2000). Many different product types can be considered under the umbrella of biopharmaceuticals, ranging from small organic molecules to proteins, nucleic acids, viral particles, and even whole cells. This chapter focuses on the production of biopharmaceutical proteins (Figure 15.1).

Downstream processing is itself usually divided into two main steps: isolation and purification. The isolation step follows immediately after harvesting of the raw material. In the isolation step, the crude raw material is refined into a clarified feed stream, that is, a process intermediate that is free from cells and other particulate matter. The unit operations employed in the isolation step depend very much on the initial raw material. Some biological materials, such as the extracellular medium from the culture of microbes, aquatic plants, or mammalian cells are already clarified to a degree, and require only limited centrifugation or filtration prior to the purification step. Wherever possible, recombinant proteins are secreted into the medium, allowing them to be collected without cell homogenization, a process which releases large amounts of particulates and soluble contaminants (Birch and Racher 2006). Where secretion is not possible, the feed stream can be extremely complex, and isolation may involve multiple operations to remove various sizes of particulates and other contaminants such as oils. This often is the case for intracellular products, where the raw material can include homogenized cells, shredded leaves or ground seeds, and complex bodily fluids such as milk (Nikolov and Woodard 2004, Nikolov et al. 2017). It may be necessary to add water to certain raw materials in order to facilitate protein extraction. This water is also considered as a contaminant and the isolation step should, therefore, achieve volume reduction as well as the clarification of the feed stream. A number of different methods may be employed during the isolation step including filtration, gravity separation, centrifugation, flocculation, evaporation, precipitation, and extraction. For certain products affinity chromatography is a key isolation technology, facilitating product capture from the raw material.

In the purification phase, the aim is to prepare a pure biopharmaceutical product from the clarified feed. This is the most challenging and expensive step in downstream processing because it is necessary to separate the desired product from other molecules with similar properties (Levine 2002, Werner

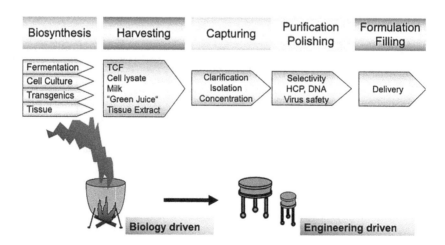

FIGURE 15.1 A generic process train for pharmaceutical protein production. HCP, host cell proteins; NA, nucleic acids; TCF, tissue culture fluid.

2004, Gottschalk 2005a, 2008). High-resolution orthogonal separation methods are required, and multiple filtration and chromatography steps are needed to remove trace impurities and replace the native solvent with a buffer suitable for storage (Sommerfeld and Strube 2005). Traditional techniques such as extraction and crystallization can also be used economically during the final stages of purification, which are collectively known as polishing (Gottschalk 2003). This chapter considers the principles and applications of different techniques that can be used for the downstream processing of proteins, and explores some of the challenges that remain in this important field.

Challenges in Protein Purification

Some of the major issues which affect protein purification include product loss, denaturation, proteolysis, and contamination with other biological molecules, especially nucleic acids, carbohydrates, and lipids (Ersson et al. 1989). In small-scale preparations, these problems are addressed through the use of an extraction buffer whose pH and ionic strength favor the solubilization of the target protein while other molecules precipitate, and through the addition of detergents, chaotropes, reducing agents, protease inhibitors, and other additives that protect the target product (Fish 2004). In large-scale industrial processes this is too expensive, and the additives themselves would only need to be removed at a later stage making additional purification steps necessary. Therefore, instead of adding components to protect the target protein, the aim in large-scale processing is to minimize the target protein's contact with potentially damaging agents by removing these agents as early as possible in the process train. Some positive measures can be implemented even in the upstream phase—for example, by ensuring a protein is secreted rather than retained in the cell, it can be recovered directly from the culture medium without lysing the cells and risking the release of oxidizing agents, proteases, and other contaminants. Where an intracellular product is unavoidable (e.g., inclusion bodies in bacteria, proteins expressed in plant leaves or seeds), there is usually a compromise between recovery and purity.

Typically, a target protein will constitute 0.1%–5% of the total soluble protein in the raw material, and after the isolation step it will be present within a mixture of many different proteins with a range of physicochemical properties, some very different from the target and some very similar (Doonan 2000). Purification exploits the unique chemical and physical properties of the target protein in order to obtain a pure and homogeneous preparation. Important properties of proteins which are exploited for separation include the following:

- Solubility
- Isoelectric point (pI)/charge
- Hydrophobicity/distribution of hydrophobic patches
- Size
- Specific binding affinity
- Presence of carbohydrate groups
- Stability under different process conditions (heat, pH, conductivity, presence of organic solvents)

Solubility differences are often exploited at an early stage in processing to separate proteins from molecules with very different physical and chemical properties, such as carbohydrates and nucleic acids (Doonan 2000). Individual proteins also show differing degrees of solubility in a salt solution due to particular surface properties (e.g., charge distribution, juxtaposition of polar and nonpolar surface patches). This means it is possible to select conditions where a desired protein remains in solution while others precipitate, or vice versa. In a complex mixture of proteins, the solubilities of individual proteins will overlap considerably, so salt fractionation (typically achieved by adding ammonium sulfate to the clarified feed) provides only a crude separation method. However, ammonium sulfate is inexpensive, so salt fractionation can be used economically on a large scale, which makes it attractive as a method for biopharmaceutical manufacturing. Occasionally, it may also be possible to achieve fractional precipitation with an organic solvent (e.g., ethanol or acetone) although this can lead to protein denaturation at high solvent concentrations. Differential solubilities can also be exploited for separation using two immiscible solvents (see the section "Extraction and Precipitation" below). A more recent innovation is the use of peptide tags which specifically exploit differences in solubility under different process conditions. For example, the elastin-like polypeptide (ELP) tag causes proteins to change from soluble to insoluble at a particular transition temperature, allowing their selective precipitation by changing the temperature of the feed (Floss et al., 2010).

The overall charge of a protein depends on the number of charged amino acid residues on its surface, so all proteins carry a net charge at all pH values except the unique pH—known as the pI—at which the positive and negative charges cancel each other out. Moreover, any proteins that have the same charge at a particular pH may differ in charge at some other pH. A number of methods have been developed to separate proteins on the basis of charge including isoelectric focusing, chromatofocusing, electrophoresis, and ion exchange chromatography. Although all these methods can be used for small-scale preparative purification, only ion exchange chromatography has the combination of simplicity and economy to allow its use in current industrial-scale processes (Jungbauer 1993, Desai et al. 2000).

The hydrophobicity of a protein is its tendency to favor nonpolar solvents. Like its charge, a protein's hydrophobicity depends on the types of amino acid residues clustered on the surface. Although the surfaces of most soluble proteins are predominantly polar, many of them have patches of hydrophobic amino acids that, under appropriate conditions (usually at high salt concentrations), can bind to hydrophobic matrices. This provides a method for separation in which proteins are dissolved in an ionic solution, passed over a hydrophobic matrix to which they bind preferentially, and eluted using an organic modifier. Methods based on this property include hydrophobic interaction chromatography (HIC) and reversed-phase chromatography (RPC), although only the former is used for the large-scale purification of proteins given that RPC uses strongly denaturing solvents (RPC may be useful, however, for the purification of small peptides). Proteins also differ from one another in size and shape. This can be exploited in size-exclusion chromatography (SEC), where the overall size of a protein determines the likelihood of it becoming trapped in a porous matrix, and in ultrafiltration methods (which utilize very fine filters).

Whereas the methods above depend on differences in protein structure there is also a set of procedures that depend essentially on differences in biological activity (Scouten 1981, Hermanson et al. 1992, Jones 2000). In the vast majority of cases, the biological activity of a protein depends on it recognizing and binding to a ligand. For example, enzymes bind to substrates and inhibitors, hormones bind to receptors, antibodies bind to antigens, and so on. This specific biological activity can be exploited by the construction of an inert substrate, such as agarose, to which the appropriate ligand is (usually covalently) attached. The passage of a protein mixture through the resulting affinity matrix should result in the binding of one or a small number of proteins that recognize the ligand. After washing to remove unbound proteins and other contaminants, subsequent elution of the bound fraction can be achieved by passing a solution of the ligand, or a suitable analog, through the column, or by using an elution buffer that disrupts the protein–ligand interaction. Methods based on this principle include immunoaffinity chromatography, protein A chromatography for the purification of antibodies, immobilized metal ion affinity chromatography for the purification of positively charged proteins, and dye-binding chromatography for proteins that recognize particular organic groups. Lectin chromatography is a specialized derivative that exploits the affinity of lectins (carbohydrate-binding proteins) to bind selectively to specific oligosaccharide groups on glycoproteins. Elution can be achieved by passage of a solution of the appropriate monosaccharide through the column.

Methods Used in Product Isolation—Low-Technology Techniques

In contemporary downstream processing, isolation often consists of capturing the product from the clarified feed, leading to a rapid and steep increase in purity and concentration early in the process. Trends include the processing of large tissue culture fluid volumes, a high dynamic capacity, high linear flow rates, and low contact times. Depending on the efficiency of capture, the purification step may involve some intermediate processing before polishing, or (if the output from the capture stage is already highly pure) two consecutive and orthogonal polishing steps (Gottschalk 2006a).

Harvesting and capture often involve a combination of filtration to remove particulates and affinity chromatography to select the target on the basis of its binding affinity, thus removing 99% of contaminants and achieving volume reduction in a single operation (Huse et al. 2002). The use of affinity chromatography at an early stage is advantageous because the desired product is rapidly separated from potentially damaging contaminants such as proteases and oxidizing agents. However, it is not always possible to develop ligands to trap the desired product, and in many cases the cost of affinity media becomes unsupportable as the scale of production increases. Therefore, before considering filtration and affinity chromatography in detail we first explore some traditional separation techniques which are increasingly used in the preparation of small-molecule drugs and could soon be adopted on a more routine basis in the manufacturing of biopharmaceutical proteins.

Gravity Separation and Centrifugation

A particle suspended in a liquid medium of lesser density tends to sediment downward due to the force of gravity. Its passage downwards is opposed by a buoyancy force equivalent to the weight of the displaced liquid, friction between particles and the liquid, and to a certain extent diffusion. Particles whose buoyancy force exceeds the gravitational force acting downwards will tend to rise to the surface and float. Gravity separation can, therefore, be used to sediment heavy particles and float buoyant particles, leaving a partially clarified liquid layer. Conventional gravity separation can be achieved either in a still tank or a stirred vessel. It is rapid and efficient for large particles but slow and inefficient as the particles get smaller, and is therefore only suitable for crude separation steps. More efficient gravity separation can be achieved using a plate separator, which comprises a set of evenly spaced plates usually inclined at an angle to provide a greater settling area in a smaller space. This allows a greater feed flow rate and minimizes the bottleneck during clarification.

Centrifugation is a mechanical process that utilizes an applied centrifugal force in place of gravity to separate the components of a mixture according to density and/or particle size. It is a well-established unit operation whose applications include cell separation from broths, removal of cell debris, separation of protein precipitates, and even the separation of dissolved macromolecules (ultracentrifugation) although this is rare in large-scale processes (Taulbee and Maroto-Valer 2000). Centrifugation is typically a batch operation at the laboratory scale (the feed is placed in a disposable tube or bottle, and the supernatant is recovered from the bottle at the conclusion of the run). However, the typical laboratory centrifuge has a small volume that is insufficient for a process-scale operation, even when scaled up. Therefore, large-scale operations tend to use continuous centrifuges, where the feed is continuously fed to a spinning rotor and the supernatant and waste pellet are continuously discharged.

Several different forms of centrifugation have been developed and each has a different application in downstream processing (Figure 15.2). *Differential sedimentation* is a form of centrifugation in which the medium within the centrifuge tube or bottle is initially homogeneous. Larger and/or denser particles sediment more rapidly in the centrifugal field and thus form a pellet on the wall or floor of the rotor faster than smaller or lighter particles, which tend to remain in the supernatant. The magnitude of the applied centrifugal force and the duration of centrifugation can be used to determine the size or density of particles that are sedimented. This approach works well when the objective is to pellet solid particles, such as cells or tissue debris, or to clarify a liquid feed stream.

Density gradient centrifugation is similar to differential sedimentation in that the principle is to exploit centrifugal force to separate feed components on the basis of particle size or density. However, the distinguishing feature is that the medium in the centrifuge tube is heterogeneous, and the density of the solution increases along the axis of rotation. This is usually achieved by varying the concentration of solute along the centrifuge tube prior to sample loading. As well as pelleting very dense particles, density gradient centrifugation also achieves the separation of particles within the density range of the solution into different bands. In *rate zonal centrifugation*, all particles will eventually form a pellet so the run must be interrupted to isolate particles in the desired density range. In *isopycnic centrifugation*, a very dense solution is used and particles or molecules in the density range will never form a pellet but will remain suspended at a specific distance along the density gradient. Such processes are common in laboratory-scale preparations but are rarely used on an industrial scale.

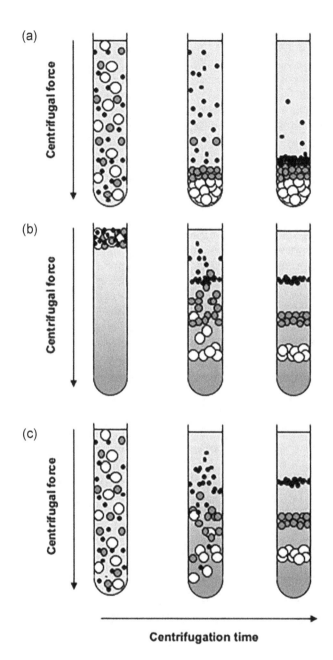

FIGURE 15.2 Principles of different forms of centrifugation. (a) Sedimentation—particles distributed uniformly in a homogeneous solution sediment according to size with the largest particles settling onto the surface of the centrifuge tube first. (b) Density gradient centrifugation—particles loaded in a thin zone above a layered solution with increasing density become distributed into density zones as long as centrifugation is not run to completion. (c) Isopycnic ultracentrifugation—particles or solute molecules distributed uniformly in a homogeneous solution will form density zones at very high centrifugation speeds as the solute itself forms a density gradient.

Several types of continuous centrifuges are incorporated into large-scale processes, and they usually have the ability to separate particles in the 0.1–200 μm diameter range (Zydney and Kuriyel 2000). A typical example is the decanter centrifuge shown in Figure 15.3a. The depicted centrifuge is of the "bowl and scroll" design, in which a rotating scroll (like a screw thread) fits tightly into a conical-shaped bowl whose apex lies at the source of the centrifugal force. The feed is introduced into the middle of the scroll. As the

(a)

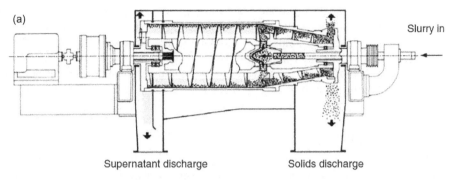

Slurry in

Supernatant discharge   Solids discharge

(b)

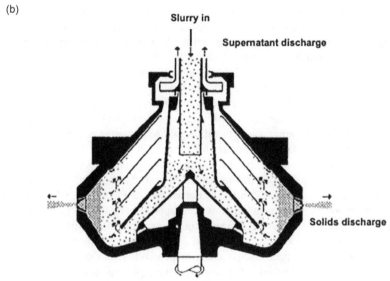

Slurry in

Supernatant discharge

Solids discharge

FIGURE 15.3 Examples of typical continuous centrifuges used in downstream processing. (a) A scroll and roll decanter centrifuge. (b) A disc stack centrifuge.

centrifuge bowl rotates, the particles in the slurry sediment upon the walls of the bowl. The accelerating force, which can be up to $10,000 \times g$, is optimized for the application and the expected composition of the solid component of the slurry. As the centrifuge spins, the scroll is rotated, scraping the solids toward the apex of the bowl where they are removed. At the same time, the clarified supernatant liquid is directed to a collection device either by gravity discharge or with discharge under pressure. This type of device is best suited to feeds with a high content of solids, such as fermentation broths or milled plant tissues.

Another continuous centrifuge device often used in large-scale processing is the disc stack centrifuge (Kempken et al. 1995) (Figure 15.3b). The disc stack centrifuge uses higher centrifugal forces than the decanter centrifuge, and is therefore suitable for slurries with a lower solids concentration and/or smaller particle sizes. The design incorporates sets of stainless steel plates (the disc stack) which provide a greater sedimentation area and significantly accelerate the separation process. The solids deposited on the plates can be removed continuously, intermittently (semi-batch mode) or regularly (batch mode) depending on the application. A typical application for semi-batch or batch mode centrifugation is the removal of mammalian cells after batch or fed-batch fermentation. Centrifuges are effective in reducing cell concentrations and removing larger particles of debris, but they tend to perform poorly in removing small cell particles and colloidal compounds which are always present in biopharmaceutical feed streams.

In laboratory-scale operations, centrifugation is often combined with filtration, such that the feed stream is centrifuged through some form of filter matrix to trap particles above a certain size and prevent their sedimentation onto the walls of the tube. Similar to conventional filtration achieved via differential pressure across a membrane or pad (see below), centrifugal filtration is driven by the pressure exerted by a liquid medium within a centrifugal field. Opposing the centrifugal pressure is the combined resistance of the porous medium and filter cake. Although spin-filters are too complex and expensive to scale up for very-large-scale processes, separators are often linked to depth filtration with lenticular filters, so that particles and debris remaining after separation are removed (see the section "Filtration Methods Used in Product Isolation and Purification" below).

Extraction and Precipitation

Extraction is the process of moving one or more components of a mixture from one phase to another, whereas precipitation is the process of removing one or more components from solution to form a solid phase (the precipitate). These are among the simplest and least expensive fractionation methods because they can be achieved by the addition or removal of salt, organic solvents, or by changes in temperature and pH.

Liquid–liquid extraction using organic and aqueous extraction media is a traditional separation operation that can be applied to the purification of biopharmaceuticals. In three-phase partitioning, proteins can be purified directly from cell homogenates by partitioning between a layer of butanol and a strong aqueous salt solution. Under these conditions, cell debris tends to separate into the organic phase and nucleic acids precipitate at the interphase while proteins remain in solution. Several proteins have been purified using this method (e.g., see Paule et al. 2004) and the selectivity of extraction can be increased through the inclusion of affinity reagents such as metal ions in the system (e.g., Roy and Gupta 2002).

Aqueous two-phase extraction (ATPE) systems are widely used in industry. They utilize a mixture of aqueous polymers and/or salts (Kula and Selber 1999). One phase generally contains polyethylene glycol (PEG) and the other contains a different polymer, such as dextran, or the salt potassium phosphate. Under ideal conditions, the desired protein can be separated into the PEG phase while the majority of contaminating proteins as well as other contaminants are trapped in the second phase, or in the interphase, and can be removed by centrifugation. Advances in the hardware used with ATPE systems have been reviewed by Banik et al. (2003) and the suitability of ATPE as a unit operation during the manufacturing of recombinant antibodies has been discussed comprehensively (Rosa et al. 2011, 2013).

Protein precipitation is a well-established but poorly understood process. Under mild conditions, protein precipitation is reversible and subsequent redissolution restores total activity. Protein precipitation may be either a product isolation step or a purification step. In the former case, precipitation and subsequent redissolution in a smaller volume of water not only reduces the processing volume, but the resulting solution also contains mostly dissolved protein, free of other soluble contaminants (Glynn, 2017). In the latter case, the differential solubility of proteins may be used for fractionation. Proteins can be precipitated by changing the pH or temperature or by adding a mild organic solvent, a salt, a multivalent metal ion, or a nonionic polymer. The chosen precipitation method depends on whether the protein precipitate that is formed can be redissolved without loss of activity, the expense of the precipitating agent and its recovery, and the effects of precipitating agent impurities in the precipitate. The following methods are widely used (Kumar et al. 2003, Hilbrig and Freitag 2003, Westoby et al. 2011):

- *Salting out.* A high salt concentration promotes protein aggregation and precipitation. Although the mechanism is not well understood, the salt is thought to remove the water of solution from the protein, thereby reducing protein solubility. The Hofmeister series represents decreasing anion effectiveness: citrate > phosphate > sulfate > acetate >> chloride > nitrate > thiocyanate. The salts at the low end of this series cause structural damage to proteins. The high solubility of ammonium sulfate in water and the position of sulfate in the Hofmeister series make it the most popular choice for salting out proteins.

- *Metal ions.* Ions such as Mn^{2+}, Fe^{2+}, Ca^{2+}, Mg^{2+}, and Ag^+ bind to different protein functional groups and can cause the protein to precipitate. They act at much lower concentrations than the ions of the Hofmeister series and are easily removed by ion exchange adsorption or chelating agents.

- *Adjusting the pH.* Proteins are soluble in water due to the interaction of their charged groups with ionized water molecules. Adjusting the pH to match the pI minimizes the solubility, because the net charge of the protein is eliminated. Most proteins have a pI < 7, and the relatively low cost of acids makes pH adjustment with acid a popular method for protein precipitation. However, too much acid or base can cause irreversible denaturation.

- *Organic solvents.* Addition of a mild organic solvent to an aqueous protein solution reduces the solvent dielectric constant, thereby inducing protein precipitation. The solvent must be completely miscible with water (e.g., ethanol and acetone). Solvent precipitation is typically performed at low temperatures (<10°C) because conformational rigidity then prevents irreversible denaturation.

- *Temperature.* Proteins precipitate and denature at different rates when the temperature is increased. However, some robust proteins are resistant to heat denaturation. Therefore, by subjecting an impure mixture to an elevated temperature for an appropriate period of time, a protein can be purified in solution due to the irreversible denaturation and precipitation of the impurities.

- *Polymers and polyelectrolytes.* Nonionic, water-soluble polymers induce protein precipitation by excluding water from the solvation structure of a protein. PEG is the most widely studied and widely used polymer, but dextrans are also used for this purpose. The effect of polymers as precipitating agents is similar to partitioning in aqueous two-phase polymer systems (see the section "Extraction and Precipitation" above). High PEG concentrations are required to precipitate low-molecular-weight proteins, whereas low concentrations are required for high-molecular-weight proteins. Polyelectrolytes such as caprylic acid, polyacrylic acid, carboxymethyl cellulose, and polyethyleneimines precipitate proteins at a much lower concentration (usually <0.1%) than nonionic polymers. They act more like flocculants and adsorb to the protein. Thus, polyelectrolytes, unlike PEG, coprecipitate with the protein and can cause irreversible denaturation.

- *Affinity precipitation.* The purification of recombinant proteins carrying affinity fusion tags has been used successfully for many years at the laboratory scale, but has been too expensive to deploy for industrial-scale manufacturing (Smith et al. 1988). However, the development of polypeptides that allow heat-dependent phase separation, such as the ELP tag mentioned above, and their conversion to a self-cleaving format, has allowed their utilization for the purification of antibodies in an industrial-scale process (Sheth et al. 2014).

Evaporation

In some biomanufacturing processes, evaporation may be a suitable volume reduction step. To minimize protein denaturation, vacuum evaporation may be used. Operating temperatures below 40°C are desirable. Foaming often causes equipment fouling and protein denaturation at the air–water interface. Ultrafiltration (see the section "Filtration Methods Used in Product Isolation and Purification" below) is a much gentler method of volume reduction for proteins, and has largely replaced evaporation in industrial-scale applications.

Flocculation

Flocculation is a similar process to coagulation, where suspended particles clump together because the attractive forces between them overcome any repulsive forces caused by like surface charges (Shaeiwitz et al. 2012). Such repulsive forces can be eliminated, for example, through the addition of inorganic electrolytes that shield the surface charges, or by the addition of polyelectrolytes that bind to and neutralize the surface charge. Flocculation is the agglomeration of particles due to the bridging effect exerted by polymers that are adsorbed to more than one particle. Coagulation and flocculation probably occur simultaneously when polymeric polyelectrolytes are added. Flocculation has been used mainly for the removal of whole cells from fermentation broth, and more recently for the removal of cell debris and proteins. Particles are often coagulated or flocculated prior to filtration to reduce the passage of small noncoagulated particles through the filter and to produce a more porous cake which is easier to remove. Various types of flocculants have been tested, including anionic polyelectrolytes such as polymethacrylic acid or polyacrylic acid, which are most often used to flocculate the product as a means to facilitate purification by precipitation (McDonald et al. 2009), and cationic flocculants such as polyamines and chitosan, which interact strongly with anionic components such as liposomes, cell debris, endotoxins, nucleic acids, and a vast majority of host cell proteins (HCPs). The flocs can form by charge bridging or charge neutralization, and achieve up to 80% HCP clearance and 99% host cell DNA removal (Peram et al. 2010). Both anionic and cationic flocculants have a limited operational window, and a more recent trend is the use of multimodal flocculants that combine electrostatic interactions, hydrogen bonds, and/ or hydrophobic interactions (Capito et al. 2013).

Filtration Methods Used in Product Isolation and Purification

Overview

In downstream processing, filtration refers to any process in which a liquid feedstock containing suspended particles or dissolved molecules is forced through a selectively permeable medium, such as a microporous membrane, such that only certain components of the feed pass through into the permeate while other components are retained on or in the filter medium (the retentate) (Jornitz and Meltzer 2004, Shukla and Suda 2017, Singh and Chollangi 2017). Filtration predominantly separates the components of a mixture according to particle or molecular size, because the minimum pore size is the most important characteristic of any filtration device. However, more sophisticated matrices have chemically modified surfaces which can specifically trap particular molecules based on their affinity or physicochemical properties, making such separations equivalent in practical terms to the corresponding chromatography steps (Etzel and Arunkumar 2017). Filtration is a mechanical process, and a driving force across the filter medium is required. The driving force can be generated by gravity, a pressure differential, the application of a vacuum, a centrifugal force (see the section "Gravity Separation and Centrifugation" above), a difference in concentration or electrical charge across the medium, a temperature differential, or in some cases a specific form of chemical attraction or repulsion (Jornitz et al. 2002).

Filtration is applied at many different stages in downstream processing, both during product isolation and purification. Filtration methods are applied widely in biomanufacturing processes because they operate at relatively low temperatures and pressures, and require no phase changes or chemical additives. Thus, these processes cause minimal denaturation, deactivation, or degradation of labile macromolecules such as proteins. Filtration methods are often subcategorized on the basis of retentate size, as summarized in Table 15.1 (Zeman and Zydney 1996).

- *Microfiltration* is used throughout the process train, for example, for cell/particulate removal during clarification and for sterile filtration toward the end of the process. When microfiltration is used as a clarification method, the product stream may comprise either the retained cells on the upstream side of the filter (containing an intracellular product) or, if the product is secreted, the filtrate on the downstream side (Jornitz et al. 2003). The membrane pore size in microfiltration ranges from 0.1–1.0 µm depending on the specific application.
- *Ultrafiltration* is similar in principle to microfiltration, but the pore sizes are an order of magnitude smaller and the filters are used for the retention of molecules in solution as well as suspended particles (Dosmar and Pinto 2008). For this reason, the retentate can be expressed

TABLE 15.1

Different Forms of Filtration Used in Downstream Processing

Method	Pore Size	Retained	Applications
Microfiltration	100 nm–10 µm	Cells, cell debris	Clarification, sterile filtration (fill and finish)
Ultrafiltration	10–100 nm (M_r 10^3–10^6)	Fine particles, viruses, large proteins	Clarification, virus clearance, size fractionation of proteins, concentration, diafiltration
Nanofiltration	1–10 nm (M_r < 10^3)	Nucleic acids, viruses, proteins	Purification of proteins, virus clearance
Reverse osmosis	0.1–1 nm (M_r < 10^3)	Salts, sugars	Water purification

either in terms of particle size or in terms of molecular weight (Table 15.1). Ultrafiltration in the lower size range can be used to size fractionate proteins, and separate target proteins from buffer components for buffer exchange, desalting, or concentration. Another important application is to ensure virus removal in later processing steps, using filters with pore sizes up to 50 nm. This requirement originated from process development for the purification of plasma proteins, as discussed by Walter et al. (1998) and Sofer (2003), as well as in relevant regulatory documents and technical guidelines (CPMP 1996, 1997, PDA 2005). The validation of virus removal by ultrafiltration is discussed by Zhou (2017).

Ultrafiltration membranes are available in many different materials that provide alternatives in terms of chemical compatibility and tendency to suffer from fouling. Low-protein-binding variants (e.g., cellulose acetate, polyacrylonitrile–polyvinylchloride copolymer, modified polyethersulfone) are designed with biopharmaceutical manufacturing in mind. The choice of membrane for different applications has been discussed (Rubin and Christy 2002, Etzel and Arunkumar 2017).

Nanofiltration and *reverse osmosis* are similar to ultrafiltration but the pore sizes are even smaller and the molecular weight cutoff points even lower. They are typically used to separate low-molecular-weight molecules from water and other solvents, for example, in desalination or the preparation of pure water. In biopharmaceutical manufacturing, such membranes are used for buffer preparation and formulation.

Configuration and Design of Filter Modules

There are two main configurations of filter devices in downstream processing (Figure 15.4). In *dead-end filtration* (also known as *normal-flow filtration*) the feed stream is perpendicular to the filter device, which is usually a membrane or pad. The filter device effectively blocks the feed, which must be forced through it under pressure. Because this configuration inevitably leads to the rapid buildup of retentate on the feed-side filter surface, it is used mainly for laboratory-scale processes if the feed contains a high concentration of the retained species. For large-scale processes, dead-end filtration is only used where the retentate load in the feed stream is anticipated to be low (e.g., sterile filtration for product filling, virus removal). Where filtration is used for clarification and size fractionation, *tangential-flow filtration* (also known as *cross-flow filtration*) is preferred. In this configuration, the feed flow is parallel to the filter medium and thus perpendicular to the flow of permeates. This allows retained species to be swept along the filter surface and out of the device, helping to maintain high flux levels even with large amounts of retentate.

Tangential-flow filter modules come in many designs. These differ in terms of channel spacing, packing density, cost, pumping energy requirements, plugging tendency, and ease of cleaning, so the design must be chosen on a case-by-case basis for each bioprocess depending on the implications of the above criteria in the context of the overall process train (Jornitz et al. 2002, Dosmar et al. 2005). Filter media can be divided into two major types: surface filters and depth filters (Figure 15.5a). *Surface filters* are essentially thin membranes containing capillary-like pores. Particles or molecules which are too big to

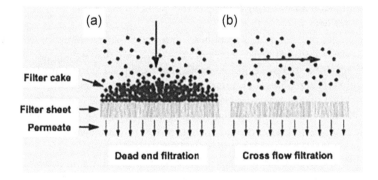

FIGURE 15.4 Comparison of (a) dead-end (normal flow) and (b) tangential (cross-flow) filtration. In each panel, the large arrow shows the direction of feed flow and the small arrows show the direction of permeate accumulation.

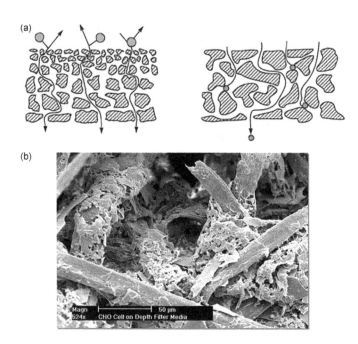

FIGURE 15.5 Comparison of membrane and depth filters. (a) The filtration mechanism of membrane filters (left panel) is absolute, with particles above a certain size rejected at the surface and smaller particles allowed through to the permeate, whereas that of depth filters (right panel) is not absolute, with particles becoming trapped in the internal matrix but some getting through. (b) Micrograph of Sartoclear® P depth filter media that has been used for the clarification of CHO cell broth, showing CHO cells trapped on the cellulose fibers.

pass through the pores are retained on the membrane surface, that is, the filtration is *absolute* at a certain particle-size cutoff and this can be validated as discussed below.

In contrast, *depth filters* have a thicker "bed" of filter medium rather than a thin membrane, and particles are trapped in the interstices of the internal structure, which describes a torturous path from one side of the filter to the other. To increase the surface area available for filtration without increasing the footprint, depth filter pads are either inserted manually into filter presses or, preferably, supplied as lenticular filters, in which multiple filter pads are preassembled in a modular housing.

The materials used to construct depth filters include cellulose fibers, inorganic filter aids, resin binders, and synthetic polymers, offering a large inner surface area and void volumes of up to 85% (Singhvi et al. 1996, Prashad and Tarrach 2006). Inorganic filter aids such as diatomaceous earth and perlite increase the permeability and retention characteristics of the filter matrix, whereas synthetic polymers and resin binders increase the strength of the filter medium and generate a net positive charge that helps to trap colloids. For these reasons, depth filters can trap particles much smaller than the maximum pore size. The retention mechanism of depth filters is not absolute, and changes during operation as retentate builds up in the filter matrix. Therefore, depth filters cannot be validated for use in sterile filtration in the same way as membrane filters, but because they are less expensive than membrane filters they are often employed in prefilter steps to remove cells and debris. For example, feed streams from mammalian cell cultures often feature two depth filters in series to clarify the fermentation broth for reactor volumes up to approximately 3,000 L. For greater volumes, a continuous centrifuge is typically used to remove the largest particles followed by depth filtration and membrane filtration in series to remove smaller particles and fines. A Sartoclear® P depth filter that has been used for the clarification of Chinese hamster ovary (CHO) cell broth is shown as an example in Figure 15.5b.

Recent innovations have increased the capacity of depth filters, which was traditionally low due to a combination of incomplete depth media utilization and limited binding capacity for HCPs and nucleic acids. New media, therefore, benefit from better utilization for capture and higher retention of impurities and reduce the levels of impurities in the permeate. For example, Clarisolve™ (EMD Millipore) provides a wide pore size distribution suitable for the broader particle size distribution found in cell suspension cultures (Tomic et al. 2015). Charged depth filters more effectively reduce the levels of HCP, DNA, and endotoxins, as well as viruses (Metzger et al. 2015).

Filtration Efficiency

The capacity of a filtration process is usually expressed in terms of *flux*, which is the volume of permeate passing through a particular membrane area per unit time (usually liters per square meter per hour) (Dosmar et al. 2005). The driving force for flux is the pressure difference between the feed side and the permeate side, which is known as the transmembrane pressure. Opposing this is the viscosity of the liquid and the hydraulic resistance of the membrane, which depends on the pore size and distribution. The permeability of the membrane is operationally defined as the inverse of its hydraulic resistance.

For a pure water feed, flux increases linearly with transmembrane pressure because resistance and viscosity remain constant. During a typical filtration process, however, the flux tends to decline over time because both viscosity and resistance increase. During cross-flow filtration, flux declines rapidly at first, then the decline slows down, and eventually a steady state is achieved. This reflects two simultaneous phenomena—cake layer build up and fouling. *Cake layer build up* occurs in microfiltration when retentate particles accumulate on the feed side and achieve a packing density that causes them to form a defined layer on top of the membrane. This has two consequences. First, the cake layer resists the flow of permeate by effectively acting as an additional filter bed, increasing the thickness of the filter membrane, and leading to increased resistance. Second, the local viscosity of the feed increases because the concentration of particles near the filter surface is higher than in the bulk feed, resulting in reduced flux. In ultrafiltration, the equivalent phenomenon is known as *concentration polarization*, where the retentate remains in solution but builds up on the feed side, increasing in concentration to such an extent that the osmotic pressure of the retained solute opposes the force driving the permeate across the membrane. At very high concentrations, the retentate can approach its solubility limit and form a gel layer on the membrane surface that also obstructs the flow of permeate (Dosmar and Pinto 2008).

Cake layer buildup and concentration polarization are both consequences of the retentate accumulating on the feed side, and both can be reversed by cleaning or back-washing, because they do not permanently affect filter performance. On the other hand, *fouling* is a distinct phenomenon in which molecules in the feed physically and chemically interact with the membrane leading to a permanent loss of function. Examples include the adsorption and deposition of macromolecules, cell fragments, or small organic molecules on the membrane surface or within the pores. Fouling increases the hydraulic resistance against permeate flow, and may also increase the observed retention of the membrane as it reduces the effective pore size. As stated above, membranes used in biopharmaceutical manufacture are designed to prevent the binding of proteins as much as possible, thereby reducing fouling and helping to avoid the loss of product through binding to the filter medium.

Validation and Integrity Testing

The suitability and reliability of a membrane filter for particular manufacturing purposes is established through basic performance and integrity tests (Jornitz and Meltzer 2003). This is important because the selectivity of a filter is determined by its largest pores and any weakness or loss of integrity could lead to contamination of the permeate with molecules or particles from the retentate, including viruses and prions (CPMP 1996, 1997, Immelmann et al. 2005, Zhou 2017). Filters for microfiltration and ultrafiltration are usually tested beyond recommended tolerances using the equipment, physical conditions, and material requirements of the intended process, according to the criteria listed below.

- Bubble point/breakthrough point testing to establish the largest pore size
- Testing for extractables (particulate or soluble contaminants originating from the filter medium or equipment)
- Flux and capacity using pure water
- Pore size, established using a range of polymers of known size.

Chromatography Techniques for Product Capture, Purification, and Polishing

Overview

Chromatography refers to any procedure in which the components of a mixture are separated by distribution between two phases for which they have differing affinities. Among the many different chromatography formats available, the one that is usually applied in large-scale downstream processing is column-based liquid chromatography, in which a liquid feed stream is passed over or through a porous, solid matrix or resin held in a column (Desai et al. 2000, Strube et al. 2019). The components of the mixture become distributed by virtue of their relative affinity for the solid and liquid phases. In most cases, this is based on selective adsorption to the resin (i.e., there is some kind of molecular interaction with the resin), although gel filtration chromatography, also known as SEC, is an exception as discussed below.

The general procedure for adsorptive chromatography is to introduce the clarified feed stream into the column under conditions where certain components bind strongly to the resin while others flow through. The composition of the buffer is chosen to favor the retention or elution of specific components. By changing the composition of this buffer, molecules that initially bind to the resin can be washed through in subsequent fractions. Chromatography columns can be run in bind-and-elute/retention mode, where the target protein is initially retained and impurities are washed through before the buffer is changed and the target is eluted, or in flow-through mode, where impurities are retained and the desired protein is eluted. Affinity chromatography is usually run in retention mode, and the interaction between the target molecule and the resin is so specific that only a few species are retained while most impurities are washed through. Elution usually occurs in a single step to recover the target protein. The other adsorption chromatography methods exploit more general physicochemical properties and both the retained fraction and the eluate are usually complex. For this reason, elution is typically performed with a gradually changing buffer composition to elute a series of fractions whose components have gradually increasing affinity for the resin. In large-scale processes, gradient elution may be replaced with stepwise gradients which are easier to automate, although programmable linear gradients are becoming more common. Adsorptive column chromatography is particularly applicable in downstream processing because short columns with a large diameter (up to 2 m) can achieve very high flow rates of 300–500 cm/h (Strube et al. 2019). The power of chromatography as a purification strategy is that two or more different operations can be carried out in series to achieve maximum separation by exploiting different principles. In this regard, the logical sequence of chromatography steps should take into account the composition of the feed and the starting and elution conditions. For example, HIC generally begins with a high-salt buffer but the elution buffer is of low ionic strength. The converse applies in ion exchange chromatography, so where both are used in a given process it makes sense to place these operations back to back.

Traditionally, the manufacturing of biopharmaceutical proteins has involved the batch production strategy, but following the lead from other manufacturing industries the benefits of continuous production have been embraced and various continuous chromatography systems have been tested (Bisschops 2017). The simplest approach is simulated moving bed chromatography, which was first adapted for the production of proteins to facilitate the affinity-based purification of enzymes (Gottschlich et al. 1996) and antibodies (Gottschlich et al. 1997). This has evolved into a variety of more complex continuous multicolumn systems such as the small-scale 3C-PCC and 4C-PCC formats (GE Healthcare) and MCSGP Contichrom® system (Chromacon/Knauer) with multiport valves, and the BioSC® (Novasep), Octave™ (Semba Biosciences) and BioSMB® (Pall Life Sciences) systems, which use distributed valve technology and are compliant with current good manufacturing practice (cGMP), the regulations that ensure the safety and quality of pharmaceutical products. Most of these systems are used at the capture step (Müller-Späth et al. 2010) but they have also been explored for the purification of bispecific antibodies (Hendriks et al. 2013) and the removal of aggregates using ion exchange or hydrophobic interaction matrices (Stock et al. 2015, Bisschops 2017).

Affinity Chromatography

In affinity chromatography, the desired product is adsorbed onto a resin containing a covalently bonded specific ligand, usually but not always reflecting the biological function of the target molecule

(Wilchek and Chaiken 2000, Chaga 2001, Turkova 2002). The ligand exploits the complexity of the target protein's structure, which consists of four basic intermolecular binding forces—electrostatic bonds (salt bridges), hydrogen bonding, hydrophobic forces, and van der Waals interactions—distributed spatially in a defined manner. The degree of accessibility and spatial presentation within the resin, and the strength of each force relative to each other, dictate whether these forces are utilized to effect the separation. The overall affinity of the biological recognition between ligand and counter-ligand reflects the sum of the various molecular interactions existing between them. However, various ligands may be found that emulate some or all of the available binding forces to various degrees. Therefore, in some cases, the ligand may be absolutely specific for a particular protein, for example, an immunoglobulin raised against a specific target, or an immobilized substrate which will capture the corresponding enzyme. In other cases, the ligand may recognize a particular family of proteins, for example, protein A will purify most immunoglobulin G (Ey et al. 1978, Suralia 1982, Huse et al. 2002). General or group-specific ligands can be used to select proteins with particular characteristics, for example, immobilized metal ions can be used to trap proteins with positively charged amino acids, as is the case for His_6-tagged recombinant proteins (Loetscher et al. 1992, Crowe et al. 1994). There are also large numbers of artificial ligands such as textile dyes and those based on rational design or the screening of chemical libraries (Curling 2004a, b). Specific interactions can be used to trap suitably labeled proteins, for example, proteins modified to contain particular epitopes or fusion partners can be trapped by corresponding antibodies or binding partners, and proteins labeled with biotin can be trapped by their affinity to avidin.

Because affinity chromatography is highly selective, it is the favored method of product capture (the initial stage of isolation). Unlike the other chromatography methods discussed below, the capacity of the resin is not compromised by the binding of hundreds of foreign proteins, because only those proteins with very specific binding affinity will adsorb to the matrix. This means that purification factors in the tens of thousands can be achieved in principle, although the actual purification factor rarely exceeds 100 in practice. In the manufacture of antibodies, for example, the isolation stage generally comprises a microfiltration step followed by protein A affinity chromatography. This results in the elimination of all particulates and 99% of soluble impurities in the first two steps (Huse et al. 2002). The eluate from the affinity chromatography column can then be applied directly to downstream chromatography steps to separate the antibody from degradation products and column extractables, such as leached protein A.

In a typical process (Figure 15.6), the column is first equilibrated with a buffer reflecting the optimum binding conditions between ligand and counter-ligand. Clarified feed is introduced into the top of the column and allowed to percolate through the resin under gravity, or with positive pressure. The feed may also be adjusted, in terms of ionic strength and pH, to optimize binding. The column is then washed with several volumes of the equilibration buffer to wash through unbound components. This step has been completed correctly when the UV absorbance of the eluate returns to the base line level.

Recovery of the bound protein is achieved by desorption, which in this case means the disruption of ligand/counter-ligand binding by changing the binding equilibrium. Depending on the ligand, this can be achieved specifically or nonspecifically. Specific desorption relies on competition for ligand-binding sites between the adsorbed protein and a free counter-ligand which is added to the elution buffer at the appropriate concentration. An example of specific desorption is the elution of bound glycoproteins from a lectin affinity column, which is achieved through the addition of competing carbohydrates. Advantages of specific desorption include the requirement for only low concentrations of the competitor (5–100 mM) and the fact that elution is carried out at the functional pH of the target protein, so denaturation does not occur. Nonspecific desorption is achieved by changing the pH or ionic strength of the buffer. Decreasing the pH to 2–4 is usually effective, although for proteins that function at low pH ranges an increase in pH may be a more suitable option. Increasing the amount of salt in the buffer disrupts electrostatic interactions, so where protein–ligand interaction is predominantly due to electrostatic bonds, salt gradient elution is a good choice. Where binding is predominantly due to hydrophobic interactions, neither salt concentration nor pH may disrupt binding. Under these circumstances, elution may be facilitated by the introduction of detergents or chaotropes into the buffer. An example is the rat biotin-binding protein, which is separated from the immobilized biotin ligand using a combination of free biotin in the elution buffer and one or more protein denaturants.

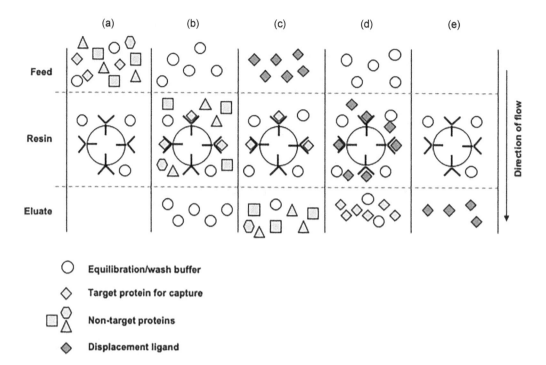

FIGURE 15.6   The principle of affinity chromatography. (a) A complex feed is passed through a column containing resin beads bearing a covalently attached ligand that recognizes the desired target protein. (b) Only the target protein binds to the ligands. (c) The nontarget proteins are washed through with buffer. (d) The elution buffer contains a counter ligand or another component which encourages desorption of the target protein from the affinity matrix, and the target protein is recovered in a substantially purified and concentrated form from the eluate. (e) The affinity matrix is stripped with NaOH and re-equilibrated.

   Although affinity chromatography involves very specific and strong interactions between ligand and target, the interactions are not covalent so column resins can be used for many cycles before replacement. Regeneration of the adsorbent involves a series of washes with reagents such as 0.1 M NaOH that remove all non-covalently bound molecules, theoretically without damaging the ligand itself, a process known as cleaning in place (CIP). This is followed by re-equilibration with the initial buffer. Eventually, column media need to be replaced due to fouling (permanent chemical modification of the ligand) and leaching (removal of the ligand from the matrix, either during a process run or during CIP). However, both these problems have been addressed by recent developments in affinity chromatography media. In the case of protein A affinity chromatography, for example, variants of the original *Staphylococcus aureus* protein A have been designed for greater stability in the alkaline environments used for CIP (Bergander et al. 2004). Alternative ligands for antibody capture have also been described, such as protein G (from *Streptococcus pyogenes*) which, unlike protein A, binds IgG3 with high affinity, and protein Z, an engineered variant of protein A. Another alternative ligand is protein L (from *Peptostreptococcus magnus*) which binds specifically to the kappa light chain (Bjorck 1998). Due to the higher cost of these reagents, some researchers have attempted to develop chemical and biomimetic ligands derived from peptide libraries, combinatorial chemistry, and rational ligand design (Mouratou et al. 2015). Ligands such as 4-mercaptoethyl pyridine (MEP), 2-mercapto-5-benzymidazole sulfonic acid (MBI) and certain triazine derivatives cost 50%–70% less than protein A and can survive over 200 cycles of binding, eluting, and CIP with more efficient cleaning reagents such as 0.5–1 M NaOH. They also operate over a greater pH range than protein A and tend not to leach into the process stream (McCormick 2005) resulting in the development of mimetic resins such as MabSorbent A2P (Prometic Biosciences, Cambridge, UK) and MEP HyperCel (Pall). These have not proven to be as efficient as protein A, but the cost savings are significant (Ferreira et al. 2007). As is the case for ion exchange chromatography and HIC, alternative separation modes have been introduced to a limited extent for affinity chromatography matrices such as protein A, including the use of membrane adsorbers to replace fixed-bed columns (Boi et al. 2005) and expanded bed chromatography (Fahrner et al. 1999).

Ion Exchange Chromatography

Whereas affinity chromatography exploits very specific interactions between the target molecule and an appropriate ligand, other forms of chromatography separate molecules on the basis of general physico-chemical properties such as size, charge, and hydrophobicity. Therefore, columns may be run in either flow-through mode or bind-and-elute/retention mode, depending on which is the most efficient for separating the target protein from contaminants. Ion exchange chromatography separates proteins on the basis of their net charge, which as discussed earlier reflects the number and nature of charged amino acid residues on the protein as well as the pH of the buffer (Boschetti and Girot 2002). The ability to control the polarity and magnitude of a protein's charge by varying the pH is exploited in ion exchange chromatography for the selective adsorption of target proteins onto a resin derivatized with charged groups. Anionic and cationic resins of varying strengths may be used to adsorb proteins of the opposite charge. Some examples of anionic and cationic exchangers are listed in Table 15.2.

The process for ion exchange chromatography is similar to that described for affinity chromatography with important differences in column capacity and elution mechanics. Initially, the column is equilibrated with a low-ionic-strength buffer containing ions of opposite charge to the resin (Figure 15.7). These counter-ions are displaced by charged molecules in the feed stream, which adsorb to the resin. When run in retention mode, the strength and selectivity of binding between the target protein and the resin are optimized by adjusting the ionic strength and pH of the buffer, and the flow rate through the column, such that maximum retention of the target is achieved. In flow-through mode, these conditions are adjusted to optimize the retention of particular contaminants. However, since many proteins will share the same charge profile and pI value as the target, numerous competing molecules will co-segregate in the appropriate fraction. In retention mode, this means that the true binding capacity of the column for the target protein is actually below the theoretical maximum. This operating capacity for the target, in the presence of impurities, is known as the dynamic capacity.

Elution from an ion exchange column is achieved by washing with buffers of gradual or stepped increases in ionic strength, or gradual or stepped changes in pH in the appropriate direction. The principle is very much the same as that employed for the elution of the adsorbed fraction from affinity columns when the affinity of target and ligand is determined mostly through electrostatic bonds. The main difference is that in affinity chromatography, the selectivity of binding is such that only one elution fraction is generally required, whereas in ion exchange chromatography it is possible to produce a number of different fractions by stepwise elution. The resolution of ion exchange chromatography is influenced by the sample load, linear flow rate, and slope of the elution gradient. The best results are obtained by adjusting gradient volumes to the resolution required.

As mentioned above in the filtration section, a more sophisticated approach to ion exchange chromatography is the use of microporous membranes with built-in ion exchange capacity (Gosh 2002, Gottschalk et al. 2004, Gottschalk 2006b). Column chromatography often involves long separation times, and the

TABLE 15.2

Some Examples of Anionic and Cationic Exchangers Used in Chromatography

Anion Exchangers	Functional Group	Comments
Diethylaminoethyl (DEAE)	$-O-CH_2-CH_2-N^+H(CH_2CH_3)_2$	Weak
Quaternary aminoethyl (QAE)	$-O-CH_2-CH_2-N^+(C_2H_5)_2-CH_2-CHOH-CH_3$	Strong
Quaternary ammonium (Q)	$-O-CH_2-CHOH-CH_2-O-CH_2-CHOH-CH_2-N^+(CH_3)_3$	Strong

Cation Exchangers	Functional Group	Comments
Carboxymethyl (CM)	$-O-CH_2-COO^-$	Weak
Sulfopropyl (S)	$-O-CH_2-CHOH-CH_2-O-CH_2-CH_2-CH_2SO_3^-$	Strong
Methylsulfonate (M)	$-O-CH_2-CHOH-CH_2-O-CH_2-CHOH-CH_2SO_3^-$	Strong

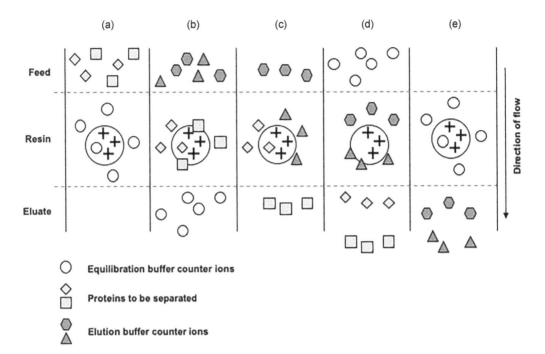

FIGURE 15.7 The principle of ion exchange chromatography, using a strong cation exchange resin in bind-and-elute/ retention mode. (a) Initially, the positively charged resin is occupied by negative counter-ions in the equilibration buffer. (b) As the feed moves through the column, negatively charged (acidic) proteins adsorb to the resin and displace the negative ions, while positively charged (basic) proteins flow through. (c) At the start of desorption, gradient ions are added to the column in the elution buffer to disrupt the weakest interactions, so weakly acidic proteins are eluted first. (d) Desorption proceeds stepwise, with the most acidic proteins eluted in the last fraction. (e) The column is then cleaned in place and regenerated with equilibration buffer.

use of membrane adsorbers can reduce process times by 100-fold compared to conventional chromatography while maintaining a flow rate of 20–40 bed volumes/min (Zhou and Tressel 2006). Figure 15.8a shows some standard chromatography media on the surface of a Sartobind Membrane Adsorber. More than 95% of binding sites are found inside conventional beads making them inaccessible. In contrast, binding sites on Sartobind membranes are found on a homogeneous film approximately 0.5–1 μm in thickness on the inner walls of the reinforced and cross-linked cellulose network. The diffusion time in such adsorbers is negligible because of the large pores and the immediate binding of target proteins to the ligands. The fluid dynamics of conventional beads and membrane adsorbers are compared in Figure 15.8b. Membrane adsorbers have become increasingly versatile over the last decade and are now key components of many downstream processes, especially anion exchange membranes. Despite their low binding capacity, they can remove trace impurities in flow through mode at higher flow rates and loading capacities than traditional resins, due to the convection-limited open pore structure of the membrane (Thömmes et al. 2017). Membrane chromatography is ideal for polishing because the loading capacity is much higher than that of packed-bed resins, HCPs and nucleic acids are retained very efficiently, and the flow rate can be increased to more than 1,000 cm/h allowing very large feed volumes to be processed (Knudsen et al. 2001, Phillips et al. 2005, Brown et al. 2010). Anion exchange membranes are available in various configurations from vendors such as Pall (Mustang Q) and Sartorius (Sartobind Q), the latter also offering a salt-tolerant primary amine ligand (Sartobind STIC).

Chromatography Methods that Exploit Hydrophobic Interactions

Many proteins are hydrophobic in nature due to the predominance of nonpolar amino acid residues on the surface. Even proteins that are polar and therefore stable in aqueous solvents may have hydrophobic

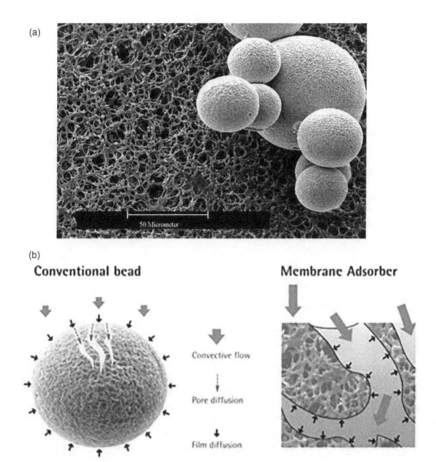

FIGURE 15.8 (a) Scanning electron micrograph showing standard ion exchange chromatography beads on the surface of a Sartobind Q membrane. Even at 500-fold magnification, pores in the beads cannot be seen, whereas the membrane pores are easily visible. (b) Transport phenomena occurring in conventional beads and in membrane adsorbers (after Gosh, 2002).

patches that allow them to interact with other proteins sharing similar characteristics. The basis of such interactions is the increase in entropy that occurs when (polar) solvent molecules are excluded from the interface. This can be exploited as a chromatography technique if a hydrophobic resin is used in concert with a strongly polar solvent—that is, a concentrated salt solution—the chromatographic equivalent of "salting out" (see the section "Chromatography Methods that Exploit Hydrophobic Interactions" above). Hydrophobic proteins then increase the entropy of the system by interacting preferentially with the hydrophobic resin (Lienqueno et al. 2007).

Like ion exchange chromatography, HIC involves the reversible adsorption of proteins to a resin and elution using a buffer which disrupts such interactions (Jennissen 2002). In this case (Figure 15.9), the resin is equilibrated in a high-salt buffer and the feed stream similarly adjusted to high ionic strength so that proteins bind preferentially to the resin. Desorption is achieved by stepwise reductions in the salt concentration of the elution buffer, sometimes in combination with a gradual increase in the concentration of an organic solvent such as ethanediol that encourages hydrophobic proteins back into solution. The most suitable ligands for HIC are C_2-C_8 alkyl groups and phenyl groups, which undergo hydrophobic interactions with most proteins but are not so hydrophobic that extreme conditions are required for elution (see the section "Chromatography Based on Size Exclusion" below). As in ion exchange chromatography, the stepwise modification of elution buffer composition results in fractions containing sequentially more hydrophobic proteins. The resolution of HIC is influenced by the sample load, linear flow rate and slope of the elution gradient, and can be optimized by decreasing the flow rate and increasing the gradient volume.

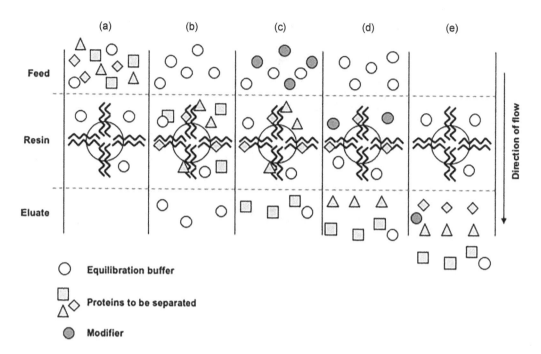

FIGURE 15.9 The principle of HIC running in bind-and-elute/retention mode. (a) Initially, the hydrophobic resin is unoccupied, and its interaction with the high salt buffer is energetically unfavorable. (b) As the feed moves through the column, hydrophobic proteins adsorb to the resin and displace salt ions, thereby increasing the entropy of the system. Meanwhile, polar proteins interact with the solvent and are washed through. (c) At the start of desorption, the amount of salt in the buffer is reduced, allowing the least hydrophobic proteins back into solution such that they are eluted first. (d) Desorption proceeds stepwise, with the most hydrophobic proteins eluted in the last fraction where the buffer has a very low ionic strength and may be supplemented with a weak organic modifier. (e) The column is then cleaned in place and regenerated with equilibration buffer.

HIC is used most often as a polishing step and is particularly useful for the removal of process-related impurities and aggregates (Lu et al. 2014) but it can also be used for the capture of proteins with hydrophobic patches (Ren et al. 2014). Although HIC resins remain the most popular format, various types of HIC membrane have been developed and these help to reduce buffer consumption (Orr et al. 2013), for example, during the purification of monoclonal antibodies from low-titer feed streams (Yu et al. 2008).

RPC is a related technique which also uses a hydrophobic interaction matrix to separate proteins. The main difference is that the resins used for RPC are much more hydrophobic than those used in HIC (e.g., C_{10}-C_{18} alkyl groups) and the elution solvents need to be stronger and usually denature the proteins which are eluted (e.g., acetonitrile or isopropanol). For this reason, RPC is rarely used for the industrial-scale processing of biopharmaceuticals unless the target protein is a polypeptide or small protein equivalent to the size of insulin or below. Large-scale RPC is more widely used for the preparation of small-molecule drugs, such as antibiotics.

Chromatography Based on Size Exclusion

SEC, also known as gel filtration chromatography, is distinct from the chromatography methods described above because it does not depend on selective absorption and desorption. Instead, the principle underlying SEC is the sieving of molecules by size as they percolate through the resin (Eriksson 2002). The column is packed with inert beads whose surfaces are covered with pores. The size selectivity of the resin depends on the size of those pores, because larger molecules cannot enter the pores and are eluted rapidly, whereas molecules smaller than the pore size will become trapped, and will move through the resin more slowly (Figure 15.10). This is known as molecular exclusion, and is distinct from the other forms of chromatography because there is no chemical interaction between the proteins in the sample and the resin.

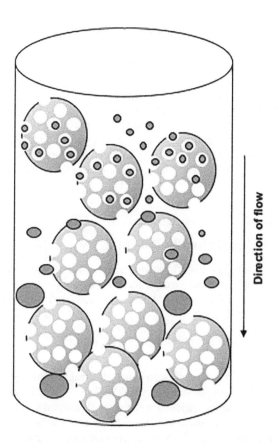

Direction of flow

FIGURE 15.10 The principle of SEC (gel filtration chromatography). A column is packed with inert beads containing pores of a certain size. As the feed percolates through the column, small molecules become trapped in the pores and are delayed, whereas molecules unable to fit in the pores travel rapidly through the gaps between beads. Different media are used to separate molecules within different size ranges.

Resins are available which separate molecules within particular size ranges (Table 15.3). SEC is therefore used for the fine fractionation of molecules by size in the same way that gel electrophoresis exploits the sieving potential of agarose and polyacrylamide gels. Indeed, many of the SEC media available commercially are based on agarose, polyacrylamide, and other polymers. An important concept in SEC is that the separation medium is the pores on the beads and not the beads themselves. Therefore, 95%–99% of the column volume remains unused in any operation, and feed volumes must be adjusted accordingly,

TABLE 15.3

Some Examples of Size-Exclusion Chromatography Media

Name	Substrate	Size Range (M_r)
Bio-Gel P-2	Acrylamide	100–1,800
Sephadex G-25	Dextran	1,000–5,000
Sephacryl S-100 HR	Dextran-acrylamide	1,000–100,000
Fractogel TSK HW-55	Hydrophilic vinyl	1,000–1,000,000
Superdex 75	Agarose-dextran	3,000–70,000
Sephacryl S-200 HR	Dextran-acrylamide	5,000–250,000
Sephacryl S-300 HR	Dextran-acrylamide	10,000–1,500,000
Sephacryl S-400 HR	Dextran-acrylamide	20,000–8,000,000
Fractogel TSK HW-65	Hydrophilic vinyl	50,000–5,000,000

representing a significant bottleneck. For this reason, SEC is often the very final stage in biopharmaceutical purification, and is used to separate the target protein from very similar molecules such as degradation products and multimers. The most important variables in SEC are the column length and linear flow rate. Slow mass transfer of macromolecules can cause peak broadening and loss of resolution, which can be addressed by reducing the flow rate.

SEC with resins suitable for molecules in the lowest size ranges ($M_r < 5,000$) is used to separate macromolecules from low-molecular-weight compounds, and is thus useful for desalting or rebuffering protein samples. This is an alternative to filtration-based methods, such as diafiltration and reverse osmosis, and has a much higher capacity and flow rate than SEC running in fine separation mode. Sample volumes in buffer exchange may reach up to 30% of the column volume, compared to the 1%–3% possible with fine separations (Strube et al. 2019).

Low-Technology Techniques Used in Polishing

Apart from high-technology filtration and chromatography methods which can be used to purify and concentrate the product, and to eliminate viruses, there are also a number of lower-technology methods which are economical to apply at this stage. Crystallization and lyophilization are considered as examples below.

Crystallization

Crystallization is the separation of a solute from a supersaturated solution (mother liquor), achieved by encouraging the formation of small aggregates of solute molecules, which then grow into crystals. The crystallization process involves the formation of a regularly structured solid phase, which impedes the incorporation of contaminants or solvent molecules, and therefore yields products of exceptional purity (Klyushnichenko 2003). It is this purity which makes crystallization particularly suitable for the preparation of pharmaceutical proteins, coupled with the realization that protein crystals enhance protein stability and provide a useful vehicle for drug delivery, as has been demonstrated with various protein drugs including antibodies (e.g., Yang et al. 2003). Protein crystallization has been developed into a proprietary technology for drug stabilization and delivery by companies such as Altus Pharmaceuticals Inc. (which has various crystalline hormones, replacement enzymes, and other protein drugs in late-stage clinical development) and Genencor International Inc. (which has received patents on technology for industrial-scale crystallization). The advantages of crystallization as a final purification and concentration step in clinical manufacturing processes include the following:

- Large-scale crystallization can replace some of the more expensive purification steps in the manufacturing process, making the whole process more affordable.
- Because reactions proceed very slowly if at all in the crystalline state, interactions between molecules are significantly retarded making crystals the ideal way to store and administer mixtures of biological macromolecules.
- Solid crystalline preparations can easily be reconstituted into very highly concentrated formulations for injection, which is particularly useful when intended for subcutaneous administration. The high concentrations required (100–200 mg/mL) are difficult to achieve in liquid formulations because of aggregation.
- Protein crystals may be used as a basis for slow release formulations *in vivo*. Characteristics of the crystal, such as size and shape, degree of cross-linking, and the presence of excipients can be manipulated so as to control the release rate.

There are numerous crystallization methods, including evaporative, cooling, precipitation, melt, and super-critical crystallization, each with specific processing methods and apparatus requirements. Evaporative, precipitation, and cooling crystallization are the most suitable for highly-soluble products, including proteins. However, the large-scale crystallization of proteins requires dedicated approaches because protein molecules are large, and sometimes easily degradable, so they require carefully designed processes (Lee and Kim 2003).

Crystallization is driven by supersaturation of the mother liquor, which may be achieved by cooling, by evaporation of the solvent, or by mixing two reactants or solvents. In all these cases, the actual concentration of the target molecule becomes higher than the equilibrium concentration, and a driving force for crystallization is achieved. Crystallization begins with nucleation, and nuclei then grow by a combination of layered solute deposition and agglomeration caused by random collision. Crystal growth is opposed by the continual dissolution of the solid phase, but conditions are chosen that favor growth over dissolution. The interplay of all these processes determines the crystal size distribution of the solid, which is an important component of the product specification because it determines the separability of particles, and how they respond to washing and drying. Because this is such an important property, the kinetic processes underlying crystallization have been extensively modeled, and can be predicted by using the population balance equation, which describes how the size distribution develops in time as a result of various kinetic processes.

Crystallization can be triggered in several ways, and these are divided into primary and secondary nucleation mechanisms. In primary nucleation, the solid phase forms spontaneously from a clear mother liquor. In cases of heterogeneous nucleation, crystals nucleate around tiny contaminating particles that are present in the solution. In a perfectly pure mother liquor there is no such substrate, and clusters of solute molecules are thought to form randomly, simply through the statistical fluctuation in their distribution (homogeneous nucleation). Secondary nucleation occurs in a mother liquor where crystallization is already in progress. It reflects the formation of tiny crystal fragments through the collision of existing crystals with each other, or with the walls of the crystallizer, which then serve as nuclei for the growth of new crystals. Most crystals are formed by primary nucleation during the initial phase of evaporative or cooling crystallization. When these have grown to form larger crystals, secondary nucleation becomes the predominant source of new crystals. For proteins with low solubility, primary nucleation tends to remain the dominant mechanism throughout crystallization because supersaturation remains high enough, and the crystals tend to be small and therefore not so prone to fragmentation.

Once nuclei have formed, crystal growth occurs by a number of mechanisms. Uniform growth from solution involves the diffusion of additional solute molecules toward the crystal/solution interface followed by their integration into the crystal surface, which creates a local concentration gradient that encourages further crystal growth, at least for highly soluble molecules. Further, nonuniform growth can occur by agglomeration, which is caused by the collision and subsequent cementing together of small crystals. Under supersaturating conditions which favor uniform crystal growth by solute deposition, the cementing of attached particles occurs through the deposition of additional solute molecules that bind the attached crystals together in a common lattice. If there is no supersaturation, attached particles tend to break apart again. The major processes by which collisions and subsequent agglomeration occur include Brownian motion, laminar or turbulent flow within the crystallizer, and gravity settling. The development of crystallization as a technique in biopharmaceutical production has been reviewed (Peters et al. 2005).

Lyophilization

Lyophilization or freeze-drying in pharmaceutical manufacturing is a process in which a pure dissolved product is frozen and then dried by exposure to conditions that cause sublimation of the ice (Oetjen 2000). With pure water as the solvent, reducing the pressure to less than 0.6 atmospheres in a vacuum chamber is sufficient to prevent the formation of liquid water when the frozen product is heated above freezing point. The general approach is therefore to freeze the product and place it on a heated shelf in a vacuum chamber. Once the chamber is evacuated to below 0.6 atmospheres, the temperature is raised to just above the freezing point of water resulting in the sublimation of the ice. At this stage, it is the bulk solvent that sublimates, and this may represent 10–100 times the volume of the dry product depending on its initial concentration. This process is known as *main drying*. Freezing and main drying are usually followed by a *secondary drying* step involving the desorption of water bound to the solid.

For pharmaceutical proteins, this means water molecules attached to the protein via hydrogen bonds. Such water molecules form a monolayer around the protein and have distinct properties to the bulk solvent. They may constitute as little as 5%–10% of the volume of the dried product, but even this amount of water can facilitate some enzymatic reactions that would cause protein degradation. Once this water has been removed, the lyophilized solid is packaged under vacuum to prevent any further exposure to water until ready for formulation.

Lyophilization, like crystallization, is a useful final-stage procedure in biomanufacturing because it provides a way to prevent the reactions that normally occur in solution. Therefore, the process can enhance the stability of a pharmaceutical protein and allow it to be stored for prolonged periods at ambient temperatures without fear of degradation or loss of activity. Lyophilization is relatively expensive to carry out for large-scale processes but the benefits of increasing drug longevity and eliminating the requirement for a cold chain can far outweigh the initial costs.

For pharmaceutical products, the lyophilization process should not impede reconstitution of the drug for formulation. For other products, such as cells, it is necessary to use cryoprotectants to prevent damage to cellular structures and membranes during freezing. For protein drugs, however, the tendency of nascent ice crystals to form pores in the solid product is actually beneficial, because this facilitates access for water molecules when the product is reconstituted and allows it to dissolve rapidly. This is important to maintain the product's structural integrity and biological activity.

Challenges and Opportunities

Expression Platform Diversity

Traditional biomanufacturing has concentrated on a small number of well-characterized upstream production systems, and downstream processes have been developed largely with these systems in mind. The most popular systems are bacterial cells (*Escherichia coli*) for the production of simple proteins (Choi and Lee 2004, Baneyx and Mujacic 2004) and mammalian cells (CHO cells and a small number of alternative rodent or human cell lines) for the production of complex proteins and glycoproteins (Wurm 2004). A few approved pharmaceutical proteins are made in yeast or in cultured insect cells. One striking characteristic of biomanufacturing in the 21st century is that a large number of novel production systems are being explored. This reflects advances in underlying gene transfer and expression technology and perceived advantages of economy and production scale made possible by the adoption of new production systems, especially those based on transgenic animals and plants (Dyck et al. 2003, Twyman et al. 2005, Buyel et al. 2015), the latter being particularly suitable for very-large-scale production (Buyel et al. 2017). The industry's faithful relationship with microbes and mammalian cells is being tested by limitations of production capacity which are becoming evident, and the costs associated with building, testing, and validating new fermenter-based production trains.

The benefits and limitations of bacterial production systems in terms of downstream processing technology are well understood. The recombinant protein is usually expressed as an intracellular product that must be recovered by cell disruption, often accomplished by concussion in a ball mill or by the application of shear forces, for example, in a homogenizer or colloid mill. Some products are expressed as soluble proteins, and in such cases microfiltration is used to remove cell debris and fines prior to capture. However, many recombinant proteins aggregate to form insoluble inclusion bodies, and in these cases continuous centrifugation may be used to separate the dense inclusion bodies from other particulate matter. Solubilization using strong denaturing buffers followed by protein refolding and renaturation are required to recover an active product, which can be time-consuming and difficult to implement on a large scale.

Similarly for eukaryotic cells, downstream processing steps have become well established. The general strategy is to secrete the product into the fermentation broth, so clarification involves separation of cells from the liquid broth by centrifugation and/or filtration and product capture from the supernatant/permeate. Although yeast cells are tough, mammalian and insect cells are fragile, so the pressure must be carefully controlled to avoid lysis. Depth filtration is widely used at this stage.

The recent proliferation of new upstream systems has challenged downstream processing to come up with complementary methods. New systems include the production of recombinant proteins in cultured plant cells, animal milk, serum or urine, silkworms, hens' eggs, and whole plant tissues such as leaves and seeds. Several pharmaceutical products produced in the milk of transgenic animals have been approved, including antithrombin (ATryn®), produced by GTC Biotherapeutics UK Limited (recently acquired by LFB Biotechnologies) in transgenic goats, and C1-esterase inhibitor (Ruconest®), produced by the Pharming Group, NV in transgenic rabbits (Maksimenko et al. 2013). Other companies are working with transgenic cattle (Monzani et al. 2016). Similarly, the first products produced in transgenic plant systems have gained approval, including recombinant glucocerebrosidase (Elylyso®) produced by Protalix Biotherapeutics in carrot cell suspension cultures (Tekoah et al. 2015) and an emergency cocktail of antibodies against Ebola virus (ZMapp®) produced by Leaf Pharmaceutical in tobacco leaves by transient expression (Na et al. 2015). Each of these systems presents new potential advantages in terms of production benefits, but also presents new challenges to downstream processing (Nikolov and Woodard 2004, Menkhaus et al. 2004, Buyel et al. 2015, Monzani et al. 2016, Nikolov et al. 2017).

There is no danger of cell lysis when proteins are expressed in animal body fluids, but each introduces a unique set of contaminants that must be dealt with early in the production train. For example, milk contains a number of endogenous proteins that compete with the recombinant product, as well as fat globules, casein micelles, and soluble lipids which can foul filters and membranes leading to poor process efficiency. The clarification of animal milk should, therefore, include a centrifugation step to remove fat droplets followed by a dedicated membrane filtration step to remove micelles (Baruah et al. 2003). Alternatively, it is possible to precipitate micelles although this can lead to the target protein becoming trapped in micelle aggregates thus reducing recovery rates. Similar principles apply to the recovery of proteins from hens' eggs—the egg white is highly viscous and unsuitable for processing without taking steps to reduce viscosity, which can be achieved through the acid precipitation of ovomucin (Rapp et al. 2003).

Plant tissue also presents challenges in the early stages of downstream processing (Menkhaus et al. 2004, Buyel et al. 2015). Seeds must be ground or milled to flour to allow the solubilization of the target protein and to maximize recovery. The processing of leaves must take into account the possibility of contamination with oxidizing agents and proteases as the tissue is shredded or pressed to remove the green juice. In small-scale processes, this can be addressed using antioxidants and protease inhibitors in the extraction buffer, but this would be too expensive on a large scale and processes must be adapted to isolate the target product rapidly from the most damaging contaminants. In the case of plant-derived pharmaceutical proteins, this may well involve the use of dedicated, chemically active membrane filters to remove particulates, fines and also specific target contaminants such as proteases, phenolics, and oxalic acid, all of which can cause damage to proteins in solution.

Integrated Process Design

Each process train should be designed *de novo* based on the optimum arrangement and juxtaposition of different operational units to suit both the upstream production system and the product. There is no perfect system suitable for all products and platforms, but the general design of a process should take into account certain rules of thumb reflecting the economy, duration, and overall safety of production (Fish 2004, Kelley 2017). In general, it makes economic sense to place the least expensive processes early in the production train, as these will bear the greatest contaminant load and the largest feed volumes. These early processes should aim to remove the bulk of the contaminants, and all of the specific contaminants that might poison later operational modules or damage the target product further downstream. The early steps should also aim to achieve volume reduction, thereby increasing the productive output of the later and more expensive separation steps. In the case of chromatography, for example, the cost of column resins and their frequency of replacement is the most significant economic factor. The lower the input volumes and the less often the resins have to be replaced or recharged due to fouling, the more economical the process.

For optimal process and cost efficiency, there should be as few process operations as possible and each should exploit, to the maximum extent, the physical and chemical differences between the recombinant

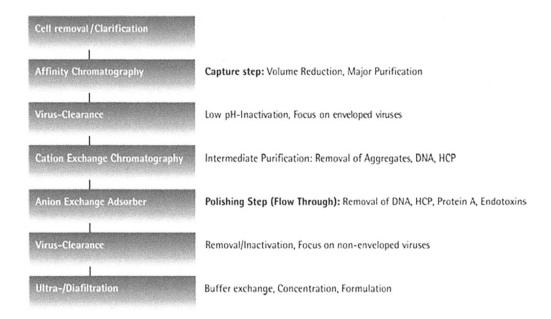

FIGURE 15.11   A generic manufacturing strategy for monoclonal antibodies. HCP, host cell protein.

product and the set of target contaminants that must be removed. These processes should be ordered in a rational manner so that consecutive separation steps exploit different separative principles (orthogonal separation). Most importantly of all, however, we need to move away from the idea of separate and independent operative units and toward the concept of an integrated production train (Gottschalk 2005c). The optimization of individual units can lead to improved output from a particular unit, but may reduce the overall efficiency of production if the impact of such changes on downstream units is not considered. Process engineering and modeling should be used to develop and refine the simplest, most efficient, and most robust processes, thus helping to overcome some of the current bottlenecks.

As an example, we can apply this concept to antibody manufacturing (Figure 15.11). It would be advantageous to employ a capture phase that utilizes the high dynamic capacity of affinity resins, followed by a filtration train for polishing, taking advantage of the properties of charged membranes (Gottschalk 2005b). Processes requiring only two columns and a filtration train would minimize costs without affecting efficiency, especially if the filtration train employed smart membranes appropriate for the removal of specific contaminants. The idea of polishing before capture is heretical, but in this example it would protect the protein A column from fouling and therefore extend its useful lifetime and operative capacity.

Economic Barriers—Upscaling and Technology Replacement

The biopharmaceutical industry is dominated by the fixed costs of production, which include the planning and development of new manufacturing processes and facilities, and the costs associated with regulatory compliance. Over the last 20 years, the spiraling costs of production have been addressed, to a certain extent, by increasing productivity. Certainly the output of key products such as monoclonal antibodies has increased over 100-fold since the first industrial processes were approved. The vast majority of this productivity increase has occurred in the upstream part of the production train, through the development of better-performing cell lines, and the use of improved media, additives, and reactor designs. Progress in downstream processing has been relatively slow in comparison, and this is perhaps the biggest challenge facing the industry at the current time. Ultimately, there are only a few ways to remove bottlenecks and increase productivity in biomanufacturing. These include upscaling current process technology, replacing current processes with more efficient ones and the more widespread adoption of disposables. These three trends are discussed below.

Upscaling

The high-end technologies of downstream processing such as chromatography are reaching their limits, both physically and economically. For example, a relatively straightforward approach to scaling up any form of chromatography is simply to increase the column diameter. The sample load is then increased proportionately, so that the linear flow rate is maintained but the overall throughput increases. Unfortunately, scaling up in this manner has a number of unpredictable effects, including zone broadening, which can reduce the overall efficiency and resolution of the separation. The largest chromatography columns in current use are some 2–3 m in diameter, which is about the maximum that can be tolerated without running into operational problems (Strube et al. 2019). We are reaching the point at which increasing the scale of each unit operation no longer leads directly to an increase in productivity, and this law of diminishing returns as the footprint of each operation increases cannot be sustained.

Further gains can be made by increasing the dynamic capacity of the resins and the linear flow rate, leading to the optimization of throughput without further scaling. However, at some stage every chromatography system will reach its optimal operational performance, thus making further increases in productivity reliant on new technological developments. Even if continued upscaling were possible without compromising efficiency, the cost of the resins and the equipment itself soon becomes unsupportable. Currently, downstream processing accounts for 50%–80% of production costs, but as ever higher capacities are demanded, this proportion is likely to increase. Downstream processing is thus suffering from the lack of technologies that are robust and scalable as well as affordable, and that do not compromise either productivity or product safety. In addition, the scaled-up processes need to be validated before they are put to use, which reveals further sets of challenges as summarized by Sofer (1996), and as discussed extensively by Sofer and Zabriskie (2000) and Rathore and Sofer (2005).

The scale-up challenge is particularly relevant as we move toward ton-scale production and beyond. Increased cell culture titers generated by extended fed-batch operations and high cell densities can now achieve batch volumes of up to 10 g/L in a 20,000-L bioreactor, yielding ~150 kg of a target protein. Although long bioreactor production phases affect facility utilization and staffing, few batches at this scale are needed to supply the market for most products. As the bioreactor production stage lengthens, the mismatch between the shorter cycle of the downstream process and the bioreactor becomes more problematic (Hagel et al. 2007). Purification costs are the dominant drivers in such very-large-scale processes but these can be reduced by ensuring that components are used to their full capacity—for example, protein A resins can be reused up to 200 times, which significantly reduces the overall cost of goods (Brorson et al. 2003).

High-tech versus Low-tech Processes

Instead of striving for scientific breakthroughs to make high-end technologies more efficient and scalable, an alternative approach is to revisit some of the robust low-end methods which are the staple of the chemical industry and are already being applied to manufacture small-molecule drugs (Gottschalk 2006a). Unlike other monologues on downstream processing, which focus on high-end technologies, equal space has been given in this chapter to approaches such as extraction, precipitation, and crystallization. These techniques may be one key to addressing the capacity crunch in downstream processing, because they are reliable, robust, scalable, and above all, economical. There is a perception that forsaking chromatography for such methods would cause regulatory issues, but this is probably unfounded. Given that such approaches are already used in the pharmaceutical industry and can be applied under cGMP standards, there seems no reason why they should not eventually be accepted for use in biopharmaceutical manufacturing. The development of crystallization as a polishing and formulation method for protein pharmaceuticals by companies such as Altus Pharmaceuticals Inc. shows that such technologies are not only viable and profitable, but also offer innovative solutions to problems such as drug delivery that have not been addressed by other methods.

Disposable Concepts

Another major challenge in downstream processing is the requirement for cleaning and validation, both of which are expensive in terms of the procedures themselves and the downtime they cause, which wastes valuable production time (Sinclair and Monge 2004, 2005). Increasingly, this is being addressed by supplementing or even replacing permanent fixtures and steel piping with disposable modules. The higher cost of such modules compared to the single purchase and installation cost of a permanent fixture is offset by the elimination of CIP and SIP (steaming in place) procedures, the validation of cleaning routines and the associated record keeping (Sinclair and Monge, 2002). Hard-piped components require cleaning, and the success of cleaning must be validated. For filters and resins, cleaning and regeneration can be expensive and time-consuming, and validation equally so. Also, CIP procedures involving harsh chemicals inevitably lead to the degradation of chromatography media and membrane chemistry, ultimately necessitating the replacement of these reagents and devices.

The rise in disposable module use marks an important paradigm shift in downstream processing, which may ultimately lead to fully modular process trains where every unit operation is disposable (Gottschalk 2005c). This would achieve one of the holy grails in downstream processing: a continuously operative and maintenance-free process train, where exhausted or malfunctioning units can simply be swapped for new ones, and where there is no need for cleaning or validation and therefore zero downtime. Each production cycle would be carried out with components that have never been in contact with previous batches, thereby avoiding all forms of cross-contamination. Disposable modules are now a staple part of laboratory work (e.g., spin columns, disposable filters) and industrial processes now frequently include not only disposable filters, but also disposable bioreactors, disposable media bags, and more recently disposable chromatography columns and membranes. Disposable process trains are particularly suitable for the production of biopharmaceuticals for clinical testing because there is no economic justification for the construction of permanent facilities to produce drugs that may not get any further than phase I development. But even in processes for established products, the benefits of disposable manufacturing are becoming more apparent. This partly reflects the diversity of available modules—it is now possible to purchase off-the-shelf filters (membranes and depth filters) covering a range of production scales and with various properties. Similarly, where disposable chromatography membranes were initially available in a limited range of chemistries and only really efficient in flow-through mode, membranes are now available to match many different chromatography resins in terms of chemical characteristics, and bind-and-elute membrane chromatography is increasingly prevalent (Brown et al. 2010, Shukla and Gottschalk 2013, Thömmes et al. 2017, Kelley 2017). In the future, we are likely to see the rapid adoption of disposable chromatography membranes, which have been shown to work as efficiently as columns but with a much smaller footprint (Zhou and Tressel 2005, Mora et al. 2006, Shukla and Gottschalk 2013). However, costs are only one benefit of disposable technology and one must also factor in the additional convenience and reduction in downtime. Polishing applications are therefore likely to be dominated by disposable membranes in the future as the cost and efficiency benefits and functional diversity become more apparent (Gottschalk 2006a).

Conclusions

In this chapter, we have considered a range of technologies which are currently used or could in the future be used in the downstream processing of protein pharmaceuticals. The challenges we face today include how to deal with ever-increasing upstream productivity and how to adapt to novel production systems, both of which have uncovered bottlenecks downstream. We have explored some of these challenges and their potential solutions, looking at tailoring downstream processes to match particular platform–product combinations, the development of an integrated process concept, and reviewing how technology can be applied in downstream processing to match the upstream demands.

At the current time, downstream processing is heavily reliant on high-technology operations such as chromatography, which is reaching its economic and physical limits. The solution to this problem is to continue with the development of novel technologies such as membrane chromatography, and marry this with the re-examination of some robust low-technology methods such as extraction, precipitation, and crystallization, which are all mainstays of the biochemical and pharmaceutical industries, and have been tried and tested for the production of small-molecule drugs. Combining this with the use of disposable modules to reduce the length of time spent off production will bring about a critically needed increase in capacity, and will hopefully remove some of the hurdles which prevent the efficient and high-throughput processing of biopharmaceutical products.

REFERENCES

Baneyx F, Mujacic M (2004) Recombinant protein folding and misfolding in *Escherichia coli. Nat Biotechnol* 22, 1399–1408.

Banik RM, Santhiagu A, Kanari B, Sabarinath C, Upadhyay NJ (2003) Technological aspects of extractive fermentation using aqueous two-phase systems. *World J Microbiol Biotechnol* 19, 337–348.

Baruah GL, Couto D, Belfort G (2003) A predictive aggregate transport model for microfiltration of combined macromolecular solutions and poly-disperse suspensions: Testing model with transgenic goat milk. *Biotechnol Prog* 19, 1533–1540.

Bergander T, Chirica L, Ljunglof A, Malmquist G (2004) Novel high capacity protein A affinity chromatography media. *3rd International Symposium on the Downstream Processing of Genetically Engineered Antibodies*, Nice, France.

Birch JR, Racher AJ (2006) Antibody production. *Adv Drug Deliv Rev* 58(5–6), 671–685.

Bisschops M (2017) The evolution of continuous chromatography: From bulk chemicals to biopharma. In: Gottschalk U (ed) *Process Scale Purification of Antibodies* (second edition). John Wiley & Sons, Inc., Hoboken, NJ, pp 409–429.

Bjorck L (1998) Protein L—A novel bacterial cell wall protein with affinity for IgL chains. *J Immunol* 140, 1194–1197.

Boi C, Facchini R, Sorci M, Giulio C, Sarti GC (2005) Characterisation of affinity membranes for IgG separation. *Desalination* 199, 544–546.

Boschetti E, Girot P (2002) Ion exchange interaction chromatography. In: Vijayalakshmi MA (ed) *Biochromatography Theory and Practice*. Taylor & Francis, Abingdon, UK, pp 24–45.

Brorson K, Brown J, Hamilton E, Stein KE (2003) Identification of protein A media performance attributes that can be monitored as surrogates for retrovirus clearance during extended re-use. *J Chromatogr A* 989, 155–163.

Brown A, Bill J, Tully T, Radhamohan A, Dowd C (2010) Overloading ion-exchange membranes as a purification step for monoclonal antibodies. *Biotechnol Appl Biochem* 56, 59–70.

Buyel JF, Fischer R, Twyman RM (2015) Extraction and downstream processing of plant-derived recombinant proteins. *Biotechnol Adv* 33, 902–913.

Buyel JF, Twyman RM, Fischer R (2017) Very-large-scale production of antibodies in plants: The biologization of manufacturing. *Biotechnol Adv* 35, 458–465.

Capito F, Bauer J, Rapp A, Schroter C, Kolmar H, Stanislawski B (2013) Feasibility study of semi-selective protein precipitation with salt-tolerant copolymers for industrial purification of therapeutic antibodies. *Biotechnol Bioeng* 110, 2915–2927.

Chaga GC (2001) Twenty-five years of immobilized metal ion affinity chromatography: Past, present and future. *J Biochem Biophys Methods* 49, 313–334.

Choi JH, Lee SY (2004) Secretory and extracellular production of recombinant proteins using *Escherichia coli. Appl Microbiol Biotechnol* 64, 625–635.

CPMP (1996) Note for guidance on virus validation studies, the design, contribution and interpretation of studies validating the inactivation and removal of viruses. CPMP/BWP/268/95, EMEA, London.

CPMP (1997) Note for guidance on quality of biotechnology products, viral safety evaluation of biotechnology products derived from cell lines of human or animal origin. CPMP/ICH/295/95, EMEA, London.

Crowe J, Dobeli H, Gentz R, Hochuli E, Stuber D, Henco K (1994) 6xHis-Ni-NTA chromatography as a superior technique in recombinant protein expression/purification. *Methods Mol Biol* 31, 371–387.

Curling J (2004a) Affinity chromatography—From textile dyes to synthetic ligands by design, Part I. *BioPharm Int* 17, 34–42.

Curling J (2004b) Affinity chromatography—From textile dyes to synthetic ligands by design, Part II. *BioPharm Int* 17, 60–66.

Desai MA, Rayner M, Burns M, Bermingham D (2000) Application of chromatography in the downstream processing of biomolecules. In: Desai AM (ed) *Downstream Processing of Proteins: Methods and Protocols*. Methods in Biotechnology 9. Humana Press, Totowa, NJ, pp 73–94.

Doonan S (2000) Essential guides for isolation/purification of enzymes and proteins. In: Wilson ID (ed) *Encyclopedia of Separation Science*. Elsevier Science, London, pp 4547–4552.

Dosmar M, Pinto S (2008) Crossflow filtration. In Jornitz MW, Meltzer TH (eds) *Filtration and Purification in the Biopharmaceutical Industry* (second edition). Informa Healthcare USA, New York, pp 495–542.

Dosmar M, Meyeroltmanns F, Gohs M (2005) Factors influencing ultrafiltration scale-up. *BioProcess Int* 3, 40–50.

Dyck MK, Lacroix D, Pothier F, Sirard MA (2003) Making recombinant proteins in animals—Different systems, different applications. *Trends Biotechnol* 21, 394–399.

Eriksson KO (2002) Gel filtration. In: Vijayalakshmi MA (ed) *Biochromatography Theory and Practice*. Taylor & Francis, Abingdon, UK, pp 9–23.

Ersson B, Ryden L, Janson JC (1989) Introduction to protein purification. In Janson JC, Ryden L (eds) *Protein Purification. Principles, High Resolution Methods and Applications*. VCH, New York, pp 3–32.

Etzel MR, Arunkumar A (2017) Charged ultrafiltration and microfiltration membranes for antibody purification. In: Gottschalk U (ed) *Process Scale Purification of Antibodies* (second edition). John Wiley & Sons, Inc., Hoboken, NJ, pp 247–268.

Ey PL, Prowse SJ, Jenkin CR (1978) Isolation of pure IgG1, IgG2b immunoglobulins from mouse serum using Protein A-Sepharose. *Immunochemistry* 15, 429.

Fahrner RL, Blank GS, Zapata GA (1999) Expanded bed protein A affinity chromatography of a recombinant humanized monoclonal antibody: Process development, operation, and comparison with a packed bed method. *J Biotechnol* 75, 273–280.

Ferreira GM, Dembecki J, Patel K, Arunakumari A (2007) A two-column process to purify antibodies without Protein A. *BioPharm Int* 20, 32.

Fish B (2004) Concepts in development of manufacturing strategies for monoclonal antibodies. In: Subramanian G (ed) *Antibodies, Volume 1: Production and Purification*. Kluwer Academic/Plenum Publishers, New York, pp 1–23.

Floss DM, Schallau K, Rose-John S, Conrad U, Scheller J (2010) Elastin-like polypeptides revolutionize recombinant protein expression and their biomedical application. *Trends Biotechnol* 28, 37–45.

Glynn J (2017) Process-scale precipitation of impurities in mammalian cell culture broth. In: Gottschalk U (ed) *Process Scale Purification of Antibodies* (second edition). John Wiley & Sons, Inc., Hoboken, NJ, pp 233–246.

Gosh R (2002) Protein separation using membrane chromatography, opportunities and challenges. *J Chromatogr A* 952, 13–27.

Gottschalk U (2003) Biotech manufacturing is coming of age. *BioProcess Int* 1, 54–61.

Gottschalk U (2005a) Biomanufacturing: Purify or perish. *EuroBioNews* 4, 33–36.

Gottschalk U (2005b) Downstream processing of monoclonal antibodies: From high dilution to high purity. *Biopharm Int* 18, 42–60.

Gottschalk U (2005c) New and unknown challenges facing biomanufacturing. *BioPharm Int* 2, 24–28.

Gottschalk U (2006a) Downstream processing in biomanufacturing: Removing economic and technical bottlenecks. *Bioforum Eur* 10, 28–31.

Gottschalk U (2006b) The Renaissance of protein purification. *BioPharm Int* 19, 8–9.

Gottschalk U (2008) Bioseparation in antibody manufacturing: The good, the bad and the ugly. *Biotechnol Prog* 24, 496–503.

Gottschalk U, Fischer-Fruehholz S, Reif O (2004) Membrane adsorbers, a cutting edge process technology at the threshold. *BioProcess Int* 2, 56–65.

Gottschlich N, Sönke W, Kasche V (1996) Continuous biospecific affinity purification of enzymes by simulated moving-bed chromatography, theoretical description and experimental results. *J Chromatogr A*, 719, 267–274.

Gottschlich N, Sönke W, Kasche V (1997) Purification of monoclonal antibodies by simulated moving-bed chromatography. *J Chromatogr A* 765, 201–206.

Hagel L, Jagschies G, Sofer G (2007) Production scenarios. In: Hagel L, Jagschies G, Sofer G (eds) *Handbook of Process Chromatography: Development, Manufacturing, Validation and Economics* (second edition). Academic Press, London, pp. 22–39.

Hendriks LJA, de Kruif J, Throsby M, Bakker ABH, Müller-Späth T, Ulmer N, Aumann L, Strohlein G, Bavand M (2013) Purifying common light-chain bispecific antibodies: A twin-column, countercurrent chromatography platform process. *Bioprocess Int* 11, 36–45.

Hermanson GT, Mallia AK, Smith PK (1992) *Immobilized Affinity Ligand Techniques*. Academic Press, London.

Hilbrig F, Freitag R (2003) Protein purification by affinity precipitation. *J Chromatogr B* 790, 79–90.

Huse K, Bö HJ, Scholz GH (2002) Purification of antibodies by affinity chromatography. *J Biochem Biophys Methods* 51, 217–231.

Huse K, Bohme HJ, Scholz GH (2002) Purification of antibodies by affinity chromatography. *J Biochem Biophys Methods* 51, 217–231.

Immelmann A, Kellings K, Stamm O, Tarrach K (2005) Validation and quality procedures for virus and prion removal in biopharmaceuticals. *BioProcess Int* 3, 38–44.

Jennissen HP (2002) Hydrophobic interaction chromatography of proteins. In: Vijayalakshmi MA (ed) *Biochromatography Theory and Practice*. Taylor & Francis, Abingdon, UK, pp 46–71.

Jones K (2000) Affinity separation. In: Wilson ID (ed) *Encyclopedia of Separation Science*. Elsevier Science, London, pp 3–17.

Jornitz MW, Meltzer TH (2003) *Filtration Handbook: Integrity Testing*. PDA Publications, Bethesda, MD.

Jornitz MW, Meltzer TH (2004) *Filtration Handbook: Liquids*. PDA Publications, Bethesda, MD.

Jornitz MW, Meltzer TH, Soelkner PG (2003) Modern sterile filtration—The economics. *Pharm Technol Eur* 15, 1–3.

Jornitz MW, Soelkner PG, Meltzer TH (2002) Sterile filtration—A review of the past and present technologies. *PDA J Sci & Technol* 56, 192–196.

Jungbauer A (1993) Preparative chromatography of biomolecules. *J Chromatogr A* 639, 3–16.

Kalyanpur M (2000) Downstream processing in the biotechnology industry: An overview. In Desai MA (ed) *Downstream Processing of Proteins: Methods and Protocols*. Methods in Biotechnology 9. Humana Press, Totowa, NJ, pp 1–10.

Kelley B (2017) Downstream processing of monoclonal antibodies: Current practices and future opportunities. In: Gottschalk U (ed) *Process Scale Purification of Antibodies* (second edition). John Wiley & Sons, Inc., Hoboken, NJ, pp 1–22.

Kempken R, Preissmann A, Berthold W (1995) Assessment of a disc stack centrifuge for use in mammalian cell separation. *Biotechnol BioEng* 46, 132–138.

Klyushnichenko V (2003) Protein crystallization: From HTS to kilogram-scale. *Curr Opin Drug Discov Devel* 6, 848–854.

Knudsen HL, Fahrner RL, Xu Y, Norling LA, Blank GS (2001). Membrane ion-exchange chromatography for process-scale antibody purification. *J Chromatogr A* 907, 145–154.

Kula M, Selber K (1999) Protein purification, aqueous liquid extraction. In: Flicker M, Drew S (eds) *Encyclopedia of Bioprocess Technology: Fermentation, Biocatalysis and Bioseperation*. Wiley, New York, pp 2179–2191.

Kumar A, Galaev IY, Mattiasson B (2003) Precipitation of proteins: Nonspecific and specific. *Biotechnol Bioproc* 27, 225–275.

Lee EK, Kim WS (2003) Protein crystallization for large-scale bioseparation. *Biotechnol Bioproc* 27, 277–320.

Levine HL (2002) Economic analysis of biopharmaceutical manufacturing. *2002 BIO International Biotechnology Convention and Exhibition*, 9–12 June, Toronto, Ontario, Canada.

Lienqueno M, Mahn A, Salgado J, Asenjo JA (2007) Current insights on protein behavior in hydrophobic interaction chromatography. *J Chromatogr B* 849, 53–68.

Loetscher P, Mottlau L, Hochuli E (1992) Immobilization of monoclonal antibodies for affinity chromatography using a chelating peptide. *J Chromatogr* 595, 113–119.

Lu Y, Williamson B, Gillespie R (2014) Recent advancement in application of hydrophobic interaction chromatography for aggregate removal in industrial purification process. *Curr Pharm Biotechnol* 1368, 155–162.

Maksimenko OG, Deykin AV, Khodarovich YM, Georgiev PG (2013) Use of transgenic animals in biotechnology: Prospects and problems. *Acta Naturae* 5, 33–46.

McCormick D (2005) Artificial distinctions: Protein a mimetic ligands for bioprocess separations. *Pharm Technol* 5, 4–7.

McDonald P, Victa C, Carter-Franklin JN, Fahrner R (2009) Selective antibody precipitation using polyelectrolytes: A novel approach to the purification of monoclonal antibodies. *Biotechnol Bioeng* 102, 1141–1151.

Menkhaus TJ, Bai Y, Zhang C-M, Nikolov ZL, Glatz CE (2004) Considerations for the recovery of recombinant proteins from plants. *Biotechnol Prog* 20, 1001–1014.

Metzger M, Peiker M, Faust S, Ebert S, Muller D, Winterfied S, Mang N (2015) Evaluating adsorptive depth filtration as a unit operation for virus removal. *BioProc Int* 13, 36–44.

Monzani PS, Adona PR, Ohashi OM, Meirelles FV, Wheeler MB (2016) Transgenic bovine as bioreactors: Challenges and perspectives. *Bioengineered* 7, 123–131.

Mora J, Sinclair A, Delmdahl N, Gottschalk U (2006) Disposable membrane chromatography: Performance analysis and economic cost model. *BioProcess Int* 4, 38–43.

Mouratou B, Béhar G, Pecorari F (2015) Artificial affinity proteins as ligands of immunoglobulins. *Biomolecules* 5, 60–75.

Müller-Späth T, Aumann L, Ströhlein G, Kornmann H, Valax P, Delegrange L, Charbaut E, Baer G, Lamproye A, Jöhnck M, Schulte M, Morbidelli M (2010) Two-step capture and purification of IgG2 using multicolumn countercurrent solvent gradient purification (MCSGP). *Biotechnol Bioeng* 107, 974–984.

Na W, Park N, Yeom M, Song D (2015) Ebola outbreak in Western Africa 2014: What is going on with Ebola virus? *Clin Exp Vaccine Res* 4, 17–22.

Nikolov ZL, Regan JT, Dickey LF, Woodard SL (2017) Purification of antibodies from plants. In: Gottschalk U (ed) *Process Scale Purification of Antibodies* (second edition). John Wiley & Sons, Inc., Hoboken, NJ, pp 631–654.

Nikolov ZL, Woodard SL (2004) Downstream processing of recombinant proteins from transgenic feedstock. *Curr Opin Biotechnol* 15, 479–486.

Oetjen GW (2000) Freeze-drying. In: Wilson ID (ed) *Encyclopedia of Separation Science*. Elsevier Science, London, pp 1023–1034.

Orr V, Zhong L, Moo-Young M, Chou C (2013) Recent advances in bioprocessing application of membrane chromatography. *Biotechnol Adv* 31, 450–465.

Paule BJA, Meyer R, Moura-Costa LF, Bahia RC, Carminati R, Regis LF, Vale VLC, Freire SM, Nascimento I, Schaer R, Azevedo V (2004) Three-phase partitioning as an efficient method for extraction/concentration of immunoreactive excreted-secreted proteins of *Corynebacterium pseudotuberculosis*. *Prot Exp Purif* 34, 311–316.

PDA (2005) *PDA Technical Report 41, Virus Filtration*. PDA Publications, Bethesda, MD.

Peram T, McDonald P, Carter-Franklin J, Fahrner R (2010) Monoclonal antibody purification using cationic polyelectrolytes: An alternative to column chromatography. *Biotechnol Prog* 26, 1322–1331.

Peters J, Minuth T, Schroder W (2005) Implementation of a crystallization step into the purification process of a recombinant protein. *Protein Expr Purif* 39, 43–53.

Phillips M, Cormier J, Ferrence J, Dowd C, Kiss R, Lutz H, Carter J (2005) Performance of a membrane adsorber for trace impurity removal in biotechnology manufacturing. *J Chromatogr A* 1078, 74–82.

Prashad M, Tarrach K (2006) Depth filtration: Cell clarification of bioreactor offloads. *FISE* 43, 28–30.

Rapp JC, Harvey AJ, Speksnijder GL, Hu W, Ivarie R (2003) Biologically active human interferon F061-2b produced in the egg white of transgenic hens. *Transgenic Res* 12, 569–575.

Rathore AS, Sofer G (eds) (2005) *Process Validation in Manufacturing of Biopharmaceuticals* (Biotechnology and Bioprocessing Series). Taylor & Francis Informa Press, Boca Raton FL.

Ren J, Yao P, Chen J, Jia L (2014) Salt-independent hydrophobic displacement chromatography for antibody purification using cyclodextrin as supramolecular displacer. *J Chromatogr A* 1369, 98–104.

Rosa PA, Azevedo AM, Sommerfeld S, Bäcker W, Aires-Barros MR (2011) Aqueous two-phase extraction as a platform in the biomanufacturing industry: Economical and environmental sustainability. *Biotechnol Adv* 29, 559–567.

Rosa PA, Azevedo AM, Sommerfeld S, Mutter M, Bäcker W, Aires-Barros MR (2013) Continuous purification of antibodies from cell culture supernatant with aqueous two-phase systems: From concept to process. *Biotechnol J* 8, 352–362.

Roy I, Gupta MN (2002) Three-phase affinity partitioning of proteins. *Anal Biochem* 300, 11–14.

Rubin D, Christy C (2002) Selecting the right ultrafiltration membrane for biopharmaceutical applications. *Pharm Technol Eur* 14, 39–45.

Scouten WH (1981) *Affinity Chromatography*. Wiley, New York.

Shaeiwitz JA, Henry JD, Ghosh R (2012) Bioseparation. In Elvers B (ed) *Ullmann's Encyclopedia of Industrial Chemistry* (seventh edition, online). doi: 10.1002/14356007.b03_11.pub2.

Sheth RD, Jin M, Bhut BV, Li Z, Chen W, Cramer SM (2014) Affinity precipitation of a monoclonal antibody from an industrial harvest feedstock using an ELP-Z stimuli responsive biopolymer. *Biotechnol Bioeng* 111, 1595–1603.

Shukla AA, Gottschalk U (2013) Single-use disposable technologies for biopharmaceutical manufacturing. *Trends Biotechnol* 31, 147–154.

Shukla AA, Suda E (2017) Harvest and recovery of monoclonal antibodies: Cell removal and clarification. In: Gottschalk U (ed) *Process Scale Purification of Antibodies* (second edition). John Wiley & Sons, Inc., Hoboken, NJ, pp 55–80.

Sinclair A, Monge M (2002) Quantitative economic evaluation of single use disposables in bioprocessing. *Pharm Eng* 22, 20–34.

Sinclair A, Monge M (2004) Biomanufacturing for the 21st century: Designing a concept facility based on single-use systems. *BioProcess Int* 2, 26–31.

Sinclair A, Monge M (2005) Concept facility based on single-use systems leads the way for biomanufacturing for the 21st century. Part 2. *BioProcess Int* 3, 51–55.

Singh N, Chollangi S (2017) Next-generation clarification technologies for the downstream processing of antibodies. In: Gottschalk U (ed) *Process Scale Purification of Antibodies* (second edition). John Wiley & Sons, Inc., Hoboken, NJ, pp 81–112.

Singhvi R, Schorr C, O'Hara C, Xie L, Wang DIC (1996) Clarification of animal cell culture process fluids using depth microfiltration. *BioPharm Int* 9, 35–41.

Smith MC, Furman TC, Ingolia TD, Pidgeon C (1988) Chelating peptide-immobilized metal ion affinity chromatography. A new concept in affinity chromatography for recombinant proteins. *J Biol Chem* 263, 7211–7215.

Sofer G (1996) Validation: Ensuring the accuracy of scaled-down chromatography models. *BioPharm Int* 9, 51–54.

Sofer G (2003) Virus inactivation in the 1990s—Part 4, culture media, biotechnology products, and vaccines. *BioPharm Int* 16, 50–57.

Sofer G, Zabriskie DW (2000) *Biopharmaceutical Process Validation* (Biotechnology and Bioprocessing Series). CRC Press, Boca Raton, FL.

Sommerfeld S, Strube J (2005) Challenges in biotechnology production: Generic processes and process optimization for monoclonal antibodies. *Chem Eng Process* 44, 1123–1137.

Stock LR, Bisschops M, Ransohoff T (2015) The potential impact of continuous processing on the practice and economics of biopharmaceutical manufacturing. In: Subramanian G (ed) *Continuous Processing in Pharmaceutical Manufacturing*. Wiley-VCH Verlag, Weinheim, Germany, pp 479–493.

Strube J, Zobel-Roos S, Ditz R (2019). Process-scale chromatography. In Elvers B (ed) Ullmann's Encyclopedia of Industrial Chemistry (seventh edition, online) doi:10.1002/14356007.b03_10.pub2.

Suralia A (1982) Interaction of Protein A with the domains of the Fc-Fragment. *Trends Biochem Sci* 7, 318.

Taulbee DN, Maroto-Valer MM (2000) Centrifugation. In Wilson ID (ed) *Encyclopedia of Separation Science*. Elsevier Science, London, pp 17–40.

Tekoah Y, Shulman A, Kizhner T, Ruderfer I, Fux L, Nataf Y, Bartfeld D, Ariel T, Gingis-Velitski S, Hanania U, Shaaltiel Y (2015) Large-scale production of pharmaceutical proteins in plant cell culture-the Protalix experience. *Plant Biotechnol J* 13, 1199–1208.

Thömmes J, Twyman RM, Gottschalk U (2017) Alternatives to packed-bed chromatography for antibody extraction and purification. In: Gottschalk U (ed) *Process Scale Purification of Antibodies* (second edition). John Wiley & Sons, Inc., Hoboken, NJ, pp 215–232.

Tomic S, Besnard L, Fürst B, Reithmeier R, Wichmann R, Schelling P, Hakemeyer C (2015) Complete clarification solution for processing high density cell culture harvests. *Sep Purif Technol* 141, 269–275.

Turkova J (2002) Affinity chromatography. In: Vijayalakshmi MA (ed) *Biochromatography Theory and Practice*. Taylor & Francis, Abingdon, UK, pp 142–224.

Twyman RM, Schillberg S, Fischer R (2005) Transgenic plants in the biopharmaceutical market. *Expert Opin Emerg Drugs* 10, 185–218.

Walter JK, Nothelfer F, Werz W (1998) Validation of viral safety for pharmaceutical proteins. In: Subramanian G (ed) *Bioseparation and Bioprocessing, Volume 1*. Wiley-VCH, Weinhemim, Germany, pp 465–496.

Werner RG (2004) Economic aspects of commercial manufacture of biopharmaceuticals. *J Biotechnol* 113, 171–182.

Westoby M, Chrostowski J, de Vilmorin P, Smelko JP, Romero JK (2011) Effects of solution environment on mammalian cell fermentation broth properties: Enhanced impurity removal and clarification performance. *Biotechnol Bioeng* 108, 50–58.

Wilchek M, Chaiken I (2000) An overview of affinity chromatography. *Methods Mol Biol* 147, 1–6.

Wurm FM (2004) Production of recombinant protein therapeutics in cultivated mammalian cells. *Nature Biotechnol* 22, 1393–1398.

Yang MX, Shenoy B, Disttler M, Patel R, McGrath M, Pechenov S, Margolin AL (2003) Crystalline monoclonal antibodies for subcutaneous delivery. *Proc Natl Acad Sci USA* 100, 6934–6939.

Yu D, McLean M D, Hall CJ, Ghosh R (2008) Purification of monoclonal antibody from tobacco extract using membrane-based bioseparation techniques. *J Membr Sci* 323, 159–166.

Zeman LJ, Zydney AL (1996) *Microfiltration and Ultrafiltration. Principles and Applications.* Marcel Dekker, New York.

Zhou JX (2017) Orthogonal virus clearance applications in monoclonal antibody production. In: Gottschalk U (ed) *Process Scale Purification of Antibodies* (second edition). John Wiley & Sons, Inc., Hoboken, NJ, pp 325–342.

Zhou JX, Tressel T (2005) Membrane chromatography as a robust purification system for large scale antibody production. *BioProcess Int* 3, 32–37.

Zhou JX, Tressel T (2006) Basic concepts in Q membrane chromatography for large-scale antibody production. *Biotechnol Prog* 22, 341–349.

Zydney AL, Kuriyel R (2000) Large-scale recovery of protein inclusion bodies by continuous centrifugation. In Desai MA (ed) *Downstream Processing of Proteins: Methods and Protocols.* Methods in Biotechnology 9. Humana Press, Totowa, NJ, pp 47–58.

16

Ultrafiltration and Crossflow Microfiltration Filtration

Michael Dosmar, Steven Pinto, and Kirsten Jones Seymour
Sartorius Stedim North America, Inc.

CONTENTS

Introduction

The application of ultrafiltration (UF) in biopharmaceuticals is a constantly shifting landscape. We can separate the applications into about seven different categories. Starting with applications using the lowest molecular weight cutoffs (MWCOs), we have the concentration and diafiltration (DF) of oligonucleotides, small proteins, and peptides like cytokines, insulin and glucagon, as well as other small chain polymers. These applications require ultrafilters with molecular cutoffs that range between 1 and 5 kD. As will be discussed later in this chapter, these applications are not very sensitive to shear velocity, but respond well to increasing pressure. The next category of applications is low concentration proteins like enzymes and monoclonal fragments like Fabs (Fragment antigen-binding) and bispecifics. These applications use membranes with MWCOs between 8 and 50 kD. These applications behave in the traditional fashion well documented in the literature. Monoclonal antibodies, especially second generation, typically utilize 30 kD ultrafilters. Monoclonal antibodies in their final formulations are concentrated to between 100 g/L and well over 250 g/L. These proteins have a tendency to become extremely viscous and require careful selection of both the processing parameters as well as selecting filters with flow paths that can accommodate products, which can exhibit very high viscosities. Category 4 includes vaccines, which use 100–300 kD ultrafilters. Category 5 is the newer applications associated with cell therapies. These applications involve the separation of viruses like adeno, adeno-associated, and lenti viruses. In the early steps of the process (harvesting), one must balance the MWCO of the membranes with the ability

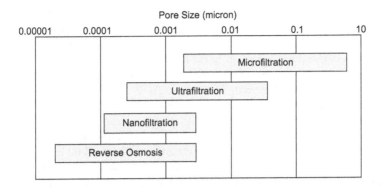

FIGURE 16.1   Typical pore sizes for membranes used in RO, NF, UF, and MF.

to clear contaminants like host cell proteins and DNA while retaining the viruses. These applications utilize ultrafilters with MWCO that range between 100 and 750 kD. Category 5 also includes the use of ultrafilters in bioreactor perfusion applications, and category 6 is the use of crossflow microfilters for cell harvesting. Category 7 is a newer modality for using ultrafilters known as SPTFF (single-pass tangential flow filtration). This is an application to date that has typically been restricted to volume reduction applications. The application of SPTFF will be discussed further in a later chapter.

In order to fully appreciate the current state of these applications, it is useful to place the technology into a historical context. Modern UF membranes have their origins in the 1950s when commercially viable reverse osmosis (RO) membranes were developed for water desalination.[1] The Loeb and Sourirajan's phase inversion process created the first highly anisotropic membranes, which is the basis of UF membranes used today.

The membrane asymmetry created by the Loeb–Sourirajan's process reduced the thickness of the membrane's rejection layer 1,000-fold less than that of previously produced symmetric membranes like those used in Microfiltration (MF).[2,3] This singular development by Loeb and Sourirajan[4] began the process of development to make it commercially practical to use these membranes in the biopharmaceutical industry today.

Membrane filters are made in a wide variety of pore sizes. Figure 16.1 shows the effective pore size for membranes used in RO, nanofiltration (NF), UF, and MF.

Filtration processes may be operated in one of the two modes. Flow may be orthogonal (dead-ended or static filtration) or tangential to the filter. Process-scale UF applications are typically performed using crossflow (XF) or tangential flow filtration (TFF), at least at a scale of operation where >10 or 50 cm^2 of membrane is used. For Laboratory R&D scale when less than 10–50 cm^2 of membrane is required, stirred cell and spin filters (centrifuge) are used where the flow is orthogonal to the filter. In crossflow or TFF, the feed stream flows parallel to the surface of the membrane. A fraction of the feed stream permeates the membrane, while the remaining retained fraction exits the filter module as retentate and is recycled back to the feed vessel.

In the absence of solute, flow through the membrane is accurately modeled by the Hagen-Poiseuille Equation, which describes liquid flow through cylindrical pores[5]:

$$J = \frac{\varepsilon \cdot r^4 \cdot \Delta p}{8 \cdot \eta \cdot \Delta x},$$
(16.1)

where,

J = liquid flux (flow rate through the membrane)

ε = membrane porosity,

r = mean pore radius,

Δp = transmembrane pressure,

η = kinematic liquid viscosity, and

Δx = pore length.

This equation states that the liquid flux is proportional to the transmembrane pressure (TMP) and inversely proportional to the liquid viscosity, which is controlled by the solute concentration and the temperature.

When solute is present in the feed stream, permeating liquid brings solute to the membrane surface by convective flow. As retained solute builds up on the membrane surface a solute layer or cake is formed (often referred to as the gel layer). The result of this added solute to the membrane's surface causes an increase in the resistance of flux through the membrane. The thickness of the solute cake is dependent on a number of factors including (a) the rate at which permeating liquid brings solute to the membrane surface, (b) the rate at which solute back diffuses into the feed stream, and (c) the hydrodynamic shear of the tangentially flowing stream transporting solute back into the bulk solution. Successful exploitation of membranes in crossflow filtration is largely dependent on effective fluid management techniques.[6] "By using hydrodynamic considerations, polarized solutes can be sheared from the membrane surface, thereby increasing back diffusion thereby reducing the decline in performance (i.e. reduction in permeation rate)."[7] Equation 16.2 has been historically used to describe flux performance in UF applications.

$$J_w = k \ln\left[\frac{C_g}{C_f}\right],$$

(16.2)

where,

J_w = liquid flux,
C_g = Solute concentration at the membrane surface,
C_f = Solute concentration of the bulk feed,
k = Mass-transfer coefficient.

However, as a practical matter, due to solute–membrane interactions it has been found that, as pressure increases, flux may become independent of pressure. When pressure (TMP—average upstream system pressure) increases, the resultant increase in flow through the membrane causes the solute cake (polarized layer) to thicken proportionally, preventing a concomitant increase in flux. Figures 16.2 and 16.3 show examples of this flux versus pressure relationship.

In plots of permeate flux verses solute concentration the mass-transfer coefficient (k) can also be determined from the slope of the line which is proportional to k. Figure 16.4 shows that k is a function of the

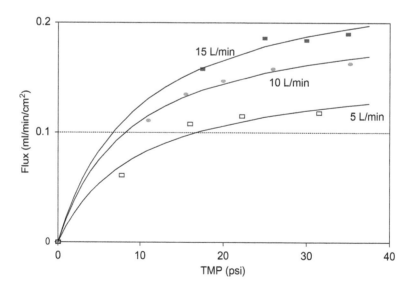

FIGURE 16.2 Bovine serum flux through a Sartorius Sartocon $0.7\,\mathrm{m}^2$ 100k PS ultrafilter cassette at three recirculation flow rates.

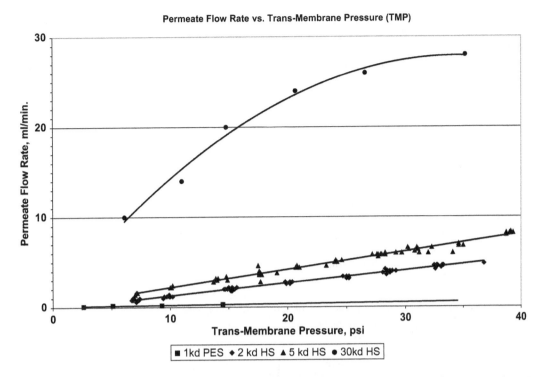

FIGURE 16.3 Milk diluted 1:5 in saline and filtered through a 1 kDa PES, 2 kDa, 5 kDa, and milk diluted 1:10 filtered through a 30 kDa Slice 200 ultrafilter cassette membranes, with 200 cm² of available surface area at a feed flow rate of 150 mL/min.

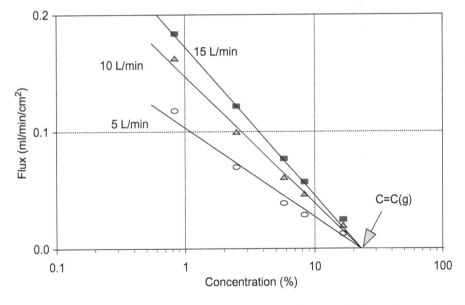

FIGURE 16.4 Flux versus concentration for UF of bovine serum using 100,000 MWCO PS membrane at three different crossflow rates (Sartorius Sartocon II, Membrane area = 7,000 cm²). Showing the convergence towards the protein's gel point where permeate flux ceases.

crossflow (recirculation flow) velocity, with k increasing as crossflow velocity (flow rate) and shear rate increases, thus reducing the gel layer.

This dependence of the mass-transfer coefficient on the shear (velocity) of the recirculating (crossflow) has been accurately correlated for 10 kDa hollow fiber filters in dairy applications.[8,9] For laminar flow the correlation is defined in equation 16.3:

$$k = 0.816 \left[\frac{\gamma}{L} D^2 \right]^{0.33}$$ (16.3)

where,

γ = shear rate,
$\gamma = 8v/d$ for flow through tubes,
$\gamma = 6v/h$ for flow through rectangular channels,
v = solution velocity,
d = tube diameter,
h = channel height,
L = length of the membrane flow path,
D = solute diffusivity.

When flow is turbulent, the mass-transfer coefficient is proportional to velocity raised to the 0.80 power instead of to the 0.33 power as in laminar flow:

$$k = 0.023 \left(\frac{1}{d_h} \right)^{0.20} \left(\frac{\rho}{\mu} \right)^{0.47} (D)^{0.67} (v)^{0.80}$$ (16.4)

where,

d_h = the hydraulic diameter and equals 4 times the cross-sectional area divided by the wetted perimeter,
ρ = liquid density,
μ = liquid's kinematic viscosity,

Because of the greater dependence on velocity when flow is turbulent, improved benefits in flux can be realized when flow is increased. The relationship between flux and velocity for both laminar and turbulent flow is shown in Figure 16.5.

This shear dependent flux relationship is particularly true for polyethersulfone (PES)-based membranes where considerable membrane fouling occurs. The consequence of protein fouling is the formation of

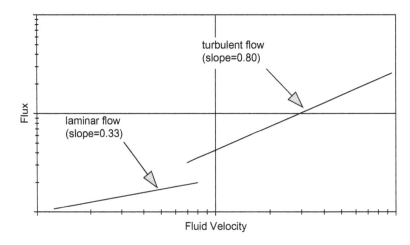

FIGURE 16.5   UF flux as a function of fluid velocity.

a protein gel that irreversibly adheres to the membrane surface. These protein gels become secondary membranes that have protein rejection characteristics that mask the intrinsic properties of the membrane. Additionally, the resistance to flow is also high through these protein gels. Once they are formed they cannot be eliminated or reduced through the control of the process hydraulics, but if the initial recirculation rates are sufficiently high the initial flux values may be higher if there is a strong dependence on the recirculation rate. When proteins do not adhere onto the membrane surface dependence on recirculation velocity becomes markedly diminished as has been reported for regenerated (RC), and modified regenerated cellulose (Hydrosart®) membranes.[10] This is true because the polarized protein layer does not have as great of a resistance to flow because the interstitial spaces between native protein is greater than that of denatured protein gels; dependence on surface shear though remains proportional to protein concentration.

Because of these flux-dependent parameters, i.e., recirculation rates and pressure profiles, it is clear that control and understanding them is important in the scale-up of any crossflow process.

Some of the conventional dogma associated with UF performance no longer seems applicable to the ultrafilters used today.

The requirements for mathematical models that are predictive of membrane performance are that the model is broadly applicable and that formulae used are robust. The predictive mathematical models established in the 1970s were elucidated using 10,000 MWCO hollow fiber polysulfone (PS) ultrafilters. The initial work used to develop these generally accepted performance profiles were performed in dairy applications on the filtration of whey. This model continued to be applicable as newer PES and cellulose triacetate (CTA) ultrafilters replaced the older PS membranes.

Today, many currently available non-fouling RC and Hydrosart® ultrafilters exhibit performance characteristics that fail to adhere to the previously established "Gel Polarization" model of the past. Membranes with MWCOs 10,000 Da and tighter typically behave according to the Hagen-Poiseuille formula and show little flux improvement as recirculation rates are increased, at least at lower product concentrations. Membranes with MWCOs greater than 10,000 Da exhibit a strong dependence on the recirculation rate as well as entering into a pressure-independent region at higher TMPs. Figure 16.3 shows an example of flux versus TMP for ultrafilter membranes both greater and lesser than 10 kDa, which support this.

UF and DF processes are developed at laboratory or process development scale. Successful implementation of these applications is the result of careful analysis of the process hydraulics (i.e., recirculation flow rates, pressure profiles, retentate flow channel, permeate flux values, and membrane surface area) and a process's dependence on shear and pressure. As these processes are scaled up from research scale to pilot scale and again to commercial scale, process engineers are often faced with limited data that at first glance may seem adequate for straight forward scale-up, but in fact are lacking critical information. The consequence of failing to recognize these critical parameters may result in predicted scale-up performance that may yield unexpected results at large(r) scale. Shortfalls in performance can have serious economic consequences arising from added labor costs and yield losses.

Applications in the Biomanufacturing Process

Traditional applications for crossflow filtration can be grouped into three basic types of operations: concentration, fractionation, and DF.

Concentration is the process of decreasing the solvent content of a solution to increase the concentration of solute. Typical concentration applications include the separation of cells from cell culture broth and recovery of the concentrated cell mass, the dewatering and subsequent concentration of proteins, peptides, olgionucleotides, carbohydrides, and the harvesting of viruses.

Fractionation may be described as a separation process where one of the solutes is separated or fractionated, one from the other by means of passing the smaller solute through the membrane while retaining the larger solute in the feed solution. Examples of membrane fractionation are depyrogenation, lysate clarification, and molecular-weight separation of poly-dispersed polymers like proteins and carbohydrates. Depyrogenation of low-molecular-weight solutions like buffers and pharmaceutical preparations is accomplished by retaining the contaminating Limulus amebocyte lysate (LAL) reactive material, i.e., Gram-negative lipopolysaccharides endotoxins (pyrogens) in the retentate and allowing the pyrogen-free product to pass through the membrane.[11] Clarification of cell lysates is the fractionation or separation of cellular debris from the products of interest. Cell lysates can be very fouling in nature, and the success of the operation is very much affected by the selection of the appropriate membrane, pore size, and operating parameters.

DF is a term combining the words dialysis and filtration. In most dialysis operations, the goal is to either exchange one buffer system for another or to wash, as in fractionation, a contaminant from the bulk.

Microfiltration Applications

Harvesting and Clarification

When evaluating crossflow for cell harvesting and clarification processes, it is usually necessary to limit the permeate flow rate using either a permeate pump or a control valve. Permeate control is used to limit the rate of solids being brought to the membrane surface via convective flow and allowing the sweeping tangential flow to lift and resuspend that material into the bulk feed so as to limit pore plugging from occurring. By controlling the TMP and monitoring the permeate pressure, one may be able to determine whether and how quickly membrane plugging is occurring.

All crossflow applications for cell processing are empirically designed and therefore may differ considerably. As a result, no particular rigorous equations have been applied consistently for MF processing.

Perfusion (Clarification)

Cell separation is one of the most difficult process steps to optimize in the production of monoclonal antibodies from recombinant cells.

The purpose of the perfusion process is to extend the cell growth phase of the cells, while either producing more extracellular products, or increasing product cell density and yields of the product in the cells. This is done by using a separation media to remove either spent or conditioned media while at the same time adding fresh media to the reactor. It must be noted that there are special requirements for separation devices used in this way. Considering that one is dealing with a cell culture the complete system must be able to be sterilized and maintained aseptically. Bioreactors and their attendant components are sterilized by means of pressurized steam. If the product is cell associated, then the cells are either removed periodically for harvesting, or collected at a predetermined time or high cell density.

Devices for this application must be able to operate at a constant permeation rate over extended periods of time. This may mean several days to several weeks of constant operation. During the development of this type of application, operating conditions must be established that assure that the microporous structure of the membrane is not altered and damaged during the sterilization process. Additionally, the membrane must not be plugged or fouled by the cells or cell debris and membranes are not fouled by antifoams during the course of the process. The permeate flux must be well controlled at all times to ensure process consistency. These systems are especially sensitive to pore plugging during process initiation. To avoid premature failure, the permeate line must be closed until the feed and retentate conditions are established.

Cell Harvesting of Extracellular products

Crossflow filtration, as a primary separation process, is especially well suited for the harvesting whole cells from a fermenter or bioreactor prior to further downstream processing. Cells harvested by crossflow filtration can be fully washed resulting is high-yield recovery of the target product in the pooled permeate.

Use of 0.45 μm or larger pore crossflow filters will generally yield a clean, cell and debris-free protein solution. Recirculation rates may range from <5 to >10 L/m²min of membrane surface area while the flux will range between 30 and 100 L/m²h (liters per square meter membrane area per hour).

Two critical parameters in processing whole cells are the pump speed as measured by the revolutions per minute (RPM) and the resulting rotor "TIP" speed and the TMP. If the rotor tip speed is too high, generally considered above 350–450 rpm, the resultant shear-induced turbulence may eventually damage or rupture the cells. Thus, most large scale crossflow systems use rotary lobe pumps operating at relatively low speeds. With increasing frequency, four piston pumps like those made by Quattroflow and ITT are being employed for these and other crossflow applications because not only are they low shear but they add little to no heat into the process. Some small single use and low pressure applications have successfully employed centrifugal pumps.

The driving force for the crossflow process is the TMP (see the section "Process Variables/Driving Force/TMP"). If the TMP exceeds a certain critical value, cells may be disrupted due to compression. Evidence of mammalian cell lysis is an increase in the levels of lactose dehydrogenase (LDH) in the extracellular media. For mammalian and insect cells, TMP values are usually maintained below 6–10 psi. Yeasts and bacteria can tolerate higher pressures and can therefore be operated at slightly higher pressures.

If yeast, fungi, or bacteria are used to produce extracellular products, then cell concentration and viscosity are usually limiting factors for crossflow.

The use of crossflow MF applied correctly to extracellular protein production containing a high percentage of whole cells should result in a cell and cell debris free product solution that can be easily processed in the downstream process train following sterile filtration.

Intracellular and Cell Wall-Associated products

When target products are cell associated, the initial fractionation processes becomes more challenging. Prior to harvesting, cells are weakened through the addition of detergents or other agents so as to release the product from the cell wall or completely lysed or homogenized in order to release the desired product from within the cells. The consequence of this mode of processing is the release of the cell's entire contents into the process batch.

When evaluating cell lysates, knowledge of the particle size distribution is very useful. Many times, the particle size is empirically "determined" by running several trial and error filtration tests on the harvest solutions. Since the target product is now mixed with the cell broth, each separation becomes somewhat unique.

Separation of disrupted cell masses requires detailed investigation. Successful harvesting of the target product may involve the use of crossflow filtration in combination with other technologies forming a process train also including centrifugation and lenticular and other microfilter membrane filters.

In instances where centrifugation is used as the primary separation step, crossflow is very effective and may offer an economic advantage over other competing technologies especially at very large scales of operations.

Ultrafilters

Concentration

The yield equation for concentration is given by equation 16.5:

$$Y = \left(\frac{V_o}{V_f}\right)^{R-1}$$

(16.5)

where,
  Y = the % yield,
  V_o = the starting volume,
  V_f = the final volume,
  R = the retention coefficient.

The flux response for most low fouling or non-fouling crossflow filters is as shown previously in Equation 16.2. That is the flux declines in a semi-log fashion with concentration factor or percent protein in solution (e.g., see Figure 16.6).

For example:

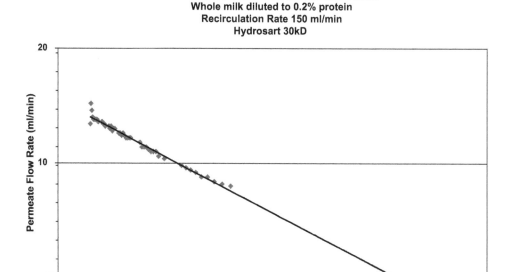

FIGURE 16.6   Permeate flow rate versus Percentage of protein on a Sartorius 200 cm² 30 kDa Hydrosart cassette.

Diafiltration

The yield equation for DF on an ultrafilter is given by equation 16.6:

$$Y = e^{\left[\left(\frac{V_d}{V_o}\right)(R-1)\right]}$$

(16.6)

where,

Y = is the % yield,
V_d = is the volume of diafiltrate buffer,
V_o = is the starting volume,
R = is the rejection coefficient.

Thus, if the rejection coefficient is high so will be the yield when utilizing DF. For rejection (R) values less than 1, then a percent of the product to be retained will pass through the membrane in accordance with the equation above and be lost to drain.

This relationship is exactly that which is utilized in crossflow MF processing as well. In both MF and UF processing, the volume of DF buffer required is empirically determined due to potential interactions between the fluid bulk characteristics and the desired product or solute passing through the membrane. The theoretical presentation of this process is shown in Figure 16.7.

Fractionation

By knowing the rejection coefficient of the target molecules and that of the process contaminants, one can exploit the differences between them. This may be accomplished through the use of Equations 16.6 and 16.7 from the previous section.

Through concentration and DF, one can fractionate a process stream if there is adequate difference between the rejection coefficients of the molecules. For this to work, there must be a large enough difference between the rejection coefficients, typically >20% (Table 16.1).

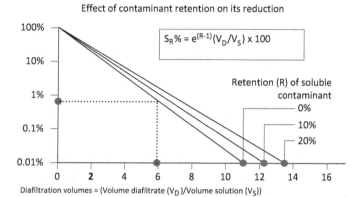

FIGURE 16.7 Theoretical contaminant dilution versus DF volume.

TABLE 16.1

The Theoretical Yield Relationships of Concentration and DF as a Function of the Rejection Coefficient and Permeate Volume

Retention Coefficient	Concentration Factor	Yield % Concentration	DF Volumes	Yield % DF
0.995	10	98.99	10	95.1
	20	98.5	20	90.5
	30	98.3	30	86.1
0.990	10	97.7	10	90.5
	20	97.0	20	81.9
	30	96.7	30	74.1
0.80	10	63.1	10	13.5
	20	54.9	20	1.83
	30	50.6	30	0.248
0.60	10	39.8	10	1.83
	20	30.2	20	0.034
	30	25.7	30	0.000

Example:* if one selects a solution which contains two proteins $P1$ and $P2$ and they have starting concentration of 1 g/L and retention coefficients of $R1 = 0.99$ and $R2 = 0.80$, we can *concentrate* the product in the first step *tenfold*. The result is given in Table 16.2. In this first step the target protein is enriched by a factor of 6.7:1.

In the second step the product is *diafiltered against ten volumes* yielding further enrichment of the target protein (10.4:1) (Table 16.3)

TABLE 16.2

The Theoretical Yield Relationships during the Tenfold Concentration of Proteins with Rejection Coefficients of 99% and 80%, Respectively

	% Yield in Retentate	Concentration in Retentate (g/L)	% in Permeate	Protein Ratio
$P1$	97.7	9.77	2.3	1.5
$P2$	63.1	6.31	46.9	

---

* Source: William Eycamp.[12]

TABLE 16.3

The Theoretical Yield Relationships during a Ten Volume Diafiltration of Proteins with Rejection
Coefficients of 99% and 80% Following a Tenfold Concentration, Respectively

	Yield in Retentate	(g) Concentration in Retentate (g/L)	% Recovery	Protein Ratio
P1	$0.905 \times 0.977 = 0.884$	$0.905 \times 9.77 = 8.84$	88.4	10.5
P2	$0.135 \times 0.631 = 0.085$	$0.135 \times 6.31 = 0.85$	8.5	

Modern Application History and membrane polymer development

In the 1970s and 1980s UF Bio/Pharma applications were primarily limited to the production of vaccines.
These solutions were relatively poorly defined and were made up of whole cell and virus fractions. It was
not uncommon to expect considerable loss of flux in these systems. During the following decade, high-
value IgG's and other Biotech products were being developed. The demand for better performing membranes resulted in the introduction of PES, CTA, and RC filters. Further, membrane improvement resulted
in improved PES and modified RC membranes featured both excellent performance and chemical stability.

Characteristics of Crossflow Membranes

Rejection Coefficient

Membranes are designated by their "Rejection Coefficient" by the various manufactures to delineate different membrane "Cut Offs" offered for use. Rejection (16.7) is a determination of the amount of target
molecule that is retained by the membrane being tested.

$$R = 1 - \left(\frac{C_p}{C_f} \right) \tag{16.7}$$

where,

   R = the rejection coefficient,
   C_p = the concentration of the target solute in the permeate,
   C_f = the concentration of the target in the feed.

Membrane MWCO values are published by the manufactures of membranes based on the rejection coefficients determined and presented by the manufacturer. The correlation to actual and reported MWCO is somewhat subjective as different suppliers may use different markers and different rejection targets. As a result,
manufacturers' determinations and designations may not be similar to one another and can only serve as a
guideline for selection. The MWCO of a membrane is determined by using either specific molecular-weight
marker molecules or the use of mixed dextrans as shown in Figure 16.8. Moreover, MWCO values are not
absolute. It is typical to refer to the MWCO as the point where the membrane (within Quality Control (QC)
acceptance limits) rejects a defined percentage of marker molecules based on the manufacturers designated
rejection levels which may range from as low as 67% to >98%. Another feature differentiating membranes
is the steepness of the rejection versus marker plot. A membrane's selectivity may be considered greater and
better defined when smaller markers have lower rejection coefficients. For example, if two, 100kDa membranes may have retention coefficients for albumin (67kDa) of 80% and 40%, respectively, then one might
consider the membrane with a albumin rejection of 40% to have greater selectivity.

By knowing the rejection coefficient of the target molecules and that of the process contaminants, one
can exploit the differences between them (see the section "Fractionation" and Tables 16.1, 16.2, and 16.3).

Protein Adsorption on UF Membranes

Protein adsorption onto the surface of a membrane is called fouling. Proteins can react with, and adhere
to, the polymer surface due to hydrophobic/hydrophobic interactions between the membrane and protein.

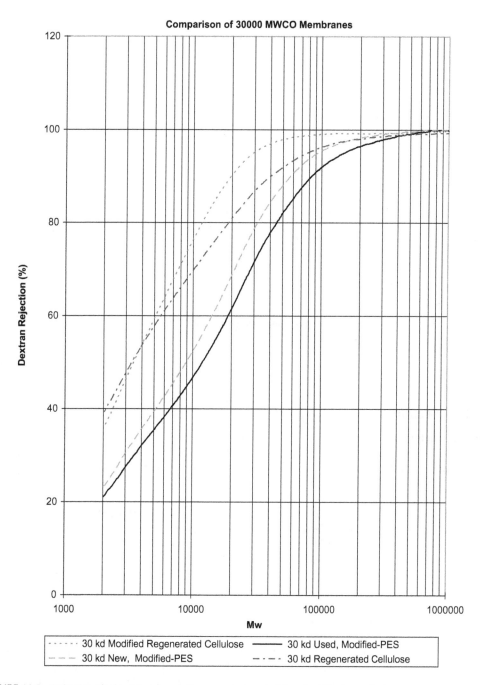

FIGURE 16.8 Rejection of mixed dextrans on three membranes as determined by size exclusion.

Fouling can also occur due to charge differences between the polymer and protein, causing the protein to adhere to the membrane surface. This problem is especially evident while running concentration or time trials to evaluate membrane for a particular process application with a more hydrophobic membrane (PS) as shown in Figure 16.9.

A truly fouling process does not follow the standard equations. Furthermore, fouled membranes may not be able to be cleaned post-use because the bond between the foulant and the membrane is irreversible. Some reactor antifoams may show such characteristics.

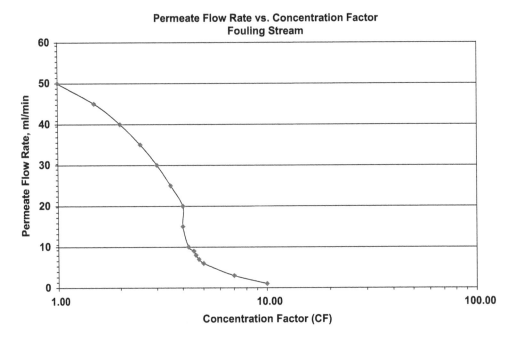

FIGURE 16.9 Example of membrane fouling, where flux does not decay linearity on the semi-log plot of permeate flow rate vs concentration factor.

Membrane Fouling

Membrane fouling is a process that results in a marked decrease in performance of ultrafilter membranes. The fouling of ultrafilters has been inextricably linked to protein processing due in part to the extended history of the membranes that have been employed. By understanding the fouling phenomenon we can often minimize or totally eliminate this problem through the proper selection of currently available membranes such as stabilized RC ultrafilters.

A consequence of protein adsorption is a decrease in membrane permeability and an increase in membrane fouling.[13,14] It has been shown that protein adsorption is greater on hydrophobic membranes than on hydrophilic membranes. Additionally, protein conformation influences membrane performance. Globular or spherical protein deposits influence flux decline less than deposition of protein sheets. Freeze-fracture and deep-etching techniques have shown that the deposition of bovine serum albumin (BSA) onto hydrophilic RC membranes is spherical in nature. The size of the deposited spheres is consistent with the accepted size of the BSA molecule. However, the deposition of BSA onto less hydrophilic PS membranes is filamentous. The conclusion is that the tertiary structure of the protein has been disrupted through the interaction of the solute and the membrane.[13]

When fouling occurs the nature of the feed stream composition can have dramatic effects on the retentive nature of the membrane. The retention of large-molecular-weight components can increase the retention of smaller-molecular-weight components. Blatt et al. (1970) demonstrated that human serum albumin (67,000 Da) retention on a 100,000 MWCO membrane was nearly zero. However, when γ-globulin (160,000 Da) was added to the feed stream, the albumin retention rose. Albumin retention showed a linearly increasing correlation to increasing concentrations of the γ-globulin.[8] Porter similarly showed that the retention of ovalbumin, chymotrypsin, and cytochrome C is increased when a 1% solution of albumin is added to the feed mixture.

The rejection of IgM on 100,000 MWCO PES membranes and stabilized RC membrane show divergently different results even though the mixed dextran rejection profiles are similar. These differences can be attributed to membrane fouling and the nature of the resultant protein cake that forms as described above.

Membrane Types

MF membranes, nanofilters, and UF membranes may differ considerably in their morphologies and can be visualized through cross-sectional cuts of these membranes using scanning electron microscopy (SEM). The symmetry of microfilters usually ranges from being uniform to being slightly asymmetric. Many are standard MF filters in crossflow format.

Modern ultrafilters, on the other hand, are either anisotropic (highly asymmetric) with the rejecting layer consisting of a tight skin (0.5–10 µm thick) supported by a thick spongy structure of a much larger pore size, or "void free" membranes cast onto an MF substructure, with no apparent "skin." Liquid generally flows through the membrane in the direction from the tight "skin side" toward the open side of the UF membrane; flow in the reverse direction can result in the delamination or separation of the UF part of the structure from the substructure of the membrane.

Nanofilters vary in their presentation forms from being composites (tight membranes cast onto a UF or MF membrane) to bi-anisotropic.

The current ultrafilter membrane materials used in the Pharma/Biotech industry today are; RC, modified RC(Hydrosart®), PES, and modified PES. The membranes used in microfilter applications include modified RC (Hydrosart®), PES, Cellulose Acetate (CA), polypropylene, and Polyvynilidine difloride (PVDF).

Figure 16.10 shows the two types of crossflow membrane structure used today, while Figure 16.11 shows typical types of MF membranes. Nanofilters or Virus retention filters are similar in structure to the "void free" UF membranes.

(a)   (b)

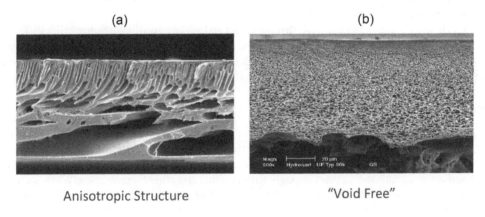

Anisotropic Structure   "Void Free"

FIGURE 16.10 UF membranes (a) anisotropic and (b) void free.

(a)   (b)

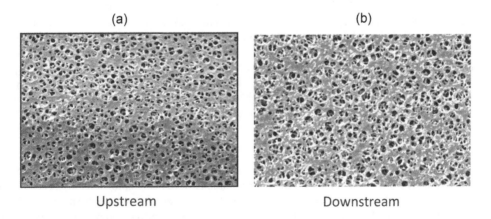

Upstream   Downstream

FIGURE 16.11 MF open foam (a) upstream and (b) downstream structure.

Membrane Polymers

UF membranes are available in a variety of polymers. Some of those polymers have surface modifications which are intended to improve their performance. Today in the pharmaceutical and biotech environment there are two primary polymer families which are in use. These are the PSs and the cellulosics.

The PSs include hydrophilic PS and PES which represent the polymers that are widely used due to the length of time that these polymers have been on the market. These membranes gained acceptance for use in validated processes in part because of their robustness and the fact that they can withstand 1N NaOH exposure. NaOH is commonly used throughout industry as a means for chemically cleaning, depyrogenating, and sanitizing process equipment. Natural PSs are hydrophobic. In the casting of these membranes, the polymer is treated with hydrophilization agents that render the polymer hydrophilic. Depending on the hydrophilizing agent and process the resulting membrane has a greater or lesser lipophilic profile.

Cellulosic membranes have also been available for many years in the form of CA, Cellulose nitrate, mixed esters of cellulose, CTA, and RC. The shortcoming of all these membranes, their chemistries notwithstanding, is their general lack of robustness and limited pH range (4–8). Because of these limitations, these membranes have been more difficult to clean in a manner acceptable to the biopharmaceutical industry. In the mid-1990s; however, stabilized RC (Hydrosart®) ultrafilters were introduced which overcame the pH limitation and extended the polymer's pH range from 4–8 to 2–14, thus allowing these membranes to be cleaned and depyrogenated using 1N NaOH. Moreover, some Hydrosart® cassettes are steam sterilizable. Cellulose ester ultrafilters are generally supplied as hollow fibers, and are often supplied in a single-use presterilized disposable format so as to overcome cleaning and sanitizing issues associated with this type of membrane.

The PVDF membranes include PVDF (hydrophobic) and surface modified (hydrophilic) PVDF supplied in a steamable format. These membranes gained acceptance for use whole cell harvesting primarily because of the open channel device format in which they were offered. Hydrophilic PVDF, however, is not compatible with 1N NaOH exposure.

Protein–Membrane Chemistry

Membrane polymer chemistry plays a crucial role in the interaction of a product being filtered and the membrane. The PSs are rich in conjugated benzene rings which serve as potential sites for hydrophobic/hydrophobic (i.e., membrane—protein) interactions. Likewise, the nitrate groups on the cellulose nitrate and mixed esters of cellulose interact strongly with proteins and other biomolecules. When such interactions occur the result is the adsorption and denaturation of proteins at the membranes' surface. The effect of the membrane polymer on a protein-containing solution has been well documented. Truskey et al. (1987) measured protein adsorption, circular dichroism, and biological activity of variety of protein solutions, i.e., insulin, IgG, and alkaline phosphatase. Truskey measured the solution's properties before and after passing the proteins through a variety of membranes. Observed shifts in circular dichroism and decreases in the activity of the enzymes were determined to be the result of conformational changes of the protein structure. This study showed clearly that membranes with the greatest degree of hydrophobicity had the greatest effect on protein adsorption and protein deformation.[15] The result of these protein–membrane interactions is that the protein's internal hydrophobic sites become exposed. These exposed hydrophobic surfaces then serve as sites for membrane–protein binding, protein–protein binding, and protein denaturation. This protein–membrane interaction ultimately leads to an overall increased rate of membrane clogging and fouling, reduced performance, and loss in product yield.

Data

Figure 16.12 shows the flux versus TMP profile for saline, 0.1% lysozyme, and 0.1% lysozyme and 0.2% BSA on 30 kDa Hydrosart® membranes. Flux determinations were made at low and high recirculation rates. The profiles for lysozyme/BSA solution and the lysozyme at the low recirculation rate showed traditional flux limited TMP-independent performance resulting from membrane fouling and protein polarization. At the higher recirculation rate, the lysozyme flux increased linearly with increasing TMP.

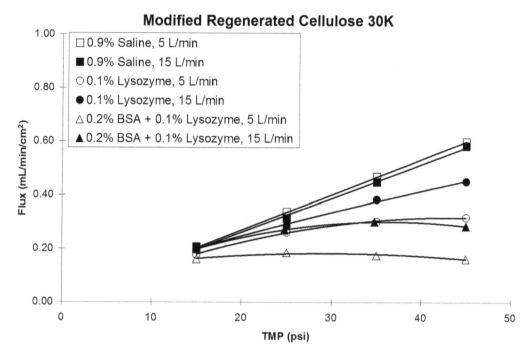

FIGURE 16.12 Flux versus TMP profiles for saline, lysozyme, and Lysozyme/BSA solutions at low and high recirculation rates.

Figures 16.13 and 16.14 are flux versus TMP curves for 10 and 30kDa membranes before and after protein (1:20 diluted skim milk) concentration and 0.1% lysozyme concentration. For the 10kDa membranes the modified RC membrane's flux was completely recovered through dilution, whereas the flux on the PES membranes remained irreversibly depressed. After the concentration of the lysozyme, flux on 10kDa modified RC, was not recovered through dilution.

Figures 16.12–16.19 examine saline flux versus TMP of the different membranes tested. Membranes are tested when new and then again after 2–3 cycles of use followed by cleaning.

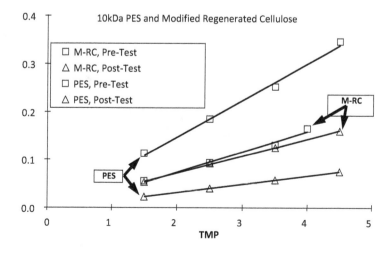

FIGURE 16.13 Saline flux on 10kDa PES and modified RC membranes before and after the 10× concentration of skim milk diluted 1:20.

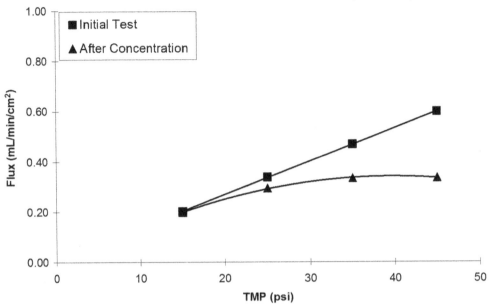

FIGURE 16.14 Saline flux versus TMP on 30 kDa modified RC membranes before and after the 10× concentration of 0.1% lysozyme.

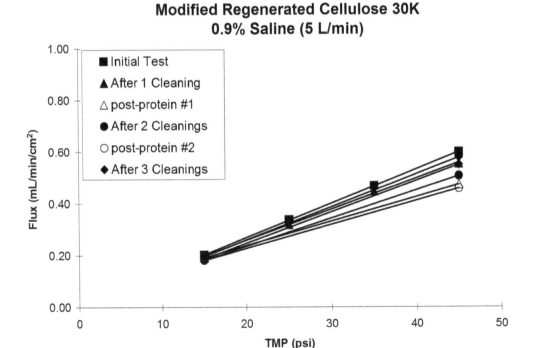

FIGURE 16.15 Saline flux on 10 kDa modified RC (Hydrosart) membranes before and after three cycles of 10× concentration of lysozyme followed by cleaning with 1 NaOH.

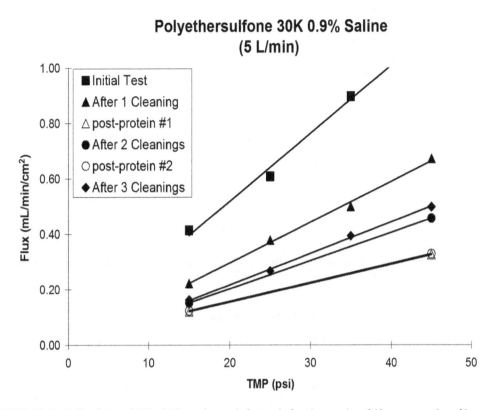

FIGURE 16.16 Saline flux on 30kDa PES membranes before and after three cycles of 10× concentration of lysozyme followed by cleaning with 1 NaOH.

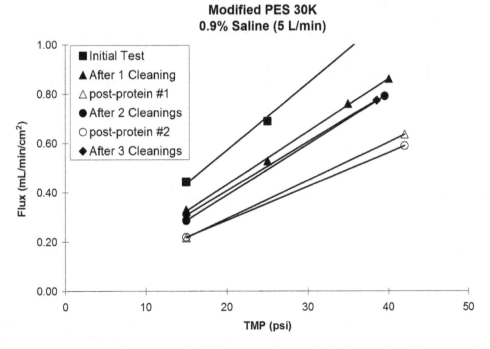

FIGURE 16.17 Saline flux on 30kDa modified PES membranes before and after three cycles of 10× concentration of lysozyme followed by cleaning with 1 NaOH.

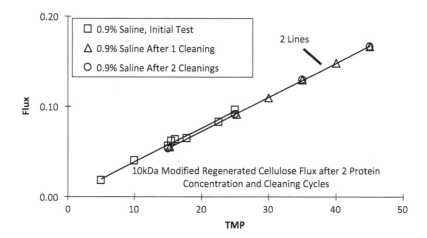

FIGURE 16.18   Saline Flux on 10 kDa modified RC (Hydrosart) membranes before and after three cycles of 10× concentration of 1:20 diluted skim milk followed by cleaning with 1 NaOH.

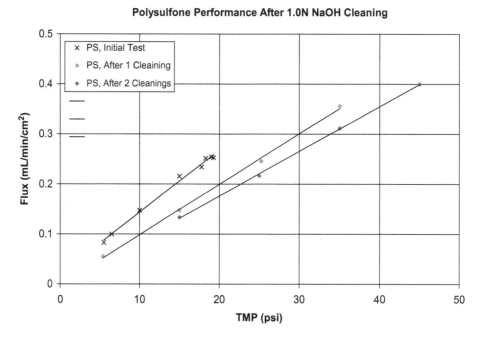

FIGURE 16.19   Saline flux on 10 kDa modified PES membranes before and after three cycles of 10× concentration of 1:20 diluted skim milk followed by cleaning with 1 NaOH.

Discussion

Post-use flux can be completely recovered after protein filtration on modified RC membranes as compared to the irreversible and permanent loss in the case of PES membranes. This fundamental difference in membrane performance is due to membrane fouling.

Depending on the membrane foulant, PES membranes can lose 75% of its flux, whereas modified RC membrane flux loss ranges from 0% to 31% after post-use rinsing. After cleaning the modified RC membrane saline flux recovery is usually between 89% and 100% versus the PES membranes, where permanent flux loss can be as high as 48%.

Conclusion

Though product loss, shifts in membrane rejection and membrane fouling have long been part of the UF process, current stabilized RC ultrafilters offer significant performance advantages over PES membranes. The increased hydrophilicity of cellulosic membranes limits the fouling process and therefore the associated product loss. This in turn minimizes the effect of the polarizing protein layer on the membrane surface. Rather than the process forming a "secondary membrane" (protein gel), which eclipses the intrinsic properties of the base membrane the properties of RC membranes are preserved. The result is improved overall performance, easier cleaning, and substantially better product and flux recovery.

Crossflow Element Design and Geometries

Turbulence-Promoting Insertions

Insertion of static mixers into the retentate flow path enhances the transition of the flow from laminar to semi-turbulent. The use of screens or meshes as static mixers in-between membranes are found in variety of crossflow devices. Screens are used in spiral-wound cartridges and in most cassette and plate-and-frame designs. These mesh-like spacers serve to disrupt the feed stream from smooth flow to a semi-turbulent state which has been shown to improve flux.[16] There is some debate as to the nature of the flow through these systems. Belfort (1987) considers the flow to be laminar through systems with screened channels, whereas Cheryan (1986) reports the flow as turbulent based on the pressure drop within the flow channel. This issue though can be resolved in a straight-forward manner by experimentally determining the slope of log-log plots of flux as a function of velocity as shown in Figure 16.2.

There are potential downsides to the indiscriminate use of turbulence-promoting insertions for bio/pharmaceutical filtrations. Specifically, some products may be caught on the mesh, creating a cleaning problem as well as causing potential occlusion of the flow channel.[17] Particulates tend to either hang up on the mesh or occlude the flow channel, so solutions with suspended solids require pretreatment of the feed. Usually 50–200 μm prefiltration of the feed will alleviate this problem. Meshes are used in construction of cassettes and spirals to keep the feed flow paths open.

Flow Path Length

The way to control the filter cake is to optimize velocity and shear forces at the membrane surface. The length of the flow path has direct and indirect bearing on these hydraulic forces. First, as shown in Equation 16.3, when flow is laminar the flux is proportional to the inverse length to the power of 0.33 $(1/L)^{0.33}$. Therefore, increasing the flow path length has the effect of decreasing flux. In turbulent flow, the length of the flow path does not have a direct bearing on flux. Second, the flow path length has an indirect bearing on flux for both laminar and turbulent flow because pressure drop through the crossflow device is proportional to the flow path length caused by frictional forces at the fluid–membrane interface. Therefore, the longer the flow path the greater the pressure drop and the lower the flux. Third, because fluid is continually permeating the membrane, as the flow path length increases the volumetric flow and velocity of the feed solution decreases. Equations 16.3 and 16.4 show that decreasing velocity causes a reduction in flux. Therefore, based on both direct and indirect reasoning, increasing the length of the flow path results in the reduction of flux. Oddly, the higher conversion of feed to permeate in some membrane devices actually results in a lower overall flux due to the reduced retentate flow if the flow path length is not taken into account during scale-down studies.

Flow Channel Height

The flow channel height also has direct and indirect bearing on flux in crossflow UF. As Equations 16.3 and 16.4 show, in laminar flow flux is proportional to the quantity $(1/dh)^{0.33}$ and in turbulent flow flux is proportional to $(1/dh)^{0.20}$. Therefore, as the channel height (or hydraulic diameter) increases the flux will decrease. The indirect consequence of changing channel height is to cause a change in the crossflow velocity, assuming constant volumetric flow rate. That is, the cross-sectional area of the flow channel divided by the volumetric flow rate gives the fluid velocity in the flow channel. By increasing the flow path channel height, the cross-sectional area is increased, resulting in a decrease in the velocity and subsequently in flux.

When possible, the channel height should be as low as practical. However, care must be taken to avoid excessive pressure drops in the flow path and not to select a channel height that might trap recirculating particles or require a pump that might damage or disrupt the product's integrity in the attempt to achieve sufficient crossflow rates.[18]

Cassettes are available with the option of different internal flow geometries. Sartocon cassettes with "E" type spacers are designed for high protein concentration applications and for viscous products, while the cassettes with "ECO" screens are designed for protein concentrations less than 15%–20% (150–200 g/L) and for other products with low viscosity [<3 cp (3 mPas)]. With current monoclonal antibody production (mAb) harvest targets of ≥5 g/L and increased use of subcutaneous dosages, protein concentrations can exceed 250 g/L. It is, therefore, important to understand when to use each type of cassette and the implications. The following data demonstrates the effect of channel height.

The effects of recirculation rate, pressure, and protein concentration on permeate flux were evaluated with Sartocon Slice 200 "E" channel and "ECO" channel cassettes. Testing was conducted using 30 kD Hydrosart ultrafilter cassettes, and the test solutions were either a 5 g/L mAb solution or 1% milk.

Results

Temperature and protein concentration have a profound influence on permeate flux. As shown in Figure 16.20, flux increases as both temperature increases and protein concentration decreases; regardless of the temperature or the protein concentration. One can see in Figure 16.20 that the influence of increasing recirculation rate is also increasing permeate flux. Furthermore, the slope of each line is the same, which means that one is able to accurately predict the performance of the cassette with the protein solution based on the process variables.

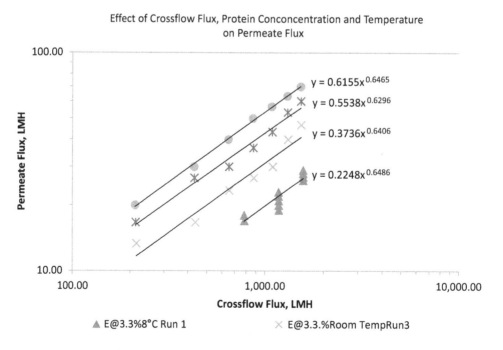

FIGURE 16.20 Permeate flux was measured at different recirculation rates between 180 and 1800 L/m²h, at 8°C and 20°C using 1% milk at protein concentrations from 0.8% to 3.3%, and A 30 kD "E" channel Slice 200 cassette.

Flow channel geometry also has a profound influence on permeate flux. In Figures 16.21 and 16.22, the thinner ECO channel cassettes achieve flux values equivalent to the E channel cassette at approximately one-third of the recirculation rate of the more open E channel cassette.

However, there are instances where the E channel cassettes fail to approach the flux values of the ECO cassette even at 3 times the recirculation flow rate. In Figure 16.23, the ECO cassette has 60% higher flux than the E channel cassette. This is typically the case when both the protein concentration and viscosity are low.

In the concentration plot (Figure 16.24) 1% milk is concentrated from 3.3% protein to 15% protein. Though the two plots are virtually superimposable, the difference is that the E channel cassette crossflow feed rate is about 2.6 times that of the ECO channel cassette.

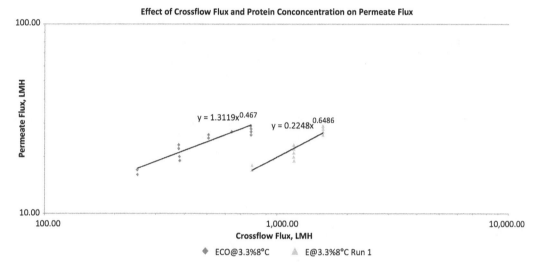

FIGURE 16.21 A 30 kD "ECO" and "E" Channel Slice 200 cassette permeate flux was measured at different recirculation rates between 180 and 1800 L/m²h at 8°C using 1% milk.

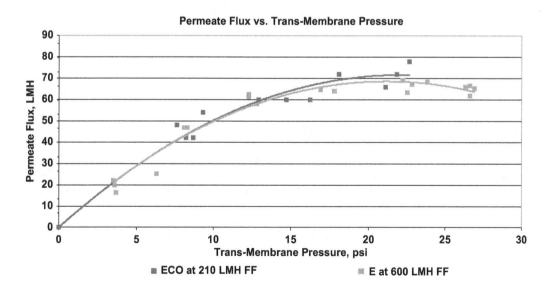

FIGURE 16.22 Permeate flux was measured at different recirculation rates between 180 and 1800 L/m²h, at 8°C and 20°C, and at protein concentrations from 0.8% to 3.3%, and A 30 kD ECO Slice 200 cassette.

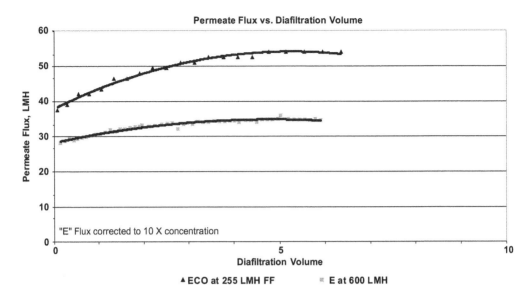

FIGURE 16.23 A 30 kD "ECO" and "E" Channel Slice 200 cassette permeate flux was measured at feed flow rates of 255 and 600 L/m²h, respectively, during the DF of a mAb at 5 g/L against citrate buffer.

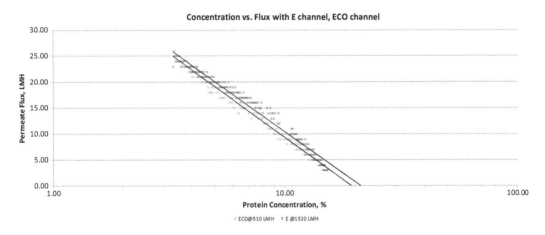

FIGURE 16.24 A 30 kD "ECO" and "E" Channel Slice 200 cassette permeate flux was measured at feed flow rates of 510 and 1320 L/m²h, respectively, during the concentration of milk fivefold from a protein concentration of 3.3%–15%.

As shown, channel height has a profound influence on both the required recirculation rate and permeate flux.

At higher protein concentrations as viscosity increases "E" channel cassette flux values rise to values equal to "ECO" channel cassettes. At high protein concentrations (>15%) "ECO" channel cassettes become impractical because of the resultant extreme pressure drop within the channel, therefore, making the "E" channel cassette the appropriate choice.

Cassette channel height selection can profoundly influence a process skid design. Pump, valve, piping, surface area, and cost can vary by a factor of two- to threefold based on the cassette selection.

Crossflow Module Types

As discussed previously, the ability to create shear and reduce concentration polarization is affected by the inherent design of the membrane module. There are numerous module designs to select for crossflow filtration. The traditional "process" designs used in the biopharmaceutical industry are cassette (plate-and-frame) modules, spiral-wound modules, and hollow fibers.

Cassette Modules

These modules consist of flat-sheet membranes mounted into a framework Figure 16.25. In the assembly of these systems each flow path is made up of two membranes that are facing each other. The upstream flow path must be sealed from the downstream permeate side of the membrane. Stacks of pairs of membranes are layered one on top of the other, and the permeate side of each membrane is supported by a rigid and porous spacer plate. In systems making use of preassembled modules, the membrane is generally glued onto the spacer plate. The spacer plate may be smooth or have surface features that give the membrane an uneven surface for turbulence promotion. Flow paths are usually open and may be parallel and or in series. In an alternative design not using rigid plates, the membrane's support is achieved by the dynamic interaction of the membranes above and below the permeate flow path (Figure 16.26).

Feed flow paths can be open, but most do use screens. Feed enters at one end of the module through a series of inlet ports and exits the other end of the module through the outlet ports. Permeate flow exits through a series of permeate ports. Preassembled cassettes come in a variety of sizes from $10\,cm^2$ up to >$7m^2$. Systems utilizing these designs may have surface areas exceeding $140\,m^2$.

Plate and Frame   Cassette   Hollow Fibers

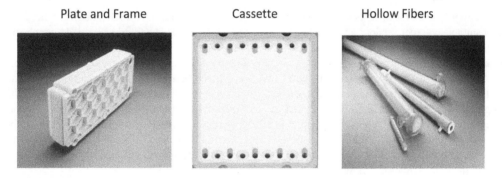

FIGURE 16.25 Cassette crossflow UF modules (Prostack Open channel module, Millipore Corp; Cassette, Sartocon II, Sartorius Corp.; Hollow Fiber module GE Health).

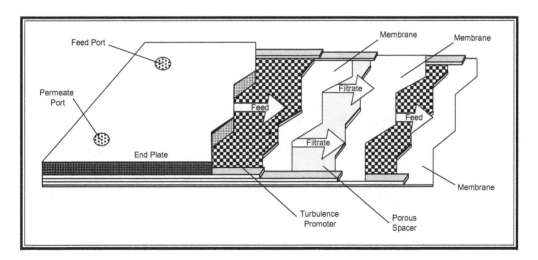

FIGURE 16.26 Schematic description of flow paths in cassette modules.

FIGURE 16.27   Cassette crossflow modules in a Sartocon 20 holder. (Courtesy of Sartorius-Stedim Biotech.)

The filter holders for these designs are usually constructed from stainless steel, though acrylic, PS and other suitable polymer versions are available for the laboratory market. The filters are sealed into the holder between two plates via a compression seal. Closure is achieved by tightening tie rods that are attached to the back plate and go through the front plate (Figure 16.27). Larger systems achieve compression by using a hydraulics that exerts a force onto a movable front plate, thereby compressing the modules in the middle.

Plate and frame systems are generally easy to clean, have relatively high membrane packing densities, support a wide variety of membrane materials, are amenable to incorporating turbulence-promoting spacers, and provide good crossflow performance. Drawbacks to this design are that fabrication of modules can be labor intensive, and thus expensive; and packing densities are not as great as hollow-fiber modules. However, the advantages to this design outweigh the disadvantages, and this design is widely used in the biopharmaceutical industry.

Spiral-Wound Modules

Spiral-wound modules utilize pairs of flat-sheet membranes bound on the up and downstream sides by screens similar to those in cassette systems. As shown in Figure 16.28, the membrane sandwich is sealed at three edges so that the feed is isolated from the permeate. The fourth side of the membrane sandwich is attached to a perforated permeate collection tube. The membrane pairs are then rolled around the perforated collection tube, thereby creating the spiral.

Feed flow enters at one end of the spiral, flows tangentially along the axis of the cartridge, and discharges at the other end. Permeate flows at a right angle to the feed flow toward the center of the spiral and is collected in the core of the spiral. Spiral-wound modules are available in a variety of surface areas, starting at $<50\,cm^2$ to $>5\,m^2$. Surface area can be increased by either increasing the number of membrane pairs, increasing the diameter of the spiral wrap, or by increasing the length of the flow path. Spiral cartridges are placed in snug fitting housings. The cartridge is sealed to the housing wall via an O-ring that allows feed flow on the outside of the cartridge. When flow is along the outside of the cartridge it is restricted by a screen so as to provide similar resistance to flow as is seen in the feed flow channels between the membranes. Laboratory devices are available preassembled in suitable plastic housings.

Spiral-wound modules can be ganged together to make filter systems of varying surface areas. Spiral systems feature relatively high membrane packing densities and low cost. This design is extremely successful for particulate-free process streams, but they are difficult to clean when particulates clog the flow paths or collect at the O-ring seals. Other drawbacks to this design include difficulty to sanitize, and long flow paths making high flow with low pressure drop impossible.

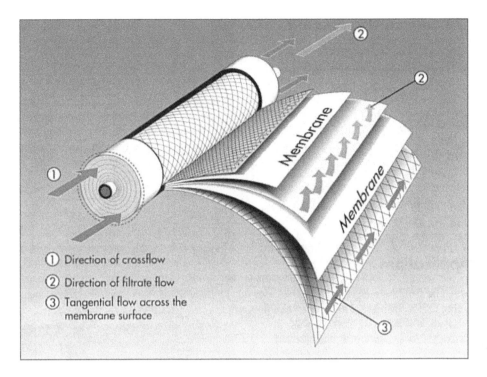

FIGURE 16.28   Spiral-wound crossflow module.

Hollow Fiber and Tubular Modules

The fundamentals of hollow fiber and tubular crossflow systems are essentially the same, with the difference being that tubes are considerably larger in diameter than hollow fibers. Figure 16.29 shows a continuum of "hollow-fiber" modules, with lumen diameters ranging in size from 0.5 to 3.0 mm. Tubular systems may also be configured with removable tubes that are inserted into individual tube holders. In ceramic tubular systems the membrane is cast as part of the ceramic tube array.

The "rejecting" layer of a hollow fiber or tube can be on the inside or outside of the fiber, with the wall of the fiber functioning to support and strengthen the rejecting layer. Liquid permeates the fiber wall, as with flat-sheet membrane, and permeate is collected on the opposite side of the fiber. Hollow fibers and tubes are grouped and sealed into tubular shells to form modules as shown in Figure 16.29. In the case

FIGURE 16.29   Hollow fiber and tubular modules containing fibers ranging in inner diameter from 0.5 to 3.0 mm. (Photo courtesy of G E Health Care.)

where the rejecting layer is on the inside (lumen) of the fiber, the feed solution enters the lumen of the fiber at one end, flows down the length of the fiber, and retentate exits at the other end. Permeate is collected on the outside (shell-side) of the fiber.

Hollow fibers are generally defined as having inner diameter of less than 1 mm. These fibers have greater pressure drop than do tubular modules; however, they also have much greater membrane surface area per volume than do tubular modules. Hollow-fiber modules are also less costly than are tubular modules. Ceramic and tubular modules have low packing densities, but because of their large lumen are able to handle very high particle loads. Because of the large lumens, they require very high feed flow rates in order to achieve sufficient shear velocity. Ceramic systems have a very high initial installation costs, but because they use inorganic membranes they may have extremely long membrane life.

Process Variables

Filtration Driving Force

Pressure is the driving force for all filtration processes. Plots of solvent flow through a membrane result in a linear increase in the permeate flow as pressure increases. When the solution to be filtered contains solute greater than the filter's pore size, then plots of flux versus pressure may become nonlinear. When resistance to flow through the membrane increases due to the buildup of a solute cake on the membrane, then the flux fails to increase with increases in pressure.

TMP

TMP is the average pressure on the upstream side of the membrane, and is one of the critical controlling factors in the performance of all crossflow filtration applications regardless of the design of the filter module (Equation 16.8).

$$TMP = \frac{P_{\text{feed}} + P_{\text{retentate}}}{2} - P_{\text{permeate}} \qquad (16.8)$$

where,
   TMP = Trans-Membrane Pressure,
   P_{feed} = Feed Pressure,
   $P_{\text{retentate}}$ = Retentate Pressure,
   P_{permeate} = Permeate Pressure.

Selecting the ideal operating pressures is the result of conducting an experiment where one plots permeate flow rates or flux as a function of the TMP as shown in Figure 16.30.

There are often three distinct regions when one plots flux versus TMP. In the first phase, flux increases proportionately with increases in pressure. Phase 2 is a transition area and Phase 3 is that portion of the plot where increasing in pressure yields no discernable increase in flux. The optimum TMP for a process is generally described as the intersection of the two tangent lines drawn through Phase 1 and Phase 3. The benefit of operating at pressures greater than this "optimal" point is offset by the requirement for greater energy input and pumping capacity especially at large scale.

Optimization experiments require that temperature, recirculation rates, and protein concentration remain constant. This is because resistance to flow increases as viscosity increases. Viscosity varies directly with concentration and the temperature of the product stream. Resistance to flow is also inversely proportional to the thickness of the solute cake.

One should be cautioned that depending on the available and type of flow measurement instrumentation used, that the recirculation flow rate will be effected as backpressure is applied into the retentate line. Pumps are only able to overcome backpressure to a point after which the recirculation rate begins to decrease. When this happens, flux will also begin to decrease in the presence of solute. Figure 16.31 shows this effect where the pressure drop decreases as backpressure is applied into the retentate line. This loss in pressure differential is an indication of the loss in recirculating flow rate, resulting in a concomitant loss in permeate flux.

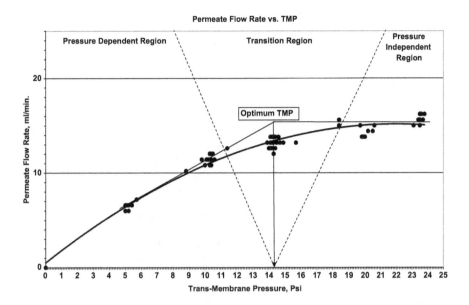

FIGURE 16.30   Flux versus TMP at 100 mL/min recirculation rate for skim milk diluted to 0.2% protein in saline filtered through a 200 cm² 30 kDa Hydrosart ultrafilter membrane.

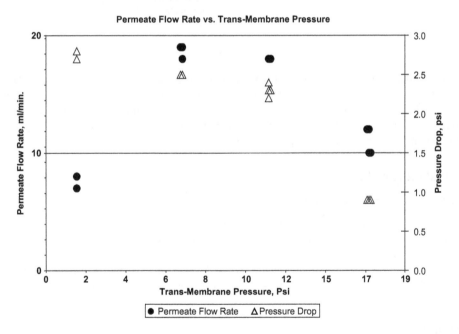

FIGURE 16.31   Permeate flow rate is plotted versus TMP and the pressure drop between the inlet and retentate with the pump set at 100 mL/min feed on the peristaltic pump for 1:10 diluted milk.

Factors Influencing Performance

See Table 16.4

Feed Stream Composition

The nature of the feed stream can have dramatic effects on the retentive nature of a filtration membrane, especially when the filter is functioning according to the adsorptive-sequestration mechanism.

TABLE 16.4

Factors Affecting Yield of a Protein Biopharmaceutical in Filtration Steps

Process Type	Filter Type	Points to Consider
Cell harvesting	Crossflow MF	• Membrane polymer • Filter preparation • Filter surface area • pK_a of the protein • Temperature • Feed pressure • Recirculation rate
Concentration	Crossflow UF	• Membrane polymer • Filter preparation • Filter surface area • pK_a of the protein • Temperature • Feed pressure • Recirculation rate
DF	Crossflow UF	• Membrane polymer • Filter preparation • Filter surface area • pK_a of the protein • Temperature • Feed pressure • Recirculation rate • Stability of protein in the buffer system

As previously discussed in the section on membrane fouling, the retention of large-molecular-weight components can increase the retention of smaller-molecular-weight components as described by Blatt et al.[8] and by Porter.[6] Similar observations have also been made regarding the microfiltraton of complex solutions. Most importantly, the actual retention capability of a specific membrane with a specific feed mixture should always be measured experimentally.

Recirculation Flow Rate

Dependence on Crossflow Rate

Generally, with solutions like buffers and water the permeate flow rate will increase with pressure in a linear fashion. For these solutions, flux is independent of the crossflow rate. Flow through the membrane is only dependent upon the TMP and temperature.

When processing solutions with retained solutes, flux may be dependent on the crossflow rate. Figure 16.32 shows a solution where there is a dependence on crossflow rate and the transition of flux from pressure dependence to pressure independence.

Temperature

The effect of temperature on filtrate flux can usually be explained by the changes in solution viscosity. Temperature has a direct effect on viscosity, i.e., as temperature is increased viscosity decreases, and as viscosity decreases flux increases. Flux is generally inversely proportional to the viscosity of the feed solution.

Biopolymer polarizing gels that form during filtration of proteinaceous solutions are gelatinous in nature. The plasticity of these components is affected by the temperature of the solution. When the solution is kept cold and viscosity is high, they behave like rigid particles; when they are warmed, they are free to deform from the stresses of the filtration process. Polarized protein cakes are compressible, and the pressure of filtration can cause the (gel) layer to collapse and completely clog the membrane.

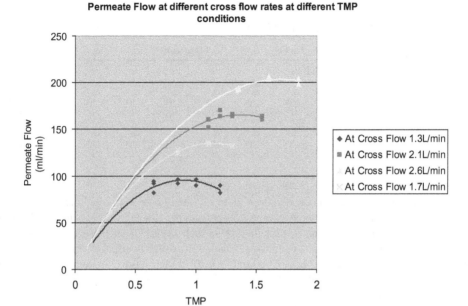

FIGURE 16.32 Flux versus TMP at several flow rates and TMP levels.

The temperature of the solution influences the compressibility of the filter cake. When the solution is kept cold (e.g., 4°C) the filter cake is less compressible than when it is warm. As a result, filtration of biopolymer-containing solutions proceeds far better when the solution is kept cold. The increased throughputs when running cold far outweigh the reduction in flux as a result of the increased viscosity of the solution.

Temperature also influences the solubility of certain proteins. Cryoglobulins are a class of serum proteins that precipitate when the temperature of the solution is lowered to a critical limit. Freezing and thawing of protein solutions also results in the generation of protein precipitates. Adding heat to the solution can cause the disruption of hydrogen bonds, causing unfolding of some portions of the protein which in turn results in the formation of aggregates that may precipitate.

If the temperature is raised, protease activity may be activated or accelerated, which will result in protein degradation and precipitation of the proteolytic fragments. Lastly, at higher temperatures the adsorption of protein to the membrane is enhanced, resulting in an increase of membrane fouling.

Normalized Clean Water Flux

$$NCWF = CWF * K \tag{16.9}$$

where,
 NCWF = Normalized clean water flux at 25°C,
 CWF = clean water flux at temperature X,
 K = correction factor for temperature x (Table 16.5).

pH and Ionic Conditions

Protein solubility generally increases as the solution pH moves away from the protein's isoelectric point and at extremes in solution ionic strength. As the isoelectric point is approached or as the solution's ionic

TABLE 16.5

Normalized Clean Water Flux: Temperature Correction Factors

Temperature °C	Correction Factor	Temperature in °C	Correction Factor
25	1.000	19	1.152
24	1.023	18	1.181
23	1.047	17	1.212
22	1.072	16	1.243
21	1.098	15	1.276
20	1.125	14	1.310

strength decreases or increases dramatically, the protein will precipitate from solution and likely foul the membrane. Moving the pH too far one way or the other from the isoelectric point charges the protein, causing increased protein–membrane or protein–protein interaction. Under these conditions, proteins may start to agglomerate or bind to the membrane, which will adversely affect the product and the process. Changes in the proteins' conformation and stability affect their adsorption to membrane surfaces. McDonogh (1990) showed that protein fouling is maximized at the protein's isoelectric point and that the phenomenon is concentration dependent.[19]

Buffer exchanges and DFs are common in the processing of protein solutions. It is important to maintain an ionic equilibrium in the solution. When a buffer or salt is exchanged, one must be sure that all of the components remain in solution during the exchange process. Failure to do this may result in protein precipitation and fouling of the system. This is especially true when proteins are being concentrated by UF, because if the salts concentrate with the proteins the proteins may start to salt out. Likewise, if the salt levels fall too far, precipitation may also take place. Calcium and phosphate are directly implicated with the formation of insoluble calcium salts that serve as bridging agents for protein deposits.[13]

Removal of certain ionic species (e.g., by DF) can also result in the formation of precipitates. This happens when the quaternary protein structure is lost, as the result of the removal of cations like magnesium, which serve to bridge the protein subunits. When serum proteins are dialyzed against distilled water, flocculation occurs as a result of the precipitation of a class of proteins called euglobulins which is comprised primarily of IgM.

Process Optimization

Optimizing Experiments

The experiments for optimizing an UF application are relatively simple and straight forward. They are primarily designed to identify the optimal feed flow rate and TMP.

Clean Water Flux

Clean water flux (CWF) values serve as benchmarks as experiments are conducted. When flux cannot be recovered through dilution we may conclude that fouling has occurred. Fouling can be described as an irreversible process whereby the product stream components become irreversibly bound to the membrane. With proteins, this manifests in the formation of a cake of denatured protein bound to the membrane surface.[20] When membranes foul, flux may only be recovered after the membranes are cleaned with NaOH or other aggressive cleaning agents. Depending on the membrane polymer CWF may exhibit a continuous decline following each cycle of use and cleaning.

CWF can be determined by determining flux at a set temperature and pressure while deadheading the filter. If the water temperature varies then one can normalize the value.

Optimizing the Pressures

As previously discussed in the section on "Process Variables/Driving force/TMP," selecting the ideal operating pressures is the result of conducting an experiment where one plots permeate flow rates or flux as a function of the TMP as shown in Figure 16.30.

There are generally three distinct regions when one plots flux versus TMP. In the first phase, flux increases proportionately with increase in pressure. Phase 2 is a transition area and Phase 3 is that portion of the graph where increasing pressure yields no discernable increase in flux. The optimum TMP for a process is generally described as the intersection of the two tangent lines drawn through Phase 1 and Phase 3. The benefit of operating at pressures greater than this "optimal" point is offset by the requirement for greater energy input and pumping capacity especially at large scale.

These experiments require that temperature, recirculation rates, and protein concentration be constant. This is because resistance to flow increases as viscosity increases. Viscosity varies directly with concentration and the temperature of the product stream. Resistance to flow is also inversely proportional to the thickness of the solute cake.

One should be cautioned that depending on the available and type of flow measurement instrumentation used, that the recirculation flow rate will be affected as backpressure is applied into the retentate line. Pumps are only able to overcome backpressure to a point after which the recirculation rate begins to decrease. When this happens, flux will also begin to decrease in the presence of solute. Figure 16.27 shows this effect where the pressure drop decreases as backpressure is applied into the retentate line. This loss in pressure differential is an indication of the loss in recirculating flow rate, resulting in a concomitant loss in permeate flux.

Excessive pressure can result the membrane substructure to compress or collapse resulting in a progressive reduction in the membrane's flux due to the occlusion of the exit pathways through the substructure.

In Figure 16.33, membrane hysteresis is observed in 1 and 5 kDa PES ultrafilters. The 1 kDa ultrafilter exhibited nearly a 40% drop in flux under the influence of a pressure of 4 bar. Under the same

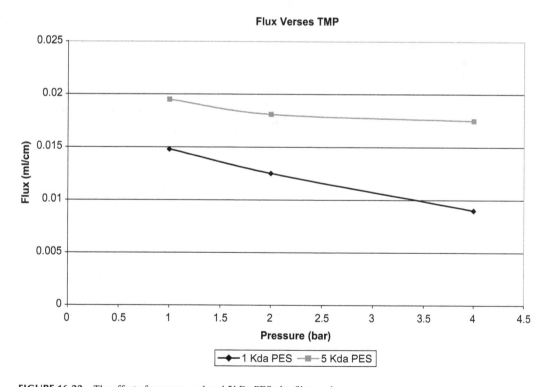

FIGURE 16.33   The effect of pressure on 1 and 5 kDa PES ultrafilters substructure.

conditions the 5 kDa PES membrane loses on 10% of its flux. Though this example may be an extreme, it does serve to illustrate and alert users that the phenomenon can occur. It should be noted that this phenomenon is less likely to be seen with membranes that have high permeation rates as exemplified by the difference between the 1 kDa membrane and the 5 kDa membranes. Furthermore, the nature of the substructure (foam versus finger) will have a significant influence on whether this phenomenon will occur at all. Membranes with a foam or supported substructure generally do not lose flux due to compaction.

Flux versus Recirculation Rate

Membrane flux is affected by the thickness of the polarized filter cake. The thickness of that cake may be controlled hydraulically. Increasing the fluid flow rate through the flow path results in an increase in the shear forces acting on the filter cake. The shear forces at any given flow rate vary with the viscosity of the product. By plotting the relationship between the permeate flux versus TMP at different feed flow rates one can assess the "cost versus benefit" of increasing the recirculation rate. For water-like products, the fluid stream will generate greater shear than for a viscous product.

Figures 16.34 and 16.35 show that as the recirculation rate increases, flux likewise increases at the same TMP.

Preparing log-log plots of flux versus velocity, shear, or recirculation rate may provide a view as to the effect of increased recirculation.

Figure 16.35 shows the effect of the membrane pore size on permeate flux and on the slope of the increase in flux with increase in recirculation rate.

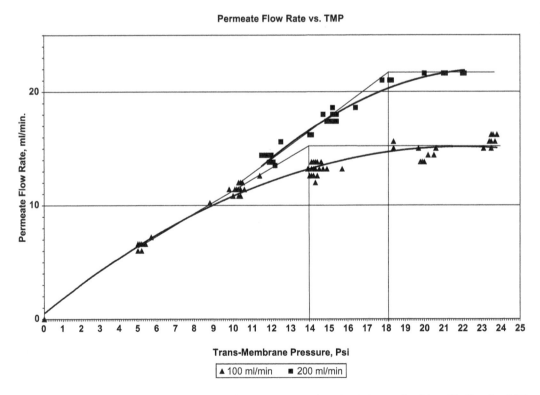

FIGURE 16.34 Permeate flow rate versus TMP at 100 and 200 mL/min recirculation rate for skim milk diluted to 0.2% protein in saline filtered through a 200 cm² 30 kDa Hydrosart ultrafilter membrane.

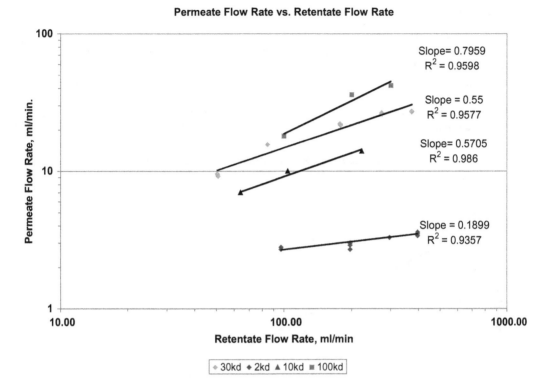

FIGURE 16.35 Permeate flow rate versus recirculation rate at a TMP of 23 PSI with skim milk diluted to 0.4% protein in saline filtered through 200 cm²: 2, 10, 30, and 100 kDa Hydrosart ultrafilter membranes (Dosmar, Emily Filtration, CPS Science Fair 2006).

If one is working with filters of differing geometries, where there are changes in either flow path length or the flow channel hydraulic diameter, plotting permeate flux and shear or velocity rather than flow rate may be more useful because it normalizes the results between the different geometries. Feed or retentate flow velocity can be calculated by dividing the volumetric flow by the hydraulic diameter.

$$V = \frac{\frac{Q}{t}}{d} \tag{16.10}$$

where,
Q/t = flow rate,
D = hydraulic diameter.

And

$$D = 4 \cdot \left(\frac{C_h \cdot C_w}{2C_h + 2C_w} \right) \tag{16.11}$$

where,
C_h = Channel Height,
C_w = Channel Width.

For cassettes the total hydraulic diameter is the hydraulic diameter for one channel multiplied by the total number of flow channels in the cassette.

Flux versus Protein Concentration

Plotting flux versus concentration at a fixed recirculation rate, fixed TMP and fixed temperature will allow one to determine where the optimal DF point might be, the required DF buffer volume, and the total time required for the process (Figure 16.36).

Extrapolating the flow decay line to where the flux line intercepts the X-axis provides a theoretical maximum solute concentration value.

Plotting runs conducted at multiple recirculation rates provides evidence as to whether the solute is fouling or not (Figure 16.37).

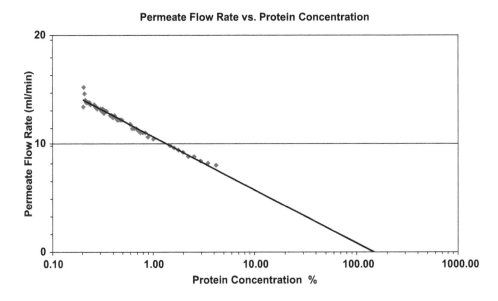

FIGURE 16.36 Permeate flow rate versus percentage of protein: Whole milk diluted to 0.2% protein in saline and then concentrated using a Sartorius 200 cm² 30 kDa Hydrosart membrane at a recirculation rate of 150 mL/min at a TMP of 18 psi.

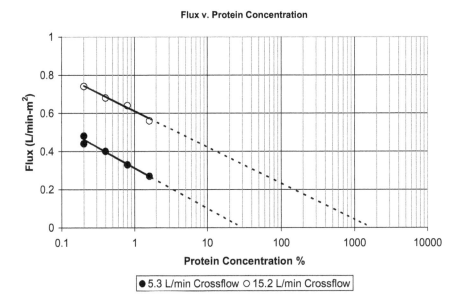

FIGURE 16.37 Flux versus protein concentration at two different recirculation rates for skim milk diluted to 0.2% protein.

Concentration decay plots are extrapolated to where flux approaches 0 (Sartorius Hydrosart 30 kDa Membrane Area = 6,000 cm²). Non-convergence of flux decay plot to a common end point provides evidence that no protein fouling is occurring. When concentration-dependent flux decay plots converge to a common end point regardless of the recirculation rate, one can conclude that the protein solute is forming a fouling protein gel.

Process Scaling

Appropriate studies should be conducted for a successful scale-up from small clinical (Phase 1–2) scale volumes to pilot (Phase 3) or commercial production scale as recommended by regulatory bodies, i.e., The European Agency for the Evaluation of Medical Products (EMEA). In the "Note for Guidance on Process Validation" section, "It is expected that during the development stage, the manufacturer of the product should gain sufficient information about the behavior and the physical and chemical properties of the drug substance, the composition of the product in terms of active ingredient(s) and key excipients, and the manufacturing process clearly define the critical steps in the manufacturing process."

Small-scale experiments conducted in the laboratory generate data that includes equipment, i.e., elbows, valves, and pumps that may skew performance expectations because of the inherent nature of the systems' plumbing. Though one may wish to minimize these effects, they cannot be disregarded.

Elucidating a process allows decision-making based on selecting optimal parameters. Experiments looking at flux versus TMP, log flux versus log recirculation rate, identifying the optimal pressures and flows for the process[21–23] must be conducted. These experiments also provide the reference values for the scaling process.

System Hydraulics

Scaling-up process piping is typically the result of determining the desired flow rate, pressure, and fluid flow velocity. Elbows, valves, and other process components within the fluids' path have calculable effects on both pressure and flow rate. Scaling-up a crossflow system, on the other hand, offers an additional hurdle that of the hydrodynamics of the fluid flow through a cassette's feed and retentate screened flow paths.[24] There are two components to a cassette's feed and retentate flow path. Those are the feed and retentate flow manifolds internal to the cassettes, which feed and receive flow from the membrane flow channels and the flow channel itself. Crossflow cassettes have screens interleaved between each membrane pair on both the feed and permeate flow channels.

These screens serve as a static mixer. Depending on the screens' designation, the gap between the membranes can vary, and with it, the pressure drop through that channel. As part of the cassette's construction, the screens and membranes make up the wall of the manifold feeding the membrane feed channel as in Figure 16.38. This internal manifold is made up of the edges of the membranes and interleaving screens; therefore, it is not smooth like process tubing. As a result, the manifold's wall increases resistance to flow because of wall drag to a much greater extent than that for process tubing. Flow rate through the feed manifold increases as one adds surface area (cassettes) because recirculating flow rate per square meter of membrane is generally kept constant as the process is scaled up. The drag at the edges of the manifold can cause the feed solution to transition from laminar to turbulent flow especially at the proximal cassette(s). As this happens pressure drop in this channel develops.

Pressure drop is directly tied to a fluid's viscosity in the flow path. Figures 16.39 and 16.40 show the effect of viscosity on pressure drop. Here, pressure drop is measured with water and with bovine serum and then plotted against surface area. Regardless of the TMP, and inlet and outlet pressures, the pressure differentials remain constant (data not shown) at any one flow rate. Reynolds numbers increase as viscosity decreases. Pressure drop likewise increases as the flow through the manifold transitions into turbulent flow. This transition occurs at lower flow rates when the viscosity is low. Cherian (1986) shows the general relationship of pressure drop (ΔP) being directly proportional to flow rate (Q). This relationship is used to determine whether flow rate is laminar or turbulent flow using Equation 16.12 where for values of $n = 1$, flow is laminar and where values of $n > 1.4$, flow becomes turbulent.

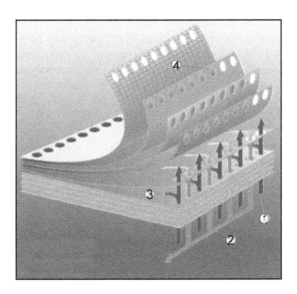

FIGURE 16.38 Diagram of a cassette where 1 is the feed flow through the feed ports of the cassette, 2 is the retentate flow, 3 is the feed flow through the membrane flow channel, and 4 is the membrane. (*Image Courtesy of* Sartorius-Stedim.)

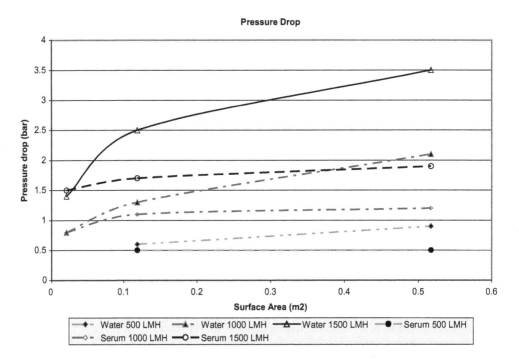

FIGURE 16.39 Observed pressure drop with water and bovine serum using Sartocon Slice 200 (200 cm²), Sartocon Slice (1,000 cm²), and Sartocon Cassette (5,200 cm²) at recirculation rates of 500, 1000, and 1500 L/m²h.

$$\Delta P \propto f(Q)^n \qquad (16.12)$$

As surface area is added the pressure required to maintain a constant recirculation rate per square meter of membrane must increase. This increase may not be linear and can vary as a function of the screen designation and flow channel gap width. In short, each membrane flow path creates a resistance to flow. As flow paths are added additional pressure is required to overcome the additive effect of the pressure drops.

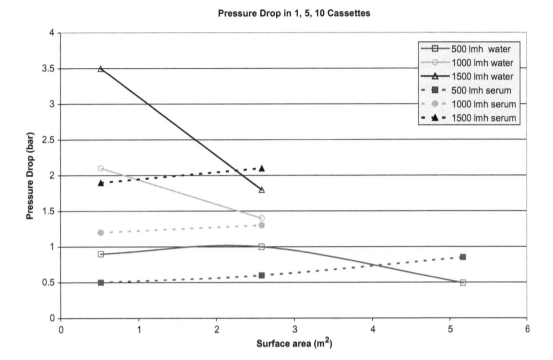

FIGURE 16.40   Pressure drop in 1, 5, 10 cassettes with water and serum.

Turbulence-Induced Pressure Drop

The pressure drop data shown in Figure 16.40 implies that with water a significant pressure drop occurs at high flow rates as a result of turbulence. This turbulence occurs at the proximal entrance into the first cassette's feed port where there are two "elbow" effects created by the change in the direction of the fluid path. Flow enters the holder and exits at a 90° angle into the cassette. A part of the flow then changes direction a second time entering into the membrane flow channel. Depending on the rate of flow and the abrupt changes in flow direction a region of turbulence can be created when the flow rate is sufficiently high. As cassettes are added, the effect is eliminated because the solution is able to transition back into laminar flow. As more cassettes are added additional flow is required to maintain a constant flow per cassette and turbulent flow can be once again reinitiated if the flow rate is sufficiently high (Figure 16.41).

The flow rate for small surface area cassettes <200 cm² relative to both the inflection distances and the port size, assures smooth flow throughout, resulting in no turbulence-induced drop in pressure. At the 1,000 cm² size turbulence-induced pressure drops can be inferred at high recirculation rates.

Since turbulence and viscosity are inextricably linked, one can see that the pressure drops seen with water are not observed with product. Depending on the nature of a product's viscosity at the start, middle, and end of a concentration run, turbulence-induced pressure drops should be accounted for and controlled.

Pressure Drop-Induced Flux Loss

When turbulence-induced pressure drops occur, the consequence is a drop in permeate flux due to loss of motive force. At low recirculation flow rates, solvent flow is greater than at higher recirculation flow rates at the same calculated TMP. This is due to the pressure drop in the feed ports. When the pressure drop occurs prior to entering the membrane flow channel, the actual pressure driving permeation is reduced even though the apparent TMPs are the same (Figure 16.42).

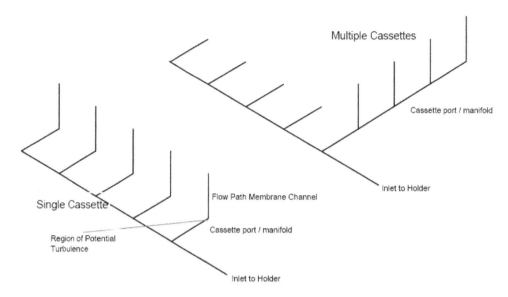

FIGURE 16.41   Diagram of flow path into a filter holder and cassettes.

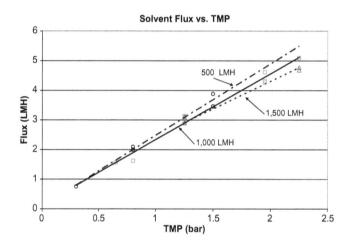

FIGURE 16.42   Solvent flux (water) is measured at recirculation flux values of 500, 1,000, and 1,500 L/m²h on a Slice 200 (200 cm²), Slice (1,180 cm²) and on 1,5, 10, and 20 Sartocon Cassettes (ea 5,200 cm²). All values are plotted together making no distinction between the devices and relative surface areas. Trend lines are automatically drawn by Excel™ through the datasets.

Surface Area

Surface area is the amount of effective membrane in a system. Commercially available "scalable" cassettes are available in surface areas from about 50 cm² to 3.5 m². Cassettes from a variety of manufactures all claim to maintain common geometries within their respective product lines making them suitable for scale-up and scale-down studies.

Sources for Variation in Flux

Surface area

Membrane surface areas reported by most manufactures of UF are in whole number increments. This being the case, rounding errors can contribute considerably to errors in scaling.

Cassettes having small amounts of surface area are subject to the variance in the actual available membrane surface area which can have a significant influence on the observed flux. As area increases these variances become less and less noticeable.

The average standard deviation as a percent of the mean normalized water flux was used to compare cassettes having different surface areas and geometries. As expected, the values increase as the cassette surface area decreases. In the analysis of multiple membrane casting lots from which >10 lots of cassettes were made of various sizes, flux range/standard deviation increased from ±6% of mean flux for a $0.7\,m^2$ cassette to ±8% for $1,000\,cm^2$ cassettes, and to ±22% for $200\,cm^2$ cassettes (Tables 16.6 and 16.7).

Case Study in Scaling

Process scaling always poses challenges. These challenges include determining whether the scale-down testing components can accurately predict performance at scale. Sartorius prides itself in being able to deliver small-scale filtration devices that are transparent to scale. However, the filters alone do not solve the issues regarding scale-up. System geometry and the system flow hydraulics can have profound influence on the performance of a process. Planning large campaigns require that small-scale studies be performed followed by intermediate and full-scale engineering runs. The following report is an example of the successful implementation of a viral vaccine process starting with initial testing with 400 mL on a $180\,cm^2$ device and successfully scaling the process to 4,000 L.

The scaling journey began with a small-scale study using 400 mL of the product and following the a standard UF optimization protocol based on the procedures of Dosmar using a Sartocon Slice 200 cassette on a Sartoflow Benchtop Crossflow system (Figure 16.43).

TABLE 16.6

Flux values for Bovine Serum on a variety of cassettes from $200\,cm^2$ to $6\,m^2$

Filter/Cassette (Actual Surface Area)	Mean Scale-Up Factor Based on Experimental Water Flux	Scale-Up Factor Based on Published Area	Scale-Up Factor Based on Experimental Serum Flux	Scale-Up Factor Based on QC Water Flux	Scale-Up Based on Actual Surface Area
Slice 200 ($180\,cm^2$)	1	1	1	1	1
Slice ($1,170\,cm^2$)	5.6	5	7.5	7.5	6.5
Sartocon 2 ($5,850\,cm^2$)	4.4	6	4.4	4.8	5

TABLE 16.7

Predicted Flux For 10 Cassettes Is Calculated by Taking the Measured Flux From a Slice 200 ($200\,cm^2$) Cassette and Multiplying It by 10 Times the Product of the QC-Based Data Scale-Up Factors from Table 16.3 for the Slice 200 to Slice (7.5) and the Slice to Sartocon (4.8)

	Flux (l/min) vs. TMP				
Cassette / TMP (bar)	1	1.5	2	2.5	3
$1 \times$ Slice 200	0.02349	0.0249	0.0253	0.0254	0.0255
$1 \times$ Slice	0.1761	0.186	0.19	0.1915	0.1905
$1 \times$ Sartocon 2	0.8	0.832	0.856	0.861	0.860
$2 \times$ Sartocon 2	1.63	1.74	1.76	1.78	1.78
$5 \times$ Sartocon 2	3.68	3.84	3.89	3.91	3.89
$10 \times$ Sartocon 2	7.78	8.08	8.25	8.34	8.35
Predicted Flux for 10 Sartocon Cassettes	8.4564	8.964	9.108	9.144	9.18
$Error\% = 1 - \dfrac{Actual\ Flux}{Predicted\ Flux}$	8%	10%	9%	9%	9%

Note: The % error (line 10) is 1 – (actual flux for 10 cassettes (line 8) divided by the predicted flux for ten cassettes (line 9)).

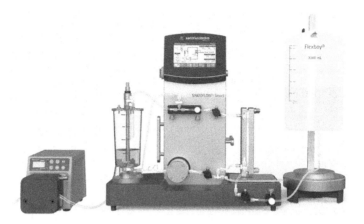

FIGURE 16.43   Sartoflow Smart Benchtop crossflow system. (*Image Courtesy of* Sartorius-Stedim.)

The initial investigation where permeate flux was measured at a variety of feed flow rates and TMP values revealed that the process was relatively insensitive to the rate of the feed flow and that a permeate flux did not increase much above a TMP of 15 psi (Figure 16.44).

Flux during the concentration phase decreased as expected (Figure 16.45).

Based on these initial experiments we used the log mean average (Equation 16.13) to calculate the expected average process flux to be ~47 LMH. We used this value to predict the process performance at manufacturing scale (Table 16.8).

$$J_{avg} = \frac{J_{initial} - J_{final}}{\ln\left(\dfrac{J_{initial}}{J_{final}}\right)} \tag{16.13}$$

where,

J_{avg} = Average Flux,
$J_{initial}$ = Flux at the start of the concentration,
J_{final} = Flux at the end of the concentration.

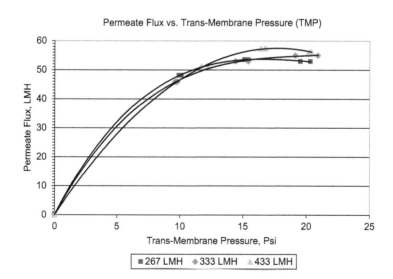

FIGURE 16.44   Permeate flux versus TMP excursion of viral vaccine at feed flux values of 267, 333, and 433 L/m²h.

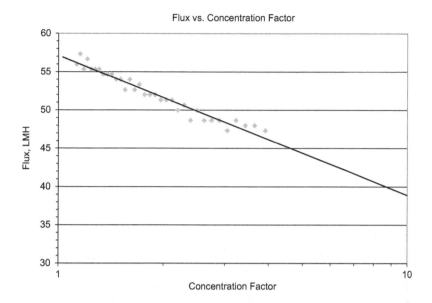

FIGURE 16.45 Permeate flux versus product concentration of the viral vaccine.

TABLE 16.8

Process Scale-up Study where the Average Process Flux is Maintained between the Initial
Laboratory Study, Pre-production Engineering Runs and Actual Full Scale Production

	Lab Scale Test	**Engineering Runs**	**Production Run**
Filter surface area (m²)	0.018	6	18
Batch size (L)	0.4	1,200	4,000
Average permeate flux (LMH)	47	51	47

Prior to full-scale testing the facility conducted three one-fourth scale engineering runs followed by a
full-scale test.

As one can see in Table 16.8, the predictive scaling data was quite accurate. Of particular note, the
membranes' performance was insensitive to product/membrane loading. The bench scale membrane
load was 22 L/m² and the production scale was 222 L/m².

Conclusion

Careful analysis of pressures and scaling factors makes it possible to predict scaled-up performance.
Scaling predictions should include both average water flux from multiple membrane lots as well as
product-specific flux.

Process Modes

Crossflow application can be operated in a variety of different modes. These include batch, modified
batch, feed and bleed, and single-pass TFF.

Batch

In batch mode, the feed solution is added to the processing vessel and the solution is recirculated through
the crossflow system returning to the tank. As the solution permeates the membrane system, the volume
concentrates in the feed tank. At the desired level (concentration factor) the system is shut down and the
retained contents are collected or discarded as dictated by the process design (Figure 16.46).

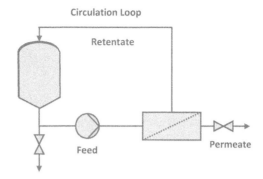

FIGURE 16.46   Batch mode schematic representation.

Modified Batch/DF

In a modified batch mode, the bulk feed solution (e.g., DF solution) is added to the processing vessel and the solution is recirculated through the crossflow system returning to the tank. As the solution permeates the membrane system, new feed solution is added to the feed tank. Feed may be either a constant rate which may or may not be equal to the rate of permeation or in aliquots until the feed/and or the diafiltrate is all transferred to the feed tank. After the transfer is complete, the process is completed as in a batch mode where the volume is allowed to concentrate in the feed tank. As before, at the desired level of concentration the system is shut down and the retentate volume is collected or discarded as dictated by the process design (Figure 16.47).

Feed and Bleed Batch

Feed and bleed is used primarily in industrial applications where the volumes are very large and high recirculation rates are required. This mode is generally not used in cGMP applications. The retentate is recirculated in a loop between the feed tank and the inlet of the recirculation pump (with or without a pressurizing pump in the line. This lowers the overall recirculation rate, thereby reducing the solution turnover rate in the feed tank. However, as the concentration in the recirculation loop increases, the loop solution must be "bled" back to the bulk feed tank to prevent the loop from becoming overconcentrated. For example, if the loop bleed rate is 10 times the permeation rate, then the loop volume will only be 5% higher than the feed tank concentration. This allows for a smaller feed pump, and small "feed" line to the system from the tank. For large systems with remote tankage this can save quite a lot of large pipes and with a small pressurizing feed pump, a large amount of energy can be saved by keeping the loop pressure high (i.e., not dropping it to zero at every pass).

The issue with feed and bleed is controlling the loop versus the return flow rates and cleaning the loop/by-pass lines to ensure proper cleaning levels. For most pharmaceutical and biotech applications this process design is usually not used (Figure 16.48).

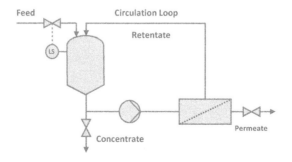

FIGURE 16.47   Modified batch mode schematic representation.

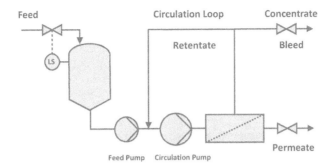

FIGURE 16.48 Feed and bleed schematic representation.

Single-Pass TFF

As mentioned earlier, SPTFF is a newer concentration modality, initially championed by Teske et al.[25] Subsequent work by Dizon-Maspat et al.[26] explored the effect of increasing flow path length and modeling the process on multistage Reverse Osmosis water treatment system configurations where the surface area decreases with each added filtration stage

In SPTFF the product of interest enters the system at one concentration and exits at the desired concentration. This approach often utilizes longer feed flow path lengths, coupled with retentate restriction. This allows for greater permeation, thereby higher protein concentration on the retentate side.

To calculate the concentration factor, divide the feed flow rate by the retentate flow rate.

$$CF = \frac{Q_{Feed}}{Q_{Retentate}} \tag{16.14}$$

where,
CF = concentration factor,
Q_{Feed} = feed flow rate,
$Q_{Retentate}$ = retentate flow rate.

Or to find the necessary retentate flow rate, divide the feed flow by the desired concentration factor.

$$Q_{Retentate} = \frac{Q_{Feed}}{CF} \tag{16.15}$$

where,
CF = concentration factor,
Q_{Feed} = feed flow rate,
$Q_{Retentate}$ = retentate flow rate.

SPTFF is typically employed in monoclonal antibody processes to reduce volume between process steps, and to highly concentrate a final product, sometimes to greater than 200 mg/mL. In conventional TFF systems, one is limited by the system's minimum working volume as there is a risk of entraining air into the drug product if the volume drops too low. This is not a concern with SPTFF as the system flow path volume is typically quite low and there is no recirculation to reduce volume, the product simply exits the system at the desired concentration.

In SPTFF, flux values often are much lower than traditional TFF modes, but because concentrated product is received almost immediately and collected, the processing times are not drastically different for an entire batch. Because it is also possible to couple SPTFF to other downstream applications as the low flow rate feed and retentate streams are available for and compatible with continuous process schemas (Figure 16.49).

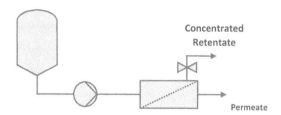

FIGURE 16.49 Single-pass TFF schematic representation.

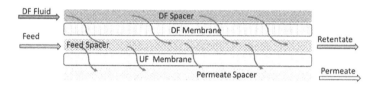

FIGURE 16.50 Concept of Sartorius-Stedim's "3-chamber-cassette 3K."

The limitation of many SPTFF configurations is that they can only be used for concentration applications. However, following the proof of concept work by Dosmar and Pinto demonstrating the ability to both concentrate and diafilter in a single pass configuration led to the development of a multistage three channel cassette (Figure 16.50).

The 3-chamber-cassette 3K design features a product feed channel, diafiltration buffer feed channel, and permeate channel. Depending on the ratio of product to buffer feed coupled with controlling the rate of retentate flow, while monitoring the rate of permeation, makes the system capable of both concentrate and diafilter to desired endpoints within limits. Depending on the protein concentration starting and desired endpoint one is able to achieve buffer clearance to seven diavolumes and concentration factors up to 10X with a single three-stage cassette. Higher values are achievable by the addition of a second cassette. Results as shown in Table 16.9 demonstrate that buffer clearance is comparable to conventional batch DF, without significantly higher buffer consumption (Table 16.9).

High Performance TFF

Another relatively recent advance in filtration was established by Robert van Reis, called high performance tangential flow filtration (HPTFF). Traditional TFF is limited to the separation of species typically with a greater than tenfold distribution of size. This severely limits the separation of individual proteins from a feed stream. HPTFF utilizes more than one MWCO membrane in a closed, multiple-stage setup to separate closely sized proteins from one another. The first stage also utilizes a co-current permeate pump to balance the level of pressure along the retentate channel to ensure optimum sieving conditions (Figure 16.51).

TABLE 16.9

22 g BSA in 10 mM K_2HPO_4 and 0.9% NaCl Diafiltered at a Feed Ratio Equivalent to 4.5 DV against 10 mM K_2HPO_4

Time (min)	P_{Feed} (bar)	$P_{Retentate}$ (bar)	P_{DF} (bar)	V_{Feed} (mL/min)	$V_{Retentate}$ (mL/min)	$V_{Permeate}$ (mL/min)	$C_{protein}$ (g/L)	X (Vol/Vol)	$LF_{Retentate}$ (ms)	Clearance actual (%)	Clearance theoritical (%)
5	1.07	1.08	1.2	20	20	90	21.3	4.5	2.28	99	99
15	1.09	1.02	1.2	22	20	90	22.4	4.5	2.18	99	99
30	1.07	1.01	1.19	22	20	88	21.5	4.5	2.17	99	99
60	1.03	0.97	1.14	21.5	20	88	23.6	4.5	2.14	99	99
90	1.01	0.95	1.12	21	20	88	25	4.5	2.16	99	99
120	1	0.95	1.12	22	20	88	22.5	4.5	2.16	99	99

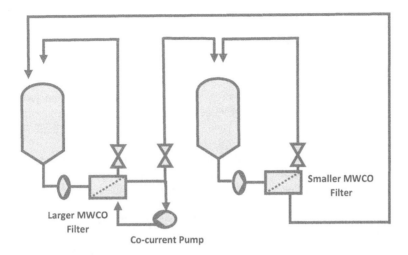

FIGURE 16.51 HPTFF schematic representation.

Membrane Cleaning

It is generally necessary to clean the membranes between filtration batches especially when fouling occurs. Methods employed to clean the membranes must not damage or alter the membrane, and the cleaning agents must be completely rinsed from the membrane prior to reuse.

The goal of the cleaning procedures is to remove product from the membrane and to assure that there is no cross-contamination between production lots and to restore the membrane's flux as close to the original starting flux as possible. The selection of a cleaning protocol must take into account the nature of the product and the agent responsible for soiling the membrane. It is critical to examine the interaction of membrane, the soil, and cleaning agent, because it is possible to irreversibly fix fouling proteins to the membrane matrix or to render a membrane unsuitable for the application that it is intended by leaving a residual charge on its surface. Also critical to the process is to be able to test for the presence of any residual cleaning or sanitizing agents because of potentially deleterious effects on subsequent production runs.[27]

Cleaning may be considered from the perspective of time, temperature, and cleaning chemicals. As a rule, the longer a cleaning agent is allowed to work the more effective it is. This is especially true when the cleaning agents contain proteases; the higher the temperature the more reactive the cleaning agents. The limitation of raising the temperature must be balanced between the reactive nature of the cleaning agent and the stability of the soils (fouling proteins). Too high a temperature can lead to protein denaturation. When proteins become denatured and precipitate on or within the membrane matrix, cleaning becomes considerably more difficult. The proper selection of cleaning chemicals and their proper use will result in the desired effect (Table 16.8). Just as one must optimize the operating parameters for production, the same can be said for the cleaning process.

The cleaning procedure should begin immediately after the end of the filtration run. Allowing protein-containing solutions to remain in a drained membrane system can lead to protein denaturation and adsorption at the protein–membrane–air interfaces. It is generally advisable to rinse out as much of the product as possible at the end of the run, prior to introducing the cleaning agents. One needs to be cognizant of the solutions used to rinse out the solution because of potential fouling by residual protein or antifoamants as a result of pH, temperature, or ionic strength. For protein-containing solutions, it is generally recommended to rinse the membranes with an isotonic solution.

Historically, certain membrane pretreatments have been shown to have profound effects on product yield. Prewashing PS 100,000 MWCO membranes with a buffered bleach solution followed by a 0.1N NaOH rinse gives considerably higher yields in the purification of polio virus than using only the NaOH (Prashad, M. Personal communication 1996). Divizia et al. (1989) improved yields of polio virus by preblocking potential membrane-binding sites using a variety of buffers of varying concentrations.[28]

Validation Issues

Process-Specific Validation Issues

The compatibility of a membrane system that is reused must look at the effects of reuse on the membranes with regard to any changes in extractables after prolonged exposures to all the fluids that the process will encounter. These include the storage, rinse, cleaning, sanitizing, and process solutions. Membrane integrity must be monitored by both direct testing of the membrane's integrity as well as by continued achievement of the desired product yield and product quality. Furthermore, the membrane's retention coefficient should also be monitored over the life of the membrane.

Retention coefficients or selectivity measurements are highly subjective. It may be best to specifically determine the membrane's retention coefficient with the products of interest by using them in the presence of normal process fluids. This then provides a practical reference by which to evaluate performance.

Membrane cleaning and sanitization from a validation standpoint must be determined to be effective. It must also be demonstrated that the cleaning agents can be removed prior to reuse. The ability to demonstrate this is important, especially considering the potentially deleterious effects of residuals on product yield and on product purity.[27] Validation of cleaning cycles can be performed through the analysis of permeate and retentate effluents after each stage of the operation. Analysis should include specific assays for compounds that have been introduced into the system. Alternative approaches are to flush the system with water for injection (WFI) and determine if the effluents continue to meet the standards for WFI. Total organic carbon analysis of effluent rinses offers yet another approach to this problem. Direct physical inspection of membrane systems provides further confirmation that cleaning procedures are adequate. After the membranes have been cleaned it is suggested that a WFI, buffer or 0.1 N NaOH flux be determined. CWF or other solution flux determinations serve as a benchmark for subsequent cleanings. Generally, the flux from a virgin membrane will never be achieved after the first production run followed by the first cleaning. It is not uncommon for the flux to drop >20% with PES membranes, though this reduced value should be retrievable after subsequent use and cleaning cycles.

If the CWF or equivalent test continues to decline after each process run and cleaning cycle, then further or different cleaning techniques need to be investigated. Certain solutions clean well (enzymes, and hypochlorite as examples) but are sometimes difficult to confirm total removal prior to subsequent uses. Continued decline in the CWF or equivalent test indicates the membranes are fouled, or the cassette may be plugging with solids. Foulants may be cleaned, but plugging is almost always irreversible, and care needs to be taken to ensure solids are filtered out before operation or filtered out during operation, or operating parameters changed to prevent precipitation during processing.

Application-Specific Validation Issues

Contaminants

During operation of a concentration process, low-level contaminants may suddenly become problematic. Two specific contaminants are of particular interest. First, protein solutions may have low levels of contaminating proteases. Though the rate of proteolysis may be undetectable in the unconcentrated bulk, after concentration the rate may be increased by the square of the concentration factor.[29] The effect of proteases on product yield can be devastating to the process. Second, endotoxins may be concentrated from below detectable limits to levels high enough to cause product-lot rejection. Apparent endotoxin content can be also influenced by the nature of the ionic content of the process fluids, which means that they may only appear after a buffer exchange step.

Reuse

Use of "single use" crossflow cassettes and process loops should make this separation and process step even more economically and process control interesting to potential users since the time-consuming membrane cleaning and validation steps are removed from the process design considerations (Table 16.10).

TABLE 16.10

Biological Foulants and Recommended Membrane Cleaning Agents

Foulant	Cleaning Agent
1. Antifoamant	1. Cold water and P3 Ultrasil 53 or Calgonite CMR or P3 Ultrasil 11 or P3 Ultrasil 91
	2. Sodium hydroxide
2. Biopolymers and	1. Isotonic saline and urea and citrate tetraborate or sodium hydroxide
3. Proteins	2. P3 Ultrasil 11
	3. P3 Ultrasil 91
4. Blood	1. Citrate solution and isotonic saline
5. Cell Debris and	1. Isotonic saline solution
6. Denatured Proteins	2. P3 Ultrasil 11 or Calgonite CMR
	3. Sodium hydroxide
	4. P3 Ultrasil 91
7. Lipids	1. P3 Ultrasil 53 or Calgonite CMR
	2. P3 Ultrasil 11
	3. P3 Ultrasil 91
8. Polysaccharides	1. Citrate tetraborate hypochlorite solution
	2. P3 Ultrasil 53 or Calgonite CMR
	3. Sodium hydroxide
	4. Hypochlorite

GLOSSARY

Membrane filters are fully characterized by both the manufacturer and the end user before they are used in the production of a protein pharmaceutical. The methods used in membrane characterization are fully described within this chapter. However, unique terminology is used in the membrane-filtration industry as it relates to the characterization and operation of membranes. These terms are defined here to assist those unfamiliar with the membrane-filtration industry.

- *Adsorption*: The retention of solutes (typically proteins) to the surfaces of pores in filtration membranes.
- *Antifoam*: A chemical added to a solution to prevent or minimize foaming of protein solutions, typically a surfactant.
- *Back Pressure*: Pressure applied to the feed side of the membrane to drive liquid through the membrane.
- *Batch Process*: A process where there are no streams flowing into or out of a controlled volume, as opposed to a continuous process. In a batch filtration process, the feed solution is reduced in volume due to permeation of filtrate through the membrane. There is no continuous addition of feed solution to the feed vessel.
- *Boundary Layer*: A stagnant layer of liquid against the surface of a membrane that forms due to friction between the membrane surface and the flowing liquid. Higher liquid velocities reduce the thickness of the boundary layer. Boundary layers are observed in crossflow filtration.
- *Bubble Point*: A pressure measurement that is directly related to the size of the largest pore in a membrane. A membrane's bubble point pressure is dependent on the membrane polymer, the membrane wetting solution, and the largest pore in the membrane.
- *Capsule*: A dead-end filtration module, typically containing flat-sheet membrane in pleated format. Membrane capsules are ready-to-use units that consist of pleated membrane encased in a molded plastic housing. The entire capsule is a disposable unit.
- *Cartridge*: A dead-end filtration module, typically containing flat-sheet membrane in pleated format. Membrane cartridges are placed in stainless-steel housings that come in various designs.
- *Cassette*: A crossflow filtration module, typically in a plate-and-frame configuration. Crossflow cassettes are stacked, one on top of another, and placed between endplates.

- *Centrifugal Filtration*: A filtration process where the driving force for liquid flow through the membrane is achieved by spinning the membrane device and generating a centrifugal force field, driving liquid outward and through the membrane filter.
- *Clean-Water Flux*: A baseline filter flow measurement performed with clean water or buffer, typically measured at 20°C.
- *Cleaning*: The process of chemically removing adsorbed, absorbed, or lodged solutes from a membrane.
- *Concentrate*: The concentrated feed solution (also known as the retentate solution) after removal of filtered liquid through the membrane.
- *Concentration Factor*: The ratio of retained solute concentration after membrane concentration to that before concentration. This factor can be easily determined from the initial feed volume and the final feed volume, assuming that the desired solute is fully rejected by the membrane. $XF = XF/C_i = V_i/V_f$.
- *Concentration Polarization*: A situation in crossflow filtration where the rejected solute concentration is much higher at the surface of the membrane than in the bulk feed solution. This occurs when the flowing filtrate solution rapidly drives solute to the membrane faster than the solute can diffuse back into the bulk feed solution.
- *Crossflow Filtration*: A membrane-filtration process where the feed solution is rapidly circulated parallel to the membrane surface, resulting in minimization of the stagnant boundary layer in the liquid adjacent to the membrane surface.
- *Dead-End Filtration*: A membrane-filtration process where there is no crossflow of feed and an attempt is made to force all of the feed solution through the membrane.
- *DF*: A crossflow filtration process where the bulk feed is washed removing solutes and or solvent by continuous or batch-wise addition of buffer to the feed solution, followed by filtration to reduce the total feed volume to its initial volume.
- *Diffusion Test*: A test for membrane integrity that involves measuring the rate of gas diffusion through a liquid-wetted membrane.
- *Dynamic Membrane*: A layer of rejected solute and/or particulate material that forms at the surface of the membrane. This dynamic membrane can have higher solute rejection than the underlying UF or MF membrane.
- *Extractables*: Chemicals used in the manufacture of a membrane or filter that are extracted into the filtered solution during use of the filter.
- *Feed*: The solution that is fed to the membrane process.
- *Filter*: A porous medium used for removal of specific sized material from a solution; also known as a membrane when the pores are very small.
- *Filtrate*: The solution that permeates a filter or membrane; also known as the permeate.
- *Flow rate*: The volumetric rate of flow of a solution; expressed in units of volume per time, e.g., L/min or gal/day.
- *Flux*: The rate of filtrate (or permeate) flow, divided by the membrane area. This parameter is used to characterize membranes. Sometimes "pressure-normalized" flux is reported, which is simply the normal flux divided by the transmembrane pressure driving force.
- *Fouling*: The process whereby solute in the feed solution blinds or blocks membrane pores, thereby reducing the filtrate flux.
- *Integrity Testing*: The process of determining if a membrane or filter has the reported pore size and solute rejection characteristics. Typically, the bubble point method, diffusion method, or water-pressure integrity test is used to determine the integrity of a membrane.
- *Log Reduction Value*: A measure of the efficiency of a sterilizing membrane to retain bacteria, defined as the logarithm (base 10) of the ratio of bacterial count in the feed stream to the bacterial count in the membrane permeate. Typically, the log reduction value is reported by membrane manufacturers for retention of *Brevundimonas diminuta*.

- *LRV*: Abbreviation for log reduction value.
- *Membrane*: A finely porous medium that is used for removal of specific sized material or solutes from a solution. Also known as a filter when the pores are fairly large, e.g., pores are greater than 0.2 μm in size.
- *Membrane Area*: The effective surface area of a membrane that is available for filtration; not the internal pore surface area, but rather the surface of one side of a membrane filter.
- *MF*: Abbreviation for microfiltration.
- *MF*: A membrane-based filtration process where the membrane pore size is in the range of 0.02–1.0 μm. MF is typically used to separate cells from solutes (e.g., proteins) in the feed solution.
- *Module*: A device that combines a large amount of membrane into a compact volume, with easily accessible feed, permeate, and possibly retentate ports.
- *MWCO*: A characteristic of membranes or filters, which specifies the average molecular weight of solutes that do not permeate the membrane. This property is dependent on the type and geometry of the solute that is used to characterize a membrane's MWCO.
- *MWCO*: Abbreviation for molecular-weight cutoff.
- *NF*: A membrane-based filtration process where the membrane pore size is 0.0001–0.002 μm. NF is typically used to concentrate fairly small molecules from water.
- *NF*: Abbreviation for nanofiltration.
- *Optimum TMP*: The TMP that maximizes the overall throughput of a membrane-filtration process. The optimum TMP should be independently determined for each unique filtration.
- *Permeability*: The liquid flux through a membrane which has been normalized to the pressure driving force or TMP.
- *Permeate*: The solution that permeates a filter or membrane; also known as the filtrate.
- *Plate-and-Frame*: A membrane-module geometry where membranes are sandwiched together one on top of another.
- *PES*: A polymer used for formation of many MF and UF membranes.
- *Pore Size*: A characteristic of a membrane that specifies the size and retention characteristics of a membrane's pores. Typically the absolute pore size is determined from integrity tests, such as bubble point tests for MF membranes and polymer-exclusion tests for UF membranes.
- *Pore Size Distribution*: The range of pore sizes in a membrane, which is centered around the membrane's average pore size.
- *Porosity*: The percentage of a membrane's volume that is occupied by air in the membrane's pores.
- *Recovery*: The mass of desired solute in the final product solution (either permeate or retentate, depending on the process), divided by the mass of desired solute in the initial feed solution, expressed as a percentage. Recovery is synonymous to yield.
- *Rejection*: The ability of a membrane to exclude solutes or particulate matter from passing a membrane.
- *Retentate*: The liquid stream, concentrated in solute that exits a crossflow membrane device. By mass balance, the flow rate of the retentate stream equals the feed flow rate minus the filtrate flow rate.
- *Retention Efficiency*: The ability of a membrane to retain a specific solute, expressed as a percentage, often synonymous with rejection.
- *RO*: A membrane-based filtration process where the membrane rejects salt from solution. Pore size is not entirely meaningful for RO membranes, as pores are often not observable by microscopic methods. RO is used to desalinate water.
- *Shear Force*: A stress on solutions that results from high velocity gradients (or differences) in solutions. A solution's viscosity is a measure of that solution's ability to resist deformation when exposed to shear forces.

- *SPTFF*: Single Pass TFF
- *Stirred-Cell Filtration*: A surrogate for crossflow filtration where shear is achieved by rapidly stirring the solution immediately adjacent to the membrane. Typically the stirring is accomplished by mechanical means, such as through the use of a stir bar or impeller.
- *TFF*: Another term for crossflow filtration.
- *Throughput*: The volume of solution that can be filtered through a specified area of membrane before filtrate flow is reduced to near zero.
- *TMP*: Abbreviation for transmembrane pressure.
- *TMP*: The pressure difference equal to the average feed stream pressure minus the average filtrate stream pressure. TMP = $(P_{feed} - P_{retentate})/2 - P_{filtrate}$.
- *UF*: Abbreviation for ultrafiltration.
- *UF*: A membrane-based filtration process where the membrane's pore size is in the range of 1,000–1,000,000 Da MWCO. UF is typically used to separate and concentrate proteins or other high molecular weight solutes from a liquid solution.
- *Velocity*: The linear rate of solution flow, equal to the solution flow rate divided by the cross-sectional area of the flow conduit. Crossflow velocity is a key parameter in determining the effectiveness of a crossflow-filtration operation.
- *Viscosity*: A solution property that is a measure of the fluid's resistance to deformation when acted upon by shear forces. Higher protein concentrations generally lead to solutions with higher viscosity.
- *Yield*: The mass of desired solute in the final product solution (either permeate or retentate, depending on the process), divided by the mass of desired solute in the initial feed solution, expressed as a percentage. Yield is synonymous to recovery.

REFERENCES

1. A.S. Michaels, *Foreword to Ultrafiltration Handbook by Munir Cheryan* 1986 Technomic Publishing Company, Inc., Lancaster, PA.
2. M. Cheryan, *Ultrafiltration Handbook* 1986 Technomic Publishing Company, Inc., Lancaster, PA. p. 13.
3. S. Loeb. The Loeb-Sourirajan Membrane: How It Came About. Synthetic Membranes Volume 1 A. Turbak (ed.) *ACS Symposium Series* 153 1981 p. 6.
4. *Preface to Ultrafiltration Handbook by Munir Cheryan* 1986 Technomic Publishing Company, Inc., Lancaster, PA.
5. M. Cheryan, *Ultrafiltration Handbook* 1986 Technomic Publishing Company, Inc., Lancaster, PA. p. 61.
6. M.C. Porter. The Effect of Fluid Management on Membrane Filtration. Synthetic Membranes Volume 1 A. Turbak (ed.) *ACS Symposium Series* 153 1981 p. 407.
7. G. Belfort. Advances in Biochemical Engineering. Chapter 10: *Membrane Separation Technology — An Overview* Bungay HR, Belford G (eds.) John Wiley & Sons: New York 1987 pp. 239–297.
8. W.F. Blatt, A. Dravid, A.S. Michaels and L. Nelsen. Solute Polarization and cake formation in membrane ultrafilters: Causes, consequences, and control techniques. *Membrane Processes in Industry and Biomedicine* Milan Beir (ed.) Plenum Press, New York 1971 pp. 65–68.
9. M. Cheryan, *Ultrafiltration Handbook* 1986 Technomic Publishing Company, Inc., Lancaster, PA. p. 89.
10. M. Dosmar. Could membrane fouling be a thing of the past. *Bioprocess International* 3(2): 62–66 (2005).
11. S. Brown and A.C. Fuller. Depyrogenation of pharmaceutical solutions using submicron and ultrafilters. *Journal of Parenteral Science and Technology* 47(6): 285–288 (1993).
12. W. Eycamp. Membrane separations. Presented at ASME Bioprocessing Course in October 1996, University of Virginia.
13. A.D. Marshall, P.A. Munro and G. Trägårdh. Effect of protein fouling in microfiltration and ultrafiltration on permeate flux, protein retention and selectivity: A literature review. *Desalination* 91: 65–108 (1993).
14. P. Levy and J. Shehan. Performance characteristics of polysulfone and cellulose membranes for the Ultrafiltration of biological process streams. *Biopharm* 5: 24–33 (1991).

15. G.A. Truskey, R. Gabler, A. DiLeo and T. Manter. The effect of membrane filtration upon protein conformation. *Journal of Parenteral Science and Technology* 41(6): 180–193 (1987).

16. M. Cheryan and B.H. Chiang. Performance and fouling behavior of hollow fibre and spiral wound ultrafiltration units processing skim milk. *Engineering and Food. Volume 1–Engineering Sciences in the Food Industry* B.M. McKenna (ed.) Elsevier Applied Science Publishers, London, UK 1984 pp. 191–197.

17. M. Cheryan, *Ultrafiltration Handbook* 1986 Technomic Publishing Company, Inc., Lancaster, PA. p. 190.

18. N. Devereaux and M. Hoare. Membrane separation of protein precipitates: Studies with cross flow in hollow fibers. *Biotechnology and Bioengineering* 28: 422–431 (1985).

19. R.M. McDonogh, H. Bauser, N. Stroh and H. Chmiel. Concentration polarisation and adsorption effects in cross-flow ultrafiltration of proteins. *Desalination* 79: 217–231 (1990).

20. M. Dosmar. Could membrane fouling be a thing of the past. *Bioprocess International* 3(2) (2005).

21. M. Dosmar and T. Scholz. Scaling up crossflow processes for biotech manufactering. *GEN* 15(15): 20 (1995).

22. D. Brose, M. Dosmar, S. Cates, and F. Hutchison. Studies on the scale-up of crossflow devices. *PDA Journal of Parenteral Science and Technology* 50(4): 252–260 (1996).

23. A. DePalma. Large scale biomanufactering operations. *GEN* 24(18): 44–47 (2004).

24. P. Wolber, M. Dosmar, and J. Banks. Cell harvesting scale-up: Parallel-leaf cross-flow microfiltration methods. *BioPharm* 1(6): 38–45 (1988).

25. C.A. Teske, B. Lebreton and R. van Reis. Inline ultrafiltration: American Institute of Chemical Engineers. *Biotechnology Progress*, 26(4): 1068–1072 (2010).

26. J. Dizon-Maspat, J. Bourret, A. D'Agostini and F. Li. Single pass tangential flow filtration to debottleneck downstream processing for therapeutic antibody production. *Biotechnology and Bioengineering*, 109(4): 962–970 (2012) (Wiley Periodicals, Inc).

27. L.E. Kirsch, R. Riggin, D.A. Gearhart, D.F. Lefber and D.L. Lytle. In-process protein degradation by exposure to trace amounts of sanitizing agents. *Journal Parenteral Science and Technology* 47: 155–160 (1993).

28. M. Divizia, A.L. Santi and A. Panà. Ultrafiltration: An efficient second step of hepatitis A virus and poliovirus concentration. *Journal of Virological Methods* 23: 55–62 (1989).

29. Industrial Perspective on Validation of Tangential Flow Filtration in Biopharmaceutical Applications. Technical Report No.15 Journal of Parenteral Science and Technology 46 Supplement 1992.

17

Virological Safety of Biopharmaceuticals: How Safe Is Safe Enough?

Hazel Aranha
Sartorius Stedim North America, Inc.

CONTENTS

Viruses were so named after the Latin for poison. Among the various descriptives used to characterize viruses, "filterable" was a key attribute. Over the past several decades, there have been phenomenal advances in membrane filtration technologies that have allowed development of membranes that retain viruses by a predominantly size-exclusion-based mechanism. Size-based (predominantly) filtration-removal of viruses is similar to removal of other viable or nonviable particulates (and several chapters in this monograph have been dedicated to its discussion). The challenge lies in the fact that many therapeutic proteins, either native or recombinant, are at the size limit of small viruses; consequently, membrane filtration for virus removal must remove viruses of concern without significantly compromising product yield.

Ensuring safety of biopharmaceuticals, in general, poses several unique challenges due to their intrinsic complex profile. They have a high level of structural complexity and heterogeneity are produced in living systems or supplemented with reagents derived from living systems, and, consequently, have a complex purity/impurity profile that poses unique analytical challenges. Additionally, biopharmaceutical production involves ten or more manufacturing stages encompassing 18–30 unit operations with several hundred process parameters. A single change could have a cascade effect; the impact on the quality, safety, and efficacy of the biopharmaceutical is not predictable. Therefore, determining what constitutes a critical process parameter (CPP) and the specific critical control points (CCPs) in the manufacturing process poses significant challenges. Nevertheless, quality and safety requirements similar to those applied to small molecules (chemical entities) are applied to biopharmaceutical products.

Initial approaches to ensuring virological safety of biologicals were responsive and disaster-led. Iatrogenic accidents resulting in virus transmission were associated primarily with vaccine contamination and occurred for several reasons: adventitious virus contamination of the production system, incomplete viral inactivation during manufacturing, and residual pathogenicity of the live attenuated virus strains (Dodet et al. 2010, Pastoret 2010). In an effort to remediate this situation several industry initiatives to enhance vaccine safety and stringent regulatory requirements were put into place. Our current approach to virus safety assurance is preemptive and focuses on disaster avoidance through efficient risk management (Miesegaes et al. 2009, 2010, Aranha 2012).

During the past few decades, pharmaceutical quality paradigms have experienced a tectonic shift. Traditional approaches were prescriptive and governed by defining set points and operating ranges for process parameters. The current quality paradigm is a risk-based approach that leverages scientific knowledge to select process parameters and unit operations that affect critical quality attributes (CQAs). This establishes design space and control strategies that are applicable throughout the life cycle of the drug product (DP, biotherapeutic).

The holy grail of virus safety is absolute absence of viral presence. However, zero risk is a myth; virological safety can only be addressed from a risk mitigation and management standpoint. Table 17.1 lists the unique issues associated with virus contamination of biopharmaceuticals. While it is highly commendable that there has been no iatrogenic transmission of viruses during biopharmaceutical administration, we need to recognize that we are not invulnerable. Virus contamination of bulk harvest has been reported; it is noteworthy that the contaminated product did not make it to the final DP stage (Kerr and Nims 2010). Also, in recent years, the industry has had issues related to adventitious agent contamination of both bulk harvests and production environments (Bethencourt 2009, Kerr and Nims 2010).

This chapter discusses issues to address in designing and incorporating adequate viral clearance strategies during the production of biologicals and biopharmaceuticals. While the focus is on safety assurance of continuous cell line (CCL)-derived products, the safety and procedural considerations as applied to plasma-derived products are also addressed.

Control of Production Processes for Virus Safety

Both regulatory groups and the pharmaceutical industry acknowledge that the quality of a finished dosage form is directly impacted by the constituents used in production. Adequate characterization of production systems and appropriate sourcing gains even more importance in the area of virus safety where it is currently impossible to test for and claim complete absence of infectious biological agents in any given product.

TABLE 17.1

Issues Unique to Viral Contamination of Biopharmaceuticals

Virus-related	• Infectious potential of even low levels of virus (e.g., HIV) • Efficient amplification of low levels of virus in cell substrates • Unknown amphitropism of unknown viral variants
Virus detection method-related	• Limited sensitivity of virus detection methods • Sampling-associated logistic limitations, i.e., inability to assay large volumes • Most virus assays are highly specific • Great diversity of viruses (and, consequently, the necessity of performing specific assays for each virus); there is no "general purpose" growth system that can be used to assay a variety of viruses (as is the case with detection of bacterial contaminants in pharmaceutical production)
Source material-related considerations	• Some source materials (e.g., cell lines used for biopharmaceutical manufacture) may harbor noninfectious retroviral particles; safety of the recombinant proteins from these substrates must be evaluated using a risk-based approach • Blood donations during the "window period," i.e., the donor is infectious but routinely mandated testing fails to detect infectious virus • In the case of plasma-derived biologicals, presence of neutralizing antibody in the plasma pool can mask detection of low levels of infectious virus

Source: Aranha (2008).

Ideally, all raw materials used in manufacturing processes must be carefully controlled; however, by its very nature source materials used in production of biologicals are complex. For plasma-derived products the source pool is highly variable and constantly changing. Blood donors enter/leave the pool at will; their health status is also not static. While blood is screened for specific pathogenic viruses (human immunodeficiency virus (HIV), hepatitis B virus (HBV), hepatitis C virus (HCV), human T-cell lymphotropic virus (HTLV)), low levels of virus may escape detection by currently used methods due to a variety of reasons: donations may be during the "window period" when the person is infectious but the screening test does not detect the virus; presence of high levels of neutralizing antibodies to a particular virus in the plasma pool (which is not controllable) is another factor that has contributed to transmission of viruses such as hepatitis A virus (HAV) and parvovirus B19 via contaminated coagulation factor concentrates (Blumel et al. 2002a, Schneider et al. 2004, Allain et al. 2009).

In the case of biotechnology-derived products, recombinant technology is a mainstream. It allows the production of high levels of the target protein to make the process commercially feasible. For recombinant products, a two-tiered system in terms of establishment of a master cell bank (MCB) and working cell bank (WCB) following current good manufacturing practice (cGMP) is the first step in ensuring the quality of a biopharmaceutical product (ICH 1997). As cell banks are extensively characterized, any viral contaminant associated with them will not be cytolytic; however, chronic or latent viruses could potentially be present. The widespread use of murine cell lines in the manufacture of monoclonal antibodies is another potential source of introduction of rodent zoonotic agents. Chinese hamster ovary (CHO) cells, a cell line frequently used in monoclonal antibody (mAb) production, may harbor contaminants such as Hantavirus. Endogenous retroviruses and retrovirus-like particles are associated with some CCLs; they are noninfectious but pose a theoretical safety concern due to their oncogenic potential. Rodent cell lines are known to express endogenous retroviral-like particles (RVLPs); these have been determined to be noninfectious to humans. Usually, two types of RVLPs have been observed by transmission electron microscopy (EM): C-type particles are most commonly observed in mammalian cell lines and the majority of these have been shown to be noninfective (e.g., in S+L-co-cultivation assays). C-type particles are commonly found in unprocessed cell culture supernatant. Monoclonal antibodies produced in human/humanized (human/mouse) cell lines are preferred from an immunological standpoint; however, due to the absence of a species barrier they raise unique viral safety considerations. Humanized cell lines are derived from human B lymphocytes, which can harbor several viruses including retroviruses, hepatitis viruses, human herpesviruses, *cytomegalovirus,* and human papilloma virus. While currently not done, use of specific viral agents, e.g., Epstein–Barr virus or Sendai virus, for cell line establishment or cell transformation also contributes to the viral load.

Source materials evaluation is a critical component of the risk minimization strategy. Cell bank source, history, and exposure to "complex" raw materials must be assessed. Cell banks for many current marketed products were established decades ago and documentation related to use of animal-derived materials (ADMs) may not be available. Detection methods will test for "known knowns" (viruses we know and suspect to be present); the potential for presence of "unknown-unknowns" (viruses that are not in our current lexicon and cannot be detected) always exists. In terms of raw materials, it is essential to look beyond the obvious. Just because a raw material is labeled recombinant or synthetic does not imply that it has not been exposed to animal-derived materials. In one report, an antibiotic with a claim of "no exposure to animal-derived materials" was, in fact, produced by bacteria grown in a medium containing bovine peptones, bile, and several other bovine constituents (Potts 2010).

Viral contaminants may be introduced adventitiously via the additives used/manipulations undertaken in production. The manufacturing process for a recombinant protein, for example, may include use of constituents such as albumin, transferrin, Tween-80, lipoproteins, and gelatin that are bovine sourced. Cell lines were often cultivated in serum-supplemented media (5%–10% serum) or reduced serum media (2%–4%). Bovine viral diarrhea virus (BVDV) has been identified as the most common contaminant of bovine serum. Porcine parvovirus is reportedly a common contaminant in preparations of porcine trypsin used for the preparation of cell cultures. Porcine circovirus (PCV) was identified as a contaminant in a marketed vaccine and was traced to the porcine trypsin used in establishment of the cell bank (Baylis et al. 2011). While serum-free media is the growth medium of choice, it must be noted that serum-free medium and mammalian supplement-free medium are not synonymous; for example, a chemically defined medium may be supplemented with recombinant growth factors produced in a serum-supplemented system. A preparation designated "protein-free" may not contain protein but filtered protein hydrolysates.

The manufacturing history of the raw material has come under increased scrutiny in the few decades. For example, yeast used for the production of yeast extract—a common additive in production processes—may be grown in a medium containing animal-derived peptones. A claim that the amino acid derived in a recombinant yeast system that contains yeast/meat extract as an additive has not been exposed to human/animal-derived components is not valid. Similarly, a chemically derivatized animal-sourced amino acid salt is not a synthetic amino acid. Table 17.2 presents a general classification of raw materials used for manufacturing biotechnology-derived products.

Supply chain management is a key consideration and it is necessary to understand the supply system and recognize the complexity and interlinking nature of the components. Replacement of ADMs with materials sourced from plants poses different challenges and risks. It is necessary to perform a comprehensive risk assessment of critical components and make risk assessment a priority with suppliers. In view of the critical nature of the raw materials used, supply chain management has gained increased focus. Additionally, there should be a program for ongoing monitoring of suppliers and application of risk mitigation as needed. Table 17.3 lists raw materials sourcing challenges. Table 17.4 emphasizes critical steps in supply chain management.

TABLE 17.2

Classification of Raw Materials Used in Manufacture of Biologicals and Biopharmaceuticals

Source	Examples
Directly sourced from animal	Bovine serum albumin (BSA), transferrin, porcine trypsin used in production; HSA used as an excipient during production of recombinant proteins such as Factor VIII
Indirectly animal-derived—fermentation product manufactured in a system supplemented with animal-derived components	Recombinant proteins produced in a bacterial/yeast system supplemented with additives like beef/meat extract.
Secondarily animal-derived: material is manufactured in a process supplemented with materials which are indirectly animal derived.	Yeast extract used in a fermentation process, e.g., amino acids, where the yeast was grown in a meat extract supplemented medium

TABLE 17.3

Raw Materials-related Challenges

Large number of components	• Components include both chemically defined and complex • Animal/plant/bacterial-derived components
Large numbers of suppliers	• Requires considerable vendor oversight • Some suppliers may have sub-suppliers
Traceability of raw materials	• Global sourcing • Some countries may not have very stringent quality practices • Are raw materials from various countries segregated/mixed?
Variability in raw materials	• Even with stringent quality management in place, inherent variability in source materials
Testing-related issues	• Contaminants may not be homogenously distributed; therefore, detection is based on probability
Materials impact	• Materials may meet specifications; however, may have detectable impact on final DP quality

TABLE 17.4

Critical Steps in Supply Chain Management

Supplier selection process	• Define requirements related to material specifications, quantity required • Vendor have enough capacity to ensure uninterrupted supply • Quality and regulatory compliance • Adherence to good distribution practices • Procurement/cost: look beyond just cost • Responsiveness and communication
Due diligence process	• Necessary for key and critical raw materials • Risk analysis, include cross-functional team • Review management history, mergers, and acquisitions
Quality assessment	• Have Quality agreement in place • Supplier/manufacturer questionnaire • Site-audits • TSE/BSE assessment • Are sub-suppliers involved • cGMP compliance history; historical performance
Change control	• Change control SOPs • Mechanism for initiation, execution, and review of change • Change communication procedures
Supply chain security	• Procedures to ensure supply chain security • Supplier changes in raw material sourcing as well as manufacturing process
Ongoing monitoring and evaluation	• Review key performance indicators: delivery, audit observations, customer complaints, failures, etc. • Re-audit frequency

Purification processes also contribute to the viral load. For example, affinity chromatography using monoclonal antibodies as ligands increases the potential for adventitious virus introduction into the product. Other ancillary sources of viral burden include breach of Good Manufacturing Practices (GMP) and consequent virus introduction from manufacturing environments or personnel; these viral contaminants would not be removed by conventional "sterilizing-grade" filters, which are intended for removal of bacterial and microbial contaminants other than viruses. The potential for viral contamination for each of the manufacturing unit operations must, therefore, be evaluated and its impact on the viral load assessed.

Virus Detection Methods

There is no all-encompassing virus method to detect all viral contaminants. Sophistication in computational power and advances in bioinformatics have proven that the concept of "virus free" is only as good as our detection method.

Conventional virus detection methods have limitations. Viral assays lack the sensitivity to detect low titers, which, even when low, may be of medical concern. Also, infectivity assays are not capable of determining *total* virus titer (concentration). Because of the diversity of viruses a specific assay must be performed for each virus. Direct testing for the absence of viral contamination from a finished product is not considered sensitive enough for detection of low levels of virus. While advanced methodologies have become available, e.g., massive parallel (deep) sequencing, degenerate polymerase chain reaction (PCR) mass spectrometry, and panmicrobial microarrays, these methods have yet to be validated. There are significant efforts underway in this regard. For example, regulatory and industry collaborative groups such as the Advanced Virus Detection Technologies Interest Group (AVDTIG) are working on appropriate standardization related to issues such as sample preparation for high throughput sequencing, spiking standards, viral database, bioinformatic analysis pipelines, and follow-up analyses for bioinformatically defined positive hits (Khan 2010, Khan et al. 2016, Khan et al. 2016).

Currently, there are several conventional virus detection methods: infectivity assays (*in vitro* and *in vivo*), molecular probes, biochemical assays, morphological assays, and antibody production tests (in animals). The particular viral detection method used will depend on the objective of the test, what is being tested and other issues. For example, the effectiveness of a virus clearance unit operation is commonly assessed using infectivity tests or validated PCR-based assays. When noninfectious retroviral burden must be estimated, assays of choice include morphological assays (EM) or biochemical assays.

Conventional infectivity assays rely on replication of the agent in a permissive system (be it tissue culture or *in vivo* tests) to detect a replication-competent virus. Infectivity assays are the gold standard and essentially involve inoculation of susceptible cell lines with the specific virus, followed by monitoring and observation of cytopathic effects, e.g., formation of plaques, focus forming units, or induction of abnormal cellular morphology, as a consequence of the infection. The two types of *in vitro* infectivity assays commonly used to estimate viral titer are the plaque (or focus) forming assay (PFA or FFA) and the 50% tissue culture infectious dose ($TCID_{50}$) assays. The PFA offers extreme sensitivity and is especially useful when the virus is present at extremely low titers. $TCID_{50}$ is defined as that dilution of virus required to infect 50% of a given batch of inoculated cell cultures. Both the plaque assay and the $TCID_{50}$ assay have been extensively validated for use in process clearance evaluation (validation) studies. While infectivity-based assays are favored due to their extreme sensitivity and specificity, the requirement for a different assay system for each virus (due to the cell culture-specific infectivity) makes biological assays cumbersome.

Molecular techniques detect the genome as a surrogate marker. Methods such as hybridization assays or PCR assays are used because of their specificity and the rapidity of the results. These methods, in general, detect the presence of nucleic acid (DNA/RNA) but cannot differentiate between infectious or noninfectious particles. Additionally, the method is applicable only when the genomic sequence of the virus is known, as in the case of retroviral genomes. PCR is especially relevant either if the viral agent cannot be grown *in vitro*, e.g., type A retroviral particles, or, for viruses such as hepatitis B and C where there are severe limitations to culturing them *in vitro*. Additionally, for example, if a unit process operation, such as chromatography, is able to effect both virus removal (resin-associated) and inactivation (low pH inactivation by the eluting buffer), PCR allows for differentiation of the contribution of each of the mechanisms. With the availability of fluorogenic 5'-nuclease-based Q-PCR, it is possible to undertake a multi-virus spike in a single preparation and measure the clearance achieved simultaneously in separate assays (Valera et al. 2003). A note of caution: while methods such as PCR have provided enhanced assay sensitivity, a negative PCR result does not prove unequivocally the absence of virions (infectious or not), due to the effect of sample size and its impact on assay sensitivity.

Morphological assays such as EM, while of limited value to assay viral load in fluids, are especially relevant for estimation of viral load in cell lines containing noninfectious particles, such as the Type A retroviral particles, which are present in several rodent cell lines used in biotherapeutics production.

Biochemical assays such as reverse transcriptase (RT) assays, radiolabel incorporation into nucleic acids, radioimmunoassays, immunofluorescence, and Western blots are also used for virus detection. However, these tests are semi-quantitative; also they detect enzymes with optimal activity under the test conditions and their interpretation may be difficult due to the presence of cellular enzymes or other background material.

Among other tests required for characterization of production cell lines at the MCB establishment stage, the antibody production test is used. Mouse antibody production tests, hamster antibody production tests, and rat antibody production tests allow detection of viruses which may be associated with the cell line and have the potential for infecting humans and other primates. Alternatives to animal testing are being investigated and are becoming more mainstream.

Several advanced methodologies have become available. Often referred to as high-throughput screening methods, they are a powerful tool especially when evaluating novel cell substrates as well as screening for adventitious agents (Khan et al. 2016). Methodologies such as massive parallel sequencing, degenerative PCR, and panmicrobial microarrays have resulted in detection of viral sequences in cell substrates and virus seed stocks (Dodet et al. 2010, Onions and Kolman 2010, Victoria et al. 2010). The significant strengths of these methods lie in their exquisite sensitivity and specificity, as well as their ability to screen for a wide variety of agents in a single test. The high sensitivity of newer methods, however, must be tempered with caution; it is necessary to evaluate the significance of the probable viral hit to determine whether there could be a nonviral source for that hit.

Currently, newer methods can supplement rather than replace conventional methods. They are not ready yet for use I first-line quality. Moreover, the newer methods require that appropriate reference materials be available. Their applications could potentially include characterization of cell banks for new cell substrates or for cases in which the history of the cell line and reagents used in establishment are unclear, as well as characterization of animal-derived raw materials.

With both conventional and new methods it is important to recognize that while positive results are meaningful, negative results are ambiguous. This is because it is not possible to determine whether the negative result reflects inadequate sensitivity of the test for the specific virus, selection of a test system (host) with too narrow a specificity, poor assay precision, limited sample size, or basically, just absence of virus. This is highlighted in cases where limited sensitivity of the screening methods, combined with masking of presence of infectious virus by neutralizing antibody in the plasma sample pool, have resulted in iatrogenic viral transmission via contaminated plasma products.

Regulatory and Risk Considerations

Clinical acceptability of biologicals and biopharmaceuticals, must, of necessity, be guided by risk-benefit analysis (Aranha 2005). Risk assessment involves process analysis to identify sources of risk and their consequence. In view of the unique considerations associated with viral contaminants (i.e., actual versus theoretical presence) and the limitations in the assay methodologies (inability to establish absolute absence of viral presence), regulatory agencies emphasize a holistic approach directed at risk minimization, which, when combined with process monitoring, constitutes an appropriate risk management program.

All guidelines and regulatory documents distinguish between well-characterized biologicals (where viral contamination is often a theoretical concern) and traditional products such as plasma derivatives (where there is a significant potential for viral presence, e.g., parvovirus B19, hepatitis viruses, HIV). Thus, for example, low levels of infectious virus in plasma products are prohibited and any virus-contaminated source material would be immediately quarantined. However, in the biotechnology industry, cell lines such as CHO cells containing endogenous retrovirus, at levels of 10^6–10^9 particles/mL (as visualized by EM), are deemed acceptable as the particles are noninfectious and pose primarily a theoretical safety concern. Clearance of these noninfectious retroviral particles is required to be demonstrated in virus clearance evaluation (validation) studies. Table 17.5 summarizes factors influencing virus risk profile of the biotherapeutic.

TABLE 17.5

Factors Influencing Virus Risk Profile

		Comments
Type of product	• Directly mammalian sourced—plasma-derived coagulation factors, immunoglobulins, other proteins and enzymes • Recombinant proteins/monoclonal antibodies	• High risk • Low risk
Production system	• Well characterized cell lines (CHO) • Advanced Therapy Materials: gene therapy products • Transgenic systems • Xenotransplantation	• Low risk • Medium/High • Low/medium • High: potential for xenosis (xenozoonoses)
Raw materials	• Animal-derived additives: BSA, transferring • Indirectly animal-derived: recombinant proteins produced in a microbial system supplemented with additives such as beef/meat extract	• High • Low/Medium

In general, the major factors influencing the viral safety of biologicals are the following: (a) the species of origin of the starting material, i.e., nonhuman viruses are less likely to initiate infection in humans due to species specificity of these viruses; the species barrier, however, is not absolute; (b) the degree of source variability of starting material (e.g., human plasma-derived products which are manufactured from pooled donations pose a higher risk compared with products derived from a well-characterized cell bank) and the possibility of testing the source material for the presence of viral contaminants (feasible for blood donation but not feasible for animal-derived products); (c) the purification and processing steps and their capacity for viral burden reduction; and (d) the existence of specific steps for viral clearance included in the process.

The current risk minimization strategy to guard against inadvertent virus exposure of patients treated with a biological is a combination of three efforts: (a) prevention of access of virus by screening of starting materials (cell banks, tissues, or biological fluids) and raw materials/supplements used in production processes (culture media, serum supplements, transferrin, etc.); (b) incorporation of robust virus clearance steps; and (c) monitoring production using a relevant screening assay. Table 17.6 presents currently used risk minimization strategies. Engineering and procedural control over facilities, equipment, and operations, as required by cGMP, are an important component of the safety paradigm.

TABLE 17.6

Risk Minimization Strategies for Virus Contamination Control

Barrier to entry	• Characterization of cell banks (MCB, WCB) • Selection and screening of donors
Raw materials sourcing	• Raw materials qualification and control program • Supply chain management
Incorporation of robust virus clearance steps	• Process unit operations, e.g., chromatography validated for virus clearance • Dedicated virus clearance steps, e.g., virus removal filtration, chemical inactivation
Testing during production to ensure absence of contaminating virus	• Testing end of production cells to ensure absence of contaminating virus • Incorporation of additional detection methods, e.g., PCR for virus surveillance
Facility operational parameters	• Adequate facility design to minimize entry of viral contaminants • Containment systems: HVAC, air flow dP • Closed systems • Restricted flow of materials/process intermediates/equipment/personnel • Effective and validated cleaning regimens • If multiproduct facility, single-use equipment (preferably), dedicated resins/membranes

How Much Viral Clearance Is "Enough"?

The extent of virus clearance required (number of logs clearance) is not provided in any prescriptive guideline but a framework approach is applied based on the evaluation of the potential for presence of any baseline viral load and incorporation of an adequate safety factor. Industry wisdom suggests that manufacturing processes must be validated to remove or inactivate ≥4–6 orders of magnitude more virus than is estimated to be present in the starting material. Extrapolating from the "Sterility Assurance Level," applied to bacterial sterility considerations, of not more than one viable microorganism (10^{-6}) in 1×10^6 volume of final product, a 6 $\log_{10}$ safety factor is routinely considered adequate. In the case of plasma-derived biologicals, there will not be any *detectable* baseline viral load (as source materials with detectable virus contamination would be immediately quarantined); for products derived from CCLs known to harbor (noninfectious) endogenous retroviruses, it is necessary to determine the theoretical viral burden per dose equivalent of the biological product and incorporate an appropriate safety margin (6 $\log_{10}$).

A key factor affecting the overall process clearance factor required for a product is the amount required to produce a single dose of product. The required level of clearance is assessed in relation to the perceived hazard to the target population and is guided by risk benefit analysis. For example, CHO cell lines containing endogenous retroviruses are deemed acceptable if the manufacturing process can be demonstrated to provide adequate retrovirus clearance. The clearance goal is usually chosen based on the product use and the risk to the patient population. The extent of product testing necessary will depend on the source and nature of the product, the stage of product development, and the clinical indication.

Risk calculations to determine retroviral load per dose are shown in Table 17.7. This example assumes a one-time dose of 1,200 mg to the patient. To achieve a conservative goal of a probability of a viral contamination event of 1 particle/million doses of product, and assuming a retroviral load of 1.62×10^7 particles/mL in the start material, the purification process for this product would have to demonstrate a minimum log clearance of 16.85 logs to achieve the stated goal of 1 viral particle/10^6 doses.

Risk and Risk Analysis Tools

Risk assessment requires integration of multiple parameters, including the nature of an extraneous agent, its target species, test limits of detection, the nature and geographical origin of raw materials, manufacturing processes and steps during production, and application of cGMPs. Risk evaluation from a virus safety standpoint must include exposures to potential sources of viral burden. This starts with selecting and establishing a MCB as well as evaluating manufacturing inputs, downstream purification reagents, and formulation excipients. For example, mammalian antibodies have been used in clonal selection, and ADMs such as porcine trypsin, bovine serum, and animal-derived growth factors have been used in manufacturing. Downstream purification reagents include antibody columns for purification. Excipients such as human serum albumin (HSA) were used in the past, and although recombinant HSA is currently used, it does not totally eliminate potential virus burden.

TABLE 17.7

Risk Calculation to Determine the Viral Load per Dose

Retrovirus-like particles/mL: 1.62×10^7 particles/mL
Antibody titer: 0.274 mg/mL
Weight of average person: 80 kg
Dose per mass: 15 mg/kg
One dose: 1,200 mg
Viral clearance factor: unknown
The total amount of retrovirus-like particles in one dose
   = [(1.62×10^7 particles/mL) (1,200 mg/dose ÷ 0.274 mg/mL)] ÷ 10^{-6} particles/dose
   = 7.09×10^{16} or 16.85 logs minimum clearance required to achieve a clearance of
      1 particle/million doses
Challenge Virus: Xenotropic Murine Leukemia Virus (X-MuLV)

Several methods for risk estimation have been proposed; their utility depends on the task at hand. Examples of these tools include fault-tree analysis, hazard operability analysis, hazard analysis and critical control points, and failure-mode effect analysis (FMEA). To maximize benefits from any tool, as with a technique, it is necessary to understand their contributions and limitations.

The FMEA approach is often used in the biopharmaceutical industry. It provides a numerical rating system for determining the severity of an event, probability of occurrence, and detectability. Severity is the potential negative impact of the risk factor on product safety and or/efficacy profile. From a virus safety standpoint, this would be high because even though not all viruses are necessarily pathogenic to humans, any contamination could prompt a facility shutdown and decontamination, a resource draining situation. Occurrence is the frequency or likelihood that contamination will happen. While this has been low historically, it is not zero. Detectability refers to the likelihood of detecting the contamination event and remediating in a timely manner. In the section "Virus Detection Methods," low detectability due to assay limitations, can result in non detection of contaminants that could be potentially infectious. On the basis of these factors, a relative risk (numerical value) is assigned. The risk priority number is a multiple of the relative risk score for each of three variables: severity, occurrence, and detection. This is done for each operating parameter of each process step. For example, once an FMEA identifies potential failure modes and potential outcomes, risk-reduction approaches can be applied to eliminate or reduce potential impacts.

Quality by Design in Virus Safety Assurance

Viral safety of the biological (DP) is an important CQA. Manufacturers of biologicals are required to demonstrate an adequate virus safety margin before clinical trials are initiated. A quality by design (QbD) approach starts with definition of CQAs of the final DP and evaluation of inputs and processes that could potentially impact the CQA. In the case of a biopharmaceutical, inputs and processes include raw materials control that requires selection and understanding of their variability and how this variability could potentially impact the manufacturing process. Evaluation of processes includes CCPs that have the potential for introduction of adventitious agents. This should then be followed by risk analysis and scientific characterization to identify those components that will have the biggest effect on process consistency and CQA.

Multiple unit operations typically contribute to the global viral clearance of the manufacturing operation. The traditional approach to evaluate viral clearance for individual unit operations involves empirical experiments with worst-case conditions when they can be clearly defined, or set-point runs when they cannot. In contrast, a QbD approach involves a more thorough investigation to establish an acceptable "process design space" for each unit operation that achieves a predefined goal.

Establishing a process-design space starts with the definition of CPP that are likely to have a significant impact on the performance of a given unit operation. This is accomplished through a formal risk analysis that draws on accumulated knowledge about each step, including in-house process development data and publicly available information, such as a database of reported viral clearance compiled by the Food and Drug Administration (FDA) (Miesegaes et al. 2010). A parameter should be included as part of a design space if performance (viral clearance) is sensitive to it, excursions are likely (inadvertently or during process improvements), and excursions are not easily detected and corrected in real time. Collectively, the CPPs produce a multidimensional space of possible operating conditions. In a QbD approach, all areas within the space where acceptable performance is achieved are defined through experimentation. A design of experiment approach is typically used because the number of factors and their potential interactions create too many conditions to test practically in a full factorial design.

Demonstration of robust viral clearance during downstream processing operations is a regulatory requirement. Parameters critical to the manufacturing process need to be explored and the robustness of the unit operation demonstrated. Multivariate analysis and other statistical techniques are applied including a design of experiments (DoE) approach. DoE reduces testing burden and goes beyond conventional "worst-case scenario" approach. Manufacturers that develop platform technologies can apply their considerable knowledge base related to their production system—cell line, raw materials, and manufacturing production and purification conditions—and leverage that information to reduce product development timelines and streamline process validation that may facilitate regulatory approval.

However, the onus of demonstration of applicability of this strategy across multiple products lies with the manufacturer.

QbD reflects the current global regulatory thinking related to pharmaceutical products. A QbD approach does not replace the need to comply with cGMPs; it is essentially a complementary methodology that builds on product and process knowledge. The overarching philosophy articulated in both the CGMP regulations *and* in current quality systems is: *Quality should be built into the product, and testing alone cannot be relied on to ensure product quality.* Nowhere is this more true than in the virus safety area where multiple considerations (see Table 17.3) preclude making an absolute claim of virus absence. Several documents discuss the current quality approach. ICH Q8 *Pharmaceutical Development* introduces QbD as "a systematic approach to development that begins with predefined objectives and emphasizes product and process understanding and process control, based on sound science and quality risk management." It provides guidance during the process of pharmaceutical development (ICH 2009). The QbD approach essentially involves identifying product attributes that are of significant importance to the product's safety and efficacy, design of the process to deliver these attributes, a robust control strategy to ensure consistent process performance, validation and filing of the process demonstrating the effectiveness of the control strategy, and finally ongoing monitoring to ensure robust process performance over the life cycle of the product. ICH Q9 *Quality Risk Management* (QRM) guideline (ICH 2015a) provides principles and examples of tools for QRM that can be applied to different aspects of pharmaceutical quality. The focus of ICH Q10 is on enablers of pharmaceutical quality system, i.e., knowledge management and QRM (ICH 2015b).

Design space is a cornerstone of the QbD paradigm and refers to the multidimensional combination of input variables and process parameters that have been demonstrated to provide assurance of product quality. ICH Q8 has established the concept of design space. Operation within the design space provides assurance that the product or process output possesses the required quality attributes. Processes analytical technology-based controls are increasingly being developed and implemented as part of routine process development.

There will be instances when the design-space concept may intersect with the development of modular viral clearance claims. For companies with robust pipelines using closely related manufacturing methods and similar starting materials, some unit operations may be amenable to thorough characterization, developing an operating range that applies generally across molecule type. The success of this approach depends on the ability to identify all CPPs that vary across feedstocks. However, when possible, the resulting cross-platform design space would provide significant efficiencies in the included development programs.

Applying a QbD approach and establishing a design space requires a significantly greater upfront investment in development than does the traditional approach. However, the benefits include operational flexibility, as future modifications to the purification method that remain within the process design space are not considered changes and do not require additional viral clearance studies. In addition, the impact of excursions during a production run can be confidently evaluated, reducing clinical and financial risk.

Are Upstream Virus Risk Minimization Barriers Necessary?

As discussed, demonstration that the operations employed in downstream processing provide an "adequate" virus safety margin is a regulatory requirement. The "adequate" safety margin is determined by several factors including the risk profile (see Table 17.5) and incorporation of a "safety assurance level" (SAL). With regard to upstream risk mitigation, given the extensive raw material supply chain for CHO manufacturing processes, and the multiple potential entry points for adventitious agents upstream of culture operations (e.g., raw material manufacture/ handling and media preparation), prevention strategies involving point-of-use barrier technologies are thought to be the most robust for adventitious agent contamination control.

Commonly used upstream risk minimization strategies include high temperature short time (HTST), gamma or UV-radiation are inactivation approaches and care must be taken to ensure that these treatments do not impact the growth promoting or target protein production. More recently, use of virus retention filters for upstream risk mitigation have become available. While filtration is noninvasive, it is important to ensure that the filtration step does not impact the cell culture performance and target protein production. The Sartorius Virosart Media filter and the Millipore Viresolve Barrier filters are recommended for upstream risk mitigation (Kleindienst 2016).

Virus Clearance Methods

An ideal clearance method should be robust and have a broad spectrum of clearance (either through inactivation or removal) of viruses (both enveloped and non-enveloped), concomitant with high product recovery. The method should be minimally invasive and non-contaminating, ie, should not involve addition of stabilizers or other additives which must be removed post treatment, and should not alter the biological integrity or reactivity of the product. The mode of action should be well characterized and the method should be scalable and amenable to process validation (clearance evaluation). The clearance strategy should be robust with respect to small/controlled changes in CPPs and be supported by a defined mechanism of action (MoA) and industrial experience.

Suitability and choice of a particular clearance method will be guided by the following considerations: the characteristics of the product, i.e., the size of the protein, its conformation, it's lability to heat or other inactivation methods; the characteristics of the potential viral contaminants, i.e., viral size, lability, presence/absence of a particular macromolecule such as a lipid envelope; and process evaluation considerations, i.e., logistics at process scale, scale-up, and scale-down considerations for process evaluation (validation), etc.

Viral clearance may be achieved as a consequence of routine processing and purification operations or strategies specifically aimed at viral clearance may be incorporated into the manufacturing process. Serendipitous (or fortuitous) virus clearance methods are operations that are part of the product purification process that offer the added bonus of viral clearance; these methods are not optimized for viral clearance but coincidentally provide viral clearance. Methods commonly used in the purification of biopharmaceutical products (clarification, centrifugation, extraction, precipitation, and filtration; and affinity, ion-exchange, gel-filtration, hydrophobic interaction, and mixed-mode exchange chromatography) may physically separate virus particles from the product (virus removal) based on size, charge, density, binding affinities, and other differences between the virus and the product. Similarly, viral inactivation may occur as a consequence of pH effects during processing, use of low pH buffers for elution of proteins from chromatography columns, and, inactivation by reagents used in the purification process. In addition to the serendipitous virus clearance afforded by downstream purification options, methods such as heat inactivation, solvent-detergent inactivation, virus filtration are deliberately introduced for virus clearance.

Clearance efficiency is evaluated in terms of the $\log_{10}$ reduction value (LRV) which is the ratio of the viral concentration per unit volume in the pretreatment suspension to the concentration per unit volume in the posttreatment suspension. Other synonyms for LRV are $\log_{10}$ titer reduction (LTR) and $\log_{10}$ reduction factor (LRF).

Unit operations that have been demonstrated to provide virus clearance fall into one of three categories (Brorson et al. 2014): (a) processes that provide "robust and reliable clearance," e.g., operations such as low pH inactivation, virus removal with large pore size virus removal filters; (b) methods that are relatively robust and provide reliable clearance, e.g., anion exchange chromatography, detergent-based inactivation; and (c) methods where there are significant gaps, and, therefore, virus clearance is not directly predictable. Nevertheless, methods described in (c) can be validated for virus clearance under the process conditions used in manufacturing. Examples here include virus clearance claimed with protein A chromatography, cation exchange chromatography, and virus filters designed for small virus removal. These unit operations are likely to be "process-dependent" at least in the near future (e.g., feedstock effects on viral clearance by protein A; small virus breakthrough related to pressure changes during parvovirus-retentive filters); nevertheless, if viral validation studies are conducted under process conditions virus clearance for the unit operation can be claimed when calculating the cumulative log reduction for the manufacturing process.

Depending on the mode of clearance, virus clearance methodologies are classified as virus removal strategies which aim at (mechanical) reduction of viral numbers, or virus inactivation methods where the objective is irreversible loss of viral infectivity. Virus inactivation steps must not compromise a product's stability, potency, biochemistry, or biological activity. The inactivation strategy used will be dictated by the following considerations: lability of the virus, the stability of the biological preparation, and the effect on other components in the preparation.

Inactivation methods are very effective in decreasing the viral burden; however, there are limitations. Heat treatment can denature certain proteins. Stabilizers (sometimes added during inactivation by heat or solvent-detergent, to ensure that the biological activity of the active moiety is not compromised), may be protective, not just to the target protein but to the virus as well. In addition to protein denaturation that may occur, the viral inactivation method has the potential to alter the functionality or antigenicity of either the active ingredient or other proteins in the product (Peerlinck et al. 1993, Suontaka et al. 2003).

One of the important considerations to be addressed in virus inactivation experiments involves evaluation of the kinetics of virus inactivation. This is important since virus inactivation is rarely linear and a persistent fraction can exist which is more resistant to inactivation than the majority of the virus population. Certain process parameters may critically impact viral clearance. Savage and colleagues (Savage et al. 1998) reported a minimum threshold moisture level requirement for efficient virus inactivation to occur during dry heat treatment of freeze-dried coagulation factor concentrates; similarly, presence of cations have been demonstrated to contribute to the thermostability of viruses (Melnick 1991).

Extrapolation of the potential for virus clearance of any given method to other viruses (e.g., within the same virus family or based on a physical characteristic such as size) must be done with extreme caution and will depend on the virus clearance method and the mechanism of virus clearance. For example, it is reasonable to infer that a virus removal filter specifically designed to remove small viruses ($\geq$20–25 nm) will be effective in removal of large viruses as well (viruses such as the hepatitis viruses, HIV, pseudorabies virus (PRV). However, in the case of virus removal by partitioning or chromatography, it is not possible to extrapolate virus behavior even within the same virus family as the physicochemical properties of the virus impact removal. In inactivation studies, different susceptibilities to low pH treatment have been demonstrated in Murine Minute Virus and parvovirus B19 (Boschetti et al. 2004). In terms of heat inactivation, in general, B19 is more sensitive to heat compared with other parvoviruses (canine parvovirus (CPV), porcine parvovirus (PPV) (Blumel et al. 2002, Yunoki et al. 2003, Prikhod'ko 2005, Yunoki et al. 2005). However, B19 heat sensitivity was shown to be dependent on other factors—heating conditions, i.e., dry heat, heating in liquid, pasteurization) (Yunoki et al. 2003).

The following paragraphs briefly summarize some commonly used inactivation and removal methods:

Inactivation Methods

Low pH Inactivation

Low pH inactivation is considered a robust inactivation method and has been employed in numerous processes based on investigational new drug and Biologics Licensing Application (BLA) submissions to the FDA and other regulatory agencies (Miesegaes et al. 2010) The CPPs for the low pH step are pH, time, and temperature. Under these conditions, robust virus clearance for retroviruses has been demonstrated ($\geq$5 $\log_{10}$)

In general, viral inactivation steps are conducted between pH 3.0 and 4.0. This is particularly compatible with mAb downstream processes in which Protein A capture columns are typically eluted at low pHs (Shukla and Aranha 2015). Very often, this low pH elution is followed by a low pH incubation step to inactivate viruses. It has been shown that robust viral inactivation requires a pH of 3.8 or below (Brorson et al. 2003). More recently, there has been a preference to conduct viral inactivation at pH 3.6 or below (Chen 2014). Understandably, a more conservative choice of pH for the pH inactivation step is dictated by the stability profile of the product. A typical time period for the low pH step can extend up to 1 h in duration. At pH 3.8 or below, viral inactivation proceeds very rapidly and is often complete within less than 10–15 min.

For all inactivation studies (e.g., low pH, detergent inactivation) kinetics of inactivation must be established. The low pH condition is typically achieved by addition of a weak acid to the protein solution (e.g., dilute HCl, or higher concentrations of citric acid or acetic acid). Higher concentrations of a strong acid can create localized low pH environments in a large tank and result in aggregation or other issues that could potentially impact product quality. Weak base solutions are typically employed for neutralization after the step is complete since prolonged exposure to low pH conditions is deemed undesirable. Solution pH has been shown to be the CPP for this step (Brorson et al. 2003).

Solvent Detergent and Detergent Only Inactivation

Products that cannot tolerate low pH conditions often employ solvent/detergent or detergent alone as chemical means of inactivating enveloped retroviruses (Yunoki et al. 2005). Solvent/detergent treatment was one of the mainstay methods in the plasma-derived products industry; it is also used for inactivating enveloped viruses in recombinant protein products, especially if the product cannot tolerate low pH conditions. Combinations of tri-n-butyl phosphate (TNBP; 0.1%–1.0%) with detergent (Triton X100 or Tween 80; 0.5%–1.0%) are commonly employed although effective retroviral inactivation can be achieved with detergent alone as well. CPPs are temperature and time, with low temperature and short time being worst-case conditions (Chen 2014, Miesegaes 2014).

Chemical inactivation requires the clearance of the agents employed for the inactivation step. As a result, this step is conducted during the early stages of the downstream process so that multiple chromatographic and filtration steps can provide clearance of the inactivating agent. It is possible that residual amounts of detergent may remain bound with the product despite these clearance steps. Another key aspect is the possibility of solvent and detergent interfering with the performance of a chromatographic step, particularly one that immediately follows the inactivation. This could manifest itself in the form of altered purification attributes for this step (as compared with the same step conducted without detergent in its load) or could result in decreased resin lifetime due to buildup of detergent on the resin. Modes of chromatography that are most successful in resisting interference from detergent include ion-exchange and affinity modes of purification such as Protein A chromatography. The latter is commonly used for Fc-fusion protein purification and can be preceded by solvent-detergent treatment in the cell culture supernatant. More hydrophobic resins such as hydrophobic interaction or mixed mode resins should typically be avoided immediately after the detergent-based viral inactivation. Another precaution that needs to be taken while evaluation of viral clearance for solvent/detergent steps is the potential for cytotoxicity to the reporter cell line used to assay for virus in the infectivity assay format. These cytotoxicity effects often necessitate significant dilution of these samples prior to analysis, resulting in a reduced reportable LRV from a solvent/detergent inactivation step.

If solvent/detergent treatment is conducted on harvested cell culture fluid, the presence of residual amounts of cell debris and lipids could potentially impact the efficacy of this step. In general, variation in lipid content due to cell culture viability variations at harvest only impacts kinetics of the viral inactivation step and produces a small effect of <0.5 LRV. It has been shown that Triton X100 is typically the most efficacious detergent for viral inactivation (Shukla and Aranha 2015).

Chromatographic Steps

Chromatographic steps can provide effective resolution of the product species from many different kinds of impurities and this can include viral particles that either flow through the column or are bound tightly on the resin. Mechanisms for viral clearance need to be established on chromatographic steps. While all chromatographic processing steps may provide some viral clearance ones that provide the most clearance and are typically validated for viral clearance include affinity chromatographic steps (e.g., Protein A) and ion-exchange chromatography, particularly anion-exchange chromatography.

Protein A chromatography provides a high degree of selectivity for mAbs and Fc-fusion proteins and is widely employed for their purification (Shukla et al. 2007). Being an affinity step makes this selective for product relative to a wide range of impurities including viral particles. Most viral particles have been shown to flow through Protein A columns without binding (Zhang et al. 2014). Protein A chromatography can routinely provide 4–5 logs of retroviral clearance (Miesegaes et al. 2010), but variability has been reported with different products. The number of logs of viral clearance on chromatographic steps is known to be highly dependent on the viral titer spike used in the load material during virus validation studies. For steps that are capable of providing good clearance, using a high titer spike in the load material can significantly increase the number of LRVs that can be claimed. Other factors that could influence the clearance may also relate to the number of column volumes of washes and their buffer composition.

A key consideration for Protein A viral clearance validation is the fact that the low pH conditions used for product elution can also inactivate retroviruses. However, if low pH viral inactivation is being claimed as a separate step, inactivation obtained during low pH is identical and the regulations stipulate that orthogonal unit operations only be included in claiming the cumulative viral clearance for the manufacturing process. In such a situation, it is important to utilize a viral assay that can detect viral particles irrespective of whether they are lysed or not due to low pH conditions (Shukla and Aranha 2015).

Quantitative PCR (q-PCR) is often employed as the analytical technique since it is based on the detection of viral nucleic acids rather than an intact viral particle capable of initiating infection I the infectivity assay (TCID$_{50}$ or plaque assay). Protein A chromatography has been shown to be a robust viral clearance step over a large number of operational cycles. It has been demonstrated that other performance attributes such as step yield and product breakthrough during the load step are more likely to decay before viral clearance begins to deteriorate. This could potentially justify not having to conduct studies on this mode of chromatography before and after the resin has been used to the full extent of its lifetime. Anion-exchange chromatography is known to be a robust means of retroviral clearance (Curtis et al. 2003, Miesegaes et al. 2010). This step can also provide >4 LRV under appropriate conditions. It has been shown that LRV on this mode of chromatography is highly dependent on the load conductivity, with higher conductivities resulting in low clearance as the viral particles begin to elute from the column. As a result, this is a preferred viral clearance step particularly for mAbs, which are typically basic proteins that can flow through anion-exchange columns. A large number of cycles (up to 120) are possible on anion-exchange chromatographic media if appropriate regeneration and storage conditions are employed. The concept of viral clearance by anion-exchange chromatography has been extended to membrane adsorbers as well (Norling et al. 2005). Greater than 5 LRV of clearance was obtained for a panel of viruses including retroviruses and parvoviruses while using a Sartobind Q membrane chromatography module. Since Q membrane chromatography requires relatively low load concentrations to enable effective binding of impurities (DNA, virus, host cell proteins (HCPs)), salt-tolerant membrane adsorbers have also been developed and launched commercially as the STIC membrane adsorbers from Sartorius-Stedim (Riordan et al. 2009). These membrane adsorbers were shown to achieve high LRVs irrespective of load salt concentrations of up to 150 mM. Additionally, adsorptive membrane chromatography is used where the matrix is composed of a filter rather than beads; these often have anion-exchange chromatography functionality. Monolithic columns in which the entire chromatography column is polymerized at one time instead of being packed with beads offer potential flow rate and throughput advantages (Ghose and Cramer 2001). Their viral clearance properties ought to be similar to those achieved on chromatographic resins and membrane adsorbers depending on the chemistry being used.

Since chromatographic resins are reused, licensure Biologics Licensing Application/Marketing Authorization Application (BLA/MAA) filings require demonstration of performance on new and used resins in terms of their viral clearance capability. This is aimed at ensuring that resins that have been used for multiple cycles are still capable of providing suitable viral clearance for the downstream process. Since it is rare for large-scale chromatographic columns to have reached the end of their predicted lifetime in terms of the number of cycles they are used for during clinical manufacturing, an artificially aged resin is often generated by operating the planned number of cycles across it at a smaller scale. The viral clearance capability of the used resin is then compared with that obtained on an unused chromatographic resin. In most cases, no significant decrease in viral clearance was observed prior to the decline of other performance attributes. Since consistency of these attributes is typically what the process is designed for, the risk to viral clearance from column reuse appears to be low. Nevertheless, providing documented evidence for this is the norm for licensure filings.

Virus Removal Filtration

Filtration through virus-retentive filters is currently a key unit operation during the production of biopharmaceuticals (Lute et al. 2004, Aranha 2005, Miesegaes et al. 2009). Next-generation virus-retentive filters for downstream processing have provided for improved flux ad throughputs without compromising virus retention by the virus-retentive filter; these include: Virosart® HF (Sartorius), Planova™ and BioEx (Asahi Kasei), Viresolve® Pro (EMD Millipore), and the Pegasus Pro (Pall).

Optimal performance of virus filters is a balance between membrane composition and construction, which is the purview of the filter manufacturer, and product characteristics/process design determined by the filter user. Differences in membrane composition and structural configuration manifest into variations in flux, product/matrix sensitivity, and virus retention performance. Process design, must be considered by the filter user for the purpose of minimizing process and product impurities and optimizing throughput and product recovery during downstream processing operations.

Careful process design and appropriate validation are critical for the successful implementation and performance of virus-retentive filters. Detailed information related to factors impacting virus clearance by virus-retentive filters and performance attributes are provided in a comprehensive technical report published by the Parenteral Drug Association (PDA 2005). While virus filtration has been demonstrated to be reliable for larger retroviral particles, removal of small viruses such as parvovirus by the small pore size filters (in the range of 15–20 nm) is less robust. Studies have to be done to ensure that there is no breakthrough of small viruses (parvovirus) under manufacturing conditions. Data for available virus-retentive filters have been summarized in a publication by Miesegaes et al. (Miesegaes et al. 2009).

Available data corroborates industry and regulatory thinking that virus filtration as a virus safety assurance unit operation is robust and reliable. However, there are several gaps in knowledge related to why small virus breakthrough is observed; additional studies will help elucidate the nuances and allow for a better understanding.

Virus Filters: Fouling and Flux Considerations

In order to retain viruses by size exclusion, virus filters must have a controlled precise pore size distribution that is not adversely impacted by minor variations in product streams (assuming these variations do not impact the critical product attributes. Both inherent characteristics of the virus filter and the process stream impact flow rates and filter fouling. When process time is predetermined and fixed, the throughput (l/m^2) is a function of the filter flux ($l/m^2/h$), which may be influenced by many different factors. Filter-associated attributes include inherent membrane permeability and transmembrane pressure. Product/process-related factors include pH, conductivity, impurity levels, aggregates, product concentration, and matrix. These factors are determined either by the purification process, biochemical/biophysical properties of the molecule, or both. Process and product impurities could potentially be process residuals, e.g., HCP, high-molecular weight species, aggregates formed during the downstream purification process, artifacts of the process design. Target protein size variations due to aggregates induced by process conditions such as pH have been correlated with the fouling behavior of monoclonal antibodies. Other process-related conditions and choice of prefilter to remove impurities will have an impact.

Positioning of the virus filter in the manufacturing process is an important consideration. Ideally, the virus filtration step is positioned relatively downstream in the process, after operations like chromatography steps that are designed primarily to increase target protein concentration and decrease process impurities. Any process step that is likely to increase product aggregates must be evaluated to determine its impact on product purity, as even product aggregates are considered process impurities, depending on the protein.

Process-operating ranges and depressurization have been reported to impact virus bleed through for virus-retentive filters designed to remove parvoviruses. Sustained pressure excursions have a greater impact on LRVs than the differential pressure (dP). Additionally, in viral spiking studies, the quality of the virus stock solution has a significant impact on the performance of virus removal filters. Highly purified stock solutions can ensure that the viral filters do not clog due to particulates from the spiked viral preparations and result in significant reductions in load filterability that does not represent what the viral filters are capable of filtering in terms of process intermediate. Since viral filters are operated solely to serve as a dedicated viral removal step, they are typically sized based on the volumetric loading during viral validation studies and not in terms of what is possible for the process intermediate alone. This can lead to a situation in which the filters need to be oversized in actual manufacturing operation reflecting the low volumetric throughput that was achieved in the validation study. A low volume spike

(0.01–00.1% v/v) is generally preferred for parvoviral grade filters to avoid clogging the membranes and artificially reducing the volumetric loading on these filters per unit surface area. An alternative strategy is based on the mechanism of viral breakthrough on these membranes. It is postulated that smaller pores clog first channeling the viral particles through the larger pores leading to viral breakthrough. This preferential clogging is reflected in the percent flux decay as compared with the initial flux and it is recommended that the viral filters be loaded to a certain percent flux decay in both viral validation and actual process operation. Since the same percent flux decay is reached much later in actual process operation as compared with the viral spike experiment, this enables process operation to continue to higher volumetric loadings. Operation of the viral filter to a specific percent flux decay level has attracted some interest although most organizations still prefer a more traditional approach relying upon volumetric loading per unit membrane surface area.

Why Optimize the Virus Filtration Step?

Virus filters represent one of the most costly consumables in biopharmaceutical manufacturing. Any approach that maximizes throughput (l/m^2) can provide significant cost savings over the lifetime of the biotherapeutic manufacture.

In view of variability in the feedstream characteristics as well as filter properties (lot-to-lot), sizing the viral filter for use in a manufacturing plant is a complex task and is not always a straightforward extrapolation. Often, in order to avoid process excursions during manufacturing, filter users tend to oversize the filters as a precautionary measure. While use of a prefilter with a virus filter is not an absolute requirement, a prefilter in front of the virus filter usually improves process economics. The prefilter may be positioned in-line with the virus filter; alternatively, it can be decoupled (off-line mode). A decoupled approach is usually preferred as it allows optimization of the prefilter to final filter ratio. Note, however, when it is decoupled, if there are significant time lapses between the prefiltration and virus filtration there is a possibility of aggregate formation which could potentially impact the process stream and virus filter performance.

The type of prefilter and the ratio of the prefilter: final filter impacts filter flux and process economics. The type of prefilter selected will depend on the type of impurity challenge. Prefilters commonly are based on mechanisms that involve primarily size exclusion, charged membranes that remove impurities primarily by adsorption, or both. The mechanism of removal of the prefilter has the potential to impact process throughputs. For example, the Sartopore XLM provides particulate retention primarily by size exclusion whereas the Virosart Max filter removes impurities by both size exclusion and adsorptive mechanisms. Alexion reported that the average throughput with the Virosart CPV when the Virosart Max prefilter was used was approximately ninefold higher than the average throughput observed when the Sartopore XLM (0.1 uM-rated) used as the prefilter. Another approach to filter optimization involves altering process conditions such as pH or ionic strength to determine impact on both product attributes and process economics.

Virus Clearance Performance of Virus Filters: Considerations Related to Small Virus Breakthrough

While virus-retentive filtration using 20 nm-rated virus filters occurs primarily by size exclusion, it is commonly acknowledged that these "small virus" removal filters do not provide absolute retention of viruses. Breakthrough of parvovirus has been reported. The precise factors that contribute to breakthrough are not well understood; however, they likely depend on a combination of factors that include virus filter characteristics (membrane chemistry/structural configuration), product matrix conditions (pH, ionic strength), and operating conditions (process interruptions, flow decay) (Miesegaes et al. 2010).

Not all filters are created equal. Studies have reported that sensitivity to process interruptions is unique to the filter brand. Broad generalizations related to performance of a virus filter cannot be applied and must be determined on a case-by-case basis under simulated manufacturing conditions. Process conditions such as low pH (pH 4.5 vs pH 8.0) and high conductivity have been shown to impact small virus (PPV) breakthrough. Process perturbations have been implicated in small virus breakthrough. In a manufacturing environment, interruptions in filtration are not uncommon. They can be a feature of the manufacturing process, as for example, before the recovery flush is applied to the virus-retentive filter. It could also potentially be an unintentional process interruption as, for example, when the system is halted due to an alarm. Considering the potential impact of process pause, duration of pause, and low pressure, it is important to evaluate the operating space across a broad range of parameters including specific product matrix conditions. In general, a lower pressure resulting in a lower flow rate leads to a local log reduction probably by allowing the virus to access other pores in the filter.

Validation study design and virus load on the filter contribute to small virus breakthrough. When designing and conducting virus validation studies, it is sometimes incorrectly assumed that using a high virus challenge will allow for claiming a higher log reduction by the virus filter. However, there is data to document virus breakthrough when high virus loads are used. It is common practice to spike a percent concentration of virus (usually 0.1%, 0.5%, or 1% virus spike) without considering the infectious units TCID50 or plaque-forming units (pfus) of the virus preparation.

Virus Clearance Evaluation (Validation) Studies

Viral clearance evaluation (validation) studies are not "validation" studies in the strict sense of the word, validation, as predetermined specifications are not set for virus clearance studies due to the unique considerations associated with demonstration of virus clearance. Nevertheless, virus validation study is a term commonly used and the terms "virus validation" and "virus clearance evaluation" are used interchangeably in this chapter.

Due to analytical limitations (See the section "Virus Detection Methods"), it is impossible to demonstrate absolute absence of viral presence. Viral validation studies are, therefore, conducted both to document clearance of viruses known to be associated with the product (e.g., HIV, hepatitis viruses, and parvovirus in the case of plasma products; endogenous retroviruses in the case of CCL-derived products) and also to estimate the robustness of the process to clear potential adventitious viral contaminants (that may have gained access to the product) by characterizing the ability of the process to clear nonspecific "model" viruses.

Process Analysis and Evaluation of Processes to Validate for Viral Clearance

Ideally, strategic planning for process validation must begin early in product development. The first steps in the validation process involve a critical analysis of the bioprocess to determine likely sources of viral contamination (including pathogenic potential of these contaminants) and process characterization to identify which steps in the manufacturing process have the potential for viral clearance.

Each process step to be tested for viral clearance should be evaluated for the mechanism by which virus clearance occurs, i.e., whether it is by inactivation, removal, or a combination of both. A "robust" step is one where the viral clearance (inactivation/removal) effectiveness is widely independent of variability in production parameters (Willkommen et al. 1999). Both serendipitous methods (those routinely used in the manufacturing process and which have coincidental viral clearance capability, e.g., chromatography and low pH-buffer elution steps) and methods deliberately incorporated for the precise purpose of viral clearance (for example, filtration and heat inactivation) are usually validated.

Regulatory guidelines (U.S. Department of Health and Human Services, Food and Drug Administration, Center for Biologics Evaluation and Research (CBER) and Center for Drug Evaluation and Research (CDER) 1998) recommend the incorporation of multiple orthogonal methods for viral clearance, i.e., methods that have independent (unrelated) clearance mechanisms. One misconception is that an entire manufacturing process which may include, for example, ion-exchange chromatography, pH inactivation, and detergent inactivation, can be tested by challenging with a large spike of virus during the first step and sampling during subsequent steps. Logistically, this is impossible for two reasons: (a) based on the product and possible contaminants, most processes require demonstration of >12–15 logs of clearance for individual viruses, and, it is not possible to grow mammalian viruses to such high concentration and (b) using a low viral challenge level will result in an initial low viral load, with each successive step in the bioprocess being challenged with fewer viral particles (assuming the previous steps are effective at inactivation/removal of viruses). This study design would also restrict the number of viral clearance steps that can be claimed and reduce the overall claim that can be established for the entire process. The best compromise is to evaluate each of the individual orthogonal steps separately and then sum the amount of clearance obtained for the entire process. While this method may have some limitations and introduce errors due to overestimation of clearance it is the only practical approach to a complex problem.

Generic and Modular Validation (i.e., Bracketing)

A generic clearance study is one in which virus removal and inactivation is demonstrated for several steps in the purification process of a model antibody/recombinant protein that can then be extrapolated to similar products. To claim this, however, each protein product must undergo the same purification and virus removal/inactivation scheme as the model antibody. A modular clearance study on the other hand, is one that demonstrates virus removal or inactivation of individual steps, such that a given step may be extrapolated to identical steps employed for other antibodies. Therefore, each "module" in the purification scheme may be treated (studied) independently of the other modules. In principle, under a modular approach, different model monoclonal antibodies may be used to demonstrate viral clearance in different modules, if necessary, and as long as the operating conditions are the same. The FDA's mAb Points To Consider (mAb PTC) document (U.S. Department of Health and Human Services Food and Drug Administration and Center for Biologics Evaluation and Research 1997) specifies acceptable conditions for both generic and modular validation. While sterilizing grade filters are validated at both the upper and lower limit, due to the considerable cost associated with conducting viral clearance evaluation studies, virus filter users generally conduct these studies at the "worst-case" condition for the specific unit operation. This demonstrates the minimum clearance a unit operation could provide. Worst-case conditions will vary depending on the method used and are determined by those factors that influence the clearance mechanism The application of modular, generic, and bracketing approaches requires a strong scientific justification based on small-scale studies, manufacturing experience, and consultation of the peer-reviewed scientific literature.

Viral Clearance Studies: Scaling Considerations and Identification of Critical Parameters

Typically, virus clearance evaluation studies are conducted at scale-down conditions due to logistic limitations. The scale-down must be a true representation of what occurs in the manufacturing process, i.e., process modeling must be accurate. Depending on the process, critical operating parameters to be conserved in scaled-down studies include volume, flow rates, contact time, and product and/or contaminant load. The composition of the test material should be similar in terms of protein concentration, pH, ionic strength, etc.; product generated by the large- and small-scale processes should be similar in terms of purity, potency, and yield. Other process parameters should also be evaluated for possible impact on viral clearance to determine if they should be included in the scaled-down study model.

Regulatory guidelines recommend use of virus validation data to set in-process limits in CPPs. While validations are usually conducted at both process extremes, viral studies being costly and time-consuming, testing at both process extremes is usually not done. Instead, testing is performed under "worst case" conditions to demonstrate the minimum clearance a step can provide. "Worst case" conditions will vary depending on the method and is determined by those factors that influence the clearance mechanism.

"Worst Case" Conditions: Virus Removal Methods

In chromatographic processes, depending on the resin and binding mode, critical variables include product/contaminant concentration, buffers, flow rate, wash volumes, temperature, etc. For example, with chromatography in the product binding mode (depending largely on the resin being evaluated), due to competitive binding for interactive sites, the kinetics of virus binding would be enhanced in the presence of the lowest product concentration (which would constitute "worst case"). Using the minimum wash volume before elution would also encourage virus to elute with the product. As with all chromatographic processes, flow rate will influence kinetics.

For chromatography in a contaminant/impurity binding mode, "worst case" contaminant conditions may be achieved by either increasing the contaminant to product ratio or loading the column with a larger volume of product than is processed during manufacture. This will provide competition between virus and the expected contaminants and impurities. Using the largest post-load wash volume expected in the manufacturing process (before the first cleaning step) will remove the maximum amount of virus from the resin along with the product and thus constitute "worst case" (Brorson et al. 2014).

In the case of filtration studies, in the direct flow (dead end) filtration mode, variables include composition of the solution to be filtered (nature of protein, protein concentration, other solution characteristics such as pH and ionic strength), process-associated factors such as dP and flux, and the appropriateness of downscaling, i.e., ratio of filter volume to filter area (Brorson et al. 2005).

"Worst-Case" Conditions: Inactivation Methods

Any viral inactivation method should result in irreversible loss of viral activity. Viral inactivation kinetics is rarely linear and sometimes a small residual fraction of the viral contaminant resistant to the inactivation strategy may persist. By performing kinetic inactivation experiments involving several time points, the rate of inactivation and thus the potential margin for safety in the actual production process can be assessed.

Variables in inactivation studies include exposure time, temperature, product concentration, presence/absence of contaminant protein, volumes, flow rates, and container equivalence. General considerations to be borne in mind are the necessity to ensure sample homogeneity prior to the treatment strategy, use of calibrated equipment (e.g., timers, chart recorders), and equipment qualification.

In the case of pH inactivation studies, low pH inactivation, in general, is considered robust at values of 3.8 or below but may be effective at different ranges for different lengths of time. Choosing a pH value closest to neutral within the range tested will provide a "worst case" challenge as will the shortest time. High protein concentrations, in general, have a protective effect, and, consequently, product (protein) concentration should be maximized (within process ranges) to ensure "worst case" conditions when conducting viral clearance studies.

Variables in the case of detergent inactivation include concentration, exposure time, and exposure temperature. Additionally, detergents being viscous, it is imperative to ensure sample homogeneity. The lowest detergent concentration combined with the shortest time provides a "worst case" condition. Temperature could be an important factor and may need to be evaluated at the extremes during development to determine its effect. In general, the lowest temperature provides the slowest kinetics. For heat inactivation studies, temperature distribution must be uniform and timing must begin only when steady state is reached. "Worst case" in heat inactivation studies would constitute the highest stabilizer concentration used, the highest product concentration, and the lowest temperature. If scaled-down studies are conducted, container equivalence must be demonstrated. Appropriately calibrated equipment, e.g., timers, chart recorders must be used; equipment qualification is mandatory.

Viral Clearance Evaluation (Validation) Studies: Virus Filtration-Related Issues

Any viral clearance process operational during manufacturing must be demonstrated to be effective under "worst case" conditions. Filter users conduct viral clearance evaluation (validation) studies often under considerably "scaled-down" conditions (100–1000X downscaled) and, therefore, process modeling must be accurate. Critical parameters will vary depending on the unit operation being evaluated. For example, in the case of filtration, filtration mode (direct flow/tangential flow), filtration-associated factors (flux, transmembrane pressure), and, product-related considerations including protein concentration and solution characteristics (pH, ionic strength) must be considered. Experimental design-associated variables will also considerably impact clearance results and the potential for erroneous clearance factors from this source must also be recognized. Virus spike-related considerations have notably been one of the key factors contributing to differences in test results; another factor is appropriateness of the process modeling in terms of downscaling, i.e., ratio of product volume to filter area. Testing process devices such as the geometry of the filter housing and the pumping device (peristaltic/gear pump, etc.) that may generate shear forces and result in viral inactivation (rather than removal) may be another contributing factor.

Viral challenges must be conducted with viral spikes that represent a "worst-case" challenge. In filtration studies, viral aggregation either due to the method of viral stock preparation, virus attachment to membrane particulates, or virus binding to proteins/other antibodies in the product, will enhance the retentive capacity of the filter and will provide false clearance values. One approach to reduce viral aggregates is to prefilter the viral-spiked product; prefiltration through "sterilizing grade" filters (0.2 μm-rated or 0.1 μm-rated) or through virus removal filters (Asahi Planova-35, Pall grade DV50, Sartorius Virosart Max) has been used.

Product load is another variable in clearance evaluation studies. In direct flow filtration, "worst case" would represent a combination of the highest mass to surface area ratio and highest product (protein) concentration. Product solution characteristics, i.e., pH and ionic strength, are another factor that can influence virus retention.

Virus aggregation, either as a consequence of the nature of the suspending medium or due to specific binding (antigen-antibody reactions, as in the case of plasma products that may contain neutralizing antibody) can enhance the observed titer reduction. For example, parvovirus B19 was efficiently eliminated by filters having nominal pore sizes larger than the diameter of the respective free virions (Omar and Kempf 2002). Yokoyama and colleagues demonstrated encephalomyocarditis virus (EMCV), parvovirus B19, and PPV aggregation in the presence of certain amino acids, which resulted in their removal by filters with pore size larger than the size of the viruses (Yokoyama et al. 2004).

In general, some common reasons for ambiguous and erroneous data with "virus-filter" evaluation studies and failure at manufacturing scale include inaccurate process modeling (inappropriate scale-down), enhanced viral retention due to gel layer/particulates that contribute to false LRVs, membrane fouling (and inability to get scaled-down volume through the small-scale device) due to additional protein load (stabilizers/serum/particulates) in virus spike, and, exceeding manufacturers recommended operating conditions in the case of filtration studies. These variables must be borne in mind when evaluating filters for virus removal and designing viral clearance evaluation studies.

Technical Aspects of Study Design

Choice of Panel of Test Viruses

Unlike bacterial sterilization where an indicator organism is specified, there is no single indicator virus that can be used in virus clearance studies. Hence, a panel of viruses is used for viral clearance studies. Choice of the appropriate panel of viruses to use will depend on the source material (plasma-derived biologicals versus cell line-derived) and on the product phase at which viral clearance testing is conducted.

In general, the panel of test viruses used should include relevant viruses (i.e., known/suspected viral contaminants), and model viruses. Relevant viruses are, for example, HIV and hepatitis B and C viruses, which are known contaminants of blood products. Some relevant viruses, e.g., hepatitis B and C viruses are difficult to propagate *in vitro*; in these cases, specific model viruses may be used. Specific model viruses are viruses that resemble known viral contaminants; for example, BVDV and Sindbis virus have been used as models for hepatitis C virus. Similarly, murine leukemia virus (MuLV) is often used as a model for noninfectious endogenous retroviruses associated with rodent cell lines. Additionally, nonspecific model viruses are also included in the test panel to characterize the theoretical clearance capability of the manufacturing process, i.e., assess the "robustness" of the process. These include viruses of different size and varied physicochemical and biophysical characteristics; they are not expected to be associated with the product but are included to address theoretical safety concerns and add confidence that the process can handle unknown or undetected viruses. Examples of viruses that have been used in virus validation studies are provided in Table 17.8.

TABLE 17.8

Test Viruses Commonly Used in Viral Clearance Evaluation Studies

Virus	Family (-viridae)	Genome	Envelope	Size (nm)	Shape
Vesicular stomatitis virus	Rhabdo-	RNA	Yes	70×175	Bullet
Parainfluenza virus	Paramyxo-	RNA	Yes	100–200 nm+	Pleomorphic/Spherical
Pseudorabies virus	Herpes	DNA	Yes	120–200	Spherical
Herpes simplex virus	Herpes	DNA	Yes	120–200	Spherical
HIV	Retro	RNA	Yes	80–100	Spherical
MuLV	Retro	RNA	Yes	80–110	Spherical
Reovirus 3	Reo	RNA	No	60–80	Spherical
Sindbis virus	Toga	RNA	Yes	60–70	Spherical
SV40	Papova	DNA	No	40–50	Icosahedral
BVDV	Toga	RNA	Yes	50–70	Pleomorphic/Spherical
Encephalomyo-carditis virus	Picorna	RNA	No	25–30	Icosahedral
Poliovirus	Picorna	RNA	No	25–30	Icosahedral
Hepatits A	Picorna	RNA	No	25–30	Icosahedral
Parvovirus (canine, murine porcine)	Parvo	DNA	No	18–24	Icosahedral

In some cases, in view of the cost-prohibitiveness of an entire virus validation package, preliminary testing with surrogates such as bacteriophages can be undertaken. Such testing is, of course, relevant only if removal is size-based, as in filtration; if clearance is dependent on a particular physicochemical or other surface characteristic of the virus, it cannot be used. The applicability of bacteriophages as surrogates for mammalian viruses in filter validation studies has been addressed elsewhere (Aranha-Creado and Brandwein 1999). While data corroborating similar retention performance with both mammalian viruses and appropriately sized bacteriophages has been available for some time, only recently has a formal assessment of their comparability been attempted. A task force report (PDA 2005) on the initiatives toward virus filter nomenclature standardization for "large pore size" virus filters provided the necessary impetus to study this issue. Bacteriophage PR 772 has been demonstrated to be an appropriately model for evaluation of "large pore size" virus-retentive filters (Lute et al. 2004) and performance of these filters from several virus filter manufacturers has been evaluated and demonstrated to be comparable (Brorson et al. 2005). While virus clearance data for regulatory submissions currently must be obtained with mammalian model viruses, the demonstration of the comparability of retention of appropriately sized bacteriophages and mammalian viruses provides a rationale for the use of bacteriophages in process development work prior to a regulatory submission.

Use of Bacteriophages as Surrogates for Mammalian Viruses in Virus Clearance Evaluation Studies

When choosing a model virus for process development studies, bacteriophages may warrant consideration over mammalian viruses. Phages are benign in the event of human contact and consequently, the required laboratory safety level is typically less than that for mammalian viruses (e.g., BSL-1 as compared to BSL-2 or above). In addition, phages can be cultured to very high titers (in excess of 109–1,010 pfu/mL). The resulting preparations are cleaner compared to those typical of some mammalian viruses. The plaque assays used to detect their presence in the filtrate requires a 24-h incubation period which allows for rapid evaluation of results. ICH Q8 has established the concept of design space. The use of a phage as a surrogate model virus when establishing a product's design space is a good starting point for reasons mentioned above. Some phage species have been fairly well characterized and possess physical properties (i.e., size, isoelectric point, etc.) close to their mammalian counterparts [19–22]. Design space conditions established with a phage will be predictive of filter clearance of the corresponding mammalian virus. Phage-based QbD studies as described above could provide a useful path forward.

Virus Stock-Related Considerations

The quality of the stock preparation and the titer of the virus spike will significantly influence the test results and the ability to make a viral clearance claim. Considering that virus spikes of varying quality were used in virus validation studies, a study group of regulatory and industry groups was convened and PDA-TR-47 was published.

In general, starting with a high viral load to challenge a process step will maximize the potential viral clearance claim. The volume of virus spiked into the challenge material and the virus stock titer combine to determine the total virus titer in the spiked product. The virus density depends primarily on the biology of the virus and can vary from virus to virus. While it is advisable to work with high titer virus stocks, keep in mind that methods used to concentrate the virus stock and achieve high stock titers may be conducive to virus aggregation.

The quality of the virus stocks in terms of presence of viral aggregates, cell debris, or other particulates can influence the results by causing a false enhancement or reduction of viral clearance. Thus, for example, with a chromatography process in a contaminant-binding mode, extra cell debris may compete with the virus for binding sites on the resin causing a decreased clearance value. In a tangential flow filtration process, use of a virus stock containing high amounts of cell debris would enhance virus retention due to the polarization of the membrane. In direct flow filtration, if the membrane clogs prematurely due to cell debris the entire load volume cannot be filtered and, therefore, the full log clearance cannot be claimed.

Viral spike volumes will impact clearance studies (especially if there are large amounts of debris), and, in general, should be maintained at 10% or less of the final volume to keep the feedstream representative of the manufacturing process (CHMP 1996).

Importance of Adequate Controls in Virus Study Design

The importance of controls cannot be overemphasized. Controls allow for attributing clearance effects to actual treatment procedures versus artifacts of the test design and methodology. The following are some common controls to be included for virus clearance evaluations.

Prior to the viral clearance assays, it is necessary to ascertain that the product does not have an inhibitory effect either on the indicator cell line (generalized cytotoxicity control) or the test virus (viral interference studies). Cytotoxicity and interference controls are often conducted considerably in advance of the actual validation study to ensure that the clearance capacity is not overestimated due to test-related considerations. The *cytotoxicity* control is included to ensure that any indicator cell cytopathology observed during the study is due to the virus alone. The cells are exposed to process components (product intermediates, buffer), in the absence of virus for the length of time the test material will be in contact with the cells; a cytopathic or morphological effect relative to the unexposed control cells is an indication of cytotoxicity. *Viral interference studies* are conducted to determine if process components interfere with the capacity of the test virus to infect the indicator cell line. Essentially, following exposure of the indicator cell line to the process component, the cells are exposed to the virus and evaluated to determine if there is any loss of infectivity and thus viral interference by the product. If either of the above two controls demonstrate positive results, one approach is dilution of the test material (in order to determine a non-inhibitory concentration); another is neutralization or other test solution adjustment if needed.

The *hold* control is included to ensure that the test virus is stable throughout the test duration in the presence of test material and essentially involves virus-spiked starting material held for process time at process temperature. This control essentially demonstrates any inactivation effect that is a consequence of the product (start material). The loss demonstrated by a hold control is not related to the clearance strategy under study and should be evaluated accordingly.

Stability and storage issues are primarily a concern if process challenges are performed at a site different from that of the virus vendor. If virus stocks are to be shipped to another location, the stocks are thawed, processed over the manufacturing step to be challenged and frozen for later shipping. This may differ from challenges performed at the vendor site in that many vendors often assay the test material immediately. This reduction may affect the final clearance claim; freeze/thaw stability should be reviewed.

Shipping controls determine if temperature changes that may have occurred during shipping affected titers when virus is shipped to a different site.

Viral Clearance Validation Studies: Pitfalls and Cautions

As discussed earlier, a "good" viral clearance validation study is the consequence of a detailed and well-designed study. Scaled-down studies are, at best, approximations of conditions achieved under manufacturing conditions and the validity of the clearance data is a direct reflection of accurate process modeling and study design. Some of the pitfalls associated with small-scale validation studies are related to the following: (a) virus-related considerations. Viral spike-related perturbations may make the process nonrepresentative of actual manufacturing conditions. Also, model viruses are used in process validation studies; these are, at best, just that—models—and the wild-type strain may not behave similar to a laboratory strain. (b) Inaccurate process modeling. Conditions in small-scale validations may not always be congruent with process-scale conditions, e.g., columns used only once for a validation may not reflect the ability of columns used repeatedly (during manufacture) to remove virus consistently; certain sites on the resins may become blocked on repeated use, reducing the effectiveness of virus removal over the resin lifetime. (c) Sample-related considerations include nonrepresentative sample used in viral validations, e.g., either the proper intermediate or actual product sample may not have been used; sample may not be representative in terms of protein concentration, pH or other solution characteristics such as ionic strength; samples may be nonhomogeneous due to inadequate mixing. (d) Assay-related considerations include failure to evaluate buffer toxicity, poor model virus selection, lack of appropriate controls, and poor standardization of viral assays. Critical assay performance criteria are accuracy, reproducibility, repeatability, linearity of range, limit of detection and limit of quantification, and must be validated.

Steps that require dilution of the product (e.g., due to viral interference or other toxicity-related considerations) will impact assay results and the ability to make a high viral clearance claim. For example, high salt concentration, pH extremes, or other sample conditions may interfere with the virus titration. Decreasing the actual volume assayed (due to dilution of the sample, e.g., tenfold) will result in decreased sensitivity and is especially important when no virus is detected and a theoretical limit titer for the sample is calculated.

In general, overall greater reduction factors can be claimed with a larger number of observations from larger volumes performed with tests with the lowest available limits of detection when complete clearance for a step is expected. Virus quantitation methods can be modified to enhance sensitivity by use of additional replicates and increased inoculation volumes. Large volume assessment can be used as a supplement to conventional titration methods to increase the probability of detection for extremely low virus concentrations.

Considerations in Data Interpretation and Estimating Viral Clearance

Establishing clearance for the entire process (overall clearance value) requires at least two orthogonal "robust" methods of viral clearance. The individual steps must possess fundamentally different mechanisms of virus removal or inactivation in order for values to be considered cumulative. Only data for the same model virus is cumulative since viruses vary greatly with regard to their inactivation or removal profiles. Clearance estimates and their variances are calculated for each orthogonal unit operation; total virus reduction is the sum of individual LRFs. In cases of complete clearance, a theoretical titer value is based on a statistical distribution (Poisson Distribution). Table 17.8 provides cumulative virus clearance values for MuLV.

The clearance goal is usually chosen based on the product use and the risk to the patient population. The extent of product testing necessary will depend on source and nature of the product, the stage of product development, and the clinical indication. Abbreviated testing may apply in serious or immediately life-threatening conditions for which no effective alternative treatment exists.

Concluding Comments

To quote Donald Rumsfeld, U.S. politician and businessman

> There are known knowns. These are things we know that we know. There are known unknowns. That is to say, there are things that we know we don't know. But there are also unknown unknowns. There are things we don't know we don't know

Nowhere is this more true than in virus safety assurance of biopharmaceuticals. While we have made significant strides in ensuring that a safe biotherapeutic is delivered to the patient, the unique considerations associated with virus safety necessitate a pragmatic paradigm. The unrelenting potential for the appearance of new viruses is enhanced by the dissolution of global boundaries. Pathogens can now travel to locations that were not previously considered indigenous to them. Because of this globalization and the many viruses still undiscovered, vigilance and the ability to clear even the viruses we cannot yet detect must remain high.

Biopharmaceutical safety is the result of multiple orthogonal barriers operating in concert. While each approach, individually, may have limitations, their use in an integrated manner provides overlapping and complementary levels of protection to recipients of recombinant and monoclonal products. Multiple orthogonal approaches for virus removal and inactivation are more effective than single steps.

Anecdotal evidence and systematic assessments have attested to the fact that biotech products have had an excellent safety record. This can largely be attributed to the viral safety tripod strictly adhered to in the industry: adequate sourcing, documentation of virus clearance evaluation (virus validation studies), and in-process testing. Newer analytical methods have demonstrated the robustness of conventional detection methods in ensuring virus safety. Nevertheless, testing gaps and alternative methods should be evaluated to continue to ensure safe, high-quality human biologicals (from a virological safety standpoint).

Application of a QbD approach to viral safety requires an in-depth understanding of the potential contamination threats in a design space as well as the capacity of the manufacturing process to clear any potential viral contaminants. Understanding how variations in processing parameters impact the capacity of the manufacturing process to remove or inactivate a potential contaminating virus allows the process to provide optimal viral clearance and to predict the impact of process changes on that clearance. By understanding the nature of potential viral contaminants, implementation of a testing program based on these potential contaminants, and an understanding of the impact of variations in processing parameters on virus clearance unit operations, the risk can be managed effectively and viral safety can be achieved.

Clinical acceptability of a biopharmaceutical is concomitant with risk assessment and guided by risk–benefit analysis. Causality assessment and management approaches for new chemical entities (small molecules/drugs) cannot be directly applied to biologicals. For a conventional drug, benefit–risk assessment usually entails investigating the problem and collating a body of data to determine conclusive evidence beyond reasonable doubt for attributing the adverse event to the drug. For biopharmaceuticals, *every* single reported case of suspected virus transmission must be considered as a potential indicator of an infectious batch, with the inherent risk of transmitting the disease to hundreds or thousands of patients.

Upstream risk mitigation and management is not a regulatory requirement. However, the significant consequences of a contamination event which is rare but catastrophic when it does occur must be balanced against the costs of incorporating appropriate risk mitigation strategies. Using virus inactivation methods (heat (HTST), UV-irradiation) and with the recent availability of virus removal filtration for upstream risk mitigation, companies are working toward ensuring that even the very low risk of upstream virus contamination is made infinitesimal.

The holy grail of virus safety is absolute absence of viral presence. Sophistication in computational power and advances in bioinformatics have proven that the concept of "virus free" is only as good as our detection method. While virus safety assurance will continue to be a moving target our only recourse is a constant vigilance combined with pragmatic regulations and guidelines that take cognizance of the latest scientific and technical information.

List of Virus Abbreviations

Bovine Polyoma Virus	BPyV
Bovine viral diarrhea virus	BVDV
Canine Parvovirus	CPV
Encephalomyocarditis virus	EMCV
Hepatitis A virus	HAV
Hepatitis B virus	HBV
Hepatitis C virus	HCV
Human immunodeficiency virus	HIV
Human T-cell Lymphotropic virus	HTLV
Infectious Bovine Rhinotracheitis virus	IBR virus
Porcine circovirus	PCV
Parainfluenza-3 virus	PI-3 virus
Severe acute respiratory syndrome Coronavirus	SARS Coronavirus
West Nile virus	WNV

List of Abbreviations

CCL	Continuous cell line
CCP	Critical control point
cGMP	Current good manufacturing practices
CHO	Chinese Hamster Ovary
CPP	Critical process parameter
CQA	Critical quality attributes
DP	Drug product
FFA	Focus forming assay
LRV, LTR, LRF	Log_{10} reduction value; Log_{10} titer reduction; and Log_{10} reduction factor (terms used interchangeably)
MCB	Master cell bank
PCR	Polymerase chain reaction
PFA	Plaque forming assay
RT assay	Reverse transcriptase assay
RVLPs	Retroviral-like particles
SAL	Safety assurance level
$TCID_{50}$ assay	50% tissue culture infectious dose assay
WCB	Working cell bank

REFERENCES

Allain, J. P., S. L. Stramer, A. B. Carneiro-Proietti, M. L. Martins, S. N. Lopes da Silva, M. Ribeiro, F. A. Proietti and H. W. Reesink (2009). Transfusion-transmitted infectious diseases. *Biologicals* **37**(2): 71–77.

Aranha, H. (2005). Virological safety of biopharmaceuticals. A risk-based approach. *Bioprocess Int* (Suppl): 17–20.

Aranha, H. (2008). Ensuring safety of biopharmaceuticals: Virus and prion safety considerations, In Jornitz M.W., Meltzer T.H. (Eds.) *Filtration and Purification in the Biopharmaceutical Industry*, Informa Healthcare USA, Inc, New York, Vol 20, pp. 543–577.

Aranha, H. (2012). Current issues in assuring virus safety of biopharmaceuticals. *Bioprocess Int* 12–17.

Aranha-Creado, H. and H. Brandwein (1999). Application of bacteriophages as surrogates for mammalian viruses: A case for use in filter validation based on precedents and current practices in medical and environmental virology. *PDA J Pharm Sci Technol* **53**(2): 75–82.

Baylis, S. A., T. Finsterbusch, N. Bannert, J. Blumel and A. Mankertz (2011). Analysis of porcine circovirus type 1 detected in Rotarix vaccine. *Vaccine* **29**(4): 690–697.

Bethencourt, V. (2009). Virus stalls Genzyme plant. *Nat Biotechnol* **27**(8): 681–681.

Blumel, J., I. Schmidt, W. Effenberger, H. Seitz, H. Willkommen, H. H. Brackmann, J. Lower and A. M. Eis-Hubinger (2002a). Parvovirus B19 transmission by heat-treated clotting factor concentrates. *Transfusion* **42**(11): 1473–1481.

Blumel, J., I. Schmidt, H. Willkommen and J. Lower (2002b). Inactivation of parvovirus B19 during pasteurization of human serum albumin. *Transfusion* **42**(8): 1011–1018.

Boschetti, N., I. Niederhauser, C. Kempf, A. Stuhler, J. Lower and J. Blumel (2004). Different susceptibility of B19 virus and mice minute virus to low pH treatment. *Transfusion* **44**(7): 1079–1086.

Brorson, K., S. Krejci, K. Lee, E. Hamilton, K. Stein and Y. Xu (2003). Bracketed generic inactivation of rodent retroviruses by low pH treatment for monoclonal antibodies and recombinant proteins. *Biotechnol Bioeng* **82**(3): 321–329.

Brorson, K., G. Miesegaes, O. Tounekti, J. Skene and J. Blumel (2014). Conference summary: Gaps, lessons learned, and areas for improvement. *PDA J Pharm Sci Technol* **68**(1): 83–89.

Brorson, K., G. Sofer and H. Aranha (2005a). Nomenclature standardization for 'large pore size' virus-retentive filters. *PDA J Pharm Sci Technol* **59**(6): 341–345.

Brorson, K., G. Sofer, G. Robertson, S. Lute, J. Martin, H. Aranha, M. Haque, S. Satoh, K. Yoshinari, I. Moroe, M. Morgan, F. Yamaguchi, J. Carter, M. Krishnan, J. Stefanyk, M. Etzel, W. Riorden, M. Korneyeva, S. Sundaram, H. Wilkommen and P. Wojciechowski (2005b). "Large pore size" virus filter test method recommended by the PDA Virus Filter Task Force. *PDA J Pharm Sci Technol* **59**(3): 177–186.

Chen, Q. (2014). Viral clearance using traditional, well-understood unit operations (Session I): Low-pH inactivation. *PDA J Pharm Sci Technol* **68**(1): 17–22.

CHMP (1996). Note for guidance on virus validation studies: the design, contribution and interpretation of studies validating the inactivation and removal of viruses (CPMP/BWP/268/95).

Curtis, S., K. Lee, G. S. Blank, K. Brorson and Y. Xu (2003). Generic/matrix evaluation of SV40 clearance by anion exchange chromatography in flow-through mode. *Biotechnol Bioeng* **84**(2): 179–186.

Dodet, B., W. Hesselink, C. Jungback, J. Lechenet, P. P. Pastoret, P. Vannier and M. Vicari (2010). Viral safety and extraneous agents testing for veterinary vaccines. *Biologicals* **38**(3): 326–331.

Ghose, S. and S. M. Cramer (2001). Characterization and modeling of monolithic stationary phases: Application to preparative chromatography. *J Chromatogr A* **928**(1): 13–23.

ICH (1997). ICH Q5D: Derivation and characterisation of cell substrates used for production of biotechnological/biological products.

ICH (2009). ICH Q8 (R2): Pharmaceutical Development. International Conference on Harmonisation of Technical Requirements for Registration of Pharmaceuticals for Human Use; Current Step 4 version, August 2009.

ICH (2015a). ICH guideline Q9 on quality risk management Step 5. September 2015. EMA/CHMP/ICH/24235/2006.

ICH (2015b). ICH guideline Q10 on pharmaceutical quality system Step 5. September 2015 EMA/CHMP/ICH/214732/2007.

Kerr, A. and R. Nims (2010). Adventitious viruses detected in biopharmaceutical bulk harvest samples over a 10 year period. *PDA J Pharm Sci Technol* **64**(5): 481–485.

Khan, A. S. (2010). Testing considerations for novel cell substrates: A regulatory perspective. *PDA J Pharm Sci Technol* **64**(5): 426–431.

Khan, A. S., S. H. S. Ng, O. Vandeputte, A. Aljanahi, A. Deyati, J. P. Cassart, R. L. Charlebois and L. P. Taliaferro (2016). A multicenter study to evaluate the performance of high-throughput sequencing for virus detection. *mSphere* **70**: 559–591.

Khan, A. S., D. A. Vacante, J. P. Cassart, S. H. Ng, C. Lambert, R. L. Charlebois and K. E. King (2016). Advanced Virus Detection Technologies Interest Group (AVDTIG): Efforts on High Throughput Sequencing (HTS) for virus detection. *PDA J Pharm Sci Technol* **70**(6): 591–595.

Kleindienst, A. M. B. (2016). Virus risk mitigation in cell culture media. *Biopharm.*

Lute, S., H. Aranha, D. Tremblay, D. Liang, H. W. Ackermann, B. Chu, S. Moineau and K. Brorson (2004). Characterization of coliphage PR772 and evaluation of its use for virus filter performance testing. *Appl Environ Microbiol* **70**(8): 4864–4871.

Melnick, J. L. (1991). Virus inactivation: Lessons from the past. *Dev Biol Stand* **75**: 29–36.

Miesegaes, G. (2014). Viral clearance by traditional operations with significant knowledge gaps (Session II): Cation Exchange Chromatography (CEX) and detergent inactivation. *PDA J Pharm Sci Technol* **68**(1): 30–37.

Miesegaes, G., S. Lute and K. Brorson (2010). Analysis of viral clearance unit operations for monoclonal antibodies. *Biotechnol Bioeng* **106**(2): 238–246.

Miesegaes G., S. Lute, H. Aranha, and K. Brorson (2009). *Virus Retentive Filters. Encyclopedia of Industrial Biotechnology*, New york, NY: John Wiley and Sons.

Norling, L., S. Lute, R. Emery, W. Khuu, M. Voisard, Y. Xu, Q. Chen, G. Blank and K. Brorson (2005). Impact of multiple re-use of anion-exchange chromatography media on virus removal. *J Chromatogr A* **1069**(1): 79–89.

Omar, A. and C. Kempf (2002). Removal of neutralized model parvoviruses and enteroviruses in human IgG solutions by nanofiltration. *Transfusion* **42**(8): 1005–1010.

Onions, D. and J. Kolman (2010). Massively parallel sequencing, a new method for detecting adventitious agents. *Biologicals* **38**(3): 377–380.

Pastoret, P. P. (2010). Human and animal vaccine contaminations *Biologicals* **38**(3): 332–334.

PDA (2005). Virus filtration. *PDA J Pharm Sci Technol* **59**(S-2): 8–42.

Peerlinck, K., J. Arnout, J. G. Gilles, J. M. Saint-Remy and J. Vermylen (1993). A higher than expected incidence of factor VIII inhibitors in multitransfused haemophilia A patients treated with an intermediate purity pasteurized factor VIII concentrate. *Thromb Haemost* **69**(2): 115–118.

Potts, B. J. (2010). TSE case studies associated with japanese and other regulatory authorities—Talk transcript. *PDA J Pharm Sci Technol* **64**(5): 442–444.

Prikhod'ko, G. G. (2005). Dry-heat sensitivity of human B19 and porcine parvoviruses. *Transfusion* **45**(10): 1692–1693.

Riordan, W. T., S. M. Heilmann, K. Brorson, K. Seshadri and M. R. Etzel (2009). Salt tolerant membrane adsorbers for robust impurity clearance. *Biotechnol Prog* **25**(6): 1695–1702.

Savage, M., J. Torres, L. Franks, B. Masecar and J. Hotta (1998). Determination of adequate moisture content for efficient dry-heat viral inactivation in lyophilized factor VIII by loss on drying and by near infrared spectroscopy. *Biologicals* **26**(2): 119–124.

Schneider, B., M. Becker, H. H. Brackmann and A. M. Eis-Hubinger (2004). Contamination of coagulation factor concentrates with human parvovirus B19 genotype 1 and 2. *Thromb Haemost* **92**(4): 838–845.

Shukla, A. and H. Aranha (2015). Viral clearance for biopharmaceutical downstream processes. *Pharm Bioprocess* **3**(2): 127–138.

Shukla, A. A., B. Hubbard, T. Tressel, S. Guhan and D. Low (2007). Downstream processing of monoclonal antibodies--application of platform approaches. *J Chromatogr B* **848**(1): 28–39.

Suontaka, A. M., M. Blomback and J. Chapman (2003). Changes in functional activities of plasma fibrinogen after treatment with methylene blue and red light. *Transfusion* **43**(5): 568–575.

U.S. Department of Health and Human Services Food and Drug Administration and Center for Biologics Evaluation and Research (1997). Points to Consider in the Manufacture and Testing of Monoclonal Antibody Products for Human Use.

U.S. Department of Health and Human Services, Food and Drug Administration, Center for Biologics Evaluation and Research (CBER) and Center for Drug Evaluation and Research (CDER) (1998). Guidance for industry: Q5A viral safety evaluation of biotechnology products derived from cell lines of human or animal origin. *Federal Register* **63**(185): 51074–51078.

Valera, C. R., J. W. Chen and Y. Xu (2003). Application of multivirus spike approach for viral clearance evaluation. *Biotechnol Bioeng* **84**(6): 714–722.

Victoria, J. G., C. Wang, M. S. Jones, C. Jaing, K. McLoughlin, S. Gardner and E. L. Delwart (2010). Viral nucleic acids in live-attenuated vaccines: Detection of minority variants and an adventitious virus. *J Virol* **84**(12): 6033–6040.

Willkommen, H., I. Schmidt and J. Lower (1999). Safety issues for plasma derivatives and benefit from NAT testing. *Biologicals* **27**(4): 325–331.

Yokoyama, T., K. Murai, T. Murozuka, A. Wakisaka, M. Tanifuji, N. Fujii and T. Tomono (2004). Removal of small non-enveloped viruses by nanofiltration. *Vox Sang* **86**(4): 225–229.

Yunoki, M., M. Tsujikawa, T. Urayama, Y. Sasaki, M. Morita, H. Tanaka, S. Hattori, K. Takechi and K. Ikuta (2003). Heat sensitivity of human parvovirus B19. *Vox Sang* **84**(3): 164–169.

Yunoki, M., T. Urayama, M. Tsujikawa, Y. Sasaki, S. Abe, K. Takechi and K. Ikuta (2005). Inactivation of parvovirus B19 by liquid heating incorporated in the manufacturing process of human intravenous immunoglobulin preparations. *Br J Haematol* **128**(3): 401–404.

Zhang, M., G. R. Miesegaes, M. Lee, D. Coleman, B. Yang, M. Trexler-Schmidt, L. Norling, P. Lester, K. A. Brorson and Q. Chen (2014). Quality by design approach for viral clearance by protein a chromatography. *Biotechnol Bioeng* **111**(1): 95–103.

18

A Rapid Method for Purifying Escherichia coli β-galactosidase Using Gel-Filtration Chromatography

Lynn P. Elwell
Wake Technical Community College

CONTENTS

A Brief History

North Carolina's economy has undergone a sea change over the past 15 years with significant job losses in the textile, tobacco, furniture, and paper industries. In the textile industry alone, over 100,000 jobs have been lost between 1997 and 2002 with an additional 70,000 apparel jobs disappearing during the same period.[1]

By contrast, a bright spot in the state's long-term employment outlook has been the emergence of biotechnology as a promising economic force. North Carolina is ranked among the five largest biotechnology industry centers in North America, with firms engaging in research and development, product development, clinical trials, pharmaceutical manufacturing and sales, bio-manufacturing, and healthcare applications. Many of the world's largest biotechnology and pharmaceutical facilities are located in North Carolina, including facilities belonging to industry leaders GlaxoSmithKline and Merck & Company. In addition, the state is home to Talecris, with the world's largest plasma-based factory; Wyeth, with a major vaccine facility; Baxter, with an intravenous solutions facility; and Biogen Idec with a large manufacturing biologics operation.

The Bionetwork Capstone Learning Center

To support North Carolina's competitive position in retaining the biomanufacturing facilities already situated in the state as well as attracting new companies, an ambitious workforce training effort has been launched. To this end, a biomanufacturing and pharmaceutical training consortium has been established. Start-up of this effort was initially funded by part of a $60 million grant from the Golden Leaf Foundation as well as additional support from local industry. The Golden Leaf Foundation is a nonprofit corporation that was created to receive a portion of the funds coming to North Carolina from the settlement agreement with cigarette manufactures.

BioNetwork is a statewide initiative providing education and customized workforce training for the biopharmaceutical industry. One component of BioNetwork is the Capstone Learning Center which is a consortium program comprised of seven regional community colleges with Wake Technical Community College (WTCC) serving as the lead institution. The Learning Center is temporarily situated at the Western Campus of WTCC in Cary, NC. It consists of a laboratory, a classroom, a mobile laboratory/BioNetwork bus, six full-time faculty members, and a fluctuating number of part-time instructors and consultants. Under the leadership of the consortium colleges, the Center currently offers five comprehensive, 2-to-5-day hands-on workshops dealing with a variety of biopharmaceutical and biotechnology-related subjects. The courses that are currently offered are: Aseptic Manufacturing, Elements in Microbial Identification, Current Good Manufacturing Practices, Gram-negative Bacterial Endotoxin Detection and Quantitation, and Operations in Biotechnology Manufacturing Processes. The last course on this list, referred to throughout this document as the "Bio-processing" course, is the subject of this chapter.

Introduction

The primary purpose of the Bioprocessing course is to familiarize students with the major unit processes that comprise the upstream and downstream elements of a typical industrial biomanufacturing operation, from both a theoretical and practical perspective. The experimental component of this course was designed to provide realistic, hands-on experience with these unit processes. An advantage of this course is that much of the equipment and instrumentation used is smaller in scale and generally more approachable than their larger and generally more complicated industrial counterparts.

In the Bioprocessing course, we begin with 2.4 L of an overnight culture of a genetically engineered *Escherichia coli* strain and approximately 5 days later the students can visualize a 99.5% homogeneous preparation of the target protein, β-galactosidase, in a sodium dodecyl sulfate (SDS)-polyacrylamide gel. The specific unit processes discussed and demonstrated include bioreactor operation and control, target protein detection and monitoring, cell harvesting, cell-disruption, protein concentration and dialysis, protein separation by gel-filtration chromatography, and protein characterization using SDS-polyacrylamide gel electrophoresis.

Figure 18.1 is a flow diagram of the overall experimental sequence for the course. As indicated in Figure 18.1, a bench-top bioreactor/fermentor may be replaced by several 1-L Erlenmeyer flasks. As a consequence, laboratories with limited equipment budgets can negotiate this course without compromising the quality of the final results.

The Target Protein: β-galactosidase

Historical Perspective

The protein we chose as our target is β-galactosidase (EC 3.2.1.23) from the bacterium *Escherichia coli*. Beta-galactosidase (lactase) hydrolyzes lactose and other β-galactosidase into their constituent monosaccharides.[2] It is widespread in nature, found in microorganisms, animals, and plants. This enzyme is one of the gene products of the *lac* operon and, as such, has a unique place in the history of molecular biology. It is an *inducible* enzyme; *E. coli* synthesizes β-galactosidase only when its inducer, lactose, is present. The molecular mechanism for this adaptive phenomenon posed a thorny and intriguing problem that attracted the interest of two French scientists, Jacques Monod and Francois Jacob, working at the Institut Pasteur in Paris in the late 1940s. Relying on time-honored, classical techniques of genetically analyzing carefully selected mutants (molecular biology had not yet been invented), Jacob and Monod postulated (a) that a specific repressor molecule exists that binds near the beginning of the β-galactosidase gene at a specific site called the *operator* and that, by binding to the operator site on the DNA, it sterically prevents RNA polymerase from commencing the synthesis of β-gal messenger RNA, and (b) that lactose acts as an inducer which, by binding to the repressor molecule, prevents the repressor from binding to the operator. Thus, in the presence of lactose, the repressor protein is inactivated and the messenger RNA is made. Upon removal of lactose, the repressor regains its ability to bind to the operator DNA sequence thereby switching "off" the *lac* operon and the synthesis of β-galactosidase.

This elegant hypothesis, explaining the adaptive phenomenon in *E. coli,* became known as the *operon model* of gene regulation and earned Francois Jacob and Jacques Monod the Nobel Prize in Physiology or Medicine in 1965.[3,4]

Molecular Characteristics

The functional form of β-galactosidase is a tetramer of four identical subunits, each consisting of 1,023 amino acid residues (monomer molecular weight = 116,000 Da). Each monomer contains an active enzymatic site and they appear to be independently active. The tetramer (molecular weight = 465,412 Da) contains four catalytic sites that show no cooperativity or allosteric effectors.[5]

The enzyme has three activities that ultimately result in the complete breakdown of the disaccharide lactose into galactose plus glucose. First, β-galactosidase cleaves lactose into galactose plus glucose. Second, the enzyme acts as a transglycosylase, converting lactose into allolactose. Third, it hydrolyzes allolactose into galactose plus glucose. Historically, it has been a puzzle as to why the β-galactosidase protein is so large and why it needs to be a tetramer. The recent elucidation of this enzyme's multiple and sequential activities may help explain its structural complexity and large mass.[6]

Commercial Uses

In addition to its significance in the history of molecular biology, and the crucial role played in unraveling the nuances of gene regulation, β-galactosidase (lactase) has both medical and commercial applications.[7] Lactase may be used as a reagent for determining lactose levels in blood and other biological fluids. In addition, β-galactosidase has important applications in food processing. Of special interest is its use in the treatment of milk to meet the needs of a large percentage of the world's population afflicted with lactose intolerance. The enzyme has been formulated in a pill form; one such product is sold under the trade name Lactaid.™ It is also used in ice cream manufacture, preventing the "sandy" texture caused by lactose crystals.

Why β-galactosidase

This particular protein has a host of advantages to recommend it as the target product for our course including, (a) it is a very stable and well-characterized protein, (b) its enzymatic activity can be easily and accurately assayed, (c) it is unusually large and therefore amenable to purification in a *single* gel-filtration chromatography step, (d) it is a therapeutically useful protein that is used to treat people who suffer from lactose intolerance, and (e) it is widely used in the food processing industry.

Assay for β-galactosidase Activity

One advantage for choosing this particular enzyme as the target protein for this course is the fact that a well-established assay exists for β-galactosidase activity.[8] A task that an entry-level bioprocess techni-cian might be expected to carryout is to monitor a fermentor or bioreactor for product yield and chances are good that this task will involve an enzymatic assay. Throughout this course, students gain valuable practical experience performing enzyme assays as well as interpreting and plotting their results.

A simple assay for β-galactosidase was originally devised by Lederberg[8] and later formalized by Miller.[9] In order to assay enzyme levels, it is first necessary to permeabilize bacterial cell walls and membranes because β-galactosidase is an *intracellular* enzyme.

Briefly, small aliquots (0.1–0.5 mL) of an overnight culture are added to enzyme assay buffer (final volume = 1.0 mL) and exposed to chloroform and SDS. The cells are vigorously agitated followed by the addition of a 4% solution of ONPG (orthonitrophenyl-β-D-galactoside) and a second agitation step. Tubes are incubated at room temperature. ONPG is a chromogenic substrate of β-galactosidase that, when cleaved, produces an intense yellow color.[10] The greater the enzyme concentration the quicker the yellow color appears and the more intensely yellow the solution ultimately becomes over time. The reac-tion can be stopped by the addition of a 1.0 M sodium carbonate solution which raises the pH to the point where the enzyme is no longer active.

The Quantitation of β-galactosidase Activity

The intensity of the yellow color is quantified by determining its absorbance at a wave length of 420 nm in a spectrophotometer. The original cell density (OD_{600}), the volume of cells assayed, the absorbance value at 420 nm and the incubation time—post-ONPG addition—can be combined to determine the units of β-galactosidase activity according to the following formula[9,11]:

$$\frac{1,000 \times OD_{420}}{t \times V \times OD_{600}} = \text{UNITS of β-galactosidase activity}$$

where:
t = the time of ONPG reaction in minutes
V = volume of culture (in mL)
OD_{600} = cell density immediately prior to the assay

Despite the molecular elegance that *E. coli* manifests in its control and regulation of β-galactosidase synthesis, it normally produces very modest amounts of this enzyme.

So little, in fact, that Anfinsen and his colleagues needed to propagate *E. coli* in 300-L lots in order to accumulate sufficient protein for subsequent analytical studies.[12] The advent of recombinant DNA technology and gene cloning techniques has provided the means for scientists to construct custom-made bacterial strains possessing whatever trait or traits a researcher might find useful; *E. coli*-PAD is a prime example of the usefulness of recombinant DNA technology.

This project would not have been possible without two critical tools namely, (a) access to a genetically modified strain of *E. coli* and (b) the technique of gel-filtration chromatography. First, we will consider the genetically manipulated bacterial strain.

The Production Strain: *Escherichia coli*-PAD

Strain Construction

E. coli-PAD (MC4100/*ppiA'-lacZ*+) harbors a recombinant plasmid, pRS415, especially constructed to overexpress the enzyme β-galactosidase. In this strain, *lacZ* (the structural gene for β-galactosidase) is under the transcriptional control of the *ppiA* promoter, a promoter that is highly expressed in Luria-Bertani (LB) growth medium. Details of the construction of the *ppi'-lacZ* fusion, using plasmid pRS415, is beyond the scope of this discussion; however, the experimental details can be found in DiGiuseppe and Silhavy[13] and Simons et al.[14]

Strain Maintenance

E. coli-PAD is a thiamine auxotroph (Dr. Natividad Ruiz, personal communication) and must be grown in LB broth or agar. It will not thrive on general purpose growth media such as trypticase soy broth or nutrient broth. In addition, this strain must be grown in the presence of ampicillin at a concentration of 125 μg/mL. The antibiotic is necessary to provide positive selective pressure for plasmid pRS415. Furthermore, it is a good idea to propagate this strain on LB agar containing 20 μg/mL x-gal. X-gal (5-Bromo-4-chloro-3-indolyl-β-D-galactoside) is a chromogenic substrate of β-galactosidase that, when cleaved, produces a blue color.[10] X-gal is commonly used for detecting β-galactosidase made by recombinant vectors such as plasmid pRS415. Individual bacterial colonies that overproduce enzyme are various shades of blue and the bluest of these colonies were preferentially selected for subculturing and subsequent experiments.

Strain Performance

In order to determine the extent to which *E. coli*-PAD overexpresses β-galactosidase, equivalent numbers of permeabilized cells from an overnight culture of *E. coli*-PAD and a wild-type *E. coli* strain were assayed for enzyme activity. Because β-galactosidase is an inducible enzyme, its synthesis needed to be *induced* in the wild-type strain thus, IPTG (isopropyl-l-thio-β-D-galactoside) was added to the culture at a final concentration of 1.0 mM. IPTG, unlike lactose, is non-metabolizable and acts directly by inhibiting the *lac* repressor. It is the generally preferred inducer for molecular studies involving the regulation and control of the *lac* operon. By contrast, *E. coli*-PAD requires no induction because the production of β-galactosidase, driven by plasmid pRS415, is constitutive.

The results of three independent assays showed that the genetically engineered strain, *E. coli*-PAD, synthesized approximately 45-times more β-galactosidase than did its wild-type counterpart. By extrapolation, a 2.4-L production culture of *E. coli*-PAD would be roughly equivalent to 108 L of an induced, wild-type *E. coli* production culture. This impressive level of enzyme overproduction played a crucially important role in the successful purification of the target protein.

As mentioned earlier, the production of significant amounts of β-galactosidase would not have been possible without the overexpressing bacterial strain and the technique of gel-filtration chromatography. We will now discuss the chromatography component of the purification strategy.

Gel-Filtration Chromatography

Introduction

Among the chromatographic techniques commonly used for protein purification, gel-filtration chromatography (also called gel-permeation, molecular sieve, gel-exclusion, and size-exclusion chromatography) is unique in that fractionation is based on the relative size of the protein molecule. In contrast to other methods such as ion-exchange, affinity, or hydrophobic interaction chromatography, none of the proteins or polypeptides is *retained* by a gel-filtration column. Since no binding is required and harsh elution conditions can be avoided, gel-filtration chromatography rarely inactivates enzymes, and is frequently used as the first step in a protein purification scheme. The disadvantage of nonbinding, however, is the fact that this property may limit the resolution of this type of chromatography. For example, Stellwagen[15] has estimated that fewer than ten proteins can be resolved from one another in the eluent from any gel-filtration column.

Principles of the Technique

Gel-filtration chromatography is a method for separating proteins and polypeptides based on their size. The chromatographic matrix consists of porous beads, and the size of the bead pores defines the size of the macromolecules that may be fractionated. Beads of differing pore sizes are available, allowing proteins of different sizes or, more precisely, *hydrodynamic diameters*, to be effectively separated. For the sake of this discussion, hydrodynamic diameter refers to the diameter of the spherical volume created by a protein as it rapidly tumbles downward in a buffer solution.[15]

To start the process, a mixture of proteins or polypeptides is applied in a discrete volume or zone at the top of a gel-filtration column and allowed to percolate through the column matrix. Those proteins or polypeptides that are too large to enter the bead pores are *excluded*, and elute from the column first (i.e., the green circles shown in Figure 18.2). A useful way to grasp the principle of this separation technique is to think in terms of buffer *accessibility*. Since large molecules do not enter the beads they have a smaller volume of buffer *accessible* to them namely, only the buffer surrounding the beads. As a consequence, large macromolecules move through the column faster and emerge from the column first. Proteins whose hydrodynamic diameter is small relative to the average pore diameter of the beads will access *all* of the internal volume and are described as being *included* in the gel matrix and emerge from the column last (i.e., the orange symbols depicted in Figure 18.2). Proteins or polypeptides whose hydrodynamic diameter is comparable to the average pore diameters of the beads will access some but not all of the internal volume and are described as being *fractionally excluded* (i.e., the blue triangles shown in Figure 18.2). These macromolecules elute from our rather idealized column in a middle position with respect to the other two proteins.

A diagrammatic representation of the principle of gel-filtration chromatography is shown in Figure 18.3. Molecules of different sizes in the far left column are separated according to size during migration through the gel-filtration matrix depicted in the three columns to the right.

Table 18.1 provides a list of some of the commercially available gel-filtration matrices and their respective chemical compositions.

TABLE 18.1

Matrices Used in Gel-Filtration Chromatography[16]

Trade Name	Supplier	Chemistry
BioGel A	Bio-Rad	Cross-linked agarose
BioGel P	Bio-Rad	Cross-linked polyacrylamide
Sepharose	Pharmacia	Cross-linked agarose
Sephacryl HR	Pharmacia	Composite: polyacrylamide/dextran
Sephadex G	Pharmacia	Composite: polyacrylamide/dextran
Ultrogel AcA	IBF	Composite: agarose/polyacrylamide
Ultrogel A	IBF	Cross-linked agarose
Macsrosorb KA	—	Composite of porous kieselguhr and agarose

Equipment Needed for Gel-Filtration Chromatography

Figure 18.3 is a depiction of the equipment required for gel-filtration chromatography. The requirements are relatively modest, but laboratories with robust equipment budgets may opt for more sophisticated systems. For example, GE Healthcare sells a compact chromatography system called AKTA™ which is designed for one-step purification of proteins at a laboratory scale. In our hands, this unit provided significant advantages in terms of speed and sample resolution. The subsequent results shown and discussed in this document were derived from the AKTA™ system. By contrast, our earlier, test-of-concept experiments were done using a 30-year-old LKB Uvicord S UV monitor and an equally ancient LKB RediRac fraction collector and these instruments performed almost as well as the more automated and technically sophisticated chromatography system.

The heart of a gel-filtration chromatographic set-up is the column, which generally consists of a glass cylinder and a column support. Columns for gel filtration are generally long and narrow, but the diameter should be at least 1.0 cm, so that potential anomalous effects from the protein and buffer interactions with the column wall can be avoided. The column used in this experiment was 2.5 cm in diameter and 30 cm long. Normally, a chromatography column is equipped with a tight-fitting adaptor on the top to allow homogeneous and efficient delivery of sample and buffer matrix bed. A buffer reservoir in combination with a peristaltic pump is frequently employed in order to control the column flow rate with a high degree of precision.

An ultraviolet (UV) wavelength detector is generally included to monitor the absorbance of the eluting sample. The signal from the monitor can be sent to either a chart recorder or a personal computer for analysis. Finally, the eluting samples are directed to a preprogrammed fraction collector that sequentially collects aliquots of eluent according to either time or volume (Figure 18.3). All of this equipment can be purchased as individual components or as an integrated chromatography system such as the AKTA™ system previously discussed.

The Matrix

The column matrix for gel filtration must be chosen carefully to allow the best-resolved separation of the protein of interest from contaminating proteins or polypeptides. The matrix should be chosen so that the target protein's molecular weight falls near the middle of the matrix fractionation range or so that contaminating components are well resolved from the macromolecule of interest. Table 18.2 outlines the fractionation ranges of a variety of commercially available gel-filtration matrices:

TABLE 18.2

Fractionation Range of Various Gel-Filtration Matrices

Trade Name	Fractionation Range[a] (kDa)
BioGel P-6	1–6
BioGel P-60	3–60
BioGel P-100	5–100
Sephacryl 100-HR	1–100
Sephacryl 200-HR	5–250
Sephacryl 300-HR	10–1,500
Sephadex G-25	1–5
Sephadex G-50	1.5–30
Sephadex G-100	4–150
Sephadex G-200	5–600
Sepharose CL-6B	10–4,000

[a] The fractionation range defines the approximate protein and peptide molecular weights that can be separated with the matrix.[17]

If a particular column matrix is not supplied as a pre-swollen slurry, the dry powder needs to be swollen in the appropriate buffer. Swelling is generally carried out by gently swirling the matrix in the appropriate buffer at room temperature. The use of a magnetic stirrer is discouraged because this strategy causes some of the beads to break into "fine" particles which subsequently cause irregularities in column packing or may reduce the column flow rate. Instead, slow agitation on a rotary shaker or occasional gentle swirling of the matrix using a clean glass rod is preferred. In addition, de-gassing of the matrix is strongly suggested in order to reduce the likelihood that air bubbles will form in the column.

The Potential Shortcomings of the Gel-Filtration Technique

The chief limitations of gel-filtration chromatography are that the separation may be slow and that the resolution of the emerging peaks is limited. The relatively low resolution occurs because none of the proteins or polypeptides is retained by the column during chromatography and because nonideal flow occurs around the beads.[17] The speed of sample elution is limited primarily by the requirement for a long, narrow column in order to permit sufficient component separation. This procedure may be accelerated by the use of matrices allowing faster flow rates and/or the use of pumps or high-pressure chromatography equipment, assuming the matrix in question is able to tolerate the additional pressure.

A further disadvantage involves the fact that size-exclusion columns are less forgiving compared with other types of chromatography. Gel-filtration columns must be poured and monitored with great care and attention to detail. For example, after packing a gel-filtration column, a visual inspection for air bubbles is necessary. Other things that can go wrong are outcomes such as matrix compaction and/or channeling. Compacting can generally be avoided by pouring the entire pre-equilibrated matrix slurry in a single step rather than incrementally. Vendors of chromatographic resins usually will provide helpful information to investigators regarding questions and problem-solving issues.

Production of β-galactosidase

Cell Growth

Only 2.4 L of an overnight culture of *E. coli*-PAD were required for the successful negotiation of this experiment. As shown in Figure 18.1, one has the option of growing the production strain in either a small bench-top fermentor (we have used a New Brunswick Scientific BioFlo-110 Benchtop Fermentor/Bioreactor System with a 3-L capacity) or in individual Erlenmeyer flasks. Laboratories with limited equipment budgets may choose the latter option without compromising their results. We routinely used individual 1-L Erlenmeyer flasks, each containing 600 mL of culture. In either case, cultures are grown overnight, with agitation, at 35°C in LB broth supplemented with 125 µg/mL ampicillin.

Cell Harvesting

After 18 h of growth, the culture was harvested by centrifugation. We used a Sorvall Super T-21 refrigerated super-speed centrifuge, an SL-250T fixed angle rotor and 250-mL capacity centrifuge bottles. Cell pellets were washed with an appropriate isotonic buffer, containing magnesium ions[18] and the final cell suspension was recentrifuged in a single pre-weighed bottle. The wet weight of the pellet was determined and the pellet stored at −20°C until further use. Generally, 2.4 L of an 18-h culture yielded 5–5.5 g of wet weight cells.

Cell Disruption

Cell disruption is a neglected area of bioprocessing, as there has been relatively little significant innovation or progress over the last several decades.[7] Cell disruption can be achieved both by *mechanical* (e.g., French press, high-speed ball mills, or sonication) and by *nonmechanical* means (e.g., simple treatment with alkali or detergents such as sodium dodecyl sulfate or Triton X-100).

Because β-galactosidase is an *intracellular* enzyme, we needed to disrupt the *E. coli* cell wall in order to release the target protein. Ideally, one would prefer to use a nonabrasive cell-disruption method in order to minimize or avoid the destruction of the target protein. However, the breaching of the cell walls and outer envelopes of gram-negative bacteria can pose thorny problems. In the first place, the liberation of large amounts of cellular DNA can increase the viscosity of the lysate to the point where it adversely affects the optimal flow through chromatography resins. As a consequence, a nucleic acid precipitation step or the addition of a nuclease during the cell-disruption process is usually recommended. Furthermore, target proteins released from cells are often subjected to degradation by cellular proteases and other hydrolytic enzymes. This adverse outcome can be minimized by the addition of enzyme inhibitors or by employing especially mutated host strains selected for reduced levels of proteases.

We used a commercially available protein extraction system called BugBuster™ supplied by Novagen Inc. (La Jolla, CA) to disrupt large numbers of *E. coli*-PAD cells. This two-component cell-lysis system consists of a protein extraction reagent—a proprietary nonionic detergent—plus a nuclease that Novagen calls Benzonase Nuclease.™ According to the manufacturer, this lysis cocktail is especially formulated to gently disrupt the cell wall of *E. coli*, resulting in the liberation of all soluble proteins with a minimum of protein denaturation.

Briefly, a 5.0 g (wet weight) cell pellet of *E. coli*-PAD was suspended in 25 mL of BugBuster™ extraction reagent followed immediately by the addition of Benzonase™ followed by the addition of phenylmethylsulfonyl fluoride, a potent protease inhibitor. The resultant cell suspension was incubated at room temperature for 20 min with gentle shaking. After incubation, the lysed cell suspension was centrifuged in order to remove cell debris. The resultant supernatant, referred to as the "total cell protein extract," was decanted into a clean tube and refrigerated.

Protein Concentration and Dialysis

A commonly employed first step in protein concentration is ammonium sulfate $(NH_4)_2SO_4$ precipitation. This classic technique exploits the fact that the solubility of most proteins is lowered at high salt concentrations. As the salt concentration is increased, a point is reached where the protein comes out of solution and precipitates.

The "total cell protein extract" was adjusted to a final concentration of 60% ammonium sulfate by the addition of a supersaturated solution of this salt. Following a short period of stirring at room temperature, the *cloudy* solution (cloudy due to precipitated protein) was refrigerated overnight. The resultant precipitate was pelleted by centrifugation and gently resuspended in a small volume of β-galactosidase assay buffer. This assay buffer contains a final concentration of 0.4 mM dithiothreitol (DTT). The reducing agent, DTT, is necessary to disrupt disulfide bonds, thereby disaggregating β-galactosidase into its constituent, enzymatically active monomers. The tetrameric form of this large enzyme (465,412 Da) would be excluded from conventional polyacrylamide gels. The suspension was exhaustively dialyzed against multiple exchanges of assay buffer and the resultant "mud"-colored suspension was transferred to a clean tube or small bottle and refrigerated until further use.

Enzyme Purification Using Gel-Filtration Chromatography

General Considerations

Chromatography is the technique of choice for high-resolution purification. These methods, normally involving glass columns containing chromatographic media, are universally used for the concentration and purification of protein preparations. In choosing the appropriate chromatographic technique a number of considerations must be taken into account. For protein products these factors include molecular mass, isoelectric point, hydrophobicity, and inherent biological affinities. Each of these properties can be usefully exploited by specific chromatographic methods that may be scaled-up for use in an industrial unit-process context.

Choice of Matrix

As discussed earlier, one of the chief limitations of gel-filtration chromatography is that the separation may be slow and that the resolution of the emerging peaks is limited.

Resolution is limited because proteins do *not bind* to the matrix. As a consequence, the column matrix for gel filtration must be chosen with great care to insure the best-resolved separation of the target macromolecule from contaminants. The matrix should be chosen so that the molecular weight of the target protein falls near the middle of the matrix fractionation range. The fractionation range defines the approximate protein or peptide molecular weights that can be separated with that particular chromatography medium. Tables 18.1 and 18.2 provide information pertinent to the selection of column media.

Sephacryl-HR Gel-Filtration Matrices

We chose a Sephacryl HR (high resolution) medium for this experiment. As shown in Table 18.1, this particular gel-filtration matrix is a cross-linked copolymer of allyl dextran and N,N-methylenebisacrylamide. According to Pharmacia, the narrow particle size distribution of this medium, together with its steep selectivity curve, make Sephacryl HR resolution matrices particularly useful for routine separations, especially when dealing with relatively large amounts of crude sample.

We specifically chose Sephacryl 300-HR for two reasons. First, the molecular weight of the β-galactosidase monomer (116,000 Da) fell within the fractionation range of this matrix (10–1,500 kDa). The second reason was that Craven et al.[12] had reported the efficient purification of *E. coli* β-galactosidase using a Sephadex G-200 column; the fractionation range for Sephadex G-200 is close to that of Sephacryl 300-HR (Table 18.2).

The large size of our target protein was advantageous with respect to its ultimate purification. Because of the relatively low resolution power of gel-filtration chromatography, it is usually relegated to a later stage in the purification process after the total number of proteins has been narrowed down to a manageable few by ion-exchange and/or affinity chromatography. Gel-filtration chromatography, as a protein purification technique, is generally considered to be most effective when the desired protein target has a molecular weight either considerably larger or smaller than that of the majority of the proteins in a mixture. Because the 116,000 molecular weight β-galactosidase monomer is relatively large compared to the majority of other proteins synthesized by *E. coli*, we reasoned that the goal of purifying it in a single gel-filtration step was very likely.

Column Preparation and Sample Loading

A Kontes glass chromatography column (30 × 2.5 cm) was packed to a height of 28 cm with buffer-equilibrated Sephacryl 300-HR beads. The *void volume* (the volume of buffer *external* to the beads) of the column was determined by allowing a 0.2% blue dextran solution to percolate through the column and elute. The void volume of this column was calculated to be approximately 60 mL. This is a very useful value to determine because our exceptionally large target protein would be expected to filter near the front in a Sephacryl HR-300 gel-filtration column.[12]

A cautionary technical note: Our experimental experience with Sephacryl 300-HR beads packed to a height of 28 centimeters has convinced us that one should pack the Kontes glass chromatography column *immediately prior* to loading the "total cell protein extract." In our hands, using "older" Sephacryl 300-HR columns has occasionally resulted in unsatisfactory elution profiles (Figure 18.4 shows an acceptable elution pattern). In several cases, "total cell protein extracts" have essentially "stalled" in mid-column and aborted the considerable previous efforts of the particular experiment. To be confident of satisfactory resolution patterns one should always use freshly poured (and pampered) Sephacryl 300-HR columns.

The packed column was secured into the AKTA™ chromatographic instrument. Approximately 3.0 mL of the dialyzed "total cell protein extract" was carefully layered onto the top of the column. The suspension was allowed to percolate into the beads, followed by the addition of 3–4 mL of assay buffer that was also allowed to percolate into the beads before the actual fractionation was initiated.

The system was sealed and the fractionation begun. Buffer was introduced into the column throughout the run by way of the instrument's built-in peristaltic pump. The AKTA™ instrument was programmed to deliver a flow rate of 1.0 mL/min and to collect the column eluent in 4.0 mL aliquots. The column was allowed to run until approximately 2-times the void volume (around 120 mL) had eluted. At the end of the run, the fraction tubes were collected and stored at refrigerator temperature until needed for further analysis.

Assaying Column Fractions for Enzyme Activity

The goal of this segment of the experiment was to identify the fraction tubes that contained *pure* β-galactosidase—free from contaminating proteins or polypeptides. To this end, the contents of selected column fraction tubes were assayed for enzyme activity employing the standard ONPG assay methodology previously described in detail.

Based upon the size of the β-galactosidase monomer (our target protein), it should elute close to the leading edge of the void volume. Given that the void volume was around 60 mL and that the eluent was collected in 4.0 mL fractions, we anticipated that we would detect β-galactosidase activity in the vicinity of fraction #15, (15×4.0 mL=60 mL). Column fractions #1 through #28 were assayed for enzyme activity. It should be noted that in these particular enzyme assays, neither chloroform nor SDS was needed because we were dealing, in this case, with *cell-free* β-galactosidase—obviating any requirement to permeabilize bacterial cell walls. The 420 nm absorbance values were determined using a spectrophotometer, whereas the 280 nm absorbance values (the total protein profile) were measured and recorded automatically by the AKTA™ instrument.

The data generated by this analysis are shown in Figure 18.4. Clearly, the main peak of enzymatic activity emerged from the column shortly after the void volume front. Our prediction as to when the target protein would emerge was realized, in that β-galactosidase activity (black squares) began to appear in column fraction #14 and persisted to column fraction #22. The bulk of the protein in the "total cell protein extract" (open squares) eluted from the column well after the enzyme activity peak. Interestingly, a large protein(s) appeared to elute *before* the β-galactosidase monomer. This apparent "retention" of the 116,000 Da β-galactosidase monomer in a gel-filtration column, was similarly observed and reported, over 50 years ago, in Anfinsen's laboratory.[12] These authors hypothesized that "this material may represent either a highly polymerized form of the protein or a fraction tightly bound to the nucleic acid components of the mixture." We made no attempt to investigate the nature of this phenomenon but, suffice it to say, the presence of this putative protein polymer or protein complex had no adverse effect on the purification of our target protein.

Fractionating the Enzyme Activity Peak

The experience gained from preliminary test-of-concept experiments showed that "pure" β-galactosidase monomer is confined to only one or two column fractions and those fractions resided exclusively within the *leading* edge of the enzyme activity peak. Based upon this knowledge, we subdivided the enzyme activity peak into three component parts representing the *leading edge* of the activity peak, the *apex* of the activity peak, and the *trailing edge* of the activity peak. Referring to the profile shown in Figure 18.4, the *leading edge* segment would include column fraction #15 through fraction #17; the *apex* of the peak would consist of column fractions #18 and #19 and the *trailing edge* would include column fractions #20 through #22.

Concentration of Selected Column Fractions

Previous experience had also shown us that samples of eluent originating directly from the gel-filtration column contained an insufficient concentration of protein to make the SDS-polyacrylamide gel electrophoresis analysis worthwhile. As a consequence, the pooled column fractions representing the *leading edge,* the *apex,* and the *trailing edge* of the enzyme activity peak were concentrated.

This was accomplished by transferring the individual pooled column fractions into dialysis bags, sealing the bags and covering them—both top and bottom—with Ficoll-400™ powder in a glass dish. Ficoll-400™ is a nonionic synthetic polymer of sucrose and is a registered trademark of Amersham Pharmacia Biotech.

The bags were incubated at room temperature and closely observed until the volumes had decreased by a predetermined amount (generally three- to fourfold). Following volume reduction, protein values for each sample were determined using the Lowry technique. If the protein concentration of the samples was found to be in the range of 300–450 µg/mL, it could be safely assumed that sample loading volumes of 5–8 µL per lane would be sufficient to produce a satisfactory gel. Figure 18.5 is an example of such a gel.

Protein Analysis by Polyacrylamide Gel Electrophoresis

The importance of the technique of SDS-polyacrylamide gel electrophoresis to monitor the step-wise progress throughout a protein purification scheme cannot be overestimated. Data derived from this important analytical tool directly informs an investigator whether he or she has purified their target protein to homogeneity—free from contaminating proteins and polypeptides.

In the interest of full disclosure, it needs to be noted that the gel photograph shown in Figure 18.5 was *not* generated from the enzyme activity peak shown in Figure 18.4. Instead, it originated from a previous iteration of this course; one in which the gel-filtration patterns of β-galactosidase activity and total protein content were very similar to the profile seen in Figure 18.4. It is because of this "disconnect" that lanes in the SDS-polyacrylamide gel shown in Figure 18.5 were labeled: *leading edge, apex of peak,* and *trailing edge* rather than assigning specific lanes of the gel the corresponding column fraction number(s) as would normally be the case.

The gel electrophoresis system we chose was the NuPAGE Novex Bis-Tris Gel System™ supplied by Invitrogen Corporation (Grand Island, NY). This multicomponent electrophoresis system comes with premixed sample buffer, sample reducing agent, gel running buffer (MOPS), preformed and ready-to-use 4%–12% Bis-Tris Gels, as well as a compact electrophoresis apparatus the manufacturer has dubbed the XCell SureLock Mini-Cell.™

The following samples were loaded onto a Bis-Tris 4%–12% gradient gel: a sample of the "total cell protein extract" (5.1 µg total protein), a sample of the *leading edge* segment of the enzyme activity peak (2.2 µg total protein), a sample of the *apex* of the enzyme activity peak (2.3 µg total protein), a sample of the *trailing edge* segment of the enzyme activity peak (1.9 µg total protein), and an authentic *E. coli* β-galactosidase standard (1.5 µg of total protein). The "total cell protein extract" sample was identical to the material originally loaded onto the chromatography column. It was included as a "baseline" indicator against which to judge the overall ability of the gel-filtration column to separate our target protein away from the host of contaminating proteins and polypeptides present in the original crude *E. coli* cell extract.

Samples were electrophoresed at 200 volts until the tracking dye reached the bottom of the gel; this generally took 50–65 min. The gel was removed from the Mini-Cell apparatus and stained for approximately 30 min in a bath of Coomassie blue protein stain. The gel was de-stained overnight in a methanol/acetic acid/water solution with frequent exchanges of de-staining solution. Following de-staining, the gel was photographed and analyzed. Figure 18.5 is a photograph of a typical gel. An analysis of this gel revealed the following:

- The lane containing the "total cell protein extract," derived from *E. coli*-PAD, contains 25–35 individual protein or polypeptide bands. The largest protein(s) visible in the "total cell protein extract" lane is slightly larger than 94 kDa according to the molecular weight protein markers.
- The largest protein(s) synthesized by *E. coli*-PAD appears to co-migrate with the sample of authentic β-galactosidase monomer standard.

- The *leading edge* segment of the enzyme activity peak contains *pure* β-galactosidase based on the observation that the only protein band visible in that lane co-migrates with authentic β-galactosidase monomer standard.
- The *apex* of the enzyme activity peak contains a significant amount of β-galactosidase. In addition, however, there also is a relatively minor amount of a contaminating protein or polypeptide with a molecular weight around 70 kDa.
- By contrast, the *trailing edge* segment of the enzyme activity peak contains only a trace amount of β-galactosidase. Most of the protein in the concentrated *trailing edge* sample contains two protein species; one is the 70 kDa protein seen in the *apex* sample whereas the second contaminating protein species has a molecular weight of around 22 kDa.

In conclusion, SDS-polyacrylamide gel electrophoretic analysis of selected fractions eluting from a Sephadex 300-HR gel-filtration column revealed that "pure" β-galactosidase monomer resided exclusively in the *leading edge* of the enzyme activity profile; 90%–95% "pure" target protein could be found at the *apex* of the enzyme activity curve whereas the β-galactosidase monomer protein virtually disappeared in the *trailing edge* of the curve. This relatively "sharp" demarcation of protein species, of varying molecular weights, was a testimony as to how effectively our *single* gel-filtration column performed its role as a protein purification tool within the experimental conditions outlined in this document.

Summary

The state of North Carolina has established a workforce training consortium aimed at providing biopharmaceutical and biotechnology-related education for new employees, incumbent workers, and individuals interested in a new career or a career change involving some aspect of biomanufacturing. An important part of this educational effort is the Capstone Learning Center, temporarily situated on the Western Campus of Wake Technical Community College. One of the courses that the Capstone Center provides is a comprehensive, hands-on bioprocessing course. During this 5-day course, students are exposed to the unit processes of a typical biomanufacturing operation, including bioreactor operation and control, protein detection and monitoring, cell harvesting, cell-disruption, protein concentration and dialysis, protein purification using gel-filtration chromatography, and protein analysis using the technique of SDS-polyacrylamide gel electrophoresis. Starting with 2.4 L of production culture, we are able to purify our target protein, *Escherichia coli* β-galactosidase, to 99.5% homogeneity in the course of four and one-half days. This was possible for two reasons: (a) we used a strain of *Escherichia coli* genetically engineered to significantly overexpress β-galactosidase compared to a normal wild-type isolate and (b) the comparatively large size of our target protein made it amenable to purification using a single gel-filtration chromatography column.

Acknowledgments

The experiments discussed in this chapter would not have been possible without the generosity and assistance of Dr. Steve Short and Leslie Walton—former colleagues of mine at the Burroughs Wellcome Co. (aka GlaxoSmithKline). Their gifts of incubators, UV monitor, fraction collector, and a variety of reagents and consumables were crucial elements in the developmental phase of this course. In addition, I am deeply indebted to Drs. Thomas Silhavy and Natividad Ruiz of the Department of Molecular Biology, Princeton University for allowing us to use their β-galactosidase overproducing strain of *Escherichia coli*. Without their strain, this course would have remained an unrealized idea. I wish to acknowledge the support, both tangible and intangible, of my colleagues at the BioNetwork Capstone Learning Center namely, Leonard Amico, Dr. Michael Morgan, Dr. Lin Wu and David Yarley. I greatly benefited from numerous discussions with Mike Morgan regarding the science involved in this course and the document itself greatly benefited from Len Amico's artful design skills which can be seen in Figures 18.1–18.3.

REFERENCES

1. Conway, P. 2004. Charting employment loss in North Carolina textiles. Data from U. S. Bureau of Labor Statistics, (Jan. 14, 2004).
2. Wallenfels, K. and Weil, R. 1972. β-galactosidase In: *The Enzymes* (3rd Edition), vol. 7, Boyer, P. D. (editor), Academic Press, New York. pp. 617–663.
3. Pardee, A., Jacob, F., and Monod, J. 1959. The genetic control and cytoplasmic expression of "inducibility" in the synthesis of β-galactosidase by *E. coli. J. Mol. Biol.*, 1: pp. 165–178.
4. Jacob, F. and Monod, J. 1961. Genetic regulatory mechanisms in the synthesis of proteins. *J. Mol. Biol.*, 3: pp. 318–356.
5. Juers, D., Jacobson, R., Wigley, D. et al. 2000. High resolution refinement of β-galactosidase in a new crystal form reveals multiple metal-binding sites and provides a structural basis for α-complementation. *Protein Sci.*, 9: pp. 1685–1699.
6. Juers, D., Heightman, T., Vasella, A. et al. 2001. A structural view of the action of *Escherichia coli* (*lacZ*) β-galactosidase. *Biochemistry*, 40: pp. 14781–14794.
7. Waites, M., Morgan, N., Rockey, J., and Higton, G. (editors), 2001. *Industrial Microbiology: An Introduction*, Blackwell Science Publ., Oxford, UK. p. 134.
8. Lederberg, J. 1950. The β-D-galactosidase of *Escherichia coli*, strain K-12. *J. Bacteriol.*, 60: pp. 381–392.
9. Miller, J. H. 1992. *A Short Course in Bacterial Genetics*, Cold Spring Harbor Laboratory Press, New York. pp. 71–74.
10. Ausubel, F. M., Brent, R., Kingston, R. E., et al. (editors), 1992. *Short Protocols in Molecular Biology* (2nd Edition), John Wiley and Sons, Inc., New York. pp. 1–10.
11. Becker, J., Caldwell, G., and Zachgo, E. 1996. *Biotechnology: A Laboratory Course* (2nd Edition), Academic Press, San Diego, CA. pp. 125–141.
12. Craven, G., Steers, E., and Anfinsen, C. 1965. Purification, composition, and molecular weight of the β-galactosidase of *Escherichia coli* K-12. *J. Biol. Chem.*, 240: pp. 2468–2476.
13. DiGiuseppe, P. and Silhavy, T. 2003. Signal detection and target gene induction by the CpxRA two-component system. *J. Bacteriol.*, 185: pp. 2432–2440.
14. Simons, R., Houman, F., and Kleckner, N. 1987. Improved single and multicopy *lac*-based cloning vectors for protein and operon fusions. *Gene*, 53: pp. 85–96.
15. Stellwagen, E. 1990. Gel filtration. In: *Methods in Enzymology*, vol. 182, Academic Press, New York, pp. 317–328.
16. Ratledge, C. and Kristiansen, B. (editors), 2001. *Basic Biotechnology* (2nd Edition), Cambridge University Press, Cambridge, UK, p. 205.
17. Bollag, D. 1994. Gel-filtration chromatography. In: *Methods in Molecular Biology*, vol. 36, Dunn, B. and Pennington, M. (editors), Humana Press, Totowa, NJ, pp. 1–9.
18. Steers, E., Cuatrecasas, P., and Pollard, H. 1971. The purification of β-galactosidase from *Escherichia coli* by affinity chromatography. *J. Biol. Chem.*, 246: pp. 196–200.

19

Membrane Chromatography

Sherri Dolan
Sartorius Stedim North America, Inc.

Susan Martin
Sartorius Stedim North America, Inc.

CONTENTS

Introduction

Due to the process optimization of cell culture, an increase in titers from upstream manufacturing is placing a demand on the downstream purification area to become more efficient at processing these high-titer products (1).

Around 1997, a relatively new method of chromatography was introduced to the market with the potential to overcome the limitations of packed bead columns. Membrane chromatography is composed of a "filter-like" backbone, such as cellulose acetate, containing pore sizes larger than conventional chromatography resins. The pore size of these membranes may be 3–5, 0.8, or 0.4 µm in size which allow large molecules to fully penetrate the stationary phase and interact with the ligands.

Membrane chromatography devices offer many advantages over conventional chromatography in terms of protein purification. Some of these advantages include a higher binding capacity for large molecules such as DNA and viruses, >10-fold faster flow rates, and a flexible single-use disposable solution which does not require reuse validation. These qualities make membrane adsorbers a perfect fit for flow-through chromatography operations.

In flow-through chromatography operations, the product of interest is loaded onto the chromatography device under conditions in which the unwanted contaminants/impurities will bind to the ligands. This is a very common operation in biopharmaceutical manufacturing using both resins and membranes and both types of chromatography will result in acceptable results. However, the membrane has an advantage over the resin for this application for many reasons. The first, as mentioned, is that the binding capacity of membranes for large molecules is much higher in membranes >10 times higher. Therefore, a much smaller membrane may be able to replace a large resin-based chromatography column. An example is shown here where a 5 L membrane replaced a 200 L column (ImClone reference). Next, since membrane chromatography is based on a more open stationary phase, higher flow rates (>10-fold), combined with lower operational pressures result in >4× faster processing times. By decreasing the process time 4×, there will be more time to reuse the membrane in cycles; therefore, productivity is increased.

An important benefit of membrane chromatography often overlooked is the reduced usage of buffer. Using membranes can save up to 95% in buffer usage (1) which along with the cost savings of the buffer, results in the ability to process in a smaller space due to not needing large amounts of buffers (and tanks) in the production suite.

In summary, membrane chromatography benefits over columns (2,3)

- Reduce 200 L column to 5 L membrane module
- Tenfold higher volumetric flow rate
- Decrease process time by >4×
- Uses 95% less buffer
- Single use: no reuse validation necessary
- Comparable virus clearance when compared to resin (assuming loading conditions are properly determined) (4)

Principles and Basic Concepts

Modern chromatography has been under development and used since the 1940s. Traditionally, this technology makes use of columns composed of innumerous bead-like porous resins as a sorbent (the beads are approximately 100 μm in diameter). It is necessary to mention that the beads have ligands attached to their surface. Ligands are molecules that possess a region that has a specific charge or affinity. The bulk of a resin's surface and inner pores are covered with ligands. This results in high binding potential and will be discussed in detail below. The spherical beads are suspended in a solution that allows them to pour more easily into columns. The solution (often referred to as a slurry) is allowed to settle and is packed via hydrostatic pressure. Since the beads are semirigid, they will not fully compress under controlled optimum pressure. This creates interstitial spaces between the beads. The entire mass of resin within a column is commonly called a resin bed, bed volume, or stationary phase. Columns have an inlet on the top and an outlet at the bottom. This allows for liquid, or a mobile phase, to pass through the interstices within the resin bed. The mobile phase is typically a complex mixture and concentration of molecules, including buffers, salts, proteins, and other biomolecular species. Each species of molecule has a specific charged group that can be bound by an oppositely charged ligand or moiety (region) that can be bound by affinity ligand.

Ion-exchange (IEX) chromatography is characterized by using positively or negatively charged ligands to bind molecules within the mobile phase as they pass through the chromatography device. There are two general subsets within IEX. They are cation-exchange (CEX) chromatography and anion-exchange (AEX) chromatography. These are named for the types of charged molecules they bind to under optimum conditions. CEX utilizes resins (or other stationary phase) with negatively charged ligands to bind positively charged molecules (cations). AEX utilizes resins (or other stationary phase) with positively charged ligands to bind negatively charged molecules (anions).

In either case CEX or AEX devices are extremely useful as purification devices. Consider a mobile phase that is a complex mixture of thousands, tens of thousands, or even millions of molecules. Only one species of these molecules in the mobile phase is a desired product or target that must be purified from the others. Usually, the target molecule is well characterized and conditions in the mobile phase can be adjusted to allow the target to bind to the stationary phase of a chromatography device and then be eluted under other conditions. However, under the same conditions, contaminant molecules are allowed to flow through and are collected as waste. After loading the product, the chromatography device is washed under equilibration conditions. The first wash solution flushes away any contaminants that remain within but not bound to the stationary phase. The wash is collected as waste. A series of salt- or pH-adjusted washes may ensue. This will strip off or elute any contaminants that are loosely associated with the ligands. However, these washes do not strip off the product. This action further removes contaminant molecules from the target product which remains bound on the stationary phase. At this point, most or all of the contaminants that have a weaker attraction to the charged ligands have been removed. However, the product molecule and contaminants that have a stronger attraction to the ligands are still bound to the stationary phase. Finally, an elution condition mobile phase is passed through the chromatography device. The elution solute has a well-characterized salt/pH and it is optimized to strip off the target product but not the contaminants that remain on the stationary phase. This elution is collected as a separate fraction and contains highly purified target molecules. The more tightly bound extant contaminants are often removed by a high salt strip and collected as waste.

What was just described above was an example of positive capture. There is a second mode of IEX that is complementary to positive capture and is rightly named, negative capture. This mode of chromatography is simpler to operate but just as powerful as its counterpart. During negative capture, target product flows through the chromatography device as contaminants bind. Typically, this type of chromatography takes place when product is in high concentration; contaminants are in very low concentration and of only a few species. This allows for high polishing power near the end of a series of chromatography devices. This does not exclude the possibility of using negative capture with complex mobile phases. In fact negative capture is used for these applications too, and is just as powerful.

Affinity chromatography is defined by using ligands that have a specific affinity for specific moieties of particular molecules. Immobilized Protein A is the most common use of affinity chromatography and is an excellent example of how this mode of chromatography operates. Protein A is a ligand that has a strong affinity for the fragment crystallizable region (Fc region) of antibodies. Under neutral pH conditions, the Fc regions of antibodies bind to Protein A. The Fc region will disassociate with Protein A when conditions in the mobile phase are changed to acidic (pH 2–4). This is a powerful purification tool when highly purified antibodies are desired and the mobile medium (process feed stream) is a complex mixture of contaminant molecules and target antibody. Contaminants flow through and antibodies bind to Protein A, as the mobile phase passes through the chromatography device. Once the entirety of antibody is bound, it can be stripped off or eluted as a separate fraction. The result is a process intermediate containing high purity antibody.

Membrane chromatography operates under similar principles that define and characterize resin-based chromatography. The major difference is that membrane chromatography has a stationary phase that is composed of flat "filter like" membranes and resin-based chromatography has a stationary phase that is composed of spherical beads (Figure 19.1). These beads are not solid; they have pores or crevices on the outermost surface. These openings on the outer surface lead to lumens, or channels, within the spherical bead. About 90% of the bead's available binding sites are within these lumens. The remainder of available binding sites (10%) is situated on the outermost surface of the bead. Chromatography resins are available in a variety of spherical diameters and pore sizes. The use of a specific resin diameter and pores size varies to suit the intended application. Both membrane- and resin-based chromatography platforms

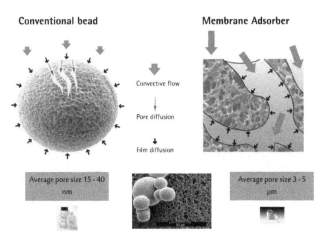

FIGURE 19.1 Diffusion-limited resins versus convection-limited membranes.

require ligands to bind either process impurities, target product, or both. These ligands are attached to the outermost layer, or throughout the layer, of the membrane if it is a membrane chromatography device; or the ligands are attached to the outermost layer of a spherical resin and upon the outermost layer present within a resin's lumens. Membrane chromatography offers a variety of ligand types (Table 19.1). Within this platform, ion-exchange ligands are by far the most widely used. However, affinity ligands are also available for use with membrane chromatography devices.

Membrane chromatography is differentiated from conventional chromatography by the configuration of its stationary phase. This difference dramatically affects how each platform is configured into a usable format. Membrane chromatography devices are available in disc, capsule, or cartridge format. These devices are static with regard to bed volume and frontal surface area (FSA). However, there are a variety of small devices (0.08–10 mL) that can be used for small-scale evaluations, mid-sized devices (10–1,000 mL) for pilot scale, and larger devices (1,000–5,000 mL) for process scale (Figure 19.2). Devices can operate in parallel or series to increase bed volume and overall binding capacity (5). Final membrane configuration in cartridges and capsules can be in "layered spiral wound" or "pleated layer" format—which varies from vendor to vendor. The raw shape of both the spiral wound and pleated format is a hollow cylinder that can be referred to as a module. Modules are welded into a plastic housing in a fashion that is similar to normal flow filters. The top of the "layered spiral wound" or "pleated layer" format is sealed closed. The module bottom is welded to a hollow disc or plate. The disc has a greater diameter than the "layered spiral wound" or "pleated layer" devices, and this provides a bottom plate ledge. A dome-like housing is placed over the module and is welded to the bottom plate ledge. The above description constitutes a disposable capsule design. This capsule design size ceases at 30 in. elements. Larger devices have a central core that is located within the "layered spiral wound" or "pleated layer" device. This core occupies a void volume and is necessary for high-resolution elution peaks, baseline separation, and low elution volumes. In both instances, feed stream enters at the top of the housing and is typically driven by a peristaltic pump. This allows the mobile phase to pass through the module from the outside toward the inside. Once the mobile medium has passed through the membrane it occupies the void volume within the cylinder. Continuous pressure from convective flow forces the mobile phase out through the opening in the bottom center of the housing. At this point, the mobile medium has exited the capsule.

TABLE 19.1

Ligands Available in Membrane Chromatography Format

Ion Exchange	
Anion-Exchange Chemistries	
Quaternary ammonium (Q)	Strong basic
Diethylamine (D)	Weak basic
Polyethyleneimine (Mustang® E®)	
Salt-tolerant primary amine (STIC)	Weak basic
Cation-Exchange Chemistries	
Sulfonic acid (S)	Strong acidic
Carboxylic acid (C)	Weak acidic
Mixed-Mode Cation Exchange: Salt-tolerant cation-exchange membrane augmented with HIC groups	
Affinity	
Protein A	
p-Aminobenzamidine pABA (pABA)	
Iminodiacetic acid (IDA)	
Cibacron blue	
Heparin	
Streptavidin	
Epoxy and aldehyde activated	

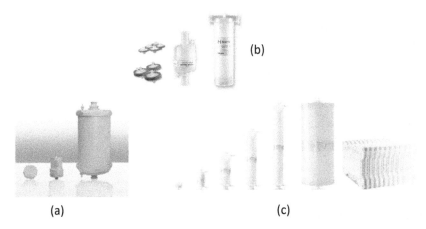

FIGURE 19.2 (a) 5 mL, 140 mL, and 5 L Mustang capsules, (b) 0.8, 15, 115, and 460 mL Natrix capsules, and (c) 1, 75, 200, 400 and 600, 2,500 and 800 mL Sartobind capsules.

Not unlike conventional chromatography, membrane chromatography devices have a FSA, bed height, and bed volume. These values can be attained from the supplier. Determination of these values is a matter of simple geometry and can be visualized in Figure 19.3.

As stated before, the raw shape of a membrane chromatography device is often a hollow cylinder. Membrane volume (MV) is determined by first calculating the total volume of the entire cylinder (including the hollow core). Then subtract the volume of the inner core from the total volume.

$$MV = V_{c1} - V_{c2}$$

$$v_{c1\&2} = \pi \times r^2 \times h$$

(19.1)

V_{c1} is the volume of the entire cylinder
V_{c2} is the volume of the inner core.

FSA* is determined by the following equation:

$$FSA = 2 \times \pi \times r \times h$$

(19.2)

Anatomy of a membrane chromatography device

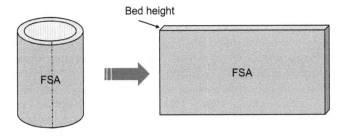

FIGURE 19.3 Cylinder on left represents raw shape of membrane. FSA and bed height are seen when cylinder is cut and laid flat.

---

* Inner surface area is less than FSA. This means the linear velocities are a fraction greater at the innermost portion of the membrane chromatography device. However, as will be discussed later, dynamic binding capacity is not affected.

Linear velocity, membrane residence time, and volume/min can be calculated if the aforementioned dimensions are known. The calculations are as follows:

Linear velocity:

$$\text{cm/h} = [(n)(60 \text{ min/h})]/\text{FSA} \tag{19.3}$$

n is nominal flow rate (mL/min)

FSA is frontal surface area (cm^2)

Residence time:

$$t_r = \left[(60)(\text{FSA})(h)\right]/n \tag{19.4}$$

FSA is frontal surface area (cm^2)

n is nominal flow rate (mL/min)

h is membrane height (cm)

Membrane volume/min:

$$\text{MV/min} = n/\text{MV} \tag{19.5}$$

n is nominal flow rate (mL/min)

MV is membrane volume (mL)

The disparity in stationary phase design explains why membrane chromatography devices are well suited for high flow rate applications, purifying large molecules, or dilute feed streams. Convective flow forces the mobile medium through the membranous stationary phase. At this point, the ligands are 100% exposed to the molecules in the mobile medium as it passes through the stationary phase. These molecules have the chance to bind immediately to the ligands without diffusing into pores. Thus, molecules bind nearly instantaneously when they are exposed to the stationary phase. The same is true for elution conditions. When the mobile phase's pH or conductivity is adjusted, bound molecules disassociate from ligands. Convective flow forces the elution buffer through the membranous stationary phase. No diffusion is needed for the elution buffer to reach the bound molecules on the membrane's surface. Thus, molecules elute instantaneously when buffer conditions are changed.

Membrane chromatography design is optimal for purifying large molecules, viral vectors, and vaccines. This is because the membranes have much wider pores than resins. The pore distribution of a membrane can be 0.2–5 μm (2,000–50,000 Å)—depending on which supplier and format is used. A resin's pore distribution can range between 100 and 5,000 Å or 0.01 μm and 0.5 μm. Even if a resin has a stated exclusion limit of 4×10^6 Daltons (5,000 Å; 0.5 μm), dynamic binding capacity for large molecules can be dramatically less than binding capacity achieved with smaller molecules. As an example, thyroglobulin has a molecular weight of 660,000 Daltons. That roughly translates to 0.09 μm molecular diameter, well below the exclusion limit of 4×10^6 Daltons. However, the dynamic binding capacity (at 75 cm/h) for this molecule is only 2.5% of what it could be if using Bovine Serum Albumin (BSA), which is 67 kD or 0.009 μm (6). In general, pore sizes ranging from 30 to 50 nm (300–500 Å) are optimal for proteins with a molecular weight between 30,000 and 100,000 Daltons (7). Larger proteins require pore sizes above 100 nm or 1,000 (8). In fact, only the outermost shell of the resin is utilized for binding capacity when large molecules are selected for purification. Some of the larger molecules may occupy or block the pores of a resin. However, these pores become occluded as large molecules diffuse into them. This restricts access to the available binding sites within the resin. As stated before, membrane chromatography provides pore sizes that range from 0.2 to 5 μm. Even so, dynamic binding capacity (at 1,200 cm/h) for thyroglobulin is only 83% of what it could be if using BSA. If the linear flow rate is 75 cm/h, dynamic binding capacity is 100% of what it could be if using BSA (6). Molecular kinetics in

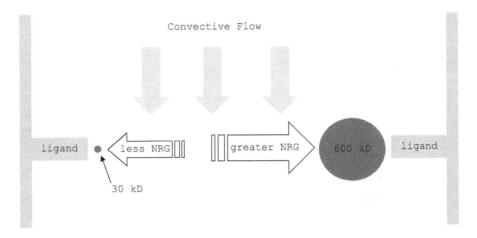

FIGURE 19.4 Larger molecule requires more energy to change their state of motion.

the mobile phase best explains why dynamic binding capacity drops when binding large molecules with membrane chromatography devices. Greater mass results in greater inertia. Molecules with a greater mass will require a stronger opposing force to change their state of motion. As an example, a large molecule passes through the stationary phase in one device and a small molecule passes through the stationary phase of another device. Linear velocity is constant. If the ligand's and molecule's net charge remains constant, it will require more energy to change to state of motion of a large molecule toward a ligand than it would require for a small molecule (Figure 19.4).

Membrane Chromatography Designs

There are three major suppliers of membrane chromatography devices. All provide similar devices but with minor differences observed in the device construction and stationary phase. These suppliers manufacture scalable devices which are suitable for use in large-scale manufacturing (Figure 19.5). Tables 19.2 and 19.3 shows the variety of ligands, formats, volumes available for use and potential applications.

One type of membrane chromatography utilizes a three-dimensional macroporous hydrogel structure that provides a high density of binding sites and rapid mass transfer rates. These membranes offer high loading capacities, even with feed sample conductivity as high as 15 mS/cm. High binding capacity and superior throughput combined with improved salt tolerance provides development flexibility and increased process robustness, which translate into improved process economics.

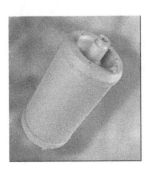

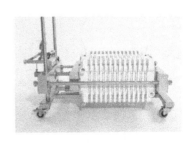

FIGURE 19.5 Pall XT 5000 (left) and Sartorius Sartobind Jumbo (middle) both have 5 L of membrane volume. Sartorius Sartobind cassettes (right) have 0.8 m² or 1.6 L of membrane volume per cassette and are designed to be stacked together.

TABLE 19.2

A Summary of Membrane Chromatography Pore Size, Format, Size, and Ligands Offered by Major Suppliers

Pore Size μm	Format: 4 mm Bed height	MV (mL)	Ligands
Sartorius® Sartobind®			
3–5	96 well plate	0.0019	Q, S, STIC, HIC
3–5	Pico	0.08	Q, S, STIC, HIC
3–5	Nano	1	Q, S, STIC
3–5	5", 10", 20", 30"	75, 200, 400, 600	Q, S, STIC
3–5	Jumbo	2,500	Q, STIC
3–5	Stackable cassette	800	Q, S, STIC

Pore Size μm	Format: 8 mm Bed height	MV (mL)	Ligands
3–5	Nano	3	Q, S, HIC
3–5	5", 10", 20", 30"	150, 400, 800, 1,200	Q, S, HIC
3–5	Jumbo	5,000	Q, S, HIC
3–5	Stackable cassette	1,800	Q, S, HIC
Pall® Mustang®			
0.2	Multiwell plate	0.0014	Q, S
0.2	Acrodisk	0.86	Q, S, E
Single Use Capsules			
0.8	CLM05, CL3	10, 60	Q, S
0.8	CLM05, CL3	10, 40	E
0.8	NP6, NP7, NP8	260, 520,780	Q, S
Reusable Capsule			
0.8	XT5, XT140, XT5000	5, 140, 5,000	Q, S
Natrix®			
NA	Mini	0.2	Q
NA	Disk	0.8, 0.87	Q, Salt-tolerant HIC
NA	Pilot	15	Q
NA	Process 150	115	Q
NA	Process 600	460	Q

TABLE 19.3

List of Available Membrane Chromatography Ligands and Their Respective Applications

Ligand	Mode of Chromatography	Application
Quaternary ammonium	Strong anion exchange	Bind and elute (purification) polishing, negative capture. DNA and endotoxin removal, virus clearance
Primary amine	Weak anion-exchange/salt tolerant	Bind and elute (purification) polishing, negative capture. DNA and endotoxin removal, virus clearance
Sulfonic acid	Strong cation exchange	Bind and elute (purification) polishing, negative capture
Phenyl	Hydrophobic interaction	Aggregate binding, product flow through
Carboxylic acid	Weak cation exchange	Bind and elute (purification) polishing, negative capture
Protein A	Affinity	Bind and elute (purification) of antibodies
parabenzamidine (pABA)	Affinity	Bind serine-based proteases
Iminodiacetic acid (IDA)	Metal chelate	Bind and elute of histine tagged proteins
E	polyethyleneimine	Endotoxin removal
Epoxy and aldehyde	NA	Ligand immobilization

A second type of membrane chromatography is based on a polyethersulfone (PES)-based membrane with a 0.8 μm nominal pore size and a surface coating of an irreversibly cross-linked polymer containing pendant Q groups. This membrane chromatography device allows access to all of the membrane binding sites for small biomolecules (mononucleotides), large biomolecules (DNA), and virus particles by direct fluid convection. These devices are constructed with 16 layers of pleated membrane into scalable devices for consistent performance and scale-up. Process capacities can be increased by linking units in parallel or series.

The last manufacturer has a stationary phase that is 3–5 μm nominal pore size and is made of stabilized reinforced cellulose; other formats include 0.45 μm membranes. The membrane is spiral wound into 15-layer capsules (4 mm bed height) for polishing applications or 30-layer (8 mm) capsules for binding and eluting applications. This type of capsule is now available in a void volume optimized format. There are several advantages to decreasing the void volume on the downstream side of the membrane. First, the improved performance is shown by sharper peaks with smaller elution volumes. Also, lower buffer requirements and higher binding capacities are noted (Figure 19.6).

Both the polyethersulfone (PESU) and cellulose base membranes are hydrophilic, this quality allows the base membrane to be very low protein binding. Thus, any removal of proteins is by a chromatographic mode of operation. Of equal importance, this attribute ensures high product recoveries and reproducible results.

Layering of membrane sheets is important for proper function of the stationary phase within membrane chromatography devices. Multiple layers of membrane provide a torturous path for molecules in the mobile medium to pass through. This allows a minimal but necessary residence time for optimal dynamic binding capacity. At high linear velocities (>1,000 cm/h) a single membrane layer may not offer enough opportunities for molecules in the mobile medium to bind to the ligands on the microporous membrane. Consider a single pass as molecules in the mobile medium maneuver through a pore in a solitary sheet of membrane. The molecules that occupy the midpoint of the pore diameter are furthest away from the ligands. From this point the distance from the molecule to the ligands is quite significant and residence times can be as low as 1/10 of a second at 1,000 cm/h. At that flow rate, the probability that a molecule occupying the center of the pore will bind to a ligand is low. Remember the ligands must provide sufficient opposing energy in order to change the molecules state of motion toward the ligand. The probability of binding increases if additional layers are added just beneath the first layer; more so, when the pores of the membrane layers are not aligned. When this occurs, a molecule in the mobile medium that may miss the opportunity to bind to ligands on the first layer, most likely will bind to a ligand on the next layers. This is because the convective flow that directs and carries the molecules in the mobile phase will move laterally in any direction in order to find the path of least resistance (Figure 19.7). The probability that the molecule will bind to a ligand is directly proportional to the number of membrane layers. The concept of increased binding capacity per unit surface area as directly proportional to number of layers was demonstrated by Knudsen et al. (9). Binding capacity was measured as gram of antibody per liter of membrane. Results are summarized in Table 19.4 and clearly demonstrates that the relationship between dynamic binding capacity and layers of membrane.

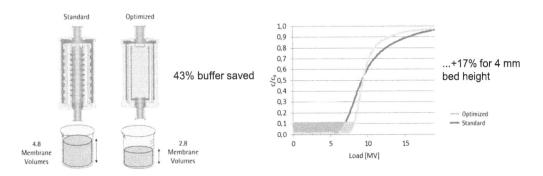

FIGURE 19.6 Void volume optimized capsules allow for sharper elution peaks, higher-binding capacity, and less buffer use.

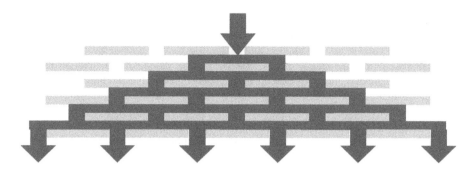

FIGURE 19.7 Cross-sectional view of stacked membranes (light gray). Flow dynamic of mobile medium (dark grey) as is passes through multiple layers of membrane. Notice how first layers are not saturated and final layers are.

TABLE 19.4

Relationship between Number of Stacked Layers, Flow Rate, and Dynamic Binding Capacity

Number of Layers	Bed Height (mm)	Flow Rate (cm/h)	~Dynamic Binding Capacity (g Antibody/L Membrane)
1	0.275	25	7
		125	
		250	
		500	
		750	
5	1.375	25	22
		125	
		250	
		500	
		750	
15	4.125	25	30
		125	
		250	
		500	
		750	

~4.5 g/L, 4.5 mS, pH 7.2, 0.5% Reo-3 Spike.

Polishing Applications

Most biopharmaceutical production processes consist of several chromatography unit operations, typically two to three chromatography steps. The mode of chromatography between the unit operations is ideally orthogonal. A typical antibody downstream purification process may consist of an affinity step followed by CEX/AEX, then hydrophobic interaction (10). The complexity or number of chromatography steps is usually dictated by the nature of the target molecule and contaminants that are present in the mobile medium, or feed stream. The later chromatography unit operations in a sequential scheme are traditionally committed to polishing applications (Figure 19.8). More specifically, these unit operations are designed to remove any trace impurities that may remain in the process bulk, after it has been processed by earlier chromatography steps (11). These impurities are divided into two categories: (a) product-related impurities and (b) process-related impurities. Product-related impurities are molecules that are associated with the final product but are not considered as such. Product dimers, fragments or clips, host-cell proteins (HCPs), and DNA are considered product-related contaminants or impurities.

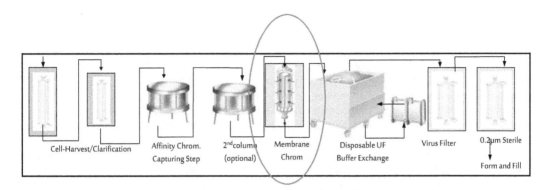

FIGURE 19.8 Typical biomanufacturing process. Polishing unit operations (circled) are commonly toward the end of the purification process.

Leached ligands and media additives are considered process-related contaminants or impurities. The bulk of these impurities express different physiochemical properties than the desired final product. These disparities allow process scientists to separate contaminants from products.

Flow-through anion exchange (FT-AEX) chromatography is a powerful step that is commonly used for polishing applications. This mode of chromatography may also be referred to as negative chromatography—not because of charge but because the product does not bind to the stationary phase (positive capture). During FT-AEX, negatively charged contaminants bind to positively charged ligands while positively charged product flows through the chromatography device. For this reason, product concentration does not change after the intermediate bulk passes through the chromatography device. Throughput values for this type of chromatography step are defined as mass of product/L of sorbent (g/L). FT-AEX is convenient because most biopharmaceutical products express a net neutral iso-electric point (pI) and most contaminants express an acidic pI (Figure 19.9). The product will be positively charged if the pH of the mobile medium is below the product pI. For neutral products the pH of the mobile medium can be as high at 6.5–7.0 and it will still be positively charged. However, contaminants with acidic pIs will be highly negative at neutral pH. Ligands of an AEX media carry a positive charge. Thus, a mobile phase that has a properly adjusted pH and conductivity will bind contaminants as product flows through. After this polishing step, the flow through is devoid of detectable contaminants or contaminants have been removed to a degree that they meet regulatory or in-house specifications. In addition to contaminant removal, FT-AEX chromatography is also useful for clearing viruses with acidic isoelectric points (12–14).

Positvely (+) charged adsorber binds negatively (-) charged contaminants

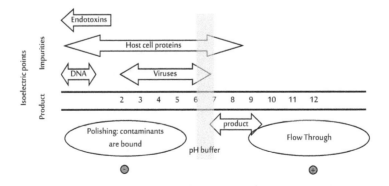

FIGURE 19.9 Approximate isoelectric points of product and impurities are listed above. If AEX chromatography is used, molecules with pI below the buffer pH will bind.

It is known that dynamic binding capacity for small molecules with membrane chromatography devices is less than bead-based chromatography. However, polishing applications are not capacity driven because product flows through and only a few grams of contaminants per several thousand liters of product may be present for removal. For this reason device size selection for this chromatography unit operation is based on flow rate and not capacity. Consider a process bulk intermediate of a monoclonal antibody that is at a volume of 1,300 L. The concentration of the antibody is 5 g/L and DNA/HCP are at 100 ppm or 500 ug/L (=6,500 g monoclonal antibody (mAb) and 1.5 g DNA/HCP in 1,300 L). Throughput capacities for *disposable* FT-AEX membrane chromatography are currently at >10 kg mAb/L of membrane (15) when there are very low levels of contaminants present in the feed stream. The 1,300 L process intermediate will require 0.6 L of membrane for capacity of DNA and HCP. The desired MV is calculated by dividing total mass of product by throughput capacity. A 0.6 L membrane chromatography device contains the MV that will accommodate this capacity. A 0.6 L device has a FSA of 1,350 cm². Linear flow rates with FT-AEX membrane chromatography devices are typically around 500 cm/h. That equals ~11 LPM (liters per minute) or 18 MV/min with a 0.6 L device. At that flow rate, it will require approximately 2 h to process 1,300 L. Flow rate is an important consideration in regards to setting up the desired equipment to process at 11 LPM.

Of course conventional chromatography will have the same, if not better overall throughput when considering capacity for DNA and HCP. What would happen if a column was sized on impurity capacity alone? A column that is 0.6 L (10 cm diameter × 8 cm high) would take approximately 9 × 24 h days to operate at linear flow rates currently used in the industry (100–200 cm/h). Column diameters must increase in order to accommodate higher nominal flow rates—usually to keep unit operations within the time frame of one work day. As a result, chromatography columns for polishing are grossly oversized with regard to capacity. For instance, a 1.2 m diameter column (11,304 cm² FSA) will achieve a nominal flow rate of ~33 LPM at 175 cm/h. Flow-through IEX columns have an average bed height of 20 cm, thus creating resin-based columns that are <200 L in sorbent volume. Roughly, 200 × larger than it needs to be for capacity alone. A 10-in. membrane chromatography device may replace a 30 L resin-based chromatography column when sizing is based on flow rate (Figure 19.10).

The advantage of using a small volume, disposable membrane chromatography device can be visualized in overall process economy and ease of use. AEX resin columns and disposable membrane chromatography devices are both capable of trace-contaminant removal and virus clearance. The difference between the two formats is load capacity at flow rates acceptable for large-scale manufacturing and disposability. Capacity and disposability are critical factors to consider when calculating unit operation costs for new products and processes.

Process lifetime can be up to 10 years: generally the lifetime of a product before generics may compete and erode its price. That 10-year process is assumed to encompass 400 batch production runs and column cycling up to 100 times (four columns, total). Consider that each batch production run stems

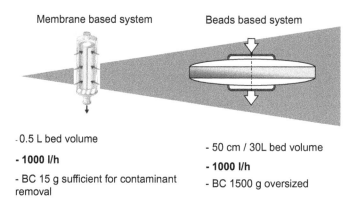

FIGURE 19.10 An example of a polishing application where the size of the chromatography device is determined based on flow rate. A 10" membrane chromatography device can replace a 30-L bead-based column (H. L. Knudsen et al., J. Chromatogr. A 907, 145–154, 2001).

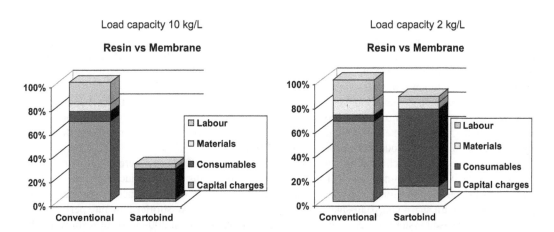

FIGURE 19.11 Graphic results from the Biopharm Services cost model. Component costs are added up to 100% for the column. Results show membrane chromatography is 80% more affordable than columns if load capacity is 10 kg mAb/L and that membrane chromatography breaks even if loaded to 2 kg mAb/L of membrane.

from a 15,000-L bioreactor. Typical mAb yield at cell harvest is 1 g/L. Thus, each batch produces 15 kg mAb—assuming a 100% process yield. The resin-based column size will be 215–225 L, and the membrane chromatography device will be 1.6 L.

Cost models that compare disposable and column-based chromatography have been developed and published in the recent past (16). Input data are from the aforementioned load capacity. Results demonstrate where cost benefits are and are not encountered. This economic model yields a 23% cost reduction when disposable membrane chromatography is used in place of resin-based chromatography. Overall, operating costs for the FT-AEX step are reduced in spite of increased consumable costs, although there is an economy of scale that was not considered in the evaluation. Media costs increase because a new membrane chromatography capsule is used for each chromatography cycle. Conversely, a column is reusable and can be cycled up to 100 times. BioPharm Services provides a cost model that allows end users to input their own data to a software program. This program demonstrates that membrane chromatography costs break even to columns when membranes are loaded to 2 kg mAb/mL and 80% less than columns if loaded to 10 kg mAb/mL. The cost model considers all aspects of a Q FT-AEX unit operation, including user interface, utilities, production, labor, consumables, materials, and capital equipment (17). Dramatic reductions in buffer consumption, labor, and overhead are a direct result of smaller membrane chromatography devices. Column volumes—or in this case MVs—are significantly reduced because a membrane chromatography device is 1.6 L, rather than 220 L. Smaller MVs translate into less buffer volume required for equilibration and wash steps while eliminating cleaning steps. In fact, buffer consumption is reduced >95%. Disposability eliminates significant upfront costs such as cleaning validation, a column lifetime study, assay development, packing studies, hardware, and columns. Those costs are not required with a disposable chromatography device. The cost benefits provided by reduced buffer consumption, processing time, and upfront costs overcompensate for the increased cost of membrane chromatography devices (Figure 19.11). Consideration of holdup volume is of equal importance and is directly related to the volume of the chromatography devices used for a unit operation. Large-scale columns can be quite large with respect to volume. Larger columns require copious volume buffer flushes for optimal recovery of product. A smaller membrane chromatography device will require less buffer to flush residual product from the device. Thus, eliminating dilution of product or sacrificing product left behind on the chromatography device.

Capture/Purification Applications

The first chromatography step in a typical sequential chromatography scheme is designed to capture the molecule of interest and remove the bulk of process and non-process-related impurities.

This chromatography step may also serve to concentrate the process stream into volumes that are more convenient to manage for further downstream purification. When using IEX chromatography in the bind and elute mode, pH and conductivity of the mobile phase are adjusted, so that product binds and impurities flow through. In order for membrane chromatography to be a viable option as a bind and elute device, products should be in low concentration and/or large in molecular weight (<300 kD).

High flow rates enable membrane chromatography devices to concentrate dilute feed streams in a short period of time. Concentration of product is critical when converting large upstream process volumes to smaller, easier to manage volumes. This strategy also proves useful in removing degrading agents or conditions from products in a short period of time.

A single 5 L membrane chromatography device can process 2,000 L of filtered low titer harvest (~100 mg/L) at 10–12 MV/min or 50–60 LPM. Within 1-h processing time, product is bound, washed, and eluted in concentrated form. Baseline separation between each of these fractions indicates very good resolution with sharp Gaussian-shaped peaks observed. To achieve similar flow rate performance using a column-based system, a 1.2–2.0 m diameter column packed with 200–300 L of resin would be required.

Purification of large molecules and particles also plays into the favor of membrane chromatography devices when compared to traditional column chromatography. Fibrinogen, plasmid DNA, viral vectors, and vaccines all fall into the category of large biomolecules or particles. Some of these molecules may be just under the exclusion limit of chromatography resins and separation can be achieved with a column-based system. However, there is still the all too familiar case of occluding pores with only a few target molecules. Once, this occurs the internal surface area of the resin is useless for capacity. Due to the large internal pore structure of membrane chromatography devices, larger molecules can bind more efficiently to the membrane and are no longer limited by diffusion through the resin pores.

Scale-Up Principles and Requirements for Large-Scale Processing

Large-scale membrane chromatography devices have proven to be effective for trace-contaminant removal (18). Conveniently, this unit operation can also be validated for virus clearance. As discussed previously, this "flow through" or "negative capture unit operation" application, defines throughput by measuring the amount of product (mass) that can pass through a unit (volume or area) of membrane (g/L). This throughput value (g/L Q membrane) is determined experimentally from small-scale experiments that accurately reflect large-scale process conditions including pH, conductivity, product concentration, flow rate, and buffer selection. The feed material used in these small-scale experiments is well characterized with a known amount of contaminants and product. Contaminants such as DNA, HCPs (CHOP), leached protein A, and endotoxins are commonly removed by Q membranes (strong basic anion exchanger). Contaminants are usually at the ppm (ng/mg of product) or ppb (pg/mg of product) level and product concentration can range from 5 g to 10 g mAb/L.

The feed material is typically an antibody pool that is a mixture of contaminants and product. At this point in the process the contaminant concentration should be at trace levels (<100 ppm). Contaminants bind to the Q ligands and product flows through as the feed material passes through the Q membrane capsule. Initially, the flow through should be devoid of contaminants until such time that the Q ligands become saturated with contaminants. When this "breakthrough" occurs, contaminants are detected in the flow through. Saturation or 100% breakthrough has occurred when the concentration of contaminants in the flow (C) through is equal to the concentration of contaminants in load (Co). Usually, the acceptable contaminant levels are left up to the discretion of the process development team. These levels may be undetected or at the throughput amount before breakthrough. On the other hand, acceptable contaminant levels may be anywhere between the start of breakthrough up to 100% breakthrough. As a rule of thumb, the current accepted levels (19) of HCP should be <5 ppm and DNA should be removed to 10 ng per dose in the final flow-through pool. These are the current specifications given by regulatory agencies. Dose amounts range in quantity. Thus, acceptable levels of DNA in the flow through can only be claimed when the dose amount is determined. A high dose of mAb is 150 mg. That means, for every 150 mg mAb there can only be 10 ng or 67 ppb of DNA.

Small-Scale Experiment Set-Up

The goal of the small-scale experiment is to accurately predict how much membrane capacity will be needed as well as what the processing time (flow rate) of the application will be during large-scale processing. Buffer conditions (pH and conductivity) suitable for the unit operation should also be determined during these experiments. Effective conditions are typically a neutral pH (0.5–1 unit below the pI of the product) and a conductivity of 5 mS/cm for Q membranes; higher conductivities are used for salt-tolerant/mixed-mode membranes. However, the most effective conditions need to be determined for each individual product based on the impurity load and requirements of the process.

Small-scale experiments should be performed using a representative scale-down model device. This device should have similar flow dynamics compared to process-scale devices. This device will behave similarly to large-scale devices and will allow for more accurate scale-up. The smallest scalable small-scale device that has the same format as large-scale devices is a pico capsule. Its total bed volume is 0.08 mL (2.9 cm²), FSA is 20 mm² and it has a 4 mm bed height.

As discussed earlier, current common throughputs for Q membranes are >10.9 kg mAb/L of membrane when used as a third chromatography step. That translates to >10.9 g of mAb/ mL of membrane—virus clearance values and trace-contaminant removal are good at this throughput. Therefore, a 0.08 mL capsule can accommodate >864 mg of mAb. Average antibody pool concentrations that are loaded onto a Q application are ~5 mg mAb/mL of process intermediate. A 0.08 mL capsule can process >172.8 mL of antibody pool. The feedstock at this point in the process (post protein A and S column) is typically >98% pure.

In order to be assured the best performance of the membrane, it is important to prefilter the load material with either a 0.45 or 0.2 μm membrane filter. This will ensure that the membrane will not foul due to large particles/aggregates which may have formed. If the membrane becomes fouled, access to the binding ligands will be hampered. Before loading the product onto the membrane, a load sample is taken so that the contaminant levels preload may be compared to the contaminant levels post-load.

The 0.08 mL capsule can be operated with a low-pressure automated chromatography system or peristaltic pump at a flow rate of 0.8–2.4 mL/min. The Q pico has a binding capacity of 29 mg/mL or 2.3 mg per pico device. The maximum operating pressure for the pico device is 6 bar. If required, a UV meter can be placed downstream of the pico capsule. This meter will give a signal to a recording device that will measure UV 260/280. The meter will not be sensitive enough to discern between contaminants and product. However, it can detect product, which is the majority of the total protein, and is useful for initial recovery data.

The membrane must be flushed with at least 100 MV (8 mL) of equilibration buffer before use. This buffer should have a pH and conductivity that is similar to the load material (antibody pool). It is important that all air is removed from the 0.08 mL capsule, as any air left within the device may negatively affect results.

Load the antibody pool (~172 mL) at 10 MV/min (0.8 mL/min). Collect the flow through in 8–10 mL sequential fractions. These fractions are used for assay detection of CHOP, DNA, leached protein A, and other contaminants.

Wash the membrane with at least 100 MV (8 mL) buffer after the entire antibody pool has been processed. If a UV meter is in line, wash the membrane until the signal returns to baseline. Collect the wash as another fraction.

For a thorough experiment, strip the membrane with at least 100 MV (8 mL) 2 M NaCl. Collect the elution/strip as a separate fraction. This will elute bound contaminants and can be used to confirm the levels of contaminants that were removed. The elution will also determine if any product was bound to the membrane during the experiment.

The fractions that were collected during the load, wash, and elution will be assayed for contaminant removal and product recovery. Contaminant levels from the load, wash, and sequential flow through fractions should be at ppm or ppb level. The first fractions of the flow-through should not have any contaminants. As the load/ flow-through volume increases, there should be a point where contaminants are

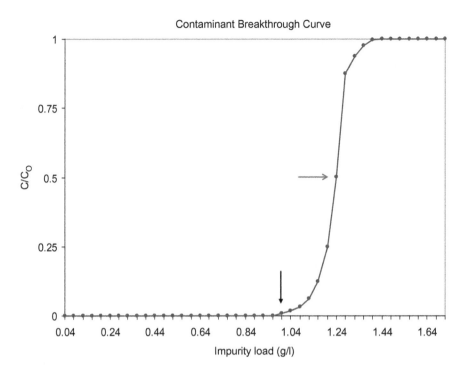

FIGURE 19.12   Breakthrough curve for CHOP. Black arrow indicates initial breakthrough, red arrow indicates point at which flow though pool has 5 ppm impurities (at 50% BT).

detected (breakthrough). Soon after breakthrough, the concentration of contaminants in the fractions will be equal to the load (100% breakthrough). Figure 19.12 demonstrates how plotting these data make up a breakthrough curve. Membrane capacity will be at a throughput volume or mass between breakthrough and 100% breakthrough. This depends on what contaminant level is acceptable.

It is imperative to differentiate between the concentrations of contaminants in the fractions versus the concentration of contaminants in the entire flow-through pool. For instance, the final fraction concentration may be 50 ppm HCP in 10 mL, or above maximum specifications. However, if all the fractions are pooled in 172 mL, the concentration will be <5 ppm, or below specification.

The above example for HCP and DNA removal can be used for scale-up. The entire 172 mL antibody pool (5 mg/mL) had an initial HCP and DNA concentration of 100 ppm. This was loaded on a 0.08 mL membrane with a bed height of 4 mm. The flow-through pool had a HCP concentration of <5 ppm and a DNA concentration <5 ppb. Thus, 0.864 g of mAb was able to pass through 0.08 mL of membrane and HCP/DNA was removed to below specifications. Flow rate was 2 mL/min (or 10.5 mL/min/cm²). This information is useful to calculate how much membrane will be used in large-scale processing and how much time the unit operation will consume during large-scale processing. Below are examples of how this is carried out.

Capacity

The ratio of product mass (kg) per L of membrane is known from small-scale studies. Divide the total mass of product at large scale by membrane capacity to determine what minimum size device can be used.

0.864 g mAb/0.08 mL membrane = 10.8 g/mL (or 10.8 kg/L)

Assuming the product to be processes is 6.5 kg batch:

6.5 kg mAb/(10.8 kg mAb/L membrane) = 0.6 L of membrane (30" capsule).

Size	Nano	5"	10"	20"	30"	Jumbo	Cassette
4 mm bed height							
Bed volume (mL)	1	75	200	400	600	2500	800
Void volume (mL)	3,5	200	540	1080	1600	7000	2500
g capacity @2 kg/L	0.2	150	400	800	1200	5000	1600
g capacity @10 kg/L	10	750	2000	4000	6000	25000	8000
g capacity @19 kg/L	19	1425	3800	7600	11400	47500	15200

FIGURE 19.13 Shows how much protein may be loaded onto a membrane absorber in the flow-through mode to remove impurities (i.e., DNA, HCP, and virus).

A device containing 0.6 L of membrane can process 6.5 kg of mAb in flow-through mode polishing applications. See Figure 19.13, which shows the loading amount of product (g) that can be processed on different sizes of the membrane absorbers.

Processing Time

The mAb pool is at a concentration of 5 mg/mL (=5 g/L). Batch size is 6.5 kg mAb (=6,500 g) which yields a pool volume of 1,300 L. The FSA of a 0.6 L membrane is 1,350 cm². The flux is 10.5 mL/min/cm², multiply this value by the total FSA of the large-scale device (1,350 cm²) to yield process flow rate. Divide total volume by process flow rate to determine process time. Add 30 min for preparation and buffer flushes.

Scale-up flow rate:

$$\left(10.5 \text{ mL/min/cm}^2\right) \times \left(1,350 \text{ cm}^2\right) = 14.175 \text{ mL/min or } 14.1 \text{ LPM}$$

Alternately, linear flow rate may be used to scale-up flow rate:

$$\text{cm/h} = \left[\left(\text{mL/min}\right)\left(60 \text{ min}\right)\right]/\text{surface area cm}^2$$

$$631 \text{ cm/h} = \left[\left(x \text{ mL/min}\right)\left(60 \text{ min}\right)\right]/1,350 \text{ cm}^2$$

$$x \text{ mL/min} = \left[\left(631 \text{ cm/h}\right)\left(1,350 \text{ cm}^2\right)\right]/60 \text{ min}$$

$$x \text{ mL/min} = 14,197 \text{ or } 14.1 \text{ LPM}$$

Processing time:

$$1,300 \text{ L}/14.1 \text{ LPM} = 92 \text{ min}$$

$$92 + 30 \text{ min for preparation and flushes} = 122 \text{ min}(\sim 2 \text{ h})$$

To summarize the scaling example presented above: It was determined from small-scale experiments that a 0.6 L of Q membrane had the ability to process 6.5 kg of mAb. The initial HCP and DNA concentration will be 100 ppm, final HCP and DNA concentrations are <5 ppm and <5 ppb, respectively, in this example. The recommendation is to use a 0.6-L capsule to process 6.5 kg mAb pool which will be at 1,300 L process volume. The 0.6-L capsule will have a flow rate of 14 LPM, and the entire pool will be processed in 92 min. About 30 min were added for preparation and buffer flushes. Thus, the total process time will be 122 min or approximately 2 h.

Validation Aspects

Contaminant removal capabilities and single-use concepts are the key drivers that characterize validation of membrane chromatography for Good Manufacturing Practice (GMP) use. Single use eliminates the need to validate multiple cycling of the membrane. Proof of a consistent, defined level of contaminant removal eliminates the need for QC testing for contaminants (20). This can happen only if the device that is removing contaminants demonstrates a power of removal that is below regulatory or in-house specifications. If the performance is predictable and robust, there is no need to test for contaminants—the processing step has been validated to effectively clear contaminants below the level of specifications. DNA and virus clearance are the two most accepted and validated applications for membrane chromatography devices thus far. The first time a membrane chromatography device was used in a validated process for a market-approved biopharmaceutical product, was in 2001 (21). The main purpose for placing the membrane chromatography device in this process was to remove excess DNA. However, since regulatory requirements state the need to show that biopharmaceutical processes can remove or inactivate many types of virus (22) the step was also validated for virus clearance. The virus clearance validation was scaled down to show effectiveness at 2,000 and 12,000 L production. Removal of DNA was validated at 3 Log Reduction Value (LRV) and virus clearance values for four model viruses was also achieved (Table 19.5). In 2004, another biopharmaceutical product utilized membrane chromatography in an approved manufacturing process for contaminant removal and was validated for DNA removal and virus clearance (23). Removal of DNA was validated at 5 LRV and virus clearance values for model viruses was also achieved (Table 19.6). Since then, numerous products have been validated for early and late phase III clinical trials.

Membrane chromatography devices are produced for optimal processing in single-use mode. Thus, it is important to consider inter- and intra-lot consistency when validating the devices for contaminant removal and virus clearance. This matter is simple and relatively affordable for process- and product-related contaminants. In this case, clearance power is determined by performing spiking experiments. The goal of these experiments is to demonstrate that the membrane chromatography device removes the known spiked contaminant to a specific, consistent, and predictable value. These validation studies are

TABLE 19.5

Virus Clearance Values for 2,000 and 12,000 L Monoclonal Antibody Production Runs

Viruses	Size (nm)	Enveloped	Clearance by Sartobind Q Factor ($\log_{10}$) Run 1	Clearance by Sartobind Q Factor ($\log_{10}$) Run 2
Simian virus-40 (SV-40)	45	No	1.25 ± 0.46	1.34 ± 0.43
Reovirus type III (Reo-3)	75–80	No	4.07 ± 0.50	3.62 ± 0.42
MuLV	80–110	Yes	3.80 ± 0.39	4.40 ± 0.56
PRV	150–250	Yes	3.97 ± 0.44	3.88 ± 0.38

TABLE 19.6

Virus Clearance Values for Large-Scale Processing Runs

Virus	Size (nm)	Enveloped	Removal of Virus from Flow through ($\log_{10}$)	Recovery of Input Virus (%)
PRV	130	Yes	≥4.13	18.5
MuLV	80–110	Yes	≥4.72	0.1
BVDV	25–40	Yes	0.4	42.5
HAV	22–30	No	≥3.84	37.5
PPV	18–26	No	≥6.98	102.5

performed using a scale-down device. These studies may also be performed using the manufacturing scale devices; however, this is not an affordable option because virus clearance runs are expensive to operate. Nonetheless, inter- and intra-lot consistency data has been generated and is provided in Table 19.7.

It is important to use representative material when performing virus clearance validation studies. Therefore, the actual amount or absence of contaminants in the feed stream must be known. Product recovery is another attribute that is equally important to achieve. This should also be consistent and measured to an acceptable level (>95%). Ultimately, log reduction values should always correlate with a throughput value achieved with the membrane chromatography device. Consider the results found in Table 19.8; log reduction values are shown for each virus at a product throughput value of 3,000 g/m² of Q membrane.

Virus clearance is a complex issue and is covered in-depth in another chapter of this text. However, there are some aspects of virus clearance with membrane chromatography devices that are worth discussing here. In brief, virus clearance is defined as the sum of all virus clearance unit operations in a biomanufacturing process, so long as the mode of operation between the unit operations is complementary to each other (24). Most virus clearance strategies use low pH/solvent detergent, virus filtration, and FT-AEX chromatography in order to gain an overall virus clearance value that is acceptable for the process. Each step eliminates virus from product in a different, orthogonal, way; thus, the virus clearance value achieved from each step can be added to the others.

Membrane chromatography devices used in validation studies prove that the mode of operation is adsorption, not size exclusion. To show this is in fact true, validation studies were performed to confirm

TABLE 19.7

Virus Clearance LRV Variability between Membrane Chromatography Lots

	Lot Number				
	521083	**521283**	**521183**	**Ave.**	**SD**
LRV–MVM[a]	6.6	6.73	6.73	6.69	0.08
LRV–Reo III[b]	3.49	3.85	3.67	3.67	0.18

[a] ~9 g/L at 600 cm/h, 4.5 mS and pH 7.2, 1% MVM Spike.

[b] ~4.5 g/L at 450 cm/h, 4.5 mS and pH 7.2, 0.5% Reo-3 Spike.

TABLE 19.8

Virus Clearance Values for Large-Scale Processing Runs

Viruses	Size (nm)	Enveloped	LRV Run 1	LRV Run 2	% Recovery
PRV	120–200	Yes	>5.58	>5.58	100
MuLV	80–110	Yes	>5.35	>5.52	70
Respiratory enteric orphan III (Reo-III)	60–80	No	>7.00	>6.94	100
Minute mouse virus (MMV)	16–25	No	>6.03	>6.03	100

Throughput value = 3,000 g/m² of membrane.

the nature of virus clearance is by adsorption. First, a known amount of product flows through a defined volume of Q membrane absorber at linear velocities approximately 500 cm/h. The product is spiked with a relevance of model virus at 0.1%–1% v/v. Thus, there is a known amount of virus in the load. The membrane is washed with wash buffer after the entire spiked load is passed over the Q membrane. This ensures the entire product is flushed out of the membrane and product recovery is high. After this, the membrane is stripped with 2 M NaCl, which will elute bound virus. Total virus in the load, flow through, wash, and eluate is determined by biological or molecular assays ($TCID_{50}$ or qPCR). Virus recovery is 100%, if the amount of virus in the load is equal to the amount in the flow through + wash + eluate. It is important to note that some viruses are not stable in high salt or are shear sensitive. Some of these particles are destroyed during elution. This reduces recovery values for these viruses. Murine leukemia virus (MuLV) is one such virus. Recovery for this virus is lower than others used as a model virus for clearance trials. However, if this is a concern, consider the size and recovery of pseudorabies virus (PRV). This virus is 40% larger than MuLV and its recovery is typically 100%. Evidence that suggests that MuLV recovery is not compromised by size exclusion.

A 100% recovery of spiked virus is not entirely necessary but does prove that the membrane chromatography device is removing virus by adsorption and not size retention. This is important to realize if there is a virus removing filter in the same process and both steps are validated for virus clearance. Virus clearance values achieved with a membrane chromatography device that is removing virus by size retention should not be added to virus clearance values achieved by virus removal filtration; the modes of operation are not orthogonal.

Disposability eliminates the risk of carryover contamination and the need for cycling studies. These attributes streamline validation efforts, reducing the amount of time and paperwork. Viruses do carry over in clearance studies that involve cycling of chromatography media (25). After a contaminant, impurity, or virus binds to a single-use device, they are disposed and will never enter the process again. Cleaning does reduce the risk but it has been shown that contaminants can carryover and, as a result, compromised batches are possible. This has occurred in the past and may occur in the future. The cause may be variable. However, process engineers and developers can make every effort to reduce this probability. Single-use device concepts provide an option to at least eliminate one cause.

Reusable chromatography media process validation should demonstrate that the level of clearance at the end of its lifetime is not dramatically different than the first cycle. This requires the process developer to commit time and resources to cycling studies with and without spiked contaminants. A reusable device may have great performance without spiked contaminants. This can be up to 100 cycles or more. Validation studies require loading spiked material during cycle one and the last cycle but there is always the chance that the last cycle will not have the same level of clearance as the first. So, intermediate cycles are spiked to determine up to how many cycles the reusable device can demonstrate the power to remove contaminants. This can be anywhere between 25% and 100% of the cycles demonstrated without spiked material. Single-use contaminant removal devices eliminate such studies, since after each run a new device is used. The question of intra- and inter-lot variability are addressed with validation studies described above and will be discussed in the next section—suppliers ensure quality by providing detailed product validation and lot release data.

A major step forward in the validation process is to show that the membrane chromatography device will consistently remove contaminants/virus from product, regardless of membrane batch (lot number). Since this is a chromatography application, conditions in the mobile phase (pH, conductivity, product concentration) must remain somewhat consistent in order for this to occur. However, flow rate can vary for reasons already discussed.

Implementation is a matter of identifying the correct-sized device for large-scale production. LRV of contaminants and virus at a given throughput is known. Simply divide the grams of product at process scale by the throughput value. The product of this equation indicates device volume and flow rates that will be used at that scale.

Manufactures provide product validation data upon request and certificates of analysis with each product. Information within validation documents gives detailed accounts of quality control concepts, technical specifications, and chemical compatibility/extractables.

Quality control concept includes a short statement and certification on the supplier's quality management system and its ability to show complete traceability. This section may also include the drug master file number for the membrane. A detailed description of the quality assurance methods is given. This includes how the filter and membrane material are inspected and tested, how protein-binding capacity and flow rate for the membrane is characterized, and how the shelf life for capsules are tested for quality assurance.

Technical specifications demonstrate the mechanism of adsorption and a description of available ligands. Other useful product information, like part numbers and product dimensions, construction, and flow pattern are also given here. If the device is autoclavable, this is where detailed directions for this process can be found. Binding capacity for each chemistry and flow rates for capsules are detailed, too. Of course, chemical compatibility and extractables information is given also.

Certificates of analysis that are supplied with each product ensure the end user that the product meets the specifications for release and quantifies those values.

Summary

Implementation of membrane chromatography in validated, large-scale biopharmaceutical processes is a reflection of how the industry is responding to bottlenecks in downstream purification. This technology provides a disposable, cleaning validation-free option that shares similar levels of contaminant clearance as conventional column chromatography. In other cases, membrane chromatography shows promise as a mechanism to rapidly concentrate and purify dilute feed streams. Membrane chromatography uses only a fraction of the time and consumables compared to that of traditional column chromatography. Advantages experienced while operating these devices translate directly or indirectly into improved process economy. Smaller footprints, disposability, reduced processing time, and ease of use feed directly into reducing cost of goods.

REFERENCES

1. Wurm, F. M. Production of recombinant proteins in therapeutics in cultivated mammalian cells. *Nat. Biotechnol.* 22 (2004) 1393–1398.
2. Gjoka, X., Gantier, R., Schofield, M. Transfer of a three step mAb chromatography process from batch to continuous: Optimizing productivity to minimize consumable requirements. *J. Chromatogr.* 242 (2017) 11–18.
3. Arunakumari, A., Wang, J., Ferreira, G. Improved downstream process design for human monoclonal antibody production. *Suppl. Biopharm. Int.* 20, (2007) (suppl), 36–40.
4. Miesegaes, G., Lute, S., Read, E., Brorson, K. Viral clearance by flow-through mode ion exchange columns and membrane adsorbers. *Biotecnol. Prog.* 30 (1) (2014).
5. Demmer, W., Nussbaummer, D. Large scale membrane chromatography. *J. Chromatogr.* 852 (1999) 73–81.
6. Karlsson, L., Brewer, J. *Protein Purification, Principles.* J.-C. Janson, L. Ryden Eds. Wiley-VCH, Weinheim, Germany, 1989: 123.
7. Rounds, Kopaciewics, W., Regnier, F. E. Factors contributing to intrinsic loading capacity in silica based packing materials for preparative anion-exchange chromatography. *J. Chromatogr. A* 362 (1986) 187–196.
8. Regnier, F. E. High performance ion exchange chromatography. *Methods Enzymol.* 10 (1984) 179–189.
9. Knudsen, H., Fahrner, R., Xu, Y., Norling, L., Blank, G. Membrane ion-exchange chromatography for process-scale antibody production. *J. Chromatogr. A.* 907 (2001) 145–154.
10. Gottschalk, U. From hunter to craftsman: Engineering antibodies with natures toolbox. *Modern Biopharmaceuticals.* J. Knablein Ed. John Wiley & Sons, Inc., Hoboken, NJ, 2005: 1105–1145.
11. Hanna, L. S., Pine, P., Revzinsky, G., Nigam, S., Omestead, D. R. Removing specific cell culture contaminants in mAb purification process. *Biopharm.* 4 (1991) 33–37.

12. Zhou, J. et al., New Q membrane scale-down model for process-scale antibody production. *J. Chromatogr. A* (2006), doi:101016/j.chroma.2006.08.064.
13. Strauss, D., Gorrell, J., Plancarte, M., Blank, G., Chen, Q., Yang, B. Anion exchange chromatography provides a robust predictable process to ensure viral safety of biotechnology products. *Biotechnol. Bioeng.* 102 (2009) 168–175.
14. Strauss, D., Lute, S., Tebaykina, Z., Frey, D., Ho, C., Blank, G., Brorson, K. Understanding the mechanism of virus removal by Q sepharose fast flow chromatography during the purification of CHO-cell derived biotherapeutics. *Biotechnol. Bioeng.* 104 (2009) 371–380.
15. Mora, J., Sinclair, A., Delmdahl, N., Gottschalk, U. Disposable membrane chromatography: Performance analysis and economic cost model. *Bioprocess Int.* 4 (6) (2006) S38–S43.
16. Zhou, J., Tressel, T. Basic concepts in Q membrane chromatography for large-scale antibody production. *Biotechnol. Prog.* 22 (2006) 341–349.
17. Sinclair, A., Mongue, M. Quantitative economic evaluation of single use disposables in bioprocessing. *Pharmaceut. Eng.* 22 (3) (2002) 20–34.
18. Walter, J. K. Strategies and considerations for advanced economy in downstream processing of biopharmaceutical proteins. *Bioseparation and Bioprocessing*, Vol. 2. G. Subramanian Ed. Wiley-VCH, Weinheim, Germany, 1998: 447–460.
19. Fahrner, R. L. Industrial purification of pharmaceutical antibodies: Development, optimization and validation of chromatography process. *Biotechnol. Gen. Eng. Rev.* 18 (2001) 301–324.
20. CPMP Position Statement on DNA & Host Cell Proteins (HCP) Impurities. Routine Testing versus Validation Studies. 1997.
21. Galliher, P., Fowler, E. Validation of Impurity Removal by the CAMPATH 1-H Biomanufacturing Process. IBC's Biopharmaceutical Production Week.
22. ICH. Q5A: Viral Safety Evaluation of Biotechnology Products Derived from Cell Lines of Human on Animal Origin. Geneva: International Conference on Harmonization: 1999.
23. Martin, J. Case study, orthogonal membrane technologies for viral and DNA clearance. In *SCI Membrane Chromatography Conference*. November 3, 2004: London, UK. http://www.sci.org/SCI/events/membrane/Martinpdf.
24. CPMP Note for Guidance on Quality of Biotechnology Production: Viral Safety Evaluation of Biotechnology Products Derived from Cell Lines of Human or Animal Origin. October 1997 (CPMP/ICH/295/95).
25. Bose, J. An introduction to viral clearance: An overview of study design, regulatory expectation and data interpretation. *Wilbio's Purification of Biological Products*. December 5–7, 2005, Santa Monica, CA. USA.

20

Expanded Polytetrafluoroethylene Membranes and Their Applications

Michael Wikol, Bryce Hartmann, Michael Debes, Cherish Robinson, Scott Ross, and Uwe Beuscher
W. L. Gore & Associates, Inc.

CONTENTS

Introduction

Expanded polytetrafluoroethylene (ePTFE) is created when polytetrafluoroethylene (PTFE)—a linear polymer consisting of fluorine and carbon molecules—is expanded. Expansion of the PTFE polymer creates a microporous membrane with very desirable characteristics including a high strength-to-weight ratio, low leachables and extractables, high thermal resistance, and chemical resistance. This unique combination of properties makes ePTFE membranes a good choice for a number of pharmaceutical

FIGURE 20.1   Examples of ePTFE membranes used for pharmaceutical and biopharmaceutical applications.

applications. Currently, ePTFE membranes are used for sterile filtration of fermentation feed air, process gases, and solvents as well as in venting and lyophilization. Figure 20.1 shows several examples of ePTFE membranes engineered for pharmaceutical and biopharmaceutical applications.

The purpose of this chapter is to:

- Explain how PTFE is made into a microporous membrane
- Discuss properties of ePTFE relevant to pharmaceutical and biopharmaceutical applications
- Describe the unique characteristics of ePTFE membranes
- Discuss the benefits of these characteristics in pharmaceutical and biopharmaceutical applications

Properties of PTFE

PTFE, commonly referred to by the DuPont trademark Teflon® or the ICI trademark Fluon®, is well known for its chemical resistance, thermal stability, and hydrophobicity. PTFE has these desirable characteristics because of its unique chemical structure, as seen in Figure 20.2.

PTFE is a simple polymer comprised of only two elements: carbon and fluorine. PTFE has a long, straight carbon backbone to which the fluorine atoms are bonded. Both the C–C and C–F bonds are extremely strong. In addition, the electron cloud of the fluorine atoms forms a uniform helical sheath that protects the carbon backbone. The even distribution of fluorine atoms along the carbon backbone makes the polymer nonpolar and nonreactive. The combination of strong bonds, a protective sheath, and nonpolarity make PTFE extremely inert and thermally stable. This explains why PTFE is compatible with nearly all the processing and cleaning fluids that are typically used in the pharmaceutical industry including acids, bases, and organic solvents.

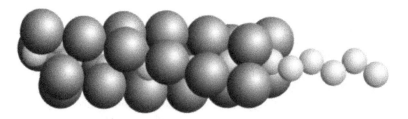

FIGURE 20.2   Chemical structure of PTFE.

TABLE 20.1

Physical Properties of PTFE

Property	
Structure	$-(CF_2CF_2)-n$
Surface free energy	18.5 dyn/cm
Melt temperature	327°C
Continuous service temperature	260°C

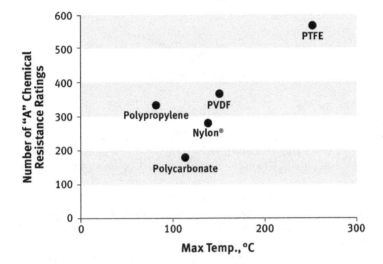

FIGURE 20.3 Chemical resistance and temperature map.

Because of the chemical inertness and low-surface energy of PTFE, it is difficult for anything to adhere to it. This is why PTFE (Teflon®) is well known as a nonstick and easy-to-clean product.

Fluorine is the most electronegative element in the periodic table; therefore, it does not want to share electrons with neighboring fluorine atoms. This results in a low-surface free energy for PTFE. The lower the surface free energy of a material, the less likely it is for the material to be wetted with high-surface tension fluids such as water. Table 20.1 summarizes some of the physical properties of PTFE.

In contrast, other polymeric membrane materials have hydrogen or other atoms attached to their backbone. This results in weaker bonds and thus a more polar, less thermally stable, reactive molecule than PTFE. This also increases the surface free energy; therefore, these polymers are less hydrophobic than PTFE.

Figure 20.3 demonstrates one high level way to look at the relative chemical and thermal compatibility of different materials (Pruett, 1983). The "Compass Corrosion Guide" rates the Chemical Resistance of Metals and Engineering Plastics from "A" to "NR" (Not Recommended). The *y* axis is simply the number of times a polymer gets the highest—or "A"—rating in a solution according to the "Compass Corrosion Guide II." The maximum continuous operating temperature is on the *x* axis.

Microporous PTFE

PTFE is chemically inert, thermally stable, and extremely hydrophobic, which makes this polymer optimal for various pharmaceutical and biopharmaceutical applications. As a microporous membrane, ePTFE is highly valuable because it has a high flow rate and high filtration efficiency.

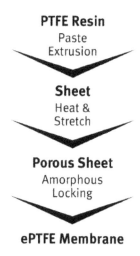

FIGURE 20.4   ePTFE process flow.

Figure 20.4 shows a schematic diagram of how an ePTFE membrane is made. In general, the process begins with pure PTFE consisting of a fine powder resin (Gore, 1980). A lubricating agent is added to the powder so that it forms a paste, which can then be extruded into sheet form. This sheet is heated and expanded under proper conditions to make a microporous membrane. The structure is stabilized in an amorphous locking step. Although most polymers fracture when subjected to a high strain rate, expansion of PTFE at extremely high rates increases the tensile strength of the polymer. The lubricating agent is extremely volatile, and it is entirely removed from the porous structure during processing. The resulting product is 100% ePTFE.

Another method used to manufacture porous PTFE membranes is a replication process in which PTFE particles are mixed with a burnable material such as paper fibers and then heated to remove the fibers (Lawrence and Dwight, 1987). PTFE membranes can also be made porous by removing a fugitive material such as a carbonate. Because these methods yield products that have lower flow rates and lower strength than the expansion method described above (ePTFE), they have found little commercial utility in the pharmaceutical industry.

The remaining topics in this chapter discuss microporous ePTFE membranes.

Figure 20.5 shows a scanning electron micrograph (SEM) of an ePTFE structure that is commonly used in pharmaceutical microfiltration.

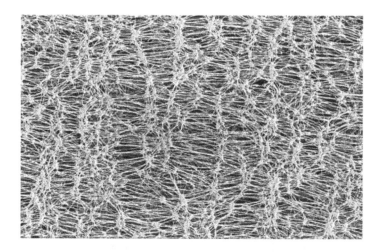

FIGURE 20.5   SEM of ePTFE.

The microstructure of an ePTFE membrane is characterized by nodes that are interconnected by fibrils. Expanded PTFE is a single, continuous structure in which all the fibrils and nodes connect. There are no loose ends and no particles to be shed or to contaminate a fluid stream. Even though this structure has a high density of thin fibrils, it retains a high flow rate because it has a high void volume (typically >85% porosity). Table 20.2 shows that the physical properties of ePTFE can vary along a broad range of pore sizes, flow rates, and water breakthrough pressures.

Membranes can be engineered and optimized to meet the needs of particular applications (Figure 20.6).

Because ePTFE membranes are extremely microporous and hydrophobic, they repel water droplets while allowing water vapor to readily pass through as illustrated in Figure 20.7.

Moisture vapor flows through an ePTFE membrane by either bulk gas flow or diffusion. If the pressure differs across the membrane, gas flows from the high- to the low pressure side. Moisture vapor also diffuses through the microporous structure if humidity or temperature varies across the membrane.

In addition, ePTFE membranes are sometimes laminated to support layers for additional structural reinforcement. The membranes can be laminated to felts and woven and nonwoven materials including polyolefins, polyesters, and fluoropolymers. The support layers added to the membrane can sometimes function as a drainage layer. Support materials are selected according to the chemical, thermal, and mechanical requirements of the application.

TABLE 20.2

Physical Properties Ranges of ePTFE

Property	Range
Porosity	1%–99%
Pore size[a]	0.03–40 μm
Isopropanol bubble point	0.25 to >100 psi
Water entry pressure	1 to >350 psi
Volumetric flux of air[b]	0.03–2,500 (L/(h·cm²))
Volumetric flux of IPA[c]	0.002–560 (L/(h·cm²))

[a] Pore size as correlated to IPA bubble point.
[b] At 21°C and 0.177 psi.
[c] At 21°C and 14.2 psi.

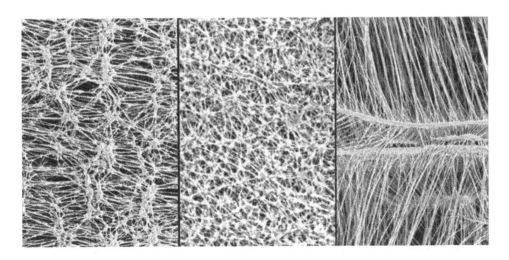

FIGURE 20.6 Examples of ePTFE structures engineered for specific applications.

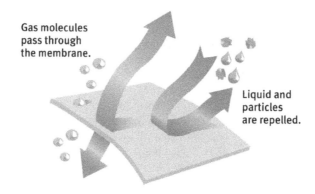

FIGURE 20.7 Functional characteristics of ePTFE.

Pore-Size Measurement

As discussed elsewhere in this volume, pore size is a relative term and often depends on the application and the test method used to measure it. SEMs show that ePTFE is a highly porous material (Figures 20.5 and 20.6) with a pore structure resembling a complex mesh-like network rather than idealized right cylindrical pores. Similar to other porous materials, ePTFE fibers are well-defined units, but the interstitial space deviates from an ideal circular pore. A common method for determining the pore size of microporous membranes such as ePTFE is the bubble point method (Figure 20.8).

In this test, a membrane is wet out with an appropriate test fluid (e.g., isopropyl alcohol). Then gas pressure is applied to one side of the membrane. The pressure at which the first steady stream of bubbles (or first measurable bulk gas flow) appears is said to be the bubble point. The inverse pressure–pore-size relationship for a cylindrical pore is expressed by the equation in Figure 20.9.

Note that the contact angle for a wetting fluid such as isopropyl alcohol is less than 90°, which keeps the $\cos\theta$ term positive. For any pore structure other than a cylinder, modifying shape factors must be added to the equation. Because most membranes including ePTFE do not have a cylindrical pore structure, a complex interaction of the wetting fluid, membrane, and test gas is actually measured. Therefore, although the general inverse relationship supports that higher bubble point pressures indicate smaller pore sizes (i.e., tighter membrane structures), an actual quantitative value for the pore size cannot be precisely determined from a bubble point measurement.

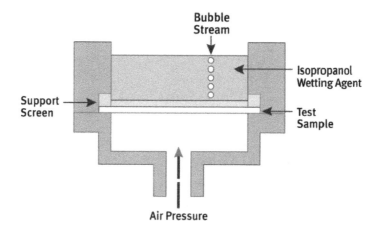

FIGURE 20.8 Bubble point method for measuring relative pore size.

$$D = \frac{4\gamma\cos\theta}{\Delta P}$$

Where

D = pore diameter
γ = surface tension of wetting fluid
θ = contact angle of wetting fluid on filter surface
ΔP = pressure difference between gas and liquid

FIGURE 20.9   Bubble point equation assuming cylindrical pore size.

The bubble point method is a reliable method with good reproducibility. However, to precisely determine the bubble point pressure of the membrane, the contribution of the diffusion of air through the liquid inside the porous structure may also have to be considered. This diffusional flow can contribute significantly to the total observed flow, particularly if the membrane is very thin or has a high porosity. In this case, the diffusional airflow provides a large background signal, which can make it challenging to differentiate and accurately determine the convective bubble flow through the largest pore. This effect can subsequently lead to an overestimate of the size of the largest pore and, therefore, may not describe the filtration behavior accurately. If overestimation of pore size is a concern for the application of interest or if the user wishes to improve the signal-to-noise ratio and reliability of the test results, enhanced bubble point test methods are available. These enhanced test methods minimize the influence and negative impact of the diffusional flow and have demonstrated sharper correlation between measured bubble point pressure and filtration behavior, particularly for sterile liquid filtration applications.

Water breakthrough or penetration pressure testing of hydrophobic membranes such as ePTFE can also be used to obtain a relative measurement of the pore size of a membrane (Dosmar et al., 1992). Water breakthrough pressure is the minimum pressure required to force water through the largest pore of a dry hydrophobic membrane, and it is illustrated in Figure 20.10.

The contact angle in this case is larger than 90°, which leads to a negative pressure difference (i.e., the liquid pressure has to be higher than the gas pressure). The water breakthrough pressure can be correlated to the pore size using the equation in Figure 20.9. Nonetheless, this method and the bubble point method have the same challenges with respect to quantitatively determining the pore size. Every hydrophobic membrane has a unique water breakthrough pressure that depends on the membrane's surface free energy, pore size, and shape.

Both bubble point and water breakthrough methods are excellent tests for relative comparisons of membranes of similar surface free energy and pore structure. For example, a higher bubble point or water breakthrough pressure indicates a tighter membrane structure and enhanced filtration capability,

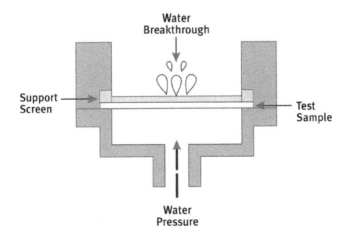

FIGURE 20.10   Water breakthrough method.

respectively. However, these test methods have limited applicability when comparing membranes made of different polymers or having different pore morphology.

Pore-Size Distribution Measurements

Recently, characterization of filtration media by pore-size distribution methods such as capillary flow porometry (or liquid porometry) and mercury porosimetry has become more common than the methods described above (Beuscher, 2017). The liquid porometry test is similar to the bubble point test previously described. However, instead of measuring only the largest pore (as in the bubble point test), the liquid porometry test continually increases pressure, which opens smaller pores and allows a measurement of pore-size distribution. The flow rate through the fraction of open pores at a given pressure is compared to the flow rate through the dry filtration media to assess the fraction of open pores at that pressure.

Mercury porosimetry is similar to the water breakthrough test. Mercury, a non-wetting liquid, is forced into the porous structure. The pressure is continually increased forcing the mercury into smaller and smaller pores according to the equation in Figure 20.9. The measured relationship of applied pressure to the volume occupied by mercury leads to a measurement of volumetric pore size distribution. It is important to recognize that the pore-size distribution measured by these two methods differ from each other. Mercury porosimetry is an equilibrium method based on the volume of the pores, whereas capillary flow porometry is a dynamic method based on the flow through the evacuated pores. In addition, the measured pore-size distribution is not only influenced by the pore sizes in the membrane but also by the connectedness of the pores and the experimental protocol, as both will change the sequence in which the pores evacuate (or fill with) the liquid.

Use and Misuse of Pore-Size Measurements

Air- and liquid filtration efficiency testing can provide information about the pore structure of a membrane. However, it is difficult to determine the actual pore size of a membrane during aerosol filtration because adsorptive effects allow the filter to capture particles that would otherwise pass easily through the structure (Grant et al., 2010). Thus, the efficiency test gives a good estimate of the pore size only if the dominant filtration mechanism is sieving or size exclusion, which is not necessarily the case for air filtration applications. However, these tests can be used to compare the relative effectiveness of different filters in a given application.

The true pore-size distribution of an air filter does not by itself determine the capture efficiency versus particle-size curve because most particles that can fit through the pores are still captured by other mechanisms to be discussed later. Moreover, practical pore-size measurement methods can only infer pore sizes indirectly and imperfectly. As pointed out previously, many methods assume that the pores are cylindrical, but microscopy shows that this is far from true. Thus, particles that are much smaller than the measured pore size of a filter are mostly surface filtered. On the other hand, a filter's pore-size rating may be claimed based on the size of the smallest particle that is captured; however, this may vary tremendously depending on test conditions for particle retention (e.g., air velocity) as well as the nature of the fluid and particle being filtered (e.g., electrostatic interactions). Air filtration efficiency for an ePTFE membrane having a nominal pore size of 5.0 μm may be better than 99.99% at 0.1 μm. For these reasons, pore size can be a confusing specification for an air filter. It is often more useful to specify the retention efficiency for the particle size and conditions of interest.

Sterilization

Materials used in pharmaceutical manufacturing may be sterilized by a variety of methods including dry heat, moist heat, ethylene oxide (EtO) gas, or ionizing radiation. Because of PTFE's thermal stability up to 260°C, ePTFE can withstand multiple cycles of thermal sterilization under typical autoclave, steam-in-place, and dry-heat oven conditions. In addition, because PTFE is chemically inert, it is unaffected by common reactive gas sterilization and cleaning methods.

EtO is widely accepted as a preferred sterilization method in many medical and pharmaceutical packaging applications. A common concern regarding the use of EtO sterilization is residuals (Biological evaluation of medical devices). The residuals that may be found after EtO sterilization include EtO, ethylene chlorohydrin (ECH) when in contact with free chloride ions and ethylene glycol (EG) when in contact with water (Jordy and Suhr, 1973). Since EtO weakly adsorbs to ePTFE and rapidly desorbs from PTFE, PTFE typically has low residuals after exposure to EtO. Although ePTFE maintains a broad compatibility with EtO and chemical sterilization methods, the compatibility of other device components or supporting layers must be considered when selecting this sterilization method.

Ionizing radiation is not generally preferred or used with PTFE materials (Rosenburg et al., 1992). Although PTFE exhibits extraordinary resistance to chemical attack from a wide range of chemical species, it has only limited resistance to ionizing radiation. This is due to chain scission of the carbon bonds in the backbone of the helical PTFE molecule. The amount of degradation will be based on the irradiation dosage.

Air Filtration Theory

Modes of Air Filtration

Air filtration occurs in two ways: surface filtration and depth filtration. Surface filtration occurs when particles are too large to fit into the pores of a filter and are trapped on the surface of the filter medium (Tien and Ramarao, 2007). Depth filtration occurs when particles are small enough to fit into the pores, but they are trapped along their path through the depth of the filter medium. Therefore, the interaction between the particle-size distribution and the pore-size distribution determines the extent to which surface and depth filtration contributes to overall filtration efficiency.

Surface Filtration Mode

Air filters sometimes work by excluding large particles from the small pores in the filter. This mechanism of particle capture is called sieving or size exclusion. Particles that are larger than the pore diameter do not enter into the depth of the filter. In air filtration, the surface filtration mode is less common than depth filtration. If a particle is bigger than the pores, the particle is collected. However, because all filters have a pore-size distribution, there is always a certain probability (which may be very small) that some of the large particles are carried through a small number of the large membrane pores. Nonetheless, if a particle does enter the depth of a filter because it is not filtered at the surface, the depth filtration mode remains available to help capture the particle.

Depth Filtration Mode

In depth filtration, particles small enough to enter the filter structure are collected by probabilistic interactions of the particles with the filter's fibers. If the structure of the filter is the same at all depths, as it is in most filters, there is an exponential decay in the particle concentration as the air passes through the depth of the filter. This filtration mode is consistent with a constant probability of collection within the next increment of depth of the filter.

Unlike surface filtration—which captures particles only by sieving—depth filtration works by several particle-capture mechanisms. Depth filtration is a two-step process: (a) transport of the particles to the internal fibers of the filter and (b) attachment of the particles to the surface of the fiber. Depth filtration mechanisms predominantly rely on van der Waals forces, electrostatic adhesion, or both to hold particles to filter fibers once the particles contact the fibers. However, there are various mechanisms of particle–fiber contact. These mechanisms are discussed in more detail elsewhere in this book and are thoroughly discussed in Hinds (1982; 1999).

In the impaction mechanism, large particles hit the membrane fibers because their momentum exceeds the airflow deviation around the fibers. In the interception mechanism, the airflow carries the particles close enough to the fiber so that contact occurs. In the diffusion mechanism, Brownian motion causes particles to move randomly thus increasing the probability of contacting a fiber (Brown, 1993). Impaction and interception work better on large particles, whereas diffusion favors small particles. Therefore, large and small particles are collected easily, whereas intermediate-size particles are difficult to collect and, hence, are described as the most penetrating particle size. Filters made of fine fibers have a smaller most-penetrating particle size than filters made of coarse fibers.

The fibrils in ePTFE membranes designed for filtration are smaller in diameter than those found in many other commonly used filtration media. Many fibrils in ePTFE membranes can be smaller than 100 nm. In comparison, most fibers in microfiber glass paper are about 1 µm, and fibers in filtration textiles are about 10 µm or more. Recently developed nanofiber materials produced by electrospinning can have similarly small fiber diameters but the density, consistency, and thickness of these fiber mats still needs to be optimized. For high air filtration efficiency, ePTFE is a nearly ideal material because of its random mesh of fine fibers distributed almost perpendicularly to the airflow and with high void fraction. Depending on the air velocity, the most penetrating particle size for ePTFE filters is approximately 0.07 µm, compared to approximately 0.30 µm for typical air filters such as high efficiency particulate air (HEPA) filters. In addition, the small fibers and high porosity in ePTFE offer low resistance to airflow providing good capture efficiency while maintaining a low pressure drop.

Pressure Increase and Cleaning in the Air Filtration Modes

The most significant implication of using surface versus depth filtration is the location of the captured particles. In surface filtration, the particles are accumulated in a thin, dense layer right at the surface of the filter, whereas in depth filtration the particles are distributed throughout the depth of the filter medium. The advantage of depositing the particles right on the surface is that they can be removed easily, and a filter's decreased airflow can be recovered by cleaning. The advantage of depth filtration is that the particles are distributed throughout a large region of the filter, which still has a large fraction of open space. In depth filtration, the filter's airflow is more easily maintained without cleaning or removing the captured particles.

When choosing a filter, it is useful to consider three different types of particle loading. When particulate loading is light, such as those experienced by high-purity, point-of-use filters or recirculation filters sealed inside computer disk drives, the effect of particle loading is less important because very few particulates are present. In this case, whether surface or depth filtration dominates is not important, and filters are chosen based on other criteria.

When particle loading is very heavy and rapid, it is necessary to clean the filter frequently and possibly thousands of times during its lifetime. An example would be baghouse or cartridge collectors for food or pharmaceutical powder collection. In this case, the surface filtration mode is crucial and should make it easy for particles to be removed thoroughly in each cleaning cycle. Expanded PTFE filters are very useful in these applications because they are easy to clean. An additional benefit of ePTFE filters is that it provides minimal adhesion between particles and the fibers, as has been discussed earlier in this chapter.

In the third type of particle loading, which is between the two extremes discussed above, the particulate loading is low enough to make cleaning unnecessary, but high enough to limit useful lifetime. Surface filtration can be disadvantageous for this situation, especially if the captured particles form a continuous sheet as this may limit airflow. In this case, membrane filters (including ePTFE membranes) acting as surface filters require a prefiltering layer to increase the overall particle capacity when performing depth filtration.

Improved Efficiency During Cleaning and Low Pressure Drop

Filters used for extremely high particulate loadings must be cleaned repeatedly. However, some filters rely on particles bridging and filter cakes forming over openings in nonwoven filter media to help capture particles. During cleaning, these particle bridges are disrupted, and particle-retention efficiency can be reduced. Relative to most filters of this type, ePTFE filters have excellent retention efficiencies even during the cleaning cycle. The surface of the ePTFE membrane serves as a permanent size-exclusion layer without the high pressure drop that is common for filters that rely on a filter cake for particle retention.

Summary of Air Filtration Theory

Compared to most other air filtration media, ePTFE membranes are unusual in several ways. They have small and consistent pores to provide surface filtration, and cleaning of surface-filtered particles is very easy. In addition, the high density of extremely fine fibrils provides very high depth filtration efficiency if needed. High porosity and fine fibrils in ePTFE membranes offer little resistance to airflow, and these membranes combine high air filtration efficiency with low pressure drop. In surface filtration mode, the filter efficiency is still high during and immediately after cleaning. This combination of properties makes ePTFE membranes a very good choice for air filtration applications.

Gas Filtration and Venting

Air, oxygen, carbon dioxide, and other gases are often fed directly into fermenters and bioreactors to increase cell growth and overall productivity. In other situations, inert process gases such as nitrogen or argon are used to minimize product oxidation in process vessels and product packaging. Additionally, vessels need to be properly vented to allow filling or emptying while maintaining aseptic conditions. These gases must be free of bacteria and particulates, which can contaminate the bioreactor, vessel, or product. Since expanded PTFE membranes are hydrophobic, high flowing and highly retentive, they are frequently the material of choice for these gas filtration and venting applications.

Fermentation Gas Filtration

Large volumes of sterile air and gases are required as a raw material in aerobic fermentation reactions. These gases require filtering to remove organisms and particulates. Exhaust gases are filtered to prevent the fermenter from contaminating the environment as well as to prevent the environment from contaminating the fermenter. During their service life (typically a year or more), these filters must undergo repeated steam sterilizations without blinding or losing their integrity. Filter failure is extremely costly in terms of product yield, product quality, maintenance, and downtime.

Historically, packed towers were used for fermentation feed air and exhaust gas filtration; however, they are relatively inefficient (Schubert, 1989), expensive to install and operate, wasteful of space, hydrophilic, and extremely difficult to test for integrity. Over time, many of these packed tower systems have been replaced by or supplemented with some type of cartridge filter. Cartridges made of glass fiber and borosilicate glass save more space than randomly packed towers. However, membrane filters containing ePTFE are achieving significant improvements in filtration efficiency, pressure drop, hydrophobicity, and integrity testability (Figure 20.11).

Because ePTFE membranes have smaller fibril diameter and a narrower pore-size distribution, they retain particles and organisms more efficiently than nonwoven depth filtration media. In addition, ePTFE is extremely hydrophobic, and (a) it remains hydrophobic through repeated sterilizations, (b) it resumes its pre-steam pressure drop with a minimal post-steaming blowdown, and (c) it is significantly less susceptible to bacterial grow-through.

Recent innovations in ePTFE membranes have further reduced pressure drop compared to ePTFE membranes previously available for fermentation feed air applications (GORE® Fermentation Air Filter Product, 2015). At typical operating conditions, the improved ePTFE membranes can provide similar retention at approximately half the pressure drop of traditional ePTFE filters. The increased performance of the improved ePTFE membranes can potentially:

- *Lower capital cost*: Capital and replacement costs are further reduced because fewer filters may be required for a desired flow rate. The installation and capital costs of heat-tracing filter housings are also reduced.
- *Lower energy cost*: The lower pressure drop of ePTFE filters can result in significant energy savings in compressor operation.

FIGURE 20.11   Filter cartridge containing ePTFE. (Courtesy of W. L. Gore & Associates, Inc.)

- *Increased productivity*: Higher airflow and/or maintaining higher vessel pressure than conventional filters may improve batch productivity for oxygen-limited processes by increasing product output or reducing batch-processing time.

The contamination, energy, maintenance, and productivity cost savings achieved by using ePTFE filters can be calculated to determine annual cost savings.

Venting

In aseptic processing, any rigid vessel that allows liquid to flow through requires venting to allow air to move in and out of the vessel as it is emptied or filled. A vent filter allows air or other gases to flow into and out of the vessel while also serving as a microbial barrier that maintains aseptic conditions in the vessel. In addition, nonrigid vessels, such as some types of flexible, rocking-type bioreactors where gas is continuously introduced to facilitate cell growth, may also require venting.

Glass wool was commonly used in the 1960s as a microbial barrier to maintain aseptic conditions in a vessel. After advancements in aseptic bioprocessing, the common practice has been to use hydrophobic membrane filters to achieve the microbial barrier needed during venting. Since publication of the PDA Technical Report No. 40 in 1995 (PDA, 2005), the use of membrane filters with liquid bacterial-retention properties has been recognized in many critical applications. Although it is recognized that the primary mechanisms of particle retention in gas streams are far more efficient than the mechanisms of particle retention in liquid streams, it has become standard practice to use vent filters with supporting liquid bacterial-retention claims especially for gas stream applications considered to be critical.

Applications

Applications for vent filters can be segmented into several categories including critical applications where the gas has contact with a liquid drug product, a close precursor, or a critical contact surface in the production of a drug product. Certain venting applications can include vessels such as bioreactors or fermenters, which typically have sparge gas, overlay gas, or both entering the vessel. This gas needs to be vented to avoid pressure buildup inside the reactor. Venting applications can be further complicated by the presence of warm moist air, which can result in condensate formation as the gas cools. The presence of condensate can result in blockage of the filter, which can lead to a reduction of gas flow or increase in back pressure through the hydrophobic membrane filter.

Critical Gas Applications

Critical applications as defined by PDA Technical Report No. 40 include the following (PDA, 2005):

Bioreactors and Fermenters

Bioreactors and fermenters often include multiple applications requiring vent and in-line filtration. Applications include filters for in-line filtration of sparge or overlay gases entering the reactor, filters for exhaust gases, and vent filters on addition bottles that introduce liquids into a reactor to maintain a proper environment for cell growth.

Exhaust filters on bioreactors and fermenters need to provide sufficient gas flow to vent sparge and overlay gases as they are introduced into the reactor. Filter blockage due to the formation of liquid condensate between the reactor and the exhaust filter—formed as a warm, moist gas when the reactor cools and water vapor condenses—should be avoided.

Water-for-Injection Tank Vents

Water-for-injection (WFI) tanks often require vent filters that can withstand elevated temperatures and perform for extended periods given the limited opportunities available for filter replacement. Typically, the filter and associated housing used to vent a WFI tank are maintained at approximately 5°C above the temperature of the WFI in the tank to prevent the formation of condensate in the exhaust filter housing.

Sizing

Selection of an appropriately sized filter is critical to the success of the venting operation. An undersized vent filter can result in the creation of a vacuum as liquid is removed from a vessel or when excessive pressure builds up as liquid is introduced into a vessel. Either situation can damage the vessel, disrupt the process, or result in loss of aseptic conditions inside the vessel.

External factors to be considered when determining the correct size of a vent filter include the maximum rate at which liquid will be introduced or discharged from the vessel being vented, the method of filter sterilization or maximum temperature of the system, the vacuum rating of the vessel, and the potential loss of filter performance due to condensate formation, among other factors.

Steam-in-place sterilization will have an impact on filter sizing because the filter will need to provide sufficient gas flow to accommodate the rapid collapse of the steam and the subsequent flow of gas required into the vessel to avoid creation of a vacuum and potential collapse of the vessel. In many cases, the main driving factor dictating the size of a vent filter in applications where the filter will be steam-in-place sterilized is the need for rapid gas flow following steam collapse and not the process conditions experienced by the filter following sterilization.

Integrity Testing

Historically, integrity testing of vent filters has been performed after use (i.e., after the filter had been removed from the vessel) using an alcohol/water mixture. More recently, the trend has been toward performing the integrity test both before use, after use, and *in situ* to more accurately assess the performance of the filter during use. The ability to test the hydrophobic vent filter *in situ* has been greatly facilitated by the development of integrity test methods that use only water and do not introduce liquids downstream of the filter during the integrity test itself. These integrity tests include water intrusion tests performed on the upstream side of the filter's membrane. These tests can be correlated to a minimum defect size or bacterial challenge tests; thus, the nondestructive (water intrusion) test can be a useful surrogate for a destructive test such as a liquid microbial challenge test.

Filters constructed of ePTFE membranes are well suited for most venting applications. The ePTFE membrane allows for a high flow rate at a low pressure drop. Expanded PTFE membrane filters can be regularly tested to verify their integrity and proper installation. Expanded PTFE is hydrophobic; therefore, ePTFE filters do not blind from repeated steam sterilization, high humidity, or incidental contact with aqueous solutions.

Lyophilization

Many biopharmaceutical products such as vaccines and monoclonal antibodies are unstable in aqueous solutions over time (Xiaolin and Michael, 2004). Although drying could enhance the shelf life of these products, many of these substances are unstable when exposed to heat. Lyophilization, also known as freeze-drying, allows these pharmaceutical products to be preserved with minimum degradation. During lyophilization, the product is first frozen to below its eutectic or glass transition temperature, usually in the range of $-40°C$ to $-60°C$. A vacuum is then applied and energy is added to the frozen product to create the proper conditions for sublimation. Removing moisture through sublimation, in which a solid (usually ice) is changed to the gaseous phase without first going through a liquid phase, provides a low-heat input method for preserving and extending the shelf life of valuable pharmaceutical products that otherwise become unstable during processing or storage.

Single-dose pharmaceutical drug products are typically lyophilized in glass vials while bulk active pharmaceutical ingredients (APIs) and drug substances are frequently lyophilized in open trays (Louis and Meagan, 2007). Bulk APIs and drug substances are often freeze-dried to increase the stability of biopharmaceuticals, enable longer shelf life, and ease transport of bulk product between manufacturing process steps. These trays can be used from early research and development, when drug product attributes, such as toxicity, are unknown through to commercial manufacturing. The main risks associated with lyophilization in open trays include contaminants entering the product in the tray or product leaving the container. Challenges relating to product leaving the container include the potential for cross-contamination, additional cost for cleaning and cleaning validation as well as risk of worker exposure.

A unique application of ePTFE membrane technology is currently being used in the pharmaceutical industry to facilitate lyophilization in a closed tray. The ePTFE membrane is attached to the trays to create a closed container during lyophilization and transport in order to provide product containment and contamination control while at the same time allowing for moisture vapor transmission during lyophilization.

There are several situations where ePTFE membrane barrier properties are beneficial. For example, during transport into the dryer liquid is contained because ePTFE is extremely hydrophobic. In R&D, it is common to have various samples freeze-dried in one batch to reduce overall development time (Barbaree and Sanchez, 1982; Barbaree et al., 1985). It is critical that the samples are covered to minimize the risk of product cross-contamination. Additionally, having a closed tray minimizes the risk of product fly-out and shortens the time required for dryer cleaning between runs. This is more important in lab and pilot scale freeze dryers where there are no Clean-in-place/Steam-in-place (CIP/SIP) systems in place and no validated cleaning procedures. Finally, the barrier properties of ePTFE minimize the risk of aerosol microbial contamination from entering the container.

While other material may have similar barriers properties, they typically have low moisture vapor rates. Expanded PTFE membranes are highly desirable for lyophilization because they have excellent barrier characteristics and are thin, strong, and highly porous to allow for high moisture vapor transmission rates. Figure 20.12 shows an example of a single use, closed lyophilization tray currently being used by pharmaceutical companies.

The application of vented freeze-dry packaging takes advantage of several unique properties of ePTFE, including barrier performance, temperature resistance, and permeability to moisture vapor.

FIGURE 20.12   GORE® LYOGUARD® Freeze-Drying Tray, a single-use lyophilization product.

Filtering Liquids

Because ePTFE membrane is chemically inert and has high flow rates, it is well suited for various liquid filtration applications such as filtration of aggressive solvents and acids that are not compatible with other types of membranes (Johnston, 1998).

Low-surface tension liquids such as alcohols (e.g., methanol or isopropanol) or solvents (e.g., methyl ethyl ketone) can readily wet ePTFE membranes. When these liquids are used in an application, no additional prewetting steps are required. On the other hand, liquids with high-surface tension (e.g., water) do not flow through hydrophobic membranes (e.g., ePTFE) at normal operating pressures (typically up to ~30 to 40 psid). If a hydrophobic membrane is used for an aqueous filtration, it must first be prewetted with a low-surface tension liquid such as isopropanol; once properly wetted, aqueous solutions can be filtered through ePTFE or other hydrophobic membranes. Depending on the application, the prewetting solution can be flushed from the filter with water or with the aqueous solution to be filtered—taking care to prevent air entrainment during and after flushing. Prewetting of ePTFE membranes is done extensively in the semiconductor industry.

Prewetting a membrane can sometimes be inconvenient; therefore, a water wettable or hydrophilic ePTFE membrane may be preferred. The surface of ePTFE membranes can be modified to render the membranes hydrophilic. Hydrophilic ePTFE membranes with high flow rates are desirable in applications where high viscosity fluids or high volumes are being processed.

Conclusion

Expanded PTFE membranes are valuable in a number of biopharmaceutical filtration, venting, and processing applications. PTFE is inherently chemically inert, thermally resistant, and extremely hydrophobic, and it can be engineered into a microporous membrane with high retention and high flow-rate properties. Because of its physical properties, ePTFE membranes are the filtration media of choice in multiple applications.

REFERENCES

Barbaree, J. M. and Sanchez, A. 1982. Cross-contamination during lyophilization, *Cryobiology* 79:443–447.
Barbaree, J. M., Sanchez, A., and Sanden, G. N. 1985. Problems in freeze-drying: II. Cross-contamination during lyophilization, *Developments in Industrial Microbiology* 26:407–409.
Beuscher, U. Investigation of the correlation between gas/liquid porometry and particle filtration using simple network models. *Presentation at Frontiers of Applied and Computational Mathematics*, Newark, NJ, June 24–25, 2017.
Biological evaluation of medical devices—Part 7: Ethylene oxide sterilization residuals. ANSI/AAMI/ISO 10993-7: 2008/(R)2012.

Brown, R. C. 1993. *Air Filtration: An Integrated Approach to the Theory and Applications of Fibrous Filters.* New York: Elsevier Science.

Dosmar, M., Wolber, P., Bracht, K., Tröger, H., and Waibel, P. 1992. The water pressure integrity test—A new integrity test for hydrophobic membrane filters, *J Parenter Sci Technol* 46(4):102–106.

Gore, R. W. 1980. Porous Products and Process Therefor. US Patent 4,187,390, filed June 21, 1977, and issued February 5, 1980.

GORE® Fermentation Air Filter Product: Validation Guide. PB-1841, rev 4. Elkton, MD: W. L. Gore and Associates Publishing, 2015.

Grant, D. C., Beuscher, U., and Ross. S. Integrity Test Method for Porous Filters. US Patent 8,689,610 B2, filed September 23, 2010, and issued April 8, 2014.

Hinds, W. C. 1999. *Aerosol Technology*, 2nd edition. New York: Wiley-Interscience.

Johnston, P. R. 1998. *Fundamentals of Fluid Filtration*, 2nd edition. Littleton, CO: Tall Oaks Publishing.

Jordy, A. and Suhr, H. 1973. Sorption process in gas sterilization in the medical sector, *Applied Microbiology* 26(4):598–607.

Lo, L. Y. and Thomas, D. J. Microporous Asymmetric Polyfluorocarbon Membranes. U.S. Patent 4,863,604 A, filed February 5, 1987, and issued September 5, 1989.

PDA International Association for Pharmaceutical Science and Technology. *Sterilizing filtration of gases.* Technical report no. 40. Parenteral Drug Association. PDA J Pharm Sci Technol. 2005 Jan-Feb; 58 (1 Suppl TR40):7–44.

Pruett, K. M. 1983. *Compass Corrosion Guide II, A Guide to Chemical Resistance of Metals and Engineering Plastics.* La Jolla, CA: Compass Publications.

Rey, L. and Gassler, M., 2007 Development of a new concept for bulk freeze-drying: LYOGUARD® freeze-dry packaging. *Freeze-Drying/Lyophilization of Pharmaceutical and Biological Products* Rey L. and Rey J.C. (Eds.), 2nd edition. New York: Informa Healthcare USA, Inc.

Rosenburg, Y., Siegmann, A., Narkis, M., and Shkolnik, S. 1992 Low dose γ-Irradiation of some fluoropolymers: Effect of polymer chemical structure, *Journal of Applied Polymer Science* 45:783–795.

Schubert, P. 1989. The Sterilization of Fermentation Inlet Air, Scientific and Technical Report, Glen Cove, NY: Pall Corporation.

Tang, X. C. and Pikal, M. J. 2004 Design of freeze-drying processes for pharmaceuticals: Practical advice, *Pharmaceutical Research* 21(2):191–200.

Tien, C. and Ramarao, B. V. 2007. *Granular Filtration of Aerosols and Hydrosols*, 2nd edition. New York: Elsevier Science.

21

Gas Filtration Applications in the Pharmaceutical Industry

Elisabeth Jander
Pall Corporation

CONTENTS

Introduction

Many applications exist for air and gas filtration in the pharmaceutical industry. The filtration required can be for bacteria and phage removal (typically achieved by employing 0.2 μm-rated hydrophobic membrane filters) or to a coarser filtration level for particulate removal. Some gas filtration applications for which bacteria and phage removal filtration is employed are fermenter (bioreactor) inlet gas, fermenter (bioreactor) vent gas, vents on water for injection tanks, and vacuum break filters on autoclaves and lyophilizers. In biotechnology alone there is a wide range of products that are produced by bacteria or mammalian cell cultures, such as antibiotics, organic acids, amino acids, vitamins, enzymes, and other proteins such as antibodies and vaccines. Coarser filtration can be employed for contamination control, such as particulate or yeast and mold removal, or as prefilter to the finer sterilizing-grade filter. Protection of the sterilizing-grade filter in moisture-loaded gas service may also be achieved by employing coalescing filters for the removal of water droplets. They may also be used to remove oil droplets from a gas stream.

This chapter will provide information on the applications for air filtration in the pharmaceutical industry and is divided into the following sections:

1. "Mechanisms Affecting Gas Filtration," describing filtration mechanisms
2. "Gas Filters Used in the Pharmaceutical Industry," describing the types of gas filters used in the pharmaceutical industry and considerations for their operation
3. "Gas Filtration Applications," describing specific air/gas filtration applications

4. "General Considerations for Operation of Gas Filters," containing recommendations and considerations for proper usage of membrane filters in the applications
5. "Disposable Systems for Bioprocesses and the Specific Challenges to Gas Filtration," discussing air/gas filtration aspects in single-use systems

Mechanisms Affecting Gas Filtration

Regardless of the filtration system used (e.g., packed towers or cartridge filters), the manners in which particles are captured and removed from an air or gas stream are the same. The removal efficiency of filtration media is dependent upon the following mechanisms:

1. Direct interception by the filter media (size exclusion)
2. Inertial impaction
3. Brownian motion or diffusional interception
4. Electrostatic attraction between the filter media and particles [1]

The filtration mechanism for direct interception is a sieving action that mechanically retains particles larger than the filter media pores, either on the outer filter media surface or in the depth of the filter media. Direct interception is independent of face velocity and any other mechanism.

Inertial impaction refers to capture of particles due to the inability of the particle to fully follow the fluid flow through a torturous flow path in the depth of the filter media. Due to their mass and resulting inertia particles may get into contact with the filter media pore walls, and may thus be removed from the fluid flow and permanently retained by adsorptive forces. As the face velocity increases, the probability of inertial impaction increases. This effect is greatest for particles with larger diameters (typically larger than 1 μm in diameter) or with high densities.

Brownian motion or diffusional interception applies to very small particles (typically less than 0.3 μm in diameter) at low face velocities. Gas molecules are in a state of random motion. Small particles suspended in the gas stream can be struck by moving air molecules and displaced. The movement of particles resulting from molecular collisions is known as Brownian motion. This phenomenon will increase sideways movement of the particles suspended in gases and increases the probability of capture of the particle by the filter media, see Figures 21.1–21.3.

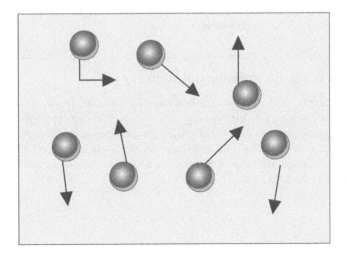

FIGURE 21.1 Moving gas molecules.

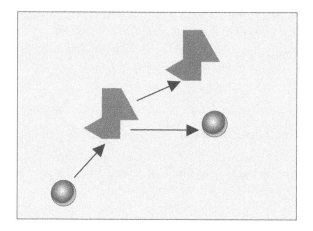

FIGURE 21.2 Brownian motion of particles in gas.

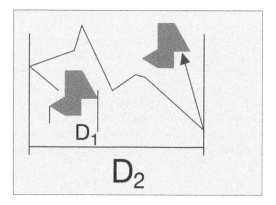

FIGURE 21.3 Particles claiming increased space in gas.

In dry air and gas streams, electrostatic charges can build up on the filter matrix and aid the attraction and thus removal and retention of particles to the filter media. This can enhance the ability of the filter to remove particles much smaller than the pore size of the filter medium. For some filter materials, this effect can be enhanced by surface modification.

Gas Filters Used in the Pharmaceutical Industry

Historically, packed towers were the first air filters used by the industry for air sterilization, i.e., the removal of bacteria from process air. As technology has advanced, sterilizing-grade membrane cartridge filters have become the major means to provide sterile gases in pharmaceutical processes. Their features include compact design, ease of use, hydrophobic (water repellent) surface properties, stable filter matrix, non-fiber releasing, and reliable retention of bacteria and phages (viruses) correlated to a nondestructive integrity test available to the filter user.

Packed Towers

Description of Packed Towers

Packed towers used to filter fermentation air are comprised of beds which can be constructed of pads of paper, cotton wool, glass wool, or mineral slag wool. The diameter of the fibrous material is typically

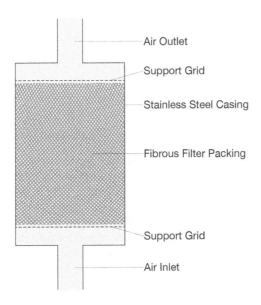

FIGURE 21.4   Design of packed tower air filter.

between 0.5 and 15 μm. The space between the fibers (the filter media pores) can be many times this size range.

Figure 21.4 illustrates a simple design of a packed tower air filter [2].

The filter consists of a steel container or housing filled with loose fibrous packing. The air inlet is on the bottom and the outlet is on the top of the filter. The packing is supported by a grid or perforated plate. When it is placed in the tower it is necessary to ensure that the appropriate packing density for the application is obtained. Proper packing must preclude movement of the fibers during use. A repositioning of fibers during use can lead to channeling of air, which will lead to an inefficient packed tower, since only a portion of the bed will be acting as a filter. Fiber movement can also lead to the dislodging of trapped microorganisms.

Once the filter has been correctly packed with fibrous material, a support grid or plate is fitted to the top of the bed to ensure that the bed remains compressed. After the first steam sterilization of a packed tower air filter, the packing will tend to settle further. It is recommended that additional fibers are added to the bed after the first steam sterilization to maintain the correct packing density.

Bonded fiber mats have been developed to use in place of loose fibers. When mats are used, it is necessary to have a good seal between the mat and the tower wall, so that channeling does not occur.

Thin sheets of small diameter fibers can also be used in packed towers. The sheets are placed on top of each other with a mesh or grid in between each sheet for support. The edges of the sheets are sealed between flanges.

Sterilization of Packed Tower Air Filters

Prior to using a packed tower for the sterilization of fermenter inlet air, the filter itself must be sterilized. There are two techniques which can be employed: steam sterilization and dry heat sterilization [3].

Passing steam at a pressure of 1 bar g (15 psig) through a packed tower for 2 h should be adequate for sterilization. Because the presence of air in the packed tower during the sterilization can prevent complete sterilization of the packing, it is best to introduce the steam at the bottom and vent out the top of the housing. A drain at the bottom of the packed tower is needed to purge the steam and to drain any residual condensate in the filter. It is necessary to remove condensate from the bed because wetted fibers are less efficient for particle and microorganism removal and may also decrease the retention efficiency of the packed tower well below its design value, particularly if channeling through the wetted media occurs.

Some fiber material, as well as material used to bond fibers, can be degraded by steam sterilization. An alternative to steam sterilization is dry heat sterilization, which will avoid the possibility of steam degradation and fiber wetting. This can be accomplished by using a heating device at the inlet of the tower and passing air at a temperature of 160°C–200°C through the bed for 2 h. During dry heat sterilization, the filter is isolated from the rest of the process. However, care must be taken because not all materials can withstand the higher dry heat temperatures needed for sterilization.

Operating Considerations for Air Sterilization by a Packed Tower

The microorganism retention efficiency of packed towers is dependent upon the velocity of the air within the tower. The relationship between air velocity and filtration efficiency has been determined experimentally in a number of studies [4]. In the example shown in Figure 21.5 [4], the particle retention efficiency may change by a factor of ten as a result of a relatively small change in the inlet air velocity. The results also show that the most difficult particles to remove are in the size range of small microorganisms. Therefore, it is quite possible to encounter air flow conditions in a packed tower which can reduce the statistical probability for the complete retention of all microorganisms.

The hydrophilic nature of the fibrous material used in packed towers (e.g., glass wool) can contribute to a reduction of the microorganism removal efficiency of the packed tower. When water vapors enter the system with the air discharge of the compressor, the air and water vapor mixture is initially at an elevated temperature. As the gas stream is cooled, water droplets may condense, be collected by the fiber matrix and wet the hydrophilic glass fibers. Due to the loss of electrostatic effects, the wetted fibers are less efficient for microorganism removal and may decrease the retention efficiency of the packed tower well below its design value, particularly if channeling through the wetted media occurs. Also, organic components present in the compressor exhaust can provide a nutrient source for the retained microorganisms and increase the possibility of bacterial growth and eventual penetration through the depth filter medium. In addition, droplet formation can result in liquid being forced through the packed tower and contaminated droplets being re-entrained in the outlet air stream thereby contaminating the downstream system.

The pressure differential across the tower may also increase significantly with wetting, increasing the energy costs. A number of approaches have been tried to overcome the wetting problem, such as heat tracing to maintain an elevated temperature, these are expensive to operate and have not consistently resolved the problem.

Although it is obvious that operating deviations such as these do reduce the reliability of a packed tower for air sterilization, there is no quantitative procedure to determine if the filtration efficiency is adequate to assure a sterile inlet air condition. The lack of such a quantitative procedure adds an element

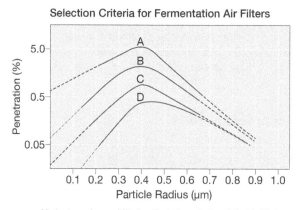

Mechanisms of aerosol filtration. Percent penetration of dioctyl phthalate
particles through a resin inpregnated glass fiber filter is plotted as a
function of particle radius and incident air velocity (cm s¹). A.0.94:
B.042: C.021: D.0.094

FIGURE 21.5 Particle retention efficiency.

of uncertainty which affects both the operation and maintenance decisions. Skilled operators are necessary to monitor the packed tower to ensure that it is packed and operating efficiently. The actual source of contamination of a production batch is often difficult to identify and the air filtration system is always suspect during a contamination outbreak. Without a technique for testing the efficiency of a packed tower, it is difficult to ascertain whether the packed tower is the cause of the contamination outbreak.

Design of Fibrous Air Filters

In order to model a fibrous air filter, several assumptions must be made. It is assumed that

1. Once a particle is trapped by a fiber, it then will remain trapped.
2. At a particular depth across the filter, the particle concentration does not vary.
3. The removal efficiency at a given depth is equivalent across the filter.

The following equation describes how the concentration of particles varies with the depth position in the filter [3]:

$$\frac{dN}{dt} = -Kx \tag{21.1}$$

where N = particle concentration, x = depth, and K = a constant.

Solving the equation between a depth of 0 and x and a particle concentration of N_0 particles entering the filter and particle concentration of N particles leaving the filter yields:

$$\ln\left(\frac{N}{N_0}\right) = -Kx \tag{21.2}$$

The relationship between depth and the logarithm of the ratio of particles removed to particles incident is known as the log-penetration relationship [3]. This relationship has been used in sizing depth filters.

The constant K in Equation 21.2 will vary with the type of packing and is dependent on linear velocity through the packed bed. If the relationship between the constant K and linear velocity through the bed is known, Equation 21.2 can be used to size a packed bed for a given log reduction of particles.

Another consideration for the design of a packed bed is the pressure drop across the bed. Typically, ΔP is linear with the linear air velocity for a given depth [3]. The pressure drop across the packed tower can be dependent upon the type of medium, the packing density, the air density, and the linear air velocity through the filter.

As an example of an equation for the pressure drop across the packed bed is given in Richards [3]:

$$\Delta P = \frac{2\rho v^2 \alpha x C}{\pi D_f} \tag{21.3}$$

where
ΔP = pressure drop
v = linear air velocity
α = ratio of filter density over fiber density
x = filter bed depth
C = drag coefficient
D_f = fiber diameter
ρ = air density

At high air velocities, the above relationship indicates that the pressure drop is proportional to the square of the linear air velocity. At low linear air velocities (<2–3 ft/s), the relationship is linear.

Transition to Cartridge Filters

The specific changes required during the retrofit process to convert from fiberglass packed towers to filter cartridges are dependent upon the condition of the existing facility. The upstream requirement to operate cartridge filters is the absence of condensate water and fine particulate material from the feed stream. Since condensate water is a more critical problem for the hydrophilic glass wool media than the hydrophobic cartridges, the existing approach (such as a coalescer or cyclone) may be sufficient. In some installations, a coalescer alone has been shown to be also adequate to remove fine particulate material without requiring a separate prefilter.

In dry air systems utilizing oil-free compressors, a coalescer typically is not required. In such cases, a dedicated air particulate prefilter upstream of the sterilizing-grade filter cartridges has also been used.

There must also be provision made to eliminate the generation of particulate contaminant in the region between the prefilter and the final sterilizing-grade filter. Stainless steel piping is recommended for this application. An evaluation of the existing system should be performed to determine the best approach to minimize the extent of contamination which may reach the final sterilizing-grade filter.

Unlike packed towers, cartridge filters are compact, easily handled, and can be used in housings or manufactured as a fully disposable capsule form. Their lack of depth is more than compensated for by their high surface area and tight particle capture specifications. Membrane filters for contamination control of process gases have thus developed to be the prevalent gas filtration tool in the pharmaceutical industry, besides high efficiency particulate air (HEPA) and ultra-low particulate air (ULPA) filters for clean room air filtration and other process applications that require extremely high airflow on process equipment. Cartridge filters are available as either prefilter (particulate rating) or sterilizing filter (bacterial rating) configurations. Prefilters in air service can be used for particulate removal or liquid aerosol removal. Prefilters are positioned upstream of the final (sterilizing) filters and are designed to protect the final filter from premature plugging, thereby prolonging significantly the life of the final filter.

Cartridge Filters for Particle and Liquid Aerosol Removal

The following are brief descriptions of the coarser cartridge filters that can be used for gas filtration. The design and qualification of sterilizing-grade membrane gas filters for the removal of bacteria and phages (viruses) from gases are described in the "Sterilizing Grade Membrane Filters for Gas Service" section.

Rating of Cartridge Filters: Nominal versus Retention Testing

Cartridge filters can have nominal or absolute ratings. A nominal rating is an arbitrary micron value assigned by the manufacturer, based upon the removal of some percentage of all particles of a given size or larger. Therefore, the direct comparison of nominally rated filters is very difficult. Nominal ratings can also be misleading, because the filter will not retain all particles at the pore size rating and can pass particles larger than the rating indicates. Many filter manufacturers use a nominal micron rating for removal efficiency. This is defined by the American National Standards Institute (ANSI) as an "arbitrary micrometer value indicated by the filter manufacturer. Due to lack of reproducibility this rating is deprecated."

An alternative method for rating filters is the Oklahoma State University (OSU) F-2 Test. This rating method [5, 6] provides a standardized rating, has received wide acceptance for use on lubricating and hydraulic fluids, and has been adapted for use in water-based tests. The test is based on continuous online particle counts of different particle sizes, both in the influent and the effluent. The filter removal efficiency is expressed as beta value or in percent removal efficiency. The beta ratio at a specific particle size is defined as β_X: the number of particles of a given size (X) and larger in the influent, divided by the number of particles of the same size (X) and larger in the effluent, where X is the particle size in microns. The percent removal efficiency can be calculated from the beta value. The percent removal efficiency is $[(\beta_X - 1)/\beta_X]\,100$ [7].

The following example beta values thus correspond to the following percentage removal efficiency:

Beta value = 2	50%
Beta value = 20	95%
Beta value = 75	98.7%
Beta value = 200	99.5%
Beta value = 1,000	99.9%
Beta value = 5,000	99.98%

Prefilters for Particle Removal

For some applications, it is essential to use a prefilter to remove particulate material or liquid aerosols present in the gas stream to prevent premature filter blocking and achieve an economical service life of the final filter. A suitable prefilter will reduce or eliminate particulate contamination within the system, for example, from the incoming steam, compressed gas or piping, or exhaust gas, thus protecting and extending the life of the final, typically sterilizing-grade filter.

Membrane filters composed of materials such as, for example, polypropylene (PP) or cellulose can effectively be used to remove particulate material from a gas stream. The filter micron ratings range from the order of 1 μm to the order of 100 μm. An appropriately selected filter will ensure the desired level of particulate contaminant removal. The following are descriptions of examples of filters that can be used as prefilters in pharmaceutical air filtration.

Porous Stainless Steel Filters

Porous stainless steel medium is made by sintering (bonding by pressure and heat) very fine particles of stainless steel or other high alloy powder to form a controlled pore size metal medium. For use as a filter medium, porous stainless steel can be formed as a flat sheet, or preferably as a seamless cylinder. This special manufacturing process produces a high dirt capacity medium which is temperature and corrosion resistant. The recommended alloy is type 316 LB, which has a higher silicon content than type 316 L and provides a stronger, more ductile product with better flow properties.

Standard porous stainless steel filters are 2⅜ in. O.D. with type 304 or 316 stainless steel flat blind endcap at one end and 1 or 1½ in. NPT connection at the other, or industrial style flat gasket open endcaps welded at each end. Porous stainless steel filter cartridges are chemically or mechanically cleanable, offering economy of reuse. For gas and steam applications, filter elements typically have absolute ratings of 0.4–11 μm. They are also very useful in sparging applications.

Cellulose-Pleated Filter Cartridges

Pleated cellulose filter cartridges are applicable as prefilters for inlet air for fermenters and bioreactors. These filter cartridges are constructed of pure cellulose medium, without resin binders, which is pleated to form a high-area filter cartridge. Cellulose media cartridges are assembled with hardware components consisting of an inner support core and an outer support cage with appropriately sized windows, and endcaps melt sealed to imbed the medium in the plastic. All hardware components are typically of PP.

PP-Pleated Filter Cartridges

PP-pleated filters are applicable as prefilters for prefiltration of inlet and exhaust gases. These process filter cartridges are constructed using nonmigrating continuous strands of nonwoven PP filaments. The filter should be described by an absolute rating for reliable selection and performance. The thin sheet of PP media is pleated and formed into a cylinder with a longitudinal side seal of melt seal PP. The cylinder is then melt sealed to molded PP endcaps to ensure no fluid bypass. PP hardware components consisting of an inner support core and an external protective outer cage with appropriately sized windows are incorporated.

Liquid aerosol Removal

A coalescer can be used for the removal of liquid aerosols containing water or oil droplets. This is desirable in compressed air systems and in fermenter (bioreactor) vent applications as a prefiltration for a sterilizing gas filter, because the liquid aerosol droplets could be removed by and entrapped in the final filter, causing reduced gas flow or filter blockage.

Coalescers operate efficiently if they are able to separate the liquid and the gas in the liquid aerosol. The three basic steps that are required are:

- Aerosol capture
- Unloading or draining of the liquid
- Separation of the liquid and gas

Sizing of liquid/air coalescers is critical to ensure that they are to perform their function. They must be matched to the air flow and that flow must be below the rate at which the coalesced droplets will be swept off the medium and re-entrained into the air exiting the unit.

Figure 21.6 is an illustration of a liquid-gas coalescer. The coalescer has a gravity separator, which allows for the removal of large liquid aerosols (typically >300 μm). The coalescer flow direction is in-to-out. The liquid is captured through the coalescence of fine aerosols (0.1–300 μm) to large droplets (1–2 mm). The coalescence of the droplets is illustrated in Figure 21.7. The large droplets flow downward from a drainage layer. The separated liquid is then drained, usually automatically, from the system. The aerosol-free air leaves the system from the top of the assembly.

Aerosol Removal Tests

A coalescer effects a separation of liquid and gas by first capturing the aerosol, then unloading or draining the liquid, and finally separating the liquid and gas. Coalescer performance can be degraded by re-entrainment of the discontinuous (or liquid) phase due to poor drainage. It is preferable, therefore, to use a coalescer performance test that employs an aerosol and parameters representative of actual

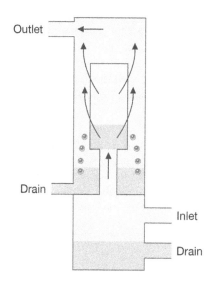

Gravity Separator: Removal of large liquid aerosols (>300 μm).
Coalescer: Flow Direction In-to-out; -prevents reintrainment.
Capture: Coalescence of fine aerosol liquids (0.1-300 μm)
to large droplets (1-2 mm).
Drainage: Downward flow of liquids from coalescer drainage layer.
Separation: Removal of liquids from housing.

FIGURE 21.6 Liquid-gas coalescer.

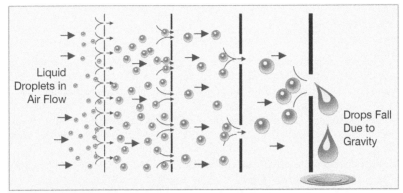

Small Liquid Droplets Coalesce to Form Larger Drops

FIGURE 21.7 Coalescence of droplets.

systems and considers the three factors (aerosol capture, medium drainage, and downstream separation) of importance for proper operation. An example of such a procedure is found in Ref. [8].

Sterilizing-Grade Membrane Filters for Gas Service

Guidelines

The U.S. Food and Drug Administration (FDA) describes key features, applications, and recommendations of gas filters used in pharmaceutical processes as follows in Ref. [9]. Many of these aspects are discussed in detail in the following sections of this chapter.

> A compressed gas should be of appropriate purity (e.g., free from oil) and its microbiological and particle quality after filtration should be equal to or better than that of the air in the environment into which the gas is introduced. Compressed gases such as air, nitrogen, and carbon dioxide are often used in cleanrooms and are frequently employed in purging or overlaying. Membrane filters can be used to filter a compressed gas to meet an appropriate high-quality standard. These filters are often used to produce a sterile compressed gas to conduct operations involving sterile materials, such as components and equipment. For example, we recommend that sterile membrane filters be used for autoclave air lines, lyophilizer vacuum breaks, and tanks containing sterilized materials. Sterilized holding tanks and any contained liquids should be held under positive pressure or appropriately sealed to prevent microbial contamination. Safeguards should be in place to prevent a pressure change that can result in contamination due to back flow of nonsterile air or liquid. Gas filters (including vent filters) should be dry. Condensate on a gas filter can cause blockage during use or allow for the growth of microorganisms. Use of hydrophobic filters, as well as application of heat to these filters where appropriate, prevents problematic moisture residues. We recommend that filters that serve as sterile boundaries or supply sterile gases that can affect product be integrity tested upon installation and periodically thereafter (e.g., end of use). Integrity tests are also recommended after activities that may damage the filter. Integrity test failures should be investigated, and filters should be replaced at appropriate, defined intervals.

Guidelines on various aspects of gas supply and filtration have been issued from organizations, such as The International Society for Pharmaceutical Engineering (ISPE). ISPE has issued the Good Practice Guide: Process Gases [10]. ISPE describes their guideline as

> providing information to allow organizations to benchmark their practices, and improve upon them.
>
> This Guide considers gases that come into direct contact with the biopharmaceutical and pharmaceutical manufacturing process streams, including:
>
> * nitrogen
> * oxygen

- argon
- carbon dioxide
- compressed air

(...) The Guide focuses on defining cost effective engineering approaches and practices used to deliver a process gas systems for a manufacturing facility in a timely manner providing clarification of issues critical to product quality for the production of biopharmaceutical and pharmaceutical drug substances and drug products.

Specifically, the Guide addresses the process of designing, constructing, commissioning, and qualifying a process gas system regulated by the FDA or other regulatory authority, such as the EMA.

This Guide provides the pharmaceutical manufacturing and engineering community with a common language and understanding of gas systems, promoting a Science and Risk-Based basis for the planning, construction, commissioning, and qualification of gas systems used to support production.

Five key concepts are applied throughout the Guide:

1. Product and Process Understanding
2. Life Cycle Approach within a Quality Management System
3. Scalable Lifecycle Activities
4. Science-Based Quality Risk Management
5. Utilizing Supplier Involvement

Risk-based approaches have developed to the key principle in pharmaceutical manufacturing.

Design of Sterilizing Grade Membrane Filters

Membrane filters used for fermenter and bioreactor sterile inlet gas and exhaust gas vents, sterile pressure gas, sterile nitrogen blankets, storage tank sterile vents, formulation tank sterile vents, lyophilizers, and sterile air for aseptic packaging usually contain a membrane made of hydrophobic materials such as polyethersulfone (PES), polyvinylidenefluoride (PVDF), or polytetrafluoroethylene (PTFE).

It should be noted that prior to the introduction of hydrophobic membrane filters, hydrophilic (e.g., polyamide (nylon), modified PVDF and PES) were used for air filtration applications in the pharmaceutical industry. While hydrophobic membrane filters are employed for most gas applications due to their water-repellent surface properties that minimize blockage by wetting, there may still be applications in which hydrophilic membrane filters are used. Hydrophilic membranes can be used for dry air and gas filtration in applications in which the moisture is minimal and thus no wetting will occur.

Hydrophobic membrane filters are preferred in sterile gas filtration applications because hydrophobic filters do not wet with water and other higher surface tension liquids. When a filter membrane is wetted, i.e., pores are filled with liquid, it will not freely pass air until the liquid-wet bubble point (BP) of the filter is exceeded. This liquid-wet BP can be greater than 3.5 bar (50 psi), depending on pore size and surface tension of the wetting liquid. The inherent hydrophobicity of membrane filters used for gas filtration allows sterilizing-grade filters to be able to remove bacteria and viruses completely from gas, even when exposed to moisture [11].

The hydrophobic membrane filter material is pleated together with layers of support material (typically nonwoven PP) on the upstream and downstream side of the membrane. These layers provide mechanical support to the membrane, ensure that the complete filter area can be utilized for fluid flow, and ensure proper drainage of the fluid. The pleated membrane pack is formed into a cylinder by a longitudinal, homogeneous melt side seal.

A rigid inner core with appropriately sized windows is present to provide support against differential operating pressure in normal (out-to-in) flow direction. An outer cage placed on the upstream side of the membrane filter pack is provided for additional support and protection during handling. The cage provides retention of structural integrity against (typically lower) differential operating pressure in reverse flow direction and accidental reverse pressure. PP and PTFE are examples of materials that can be used for the cage, core, and support material in a hydrophobic membrane filter.

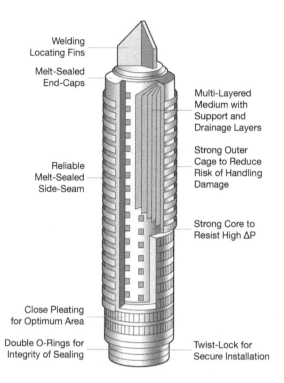

Welding
Locating Fins

Melt-Sealed
End-Caps

Multi-Layered
Medium with
Support and
Drainage Layers

Strong Outer
Cage to Reduce
Risk of Handling
Damage

Reliable
Melt-Sealed
Side-Seam

Strong Core to
Resist High ΔP

Close Pleating
for Optimum Area

Double O-Rings for
Integrity of Sealing

Twist-Lock for
Secure Installation

FIGURE 21.8   Construction of a membrane filter.

Endcaps are attached by melt sealing to imbed the membrane pack in the plastic. Several (typically up to four) modules can be welded together end-to-end to produce larger filter cartridges. Membrane filters are available in a large variety of shapes and sizes. The most typical configuration for pharmaceutical air applications is 10-in. elements. In single-use systems, filter capsules are utilized that can be sterilized by gamma irradiation. A typical membrane filter is illustrated in Figure 21.8.

Membrane filters may be assessed for integrity by a nondestructive physical integrity test correlated to filter retention performance that is performed by the filter user prior to and/or after use in order to assure that the filter will perform/has performed to its specified function. Integrity testing and its correlation to filter performance, such as bacteria removal, is further described in Chapters 11 and 13 of this book.

Qualification Tests for Sterilizing-Grade Membrane Filters

Organism Retention Tests

Microorganism retention tests can be conducted to verify that membrane filters effectively remove all bacteria from a gas stream. Liquid challenge tests with *Brevundimonas diminuta* (American-Type Culture Collection (ATCC) 19146), measuring about $0.3 \times 0.6\text{--}0.8\,\mu m$, is a standard challenge test for the validation of sterilizing-grade filters ($0.2\,\mu m$) in the pharmaceutical industry. Aerosol challenges with T_1 bacteriophage ($0.05 \times 0.1\,\mu m$), *PP7* bacteriophage (25 nm), or *MS-2* (23 nm) bacteriophage can provide a test of a filter's retention efficiency of extremely small contaminants in gas service.

The retention efficiency of a given filter is less when a liquid challenge is used instead of an aerosol challenge due to the lack of Brownian motion in liquids and thus the absence of diffusional interception. Thus, a liquid challenge test is a more stringent test of a filter's retention capability. A liquid challenge test can also provide retention information for process conditions such as extreme moisture after sterilization or air entrained with water drops. An example of the technique used to perform a liquid bacterial challenge on sterilizing-grade membrane cartridges is found in Refs. [12, 13].

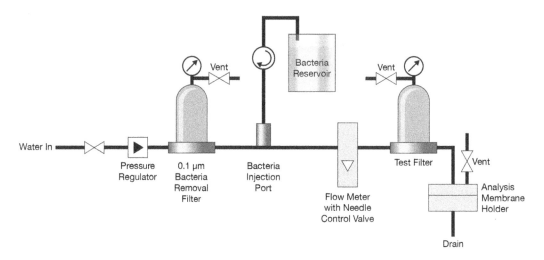

FIGURE 21.9   Liquid bacterial challenge test rig.

The industry standard liquid test for sterilizing-grade filters involves challenging a test filter with a known quantity of *Brevundimonas diminuta*, no less than 1×10^7 colony-forming units (cfu) per cm^2 of filter area. The challenge organisms are passed through the filter suspended in sterile water at a defined flow rate and time. All effluent from the test filter is passed through an analysis membrane. The analysis membranes are removed from the filter disc holder and placed on an appropriate agar growth medium and incubated for the specified time and temperature. After incubation, the plate is examined for the presence or absence of microbial colonies. Figure 21.9 illustrates a typical liquid bacterial challenge test stand.

The aerosol challenge test system can consist of a nebulizer loaded with the challenge microorganism suspension, a separate line for dry air makeup, and split stream impingers to sample the aerosol challenge with and without the test filter. A schematic of a test stand that can be used for the aerosol challenge procedure described is given in Figure 21.10. Detailed descriptions of the aerosol test protocols for *Brevundimonas diminuta*, *PP7*, and *MS-2* bacteriophages can be found in Ref. [12].

During the aerosol challenge, an aerosol is generated with a nebulizer. The aerosol is introduced into the test filter at a given flow rate. The filter effluent is collected in dual liquid impingers. Controls are performed simultaneously via a split stream by using a two-channel timer to direct air flow, on an alternating basis, from the test side filter impingers to the unfiltered control side impingers for recovery.

The impingers contain sterile buffer and after the challenge is completed, the buffer can be analyzed for the test organism. If *Brevundimonas diminuta* is the test organism, then the buffer is analyzed by filtering the buffer solutions through an analysis membrane, placing the membrane on Mueller Hinton Agar for 48 h, and counting the cfu. If a bacteriophage is the test organism, then samples of the buffer are diluted with a suitable broth, mixed with liquid nutrient agar (0.7% agar concentration; 48°C) and the respective bacteria host in the log phase of growth. After mixing all three components, the mix is poured over nutrient agar plates and incubated for a suitable temperature, so that the plaques can be counted.

DOP/PAO Test

The DOP (dioctylphthalate) aerosol test has seen extensive use in measuring the efficiency of HEPA and ULPA filters used to provide air to clean rooms, and for similar applications. DOP was used when the test was first developed but this has been superseded by other less toxic materials, such as Poly Alpha Olefin (PAO). During the test, the oil is aerosolized to form droplets which have a mean diameter of 0.3 μm. The droplets are then carried at high concentration, in a gas stream to the filter under test. Any droplets which pass through the filter are detected and counted by either a light scattering photometer or laser particle counter, attached to the downstream side of the filter under test, giving a percentage penetration when compared to the upstream concentration. For a filter to be rated as a HEPA filter it must meet or exceed

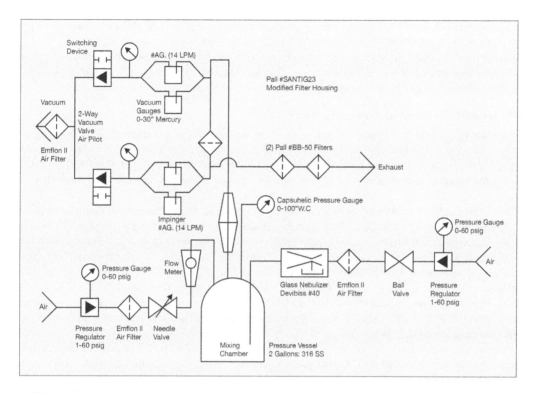

FIGURE 21.10 Aerosol challenge test stand.

the Military Standard, MIL-STD-2821 [14] and must retain 99.97% of 0.3 μm particles. For a filter to be rated as an ULPA filter it must meet or exceed 99.999% retention of particles at 0.12 μm. The commercially available equipment operates at 4 cubic feet per minute (CFM), and cannot detect fractional penetration by 0.3 μm droplets of 10^{-6} (0.0001%). Using microbiological terminology, the method, at 4 CFM, is able to measure titer reduction (defined as the ratio of upstream to downstream cfus) of 10^6. It cannot, for example, distinguish between two filters having respective titer reductions of 10^8 and 10^6, nor can it detect a minor defect that could compromise sterility of the gas filtered.

A typical air flow for a fermenter air filter, such as a sterilizing grade 0.2 μm-rated membrane filter, is about 50–100 standard cubic feet per minutes (SCFM) per 10-in. module (85–170 Nm³/h). To test a single module at 50 SCFM, for example, the DOP method requires a 12.5-fold dilution with air, reducing the sensitivity to a titer reduction of 8×10^4. To test *in situ* at a 1,000 CFM rate reduces sensitivity further to 4×10^3. A titer reduction of 10^4 corresponds to a removal efficiency of 99.99%. This means that this test is basically a qualitative check for filter damage when used with all but the smallest housings.

As an example, the bacteria content for the compressed air incident on a filter could range from 10^1 to 10^4 per cubic foot, depending on the cleanliness of the system. Assuming a level of 10^2 organisms per cubic foot, a single 10-in. module runs at 50 SCFM for 180 h would have approximately 5.4×10^7 bacteria incident on it. A filter able to meet the DOP test sensitivity of 8×10^4 (~99.998%) could theoretically pass 6.8×10^2 bacteria cells during the 180 h period (1 every 15 min).

By contrast, the bacteria challenge test and its relationship to the industry standard integrity tests, the forward flow, water intrusion, and bubble point, provide reliable and convenient means to test the integrity of a sterilizing-grade filter and may be correlated to its retention performance. These are the methods upon which most filter manufacturers' validation data is based.

As with the liquid challenge test, for a filter cartridge to pass an aerosol challenge, all incident organisms must be retained. The test reliability is such that a single-organism downstream can be detected. Thus, using the aerosol challenge tests a titer reduction of $>10^{10}$ for *Brevundimonas diminuta* (size: 0.3 μm × 0.8 μm) and titer reductions of $>10^{11}$ for *PP7 and MS-2* bacteriophage (size: 25 and 23 nm) can be demonstrated. A DOP/PAO test, under the same conditions, would only be able to demonstrate a titer reduction of about 8×10^4 (efficiency of 99.998%), due to the limited sensitivity of the test.

Furthermore, frequent DOP testing of a membrane filter cartridge may reduce the service life of the filter. An accumulation of the DOP/surrogate oil droplets generated during the test can be deposited on the filter, accumulate as an oil film, and block the pores of the media.

Integrity Tests for Membrane Filter Cartridges

For sterilization filtration, it is necessary to achieve the highest possible assurance of filter integrity and removal efficiency. The installation of integrity-testable filters and the performance of routine integrity testing by the user is essential to demonstrate that the system is performing to specification. Tests which qualify the retention characteristics of a membrane filter can be defined as destructive or nondestructive tests.

Destructive tests are performed using an appropriate contaminant to meet a specific claim for retention of the contaminant. The test procedure must be sensitive enough to detect the passage of contaminants of interest. For sterilizing grade $0.2\,\mu m$ membrane filters, the industry standard test organism (i.e., contaminant) is *Brevundimonas diminuta* (ATCC 19146). The organism and minimum challenge level ($10^7\,cfu/cm^2$ filter area) are specified in the ASTM standard F383-2015 and referenced in the FDA Guideline for Industry—Sterile Drug Products Produced by Aseptic Processing (1987). The current (2004) FDA Guideline for Industry—Sterile Drug Products Produced by Aseptic Processing—Current Good Manufacturing Practice specifies that a sterilizing-grade filter is one that removes all microorganisms present in the product being processed.

Because most filter users would not want to perform a destructive test in a process environment, nondestructive tests (forward flow, bubble point, water intrusion) related to the retention results of the destructive test are used instead.

Pall Corporation developed the forward flow test for quantitative integrity testing. This integrity test is presented in detail in Pall Publication [15]. The forward flow test quantitatively measures the gas (typically air or nitrogen) flow through a wetted filter at a predetermined and fixed gas test pressure. The filter is deemed integral if the measured gas flow rate is lower than the manufacturer's specified maximum value. BP testing utilizing commercially available integrity test devices assesses a rapid change in gas flow through a wetted filter, while the test pressure is increased in predefined increments. The increase in gas flow occurs when the capillary forces of the largest pores in the filter membrane are exceeded and the wetting fluid is expelled from the filter membrane at this pressure point (BP). Thus, details of the test execution by the device and the employed test algorithm influence the test result. The filter is deemed integral if the determined BP pressure is higher than the manufacturer's specified minimum value.

The water intrusion test (WIT) quantitatively measures the water flow across a non-wetted hydrophobic filter when the water-filled filter housing is subjected to a predefined test pressure [15]. The filter is deemed integral if the measured water intrusion flow rate is lower than the manufacturer's specified maximum value. Studies suggest that the water intrusion flow largely consists of water vapor flow that pass through the non-wetted membrane driven by the pressure gradient across the filter during testing [16].

From the relationship developed between these nondestructive integrity tests and the destructive microbial challenge test, membrane filter performance can be safely and conveniently verified in the production environment. The relationship between a nondestructive integrity test and the assurance of bacterial retention constitutes an essential part of the sterilizing-grade filter validation study, and is extremely important for microbial retentive filters used in critical fluid processes. A discussion of nondestructive tests for gas membrane filters is included in "Integrity Testing of Gas Filters" section of this chapter.

Certificate on Filter Quality

To verify and document the filter design, the materials of construction (MoC), and quality assurance testing of filters designed and manufactured for pharmaceutical use, the vendor shall provide a certificate with each sterilizing-grade filter. This might be a called a certificate of conformance or a certificate of test. Typical and desired element of such a quality certificate are:

- Part number
- Pore rating
- Batch number
- Specification of membrane employed in the filter
- Filter supplied sterile or non-sterile
- Date of manufacturing
- The quality system certification under which the product was manufactured
- MoC

    All materials used in the manufacture of filters optimized for pharmaceutical use shall be traceable. All filter components shall be made from materials listed for food contact usage per Title 21 of the U.S. Code of Federal Regulations (CFRs), parts 170–199. These materials shall also meet the specifications for biological tests listed in the latest revision of the United States Pharmacopeia (USP) for Class VI plastics at 121°C. They should not contain materials that are considered specified transmissible spongiform encephalopathies (TSE)- or bovine spongiform encephalopathies (BSE)-risk materials according to current legislation and guidelines (reference European CPMP EMA/410/01 and Title 21 of the U.S. Code of Federal Regulations, Part 189.5).

- Element Integrity

    All sterilizing-grade filter elements shall be 100% integrity tested by a nondestructive integrity test during manufacture, such as the forward flow test, to confirm the integrity of the filter element "as manufactured." The integrity test procedure shall be correlated to a bacterial challenge test and the manufacturing test limit provide a safety margin when compared to the user limit.

- Retention Testing

    Any retention testing performed on samples of the products, such as bacteria challenge testing with *Brevundimonas diminuta* (ATCC 19146), using internal procedures and ASTM Standard Test Method F838-15, in conformance with the applicable requirements of the FDA Guideline Sterile Drug Products Produced by Aseptic Processing—Current Good Manufacturing Practice (September 2004).

- Effluent Quality

    Filter samples from each manufacturing lot shall undergo the following tests to assure the highest level of effluent quality:

    - *Cleanliness*: Shall meet with an adequate safety margin the USP limits under particulate matter in injections with effluent counts determined microscopically. Counts shall serve to document conformance with the requirements for a non-fiber releasing filter per 21 CFR 211.72 and 210.3 (b) (6).
    - *Oxidizables*: Shall meet the current USP requirements, after flushing, under sterile purified water, as determined by a potassium permanganate test. Alternatively, the filter shall meet the current USP requirements under purified water for total organic carbon (TOC) and conductivity.
    - *pH*: Shall meet current requirements under USP water for injection or meet internal specifications after flushing, such as upstream versus downstream differential not to exceed ±0.5 pH units, when tested in accordance with USP <791> pH [17].
    - *Pyrogens/Endotoxins*: Shall meet current requirements under USP water for injection, 0.25 EU/mL, or a similar limit, when an aliquot from a soak solution is tested using Limulus Amoebocyte Lysate (LAL) reagent in accordance with USP <85> Bacterial Endotoxins Test [18].

Sterilization of Sterilizing-Grade Membrane Filters

During their life cycle, hydrophobic membrane process filter cartridges may be subjected to multiple cycles of use, including repeated sterilization. Therefore, they must be designed to be repeatedly steam sterilized in either direction of flow or repeatedly autoclaved. The vendor can provide guidelines on filter cartridge sterilization and use limitations (for example, regarding time and temperature exposure). Typically, these filters are capable of withstanding multiple autoclaving or *in-situ* steam sterilizations of over 100 cumulative hours at up to 140°C.

Because the filters are hydrophobic, drying time is usually not required after steam sterilization or autoclaving prior to starting the gas flow in the system. It is necessary, for membrane filters, as well as for packed towers, to drain the entrained condensate on the inlet side of the filter. Installation of suitable steam condensate traps in the system and maintaining steam as dry as possible is essential to prevent condensate filling the housings and blocking air flow. Procedures and aspects of steam sterilization are described in more detail in the "Steam Sterilization Guidelines for Sterilizing Grade Membrane Filters" section of this chapter.

Filter Housings for Cartridge Filters

General Considerations

It is also necessary to consider the performance requirements of sanitary gas service filter housings for replaceable filter cartridges. Housing size should be adequate for the flow and differential pressure requirements. Filter housings for pharmaceutical applications are typically constructed of stainless steel (e.g., 304, 316, 316L, etc.) or carbon steel, with 316 series stainless steel internal hardware and cartridge seating surfaces. Internal hardware includes tube sheet adapters, tie rods, and seal nuts. Housing closures should utilize quick release mechanisms such as V-band clamps or fast-action swing bolts to facilitate filter change-outs.

Design operating pressure of all filter housings should be specified as maximum psig (barg), and, where needed, rated for full vacuum service. Design maximum operating temperature of the housing should also be specified. The housings or pressure vessels which are within the scope of the American Society of Mechanical Engineers (ASME) [19] should be designed and U-stamped per the code. The respective European guideline is Pressure Equipment Directive (PED) 2014/68/EU. Tungsten inert gas (TIG) weld construction should be used in sanitary style housings to minimize weld porosity and insure high quality, clean joints, with all internal welds ground smooth and flush. All weld procedures and welders should be qualified [20, 21]. In addition, the finished surface should be polished to the level demanded by the end use application up to and including electropolish.

Housings should be capable of *in-situ* steam sterilization in accordance with the manufacturer's recommended procedures and housing or system design should provide for condensate drainage. Gasket material and O-ring elastomers must also be capable of withstanding repeated steam sterilization cycles, along with being compatible with process fluids.

Industrial style housings provide cartridge mounting on a tie rod and sealing to the tie rod assembly by use of a seal nut at the top of the assembly. Tube sheet adapters should be seal welded to the tube sheet to prevent fluid bypass. Filter cartridges are thereby sealed in the housing independent of any cover assembly, ensuring positive sealing and no fluid bypass. Filter cartridges should be seated on the tube sheet adaptor assemblies above the tube sheet to ensure complete drainage of non-filtered fluid prior to cartridge replacement. This prevents potential contamination of downstream surfaces during change-out of filter elements.

Stainless Steel Housings for Gas Service for Sterilization Applications

Gas service housings should be designed to maximize gas flow with minimal pressure drops and effective liquid and condensate drain from the filter cartridge and housing. They should allow for *in-situ* integrity testing. The preferred material of construction is again type 316L stainless steel where in contact with the fluid stream. An aseptic design calls for electropolished internal surface with low Ra-Values (such as <0.4μm/<15μin), without crevices or dead-legs and fully self-draining. External surfaces can be electropolished with typical Ra-Values <0.8 μm/<30 μin), or mechanically polished with Ra-Values <1.2 μm/<48 μin) and passivated. Inlet and outlet fittings for gas service housings should either be butt weld or clamp couplings. Vent and drain ports should be stainless steel fittings with appropriate thread diameters for the housing size. Vent and drain ports in critical applications should be designed for *in-situ* integrity testing.

Gas Filtration Applications

General Considerations and List of Application Examples

Gas filters are critical components for the production of pharmaceutical drugs. Especially in biotechnology and aseptic processing, reliable, efficient, and safe contamination control of gases is of utmost importance. The following processes are examples for critical gas filtration applications:

- Fermentation (bioreactor) inlet gas
- Fermentation (bioreaction) exhaust/off gas
- Product contact gases
- Venting on compendial water tanks (including hot and ozonated)
- Venting on product holding tanks
- Vacuum break at autoclaves and lyophilizers

For each of the above steps, sterilizing grade 0.2 μm hydrophobic membrane filters are typically employed as they provide reliable effective contamination control, maintain their flow characteristic in moist operating conditions, and allow user integrity testing correlated to retention performance prior and/or after use.

The Parenteral Drug Association (PDA) Gas Filtration Committee has defined the desirable characteristics of gas filters for these applications in the document [22]. The committee issued guidelines for use of hydrophobic filters in eight applications (A–H) as follows:

> Most applications for hydrophobic membrane filters can be satisfied with a filter that meets as many of the following ideal characteristics as possible:
> - The filter must retain microorganisms, even under adverse conditions such as high humidity.
> - The filter should have high thermal and mechanical resistance, sufficient to endure long-term applications under demanding use conditions.
> - The filter should withstand multiple steam sterilization cycles.
> - The filter should allow high gas flow rates at low differential pressures.
> - The membrane should be hydrophobic to resist blockage by condensate.
> - The filter construction should be optimized for long, dependable service life.
> - The filter must not release fibers.
> - The filter must be integrity testable with a test correlated to removal efficiency.
> - The filter should be easy to install and maintain.
> - The filter's materials of construction should be compatible with the proposed application (e.g. oxygen service)
>
> The relative importance or need for such properties can best be illustrated by a few sample applications.

1. *Product Contact Gases*: The broadest, most critical use of sterilizing grade hydrophobic membrane filters is for gases that are in direct contact with pharmaceutical products. For example, nitrogen gas is widely used to blanket oxygen sensitive solutions to reduce degradation. Any gas that comes in contact with solutions should be sterile to maintain low bioburden in terminally sterilized products or to maintain sterility in aseptically filled products. This includes process gases used in tanks or headspace gases used to flush product vials and ampoules.

Due to the critical nature of these applications, hydrophobic membrane filters that are validated to a rigorous liquid-based microbial retention challenge are recommended. In many critical applications, redundant filters in series are frequently employed, but not required. Filters must be routinely integrity tested in use to assure their efficacy. Membrane materials should be chosen to reflect the conditions of use, especially if filters units are steamed- or sterilized-in-place.

2. *Fermentor Inlet Air*: The volume of air required to maintain the fermentation process depends on the process and the volume of the culture, and filtration systems should be sized accordingly. In large fermentor applications, the air supply may be millions of cubic meters per year and require large filter assemblies. The air supply needs to be reliable to provide proper oxygenation of the culture and sterile in order to avoid costly contamination problems in the process. Filters used in fermentation processes should meet high microbial retention standards and provide high flow rates at a relatively low pressure drop (1–5 psig). Membrane materials for such applications should be hydrophobic, of high void volume, yet show reliable microbial retention capability. Construction of the filter cartridges is optimized to avoid water blockage. The elements also require a high thermal and mechanical stability, because for the process to be economical, they have to withstand many sterilization cycles at elevated temperatures.

3. *Fermentor Off-Gas*: Membrane filters are employed increasingly for fermentor off-gas applications. The challenges in this application are the high moisture content and the high level of microbial contamination of the fermentor exhaust gases. As the gas stream cools, condensation occurs. This, in turn, can result in an undesirable increase of the head pressure within the fermentor. Water blockage can be avoided by choosing the proper design, protecting the final filter with coalescing pre-filters and heat tracing the filter housings to avoid condensation. Off-gas systems should be designed to prevent condensate and coalesced aerosols from reaching the filter. This is often accomplished by having the off-gas condensate drain back into the fermentor.

Also, there is a potential for foam to be carried over into the off-gas, which can lead to blockage of the filter. Therefore, systems should be designed and operated to avoid foaming. Foaming is typically reduced with addition of anti-foam agents or modification of the fermentation media. In difficult processes, it may be necessary to install a mechanical separator to eliminate foam and the potential for filter blockage.

4. *Vent Filters on Compendial Water and Product Holding Tanks*: When liquid is added to or drawn from a tank, an equivalent volume of air is displaced from or into the tank. To avoid bacterial contamination of the contents in critical applications, the air has to be filtered through a sterilizing grade vent filter. The same is true when a holding or transport tank is steam sterilized, because the air that enters the tank at the end of the sterilization cycle has to be sterile. In addition to the rigor of the steam cycle, another challenge presented by this application is blockage of flow due to entrapment of moisture within the membrane.

The need to avoid blockage of flow through the vent filter is particularly important at the end of a steaming cycle. As the tank cools, condensation of steam creates a vacuum that can be estimated from the ideal gas law or steam tables [23, 24]. At 100°C, for instance, each liter of steam that condenses will occupy only about 0.6 mL, an almost 1700-fold decrease in volume. Because the bulk of the condensation will take place rapidly, the vent filter should be properly sized to deliver the equivalent of the tank volume of air in a small period of time. If no appropriate measures are taken to prevent the disruption of air flow through the vent filter, the resulting vacuum in the tank may damage the tank. The issue is less problematic in tanks that are vacuum rated, a feature that makes them considerably more expensive.

Other design features can also prevent tank implosion. For instance, the vent filter can be connected to a source of compressed air, at a pressure high enough to displace the moisture lodged within the pore structure. Preventive measures such as heat traced housings should be seriously considered. Special care needs to be exercised in the sizing of the filter to avoid the problems associated with blockage in this application. It is also prudent to fit sealed tanks with a suitable rupture/implosion disc. However, reliance on this feature risks product loss and implies a significant amount of downtime to replace the disc, as well as repeating the cleaning and steaming process.

5. *Lyophilizer and Autoclave Vacuum Break*: The air (gas) that enters the chamber of a lyophilizer will come into direct contact with the sterile product. Likewise, the air that enters an autoclave will come in contact with sterile commodities or equipment. Hence, the gas supplied to reduce/ break the vacuum at the end of the lyophilization/autoclave cycle must be sterile in these cases. Disruption of air flow due to condensation can adversely impact the operation, and appropriate measures to prevent this should be taken. The filter element in such applications needs to be sterilized, most often by steaming in place. The filter manufacturer's recommendations for steaming or sterilization should be adhered to, particularly if steaming in the reverse direction is required. Because the filter may be subjected to repeated steaming or sterilization cycles in such applications, it should be durable, and should be integrity tested on a regular basis to assure the expected microbial retention level. Ease of integrity testing, placement of the filter, and easy access to the filter are critical in this application.

6. *Gas Used for Drying and Transfer/Fill Line*: Some components (such as rubber stoppers and large equipment such as holding tanks) are typically rinsed in WFI and dried after steaming. Drying is especially critical if they are to be used in oil-based sterile product formulations. Often, compressed air is used to accelerate the drying process.

   In addition, in many processes, the sterile bulk product must be transferred from the sterile holding tank to the filling line. This is often accomplished by pressurizing the head space in the holding tank with a suitable gas.

   The gas in such critical applications must be sterile and free of particles, and a suitable filter must be chosen. Filters in such applications should be routinely sterilized and integrity tested to assure the expected microbial retention capability.

7. *Blow-Fill-Seal Equipment*: Large amounts of sterile compressed air are needed to run blow-fill-seal operations. Often, the equipment is fitted with several different air filtration systems in order to provide sterile air to individual process steps, such as in molding the primary container or shielding critical portions of the machine to prevent the ingress of environmental air containing bacteria and particulate matter. The filtered air contacts critical surfaces as well as the product during the filling step, thus, a high level of bacteria retention must be assured through proper filter selection and validation. Form-fill-seal operations are typically run for extended times, thus the filters used must be durable and reliable. The filters must be routinely sterilized and integrity tested to assure the expected retention performance.

8. *Environmental Air in Isolators*: Isolator technology has been gaining popularity over the past few decades for critical applications, such as sterility testing, aseptic filling, weighing and handling of sterile and even non-sterile potent compounds. Depending on the application, isolators can be run at positive or negative pressure relative to the surrounding environment. Whichever the mode of operation, filtration of make-up and exhaust air plays an important role. Hydrophobic membrane filters can be used as an alternative to conventional depth filters, such as HEPA filters to accomplish the air exchange between isolators and the surrounding environment. The more demanding the operation, whether it be retention of toxic powders from the exhaust or the admission of sterile air, the more demanding the retention validation and integrity test program that should be implemented.

Fermentation Inlet Gas

Overview

During a fermentation process a specific cell (yeast, bacteria or mammalian) is grown to provide a desired product. Products can include cells, antibiotics, amino acids, recombinant proteins, viruses, and many more. There can be a wide variety of sizes for the fermenter, ranging from very small (a few liters or less) cell culture reactors to very large-scale antibiotic production (100,000L). In these applications,

TABLE 21.1

Filter Recommendations for Fermentation and Bioreactor Gas Applications

Application	Filter Type	Typical Micron Rating (μm)	Typical Gas Flow Rate per 10 in. Module (SCFM)	Typical Gas Flow Rate per 10 in. Module (Nm³/h)
Prefiltration of gas to sterilizing filter for particulate removal	Cellulose Pleated	8.0	75	127
	PP Pleated	2.5	2	
Prefiltration of gas to sterilizing filter for oil droplet removal (coalescer)	Coalescer	0.3	00–400	340–680
Sterile filtration of gas for fermenter and bioreactors	Hydrophobic membrane	0.2	75–100	127–170
Sparging	Porous stainless steel	3.0		
Prefiltration of exhaust gas from fermenters and bioreactors	PP pleated	1.2	40	68
Sterile filtration of exhaust gas from fermenters and bioreactors	Hydrophobic membrane	0.2	40	68
Tank venting	Hydrophobic membrane	0.2	75–100	127–170
Steam for cleaning and sterilizing	Porous stainless steel	18	2 bar (30 psig) saturated steam (130 Lb/h)	2 bar (30 psig) saturated steam (130 Lb/h)

it is typically the need to maintain sterility in both, liquid and gas feeds, to support growth of the desired cells and avoid undesired contamination.

Gas filtration applications for fermentation are shown in Table 21.1 and illustrated in Figure 21.11. The applications specific to fermentation are described below, while filtration of utilities used in fermentation such as steam, air, and water are discussed in the "Utilities" section of this chapter.

The indicated gas flow rates per 10-in. filter module can be considered as typical achievable gas flow rates in these applications in typical filter installations. They can be used to select the appropriate number of 10-in. modules for the desired gas flow. For applications such as venting, installations prone to gas flow loss due to contamination load, and where the pressure rating of the installation components is limited, an appropriate safety margin should be applied.

Prefiltration of Fermentation Inlet Gas

Compressors are used to generate air flow for the manufacturing facility. There are two types of compressors, oil free and oil lubricated. In older facilities where oil lubricated air compressors are commonly used, prefiltration of inlet air is necessary for removal of oil droplets. A coalescing filter can provide greater than 99.9% removal of oil and water droplets in the 0.01–0.5 μm range and larger. This also acts as an excellent prefilter for the hydrophobic membrane-pleated filters that are commonly used for sterilizing the inlet gas to the fermenter.

For oil-free compressors, a prefilter acts to remove dirt in the gas system, extending the service life of the final filter. For use with fermentation gas, a cellulose-pleated filter with an absolute rating of 8.0 μm is often employed. Alternately, PP-pleated filters (2.5 μm rated) also serve as excellent prefilters for this application.

Sterile Filtration for Fermenter Inlet Gas

One of the largest applications for sterile gas filtration is the gas used for an aerobic bioreactor or fermenter during a typical production cycle. Typically, one volume of gas per volume of broth per minute is used. Thus, for a 10,000 L fermenter online for 48 h a total of 1×10^6 ft³ (2.8×10^4 sm³) of gas requires sterilization.

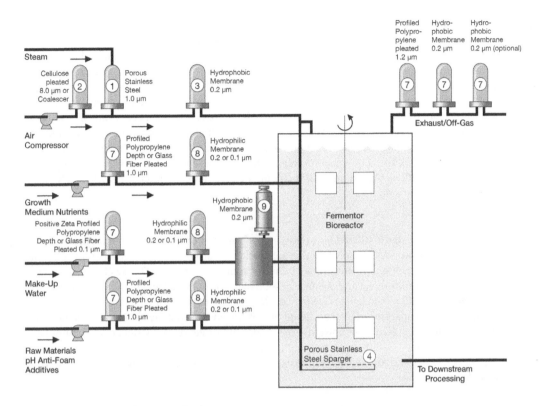

FIGURE 21.11 Fermentation gas applications.

The contaminants present in compressed air can include the following: dust, lubricating oil, hydrocarbons, water, rust, and microorganisms including molds, bacteria, and viruses. Microorganisms in air are often associated with carrier particles, such as dust. Water and oil can be present as bulk liquid, vapor, or an aerosol. The gas distribution system can give rise to contaminants such as rust and water. The concentration and size distribution of particles in compressed air are variable. The size range is generally between 0.001 and 30 μm, with a concentration between 10^{-2} and 10^{-4} g/m^3 [1, 3, 25].

Bacteria and bacteriophage when present in gas feeds can enter fermentation tanks or bioreactors and contaminate the product. Bacteriophage or other viruses can destroy the producing cells and reduce yields.

The process requirements to supply this sterile gas are quite restrictive. The gas sterilization process must

1. Process a large volume of compressed air/gas
2. Provide a high degree of reliability
3. Operate economically

Several methods have been considered for the sterilization of fermenter inlet gas and gas systems. These include filtration, heat, irradiation, washing with sterilizing chemicals, and electrostatic precipitation. Washing and electrostatic precipitation are not effective for the removal of microorganisms. Heat and irradiation are not economical. Filtration is the only technique that meets all the requirements for sterilizing bioreactor and fermenter inlet gas.

An early filtration approach, packed towers were employed widely in the industry. Since the early 1980s, filtration technology has advanced [26] and there has been an ongoing trend to replace depth filters with hydrophobic membrane cartridge filters [11, 27].

The recommended filters for sterilization of air feeds to fermenters and bioreactors are the hydrophobic membrane-pleated filters. The hydrophobic (water repelling) nature of these membranes can provide for bacteria and bacteriophage removal with 100% efficiency under moist or dry operating conditions. This is an important benefit over fiber glass towers and cartridges. Filters for sterile gas feeds should have a 0.2 µm rating and provide full bacterial retention in liquids and a 0.01 µm particulate rating in air service, as demonstrated by phage retention and sodium chloride aerosols as described in Ref. [12].

For some fermentations, the requirement may be for the filtration of fermenter gas at an elevated temperature. If an application involves hot air and a longer service life is desired, then a filter that can withstand the elevated temperature is required. Specially designed high-temperature filters are available and can be used in continuous service at a temperature up to 120°C. These filters have a 0.2 µm microbial rating in liquid service and a particulate removal rating of 0.01 µm in gas service. The filter membrane is made of inherently hydrophobic PTFE and the support layers, cage, core, and endcaps are specifically designed for high-temperature applications. An example for such a high-temperature gas filter is described in Ref. [28].

Sparging

Sparging acts to disperse sterile filtered air evenly in the fermenter or bioreactor containing the growth media and product. The product of choice for this application is porous stainless steel sparging elements, which can provide an exceptionally uniform and fine aeration gas dispersion. These elements are fabricated with one face of porous metal and one face of solid metal. If both surfaces of the sparging elements were porous, bubbles from the under surface may coalesce with bubbles from the top surface.

Porous stainless steel sparging elements should be positioned horizontally in the fermentation tank, with the porous stainless steel facing upward. Fine grades of porous stainless steel (e.g., 3.0-µm liquid rated based on beta value >5,000) are ideal even for shear-sensitive mammalian cell cultures because of their high gas transfer and low shear aeration capability. Elements are typically available in standard and custom designs.

Filtration of Enriched Air or Pure Oxygen for Bioreactors

Modern aeration concepts are increasingly using enriched or pure gaseous oxygen to improve cell culture productivity. However, many materials such as organic matter, plastics, or even metals can potentially ignite when in contact with oxygen, particularly if also subjected to static discharges, high temperatures, pneumatic shocks, or mechanical impact. In addition to the above safety aspects, oxygen or enriched oxygen gases can lead to accelerated oxidation or corrosion of component materials. Both aspects are discussed in some more detail below.

Ignition Risk

To address the risk of ignition, installations for gaseous oxygen including those for filtration need a dedicated risk assessment prior to use. There may also be mandatory requirements in some countries. For example, there are special safety requirements in Europe for the operation of oxygen systems (e.g., [29]).

Sparged air often contains oil from the compressor which, if mixed with oxygen in a common transfer pipe, presents a potential fire hazard. Therefore, air from compressors must be oil free or use oxygen suitable oils.

If any oils or liquid hydrocarbons are present and collect on the filter, they can ignite spontaneously (especially in a hot system) or be ignited by a spark. A filter membrane should, therefore, be free of flammable residues to avoid fire hazards. Oils are available specifically for use in oxygen service.

The German BGR 500, Kapitel 2.32 Betreiben von Sauerstoffanlage [29] instructs that impurities should be ruled out; therefore, avoidance of organic traces as combustible substrate on the filter surface. Single use of sterilizing-grade gas filters is therefore recommended, also the use of "clean" filters, i.e., free of organic contamination. Special instructions on filter installation and operation is also required. Oil, aerosol, and particle-free pressurized airline can be supported by usage of coalescers, stainless steel, and particle filters.

Static discharge presents a risk. At low flow rates, the risk of static buildup and spark formation is small. With high flow rates in dry or low humidity gases, static charge buildup risks are higher. Static discharge has been observed in dry air systems even at flows of 200 Nm^3/h (117 SCFM) or less per 10-in. module. The housing size, grounding, tie rod position and number, and other factors play a role.

To avoid static discharging that may lead to membrane damage, ignition, and combustion of filters, the following measures are recommended:

- Grounding of housings
- Only low flow rates (ca. 85 Nm³/h (50 SCFM) per 10-in. module) by generous sizing
- Minimized linear velocities by generous sizing

Corrosion (Degradation of Filter Materials)

Sterilizing-grade gas filters for this application (preventing spoilage of bioreactors by organisms and contaminants in the incoming and outgoing air and oxygen streams) should be integrity testable by means of a WIT and display sufficient corrosion resistance when exposed to oxygen-enriched air or even pure oxygen. Hydrophobic PTFE membrane filters with suitably stabilized PP hardware and support materials have found suitably resistant and thus become the preferred choice.

Filters for this demanding application should be qualified by the filter vendor as described in the example below, but also user application specifically, as each system and application presents different operating conditions for the filter.

Filter vendor Pall Corporation offers such a more oxidation resistant filter and described it in Ref. [28]. These filters employ support layers from oxidation-resistant polyphenylene sulfide (PPS) polymer, rather than PP. Pall Corporation has qualified this filter type for the sterilizing filtration of pure gaseous oxygen or oxygen-enriched air with an application-relevant series of tests [30]. These tests were performed vendor-internally and by the German Bundesanstalt für Materialforschung und -prüfung (BAM) (Federal Institute for Materials Research and Testing). The construction materials of Emflon HTPFR filters have been subjected to a series of standard pressure shock tests [31] with 100% gaseous oxygen at 10 bar (145 psi) pressure at 60°C (140°F) as described in the Pall publication:

BAM Reactivity Test Method

The materials are placed into a heatable steel tube. The sample tube is then connected by long pipe with a pneumatically operated quick opening valve to a high-pressure oxygen accumulator. A heater enables the sample tube to be set to a defined test temperature. After the tube and pipe are at starting pressure, usually atmosphere pressure, the quick opening valve is opened and preheated oxygen of 60°C (140°F) at pre-set pressure flows abruptly into the pipe and tube. In this way, the oxygen in the tube and pipe is almost adiabatically compressed and heated. If there is a reaction of the sample with oxygen, indicated by a steep temperature rise in the tube, further tests with a new sample are performed at a lower pressure ratio. If, however, no reaction of the sample with oxygen can be detected after a waiting period of 30 seconds, the tube is de-pressurized and the test is repeated (up to four times) until a reaction takes place. This means each test series consists of a maximum of five single tests with the same material under the same conditions. If no reaction can be observed, even after the fifth single test of a test series, testing is continued with new samples at greater pressure ratios, until finally that pressure ratio is determined, at which no reaction can be observed within a test series of five single tests. If the repetition of that test series with a new sample shows the same result, the test can be finished or continued at a different test temperature.

The Pall publication further states:

The evaluation of component materials both unused and previously exposed to oxygen for 14 and 28 days respectively showed that Emflon HTPFR filter materials passed the reactivity tests with 100% gaseous oxygen at 10 bar pressure at 60°C (140°F).

Providing that the user performs an adequate risk assessment as described earlier, Emflon HTPFR filters may be considered for gaseous oxygen service in applications such as:

- Feed of oxygen enriched air or gaseous oxygen at maximum temperature up to 40°C and a maximum pressure of 3 bar for a maximum service life of 28 days, or
- Exhaust gas at maximum temperature up to 60°C for a maximum service life of 28 days in microbial and mammalian cell culture.

These conditions are slightly less severe than the conditions applied to filter material parts during the above described reactivity tests. Also, process temperatures, excess gas pressures, contact times and oxygen concentration in the feed and exhaust air employed for cell culture applications where sterilizing grade gaseous oxygen filtration must be applied are typically even less severe, thus allowing for an additional safety margin.

Fermenter Exhaust Gas Filtration

The purpose of a vent filter on a sterile fermentation/bioreactor tank is twofold: to prevent contamination of the tank and to provide containment of the material inside the tank. Prevention of contamination in the tank is desirable for processes that involve long fermentation cycles or require a sensitive fermentation medium (e.g., tissue culture medium). Genetic engineering techniques, as well as fermentation of pathogenic organisms (such as organisms used for the manufacture of vaccines), have made it necessary to protect the environment and prevent the escape of microorganisms from the fermentation tank. The exhaust filtration system for a recombinant or mammalian cell fermenter/bioreactor must yield sterile and often also virus-free gas to the environment and provide a reliable barrier to prevent ingression of contaminants. Additionally, it must be *in-situ* steam sterilizable and should typically have a clean differential pressure less than 0.07 bard (1 psid).

The removal efficiencies for depth filters (as described above) are typically poor under wet or variable flow conditions. Therefore, membrane filters are recommended for critical vent filtration applications.

The fermenter/bioreactor exhaust gas line can be contaminated with microorganisms or cells, growth medium components expelled from the fermenter/bioreactor as droplets or as solid particles, and aerosol condensate droplets formed during cooling of the gas in the exhaust system. These aerosol droplets, when present, can potentially block the final filter and must thus be removed prior to reaching the final filter. Mechanical separation devices, e.g., cyclones, condensers, and demisters, may not achieve effective aerosol removal below 5 μm [32]. Removal efficiencies and pressure drops also vary significantly with flow rate in such equipment. Studies have shown that aerosols in exhaust lines are predominantly in the very fine 1–5 μm range [33].

The contaminants present will depend upon the fermentation conditions, the growth medium, and the design of the exhaust gas system. The basic requirements for a vent filter are:

- Ability to remove all undesired organisms from the gas stream
- Low pressure drop (high flow rate at a given differential pressure)
- *In-situ* steam sterilizable
- Integrity testable, preferably *in-situ*.

The recommended exhaust filtration system design entails two stages using a PP-pleated depth filter cartridge as a prefilter to a 0.2 μm sterilizing-grade hydrophobic membrane-pleated filter cartridge. The purpose of the prefilter (typically 1.2 μm-rated based on beta >5,000) is to remove aerosolized particles and liquid droplets containing cells and/or growth media from the fermenter/bioreactor exhaust gas. This serves to extend the service life of the final sterilizing-grade filter. If the medium contains only fully dissolved components, such as with a sterile filtered cell culture medium, and if the fermentation is run at low temperatures (<30°C) and low aeration rate (1–1.5 vessel volumes per minute (VVM)), the prefilter may be optional.

Like the final sterilizing-grade filter, the pleated PP prefilter should be resistant to multiple steam cycles. As additional benefit, the prefilter is also acting as a coalescer to retard "foam-outs" from reaching the final sterilizing filter.

Sterilizing grade 0.2 μm absolute rated hydrophobic membrane-pleated final filters, with PVDF or PTFE membranes, can prevent organisms from entering or leaving the controlled reaction zone, even in the presence of water droplets and saturated gas [11, 34]. Steam sterilizability and integrity test values correlated to microbial retention studies under "worst case" liquid challenge conditions provide the highest degree of assurance performance. Redundant systems using a second 0.2 μm-rated sterilizing filter in series are recommended for high-risk recombinant or pathogenic organisms.

TABLE 21.2

Filter Recommendations for Downstream Processing Gas Filtration Applications

Application	Filter Type	Micron Rating (μm)	Typical Gas Flow Rate per 10-in. Module SCFM	Typical Gas Flow Rate per 10-in. Module (Nm³/h)
Sterile nitrogen blanket	Hydrophobic membrane	0.2	75–100	127–170
Tank venting	Hydrophobic membrane	0.2	75–100	127–170
Vacuum break	Hydrophobic membrane	0.2	75–100	127–170
Sterile air for container and closure cleaning	Hydrophobic membrane	0.2	75–100	127–170

Condensate control is usually the most critical consideration for this application. In cases in which there is condensate accumulation and if the fermenter is operated with overpressure in the fermenter head, the amount of condensate accumulation can be reduced if a pressure control valve is placed at the fermenter exit, upstream of the exhaust gas filter. An alternative technique for the prevention of condensate accumulation is to use a heating section in the exhaust gas pipe before the filter installation so that the exhaust gas temperature at the filter train is higher than at the fermenter exit. The heater must be properly sized based on the process parameters. Condensate accumulation at the exhaust filter cartridge can also be avoided by employing steam jacketing on the exhaust filter housings.

Gas Filter Applications in Downstream Processing

General Considerations

Starting with the cells and conditioned broth medium from the fermenter/bioreactor, the objective of downstream processing is to produce a highly purified, biologically active product, free of contaminants such as endotoxins, bacteria, particles, or other biologically active molecules. This phase of bioprocessing typically comprises a series of unit operations including cell and cell debris separation, fluid clarification and polishing, concentration and purification, virus clearance, and membrane filtration sterilization of the purified product.

Cartridge filters are used in many stages of downstream processing, involving filtration of both the harvest fluid and product intermediates, as well as filtration of air and gases required throughout the process. Air filtration applications include vacuum break filters for lyophilizers, sterile nitrogen blankets, tank vents, and sterile air for container cleaning. Table 21.2 lists these typical applications, the recommended filters and their typical gas flow rates that can be used for selecting the appropriate number of 10-in. modules for gas filtration. The indicated gas flow rates can be considered as typical achievable gas flow rates in these applications in typical filter installations. For tank venting, an appropriate safety margin should be applied.

Venting Applications

Absolute rated cartridge filters eliminate contaminants and impurities from air, nitrogen, and other gases used in downstream processing, to prevent contamination of product and further protect concentration and purification equipment. Vent filtration ensures containment and freedom from product contamination during fluid transfer operations and protects processing equipment during sterilization cycles.

In fermentation, cartridge filters are used to maintain the sterility of the makeup water, feeds, additives, media in holding tanks, and in fermenter/bioreactor exhaust gas. Cartridge filters are typically used in downstream processing for

- filtration of air and process gases in pressurized gas lines
- venting applications when it is necessary to vent tanks during fluid transfers
- pressurizing tanks using inert gases such as nitrogen and argon

- protect vacuum lines
- sterile vent holding tanks and lyophilizers
- gas purging
- gas blanketing
- drying
- when sterilizing equipment by *in-situ* steaming or autoclaving.

The recommended filters for non-sterile particulate removal applications are PP-pleated filters. Hydrophobic membrane-pleated filters with a rating of 0.2 μm such as PVDF or PTFE are recommended for aseptic processing. The removal performance of the latter filters should be sterilizing grade when challenged with a bacteria liquid challenge suspension.

Venting applications require careful management of condensate on the vent filter to maintain a sufficient level of gas flow, during use but also during steam sterilization. Water vapor can condense on a vent filter membrane during use if the fluid in the tank or fermenter/bioreactor is water based and the temperature of the filter is lower than the dew point of the fluid in the tank. A recommended procedure for avoiding of the formation of condensate on the membrane is to maintain the filter assembly at a temperature slightly above the dew point of the liquid in the vessel. Formation of condensate can be prevented by fitting a heating section on the vent gas line between the fluid vessel and the filter, or a heating jacket around the filter housing. The purpose of the heater is to ensure that the temperature of the exhaust gas at the filter is above the temperature of the exhaust gas from the system. The effect of the heating unit is to lower the relative air humidity from 100% at the tank or fermenter/bioreactor outlet to 20%–50% downstream of the heating unit at the filter housing inlet.

NOTE: Unnecessarily high heating temperature will limit filter life due to the degradation of the filter polymers (see also the section "Vacuum Break Filters on Lyophilizers and Sterilizers"). Generally, if the temperature of the heating needs to exceed 60°C, the use of a high-temperature membrane filter may be advisable for this continuous service.

In fermenter exhaust gas with a high flow rate, the amount of condensate that can accumulate in the exhaust filter is related to the exhaust gas flow velocity. At a higher flow velocity, the amount of moisture that reaches the exhaust filter, will increase. Thus, if there is any way in which the flow velocity of the exhaust gas can be reduced, the amount of condensate at the filter can be lowered. One possible solution would be to fit the exhaust gas line with a section of wider diameter piping.

Figures 21.12–21.14 illustrate steps that can be required in downstream processing applications. The following discussion is on the air or gas filters required in these applications.

Figure 21.12 illustrates a cell and cell debris separation and clarification process, which is broken into a primary separation, secondary separation, and a cell concentrate section. During primary separation, a cyclone can be used for particle removal. Applications for 0.2 μm-rated sterilizing-grade hydrophobic gas filters include:

- Vent on the cyclone
- Venting of solvent/buffer tanks used throughout the process
- Venting of product holding and receiving tanks
- Provision of a sterile nitrogen blanket

Figure 21.13 shows a general process for concentration and purification of clarified harvest fluid. Applications for 0.2 μm-rated sterilizing-grade hydrophobic gas filters include:

- Venting of solvent/buffer tanks used throughout the process
- Venting of product holding tanks

The final pharmaceutical product will typically need to be packaged. Figure 21.14 shows a generalized filling operation. Applications for 0.2 μm-rated sterilizing-grade hydrophobic gas filters include in this process step:

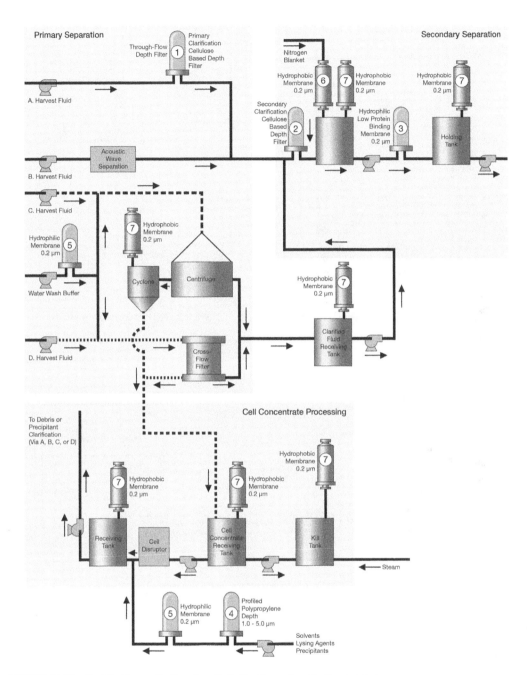

FIGURE 21.12 Air filtration applications in cell clarification and purfication processes.

- Provision of a sterile nitrogen blanket
- Provision of sterile air or nitrogen for container cleaning
- Venting of product-holding tanks
- Vacuum break

The operation of vacuum break filters and filters employed in a Blow Fill Seal operation are addressed in some more detail below.

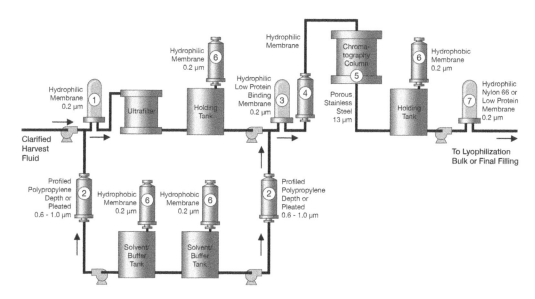

FIGURE 21.13 Air filtration applications in concentration and purification of clarified cell harvest.

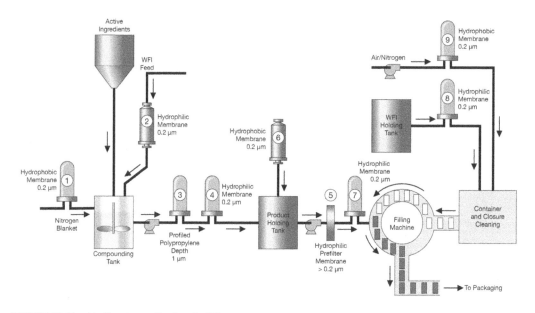

FIGURE 21.14 Air filtration applications in filling processes.

Vacuum Break Filters on Lyophilizers and Sterilizers

0.2 μm-rated sterilizing-grade hydrophobic gas filters are employed in freeze dryer installations to filter the gases used to maintain the chamber pressure and to break vacuum during operation, and in sterilizers for vacuum break purposes.

As an example, the operation steps required for a sterilizing filter used in a lyophilizer as a vacuum break is described below. The system is illustrated in Figure 21.15.

1. *In-situ steam sterilization*: The filter assembly and the receiving vessel and vent filter attached on the vessel are *in-situ* steam sterilized

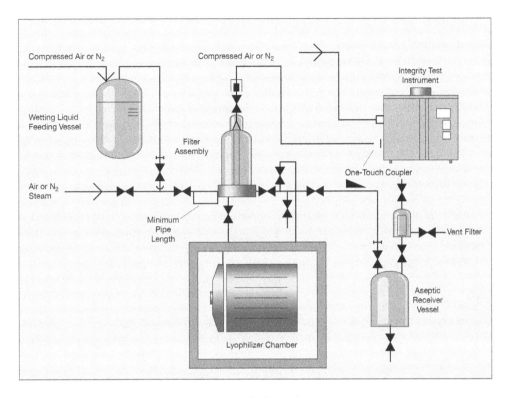

FIGURE 21.15   Air filtration applications in a vacuum break application (lyophilizer).

2. *Cooling*: After the sterilization, the steam is shut off and air or nitrogen is immediately added to the system. Air or nitrogen gas is used to prevent a collapse situation (reverse pressurization – see below) and to cool the system and filter.

3. *Addition of integrity test fluid*: Forward flow and BP integrity test methods require a fully wetted filter. Hydrophobic membrane filters require wetting with a low surface tension fluid, such as an alcohol/water mix. The solution is placed in the wetting solution feed vessel. Compressed air or nitrogen pressure can be used to flow liquid through the filter cartridge in order to fully wet the filter for forward flow or BP integrity testing. The wetting fluid is collected in a receiving vessel. To avoid use of alcohol in these applications and wetting of the filter membrane that prevents free gas flow through the filter, the WIT method is often preferred. For this test, water needs to be introduced on the upstream side of the filter.

4. *Integrity test*: A filter integrity test instrument is connected for the performance of the integrity test. The use of an automated instrument connected to the control system allows for remote operation. If the filter fails the integrity test, it should not be used for operation but removed and replaced with a new filter. This would require repeat of steps 1–4.

5. *Drying*: After the test, the membrane filter is dried to remove the wetting fluid utilized to perform forward flow or BP testing to ensure free gas flow and avoid contamination of the sterilized or vacuum-dried goods. After water intrusion testing the filter allows free gas flow that is sufficient for many applications, as the membrane has not been wetted, although the filter and housing will still hold some water, for example, between filter pack pleats and in the support layers. For freeze dryers, the presence of water is typically not desired on the vacuum break filter; hence, drying of the filter after water intrusion testing is still required. Compressed air or nitrogen can be used for drying.

6. *Lyophilization*: At this point the system is ready for the lyophilization operation.

Gas Filtration in Blow-Fill-Seal Filling Operations

Blow-Fill-Seal (BFS) technology is a widely used, fully automated aseptic filling technique for production of small to large volume liquid-filled containers. The process involves extrusion of a suitable grade plastic material (polyethylene or PP) to a tube ("parison") that is then enclosed with a mold, cut, and transferred to the filling zone of the machine. The filling needles are used to inflate ("Blow") the tube with gas/air to a container, that is then filled with liquid ("Fill") and the container is then heat sealed ("Seal"). Effective contamination control regarding particulates and microorganisms by filtration is essential for this filling operation. A typical arrangement of filters in a BFS machine is illustrated in Figure 21.16. Typical requirements for the filters used in the BFS machines include that the filters can be steam sterilized *in-situ*, are integrity testable, and appropriately sized for adequate gas flow. Therefore, 0.2 µm-rated sterilizing-grade hydrophobic gas filters are the filters of choice. Their applications in this process includes

- Provision of sterile blanket gas (also called gas cushion or buffer tank gas) for the buffer tank on the BFS machine to drive the sterile product liquid through the pneumatically controlled dosing system (gas cushion)
- Provision of sterile gas to form the plastic container in the "Blow" operation

Utilities

There are a number of peripheral unit operations required during a sterile process. The section below describes the gas filtration applications for these unit operations.

Venting of Hot and Ozonated Water Tanks and Systems

Many pharmaceutical processes require large volumes of water. It is critical that the pharmaceutical grade water used is protected from particulate or microorganism contamination to ensure that the process operations do not become inadvertently contaminated. There are several approaches that can be used to ensure that the water remains free from contamination, including the storage of purified water, highly purified water or water for injection (WFI), at a minimum temperature of 80°C (176°F) to discourage microbial growth in the storage system. Another approach is to add ozone, which acts as an

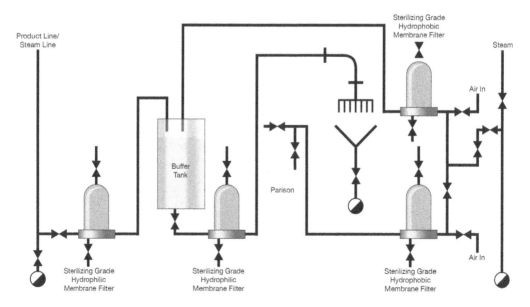

FIGURE 21.16 Air filtration applications in a BFS operation.

antimicrobial and oxidizing agent, to ambient as well as to hot water storage and distribution systems. Usually, the water is stored in tanks fitted with a 0.2 µm-rated sterilizing-grade hydrophobic vent filter to ensure that the tank can be properly vented for filling and emptying without the risk of a secondary contamination from the tank environment.

It is known that standard vent filters can show evidence of oxidative degradation of the PP components from exposure to ozone after 3–6 months in hot and ozonated water tank applications. The PP drainage layers became brittle and powdery due to oxidative attacks from the ozone or the hot air above the water. This type of degradation can lead to:

- Material and particle input into WFI or pure water storage tanks
- Passage of microorganisms through damaged cartridge components
- Failure of cartridge integrity test

For this reason, the use of standard vent filter cartridges in elevated temperature oxidative conditions requires a frequent change-out of filter cartridges in order to avoid degradation of the filter materials. To provide a longer vent filter service life in applications that involve a highly oxidative environment, PTFE membrane filters have been developed with a special support and drainage material which is more robust in oxidative environment. In addition, the PP hardware used for these filters has been optimized to have good resistance to oxidation after longer exposure times.

An example of such a more oxidation-resistant filter has been mentioned above (Pall Corporation Emflon® HTPFR Filter Cartridges) and feature support layers from oxidation-resistant PPS polymer, rather than PP. The higher oxidation resistance of these filter is described in Ref. [35]. The test data in this publication demonstrate that "Emflon HTPFR filters have a higher degree of resistance to oxidation than Emflon II and Emflon PFR filters in vent filter systems on ozonated water tanks." These filters have been found "ideal as sterilizing-vent filters in water systems operated with:

- 20–100 ppb ozone in water at temperature of 20°C–40°C for a minimum of 25 weeks' use
- 100 ppb ozone in water at ambient temperatures for a minimum of 6 months' use"

In even more extreme oxidizing conditions of use, the use of all-fluoropolymer filter constructions should be considered. Such applications include water charged with significantly higher ozone concentrations than 100 ppb, or hot water installations that use ozone in addition as disinfectant. Such all-fluoropolymer filters may employ a 0.2 µm-rated PTFE membrane. While they typically do not fulfil the bacteria retention requirements for a sterilizing-grade filter in a liquid bacteria challenge using *Brevundimonas diminuta* (ATCC 19146) as challenge organism at a challenge level of 10^7 cfu/cm^2 of filter area, they can provide very high titer reductions when used as gas filter. This is due to the filtration mechanism diffusional interception that has been described and discussed in earlier sections of this chapter.

Sterilizing-grade membrane filters can be used in vent applications in which the fluid in the tank is at an elevated temperature. One such application is the vent used to prevent contamination in a WFI tank. The water is at 80°C or higher. When a sterilizing-grade air filter is used for this type of vent service, a steam-jacketed housing is typically used. It is only necessary to maintain the temperature of the filter cartridge at a temperature *slightly above* the dew point of the vapor. The steam introduced into the jacket should be at ambient pressure. Continuous operation of the jacket at a significantly higher steam pressure and temperature can reduce the service life of the filter due to accelerated aging of the hardware by oxidation.

Aging of the filters by oxidation depends on the status of the system. Oxidation does not occur when the cartridge is being steamed, since there should be no air present in a properly operating steam-in-place system. If a cartridge is exposed to air at an elevated temperature, oxidation of the material in the filter, such as PP hardware, will be accelerated. Oxidation will also occur when the filter is in a stagnant situation, i.e., it has no air flow going through it. The flow of air through a filter can moderate the temperature environment, whereas under stagnant conditions the temperature of the filter will rise to the temperature of the housing. Stagnant conditions can exist when the tank is not being used or when the tank is empty.

To prolong service life, it is recommended that the steam jacket is turned off when there is no air flow through the filter for extended periods of time, when operating conditions permit.

For any application for vent filtration when the temperature of the air is above 60°C and/or ozone is present the filter used either has to be specifically designed for this application or should be inspected very frequently to track filter life and to detect the start of the oxidative damage process to set change-out parameters.

Hot Air

Hot air is an oxidizing environment. Thus, similar considerations apply to this application that those given in "Venting of Hot and Ozonated Water Tanks and Systems" section. If an application involves hot air and a longer service life is desired, then high-temperature filters can be used that display a superior oxidation resistance compared to standard gas filters. High-temperature filters can be used in continuous service at a temperature up to 120°C. These filters have a 0.2 μm-rated hydrophobic membrane and fulfill the bacteria retention requirements for a sterilizing-grade filter in a liquid bacteria challenge using *Brevundimonas diminuta* (ATCC 19146) as challenge organism at a challenge level of 10^7 cfu/cm^2 of filter area. Their retention efficiency in gases reaches a particulate removal rating of 0.01 μm in gas service and provide high titer reductions for phages, as described in earlier sections of this chapter. The filter membrane is made of inherently hydrophobic PTFE and the cage, core, and endcaps and support layers are specifically designed for high-temperature applications. For hot dry air, high-temperature filter cartridges are expected to have a service life of up to 1 year at 100°C. However, change-out should be set for actual service conditions. Considerations on the safe use of filters in such environment can be found in Ref. [36].

Steam Filtration

Process equipment and final filters are frequently sterilized by direct steam flow *in-situ*, during the normal line sterilizing cycle. This eliminates the need for making aseptic connections and risking recontamination. Filtered steam is required for this "sterilize in place" of filters, piping, vessels, and filling equipment. Steam is also required for general equipment cleaning and sterilizing. The steam often contains significant amounts of pipe scale and other corrosion products. This particulate material should be removed in the interest of overall cleanliness and to avoid burdening the prefilters and final filters.

Particulate contamination in process steam is efficiently retained by porous stainless steel filters with a removal rating in gases based on beta values of >5,000 of about 1 μm. Even finer stainless steel filters are available on the market with a removal rating of 0.1 μm in gases based on beta values of >5,000. These filters are typically used for the filtration of high purity steam. Porous stainless steel filter assemblies rated 1.0 μm are typically sized at steam flow rates of 30–40 actual cubic feet per minute (60–90 m^3/h) per square foot of filter medium.

General Considerations for Operation of Gas Filters

Integrity Testing of Gas Filters

Guidelines

The U.S. FDA states in their "Guidance for Industry" [9], in Chapter D "Air Filtration," Section 1 "Membrane" (page 8):

> We recommend that filters that serve as sterile boundaries or supply sterile gases that can affect product be integrity tested upon installation and periodically thereafter (e.g., end of use). Integrity tests are also recommended after activities that may damage the filter. Integrity test failures should be investigated, and filters should be replaced at appropriate, defined intervals.

The guideline further states on page 28:

> It is important that integrity testing be conducted after filtration to detect any filter leaks or perforations that might have occurred during the filtration. Forward flow and bubble point tests, when appropriately employed, are two integrity tests that can be used. A production filter's integrity test specification should be consistent with data generated during bacterial retention validation studies.

While the statement on page 28 of the FDA 2004 Guidance for Industry refers to the actual product (liquid) sterilizing-grade filter, the principle is also applicable to sterilizing-grade gas filters, i.e. the non-destructive integrity test should be correlated to the bacteria retention that were performed by the filter manufacturer during filter development and validation, and thus be predictive of filter retention performance.

Implications of Guideline Statements

The recommendation of the FDA 2004 Guidance for Industry implies a risk-based approach for integrity testing of gas filters, depending on their criticality in the process, operating conditions, and duration of use. A risk assessment of these parameters combined with considerations on economics and the practicalities of the process will lead to a wide range of possible approaches to integrity testing gas filters and combinations of tests in the various process stages:

1. **Possible Stages of Integrity Testing in a Process**
   - Do not test filters at any stage
   - Process stage: Installation (pre-sterilization)
     - Test filters off-line prior to installation
     - Test filters *in-situ* after installation
   - Process stage: Sterilization
     - Test filters *in-situ* after sterilization
   - Process Stage: After Use (Filtration)
     - Test filters off-line after use
     - Test filters *in-situ* after use
2. **Cadence of Testing**
   - Only in first cycle of use
   - Periodically after a predefined number of cycles
   - In each cycle of use
3. **Number of Installed Filters**
   - Single filter
   - Redundant filters (two or more in series)
   - Parallel filters so that while one filter is in use the other filter can be tested
4. **Criteria for Filter Change-Out**
   - Based on generic data such as steam sterilization specification for the filter
   - Based on integrity test results for the application (i.e., upon failure)
   - Based on integrity test results for the application but including an appropriate safety margin (i.e., use for less cycles than the typical life time in the application)
   - Change-out after each cycle of use

These considerations will lead to an application-specific pattern of system installation, integrity testing, and number of use cycle for a given gas filter.

The number of cycles for a gas filter is largely dependent on the steam sterilization conditions and the robustness of the filter to the steam sterilization, as the filters would typically not block during use, unlike filters used for liquid filtration applications. An exception are applications with highly challenging (oxidizing) conditions of use, such as hot air or ozone exposure, where the chemical stability of the filter MoC may be the limiting factor for the actual duration of use. During steam sterilization, temperature, differential pressure (especially in reverse direction where the filter is less robust) and condensate management are the most critical parameters that determine filter life. A filter life study data or a periodic integrity test regimen can thus be used only if the filter sterilization procedure is validated and in control.

Integrity Test Methods for Gas Filters and Practical Considerations

Forward Flow and BP

The PDA Technical Report No.40 "Sterilizing filtration of gases" [22] provides an extensive overview of integrity test methods that are available for the integrity testing of gas filters. Tests like forward flow and BP require the use of a low surface tension solvent, such as alcohol/water mixes (isopropanol (IPA)/water 60/40%, v/v and 70/30%, v/v are widely used) to fully wet the hydrophobic filter membrane. Forward flow testing is performed on a wetted filter, i.e., all pores are filled with a suitable wetting liquid and a fixed gas test pressure lower than the BP pressure is applied to the gas phase upstream of the wetted filter. This gas test pressure drives a gas transport across the wetted filter membrane following the pressure differential, see Figure 21.17.

BP testing assesses the pressure at which a significant increase in gas flow is detected when applying increments of increasing gas test pressure. After both these integrity test methods, the filter is not ready for gas filtration, as free gas flow is hindered by the wetting liquid in the membrane pores that requires significant pressure to be expelled. This is also true after BP testing. Therefore, these tests require removal of the wetting liquid and drying of the filters prior to gas filtration use. They are thus of limited practical use for gas filters after sterilization.

Water Intrusion Test

An alternative test that has found wide acceptance for integrity testing of hydrophobic gas filters is the WIT. The WIT relies on the water-repellent properties of the hydrophobic filter membrane of a gas filter. The filter housing is filled with water, a fixed gas pressure is applied and the small flow of water that occurs in this test situation across the filter is assessed, see Figure 21.18. As mentioned in an

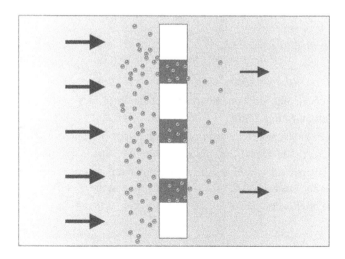

FIGURE 21.17   Gas test pressure and gas flow during forward flow testing.

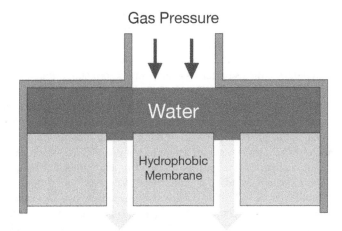

FIGURE 21.18   Water vapor flow during water intrusion testing.

earlier section, studies suggest that the water intrusion flow largely consists of water vapor flow that pass through the non-wetted membrane driven by the pressure gradient across the filter during testing [16].

After the test, the water is drained from the housing. After water intrusion testing the filter allows free gas flow that is sufficient for many applications, as the membrane has not been fully wetted. Water intrusion testing has been found correlatable to bacterial challenge (for example [12]). Thus, water intrusion testing is often the test of choice for after sterilization-preuse (PUPSIT) integrity testing of gas filters.

Water intrusion testing can also be employed after use. Limitations might occur in applications such as fermenter exhaust, where the filter might be loaded with contaminants. As the test relies on the hydrophobic properties of the filter membrane, foreign substances on the membrane that compromise the hydrophobic surface properties, may lead to partial wetting that results in an increased water flow across the membrane during testing and cause the test to fail, although the filter might be integral (see Figure 21.19).

Such partial wetting might also be caused by physical events (condensation, pressure above the water intrusion pressure, localized wetting of the membrane due to contact with a low surface tension liquid). These would also lead to WIT failure although the filter is integral. Partial wetting may be removed by drying the filter. If the critical surface energy of the filter membrane was not permanently altered, a subsequent WIT might be passed.

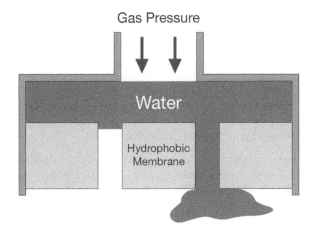

FIGURE 21.19   WIT failure due to partial wetting.

Many commercially available integrity test devices can perform a water intrusion-type test. Different vendors may have different names for the test but the test principle is the same. The filter housing is filled with water and a gas test pressure applied to the water-filled housing. As a flow is occurring across the filter, the devices maintain a constant gas test pressure to the water-filled housing. In doing so, they assess the flows measured during the test after an appropriate stabilization time.

WIT is typically two orders of magnitude lower than those measured during forward flow testing for the same hydrophobic filter. Thus, any small system leaks and environmental influences, such as temperature fluctuations, may cause a negative integrity test result for an integral filter. Especially temperature fluctuations that cause pressure changes in the gas-filled measuring system upstream of the water-filled filter housing can interfere with an accurate test result. Thus, great care must be taken to employ a leak-free system and perform the test in an environment with stable temperature conditions.

These challenges have been addressed by a vendor (Pall Corporation) by developing an automated integrity test system (AquaWIT, see Ref. [15]. This system incorporates their standard integrity test device but brings the gas room, where the measurement during water intrusion testing takes place, into the protected integrity test system. The water-filled system thus extends beyond the housing to the integrity test system via a hydraulic bridge.

This vendor has published a best practice guide for water intrusion testing [37]. The factors to consider for a successful and reliable WIT are given as follows:

1. **Installation/Handling Best Practice:**
   - Use of Gloves
   - Use only de-ionized water for lubrication of O-rings prior to installation of the filter cartridge
   - Ensure the filter is completely covered with water prior to WIT
   - If a sanitizing solution is used to wipe down the filter bag prior to opening, it must be completely dried before opening
   - Filter should be in the correct position for filling and testing
2. **Water Best Practice:**
   - Should be at room temperature (18–22°C)
   - Should be de-ionized or better quality
   - Water should be filled from the bottom of the housing to the vent
   - Use a pump for filling filter assembly with water – NOT a pressure can
3. **Air Best Practice:**
   - Should be clean dry air (CDA) or nitrogen gas
   - Should be at ambient temperature
4. **Integrity Test Instrument – Palltronic Flowstar IV and AquaWIT IV Best Practice**
   - Should be placed away from heat sources and HVAC registers
   - An additional pre-stabilization time can be set to 10 minutes at the normal water intrusion test pressure

In summary, there are a number of integrity tests possible for a hydrophobic air filter. The selection of the appropriate test and the appropriate test schedule depends upon the specific application.

Drying of Filter Cartridges Used for Gas Filtration

After forward flow or BP integrity test has been completed, it is typically desirable to remove the wetting fluid from the filter so that the filter can be used again for gas filtration. Filter drying after water intrusion testing is easier to accomplish as the filter membrane pores remain free of water during the test. *In-situ* drying can be accomplished by blowing clean, dry (–40°C dew point) air or nitrogen through the filter, ideally assisted by a somewhat elevated temperature, as this will speed up the drying process. It is necessary to qualify the drying procedure for a specific application, since every system is different.

The desired degree of dryness will depend on the application. For many applications, it will be sufficient to dry the filter such that it delivers sufficient gas flow. Other applications require a high degree of complete dryness to avoid moisture ingression into the system. The latter might be qualified be drying the filters to constant weight:

- Determine weight of filter out-of-box by weighing on a scale.
- Dry in a fan-assisted oven at a suitably high temperature (for example, 80°C) and periodically determine filter weight to confirm the filter is fully dry.
- Install the filter in the system.
- Execute all process steps up to the point of filter drying.
- Apply a minimum initial air or nitrogen pressure of at least 2 barg (25 psig) to a wetted filter so that the BP is exceeded and the wetting liquid expelled from the membrane pores.
- Blow air through the filter, as a starting point, 75 ft³ of dry air per square foot of filter area. The vent on the housing can be opened slightly to facilitate rapid drying of the housing and filter membrane.
- As flow is initiated the pressure can be reduced if desired.
- Periodically determine the weight of the filter by weighing on a scale.
- Continue with the drying process until the weight of the processed filter reaches weight of the dry filter. A difference in weight is indicative of residual liquid in the filter system.
- A safety factor can be added on the drying cycle if required.

Over drying can also be applied to filter that can be dried off-line. Filters that are alcohol wet should be flushed with water prior to oven drying for safety reasons. The actual drying times will depend upon the filter cartridge style (i.e., cartridge length, closures) as well as the operating conditions of the oven (temperature, air velocity, relative humidity). Therefore, the actual drying time needs to be determined load-specifically. Oven loads should be qualified by drying to constant weight, if critical for the application, as described above for *in-situ* drying.

It is important to emphasize that the temperature maximum for the filter must not be exceeded and that the oven environment should not cause degradation to the filter components.

Filter Service Life

Filter cartridge change-out can be based on a variety of considerations, depending on the criticality of the application. As mentioned in the earlier section, the definition of service intervals and filter change-out should be driven by a risk-based approach. Criteria for change-out can be based on (in the order of increasing criticality):

- Generic data such as steam sterilization specification for the filter
- Generic data for the actual application in case of hot air service or ozone exposure
- Visual inspection criteria, such as discoloration (see also below)
- Integrity test results for the application (i.e., upon failure)
- Integrity test results for the application but including an appropriate safety margin (i.e., use for less cycles than the typical life time in the application)
- Change-out after each cycle of use

Visual appearance of a gas filter after some time of use can be a very helpful and simple tool for defining change-out intervals. Sign to look out for are:

- Discoloration (yellowing)
- Shiny surfaces turning matt
- Disintegration of compounds

Yellowing

Gas filters typically employ PP compounds as material of construction. PP for such applications is chemically stabilized by addition of an antioxidant system to the resin formulation to protect the base polymer during processing and end use. Such commercially available antioxidants sacrificially enable polymers to better resist oxidative chain scission and degradation of the base polymer during molding, sterilization, or exposure to oxidizing conditions during use, such as high temperature or ozone exposure. Additionally, antioxidants are typically added in combination of primary antioxidants such as hindered phenols that stabilize the polymer over the life cycle of the finished good, and secondary process stabilizers such as phosphites or thioesters that stabilize the product through repeated heat exposure. Phenolic discoloration or "yellowing" of the finished good is a well-described process involving oxidative transformation of the hindered phenolic antioxidants into yellow chromophores. The characteristic example of this reaction involves the oxidation of butylated hydroxytoluene to a quinomethide intermediate, which dimerizes and subsequently forms a yellow chromophore, stilbenquinone structure [38–41].

Yellowing of filter hardware compounds is thus indicative of the reaction of the antioxidants in the PP compounds to yellow chromophores and therefore their increasing consumption. Once they are used up, the polymer is no longer protected against oxidation and may deteriorate very quickly after the point of consumption, comparable to the rapid pH change of a buffer solution, when its buffer capacity is exceeded. In the stage of yellowing they might still be able to protect the PP against degradation for a slightly longer time. However, yellowing during visual inspection after a certain time of filter use should be an immediate trigger to exchange the filter and limit cycle numbers.

Shiny Surfaces Turning Matt

PP molded components often have a shiny surface as made. Matting of these surfaces is indicative of beginning polymer degradation and should also be considered a trigger for filter change-out.

Disintegration of Compounds

Filter compounds with a high surface-to-mass ratio, i.e., thin structures with a high surface such as nonwoven materials that are often used a support layers for the filter membrane, are typically the first to become brittle and disintegrate when the polymer is degraded. Filters in this condition would shed high amounts of particles that could contaminate system and drug product or utility streams. Filter change-out should thus occur long before such material disintegration takes place.

Integrity test failure may occur long after yellowing, surface matting, and even material disintegration, especially in the case of PTFE membrane filters, where the PTFE membrane has an extremely high oxidation resistance. There are instances where a filter element has passed forward flow integrity testing, although the filter has been completely stripped off its nonwoven support layers during use due to the embrittlement of these support layers.

Inspection intervals on a monthly basis, for filters used in highly oxidizing applications such as hot air or ozone exposure, on a biweekly is a good starting point. This should be supplemented by monitoring the pressure drop across the filters during operation to determine if the filters are plugging. Integrity testing can complement visual inspection.

Alternatively, dedicated filter life studies outside the actual application system could also be used to set a change-out schedule. Actual conditions of use for each application need to be used during such filter life studies, hence potentially making these a labor and equipment-intensive exercise.

Steam Sterilization Guidelines for Sterilizing-Grade Membrane Filters

Membrane filters can be sterilized by chemical sterilants (such as ethylene oxide, hydrogen peroxide in vapor form, propylene oxide, formaldehyde, and glutaraldehyde), radiant energy sterilization (such as gamma or beta irradiation) or steam sterilization. The most common method of sterilization, except for single-use systems, where gamma irradiation is typically used, is steam sterilization and it will be the focus of further discussion regarding the usage of steam sterilization for membrane filters used for gas filtration.

Points to Consider for Steam Sterilization of Membrane filters

1. *The effect of reverse pressurization*: Reverse pressurization is the most critical condition during steam sterilization of a membrane filter, as the high temperature impacts the mechanical strengths of the MoC and the filter construction will typically lead to less pressure resistance in the reverse direction than in the forward (the actual flow) direction. Many of the following recommendation aim at avoiding reverse pressurization.

2. *Starting the steaming cycle*: Generally, the steam shall be introduced into the filter housing in a procedure which displaces the air from the housing, either through the actual (non-wetted) filter membrane, or through a vent valve, and then permits the steam to flow through the filter and exit through the downstream outlet of the system for the duration of the desired sterilization time.

3. *Avoiding condensation vacuum by gas ballasting*: Ending the sterilization cycle is the most challenging phase of the steaming procedure. It is typically not recommended to simply close the steam valve and let the system cool without gas ballasting. The steam, which is water vapor, will cool and collapse to liquid water of a much smaller volume when it reaches a temperature below 100°C. The collapse will cause the rapid formation of a condensation vacuum. The rapid pressure change may not only cause damage to the filter but also compromise system sterility due to the pressure gradient from the environment to the interior of the sterilized system. Due to differential heat transfer during the cooling cycle, steam condenses to liquid water at different rates upstream and downstream of the filter. As a consequence, significant pressure differences up to 1 bar (14.5 psi) across the filter may develop. This condition may exist for a short duration until the pressure across the filter has equalized; however, this period is sufficient for permanent damage to be done to the filter.

   It is, therefore, highly recommended to introduce a non-condensable gas, such as regulated air or nitrogen, into the housing immediately after the steam valve is closed to prevent a vacuum from being formed in the steamed system. The gas pressure should be about 200 mbar (3 psi) higher than the steam pressure. The upstream vent valve may be carefully opened when gas is introduced after steaming. This will facilitate cooling, by flushing the steam from the system. After venting, the valve may be closed.

   This procedure is also referred to as gas ballasting and its executing is described further below under the steam sterilization procedures.

4. *Executing condensate control*: Condensate can form on filter membranes during the SIP (steam-in-place) procedure. The following measures can be used to minimize the accumulation of condensate on a filter for both air and vent filters.

   a. Filter installation design considerations for condensate control:

      Figure 21.20, derived from Ref. [42] illustrates a recommended system configuration for steam sterilization. Recommended locations of drains are indicated (Drains D, I, and J). The following aspects should be considered for the design of the filter installation:

      - Pressure gauges and temperature sensors in the system should be checked on a routine basis for accuracy.
      - Steam traps should be checked periodically to make sure that they are working properly.
      - A temperature sensor should be installed on the downstream side of the filter to verify that the steam is at the correct temperature.

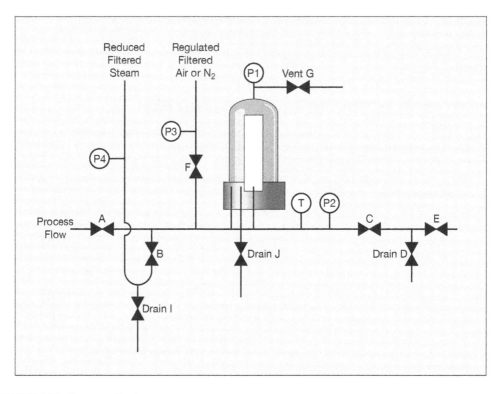

FIGURE 21.20   Steam sterilization arrangement.

- Condensate traps should be located as close to the inlet of the filter housing as possible.
- The filter cartridge should be positioned so that the open end is facing down in order to permit condensate to drain. The housing should be installed vertically to prevent condensate from accumulating on the upstream side of the filter.
- Pressure gauges (accurate over the range of 0–3 bar (45 psi)) should be installed both up and downstream of the filter housing, so that the pressure differential (ΔP) across the filter can be monitored. The pressure differential across the filter should not exceed 300 mbard (4.5 psid). A higher ΔP can cause damage to the filter when it is at elevated temperatures during the steam sterilization process. If a filter is blocked with condensate and steam is introduced, the ΔP can rapidly exceed that recommended differential pressure.
- It is recommended that the filter housing has a vent valve and a drain valve on the upstream side of the housing for the removal of condensate (Figure 21.20: Vent G and Drain J). These valves should be partially open during steaming to prevent the accumulation of condensate.

b.   Steam quality for condensate control:
- Dry, saturated steam should be used in order to prevent excess condensate from entering the system. Super-heated steam should **not** be used, because it could subject the filter to an excessively high temperature and cause damage to the filter.
- The inlet pressure of the steam must be checked to verify that the required steam pressure is being delivered to the system to ensure that the system is properly being sterilized.
- Condensate should be drained from the steam line before introducing steam flow into the filter housing. This can be accomplished by ensuring that condensate drains in the upstream lines and in the housing are opened and functional so that condensate is removed before steam flow is initiated through the filter.

    c.   Steam cycle operation for condensate control:

        During the steaming cycle, the drains and steam traps must be partially opened to prevent a buildup of condensate.

5. *Use of post-sterilization preuse integrity testing (PUPSIT)*: At the conclusion of the sterilization cycle, an integrity test may be conducted in order to ensure that the filter has not been damaged during the steam procedure. While regulatory authorities in some regions, such as Europe, state for sterilizing-grade liquid filters [43]: "The integrity of the sterilised filter should be verified before use and should be confirmed immediately after use by an appropriate method such as bubble point, diffusive flow or pressure hold test...." this mandatory requirement for PUPSIT is not voiced for sterilizing-grade gas filters.

However, steam sterilization can still be considered as one of the process steps with significant potential for filter damage. Application of PUPSIT might thus be in the commercial interest of the drug manufacturer for processes where filter damage might bear the risk of a high commercial loss.

Sterilization Procedure for a Non-Wetted Membrane Gas Filter in Flow Direction

Steam sterilization of a non-wetted membrane filter can be accomplished either by an autoclave or by *in-situ* steam sterilization. *In-situ* steam sterilization can be effectively accomplished by a variety of different process arrangements. Below is an example of an effective procedure that can be used as a guideline for *in-situ* steam sterilization. Procedure and figure (Figure 21.20) is derived from Ref. [42]. Steam sterilization is often the most critical portion of the process and it is important that the procedures followed lead to sterilization of the system and do not impart any damage to the membrane filters.

1. Start with ALL valves closed.
2. Fully open valve C.
3. Fully open condensate drain trap or valve I, housing drain valve J, and housing vent valve G.
4. Preset steam pressure (P4) to 300 mbar (4.3 psig) above the steam pressure required at the filter assembly.
5. After condensate has been expelled from valve I, partially close valve I (if necessary).
6. Slowly open valve B to admit stream to system.
7. After condensate has expelled from J, partially close valve J.
8. When steam flow is evident.
    a. Partially close vent valve G.
    b. Ensure that the pressure at P2 remains within 300 mbard (4.3 psid) of the pressure at P1.
      Note: Adhere to product specifications for maximum steam conditions and differential pressure variations.
9. Partially open drain valve D to drain condensate.
10. Permit steam to flow through the system until stream pressure is stabilized.
11. Adjust the regulated steam supply until the validated temperature is achieved at position T.
12. Monitor the temperature at T for the necessary sterilization time.
13. Ensure that the pressure at P2 remains within 300 mbard (4.3 psid) of the pressure at P1.
      Note: Adhere to product specifications for maximum steam conditions and differential pressure variations.
14. When sterilization is complete:
    a. Close drain valve D, J, and I and vent valve G.
    b. Close steam valve B.

    c. Allow the assembly to cool to ambient temperature or process fluid temperature.

    d. Open vent valve G to compensate for any differential pressure between the pressure within the assembly and ambient pressure.

The filter assembly is now ready for use.

    An alternative approach is ballasting with air or nitrogen instead of step 14 in the above procedure. Air ballasting may be used after steam sterilization in order to avoid condensation vacuum in the system as follows.

Instead of Step 14

    a. Preset the pressure (P3) of regulated air or N2 at 200 mbarg (2.9 psig) above steam pressure (P4).

    b. Close drain valves D, J, and I and vent valve G.

    c. Close steam valve B.

    d. Immediately introduce pre-regulated air or N2 through valve F.

    e. To assist cooling, steam may be flushed from the assembly by carefully opening vent valve G and drain valve J.

    f. Allow the assembly to cool to ambient temperature or process-fluid temperature.

    g. Close valves G and J after flushing.

    h. Close the air or nitrogen valve F.

    i. Relieve the gas pressure in the filter assembly via vent valve G.

Sterilization Procedure for a Non-Wetted Membrane Gas Filter in Reverse Direction (Such as Vent Filters on Tanks)

In-situ steam sterilization of filters mounted on tanks can present a significant challenge. Steaming in the reverse direction requires careful control of the differential pressure across the filter. Equally, the sterilization of the equipment assemblies requires very careful control since the required steaming cycle is influenced by the equipment configuration, MoC, heat capacity, and volume of the system that is vented by the gas filter.

    It might be preferable to sterilize the filter and downstream components separately. However, if the filters and downstream equipment are steamed simultaneously, appropriate vacuum relief safety devices must be fitted on downstream vessels which cannot withstand negative pressure without collapse.

    Figure 21.21 and the procedure indicated below are again derived from Ref. [42] and present a suitable steaming set-up for steaming a hydrophobic filter in the reverse direction.

    1. Ensure that all valves are closed.

    2. Fully open the condensate drain trap or valve A and housing drain valve C.

    3. Slowly open valve B.

        Note: Ensure that pressure at P2 remains within 200 mbard (2.9 psid) of pressure at PI.

        Note: Adhere to product specifications for maximum steam conditions and differential pressure variations.

    4. Allow condensate to drain from housing drain valve C.

    5. When steam flow is evident from valve C, partially dose valve C.

    6. Partially open vent valve D and E.

        Note: Ensure that the differential pressure (P2–PI) does not exceed 200 mbard (2.9 psid).

    7. Permit steam to flow through the system until the steam pressure is stabilized.

    8. Adjust the regulated steam supply until the validated temperature is achieved at position T.

    9. Monitor the temperature at *T* for the necessary sterilization time.

        Note: Ensure that the pressure at P2 remains within 200 mbard (2.9 psid) of the pressure at Pl. It is recommended that steam sterilization be followed by air ballasting.

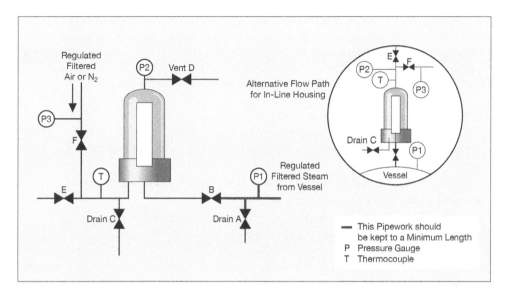

FIGURE 21.21 Recommended filter installation for *in-situ* steam sterilization of filter assembly in the reverse direction.

10. When sterilization is complete:

  a. Close valve E, drain valve A, housing drain valve C, and vent valve D.

  b. Close the vessel steam supply valve (not shown) and immediately introduce pre-regulated air or N2 through valve F.

  c. Allow the assembly to cool to ambient temperature or process-fluid temperature.

  d. Open valve D to compensate for any differential between the pressure within the assembly and ambient pressure.

The filter assembly is now ready for use.

Post-Steaming Filter Drying

After an *in-situ* sterilization cycle, a hydrophobic membrane gas filter will typically be readily useable for gas filtration, as the hydrophobic membrane will not wet out with condensate, although some condensate might remain trapped in the filter construction and slightly diminish the gas flow. The filter should be appropriately sized to account for this effect so that it will still be able to deliver the desired gas flow directly post-steaming.

However, some applications might require the actual absence of water. These cases, *in-situ* drying can be accomplished by blowing clean, dry (−40°C dew point) air or nitrogen through the filter, ideally assisted by a somewhat elevated temperature, as this will speed up the drying process as mentioned in "Drying of Filter Cartridges Used for Gas Filtration" section. It is necessary to qualify the drying procedure for a specific application and system as per the recommendations also given in "Drying of Filter Cartridges Used for Gas Filtration" section.

Disposable Systems for Bioprocesses and the Specific Challenges to Gas Filtration

General Considerations on Single-Use Systems and Bioprocesses

Integrated single-use technologies for bioprocess systems can play an integral role in helping companies bring their drug products to market faster than ever before. They offer many advantages to drug manufacturers by eliminating or significantly reducing sterilization or cleaning procedures, reducing risk of contamination between different processes or batches, and providing lower initial capital cost [44, 45]. Single-use technologies for bioprocesses include bioreactors, bag systems, mixing systems, tubing, filters, and aseptic connections.

The benefits that are typically associated with single-use systems and compounds are:

- Eliminating cleaning and cleaning validation
- Eliminate SIP system sterilization and validation
- Eliminating cost of cleaning-in-place including use of caustic chemicals, detergents, and WFI consumption
- Efficient use of space: smaller overall footprints and reduced storage requirements
- Reducing cross-contamination between batches
- Reducing downtime associated with stainless steel assembly and labor
- Ability/flexibility to increase production capacity

Figure 21.22 shows a general bioprocess flow diagram for the production of monoclonal antibiotics equipped with single-use components.

Gas Filtration Applications in Single-Use Bioprocesses

Figures 21.23 and 21.24 show examples of upstream cell culture process and buffer and media prep process equipped with single-use components and indicate where gas filtration in this process step typically arises. This is mainly at

- Bioreactors
- Mixers

Typical mAb Production Process Flow

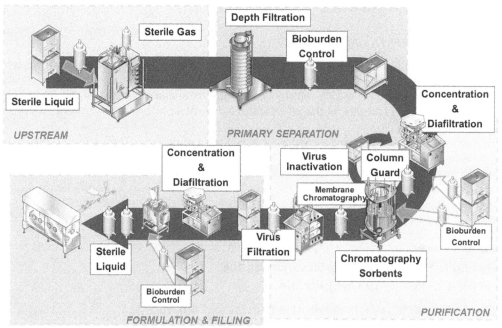

FIGURE 21.22   Typical process flow: production of monoclonal antibiotics equipped with single-use components.

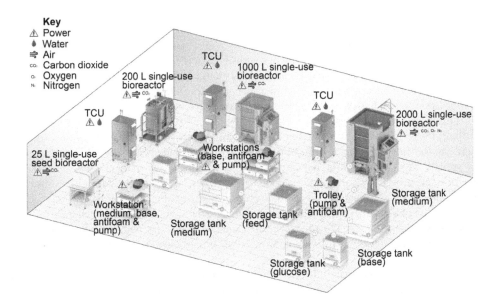

FIGURE 21.23 Cell culture process in single use.

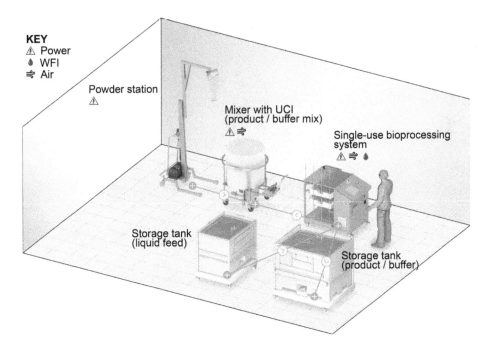

FIGURE 21.24 Buffer and media preparation in single use.

Biocontainer ("bag") systems for liquids storage typically do not require venting, as folded empty bags do not contain air and will unfold and collapse upon filling and draining.

Several key challenges arise for gas filter use in single-use systems that are discussed below:

- Sterilization by gamma irradiation
- Low pressure rating and low flow rates
- Filtration of oxygen or oxygen-enriched gas

Sterilization by Gamma Irradiation

Single-use systems have, like stainless steel systems, the requirement of low bioburden or sterility. Many of the single-use compounds, however, will not withstand sterilization by *in-situ* steaming, or auto-claving. The sterilization method employed is typically gamma irradiation. The single-use systems are preassembled by the compound manufacturer or a subcontractor (integrator) who submits the system for gamma irradiation so that it arrives presterilized to the drug manufacturer.

Gamma irradiation poses specific requirements for the MoC of the single-use components. They need to be sufficiently permeable for the gamma rays and sufficiently resistant to gamma rays so that the compound can still fulfill its intended function, is safe to operate, and does not cause unwanted effect to the drug product. This must be ensured over the complete lifetime of the component.

Filters for single use are typically constructed as capsule filter, i.e., the filter element is encapsulated in a polymeric filter housing so that it is disposed together with the filter element (Figure 21.25).

Gamma stability of a polymeric material can be inherent to the actual polymer, or achieved by addition of suitable antioxidant systems to the polymer resin. Generally, polymers with conjugated double bonds display a high resistance to gamma irradiation, while aliphatic carbohydrates are typically poorly gamma resistant.

Commonly used polymeric materials for filter construction that display a good amount, or at least sufficient, of gamma irradiation resistance for use in single-use systems are:

- PES
- PVDF
- PP when stabilized with a suitable antioxidant system

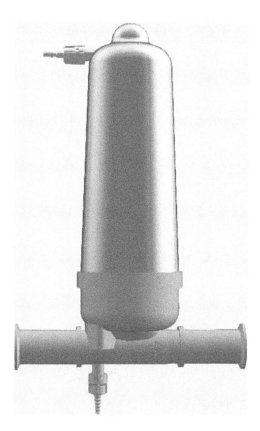

FIGURE 21.25   Example of a polymeric filter capsule.

Polytetrafluorethylene (PTFE) that is a most commonly used material for hydrophobic filters is poorly gamma irradiation resistant so that its use in pleated membrane filters is prohibited, if these filters undergo gamma irradiation. For gas filters, naturally hydrophobic PVDF membranes are thus the most widely employed material for single-use gas filters. Other filter compounds such as support materials, cage, core, adapters, and filter capsule typically employ suitable gamma-resistant grades of PP.

Gamma irradiation doses of 25 kGy are typically considered the minimum dose to achieve the required sterility assurance safety margin for the sterilized component. Single-use system will typically require higher doses due to their complexity and potentially higher bioburden levels [46]. Filters integrated in single-use system should thus be able to withstand gamma doses up to 50 kGy without impact to their function. A respective generic and potentially system or application-specific validation is required.

While hydrophobic PVDF is the material of choice for gas filters in single-use systems due to its gamma irradiation resistance, the inherent critical wetting surface tension of such PVDF membranes typically prevents employing water intrusion testing as integrity test, i.e., these membranes are less hydrophobic than PTFE membranes [22]. Integrity test methods such as forward flow or BP that require wetting the filter membrane with a solvent or a solvent/water mix are not preferred for preuse testing of gas filters due to challenge to eliminate the wetting fluid (see also earlier sections of this chapter). This challenge is further increased in a single-use system due to their inherent volume and pressure limitations.

This challenge and limitation for the use of the traditional hydrophobic membrane materials PTFE and PVDF in single-use systems has recently driven the development of alternative membrane materials, such a hydrophobic PES for gas filtration applications in single-use systems (Gamma Stable Opticap® XL Capsule Filters with Millipore Express® SPG Hydrophobic Membrane). This filter product is resistant to gamma irradiation and is specified to be integrity testable with a WIT method (HydroCorr™ Test; HydroCorr is a Millipore trademark).

Low Pressure Rating and Low Flow Rates

Single-use systems equipped with single-use components typically have a very low pressure rating, or need to be operated without system pressure. Especially biocontainers ("bags") shall be operated without system pressure to avoid leaks and burst. This is generally tackled by generous sizing of filters and other system components (bags) and slow flow rates. The interior of a bioreactor would also be at atmospheric system pressure.

Typical sizing for filters on bioreactors of increasing scale and can be found in Table 21.3.

Filtration of Oxygen or Oxygen-Enriched Gas

The desire to foster cell growth by supplying oxygen-enriched gas or pure oxygen to the cell culture also arises in single-use bioreactors. As outlined before, PTFE membrane filters especially constructed for increased oxidation resistance are the filters of choice for the filtration of these gases; however, pleated PTFE membranes filters are not suitable for gamma irradiation that is a requirement for filters used in single-use systems. This appears a conflict that cannot be easily technically reconciled.

TABLE 21.3

Typical Sizing of Gas Filter on Bioreactors

	Bioreactor Volume		
Application	**500 L**	**2,500 L**	**12,500 L**
Sparge	5 in. filter	5 in. filter	5 in. filter
Overlay	5 in. filter	10 in. filter	20 in. filter
Exhaust	10 in. filter	30 in. filter	40 in. filter
Titrant air header	N/A	10 in. filter	10 in. filter
Sample air	5 in. filter	5 in. filter	5 in. filter

The low operating pressure and flow rates that are typical for the operation of filters in single-use systems and bioreactors, however, present not only limitation but also chances for this specific application. To address the requirements for a sterilizing-grade gas filter that can be integrated into single-use systems and sterilized by gamma irradiation, but is also resistant to the use in oxygen-enriched air and oxygen service, a vendor has qualified their PVDF membrane filter capsules under the specific conditions of use in these applications:

Pall Corporation has exposed Kleenpak™ capsules with Emflon II media [47] with part numbers KA2V002PV2G and KA3V002PV2G to supply of gaseous oxygen at a flow rate of 1 L/min. The KA3V002PV6G filters were maintained at a temperature of 60°C using an electric heating blanket, while the KA2V002PV2G were maintained at ambient temperature of approximately 20°C. After oxygen exposure, the capsule filters underwent a range of applicable testing, such as forward flow integrity testing and pressure burst testing. The capsules were found to meet all acceptance criteria, thus demonstrating that filter bacteria retention performance that is correlated to forward flow integrity testing, and operational safety of the capsule housing were satisfactorily maintained [48].

The MoC of these filters were also submitted to the German BAM (Federal Institute for Materials Research and Testing) and underwent compatibility testing in gaseous oxygen at 60°C (oxygen reactivity test with 100% gaseous oxygen at 10 bar pressure at 60°C). The materials were found to meet the reactivity test under these conditions [49], thus demonstrating the suitability of the filter materials for this application.

Summary

This chapter has provided information on gas filtration products and a variety of gas filtration applications in biotechology processes, such as gases going into and out of fermenters/bioreactors, venting of tanks, and vacuum break filters. It included traditional filtration technology (packed beds), current prevalent technology (membrane filters), and pointed to production trends that will gain more and more share in biotechnology (single-use systems). In addition to a description of the air filtration applications, considerations and guidelines were provided on the usage of the filters in these applications.

REFERENCES

1. Bruckshaw NB. Removal of contamination from compressed air. *Filtr. Sep.* 1973; 10(3):296–302.
2. Stanbury PF, Whitaker A. *Principles of Fermentation Technology.* Oxford: Pergamon Press; 1984.
3. Richards JW. *Introduction to Industrial Sterilization.* London and New York: Academic Press; 1968.
4. Fuchs NA. In: Davies CN, ed. *The Mechanics of Aerosols.* New York: Macmillan; 1964.
5. ISO 4572:1981 Hydraulic Fluid Power—Filters—Multi Pass Method for Evaluating Filtration Performance.
6. ANSI B93.31 73rd Edition, 1987 Multi-Pass Method for Evaluation the Filteration Performance of a Fine Hydraulic Fluid Poer Filter Element.
7. Uberoi T. Effectively select in-line filters. *Chem. Eng. Prog.* 1992; 88(3):75–80.
8. Williamson K, Tousi S, Hashemi R. Recent developments in performance rating of gas/liquid coalescers. *Fluid/Part. Sep. J.* 1988; 1(2):111.
9. U.S. Food and Drug Administration (FDA) September 2004 Guidance for Industry Sterile Drug Products Produced by Aseptic Processing—Current Good Manufacturing Practice.
10. The International Society for Pharmaceutical Engineering (ISPE). ISPE has Issued the Good Practice Guide: Process Gases (July 2011).
11. Bruno CF, Szabo LA. Fermentation air filtration upgrading by use of membrane cartridge filters. *Biotechnol. Bioeng.* 1983; 25(5):1223–1227.
12. Pall Publication USTR2114 Validation Guide for Pall Emflon PFR Filter Cartridges (Pall Corporation, 2003).
13. American Society for Testing and Materials (ASTM), Standard Test Method for Determining Bacterial Retention of Membrane Filters Utilized for Liquid Filtration, ASTM Standard F838-15 (2015).

14. Military Standard, MIL-STD-282, Filter Units, Protective Clothing, Gas-Mask Components and Related Products; Performance Test Methods, (1952).
15. Pall Publication USTR 2184b Validation Guide Palltronic Flowstar and AquaWIT Integrity Test Instruments (Pall Corporation, 2010).
16. Pall Publication USTR 2047 Water Intrusion Test—Studies on the Theoretical Basis of the Water Intrusion Test (WIT) (R. Jaenchen, J. Schubert, S. Jafari, A. West; Pall Corporation 2002).
17. USP. 2017 <791> pH, The United States Pharmacopeial Convention, 12601 Twinbrook Parkway, Rockville, MD.
18. USP. 2017 <85> Bacterial Endotoxins The United States Pharmacopeial Convention, 12601 Twinbrook Parkway, Rockville, MD.
19. American Society of Mechanical Engineers (ASME) Boiler and Pressure Vessel Code (BPVC), Section VIII—Rules for Construction of Pressure Vessel, Division 1.
20. American Society of Mechanical Engineers (ASME) Boiler and Pressure Vessel Code (BPVC), Section IX—Welding, Brazing and Fusing Qualifications.
21. ISO 15614-1:2017 Specification and Qualification of Welding Procedures for Metallic Materials—Welding Procedure Test—Part 1: Arc and Gas Welding of Steels and Arc Welding of Nickel and Nickel Alloys.
22. Parenteral Drug Association (PDA) Technical Report No.40 Sterilizing Filtration of Gases vol. 58, No. S-1; 2005.
23. Cole, JC. Consideration in applications of bacteria retentive air vent filters. *Pharm. Tech.* 1977; 1:49–53.
24. Meltzer, TH. *Filtration in the Pharmaceutcal Industry*. New York: Marcel Decker; 1987.
25. Jornitz MW. *Aspects of Air and Gas Filtration in the Biopharmaceutical Industry, in Filtration in the Biopharmaceutical Industry*. New York: Marcel Dekker; 1998.
26. Conway RS. State of the art in fermentation air filtration. *Biotechnol. Bioeng.* 1984; 26(8):844–847.
27. Perkowski CA. Fermentation process air filtration via cartridge filters. *Biotechnol. Bioeng.* 1983; 25:1215–1221.
28. Pall Publication USTR 2863a Validation Guide Emflon® HTPFR Filter Cartridges (Pall Corporation, 2013).
29. Berufsgenossenschaftliche Regeln (BGR) 500, Kapitel 2.32 Betreiben von Sauerstoffanlagen (Inhalte aus vorheriger VGB 62) Fachausschuss „Chemie" der Deutschen Gesetzlichen Unfallversicherung (DGUV), Stand: März 2008 (Germany: Operation of Oxygen Systems, March 2008).
30. Pall Publication USTR 2311a Application Note Sterilizing Filtration of Enriched and Pure Gaseous Oxygen Employed in Cell Culture Applications, 2013.
31. Bundesanstalt für Materialforschung und -prüfung (BAM) (Federal Institute for Materials Research and Testing) Report on Testing of Emflon HTPFR Filter Materials for Reactivity with Oxygen (BAM reference 2–993/2012–E).
32. Porter HF. Gas-solid systems, Chapter 20. In: Chilton CH, Perry RH, eds. *Perry's Chemical Engineers' Handbook*, 5th edn. New York: McGraw-Hill; 1973.
33. Jaenchen R, Dellweg R. Pall Corporation Publication STR PUF 13. Process Parameters for an Economic Use of Membrane Filters in Fermentation Exhaust Gas Filtration. East Hills, NY: Pall Ultrafine Corp, East Hills; 1989.
34. Cooney C, ed. *Comprehensive Biotechnology*. New York: Academic Press; 1984.
35. Pall Publication USD2330a Application Note Sterile Vent Filtration on Ozonated Water Tanks (M Cardona, J Schubert Pall Corporation, 2015).
36. Pall Publication USD3087 Application Note Safety Considerations for Gas Filtration in High-Temperature and Oxygen Enrichment Applications (Pall Corporation, 2015).
37. Pall Corporation USD 3033 Application Note: Best Practices for Successful Integrity Testing Using the Water Intrusion Test (WIT), 2015.
38. Bart JCJ. *Polymer Additive Analytics: Industrial Practice and Case Studies*. Firenze: Firenze University Press; 2006.
39. van Beusichem B, Ruberto MA. Introduction to Polymer Additives and Stabilization, Product Quality Research Institute (PQRI). http://www.pqri.org/workshops/leach_ext/imagespdfs/posters/polymer_additives_pqri_poster.pdf.
40. Yellowing and Pinking of White PE/PP, Ampacet FAQ, Dec 2014. http://www.ampacet.com/faqs/yellowing-and-pinking-white-pe-pp/.

41. Bart JCJ. *Additives in Polymers: Industrial Analysis and Applications.* John Wiley & Sons, Ltd; 2006.
42. Pall Publication USTR 805 Rev K Steam Sterilization of Pall Filter Assemblies Utilizing Replaceable Filter Cartridges (Pall Corporation, 2008).
43. EudraLex Volume 4, EU Guidelines to Good Manufacturing Practice Medicinal Products for Human and Veterinary Use, Annex 1, Manufacture of Sterile Medicinal Products, Brussels, 2008.
44. Martin J. Reducing the risk of microbial contamination. *Pharm. Technol. Eur.* 2010. http://www. pharmtech.com/reducing-risk-microbial-contamination?__hstc=126692114.6399a694bdece98431270 c9605d20a10.1550698412111.1550698412111.1550758151720.2&__hssc=126692114.1.1550758151720 &__hsfp=2182710941
45. Boehm J, Bushnell B. Contamination prevention: How single-use systems can ensure a safe, clean, and efficient bioprocess environment. *Pharm. Technol.* 2008; 32(6). http://www.pharmtech.com/ contamination-prevention-how-single-use-systems-can-ensure-safe-clean-and-efficient-bioprocess-envir
46. Martin JM. Understanding gamma sterilization. *Biopharm. Int.* 2012; 25(2).
47. Pall Publication SD 1127c. Emflon II Filters. 1994.
48. Pall Corporation, Internal Confidential Research and Development Report (R&D) Report Number 12/17.
49. Bundesanstalt für Materialforschung und -prüfung (BAM) (Federal Institute for Materials Research and Testing) Report Reference Number: 2–2462/2013 E.

22

Sterility Testing by Filtration in the Pharmaceutical Industry

Olivier Guenec
Sartorius Biohit Liquid Handling Oy

CONTENTS

Introduction

- *Definition of sterility:* The absence of viable and actively multiplying microorganisms.
- *Test for sterility:* The test described in the International Pharmacopeias consists in searching for microbiological contamination in a representative sample of a sterile product.

In order to comply with the regulations, the test for sterility must be qualified in performance especially when there is a risk of inhibition of the growth of microorganisms (e.g., test of antibiotics).

Although the test for sterility, as it is described in the current regulations, has statistical limitations, it remains the only microbiological batch release test of sterile products in the pharmaceutical industry.

Regulatory Context: Description, Analysis, and Interpretation

International Pharmacopeias

Knowing the International Pharmacopeias is essential to understand the test for sterility of pharmaceutical sterile products.

There are three major pharmacopeias describing the requirements of sterility testing:

- The United States Pharmacopeia Chapter <71> (USP 2016)
- The European Pharmacopoeia Chapter 2.6.1 (EP 2005)
- The Japanese Pharmacopoeia. Not discussed here.

These texts have been partially harmonized which helps international companies to rationalize the test procedures and validation protocols when exporting to foreign countries where different regulations are in place. Nevertheless, some minor discrepancies still remain.

Environment of the Test

The test environment is not clearly specified in details in the pharmacopeias as it is in the FDA Guidance for Industry or the Pharmaceutical Inspection Convention and the Pharmaceutical Inspection Co-operation Scheme (PIC/S) Guide to good manufacturing practice (GMP) texts (see "FDA Guidance for Industry" and "PIC/S: PI 012-3 September 2007" sections). Nevertheless, it is obvious that the quality of the test environment can impact the result of the test and must be monitored in a proper way to minimize risks of false positive and false negative results.

Sterility test is generally performed in a class A laminar air flow cabinet within a class B, in a class A clean room if available or in an isolator. More and more users take advantage of isolator technologies as it creates a higher assurance that false positive tests do not happen. These enclosed systems have a very high reliance and create a clean environment without user intervention. Any space the sterility test is performed in requires routine air sampling and monitoring for organisms to assure that such airborne contaminants do not influence the outcome of the sterility test adversely.

Culture Media

In order to allow the growth of most of the microorganisms, yeasts, molds, aerobes and anaerobes, spore-forming and nonspore-forming organisms, two culture media and several microorganisms have been selected in the International Pharmacopeias.

- *Fluid Thioglycollate medium* allows the growth of anaerobic and aerobic bacteria.
- *Soybean-Casein Digest medium* is used for the detection of fungi and aerobic bacteria.

In other terms, both media complement each other and provide an overlap of nourishment for aerobic bacteria in order to optimize the overall recovery of the test.

United States Pharmacopeia (USP) and European Pharmacopoeia (EP) clearly define the media compositions as well as a test, called growth promotion test, which consists in growing several strains of microorganisms in a maximum time period.

Tables 22.1 and 22.2, listing the test microorganisms, are compiled from the USP and the EP.

The slight discrepancy between the EP and the USP probably lies in a separate official FDA Code of Federal Regulation 21 CFR 610.12, where different microorganisms are listed.

In the 21 CFR 610.12 Pseudomonas aeruginosa, Staphylococcus aureus, and Aspergillus niger are not listed and only one ATCC number is defined for each microorganism.

This might be of importance for pharmaceutical companies selling their drugs in the United States, whether they produce in the United States or anywhere else in the world.

A special note states that the "… viable microorganisms used for inoculation are not more than five passages removed from the original master seed lot." As a matter of fact, old cultures might not grow as well as younger ones.

TABLE 22.1

USP and EP Test Micoorganisms

	EP		USP
Aerobic Bacteria			
Staphylococcus aureus	ATCC 6538, CIP 4.83, NCTC 10788, NCIMB9518	Staphylococcus aureus[a]	ATCC 6538, CIP 4.83, NCTC 10788, NCIMB9518
Bacillus subtilis	ATCC 6633, CIP 52.62, NCIMB 8054	Bacillus subtilis	ATCC 6633, CIP 52.62, NCIMB 8054
Pseudomonas aeruginosa	ATCC 9027, NCIMB 8626, CIP 82.118	Pseudomonas aeruginosa[b]	ATCC 9027, NCIMB 8626, CIP 82.118
Anaerobic Bacteria			
Clostridium sporogenes	ATCC 19404, CIP 79.3, NCTC 532, ATCC 11437	Clostridium sporogenes[c]	ATCC 19404, CIP 79.3, NCTC 532, ATCC 11437
Fungi			
Candida albicans	ATCC 10231, IP 48.72, NCPF 3179	Candida albicans	ATCC 10231, IP 48.72, NCPF 3179
Aspergillus niger	ATCC 16404, IP 1431.83, IMI 149007	Aspergillus niger	ATCC 16404, IP 1431.83, IMI 149007

[a] or Bacillus subtilis as an alternative.
[b] or Micrococcus luteus (Kocuria rhizophila) as an alternative.
[c] or Bacteroides vulgatus as an alternative when a nonspore-forming microorganism is desired.

TABLE 22.2

Recommended Limits for Microbial Contamination

	Recommended Limits for Microbial Contamination			
Grade	Air Sample cfu/m^3	Settle Plates (Diam. 90 mm) cfu/4 h	Contact Plates (Diam. 55 mm) cfu/Plate	Glove Print 5 Fingers cfu/Glove
A	<1	<1	<1	<1
B	10	5	5	5
C	100	50	25	—
D	200	100	50	—

Sampling

Sampling parameters like the number of items to be tested in each batch of product and the quantity of product in each container are clearly defined in the pharmacopeias.

The rules are based on the size of the batch, the volume of the container, and the type of product. In general, the bigger the batch size, the higher the number of containers to be tested. Nevertheless, over a batch size of 500 items, which is very often the case, the number of items to be tested does not exceed 10 or 20, depending on the type of product. Users generally do not take more samples although this is perfectly allowed. Quantity of product to be tested per container depends on the volume of product in each container and the type of product. In general, when the total volume of product in the container is small, the whole content is tested. When the total volume is large, only a part of it is tested. Specific rules apply depending on the nature of the product to be tested.

Validation Test

The validation test is based on the incorporation of selected microorganisms (the same strains used for the growth promotion test) during the sterility test procedure in order to check whether they will grow in a visually comparable way to a positive control. In other terms, this test demonstrates that the procedure of sterility testing does not affect the growth of microorganisms. For instance, if the product to be tested has inherent antimicrobial activity (e.g., antibiotics or drugs containing preservatives), it is important to demonstrate that the established procedure does not allow a risk of inhibition of the growth of the referenced microorganisms. The antimicrobial activity is removed using an appropriate rinsing procedure or neutralized (e.g., using of β-lactamase for neutralizing the activity of penicillins or cephalosporins).

The accuracy of this validation test is certainly not optimal as it mainly consists in comparing turbidity in the test and positive control containers. As a matter of fact, it is not clearly demonstrated that a moderate microorganism inhibition will be identified by comparing turbidity in a liquid culture media. On the other hand, the microorganisms listed in the USP and EP are not selected based on their specific sensitivity to a defined antimicrobial substance, sterilizing agent, or antibiotic. Then, it might be informative to select sensitive microbes for running validations studies depending on the type of antimicrobial agent in the sample.

Besides, the informational chapter <1227>—Validation of Neutralization Methods—Recovery comparisons of the USP describes a test based on colony enumeration on the filter plated on agar compared to a positive control which has not been in contact with the product sample (USP 2012a).

This test might give a more quantitative answer although microbial colony-forming units enumeration is subject to limitations in accuracy. This chapter also indicates that at least three validation runs have to be performed independently.

Membrane Filtration

As written in the USP and the EP, personnel performing sterility tests must use:

> Membrane filters having a nominal pore size not greater than 0.45 μm whose effectiveness to retain microorganisms has been demonstrated.

In general, any filter membrane named 0.45 μm should comply with the requirement as long as its retention efficiency has been demonstrated. Here, the technician working in the quality control (QC) laboratory might already need some assistance to understand what's written between lines.

Publications describing retention mechanisms and ratings are widely available and could shed light of what is a true retention rating and what might need to be evaluated (Jornitz and Meltzer, 2001).

In order to summarize, 0.45 μm was the nominal pore size of sterilizing grade filters before the 1960s when Bowman (1960) and Bowman and Holdowsky (1960) demonstrated that 0.45 μm filters failed to retain *Brevundimonas diminuta* formerly known as *Pseudomonas diminuta*.

Questions have been often asked why 0.45 μm and not 0.2 μm which is the sterilizing grade-retention rating of filter cartridges used in production. When raised, most of the discussions drift to the experience level one has with 0.45 µm-rated membranes. The advantage of this pore size over a 0.2 µm-rated membrane is the enhanced ability of the growth media diffusion through the larger pore structure of the 0.45 µm membrane. Furthermore, most of the sterility test membranes are highly adsorptive polymeric materials which capture the organisms not only by sieve retention, impaction, but also by adsorptive sequestration. So higher flow rate and better recovery might be obtained with 0.45 µm-rated analytical filters without the loss of retentivity. Having said this, the debate over 0.45 versus 0.2 µm will never end. It is probably more a preference issue than a scientific exercise.

The more important issue is the proper validation of the sterility test membrane within the user's processes. This often does not include the retention capabilities of the membrane with the actual drug product. Often there is an exaggerated reliance on the manufacturer's data and certificates, which has been abolished in the sterilizing grade filter field as incomplete validation effort. It might be advantageous for the end user to obtain answers whether or not the retentivity of the sterility test membrane is truly given with the drug product tested. It well be that the drug product components influence the previously mentioned adsorptive capture (Jornitz and Meltzer, 2001). The retentivity efficiency and possible adverse influences of the product can be determined by the use of bacteria challenge tests. The 0.45 µm membrane could be challenged with specific test organisms inoculated in the drug product. If the drug product has an influence on the capture mechanism the organism might penetrate the sterility test membrane. Such possibility should be determined within the validation process. If not so done, how does one know what one captures or not.

Observation and Interpretation of Results

Both EP and USP specify that canisters containing media have to be incubated for 14 days. At intervals (see the section "Culture Media") and at the end of the incubation period, the macroscopic evidence of microbial proliferation must be examined in both canisters.

When, after 14 days, both media do not present any evidence of microbial growth, the tested product complies with the test for sterility.

In instances further tests are applicable. At that point at least 1 mL of culture media should be transferred to fresh vessels of medium and incubated for at least 4 additional days together with the original canisters.

When growth is observed in the culture medium, the test may be considered invalid unless a fault, for example, handling mistake, can be unequivocally demonstrated (details are given in "Investigation of Positive Results" subsection).

FDA Guidance for Industry—Sterile Products Produced by Aseptic Processing Current Good Manufacturing Practice

This document from September 2004, while giving recommendations on Aseptic Processing operations also includes a chapter dedicated to sterility testing.

Environment

In the Introduction, readers can find a very specific statement about the environment of the test which should compare to the environment used for aseptic processing operations. Mainly, based on historical reporting of false positive sterility testing, this statement also clearly highlights the use of isolators in order to minimize the risk of false positive results. It certainly is in the interest of the user to avoid false positive results, as such, result would require extensive investigation and out-of-specification reports. Therefore, everything needs to be done to eliminate the potential for false positive tests, being a clean environment to train the user. This topic will be addressed later in section "PIC/S: PE009-13 (Part I and Annexes) January 2017 Guide to GMP for Medicinal Products" regarding trends in sterility testing.

Training and Qualification

An important recommendation is done about personnel qualification and training as part of a written program allowing regular update.

Companies providing sterility test units, systems, and consumables are aware of this and provide training and qualifying sessions on a regular basis. Training and qualifying personnel can also be performed by internal resources. Actually, it has been often found that in a team of several technicians performing sterility tests in a QC laboratory, there are some "experts" who are also responsible for maintaining a sufficient level of understanding of the application for others and especially new personnel.

As stated this issue is highly important to minimize the risks of sterility test failures and false positive results.

Sampling

Principally based on the statistical weakness of the test, due to the small size of the sample compared to the batch size, it is very important to test a representative sample.

Although a definition of a representative sample is given in the 21 CFR 210.3 (b) (21), the common practice matching the FDA Guidance for industry's recommendation is to sample at the beginning, middle, and end of manufacturing process. Besides, in case of unusual interventions on the production line during processing, samples should also be taken.

Investigation of Positive Results

When a positive result is found (growth in the culture media) an investigation is necessary in order to demonstrate whether the microbial growth comes from the product or lies in an error which generated a contamination during sampling or the sterility-testing procedure. This event is commonly named a "false positive result."

Until the full investigation is conducted and accomplished, the lot is considered nonsterile.

It must be mentioned here that it is extremely difficult to demonstrate the invalidity of the first result because the regulatory bodies hardly accept it. As a matter of fact, and although it is not clearly written in the regulations, this strictness finds its root in the increasing safety of the environment and disposable closed systems used for sterility testing.

The investigation should at least include:

1. *Microbial identification:* This helps to compare the identified strain(s) to the commonly found strain during environmental monitoring in the laboratory and the production environment.
2. *Review of laboratory tests and deviations:* This helps to define whether the laboratory regularly finds the identified microbe(s) in the laboratory monitoring. The analysis of deviations is essential and operators should stop the procedure before incubation if they think a deviation should have compromised the integrity of the test. It is common practice to perform multiple sampling in order to allow a second opportunity to perform the test again in this case.
3. *Investigation of process and process environment:* As the source of growth found in the culture media could find its root in the production itself or in the production environment, the complete aseptic process should be deeply analyzed.

Besides, monitoring personnel, product presterilization bioburden, production record review, and manufacturing history should be deeply investigated.

It is then a very hard task to investigate a sterility positive creating a lot of additional work for the laboratory. Of course, this favors the implementation of technical solutions to minimize the risk of false positives like isolators and closed disposable filtration devices.

PIC/S: PI 012-3 September 2007: Recommendation on Sterility Testing

PIC/S

The PIC/S is international instruments helping the cooperation between countries and authorities in the definition of good manufacturing practice.

The PI 012-3 provides guidance for GMP inspectors to be used for training and preparation of inspections. It is also a very informative document for companies wanting to prepare for a GMP inspection of their sterility-testing activities.

Among others, here are some aspects of sterility testing described in this document:

Training

In addition to what is found in the previously commented FDA Guidance for Industry (see the "International Pharmacopeias" section) a special highlight is given in regards to the examination of the growth during and at the end of the incubation period. Actually, the growth of microbes is not always appearing in the same shape in a canister. For instance, growth sometimes occurs at the bottom of the canister where it is not easy to observe. Besides, as most of the time tests are negative, laboratory technicians do not often see a microbial growth and need to be trained.

To mirror the need to qualify the operators in the previous FDA Guidance, the term of certification is used instead.

Environment

The sterility test should be performed in a class A laminar airflow cabinet located within a class B clean room, a class A clean room if available or in an isolator.

Validation

"Validation (Bacteriostasis and Fungistasis)" section of the PI 012-3 mirrors what is found in the international pharmacopeias but also recommends, as it is good practice, to revalidate every 12 months.

As this last recommendation is not a pharmacopeial requirement, revalidation of sterility testing is generally not repeated.

"Positive Test Controls" section clearly states that the positive controls (including validation) should be performed in a laboratory environment separate from the one where the product is tested. In other terms, it is not recommended at all to introduce microorganisms intentionally in the sterile test environment, even when it is part of a validation study. This seems obvious, but at least this recommendation makes sense, particularly when it is not available in many other official texts.

PIC/S: PE009-13 (Part I and Annexes) January 2017
Guide to GMP for Medicinal Products

The guide to GMP gives essential information related to manufacturing and some general indications in regards to sterility testing, although the Head of Quality Control is considered in this document as key personnel.

Sampling

In page 36 of the guide (chapter Quality Control) some indications are given about sampling:

samples should be representative of the batch of materials or products from which they are taken. Other samples may also be taken to monitor the most stressed part of a process (e.g., beginning or end of a process). The sampling plan used should be appropriately justified and based on a risk management approach.

Environment

No specific recommendation is given related to the environment of sterility testing but the meaning of A, B, C, and D classification is given in the "Annexes" document and displayed in Table 22.2.

Realization of the Test According to Regulations and Troubleshooting

Introduction

Today, the method of choice for testing the sterility of sterile product by filtration is the disposable sterility-testing device.

A filtration device (Figure 22.1) consists of two closed filtration canisters (Figure 22.2) each containing a membrane filter and attached to a tubing allowing the filtration of products and incorporation of liquid culture media applied by a peristaltic pump (Figure 22.3). At the end of the tubing set, an adaptor, commonly a collection needle is attached in order to withdraw the liquid from the container in safe conditions. Depending on the container properties and design, several adaptors are available (See Figures 22.4–22.6). Here are some examples:

FIGURE 22.1   Sterility testing device.

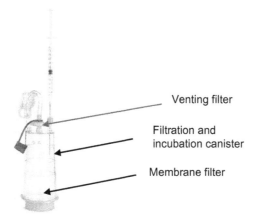

Venting filter

Filtration and incubation canister

Membrane filter

FIGURE 22.2   Sterility testing canister. (Pictures courtesy of Sartorius.)

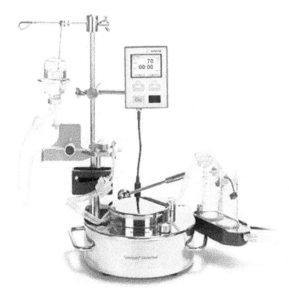

FIGURE 22.3 Sterility testing peristaltic pump. (Pictures courtesy of Sartorius.)

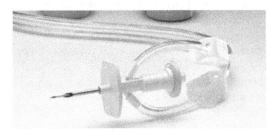

FIGURE 22.4 Adaptor for large-volume parenterals in closed containers with integrated sterilizing grade filter (Picture courtesy of Sartorius).

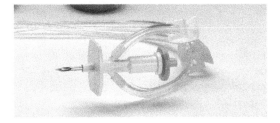

FIGURE 22.5 Adaptor for small-volume parenterals in closed containers with integrated sterilizing grade filter (Picture courtesy of Sartorius).

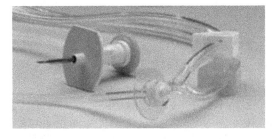

FIGURE 22.6 Adaptor for prefilled syringes (Picture courtesy of Sartorius).

The product to be tested is filtered simultaneously on both membranes and culture media is introduced in each canister thanks to a set of preinstalled clamps. At the end of the procedure, one canister contains fluid thioglycollate medium and the other Soybean-Casein Digest medium.

The tubing is cut and clamps are closed on top of the canisters to allow incubating in closed sterile conditions.

Preconditioning the Membranes

Reading the EP or USP, users should transfer a small quantity of a sterile diluent onto the membrane in the apparatus and filter. No clear reason is given in the pharmacopeias to justify this step, as it is only written "If appropriate."

Nevertheless, there are some explanations available and membrane preconditioning might be useful in one special case and for two main reasons.

First, it must be mentioned that laboratories dealing with the test for sterility of antibiotics or products having inherent antimicrobial activity are used to condition the membrane filters before filtration.

The first reason is linked to the probability for liquids to find difficult to rinse voids in the canister. If such voids are likely to be present, and if no preconditioning of the membrane is applied, antimicrobial substances could hide there and would be very difficult to remove as it is not truly accessible to the liquid flow during the rinsing steps.

The second reason is more related to chemistry than to physics.

Standard membranes generally made of mixed esters of cellulose contain strong polar groups and are a good support for hydrophobic interactions. These properties generate a nonspecific absorption capability that could help to bind antimicrobial substances, making them difficult or impossible to rinse. Of course in such a case, the risk of generating inhibition of microbial growth could be high enough to create false negative results.

Preconditioning of membranes, when done with fluid A according to USP or a neutral solution of meat or casein peptone at 1 g/L according to EP, will create a protein layer as peptone proteins will bind to the active available groups of the filter material.

It will be then much more difficult for other substances to bind to the membrane later on.

General usage is 50 mL of fluid A according to USP or 50 mL of a neutral solution of meat or casein peptone at 1 g/L according to EP.

Sample Filtration

The sample is then filtered immediately.

This is not mentioned in the regulations but the pump speed has to be adjusted to avoid product foaming and splashing in the canister.

As a matter of fact, product foaming could lead to a blockage of the filter vent creating pressure in the canister and damaging the integrity of the filter vent.

Product splashing, when having inherent antimicrobial properties could leave difficult to rinse drops that could be released in the culture media during incubation, generating a risk of false negative results.

The internal part of the canister is sometimes designed to guide the liquid along the wall, then limiting splashing and foaming.

When lyophilized antibiotics (powders) have to be filtered after dissolution, the users should make sure that all powder particles are dissolved. Undissolved particles could remain in the filter structure and be difficult to rinse, generating a risk of false negative results.

Membrane and Device Rinsing

When the product has antimicrobial properties, the membranes and devices must be rinsed not less than 3 times but not more than 5 times for 200 mL. Generally users apply 3 times for 100 mL of fluid A.

During the rinsing procedure, users must make sure that the complete portion of sample remaining on the canister surfaces and in the membrane will be rinsed. Generally, the diluent is introduced

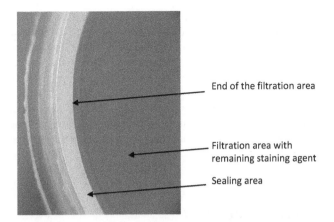

End of the filtration area

Filtration area with remaining staining agent

Sealing area

FIGURE 22.7 Membrane sealing zone. (Picture courtesy of Sartorius.)

in the canisters while the vents are open to allow the introduction of a big amount of diluent in the canister.

Besides, in order to avoid any retention of antimicrobial substances in the sealing ring (Figure 22.7) of the membrane, the design of the canister is of major importance.

Culture Media Introduction

After rinsing, the culture media are introduced separately in each canister and the tubes are cut on top of each canister.

Although the volume of culture media is not given in the EP or USP, the common practice is to use 100 mL. The volume of culture media is anyway part of the validation.

Incubation of the Canister and Growth Examination

The canisters are incubated for 14 days as mentioned in the regulations.

Thioglycollate media at $32.5 \pm 2.5°C$

Soybean Casein Digest at $22.5 \pm 2.5°C$

At intervals during the incubation users should examine the media for growth of microorganisms. The definition of intervals depends on the laboratory organization; if possible, a daily observation is preferred. Examples of growth are shown in Figure 22.8.

A particular attention has to be paid concerning the Thioglycollate media. This media contains agar to limit the diffusion of oxygen into it, in order to allow the growth of anaerobes. The fluid also contains a

(a)   (b)

FIGURE 22.8 Examples of growth of Clostridium sporogenes (a) and Staphylococcus aureus (b) after 2 days in Thioglycollate media compared to negative control (left canister on each picture). (Pictures courtesy of Sartorius AG.)

color indicator (Resazurin sodium) which turns pink when exposed to oxygen. Users have to make sure that at the end of the incubation period, not more than the half upper part of the culture media has turned pink. This would mean that the oxygenation is too high and might lead to the inhibition of anaerobes, generating a risk of false negative results. Besides, in fresh or stored media, not more than the upper third of the media should have turned pink. If so, the media must be restored by heating and cooled down promptly.

Ready-to-use Thioglycollate media in bottles is generally filled by the producer under inert gas (e.g., Nitrogen) in order to avoid adverse oxygen intake during transportation and storage.

Shaking the canister containing Thioglycollate media is generally not recommended as it would unnecessarily oxygenate the media.

Review of Warning Letters 2012–2017

The following statistical analysis about failures related to sterility has been performed by looking at the FDA Warning Letters of the last 6 years (2012–Sep 2017) when sterility test was mentioned. Such warning letters can serve as an indicator for the user to train the personnel or see what has to be focused on to eliminate any problems.

Of a total of 3,879 warning letters issued by the FDA from 2012 to Sep 2017, 84 letters refer to sterility testing, ranging between 1.5% and 2.3%. However, the percentage increased until Sep 2017, reaching 4.32% (Graph 22.1).

Graph 22.2 shows a ranking of the most commonly criticized points mentioned in warning letters concerning sterility testing.

A total of 80% of the statements and remarks related to sterility testing refer to validation and procedure. Out of this, 45% criticize the procedure and 35% the validation. Whether there is a need of improvement of validation and regulatory requirements understanding is not demonstrated but likely to be. On the other hand, proper training in handling and knowledge of regulatory needs, as suggested in nearly all regulations, could clearly help to get a better picture and reduce the number of apparitions of sterility testing remarks in FDA's warning letters.

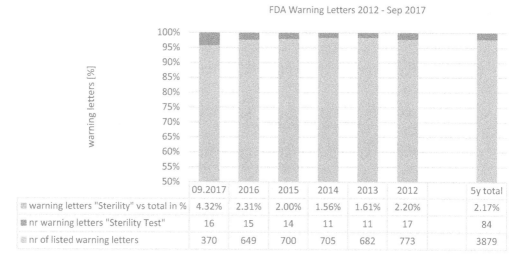

FDA Warning Letters 2012 - Sep 2017

	09.2017	2016	2015	2014	2013	2012		5y total
warning letters "Sterility" vs total in %	4.32%	2.31%	2.00%	1.56%	1.61%	2.20%		2.17%
nr warning letters "Sterility Test"	16	15	14	11	11	17		84
nr of listed warning letters	370	649	700	705	682	773		3879

GRAPH 22.1 Importance of FDA warning letters mentioning sterility test.

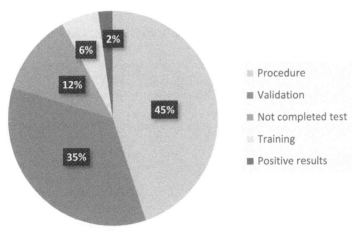

Critized points
in the 84 Warning Letters regarding "Sterility Test"

- Procedure
- Validation
- Not completed test
- Training
- Positive results

GRAPH 22.2 Importance of criticized procedures in the warning letters associated with sterility test.

Trends in Sterility Testing

Trend Toward Usage of Closed Systems in Class A Environment to Minimize the Risks of False Positive and False Negative Results

Most of the sterility tests are currently performed using a closed ready to use and disposable filtration set in laminar air flow (LAF) cabinets or in isolators. However, there is still a part of the tests which is performed with reusable filtration systems mainly due to economical reasons. Using reusable sterility test equipment increases the risk of secondary contamination leading to potential difficult to prove false positive results.

Besides, the environment of the test for sterility of pharmaceutical sterile products is of major importance. Microbiological quality of the environment around the test must be controlled in a proper way and is according to regulations classified as a class A (ISO 5) LAF cabinet within a class B (ISO 7), an isolator or a class A (ISO 5) clean room when available.

This means that the quality required is closed to sterility (see the section "PIC/S: PE009-4 June 2006 Guide to Good Manufacturing Practice for Medicinal Products").

Maintaining this quality is essential for minimizing the risks of introducing microorganisms from the environment into the canisters.

As the retest of a product batch is extremely problematic, users need more and more to improve the quality of the environment targeting the lowest risk of obtaining false positive results. This is why class A LAF must be within a class B environment and why isolators are constantly gaining interest for the sterility test application.

More, recently the FDA clearly stated in its "FDA Guidance for Industry—Sterile Products Produced by Aseptic Processing Current Good Manufacturing Practice" (see the *s*ection "FDA Guidance for Industry—Sterile Products Produced by Aseptic Processing Current Good Manufacturing Practice") that: "the use of isolators for sterility testing minimizes the chance of a false positive test result."

As a matter of fact, the isolator technology allows personnel to work outside the critical area by using gloves and sleeves or half suits. It is well known that the major source or microorganism in sterility testing laboratory is personnel; any mean providing a physical separation between the working place and the analyst will with no doubt limit the risk of microorganism release at the critical point.

There are many isolator suppliers on the market and several technologies can be found.

One of them is the soft wall isolator (Figure 22.9) equipped with one or several half suits or with gloves and allowing the introduction of material and consumables through transfer ports connecting the work station to transfer isolators used for gas decontamination.

The same isolation concept can also be found with rigid walls.

This concept allows some flexibility for transfer operations and a reduced frequency of gas decontamination of the work station.

Another concept consists of a work station which can be fully opened, generally in front of it, but not using transfer isolators connected to the work station (Figure 22.10).

In this case, the main work station must be decontaminated after each loading of material and samples required for the test.

Although the advantages of isolation technology are undeniable, it generates some challenges for QC personnel.

FIGURE 22.9 Getinge isolator with soft walls.

FIGURE 22.10 SKAN rigid wall isolator.

One of them lies in the use of chemical agents for the decontamination of material and consumables. Generally, isolators are decontaminated with vapor phase hydrogen peroxide or a mixture of hydrogen peroxide and peracetic acid.

Packaging material, culture media bottles, and other consumables and reagents which are necessary for performing the test are in direct contact with the chemicals during the decontamination process. In case the chemicals penetrate inside the packaging, this could have an adverse effect on the growth of microorganisms, potentially generating a risk of inhibition, giving false negative results. In the USP chapter <1208> Package Integrity Verification, the risk of penetration of chemicals used for decontamination of isolators inside canisters used for sterility testing is clearly specified (USP 2012b).

Besides, the FDA Guidance for Industry—"Sterile Products Produced by Aseptic Processing Current Good Manufacturing Practice," states that users should validate that there is no risk of false negatives.

To minimize this risk, the packaging material should be adapted and technical solutions are already available. The trend is to get consumables packed in multilayer plastic packaging or multilayer plastic and aluminum packaging.

Rapid Detection

The compendial growth-based method of sterility testing based on visual inspection takes more than 14 days to get a result, until then, final products are in quarantine and cannot be released. There is a need to release products faster to avoid drug shortages and/or to optimize the cash-to-cash cycle of companies. During the last years, several methods and systems have been adopted from other industries such as clinic, food, or cosmetics to enable companies to get a faster time to result. To name a few, the ATP-based detection via the Celsis System from Charles River claims to provide results in 7 instead of 14 days. This system can be used for faster sterility testing of directly inoculated or filtered products. The BactAlert from Biomerieux can be used to gain faster results for products that are tested for sterility by direct inoculation. Similar to BactAlert is the Bactec from BD. BDs Bactec repeatedly reads pH shift in the inoculated media and automatically provides alarm if a positive result is found. The growth direct system from Rapid Micro Biosystems is designed for Microbial Enumeration, but the extension for the usage of sterility testing is currently in development.

The named systems differ in their level of automation, capacity, and detection method.

Obtaining the results very early compared to the compendial 14 days can be highly valuable when the sterile product has a very short shelf life (a few days only). It is then impossible to apply the traditional method.

Generally speaking, the introduction of alternative microbiology methods for sterility testing is so far limited to some specific cases, and it is not really clear how long the compendial traditional way will remain the preferred method. However, the new technologies have gained an increased interest and even found the ways of FDA approvals in a supposed very conservative environment.

Conclusion

Sterility testing is still considered a critical analytical step for drug product release. Since it is as critical and manifested in the release criteria of a batch any false positive result can be extremely disturbing, especially as full-scale investigation are lengthy and would delay the release of a batch. In instances, such investigation can be inconclusive which would jeopardize such batch.

For this reason, it is of importance to utilize best practices to avoid any potential cross-contaminant. New disposable device technologies to perform sterility tests with a lower risk of a false positive result, as well as isolator technology which creates an even cleaner environment support such practice. Certainly, new equipment technologies enhanced the accuracy of the sterility test, but still the well-established membrane sterility test method is lengthy. New rapid microbial detection technologies will be developed and approved.

In any case, the accuracy of a sterility test is only as good as the responsible analytical personnel performing such test. Training should never be forgotten, as the equipment is only being as good as the user of such.

This chapter described the common regulatory practices, but also detailed what is required to perform an appropriate sterility test and interpret such test. Equipment designs, especially in regard to disposable canisters are essential in critical application like the sterility testing of bactericidal or bacteriostatic solutions.

Other topics, not yet concluded were also described; one of such being the validation of the sterility test membrane. So far, there is no challenge standard to verify that the pore size rating quoted has the reduction value required. However, such challenge test verification would be supportive for any validation process.

REFERENCES

Bowman, F.W., (1966). Application of membrane filtration to antibiotic quality control sterility testing, *J Pharm. Sci.*, 55:818–821.

Bowman, F.W., and Holdowsky, S., (1960). Production and control of a stable penicillinase, *Antibiot. Chemother.*, 8:508.

The European Pharmacopoeia (2005) 2.6.1 Sterility, EDQM - Council of Europe, 7 allée Kastner, CS 30026 F-67081 Strasbourg, France.

FDA Code of Federal Regulation 21 CFR 610.12.

FDA Guidance for Industry—Sterile products Produced by Aseptic Processing—Current Good Manufacturing Practice—September 2004.

Jornitz, M.W., and Meltzer, T.H. 2001. *Sterile Filtration—A Practical Approach*, Marcel Dekker, New York.

PIC/S: PI 012-3 September 2007: Recommendation on Sterility Testing.

PIC/S: PE009-13 January 2017 Guide to Good Manufacturing Practice for Medicinal Products (Part I and Annexes).

The United States Pharmacopoeia (USP). 2012a. <1227>—Validation of Neutralization Methods—Recovery comparisons—Recovery by Membrane Filtration.

The United States Pharmacopoeia (USP). 2012b. <1208> Sterility Testing - Validation of Isolator Systems, The United States Pharmacopeial Convention, 12601 Twinbrook Parkway, Rockville, MD.

The United States Pharmacopoeia (USP). 2016. <71> Sterility Tests.

23

Bacterial Biofilms in Pharmaceutical Water Systems

Marc W. Mittelman
Mittelman and Associates, LLC

CONTENTS

Introduction

The majority of natural and industrial aquatic environments are nutrient limited, and microorganisms—principally, bacteria—have developed a number of survival strategies that enable their survival and replication. While planktonic microorganisms exist in oligotrophic environments, the predominant mode of survival and growth is associated with biofilms. There are a number of similarities between the physico-chemistry of pharmaceutical water systems and some natural aquatic ecosystems, and these similarities extend to the microbial populations and the survival mechanisms that are employed. Bacterial contamination of purified waters continues to present a challenge to pharmaceutical, biotechnology, medical device, and cosmetic manufacturers. Biofilms are ubiquitous in other types of industrial water systems, and create similar health-related and economic problems (Mittelman and Jones 2016). The presence of bacteria and their associated endotoxins (bacterial pyrogens) in pharmaceutical waters poses the single greatest threat to product quality.

The majority of FDA recalls are associated with product contamination, accounting for 36.5%, 55.9%, and 22.1% of class I, II, and III recalls, respectively, between 2012 and 2014 (Hall et al. 2016). Regulatory recalls directly related to bacterial bioburden are often associated with contamination of Purified Water and Water for Injection; reviews of the impact have been published by a number of authors (Mittelman 1995; Weyandt 2001; Jimenez 2007; Torbeck et al. 2011; Sutton and Jimenez 2012; Ahearn and Stulting 2014).

While the abiological particle loading of a given system usually remains relatively constant, small changes in environmental conditions can drastically influence the number and type of microorganisms present. Regardless of the prevailing conditions, however, the majority of bacteria in pharmaceutical water systems are associated with surfaces as biofilms. Biofilms may be described as surface accretions of bacteria, extracellular polymeric substances (slime), and entrained organic and inorganic detrital material. Desorption of bacteria and bacterial aggregates from biofilms gives rise to the majority of bulk-phase (planktonic) bacteria in fluid-handling systems.

Although microporous membrane filters are designed to reduce or eliminate planktonic bacterial numbers, it is important to recognize that filtration efficacy and effective filter life are inextricably linked to bacterial biofilms associated with various surfaces. The high surface area/volume ratios associated with the many components of a purified water system create considerable niches for biofilms and, by extension, generate water system bioburden. It is this bioburden generated at surfaces that is most often responsible for transmembrane pressure increases resulting from fouling of microporous membrane feedwater surfaces (Figure 23.1).

The Microbial Ecology of Purified Waters

As in most natural aquatic ecosystems, the vast majority of bacteria isolated from purified water systems are Gram-negative, non-fermentative bacilli. Similarly, diverse populations are often found in potable waters and other treated and untreated water systems. These bacteria are heterotrophic, requiring the presence of reduced assimilable organic carbon (AOC) compounds as energy sources. The Gram-negative cell wall consists of multiple layers of phospholipids surrounded by a lipopolysaccharide (LPS) structure. This multilaminated structure may afford the cell protection from the extremely hypotonic environment that is intrinsic to purified water systems. Therefore, these compounds serve as limiting growth factors in purified water systems. The term "oligotroph" has been assigned to organisms that are capable of growth in media containing <1 mg/L organic carbon (Ishida and Kadota 1981). Therefore, these compounds serve as limiting growth factors in purified water systems. In general, a positive correlation exists between AOC levels and planktonic bacterial numbers in natural environments and in industrial water systems. Kulakov et al. investigated the bacterial communities of six different ultrapure

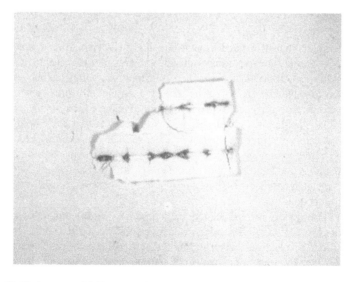

FIGURE 23.1 *Burkholderia cepacia* biofilm on the feedwater surface of a 0.45-μm microporous membrane filter located within a USP Purified Water system.

water systems, which are summarized in Table 23.1. Similar groups of bacteria have been isolated from purified waters in a variety of industries (Bohus et al. 2010; Bohus et al. 2011; Mijnendonckx et al. 2013; Minogue et al. 2013).

Fungal contamination of and growth in potable waters has been described (Arvanitidou et al. 1999; Cabral and Pinto 2002; Al-Gabr et al. 2014), and is often associated with higher AOC levels, i.e., >1 mg/L. While molds and yeasts have occasionally been isolated from industrial and health-care system purified water systems (Montagnac et al. 1991a, b; Falcao et al. 2012), their presence is likely due to allochthonous introduction, e.g., airborne. Growth in purified waters used in industrial and health-care applications has only rarely been reported (Ahearn and Stulting 2014).

The International Space Station has a number of "purified" water systems associated with both space-craft operations and crew usage. The types of microorganisms and their distribution on surfaces are very similar to those found in pharmaceutical water systems (Novikova et al. 2006). In addition to the concerns of bioburden and endotoxins as a direct health threat, microbially influenced corrosion is also of concern (Roman et al. 2001). "Ultrapure" water systems found in the semiconductor (Kim et al. 1997; Kim et al. 2000) and nuclear power (Chicote et al. 2004; Sarro et al. 2005) industries are also susceptible to bioburden contamination resulting from biofilm development. Again, the types and distributions of microbial populations are similar in these various water systems.

TABLE 23.1

16S rRNA-based Identification of Cultures from Six Different Ultrapure Water Systems

Water System	Sample Site	Isolates Recovered	Isolates (% of Total)
UPWS-1	Before UV254 (polishing loop)	*Ralstonia pickettii*	8 (13)
		Bradyrhizobium sp.	3 (5)
		Flavobacterium sp.	3 (5)
		Burkholderia sp.	4 (6.7)
		Stenotrophomonas sp.	5 (8.3)
		Mycobacterium sp.	4 (6.7)
		Bacillus sp.	8 (13.3)
		Other	25 (41)
UPWS-1	Distribution system	*Ralstonia pickettii*	8 (24)
		Bradyrhizobium sp.	12 (36)
		Pseudomonas saccharophila	4 (12)
		Other	9 (27)
UPWS-2	After UV254, UV185, and final filters (0.1 μm)	*Bradyrhizobium* sp.	6 (60)
		Other	4 (40)
UPWS-3	Distribution system	*Ralstonia pickettii*	4 (66)
		Bradyrhizobium sp.	1 (17)
		Other	1 (17)
UPWS-4	Distribution system and distribution system (return loop)	*Bradyrhizobium* sp.	4 (25)
		Pseudomonas saccharophilia	4 (25)
		Sphingomonas sp.	4 (25)
		Other	4 (25)
UPWS-5	Distribution system	*Ralstonia pickettii*	6 (100)
UPWS-6	Distribution system, storage tank, before UV254 and after UV254	*Pseudomonas fluorescens*	6 (28)
		Ralstonia pickettii	5 (24)
		Pseudomonas saccharophila	1 (5)
		Bradyrhizobium sp.	2 (10)
		Sphingomonas sp.	3 (14)
		Other	4 (19)

Source: Kulakov et al. (2002).

Population densities in distilled water have been reported to exceed 10^6 colony-forming units (cfu) per mL (Carson et al. 1973). McFeters et al. (McFeters et al. 1993) found 10^2–10^3 cfu/mL in a model laboratory water system, with many of the same system components (deionization beds, UV, and microporous membrane filters) that are seen in pharmaceutical-grade purified water systems. Like a number of other workers (Mittelman et al. 1987; Patterson et al. 1991; Martyak et al. 1993), this group found that significantly greater numbers of bacteria (ranging up to 10^5 cfu/cm^2) were associated with various surfaces within the water production and distribution systems.

Starvation and Survival in Purified Waters

When one or more essential growth factors are limited, as is often the case in natural environments and purified water systems, bacteria use a number of strategies designed to ensure their survival. In the short term, "starved" bacterial tend to use endogenous energy reserves for replication; therefore, one strategy for survival involves replication to increase the probability of species survival once additional energy sources become available (Novitsky and Morita 1978). In marine systems, limited in assimilable nutrients, some bacteria reduce their cell volume, forming "ultramicrobacteria." Tabor et al. (Tabor et al. 1981) demonstrated that these organism, many of which were <0.3 μm in diameter, were capable of passing through 0.45-μm pore microporous membrane filters. Chen et al. (Chen et al. 2012) reported that *Leptospira licerasiae* was isolated from cell culture media at a major U.S. pharmaceutical operation. The bacterium, which likely originated in surface waters used for production of purified water, was found to be capable of passing through 0.1 μm pore-sized microporous membrane filters. Their findings tend to corroborate the work of Christian and Meltzer (Christian and Meltzer 1986) and others regarding bacterial penetration of "sterilizing grade" microporous membrane filters.

Changes to cellular morphology are a common response to the starvation–survival mechanism triggered among Gram-negative bacteria. Cells typically become more coccoid in shape, reduce cell length, may develop flagella for locomotion, and transition to ultramicrocells (Tabor et al. 1981; Hartke et al. 1998). *Vibrio* species have been shown to reduce in volume to 0.03 μm^3 (Hartke et al. 1998). These resulting "ultramicrobacteria" maximize their surface area to volume ratio to increase the efficiency of cellular transport processes, and the smaller size reduces predation rates. Ultramicrobacteria are considered the normal state of bacterial cells in oligotrophic aquatic, marine, and terrestrial environments (Moyer and Morita 1989; Moyer and Morita 1989). Size considerations, including aspect ratios of bacteria in water, significantly influence microporous membrane retention characteristics (Sundaram et al. 2001a, b, c; Schroeder 2005; Lee et al. 2010a, b).

Natural oligotrophic environments are often defined as containing less than 0.5 mg/L of dissolved organic carbon (DOC) (Amy and Morita 1983; Amy et al. 1983; Cavicchioli et al. 2002), or 0.1–50 nanomolar concentrations of low molecular weight (LMW) organic compounds such as amino acids and sugars (Fuhrman 1987; Williams 2000). A significant portion of this DOC in oligotrophic environments is often considered recalcitrant and not bioavailable (Barber 1968). Nonetheless, microbial density and diversity in oligotrophic aquatic environments can be high, with up to 10^5–10^6 cells/mL (Cavicchioli et al. 2002; Hobbie and Hobbie 2013), with growth rates of less than 0.01/day in oligotrophic waters (Crump et al. 2013).

Despite the nutritional constraints of oligotrophic environments, microorganisms have adopted a number of starvation–survival mechanisms, which include nutritional versatility, cellular morphological changes, viable but non-culturable (VBNC) state, formation of cysts and spores, and biofilm formation. These mechanisms can be triggered by environmental stressors such as low DOC, temperature extremes, salinity, low-nutrient concentration, and light extremes. A single environmental stressor will likely trigger any one of the starvation–survival mechanisms available, while multiple stressors may favor a VBNC starvation–survival mechanism (Morita 1997; del Mar Lleò et al. 2005). The starvation–survival mechanisms used are species-dependent and can also be dependent on whether the microorganism can form cysts or spores (McDougald et al. 2006). Exposure to one stressor typically provokes a starvation–survival mechanism which may provide resistance against other, unrelated, environmental stressors (Hartke et al. 1998). Microbial starvation–survival mechanisms in response to oligotrophy in the natural environment are variable and highly effective in reducing respiration rates and reducing microbial cell densities while enabling microbial cells to retain viability, which is of critical importance in high purity industrial waters used in pharmaceutical and other biomedical processes.

A number of investigators have described bacterial growth and biofilm formation in "ultrapure" water (18 MΩ cm; <10 μg/L TOC). Kim (Kim et al. 2000) described bacteria with a wide range of AOC utilization capabilities in semiconductor waters. Similar types of bacteria were recovered from "ultrapure" water (Chicote et al. 2005), and from biofilms (Chicote et al. 2004; Sarro et al. 2005) in spent nuclear fuel pools.

Objectionable Organisms

The U.S. Pharmacopeia stipulates that purified water and other pharmaceutical waters not contain objectionable organisms (USP 2014a). Included in this group are coliform bacteria, which by compendial requirement cannot exceed limits promulgated by the U.S. EPA. Currently, a limit of <1 cfu/100 mL total coliforms is in place. In addition, it is important to consider that changes in the microbial ecology of both the feedwater and the manufacturing environment may occur at any time. The significance of organisms in non-sterile drug forms requires an evaluation with respect to the product's intended use, the nature of the preparations, and potential hazard to the user.

Increasingly, however, noncoliform, heterotrophic bacteria previously considered "normal inhabitants" of purified waters are considered objectionable. Indeed, the prevailing view among manufacturers and the FDA is that objectionable organisms (other than the stipulated prohibition against coliform bacteria) are product application-defined (USP 2014b, c). For example, purified water used in the manufacture of non-sterile ophthalmic preparations should be free of *Pseudomonas aeruginosa* and *Burkholderia cepacia*. The definition of "objectionable organisms" in pharmaceutical waters is likely to broaden in the future: As new products and product applications are introduced, it follows that a number of existing and emerging environmental bacteria will be proscribed.

With an increasing recognition of the role of bacterial biofilms plays in the generation of water systems bioburden, it is likely that limits will eventually be placed on both "normal inhabitants" and "objectionable organisms" associated with surfaces. Current limitations associated with sampling and enumeration techniques for this significant subpopulation of water systems bioburden prevent the establishment of concern and action limits. Biofilms have been implicated as a reservoir for pathogenic bacteria in drinking water distribution conduits (Liu et al. 2016; Wang et al. 2017), hospital water systems (Alary and Joly 1992; Walker and Moore 2015; Muchesa et al. 2016; Garvey et al. 2017), hemodialysis water systems (Phillips et al. 1994; Chen et al. 2017), and dental treatment units (Schulze-Robbecke et al. 1995; Shearer 1996; Huntington 2010; Lal et al. 2017). To date, no comprehensive studies on the microbial ecology of pharmaceutical grade water systems biofilm communities have been carried out.

The specific physicochemical environment associated with purified water systems is the primary determinant of the microbial ecology (Mittelman and Jones 2016). As was previously noted, similar types of bacteria are found in purified water systems associated with the pharmaceutical, dialysis, semiconductor, and aerospace industries. Unless these waters are maintained sterile—free of any viable microorganisms—it is not possible to exclude bacteria that are adapted to life in an extremely oligotrophic environment. Many of these organisms include *Pseudomonas spp.* and other microorganisms that are of concern to the pharmaceutical industry.

Genesis of Bacterial Biofilms

Perhaps the most significant adaptive mechanism used by nutrient-limited purified water bacteria involves adhesion to surfaces. Indeed, the majority of bacteria in a nutrient-limited environment, such as an ultrapure water system, are attached to surfaces (Figure 23.2). Surfaces afford these organisms three major advantages relative to life in a bulk-phase environment:

1. Trace organics, which can serve as nutrient sources, concentrate on clean surfaces shortly after their immersion.
2. Surface-associated bacteria tend to produce extracellular polymeric substances (EPSs), which can further concentrate trace growth factors.
3. Bacteria in biofilms are afforded some protection from antagonistic agents such as antimicrobial compounds, heat treatments, and other inhibitory factors.

Adhesion may be defined as the discrete association between a bacterium and a surface. If a bacterium has adhered to a surface, energy is required to effect a separation (Mittelman 1999a, b). A biofilm is comprised of these adherent cells, EPS produced by the attached organisms, and entrained organic and inorganic material from the fluid milieu. Attachment to surfaces is mediated and stabilized by EPS (Figure 23.3). At the molecular level, bacteria and fungi adhere to surfaces by a combination of electrostatic and hydrophobic interactions. The nature of these interactions is dependent upon a combination of physicochemical factors, including pH, temperature, ionic strength, ligand density, dipole moment, and charge density (Donlan 2002). The size and charge of bacteria are in the same range as colloidal solutes. Therefore, bacteria can exist as lyophobic or lyophilic solutions, association colloids, gels, or as part of an emulsion.

Several workers have shown that nutrient-limiting environments promote the attachment of bacteria to surfaces (Mittelman et al. 1987; Marshall 1988). The relatively high surface area/volume ratio associated with industrial water systems provides ample space for bacterial attachment. Any one of the many systems used in the purification of feedwaters is therefore a potential reservoir for contamination. In terms of biological generation, however, granular-activated carbon columns (Johnston and Burt 1976; Collentro 1986), reverse osmosis (RO) and ultrafiltration membranes (Ridgway et al. 1985; Laurence and Lapierre 1995), ion-exchange (DI) systems (Flemming 1987), RO/DI water storage tanks (Collentro 1996), and microporous membrane filters (Collentro 1996), are the most significant areas of concern.

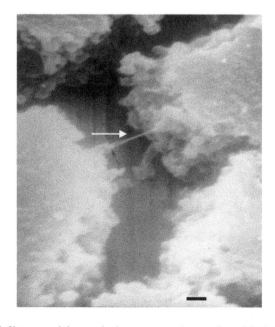

FIGURE 23.2 Bacterial biofilm on a stainless steel substrate; arrow shows collapsed EPS. Bar = 1 μm.

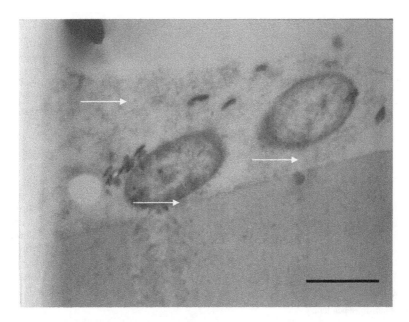

FIGURE 23.3 Transmission electron micrograph of bacteria adhering to a polymeric substrate; attachment mediated by EPS (shown by arrows). Bar= 1 µm. (Courtesy of Dr. Gill Geesey.)

Biofilm Development

Development of bacterial biofilms in aqueous environment proceeds in a three-step process: (a) accretion of trace organics on the surface, (b) primary ("reversible") adhesion, and (c) surface colonization (*in situ* division of adherent bacteria). Bacteria form microcolonies on surfaces that are discontinuous and heterogeneous in their distribution. Although biofilms are known to be the source of bulk-phase or planktonic bacteria in a water system, there is no discrete relationship known between the relative population sizes. This is due to the stochastic nature of adhesion, colonization, and desorption, all of which are affected by a number of interrelated physiochemical factors (Table 23.2).

The elaboration of EPS by reversibly bound bacteria stabilizes the initial adhesion event. Extracellular polymeric substances often carry a strong net negative charge, which may be important in the stabilization of succeeding adherent organisms. Microbial cells may also become more hydrophobic and adhesive through secretion of EPSs that increase the rate of co-aggregation of cells (Declerck 2010). Increases in co-aggregation and ultimately biofilm formation provide additional protection against predation and impacts from other environmental stressors as well as enabling the recycling of LMW organic compounds secreted from or lyzed by neighboring cells (Álvarez et al. 2008). It is the presence of EPS that affords bacteria in pharmaceutical water systems some protection from chemical treatments and, possibly, flowing steam/hot water treatment. EPS can constitute a significant fraction of the total surface biomass (bioburden) as is shown in Figure 23.3. Significantly, EPS can be an important contributor to fouling processes associated with both microporous and RO membranes (Ridgway et al. 1985; Roth et al. 1998; Ridgway et al. 1999; Berman et al. 2011).

Biofilm formation is also controlled, in part, by quorum sensing, a bacterium–bacterium communication mechanism that is related to population density. (Costerton et al. 2005; Fux et al. 2005; Jakobsen et al. 2017; Li et al. 2017). Inhibiting precursor molecules involved with this mechanism may prevent/disrupt bacterial biofilm formation. However, to date, the applications for disruptive treatments of this nature have been limited to the clinical environment, e.g., device-related infections.

Endotoxins present in pharmaceutical water systems—like planktonic bacteria—originate with bacterial biofilms. Rioufol (Rioufol et al. 1999) found >1,000 endotoxin units/cm^2 of surface were associated with a medical device biofilm. Endotoxin is present in both free and bound forms, and is continually

TABLE 23.2

Environmental Effects on Bacterial Adhesion Parameters

Bulk-phase Environmental Parameters	Effect(s) on Bacterial Adhesion in Aqueous Environments	Conditions Minimizing Adhesion[a]	References
pH	Cell surface charge, adhesion to surfaces, binding capacity of cell surface, extracellular polymer stability	<6	Herald and Zottola (1987), Characklis (1990), Richards et al. (1993)
Temperature	Metabolic activity, heat-shock protein analysis	>40°C to minimize viscosity	Hoadley (1981), Aranha and Meeker (1995)
Ionic Strength/ osmolarity	Cell surface charge, adhesion to surfaces	Greater ionic strength increases bacterial cell surface negative charge densities	Baldwin et al. (1988), Fletcher (1988), Geertsema-Doornbusch et al. (1993), Baldwin et al. (1995a), Baldwin et al. (1995b)
Assimilable carbon	Metabolic activity, organism size, cell surface hydrophobicity	Decreasing carbon and starvation result in shrinking cell size and increases in cell surface hydrophobicity	Novitsky and Morita (1978), Dahlback et al. (1981), Morita (1982), Morita (1985), Nystrom et al. (1992)

[a] Surface- and organism-dependent.

sloughed-off from growing Gram-negative bacteria. Removal of biofilms from surfaces also results in the elimination of most endotoxins from the bulk-phase water (Shinoda 2004).

Influence of Surface Characteristics

The influence of surface roughness and surface energetics on the development of bacterial biofilms has been examined by a number of investigators. Vanhaecke and Van den Haesevelde (Vanhaecke and Van den Haesevelde 1991) and Vanhaecke et al. (Vanhaecke et al. 1990) reported that surface roughness can have an influence on the adhesion kinetics of some bacteria. They suggest that hydrophobic strains of *P. aeruginosa* show greater adhesion to electropolished stainless steel than strains possessing more hydrophilic cell surfaces. Indeed, the kinetics of adhesion for the former strain types were similar on 120 grit polished or electropolished stainless steels. Other investigators have reported significantly different "adhesion kinetics" for the same organisms (Pedersen 1990; Quirynen et al. 1993; Verheyen et al. 1993). Conversely, Arnold and Suzuki (Arnold and Suzuki 2003) have suggested that bacterial adhesion to electropolished stainless steel surfaces is significantly reduced relative to "rougher" steels. Riedewald (Riedewald 2006) has evaluated the literature concerning the influence of surface roughness on bacterial adhesion: he concludes that there is no real benefit to specifying highly polished (i.e., smooth) surfaces if the desired outcome is reduced bacterial attachment. In particular, he notes that, "the roughness of stainless steel surfaces in the range of 0.01–3.3 μm Ra has no significant influence in cleanability."

It is apparent that surface characteristics are important during the initial stages of adhesion (Marshall et al. 1971; Dahlback et al. 1981). It is unlikely, however, that surface structure or free energy considerations play important roles following the initial adhesion event. Following the initial adhesion event, succeeding bacteria may not contact the underlying surface. Similar findings have been reported for fluid hydraulic effects. Characklis (Characklis 1990) showed that fluid hydraulics can affect the initial rate of colonization; however, following this initial "lag" phase, biofilm development appears to proceed somewhat independently of fluid flow.

Flow Effects

As with surface roughness, there is much debate surrounding the influence of flow on the formation and stability of biofilms. The often-stated "recommended" minimum flow rate of 5–7 ft/s does not appear to have any scientific support, and is based on a "standard" 2″ diameter pipe (Meltzer and Jornitz 2006a).

Indeed, most of the peer-reviewed literature suggests that flow rates have a minimal effect on biofilm development and stability. Neither biofilm development or planktonic cell numbers were significantly influenced by purified water flowing at 1.5–5.2 m/s and the corresponding shear stresses of 9.1–84 N/m² (Soini et al. 2002; Rickard et al. 2004; Tsai et al. 2004; Ramasami and Zhang 2005; Rupp et al. 2005). One report by Florjanic and Kristi (Florjanic and Kristl 2011) suggested that greater numbers of planktonic cells were generated in a "stagnant" simulated pharmaceutical water system than by one in which shear force was generated. However, Saur et al. (Saur et al. 2017) found greater numbers of attached cells at higher shear levels in a different experimental system. There is also evidence to suggest that "stronger" biofilms may form at higher shear forces, up to a critical shear force (Liu and Tay 2001).

Given the submicron size range of bacterial footprints on surfaces, which place attached cells within a viscous fluid sublayer under most flow regimes, it is unlikely that maintenance of a high flow rate alone would retard adhesion and biofilm development. There may be a benefit to increased flow rates where UV, microporous membrane filtration, or other planktonic bacterial treatments are employed. In these cases, higher flow rates would increase the frequency of interaction between planktonic cells and the treatment device.

Biofilm Detection

Since biofilm-associated bacteria are not detected by current compendial test methodologies, serious underestimates of contaminating populations result. In addition, this inability to detect the major source of bulk-phase biological contaminants can result in an overestimate of treatment efficacies. Biofilm bacteria can be quantitatively recovered and enumerated from surfaces by using classical cultural techniques (Martyak et al., 1993; Patterson et al., 1991). Pipe surfaces may be swabbed with sterile cotton applicators, then plated onto the appropriate medium (R2A, etc.). However, the difficulty in reproducibly sampling surfaces has precluded more widespread testing of pharmaceutical systems. Currently, there are no commercially available biofilm samplers available for the pharmaceutical industry. Sacrificial pipe sections, including a modified Robbins device, have been used for recovery of biofilm bacteria in purified water systems (Mittelman et al. 1987; Martyak et al. 1993). However, these types of sampling systems and the associated analytical techniques are somewhat cumbersome and time-consuming.

While dedicated biofilm sampling devices are not currently available, there are methods available for evaluating the influence of bulk-phase physicochemical, substratum, and fluid hydraulic properties on biofilm development. In particular, two ASTM methods have been developed to facilitate these types of studies: E2799-11 and E2562-12 (ASTM 2011, 2012). The Parenteral Drug Association has also published a Technical Report, TR 69, which reviews biofilm sampling, recovery, and characterization methods (PDA 2015).

Techniques for recovering biofilm bacteria from surfaces usually involve mechanical disruption through physical scraping or sonication. These techniques result, at best, in semiquantitative assessments of biofilm population sizes. This is due in part to the small size of bacteria, which often are smaller than the surface Ra. In addition, many biofilms are tightly adhered to surfaces and effective removal of cells (via sonication and surfactant application, for example) may kill otherwise viable organisms. Although the techniques for removal and enumeration of biofilm bacteria are evolving, some methods have been described that may have applications for pharmaceutical water systems (Mittelman 1998; McFeters et al. 1999; Mittelman 1999a, b; Haberer and Mittelman 2003; Marion-Ferey et al. 2003).

In any process, it is important to monitor possible contamination so corrective action can be initiated as rapidly as possible. The ideal monitors should be nondestructive so they will not inhibit or damage the biofilm. If the test systems can be placed in a supply lines or in the system upstream of purification/disinfection systems, then treatments can be modified to maintain microbiological control. A number of emerging online detection systems have previously been reviewed (Mittelman et al. 1993; Mittelman 1994; Mittelman 1998; Mittelman 1999a, b; Flemming 2003; Haberer and Mittelman 2003); three technologies with potential applications for the pharmaceutical industry are described below.

Characterization of biofilm biomass constituents may be performed using a variety of analytical techniques, including rapid methods (Verdonk et al. 2010; Shintani et al. 2011; Nemati et al. 2016;

Stubiger et al. 2016). The Parenteral Drug Association has also published a Technical Report, TR 33, which reviews advances in rapid microbiological methods (PDA 2013). The FDA's Manual for Pharmaceutical Microbiology (FDA 2014) includes descriptions of a number of rapid methods for microbial detection and characterization. Improvements to adenosine triphosphate (ATP) measurements have increased the sensitivity of this technique for biofilm characterization (Lee et al. 2010a, b), although its utility for detecting the presence of low numbers of bacteria on surfaces is limited at this time.

Fourier Transform Infrared Spectrometry

Fourier transform infrared (FTIR) spectrometry operated in the attenuated total reflectance mode allows the detection of bacterial biofilms as they form on a crystal of zinc selenide or germanium (Nichols et al. 1985; Schmitt and Flemming 1998). The amide stretching of the proteins and ether stretch of the carbohydrates are clearly detectable when bacteria attach to surfaces. Often the nutrients attracted to the surface from the bulk phase are also clearly indicated by their infrared fingerprint. If the water system contained IR "windows," biofilm formation could be monitored and an indication of the chemical nature of the contamination would be apparent. Periodically, some mechanism for cleaning the "window" would have to be provided. A detection limit of approximately 5×10^5 *Caulobacter crescentus* cells/ cm^2 was obtained using a germanium substratum monitored in an ATR flow cell (Nivens et al. 1993a). This nondestructive technique holds promise as an online monitoring tool for bacterial colonization compounds in purified water systems (Holman et al. 2009; Quiles et al. 2010). The ability to monitor biomass "signature compounds" may be of particular utility in assessing chemical treatment efficacies against purified water system foulants.

Fluorometry

The use of fluorometry for online monitoring of biofilm development has been described for monitoring of antifouling (Mittelman et al. 1993) and uncoated stainless-steel surfaces (Khoury et al. 1992). Reduced nicotinamide adenine dinucleotide (NAD) compounds along with aromatic amino acids (e.g., tyrosine and tryptophan) can be monitored as indicators of cell energy charge and biomass, respectively. As with FTIR spectrometry and quartz crystal microgravimetry (described below), this technique holds promise for application to monitoring purified water system fouling (Tajima et al. 2010; Corcoll et al. 2011; Tiam et al. 2015). Detection limits remain relatively poor, however, in the range of approximately 10^5 cells/cm^2.

Costanzo (Costanzo et al. 2002) have described the application of the Scan RDI system for detecting bacteria and other microorganisms on membrane surfaces. Individual cells or aggregated cells can be detected at a resolution of approximately 0.1 μm. Fluorometry has also been applied to the detection of specific clinical and environmental bacteria, some of which also have significance for biodefense applications (Chuang et al. 2001; Ji et al. 2004). Jun et al. (Jun et al. 2010) have described a fluorescence-based biofilm technology for food-contact surfaces, which may have pharmaceutical applications.

Quartz Crystal Microbalance

The presence of material of a significantly different intrinsic viscosity than that of the water can be detected as a change in frequency of a vibrating quartz crystal in quartz crystal microbalance (QCM) technology (Sprung et al. 2009; Olsson et al. 2015). The surface can also be used as an electrode to produce both the microbalance and electrochemical signals (Deakin and Buttry 1989). This technique was applied to monitoring biofilm formation in a simulated purified water system for the space station project. Detection limits of approximately 10^5 cells/cm^2 were obtained using an AT-cut quartz crystal (Nivens et al. 1993a).

Treatment

Inactivation and removal of bulk-phase bacteria following the most commonly employed physical and chemical treatments is usually effective. Within days or weeks of treatment, however, bulk-phase bacterial levels are often as high or higher than pretreatment levels. Bacteria existing in sessile biofilms are protected from the effects of some antimicrobial agents and, to some extent, physical treatments (e.g., steam, hot water). This resistance to inactivation is very different from that associated with classical antibiotic resistance, which involves specific mechanisms of resistance that are often unique to individual microbial species (Costerton et al. 2005; Fux et al. 2005). Again, this resistance is not absolute, and it is possible to inactive and remove biofilm biomass from surfaces. A number of studies have shown that repopulation of purified and other industrial water systems is mediated by the presence of adherent bacterial populations (Mittelman and Geesey 1987). The key to effective treatments, therefore, is inactivation and removal of this population of contaminating biological particulates.

Any treatment employed must be compatible with water system materials of construction. For example, although application of sodium hypochlorite can be a very effective means of inactivating and removing biofilm, this chemical compound can cause chloride-induced stress cracking of stainless steels (Meltzer and Jornitz 2006b). Understanding component compatibility is also essential to the development of an effective equipment cleaning program. The Parenteral Drug Association has also published a Technical Report, TR 69, which reviews approaches for biofilm and bioburden treatment (PDA 2015).

Physical Treatments

Empirical experience has demonstrated the efficacy of frequent flowing steam or hot water treatments of pharmaceutical water systems (Agalloco 1990) and in other industrial water systems (Pflug et al. 2001). Most vegetative bacteria (nonspore-forming) are killed at temperatures between 50°C and 65°C (Bader 1986; Assar and Block 2001). As with any type of antimicrobial treatment, the two key parameters are contact time and concentration (or temperature). Although there have been no reports of heat-resistant populations of bacteria in pharmaceutical water systems, problems with heat inactivation efficacy have been described for *Legionella spp.* in distribution systems for portable water (Stout et al. 1986) and *Listeria monocytogenes* in dairy products (Lee and Frank 1990).

While both flowing steam and hot water (80°C) appear to be effective at inactivating biofilm bacteria in pharmaceutical waters, neither treatment will effectively remove the biomass from surfaces, including EPSs and constituent endotoxins. However, it is clear that combining heat treatment with the appropriate chemical treatment results in a synergistic effect in terms of bioburden reduction (Holmes et al. 2004). Depyrogenation of surfaces cannot be reliably accomplished using hot water or steam-in-place (SIP) treatments. Bacterial LPSs are notoriously difficult to remove from surfaces (Novitsky 1984; Ludwig and Avis 1990). A significant number of problems with pyrogens have been reported in hemodialysis facilities with improperly treated purified water systems (Murphy et al. 1987; Laurence and Lapierre 1995).

Ultraviolet irradiation at 185 or 254 nm is an effective process for inactivating planktonic microorganisms in pharmaceutical and other industrial waters (McAlister et al. 2002; Anderson et al. 2003). However, UV has not been shown to be effective against attached bacteria in biofilms. In part, this is due to the poor penetration of UV, either at 185 or 254 nm, with the energy available for cell interaction decreasing by the square of the distance from the UV source. Meltzer (Meltzer 1997) has described UV applications for pharmaceutical water systems.

Chemical Treatments

The development of process- and product-compatible biofouling treatments has long challenged manufacturers of critical products that require purified water as a raw material. Of all the physical and biocidal treatments applied to pharmaceutical grade purified water systems, ozone appears to hold the greatest promise as an effective product-compatible antimicrobial treatment. A number of publications have described ozone-associated biofilm inactivation efficacy (Characklis 1990; Smeets et al. 2003; Bott and Tianqing 2004; Dosti et al. 2005; Florjanic and Kristl 2006; Baumann et al. 2009). It is unlikely, however, that water systems ozone dosing, which is limited by the relatively poor solubility of ozone in water, is effective against heavily fouled systems. That is, precleaning with a surface-active agent and/or oxidizing antimicrobial may be required. With the development of fluoropolymer-based microporous membranes for pharmaceutical applications, ozone can be applied throughout a USP purified or water-for-injection

(WFI) system. The technology is currently available for inactivation of residual ozone levels *in situ* via UV irradiation (Meltzer 1993). Most of the problems with ozone application to purified water systems have been in the realm of component compatibility. Since ozone is an extremely reactive oxidant, its use is confined to systems constructed of such inert materials as Teflon and other fluoropolymers.

Hydrogen peroxide, a commonly employed purified water system treatment chemical, can also be readily degraded by ultraviolet light. However, it has relatively little activity against attached bacteria in biofilms. There is also evidence that suggests that hydrogen peroxide requires catalytic concentrations of Fe^{2+}, Ni^{2+}, or Cu^{2+} for optimal antimicrobial efficacy (Block 2001).

Surfactants such as the quaternary ammonium compounds have excellent antimicrobial activity in addition to their intrinsic detergency. Synergistic combinations of chlorinated or brominated compounds with surfactants may provide additional activity against bacterial biofilm populations. Their ability to interact with surfaces does, however, create problems related to removal of these compounds following application. Larger volumes of rinse water are required for the surfactant compounds than, for example, for hydrogen peroxide.

Peracetic acid, 0.02% (v/v), has been found to be an effective treatment agent for both deionization resins and associated water system components (Flemming 1984; Alasri et al. 1993; Mazzola et al. 2006; Farhat et al. 2011). This compound is sometimes used in synergistic combinations with hydrogen peroxide and/or UV irradiation (Henthorne and Amer Desalting 1996; Mazzola et al. 2006; Sacchetti et al. 2009). Along with its true biocidal properties (i.e., sporicidal activity), peracetic acid is an effective depyrogenating agent and is used extensively in the hemodialysis industry, both for water system disinfection and for ultrafilter sterilization/depyrogenation.

Citric acid has been evaluated for its ability to inactivate and remove biofilms from water distribution systems. Tsai (Tsai et al. 2003) showed that 10,000 mg/L solutions of citric acid removed 99.999% of heterotrophic bacteria from surfaces in a simulated potable water system. Citric acid has also been used as part of a passivation system for stainless steels (Meltzer and Jornitz 2006b, c).

Although formaldehyde and glutaraldehyde have been shown to be effective agents against biofilm bacteria in water systems, their use is now extremely limited due to occupational safety and environmental disposal concerns. More recently, orthophthalaldehyde (OPP) has been evaluated as a biofilm treatment agent (Simoes et al. 2003). OPP is reportedly less toxic than other aldehyde compounds, and has been used for sterilizing heat-labile medical devices. The results of studies with *P. aeruginosa* biofilms showed that OPP was effective at inactivating cells, but did not effectively remove biofilms from the underlying surface.

The so-called bacterial regrowth phenomenon following chlorine treatments of purified and potable water systems is likely a function of biofilm formation rather than resistance in the classical sense of antibiotic resistance (Wolfe et al. 1988). A combination of the polyanionic nature of many EPS moieties coupled with the inherent biocide demand associated with extracellular slime matrices may act as an inhibitor of various treatment agents. To date, the most effective chemical agents used in the control of bacterial biofilms in pharmaceutical grade water systems have been the oxidizing compounds such as chlorine (Rutala and Weber 1997), hydrogen peroxide (Kim et al. 2000; Kim et al. 2002), and peracetic acid (Gorke and Kittel 2002). Table 23.3 lists some of the more commonly applied chemical treatments along with typical dosage regimes. Alkaline or acid treatments, combined with surfactants and antimicrobial agents, have shown efficacy in biofilm removal from a variety of water systems and materials of construction (Parkar et al. 2004; Hadi et al. 2010).

As with any type of chemical treatment, the compatibility of water system components (including microporous membrane filters) should be verified with the appropriate manufacturers. Handling and disposal of water treatment and other chemical agents require a familiarity with local health, safety, and environmental regulations.

Summary

Pharmaceutical water systems contain very low AOC and present significant physicochemical challenges to microorganisms. Microbial strategies for survival in these water systems are similar to

TABLE 23.3

Examples of Chemical Treatment Regimes

Treatment Agent	Dosage Regime	Treatment Time (h)
Quaternary ammonium compounds	300–1,000 mg/L	2–3
Sodium hypochlorite	50–100 mg/L	2–3
Peracetic acid/peroxide	0.02–0.05% (v/v)	2
Iodine	50–100 mg/L	1–2
Hydrogen peroxide	10% (v/v)	2–3

strategies used in natural oligotrophic environments, and include combinations of nutritional versatility, cellular morphological changes, VBNC state, cysts and spores, and—most importantly—growth in biofilm. These strategies enable survival in a variety of pharmaceutical and biotechnology water systems. Microorganisms isolated from these systems are typically Gram-negative, non-fermentative bacilli, although other microbes including fungi can be isolated as well. Microbial growth, particularly as biofilms, can result in significant and periodic microbial bioburden development. The significance of the resulting deleterious effects of microbial contamination can range from increased morbidity and mortality in health-care settings to the financial burden of product recalls. Detection and control of microbial biofilm in pharmaceutical water systems are essential for bioburden control: biofilms are the source of planktonic organisms responsible for product and process contamination events.

REFERENCES

Agalloco, J. P. 1990. Steam sterilization-in-place technology, *Journal of Parenteral Science and Technology* 44: 253–256.

Ahearn, D. G. and R. D. Stulting. 2014. Fungi associated with drug recalls and rare disease outbreaks, *Journal of Industrial Microbiology and Biotechnology* 41(11): 1591–1597.

Al-Gabr, H. M., T. L. Zheng and X. Yu. 2014. Fungi contamination of drinking water, in *Reviews of Environmental Contamination and Toxicology, Vol 228*. D. M. Whitacre (ed.). 121–139. Switzerland: Springer.

Alary, M. and J. R. Joly. 1992. Factors contributing to the contamination of hospital water distribution systems by *Legionellae, Journal of Infectious Disease* 165: 565–569.

Alasri, A., M. Valverde, et al. 1993. Sporocidal properties of peracetic acid and hydrogen peroxide, alone and in combination, in comparison with chlorine and formaldehyde for ultrafiltration membrane disinfection, *Canadian Journal of Microbiology* 39: 52–60.

Álvarez, B., M. M. López and E. G. Biosca. 2008. Survival strategies and pathogenicity of Ralstonia solanacearum phylotype II subjected to prolonged starvation in environmental microcosms, *Microbiology* 154: 3590–3598.

Amy, P. S. and R. Y. Morita. 1983. Starvation-survival patterns of 16 freshly isolated open-ocean bacteria, *Applied and Environmental Microbiology* 45(3): 1109–1115.

Amy, P. S., C. Pauling and R. Y. Morita. 1983. Starvation-survival processes of a marine vibrio, *Applied and Environmental Microbiology* 45(3): 1041–1048.

Anderson, W. B., P. M. Huck, D. G. Dixon and C. I. Mayfield. 2003. Endotoxin inactivation in water by using medium-pressure UV lamps, *Applied and Environmental Microbiology* 69(5): 3002–3004.

Aranha, H. and J. Meeker. 1995. Microbial retention characteristics of 0.2-microns-rated nylon membrane filters during filtration of high viscosity fluids at high differential pressure and varied temperatures, *Journal of Pharmaceutical Science and Technology* 49: 67–70.

Arnold, J. W. and O. Suzuki. 2003. Effects of corrosive treatment on stainless steel surface finishes and bacterial attachment, *Transactions of the ASAE* 46: 1595–1602.

Arvanitidou, M., K. Kanellou, T. C. Constantinides and V. Katsouyannopoulos. 1999. The occurrence of fungi in hospital and community potable waters, *Letters in Applied Microbiology* 29(2): 81–84.

Assar, S. K. and S. S. Block. 2001. Survival of microorganisms in the environment, in *Disinfection, Sterilization, and Preservation, 5th ed.* S. S. Block (ed.). 1221–1242. Philadelphia, PA: Lippincott.

ASTM (2011). E2799-11: Standard Test Method for Testing Disinfectant Efficacy against *Pseudomonas aeruginosa* Biofilm Using the MBEC Assay. ASTM.

ASTM (2012). E2562-12: Standard Test Method for Quantification of *Pseudomonas aeruginosa* Biofilm Grown with High Shear and Continuous Flow Using CDC Biofilm Reactor. ASTM.

Bader, F. G. 1986. Sterilization: Prevention of contamination, in *Manual of Industrial Microbiology and Biotechnology*. A. L. Demain and N. A. Solomon (eds.). 345–362. Washington, DC: American Society for Microbiology.

Baldwin, W. W., R. Myer, T. Kung, E. Anderson and A. L. Koch. 1995a. Growth and buoyant density of *Escherichia coli* at very low osmolarities, *Journal of Bacteriology* 177: 235–237.

Baldwin, W. W., R. Myer, N. Powell, E. Anderson and A. L. Koch. 1995b. Buoyant density of *Escherichia coli* is determined solely by the osmolarity of the culture medium, *Archives of Microbiology* 164: 155–157.

Baldwin, W. W., J. T. M. Sheu, P. W. Bankston and C. L. Woldringh. 1988. Changes in buoyant density and cell size of *Escherichia coli* in response to osmotic shocks, *Journal of Bacteriology* 170(452–455): 170–177.

Barber, R. T. 1968. Dissolved organic carbon from deep waters resists microbial oxidation, *Nature* 220: 274–275.

Baumann, A. R., S. E. Martin and H. Feng. 2009. Removal of Listeria monocytogenes biofilms from stainless steel by use of ultrasound and ozone, *Journal of Food Protection* 72(6): 1306–1309.

Berman, T., R. Mizrahi and C. G. Dosoretz. 2011. Transparent exopolymer particles (TEP): A critical factor in aquatic biofilm initiation and fouling on filtration membranes, *Desalination* 276(1–3): 184–190.

Block, S. S. 2001. Peroxygen compounds, in *Disinfection, Sterilization, and Preservation*. S. S. Block (ed.). 185–204. Malvern, PA: Lippincott Williams & Wilkins.

Bohus, V., Z. Keki, et al. 2011. Bacterial communities in an ultrapure water containing storage tank of a power plant, *Acta Microbiologica Et Immunologica Hungarica* 58(4): 371–382.

Bohus, V., E. M. Toth, et al. 2010. Microbiological investigation of an industrial ultra pure supply water plant using cultivation-based and cultivation-independent methods, *Water Research* 44(20): 6124–6132.

Bott, T. R. and L. Tianqing. 2004. Ultrasound enhancement of biocide efficiency, *Ultrasonics Sonochemistry* 11(5): 323–326.

Cabral, D. and V. E. F. Pinto. 2002. Fungal spoilage of bottled mineral water, *International Journal of Food Microbiology* 72(1–2): 73–76.

Carson, L. A., M. S. Favero, W. W. Bond and N. J. Peterson. 1973. Morphological, biochemical, and growth characteristics of *Pseudomonas cepacia* from distilled water, *Applied Microbiology* 25: 476–483.

Cavicchioli, R., M. Ostrowski, F. Fegatella, A. Goodchild and N. Guixa-Boixercu. 2002. Life under nutrient limitation in oligotrophic marine environments: An eco/physiological perspective of Sphingopyxis alaskensis (formerly Sphingomonas alaskensis), *Ecology* 45: 203–217.

Characklis, W. G. 1990. Microbial biofouling control, in *Biofilms*. W. G. Characklis and K. C. Marshall (eds.). 585–633. New York: John Wiley & Sons.

Chen, J., J. Bergevin, et al. 2012. Case study: A novel bacterial contamination in cell culture production— *Leptospira licerasiae*, *PDA Journal of Pharmaceutical Science and Technology* 66(6): 580–591.

Chen, L. H., X. Zhu, et al. 2017. Profiling total viable bacteria in a hemodialysis water treatment system, *Journal of Microbiology and Biotechnology* 27(5): 995–1004.

Chicote, E., A. M. Garcia, et al. 2005. Isolation and identification of bacteria from spent nuclear fuel pools, *Journal of Industrial Microbiology and Biotechnology* 32(4): 155–162.

Chicote, E., D. A. Moreno, et al. 2004. Biofouling on the walls of a spent nuclear fuel pool with radioactive ultrapure water, *Biofouling* 20(1): 35–42.

Christian, D. A. and T. H. Meltzer. 1986. The penetration of membranes by organism grow-through and its related problems, *Ultrapure Water* 3: 39–44.

Chuang, H., P. Macuch and M. B. Tabacco. 2001. Optical sensors for detection of bacteria. 1. General concepts and initial development, *Analytical Chemistry* 73(3): 462–466.

Collentro, W. V. 1986. Pretreatment part II: Activated carbon filtration, *Ultrapure Water* 3: 39–44.

Collentro, W. V. 1996. USP purified water systems—Case histories, part I, *Pharmaceutical Technology*. September: 148–168.

Corcoll, N., B. Bonet, M. Leira and H. Guasch. 2011. Chl-a fluorescence parameters as biomarkers of metal toxicity in fluvial biofilms: An experimental study, *Hydrobiologia* 673(1): 119–136.

Costanzo, S. P., R. N. Borazjani and P. J. McCormick. 2002. Validation of the Scan RDI for routine micro-biological analysis of process water, *PDA Journal of Pharmaceutical Science and Technology* 56(4): 206–219.

Costerton, J. W., L. Montanaro and C. R. Arciola. 2005. Biofilm in implant infections: Its production and regulation, *International Journal of Artificial Organs* 28(11): 1062–1068.

Crump, B. C., H. W. Ducklow and J. E. Hobbie. 2013. Estuarine microbial food webs, in *Estuarine Biology*. J. W. Day, B. C. Crump, W. M. Kemp and A. Yàñez-Arancibia (eds.). 263–284: Wiley-Blackwell, Hoboken, NJ.

Dahlback, B., M. Hermannsson, S. Kjelleberg and B. Norkrans. 1981. The hydrophobicity of bacteria—An important factor in the initial adhesion at the air-water interface, *Archives of Microbiology* 128: 267–270.

Deakin, M. R. and D. A. Buttry. 1989. Electrochemical applications of the quartz crystal microbalance, *Analytical Chemistry* 61: 1147–1154.

Declerck, P. 2010. Biofilms: The environmental playground of *Legionella pneumophila*, *Environmental Microbiology* 12(3): 557–566.

del Mar Lleò, M., B. Bonato, D. Benedetti and P. Canepari. 2005. Survival of enterococcal species in aquatic environments, *FEMS Microbiology Ecology* 54: 189–196.

Donlan, R. M. 2002. Biofilms: Microbial life on surfaces, *Emerging Infectious Diseases* 8(9): 881–890.

Dosti, B., Z. Guzel-Seydim and A. K. Greene. 2005. Effectiveness of ozone, heat and chlorine for destroy-ing common food spoilage bacteria in synthetic media and biofilms, *International Journal of Dairy Technology* 58(1): 19–24.

Falcao, F., A. Santos, et al. 2012. Fungal contamination in reverse-osmosis treated water, *Mycoses* 55: 322–323.

Farhat, M., M.-C. Trouilhe, et al. 2011. Chemical disinfection of Legionella in hot water systems biofilm: A pilot-scale 1 study, *Water Science and Technology* 64(3): 708–714.

FDA 2014. Pharmaceutical microbiology manual, 2014: 91 pp. http://www.fda.gov/downloads/scienceresearch/fieldscience/ucm397228.pdf

Flemming, H. C. 1984. Peracetic acid as disinfectant—A review, *Zentralblatt Fur Bakteriologie Und Hygiene* 179: 97–116.

Flemming, H. C. 1987. Microbial growth on ion exchangers, *Water Research* 21: 745–756.

Flemming, H. C. 2003. Role and levels of real-time monitoring for successful anti-fouling strategies—An overview, *Water Science and Technology* 47(5): 1–8.

Fletcher, M. 1988. Attachment of *Pseudomonas fluorescens* to glass and influence of electrolytes on bacterium-substratum separation distance, *Journal of Bacteriology* 170: 2027–2030.

Florjanic, M. and J. Kristl. 2006. Microbiological quality assurance of purified water by ozonization of storage and distribution system, *Drug Development and Industrial Pharmacy* 32(10): 1113–1121.

Florjanic, M. and J. Kristl. 2011. The control of biofilm formation by hydrodynamics of purified water in industrial distribution system, *International Journal of Pharmaceutics* 405(1–2): 16–22.

Fuhrman, J. 1987. Close coupling between release and uptake of dissolved free amino acids in seawater stud-ied by an isotope dilution approach, *Marine Ecology Progress Series* 37: 45–52.

Fux, C. A., J. W. Costerton, P. S. Stewart and P. Stoodley. 2005. Survival strategies of infectious biofilms, *Trends Microbiology* 13(1): 34–40.

Garvey, M. I., C. W. Bradley, E. Holden and M. Weibren. 2017. Where to do water testing for Pseudomonas aeruginosa in a healthcare setting, *Journal of Hospital Infection* 97(2): 192–195.

Geertsema-Doornbusch, G. I., H. C. V. D. Mei and H. J. Busscher. 1993. Microbial cell surface hydrophobic-ity. The involvement of electrostatic interactions in microbial adhesion to hydrocarbons, *Journal of Microbiological Methods* 18: 61–63.

Gorke, A. and J. Kittel. 2002. Routine disinfection of the total dialysis fluid system, *EDTNA ERCA Journal* 28(3): 130–133.

Haberer, K. and M. W. Mittelman. 2003. Microbiological methods of the pharmacopoeia: Growth and recov-ery of microorganisms from pharmaceutical manufacturing environments, in *Rapid Microbiological Methods in the Pharmaceutical Industry*. M. Easter (ed.). 19–40. Boca Raton, FL: CRC Press.

Hadi, R., K. Vickery, A. Deva and T. Charlton. 2010. Biofilm removal by medical device cleaners: Comparison of two bioreactor detection assays, *Journal of Hospital Infection* 74(2): 160–167.

Hall, K., T. Stewart, J. Chang and M. K. Freeman. 2016. Characteristics of FDA drug recalls: A 30-month analysis, *American Journal of Health-System Pharmacy* 73(4): 235–240.

Hartke, A., J.-C. Giard, J.-M. Laplace and Y. Auffray. 1998. Survival of Enterococcus faecalis in an oligo-trophic microcosm: Changes in morphology, development of general stress resistance, and analysis of protein synthesis, *Applied and Environmental Microbiology* 64(11): 4238–4245.

Henthorne, L. R. and A. Amer Desalting. 1996. Long-term storage of reverse osmosis membranes in three biocides. 348–367 pp. http://citeseerx.ist.psu.edu/viewdoc/download?doi=10.1.1.625.1274&rep=rep1&t ype=pdf

Herald, P. J. and E. A. Zottola. 1987. Attachment of *Listeria monocytogenes* and *Yersinia enterocolitica* to stainless steel at various temperatures and pH values, *Journal of Food Protection* (abstract) 50: 894.

Hoadley, A. W. 1981. Effects of injury on the recovery of bacteria on membrane filters, in *Membrane Filtration: Application, Techniques, and Problems*. B. J. Dutka (ed.). 413–450. New York: Marcel Dekker.

Hobbie, J. E. and E. A. Hobbie. 2013. Microbes in nature are limited by carbon and energy: The starving-survival lifestyle in soil and consequences for estimating microbial rates, *Frontiers in Microbiology* 4: 1–11.

Holman, H. Y. N., R. Miles, et al. 2009. Real-time chemical imaging of bacterial activity in biofilms using open-channel microfluidics and synchrotron FTIR spectromicroscopy, *Analytical Chemistry* 81(20): 8564–8570.

Holmes, C. J., A. Degremont, W. Kubey, P. Straka and N. K. Man. 2004. Effectiveness of various chemical disinfectants versus cleaning combined with heat disinfection on Pseudomonas biofilm in hemodialysis machines, *Blood Purification* 22(5): 461–468.

Huntington, M. K. 2010. Microbiology of dental waterlines. 181–213 pp.

Ishida, Y. and H. Kadota. 1981. Growth patterns and substrate requirements of naturally occurring obligate oligotrophs, *Microbial Ecology* 7: 123–130.

Jakobsen, T. H., T. Tolker-Nielsen and M. Givskov. 2017. Bacterial biofilm control by perturbation of bacterial signaling processes, *International Journal of Molecular Sciences* 18(9): 1–27.

Ji, J., J. A. Schanzle and M. B. Tabacco. 2004. Real-time detection of bacterial contamination in dynamic aqueous environments using optical sensors, *Analytical Chemistry* 76(5): 1411–1418.

Jimenez, L. 2007. Microbial diversity in pharmaceutical product recalls and environments, *PDA Journal of Pharmaceutical Science and Technology* 61(5): 383–399.

Johnston, P. R. and S. C. Burt. 1976. Bacterial growth in charcoal filters, *Filtration Separation* 13: 240–244.

Jun, W., M. S. Kim, et al. 2010. Microbial biofilm detection on food contact surfaces by macro-scale fluores-cence imaging, *Journal of Food Engineering* 99(3): 314–322.

Khoury, A. E., K. Lam, B. Ellis and J. W. Costerton. 1992. Prevention and control of bacterial infections asso-ciated with medical devices, *ASAIO Journal* 38: 174–178.

Kim, B. R., J. E. Anderson, S. A. Mueller, W. A. Gaines and A. M. Kendall. 2002. Literature review—Efficacy of various disinfectants against *Legionella* in water systems, *Water Research* 36(18): 4433–4444.

Kim, I. S., S. E. Kim and J. S. Hwang. 1997. Nutritional flexibility of oligotrophic and copiotrophic bacteria isolated from deionized-ultrapure water made by high-purity water manufacturing system in a semicon-ductor manufacturing company, *Journal of Microbiology and Biotechnology* 7: 200–203.

Kim, I. S., G. H. Lee and K. J. Lee. 2000. Monitoring and characterization of bacterial contamination in a high-purity water system used for semiconductor manufacturing, *Journal of Microbiology* 38: 99–104.

Kulakov, L. A., M. B. McAlister, K. L. Ogden, M. J. Larkin and J. F. O'Hanlon. 2002. Analysis of bacteria contaminating ultrapure water in industrial systems, *Applied and Environmental Microbiology* 68(4): 1548–1555.

Lal, S., M. Pearce, et al. 2017. Developing an ecologically relevant heterogeneous biofilm model for dental-unit waterlines, *Biofouling* 33(1): 75–87.

Laurence, R. A. and S. T. Lapierre. 1995. Quality of hemodialysis water: A 7-year multicenter study, *American Journal of Kidney Diseases* 25: 738–750.

Lee, A., J. McVey, et al. 2010a. Use of *Hydrogenophaga pseudoflava* penetration to quantitatively assess the impact of filtration Parameters for 0.2-micrometer-Pore-size filters, *Applied and Environmental Microbiology* 76(3): 695–700.

Lee, H. J., M. R. Ho, et al. 2010b. Enhancing ATP-based bacteria and biofilm detection by enzymatic pyro-phosphate regeneration, *Analytical Biochemistry* 399(2): 168–173.

Lee, S. H. and J. F. Frank (1990). Resistance of *Listeria monocytogenes* biofilms to hypochlorite and heat. *Proceedings XXIII International Dairy Congress*, Montreal, QC, Canada.

Li, Q., P. F. Xia, Z. Y. Tao and S. G. Wang. 2017. Modeling biofilms in water systems with new variables: A review, *Water* 9(7): 462.

Liu, S., C. Gunawan, et al. 2016. Understanding, monitoring, and controlling biofilm growth in drinking water distribution systems, *Environmental Science Technology* 50(17): 8954–8976.

Liu, Y. and J. H. Tay. 2001. Metabolic response of biofilm to shear stress in fixed-film culture, *Journal of Applied Microbiology* 90(3): 337–342.

Ludwig, J. D. and K. E. Avis. 1990. Dry heat inactivation of endotoxin on the surface of glass, *Journal of Parenteral Science and Technology* 44: 4–12.

Marion-Ferey, K., F. Enkiri, M. Pasmore, G. P. Husson and R. Vilagines. 2003. Methods for biofilm analysis on silicone tubing of dialysis machines, *Artificial Organs* 27(7): 658–664.

Marshall, K. C. 1988. Adhesion and growth of bacteria at surfaces in oligotrophic environments, *Canadian Journal of Microbiology* 34: 503–506.

Marshall, K. C., R. Stout and R. Mitchell. 1971. Mechanisms of the initial events in the sorption of marine bacteria to surfaces, *Journal of General Microbiology* 68: 337–348.

Martyak, J. E., J. C. Carmody and G. R. Husted. 1993. Characterizing biofilm growth in deionized ultrapure water piping systems, *Microcontamination* 11(1): 39–44.

Mazzola, P. G., A. M. S. Martins and T. C. V. Penna. 2006. Chemical resistance of the gram-negative bacteria to different sanitizers in a water purification system, *BMC Infectious Diseases* 6: 131.

McAlister, M. B., L. A. Kulakov, J. F. O'Hanlon, M. J. Larkin and K. L. Ogden. 2002. Survival and nutritional requirements of three bacteria isolated from ultrapure water, *Journal of Industrial Microbiology and Biotechnology* 29(2): 75–82.

McDougald, D. M., S. A. Rice, D. Weichart and S. Kjelleberg. 2006. Nonculturability: Adaptation or debilitation, *FEMS Microbiology Ecology* 25(1): 1–9.

McFeters, G. A., S. C. Broadaway, B. H. Pyle, K. K. Siu and Y. Egozy. 1993. Bacterial ecology of operating laboratory water purification systems, *Ultrapure Water* 10: 32–37.

McFeters, G. A., B. H. Pyle, J. T. Lisle and S. C. Broadaway. 1999. Rapid direct methods for enumeration of specific, active bacteria in water and biofilms, *Symposium Series* (*Society for Applied Microbiology*) 85(28): 193S–200S.

Meltzer, T. H. 1993. *High-Purity Water Preparation for the Semiconductor, Pharmaceutical, and Power Industries.* Littleton, CO: Tall Oaks Publishing, Inc. 833 pp.

Meltzer, T. H. 1997. Ultraviolet radiation and its applications, in *Pharmaceutical Water Systems.* T. H. Meltzer (ed.). 165–188. Littleton, CO: Tall Oaks Publishing, Inc.

Meltzer, T. H. and M. W. Jornitz. 2006a. The fluid vehicle, in *Pharmaceutical Filtration, the Management of Organism Removal.* T. H. Meltzer and M. Jornitz (eds.). 113–122. Bethesda, MD: PDA.

Meltzer, T. H. and M. W. Jornitz. 2006b. Passivation and electropolishing, in *Pharmaceutical Filtration, the Management of Organism Removal.* T. H. Meltzer and M. Jornitz (eds.). 215–227. Bethesda, MD: PDA.

Meltzer, T. H. and M. W. Jornitz. 2006c. The stainless steels and rouging, in *Pharmaceutical Filtration, the Management of Organism Removal.* T. H. Meltzer and M. W. Jornitz (eds.). 195–214. Bethesda, MD: PDA.

Mijnendonckx, K., A. Provoost, et al. 2013. Characterization of the survival ability of *Cupriavidus metallidurans* and *Ralstonia pickettii* from space-related environments, *Microbial Ecology* 65(2): 347–360.

Minogue, E., K. Reddington, et al. 2013. Diagnostics method for the rapid quantitative detection and identification of low-level contamination of high-purity water with pathogenic bacteria, *Journal of Industrial Microbiology and Biotechnology* 40(9): 1005–1013.

Mittelman, M. W. 1994. Emerging techniques for the evaluation of bacterial biofilm formation and metabolic activity in marine and freshwater environments, in *Recent Developments in Biofouling Control.* D. Morse (ed.). 49–56. London: Oxford University Press.

Mittelman, M. W. 1995. Biofilm development in purified water systems, in *Microbial Biofilms.* H. L. Lappin-Scott and J. W. Costerton (eds.). 133–147. London: Cambridge University Press.

Mittelman, M. W. 1998. Laboratory studies of bacterial biofilms, in *Techniques in Microbial Ecology.* R. Burlage (ed.). 337–353. London: Oxford University Press.

Mittelman, M. W. 1999a. Recovery and characterization of biofilm bacteria associated with medical devices, in *Methods in Enzymology.* R. J. Doyle (ed.). 534–551. San Diego, CA: Academic Press.

Mittelman, M. W. 1999b. Recovery and characterization of biofilm bacteria associated with medical devices, *Biofilms* 310: 534–551.

Mittelman, M. W. and G. G. Geesey. 1987. *Biological Fouling of Industrial Water Systems: A Problem Solving Approach*. San Diego, CA: Water Micro Associates. 375 pp.

Mittelman, M. W., R. Islander and R. M. Platt. 1987. Biofilm formation in a closed-loop purified water system, *Medical Device and Diagnostic Industry* 10: 50–55; 75.

Mittelman, M. W. and A. D. Jones. 2016. A pure life: The microbial ecology of high purity industrial waters, *Microbial Ecology* 71(2): 257–266.

Mittelman, M. W., J. Packard, et al. 1993. Test systems for evaluating antifouling coating efficacy using on-line detection of bioluminescence and fluorescence in a laminar-flow environment, *Journal of Microbiological Methods* 18: 51–60.

Montagnac, R., F. Schillinger, M. F. Roquebert, J. C. Croix and C. Eloy. 1991a. Fungal contamination of a dialysis water-supply, *Nephrologie* 12(1): 27–30.

Montagnac, R., F. Schillinger, M. F. Roquebert, J. C. Croix and C. Eloy. 1991b. Fungal contamination of a water delivery system in a self-dialysis unit, *Medecine Et Maladies Infectieuses* 21(4): 261–265.

Morita, R. Y. 1982. Starvation-survival of heterotrophs in the marine environment, *Advances in Microbial Ecology* 6: 171–198.

Morita, R. Y. 1985. Starvation and miniaturization of heterotrophs, with special emphasis on maintenance of the starved viable state, in *Bacteria in the Natural Environments: The Effect of Nutrient Conditions*. M. Fletcher and G. Floodgate (eds.). 111–130. London: Soc. Gen. Microbiol.

Morita, R. Y. 1997. *Bacteria in Oligotrophic Environments: Starvation-Survival Lifestyle*. London: Chapman and Hall. 529 pp.

Moyer, C. L. and R. Y. Morita. 1989. Effect of growth-rate and starvation-survival on cellular DNA, RNA, and protein of a psychrophilic marine bacterium, *Applied and Environmental Microbiology* 55(10): 2710–2716.

Muchesa, P., M. Leifels, L. Jurzik, T. G. Barnard and C. Bartie. 2016. Free-living amoebae isolated from a hospital water system in South Africa: A potential source of nosocomial and occupational infection, *Water Science and Technology-Water Supply* 16(1): 70–78.

Murphy, J. J., L. A. Bland, et al. (1987). Pyrogenic reactions associated with high-flux hemodialysis. *Proceedings of ICAAC '87*.

Nemati, M., A. Hamidi, S. M. Dizaj, V. Javaherzadeh and F. Lotfipour. 2016. An overview on novel microbial determination methods in pharmaceutical and food quality control, *Advanced Pharmaceutical Bulletin* 6(3): 301–308.

Nichols, P. D., J. M. Henson, J. B. Guckert, D. E. Nivens and D. C. White. 1985. Fourier transform-infrared spectroscopic methods for microbial ecology: Analysis of bacteria, bacteria-polymer mixtures, and bio-films, *Journal of Microbiological Methods* 4: 79–94.

Nivens, D. E., J. Q. Chambers, et al. 1993a. Monitoring microbial adhesion and biofilm formation by attenu-ated total relection/Fourier transform infrared spectroscopy, *Journal of Microbiological Methods* 17: 199–213.

Nivens, D. E., J. Q. Chambers, T. R. Anderson and D. C. White. 1993b. Long-term, on-line monitoring of microbial biofilms using a quartz crystal microbalance, *Analytical Chemistry* 65: 65–69.

Novikova, N., P. De Boever, et al. 2006. Survey of environmental biocontamination on board the International Space Station, *Research in Microbiology* 157(1): 5–12.

Novitsky, J. A. and R. Y. Morita. 1978. Possible strategy for the survival of marine bacteria under starvation conditions, *Marine Biology* 48: 289–295.

Novitsky, T. J. 1984. Monitoring and validation of high purity water systems with the Limulus amebocyte lysate test for pyrogens, *Pharmaceutical Engineering* 4: 21–33.

Nystrom, T., R. M. Olsson and S. Kjelleberg. 1992. Survival, stress resistance, and alterations in protein expression in the marine *Vibrio* sp. strain s14 during starvation for different individual nutrients, *Applied and Environmental Microbiology* 58: 55–65.

Olsson, A. L. J., M. R. Mitzel and N. Tufenkji. 2015. QCM-D for non-destructive real-time assessment of *Pseudomonas aeruginosa* biofilm attachment to the substratum during biofilm growth, *Colloids and Surfaces B-Biointerfaces* 136: 928–934.

Parkar, S. G., S. H. Flint and J. D. Brooks. 2004. Evaluation of the effect of cleaning regimes on biofilms of thermophilic bacilli on stainless steel, *Journal of Applied Microbiology* 96(1): 110–116.

Patterson, M. K., G. R. Husted, A. Rutkowski and D. C. Mayett. 1991. Bacteria: Isolation, identification, and microscopic properties of biofilms in high-purity water distribution systems, *Ultrapure Water* 8(4): 18–24.

PDA (2013). Evaluation, validation and implementation of alternative and rapid microbiological methods. PDA Technical Report 33. Bethesda, MD: 59 pp.

PDA (2015). Bioburden and biofilm management in pharmaceutical manufacturing operations. PDA Technical Report 69. Bethesda, MD: 73 pp.

Pedersen, K. 1990. Biofilm development on stainless steel and PVC surfaces in drinking water, *Water Research* 24: 239–243.

Pflug, I. J., R. G. Holcomb and M. M. Gomez. 2001. Principles of the thermal destruction of microorganisms, in *Disinfection, Sterilization, and Preservation*. S. S. Block (ed.). 79–129. Malvern, PA: Lippincott Williams & Wilkins.

Phillips, G., S. Hudson and W. K. Stewart. 1994. Persistence of microflora in biofilm within fluid pathways of contemporary haemodialysis monitors (Gambro AK-10), *Journal of Hospital Infection* 27: 117–125.

Quiles, F., F. Humbert and A. Delille. 2010. Analysis of changes in attenuated total reflection FTIR fingerprints of *Pseudomonas fluorescens* from planktonic state to nascent biofilm state, *Spectrochimica Acta Part a-Molecular and Biomolecular Spectroscopy* 75(2): 610–616.

Quirynen, M., H. C. van der Mei, et al. 1993. An in vivo study of the influence of the surface roughness of implants on the microbiology of supra- and subgingival plaque, *Journal of Dental Research* 72: 1304–1309.

Ramasami, P. and X. Zhang. 2005. Effects of shear stress on the secretion of extracellular polymeric substances in biofilms, *Water Science and Technology* 52: 217–223.

Richards, G. K., R. F. Gagnon, G. Obst and G. B. Kostiner. 1993. The effect of peritoneal dialysis solutions on rifampin action against *Staphylococcus epidermidis* in the fluid and biofilm phases of growth, *Peritoneal Dialysis International* 9: 183–186.

Rickard, A. H., A. J. McBain, A. T. Stead and P. Gilbert. 2004. Shear rate moderates community diversity in freshwater biofilms, *Applied and Environmental Microbiology* 70(12): 7426–7435.

Ridgway, H., K. Ishida, et al. 1999. Biofouling of membranes: Membrane preparation, characterization, and analysis of bacterial adhesion, in *Meth. Enzymol., Biofilms*, R.J. Doyle(ed.). San Diego, CA: Academic Press, 463–494.

Ridgway, H. F., M. G. Rigby and D. G. Argo. 1985. Bacterial adhesion and fouling of reverse osmosis membranes, *Journal of the American Water Works Association* 77: 97–106.

Riedewald, F. 2006. Bacterial adhesion to surfaces: The influence of surface roughness, *PDA Journal of Pharmaceutical Science and Technology* 60: 164–170.

Rioufol, C., C. Devys, G. Meunier, M. Perraud and D. Goullet. 1999. Quantitative determination of endotoxins released by bacterial biofilms, *Journal of Hospital Infection* 43(3): 203–209.

Roman, M. C., O. J. van der Schijff, P. Macuch and M. W. Mittelman. 2001. Preliminary assessment of microbial adhesion on the surface of materials from the ISS internal thermal control system: Results of an accelerated 60-d study, *Society of Automotive Engineering Journal* 2337: 1–11.

Roth, E., B. Fabre, A. Accary and B. Faller. 1998. Study of fouling of reverse osmosis membranes used to produce water for hemodialysis, *Revue des Sciences de l'Eau* 11(3): 409–427.

Rupp, C. J., C. A. Fux and P. Stoodley. 2005. Viscoelasticity of Staphylococcus aureus biofilms in response to fluid shear allows resistance to detachment and facilitates rolling migration, *Applied and Environmental Microbiology* 71(4): 2175–2178.

Rutala, W. A. and D. J. Weber. 1997. Uses of inorganic hypochlorite (bleach) in health-care facilities, *Clinical Microbiology Reviews* 10(4): 597–610.

Sacchetti, R., G. De Luca and F. Zanetti. 2009. Control of *Pseudomonas aeruginosa* and *Stenotrophomonas maltophilia* contamination of microfiltered water dispensers with peracetic acid and hydrogen peroxide, *International Journal of Food Microbiology* 132(2–3): 162–166.

Sarro, M. I., A. M. Garcia and D. A. Moreno. 2005. Biofilm formation in spent nuclear fuel pools and bioremediation of radioactive water, *International Microbiology* 8(3): 223–230.

Saur, T., E. Morin, F. Habouzit, N. Bernet and R. Escudie. 2017. Impact of wall shear stress on initial bacterial adhesion in rotating annular reactor, *PLoS One* 12(2): 19.

Schmitt, J. and H. C. Flemming. 1998. FTIR-spectroscopy in microbial and material analysis, *International Biodeterioration and Biodegradation* 41: 1–11.

Schroeder, H. G. 2005. Sterility failure analysis, *PDA Journal of Pharmaceutical Science and Technology* 59(2): 89–95.

Schulze-Robbecke, R., C. Feldmann, et al. 1995. Dental units: An environmental study of sources of potentially pathogenic mycobacteria, *Tubercle and Lung Disease* 76: 318–323.

Shearer, B. G. 1996. Biofilm and the dental office, *Journal of the American Dental Association* 127: 181–189.

Shinoda, T. 2004. Clean dialysate requires not only lower levels of endotoxin but also sterility of dilution water, *Blood Purification* 22(Suppl 2): 78–80.

Shintani, H., A. Sakudo and G. E. McDonnel. 2011. Methods of rapid microbiological assay and their application to pharmaceutical and medical device fabrication, *Biocontrol Science* 16(1): 13–21.

Simoes, M., H. Carvalho, M. O. Pereira and M. J. Vieira. 2003. Studies on the behaviour of *Pseudomonas fluorescens* biofilms after ortho-phthalaldehyde treatment, *Biofouling* 19(3): 151–157.

Smeets, E., J. Kooman, et al. 2003. Prevention of biofilm formation in dialysis water treatment systems, *Kidney International* 63(4): 1574–1576.

Soini, S. M., K. T. Koskinen, M. J. Vilenius and J. A. Puhakka. 2002. Effects of fluid-flow velocity and water quality on planktonic and sessile microbial growth in water hydraulic system, *Water Research* 36(15): 3812–3820.

Sprung, C., D. Wahlisch, et al. 2009. Detection and monitoring of biofilm formation in water treatment systems by quartz crystal microbalance sensors, *Water Science and Technology* 59(3): 543–548.

Stout, J. E., M. Best and V. L. Yu. 1986. Susceptibility of members of the family *Legionellaceae* to thermal stress: Implications for heat eradication methods in water distribution systems, *Applied and Environmental Microbiology* 52: 396–399.

Stubiger, G., M. Wuczkowski, et al. 2016. Characterization of yeasts and filamentous fungi using MALDI lipid phenotyping, *Journal of Microbiological Methods* 130: 27–37.

Sundaram, S., J. Eisenhuth, G. Howard and H. Brandwein. 2001a. Method for qualifying microbial removal performance of 0.1 micron rated filters part I: Characterization of water isolates for potential use as standard challenge organisms to qualify 0.1 micron rated filters, *PDA Journal of Pharmaceutical Science and Technology* 55(6): 346–372.

Sundaram, S., J. Eisenhuth, M. Steves, G. Howard and H. Brandwein. 2001b. Method for qualifying microbial removal performance of 0.1 micron rated filters part II: Preliminary characterization of hydrogenophaga (formerly pseudomonas) pseudoflava for use as a standard challenge organism to qualify 0.1 micron rated filters, *PDA Journal of Pharmaceutical Science and Technology* 55(6): 373–392.

Sundaram, S., S. Mallick, J. Eisenhuth, G. Howard and H. Brandwein. 2001c. Retention of water-borne bacteria by membrane filters—Part II: Scanning electron microscopy (SEM) and fatty acid methyl ester (FAME) characterization of bacterial species recovered downstream of 0.2/0.22 micron rated filters, *PDA Journal of Pharmaceutical Science and Technology* 55(2): 87–113.

Sutton, S. and L. Jimenez. 2012. A review of reported recalls involving microbiological control 2004–2011 with emphasis on FDA considerations of objectionable organisms, *American Pharmaceutical Review* 15(1): 42–57.

Tabor, P. S., K. Ohwada and R. R. Colwell. 1981. Filterable marine bacteria found in the deep sea: Distribution, taxonomy, and response to starvation, *Microbial Ecology* 7: 67–83.

Tajima, Y., T. Yamaguchi, R. Takagi, T. Nakajima and Y. Kominato. 2010. Comparison of methods of detecting bacterial biofilm, *Clinical Laboratory* 56(3–4): 143–147.

Tiam, S. K., M. Laviale, et al. 2015. Herbicide toxicity on river biofilms assessed by pulse amplitude modulated (PAM) fluorometry, *Aquatic Toxicology* 165: 160–171.

Torbeck, L., D. Raccasi, D. E. Guilfoyle, R. L. Friedman and D. Hussong. 2011. *Burkholderia cepacia*: This decision Is overdue, *PDA Journal of Pharmaceutical Science and Technology* 65(1): 535–543.

Tsai, Y. P., T. Y. Pai, J. Y. Hsin and T. J. Wan. 2003. Biofilm bacteria inactivation by citric acid and resuspension evaluations for drinking water production systems, *Water Science and Technology* 48(11–12): 463–472.

Tsai, Y. P., T. Y. Pai and J. M. Qiu. 2004. The impacts of the AOC concentration on biofilm formation under higher shear force condition, *Journal of Biotechnology* 111(2): 155–167.

USP. 2014a. *USP 37, <61>*. Taunton, MA: United States Pharmacopeial Convention/Rand McNally. 1–7.

USP. 2014b. *USP 37, <1111>*. Taunton, MA: United States Pharmacopeial Convention/Rand McNally. 1–2.

USP. 2014c. *USP 37, <1231>*. Taunton, MA: United States Pharmacopeial Convention/Rand McNally. 1–36.

Vanhaecke, E. and K. Van den Haesevelde. 1991. Bacterial contamination of stainless steel equipment, in *Sterile Pharmaceutical Manufacturing*. M. J. Groves, W. P. Olson and M. H. Anisfeld (ed.). 141–162. Buffalo Grove, IL: Interpharm Press.

Vanhaecke, E., J. P. Remon, et al. 1990. Kinetics of *Pseudomonas aeruginosa* adhesion to 304 and 316-L stainless steel: Role of cell surface hydrophobicity, *Applied and Environmental Microbiology* 56: 788–795.

Verdonk, G., M. J. Willemse, S. G. G. Hoefs, G. Cremers and E. R. van den Heuvel. 2010. The Most Probable Limit of Detection (MPL) for rapid microbiological methods, *Journal of Microbiological Methods* 82(3): 193–197.

Verheyen, C. C., W. J. Dhert, et al. 1993. Adherence to a metal, polymer and composite by *Staphylococcus aureus* and *Staphylococcus epidermidis*, *Biomaterials* 14: 383–391.

Walker, J. and G. Moore. 2015. *Pseudomonas aeruginosa* in hospital water systems: Biofilms, guidelines, and practicalities, *Journal of Hospital Infection* 89(4): 324–327.

Wang, H., E. Bedard, et al. 2017. Methodological approaches for monitoring opportunistic pathogens in premise plumbing: A review, *Water Research* 117: 68–86.

Weyandt, R. G. 2001. Microbiological aspects of ultra pure water units in the pharmaceutical industry—An up-to-date literature review, *Pharmazeutische Industrie* 63(12): 1295–1307.

Williams, P. J. L. 2000. Heterotrophic bacteria and the dynamics of dissolved organic matter, in *Microbial Ecology of the Oceans*. D. L. Kirchman (ed.). 153–200: New York: Wiley-Liss.

Wolfe, R. L., N. R. Ward and B. H. Olsen. 1988. Inorganic chloramines as drinking water disinfectants: A review, *Journal of the American Water Works Association* 76: 74–88.

24

Ozone Applications in Biotech and Pharmaceuticals

Joseph Manfredi
GMP Systems, Inc.

CONTENTS

Introduction

Sanitization in any healthcare-related environment is one of the most important, if not the most important, aspect of patient care or product integrity. Virtually all advances in pharmaceuticals, devices, and treatment would be for naught if sanitary conditions could not be maintained and infections inevitably resulted, because of, or in spite of treatment.

Since the foundations of scientific microbiology were laid by Robert Koch in the late 1800s, as a result of his Nobel Prize winning work at the Institute for Infectious Diseases in Berlin, we have had a clearer understanding of the mechanisms of infection and disease. Koch's "Germ Theory" and his epidemiologic work were critically important in developing appropriate regimes for patient care and treatment. Over time, practical solutions for the maintenance of sanitary conditions developed, which included appropriate application and use of materials and enhanced cleanliness standards utilizing heat as well as materials such as iodine, alcohol, formaldehyde, peroxide, ozone, and chlorine.

Chlorine has become the most common sanitant used for treatment of potable water in the United States and is also often used for non-potable water applications, both of these uses are based on its oxidative strength and low relative cost. Ozone sanitization of potable water is far less common except in Europe where it has been in continuous use in many locales for more than 100 years. Within the pharmaceutical industry, it is common to see chlorine employed for supplemental water treatment using the sodium hypochlorite (NaClO) form. More recently, for drinking water, chloramines have seen increased utility since chlorine-ammonia compounds are more stable, offering extended protection against microbial proliferation. Chlorine compounds however, can result in the development of trihalomethanes (THMs), which are considered to be carcinogenic, and hence obviously undesirable. The development of THMs has been referred to as "induced contamination"[1] since the chlorine that is added for sanitization reacts with naturally occurring organic precursor compounds, such as humic and fulvic acids as well as algal by-products, resulting in organohalogens, some of which are listed in Table 24.1. Many of these haloforms have the general formula CHX_3 where X represents chlorine, bromine, etc.

There are two possible explanations for the presence of bromide compounds, one being that bromine is introduced during chlorination as an impurity present in industrial grade chlorine. Alternatively, and more frequently, bromides present in raw water are oxidized to HOBr, which is highly reactive in the presence of organic matter[1]. Although ozone does not result in the formation of THMs, other disinfection by-products of ozone, such as bromate, can be potentially hazardous.

TABLE 24.1

List of Organohalogens

Chloroform	$CHCL_3$
Bromodichloromethane	$CHBrCl_2$
Dibromochloromethane	$CHBr_2Cl$
Bromoform	$CHBr_3$
Carbon tetrachloride	CCl_4
Trichloroethylene	C_2HCl_3
Chlorobromomethane	CH_2BrCl
Tetrachloroethylene	C_2Cl_4
Dichloroethane	$CH_2Cl\text{-}CH_2Cl$

The potential for trihalomethane formation (THMFP) "refers to the maximum quantity of THMs that will be produced by the precursors present in the water, taking into account the conditions most favorable to THM formation (excessive free chlorine combined with a 3- or even a 5-day contact time)[1]." Determining the potential for THM formation in raw water is of critical importance for the health and safety of the public as well as for the design and implementation of specialized treatment, as is required for pharmaceutical water production. Additionally, ozone can be used in the form of pretreatment to oxidize THM precursors prior to the application of chlorine in a water treatment facility.

The use of chlorine as a disinfectant grew substantially after World War I, based primarily on cost; however, chlorine compounds also offer the benefit of residual action as they continue their sanitizing action throughout distribution piping, up to the point of use in individual residences. This is especially important for large municipal distribution networks as regrowth could occur in the piping if localized disinfection was the sole method employed.

Heat, although impractical for residential use, except in emergencies, has been the most accepted and reliable method of sanitization utilized in healthcare applications, including surgical tool sterilization, as well as for biotech and pharmaceutical production. Dry heat is effective for sterilization and also for depyrogenation using specialized ovens. Alternatively, wet heat can also be employed. Pure steam as utilized in autoclaves may also be directly injected into equipment and piping systems to provide effective sterilization. Heat can also be applied indirectly to raise the temperature of liquid product above 60°C, provided heat sensitivity is not of concern. The use of heat is extremely common as it can reliably eliminate most viable species of microbial contamination; however, the cost of heat sanitization has prompted investigation and use of alternative methods.

Within the healthcare industry, water is the single largest commodity employed, finding use in product formulation, laboratory analysis, cleaning, and product manufacture. Hence, control of bacteriologic purity is critical. As such, it is important to note that significant differences exist between requirements for potable water and for water associated with drug products. Potable water microbial standards, promulgated by the U.S. Environmental Protection Agency and defined within National Primary Drinking Water Regulations (NPDWR), allow for as high as 500 colony-forming units per milliliter (cfu/mL), while the United States Pharmacopeia (USP) lists action limits for microbial contamination in varying grades of bulk pharmaceutical waters from 100 cfu/mL to 10 cfu/100 mL. Microbial limits for products and excipients may be lower based on application, such that it is not uncommon for sterility to be required, especially for parenteral (injectable) products. Sterility can be accomplished using dry heat, wet heat, gas sterilization (i.e., ethylene and propylene oxide), ionizing radiation (i.e., gamma and cathode ray), and via filtration.

Although not recognized as a sterilizing agent, ozone has gained significant acceptance in the United States for use in sanitization since it offers a number of advantages and is useful in a multitude of applications. It should be noted that acceptance in the United States has been slower and is less widespread than in Europe, with ozone use in Europe far more extensive with many long-term applications.

Ozone, commonly designated O_3, is a gaseous triatomic allotrope of oxygen that is extremely unstable, and as a result it is one of the most powerful commercially applied oxidizing agents in use. Ozone can be formed in various ways with the most common commercial methods based on the application of

TABLE 24.2

Relative Strength of Ozone[2-4]

Oxidizing Agent	EOP* (volt)	EOP versus Cl_2
Fluorine	3.06	2.25
Hydroxyl radical	2.80	2.05
Oxygen (atomic)	2.42	1.78
Ozone	2.08	1.52
Hydrogen peroxide	1.78	1.30
Hypochlorite	1.49	1.10
Chlorine	1.36	1.00
Chlorine dioxide	1.27	0.93
Oxygen (molecular)	1.23	0.90

*EOP, Electrical Oxidation Potential.

electricity to oxygen. The relative oxidative strength of ozone can be readily seen in Table 24.2 making it more powerful than chlorine or peroxide.

As such, ozone is considered a hazardous material and must be handled in appropriate fashion. However, unlike heat that scalds on contact, ozone is somewhat more subtle in that its pungent odor and acridity is obvious even at levels well below Occupational Safety and Health Administration (OSHA) threshold limits for exposure. This is an obvious advantage as many deadly gases are odorless and hence difficult to detect.

Based on its reactivity, high concentrations of ozone can be explosive. Although concentrations at these levels are usually unachievable with standard commercial equipment, certain improper application of equipment and materials, such as carbon stripping of an ozonated gas stream (ozone in air) can result in an increased risk of fire or explosion.

Atmospheric ozone is created by ultraviolet (UV) irradiation; however, this method is generally too inefficient for most commercial purposes. For relatively large-volume commercial production, various electric discharge technologies are the most commonly employed manufacturing techniques. The two most often implemented for pharmaceutical site production of ozone are termed "Corona Discharge" or "Cold Generation" whereby ozone is produced from a gaseous feed of either air or oxygen, and "Electrolytic" where oxygen from the dissociation of pure water is the feed source. Each methodology will be discussed in additional detail in the following pages for the purpose of providing background information salient to the topic.

Based upon its unstable nature and short half-life, ozone cannot be stored in containers for subsequent use; hence, it is generated relatively close to the point of application or delivery, typically for immediate use. Ozone's half-life has been estimated to be approximately 25 min at 20°C in distilled water[5]; however, many factors can influence its rate of decomposition, including temperature, pH, and the presence of oxidizable substances. As well, "ozone is only sparingly soluble in water, in general about 13 times more soluble than oxygen[5]," with a high rate of off-gassing anticipated.

As an oxidizing agent, ozone can be problematic relative to materials of construction, especially plastics, because of its basic ability to break double-carbon bonds and as it degrades to hydroxyl radicals (OH^0 and HO_2^0) to break higher carbon bonds, before finally reverting back to a simple oxygen (O_2) molecule. Ozone is also very aggressive in its attack of metallics, with the exception of gold, platinum, and iridium, as it creates metal oxides in the highest oxidation state. Alternatively, certain metal alloys can easily withstand ozone contact in typical concentrations including the class III, 300 series, austenitic stainless steels commonly specified by the biotech and pharmaceutical industries. As an unanticipated benefit, ozone's eventual degradation back to oxygen is thought to assist with maintenance of the passive film that forms on stainless steel, reducing the development of rouge and increasing the interval between re-passivations. Further discussion of materials compatibility with ozone will follow in subsequent sections of this chapter and discussion of stainless steel passivation may be found in Chapter 8.

In addition to its oxidative capacity, ozone also serves as a disinfectant and a sanitant as it kills cells by lysing, or causing the cell wall to rupture. Ozone also has the capacity to decompose microbial by-products, including those constituents known as endotoxin. Ozone is effective against all bacteria, virus, cysts, and spores in varying degrees depending on the concentration, contact time, and other physical conditions, serving as an excellent biocide.

More than 99.9% of the bacteria present in any system exist in biofilms. Free-floating, or planktonic, microbiological organisms originate from an upstream biofilm and are easily destroyed; however, sessile organisms resident in a biofilm are more resilient due to the extracellular polymeric substance (EPS) matrix that is formed partially shielding those resident organisms from the effects of most sanitizers.

Ozone's aggressive oxidative nature does allow it to attack biofilm; however, ozone contact time may be significant for a well-established biofilm. Hence, it is far more prudent to restrict biofilm development rather than address its removal after it has become substantial. Additional details related to biofilm can be found in Chapter 23.

Ozone is also rapidly degraded to oxygen by UV irradiation at the 254 nanometer (nm) wavelength, offering the added advantage of simple and inexpensive removal, using a technology already embraced in both the biotech and pharmaceutical arenas, and which itself offers an added degree of microbial reduction.

UV irradiation, in addition to destroying ozone, has been shown to have excellent germicidal effect at the 185 nm wavelength, and based on wavelength and intensity is also suitable for reduction of total organic carbon or total oxidizable carbon (TOC), chlorine, and organics. Dosing for ozone decomposition is usually in the range of three times that used for bacterial destruction, with a 90 mJ/cm^2 UV dose typically effective for removal of 1 mg/L ozone in high purity water to below detectable limits. The action of the UV radiation produces OH^0 radicals (short-lived) and oxygen (O_2). It should be noted that UV bulbs cannot be manufactured such that only a single wavelength is emitted; hence, bulbs with specific wavelength ratings may be predominant at those wavelengths, based on masking; however, other wavelengths cannot be completely excluded. Therefore, bulbs rated for ozone destruction also provide some amount of germicidal effect as well.

UV equipment is also available with both low and medium pressure bulbs, albeit not from every vendor. The intensity of medium pressure bulbs allows for, in many instances, significant downsizing of the equipment and higher flows per bulb; however, there is a trade-off in that the bulbs are significantly more expensive, control cabinets are substantially larger and require more power, and bulb life is shorter creating a situation where operating costs may offset anticipated savings.

When compared to heat, ozone offers a number of distinct advantages not the least of which is low relative operating cost. As a matter of fact, as the cost of energy continues to rise, current high energy practices such as heat sanitization (especially when subsequent cooling is required) will come under increased scrutiny, and ozone is likely to see more opportunities for use. As such, it is already of increasing interest to designers, manufacturers, and operators. This statement must be kept in perspective since it is not applicable to other industries especially commercial water treatment, where the comparison must be made to chlorine injection. In these cases, ozonation may be considered more energy intensive and hence more costly.

There are no accepted standards for ozone concentrations expected to result in complete microbial elimination primarily due to the variance in water chemistry and microbial loading. Current practices vary from below 0.01 to higher than 2.0 mg/L (ppm) with the vast majority operating between 0.10 and 0.30 mg/L. The International Society for Pharmaceutical Engineering (ISPE) has issued a baseline guide for water and steam that indicates it is common for system ozone residual to be set between 0.08 and 0.2 mg/L[6]. Lower levels obviously result in lower cost operation and it has been noted that higher concentrations can often result in a shift of pH to the acidic side potentially compromising the ability to meet compendial standards. This is judged to be the result of reaction by the ozone with trace amounts of resident organics present but below the levels expected to cause failure based on TOC alone (Figure 24.1).

The use of ozone for commercial pharmaceutical applications began in earnest in the United States during the early to middle 1980s; however, there may have been earlier functional installations unrecognized due to confidentiality. After the initial barriers to its application were removed, the use of ozone grew slowly but steadily, gaining ground as a reliable sanitant, although it has yet to gain universal acceptance or quell all of its detractors.

Early installations at Lederle Laboratories (now Pfizer) and Richardson-Vicks helped to lead the industry by example, and in spite of minor flaws, these and other systems were milestones for the use of ozone as well as the development of pharmaceutical water system technology. In its 1993 Guide to the Inspection of High Purity Water Systems, the FDA acknowledged the use of ozone, commented on

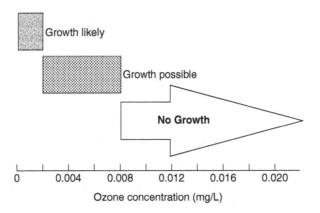

FIGURE 24.1 Microbial growth versus ozone concentration. (Hoffmann-LaRoche[2] (Swiss Pharma (1983).)

its functionality, and through the use of examples noted limitations that can become problematic if not properly addressed, paving the way for ozone's further use.

Ozone, unlike chlorine, leaves no residual after its decay to oxygen. Hence, any regrowth of organisms will be unimpeded, unless ozone contact is virtually continuous. The FDA Guide makes note of microbial contamination in ozonated systems and includes a system schematic in which ozone is apparently added only to treated water entering the storage vessel and also mentions another wherein for safety reasons, "ozone was removed from the water prior to placing it in their recirculating system[7]." These issues have been successfully addressed in current system designs with continuous ozonation of storage volumes and frequent ozonation of distribution piping, facilitated by enhanced controls that lock-out use-points during periodic sanitizations. Since distribution loop sanitizations can easily be automated and require little time, daily sanitizations are considered ideal with even higher frequency sometimes selected; however, some users have successfully validated the use of weekly or even less frequent sanitizations.

Unfortunately, ozone and its value have always been shrouded in controversy even to this day, apparently because ozone research has been limited and extremely focused. A search of the Internet yields literally thousands of articles relating to global warming ostensibly a result of depletion of ozone in the earth's upper atmosphere. There, ozone, produced by UV radiation, filters shorter wavelengths (<320 nm) of UV light that would otherwise reach our planet's surface, potentially harming most forms of life. Depletion of the ozone in the stratosphere allows this radiation to pass and appears to also result in surface temperature increases with global repercussions. It has been postulated and is widely believed that the recorded ozone depletion is caused by "greenhouse" gases such as chlorofluorocarbons (CFCs) as well as from automotive and industrial emissions rather than by normal cyclic planetary environmental activity. However, it should be recognized that there are also many who doubt that the changes in the ozone layer are the result of human activity, alternatively believing it to be normal climatic cycling. This debate, although interesting and of significant concern, is beyond the scope of this volume.

Interestingly, continued searches of the Web reveal a vast array of material that might be best characterized as lively debate covering a wide range of applications and issues relating to ozone beyond that of global warming. Issues such as air and water purification, ozone-based insecticides, and medical therapies using ozone, elicit a surprising range of responses from: (a) "...vaccination offers no protection against disease"....instead, "...create ozone from pure oxygen and bring that into the body"[8] to (b) "Ozone is bad news"[9] and (c) "Ozone has been proven to form...metabolites...thought to facilitate heart disease"[10,11] to (d) "Down and dirty: Airborne ozone can alter forest soil[12]."

Most interesting is the range of beliefs relating to ozone human therapy including venous ozone injection, ozone inhalation, and even rectal, otic, and vaginal insufflation for treatment of all manner of conditions including infection, cancer, and HIV. Although technically illegal in the United States, since it is not approved by the FDA, at least 12 states have passed legislation allowing alternative therapies that include ozone and no less than 16 other nations, including France, Germany, Israel, Italy, and Russia allow medical ozone therapy on a regular basis. Notwithstanding, at least one death has been reported in the United

States as a result of insufflation. Additionally, surface ozone has been determined to irritate the respiratory system and potentially harm lung function. Ozone has also been found to convert cholesterol in the bloodstream into plaque, hardening and narrowing arteries, and is also implicated in Alzheimer's disease[1].

Returning to pharma application, ozone generated by corona discharge occurs when a feed gas, often air, containing oxygen is passed through a properly sized gap between a dielectric-covered high-voltage electrode and a ground electrode. When power is applied the electrical current generated excites the stable O_2 molecules forcing a portion to become reconfigured as ozone and resulting in a mixture of feed gas and ozone, the percentage of which determines the ozone concentration. Impurities in the feed gas may tend to reduce the ozone concentration as they compete to become reactants within the electrical field. The maximum ozone concentration produced by a generator that uses air as its feed is $50\,g/m^3$ and the maximum solubility concentration of ozone in ambient temperature water is approximately $40\,mg/L$[13]. If the feed gas stream consists primarily of oxygen (O_2) then a higher concentration of ozone (O_3) molecules will be produced and a lesser amount of contaminants will typically interfere with ozone purity and volume. Inherent with the corona discharge process and in spite of the "Cold Generation" name, is the generation of heat which must be dissipated by some means, usually water or air cooling, since ozone production is severely restricted by elevated temperatures, especially 100°F and above. Additionally, the quality of the feed gas is critical not just from an overall purity perspective but also based on dryness. Feed gas quality will be discussed in more detail in the section "Generation and Control." Dielectric life can be improved hence improving overall generator performance through the use of low relative operating voltages, (i.e., less than 4,000 volts) and by avoidance of design or operation near the dielectric breakdown voltage (Figures 24.2 and 24.3).

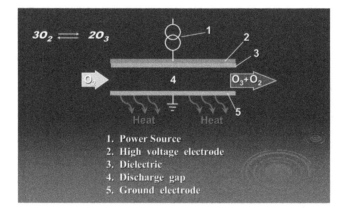

FIGURE 24.2   Corona discharge ozone generation. (Graphic courtesy of Suez Treatment Solutions (formerly Ozonia, NA).)

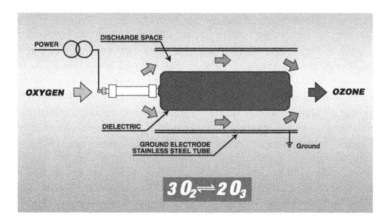

FIGURE 24.3   Tubular corona discharge O_3 generator. (Graphic courtesy of Suez Treatment Solutions (formerly Ozonia, NA).)

Alternatively, electrolytic ozone production uses pure water as the source for oxygen to convert to ozone eliminating the potential for contaminants common to gaseous feeds. In a typical electrolytic cell, the anode and cathode are separated by a solid polymeric membrane that serves as an electrolyte. A side stream of the process water flow is connected to the anode side of the cell where some of the water is split into hydrogen and oxygen and then a portion of the oxygen is subsequently converted to ozone by electrical current. The developed ozone is immediately dissolved into the water which, along with any residual oxygen, is then reintegrated with the main process flow allowing the dissolved ozone to distribute throughout the process. "Waste" streams from the cathode side of the cell include a small amount of water and hydrogen residual from the disassociation of the water used to make the ozone. Since ozone is dissolved immediately in the process stream, undissolved ozone gas is not available for venting, possibly mitigating the need for ambient ozone leak detection systems in some instances. The amount of ozone added to the process stream can be precisely controlled as the production rate, according to Faraday's Law, is proportional to the current flowing through the cell (Figure 24.4).

Generally, the credit for the discovery of ozone is given to C. F. Schönbein, whose 1840 paper entitled "Research on the nature of the odor in certain chemical reactions" named ozone after the Greek word "ozein," meaning to smell. However, a Dutch chemist, Van Marum, was probably the first person to detect and note ozone's characteristic odor sensorially (in the vicinity of his electrifier) during his research[14]. Other historical data relating to ozone is rather limited, although J. L. Soret is credited with determining the molecular structure of ozone, Werner von Siemens is credited with development of the first ozone generator in 1857, and Marius Paul Otto appears to be the first to begin a specialized firm, Compagnie des Eaux et de l'Ozone, in France based on ozone as its primary product.

Apparently, ozone's use as a disinfectant was recognized quickly, although it does not appear any one individual was primarily credited with that determination. Many studies followed von Siemens' invention with the first installation of ozone to disinfect drinking water at Oudshoorn in the Netherlands in 1893. Subsequently, ozonation of drinking water was implemented in Nice, France, in 1906, where it has continued without interruption for more than 100 years. Kramer and Leung note that during the same year, New York City's 773,000,000 gallon Jerome Park Reservoir also began ozonation to control taste and odor; however, it does not appear the practice was continued long term[15].

Use of ozone grew in the early 1900s; however, the post-World War I world saw it replaced, primarily by chlorine variants based on overall cost, ease of application, and higher yield. By 1940, there were only 119 ozonated drinking water applications worldwide and this figure had only grown to 1,043 by 1977 with more than 50% of these located in France[16]. In 1987, there were only five water treatment facilities using ozone in the United States. Not surprisingly, there has been a resurgence of interest in drinking water disinfection using ozone based on the discovery of THMs as a harmful disinfection by-product of chlorine-related sanitization.

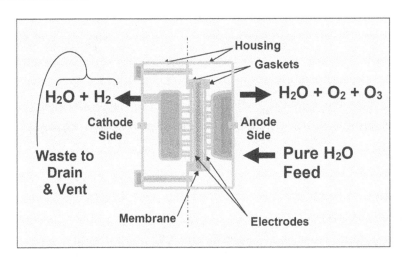

FIGURE 24.4 Electrolytic ozone cell. (Graphic courtesy of Suez Treatment Solutions (formerly Ozonia, NA).)

Practical Issues Relating to the Use of Ozone

The competitive nature and resulting confidentiality within the healthcare industry has done little to allow for documented historical perspective relative to ozone usage, hence the following discussion is based on recognized industrial trends and reasonably available information; however, all site-specific installation data may not be included if it has been deemed to be of a proprietary nature, has remained undisclosed, or is unverified.

The application of ozone for sanitization of pharmaceutical water systems within the United States began in earnest during the 1980s with installations including both corona discharge and electrolytic technologies. Equipment available at that time was typically less than robust with the higher quality componentry available from Europe where the use of ozone was more prevalent. Implementation of ozone within a system creates interesting and unique challenges not just from ozone's application but based on traditional practices within the drug manufacturing arena.

Equipment necessary to generate ozone is only the starting point as the ozone must then be introduced into the process environment, monitored, controlled, and removed before use, all without impacting materials of construction, operator safety, final product quality and efficacy, or patients. Feed gas quality, temperature, ozone concentration, off-gassing, leakage, and other issues must be adequately addressed as well, for a safe and effective installation. Although ozone application is not limited to process water, for the purposes of this discussion we will focus on that specific area. The reader is encouraged to review additional available material regarding ozone sterilization of surgical suites, swimming pool sanitization, use in aquariums, direct human therapy, bottled beverages, drinking water, and the plethora of other applications available.

Initially, corona discharge generation was most prevalent based on its lower price and availability. Generators of that era were often constructed using a plate configuration for the ozone cell, with inherent flaws that manifested in frequent failures and resulted in substantial downtime, high maintenance costs, and leaks that posed potential injury to personnel. Ozone monitors, for both gaseous ambient ozone as well as dissolved ozone, varied in their technologic approach to measurement, were expensive, unreliable, and difficult to maintain. Controls were unsophisticated and often capable of only on-off functionality compounding operational and reliability issues. Materials of construction and operational learning curves resulted in a significant number of failures that compromised the ability of many plants to produce finished product while problems were being resolved. Off-gassing and ozone venting caused possible environmental concerns and leaks posed risks to personnel. Monitoring limits and other uncertainties created an added level of complexity that might have been expected to radically limit the roster of those willing to take on the added burden associated with implementation of an ozonated system.

Instead, the use of ozone has increased based on its efficacy and in spite of these noted problems, many of which have been fully or partially resolved. Today, systems incorporating ozone are considered reliable, cost-effective, practical, and trusted for Purified Water, USP (PW) production and for waters that serve as feed to Water for Injection (WFI) systems. The FDA has given tacit approval for ozone application and many of ozone's vocal detractors have been silenced by the lack of operational problems and because the predictions of carcinogenic by-product development have not come to fruition.

To fully understand the evolution that has taken place over the past three decades, it is prudent to track the changes and developments that have occurred; hence, a brief review will follow discussing the improvements that have brought us to the current state-of-the-art. Details of each development including technological improvements are beyond the scope of this section; however, materials listed in the bibliography can provide additional detail and support information.

Generation and Control

Many of the early generations of ozone equipment, especially corona discharge, utilized on-off control and employed printed circuit boards that were proprietary in design. The inability of this equipment to accept control input ultimately resulted in systems that exhibited erratic behavior and wide fluctuations in dissolved ozone levels. As a result, the technology was not viewed as robust or reliable, and systems were operated so that the lowest level of dissolved ozone that might be expected was still far above some arbitrary minimum selected as a baseline, with actual levels usually far above those needed to maintain control of organisms. These excessive levels commonly produced negative results including pH shifts in product water and failures to meet quality standards. Excessive levels of dissolved ozone also resulted in accelerated attack of materials, especially gaskets, filter elements, and other less resistant materials. In addition, the previously noted design flaws compounded reliability issues as did the lack of ozone operating and maintenance experience. There were literally dozens of system failures from water entering the ozone generators based on poor injection design and poor piping techniques, both of which will be discussed further.

Minor pressure fluctuations caused plate-type ozone generation cells to flex resulting in broken seals and leaks that jeopardized operators and systems alike. Vendors were marginally more experienced than users and not equipped to provide reasonable service response. As well, parts were seldom available from vendors stock increasing user frustration and cost. Feed gas, critical to ozone generator operation, was typically from either an existing plant compressed air supply or from a dedicated oxygen generator. During that period it was uncommon for either source to be monitored for quality and as a result any failures that occurred were typically attributed to the ozone generator.

However, once the impact of these systems was fully understood and monitoring systems installed, overall reliability began to steadily increase. In should be reemphasized that oxygen feed to corona discharge technology results in higher ozone concentration, reduced levels of undesired contaminants, and ultimately in lower operating costs. On-off control was exacerbated by demand issues such that storage/contact tank levels and rate of fill often determined the amplitude of the dissolved curve and the amount by which levels overshot or undershot the desired set point.

Ozone monitoring and control instrumentation was also less than ideal during this period with both accuracy and reliability issues complicating the situation. Unfortunately, this was the case for both dissolved and ambient monitors alike. Ambient monitors serve as leak detectors to protect personnel; however, in one reported instance, the sample pump within the monitor failed with the monitor continuing to report "zero" levels of ambient ozone for almost 2 years before the problem was discovered. Obviously, the user was primarily at fault; however, the situation caused the manufacturer to reevaluate the unit design incorporating additional safety features in the future.

Although less likely to cause personnel injury, dissolved ozone monitors, including those manufactured in Europe where ozone use was more commonplace, also required modification to improve functionality. Problems with instrument reliability were caused by normal system pressure fluctuations or instrument drift resulting in out-of-calibration conditions far more frequently than predicted by the instrument manufacturer. Oftentimes, expensive pressure regulating valves are required to minimize the impact of pressure fluctuations even today, while many instruments require frequent recalibration to ensure they are consistently operating within specifications.

The prevalent technology for ozone monitoring incorporates electrochemical (EC) sensors and accounts for approximately 90% of installed applications. Alternatively, UV spectroscopic absorption units measuring either through the water matrix or by stripping the gas and measuring in the gas phase are also employed[17]. Although UV sensors are excellent for high concentration gaseous measurement, they are not considered the best for dissolved ozone measurement primarily based on interferences and stripping complexities[17].

EC sensors rely on the polarographic principal and the cell consists of 2–3 electrodes, including an anode, a cathode, and possibly a guard-ring electrode submerged in an electrolyte, "A specific potential is applied to the cathode that will selectively reduce the gas analyte of interest[17]." The electrodes are covered by a gas-permeable membrane that will separate the gas from the liquid based on Henry's Law, "which asserts that gases seek to be balanced across a permeable barrier[17]." Because the cathode chemically changes the gas, the effective concentration in the electrolyte always remains zero, thus keeping a constant permeation of gas into the cell. The current generated by the reduction of ozone at the cathode is proportional to the concentration of the ozone outside the cell, and adjusting for temperature and solubility yields a dissolved value[17].

As previously mentioned, accuracy of dissolved ozone measurement has been a recurring problem. This has most often been associated with off-gassing, as EC sensors cannot respond to mixed-phase samples. Henry's Law of partial pressures applies and off-gassing will occur when pressure fluctuations are present within the system as a result of equipment configuration and operational activity. Severe pressure gradients as well as pulsation and cavitation can even dislodge or damage (tear) the membrane resulting in erroneous readings and loss of process control.

Sensor locations within recirculated systems are important and worthy of mention. The primary sensor is normally located in the distribution piping after storage but before UV decomposition, normally after the distribution pump(s) to assure positive pressure. This sensor is linked to the ozone generator via the control system and modulates the generator output to maintain constant dissolved ozone levels based on set point. A second monitor is typically located immediately after the ozone destruct UV light. This monitor is used commonly to ensure that ozone is not allowed to reach points-of-use during normal operation and may be interlocked with use-points through the control system to restrict opening if ozone is present in the effluent. Conversely, this monitor can also be used to confirm that ozone is present, and its level, during sanitizations of the distribution system. Finally, a third monitor is also commonly included to measure and confirm proper return-loop ozone levels during sanitization as well as for back-up of the post-UV monitor.

Ambient ozone monitors are recommended for application in any areas where ozone gas leaks might pose a hazard to personnel, especially adjacent to the ozone generation system and/or ozone contact vessel. In this regard, it is also common and considered good engineering to isolate the ozone gas generation system (in a dedicated containment space) wherever practical and to include interlocks such that electrical power to the generator is disconnected and a room exhaust fan is activated if a leak occurs. As well, an illuminated warning light should caution personnel not to enter the containment if a leak is present, while also alerting appropriate individuals and creating an event log.

Calibration of ozone monitoring cells is an area of concern for metrology groups and operations personnel alike. There are two methods for calibrating EC sensors: titration and air calibration. Both of these are indirect calibration methods as no bottled standards could be created and delivered based on ozone's half-life. Blonshine[18] mentions various titrants that are available to measure dissolved ozone including sodium arsenite, potassium iodine, and N,N-diethyl-p-phenylenediamine; however, the International Ozone Association (IOA), the American Water Works Association (AWWA), and the U.S. Environmental Protection Agency (USEPA) all recognize the indigo trisulfonate colorimetric method commonly called the "Indigo Method." The Indigo Method is relatively easy to perform but does require access to laboratory hardware and careful attention to detail, including sample temperature, ozone half-life, pH, water purity, exposure to light, and reference interferences (such as chlorine). Within these constraints, accuracies of ± 10 ppb are achievable.

Air calibration, invented by Hale, is not only a reasonable alternative but in many cases a more accurate one. Hale recognized that oxygen could be measured with the same probe as used for ozone if the electrode potentials were changed and based on the many commonalities shared by ozone and oxygen. Accuracies of ± 5 ppb are possible making air calibration more accurate than titration. Unfortunately, even though air calibration has the added benefit of using no reagents, it can be problematic as the readjustment required from air back to dissolved ozone can take hours.

As a natural result of ozonation, undissolved gas, as well as gas liberated from the water requires venting which normally occurs from the storage/contact vessel. When permitted by code, ozone may be discharged directly to the atmosphere where it reverts to oxygen (O_2) molecules relatively quickly. However, code notwithstanding, care must be taken not to discharge near building air intakes and windows, onto roofing materials or other unsuitable construction materials, or at points where impact to vegetation, animals, or humans might occur. This type of venting, of necessity, typically occurs using a vent tube or pipe that discharges outside of a building; however, protection of the vessel contents remains a concern.

Alternatively, when direct discharge is not allowed or when discharge within a building is necessary or desired, ozone must be removed to avoid damage to property or personnel injury. For these instances, ozone vent decomposers are typically installed. Vent decomposers usually contain a catalyst, most often manganese dioxide, which is used to speed the reaction of the ozone back to oxygen. Units may also utilize fans to facilitate flow and many are equipped with heaters to reduce moisture that may cause operating problems. Moisture from the vent stream or from ambient outside air can cause the catalyst to solidify, mitigating its effect or worse, plugging the vent such that pressure or vacuum within the vessel causes operational issues, damage to equipment, or even injury. With vent decomposers typically mounted at the top of storage/contact vessels, service was often difficult at best and ignored at worst, compounding a complex and possibly dangerous situation. Even pressure and vacuum-rated vessels were not immune from problems as interior pressure and vacuum could affect proper operation of pressure and level sensors, cause pump cavitation, and damage accessory equipment including the vent decomposer itself. Traditional vessel design relied on tall slender vessels (large H to D ratio) to improve mass transfer; however, equipment and application improvements today allow for far more flexibility for new systems.

There are many options for introduction of ozone into the system from corona discharge generators; however, many of the earliest were rife with problems. Some of these early designs utilized porous ceramic disks or "stones," similar to those used in fish tanks, to bubble the ozone gas into the bottom of the vessel. Bubbles were allowed to rise through the vertical column of water to enhance mass transfer; however, these diffusers were contrary to sanitary design as they included threads, were not cleanable, and were fragile with breakage causing reduction of dissolved ozone and downtime required for repairs. Other design difficulties included use of silicone gasketing (used because of the softness/low durameter) often with a severely limited life in ozone contact and an extremely narrow application range (small tank diameter) since stones were typically only 8in. in diameter (approximately), requiring multiple units for larger diameter tanks thus posing serious problems for balancing gas flow through each stone.

Subsequently, sparge tubes began to replace ceramic bubblers; however, these only circumvented a portion of the issues relating to physical design but still required the ozone generator pressure to drive injection and the necessity for low-point injection to assure intimate contact between the bubbles and the bulk water. Current designs may utilize a venturi eductor system that minimizes the need for the ozone generator to overcome line pressure, and are often coupled with an in-line static mixer and one or more spargers to ensure suitable ozone distribution.

These advancements result in higher levels of dissolved ozone, lower ozone production, and more even gas distribution at minimal additional cost and while reducing the likelihood water will flood the ozone cell causing damage to the generator. As a result, vessels are no longer required to be tall and thin to aid ozone contact time offering more flexible installation options and system configurations, including the use of horizontal vessels. When "bubbling" is necessary for the dissolution of ozone, basic mass transfer rules are applicable such that smaller bubbles result in greater exposed surface area and better transfer characteristics. High-quality "stones" are capable of bubble sizes of about 30 micron.

It should be noted that in spite of improvements in ozone injection and in generator design, it remains an appropriate design practice to ensure the ozone feed line to the vessel is routed in a fashion such that it is higher than the water level in the vessel. This will assure that in a system-wide failure, water will not flood the generator causing additional damage.

As previously cautioned, ozone venting must be addressed; however, this issue is complicated by the necessity to protect the vessel contents from microbial contamination. Under dynamic conditions, water will continually fill and empty from the system. This situation will result in tank level fluctuation including air in-rush during emptying and combined air and ozone venting during filling, unless nitrogen blanketing is installed. Air entering the vessel may contain particulate as well as bacteria that could compromise the water quality and as a result, a microbially retentive filter may be included in the design scheme. This topic is the subject of considerable debate for many reasons, including the hostile microbiological environment created by ozone inside the tank and water regulations that do not necessitate sterility. For permitted applications a vent filter, typically rated at 0.2 micron "absolute" retention can be placed in the vent line to clean the air entering the vessel. This unit must be compatible with ozone gas, must be hydrophobic to avoid plugging from moisture, and may require a heating jacket as well as other accessories such as vent and drain valves to ensure proper operation and testing. Alternatively, when used with a vent decomposer, the vent filter should be placed below the vent decomposer to perform the tasks mentioned above and to minimize the potential for particulate, catalyst, and other foreign matter from the decomposer to enter the tank including any resident microbes. The added benefit of this arrangement is that the sanitary vent filter serves as a barrier between the non-sanitary vent decomposer (as of this writing, sanitary designed vent decomposers have yet to become available) and all other portions of the sanitary system. It would be prudent to mention that numerous system failures have occurred over the years as a result of ozone vent decomposer failures including microbial contamination, collapsed tanks, and catalyst resin suspended in product water distributed to use-points throughout the facility.

Vent filter elements are typically constructed of plastic materials many including a polypropylene frame that has limited functional life in ozone environments. This limitation necessitates frequent testing and change-out at significant cost. Sintered metal filters, rated at 0.45 micron in a gas stream and 1 micron in a liquid stream (approximately) may be considered inadequate although their stainless steel construction could last indefinitely under even the harshest ozone concentrations. Recently, one manufacturer introduced filter elements constructed entirely of Teflon™, including both the media and support structure, albeit at relatively high cost. These new types of elements eliminate the issues related to vent filter failure from ozone attack of materials and may be validated for extended periods provided the local environment does not cause failure from particulate plugging.

It may be surmised that the market for ozone-resistant vent filter elements is not large enough to justify a significant investment in research and development by other suppliers to bring suitable competing products to the marketplace and there may be little added motivation on the part of some filter manufacturers who will likely see a reduction in sales if this were to occur. Based on the limited number of sources, cost, and the tendency by pharmaceutical companies to maintain the status quo, change may come about very slowly.

For drinking water applications, additional concerns such as those relating to fertilizers, herbicides, and pesticides are prevalent. Atrazine and other triazines merit special mention as they are difficult to remove. However, the addition of hydrogen peroxide to ozone ($O_3 + H_2O_2$) produces hydroxyl radicals effective in the destruction of these undesired compounds. As well, the combination of ozone and hydrogen peroxide can be effective in elimination of unpleasant tastes and odors. Although the free radical ($HO°$) produced from the combination of ozone and hydrogen peroxide is effective in removing trace organics, it must be noted that this activity usually leaves no residual ozone remaining for downstream disinfection, a situation that obviously cannot be overlooked.

For more than five decades, chlorination of raw water was the method of choice to prevent virtually all biologic activity, primarily based on cost and also because of our ignorance relating to the formation and impact of THMs. Today, ozonation has become fairly common in European drinking water treatment as cost differences have become less substantial and in light of the discoveries relating to the disadvantages of chlorination by-products. Ozonation of raw water as part of drinking water preparation is, however, significantly different than pre-ozonation in a pharmaceutical water system in the United States since it would be expected that feedwater to most pharmaceutical water systems contains chlorine, in at least minimum amounts.

Most public suppliers of potable water view their constituency primarily as residential users who are uneducated and unconcerned, who trust that they are being protected, and who require little information about the methods being employed. As a result, when treatment technology is modified, as in the change from chlorine to chloramines, there is little fanfare or publicity. For residential users these changes seldom have significant impact and are most often overlooked. However, on the commercial and industrial side, these changes can have tremendous effect ranging from equipment sizing to materials-of-construction issues. As an example, granular activated carbon (GAC) filters, used for chlorine and organics removal, may be undersized for chloramine removal if they were originally sized for normal and expected levels of chlorine. Situations of this type have occurred often over the past two decades as suppliers of potable water convert to chloramine without notice to users, affecting systems designed and installed 5–20+ years ago based on then-current data and technology. As well, more recent systems may utilize UV irradiation for chlorine removal to protect downstream equipment, and these too may be undersized if a change to chloramines is surreptitiously implemented, irreversibly damaging expensive RO membranes and causing system outages with associated lost time and ruined product.

Additionally, changes to chloramines can have other surprising effects on system performance and materials. In two documented cases, systems originally designed with stainless steel pretreatment hardware operated successfully for many years with residual chlorine from the treatment source and in-plant pre-ozonation. However, when chloramine was introduced these systems experienced major component failures within a short period after conversion to chloramine. The failure mode was accelerated chloride attack of the stainless steel as confirmed by an independent laboratory. Both systems had operated for many years without failure in spite of the combined chlorine and ozone. Yet, within very short periods (in one case, as little as 48 h.) after conversion to chloramines, stainless steel components failed catastrophically exhibiting classic signs of chloride-based crevice corrosion. Since the simple conversion to chloramine has not induced failure in other stainless systems and since the combination of chlorine and ozone had not resulted in previous failures, it has been deduced that the replacement of chlorine by chloramine in an ozonated environment resulted in accelerated attack and the noted failures. Although significant further study did not occur, repeated short-term failures of individual components served to confirm the assertion that the combination of ozone and chloramine led to accelerated metallic attack, possibly enhanced by other contributing but undetected factors.

Ozone's use as an organic oxidant is primarily based on the cleavage of the carbon double bond which acts as a nucleophile or a specie having excess electrons[19]. As a result, ozone will always react directly with organic compounds and also by reaction of free hydroxyl radicals. This dual reaction model was described by Hoigné in 1975 and is reproduced for clarification (Figure 24.5).

As well, Aeppli and Dyer-Smith noted that "the consumption of ozone by direct reaction can be written as a pseudo first order reaction if the solute concentration is higher than the ozone concentration (Figure 24.6)"[20].

It should be noted that direct reaction is heavily dependent upon the organic compound's chemical nature, while the reaction of the radical is primarily independent although a few orders higher than those of the direct reaction[20]. Reaction rate constants for various ozone and hydroxyl radical reactions with organic compounds are listed in Table 24.3.

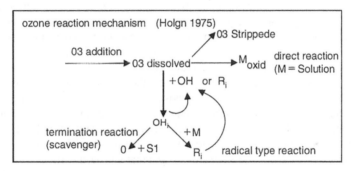

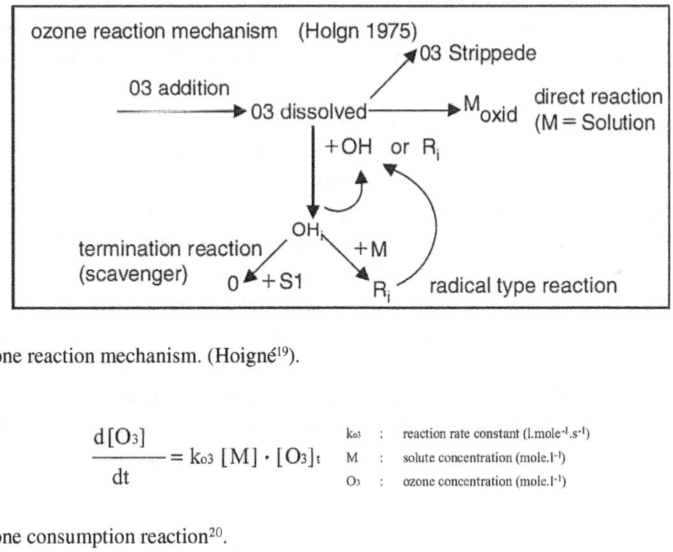

FIGURE 24.5 Ozone reaction mechanism. (Hoigné[19]).

$$\frac{d[O_3]}{dt} = k_{O3}[M] \cdot [O_3]_t$$

k_{O3} : reaction rate constant (l.mole^{-1}.s^{-1})
M : solute concentration (mole.l^{-1})
O_3 : ozone concentration (mole.l^{-1})

FIGURE 24.6 Ozone consumption reaction[20].

TABLE 24.3

Reaction Rate Constants k of Ozone and Hydroxyl Radicals with Organic Compounds[20]

Compound	k, in L.mole^{-1}.s^{-1} O_3	$^{\circ}OH$
Olefins	$1,000–4.5 \times 10^5$	$10^9–10^{11}$
S-organics	$10–1.6 \times 10^3$	$10^9–10^{10}$
Phenols	10^3	10^9
N-organics	$10–10^2$	$10^8–10^{10}$
Aromatics	$1–10^2$	$10^8–10^{10}$
Acetylenes	50	$10^8–10^9$
Aldehydes	10	10^9
Ketones	1	$10^8–10^9$
Alcohols	$10^{-2}–1$	$10^9–10^{10}$
Alkanes	10^{-2}	$10^6–10^9$

Aeppli and Dyer-Smith were also careful to note that in the reaction chain, species of aldehydes or ketones appeared twice as reaction products and the carboxylic acids only once as further oxidation of these products, based on their low reaction rate constants, will not easily occur. As well, aldehydes and ketones are known nutrients for bacteria making organic loading an important consideration when considering ozone in pretreatment. This is obviously less of concern after purification, especially for pharmaceutical applications with TOC limitations; however, it should not be ignored completely as it cannot be considered insignificant.

The application of corona discharge for ozone production requires careful consideration of the feed gas quality as it is the most critical aspect involved in creating pure gaseous ozone that is not laden with contaminants, moisture, or reactants, any of which can hamper the effectiveness, ultimately reduce the degree of microbial kill, and potentially contaminate the products it contacts.

It can be appropriate to use either air or oxygen to produce ozone; however, for high purity applications, including pharmaceuticals, oxygen-rich (90+ %) feed gas is highly recommended by equipment manufacturers. It is also recommended that the feed gas be clean and particle free above 0.4 micron, dry to −60°C dew point or lower, and oil and hydrocarbon free. It is also extremely important that the feed gas be plumbed using appropriate materials of construction to avoid contamination, especially particulate that can either react with ozone, compromise the process, or both. With lower levels of impurities in the feed gas, higher concentrations (wt. %) of ozone can be achieved, and as a result, increased gas absorption into the water is possible resulting in more effective disinfection, lower operating cost, and possibly even lower costs for capital equipment based on physical size and purchase expense. Although lower concentrations of ozone are common, in the range of 5%, higher concentrations, in the range of 10%–12% by weight are considered optimal. As an example, note the difference in oxygen (O_2) required to produce ten pounds of O_3 at 5% concentration (200#) versus that required at 12% concentration (83#).

Appropriately sized compressed air systems that meet the purity requirements noted above can be used to produce ozone, however, many facilities chose an alternate route since upgrading and maintaining a large diverse system simply to accommodate a single user may prove cost prohibitive. Plant compressed air systems are seldom categorized critical direct contact systems although that status would most likely change if ozone production were added to the list of uses. Therefore, it is not uncommon for system design to include a dedicated source of oxygen that has been earmarked solely for supply of oxygen to the ozone generation system. One possible method of providing oxygen for the ozone system is from the vaporization of liquid oxygen (LOX) stored on-site in cylinders or in a bulk storage vessel. This can become expensive and can also result in outages if refilling is delayed. Furthermore, reliance on a vendor for delivery combined with the requirements for vendor qualification and subsequent auditing can substantially increase the per-unit cost making this option less desirable.

Alternatively, oxygen generation equipment can be sized and selected solely to supply oxygen to the ozone generation system. Two primary types of oxygen generators are produced and they are designated as pressure swing adsorption (PSA)-type and vacuum swing adsorption (VSA)-type generators. For smaller applications, and most pharmaceutical applications fall into this category, PSA generation is most practical. PSA technology involves the passage of compressed (30–90 psig) air through a vessel containing molecular sieve material. The sieve, having a greater affinity for nitrogen and other gasses, including moisture, retains all but the oxygen and about 4% argon. Prior to becoming fully saturated, the sieve, is regenerated by depressurization (desorption) followed by an oxygen purge. The majority of PSA generators utilize at least two pressure vessels, also known as adsorbers or beds, to allow one vessel to be regenerated while the other is in service. An oxygen receiver tank connected to the outlet of the system stores the 90%–95% pure oxygen at constant pressure to eliminate fluctuations and possible downtime. The product oxygen is typically produced between 5 and 60 psig, has a dew point of approximately −100° Fahrenheit and is 90%–95% pure.

VSA, also known as vacuum pressure swing adsorption (VPSA) is similar to PSA; however, low pressure, high-volume blowers are utilized for the adsorption and vacuum blowers are used for desorption. Reduced air inlet pressure translates to lower oxygen output pressure, most commonly in the range of 3–5 psig unless an oxygen booster or compressor is added. Oxygen produced is in the range of 88%–94% pure and a dew point at −100°F parallels that from the PSA generator. Both PSA and VSA/VPSA employ the same 3:1 ratio of adsorption pressure to regeneration pressure, although the regeneration pressure for VSA is below atmospheric. VSA also commonly employs dual adsorbers and can be well suited to large-volume applications where ambient air is simply drawn into the pressure blower with minimal prefiltration.

For large applications, such as 10,000–80,000 SCFH, VSA/VPSA is the more practical alternative and when lower purity and pressure is acceptable VSA is generally in the range of 30% more energy efficient. PSA oxygen generators are typically fed from a plant compressed air source and are less expensive on a first-cost basis. In addition, they are also more compact, quieter, more reliable, and less maintenance intensive than the VSA/VPSA alternative, providing feed gas temperature is below 122°F.

As mentioned previously, ozone can be formed by electrical discharge such as lightning but also from high energy electromagnetic radiation. In addition, electrical equipment can generate significant amounts of ozone when high voltages are employed such as is common in laser printers, photocopiers, electric motors, and welding systems. This has given rise to concerns for employee safety in the workplace not just for those operating and maintaining heavy equipment but also for office employees surrounded by computer-related electronic equipment resident in their workspace.

Summary

Ozone is an effective sanitizing agent appropriate for use in pharmaceutical, biotech, and other healthcare-related applications. Ozone is especially suited for microbial control in water systems including those that must comply with monographs promulgated within the U.S. Pharmacopeia[21] and also with FDA requirements. Based on its oxidative strength, ozone is extremely useful but poses certain challenges including selection and maintenance of proper materials of construction and suitable design for the protection of personnel and products. There is a continually expanding body of knowledge relating to ozone's application and use which must be clearly understood if ozone's full benefit is to be derived. Sources of this information include USP Informational Chapter <1231> and the *ISPE Good Practice Guide: Ozone Sanitization of Pharmaceutical Water Systems.*[22]

Ozone has the capacity to offer reliable, cost-effective treatment for microbial control and as expenditures for pharmaceutical and healthcare products continue to rise, traditional technologies will experience increased scrutiny, and ozone will most likely continue to gain in popularity with greatly expanded use and further development of applications and technical information.

REFERENCES

1. Ozonia: Ozone in the Advancement of Drinking Water Treatment Technology. The Clean Technology. CH-O 9727 E, 1997. p. 2.
2. Stanley, B.T. *Electrolytic Ozone Generation and Its Application in Pure Water Systems.* Zürich, Switzerland: Ozonia Ltd., 2004. p. 4.
3. Meltzer, T.H. *High-Purity Water Preparation for the Semiconductor, Pharmaceutical, and Power Industries.* Littleton, CO: Tall Oaks Publishing, 1993. p. 103.
4. Meltzer, T.H. *Pharmaceutical Water Systems.* Littleton, CO: Tall Oaks Publishing, 1997. p. 127.
5. Meltzer, T.H. *Pharmaceutical Water Systems.* Littleton, CO: Tall Oaks Publishing, 1997. p. 129.
6. ISPE. *Baseline Pharmaceutical Engineering Guide for New and Renovated Facilities Volume 4—Water & Steam Systems*, 2nd Edition. Tampa, FL: International Society for Pharmaceutical Engineering, 2011. p. 226.
7. FDA. *Guide to the Inspections of High Purity Water Systems.* U.S. Food & Drug Administration. Division of Field Investigations, Rockville, MD: Office of Regional Operations, Office of Regulatory Affairs, 1993. p. 11.
8. *Medical Use of Ozone—The Story of Ozone*, 6th Edition. O3zontechnik. S. Pressman. http://www. ozonio.com.br. p. 49–50.
9. Ozone. Silent Menace. September 9, 2006. http://www.landmark.org/ozone.html. p. 1.
10. Ozone and Cholesterol Combine to Cause Heart Disease. May 31, 2006. Scientific American.com. p. 1.
11. Ozone. Last modified May 28, 2019. http://en.wikipedia.org/wiki/Ozone.
12. Down and Dirty: Airborne Ozone Can Alter Forest Soil. September 9, 2006. http://www.innovations-report.com/html/reports/agricultural_sciences/report 22474.html. p. 1.

13. Kramer, S. and Leung, S. Ozonation Disinfection: Disinfection with Ozone. September 10, 2006. http://ewr.cee.vt.edu/environmental/teach/wtprimer/ozone/ozone.html. p. 3.

14. *Lenntech: History of Ozone.* Netherlands: Lenntech Water Treatment & Air Purification, 2005. p. 1.

15. Kramer, S. and Leung, S. Ozonation Disinfection: Disinfection with Ozone. September 10, 2006. http://ewr.cee.vt.edu/environmental/teach/wtprimer/ozone/ozone.html. p. 1.

16. *Lenntech: History of Ozone.* Netherlands: Lenntech Water Treatment & Air Purification, 2005. p. 2.

17. Blonshine, T. Dissolved ozone in pharmaceutical water systems: How and where to measure dissolved ozone. *Pharmaceutical Technology.* April 13, 2006. http://www.pharmtech.com/pharmtech/content/printcontentpopup.jsp?id=316163. p. 2.

18. Blonshine, T. Dissolved ozone in pharmaceutical water systems: How and where to measure dissolved ozone. *Pharmaceutical Technology.* April 13, 2006. http://www.pharmtech.com/pharmtech/content/printcontentpopup.jsp?id=316163. p. 3.

19. Aeppli, J. and Dyer-Smith, P. Ozonia: Ozonation and Granular Activated Carbon Filtration the Solution to Many Problems. First Australasian Conference: International Ozone Association Down Under, 1996. p. 5.

20. Aeppli, J. and Dyer-Smith, P. Ozonia: Ozonation and Granular Activated Carbon Filtration the Solution to Many Problems. First Australasian Conference: International Ozone Association Down Under, 1996. p. 6.

21. *US Pharmacopeia/National Formulary*, 41st Edition. Rockville, MD: United States Pharmacopeial Convention, Inc., 2018.

22. ISPE. *Good Practice Guide: Ozone Sanitization of Pharmaceutical Water Systems.* Tampa, FL: International Society for Pharmaceutical Engineering, 2012.

BIBLIOGRAPHY

Aeppli, J. and Dyer-Smith, P. Ozonia: Ozonation and Granular Activated Carbon Filtration the Solution to Many Problems. First Australasian Conference: International Ozone Association Down Under, 1996.

Allaby, M. Photochemical smog. *Encyclopedia of Weather and Climate.* New York: Facts on File, Inc., 2002. Science Online. August 26, 2006. http://www.fofweb.com

Angelo, J.A. Oxidizer. *Facts of File Dictionary of Space Technology*, Revised Edition. New York: Facts on File, Inc., 2003. Science Online. August 26, 2006. http://www.fofweb.com

Blonshine, T. Dissolved ozone in pharmaceutical water systems: How and where to measure dissolved ozone. *Pharmaceutical Technology.* April 13, 2006. http://www.pharmtech.com/pharmtech/content/printcontentpopup.jsp?id=316163

Cho, M., Chung, H., and Yoon, J. Disinfection of Water Containing Natural Organic Matter by Using Ozone-Initiated Radical Reactions. August 20, 2006. http://www.pubmedcentral.nih.gov/articlerender.fcgi?artid=145773

Down and Dirty: Airborne Ozone Can Alter Forest Soil. September 9, 2006. http://www.innovations-report.com/html/reports/agricultural_sciences/report22474.html

Entrez PubMed: 150 Years since the Birth of R. Koch-His Life and Work. August 20, 2006. http://www.ncbi.nlm.nih.gov

EPA, Identification of New Disinfection By-Products Formed by Alternative Disinfectants: Exposure Research. July 6, 2006. August 20, 2006. http://www.epa.gov/nerl/research/2000/html/g2-1.html

Epidemiology. Last modified May 25, 2019. http://en.wikipedia.org/wiki/Epidemiology

FDA. *Guide to the Inspections of High Purity Water Systems.* U.S. Food & Drug Administration. Division of Field Investigations, Rockville, MD: Office of Regional Operations, Office of Regulatory Affairs. 1993. p. 11.

Geering, F. 1999 Ozone Applications: The state-of-the-art in Switzerland. *Ozone Science and Engineering* 21:187–200.

Hennessy, J. PSA Verses VPSA Oxygen Generation. E-mail from Hennessy of AirSep Corporation. September 27, 2006.

Hoeger, S.J., Dietrich, D.R., and Hitzfeld, B.C. 2002. Effect of ozonation on the removal of cyanobacterial toxins during drinking water treatment. *Environmental Health Perspectives* 110(11):1127–1132.

Hozalski, R.M., Bouwer, E.J., and Goel, S. 1999 Removal of natural organic matter (NOM) from drinking water supplies by ozone-biofiltration. *Water Science and Technology* 40:157–163.

Hundley, P. *Ozone Use in Recirc Systems*. Systems Engineering Newsletter, Charleston, SC: Aquasales, 1990.

ISPE. *Baseline Pharmaceutical Engineering Guide for New and Renovated Facilities Volume 4—Water & Steam Systems*. 2nd Edition. Tampa, FL: International Society for Pharmaceutical Engineering. 2011. p. 226.

ISPE. *Good Practice Guide: Ozone Sanitization of Pharmaceutical Water Systems*. Tampa, FL: International Society for Pharmaceutical Engineering, 2012.

Johansen, B.E. *The relationship of Ozone Depletion and the Greenhouse Effect*. Greenwood Press: *The Global Warming Desk Reference*. September 9, 2006. http://www.ratical.org/ratville/ozoneDepletion.html

Kirk-Othmer. *Encyclopedia of Chemical Technology*, 4th Edition, Volume 17. New York: John Wiley & Sons, 1996. p. 953–994.

Kramer, S. and Leung, S. Ozonation Disinfection: Disinfection with Ozone. September 10, 2006. http://ewr.cee.vt.edu/environmental/teach/wtprimer/ozone/ozone.html

Kusky, T. Life's Origins and Early Evolution. *Encyclopedia of Earth Science*. New York: Facts on File, Inc., 2005. Science Online. August 26, 2006. http://www.fofweb.com

Langlais, B., Reckhow, D.A., and Brink, D.R. *Ozone in Water Treatment. Application and Engineering*. Denver, CO/Chelsea, MI: American Water Works Association Research Foundation/Lewis Publishers, Inc, 1991.

Lenntech: History of Ozone. Delfgauw, Netherlands: Lenntech Water Treatment & Air Purification, 2005.

Levine, S., Dr. Oxygen Deficiency: A Concomitant to All Degenerative Illness, The Vitamin Supplement, 1987.

Medical Use of Ozone—The Story of Ozone, 6th Edition. O$_3$zontechnik. S. Pressman, et al. http://www.ozonio.com.br

Medicine 1905: The Nobel Prize in Physiology or Medicine 1905. August 20, 2006. http://nobelprize.org/nobel_prizes/medicine/laureates/1905/

Meltzer, T.H. January/February 2004. Pharmaceuticals: FDA on Filters in Water Systems at Point-of-use, Storage, and Distribution. *Ultrapure Water* 21(1):40–42.

Meltzer, T.H. *High-Purity Water Preparation for the Semiconductor, Pharmaceutical, and Power Industries*. Littleton, CO: Tall Oaks Publishing, 1993.

Meltzer, T.H. *Pharmaceutical Water Systems*. Littleton, CO: Tall Oaks Publishing, 1997.

Meltzer, T.H. and Rice, R. Ultraviolet and ozone systems. In: Mittleman, Marc W and Geesey, Gill G (eds.). *Biological Fouling of Industrial Water Systems: A Problem Solving Approach*. San Diego, CA: Water Micro Associates, 1987. pp. 97–137.

Osmonics Enhances Control Precision on New Ozone Generator. August 20, 2006. http://www.bevnet.com/news/2002/01-29-2002-osmonics.asp

Oxygen. Facts on File, Inc. Science Online. August 26, 2006. http://www.fofweb.com

Ozonia: Ozone in the Advancement of Drinking Water Treatment Technology. The Clean Technology. CH-O 9727 E, 1997, p. 2.

Ozone. Last modified May 28, 2019. http://en.wikipedia.org/wiki/Ozone

Ozone and Cholesterol Combine to Cause Heart Disease. May 31, 2006. Scientific American.com

Ozone Disinfection. Environmental Technology Initiative National Small Flows Clearinghouse, Wikipedia, 1998. Last Modified May 2019.

Ozone. *The Columbia Encyclopedia*, 6h Edition. New York: Columbia University Press, 2004.

Ozone: Silent Menace. September 9, 2006. http://www.landmark.org/ozone.html

Ministry of Health. *Public Health Risk Management Plan Guide: Treatment Processes-Ozone Disinfection*. Wellington, New Zealand: Ministry of Health (author), Version 1, RefP7.3. June 2001.

Rasplicka, D. (Zdenek) ed. *Ozone Safety Limits: Ozone Levels and Their Effects*. International Ozone Association (IOA).

Rittner, D., and Bailey, R.A. *Ozone. Encyclopedia of Chemistry*. New York: Facts on File, Inc., 2005. Science Online. August 26, 2006. http://www.fofweb.com

Rowland Lecture: Scientist Who Discovered Ozone Problem to Deliver Lectures. April 3, 1989. http://www.rochester.edu/pr/releases/chem/ozone.htm. September 2006.

Salawitch, R.J. Ozone Milestones: Historic. September 9, 2006. http://remus.jpl.nasa.gov/milestones.htm

Schöbein, Christian Fredrich. September 9, 2006. http://dictionary.laborlawtalk.com/Christian_Fredrich_Schonbein

Stanley, B.T. *Electrolytic Ozone Generation and its Application in Pure Water Systems*. Zürich, Switzerland: Ozonia Ltd, 2004.

Stark, C. 2006. Ozone: Use of Electrolytically Generated Ozone for the Disinfection of Pure Water. *Water Conditioning & Purification* 48(8):40–44.

Trihalomethane Reduction (THMs): How Ozone Technology Reduces Disinfection Byproducts. Parker, CO: BioOzone Corporation, 2006. August 20, 2006. http://www.biozone.com/trihalomethanes.html

Tuhkanen T., Kainulainen T, Vartiainen T., and Kalliakeski P. 1994. The effect of preozonation, ozone/hydrogen peroxide treatment, and nanofiltration of the removal of organic matter from drinking water. *Ozone Science and Engineering* 16:367–383.

US Pharmacopeia. *US Pharmacopeia/National Formulary*, 41st Edition. Rockville, MD: United States Pharmacopeial Convention, Inc., 2016.

Valacchi Giuseppe, Fortino Vittoria, and Bocci Velio. The Dual Action of Ozone on the Skin. September 9, 2006. http://www.medscape.com/viewarticle/518529

von Siemens, Ernst Werner. September 10, 2006. http://chem.ch.huji.ac.il/~eugeniik/history/siemens.html

Wyman, B. and Stevenson, H.L. Ozonation. *The Facts on File Dictionary of Environmental Science*, New Edition. New York: Facts on File, Inc., 2001. Science Online. August 26, 2006. http://www.fofweb.com

25

Disposable Equipment in Advanced Aseptic Technology

Maik W. Jornitz
Sartorius Stedim North America, Inc.

Peter Makowenskyj
G-CON Manufacturing, Inc.

CONTENTS

Disposable Unit Operations

Aseptic processing gains an increasing importance within the biotech industry due to the fact that cold sterilization by membrane filtration is the only option to sterilize biological solutions. Any heat treatment would destructively affect the drug product and target protein. To assure that the sterile filtered product maintains its sterile state, disposable process solutions are used increasingly to process or store the resulting filtrate. In addition, there are certain processes where sterile filtration is not possible, as it would remove the drug substance. In those instances, such as cell therapies or certain viral product in (oncolytic) vaccines, the entire process must be handled in an aseptic fashion to mitigate foreign contaminants.

Liquid Hold Bags

Fluid holding or storage bags are not new to the industry, but are in use for decades in the form of blood bags or infusion solution bags, which were most often only of small volume size. Yet, within a manufacturing process multiple fluid holding steps might be involved, storing either water, media, buffer, or the actual drug product. Traditionally, these holding steps are handled by the use of stainless steel tanks or glass vessel. Nevertheless, the capital investment, footprint, downtime, and cleaning/set-up costs were a concern and the industry started looking for alternatives, found in disposable bags of larger volumes. These bags range from the milliliter range to now +3,000 L in volume and can either be standard configuration or custom made. Filled small volume bags are commonly stored in trays and can be interconnected during filling to portion any large liquid volume. Small holding bags cause convenience when, for example, large volumes of media or buffer require to be divided into smaller volumes to be fed into either bioreactor systems (media) or wash/elution processes (buffer). Large volume bags can be placed in either plastic totes or more reliable stainless steel tank systems. The stainless steel tank systems are design to avoid friction or pressure points or bag folding to evade any damage to the bag (Figure 25.1). Furthermore, certain tank holders allows for stacking of these systems to reduce footprint requirements. Some tanks have also load cells included to be able to verify volume intake or outflow.

Since hold bags are also used to store and transport bulk drug product, the design and construction of such bags are critical. Welds, dimensions, bag film thickness, and layering have to be well developed to gain the best mechanical robustness. The bag film is often a multilayer of different polymers to obtain low extractable levels by the product contact film, mechanical stability, and gas barrier by the different layers supporting the inner film. The inner film is most commonly a low-density polyethylene film, where polyamide creates mechanical strength and ethyl vinyl a gas barrier.

Mixing

Mixing within the biopharmaceutical industry is an essential step in multiple process operations. For example, buffer and media mixing is a very common unit operation. The cleaning of stainless steel mixing system is tedious and requires appropriate attention to avoid any contaminating residues. For this reason, disposable mixing systems were designed and eagerly utilized. These systems can be interconnected with filtration systems or hold bags. Disposable mixing systems are available from <10 to +3,000 L

FIGURE 25.1 Example of a storage tank.

and most commonly used for buffer and media preparation, pH adjustments such as viral inactivation, drug substance intermediates, UF/DF loops, protein folding, product compounding, or final formulation purposes. Mixing bags are now being integrated with more single-use sensor technology to implement process analytical technology (PAT). Sensors such as single-use pH, conductivity, flow meters, etc. are common place for single-use systems. Various modes of single-use mixing exist such as recirculation, pulsation of the mixing bag, magnetic impellers, stirrer bars or paddles, rocking, and levitation mixer. Each mixing systems will have various benefits associated with them and are typically chosen per application. For example, magnetic mixing is more common for buffer/media preparation when higher impeller rotation per minute (RPM) are needed levitating mixing is more common downstream as this avoids any friction of the bag material, while showing fast and thorough mixing results.

Liquid and Component Transfer

Within biopharmaceutical processes, bulk raw materials and process intermediates might be shipped over long distances or production processes require a product hold step due to downstream equipment bottlenecks. In both instances, specific operations are required to avoid any protein degradation, which can happen due to enzymatic attack, temperature, pH, concentration, or gas conditions within the hold or transport step. To avoid such yield losses, the end users decided on 2°C–8°C cold storage or freeze steps to keep the product stabile over an extended period of time. Depending on the solution makeup, protein stability and other factors, certain methods may be chosen over others. In the case of freezing, this process can either be controlled or uncontrolled. Uncontrolled freeze, such as blast freezers may result in freeze concentration, pH shifts, aggregation, and ice crystals within the frozen material or hold bag damages. To avoid such damaging conditions, disposable-controlled freeze/thaw devices have been established. These devices utilize a hold bag within a frame and a freeze/thaw module that uses heat exchanger plates, which assure a unified controlled freeze and thaw process. Component transfers of solids or liquids can also be performed using disposable bags or single-use systems. Solid components, such as stoppers, are placed into the transfer bag and the system is gamma irradiated. The transfer bag has an aseptic transfer port which allows the bag with the sterile content being connected to the transfer port installed on a production isolator. Once connected to the aseptic transfer port the bag is opened and the sterilized stoppers can be transferred into the hopper inside the isolator. The contaminated surface of the transfer port of the bag is covered by the counter-connection on the port of the isolator, so neither the inside of the isolator nor bag will come in contact with the environment. Transfers of liquids into different ISO classifications or to/from BSL 2 spaces could likewise occur over an aseptic transfer system.

Upstream Technologies

There have been significant improvements in single-use upstream technology since the first rocking motion bioreactor was launched in the late 1990s. Disposable process steps upstream now include stirred tank reactors, single-use retention devices for perfusion such as the alternate tangential flow (ATF) system, single-use centrifuges, and diatomaceous earth (DE) filters.

Aside from centrifugation, most of these technologies have a high percentage of adoption. Through process intensification, the 2,000 L SU bioreactor has now been established as the platform scale of choice for production bioreactors. Rather than scale-up, scale-out at this volume is the new norm. Recently, a 4,000 L SU bioreactor was launched and it will be interesting to see the level of disruption this larger scale single-use (SU) can create. Additionally, the ATF system has been a major enabler in migration from batch to perfusion processes upstream by creating a relatively clean product stream off the filter, often eliminating any need of centrifugation and/or DE depth filtration.

Downstream Technologies

Disposable process steps in downstream processing include tangential flow ultra filtration/dia-filtration (UF/DF) steps, intermediate or column protection filtration, viral inactivation and filtration, and membrane chromatography.

The most commonly found disposable chromatographic separations are membrane adsorbers, which prove to be an economical alternative to traditional resin and column-based operations (Gottschalk, 2008). Microporous membranes with pore sizes ranging from 0.8–3 µm drastically reduce diffusion-related mass transfer effects enabling higher linear velocities and are primarily used for the adsorptive removal of contaminants such as HCP, DNA, endotoxin, and viruses in flow-through mode (polishing). While reusable resin columns require a complex periphery including a packing station and a chromatography skid, this is not the case for disposable membrane chromatography or prepacked columns, the impact of which can be verified by the utilization of process cost models (Sinclair and Monge, 2002). In addition to cost advantages, however, there are many additional benefits, including significantly shorter cycle times and superfluous carryover studies in process validation, making adsorptive virus clearance much more straightforward.

A broad range of functional chemistries, including various ion exchange and affinity ligands, are currently available in disposable membrane formats with typical dynamic binding capacities of 30 g/L for proteins and up to 10 g/L for DNA. Protein A chromatography, while possible in membrane format, remains economically impractical at production scales and the use of traditional resin-based columns are recommended. However, the trend toward disposable chromatography is ongoing and is trending toward the platform technology of polishing applications. Other chromatography systems are classical, prepacked, pre-sanitized columns. These units contain classical chromatography resins, but the end user benefit is that the columns just need to be connected into the fluid stream, without packing or testing. The sanitization agents used for such columns are either sodium hydroxide and/or isopropyl alcohol. As with membrane chromatography units, if disposability is not aspired the systems can be cleaned and reused.

Another step within the purification process is viral clearance. Integrated disposable mixing, filter, and bag assemblies are used for pH titration and low-pH hold viral inactivation. Column eluate is titrated down to a low-pH by adding acid through a second filter to the eluate bag. The solution is then transferred via peristaltic pump to a second bag for low-pH hold for viral inactivation. After the hold, buffer is added to raise the pH. Disposable virus filtration has been developed for the removal of relevant, as well as adventitious viruses. Virus filters are available in a variety of capsule sizes, so processing of batch sizes of 1,000 L or more are possible. In order to protect the viral filter, a 0.1 µm viral prefilter is commonly used. The entire fluid path is disposable, including the viral prefilter, viral filter, collection bag, and all tubing.

Single-use concepts in cross-flow applications have recently become very popular in vaccine manufacturing and are currently being evaluated in monoclonal antibody production also. Ultrafiltration steps to diafilter and concentrate process intermediates are very common to exchange buffers and reduce fluid volumes. Cleaning of such membrane structures is tedious and requires thorough cleaning validation. It has to be assured that all product and cleaning agent residues are removed from the ultrafilter membrane structure. Cross-flow systems with entirely disposable fluid paths are standard or customizable depending on batch size, concentration factor, and required processing time. Ultrafiltration membranes have molecular weight cutoff from 1 to 100 kD.

Filtration

Disposable filter devices are commonly filter elements, membrane, and prefilter, which are encapsulated by a plastic housing (Figure 25.2). These units are available in different sizes (filtration areas from 1.5 to 30 ft²), with different connectors (hose barb, sanitary flange, threaded) and design (in-line or T-style). These filter units are either supplied presterilized by gamma irradiation or autoclaving or as bulk shipment to be sterilized by the end user. Since most manufacturers analyze the extractable release of such filters after sterilization and flush the filters within their production processes, these filters can be used without or limited rinsing. Limited rinse volume needs the connectivity of filter capsules and the lack of filter assembly reduces the setup time within the production process greatly. Furthermore, the filter units are often connected to tubing and aseptic connection devices, which reduce the possibility of filtrate contamination. Since the filter devices are disposable and encapsulated, the end user will not come in contact with the spent filter, i.e., neither the filtered product, which could be cytotoxic or of elevated potency nor the separated contaminants on the upstream side of the filter. The end user safety is therefore improved.

FIGURE 25.2   Different encapsulated filter devices: sizes and connectors.

Filter capsules are often regarded as cost-intensive devices, which require to be replaced after every filtration and therefore elevate the running costs. Having said this, capital expenses necessary for the purchase of stainless steel housings, depreciation, and cleaning costs are avoided. Cleaning costs of filter housings, when analyzed appropriately, might exceed the cost of an encapsulated filter, depending on the flush volumes of water for injection, the man power required, cleaning agent costs, and energy requirements to sterilize the filter system. These costs do not include any production capacity losses due to prolonged setup time, which would be void with capsule filters. Cleaning validation, which needs to be performed with fixed equipment like filter housings, would be greatly reduced or eliminated.

Sterile Connections

Commonly, assemblies of filter capsules and bags are connected via tubing and gamma irradiated. The assembly itself has to be connected to a feed stream, for example, a disposable mixing system or the hold bag could be connected to a bioreactor or fill line. In all cases, the desire is to connect the equipment or process units aseptically to achieve a high sterility assurance. Fittings of all different designs, whether hose barb or sanitary flange may be used, but often do not address the criticality of the aseptic connection. The lack of appropriate aseptic connectivity has been recognized and addressed with newer more effective designs. These designs assure the connections are aseptic due to the fact that these connectors are presterilized by gamma irradiation and the fluid paths do not come in contact with the exterior environment. The integrity of those devices toward the external environment is ensured via either sterilizing-grade membranes or solid plugs. These aseptic connector devices are generally 100% integrity tested after production by manufacturers. Aseptic connectors allow performing aseptic connection between two disposable systems without the use of a laminar airflow. They are available from 1/4" to 1" tubing and can be sterilized by both gamma radiation and autoclaving.

To verify the appropriate functionality of these connectors, rigorous tests have to be performed under worst-case operating conditions, for example, bacterial ingress tests. Test data can commonly be obtained from the vendor and might be useful within the user's own qualification process.

Other aseptic connections are performed by welding thermoplastic tubing together. The weld process cuts the tubing and welds the both cut-ends together. Tubes of different diameters from 1/8" to 3/4" can be welded, each diameter requiring individual weld parameters commonly programmed into the welder unit. The blade used to weld the tubing heats up to over 700°F and therefore is sterilized during this process. The welding process requires being qualified within the end user process to assure that the weld strength is according to specifications. Any wet or filled tubing cannot be welded. The tubing requires to be dry to achieve an even heat distribution. Welders are used for years in the biopharmaceutical industry with great success.

Filling

Single-use systems for filling of drug product have progressed significantly. This is very critical in autologous processes where the entire process is often single use. Various options are now developed to integrate single-use assemblies into filling lines. Extreme diligence must be taken in the materials of construction for such assemblies as establishing an extractable/leachable profile is critical in drug product. Such assemblies must also have very tight tolerances to ensure repeatable dosing into vials or syringes. A high level of integration is required with the hardware to ensure for proper validation of the system.

Continuous Manufacturing

Continuous manufacturing has been a growing area of interest in biotech. While this has been commercially successful for oral solid dosage (OSD) applications, this is yet the case for biotech. However, limiting unit operations such as chromatography, viral inactivation, tangential flow filtration, and PAT are being addressed through innovation. As these technologies are being adopted and tested within R&D and process development, it is just a matter of time before the first commercial continuous manufacturing process is launched.

Plant Layout and Process Design

Disposable systems utilization creates the possibility to exploit either the entire or parts of the process for multiproduct processing purposes. Hard-piped processes, even when cleaned diligently, are often restricted to a specific product due to the potential risk of cross-contamination. However, this also means that some processes could be underutilized, resulting in value losses. If a process step could be utilized by a multitude of product streams, a disposable version of this step would be advisable as cross-contamination by the disposal of any product contact area would be eliminated. Additionally, disposable systems can be self-containing and are qualified to assure that risk from contaminant ingress from the environment is mitigated. Migration to single-use systems has allowed for closed processing which has allowed for lower clean room classifications. Process validation has to verify that the disposable unit operation works according to specifications within that clean room class, but the feasibility is given. Advancements in single-use technology have had a heavy influence on facility design allowing for larger open ballroom concepts. However, such practice requires higher investment into quality and procedures and never fully eliminating risk; thus, the need to strike a proper level of segregation and relaxed ISO standards to fully manage risk against operating expense (OPEX).

High adaptation of single-use system has allowed for a more flexible facility. However, traditional facilities are often bound to their original design and high CAPEX to retrofit due to their interconnected nature. However, facilities have also been evolving away from their traditional brick and mortar and fixed design to becoming truly flexible in nature through mobility and autonomy. This has allowed for facilities to adapt to different modalities through easier redesign of both clean room space and process equipment. The autonomous nature of cleanrooms additionally enhances how a facility can scale-out or down as capacity needs to adapt.

Regulatory and Validation Requirements

The usability of particular components, like a capsule filter, depends on the requirements of the end user. Parameters, like flow, temperature, pressure conditions, of the application and process will determine the rational of specific design criteria and component choices. The user needs to have detailed know-how of all process parameters to be able to predefine the needs of particular assembly designs and component robustness. Without precise user requirement specifications (URSs), a disposable assembly could be unsuitable for a process. Parameters which are critical for an assembly design are:

- Flow rate
- Pressure conditions
- Temperature conditions
- Filter pore size requirements
- Product volumes
- Process time
- Filter size (established in previously performed throughput trials)
- Fluid properties (compatibility issues)
- Integrity test methods and needs

Bag Validation

Basically, the validation requirements for a disposable aseptic processing are not different than that of a traditional stainless steel process. Because single-use systems are preassembled and sterilized by vendors, there is a higher level of involvement of the supplier in the validation work. End users and suppliers work together at specifying the expected product performance for a given application and agree on the level of validation and certification required for the specific assembly. To be a qualified vendor of single-use aseptic processing, therefore, requires an in-depth understanding and the application of current regulatory and good manufacturing practise (GMP) requirements.

Since most disposable devices are gamma irradiated, between 25 and 50 kGy short- and long-term stability studies with the irradiated devices have to be performed. The irradiation commonly reduces the shelf life of such devices and it has to be determined what the limits are. Furthermore, the irradiation step could accelerate the degradation of the polymeric substances used, which can impact leachable/extractable levels. To determine the effects of irradiation and the stability of the polymer used, manufacturer subject the devices to a considerable regime of qualification tests, before the device is launched. The qualification tests can be utilized as a guidance by the end user and commonly encompass, but are not limited to, following tests:

- Biocompatibility testing
  - USP<87> (2017b): Biological reactivity tests, *in vitro*
  - USP<88> (2017c): Biological reactivity tests, *in vivo*
- Mechanical properties
  - Tensile strength
  - Elongation at break
  - Seal strength
  - Air leak test
- Gas transmission properties
  - ASTM D3985: Oxygen
  - ASTM F1249: Water Vapor
- USP <661> (2017a) Test for Plastics
- E.P. 3.1.7.: EVA for containers and tubing
- E.P. 5.2.8. on TSE-BSE
- TOC analysis
- pH/conductivity
- Extractable/leachable tests with standard solutions

- Chemical compatibility testing
- Protein adsorption studies
- Endotoxin testing
- Gamma irradiation sterilization validation
- Bacterial ingress test

These tests are performed under standard settings with standard solutions. The data of these tests are available from the manufacturer.

Since qualification tests run under standard conditions, possible process-specific validation requirements need to be met. Such validation studies can be supported by the services of the vendor. Process validation studies would, for example, utilize a model solvent and simulate the process parameters within the end users' specifications. Leachable testing with product cannot always be achieved since the product would cover any potential peaks. For this reason, model solvents are often used which are similar to the solvent used within the product stream. However, possible influences by the environmental conditions used within the end users' processes require to be tested to assure that the disposable device performs to specifications (Meyer and Vargas, 2006; Uettwiller, 2006).

The process validation steps vary as the disposable devices have different purposes. Sterilizing-grade filters have to undergo a product bacteria challenge test under end users' process conditions. If the actual fluid is bactericidal or bacteriostatic, a placebo solution could be used. In any case, the influence of the process conditions and fluid toward the challenge organisms or separation mechanisms need to be determined. Product hold bags or mixing bags do not have to undergo bacteria challenge tests, but possibly bacteria ingress tests. Both filter and bag systems require to be tested for leachable or extractable. As mentioned, the end user should take advantage of the vendor's services, which support by the qualification documentation and process validation.

Equipment Qualification

Disposable aseptic processing bag assemblies need to be installed in stainless steel or plastic totes to support the functional filling, draining, storage, transportation, and transfer operations. Jacketed bag holders may be required to offer thermoregulation and temperature control and other single-use sensors such as pH, conductivity, and dissolved oxygen probes can be involved to control a single-use aseptic process. Also weighing load cells and automatic pinch valves can be integrated into these single-use units to offer filling and draining automation and controls. All process hardware, control devices, monitoring instruments, and probes used for the process will need to undergo the traditional installation qualification (IQ), operational qualification (OQ), and performance qualification (PQ). Here again, the approach is not different from that utilized to qualify traditional stainless steel systems but the validation burden is significantly reduced since cleaning validation is not required and gamma sterilization is already validated by the supplier of the disposable assembly. Suppliers of single systems generally offer factory acceptance test (FAT), site acceptance test (SAT), and IQ and OQ services while PQ is the responsibility of the end user.

During IQ and PQ, a validation expert team usually composed of personnel from the supplier and the end user ensure that the hardware, the instruments, and the disposable assemblies are designed and installed according to the URS. Critical dimensions, component design and part numbers, conformance to technical drawings, and functionalities are checked and documented in a preestablished IQOQ protocol: the verification that the appropriate operating and maintenance documentation is also carried out.

The calibration of instruments and probes is also checked during IQOQ.

The equipment qualification is then complete by an in-depth training of the operators in charge of the system and the establishment of standard operating procedures (SOPs).

If a disposable filling system is used, filling accuracy and reproducibility tests using three different disposable set-ups will be required to qualify the filling equipment.

Mixing Qualification

Disposable mixing systems comprise a single-use bag and mixing device assembly and the associated tubing, sensors, filters, and connectors. Like for disposable bags, single-use mixing systems involve a stainless steel or plastic container and a drive unit to actuate the impeller at the desired speed measured in RPM. Thermoregulation, pH, and conductivity controls are commonly applied and monitoring instrumentation is very often adjacent to single-use mixers. The mixing hardware, drive unit, instruments, and probes are also subject to traditional IQ, OQ, and PQ procedures to verify that the system is installed and that it operates according to manufacturer and URS and that it offers the expected end user mixing performances. Beyond classical equipment qualification steps, the major aspect of mixer qualification is the PQ carried out with the solution to be mixed or homogenized or with the powder to be dissolved. The PQ is performed under normal production conditions and will establish the mixing process parameters such as mixing time, temperature, and RPM that need to be observed during production. When in-line monitoring is applied, the PQ will also define the pH or conductivity set limits to be obtained to guaranty the reproducibility of the mixing process.

Generally, three consecutive successful PQ test must be achieved to validate the disposable mixing process.

Operator training and SOP development ultimately generate a fully validated process. No cleaning validation is required like with any other disposable unit operations (Figure 25.3).

Transfer Qualification

The final aseptic transfer of liquids and solid goods such as vial stoppers, syringe stoppers and plungers, monitors, and other items necessary for the aseptic process is certainly one of the most critical operations. Disposable aseptic transfer systems made of a single-use connector and a bag that contains the components to be transferred are either gamma sterilized by suppliers or by autoclaved at end users. In

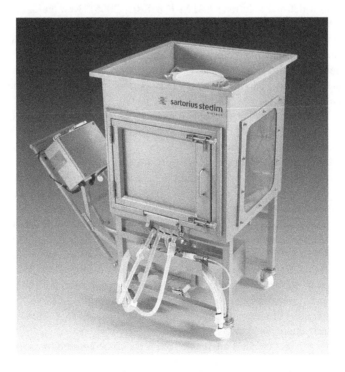

FIGURE 25.3 Example of a levitating disposable mixing unit design including a container, a mixing and drive unit.

the latest case, autoclave sterilization needs to be validated by end users using spore strips of *Bacillus stearothermophilus*.

The aseptic transfer door installed onto the isolator, the restricted access barrier system (RABS) or the wall of the clean room needs to undergo IQ, OQ, and PQ according to a predefined validation protocol.

The IQ and OQ steps are generally supported by the supplier of the aseptic transfer door in collaboration with the supplier of the isolator, RABS, or clean room and the end user.

Ideally, the qualification of the aseptic transfer system should be integrated in the overall qualification of the isolator or RABS to provide a completely validated process solution. Dimensional checks, conformity to technical drawings, functional flow of components through the installed aseptic transfer door and integrity of the bag and the connection are the main qualification tests requirements.

Following the qualification of the equipment and the disposable, three consecutive successful media fills must be obtained to validate the transfer process together with the entire aseptic process. Since multiple transfers can occur during a normal production campaign, it is very critical that the maximum number of transfers is performed during the media fill validation so as to offer worst-case conditions.

All tests performed for the qualification of the aseptic transfer system, including the hardware and the disposable components are documented in a final validation report and signed off for approval by the quality and or validation management.

Filter Validation

Pharmaceutical and biopharmaceutical processes are validated processes to assure a reproducible product within set specifications. Equally important is the validation of the filters used within the process, especially the sterilizing-grade filters, which often enough are used before filling or final processing of the drug product (Akers, 2008). In its Guideline on Sterile Drug Products produced by aseptic processing (2004), the Food and Drug Administration (FDA, 2004) describes that the validation of sterile processes is required by the manufacturers of sterile products (PDA, 2008).

Sterilizing-grade filters are determined by the bacteria challenge tests. This test is performed under strict parameters and a defined solution (ASTM F 838-05, 2005). New guidances, including FDA, nowadays require also evidence that the sterilizing-grade filter will create a sterile filtration, no matter of the process parameters, fluid, or bioburden found (PDA, 1995). This means that bacteria challenge tests have to be performed with the actual drug product, possibly native bioburden, if different or known to be smaller than *Brevundimonas diminuta* and the process parameters involved. The reason for the requirement of a product bacteria challenge test is threefold. First, the influence of the product and process parameters to the microorganism has to be tested. There may be cases of either shrinkage of organisms due to a higher osmolarity of the product or prolonged filtration times. Second, the filters compatibility with the product and the process parameters has to be tested. The filter should not show any sign of degradation due to the product filtered. Additionally, rest assurance is required that the filter used will withstand the process parameters, e.g., pressure pulses, if happening, should not influence the filters performance. Third, there are two separation mechanisms involved in liquid filtration: sieve retention and retention by adsorptive sequestration. In sieve retention, the smallest particle or organism size is retained by the biggest pore within the membrane structure. The contaminant will be retained, no matter of the process parameters. This is the ideal. However, retention by adsorptive sequestration depends on the filtration conditions. Contaminants smaller than the actual pore size penetrate such and may be captured by adsorptive attachment to the pore wall. This effect is enhanced using highly adsorptive filter materials, for example, Glassfibre as a prefilter or polyamide as a membrane (Tanny et al, 1979; Emory et al, 1993). Nevertheless, certain liquid properties can minimize the adsorptive effect, which could mean penetration of organisms. Whether the fluid has such properties and will lower the effect of adsorptive sequestration and may eventually cause penetration has to be evaluated in specific product bacteria challenge tests.

Before performing a product bacteria challenge test, it has to be assured that the liquid product does not have any detrimental, bactericidal or bacteriostatic, effects on the challenge organisms. This is done utilizing viability tests. The organism is inoculated into the product to be filtered at a certain bioburden level. At specified times, the log value of this bioburden is tested. If the bioburden is reduced due to the fluid properties different bacteria challenge test mode become applicable. If the mortality rate is low the challenge test will be performed with a higher bioburden, bearing in mind that the end challenge level should reach $10^7/cm^2$. If the mortality rate is too high the toxic substance is either removed or product properties are changed. This type of challenge fluid is called a placebo. Another methodology would circulate the fluid product through the filter at the specific process parameters as long as the actual processing time would be. Afterwards, the filter is flushed extensively with water and the challenge test, as described in ASTM F838-05, performed.

In addition to the product bacteria challenge test, tests determining the release of leachable substances or particulates have to be performed. Extractable measurements and the resulting data are available from filter manufacturers for the individual filters. Nevertheless, depending on the process conditions and the solvents used, explicit leachable tests have to be performed. These tests are commonly done only with the solvent or diluent used, but not with the actual drug product, as the drug product usually covers any leachable/extractables during measurement. Often, such tests are conducted by the validation services of the filter manufacturers using sophisticated separation and detection methodologies, as GC-MS, FTIR, and RP-HPLC. These methodologies are required due to the fact that the individual components possibly released from the filter have to be identified and quantified. Elaborated studies, performed by filter manufacturers showed that there is neither a release of high quantities of extractables (the range is ppb to maximum ppm per 10-in. element) nor have been toxic substances been found (Reif et al, 1996). Particulates are critical in sterile filtration, specifically of injectables. The USP (United States Pharmacopeia) and BP (British Pharmacopeia) define specific limits of particulate level contaminations for specific particle sizes. These limits have to be met by sterilizing-grade filters. Filters are routinely tested within the manufacturers release control, evaluating the filtrate with laser particle counters. Such tests are also performed with the actual product under process conditions to prove that the product, but especially process conditions do not result in an increased level of particulates within the filtrate.

Furthermore, within specific applications the loss of yield or product ingredients due to adsorption requires to be determined. For example, preservatives, like benzalkoniumchloride or chlorhexadine, can be adsorbed by filter membrane polymers like polyamide (Brose and Henricksen, 1994). Such membranes need to be saturated by the preservative to avoid preservative loss within the actual product. This preservative loss, e.g., in contact lens solutions, can be detrimental due to long-term use of such solutions. Similarly, problematic would be the adsorption of targeted proteins within a biological solution (Hawker and Hawker, 1975). To optimize the yield within an application, adsorption trials have to be performed to find the optimal membrane material and filter construction.

In cases of using the actual product as a wetting agent to perform integrity tests require the evaluation of product integrity test limits. The product can have an influence on the measured integrity test values due to surface tension or solubility. A lower surface tension, for example, would shift the bubble point value to a lower pressure and could result in a false negative test. The solubility of gas into the product could be reduced, which could result in false positive tests. Therefore, a correlation of the product as wetting agent to the, by the filter manufacturer established, water wet values has to be done. This correlation is carried out by using a minimum of three filters of three filter lots. Depending on the product and its variability, one or three product lots are used to perform the correlation. The accuracy of such correlation is enhanced by automatic integrity test machines. These test machines measure with highest accuracy and sensitivity and do not rely on a human judgment as with a manual test. Multipoint diffusion testing offers the ability to test the filters' performance, but especially to plot the entire diffusive flow graph through the bubble point. The individual graphs for a water wet integrity test can now be compared to the product wet test and a possible shift evaluated. Furthermore, the multipoint diffusion test enables an improved statistical base to determine the product wet versus water wet limits.

SOP Development and Operator Training

Following the IQ, OQ, and PQ of hardware, disposable components and instruments involved in the different unit operations, the training of operators in charge of those operations and the development of the associated SOPs will terminate the validation work. Because disposable technologies such as bag assemblies, bioreactors, filling systems, or mixers are not yet broadly understood by operators who have historically been trained and certified to stainless steel process, operator training takes a critical importance.

Validation scientists and application specialist from the key suppliers of disposable assemblies provide expert validation, SOP development, and training support to the industry.

The handling of disposable bags requires specific skills and hands-on experience to ensure that the bags are properly installed into their totes. The installation of the bag and the filling and draining processes are critical for the integrity of the disposable bag throughout the entire process. Well-documented IQ, OQ and PQ, optimal SOP development, and in-depth operator training carried out in collaboration with expert suppliers will guaranty the safety and the robustness of the disposable aseptic process.

REFERENCES

Akers, J.E. (2008) Microbiological Considerations in the Selection and Validation of Filter Sterilization, Chapter 6 in Jornitz, M.W. and Meltzer, T.H., (Eds.)., *Filtration and Purification in the Biopharmaceutical Industry.* informa, New York, ISBN: 0-8493-7953-9.

ASTM F 838-05 (2005) *Standard Test Method for Determining Bacterial Retention of Membrane Filters Utilized for Liquid Filtration.* ASTM, West Conshohocken, PA.

Brose, D.J. and G. Henricksen (1994) A quantitative analysis of preservative adsorption on microfiltration membranes. *Pharmaceutical Technology Europe* 18: 42–49.

Emory, S.F., Y. Koga, N. Azuma, and K. Matsumoto (1993) The effects surfactant types and latex-particle feed concentration on membrane retention. *Ultrapure Water* 10(2): 41–44.

FDA (2004) *Guidance for Industry, Sterile Drug Products Produced by Aseptic Processing.* Center for Drugs and Biologics and Office of Regulatory Affairs, Food and Drug Administration, Rockville, MD.

Gottschalk, U. (2008) Bioseparation in antibody manufacturing: the good, the bad and the ugly. *Biotechnology Progress* 24(3): 496–503. ACS & AICE BP070452G.

Hawker, J. and L.M. Hawker (1975) Protein losses during sterilization by filtration. *Laboratory Practices* 24: 805–814.

Meyer, B.K. and D. Vargas (2006) Impact of tubing material on the failure of product-specific bubble points of sterilizing-grade filters. *PDA Journal of Pharmaceutical Science and Technology* 60(4): 248–253.

PDA Special Scientific Forum (1995) *Validation of Microbial Retention of Sterilizing Filters.* Bethesda, MD; July 12–13.

PDA Technical Report 26 (2008) *Liquid Sterilizing Filtration.* Parenteral Drug Association, PDA: Bethesda, MD.

Reif, O.W., P. Sölkner, and J. Rupp (1996) Analysis and evaluation of filter cartridge extractables for validation in pharmaceutical downstream processing. *PDA Journal of Pharmaceutical Science and Technology* 50: 399–410.

Sinclair, A. and M. Monge (2002) Quantitative economic evaluation of single use disposables in bioprocessing. *Pharmaceutical* Engineering 22(3), 20–34.

Tanny, G.B., D.K. Strong, W.G. Presswood, and T.H. Meltzer (1979) Adsorptive retention of *Pseudomonas diminuta* by membrane filters. *Journal of Parenteral Drug Association* 33: 40–51.

Uettwiller, I. (2006) Testing & validation of disposable systems. *Genetic Engineering News* 26(3).

USP. (2017a) <661> Plastic Packaging Systems and Their Materials of Construction, The United States Pharmacopeial Convention, 12601 Twinbrook Parkway, Rockville, MD.

USP. (2017b) <87> Biological Reactivity Tests, In Vitro, The United States Pharmacopeial Convention, 12601 Twinbrook Parkway, Rockville, MD.

USP. (2017c) <88> Biological Reactivity Tests, In Vivo, The United States Pharmacopeial Convention, 12601 Twinbrook Parkway, Rockville, MD.

Index

A

Absolute filter, 24, 75–76
Absolute retention, 126, 297
Absolute zero, 97
Accurate scale-up operation, 159
Activated carbon, 8, 12
Active pharmaceutical ingredients (APIs), 12, 295, 516
Adenosine triphosphate (ATP), 596
Adhesion kinetics, 594
ADMs, *see* Animal-derived materials (ADMs)
Adsorption, 23
    blocking, 205–206
    in microporous membranes, 24
    of organisms, 83–84
    of proteins, 123–124, *see also* Protein adsorption
    salt addition effect on, 35
Adsorptive bonding, 98–99
Adsorptive chromatography, 362, 451
Adsorptive effects, 82–84, 208
Adsorptive forces, 191, 208
Adsorptive interactions, 7
Adsorptive sequestration, 82, 88–90, 92–94, 99
    effect of ionic strengths, 202
    practical implications of, 125–127
    removal of suspended matter, 231
    retention by, 296–297, 304–305
Advanced Virus Detection Technologies Interest Group (AVDTIG), 442
Aerobic fermentation reaction, 513
Aerosol challenge test system, 532
Aerosol microbial contamination, 516
Aerosol removal test, 528–529
AES, *see* Auger electron spectroscopy (AES)
AEX chromatography, *see* Anion-exchange (AEX) chromatography
Affinity chromatography, 353, 362–365, 441, 483
Affinity precipitation, 357
Air filters
    filtration modes, 511–512
    pore-size distribution of, 510
    redrying of, 267–268
AKTA™ system, 473, 476–477
Albumin retention, 16, 203, 396
Altus Pharmaceuticals Inc., 370, 375
Ambient temperature, 150
American National Standards Institute (ANSI), 526
American Society for Testing Materials (ASTM), 178
American Society of Mechanical Engineers (ASME), 536
American Water Works Association (AWWA), 618
Analytical interference removal, 324–325
Animal-derived materials (ADMs), 440
Anion-exchange (AEX) chromatography, 482
Anisotropic pore structures, 245

Anthropomorphism, 125
Antibody manufacturing, 374
Antimicrobial peculiarity, 185
Antioxidants, 311, 558
APIs, *see* Active pharmaceutical ingredients (APIs)
Application-specific validation issues, 430
Aqueous two-phase extraction (ATPE) system, 356
Archetypical hydrophobic membranes, 261–262
Asbestos filters, 21, 30
Aseptic processing, 627
Aseptic Processing Guidance (FDA), 225, 297
ASME, *see* American Society of Mechanical Engineers (ASME)
Assimilable organic carbon (AOC), 588
Asymmetric diffusive flow test, 241–244
ASTM, *see* American Society for Testing Materials (ASTM)
Asymmetric membranes, 245, 343
ATPE system, *see* Aqueous two-phase extraction (ATPE) system
Attenuation of repulsive forces, 114–115
Attractive forces, 99–100, 111, 112, 114, 201
Auger electron spectroscopy (AES), 173
Austenitic stainless steels, 172, 176
Automated production processes, 283
Automated water intrusion test machine, 265, 266
Automated welding, 180–182
Automatic integrity testing, 271–273

B

Bacillus prodigiosus, 90
Bacteria and phage removal filtration, 520
Bacteria challenge test, 636
    mortality rate, 637
    water intrusion value and, 266
Bacterial adhesion to surfaces, 116–117
Bacterial adsorptions, 200
Bacterial challenge testing, 297, 302–303
Bacterial filters, 82
Bacterial fouling, 201
Bacterial regrowth phenomenon, 598
Bacterial retention mechanism, 66
Bacteriophages, 458
Bag validation, 633–634
Batch mode operation, 425, 426
Batch sizing, 19
B. diminuta, see Brevundimonas diminuta (B. diminuta)
Benzonase Nuclease™, 475
Beta-galactosidase (β-galactosidase)
    activity
        assay for, 470, 477–478
        quantitation of, 470–471
    commercial uses, 469–470

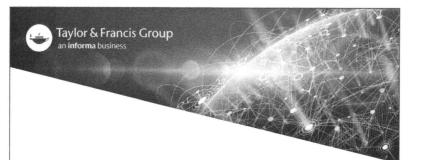